Actors' Television Credits
1950–1972

by
JAMES ROBERT PARISH

Editing Associates:
Paige Lucas, Florence Solomon,
T. Allan Taylor

The Scarecrow Press, Inc.
Metuchen, N.J.   1973

Library of Congress Cataloging in Publication Data

Parish, James Robert.
  Actors' television credits (1950-1972)
    1. Actors, American. 2. Television programs--
United States. I. Title.
PN2285.P3   791.45'028'0922   73-9914
ISBN 0-8108-0673-8

To

JAWBU

Whose Patience Made This Book Possible

CONTENTS

v

Foreword

Widespread commercial television in the United States is less than three decades old, but already much of the basic data, particularly concerning live video drama, is irretrievably lost.

The purpose of this volume is to present detailed credits on a spectrum of television players, focusing on those performers who have contributed most uniquely to the industry. Due to space limitations, the author had selectively to eliminate some of the more hard-working but less essential actors who have populated the small screen over the years. (Thus one will search in vain, for example, for the credits of Robert Emhardt, Madge Blake, or Dick Van Patten.)

Obviously the most essential source available for preparing this checklist volume was TV Guide (New York City market edition), which I indexed issue by issue from 1950-1972, omitting all repeats, theatrical feature films, and all other non-entertainment or non-situation comedy/drama programming. The reader is warned that in the early 1950s, very frequently there was no designation in available programming listings when a video series returned to the telewaves after a summer hiatus; so the absence of a "sr ret" entry for any particular performer does not necessarily mean it was a one-season program. Also unavailable in the early days of live television were detailed cast lists of players for episode entries; thus should Steve McQueen, being unknown to the general public in, say, 1953, have appeared on an entry of Kraft Theatre, there is no record of same.

When utilizing this volume, it is suggested that the reader take advantage of the following supplementary volumes:

TV Guide (New York City market edition).

Broadcast Information Bureau--TV Series Source Book (New York City, Semi Annual Updates).

vii

The Emmy Awards: A Pictorial History (Crown, 1971).

How Sweet It Was (Shorecrest, 1966).

A Pictorial History of Television (Chilton/Bonanza, 1959).

Please keep in mind that the author utilized published source materials for his credit listings, trying to eliminate errors whenever possible, but often unable to cross-reference when a particular special news event (e.g., the Assassination of Martin Luther King, Astronaut Space Flights, etc.) might preempt an evening's programming, with no rescheduled telecastings noted in later time logs.

For future editions of this volume, the author would be grateful for data concerning corrections, additions, and amplifications of published entries.

James Robert Parish
2039 Broadway 17F
New York City 10023

January 15, 1973

Acknowledgments

Broadcast Information Bureau Inc. (Avra Fleigelman)

James W. Buchanan

John Robert Cocchi

Doug McClelland

Jack E. Nolan

Jeanne Passalacqua

Michael R. Pitts

Television Program Analysis Departments of ABC, CBS, NBC.

and special thanks to Paul Myers, curator of the Theatre Collection at the Lincoln Center Library for the Performing Arts (NYC) and his staff: Monty Arnold, Rod Bladel, Donald Fowle, Stephen Ross, Maxwell Silverman, Dorothy Swerdlove, Betty Wharton, and page, Juan Hodelin.

KEY

ep	episode
ep hos	episode host/hostess
nar	narrator
NN	Non-Network
pt	pilot
sh	series host/hostess
sh/sr	series host/series regular
Sp	Special
sr	series regular
sr ret	series regular returning for another season
tf	telefeature

AREAS NOT COVERED WITHIN THIS VOLUME

Documentaries

Game Shows

Live Special Events

News Shows

Quiz Shows

Sports Shows

Talk Shows

Theatrical Motion Pictures

Variety Shows

***Repeats of any type of any show are not tabulated.

AAKER, LEE

Jewelers Showcase   ep   Teacher of the Year   12. 2. 52
CBS
A Letter to Loretta   ep   Kid Stuff   11. 8. 53 NBC
Fireside Theatre   ep   The Boy Down the Road   12. 8. 53
NBC
Ford Theatre   ep   And Suddenly You Knew   12. 10. 53
NBC
Schlitz Playhouse of Stars   ep   Pearl-Handled Guns
1. 15. 54 CBS
Rin Tin Tin   sr 10. 15. 54 ABC
Rin Tin Tin   sr ret   9. 9. 55 ABC
Screen Directors Playhouse   ep   The Bush Roper
11. 23. 55 NBC
Loretta Young Show   ep   The Refinement of Abe   5. 13.
56 NBC
The Millionaire   ep   Millionaire Henry Banning   4. 1. 59
CBS
Danny Thomas Show   ep   5. 16. 60 CBS

ABBOTT, BUD

Abbott and Costello Show   sr   12. 5. 52 CBS
Abbott and Costello Show   sr ret   fall 1953 CBS
G. E. Theatre   ep   The Joke's on Me   4. 16. 61 CBS

ABBOTT, GEORGE

The Skin of Our Teeth   Sp   9. 11. 55 NBC

ABEL, WALTER

Masterpiece Playhouse   ep   Hedda Gabler   7. 23. 50 NBC
Masterpiece Playhouse   ep   Uncle Vanya   9. 3. 50 NBC
Family Playhouse   ep   10. 24. 50 CBS
Video Theatre   ep   The Lovely Menace   12. 11. 60 CBS
Robert Montgomery Presents   ep   Kiss and Tell   1. 1. 51
NBC
Tales of Tomorrow   ep   Enemy Unknown   11. 23. 51
ABC
Prudential Playhouse   ep   Ruggles of Red Gap   2. 27. 51
CBS

1

Celanese Theatre ep Yellow Jack 5. 28. 52 ABC
Robert Montgomery Presents ep Penny 6. 9. 52 NBC
Tales of Tomorrow ep The Chase 9. 19. 52 ABC
Tales of Tomorrow ep The Tomb of King Tarus 10. 31. 52 ABC
Ford Theatre ep There's No Place Like Home 6. 4. 53 NBC
Studio One ep Twelve Angry Men 9. 20. 54 CBS
Climax ep The Midas Touch 10. 18. 56 CBS
Playhouse 90 ep Sincerely, Willis Wayde 12. 13. 56 CBS
On Trial ep The Person and Property of Margery Hay 12. 7. 56 NBC
20th Century-Fox Hour ep The Great American Hoax 5. 15. 57 CBS
Kraft Theatre ep Heroes Walk on Sand 12. 11. 57 NBC
Suspicion ep Meeting in Paris 2. 10. 58 NBC
Suspicion sh 6. 14. 59 NBC
Play of the Week ep The Enchanted 4. 11. 60 NN
Drama ep A Question of Chairs 1. 15. 61 CBS
Defenders ep A Book for Burning 3. 30. 63 CBS
East Side/West Side ep Here Today 4. 27. 64 CBS
Bob Hope Chrysler Theatre ep And Baby Makes Five 10. 5. 66 NBC

ADAIR, JEAN
Summer Theatre ep At Mrs. Beam's 7. 30. 51 CBS
Kraft Theatre ep Never Be the Same 11. 14. 51 NBC
Broadway Theatre ep Outward Bound 11. 24. 52 NN

ADAMS, DON
Bill Dana Show sr 9. 22. 63 NBC
Bill Dana Show sr ret 9. 20. 64 NBC
Get Smart sr 9. 18. 65 NBC
Get Smart sr ret 9. 17. 66 NBC
Get Smart sr ret 9. 16. 67 NBC
Danny Thomas Show ep Instant Money 9. 18. 67 NBC
Get Smart sr ret 9. 21. 68 NBC
Get Smart sr ret 9. 26. 69 CBS
Partners sr 9. 18. 71 ABC

ADAMS, EDIE
Appointment With Adventure ep The Royal Treatment 8. 14. 55 CBS
Cinderella Sp 3. 31. 57 CBS
Suspicion ep If I Die Before I Live 2. 24. 58 NBC
G. E. Theatre ep The Falling Angel 11. 16. 58 CBS

Lucille Ball-Desi Arnaz Hour   ep   Lucy Meets the
    Moustache   4.1.60 CBS
Theatre 62   ep   The Spiral Staircase   10.4.61 NBC
Dick Powel Theatre   ep   Thunder in a Forgotten Town
    3.5.63 NBC

ADAMS, JULIE
Lux Video Theatre   ep   Appointment with Love   11.3.55
    NBC
Studio One   ep   Circle of Guilt   2.20.56 CBS
Lux Video Theatre   ep   Just Across the Street   1.10.57
    NBC
Climax   ep   Two Tests for Tuesday   11.14.57 CBS
Loretta Young Show   ep   The Hidden One   1.19.58
    NBC
Zane Grey Theatre   ep   Man of Fear   3.14.58 CBS
Playhouse 90   ep   The Dungeon   4.17.58   CBS
Alfred Hitchcock Presents   ep   Little White Rock
    6.29.58 CBS
Yancy Derringer   ep   10.2.58 CBS
Zane Grey Theatre   ep   The Tall Shadow   11.20.58
    CBS
Loretta Young Show   ep   Strange Money   12.14.58 NBC
Maverick   ep   The Brass Spur   2.22.59 ABC
Ellery Queen   ep   The Curse of Aden   5.1.59 NBC
77 Sunset Strip   ep   The Canina Caper   5.15.59 ABC
Alcoa Presents   ep   Epilog   7.7.59 ABC
Alfred Hitchcock Presents   ep   Dead Weight   11.22.59
    CBS
Alaskans   ep   Doc Booker   12.6.59 ABC
Cheyenne   ep   Gold, Glory and Custer   1.4.60, 1.11.
    60 ABC
Maverick   ep   The White Widow   1.24.60 ABC
Alcoa Theatre   ep   Minister Accused   2.8.60 NBC
77 Sunset Strip   ep   Safari   3.4.60 ABC
Hawaiian Eye   ep   Murder Anyone   4.13.60 ABC
Rifleman   ep   5.24.60 ABC
Tate   ep   The Mary Hardin Story   9.21.60 NBC
Checkmate   ep   Face in the Window   10.22.60 CBS
Michael Shayne   ep   This Is It, Michael Shayne   11.18.
    60 NBC
Bonanza   ep   The Courtship   1.7.61 NBC
Alfred Hitchcock Presents   ep   Summer Shade   1.10.61
    NBC
Surfside 6   ep   The Facts on the Fire   1.16.61 ABC
Hawaiian Eye   ep   Robinson Koyoto   1.25.61 ABC
77 Sunset Strip   ep   Open and Close in One   3.17.61

ABC
Surfside 6   ep   Laugh for the Lady   10. 30. 61 ABC
Andy Griffith Show   ep   3. 19. 62 CBS
Dr. Kildare   ep   Horn of Plenty   4. 19. 62 NBC
Checkmate   ep   The Someday Man   5. 2. 62 CBS
Gallant Men   ep   A Taste of Peace   3. 16. 63   ABC
Perry Mason   ep   The Case of the Lover's Leap   4. 4.
    63 CBS
Cheyenne   ep   Gold, Glory and Custer, Requiem   4. 19.
    63 ABC
Perry Mason   ep   The Case of the Deadly Verdict   10.
    3. 63 CBS
Arrest and Trial   ep   Inquest into a Bleeding Heart
    11. 10. 63 ABC
77 Sunset Strip   ep   Alimony League   1. 10. 64 ABC
Kraft Suspense Theatre   ep   The Robrioz Ring   5. 28. 64
    NBC
Perry Mason   ep   The Case of the Missing Bottle   9.
    24. 64   CBS
Perry Mason   ep   The Case of the Fatal Fortune   9. 19.
    65 CBS
12 O'Clock High   ep   Big Brother   10. 11. 65 ABC
Amos Burke   ep   Deadlier than the Male   11. 17. 65
    ABC
The Long Hot Summer   ep   Bitter Harvest   11. 18. 65
    ABC
Virginian   ep   No Drums, No Trumpets   4. 6. 66 NBC
Big Valley   ep   10. 31. 66 ABC
Big Valley   ep   Emperor of Rice   2. 12. 68   ABC
Mod Squad   ep   You Can't Tell the Players without a
    Programmer   10. 29. 68 ABC
Ironside   ep   I the People   10. 31. 68 NBC
Outsider   ep   One Long-Stemmed American Beauty   11.
    20. 68 NBC
My Friend Tony   ep   1. 19. 69 NBC
Doris Day Show   ep   10. 6. 69 CBS
Marcus Welby, M. D.   ep   Don't Ignore the Miracles
    10. 7. 69 ABC
FBI   ep   Blood Ties   11. 9. 69 ABC
General Hospital   sr   1970 ABC
Dan August   ep   Epitaph for a Swinger   11. 18. 70 ABC
Bold Ones   ep   An Absence of Loneliness   1. 24. 71
    NBC
Young Lawyers   ep   All the Walls Came Tumbling Down
    2. 24. 71 ABC
Jimmy Stewart Show   sr   9. 19. 71 NBC
The Trackers   tf   12. 14. 71 ABC

Night Gallery ep The Miracle at Camefeo 1.19.72
  NBC
Cannon ep 11.15.72 CBS

ADAMS, NICK
  People's Choice ep 1.12.56 NBC
  Playhouse 90 ep The Troublemakers 11.21.57 CBS
  Zane Grey Theatre ep Sundown at Bitter Creek 2.14.
    58 CBS
  Richard Diamond ep Juvenile Jacket 3.13.58 CBS
  Wagon Train ep The Marie Dupree Story 3.19.58
    NBC
  Wanted Dead or Alive ep 9.6.58 CBS
  Cimarron City ep Twelve Guns 11.1.58 NBC
  Steven Canyon ep Operator B-52 12.6.58 NBC
  Zane Grey Theatre ep A Thread of Respect 2.12.59
    CBS
  Trackdown ep 2.25.59 CBS
  Tales of Wells Fargo ep The Tired Gun 3.30.59
    NBC
  Trackdown ep 4.15.59 CBS
  Rebel sr 10.4.59 ABC
  Rebel sr ret 9.18.60 ABC
  Dick Powell Theatre ep Who Killed Julie Greer 9.26.
    61 NBC
  G.E. Theatre ep A Voice on the Phone 11.19.61
    CBS
  Wagon Train ep The Traitor 12.13.61 NBC
  Joey Bishop Show ep The Big Date 2.28.62 NBC
  Checkmate ep A Chant of Silence 3.21.62 CBS
  Dick Powell Theatre ep Savage Sunday 5.1.62 NBC
  Saints and Sinners sr 9.17.62 NBC
  Combat ep Bridgehead 9.24.63 ABC
  77 Sunset Strip ep By His Own Verdict 11.15.63
    ABC
  Burke's Law ep Who Killed Eleanor Davis 12.20.63
    ABC
  Arrest and Trial ep A Roll of the Dice 2.23.64 ABC
  Outer Limits ep Fun and Games 3.30.64 ABC
  Reporter ep How Much for a Prince 10.9.64 CBS
  Burke's Law ep 10.21.64 ABC
  Voyage to the Bottom of the Sea ep Turn Back the
    Clock 10.26.64 ABC
  Burke's Law ep Who Killed Merlin the Great 12.2.64
    ABC
  Rawhide ep Corporal Dasovik 12.4.64 CBS
  Burke's Law ep 2.3.65 ABC

Ben Casey ep Three Li'l Lambs 3.29.65 ABC
Wild Wild West ep The Night of the Two-Legged Buffalo 3.11.66 CBS
World of Disney ep Willie and the Yank 1.8.67, 1.15.67, 1.22.67 NBC
The Monroes ep 1.25.67 ABC
Combat ep 2.14.67 ABC
Hondo ep 10.13.67 ABC
Hondo ep 12.22.67 ABC
Wild Wild West ep 1.12.68 CBS

ADLER, LUTHER
U.S. Steel Hour ep Hedda Gabler 1.5.54 ABC
Studio One ep A Criminal Design 1.18.54 CBS
Motorola TV Hour ep Nightmare in Algiers 3.23.54 ABC
Center Stage ep The Day Before Atlanta 9.7.54 ABC
G.E. Theatre ep Nora 9.26.54 CBS
G.E. Theatre ep A Man with a Vengeance 5.15.55 CBS
Robert Montgomery Presents ep The Killers 6.6.55 NBC
Star Stage ep The Sainted General 4.6.56 NBC
U.S. Steel Hour ep The Partners 7.18.56 CBS
Studio One ep Cauliflower Heart 9.10.56 CBS
Playhouse 90 ep Last Clear Chance 3.6.58 CBS
Playhouse 90 ep The Plot to Kill Stalin 9.25.58 CBS
Playhouse 90 ep Rank and File 5.28.59 CBS
Play of the Week ep A Month in the Country 11.9.59 NN
Desilu Playhouse ep Meeting at Appalachin 1.22.60 CBS
Twilight Zone ep Man in the Bottle 10.7.60 CBS
Untouchables ep Nicky 11.3.60 ABC
Naked City ep The Man Who Bit the Diamond in Half 12.14.60 ABC
Islanders ep Escape from Kaledau 1.29.61 ABC
Dupont Show of the Month ep The Lincoln Murder Case 2.18.61 CBS
Untouchables ep Murder under Glass 3.23.61 ABC
Naked City ep A Memory of Crying 4.12.61 ABC
Ben Casey ep The Insolent Heart 10.16.61 ABC
Naked City ep The Fingers of Henri Tourelle 10.18.61 ABC
Target Corruptors ep Silent Partner 12.8.61 ABC
Untouchables ep Takeover 3.1.62 ABC
Target Corruptors ep The Wrecker 3.2.62 ABC

Route 66   ep   Man out of Time   10.5.62 CBS
Naked City   ep   Make It Fifty Dollars and Add Love to
     Nona   11.14.62 ABC
Ben Casey   ep   The White Ones Are Dolphins   3.11.63
     ABC
Mission Impossible   ep   2.8.70 CBS
Name of the Game   ep   Tarot   2.13.70   NBC
The Psychiatrist: God Bless the Children   tf   12.14.70
The Psychiatrist   sr   2.3.71 NBC
Hawaii Five-O   ep   11.14.72, 11.21.72, 11.28.72 CBS

AGAR, JOHN
     Fireside Theatre   ep   The Next to Crash   9.30.52 NBC
     The Unexpected   ep   Desert Honeymoon   11.12.52 NBC
     Ford Theatre   ep   The Old Man's Bride   2.12.53 NBC
     Fireside Theatre   ep The Farnsworth Case   3.9.54 NBC
     Schlitz Playhouse of Stars   ep   Little War in San Dede
          5.28.54   CBS
     Climax   ep   The First and the Last   4.28.55   CBS
     Loretta Young Show   ep   Earthquake   6.24.56 NBC
     G.E. Theatre   ep   Thousand Dollar Gun   10.20.57 CBS
     Perry Mason   ep   The Case of the Caretaker's Cat   3.7.
          59 CBS
     Rawhide   ep   Incident of the Slave Master   10.11.60
          CBS
     Best of the Post   ep   Band of Brothers   1.28.61 ABC
     Bat Masterson   ep   Farmer with a Badge   5.18.61
          NBC
     Death Valley Days   ep   2.29.64. ABC
     Virginian   ep   Walk in Another's Footsteps   3.11.64
          NBC
     Branded   ep $10,000 for Durango   11.28.65 NBC
     Combat   ep   The Mockingbird   1.4.66 ABC
     Hondo   ep   11.3.67   ABC
     Name of the Game   ep   Nightmare   10.18.68 NBC
     Virginian   ep   12.4.68 NBC

AHERNE, BRIAN
     Theatre Hour   ep   Dear Brutus   3.24.50 CBS
     Armstrong Circle Theatre   ep   The Magnificent Gesture
          6.6.50 NBC
     Robert Montgomery Presents   ep   11.6.50 NBC
     Video Theatre   ep   A Well-Remembered Voice   1.1.51
          CBS
     Pulitzer Prize Playhouse   ep   The Buccaneer   6.15.51
          ABC
     Video Theatre   ep   Two for Tea   1.5.53 CBS

Robert Montgomery Presents   ep   Element of Risk
   2. 2. 53 NBC
Robert Montgomery Presents   ep   Breakdown   10. 5. 53
   NBC
Drama   ep   The Old Flame   1. 16. 55 CBS
G. E. Theatre   ep   The Martyr   1. 23. 55 CBS
Rheingold Theatre   ep   The Round Dozen   3. 19. 55 NBC
Producers Showcase   ep   Reunion in Vienna   4. 4. 55
   NBC
Crossroads   ep   Chinese Checkers   12. 16. 55 ABC
Rheingold Theatre   ep   Appearance and Reality   2. 11. 56
   NBC
Crossroads   ep   The Sacred Trust   3. 16. 56 ABC
Climax   ep   Night Shriek   11. 15. 56 CBS
Dupont Theatre   ep   Pursuit of a Princess 12. 4. 56 ABC
Crossroads   ep   The Lamp of Father Cataldo   12. 7. 56
   ABC
Twilight Zone   ep   The Trouble with Templeton   12. 9.
   60 CBS
Wagon Train   ep   The Bruce Saybrook Story   11. 22. 61
   NBC
Rawhide   ep   The Gentleman's Gentleman   12. 15. 61
   CBS
World of Disney   ep   The Waltz King   10. 27. 63   NBC

AHN, PHILIP
Four Star Playhouse   ep   Stuffed Shirt 1. 13. 55 CBS
TV Reader's Digest   ep   Mr. Pak Takes Over   6. 13. 55
   ABC
TV Reader's Digest   ep   The Brainwashing of John Hayes
   11. 7. 55 ABC
Crossroads   ep   The Good Thief   11. 25. 55 ABC
Schlitz Playhouse of Stars   ep   Dealer's Choice   1. 13. 56
   CBS
Crossroads   ep   Calvary in China   1. 13. 56 ABC
Navy Log   ep   Operation Typewriter   1. 17. 56 CBS
Captain Midnight   ep   The   Arctic Avalanche   2. 25. 56
   CBS
Four Star Playhouse   ep   Wall of Bamboo   4. 19. 56
   CBS
Hey, Jeannie   ep   12. 15. 56 CBS
Alcoa Hour   ep   The Last Train to Pusan   3. 3. 57 NBC
Hey Jeannie   ep   Jeannie the Proprietor   4. 20. 57 CBS
Dragnet   ep   1. 2. 58 NBC
Eve Arden Show   ep   3. 4. 58   CBS
Californians   ep   Death by Proxy   3. 18. 58 NBC
Lawman   ep   The Intruders   12. 7. 58   ABC

Rin Tin Tin ep The Ming Vase 3.13.59 ABC
Gale Storm Show ep Made in Hong Kong 3.10.60 ABC
Tightrope ep The Chinese Pendant 3.29.60 CBS
Rebel ep Blind Marriage 4.17.60 ABC
Mr. Garlund sr 10.7.60 CBS
Adventures in Paradise cp One Little Pearl 11.28.60
   ABC
Pete and Gladys ep 12.12.60 CBS
Islanders ep The Generous Politician 1.15.61 ABC
Hong Kong ep Lady Godiva 2.8.61 ABC
Hawaiian Eye ep The Manchu Formula 5.3.61 ABC
Hong Kong ep The Dragon Cup 5.31.61 ABC
Adventures in Paradise ep Command at Sea 6.5.61
   ABC
Alcoa Premiere ep The Fortress 10.24.61 ABC
Bonanza ep Day of the Dragon 12.3.61 NBC
Follow the Sun ep Ghost Story 1.21.62 ABC
Hawaiian Eye ep The Broken Thread 10.23.62 NBC
Ensign O'Toole ep Operation Intrigue 1.13.63 NBC
I Spy ep Carry Me Back to Old Tsing-Tao 9.29.65
   NBC
Wild Wild West ep The Night the Dragon Screamed
   1.14.66 CBS
The Man from U.N.C.L.E. ep The Abominable Snow-
   man Affair 12.9.66 NBC
Time Tunnel ep 1.6.67 ABC
The Girl from U.N.C.L.E. ep 2.7.67 NBC
The Man from U.N.C.L.E. ep. 3.31.67, 4.7.67 NBC
I SPY ep American Princess 12.25.67 NBC
Mission Impossible ep Doomsday 2.16.69 CBS
Ironside ep Love My Enemy 10.23.69 NBC
Hawaii Five-O ep Sweet Terror 11.5.69 CBS
Kung Fu tf 2.22.72 ABC
Hawaii Five-O ep Journey out of Limbo 10.31.72
   CBS

ALBERGHETTI, ANNA MARIA
Danny Thomas Show ep 12.21.54 ABC
Ford Theatre ep Never Lend Money to a Woman
   1.19.56 NBC
G.E. Theatre ep The Song Caruso Sang 2.5.56 CBS
Ford Star Jubilee ep A Bell for Adano 6.2.56 CBS
Climax ep The Secret Thread 11.29.56 CBS
Schlitz Playhouse of Stars ep The Enchanted 1.25.57
   CBS
Loretta Young Show ep Emergency 3.24.57 NBC
Climax ep Bait for the Tiger 5.16.57 CBS

Climax ep The Mystery of the Red Room 9. 12. 57
CBS
Dupont Show of the Month ep Aladdin 2. 21. 58 CBS
Roberta Sp 9. 19. 58 NBC
Wagon Train ep The Conchita Vasquez Story 3. 18. 59
NBC
Desilu Playhouse ep A Diamond for Carla 9. 14. 59
CBS
Ford Star Time ep The Jazz Singer 10. 13. 59 NBC
Checkmate ep Runaway 10. 29. 60 CBS
Kismet Sp 10. 24. 67 ABC

ALBERT, EDDIE
Somerset Maugham Theatre ep Smith Serves 12. 10.
51 NBC
Leave It to Lester sr 10. 14. 52 CBS
Schlitz Playhouse of Stars ep Enchanted Evening 10.
31. 52 CBS
The Early Bird 12. 23. 52 CBS
Studio One ep The Trial of John Peter Zenger 1. 12.
53 CBS
Suspense Theatre ep Murder Below 2. 3. 53 CBS
Danger ep Subpoena 5. 26. 53 CBS
Revlon Theatre ep The Little Wife 6. 23. 53 NBC
Summer Studio One ep 1984 9. 2. 53 CBS
The American Hour ep Outlaw's Reckoning 11. 3. 53
ABC
U. S. Steel Hour ep Tin Wedding 11. 23. 53 ABC
Loretta Young Show ep Act of Faith 2. 14. 54 NBC
Medallion Theatre ep Voyage Back 2. 20. 54 CBS
Medallion Theatre ep Homestead 2. 27. 54 CBS
Loretta Young Show ep The Count of Ten 3. 14. 54
NBC
G. E. Theatre ep I'm a Fool 11. 14. 54 CBS
A Connecticut Yankee Sp 3. 12. 55 NBC
G. E. Theatre ep Into the Night 5. 8. 55 CBS
Schlitz Playhouse of Stars ep Too Many Nelsons 5.
13. 55 CBS
Chocolate Soldier Sp 6. 4. 55 NBC
TV Reader's Digest 6. 6. 55 ABC
Front Row Center ep Johnny Belinda 6. 29. 55 CBS
Robert Montgomery Presents ep The World to Noth-
ing 11. 7. 55 NBC
Philco Playhouse ep Rise Up and Walk 1. 1. 56 NBC
Climax ep Burst of Violence 9. 13. 56 CBS
Zane Grey Theatre ep Stage for Tucson 11. 16. 56
CBS

Climax   ep   Let It Be Me   3.21.57 CBS
Zane Grey Theatre   ep   Fugitive   3.22.57 CBS
Alcoa Hour   ep   No License to Kill   9.1.57 NBC
Wagon Train   ep   The John Darro Story   11.6.57 NBC
Climax   ep   Murder Has a Deadline   11.28.57 CBS
Zane Grey Theatre   ep   A Gun for My Bride   12.27.57
    CBS
Schlitz Playhouse of Stars   ep   Pattern for Death   12.
    27.57 CBS
Schlitz Playhouse of Stars   ep   Last Edition   11.21.58
    CBS
Zane Grey Theatre   ep   The Vaunted   11.27.58 CBS
Loretta Young Show   ep   The Last Witness   11.30.58
    NBC
Desilu Playhouse   ep   The Night the Phone Rang   12.
    15.58 CBS
Playhouse 90   ep   The Dingaling Girl   2.26.59 CBS
David Niven Theatre   ep   The Promise   5.5.59 NBC
Goodyear Theatre   ep   Lazarus Walks Again   6.22.59
    NBC
U.S. Steel Hour   ep   Apple of His Eye   7.1.59 CBS
The Ballad of Louie the Louse   Sp   10.17.59 CBS
Playhouse 90   ep   The Silver Whistle   12.24.59 CBS
G.E. Theatre   ep   Louise and the Horseless Buggy
    4.30.61 CBS
U.S. Steel Hour   ep   Famous   5.31.61 CBS
Theatre 62   ep   The Spiral Staircase   10.4.61 NBC
Frontier Circus   ep   The Hunter and the Hunted   11.2.
    61 CBS
Ben Casey   ep   An Uncommonly Innocent Killing   5.7.
    62 ABC
New Breed   ep   A Motive Named Walter   5.8.62 ABC
Naked City   ep   Robin Hood and Clarence Darrow   1.9.
    63 ABC
Dupont Show of the Month   ep   Windfall   1.13.63 NBC
Wide Country   ep   2.21.63 NBC
Sam Benedict   ep   Accomplice   3.9.63 NBC
Eleventh Hour   ep   I Feel Like a Rutabaga   4.24.63
    NBC
The Greatest Show on Earth   ep   The Loser   10.22.63
    ABC
COMBAT   ep   Doughboy   10.29.63 ABC
Dr. Kildare   ep   Voice of Confidence   12.26.63 NBC
Lieutenant   ep   O'Rourke   1.4.64 NBC
Voyage to the Bottom of the Sea   ep   Eleven Days to
    Zero   9.14.64 ABC
Outer Limits   ep   Cry of Silence   10.24.64 ABC

Rawhide   ep   The Photographer   12.11.64 CBS
Kraft Suspense Theatre   ep   The Gun 12.24.64 NBC
Rogues   ep   The Golden Ocean   1.24.65 NBC
Burke's Law   ep   Who Killed Rosie Sunset   1.27.65
   ABC
The Man From U.N.C.L.E.   ep   The Love Affair   3.
   29.65 NBC
Green Acres   sr   9.15.65 CBS
Green Acres   sr ret   9.14.66 CBS
Green Acres   sr ret   9.6.67 CBS
Green Acres   sr ret   9.25.68 CBS
Green Acres   sr ret   9.27.69 CBS
Green Acres   sr ret   9.15.70 CBS
See the Man Run   tf   12.11.71 ABC
Fireball Foreward   tf   3.5.72 ABC
McCloud   ep   The Park Avenue Rustlers   12.24.72 NBC

ALBRIGHT, LOLA
   Video Theatre   ep   Inside Story   6.18.51 CBS
   Video Theatre   ep   Stolen Years   11.19.51 CBS
   Tales of Tomorrow   ep   The Miraculous Serum   6.20.
      52 ABC
   Fireside Theatre   ep   Invitation to Marriage   4.6.54
      NBC
   Pepsi Cola Playhouse   ep   Borrow My Car   4.9.54
      ABC
   Bob Cummings Show   ep   Too Many Cooks   10.13.55
      CBS
   Screen Directors Playhouse   ep   Arroyo   10.26.55 NBC
   It's a Great Life   ep   Double Date   10.30.55 NBC
   Gunsmoke   ep   12.31.55 CBS
   Bob Cummings Show   ep   The Letter   1.5.56 CBS
   Laredo   ep   Above the Law   1.13.66 NBC
   Four Star Playhouse   ep   No Limit   2.16.56 CBS
   The Falcon   ep   The Golden Phony   4.13.56 ABC
   People's Choice   ep   5.3.56 NBC
   No Warning   ep   Fingerprints   6.22.58 NBC
   Peter Gunn   sr   9.22.58 NBC
   Target   ep   The Jewel Thief   3.21.59 CBS
   Michael Shayne   ep   Framed in Blood   10.28.60 NBC
   U.S. Steel Hour   ep   Famous   5.31.61 CBS
   G.E. Theatre   ep   Cat in the Cradle   10.1.61 CBS
   King of Diamonds   ep   The Wizard of Ice   10.6.61 ABC
   Adventures in Paradise   ep   One-Way Ticket   12.3.61
      ABC
   Detectives   ep   The Queen of Craven Point   12.22.61
      NBC

Alfred Hitchcock Theatre   ep   The Woman Who Wanted
   to Live   2.6.62 NBC
The Mighty O   pt   8.21.62 CBS
Saints and Sinners   ep   Dear George, The Siamese Cat
   Is Missing   9.17.62 NBC
Alfred Hitchcock Theatre   ep   Black Curtain 11.15.62
   CBS
My Three Sons   ep   Going Steady   12.20.62 ABC
Mystery Theatre   ep   Go Look at Roses   9.11.63 NBC
Eleventh Hour   ep   Cold Hands, Warm Heart   10.2.63
   NBC
Burke's Law   ep   Who Killed Harris Crown   10.11.63
   ABC
Burke's Law   ep   9.30.64 ABC
Alfred Hitchcock Theatre   ep   Misadventure   12.7.64
   NBC
Wagon Train   ep   Those Who Stay Behind   11.8.64 ABC
Mr. Broadway   ep   Sticks and Stones May Break My
   Bones   12.12.64 CBS
Burke's Law   ep   Who Killed Mother Goose   1.13.65
   ABC
Bonanza   ep   The Search   2.14.65 NBC
Burke's Law   ep   3.3.65 ABC
Rawhide   ep   The Gray Rock Hotel   5.21.65 CBS
Branded   ep   Mightier than the Sword   9.26.65 NBC
Branded   ep   Cowards Die Many Times   4.17.66 NBC
Bob Hope Chrysler Theatre   ep   Runaway Bay   5.25.66
   NBC
How I Spent My Summer Vacation   tf   1.7.67 NBC
Bonanza   ep   1.15.67 NBC
Bob Hope Chrysler Theatre   ep   To Sleep, Perchance
   to Scream   5.10.67 NBC
The Man From U.N.C.L.E.   ep   The Prince of Dark-
   ness Affair   10.2.67, 10.9.67 NBC
Cimarron Strip   11.30.67 CBS
Medical Center   ep   9.27.72 CBS

ALBRITTON, LOUISE
   Tele-Theatre   ep   Hart to Heart   1.2.50 NBC
   Studio One   ep   The Rockingham Tea Set   1.23.50 CBS
   Stage Door   sr   2.7.50 CBS
   Robert Montgomery Presents   ep   The Champion   6.5.50
      NBC
   Armstrong Circle Theatre   ep   The Other Woman   9.19.
      50 NBC
   Armstrong Circle Theatre   ep   The Darkroom   4.15.52
      NBC

Armstrong Circle Theatre   ep   City Editor   7. 1. 52
   NBC
Concerning Miss Marlowe   sr   7. 5. 54 NBC
Appointment with Adventure   ep   Stage Fright   11. 13.
   55 CBS
Alfred Hitchcock Presents   ep   Never Again   4. 22. 56
   CBS
Naked City   ep   Show Me the Way to Go Home   11. 22.
   61 ABC

ALDA, ALAN
Phil Silvers Show   ep   Bilko, the Art Lover   3. 7. 58
   CBS
The Nurses   ep   Many a Sullivan   1. 17. 63 CBS
Route 66   ep   Soda Pop and Paper Flags   5. 31. 63 CBS
Trials of O'Brien   ep   Picture Me a Murder   11. 27. 65
   CBS
Where's Everett   pt   4. 18. 66 CBS
Coronet Blue   ep   Six Months to Mars   8. 14. 67 CBS
Higher and Higher   pt   9. 9. 68 CBS
The Glass House   tf   2. 4. 72 CBS
M. A. S. H.   sr   9. 17. 72 CBS
Playmates   tf   10. 3. 72 ABC

ALDA, ROBERT
Faith Baldwin Playhouse   ep   Inspiration   8. 11. 51 ABC
Drama   ep   The Substitute   12. 15. 50 NN
Video Theatre   ep   I Can't Remember   6. 30. 52 CBS
Tales of Tomorrow   ep   Youth on Tap   9. 26. 52 ABC
Robert Montgomery Presents   ep   Tomorrow Will Sing
   3. 16. 53 NBC
Secret File U. S. A.   sr   10. 29. 54 NN
Schlitz Playhouse of Stars   ep   Curfew at Midnight 6.
   27. 58 CBS
Pursuit   ep   Eagle in the Cage   12. 3. 58 CBS
Alfred Hitchcock Presents   ep   The Morning After 1. 11.
   59 CBS
The Millionaire   ep   Millionaire Julia Conrad   1. 28. 59
   CBS
The Vikings   ep   Shipwreck   4. 3. 60 ABC
The Lucy Show   ep   Lucy Goes to Art Class   1. 13. 64
   CBS
Ironside   ep   The Taker   10. 12. 67 NBC
Judd for the Defense   ep   12. 15. 67 ABC
That Girl   ep   3. 28. 68   ABC
Ironside   ep   The Sacrifice   10. 3. 68 NBC
N. Y. P. D.   ep   Case of the Shady Lady   11. 19. 68 ABC

Ironside   ep   A Bullet for Mark   10.16.69 NBC
Here's Lucy   ep   Secretary Beautiful   3.2.70 CBS
Name of the Game   ep   3.6.70 NBC
Mission Impossible   ep   9.26.70 CBS
Here's Lucy   ep   2.22.71 CBS

ALEXANDER, BEN
  Dragnet   sr   12.16.51 NBC
  Dragnet   sr ret fall, 1952 NBC
  Dragnet   sr ret fall, 1953 NBC
  Dragnet   sr ret fall, 1954 NBC
  Dragnet   sr ret   9.1.55 NBC
  Dragnet   sr ret fall, 1956 NBC
  Dragnet   sr ret fall, 1957 NBC
  Dragnet   sr ret fall, 1958 NBC
  Felony Squad   sr   9.12.66 ABC
  Felony Squad   sr ret   9.67 ABC
  Felony Squad   sr ret 9.27.68

ALEXANDER, JANE
  Repertory Theatre   ep   St. Patrick's Day   3.21.65 NN
  N.Y.P.D.   ep   The Night Watch   1.21.69 ABC
  Welcome Home, Johnny Bristol   tf   1.30.72 CBS

ALLEN, FRED
  Armstrong Circle Theatre   ep   Fred Allen's Sketchbook
    11.9.54 NBC

ALLEN, GRACIE
  George Burns-Gracie Allen Show   sr   10.12.50 CBS
  George Burns-Gracie Allen Show   sr ret fall, 1951 CBS
  George Burns-Gracie Allen Show   sr ret fall, 1952 CBS
  George Burns-Gracie Allen Show   sr ret fall, 1953 CBS
  George Burns-Gracie Allen Show   sr ret   10.4.54 CBS
  George Burns-Gracie Allen Show   sr ret   10.3.55 CBS
  George Burns-Gracie Allen Show   sr ret fall, 1956 CBS
  George Burns-Gracie Allen Show   sr ret fall, 1957 CBS

ALLEN, STEVE
  Danger   ep   Five Minutes to Die   9.15.53 CBS
  Danger   ep   Flamingo   11.10.53 CBS
  Follies of Susy   Sp   10.23.54 NBC
  Kraft Theatre   ep   Man on Roller Skates   2.15.56 NBC
  Bob Cummings Show   ep   1.20.59 NBC
  G.E. Theatre   ep   The Man Who Thought for Himself
    9.18.60 CBS
  June Allyson Show   ep   Play Acting   10.27.60 CBS

Now You See It, Now You Don't   tf   11. 11. 68 NBC
Love American Style   ep   2. 20. 70   ABC

ALLISON, FRAN
Kukla, Fran and Ollie   sr   1949-1957, NBC, ABC
Many Moons   Sp   12. 25. 54 ABC
Pinocchio   Sp   10. 13. 57 NBC
Damn Yankees   Sp   4. 8. 67 NBC

ALLYSON, JUNE
June Allyson Show   sh/sr   9. 21. 59 CBS
June Allyson Show   sh/sr ret   9. 29. 60 CBS
Zane Grey Theatre   ep   Cry Hole! Cry Hate! 10. 20.
    60 CBS
Dick Powell Theatre   ep   A Time to Die   1. 9. 62 NBC
Dick Powell Theatre   ep   Special Assignment 9. 25. 62
    NBC
Dick Powell Theatre   ep   The Third Side of the Coin
    3. 26. 63 NBC
Dick Powell Theatre   ep hos   4. 23. 63 NBC
Burke's Law   ep   12. 27. 63 ABC
Name of the Game   ep   High on a Rainbow   12. 6. 68
    NBC
See the Man Run   tf   12. 11. 71 ABC
Sixth Sense   ep   10. 7. 72 ABC

AMECHE, DON
High Button Shoes   Sp   11. 24. 56 NBC
Goodyear Playhouse   ep   Your Every Wish   6. 16. 57
    NBC
Dupont Show of the Month   ep   Junior Miss   12. 20. 57
    CBS
Climax   ep   Albert Anastasia   2. 27. 58 CBS
Don Ameche Theatre   sh   5. 3. 58 CBS
Too Young to go Steady   sr   5. 14. 59 NBC
Our American Heritage   ep nar   Woodrow Wilson and
    the Unknown Soldier   5. 13. 61   NBC
The Greatest Show on Earth   ep   The Glorious Days of
    Used to Be   3. 31. 64 ABC
Burke's Law   ep   4. 10. 64 ABC
Shadow Over Elveron   tf   3. 5. 68 NBC
Alias Smith and Jones   ep   Dreadful Sorry, Clementine
    11. 17. 71 ABC
Columbo   ep   11. 17. 71 NBC
Gidget Gets Married   tf   1. 4. 72 ABC

AMES, LEON
    Twilight Theatre   ep   Ace of Spades   8.10.53 ABC
    Life with Father   sr   11.22.53 CBS
    Life with Father   sr ret   8.24.54 CBS
    Front Row Center   ep   Ah, Wilderness!   6.15.55 CBS
    Screen Directors Playhouse   ep   Want Ad Wedding   11.
        2.55 NBC
    Matinee Theatre   ep   Daught of the Seventh   10.3.56
        NBC
    Lux Video Theatre   ep   Adam Had Four Sons 4.4.57 NBC
    Studio One   ep   Tongues of Angels   3.17.58 CBS
    No Warning   ep   Amnesiac   5.25.58 NBC
    Maggie   pt   8.29.60 CBS
    Please Don't Eat the Daisies   ep   The Monster in the
        Basement   2.1.66 NBC
    Beverly Hillbillies   ep   10.12.66 CBS
    Andy Griffith Show   ep   11.14.66 CBS
    My Three Sons   ep   11.9.68 CBS
    G.E. Theatre   ep   The Odd Ball   12.28.58   CBS
    Playhouse 90   ep   The Raider   2.19.59 CBS
    G.E. Theatre   ep   Adams' Apple   4.24.60 CBS
    Barbara Stanwyck Theatre   ep   The Assassin 5.15.61
        NBC
    Father of the Bride   sr   9.29.61 CBS
    Mister Ed   sr   fall, 1963 CBS
    The Lucy Show   ep   Lucy and the Military Academy
        12.9.64 CBS
    Bewitched   ep   2.12.70 ABC
    The Ghost and Mrs. Muir   ep   3.13.70 ABC
    Storefront Lawyers   ep   10.7.70 CBS
    Name of the Game   ep   Capitol Affair   2.12.71 NBC

AMSTERDAM, MOREY
    Oh Susanna   ep   Checkmate   2.9.57 CBS
    Danny Thomas Show   ep   10.14.57 CBS
    Jim Bowie   ep   Choctaw Honor   1.3.58 ABC
    Schlitz Playhouse of Stars   ep   I Shot a Prowler   3.28.
        58 CBS
    Have Gun Will Travel   ep   The Moor's Revenge   12.27.
        58 CBS
    Ellery Queen   ep   Dance into Death   5.15.59 NBC
    Pete and Gladys   ep   1.2.61 CBS
    Dick van Dyke Show   sr   10.3.61 CBS
    Dick van Dyke Show   sr ret   9.26.62 CBS
    Mr. Magoo's Christmas Carol   Sp (voice only)   12.18.
        62 NBC
    Dick van Dyke Show   sr ret   9.25.63 CBS

Dick van Dyke Show   sr ret   9.23.64 CBS
Dick van Dyke Show   sr ret   9.15.65 CBS
That's Life   ep   Life in Suburbia   11.12.68 ABC
Love American Style   ep   Love and Mother   12.1.69
   ABC
Adam-12   ep   3.18.71 NBC

ANDERSON, BARBARA
Virginian   ep   The Challenge   10.19.66 NBC
Road West   ep   12.5.66 NBC
Star Trek   ep   12.8.66 NBC
Road West   ep   3.6.67 NBC
Laredo   ep   2.10.67 NBC
Ironside   tf   3.28.67 NBC
Ironside   sr   9.14.67 NBC
Mannix   ep   The Name Is Mannix   9.16.67 CBS
Ironside   sr ret   9.19.68 NBC
Ironside   sr ret   9.18.69 NBC
Paris 7000   ep   Call Me Lee   2.5.70 ABC
Paris 7000   ep   Call Me Ellen   3.26.70 ABC
Ironside   sr ret   9.17.70 NBC
Marcus Welby, M.D.   ep   To Get Through the Night
   10.26.70 ABC
Mission Impossible   ep   9.16.72 CBS
Mission Impossible   ep   10.14.72, 10.21.72 CBS
Night Gallery   ep   10.15.72 NBC
Mission Impossible   ep   11.4.72, 11.11.72, 11.18.72
   NBC
Night Gallery   ep   12.10.72 NBC

ANDERSON, EDDIE (ROCHESTER)
Hallmark Hall of Fame   ep   The Green Pastures   10.
   17.57 NBC
Bachelor Father   ep   Pinch that Penny   1.30.62 ABC
Dick Powell Theatre   ep   Last of the Private Eyes   4.
   30.63 NBC
Love American Style   ep   9.29.69 ABC

ANDERSON, JUDITH (DAME)
Pulitzer Prize Playhouse   ep   The Silver Cord   1.26.51
   ABC
Motorola TV Hour   ep   Black Chiffon   4.20.54 ABC
Light's Diamond Jubilee   ep   10.24.54 ABC, CBS, NBC
Hallmark Hall of Fame   ep   Macbeth   11.28.54 NBC
Elgin Hour   ep   Yesterday's Magic   12.14.54 ABC
Christmas Story   Sp   12.25.54 CBS
Rheingold Theatre   ep   Louise   2.19.55 NBC

Rheingold Theatre   ep   Virtue   4.30.55 NBC
Neighbor Theatre   ep   The Senora   8.14.55 NBC
Rheingold Theatre   ep   The Creative Impulse   12.3.55
    NBC
Producers Showcase   ep   Caesar and Cleopatra   3.5.56
    NBC
Hallmark Hall of Fame   ep   The Cradle Song   5.6.56
    NBC
Climax   ep   The Circular Staircase   6.21.56 CBS
Playhouse 90   ep   The Clouded Image   11.7.57 CBS
Telephone Time   ep   Abby, Julia and the Seven Pet
    Cows   1.7.58 ABC
Dupont Show of the Month   ep   The Bridge of San Luis
    Rey   1.21.58 CBS
Playhouse 90   ep   Second Happiest Day   6.25.59 CBS
Play of the Week   ep   Medea   10.12.59 NN
Moon and Sixpence   ep   10.30.59 NBC
Wagon Train   ep   The Felezia Kingdom Story 11.18.59
    NBC
Playhouse 90   ep   To the Sounds of Trumpets   2.9.60
    CBS
Our American Heritage   ep   Millionaire's Mite   4.10.
    60 NBC
Hallmark Hall of Fame   ep (restaged)   The Cradle Song
    4.10.60 NBC
Hallmark Hall of Fame   ep (restaged)   Macbeth   11.20.
    60 NBC
Hallmark Hall of Fame   ep   Elizabeth the Queen   1.31.
    68 NBC
Hallmark Hall of Fame   ep   The File on Devlin   11.21.
    69 NBC

ANDERSON, WARNER
    The Doctor   sr   8.24.52 NBC
    Ford Theatre   ep   Alias Nora Hale   12.31.53 NBC
    The Lineup   sr   10.1.54 CBS
    The Lineup   sr ret   9.30.55 CBS
    Climax   ep   Nightmare by Day   2.23.56 CBS
    The Lineup   sr ret   fall, 1956 CBS
    Climax   ep   The Gorsten Case   9.20.56 CBS
    The Lineup   sr ret   fall, 1957 CBS
    The Lineup   sr ret   9.26.58 CBS
    The Lineup   sr ret   9.30.59 CBS
    Play of the Week   ep   Night of the Auk   5.2.60 NN
    Peyton Place   sr   9.15.64 ABC
    Gidget Grows Up   tf   12.30.69 ABC

ANDES, KEITH
    Ford Theatre ep Pretend You're You 2.10.55 NBC
    Ford Theatre ep Johnny, Where Are You 11.3.55
    NBC
    The Great Waltz Sp 11.5.55 NBC
    Loretta Young Show ep The Challenge 1.15.56 NBC
    Producers Showcase ep Bloomer Girl 5.28.56 NBC
    Holiday Sp 6.9.56 NBC
    Conflict ep Blind Drop 1.22.57 ABC
    Playhouse 90 ep Homeward Borne 5.9.57 CBS
    Eve Arden Show ep 12.3.57 CBS
    Jane Wyman Show ep The Doctor Was a Lady 3.27.
    58 NBC
    Goodyear Theatre ep The Lady Takes a Stand 5.12.
    58 NBC
    Alcoa Theatre ep Ten Miles to Doomsday 4.20.59
    NBC
    This Man Dawson sr 9.59 NN
    Have Gun Will Travel ep 11.11.61 CBS
    Follow the Sun ep Marine of the Month 5.6.62 ABC
    G.E. True ep Firebug 1.27.63 CBS
    Perry Mason ep The Case of the Skeleton's Closet
    5.2.62 CBS
    Hide and Seek pt 8.5.63 CBS
    Glynis sr 9.25.63 CBS
    77 Sunset Strip ep The Target 1.24.64 ABC
    Perry Mason ep The Case of the Illicit Illusion 4.9.
    64 CBS
    The Lucy Show ep Lucy Goes Duck Hunting 5.18.64
    CBS
    The Lucy Show ep 10.5.64 CBS
    Outer Limits ep Expanding Human 10.10.64 ABC
    Death Valley Days ep Paid in Full 2.12.65 NN
    The Lucy Show ep 10.11.65 CBS
    Run for Your Life ep Where Mystery Begins 11.1.65
    NBC
    Daniel Boone ep 1.19.67 NBC
    I Spy ep A Room with a Rack 2.8.67 NBC
    I Spy ep Laya 9.25.67 NBC
    Star Trek ep The Apple 10.13.67 NBC
    I Spy ep 10.23.67 NBC
    Dan August ep The Manufactured Man 3.11.71 ABC
    Cannon ep A Deadly Quiet Town 2.15.72 CBS

ANDRESS, URSULA
    Thriller ep La Strega 1.15.62 NBC

ANDREWS, DANA
Playhouse 90   ep   The Right Hand Man   3.20.58 CBS
Playhouse 90   ep   Alas, Babylon   4.3.60 CBS
G.E. Theatre   ep   The Playoff   11.20.60 CBS
Barbara Stanwyck Theatre   ep   5.1.61 NBC
Checkmate   ep   Trial by Midnight   3.28.62 CBS
Dupont Show of the Month   ep nar   Emergency Ward
   11.18.62 NBC
Dupont Show of the Month   ep   Mutiny   12.2.62 NBC
Dick Powell Theatre   ep   Crazy Sunday   12.18.62 NBC
Twilight Zone   ep   No Time like the Past   3.7.63 CBS
Alcoa Premiere   ep   The Town that Died   4.25.63 ABC
Ben Casey   ep   The Light that Loses, the Light that
   Wins   1.1.64 ABC
Bob Hope Chrysler Theatre   ep   A Wind of Hurricane
   Force   2.7.64 NBC
Bright Promise   sr   1970 NBC
The Failing of Raymond   tf   11.27.71 ABC
Night Gallery   ep   The Different Ones   12.29.71 NBC

ANDREWS, JULIE
Ford Star Jubilee   ep   High Tor   3.10.56 CBS
Cinderella   Sp   3.31.57 CBS

ANGEL, HEATHER
World of Disney   ep   Alice in Wonderland   11.3.54 ABC
Studio 57   ep   Stopover in Bombay   2.23.58 NN
Perry Mason   ep   The Case of the Lucky Loser   9.27.
   58 CBS
Mr. Novak   ep   The Tower   3.10.64 NBC
Peyton Place   sr   9.65 ABC
Family Affair   ep   9.12.66 CBS
Family Affair   ep   3.13.67 CBS
Family Affair   ep   Where Do They Find Babies   9.11.67
   CBS
Guns of Will Sonnett   ep   3.8.68 ABC
Family Affair   ep   1.14.71 CBS

ANGELI, PIER
Desilu Playhouse   ep   Bernadette   10.13.58 CBS

ANKERS, EVELYN
Cavalcade of America   ep   Sam and the Whale   9.29.53
   ABC
G.E. Theatre   ep   The Hunter   11.15.53 CBS
Screen Directors Playhouse   ep   The Silent Partner 12.
   21.55 NBC

20th Century-Fox Hour   ep   The Empty Room   5.30.56
CBS
Cheyenne   ep   1.28.58 ABC

ANN-MARGRET
Flintstones   ep (voice only)   9.19.63 ABC
Here's Lucy   ep   2.2.70 CBS
Family Theatre   ep   Dames at Sea   11.15.71 NBC

ANSARA, MICHAEL
Dragnet   ep   12.30.54 NBC
Medic   ep   The Laughter and the Weeping   1.16.56 NBC
Alfred Hitchcock Presents   ep   Shopping for Death   1.
29.56 CBS
Alfred Hitchcock Presents   ep   The Orderly World of
Mr. Appleby   4.15.56 CBS
Alfred Hitchcock Presents   ep   The Baby Sitter   5.6.56
CBS
Broken Arrow   sr   9.25.56 ABC
77th Bengal Lancers   ep   The Traitor   5.5.57 NBC
Broken Arrow   sr ret   9.57 ABC
Rifleman   ep   The Indian   2.17.59 ABC
Naked City   ep   A Running of Bulls   3.24.59 ABC
Zane Grey Theatre   ep   The Law and the Gun   6.4.59
CBS
Playhouse 90   ep   The Killers of Mussolini   6.4.59 CBS
Rifleman   ep   The Raid   6.9.59 ABC
(Law of the) Plainsman   sr   10.1.59 NBC
Rebel   ep   The Champ   10.2.60   ABC
Untouchables   ep   Nicky   11.3.60 ABC
Barbara Stanwyck Theatre   ep   Night Visitors   1.9.61
NBC
Wagon Train   ep   The Patience Miller Story   1.11.61
NBC
Untouchables   ep   Jamaica Ginger   2.2.61 ABC
Tales of Wells Fargo   ep   Money Run   1.6.62 NBC
Wide Country   ep   A Devil in the Chute   11.8.62 NBC
Wagon Train   ep   The Adam MacKenzie Story   3.27.63
ABC
Rawhide   ep   Incident at Rio Doloroso   5.10.63 CBS
Rawhide   ep   Incident of Iron Bull   10.3.63 CBS
Kraft Suspense Theatre   ep   A Truce to Terror   1.9.64
NBC
Burke's Law   ep   2.14.64 ABC
Perry Mason   ep   The Case of the Antic Angel   4.16.64
CBS
Outer Limits   ep   Soldier   9.19.64 ABC

Voyage to the Bottom of the Sea   ep   Hot Line   11. 9. 64
   ABC
Virginian   ep   Showdown   4. 14. 65 NBC
Wackiest Ship in the Army   ep   10. 3. 65 NBC
Ben Casey   ep   Run for Your Lives   10. 4. 65 ABC
The Man from U. N. C. L. E.   ep   The Arabian Affair
   10. 29. 65 NBC
Voyage to the Bottom of the Sea   ep   The Hunters   1. 2.
   66 ABC
Shenandoah   ep   Rope's End   1. 17. 66 ABC
Gunsmoke   ep   3. 5. 66 CBS
I Dream of Jeannie   ep   9. 12. 66 NBC
The Girl from U. N. C. L. E.   ep   The Prisoner of Zala-
   mar Affair   9. 20. 66 NBC
Bewitched   ep   10. 13. 66 ABC
How I Spent My Summer Vacation   tf   1. 7. 67 NBC
Gunsmoke   ep   2. 18. 67 CBS
Fugitive   ep   3. 14. 67 ABC
Time Tunnel   ep   3. 24. 67 ABC
Road West   ep   A War for the Gravediggers   4. 10. 67
   NBC
Tarzan   ep   Trek to Terror   2. 9. 68 NBC
Cowboy in Africa   ep   4. 1. 68 ABC
Star Trek   ep   Day of the Dove   11. 1. 68 NBC
Here Come the Brides   ep   1. 22. 69 ABC
High Chaparral   ep   For the Love of Carlos   4. 3. 69
   NBC
Governor and J. J.   ep   12. 16. 69 CBS
Survivors   ep   12. 29. 69 ABC
Name of the Game   ep   1. 23. 70 NBC
Lancer   ep   Lamp in the Wilderness   3. 10. 70 CBS
Mod Squad   ep   A Double for Danger   2. 23. 71 ABC
World of Disney   ep nar   Hamad and the Prince   3. 7.
   71, 3. 14. 71 NBC
McMillan and Wife   ep   An Elementary Case of Mur-
   der   3. 1. 72 NBC
Hawaii Five-O   ep   9. 12. 72 CBS
Streets of San Francisco   ep   12. 9. 72 ABC

ARDEN, EVE
   Starlight Theatre   ep   Julie   2. 8. 51 CBS
   Our Miss Brooks   sr   10. 3. 52 CBS
   Our Miss Brooks   sr ret   10. 2. 53 CBS
   Our Miss Brooks   sr ret   10. 1. 54 CBS
   Our Miss Brooks   sr ret   10. 7. 55 CBS
   Our Miss Brooks   sr ret   10. 56 CBS
   It Gives Me Great Pleasure (a. k. a. The Eve Arden Show)

sr   9. 17. 57 CBS
Checkmate   ep   Death by Design   5. 20. 61 CBS
Laredo   ep   Which Way Did They Go   11. 18. 65 NBC
Bewitched   ep   1. 13. 66 ABC
Run for Your Life   ep   Who's Watching the Fleshpot
     3. 7. 66 NBC
The Man from U. N. C. L. E.   ep   The Minux "X" Affair
     4. 8. 66 NBC
Mothers-in-Law   sr   9. 10. 67 NBC
Mothers-in-Law   sr ret   9. 15. 68 NBC
In Name Only   tf   11. 25. 69 ABC
Love American Style   ep   2. 12. 71 ABC
Love American Style   ep   12. 31. 71 ABC
All My Darling Daughters   tf   11. 22. 72 ABC

ARKIN, ALAN
     East Side/West Side   ep   The Beatnik and the Politician
          1. 20. 64 CBS
     ABC Stage 67   ep   The Love Song of Barney Kempinski
          9. 14. 66 ABC

ARLEN, RICHARD
     Loretta Young Show   ep   He Always Comes Home   4.
          10. 55 NBC
     Science Fiction Theatre   ep   Out of Nowhere   4. 29. 55
          NBC
     The Whistler   ep   Cancelled Flight   6. 26. 55 NN
     TV Reader's Digest   1. 2. 56 ABC
     Crossroads   ep   St. George and the Dragon   1. 20. 56
          ABC
     Climax   ep   Flight to Tomorrow   11. 8. 56 CBS
     Crossroads   ep   Week-end Minister   1. 11. 57 ABC
     20th Century-Fox Hour   ep   Deep Water   5. 1. 57 CBS
     Playhouse 90   ep   Child of Trouble   5. 2. 57 CBS
     Crossroads   ep   9:30 Action   5. 24. 57 ABC
     Lawman   ep   The Gunman   2. 15. 59 ABC
     Yancy Derringer   ep   A State of Crisis   4. 30. 59 CBS
     Bat Masterson   ep   Death and Taxes   11. 26. 59 NBC
     Lawman   ep   Last Stop   1. 3. 60 ABC
     Bat Masterson   ep   The Price of Paradise   1. 19. 61
          NBC
     Lawman   ep   The Man from New York   3. 19. 61 ABC
     Perry Mason   ep   The Case of the Misguided Missile
          5. 6. 61 CBS
     Branded   ep   Coward Step Aside   3. 7. 65 NBC
     The Lucy Show   ep   12. 11. 67 CBS

ARMSTRONG, LOUIS
    Producers Showcase ep The Lord Don't Play Favor-
    ites 9. 17-56 NBC

ARNAZ, DESI
    I Love Lucy   sr   10. 15. 51 CBS
    I Love Lucy   sr ret   9. 15. 52 CBS
    I Love Lucy   sr ret   10. 5. 53 CBS
    I Love Lucy   sr ret   10. 4. 54 CBS
    I Love Lucy   sr ret   10. 3. 55 CBS
    December Bride   ep   2. 20. 56 CBS
    Lucille Ball-Desi Arnaz Hour   sr   11. 6. 57 CBS
    Lucille Ball-Desi Arnaz Hour   sr ret   10. 6. 58 CBS
    Danny Thomas Show   ep   1. 5. 59 CBS
    Lucille Ball-Desi Arnaz Hour   sr ret   9. 25. 59 CBS
    Desilu Playhouse   sh/sr   10. 58 CBS
    Desilu Playhouse   sh/sr ret   10. 2. 59 CBS
    Mothers-in-Law   ep   A Night to Forget   10. 1. 67 NBC
    Mothers-in-Law   ep   12. 24. 67 NBC
    Mothers-in-Law   ep   1. 14. 68, 1. 21. 68 NBC
    Mothers-in-Law   ep   10. 27. 68 NBC
    Men from Shiloh   ep   The Best Man   9. 23. 70 NBC

ARNAZ JR. , DESI
    Mothers-in-Law   ep   1. 21. 68 NBC
    Here's Lucy   sr   9. 23. 68 CBS
    Here's Lucy   sr ret   9. 22. 69 CBS
    Here's Lucy   sr ret   9. 14. 70 CBS
    Night Gallery   ep   9. 22. 71 NBC
    Mr. and Mrs. Bo Jo Jones   tf   11. 16. 71 ABC
    Mod Squad   ep   Feet of Clay   12. 14. 71 ABC
    Love American Style   ep   12. 31. 71 ABC
    Here's Lucy   ep   10. 9. 72 CBS

ARNAZ, LUCIE
    The Lucy Show   ep   Lucy Is a Chaperone   4. 8. 63 CBS
    The Lucy Show   ep   10. 9. 67 CBS
    The Lucy Show   ep   10. 30. 67 CBS
    Here's Lucy   sr   9. 23. 68 CBS
    Here's Lucy   sr ret   9. 22. 69 CBS
    Here's Lucy   sr ret   9. 14. 70 CBS
    Here's Lucy   sr ret   9. 13. 71 CBS
    Here's Lucy   sr ret   9. 11. 72 CBS

ARNESS, JAMES
    Lux Video Theatre   ep   The Chase   12. 30. 54 NBC
    Gunsmoke   sr   9. 10. 55 CBS
    Gunsmoke   sr ret   fall, 1956 CBS

```
Gunsmoke    sr ret   fall, 1957 CBS
Gunsmoke    sr ret   fall, 1958 CBS
Gunsmoke    sr ret   fall, 1959 CBS
Gunsmoke    sr ret   fall, 1960 CBS
Gunsmoke    sr ret   fall, 1961 CBS
Gunsmoke    sr ret   9. 15. 62 CBS
Gunsmoke    sr ret   9. 63 CBS
Gunsmoke    sr ret   9. 26. 64 CBS
Gunsmoke    sr ret   9. 18. 65 CBS
Gunsmoke    sr ret   9. 17. 66 CBS
Gunsmoke    sr ret   9. 11. 67 CBS
Gunsmoke    sr ret   9. 23. 68 CBS
Gunsmoke    sr ret   9. 22. 69 CBS
Gunsmoke    sr ret   9. 14. 70 CBS
Gunsmoke    sr ret   9. 13. 71 CBS
Gunsmoke    sr ret   9. 11. 72 CBS
```

ARNO, SIG
December Bride   ep   1. 10. 55 CBS
Counterpoint   ep   The Wedding   2. 18. 55 NN

ARNOLD, EDWARD
Pulitzer Prize Playhouse   ep   Our Town   12. 1. 50 ABC
Ford Theatre   ep   Junior   10. 9. 52 NBC
Hollywood Opening Night   ep   Thirty Days   11. 10. 52
  NBC
Schlitz Playhouse of Stars   ep   Lost and Found   9. 11. 53
  CBS
Ford Theatre   ep   Since the Day   12. 24. 53 NBC
G. E. Theatre   ep   Walking John Stopped Here   1. 24. 54
  CBS
Ford Theatre   ep   The Tryst   6. 17. 54 NBC
Studio One   ep   12 Angry Men   9. 20. 54   CBS
Edward Arnold Theatre   sh   10. 10. 54 NN
Climax   ep   South of the Sun   3. 3. 55 CBS
Eddie Cantor Theatre   ep   7. 11. 55 ABC
Climax   ep   Deal a Blow   8. 25. 55 CBS
Ford Theatre   ep   Twelve to Eternity   10. 27. 55 NBC
Ethel Barrymore Theatre   ep   The Victim   12. 28. 56 NN
Strange Stories   sh summer, 1960 NN

ARQUETTE, CLIFF
Dennis Day Show   (a. k. a. RCA Victor Show)   sr   10. 3.
  52 NBC
Drama at Eight   ep   Uncle Charley   7. 30. 53 NN
Dennis Day Show   sr ret   10. 5. 53 NBC

ARTHUR, JEAN
Gunsmoke   ep   3.6.65 CBS
The Jean Arthur Show   sr   9.12.66 CBS

ASHLEY, ELIZABETH
Dupont Show of the Month   ep   Heaven Can Wait   11.
16.60 CBS
U.S. Steel Hour   ep   The Big Splash   2.8.61 CBS
Defenders   ep   The Prowler   12.16.61 CBS
Nurses   ep   The Barb Bowers Story   10.18.62 CBS
Ben Casey   ep   And Even Death Shall Die   11.19.62
ABC
U.S. Steel Hour   ep   The Young Avengers   1.9.63 CBS
Sam Benedict   ep   Season of Vengeance   3.30.63 NBC
Stoney Burke   ep   Tigress by the Tail   5.6.63 ABC
Run for Your Life   ep   The Grotenberg Mask   10.24.66
NBC
Hallmark Hall of Fame   ep   The File on Devlin   11.21.
69 NBC
Love American Style   ep   2.6.70 ABC
Men from Shiloh   ep   9.16.70 NBC
Medical Center   ep   Brink of Doom   9.16.70 CBS
Harpy   tf   3.13.71 CBS
Mission Impossible   ep   10.30.71 CBS
When Michael Calls   tf   2.5.72 ABC
Second Chance   tf   2.8.72 ABC
Ghost Story   ep   9.29.72 NBC
The Heist   tf   11.29.72 ABC
Your Money or Your Wife   tf   12.19.72 CBS

ASTAIRE, FRED
G.E. Theatre   ep   Imp on a Cobweb Leach   12.1.57
CBS
G.E. Theatre   ep   Man on a Bicycle   1.1.59 CBS
Alcoa Premiere   sh/sr   10.10.61 ABC
Alcoa Premiere   sh/sr ret   10.4.62 ABC
Bob Hope Chrysler Theatre   ep   Think Pretty   10.2.64
NBC
Dr. Kildare   ep   Fathers and Daughters   11.22.65, 11.
23.65, 11.29.65, 11.30.65 NBC
It Takes a Thief   sr   10.16.69 ABC
The Over the Hill Gang Rides Again   tf   11.17.70 ABC
Santa Claus Is Coming to Town   Sp (voice only)   12.3.
71 ABC

ASTHER, NILS
Ellery Queen   ep   Ticket to Nowhere   12.16.51 ABC

Studio One   ep   The Magic Lantern   4.13.53 CBS

ASTIN, JOHN
Donna Reed Show   ep   Mouse at Play   10.5.61 ABC
I'm Dickens ... He's Fenster   sr   9.28.62 ABC
Route 66   ep   Journey to Nineveh   9.28.62 CBS
Farmer's Daughter   ep   Bless our Happy Home   2.19.
   64 ABC
Destry   ep   The Infernal Triangle   5.1.64 ABC
Addams Family   sr   9.18.64 ABC
Addams Family   sr ret   9.17.65 ABC
Phyllis Diller Show   sr   1.13.67 ABC
Batman   ep   2.8.67, 2.9.67 ABC
Hey Landlord   ep   4.9.67 NBC
Sheriff Who   ep   9.5.67 NBC
Flying Nun   ep   10.12.67 ABC
Gunsmoke   ep   10.23.67 CBS
He and She   ep   11.15.67 CBS
CBS Playhouse   ep   The Experiment   2.25.69 CBS
Bonanza   ep   Abner Willoughby's Return   12.21.69 NBC
Love American Style   ep   12.4.70 ABC
Night Gallery   ep   Pamela's Voice   1.13.71 NBC
Men from Shiloh   ep   Jump-Up   3.24.71 NBC
Night Gallery   ep   The Girl with the Hungry Eyes   10.
   1.72 NBC
Temperatures Rising   ep   10.10.72 ABC
McMillan and Wife   ep   11.19.72 NBC

ASTOR, MARY
Kraft Theatre   ep   The Missing Years   2.3.54 NBC
Studio One   ep   Jack Sparling, 46   4.12.56 CBS
Danger   ep   Circle of Doom   11.23.54 CBS
Best of Broadway   ep   The Philadelphia Story   12.8.54
   CBS
Philco Playhouse   ep   Miss America of 1955   12.26.54
   NBC
U.S. Steel Hour   ep   The Thief   1.4.55 ABC
Kraft Theatre   ep   The Hickory Limb   1.13.55 ABC
Producers Showcase   ep   The Women   2.7.55 NBC
Elgin Hour   ep   The $1,000 Window   3.22.55 CBS
Front Row Center   ep   Dinner at Eight   6.1.55 CBS
Climax   ep   Wild Stallion   7.7.55 CBS
Studio 57   ep   A Farewell Appearance   2.5.56 NN
Climax   ep   Nightmare by Day   2.23.56 CBS
Star Stage   ep   I Am Her Nurse   3.2.56 NBC
Playwrights '56 ep   You and Me and the Gatepost   4.10.
   56 NBC

Matinee Theatre ep The Catamaran 5.10.56 NBC
Climax ep Phone Call for Matthew Quade 7.5.56
   CBS
Robert Montgomery Presents ep Sunset Boulevard
   12.3.56 NBC
Zane Grey Theatre ep Black Is for Grief 4.12.57
   CBS
Lux Video Theatre ep The Man Who Played God 4.
   25.57 NBC
Climax ep The High Jungle 7.25.57 CBS
Playhouse 90 ep Mr. and Mrs. McAdam 1.10.57
   CBS
Playhouse 90 ep The Troublemakers 11.21.57 CBS
Studio One ep The Lonely Stage 2.24.58 CBS
U.S. Steel Hour ep The Littlest Enemy 6.18.58 CBS
Playhouse 90 ep The Return of Ansel Gibbs 11.27.58
   CBS
Alfred Hitchcock Presents ep Mrs. Herman and Mrs.
   Fenimore 12.28.58 CBS
Alfred Hitchcock Presents ep The Impossible Dream 4.
   19.59 CBS
Playhouse 90 ep Diary of a Nurse 5.7.59 CBS
G.E. Theatre ep The Last Dance 11.22.59 CBS
The Philadelphia Story Sp 12.7.59 NBC
U.S. Steel Hour ep The Women of Hadley 2.24.60
   CBS
U.S. Steel Hour ep Revolt in Hadley 3.9.60 CBS
Playhouse 90 ep Journey to the Day 4.22.60 CBS
Thriller ep Rose's Last Summer 10.11.60 NBC
Rawhide ep Incident of the Promised Land 2.3.61
   CBS
Checkmate ep Brooding Fixation 3.14.62 CBS
Dr. Kildare ep Operation Lazarus 5.24.62 NBC
Defenders ep 1.26.63 CBS
Dr. Kildare ep Face of Fear 3.7.63 NBC
Burke's Law ep Who Killed Cable Roberts 10.4.63
   ABC
Ben Casey ep Dispel the Black Cycle 11.27.63 ABC

ATES, ROSCOE
   Champion ep 2.10.56 CBS

AUBREY, SKYE
   Love American Style ep 11.24.69 ABC
   Marcus Welby, M.D. ep The Merely Syndrome 3.3.
      70 ABC
   Interns ep Some Things Don't Change 10.2.70 CBS

Most Deadly Game   ep   The Classic Burial Position
   1. 2. 71 ABC
Vanished   tf   3. 8. 71, 3. 9. 71 NBC
Ellery Queen: Don't Look Behind You   tf   11. 19. 71
   NBC
The Longest Night   tf   9. 12. 72 ABC
Emergency   ep   10. 7. 72 NBC
Assignment Vienna   ep   Hot Potato   10. 19. 72 ABC
Jigsaw   ep   11. 2. 72 ABC
Owen Marshall   ep   Who Saw Him Die   11. 2. 72 ABC
Banyon   ep   12. 15. 72 NBC

AUMONT, JEAN PIERRE
Celanese Theatre   ep   No Time for Comedy   12. 12. 51
   ABC
Robert Montgomery Presents   ep   A Christmas Gift
   12. 17. 51 NBC
Goodyear Theatre   ep   A Softness in the Wind   1. 6. 52
   NBC
Studio One   ep   Letter to an Unknown Woman   2. 25. 52
   CBS
Omnibus   ep   Arms and the Man   5. 3. 53 CBS
Philco Playhouse   ep   The Way of the Eagle   6. 7. 53
   NBC
Orient Express   ep   European Edition   11. 5. 54 NN
Climax   ep   The Sound of Silence   3. 1. 56 CBS
Studio 57   ep   Integrity   4. 15. 56 NN
Errol Flynn Theatre   ep   First Come, First Love
   7. 23. 57 NN
Kraft Theatre   ep   Sing a Song   8. 28. 57 NBC
Playhouse 90   ep   Word from a Sealed-Off Box   10. 30.
   58 CBS
U. S. Steel Hour   ep   Family Happiness   2. 11. 59 CBS
Loretta Young Show   ep   The Eternal Now   5. 5. 60, 5.
   12. 60 NBC
U. S. Steel Hour   ep   The Imposter   6. 15. 60 CBS
Theatre 62   ep   Intermezzo   11. 19. 61 NBC
World of Disney   ep   The Horse Without a Head   9. 29.
   63, 10. 5. 63 NBC

AUTRY, GENE
Gene Autry Show   sr   1950-1951 CBS

AVALON, FRANKIE
Eleventh Hour   ep   A Tumble from a High White Horse
   2. 27. 63 NBC
Rawhide   ep   Incident at Faragut Pass   10. 31. 63 CBS

Burke's Law   ep   Who Killed Cynthia Royal   12.13.63
   ABC
Mr. Novak   ep   A Thousand Voices   12.17.63 NBC
Patty Duke Show   ep   A Foggy Day in Brooklyn Heights
   9.15.65 ABC
The Lucy Show   ep   10.2.67 CBS
Off to See the Wizard   ep   Who's Afraid of Mother
   Goose   10.13.67 ABC
It Takes a Thief   ep   11.27.69 ABC
Love American Style   ep   12.3.71 ABC

AVERY, PHYLLIS
The Unexpected   ep   House of Shadows   5.7.52 NBC
Meet Mr. McNultey   sr   9.17.53 CBS
Ray Milland Show   sr   9.15.54 CBS
The Millionaire   ep   The Story of Vickie Lawson   6.8.
   55 CBS
Schlitz Playhouse of Stars   ep   The Girl Who Scared
   Men off   10.21.55 CBS
Schlitz Playhouse of Stars   ep   Christmas Guest   12.23.
   55 CBS
Telephone Time   ep   The Intruder   3.3.57 CBS
Jane Wyman Theatre   ep   The Man on the 35th Floor
   10.10.57 NBC
G.E. Theatre   ep   Mr. Kensington's Finest Hour   10.
   27.57 CBS
Playhouse 90   ep   The Jet-Propelled Couch   11.14.57
   CBS
Broken Arrow   ep   11.19.57 ABC
Trackdown   ep   Look for the Woman   12.6.57 CBS
Studio One   ep   The Other Place   1.13.58 CBS
G.E. Theatre   ep   Silent Ambush   1.26.58 CBS
Perry Mason   ep   The Case of the Half-Weekend Wife
   3.15.58 CBS
Schlitz Playhouse of Stars   ep   Bluebeard's Seventh Wife
   3.21.58 CBS
Richard Diamond   ep   The Torch Carrier   4.3.58 CBS
Richard Diamond   ep   6.21.59 CBS
Rawhide   ep   Incident in No Man's Land   6.12.59 CBS
Richard Diamond   ep   9.20.59 CBS
Rifleman   ep   The Baby-Sitter   12.15.59 ABC
Deputy   ep   Queen Bea   2.20.60 NBC
Broken Arrow   ep   4.3.60 ABC
Peter Gunn   ep   Send a Thief   5.16.60 NBC
Clear Horizon   sr   7.11.60 CBS
Laramie   ep   Ride into Darkness   10.18.60 NBC
Perry Mason   ep   The Case of the Brazen Bequest

12.2.61 CBS
Have Gun Will Travel   ep   3.24.62 CBS
I Love My Doctor   pt   8.14.62 CBS
Alcoa Premiere   ep   Guest in the House   10.11.62 ABC
Sam Benedict   ep   The View from the Ivory Tower   11.
24.62 NBC
Laramie   ep   The Fugitives   2.12.63 NBC
Virginian   ep   If You Have Tears   2.13.63 NBC
Eleventh Hour   ep   The Wings of the Morning   3.20.63
NBC
Have Gun Will Travel   ep   5.4.63 CBS
Dr. Kildare   ep   Four Feet in the Morning   11.21.63
NBC
The Greatest Show on Earth   ep   Man in a Hole   2.18.
64 ABC
The Human Comedy   pt   9.19.64 CBS
O.K. Crackerby   ep   10.28.65 ABC
Bob Hope Chrysler Theatre   ep   Massacre at Ft. Phil
Kearney   10.26.66 NBC
Daniel Boone   ep   9.28.67 NBC

AYRES, LEW
Omnibus   ep   Nothing So Monstrous   1.24.54 CBS
Screen Directors Playhouse   ep   One Against Many
3.7.56 NBC
Playhouse 90   ep   The Family Nobody Wanted   12.20.56
CBS
Schlitz Playhouse of Stars   ep   A Light in the Desert
12.21.56 CBS
Dupont Theatre   ep   The Man Who Asked No Favors
3.5.57 ABC
Zane Grey Theatre   ep   A Man to Look up To   11.29.
57 CBS
Climax   ep   The Thief with the Big Blue Eyes   3.6.58
CBS
Alcoa Theatre   ep   Johnny Risk   6.16.58 NBC
Frontier Justice   sh   7.14.58 CBS
Desilu Playhouse   ep   The Case for Dr. Mudd   10.20.
58 CBS
Pursuit   ep   The Silent Night   12.24.58 CBS
Alcoa Theatre   ep   Corporal Hardy   2.23.59 NBC
Route 66   ep   The Man on the Monkey Board   10.28.60
CBS
June Allyson Show   ep   A Thief or Two   12.1.60 CBS
Zane Grey Theatre   ep   The Scar   3.2.61 CBS
Barbara Stanwyck Theatre   ep   Adventure on Happiness
Street   3.20.61 NBC

Bus Stop   ep   The Opposite Virtues   2.18.62 ABC
Saints and Sinners   ep   Judgment in Jazz Alley   10.8.
    62 NBC
Laramie   ep   Time of the Traitor   12.11.62 NBC
Channing   ep   A Rich, Famous, Glamorous Folk Singer
    Like Me   1.8.64 ABC
Ben Casey   ep   For a Just Man Falleth Seven Times
    4.15.64 ABC
I Spy   ep   Tiger   1.5.66 NBC
FBI   ep   The Tormentors   4.10.66 ABC
ABC Stage 67   ep   The People Trap   11.9.66 ABC
Gunsmoke   ep   9.25.67 CBS
Big Valley   ep   The Disappearance   11.6.67 ABC
Big Valley   ep   Presumed Dead   10.7.68 ABC
Here Come the Brides   ep   2.21.69 ABC
Marcus Welby, M.D.   tf   3.26.69 ABC
Doris Day Show   ep   2.23.70, 3.2.70 CBS
My Three Sons   ep   3.14.70 CBS
Doris Day Show   ep   10.12.70   CBS
Men from Shiloh   ep   The Price of the Hanging   11.11.
    70 NBC
San Francisco International Airport   ep   Supersonic
    Transport   11.25.70 NBC
Interns   ep   The Guardian   3.5.71 CBS
She Waits   tf   1.28.72 CBS
Owen Marshall   ep   10.5.72 ABC

                        -B-

BACALL, LAUREN
    Light's Diamond Jubilee   ep   The Girls in their Summer
        Dresses   10.24.54 ABC, CBS, NBC
    Producers Showcase   ep   The Petrified Forest   5.30.55
        NBC
    Ford Star Jubilee   ep   Blithe Spirit   1.14.56 CBS
    Dr. Kildare   ep   The Oracle   12.19.63 NBC
    Mr. Broadway   ep   Something to Sing about   12.19.64
        CBS
    Bob Hope Chrysler Theatre   ep   Double Jeopardy   1.8.
        65 NBC

BACKUS, JIM
    I Married Joan   sr   10.15.52 NBC

I Married Joan   sr ret   fall, 1953 NBC
I Married Joan   sr ret   9. 29. 54 NBC
TV Reader's Digest   ep   If I Were Rich   11. 28. 55 ABC
Front Row Center   ep   Uncle Barney   2. 26. 56 CBS
Warner Bros. Show   ep   Survival   3. 13. 56 ABC
Matinee Theatre   ep   A Family Affair   5. 14. 56 NBC
Robert Montgomery Presents   ep   Reclining Figure
    2. 25. 57 NBC
Climax   ep   The Mad Bomber   4. 18. 57 CBS
Studio One   ep   In Love with a Stranger   7. 22. 57 CBS
The Pied Piper of Hamlin   Sp   11. 26. 57 NBC
Studio One   ep   The McTaggart Succession   5. 5. 58 CBS
Playhouse 90   ep   Free Week-End   12. 4. 58 CBS
Goodyear Theatre   ep   Success Story   2. 16. 59 NBC
The Millionaire   ep   Millionaire Henry Banning   4. 1. 59
    CBS
Untouchables   ep   The Star Witness   1. 21. 60 ABC
Danny Thomas Show   ep   4. 11. 60 CBS
Jim Backus Show   sr   9. 28. 60 ABC
Maverick   ep   Three Queens Full   11. 12. 61 ABC
Follow the Sun   ep   The Inhuman Equation   3. 11. 62 ABC
Mr. Magoo's Christmas   Sp (voice only)   12. 18. 62 NBC
Dick Powell Theatre   ep   Charlie's Duet   3. 19. 63 NBC
Burke's Law   ep   Who Killed Mr. "X"   9. 27. 63 ABC
Mr. Magoo's Christmas Carol   Sp (voice only)   12. 13.
    63 NBC
Burke's Law   ep   2. 14. 64 ABC
Dupont Show of the Month   ep   Jeremy Rabbit, the Se-
    cret Avenger   4. 5. 64 NBC
Arrest and Trial   ep   Birds of a Feather   4. 19. 64 ABC
Espionage   ep   A Tiny Drop of Poison   5. 20. 64 NBC
Mr. Magoo   sr (voice only)   9. 19. 64 NBC
Burke's Law   ep   9. 23. 64 ABC
Gilligan's Island   sr   9. 26. 64 ABC
Gilligan's Island   sr ret   9. 16. 65 CBS
Gilligan's Island   sr ret   9. 12. 66 CBS
Damn Yankees   Sp   4. 8. 67 NBC
Accidental Family   ep   11. 24. 67 NBC
Daniel Boone   ep   1. 4. 68 NBC
I Spy   ep   2. 26. 68 NBC
Wild Wild West   ep   2. 7. 69 CBS
Good Guys   ep   3. 12. 69 CBS
Wake Me When the War Is Over   tf   10. 14. 69 ABC
Uncle Sam Magoo   Sp (voice only)   2. 15. 70 NBC
Nanny and the Professor   ep   The Tyrannossurus Tibia
    3. 18. 70 ABC
Brady Bunch   ep   9. 22. 71 NBC

Alias Smith and Jones   ep   The Biggest Game in the
    West   2.3.72 ABC
Of Thee I Sing   ep   10.24.72 CBS
Magic Carpet   tf   11.6.72 NBC
Getting Away from It All   tf   11.18.72 ABC

BAILEY, JIM
    Here's Lucy   ep   11.6.72 CBS

BAIN, BARBARA
    Richard Diamond   ep   6.28.59 CBS
    Alcoa Theatre   ep   Small Bouquet   11.16.59 NBC
    Perry Mason   ep   The Case of the Wary Wildcatter
        2.20.60 CBS
    Adventures in Paradise   ep   Prisoner in Paradise   2.29.
        60 ABC
    Law and Mr. Jones   ep   Christmas Is a Legal Holiday
        12.23.60 ABC
    Straightaway   ep   The Craziest Race in Town   3.21.62
        ABC
    Hawaiian Eye   ep   Two Million Too Much   2.26.63 ABC
    Dobie Gillis   ep   I Was a Spy for the F.O.B.   5.8.63
        CBS
    Dick van Dyke Show   ep   5.22.63 CBS
    Lieutenant   ep   A Touch of Hands   10.26.63 NBC
    77 Sunset Strip   ep   By His Own Verdict   11.15.63 ABC
    Wagon Train   ep   12.30.63 ABC
    The Greatest Show on Earth   ep   3.10.64 ABC
    Perry Mason   ep   The Case of the Nautical Knot   10.29.
        64 CBS
    My Mother the Car   ep   10.19.65 NBC
    Get Smart   ep   10.30.65 NBC
    Mission Impossible   sr   9.17.66 CBS
    Mission Impossible   sr ret   9.10.67 CBS
    Mission Impossible   sr ret   9.29.68 CBS
    Goodnight My Love   tf   10.17.72 ABC

BAINTER, FAY
    Video Theatre   ep   A Child Is Born   12.25.50 CBS
    Schlitz Playhouse of Stars   ep   Two Living and One
        Dead   11.30.51 CBS
    Robert Montgomery Presents   ep   O Evening Star   4.7.
        52 NBC
    Video Theatre   ep   Ile   9.8.52 CBS
    Schlitz Playhouse of Stars   ep   Jenny   1.2.53 CBS
    Studio One   ep   Black Rain   1.5.53 CBS
    Suspense   ep   Career   1.27.53 CBS

Armstrong Cirlce Theatre   ep   2.3.53 ABC
Robert Montgomery Presents   ep   All Things Glad and Beautiful   5.25.53 NBC
Ford Theatre   ep   The Happiest Day   1.21.54 NBC
Video Theatre   ep   Shall Not Perish   2.11.54 CBS
Hallmark Hall of Fame   ep   The Story of Ruth   4.18.54 NBC
Ford Theatre   ep   The Unlocked Door   6.3.54 NBC
The Web   ep   The Face on the Shadow   9.19.54 CBS
Goodyear Playhouse   ep   Guilty Is the Stranger   9.26.54 NBC
Armstrong Circle Theatre   ep   The Runaway   10.5.54 NBC
Elgin Hour   ep   Family Crisis   10.19.54 ABC
Lux Video Theatre   ep   My Name is Julia Ross   3.31.55 NBC
Robert Montgomery Presents   ep   Bella Fleace Gave a Party   5.2.55 NBC
Damon Runyon Theatre   ep   Teacher's Pet   7.2.55 CBS
Kraft Theatre   ep   The Sears Girl   1.11.56 NBC
Matinee Theatre   ep   The Book of Ruth   3.30.56 NBC
Studio One   ep   The Dark Corner   1.14.57 CBS
Thriller   ep   Girl with a Secret   11.15.60 NBC
Dr. Kildare   ep   Sister Mike   3.14.63 NBC
Bob Hope Chrysler Theatre   ep   Out on the Outskirts of Town   11.6.64 NBC
Alfred Hitchcock Theatre   ep   Power of Attorney   4.5.65 NBC

BAKER, CARROLL
Danger   ep   Season for Murder   3.29.55 CBS

BAKER, DIANE
Della   tf   1959 NN
Playhouse 90   ep   In Lonely Expectation   4.2.59 CBS
The Killers   Sp   11.19.59 CBS
Dupont Show of the Month   ep   Arrowsmith   1.17.60 CBS
Adventures in Paradise   ep   Passage to Tua   4.11.60 ABC
Follow the Sun   ep   Journey into Darkness   10.8.61 ABC
Bus Stop   ep   The Resurrection of Annie Ahern   10.8.61 ABC
Adventures in Paradise   ep   Vendetta   10.15.61 ABC
Lloyd Bridges Show   ep   The Courtship   3.5.63 CBS
Route 66   ep   The Cruelest Sea of All   4.5.63 CBS

Nurses   ep   Field of Battle   5. 30. 63 CBS
Route 66   ep   Come out, Come out   10. 11. 63 CBS
Dr. Kildare   ep   The Heart, An Imperfect Machine 10.
     17. 63 NBC
Mr. Novak   ep   A Feeling for Friday   11. 19. 63 NBC
Wagon Train   ep   The Alice White Tree Story   11. 1. 64
     ABC
Hallmark Hall of Fame   ep   Inherit the Wind   11. 18. 65
     NBC
Convoy   ep   The Heart of an Enemy   11. 19. 65 NBC
Dr. Kildare   ep   The Atheist and the True Believer
     1. 3. 66, 1. 4. 66, 1. 10. 66, 1. 11. 66, 1. 17. 66, 1. 18. 66
     NBC
Big Valley   ep   1. 5. 66 ABC
Hawk   ep   The Longest Chronicle   9. 15. 66 ABC
Virginian   ep   11. 30. 66 NBC
FBI   ep   The Camel's Noise   12. 11. 66 ABC
The Dangerous Days of Kiowa Jones   tf   12. 25. 66 ABC
Invaders   ep   Beachhead   1. 10. 67 ABC
Bonanza   ep   A Woman in the House   2. 19. 67 NBC
Bob Hope Chrysler Theatre   ep   Free of Charge   3. 22.
     67 NBC
FBI   ep   11. 24. 68 ABC
FBI   ep   9. 14. 69 ABC
Virginian   ep   10. 29. 69 NBC
Name of the Game   ep   Give Till it Hurts   10. 31. 69
     NBC
The D. A. :   Murder One   tf   12. 8. 69 NBC
Mission Impossible   ep   The Falcon   1. 4. 70, 1. 11. 70,
     1. 18. 70 CBS
Paris 7000   ep   Journey to Nowhere   2. 12. 70 ABC
The Old Man Who Cried Wolf   tf   10. 13. 70 ABC
Medical Center   ep   Deadly Encounter   11. 18. 70 CBS
Men from Shiloh   ep   1. 6. 71 NBC
Do You Take This Stranger   tf   1. 18. 71 NBC
Night Gallery   ep   They're Tearing Down Tim Riley's
     Bar   1. 20. 71 NBC
Sarge: The Badge or the Cross   tf   2. 22. 71 NBC
Congratulations, It's a Boy   tf   9. 21. 71 ABC
Killer by Night   ep   1. 7. 72 CBS
Love American Style   2. 4. 72 ABC
Wheeler and Murdoch   pt   3. 27. 72 ABC

BAKER, STANLEY
     Who Has Seen the Wind   tf   2. 19. 65 ABC
     Bob Hope Chrysler Theatre   ep   After the Lion, Jackals
          1. 26. 66 NBC

Bob Hope Chrysler Theatre ep Code Names: Heraclitus 1.4.67, 1.11.67 NBC

BALIN, INA
Kraft Theatre ep Angry Harvest 4.23.58 NBC
Dupont Show of the Month ep Count of Monte Cristo
10.28.58 CBS
U.S. Steel Hour ep Bride of the Fox 8.24.60 CBS
Our American Heritage ep The Invincible Teddy 1.13.
61 NBC
Westinghouse Presents ep Come Again to Carthage
12.8.61 CBS
Adventures in Paradise ep Once There Was a Prin-
cess 1.14.62 ABC
Dupont Show of the Month ep The Interrogator 9.23.
62 NBC
Stoney Burke ep Child of Luxury 10.15.62 ABC
Lieutenant ep A Touching of Hands 10.26.63 NBC
Voyage to the Bottom of the Sea ep Time Bomb 9.26.
65 ABC
Bonanza ep Devil on her Shoulder 10.17.65 NBC
Dick van Dyke Show ep Draw Me a Pear 10.20.65
CBS
Run for Your Life ep A Girl Named Sorrow 11.22.65
NBC
12 O'Clock High ep We're Not Coming Back 11.29.65
ABC
Loner ep The West of Eden 1.1.66 CBS
Get Smart ep 10.14.67 NBC
Run for Your Life ep 2.21.68 NBC
It Takes a Thief ep 4.9.68 ABC
FBI ep The Maze 2.9.69 ABC
The Lonely Profession tf 10.21.69 NBC
Name of the Game ep The Tradition 1.2.70 NBC
Alias Smith and Jones ep 12.30.71 ABC
Search ep 11.1.72 NBC
Cool Million ep 12.20.72 NBC

BALL, LUCILLE
I Love Lucy sr 10.15.51 CBS
I Love Lucy sr ret 9.15.52 CBS
I Love Lucy sr ret 10.5.53 CBS
I Love Lucy sr ret 10.4.54 CBS
I Love Lucy sr ret 10.3.55 CBS
Lucille Ball-Desi Arnaz Hour sr 11.6.57 CBS
Lucille Ball-Desi Arnaz Hour sr ret 10.6.58 CBS
Desilu Playhouse ep K.O. Kitty 11.17.58 CBS

Danny Thomas Show ep 1.5.59 CBS
Lucille Ball-Desi Arnaz Hour sr ret 9.25.59 CBS
Ann Sothern Show ep 10.5.59 CBS
The Lucy Show sr 10.1.62 CBS
The Lucy Show sr ret 9.30.63 CBS
The Greatest Show on Earth ep Lady in Limbo 12.10.
    63 ABC
The Lucy Show sr ret 9.21.64 CBS
The Lucy Show sr ret 9.13.65 CBS
The Lucy Show sr ret 9.12.66 CBS
The Lucy Show sr ret 9.11.67 CBS
Here's Lucy sr 9.23.68 CBS
Here's Lucy sr ret 9.22.69 CBS
Here's Lucy sr ret 9.14.70 CBS
Here's Lucy sr ret 9.13.71 CBS
Here's Lucy sr ret 9.11.72 CBS

BALL, SUZAN
    Video Theatre ep 5.27.54 CBS

BALLARD, KAYE
    Mothers-in-Law sr 9.10.67 NBC
    Mothers-in-Law sr ret 9.15.68 NBC
    Love American Style ep 1.23.70 ABC
    Doris Day Show ep 2.9.70 CBS
    Doris Day Show ep 12.7.70 CBS
    Here's Lucy ep 9.27.71 CBS

BALSAM, MARTIN
    Philco Playhouse ep Statute of Limitations 2.21.54
        NBC
    Philco Playhouse ep The Joker 5.2.54 NBC
    Goodyear Playhouse ep Last Boat to Messina 12.5.54
        NBC
    U.S. Steel Hour ep Freighter 2.15.55 ABC
    Goodyear Playhouse ep The Taker 8.14.55 NBC
    Philco Playhouse ep The Man Is Ten Feet Tall 10.2.
        55 NBC
    Studio One ep The Defender 2.25.57, 3.4.57 CBS
    Alfred Hitchcock Presents ep The Equalizer 2.9.58
        CBS
    Kraft Theatre ep Dog in a Bus Tunnel 3.5.58 NBC
    Studio One ep The Desperate Age 4.21.58 CBS
    Playhouse 90 ep Bomber's Moon 5.22.58 CBS
    Desilu Playhouse ep Time Element 11.24.58 CBS
    Desilu Playhouse ep Man in Orbit 5.11.59 CBS
    Drama ep The Final Ingredient 4.19.59 ABC

Ellery Queen   ep   Dance into Death   5.15.59 NBC
Brenner   ep   Family Man   6.20.59 CBS
Ellery Queen   ep   Cartel for Murder   7.3.59 NBC
Playhouse 90   ep   Free Week-End   7.23.59 CBS
Dupont Show of the Month   ep   Body and Soul   9.28.59
    CBS
Zane Grey Theatre   ep   Lone Woman   10.8.59 CBS
Twilight Zone   ep   The 16mm. Shrine   10.23.59 CBS
Hallmark Hall of Fame   ep   Winterset   10.26.59 NBC
Five Fingers   ep   Search for Edward Stoyar   1.9.60
    NBC
Goodyear Theatre   ep   Birthright   1.18.60 NBC
Sacco-Vanzetti Story   Sp   6.30.60, 6.10.60 NBC
Have Gun Will Travel   ep   10.8.60 CBS
Naked City   ep   New York to L.A.   4.19.61 ABC
Way Out   ep   The Overnight Case   6.16.61 CBS
Route 66   ep   First Class Moulisk   10.20.61 CBS
Untouchables   ep   Tunnel of Horrors   10.26.61 ABC
Naked City   ep   Which Is Joseph Creeley   11.15.61 ABC
New Breed   ep   Lady Killer   12.7.61 ABC
Defenders   ep   The Best Defense   12.30.61 CBS
Cain's Hundred   ep   Take a Number   1.9.62 NBC
Westinghouse Presents   ep   Footnote to Fame   2.3.62
    CBS
Dr. Kildare   ep   The Glory Hunter   2.8.62 NBC
Naked City   ep   Without Stick or Sword   3.28.62 ABC
Untouchables   ep   Man in the Middle   4.5.62 ABC
Target Corruptors   ep   A Book of Faces   4.27.62 ABC
Route 66   ep   Somehow It Gets to Be Tomorrow   2.15.
    63 CBS
Eleventh Hour   ep   Something Crazy's Going on in the
    Back Room   4.3.63 NBC
Twilight Zone   ep   The New Exhibit   4.4.63 CBS
Breaking Point   ep   A Pelican in the Wilderness   11.4.
    63 ABC
Arrest and Trial   ep   Signal of an Ancient Flame   1.12.
    64 ABC
Espionage   ep   The Final Decision   1.22.64 NBC
Bob Hope Chrysler Theatre   ep   Two Is the Number
    1.31.64 NBC
Wagon Train   ep   The Whipping   3.23.64 ABC
Mr. Broadway   ep   Something to Sing about   12.19.64
    CBS
The Man from U.N.C.L.E.   ep   The Odd Man Affair
    4.19.65 NBC
Dr. Kildare   ep   The Taste of Crow   2.22.66, 2.28.66,
    3.6.66, 3.7.66 NBC

Fugitive   ep   2.7.67 ABC
Among the Paths to Eden   Sp   12.17.67 ABC
Name of the Game   ep   10.18.68 NBC
Hunters Are for Killing   tf   3.12.70 CBS
The Old Man Who Cried Wolf   tf   10.13.70 ABC
Night of Terror   tf   10.10.72 ABC

BANCROFT, ANNE
   Kraft Theatre   ep   To Live in Peace   12.16.53 NBC
   Video Theatre   ep   A Medal for Benny   11.25.54 CBS
   Lux Video Theatre   ep   Hired Wife   2.23.56 NBC
   Lux Video Theatre   ep   The Corrigan Case   6.21.56
      NBC
   Climax   ep   Fear Is the Hunter   7.12.56 CBS
   Alcoa Hour   ep   Key Largo   10.14.56 NBC
   Playhouse 90   ep   So Soon to Die   1.17.57 CBS
   Playhouse 90   ep   Invitation to a Gunfighter   3.7.57
      CBS
   ABC Stage 67   ep   I'm Getting Married   3.16.67 ABC
   Climax   ep   The Mad Bomber   4.18.57 CBS
   Alcoa Hour   ep   Hostages to Fortune   7.7.57 NBC
   Frank Sinatra Show   ep   A Time to Cry   1.17.58 ABC
   Bob Hope Chrysler Theatre   ep   Out on the Outskirts
      of Town   11.6.64 NBC

BANG, JOY
   The Kowboys   pt   7.13.70 NBC
   The Psychiatrist: God Bless the Children   tf   12.14.70
      NBC

BANKHEAD, TALLULAH
   U.S. Steel Hour   ep   Hedda Gabler   1.5.54 ABC
   Schlitz Playhouse of Stars   ep   The Hold Card   11.8.57
      CBS
   Lucille Ball-Desi Arnaz Hour   ep   12.3.57 CBS
   G.E. Theatre   ep   Eyes of a Stranger   12.8.57 CBS
   Batman   ep   3.15.67, 3.16.67 ABC

BANNEN, IAN
   Johnny Belinda   Sp   10.22.67 ABC

BARAGREY, JOHN
   Philco Playhouse   ep   The Sudden Guest   2.5.50 NBC
   Studio One   ep   The Scarlet Letter   4.3.50 CBS
   Studio One   ep   Torrents of Spring   4.17.50 CBS
   Philco Playhouse   ep   Brat Farrar   5.14.50 NBC
   Philco Playhouse   ep   Sense and Sensibility   6.4.50 NBC

Studio One ep Little Women 12. 18. 50, 12. 25. 50 CBS
Philco Playhouse ep Jefferson Davis 1. 7. 51 NBC
Kraft Theatre ep Hilda McKay 8. 1. 51 NBC
Kraft Theatre ep John Wilkes Booth 8. 15. 51 NBC
Robert Montgomery Presents ep To Walk the Night
    10. 8. 51 NBC
Suspense ep Moonfleet 11. 6. 51, 11. 13. 51 CBS
The Web ep Model Murder 12. 26. 51 CBS
Suspense ep The Mystery of Edwin Drood 3. 18. 52,
    3. 25. 52 CBS
Kraft Theatre ep She Stoops to Conquer 5. 7. 52 NBC
Goodyear Playhouse ep Four Meetings 6. 8. 52 NBC
Suspense ep Night of Reckoning 6. 24. 52 CBS
The Doctor ep The Trusting Heart 11. 30. 52 NBC
Broadway Television Theatre ep The Acquittal 1. 26.
    53 NN
The Mirror ep The Enormous Radio 7. 21. 53 NBC
Kraft Theatre ep Blind Spot 7. 15. 53 NBC
Suspense ep The Dance 7. 28. 53 CBS
U. S. Steel Hour ep Hedda Gabler 1. 5. 54 ABC
TV Soundstage ep The Green Convertible 3. 19. 54
    NBC
Kraft Theatre ep Spring 1600 4. 22. 54 ABC
Kraft Theatre ep The Stake 5. 12. 54 NBC
Studio One ep A Man and Two Gods 5. 24. 54 CBS
Producers Showcase ep Tonight at 8:30 10. 18. 54
    NBC
Danger ep Murder on 10th Street 2. 8. 55 CBS
Philco Playhouse ep Watch Me Die 4. 3. 55 NBC
Pond's Theatre ep Candle Light 5. 5. 55 ABC
Appointment with Adventure ep Never to Know 8. 7. 55
    CBS
Studio One ep The Secret 8. 15. 55 CBS
Climax ep Silent Decision 9. 15. 55 NBC
Robert Montgomery Presents ep The Stranger 10. 3.
    55 NBC
Studio One ep Uncle Ed and Circumstances 10. 10. 55
    CBS
Studio 57 ep The Girl in the Bathing Suit 11. 27. 55
    NN
Fireside Theatre ep Women at Sea 11. 29. 55 NBC
Front Row Center ep Deadlock 2. 5. 56 CBS
Alfred Hitchcock Presents ep Portrait of Jocelyn
    4. 8. 56 CBS
Star Stage ep The Shadowy Third 4. 20. 56 NBC
Fireside Theatre ep The Past Is Always Present 4.
    17. 56 NBC

Star Stage   ep   Foundation   5.25.56 NBC
Climax   ep   Burst of Violence   9.13.56 CBS
On Trial   ep   Libel in the Wax Museum   1.18.57 NBC
Alfred Hitchcock Presents   ep   One for the Road   3.3.
   57 CBS
G.E. Theatre   ep   With Malice Toward One   3.10.57
   CBS
Schlitz Playhouse of Stars   ep   The Traveling Corpse
   5.3.57 CBS
Ford Theatre   ep   Torn   5.29.57 NBC
Climax   ep   False Witness   7.4.57 CBS
Goodyear Playhouse   ep   Rumbin Galleries   7.28.57
   NBC
Playhouse 90   ep   The Mystery of Thirteen   10.24.57
   CBS
Climax   ep   Two Tests for Tuesday   11.14.57 CBS
Jane Wyman Theatre   ep   The Elevator   1.2.58 NBC
Studio One   ep   The Brotherhood of the Bell   1.6.58
   CBS
The Millionaire   ep   The Jonathan Bookman Story   1.22.
   58 CBS
Suspicion   ep   A World Full of Strangers   3.10.58 NBC
Goodyear Theatre   ep   Fix a Frame for Mourning   4.
   14.58 NBC
U.S. Steel Hour   ep   The Public Prosecutor   4.23.58
   CBS
G.E. Theatre   ep   The Stone   1.18.59 CBS
Playhouse 90   ep   The Wings of the Dove   1.8.59 CBS
Our American Heritage   ep   Shadow of a Soldier   2.21.
   60 NBC
Naked City   ep   Death of Princes   10.12.60 ABC
Thriller   ep   A Wig for Miss Devore   1.29.62 NBC
Checkmate   ep   The Yacht Club Gang   1.31.62 CBS
New Breed   ep   Wings for a Plush Horse   2.20.62 ABC
Dupont Show of the Month   ep   Mutiny   12.2.62 NBC
Defenders   ep   Black List   1.18.64 CBS
East Side/West Side   ep   Nothing But the Truth   3.20.64
   CBS
Defenders   ep   A Matter of Law and Disorder   4.8.65
   CBS
The Secret Storm   sr   1967 CBS

BARI, LYNN
   Detective's Wife   sr   1.14.50 ABC
   Bigelow Theatre   ep   Agent from Scotland Yard   2.11.51
      CBS
   Video Theatre   ep   Weather for Today   6.11.51 CBS

Pulitzer Prize Playhouse ep 6.29.51 ABC
Boss Lady sr 7.1.52 NBC
Schaefer Century Theatre ep The Other Woman 9.9. 52 NBC
Ford Theatre ep All's Fair in Love 2.26.53 NBC
Playhouse ep Stake My Life 5.8.55 ABC
Science Fiction Theatre ep Hour of Nightmare 7.1.55 NBC
Screen Directors Playhouse ep Arroyo 10.26.55 NBC
Studio 57 ep A Tombstone for Taro 3.25.56 NN
Climax ep An Episode of Sparrows 3.29.56 CBS
World of Disney ep Effego Baca, Attorney at Law 5. 15.59 ABC
Overland Trail ep Perilous Passage 2.7.60 NBC
Plainsman ep The Matriarch 2.18.60 NBC
Aquanauts ep 10.12.60 CBS
Michael Shayne ep The Heiress 2.3.61 NBC
Checkmate ep Good-By Griff 4.15.61 CBS
New Breed ep The Butcher 11.14.61 ABC
Ben Casey ep A Certain Time, a Certain Darkness 12.11.61 ABC
Perry Mason ep The Case of the Acousted Accountant 1.9.64 CBS
Perry Mason ep The Case of the Fatal Fetish 3.4.65 CBS
The Girl from U.N.C.L.E. ep 3.14.67 NBC
FBI ep 11.26.67 ABC

BARKER, LEX
Lux Video Theatre ep Hired Wife 2.23.56 NBC
Studio 57 ep The Old Lady's Tears 5.13.56 NN
It Takes a Thief ep 11.20.69 ABC
FBI ep Three Way Split 3.21.71 ABC

BARNES, BINNIE
Donna Reed Show ep The Wedding 1.3.63 ABC
Donna Reed Show ep 3.19.66 ABC

BARRIE, WENDY
Islanders ep Escape from Kaledau 1.29.61 ABC

BARRY, GENE
Loretta Young Show ep Something about Love 11.21.54 NBC
Ford Theatre ep Touch of Spring 2.3.55 NBC
Science Fiction Theatre ep Spider, Incorporated 6.2. 55 NBC

Appointment with Adventure   ep   Ride the Comet   6.19.
    55 CBS
Loretta Young Show   ep   Something about George   6.26.
    55 NBC
Science Fiction Theatre   ep   The World Below   8.26.55
    NBC
Alfred Hitchcock Presents   ep   Triggers in Leash   10.
    16.55 CBS
Fireside Theatre   ep   Nailed Down   11.1.55 NBC
Alfred Hitchcock Presents   ep   Salvage   11.6.55 CBS
Ford Theatre   ep   The Blue Ribbon   11.10.55 NBC
The Millionaire   ep   The Story of Steve Carey   11.30.
    55 CBS
Our Miss Brooks   sr   12.20.55 CBS
Damon Runyon Theatre   ep   The Good Luck Kid   1.21.
    56 CBS
Ford Theatre   ep   The Woman Who Dared   11.14.56
    ABC
Jane Wyman Theatre   ep   A Place on the Bay   12.25.
    56 NBC
Jane Wyman Theatre   ep   The Pendulum   3.12.57 NBC
20th Century-Fox Hour   ep   Threat to a Happy Ending
    5.29.57 CBS
Playhouse 90   ep   Ain't No Time for Glory   6.20.57
    CBS
Bat Masterson   sr   10.8.58 NBC
Wagon Train   ep   Dynamite Blows Two Ways   10.22.58
    NBC
Bat Masterson   sr ret   fall, 1959 NBC
Bat Masterson   sr ret   9.29.69 NBC
Pete and Gladys   ep   9.18.61 CBS
Dick Powell Theatre   ep   Seeds of April   2.13.62 NBC
G.E. Theatre   ep   The Roman Kind   4.8.62 CBS
Alfred Hitchcock Theatre   ep   Dear Uncle George   5.10.
    63 CBS
Burke's Law   sr   9.20.63 ABC
Burke's Law   sr   9.16.64 ABC
Amos Burke   sr   9.15.65 ABC
Prescription: Murder   tf   2.20.68 NBC
Name of the Game   sr   9.20.68 NBC
Istanbul Express   tf   10.22.68 NBC
Name of the Game   sr ret   9.19.69 NBC
Name of the Game   sr ret   9.25.70 NBC
Do You Take This Stranger   tf   1.18.71 NBC
The Devil and Miss Sarah   tf   12.4.71 ABC
Adventurer   sr   9.16.72 NBC

BARRYMORE, DIANA
Modern Romance   ep   hos   5.5.58 NBC

BARRYMORE, ETHEL
Hollywood Opening Night   ep   Mysterious Ways   12.8.52
  NBC
Climax   ep   The Thirteenth Chair   10.14.54 CBS
Remember   ep   White Oaks   6.19.55 NBC
Svengali and the Blonde   Sp   7.30.55 NBC
G.E. Theatre   ep   Prosper's Old Mother   11.20.55 CBS
Ethel Barrymore Theatre   sh/sr   9.21.56 NN
Playhouse 90   ep   Eloise   11.22.56 CBS

BARRYMORE JR., JOHN
Schlitz Playhouse of Stars   ep   Boomerang   9.18.53 CBS
Matinee Theatre   ep   The Runaways   2.21.56 NBC
Climax   ep   The Secret Thread   11.29.56 CBS
Matinee Theatre   ep   End of the Rope   4.1.57 NBC
Playhouse 90   ep   Ain't No Time for Glory   6.20.57
  CBS
Climax   ep   Two Tests for Tuesday   11.14.57 CBS
Wagon Train   ep   The Ruttledge Munroe Story   5.21.58
  NBC
Desilu Playhouse   ep   Silent Thunder   12.8.58 CBS
Rawhide   ep   Incident of the Haunted Hills   11.6.59 CBS
Rawhide   ep   Corporal Dasovik   12.4.64 CBS
Gunsmoke   ep   1.23.65 CBS
Gunsmoke   ep   9.18.65 CBS
Run for Your Life   ep   Hoodlums on Wheels   2.21.66
  NBC
Road West   ep   This Savage Land   9.12.66, 9.19.66
  NBC
Winchester 73   tf   3.14.67 NBC
Dundee and the Culhane   ep   The Turn the Other Cheek
  Brief   9.6.67   CBS

BARTOK, EVA
G.E. Theatre   ep   Bargain Bride   4.7.57 CBS

BASEHART, RICHARD
Playhouse 90   ep   So Soon to Die   1.17.57 CBS
Studio One   ep   Mutiny on the Shark   9.23.57, 9.30.57
  CBS
Zane Grey Theatre   ep   Medal for Valor   12.25.58 CBS
Playhouse 90   ep   A Dream of Treason   1.21.60 CBS
Playhouse 90   ep   The Hiding Place   3.22.60 CBS
Dupont Show of the Month   ep   Men in White   9.30.60
  CBS

Bob Cummings Show   ep   10.14.60 CBS
Hallmark Hall of Fame   ep   Shangri-La   10.24.60 NBC
Play of the Week   ep   He Who Gets Slapped   1.30.61
    NN
Family Classics   ep   The Light that Failed   3.16.61
    CBS
Rawhide   ep   Black Sheep   11.10.61 CBS
Theatre 62   ep   The Paradine Case   3.11.62 NBC
Laf Hit   ep   Black Curtain   11.15.62 CBS
Naked City   ep   Dust Devil on a Quiet Street   11.28.62
    ABC
Route 66   ep   You Can't Pick Cotton in Tahiti   1.11.63
    CBS
Dick Powell Theatre   ep   The Judge   2.5.63 NBC
Rawhide   ep   Incident of the Black Sheep   2.15.63 CBS
Combat   ep   The Long Way Home   10.8.63, 10.15.63
    ABC
Twilight Zone   ep   Probe Seven   11.28.63 CBS
Arrest and Trial   ep   In Question to a Bleeding Heart
    11.10.63 ABC
Ben Casey   ep   Light up the Dark Corners   11.6.63
    ABC
Voyage to the Bottom of the Sea   sr   9.14.64 ABC
Voyage to the Bottom of the Sea   sr ret   9.19.65 ABC
Voyage to the Bottom of the Sea   sr ret   9.18.66 ABC
Voyage to the Bottom of the Sea   sr ret   9.17.67 ABC
Hans Brinker   Sp   12.13.69 NBC
Hollywood Television Theatre   ep   The Andersonville
    Trial   5.17.70 NN
Dan August   ep   12.16.70 ABC
Gunsmoke   ep   Captain Sligo   1.4.71 CBS
City Beneath the Sea   tf   1.25.71 NBC
The Birdmen   tf   9.18.71 ABC
Assignment: Munich   tf   4.30.72 ABC
Bold Ones   ep   9.26.72 NBC
The Bounty Man   tf   10.31.72 ABC
Columbo   ep   11.26.72 NBC

BATES, FLORENCE
    Danger   ep   The Honeymoon Is Over   9.29.53   CBS
    Ozzie and Harriet   ep   The Ladder   12.31.58 ABC

BAXLEY, BARBARA
    Broadway Television Theatre   ep   It Pays to Advertise
        10.13.52 NN
    Robert Montgomery Presents   ep   Keane Vs Keane
        10.20.52 NBC

Armstrong Circle Theatre   ep   A Volcano Is Dancing
    Here   11. 18. 52 CBS
Kraft Theatre   ep   The Twilight Road   5. 27. 53 NBC
Mirror Theatre   ep   One Summer's Rain   8. 25. 53 NBC
Goodyear Playhouse   ep   Moment of Panic   1. 3. 54 NBC
Philco Playhouse   ep   Statute of Limitations   2. 21. 54
    NBC
Robert Montgomery Presents   ep   Paradise Cafe   3. 8.
    54 NBC
U. S. Steel Hour   ep   Late Date   4. 13. 54 ABC
Philco Playhouse   ep   Write Me out Forever   6. 20. 54
    NBC
Danger   ep   Obsession   10. 5. 54 CBS
Climax   ep   The Dance   6. 30. 55 CBS
Studio One   ep   Three Empty Rooms   9. 26. 55 CBS
Telephone Time   ep   She Sette Her Little Foote   10. 21.
    56 CBS
Alfred Hitchcock   ep   Nightmare in 4-D   1. 13. 57   CBS
Kaiser Aluminum Hour   ep   The Story of a Crime   3.
    12. 57 NBC
Alfred Hitchcock Presents   ep   The Three Dreams of
    Mr. Findlater   4. 21. 57 CBS
True Story   ep   Marriage of Convenience   9. 14. 57 NBC
Shirley Temple's Story Book   ep   Beauty and the Beast
    1. 12. 58 NBC
Have Gun Will Travel   ep   3. 22. 58 CBS
Telephone Time   ep   Man of Principle   3. 25. 58 ABC
Studio One   ep   The Strong Man   6. 9. 58 CBS
Alfred Hitchcock Presents   ep   Design for Loving   11.
    9. 58 CBS
Alfred Hitchcock Presents   ep   Anniversary Gift   11. 1.
    59 CBS
Alfred Hitchcock Presents   ep   Across the Threshold
    2. 28. 60 CBS
Play of the Week   ep   A Plum Tree in a Rose Garden
    4. 4. 60 NN
Have Gun Will Travel   ep   5. 14. 60 CBS
Diagnosis Unknown   ep   A Sudden Stillness   8. 9. 60 CBS
Bus Stop   ep   The Covering Darkness   1. 22. 61 ABC
Special for Women   ep   The Single Woman   2. 9. 61 NBC
Way Out   ep   The Overnight Case   6. 16. 61 CBS
Cain's Hundred   ep   King of the Mountain   10. 24. 61
    NBC
New Breed   ep   To None a Deadly Drug   10. 24. 61 ABC
Alfred Hitchcock Theatre   ep   Case of M. J. H.   1. 23. 62
    NBC
D. Kildare   ep   Solomon's Choice   3. 29. 62 NBC

Armstrong Circle Theatre   ep   The Secret Crime   5.
   23.62 ABC
Defenders   ep   The Seven Ghosts of Simon Gray   10.6.
   62 CBS
Twilight Zone   ep   Mute   1.31.63 CBS
Defenders   ep   Claire Cheval Died in Boston   11.23.63
   CBS
Fugitive   ep   11.22.66 ABC
Streets of San Francisco   ep   The Takers   12.22.72
   ABC

BAXTER, ANNE
   G.E. Theatre   ep   Bitter Choice   4.21.57 CBS
   Playhouse 90   ep   The Right Hand Man   3.20.58 CBS
   G.E. Theatre   ep   Stopover   4.27.58 CBS
   Lux Playhouse   ep   The Four   10.17.58 CBS
   Wagon Train   ep   The Kitty Angel Story   1.7.59 NBC
   Riverboat   ep   Race to Cincinnati   10.4.59 NBC
   Zane Grey Theatre   ep   Hand on the Latch   10.29.59
      CBS
   June Allyson Show   ep   The Dance Man   10.6.60 CBS
   G.E. Theatre   ep   Good-By My Love   10.16.60 CBS
   U.S. Steel Hour   ep   The Shame of Paula Marsten   4.19.
      61 CBS
   Alfred Hitchcock Theatre   ep   A Nice Touch   10.4.63
      CBS
   Dr. Kildare   ep   A Day to Remember   4.2.64 NBC
   Batman   ep   Zelda   1.26.66, 1.27.66 ABC
   Cowboy in Africa   ep   10.9.67 ABC
   Stranger on the Run   tf   10.31.67 NBC
   My Three Sons   ep   11.4.67 CBS
   Batman   ep   11.2.67, 11.9.67   ABC
   Danny Thomas Show   ep   Measure of a Man   1.22.68
      NBC
   FBI   ep   Region of Peril   2.25.68 ABC
   Run for Your Life   ep   3.13.68 NBC
   Ironside   ep   An Obvious Case of Guilt   11.14.68 NBC
   Name of the Game   ep   The Protector   11.15.68 NBC
   Companion in Nightmare   tf   11.23.68 NBC
   Virginian   ep   12.11.68 NBC
   Big Valley   ep   The 25 Graves of Midas   2.3.69 ABC
   Name of the Game   ep   The Bobby Currier Story   2.21.
      69 NBC
   Marcus Welby, M.D.   tf   3.26.69 ABC
   The Challengers   tf   3.28.69 CBS
   Ironside   ep   Programmed to Death   11.20.69 NBC
   Paris 7000   ep   1.22.70 ABC

Name of the Game   ep   The Takeover   1.23.70 NBC
Ritual of Evil   tf   2.23.70 NBC
Bracken's World   ep   3.13.70 NBC
Name of the Game   ep   All the Old Familiar Faces
    11.13.70 NBC
If Tomorrow Comes   tf   12.7.71 ABC

BEAL, JOHN
Musical Comedy Time   ep   Hit the Deck   12.11.50 NBC
Airflyte Theatre   ep   The Professor's Punch   3.15.51
    CBS
Goodyear Playhouse   ep   Tigers Don't Sing   3.30.52
    NBC
Schlitz Playhouse of Stars   ep   Double Exposure   8.15.
    52 CBS
Kraft Theatre   ep   The Intruder   7.29.53 NBC
Ford Theatre   ep   Good of His Soul   3.4.54 NBC
Inner Sanctum   ep   Catcalls   3.19.54 NN
G.E. Theatre   ep   You Are Young Only Once   6.6.54
    CBS
Studio One   ep   Twelve Angry Men   9.20.54 CBS
Studio One   ep   The Boy Who Changed the World   10.
    18.54 CBS
Elgin Hour   ep   High Man   11.2.54 ABC
Inner Sanctum   ep   Watcher by the Dead   5.6.55 NN
Robert Montgomery Presents   ep   The Long Way Home
    3.26.56 NBC
Goodyear Playhouse   ep   The Princess Back Home
    2.24.57 NBC
Studio One   ep   The Human Barrier   7.29.57 CBS
U.S. Steel Hour   ep   Little Charlie Don't Want a Saddle
    12.18.57 CBS
Matinee Theatre   ep   Anxious Night   3.18.58 NBC
Suspicion   ep   The Bull Skinner   4.7.58 NBC
The Millionaire   ep   The Paul Taylor Story   5.21.58
    CBS
Ann Sothern Show   ep   1.19.59 CBS
U.S. Steel Hour   ep   Whisper of Evil   6.3.59 CBS
Bonanza   ep   The Dieschimer Story   10.31.59 NBC
Alcoa Premiere   ep   The Lovers   2.16.60 ABC
Alaskans   ep   The Bride Wore Black   4.10.60 ABC
Road to Reality   sr   10.17.60 ABC
Nurses   ep   The Barbara Bowers Story   10.18.62 CBS
Defenders   ep   Madman   10.20.62, 10.27.62 CBS
Nurses   ep   Two Black Candles   11.22.62 CBS
U.S. Steel Hour   ep   Farewell to Innocence   11.28.62
    CBS

Eleventh Hour   ep   Try to Keep Alive until Next Tues-
   day   4.17.63 NBC
East Side/West Side   ep   The Beatnik and the Politician
   1.20.64 CBS
Look Up and Live   ep   Separates   4.4.65 CBS
For the People   ep   With Intent to Influence   4.11.65
   CBS
Directions '66   ep   The Easter Angel   4.10.66 ABC
Coronet Blue   ep   6.5.67 CBS
N.E.T. Playhouse   ep An Evening's Journey to Conway,
   Mass.   11.3.67 NN
On Stage   ep   This Town Will Never Be the Same   4.
   23.69 NBC

BEAN, ORSON
   Broadway Television Theatre   ep   Three Men on a
      Horse   4.21.52 NN
   Broadway Television Theatre   ep   Nothing But the Truth
      6.9.52 NN
   Studio One   ep   The Square Peg   9.29.52 CBS
   U.S. Steel Hour   ep   Good for You   6.8.54 ABC
   Robert Montgomery Presents   ep   It Happened in Paris
      7.19.54 NBC
   Studio One   ep   Joye   11.22.54 CBS
   U.S. Steel Hour   ep   The Fifth Wheel   10.26.54 ABC
   Best of Broadway   ep   Arsenic and Old Lace   1.5.55
      CBS
   Elgin Hour   ep   San Francisco Fracas   5.17.55 ABC
   Studio One   ep   A Christmas Surprise   12.24.56 CBS
   Kraft Theatre   ep   A Traveler from Brussels   2.27.57
      NBC
   Playhouse 90   ep   Charley's Aunt   3.28.57 CBS
   Phil Silvers Show   ep   Bilko's Insurance Company   5.
      20.58 CBS
   The Millionaire   ep   The Newman Johnson Story   11.12.
      58 CBS
   The Man in the Dog Suit   Sp   1.8.60 NBC
   Twilight Zone   ep   Mr. Bevis   6.3.60 CBS
   Play of the Week   ep   Once Around the Block   11.7.60
      NN
   Miracle on 34th Street   SP   11.27.60 NBC
   June Allyson Show   ep   The Secret Life of James Thur-
      ber   3.20.61 CBS
   Naked City   ep   To Walk like a Lion   2.28.62 ABC
   U.S. Steel Hour   ep   Don't Shake the Family Tree   5.
      15.63 CBS
   N.E.T. Playhouse   ep   The Star Wagon   6.2.67 NN

Ghostbreaker pt 9. 8. 67 NBC
Love American Style ep 2. 13. 70 ABC

BEATTY, WARREN
Kraft Theatre ep The Curly-Headed Kid 6. 26. 57 NBC
Studio One ep The Night America Trembled 9. 9. 57
  CBS
Suspicion ep Heartbeat 11. 11. 57 NBC
Dobie Gillis sr 9. 29. 59 CBS

BEAUMONT, HUGH
Teledrama ep Danger Zone 7. 24. 53 CBS
Fireside Theatre ep The Traitor 9. 1. 53 NBC
Studio 57 ep Trap Mates 10. 5. 54 NN
Four Star Playhouse ep The Adolescent 10. 28. 54 CBS
Lineup ep Cop Shooting Story 12. 10. 54 CBS
Playhouse ep Stake My Life 5. 8. 55 ABC
Four Star Playhouse ep The Frightened Woman 6. 23.
  55 CBS
Cavalcade Theatre ep A Time for Courage 9. 13. 55
  ABC
Four Star Playhouse ep The Firing Squad 10. 6. 55
  CBS
Crossroads ep With All My Love 10. 28. 55 ABC
Medic ep The World So High 12. 26. 55 NBC
Cavalcade Theatre ep The Boy Who Walked to Amer-
  ica 1. 3. 56 ABC
Ford Theatre ep The Silent Stranger 2. 9. 56 NBC
Four Star Playhouse ep Command 2. 23. 56 CBS
Schlitz Playhouse of Stars ep Web of Circumstance
  3. 9. 56 CBS
Science Fiction Theatre ep Conversation with an Ape
  3. 9. 56 NBC
Loretta Young Show ep But for God's Grace 4. 1. 56
  NBC
Loretta Young Show ep The Refinement of Ab 5. 13.
  56 NBC
Loretta Young Show ep The Bronte Story 6. 10. 56
  NBC
Loretta Young Show ep Take Care of My Child 11. 4.
  56 NBC
Loretta Young Show ep The Girl Who Knew 6. 16. 57
  NBC
Meet McGraw ep Border City 7. 23. 57 NBC
Leave It to Beaver sr 10. 4. 57 CBS
Leave It to Beaver sr ret 9. 58 ABC
Leave It to Beaver sr ret 9. 59 ABC

Leave it to Beaver   sr ret   9. 60 ABC
Leave it to Beaver   sr ret   9. 61 ABC
Leave it to Beaver   sr ret   9. 62 ABC
Wagon Train   ep   2. 24. 64 ABC
Petticoat Junction   ep   4. 19. 66 CBS
Petticoat Junction   ep   10. 28. 67, 11. 4. 67 CBS
Virginian   ep   1. 17. 68 NBC
Mannix   ep   10. 19. 68 CBS
Virginian   ep   12. 11. 68 NBC
Mannix   ep   War of Nerves   3. 14. 70 CBS
Most Deadly Game   ep   The Classic Burial Position 1.
    2. 71 ABC

BEAVERS, LOUISE
Beulah   sr   4. 29. 52 ABC
Beulah   sr ret   9. 2. 52 ABC
Star Stage   ep   Cleopatra Collins   3. 9. 56 NBC
Playhouse 90   ep   The Hostess with the Mostess   3. 21.
    57 CBS
World of Disney   sr   The Swamp Fox   10. 23. 59 ABC

BECKETT, SCOTTY
Armstrong Circle Theatre   ep   Before Breakfast   1. 20.
    53 NBC
Drama   ep   Backbone of America   12. 29. 53 NBC
Rocky Jones, Space Ranger   sr   2. 27. 54 NBC
Telephone Time   ep   Away Boarders   4. 29. 56 CBS
George Sanders Theatre   ep   The Night I Died   8. 31. 57
    NBC

BEDELIA, BONNIE
CBS Playhouse   ep   My Father and My Mother   2. 13. 68
    CBS
Judd for the Defense   ep   The Death Farm   11. 1. 68
    ABC
High Chaparral   ep   11. 15. 68 NBC
Then Came Bronson   tf   3. 24. 69 NBC
Bonanza   ep   4. 6. 69 NBC
Bonanza   ep   9. 12. 72 NBC
Sandcastles   tf   10. 17. 72 CBS

BEGLEY, ED
Lights Out   ep   The Posthumous Dead   10. 2. 50 NBC
Armstrong Circle Theatre   ep   Super Highway   2. 6. 51
    NBC
Drama   ep   The Early Bird   12. 23. 52 CBS
Armstrong Circle Theatre   ep   Before Breakfast 1. 20. 53
    NBC

Goodyear Playhouse ep Ernie Barger Is Fifty 8.9.53 NBC

Armstrong Circle Theatre ep Tour of Duty 10.6.53 NBC

Motorola TV Hour ep The Muldoon Matter 2.23.54 ABC

Robert Montgomery Presents ep Big Boy 4.19.54 NBC

Armstrong Circle Theatre ep Gang-Up 4.27.54 ABC

Armstrong Circle Theatre ep The Use of Dignity 5. 25.54 ABC

Treasury Men in Action ep The Case of the Broken Bond 12.30.54 ABC

Kraft Theatre ep Patterns 1.12.55 NBC

Kraft Theatre ep Boys Will Be Boys 1.26.55 NBC

Kraft Theatre ep (restaged) Patterns 2.9.55 NBC

Pond's Theatre ep A Second Chance 2.24.55 ABC

Goodyear Playhouse ep The Takers 8.14.55 NN

Justice ep Positive Identification 10.2.55 NBC

Philco Playhouse ep This Land Is Mine 1.15.56 NBC

Alcoa Hour ep Man on Fire 3.4.56 NBC

Alcoa Hour ep The Big Vote 8.19.56 NBC

U.S. Steel Hour ep Windfall 9.11.57 CBS

Kraft Theatre ep Smart Boy 10.9.57 NBC

U.S. Steel Hour ep Walk with a Stranger 2.26.58 CBS

Kraft Theatre ep Look What's Going On 3.19.58 NBC

Climax ep The Big Success 5.8.58 CBS

U.S. Steel Hour ep The Enemies 12.3.58 CBS

Desilu Playhouse ep City in Bondage 5.13.60 CBS

U.S. Steel Hour ep The Great Gold Mountain 6.29.60 CBS

Cain's Hundred ep Blue Water, White Beach 10.3.61

Target Corruptors ep Bite of a Tiger 11.3.61 ABC

My Three Sons ep Romance of the Silver Pines 1.11. 62 ABC

New Breed ep Policemen Die Alone 1.30.62 ABC

Ben Casey ep Victory Wears a Cruel Smile 2.12.62 ABC

Cain's Hundred ep Blood Money 2.13.62 NBC

Empire ep Ballard Number One 10.2.62 NBC

Defenders ep The Seven Ghosts of Simon Gray 10.6. 62 CBS

Naked City ep Make It Fifty Dollars and Add Love to Nona 11.4.62 ABC

Dick Powell Theatre ep The Court-Martial of Captain Wycliff 12.11.62 NBC

Going My Way ep My Son, the Social Worker 1.9.63
    ABC
Route 66 ep In the Closing of a Trunk 3.8.63 CBS
Ben Casey ep Hang No Hats on Dreams 5.13.63 ABC
Dupont Show of the Month ep The Last Hangman 9.15.
    63 NBC
Burke's Law ep Who Killed Julian Buck 10.18.63 ABC
Wagon Train ep The Sam Spicer Story 10.28.63 ABC
Virginian ep The Invaders 1.1.64 NBC
Wagon Train ep 5.11.64 ABC
Fugitive ep Man in a Chariot 9.15.64 ABC
Burke's Law ep 10.21.64 ABC
Alfred Hitchcock Theatre ep Triumph 12.14.64 NBC
Burke's Law ep Who Killed Supersleuth 12.16.64 ABC
Dr. Kildare ep Make Way for Tomorrow 2.18.65
    NBC
Fugitive ep Runner in the Dark 3.30.65 ABC
Burke's Law ep 4.28.65 ABC
Bonanza ep The Other Son 10.3.65 NBC
Gunsmoke ep 10.16.65 CBS
Hallmark Hall of Fame ep Inherit the Wind 11.18.65
    NBC
FBI ep The Sacrifice 1.16.66 ABC
Vriginian ep Chaff in the Wind 1.26.66 NBC
Slattery's People ep Is Democracy Too Expensive 2.
    25.66 CBS
Bob Hope Chrysler Theatre ep In Pursuit of Excel-
    lence 6.22.66 NBC
Bonanza ep A Time to Step Down 9.25.66 NBC
Invaders ep 3.28.67 ABC
The Lucy Show ep 9.26.66 CBS
Invaders ep Labyrinth 11.21.67 ABC
Gunsmoke ep 2.26.68 CBS
High Chaparral ep 10.4.68 NBC
Name of the Game ep Lola in Lipstick 11.8.68 NBC
World of Disney ep Secrets of the Pirate's Inn 11.23.
    69, 11.30.69 NBC
The Silent Gun tf 12.16.69 ABC
Hallmark Hall of Fame ep Neither Are We Enemies 3.13.
    70 NBC
Name of the Game ep 4.10.70 NBC

BELAFONTE, HARRY
    Three for Tonight Sp 6.22.55 CBS
    G.E. Theatre ep Winner by Decision 11.6.55 CBS

BEL GEDDES, BARBARA

Robert Montgomery Presents ep Rebecca 5.22.50
NBC
Robert Montgomery Presents ep The Philadelphia Story
12.4.50 NBC
Airflyte Theatre ep Molly Morgan 12.21.50 CBS
TV Soundstage ep Isn't Everything 4.9.54 NBC
On Trial ep The Gentle Voice of Murder 5.24.57
NBC
Schlitz Playhouse of Stars ep Fifty Beautiful Girls
6.21.57 CBS
Studio One ep The Morning Face 10.7.57 CBS
Schlitz Playhouse of Stars ep French Provincial 12.
13.57 CBS
Alfred Hitchcock Presents ep Fog Horn 3.16.58 CBS
Playhouse 90 ep Rumors of Evening 4.10.58 CBS
Alfred Hitchcock Presents ep Lamb to the Slaughter
4.13.58 CBS
Studio One ep The Desperate Age 4.21.58 CBS
U.S. Steel Hour ep Mid-Summer 10.8.58 CBS
Dupont Show of the Month ep The Hasty Heart 12.18.
58 CBS
Alfred Hitchcock Presents ep The Morning of the Bride
2.15.59 CBS
Riverboat ep Payment in Full 9.13.59 NBC
Great Mysteries ep The Burning Court 4.24.60 NBC
Alfred Hitchcock Presents ep Sybilla 12.6.60 NBC
Dr. Kildare ep Miracle for Margaret 2.25.66 NBC
CBS Playhouse ep Secrets 5.15.68 CBS
Journey to the Unknown ep The Madison Equation 1.
30.69 ABC
Daniel Boone ep 4.17.69 NBC

BELLAMY, RALPH

Man Against Crime sr 1949-1950 CBS
Man Against Crime sr ret 8.10.51 CBS
Man Against Crime sr ret 10.15.52 CBS
Man Against Crime sr ret fall, 1953 CBS
U.S. Steel Hour ep Fearful Decision 6.22.54 ABC
Elgin Hour ep High Man 11.2.54 ABC
Studio One ep Like Father, Like Son 9.19.55 CBS
G.E. Theatre ep Outpost of Home 10.23.55 CBS
Philco Playhouse ep The Mechanical Heart 11.6.55
NBC
Hallmark Hall of Fame ep The Devil's Disciple 11.
20.55 NBC
Star Stage ep Articles of War 1.20.56 NBC

Philco Playhouse   ep   The Starlet   1.29.56 NBC
U.S. Steel Hour   ep   The Candidate   3.14.56 CBS
Ford Theatre   ep   Alibi   4.26.56 NBC
Climax   ep   Sit Down with Death   4.26.56 CBS
Playwrights '56   ep   Honor   6.19.56 NBC
Goodyear Playhouse   ep   The Film Maker   7.1.56 NBC
Climax   ep   The Fog   9.27.56 CBS
Playhouse 90   ep   Heritage of Anger   11.15.56 CBS
Ford Theatre   ep   Model Wife   12.26.56 ABC
Zane Grey Theatre   ep   Stars over Texas   12.28.56
   CBS
Schlitz Playhouse of Stars   ep   The Big Playoff   12.28.
   56 CBS
Studio One   ep   2.25.57 CBS
Kaiser Aluminum Hour   ep   Hollywood Award Winner
   3.26.57 NBC
Alcoa Hour   ep   Nothing to Lose   4.14.57 NBC
Climax   ep   Reunion on Broadway   6.6.57 CBS
Kraft Theatre   ep   Triumph   9.4.57 NBC
U.S. Steel Hour   ep   The Locked Door   11.6.57 CBS
Suspicion   ep   The Sparkle of Diamonds   11.18.57 NBC
Our American Heritage   ep   Not without Honor   10.21.
   60 NBC
Barbara Stanwyck Theatre   ep   The Miraculous Journey
   of Tadpole Chan   11.14.60 NBC
June Allyson Show   ep   The Haven   3.6.61 CBS
Dinah Shore Show   ep   Brief Encounter   3.26.61 NBC
Checkmate   ep   Portrait of a Man Running   10.4.61
   CBS
Rawhide   ep   Judgment at Hondo Seco   10.20.61 CBS
Westinghouse Presents   ep   The Dispossessed   10.24.
   61 CBS
Golden Showcase   ep   Saturday's Children   2.25.62 CBS
Westinghouse Presents   ep   The First Day   6.20.62
   CBS
Alcoa Premiere   ep   Impact of an Execution   1.3.63
   ABC
Alcoa Premiere   ep   Chain Reaction   2.21.63 ABC
Eleventh Hour   sr   10.2.63 NBC
Dr. Kildare   ep   Four Feet in the Morning   11.21.63
   NBC
Death Valley Days   ep   The Vintage Years   11.23.63
   ABC
Rawhide   ep   The Pursuit   11.9.65 CBS
Bob Hope Chrysler Theatre   ep   A Time to Love 1.11.
   67 NBC
12 O'Clock High   ep   1.13.67 ABC

Wings of Fire tf 2.14.67 NBC
Run for Your Life ep Trip to the Far Side 10.11.67
NBC
Gunsmoke ep 12.4.67 CBS
CBS Playhouse ep My Father and My Mother 2.13.68
CBS
Virginian ep 9.18.68 NBC
FBI ep The Butcher 12.8.68 ABC
Survivors sr 9.29.69 ABC
The Immortal tf 9.30.69 ABC
Most Deadly Game sr 10.10.70 ABC
Something Evil tf 1.21.72 CBS

BENADERET, BEA
George Burns-Gracie Allen Show sr 10.12.50 CBS
George Burns-Gracie Allen Show sr ret fall, 1951 CBS
George Burns-Gracie Allen Show sr ret fall, 1952 CBS
George Burns-Gracie Allen Show sr ret fall, 1953 CBS
George Burns-Gracie Allen Show sr ret 10.4.54 CBS
The Lineup ep The Falling out of Thieves 4.15.55
CBS
George Burns-Gracie Allen Show sr ret 10.3.55 CBS
Screen Directors Playhouse ep A Midsummer Day-
dream 10.19.55 NBC
Bob Cummings Show ep Scramble for Grandpa 5.24.
56 CBS
George Burns-Gracie Allen Show sr ret fall, 1956 CBS
Bob Cummings Show ep 3.21.57 CBS
George Burns-Gracie Allen Show sr ret fall, 1957 CBS
George Burns Show sr 10.21.58 NBC
Restless Gun ep Mme. Brimstone 5.4.59 NBC
77 Sunset Strip ep Ten Cents a Dance 1.29.60 ABC
Peter Loves Mary sr 10.12.60 NBC
Flintstones sr (voice only) 9.60 ABC
Chevy Show ep The Happiest Day 4.23.61 NBC
Dobie Gillis ep Spaceville 4.25.61 CBS
Flintstones sr ret (voice only) 9.61 ABC
New Breed ep A Motive Named Walter 5.8.62 ABC
Flintstones sr ret (voice only) 9.62 ABC
Beverly Hillbillies sr 9.26.62 CBS
Flintstones sr ret (voice only) 9.63 ABC
Petticoat Junction sr 9.24.63 CBS
Flintstones sr ret (voice only) 9.17.64 ABC
Petticoat Junction sr ret 9.22.64 CBS
Flintstones sr ret (voice only) 9.17.65 ABC
Petticoat Junttion sr ret 9.14.65 CBS
Petticoat Junction sr ret 9.13.66 CBS

Petticoat Junction sr ret 9. 9. 67 CBS
Petticoat Junction sr ret 9. 29. 68 CBS

BEN AMI, JACOB
   Studio One ep Rudy 8. 19. 57 CBS
   Look Up and Live ep The Song of Freedom 3. 30. 58
      CBS
   Play of the Week ep The Rope Dancers 3. 14. 60 NN

BENDIX, WILLIAM
   Lights Out ep The Hollow Man 9. 29. 52 NBC
   Hollywood Opening Night ep Terrible Tempered Tolli-
      ver 10. 6. 52 NBC
   Life of Riley sr 1. 2. 53 NBC
   Life of Riley sr ret 9. 18. 53 NBC
   Video Theatre ep 6. 3. 54 CBS
   Life of Riley sr ret fall, 1954 NBC
   Ford Theatre ep 10. 21. 54 NBC
   Fireside Theatre ep Sgt. Sullivan Speaking 1. 11. 55
      NBC
   Fireside Theatre ep Mr. Onion 2. 8. 55 NBC
   Life of Riley sr ret 9. 16. 55 NBC
   Goodyear Playhouse ep Footlight Frenzy 4. 8. 56 NBC
   Life of Riley sr ret 9. 14. 56 NBC
   Robert Montgomery Presents ep The Misfortunes of
      Mr. Minihan 11. 19. 56 NBC
   20th Century-Fox Hour ep Threat to a Happy Ending
      5. 29. 57 CBS
   Life of Riley sr ret fall, 1957 NBC
   Jane Wyman Theatre ep Prime Suspect 2. 27. 58 NBC
   Decision ep High Air 9. 7. 58 NBC
   Wagon Train ep Around the Horn 10. 1. 58 NBC
   Desilu Playhouse ep Time Element 11. 24. 58 CBS
   Playhouse 90 ep A Quiet Game of Cards 1. 29. 59 CBS
   Schlitz Playhouse of Stars ep Ivy League 3. 13. 59
      CBS
   Ransom of Red Chief Sp 8. 16. 59 NBC
   Riverboat ep The Barrier 9. 20. 59 NBC
   Untouchables ep The Tri-State Gang 12. 10. 59 ABC
   Overland Trail sr 2. 7. 60 NBC
   G. E. Theatre ep We're Holding our Son 12. 31. 61
      CBS
   Follow the Sun ep Sgt. Kochak Fades Away 1. 28. 62
      ABC
   Dick Powell Theatre ep 330 Independence S. W. 3. 20.
      62 NBC
   Dick Powell Theatre ep Last of the Private Eyes

4. 30. 63 NBC
Burke's Law ep 9. 30. 64 ABC

BENJAMIN, RICHARD
My Lucky Penny pt 8. 8. 66 CBS
He and She sr 9. 6. 67 CBS

BENNETT, BRUCE
Ford Theatre ep So Many Things Happen 12. 18. 52 NBC
A Letter to Loretta ep Prisoner at One O'Clock 10. 4. 53 NBC
Jewelers Showcase ep The Hand of St. Pierre 10. 27. 53 NN
Fireside Theatre ep Man of the Comstock 11. 3. 53 NBC
Fireside Theatre ep The Uncrossed River 1. 26. 54 NBC
Ford Theatre ep For the Love of Kitty 2. 11. 54 NBC
Cavalcade of Stars ep Moonlight Witness 11. 2. 54 ABC
Schlitz Playhouse of Stars ep Mystery of Murder 11. 26. 54 CBS
Science Fiction Theatre ep Beyond 4. 5. 55 NBC
Damon Runyon Theatre ep Pick the Winner 4. 16. 55 CBS
Playhouse ep The Nightingale 6. 25. 55 ABC
Loretta Young Show ep Prisoner at One O'Clock 3. 11. 56 NBC
Crossroads ep False Prophet 6. 29. 56 ABC
Science Fiction Theatre ep Survival in Box Canyon 10. 12. 56 NBC
Playhouse 90 ep Ain't No Time for Glory 6. 20. 57 CBS
West Point ep White Fury 2. 4. 58 ABC
No Warning ep Survivors 5. 18. 58 NBC
Perry Mason ep The Case of the Lucky Loser 9. 27. 58 CBS
77 Sunset Strip ep 12. 26. 58 ABC
Laramie ep Hour after Dawn 3. 15. 60 NBC
Perry Mason ep The Case of the Misguided Missile 5. 6. 61 CBS
Perry Mason ep The Case of the Roving River 12. 30. 61 CBS
Perry Mason ep The Case of the Reckless Rock Hound 11. 26. 64 CBS
Kraft Suspense Theatre ep The Last Clear Chance

3.11.65 NBC
Branded   ep   I Killed Jason McCord   10.3.65 NBC
Perry Mason   ep   The Case of the Carefree Coronary
   10.17.65 CBS
Virginian   ep   1.8.67 NBC
O'Hara, U.S. Treasury   ep   10.22.71 CBS

BENNETT, CONSTANCE
   Faith Baldwin Show   ep   Love Letters   7.14.51 ABC
   Robert Montgomery Presents   ep   Sinora Isobel   10.6.
   52 NBC
   Broadway Television Theatre   ep   Twentieth Century
   10.12.53 NN
   Robert Montgomery Presents   ep   Onions in the Stew
   9.17.56 NBC
   Ann Sothern Show   ep   2.23.61 CBS
   The Reporter   ep   The Man Behind the Badge   11.6.64
   CBS

BENNETT, HYWEL
   N.E.T. Playhouse   ep   The Traveller   6.21.68 NN

BENNETT, JOAN
   Airflyte Theatre   ep   Peggy   2.8.51 CBS
   Somerset Maugham Theatre   ep   The Dream   2.14.51.
   CBS
   Danger   ep   A Clear Case of Suicide   5.22.51 CBS
   G.G. Theatre   ep   You Are Young only Once   6.6.54
   CBS
   Best of Broadway   ep   The Man Who Came to Dinner
   10.13.54 CBS
   Ford Theatre   ep   Letters Marked Personal   1.27.55
   NBC
   Shower of Stars   ep   The Dark Fleece   6.16.55 CBS
   Ford Theatre   ep   Dear Diane   1.12.56 NBC
   Playhouse 90   ep   The Thundering Wave   12.12.57 NBC
   Dupont Show of the Month   ep   Junior Miss   12.20.57
   CBS
   Pursuit   ep   Epitaph for a Golden Girl   1.14.59 CBS
   Too Young to Go Steady   sr   5.14.59 NBC
   Mr. Broadway   ep   Don't Mention My Name in Sheboy-
   gan   10.7.64 CBS
   Burke's Law   ep   3.3.65 ABC
   Dark Shadows   sr   1968 ABC
   Governor and J. J.   ep   11.11.70, 11.18.70 CBS

Love American Style   ep   2.12.71 ABC
Gidget Gets Married   tf   1.4.72 ABC
The Eyes of Charles Sand   tf   2.29.72 ABC

BENNY, JACK
Private Secretary   ep   3.1.53 CBS
G.E. Theatre   ep   The Face Is Familiar   11.21.54
   CBS
Four Star Playhouse   ep   The House Always Wins   4.
   28.55 CBS
G.E. Theatre   ep   The Honest Man   2.19.56 CBS
G.E. Theatre   ep   The Fenton Touch   3.3.57 CBS
Danny Thomas Show   ep   10.6.58   CBS
Jack Benny Show   ep   Autolight   1.11.59 CBS
Danny Thomas Show   ep   1.11.60 CBS
The Slowest Gun in the West   Sp   5.7.60 CBS
Checkmate   ep   A Funny Thing Happened to Me on the
   Way to the Game   1.3.62 CBS
Jack Benny Show   ep   The Mikado   3.26.63 CBS
Here's Lucy   ep   9.30.68 CBS
Here's Lucy   ep   11.23.70 CBS

BERG, GERTRUDE
The Goldbergs   sr   1949-1950 CBS
The Goldbergs   sr ret   9.25.50 CBS
The Goldbergs   sr ret   7.3.53 NBC
U.S. Steel Hour   ep   Morning Star   3.2.54 ABC
The Goldbergs   sr ret   4.13.54 NN
Elgin Hour   ep   Hearts and Hollywood   11.30.54 ABC
U.S. Steel Hour   ep   Six O'Clock Call   2.1.55 ABC
Elgin Hour   ep   Mind over Mama   5.31.55 ABC
The Goldbergs   sr ret   9.22.55 NN
Alcoa Hour   ep   Paris and Mrs. Perlman   4.29.56 NBC
Matinee Theatre   ep   The Golden Door   6.4.57 NBC
U.S. Steel Hour   ep   Trouble in Law   4.8.59 CBS
Play of the Week   ep   The World of Sholom Aleichem
   12.14.59 NN
Mrs. G. Goes to College   sr   10.4.61 CBS
Hennesey   ep   Aunt Sarah   10.30.61 CBS

BERGEN, CANDICE
Coronet Blue   ep   The Rebel   6.19.67 CBS

BERGEN, EDGAR
Kraft Theatre   ep   A Connecticut Yankee in King Ar-
   thur's Court   7.8.54 ABC
Shower of Stars   ep   Lend an Ear   10.28.54 CBS
Five Fingers   ep   Dossier   10.10.59 NBC

June Allyson Show ep Moment of Fear 1.25.60 CBS
Dick Powell Theatre ep Who Killed Julie Greer?
  9.26.61 NBC
Dick Powell Theatre ep A Time to Die 1.9.62 NBC
Bachelor Father ep A Visit to the Bergens 3.27.62
  ABC
Dick Powell Theatre ep Special Assignment 9.25.62
  NBC
Burke's Law ep Who Killed Victor Barrows 1.17.64
  ABC
The Greatest Show on Earth ep There Are No Prob-
  lems, only Opportunities 4.21.64 ABC
Burke's Law ep 10.28.64 ABC
The Hanged Man tf 11.18.64 NBC
Burke's Law ep 2.3.65 ABC
The Homecoming Sp 12.19.71 CBS
My Sister Hank pt 3.31.72 ABC

BERGEN, POLLY
Schlitz Playhouse of Stars ep The Haunted Heart 3.7.
  52 CBS
Schlitz Playhouse of Stars ep Autumn in New York 5.
  16.52 CBS
Playhouse sh 10.3.54 ABC
Studio One ep Fatal in My Fashion 10.25.54 CBS
Elgin Hour ep Falling Star 12.28.54 ABC
Appointment with Adventure ep Rendezvous in Paris
  5.1.55 CBS
Elgin Hour ep San Francisco Fracas 5.17.55 ABC
G.E. Theatre ep Letter from the Queen 3.4.56 CBS
Star Stage ep Foundation 5.25.56 NBC
Playhouse 90 ep Helen Morgan 4.16.57 CBS
Lux Playhouse ep The Best House in the Valley 10.
  3.58 CBS
U.S. Steel Hour ep The Great Gold Mountain 6.29.60
  CBS
Alfred Hitchcock Presents ep You Can't Trust a Man
  5.9.61 NBC
Wagon Train ep The Kitty Allbright Story 10.4.61
  NBC
Dick Powell Theatre ep Tissue of Hate 2.26.63 NBC
Dr. Kildare ep The Dark Side of the Mirror 3.28.63
  NBC
Bob Hope Chrysler Theatre ep The Loving Cup 1.29.
  65 NBC

BERGER, SENTA
   World of Disney   ep   The Waltz King   10. 27. 63, 11. 3.
      63 NBC
   Bob Hope Chrysler Theatre   ep   White Snow, Red Ice
      3. 13. 64 NBC
   See How They Run   tf   10. 7. 64 NBC
   The Man from U. N. C. L. E.   ep   The Double Affair 11.
      17. 64 NBC
   The Poppy Is Also a Flower   tf   4. 22. 66 ABC
   It Takes a Thief   ep   1. 9. 68 ABC
   Name of the Game   ep   Collector's Edition   10. 11. 68
      NBC
   Istanbul Express   tf   10. 22. 68 NBC
   It Takes a Thief   ep   Flowers for Alexander   10. 23. 69
      ABC

BERGERAC, JACQUES
   Alfred Hitchcock Presents   ep   Safe Conduct   2. 19. 56
      CBS
   Alfred Hitchcock Presents   ep   The Legacy   5. 27. 56
      CBS
   Playhouse 90   ep   Made in Heaven   12. 6. 56 CBS
   Climax   ep   The Long Count   2. 21. 57 CBS
   G. E. Theatre   ep   I Will Not Die   4. 28. 57 CBS
   Alfred Hitchcock Presents   ep   Return of the Hero   3.
      2. 58 CBS
   Matinee Theatre   ep   The Vagabond   3. 27. 58 NBC
   Studio One   ep   Mrs. 'arris Goes to Paris   4. 14. 58
      CBS
   Gale Storm Show   ep   Heaven Scent   10. 25. 58 CBS
   David Niven Theatre   ep   The Lady from Winnetka   5.
      26. 59 NBC
   77 Sunset Strip   ep   Secret Island   12. 4. 59 ABC
   G. E. Theatre   ep   The Free Wheelers   2. 18. 62 CBS
   Perry Mason   ep   The Case of the Fifty Millionth
      Frenchman   2. 20. 64 CBS
   Run for Your Life   ep   The Cold, Cold War of Paul
      Bryan   9. 13. 65 NBC
   Bob Hope Chrysler Theatre   ep   Mr. Governess 11. 10.
      65 NBC
   Batman   ep   2. 23. 67 ABC
   Daniel Boone   ep   11. 16. 67 NBC
   The Lucy Show   ep   12. 18. 67 CBS
   Get Smart   ep   2. 17. 68 NBC
   Run for Your Life   ep   3. 13. 68 NBC
   Batman   ep   3. 14. 68 ABC

BERGHOFF, HERBERT
The Trap   ep   Stan, the Killer   5.20.50 CBS
Suspense   ep   The Valley of the Kings   10.20.53 NBC
Producers Showcase   ep   Reunion in Vienna   4.4.55
    NBC
Studio One   ep   The Judge and His Hangman   11.14.55
    CBS
Kraft Theatre   ep   Once a Genius   11.30.55 NBC
Desilu Playhouse   ep   Chez Rouge   2.16.59 CBS
Playhouse 90   ep   For Whom the Bells Toll   3.12.59,
    3.19.59 CBS

BERGMAN, INGRID
Ford Star Time   ep   The Turn of the Screw   10.20.59
    NBC
24 Hours in a Woman's Life   Sp   3.20.61 CBS
Hedda Gabler   Sp   9.20.63 CBS
ABC Stage 67   ep   The Human Voice   5.4.67 ABC

BERLE, MILTON
Kraft Theatre   ep   Material Witness   2.19.58 NBC
Lucille Ball-Desi Arnaz Hour   ep   Milton Berle Hides
    out at the Ricardos   9.25.59 CBS
Danny Thomas Show   ep   12.7.59 CBS
Barbara Stanwyck Theatre   ep   Dear Charlie   12.23.61
    NBC
Dick Powell Theatre   ep   Doyle against the House   10.
    24.61 NBC
Joey Bishop Show   ep   A Show of His Own   5.2.62 NBC
Joey Bishop Show   ep   9.14.63 NBC
Bob Hope Chrysler Theatre   ep   The Candidate   12.6.
    63 NBC
Defenders   ep   Die Laughing   4.11.64 CBS
Kraft Suspense Theatre   ep   That He Should Weep for
    Me   11.5.64 NBC
The Lucy Show   ep   12.6.65 CBS
F Troop   ep   The Great Troop Robbery   10.6.66 ABC
The Lucy Show   ep   9.11.67 CBS
Big Valley   ep   A Flock of Trouble   9.25.67 ABC
I Dream of Jeannie   ep   9.26.67 NBC
Batman   ep   10.26.67 ABC
Batman   ep   1.11.68 ABC
Ironside   ep   I the People   10.31.68 NBC
Seven in Darkness   tf   9.23.69 ABC
Here's Lucy   ep   11.17.69 CBS
Love American Style   ep   11.5.71 ABC
Mod Squad   ep   11.23.71 ABC

Mannix ep 12.29.71 CBS
Evil Roy Slade tf 2.18.72 NBC
McCloud ep Give My Regards to Broadway 2.23.72 NBC
Bold Ones ep A Purge of Madness 12.5.72 ABC

BERNARDI, HERSCHEL
Walter Winchell Show ep Terror 1.3.58 ABC
Suspicion ep Comfort for the Grave 1.27.58 NBC
Court of Last Resort ep The Allen Cutler Case 4.11.58 NBC
Matinee Theatre ep Much Ado about Nothing 5.20.58 NBC
Richard Diamond ep Hit and Run 6.5.58 CBS
Peter Gunn sr 9.22.58 NBC
M Squad ep The Executioner 12.5.58 NBC
Bonanza ep The Smiler 9.24.61 NBC
Dr. Kildare ep Winter Harvest 10.19.61 NBC
Cain's Hundred ep Penitent 10.31.61 NBC
Dr. Kildare ep My Brother, the Doctor 1.4.62 NBC
Untouchables ep Fall Guy 1.11.62 ABC
Checkmate ep The Renaissance of Gussie Hill 1.17.62 CBS
Dick Powell Theatre ep Squadron 1.30.62 NBC
Detectives ep The Con Man 3.16.62 NBC
Route 66 ep Between Hello and Goodbye 5.11.62 CBS
Naked City ep Hold for Gloria Christmas 9.19.62 ABC
Untouchables ep Bird in the Hand 10.30.62 ABC
Sam Benedict ep Twenty Aching Years 10.20.62 NBC
Naked City ep Five Cans for Winter 10.24.62 NBC
Eleventh Hour ep Like a Diamond in the Sky 2.13.63 NBC
Dick Powell Theatre ep The Last of the Big Spenders 4.16.63 NBC
Mr. Novak ep I Don't Even Live Here 10.8.63 NBC
Defenders ep Claire Cheval Died in Boston 11.23.63 CBS
Eleventh Hour ep There Should Be an Outfit Called Families Anonymous 12.11.63 NBC
Route 66 ep Child of a Night 1.3.64 CBS
Grindl ep The Lucky Piece 1.5.64 NBC
Burke's Law ep 2.28.64 ABC
Kraft Suspense Theatre ep Their Own Executioner 4.23.64 NBC
Defenders ep The Sixth Alarm 5.23.64 CBS
Profiles in Courage ep 3.21.65 NBC

Doctors/Nurses   ep   The Witness   4.27.65 CBS
Honey West   ep   9.25.65 CBS
Fugitive   ep   Landscape with Running Figures   11.16.
   65 ABC
A Hatful of Rain   Sp   3.3.68 ABC
Arnie   sr   9.19.70 CBS
But I Don't Want to Get Married   tf   10.6.70 ABC
Arnie   sr ret   9.13.71 CBS
No Place to Run   tf   9.19.72 ABC
Sandcastles   tf   10.17.72 CBS

BESSELL, TED
   It's a Man's World   sr   9.17.62 NBC
   Lieutenant   ep   Alert   12.14.63 NBC
   Great Adventure   ep   Rodger Young   1.24.64
   The Greatest Show on Earth   ep   You're All Right Ivy
      4.28.64 ABC
   Ben Casey   ep   August Is the Month before Christmas
      9.14.64 ABC
   Bill Dana Show   ep   1.3.65 NBC
   That Girl   sr   9.7.67 ABC
   That Girl   sr ret   9.26.68 ABC
   That Girl   sr ret   9.18.69 ABC
   Love American Style   ep   11.17.69 ABC
   That Girl   sr ret   9.25.70 ABC
   Two on a Bench   tf   11.2.71 ABC
   Marcus Welby, M.D.   ep   Echo from Another World
      11.9.71 ABC
   Me and the Chimp   ep   Romeo and Juliet   2.3.72 CBS
   Your Money or Your Wife   tf   12.19.72 CBS

BEST, EDNA
   Pulitzer Prize Playhouse   ep   The Pen   6.22.51 ABC
   Celanese Theatre   ep   Old Acquaintance   11.14.51 ABC
   Philco Playhouse   ep   Magic Morning   12.28.52 NBC
   Way of the World   ep   1.28.55 NBC
   Robert Montgomery Presents   ep   P.J. Martin and Son
      4.18.55 NBC
   Way of the World   ep   4.25.55 NBC
   U.S. Steel Hour   ep   Counterfeit   8.31.55 CBS
   Ford Star Jubilee   ep   This Happy Breed   5.5.56 CBS
   Hallmark Hall of Fame   ep   Berkeley Square   2.5.59
      NBC

BETHUME, ZINA
   Kraft Theatre   ep   Three Plays by Tennessee Williams
      4.16.58 NBC

Little Women Sp 10.16.58 CBS
U.S. Steel Hour ep Call It a Day 5.20.59 CBS
Sunday Showcase ep People Kill People 9.20.59 NBC
Route 66 ep The Swan Bed 10.21.60 CBS
U.S. Steel Hour ep Famous 5.31.61 CBS
Cain's Hundred ep The Swinger 4.3.62 NBC
Route 66 ep Kiss the Maiden All Forlorn 4.13.62
  CBS
Nurses sr 9.27.62 CBS
Nurses sr ret 9.26.63 CBS
Nurses sr ret 9.22.64 CBS
Invaders ep The Prophet 11.14.67 ABC
Love of Life sr 1970 CBS

BETTGER, LYLE
  TV Reader's Digest ep Return from Oblivion 2.20.56
    ABC
  Schlitz Playhouse of Stars ep Showdown at Painted
    Rock 3.2.56 CBS
  Ford Theatre ep Appointment with Destiny 5.5.55
    NBC
  Warner Bros. Presents ep Explosion 3.27.56 ABC
  Schlitz Playhouse of Stars ep Step Right up and Die
    4.27.56 CBS
  20th Century-Fox Hour ep End of a Gun 1.9.57 CBS
  Ford Playhouse ep House of Glass 3.27.57 ABC
  Court of Last Resort sr 10.4.57 NBC
  Tales of Wells Fargo ep John Wesley Hardin 9.30.57
    NBC
  Cimarron Strip ep 2.21.67 CBS
  Wagon Train ep The Sally Potter Story 4.9.58 NBC
  Zane Grey Theatre ep Threat of Violence 5.23.58
    CBS
  Tales of Wells Fargo ep The Gunfighter 11.17.58 NBC
  Pursuit ep Last Night in August 12.17.58 CBS
  Plainsman ep Full Circle 1.8.59 NBC
  Zane Grey Theatre ep The Law and the Gun 6.4.59
    CBS
  Grand Jury sr 10.6.59 CBS
  Laramie ep Night of the Quiet Man 12.22.59 NBC
  June Allyson Show ep Moment of Fear 1.25.60 CBS
  Laramie ep The Lawless Seven 12.26.61 NBC
  Rifleman ep Skull 1.1.62 ABC
  Bonanza ep The Guilty 2.25.62 NBC
  Laramie ep Beyond Justice 11.27.62 NBC
  Grindl ep Grindl, Femme Fatale 10.20.63 NBC
  Kraft Suspense Theatre ep A Truce to Terror 1.9.64
    NBC

Death Valley Days ep Graydon's Charge 1.11.64 ABC
Rawhide ep Incident of the Dowry Dundee 1.23.64
    CBS
Gunsmoke ep 2.29.64 CBS
Combat ep A Rare Vintage 12.8.64 ABC
Blue Light ep Traitor's Blood 2.9.66 ABC
Bonanza ep Something Hurt, Something Wild 9.11.66
    NBC
Time Tunnel ep Invasion 12.23.66 ABC
Daniel Boone ep 1.16.69 NBC
Hawaii Five-O ep 11.26.69 CBS
Men from Shiloh ep Nightmare at New Life 11.16.70
    NBC
O'Hara, U.S. Treasury ep 1.14.72 CBS

BETTIS, VALERIE
Studio One ep Room Upstairs 5.22.50 CBS
Philco Playhouse ep Kitty Doone 2.11.51 NBC
Philco Playhouse ep Come Alive 8.19.51 NBC
Philco Playhouse ep Wings on My Feet 2.22.53 NBC
Producers Showcase ep The Women 2.7.55 NBC
Elgin Hour ep Black Eagle Pass 4.5.55 ABC
Playwrights '56 ep The Sound and the Fury 12.6.55
    NBC
Studio One ep The Drop of a Hat 5.7.56 CBS
Directions '61 ep The Rag Tent 12.25.60 ABC
Naked City ep To Dream without Sleep 5.24.61 ABC

BETZ, CARL
Kraft Theatre ep Party for Jonathan 9.8.54 NBC
Robert Montgomery Presents ep Two Wise Women
    10.4.54 NBC
Appointment with Adventure ep Suburban Terror 1.15.
    56 CBS
Crusader ep The Boy on the Brink 12.14.56 CBS
Gunsmoke ep 2.9.57 CBS
The Millionaire ep The Story of Rose Russell 3.27.
    57 CBS
Alfred Hitchcock Presents ep The Motive 1.26.58
    CBS
The Millionaire ep The Jack Garrison Story 5.14.58
    CBS
Donna Reed Show sr 9.24.58 ABC
Donna Reed Show sr ret 9.59 ABC
Donna Reed Show sr ret 9.15.60 ABC
Donna Reed Show sr ret 9.61 ABC
Donna Reed Show sr ret 9.20.62 ABC

Donna Reed Show   sr ret   9.19.63 ABC
Donna Reed Show   sr ret   9.17.64 ABC
Donna Reed Show   sr ret   9.16.65 ABC
Judd for the Defense   sr   9.8.67 ABC
Judd for the Defense   sr ret   9.27.68 ABC
FBI   ep   10.5.69 ABC
The Monk   tf   10.21.69 ABC
Love American Style   ep   11.24.69 ABC
Bracken's World   ep   1.9.70 NBC
Mission Impossible   ep   3.8.70 CBS
Medical Center   ep   The V.D. Story   3.25.70 CBS
McCloud   ep   9.16.70 NBC
Ironside   ep   The Lonely Way to Go   10.22.70 NBC
Night Gallery   ep   The Dead Man   12.16.70 NBC
Mod Squad   ep   A Bummer for R.J.   1.19.71 ABC
FBI   ep   Downfall   2.21.71 ABC
In Search of America   tf   3.23.71 ABC
The Deadly Dream   tf   9.25.71 ABC
Mission Impossible   ep   9.16.72 CBS
Bold Ones   ep   10.24.72 ABC
Cannon   ep   12.13.72 CBS
Streets of San Francisco   ep   12.16.72 ABC

BEYMER, RICHARD
Navy Log   ep   The Soapbox Kid   2.27.58 ABC
Jane Wyman Theatre   ep   On the Brink   5.1.58 NBC
World of Disney   ep   Boston Tea Party   11.21.58 ABC
Schlitz Playhouse of Stars   ep   On the Brink   2.27.59
   CBS
Playhouse 90   ep   Dark December   4.30.59 CBS
Virginian   ep   You Take the High Road   2.17.65 NBC
Kraft Suspense Theatre   ep   The Easter Breach   5.13.
   65 NBC
Virginian   ep   Show Me a Hero   11.17.65 NBC
Bob Hope Chrysler Theatre   ep   Guilty or Not Guilty
   3.9.66 NBC
Dr. Kildare   ep   A Strange Sort of Accident   3.29.66
   NBC
Dr. Kildare   ep   New Doctor in Town   4.4.66, 4.5.66
   NBC
The Man from U.N.C.L.E.   ep   The Survival School
   Affair   11.20.67 NBC
Death Valley Days   ep   3.3.68 NN

BIBERMAN, ABNER
Hec Ramsey   ep   10.29.72 NBC

BICKFORD, CHARLES
    Ford Theatre ep Sunk 11.20.52 NBC
    Schlitz Playhouse of Stars ep The Copper Ring 5.8.
      53 CBS
    Schlitz Playhouse of Stars ep The Viking 10.1.54
      CBS
    Ford Theatre ep The Woman at Fog Point 4.14.55
      NBC
    Man Behind the Badge sh/sr 5.55 CBS
    Screen Directors Playhouse ep Lincoln's Doctor's Bag
      12.14.55 NBC
    Playhouse 90 ep Forbidden Area 10.4.56 CBS
    Ford Theatre ep Front Page Father 12.5.56 ABC
    Playhouse 90 ep Sincerely, Willis Wayde 12.13.56
      CBS
    20th Century-Fox Hour ep The Man Who Couldn't Wait
      3.20.57 CBS
    Playhouse 90 ep Clipper Ship 4.4.57 CBS
    Climax ep The High Jungle 7.25.57 CBS
    Wagon Train ep The Ralph Barrister Story 4.16.58
      NBC
    Playhouse 90 ep The Days of Wine and Roses 10.2.58
      CBS
    Playhouse 90 ep Free Week-End 12.4.58 CBS
    Playhouse 90 ep Out of Dust 5.21.59 CBS
    Hallmark Hall of Fame ep Winterset 10.26.59 NBC
    Playhouse 90 ep Tomorrow 3.7.60 CBS
    Hallmark Hall of Fame ep The Cradle Song 4.10.60
      NBC
    Drama ep The Gambler, the Nun and the Radio 5.19.
      60 CBS
    Checkmate ep Target...Tycoon 11.5.60 CBS
    Barbara Stanwyck Theatre ep Ironback's Bride 11.28.
      60 NBC
    Islanders ep The Cold War of Adam Smith 12.4.60
      ABC
    American ep Long Way Back 4.24.61 NBC
    Dr. Kildare ep Winter Harvest 10.19.61 NBC
    Dick Powell Theatre ep The Geetas Box 11.14.61
      NBC
    Theatre '62 ep The Farmer's Daughter 1.14.62 NBC
    Virginian ep The Devil's Children 12.5.62 NBC
    Alcoa Premiere ep Million Dollar Hospital 4.18.63
      ABC
    Dick Powell Theatre ep Old Man and the City 4.23.63
      NBC
    Virginian ep The Devil's Children 5.29.63 NBC

Eleventh Hour   ep   The Silence of Good Men   10.9.63
  NBC
Suspense Theatre   ep   I Christopher Bell   3.25.64 CBS
Virginian   sr   9.14.66 NBC
Virginian   sr ret   9.13.67 NBC

BIKEL, THEODORE
U.S. Steel Hour   ep   Scandal at Peppernut   3.29.55
  ABC
Studio One   ep   Passage of Arms   4.11.55 CBS
Appointment with Adventure   ep   The Fateful Pilgrimage
  4.17.55 CBS
Goodyear Playhouse   ep   Visit to a Small Planet   5.8.
  55 NBC
Elgin Hour   ep   San Francisco Fracas   5.17.55 ABC
Armstrong Circle Theatre   ep   Perilous Night   5.31.55
  NBC
Star Tonight   ep   Foot Falls   7.7.55 ABC
Appointment with Adventure   ep   Return of the Stranger
  7.17.55 CBS
Studio One   ep   Julius Caesar   8.1.55 CBS
Producers Showcase   ep   The King and Mrs. Candle
  8.22.55 NBC
Justice   ep   Track of Fear   12.11.55 NBC
Goodyear Playhouse   ep   A Patch on Faith   1.22.56
  NBC
Studio One   ep   The Power   6.4.56 CBS
Goodyear Playhouse   ep   Sound the Pipes of Pan   6.17.
  56 NBC
U.S. Steel Hour   ep   Hunted   12.5.56 CBS
Kraft Theatre   ep   Six Hours of Terror   1.9.57 NBC
Hallmark Hall of Fame   ep   There Shall Be No Night
  3.17.57 NBC
Climax   ep   The Mad Bomber   4.18.57 CBS
Alfred Hitchcock Presents   ep   The Hands of Mr. Ot-
  termole   5.5.57 CBS
Studio One   ep   Death and Taxes   7.1.57 CBS
Dupont Show of the Month   ep   The Bridge of San Luis
  Rey   1.21.58 CBS
Kraft Theatre   ep   Angry Harvest   4.23.58 NBC
Playhouse 90   ep   Word from a Sealed-Off Box   10.30.
  58 CBS
Hotel de Paree   ep   10.2.59 CBS
Play of the Week   ep   The Dybbuk   10.3.60 NN
Naked City   ep   Murder Is a Face I Know   1.11.61 ABC
Naked City   ep   Portrait of a Painter   1.10.62 ABC
Dick Powell Theatre   ep   The Prison   2.6.62   NBC

Twilight Zone   ep   Four O'Clock   4.6.62 CBS
G.E. Theatre   ep   The Bar Mitzvah of Major Orlovsky
   4.15.62 CBS
Dr. Kildare   ep   The Visitors   10.11.62 NBC
Dick Powell Theatre   ep   Pericles on 31st Street   12.
   4.62 NBC
Route 66   ep   Only by Cunning Glimpses   12.7.62 CBS
Sam Benedict   ep   So Various, So Beautiful   12.15.62
   NBC
Alcoa Premiere   ep   The Potentate   12.20.62 ABC
Dupont Show   ep   Diamond Fever   3.24.63 NBC
East Side/West Side   ep   No Wings at All   10.28.63
   CBS
Bob Hope Chrysler Theatre   ep   Corridor Four Hun-
   dred   12.27.63 NBC
Nurses   ep   The Forever Child   3.19.64 CBS
Combat   sr   9.15.64 ABC
Gunsmoke   ep   2.13.65 CBS
Who Has Seen the Wind?   tf   2.19.65 ABC
Trials of O'Brien   ep   The Trouble with Archie   11.6.
   65 CBS
ABC Stage 67   ep   Noon Wine   11.23.66 ABC
Diary of Anne Frank   Sp   11.26.67 ABC
Hallmark Hall of Fame   ep   St. Joan   12.4.67 NBC
Mission Impossible   ep   11.17.68 CBS
Hawaii Five-O   ep   Sweet Terror   11.5.69 CBS
Ironside   ep   The Summer Soldier   3.4.71 NBC
Killer by Night   tf   1.7.72 CBS
Cannon   ep   Blood on the Vine   1.18.72 ABC

BILL, TONY
Ben Casey   ep   A Boy Is Standing outside the Door   1.
   4.65 ABC
Mr. Novak   ep   An Elephant Is Like a Tree   1.12.65
   NBC
For the People   ep   Dangerous to the Public Peace and
   Safety   3.21.65 CBS
Loner   ep   An Echo of Bugles   9.18.65 CBS
Dr. Kildare   ep   The Bell in the School House Tolls for
   Thee, Kildare   9.27.65, 9.28.65, 10.4.65, 10.5.65,
   10.11.65, 10.12.65, 10.18.65 NBC
Run for Your Life   ep   The Time of the Sharks
Virginian   ep   Chaff in the Wind   1.26.66 NBC
Bonanza   ep   11.20.66 NBC
I Spy   ep   12.21.66 NBC
Road West   ep   1.23.67 NBC
Bob Hope Chrysler Theatre   ep   Dead Wrong   4.5.67
   NBC

The Man from U. N. C. L. E.   ep   The Seven Wonders of
the World Affair   1. 8. 68,   1. 15. 68 NBC
Bracken's World   ep   9. 18. 70 NBC

BILLINGSLEY, BARBARA
Schlitz Playhouse of Stars   ep   The Doctor Goes Home
7. 31. 53 CBS
Four Star Playhouse   ep   Sound Off, My Love   8. 13. 53
CBS
Cavalcade of America   ep   The Stolen General   10. 6. 53
ABC
Schlitz Playhouse of Stars   ep   The Jungle Trap   2. 19.
54 CBS
Fireside Theatre   ep   The Whole Truth   6. 1. 54 NBC
Schlitz Playhouse of Stars   ep   Some Delay at Ft. Bess
9. 3. 54 CBS
Star Theatre   ep   Golden Opportunity   8. 14. 54 CBS
Professional Father   sr   1. 8. 55 CBS
Four Star Playhouse   ep   Breakfast in Bed   1. 20. 55
CBS
Schlitz Playhouse of Stars   ep   Gift of Life   11. 4. 55
CBS
Loretta Young Show   ep   Tightwad Millionaire   2. 19. 56
NBC
Cavalcade Theatre   ep   The Stolen General   4. 24. 56
ABC
The Brothers   sr   10. 4. 56   CBS
Dupont Theatre   ep   Frightened Witness   2. 19. 57 ABC
Panic   ep   The Subway   3. 26. 57 NBC
Mr. Adams and Eve   ep   That Magazine   4. 12. 57 CBS
Leave It to Beaver   sr   10. 4. 57 CBS
Leave It to Beaver   sr ret   9. 58 ABC
Leave It to Beaver   sr ret   9. 59 ABC
Leave It to Beaver   sr ret   9. 60 ABC
Leave It to Beaver   sr ret   9. 61 ABC
Leave It to Beaver   sr ret   9. 62 ABC
FBI   ep   The Fatal Connection   1. 31. 71 ABC

BISHOP, JOEY
Dupont Show of the Month   ep   Heaven Can Wait   11.
16. 60 CBS
Danny Thomas Show   ep   Everything Happens to Me
3. 27. 61 CBS
Joey Bishop Show   sr   9. 20. 61 NBC
Joey Bishop Show   sr ret   9. 15. 62 NBC
Dick Powell Theatre   ep   Thunder in a Forgotten Town
3. 5. 63 NBC

Joey Bishop Show   sr ret   9. 14. 63 NBC
Joey Bishop Show   sr ret   9. 27. 64 CBS

BISHOP, JULIE
My Hero   sr   11. 8. 52 NBC
Fireside Theatre   ep   Juror on Trial   5. 25. 54 NBC
Bob Cummings Show   ep   The Sergeant Wore Skirts
    5. 10. 56 CBS
Warner Bros Presents   ep   Survival   3. 13. 56 ABC

BISHOP, WILLIAM
Schlitz Playhouse of Stars   ep   Drawing Room A   10.
    24. 52 CBS
Easy Chair Theatre   ep   Brown of Calaveras   3. 2. 53
    NN
Fireside Theatre   ep   Unexpected Wife   3. 24. 53 NBC
Fireside Theatre   ep   Mission to Algeria   4. 21. 53
    NBC
Cavalcade of America   ep   Pirate's Choice   5. 27. 53
    ABC
Fireside Theatre   ep   Bless the Man   9. 8. 53 NBC
Ford Theatre   ep   Mantrap   1. 28. 54 NBC
Schlitz Playhouse of Stars   ep   Night Ride to Butte
    2. 26. 54 CBS
Pepsi Cola Playhouse   ep   And the Beasts Were There
    4. 30. 54 ABC
Cavalcade Theatre   ep   Spindletop   5. 11. 54 ABC
Pepsi Cola Playhouse   ep   Grenadine   5. 28. 54 ABC
I Married Joan   ep   Double Wedding   6. 30. 54 NBC
It's a Great Life   sr   9. 7. 54 NBC
Hallmark Hall of Fame   ep   Ethan Allen   4. 3. 55 NBC
Science Fiction Theatre   ep   Hour of Nightmare 7. 1. 55
    NBC
Playhouse 90   ep   The Star-Wagon   1. 24. 57 CBS
20th Century-Fox Hour   ep   The Marriage Broker   6.
    12. 57 CBS
The Millionaire   ep   The Peter Hopper Story   12. 10. 58
    CBS
G. E. Theatre   ep   The Lady's Choice   3. 22. 59 CBS
Rifleman   ep   Outlaw's Inheritance   6. 16. 59 ABC
Riverboat   ep   Payment in Full   9. 13. 59 NBC

BIXBY, BILL
Bachelor Father   ep   The Law and Kelly Gregg   12. 26.
    61 ABC
Checkmate   ep   To the Best of My Knowledge   12. 27.
    61 CBS

Joey Bishop Show   ep   Home Sweet Home   1.10.62 NBC
Andy Griffith Show   ep   1.15.62 CBS
Joey Bishop Show   ep   A Man's Best Friend   2.14.62
    NBC
Alcoa Premiere   ep   The Voice of Charlie Pont   10.25.
    62 ABC
Eleventh Hour   ep   Try to Keep Alive until Next Tues-
    day   4.17.63 NBC
Danny Thomas Show   ep   5.6.63 CBS
Lieutenant   ep   A Million Miles from Clary   9.14.63
    NBC
My Favorite Martian   sr   9.29.63 CBS
My Favorite Martian   sr ret   9.27.64 CBS
My Favorite Martian   sr ret   9.12.65 CBS
Combat   ep   The Losers   9.20.66 ABC
Iron Horse   ep   Appointment with an Epitaph   2.13.67
    ABC
That Girl   ep   10.5.67 ABC
Danny Thomas Show   ep   Two for Penny   3.11.68 NBC
It Takes a Thief   ep   3.26.68 ABC
Ghost and Mrs. Muir   ep   10.12.68 NBC
Ironside   ep   12.12.68 NBC
Courtship of Eddie's Father   sr   9.17.69 ABC
Love American Style   ep   10.20.69 ABC
Ironside   ep   Tom Dayton Is Loose among Us   4.9.70
    NBC
Courtship of Eddie's Father   sr ret   9.23.70 ABC
Love American Style   ep   10.30.70 ABC
Hollywood Television Theatre   ep   Big Fish, Little Fish
    1.5.71 NN
Love American Style   ep   2.12.71 ABC
Courtship of Eddie's Father   sr ret 9.15.71 ABC
Congratulations It's a Boy   tf   9.21.71 ABC
Night Gallery   ep   Last Rites for a Dead Druid   1.26.
    72 NBC
Night Gallery   ep   9.24.72 NBC
Love American Style   ep   9.29.72 ABC
Search   ep   11.15.72 NBC
The Couple Takes a Wife   tf   12.5.72 ABC
Of Men and Women   ep   Why He Was Late to Work   12.
    17.72 ABC
Medical Center   ep   12.20.72 CBS

BLACK, KAREN
Run for Your Life   ep   Tell It to the Dead   4.10.67
    NBC
Second Hundred Years   ep   10.18.67 ABC

Second Hundred Years   ep   12. 6. 67 ABC
Iron Horse   ep   The Prisoners   12. 30. 67 ABC
Invaders   ep   12. 12. 67 ABC
Mannix   ep   License Kill-Limit Three People   1. 13. 68
    CBS
Judd for the Defense   ep   Devil's Surrogate   2. 23. 68
    ABC
Adam-12   ep   1. 30. 68 NBC
Ghost Story   ep   10. 6. 72 NBC

BLACKMAN, HONOR
    The Vise   ep   Dead Man's Evidence   11. 18. 55 ABC
    Saber of London   ep   The Lady Doesn't Scare   12. 21. 58
        NBC
    Present Laughter   Sp   2. 28. 68 ABC
    Name of the Game   ep   An Agent of the Plaintiff   3. 21.
        69 NBC
    Columbo   ep   11. 26. 72 NBC

BLACKMER, SIDNEY
    Pulitzer Prize Playhouse   ep   The Pen   6. 22. 51 ABC
    Armstrong Circle Theatre   ep   Last Chance   7. 17. 51
        NBC
    Philco Playhouse   ep   Television Story   7. 29. 51 NBC
    Suspense   ep   This Is Your Confession   8. 21. 51, 8. 28.
        51 CBS
    Tales of Tomorrow   ep   The Dark Angel   9. 28. 51 ABC
    The Web   ep   Kill with Kindness   5. 14. 52 CBS
    Broadway Television Theatre   ep   The Barker   6. 16. 52
        NN
    Robert Montgomery Presents   ep   Victory   12. 15. 52
        NBC
    The Web   ep   The Tower   12. 28. 52 CBS
    Goodyear Playhouse   ep   Fadeout   8. 23. 53 NBC
    Hallmark Hall of Fame   ep   Never Kick a Man Upstairs
        10. 25. 53 NBC
    Armstrong Circle Theatre   ep   The Military Heart   3.
        30. 54 NBC
    U. S. Steel Hour   ep   The Notebook Warrior   9. 14. 54
        ABC
    Ford Theatre   ep   Shadow of Truth   10. 14. 54 NBC
    Damon Runyon Theatre   ep   The Big Fix   7. 23. 55 CBS
    Robert Montgomery Presents   ep   Paper Town   10. 10.
        55 NBC
    Alfred Hitchcock Presents   ep   Don't Come Back Alive
        10. 23. 55 CBS
    Front Row Center   ep   Strange Suspicion   1. 15. 56 CBS

Rheingold Theatre ep Arab Tool 2. 18. 56 NBC
Climax ep Flame-Out on T-6 5. 17. 56 CBS
Star Stage ep Dr. Jordan 6. 8. 56 NBC
Robert Montgomery Presents ep One Bright Day 10.
    29. 56 NBC
Hallmark Hall of Fame ep The Little Foxes 12. 16.
    56 NBC
Climax ep Scream in Silence 1. 2. 58 CBS
Jim Bowie ep 2. 14. 58 ABC
Zane Grey Theatre ep The Sharpshooter 3. 7. 58 CBS
Jim Bowie ep Horse Thief 3. 21. 58 ABC
Matinee Theatre ep The Cause 5. 12. 58 NBC
Desilu Playhouse ep The Night the Phone Rang 12.
    15. 58 CBS
Sunday Showcase ep What Makes Sammy Run 9. 27.
    59, 10. 4. 59 NBC
Name of the Game ep Chains of Command 10. 17. 69
    NBC
Best of the Post ep Early Americana 12. 31. 60 ABC
Bonanza ep The Dream Riders 5. 20. 61 NBC
Thriller ep Premature Burial 10. 2. 61 NBC
Cain's Hundred ep The Manipulator 1. 30. 62 NBC
Target Corruptors ep The Malignant Hearts 3. 23. 62
    ABC
Dr. Kildare ep Operation Lazarus 5. 24. 62 NBC
Alfred Hitchcock Theatre ep The Faith of Aaron Mene-
    fee 1. 20. 63 NBC
Dupont Show of the Month ep Diamond Fever 3. 24. 63
    NBC
Outer Limits ep The Hundred Days of the Dragon 9.
    23. 63 ABC
Defenders ep The Empty Heart 10. 5. 63 CBS
Profiles in Courage ep 11. 8. 64 NBC
The Reporter ep A Time to Be Silent 12. 4. 64 CBS
Ben Casey ep For San Diego You Need a Different
    Bus 1. 17. 66 ABC
Ben Casey ep Smile, Baby, Smile 1. 24. 66 ABC
Ben Casey ep Fun and Games and Other Tragic Things
    1. 31. 66 ABC
Ben Casey ep Weave Nets to Catch the Wind 2. 7. 66,
    2. 14. 66 ABC
The Girl from U. N. C. L. E. ep 11. 15. 66 NBC
Bonanza ep 3. 3. 68 NBC
Name of the Game ep Pineapple Rose 12. 20. 68 NBC
Do You Take This Stranger tf 1. 18. 71 NBC

BLAINE, VIVIAN
   Philco Playhouse   ep   Double Jeopardy   1.4.53 NBC
   Center Stage   ep   The Heart of a Clown   9.20.54 ABC
   Damon Runyon Theatre   ep   Pick the Winner   4.16.55
      CBS
   Hallmark Hall of Fame   ep   Dream Girl   12.11.55
      NBC
   Lux Video Theatre   ep   The Undesirable   2.7.57 NBC
   Route 66   ep   A Bunch of Lonely Pagliaccis   1.4.63
      CBS

BLAIR, BETSY
   Philco Playhouse   ep   The Charmed Circle   5.21.50
      NBC
   Goodyear Playhouse   ep   A Will to Live   5.12.57 NBC

BLAIR, JANET
   Armstrong Circle Theatre   ep   The Beautiful Wife   8.
      31.54 NBC
   Elgin Hour   ep   Flood   10.5.54 ABC
   U.S. Steel Hour   ep   King's Pawn   11.23.54 ABC
   Goodyear Playhouse   ep   Doing Her Bit   1.16.55 NBC
   A Connecticut Yankee   Sp   3.12.55 NBC
   Climax   ep   The Dance   6.30.55 CBS
   Front Row Center   ep   Kitty Foyle   7.13.55 CBS
   One Touch of Venus   Sp   8.27.55 NBC
   Ford Theatre   ep   The Payoff   5.3.56 NBC
   Alcoa Theatre   ep   The First Star   12.1.58 NBC
   Strawberry Blonde   Sp   10.18.59 NBC
   Chevy Show   ep   Around the World with Nellie Bly   1.
      3.60 NBC
   Mystery Show   ep   Femme Fatale   8.28.60 NBC
   Chevy Show   ep   Arabian Nights   11.27.60 NBC
   Shirley Temple Theatre   ep   Tom and Huck   10.9.60
      NBC
   Outer Limits   ep   Tourist Attraction   11.25.63 ABC
   Burke's Law   ep   Who Killed Purity Mather   12.6.63
      ABC
   Bob Hope Chrysler Theatre   ep   Wake up Darling   2.
      21.64 NBC
   Burke's Law   ep   Who Killed Merlin the Great   12.2.64
      ABC
   Ben Casey   ep   Then, Suddenly, Panic   3.21.66 ABC
   Marcus Welby, M.D.   ep   The Legacy   1.27.70 ABC
   Smith Family   sr   1.20.71 ABC
   Smith Family   sr ret   9.21.71 NBC

BLAKE, AMANDA
  Schlitz Playhouse of Stars   ep   Double Exposure   8.15.
    52 CBS
  Fireside Theatre   ep   Nine Quarts of Water   4.20.54
    NBC
  Four Star Playhouse   ep   Vote of Confidence   11.11.54
    CBS
  Gunsmoke   sr   9.10.55 CBS
  Gunsmoke   sr ret   fall, 1956 CBS
  Matinee Theatre   ep   Sound of Fear   6.13.57 NBC
  Gunsmoke   sr ret   fall, 1957 CBS
  Gunsmoke   sr ret   fall, 1958 CBS
  Gunsmoke   sr ret   fall, 1959 CBS
  G.E. Theatre   ep   Night Club   10.11.59 CBS
  Gunsmoke   sr ret   9.30.61 CBS
  Gunsmoke   sr ret   9.15.62 CBS
  Gunsmoke   sr ret   9.63 CBS
  Gunsmoke   sr ret   9.26.64 CBS
  Gunsmoke   sr ret   9.18.65 CBS
  Gunsmoke   sr ret   9.17.66 CBS
  Gunsmoke   sr ret   9.11.67 CBS
  Gunsmoke   sr ret   9.23.68 CBS
  Gunsmoke   sr ret   9.22.69 CBS
  Gunsmoke   sr ret   9.14.70 CBS
  Gunsmoke   sr ret   9.13.71 CBS
  Gunsmoke   sr ret   9.11.72 CBS

BLAKE, ROBERT
  Favorite Story   ep   Born unto Trouble   4.26.53 NBC
  Fireside Theatre   ep   Night in the Warehouse   6.23.53
    NBC
  It's a Great Life   ep   8.2.55 NBC
  Court of Last Resort   ep   The Case of Tomas Mendoza
    10.11.57 NBC
  Black Saddle   ep   2.21.59 NBC
  Rebel   ep   He's Only a Boy   2.28.60 ABC
  Alcoa Premiere   ep   Gypsy   5.17.60 ABC
  Have Gun Will Travel   ep   10.29.60 CBS
  Bat Masterson   ep   The Amnesty for Death   3.30.61
    NBC
  Naked City   ep   New York to L.A.   4.19.61 ABC
  Wagon Train   ep   The Joe Muharich Story   4.19.61
    NBC
  Laramie   ep   Wolf Cub   11.21.61 NBC
  Ben Casey   ep   Imagine a Long Bright Corridor   1.15.
    62 ABC
  Straightaway   ep   A Moment in the Sun   1.17.62 ABC

New Breed   ep   My Brother's Keeper   5.1.62 ABC
Have Gun Will Travel   ep   10.6.62 CBS
Slattery's People   ep   Does Nero Still at Ringside Sit
    2.5.65 CBS
Rawhide   ep   The Winter Soldier   3.12.65 CBS
Trials of O'Brien   ep   9.25.65 CBS
FBI   ep   The Price of Death   9.18.66 ABC
12 O'Clock High   ep   A Distant Cry   10.7.66 ABC

BLANE, SALLY
    Pepsi Cola Playhouse   ep   Grenadine   5.28.54 ABC
    Star Stage   ep   On Trial   9.23.55 NBC
    Loretta Young Show   ep   Oh, My Aching Heart   2.5.56
        NBC

BLOCKER, DAN
    Restless Gun   ep   The Child   12.23.57 NBC
    Thin Man   ep   The Departed Doctor   4.4.58 NBC
    Sgt. Preston   ep   Underground Ambush   4.24.58 CBS
    Restless Gun   ep   Mercy Day   10.6.58 NBC
    Jefferson Drum   ep   Stagecoach Episode   10.10.58 NBC
    Cimarron City   sr   10.11.58 NBC
    Gunsmoke   ep   10.18.58 CBS
    Restless Gun   ep   Take Me Home   12.29.58 NBC
    Bonanza   sr   9.12.59 NBC
    Rebel   ep   10.4.59 ABC
    Troubleshooters   ep   Tiger Culhane   10.9.59 NBC
    Bonanza   sr ret   9.10.60 NBC
    Bonanza   sr ret   9.24.61 NBC
    Mystery Theatre   ep   Chez Rouge   8.8.62 NBC
    Bonanza   sr ret   9.23.62 NBC
    Bonanza   sr ret   9.63 NBC
    Bonanza   sr ret   9.20.64 NBC
    Bonanza   sr ret   9.12.65 NBC
    Bonanza   sr ret   9.11.66 NBC
    Bonanza   sr ret   9.67 NBC
    Bonanza   sr ret   9.15.68 NBC
    Bonanza   sr ret   9.14.69 NBC
    Bonanza   sr ret   9.13.70 NBC
    Bonanza   sr ret   9.19.71 NBC

BLODGETT, MICHAEL
    Bonanza   ep   10.22.67 NBC
    To Rome with Love   ep   9.22.70 CBS
    Night Gallery   ep   The Dead Man   12.16.70 NBC
    Ironside   ep   1.7.71 NBC

BLONDELL, JOAN
  Airflyte Theatre ep Pot of Gold 1.18.51 CBS
  Tales of Tomorrow ep Little Black Bag 5.30.52 ABC
  Schlitz Playhouse of Stars ep The Pussyfootin' Rocks
    11.21.52 CBS
  Suspense ep Vacancy for Death 1.20.53 CBS
  Video Theatre ep Tango 7.9.53 CBS
  Fireside Theatre ep Sgt. Sullivan Speaking 1.11.55
    NBC
  Shower of Stars ep Burlesque 3.17.55 CBS
  G.E. Theatre ep Star in the House 6.5.55 CBS
  U.S. Steel Hour ep White Gloves 12.21.55 CBS
  Playhouse 90 ep Child of Trouble 5.2.57 CBS
  Studio One ep The Funny-Looking Kid 5.19.58 CBS
  Playhouse 90 ep A Marriage of Strangers 5.14.59
    CBS
  Adventures in Paradise ep Forbidden Sea 4.4.60
    ABC
  Witness ep 1.12.61 CBS
  Untouchables ep The Underground Court 2.16.61 ABC
  Barbara Stanwyck Theatre ep Sign of the Zodiac 4.3.
    61 NBC
  Dick Powell Theatre ep The Big Day 12.25.62 NBC
  Virginian ep To Make this Place Remember 9.25.63
    NBC
  Burke's Law ep Who Killed Harris Crown 10.11.63
    ABC
  Wagon Train ep The Bleecker Story 12.9.63 ABC
  Twilight Zone ep What's in the Box 3.13.64 CBS
  The Greatest Show on Earth ep You're All Right Ivy
    4.28.64 ABC
  Burke's Law ep 5.84.64 ABC
  Bonanza ep The Pressure Game 5.10.64 NBC
  Dr. Kildare ep 5.21.64 NBC
  World of Disney ep Kilroy 4.4.65 NBC
  The Lucy Show ep 10.11.65 CBS
  My Three Sons ep 10.28.65 CBS
  Slattery's People ep The Last Commuter 11.19.65
    CBS
  Baby Crazy pt 9.19.66 ABC
  Bob Hope Chrysler Theatre ep The Blue-Eyed Horse
    11.23.66 NBC
  The Man from U.N.C.L.E. ep 11.25.66 NBC
  The Girl from U.N.C.L.E. ep The UFO Affair 1.3.
    67 NBC
  Winchester .73 tf 3.14.67 NBC
  Family Affair ep 12.11.67 CBS

Petticoat Junction ep   2.3.68 CBS
That Girl ep   3.28.68 ABC
Here Come the Brides sr   9.25.68 ABC
Outsider ep   There Was a Little Girl   12.25.68 NBC
Here Come the Brides sr   9.26.69 ABC
Name of the Game ep   10.9.70 NBC
McCloud ep   11.3.71 NBC
Banyon sr   9.15.72 NBC

BLOOM, CLAIRE
Producers Showcase ep Cyrano de Bergerac 10.17.55
    NBC
Producers Showcase ep Caesar and Cleopatra 3.5.56
    NBC
Producers Showcase ep Romeo and Juliet 3.4.57
    NBC
Goodyear Playhouse ep First Love 3.24.57 NBC
Robert Montgomery Presents ep Victoria Regina 4.8.
    57 NBC
Shirley Temple's Story Book ep Beauty and the Beast
    1.12.58 NBC
Playhouse 90 ep Misalliance 10.29.59 CBS
Checkmate ep Through a Dark Glass 11.1.61 CBS
BBC Drama ep Anna Karenina 4.22.64 NN
Bob Hope Chrysler Theatre ep A Time to Love 1.11.
    67 NBC
Hallmark Hall of Fame ep Soldier in Love 4.26.67
    NBC
Ivanov Sp 5.20.67 CBS

BLORE, ERIC
Story Theatre ep An Old, Old Story 3.2.51 NN
World of Disney ep (voice only) Mr. Toad 2.2.55 ABC

BLYDEN, LARRY
Goodyear Playhouse ep Suitable for Framing 7.4.54
    NBC
Elgin Hour ep The $1,000 Window 3.22.55 CBS
Joe and Mabel sr 9.20.55 CBS
Playwrights '56 ep You Sometimes Get Rich 5.8.56
    NBC
Joe and Mabel sr ret 6.26.56 CBS
Playhouse 90 ep One Coat of White 2.21.57 CBS
Playhouse 90 ep Three Men on a Horse 4.18.57 CBS
Alcoa Hour ep He's for Me 7.21.57 NBC
Kraft Theatre ep The Old Ticker 9.11.57 NBC
U.S. Steel Hour ep Never Know the End 1.29.58 CBS

U.S. Steel Hour ep Be My Guest 8.27.58 CBS
Dupont Show of the Month ep Harvey 9.22.58 CBS
Sunday Showcase ep What Makes Sammy Run 9.27.59, 10.4.59 NBC
Play of the Week ep Thieves' Carnival 12.21.59 NN
Sunday Showcase ep One Loud Clear Voice 1.17.60 NBC
Play of the Week ep A Very Special Baby 2.22.60 NN
Twilight Zone ep A Nice Place to Visit 4.15.60 CBS
Play of the Week ep The Girls in 509 4.18.60 NN
Mystery Show ep The Machine Calls It Murder 5.29.60 NBC
Moment of Fear ep Conjure Wife 7.8.60 NBC
Omnibus ep He Shall Have Power 11.13.60 NBC
Thriller ep Choose a Victim 1.24.61 NBC
Loretta Young Show ep Double Edge 2.19.61 NBC
Loretta Young Show ep Thirteen Donner Street 4.30.61 NBC
Target Corruptors ep The Golden Carpet 11.24.61 ABC
G.E. Theatre ep Call to Danger 12.10.61 CBS
U.S. Steel Hour ep My Wife's Best Friend 12.13.61 CBS
Twilight Zone ep Showdown with Rance McGrew 2.2.62 CBS
Cain's Hundred ep Blood Money 2.13.62 NBC
Adventures in Paradise ep The Dream Merchant 3.18.62 ABC
U.S. Steel Hour ep Male Call 8.8.62 CBS
Dick Powell Theatre ep Tomorrow the Man 10.2.62 NBC
Sam Benedict ep Hear the Mellow Wedding Bells 11.3.62 NBC
Dupont Show of the Month ep Two Faces of Treason 2.10.63 NBC
Harry's Girls sr 9.13.63 NBC
Route 66 ep 1.17.64 CBS
The Reporter ep Murder by Scandal 11.27.64 CBS
Dr. Kildare ep Take Care of My Little Girl 1.14.65 NBC
Alfred Hitchcock Theatre ep Wally the Bear 3.1.65 NBC
12 O'Clock High ep Mutiny at 10,000 Feet 3.26.65 ABC
Defenders ep The Prosecutor 4.29.65 CBS
Kraft Suspense Theatre ep Twixt the Cup and the Lip

6.3.55 NBC
Fugitive ep Crack in a Crystal Ball 9.28.65 ABC
Slattery's People ep The Hero 11.5.65 CBS
The Man from U.N.C.L.E. ep The Waverly Ring Af-
    fair 1.28.66 NBC
ABC Stage 67 ep Olympus 7-000 9.28.66 ABC
Ghostbreaker pt 9.8.67 NBC
FBI ep The Innocents 11.1.70 ABC
Mod Squad ep 11.9.71 ABC
Medical Center ep Terror 1.26.72 CBS
Cannon ep 2.29.72 CBS

BLYTH, ANN
RCA Victor Show ep 6.23.53 NBC
Video Theatre ep A Place in the Sun 1.28.54 CBS
Wagon Train ep The Jenny Tannen Story 6.24.59
    NBC
Wagon Train ep The Martha Barhman Story 11.4.59
    NBC
June Allyson Show ep Suspected 1.28.59 CBS
The Citadel Sp 2.19.60 ABC
Wagon Train ep The Clementine Jones Story 10.25.
    61 NBC
Dick Powell Theatre ep Savage Sunday 5.1.62 NBC
Wagon Train ep The Eve Newhope Story 12.5.62
    ABC
Saints and Sinners ep The Year Joan Crawford Won
    the Oscar 1.21.63 NBC
Wagon Train ep The Ft. Pierce Story 9.23.63 ABC
Twilight Zone ep Queen of the Nile 3.6.64 CBS
Burke's Law ep 3.13.64 ABC
Burke's Law ep Who Killed Mother Goose 1.13.65
    ABC
Kraft Suspense Theatre ep Jungle of Fear 4.22.65
    NBC
Name of the Game ep Swingers Only 1.10.69 NBC

BOEHM, KARL
World of Disney ep The Magnificent Rebel 11.18.62,
    11.25.62 NBC
Virginian ep The Golden Door 3.13.63 NBC
Burke's Law ep Who Killed Julian Buck 10.18.63 ABC
Combat ep The Wounded Don't Cry 10.22.63 ABC

BOGARDE, DIRK
Hallmark Hall of Fame ep Little Moon of Alban 3.18.
    64 NBC

BOGART, HUMPHREY
   Producers Showcase   ep   The Petrified Forest   5.30.55
   NBC

BOLAND, MARY
   Masterpiece Playhouse   ep   The Rivals   8.6.50 NBC
   Musical Comedy Time   ep   Mme. Modiste   2.5.51 NBC
   Armstrong Circle Theatre   ep   The First Born   9.7.54
   NBC
   Producers Showcase   ep   The Women   2.7.55 NBC
   Best of Broadway   ep   The Guardsman   3.2.55 CBS

BOLGER, RAY
   Where's Raymond   sr   10.8.53 ABC
   Ray Bolger Show   sr   9.17.54 ABC
   G.E. Theatre   ep   The Girl with the Flaxen Hair   12.
   14.58 CBS
   G.E. Theatre   ep   Silhouette   12.27.59 CBS
   Jean Arthur Show   ep   10.10.66 CBS

BOND, WARD
   Silver Theatre   ep   My Brother's Keeper   2.20.50 CBS
   Schlitz Playhouse of Stars   ep   Apple of His Eyes   2.
   29.52 CBS
   Gulf Playhouse   ep   You Can't Look It up   10.10.52 NBC
   Ford Theatre   ep   Gun Job   12.17.53 NBC
   G.E. Theatre   ep   Winners Never Lose   9.13.53 CBS
   Ford Theatre   ep   Segment   10.21.54 NBC
   Cavalcade of America   ep   The Marine Who Was 200
   Years Old   1.4.55 ABC
   Climax   ep   The Mojave Kid   1.27.55 CBS
   Screen Directors Playhouse   ep   Rookie of the Year
   12.7.55 NBC
   Star Stage   ep   The Marshal and the Mob   1.6.56 NBC
   Schlitz Playhouse of Stars   ep   Plague Ship   5.11.56
   CBS
   Dupont Theatre   ep   Once a Hero   12.11.56 ABC
   Wagon Train   sr   9.18.57 NBC
   Wagon Train   sr ret   9.24.58 NBC
   G.E. Theatre   ep   A Turkey for the President   11.23.
   58 CBS
   Wagon Train   sr ret   9.30.59 NBC
   Wagon Train   sr ret   9.28.60 NBC

BONDI, BEULAH
   Medallion Theatre   ep   Gran'ma Rebel   10.31.53 CBS
   Alfred Hitchcock Presents   ep   Our Cook's a Treasure

11. 20. 55 CBS
Front Row Center   ep   Finley's Fan Club   1. 8. 56 CBS
Climax   ep   The Secret of River Lane   1. 26. 56 CBS
Climax   ep   Circle of Destruction   1. 24. 57 CBS
Zane Grey Theatre   ep   Black Is for Grief   4. 12. 57
   CBS
Hallmark Hall of Fame   ep   On Borrowed Time   11. 17.
   57 NBC
Climax   ep   Hurricane Diane   12. 12. 57 CBS
Playhouse 90   ep   Tomorrow   3. 7. 60 CBS
Play of the Week   ep   Morning's at Seven   4. 25. 60 NN
Harrigan and Son   ep   Non Compos Mentis   12. 30. 60
   ABC
Wagon Train   ep   The Prairie Story   2. 1. 61 NBC
Best of the Post   ep   Antidote for Hatred   3. 18. 61 ABC
Route 66   ep   Burning for Burning   12. 29. 61 CBS
Alcoa Premiere   ep   The Hands of Danofrio   11. 29. 62
   ABC
Perry Mason   ep   The Case of the Nebulous Nephew
   9. 26. 62 CBS
Jimmy Stewart Show   ep   10. 31. 71 NBC
She Waits   tf   1. 28. 72 CBS

BOONE, PAT
Dick Powell Theatre   ep hos   4. 2. 63 NBC
The Pigeon   tf   11. 4. 69 ABC

BOONE, RICHARD
Medic   sr   9. 13. 54 NBC
G. E. Theatre   ep   Love Is Eternal   2. 13. 55 CBS
Medic   sr ret   fall, 1955 NBC
Matinee Theatre   ep   Wuthering Heights   11. 30. 55 NBC
Climax   ep   Bail Out at 43, 000   12. 29. 55 CBS
Climax   ep   The Shadow of Evil   5. 24. 56 CBS
Lux Video Theatre   ep   A House of His Own   6. 14. 56
   NBC
Studio One   ep   Dead of Noon   1. 28. 67 CBS
Climax   ep   Don't Ever Come Back   2. 28. 57 CBS
Have Gun Will Travel   sr   9. 14. 57 CBS
Climax   ep   To Walk the Night   12. 19. 57 CBS
Have Gun Will Travel   sr ret   fall, 1958 CBS
U. S. Steel Hour   ep   Little Tin God   4. 22. 59 CBS
Have Gun Will Travel   sr ret   fall, 1959 CBS
Playhouse 90   ep   The Tunnel   12. 10. 59 CBS
Playhouse 90   ep   Tomorrow   3. 7. 60 CBS
U. S. Steel Hour   ep   The Charlie and Kid   3. 23. 60
   CBS

Have Gun Will Travel   sr ret   9.10.60 CBS
The Right Man Sp 10.24.60 CBS
Have Gun Will Travel   sr ret   9.16.61 CBS
John Brown's Body Sp 1.14.62 CBS
Have Gun Will Travel   sr ret   9.15.62 CBS
Richard Boone Show sh/sr 9.24.63 NBC
Cimarron Strip ep The Roarer 11.2.67 CBS
Deadly Harvest tf 9.26.72 CBS
Hec Ramsey sr   10.8.72 NBC
Goodnight My Love tf 10.17.72 ABC

BOOTH, SHIRLEY
Playhouse 90 ep The Hostess with the Mostess 3.21.
   57 CBS
U.S. Steel Hour ep Welcome Home 3.22.61 CBS
U.S. Steel Hour ep The Haven 6.28.61 CBS
Hazel sr 9.28.61 NBC
Hazel sr ret 9.20.62 NBC
Hazel sr ret 9.19.63 NBC
Hazel sr ret 9.17.64 NBC
Hazel sr ret 9.13.65 CBS
Glass Menagerie sp 12.8.66 CBS
CBS Playhouse ep Do Not Go Gentle into That Good
   Night 10.17.67 CBS
The Smugglers tf 12.24.68 NBC
The Ghost and Mrs. Muir ep spring, 1970 ABC

BORDONI, IRENE
Musical Comedy Time ep Louisiana Purchase 1.22.
   51 NBC

BORGNINE, ERNEST
Ford Theatre ep Night Visitor 4.29.54 NBC
Fireside Theatre ep The Poachers 3.8.55 NBC
Zane Grey Theatre ep Black Creek Encounter 3.8.57
   CBS
Wagon Train ep The Willy Moran Story 9.18.57
   NBC
Schlitz Playhouse of Stars ep Two Lives Have I 2.
   28.58 CBS
Navy Log ep Lost Human Bomb 4.10.58
   ABC
Wagon Train ep Around the Horn 10.1.58
   NBC
Laramie ep Circle of Fire 9.29.59 NBC
Wagon Train ep The Staban Zamora Story 10.
   21.59 NBC

Zane Grey Theatre   ep   A Gun for Willie   10.6.60 CBS
Laramie   ep   Ride the Wild Wind   10.11.60 NBC
Wagon Train   ep   The Earl Packer Story   1.4.61 NBC
G.E. Theatre   ep   2.12.61 CBS
Alcoa Premiere   ep   Seven Against the Sea   4.3.62
   ABC
G.E. Theatre   ep   The Bar Mitzvah of Major Orlovsky
   4.15.62 CBS
McHale's Navy   sr   10.11.62 ABC
McHale's Navy   sr ret   9.7.63 ABC
McHale's Navy   sr ret   fall, 1964 ABC
McHale's Navy   sr ret   fall, 1965 ABC
Bob Hope Chrysler Theatre   ep   The Blue-eyed Horse
   11.23.66 NBC
Run for Your Life   ep   12.19.66 NBC
Sam Hill: Who Killed the Mysterious Mr. Foster   2.1.
   71 NBC
The Trackers   tf   12.14.71 ABC

BOTTOMS, TIMOTHY
   CBS Playhouse 90   ep   Look Homeward, Angel   2.25.
   72 CBS

BOUVIER, LEE
   Laura   Sp   1.24.68 ABC

BOWMAN, LEE
   Silver Theatre   ep   Bad Guy   4.24.50 CBS
   Robert Montgomery Presents   ep   The Awful Truth   9.
   11.50 NBC
   Studio One   ep   The Blonde Comes First   11.6.50 CBS
   Airflyte Theatre   ep   Suppressed Desires   11.16.50
   CBS
   Ellery Queen   sr   1.18.51 NN
   Video Theatre   ep   Weather for Today   6.11.51 CBS
   Ellery Queen   sr ret   9.13.51 NN
   Robert Montgomery Presents   ep   The Glass Cage   4.
   13.53 NBC
   Love Story   ep   The Arms of the Law   5.11.54 NN
   Robert Montgomery Presents   ep   Halfway House   2.21.
   55 NBC
   Stage 7   ep   Emergency   4.17.55 CBS
   Robert Montgomery Presents   ep   The Great Gatsby
   5.9.55 NBC
   Robert Montgomery Presents   ep   Quality Town   12.19.
   55 NBC
   Robert Montgomery Presents   ep   All Expenses Paid

5. 21. 56 NBC
Lux Video Theatre   ep   The Top Rung   9. 13. 56 NBC
Schlitz Playhouse of Stars   ep   Top Secret   9. 21. 56
   CBS
Loretta Young Show   ep   New Slant   10. 14. 56 NBC
Loretta Young Show   ep   Bad Apple   2. 3. 57 NBC
Suspicion   ep   Someone Is After Me   1. 6. 58 NBC
Studio One   ep   The Laughing Willow   2. 3. 58 CBS
Miami Undercover   sr   1. 23. 61 NN
77 Sunset Strip   ep   The Raiders   11. 2. 62 ABC
Fame Is the Name of the Game   tf   11. 26. 66 NBC
Judd for the Defense   ep   1. 5. 68, 1. 12. 68 ABC

BOYD, STEPHEN
Playhouse 90   ep   To the Sounds of Trumpets   2. 9. 60
   CBS
G. E. Theatre   ep   The Wall Between   1. 7. 62 CBS
Bob Hope Chrysler Theatre   ep   War of Nerves   1. 3. 64
   NBC
The Poppy Is Also a Flower   tf   4. 22. 66 ABC
Carter's Army   tf   1. 27. 70 ABC
Hallmark Hall of Fame   ep   The Hands of Cormac
   Joyce   11. 17. 72 NBC

BOYD, WILLIAM
Hopalong Cassidy   sr   1948-1951 NBC

BOYER, CHARLES
Four Star Playhouse   sr   9. 25. 52 CBS
Four Star Playhouse   sr ret   10. 8. 53 CBS
Four Star Playhouse   sr ret   9. 30. 54 CBS
Four Star Playhouse   sr ret   10. 20. 55 CBS
I Love Lucy   ep   3. 5. 56 CBS
Hallmark Hall of Fame   ep   There Shall Be No Night
   3. 17. 57 NBC
Alcoa Theatre   ep   Guests for Dinner   11. 4. 57 NBC
Alcoa Theatre   ep   Even a Thief Can Dream   3. 10. 58
   NBC
Alcoa Theatre   ep   The Clock Strikes Twelve   6. 2. 58
   NBC
Dick Powell Theatre   ep   The Prison   2. 6. 62 NBC
Dick Powell Theatre   ep   Days of Glory   11. 14. 62 NBC
Rogues   sr   9. 13. 64 NBC
Name of the Game   ep   The Emissary   10. 10. 69 NBC

BRACKEN, EDDIE
Gulf Playhouse   ep   A Question of Rank   11. 7. 52 NBC

Gulf Playhouse   ep   Mr. Breger 12.26.52 NBC
Ford Theatre   ep   It Happened in a Pawn Shop 1.8.53
   NBC
Video Theatre   ep   The Corporal and the Lady 7.16.
   53 CBS
Schlitz Playhouse of Stars   ep   Simplon Express 8.7.53
   CBS
Goodyear Playhouse   ep   Suit Yourself 9.11.55 NBC
Studio One   ep   A Likely Story 10.3.55 CBS
20th Century-Fox Hour   ep   Mr. Belvedere 4.18.56
   CBS
Schlitz Playhouse of Stars   ep   Formosa Patrol 5.4.56
   CBS
Ethel Barrymore Theatre   ep   The Peabodys 10.19.56
   NN
Ford Theatre   ep   The Marriage Plan 12.12.56 ABC
Alcoa Hour   ep   Awake with Fear 6.23.57 NBC
Climax   ep   False Witness 7.4.57 NBC
Studio One   ep   The Award Winner 3.24.58 CBS
David Niven Theatre   ep   A Day of Small Miracles 5.
   19.50 NBC
Strawberry Blonde   Sp   10.18.59 NBC
Play of the Week   ep   Archy and Mehitabel 5.16.60 NN
Roaring 20s   ep   Another Time, Another War 11.4.61
   ABC
Going My Way   ep   Like My Own Brother 11.7.62
   ABC
Rawhide   ep   Incident of the Clown 3.29.63 CBS
Burke's Law   ep   1.31.64 ABC
Rawhide   ep   Incident of the Pied Piper 2.6.64 CBS
Burke's Law   ep   5.5.65 ABC

BRADY, SCOTT
   Ford Theatre   ep   Just What the Doctor Ordered 4.9.
      53 NBC
   Video Theatre   ep   Return to Alsace 9.24.53 CBS
   Ford Theatre   ep   Tangier Lady 10.1.53 NBC
   Schlitz Playhouse of Stars   ep   Rim of Violence 1.8.54
      CBS
   Ford Theatre   ep   Wonderful Day for a Wedding 5.15.
      54 NBC
   Studio One   ep   Millions of Georges 3.75.55 CBS
   Damon Runyon Theatre   ep   All Is Not Gold 4.30.55
      CBS
   Ford Theatre   ep   The Blue Ribbon 11.10.55 NBC
   Schlitz Playhouse of Stars   ep   Night in the Big Swamp
      11.18.55 CBS

Studio 57   ep   Night Tune   12.4.55 NN
Loretta Young Show   ep   Man in the Ring   12.11.55
   NBC
Lux Video Theatre   ep   Tabloid   4.5.56 NBC
Schlitz Playhouse of Stars   ep   Roustabout   6.8.56
   CBS
Climax   ep   The 78th Floor   8.16.56 CBS
Zane Grey Theatre   ep   Man on the Run   6.21.57 CBS
Playhouse 90   ep   Lone Woman   12.26.57 CBS
Schlitz Playhouse of Stars   ep   Papa Said No   4.4.58
   CBS
Climax   ep   The Big Success   5.8.58 CBS
Schlitz Playhouse of Stars   ep   The Salted Mine   3.27.
   59 CBS
Shotgun Slade   sr   11.11.59 NN
Checkmate   ep   Voyage into Fear   5.6.61 CBS
G.E. Theatre   ep   We're Holding Your Son   12.3.61
   CBS
Untouchables   ep   The Floyd Gibbons Story   12.11.62
   ABC
Alfred Hitchcock Theatre   ep   Run for Doom   5.17.63
   CBS
Judd for the Defense   ep   9.29.67 ABC
Felony Squad   ep   1.8.68 ABC
Virginian   ep   The Storm Gate   11.13.68 NBC
Name of the Game   ep   The High on a Rainbow   12.6.
   68 NBC
Bracken's World   ep   9.26.69 NBC
The D.A.: Murder One   tf   12.8.69 NBC
Mannix   ep   1.17.70 CBS
Lancer   ep   2.17.70 CBS
High Chaparral   ep   10.9.70 NBC
Name of the Game   ep   10.30.70 NBC
San Francisco Airport   ep   Hostage   11.11.70 NBC
The Immortal   ep   Paradise Bay   12.10.70 ABC
Men from Shiloh   ep   1.20.71 NBC

BRAND, NEVILLE
Footlights Theatre   ep   The Man Who Had Nothing to
   Lose   8.22.52 CBS
Schlitz Playhouse of Stars   ep   The Edge of Battle   3.
   26.54 CBS
Schlitz Playhouse of Stars   ep   The Dumbest Man in
   the Army   12.31.54 CBS
Appointment with Adventure   ep   The Quiet Gun   4.24.
   55 CBS
Stage 7   ep   Armed   5.1.55 CBS

Screen Directors Playhouse   ep   Arroyo   10. 26. 55 NBC
Fireside Theatre   ep   Ride with the Executioner   11. 8.
    55 NBC
Studio One   ep   Blow up at Cortland   12. 5. 55 CBS
Schlitz Playhouse of Stars   ep   On the Nose   12. 9. 55
    CBS
Jane Wyman Theatre   ep   Between Jobs   10. 30. 56 NBC
Climax   ep   Ten Minutes to Curfew   12. 27. 56 CBS
Jane Wyman Theatre   ep   Harbor Patrol   4. 23. 57 NBC
Kraft Theatre   ep   Run, Joe, Run   1. 29. 58 NBC
Kraft Theatre   ep   All the King's Men   5. 14. 58, 5. 21.
    58 NBC
G. E. Theatre   ep   The Coward of Ft. Bennett   3. 16. 58
    CBS
Kraft Theatre   ep   Look What's Going on   3. 19. 58 NBC
Playhouse 90   ep   Galvanized Yankee   7. 3. 58 CBS
Texan   ep   Law of the Gun   9. 29. 58 CBS
U. S. Steel Hour   ep   Goodbye... But It Doesn't Go Away
    12. 31. 58 CBS
Zane Grey Theatre   ep   Trouble at Tres Cruces 3. 26. 59
    CBS
Desilu Playhouse   ep   The Untouchables   4. 20. 59, 4. 27.
    59 CBS
Texan   ep   6. 22. 59 CBS
Dupont Show of the Month   ep   Body and Soul 9. 28. 59 CBS
Rawhide   ep   Incident of the Devil and His Duel   1. 22. 60
    CBS
Bonanza   ep   The Last Viking   11. 12. 60 NBC
Untouchables   ep   The Big Train   1. 5. 61, 1. 12. 61 ABC
Straightaway   ep   The Tin Caesar   10. 13. 61 ABC
Cain's Hundred   ep   The Debasers   1. 16. 62 NBC
Joey Bishop Show   ep   Double Exposure   2. 7. 62 NBC
Naked City   ep   Lament for a Dead Indian   4. 11. 62 ABC
Ben Casey   ep   Will Everyone Who Believes in Terry
    Dunne Please Applaud   3. 18. 63 ABC
Rawhide   ep   Incident of the Red Wind   9. 26. 63 CBS
Lieutenant   ep   The Two-Star Giant   10. 5. 63 NBC
Bob Hope Chrysler Theatre   ep   Seven Miles of Bad
    Roads   10. 18. 63 NBC
Arrest and Trial   ep   An Echo of Consciences 1. 26. 64 ABC
Destry   ep   The Solid Gold Girl   2. 14. 64 ABC
Wagon Train   ep   4. 20. 64 ABC
Suspense Theatre   ep   The Savage   4. 22. 64 CBS
Combat   ep   Fly Away Home   11. 17. 64 ABC
Virginian   ep   We've Lost a Train   4. 21. 65 NBC
Laredo   sr   9. 16. 65 NBC
Gunsmoke   ep   10. 23. 65 CBS
Laredo   sr ret   9. 16. 66 NBC

Tarzan   ep   3. 22. 68 NBC
Men from Shiloh   ep   Gun Quest   10. 21. 70 NBC
Bonanza   ep   The Buck of Pepper Shannon   11. 22. 70 NBC
Lock Stock and Barrel   tf   9. 24. 71 NBC
Chicago Teddy Bears   ep   10. 1. 71 CBS
Alias Smith and Jones   ep   Shootout at Diablo Station
   12. 2. 71 ABC
Bonanza   ep   The Rattlesnake Brigade   12. 5. 71 NBC
Longstreet   ep   1. 7. 72 ABC
McCloud   ep   Fifth Man in a String Quartet   2. 2. 72
   NBC
Alias Smith and Jones   ep   Which Way to the OK Cor-
   ral   2. 10. 72 ABC
The Adventures of Nick Carter   tf   2. 20. 72 ABC
Marcus Welby, M. D.   ep   Don't Talk about Darkness
   2. 22. 72 ABC
Two for the Money   tf   2. 26. 72 ABC
No Place to Run   tf   9. 19. 72 ABC

BRANDO, JOCELYN
Kraft Theatre   ep   Ben Franklin   5. 30. 51 NBC
U. S. Steel Hour   ep   Freighter   2. 15. 55 ABC
U. S. Steel Hour   ep   Thirty Year Man   3. 28. 56 CBS
Wagon Train   ep   The Sally Potter Story   4. 9. 58 NBC
Richard Diamond   ep   Lost Testament   5. 1. 58 CBS
Alcoa Premiere   ep   Emergency Only   2. 4. 59 ABC
Accused   ep   2. 25. 59 ABC
Buckskin   ep   Mail Order Groom   4. 20. 59 NBC
Alfred Hitchcock Presents   ep   True Account 6. 7. 59
   CBS
Lux Playhouse   ep   The Miss and the Missiles   6. 12.
   59 CBS
Alcoa Premiere   ep   Emergency Only   6. 23. 59 ABC
Alfred Hitchcock Presents   ep   Graduating Class   12.
   27. 59 CBS
Riverboat   ep   The Night of the Faceless Men   3. 28.
   60 NBC
Laramie   ep   Cemetery Road   4. 13. 60 NBC
Markham   ep   The Man from Saltzberg   6. 2. 60 CBS
G. E. Theatre   ep   The Money Driver   12. 18. 60 CBS
Laramie   ep   Man from Kansas   1. 10. 61 NBC
Checkmate   ep   One for the Book   3. 18. 61 CBS
Wagon Train   ep   The Kitty Allbright Story   10. 4. 61
   NBC
Alcoa Premiere   ep   People Need People   10. 10. 61
   ABC
Frontier Circus   ep   The Hunter and the Hunted   11.
   2. 61 CBS

87th Precinct ep My Friend, My Enemy 11.27.61
   NBC
Thriller ep Till Death Do Us Part 3.12.62 NBC
Wagon Train ep The Michael McGoo Story 3.20.63
   ABC
Wagon Train ep The Sam Pulaski Story 11.4.63 ABC
Dr. Kildare ep The Oracle 12.19.63 NBC
My Three Sons ep 12.31.64 ABC
Virginian ep 3.22.67 NBC
Love of Life sr 1968 CBS

BRANDON, MICHAEL
   Man in the Middle pt 4.14.72 CBS
   Owen Marshall ep 10.12.72 ABC
   The Strangers in 1A 10.14.72 CBS
   Love American Style ep 12.8.72 ABC

BRASSELLE, KEEFE
   Ford Theatre ep Shadow of Truth 10.14.54 NBC
   Rheingold Theatre ep A Matter of Courage 4.2.55
      NBC
   Lux Video Theatre ep The Eyes of Father Tomasino
      9.22.55 NBC
   Ford Theatre ep Never Lend Money to a Woman 1.
      19.56 NBC
   Loretta Young Show ep Conflict 3.2.58 NBC
   Phil Silvers Show ep Bilko vs. Cowington 10.24.58
      CBS
   David Niven Theatre ep Good Deed 7.7.59 NBC
   U.S. Steel Hour ep The Go-Between 4.18.62 CBS

BRAZZI, ROSSANO
   Rheingold Theatre ep Big Nick 9.7.55 NBC
   June Allyson Show ep Slip of the Tongue 4.11.60 CBS
   June Allyson Show ep Our Man in Rome 3.27.61 CBS
   Run for Your Life ep Keep My Share of the World
      2.7.66 NBC
   Bob Hope Chrysler Theatre ep 4.19.67 NBC
   Survivors sr 10.6.69 ABC
   Honeymoon with a Stranger tf 12.23.69 ABC
   Name of the Game ep The Skin Game 2.27.70 NBC

BRENNAN, WALTER
   Schlitz Playhouse of Stars ep Lucky Thirteen 11.13.53
      CBS
   Light's Diamond Jubilee ep The Leader of the People
      10.24.54 ABC, CBS, NBC

Schlitz Playhouse of Stars   ep   Mr. Ears   4. 8. 55 CBS
Screen Directors Playhouse   ep   The Brush Roper   11.
   23. 55 NBC
Schlitz Playhouse of Stars   ep   The Happy Sun   7. 13. 56
   CBS
Ethel Barrymore Theatre   ep   The Gentle Years   9. 28.
   56 NN
Dupont Theatre   ep   Woman's Work   11. 20. 56 ABC
Zane Grey Theatre   ep   Vengeance Canyon   11. 30. 56
   CBS
Ford Theatre   ep   Duffy's   12. 19. 56 ABC
Real McCoys   sr   10. 3. 57 ABC
Zane Grey Theatre   ep   Ride a Lonely Trail   11. 1. 57
   CBS
Real McCoys   sr ret   fall, 1958 ABC
Real McCoys   sr ret   fall, 1959 ABC
Real McCoys   sr ret   9. 29. 60 ABC
Real McCoys   sr ret   9. 28. 61 ABC
Real McCoys   sr ret   9. 30. 62 ABC
Tycoon   sr   9. 15. 64 ABC
Guns of Will Sonnett   sr   9. 8. 67 ABC
Guns of Will Sonnett   sr ret   9. 27. 68 ABC
The Over the Hill Gang   tf   10. 7. 69 ABC
The Young Country   tf   3. 17. 70 ABC
To Rome with Love   sr   9. 15. 70 CBS
The Over the Hill Gang Rides Again   tf 11. 17. 70 ABC
Alias Smith and Jones   ep   9. 16. 71 ABC
Alias Smith and Jones   ep   1. 6. 72 ABC
Two for the Money   tf   2. 26. 72 ABC
Home for the Holidays   tf   11. 28. 72 ABC

BRENT, GEORGE
Ford Theatre   ep   Double Exposure   3. 26. 53 NBC
Schlitz Playhouse of Stars   ep   Medicine Woman   5. 1.
   53 CBS
Mirror Theatre   ep   Key in the Lock   11. 14. 53 CBS
Ford Theatre   ep   Unbroken Promise   12. 30. 54 NBC
Fireside Theatre   ep   The Indiscreet Mrs. Jarvis   1. 4.
   55 NBC
Gloria Swanson Theatre   ep   A Fond Farewell 1. 25. 55
   ABC
Fireside Theatre   ep   Return in Triumph   3. 1. 55 NBC
Fireside Theatre   ep   It's Easy to Get Ahead   3. 29. 55
   NBC
Stage 7   ep   The Mativ Hat   4. 24. 55 CBS
Star Playhouse   ep   Medicine Woman   6. 7. 55 NN
Studio 57   ep   Diagnosis of a Selfish Lady   10. 23. 55 NN

Studio 57   cp   Death Dream   11.13.55 NN
Science Fiction Theatre   ep   The Long Day   12.23.55
   NBC
Crossroads   ep   The Inner Light   2.3.56 ABC
Wire Service   sr   10.4.56 ABC
Crossroads   ep   The Kid Had a Gun   12.28.56 ABC
Rawhide   ep   Incident of the Chubasco   4.3.59 CBS
Mystery Show   ep   I Know What I'd Have Done   7.24.60
   NBC

BRENT, ROMNEY
   Armstrong Cirlce Theatre   ep   The Perfcct Type   11.21.
      50 NBC
   Billy Rose's Playbill   ep   The Benefit of the Doubt   12.
      4.50 NN
   Somerset Maugham Theatre   ep   The Moon and Sixpence
      4.30.51 NBC
   Summer Theatre   ep   Stan, the Killer   9.1.52 CBS
   Omnibus   ep   King Lear   10.18.53 CBS
   Studio One   ep   Camille   11.9.53 CBS
   Schlitz Playhouse of Stars   ep   The Man Who Escaped
      from Devil's Island   6.25.54 CBS
   Omnibus   ep   The Trial of St. Joan   1.2.55 CBS
   Studio One   ep   Sane as a Hatter   7.11.55 CBS
   Loretta Young Show   ep   Father Happe   3.4.56 NBC
   Playhouse 90   ep   Confession 11.29.56 CBS

BRESLIN, PAT
   Broadway Television Theatre   ep   Rebecca   9.1.52 NN
   Suspense Theatre   ep   The Deadly Lamb   12.23.52 CBS
   Armstrong Circle Theatre   ep   Black Wedding   1.27.53
      NBC
   TV Sound Stage   ep   Exit Laughing   9.18.53 NBC
   Broadway Television Theatre   ep   Room Service 1.11.54
      NN
   Studio One   ep   Man of Extinction   2.8.54 CBS
   Armstrong Circle Theatre   ep   My Client, McDuff   4.6.
      54 NBC
   The Mask   ep   Party Night   4.11.54 ABC
   The Mask   ep   Royal Revenge   4.25.54 ABC
   Studio One   ep   Fear Is No Stranger   5.10.54 CBS
   Kraft Theatre   ep   See You on Sunday   6.24.54 ABC
   Best of Broadway   ep   Arsenic and Old Lace   1.5.55
      CBS
   People's Choice   sr   10.6.55 NBC
   People's Choice   sr ret   fall, 1956 NBC
   People's Choice   sr ret   fall, 1957 NBC

Alfred Hitchcock Presents ep The Crooked Road 10. 26.58 CBS

Schlitz Playhouse of Stars ep False Impression 11.7. 58 CBS

Maverick ep Yellow River 2.8.59 ABC

The Millionaire ep Millionaire Susan Ballard 5.6.59 CBS

Hotel de Paree ep Sundance and the Fallen Sparrow 5.27.60 CBS

Outlaws ep Ballad for a Badman 10.6.60 NBC

Perry Mason ep The Case of the Lavender Lipstick 10.15.60 CBS

Alfred Hitchcock Presents ep Oh Youth and Beauty 11. 22.60 NBC

Detectives ep 11.25.60 ABC

Rifleman ep Flowers by the Door 1.10.61 ABC

June Allyson Show ep The Haven 3.6.61 CBS

Rebel ep Miz Purdy 4.2.61 ABC

New Breed ep Sweet Bloom of Death 11.28.61 ABC

Perry Mason ep The Case of the Poison Pen Pal 2. 10.62 CBS

Adventures in Paradise ep The Dream Merchant 3. 18.62 ABC

Alfred Hitchcock Theatre ep Apex 3.20.62 NBC

Bonanza ep The Miracle Worker 5.20.62 NBC

Alfred Hitchcock Theatre ep Night of the Owl 10.4. 62 CBS

Stoney Burke ep Point of Honor 10.22.62 ABC

Perry Mason ep The Case of The Prankish Professor 1.17.63 CBS

Twilight Zone ep No Time Like the Past 3.7.63 CBS

Dr. Kildare ep Vote of Confidence 12.26.63 NBC

The Greatest Show on Earth ep Corsicans Don't Cry 1.14.64 ABC

Alfred Hitchcock Theatre ep Anyone for Murder 3.13. 64 CBS

Virginian ep The Long Quest 4.8.64 CBS

General Hospital sr 19.69 ABC

BRIAN, DAVID

Schlitz Playhouse of Stars ep 19 Rue Marie 3.13.53 CBS

Mirror Theatre ep Flight from Home 10.10.53 CBS

G.E. Theatre ep That Other Sunlight 3.14.54 CBS

Ford Theatre ep Taming of the Shrewd 3.25.54 NBC

Mr. District Attorney sr 4.3.54 CBS

Mr. District Attorney sr ret fall, 1954 CBS

Crossroads   ep   Timberland Preacher   11.16.56 ABC
Crossroads   ep   The Wreath   5.3.57 ABC
Alcoa Theatre   ep   Shadow of Evil   11.30.59 NBC
Desilu Playhouse   ep   Murder Is a Private Affair   6.10. 60 CBS
Untouchables   ep   The St. Louis Story   6.30.60 ABC
G.E. Theatre   ep   Labor of Love   3.26.61 CBS
Untouchables   ep   Testimony of Evil   3.30.61 ABC
Rawhide   ep   Incident of the Painted Lady   5.12.61 CBS
Cain's Hundred   ep   10.17.61 NBC
Target Corruptors   ep   One for the Road   1.12.62 ABC
Laramie   ep   Protective Custody   1.15.63 NBC
Dakotas   ep   Fargo   2.25.63 ABC
Death Valley Days   ep   The Peacemaker   11.2.63 ABC
Kraft Suspense Theatre   ep   Who Is Jennifer   1.16.64 NBC
Daniel Boone   ep   The Choosing   10.29.64 NBC
Profiles In Courage   ep   4.25.65 NBC
Laredo   ep   Three's Company   10.14.65 NBC
I Dream of Jeannie   ep   The Yacht Murder Case   10.23. 65 NBC
Honey West   ep   The Perfect Un-Crime   1.28.66 ABC
Branded   ep   Call to Glory   2.28.66, 3.6.66, 3.13.66 NBC
Please Don't Eat the Daisies   ep   A-Hunting We Will Go 10.1.66 NBC
Iron Horse   ep   11.7.66 ABC
Love on a Rooftop   ep   1.3.67 ABC
Hondo   ep   11.24.67 ABC
Star Repertory Theatre   ep   Patterns of Force   2.16.68 NBC
Cimarron Strip   ep   The Greeners   3.7.68 CBS
Mannix   ep   Night out of Time   12.7.68 CBS
Gunsmoke   ep   12.16.68 CBS
Name of the Game   ep   Keep the Doctor Away   2.14.69 NBC
Gunsmoke   ep   11.30.70 CBS
O'Hara, U.S. Treasury   ep   11.5.71 CBS
Mission Impossible   ep   11.4.72 NBC
Search   ep   11.8.72 NBC

BRIDGES, BEAU
My Three Sons   ep   Brotherly Love   10.27.60 ABC
Sea Hunt   ep   11.26.60   CBS
Zane Grey Theatre   ep   Image of a Drawn Sword   5.11. 61 CBS
Sea Hunt   ep   10.14.61 CBS

My Three Sons ep A Lesson in any Language 11.16.
61 ABC
Ensign O'Toole sr 9.23.62 NBC
Lloyd Bridges Theatre ep 10.2.62 CBS
Lloyd Bridges Theatre ep 2.12.63 CBS
Lloyd Bridges Theatre ep A Pair of Boots 4.23.63
CBS
Ben Casey ep The Echo of A Silent Cheer 10.16.63,
10.23.63 ABC
Rawhide ep Incident at Paradise 10.24.63 CBS
Mr. Novak ep Sparrow on the Wire 1.21.64 NBC
Eleventh Hour ep Cannibal Plants, They Eat You Alive
2.5.64 NBC
Dr. Kildare ep The Child Between 3.5.64 NBC
Combat ep The Short Day of Private Putnam 3.24.64
ABC
Mr. Novak ep Honor--and All That 3.23.65 NBC
12 O'Clock High ep Then Came the Mighty Hunter 9.
27.65 ABC
FBI ep An Elephant Is Like a Rope 12.5.65 ABC
Fugitive ep Stroke of Genius 2.1.66 ABC
Loner ep The Mourners for Johnny Starp 2.5.66 CBS
Branded ep Nice Day for a Hanging 2.6.66 NBC
Gunsmoke ep 2.12.66 CBS
Frank Merriwell pt 7.25.66 CBS
Bonanza ep 1.8.67 NBC
Fugitive ep 1.9.67 ABC
World of Disney ep Atta Girl Kelly 3.5.67, 3.12.67,
3.19.67 NBC
Cimarron Strip ep 9.14.67 CBS
Felony Squad ep 12.4.67 ABC

BRIDGES, JEFF
Lloyd Bridges Theatre ep To Walk with the Stars 2.
26.63 CBS
FBI ep 10.4.69 ABC
Most Deadly Game ep Nightbirds 12.12.70 ABC
In Search of America tf 3.23.71 ABC

BRIDGES, LLOYD
Bigelow-Sanford Theatre ep A Man's First Debt 9.27.
51 NN
Robert Montgomery Presents ep Rise up and Walk
2.4.52 NBC
Studio One ep International Incident 6.16.52 CBS
Suspense ep Her Last Adventure 8.19.52 CBS
Schlitz Playhouse of Stars ep This Plane for Hire
10.17.52 CBS

Goodyear Playhouse ep A Long Way Home 3.19.53
  NBC
Teledrama ep Secret Service Investigator 6.19.53
  CBS
Shower of Stars ep The Dark Fleece 6.16.55 CBS
Climax ep Edge of Terror 8.11.55 CBS
Front Row Center ep The Ainsley Case 1.29.56
  CBS
Studio One ep 2.6.56 CBS
Alcoa Hour ep Tragedy in a Temporary Town 2.19.
  56 NBC
Climax ep The Sound of Silence 3.1.56 CBS
Studio 57 ep The Regulators 4.8.56 NN
Climax ep Figures in Clay 5.31.56 CBS
Studio One ep American Primitive 10.29.56 CBS
Playhouse 90 ep Heritage of Anger 11.15.56 CBS
Zane Grey Theatre ep Time of Decision 1.18.57
  CBS
Climax ep Disappearance of Amanda Hale 5.30.57
  CBS
Playhouse 90 ep Clash by Night 6.13.57 CBS
U.S. Steel Hour ep They Never Forget 1.30.57 CBS
Studio 57 ep Man on the Outside 9.22.57 NN
Sea Hunt sr 1.11.58 CBS
Frank Sinatra Show ep A Time to Cry 1.17.58 ABC
Zane Grey Theatre ep Wire 1.13.58 CBS
Sea Hunt sr ret fall, 1958 CBS
Zane Grey Theatre ep Time of Decision 5.7.59 CBS
Sea Hunt sr ret fall, 1959 CBS
Desilu Playhouse ep Lepke 11.20.59 CBS
The Valley of Decision Sp 3.20.60 NBC
Sea Hunt sr ret fall, 1960 CBS
Zane Grey Theatre ep Ransom 11.17.60 CBS
June Allyson Show ep Death of the Temple Bay 4.3.
  61 CBS
Zane Grey Theatre ep Image of a Drawn Sword 5.11.
  61 CBS
Dick Powell Theatre ep Who Killed Julie Greer 9.26.
  61 NBC
Alcoa Premiere ep The Fortress 10.24.61 ABC
G.E. Theatre ep Star Witness 11.12.61 CBS
Lloyd Bridges Show sh/sr 9.11.62 CBS
Kraft Suspense Theatre ep A Hero for Our Times
  10.31.63 NBC
Great Adventure ep Wild Bill Hickock 1.3.64 CBS
Eleventh Hour ep Cannibals Plants, They Eat You Alive
  2.5.64 NBC

Loner   sr   9.18.65 CBS
Mission Impossible   ep   12.3.66 CBS
A Case of Libel   Sp   2.11.68 ABC
CBS Playhouse   ep   The People Next Door   10.15.68
  CBS
The Silent Gun   tf   12.16.69 ABC
Silent Night, Lonely Night   tf   12.16.69 NBC
The Love War   tf   3.10.70 ABC
San Francisco International Airport   sr   10.20.70 NBC
Do You Take This Stranger   tf   1.18.71 NBC
The Deadly Dreams   tf   9.25.71 ABC
Here's Lucy   ep   9.11.72 CBS
Haunts of the Very Rich   tf   9.20.72 ABC

BRITT, MAY

Danny Thomas Show   ep   Fear Is the Chain   2.19.68 NBC
Mission Impossible   ep   10.5.69 CBS
Most Deadly Game   ep   The Lady from Praha   1.9.71 ABC

BRITTON, BARBARA

Robert Montgomery Presents ep Mrs. Mike 12.18.50 NBC
Armstrong Circle Theatre   ep   Christopher Beach   12.
  26.50 NBC
Pulitzer Prize Playhouse   ep   Haunted House   3.9.51 ABC
Video Theatre   ep   Treasure Trove   3.26.51 CBS
Schlitz Playhouse of Stars   ep   Say Hello to Pamela
  6.20.52 CBS
Robert Montgomery Presents   ep   Til Next We Meet
  6.23.52 NBC
Mr. and Mrs. North   sr   10.3.52 CBS
Mr. and Mrs. North   sr ret   2.2.54 NBC
Mr. and Mrs. North   sr ret   2.25.55 NN
Climax   ep   Flight 951   4.21.55 CBS
Robert Montgomery Presents   ep   Now or Never   5.30.
  55 NBC
Appointment with Adventure   ep   Five Star Crisis   8.21.
  55 CBS
Robert Montgomery Presents   ep   The Stranger   10.3.55
  NBC
Ford Theatre   ep   Twelve to Eternity   10.27.55 NBC
Ford Theatre   ep   The Fabulous Sycamores   12.1.55 NBC
Head of the Family   pt   7.19.60 CBS

BROLIN, JAMES

Patty Duke Show   ep   12.8.65 ABC
The Long Hot Summer   ep   Man with Two Faces   4.13.
  66 ABC
Batman   ep   The Cat and the Fiddle   9.14/15.66   ABC

The Monroes   ep   Incident of the Hanging Tree   10.12.
   66 ABC
The Monroes   ep   11.23.66 ABC
The Monroes   ep   12.21.66 ABC
The Monroes   ep   1.4.67 ABC
Marcus Welby, M.D.   tf   3.26.69 ABC
Marcus Welby, M.D.   sr   9.23.69 ABC
Marcus Welby, M.D.   sr ret   9.23.69 ABC
Marcus Welby, M.D.   sr ret   9.22.70 ABC
Marcus Welby, M.D.   sr ret   9.14.71 ABC
Owen Marshall   ep   2.3.72 ABC
Marcus Welby, M.D.   sr ret   9.12.72 ABC
Short Walk to Daylight   tf   10.24.72 ABC

BRONSON, BETTY
   Dr. Kildare   ep   Hastings' Farewell   11.1.62 NBC
   Marcus Welby, M.D.   ep   Best Is Yet to Be   11.16.71
      ABC

BRONSON, CHARLES
   The Doctor   ep   Take the Odds   1.18.53 NBC
   Four Star Playhouse   ep   The Witness   7.22.54 CBS
   Man Behind the Badge   ep   2.19.55 CBS
   Public Defender   ep   Cornered   3.24.55 CBS
   Treasury Men in Action   ep   The Case of the Deadly
      Dilemma   3.24.55 ABC
   Stage 7   ep   The Time of Day   5.29.55 CBS
   Treasury Men in Action   ep   The Case of the Shot in
      the Dark   6.9.55 ABC
   Playhouse   ep   Woman in the Mine   6.12.55 ABC
   Crusader   ep   A Boxing Match   10.21.55 CBS
   Cavalcade Theatre   ep   Chain of Hearts   11.1.55 ABC
   G.E. Theatre   ep   Prosper's Old Mother   11.20.55
      CBS
   Alfred Hitchcock Presents   ep   And so Died Riabouchin-
      ska   2.12.56 CBS
   Crusader   ep   Freeze Out   2.17.56 CBS
   Medic   ep   Who Search for Truth   2.27.56 NBC
   Alfred Hitchcock Presents   ep   There Was an Old Wom-
      an   3.18.56 CBS
   Warner Bros. Presents   ep   Explosion   3.27.56 ABC
   Gunsmoke   ep   5.26.56 CBS
   The Millionaire   ep   The Story of Jerry Bell   2.27.57
      CBS
   Hey Jeannie   ep   Jeannie the Policewoman   3.2.57 CBS
   Studio 57   ep   Outpost   9.1.57 NN
   Richard Diamond   ep   The Peter Rocco Case   9.9.57
      CBS

Have Gun Will Travel   ep   9.21.57 CBS
Colt .45   ep   Young Gun   12.13.57 ABC
M Squad   ep   Fight   4.18.58 NBC
Sugarfoot   ep   The Bullet and the Cross   5.27.58 ABC
Have Gun Will Travel   ep   9.27.58 CBS
Man with a Camera   sr   10.10.58 ABC
Gunsmoke   ep   11.1.58 CBS
U.S. Marshal   ep   Pursuit   5.25.59 NBC
Playhouse 90   ep   Rank and File   5.28.59 CBS
Man with a Camera   sr ret   10.19.59 ABC
Colt .45   ep   Young Gun   1.7.60 ABC
Playhouse 90   ep   The Cruel Day   2.24.60 CBS
Laramie   ep   Street of Hate   3.1.60 NBC
Hennesey   ep   10.17.60 CBS
Aquanauts   ep   The Cave Divers   12.7.60 CBS
Riverboat   ep   Zigzag   12.26.60 NBC
Alcoa Premiere   ep   The Last Round   1.10.61 ABC
Islanders   ep   The Generous Politician   1.15.61 ABC
G.E. Theatre   ep   Memory in White   1.8.61 CBS
Loretta Young Show   ep   Wood Lot   3.26.61 NBC
Laramie   ep   Run of the Hunted   4.4.61 NBC
Hennesey   ep   The Nogoodnik   4.17.61 CBS
Have Gun Will Travel   ep   10.14.61 CBS
Have Gun Will Travel   ep   11.18.61 CBS
New Breed   ep   The Valley of the Three Charlies   12.
    15.61 ABC
Cain's Hundred   ep   Dead Load   11.21.61 NBC
Adventures in Paradise   ep   Survival   12.31.61 ABC
Alfred Hitchcock Theatre   ep   The Woman Who Wanted
    to Live   2.6.62 NBC
Untouchables   ep   The Death Tree   2.15.62 ABC
Empire   ep   The Day the Empire Stood Still   9.25.62
    NBC
Have Gun Will Travel   ep   1.5.63 CBS
Empire   sr   2.26.63 NBC
Dr. Kildare   ep   Who Ever Heard of a Two Headed
    Doll   9.26.63 NBC
Bonanza   ep   The Underdog   12.13.64 NBC
Combat   ep   Heritage   4.13.65 ABC
Big Valley   ep   11.10.65 ABC
Virginian   ep   Nobility of Kings   11.10.65 NBC
Rawhide   ep   Duet at Daybreak   11.16.65 CBS
Fugitive   ep   1.17.67 ABC
Virginian   ep   9.13.67 NBC

BROOK, CLIVE
    Pulitzer Prize Playhouse   ep   Second Threshold   2.27.51
    ABC

BROOKE, HILLARY
    Racket Squad   ep   Fair Exchange   2.14.52 CBS
    My Little Margie   sr   6.16.52 CBS
    My Little Margie   sr ret   10.4.52 NBC
    Abbott and Costello Show   sr   12.5.52 CBS
    My Little Margie   sr ret   1.1.53 CBS
    Dark Adventure   ep   Second Mrs. Sands   3.2.53 ABC
    Four Star Playhouse   ep   The Ladies on His Mind   5.
      21.53 CBS
    Twilight Time   ep   That Time in Boston   7.13.53 ABC
    My Little Margie   sr ret   9.2.53 NBC
    Four Star Playhouse   ep   Backstage   5.20.54 CBS
    Pepsi Cola Playhouse   ep   Before the Police Arrive
      6.25.54 ABC
    Cavalcade Theatre   ep   A Man's Home   12.28.54 ABC
    Big Town   ep   12.20.54 NBC
    Public Defender   ep   Jackpot   2.24.55 CBS
    Fireside Theatre   ep   Luxurious Ladies   4.19.55 NBC
    Ford Theatre   ep   Cardboard Casanova   5.26.55 NBC
    The Millionaire   ep   The Story of Vickie Lawson   6.8.
      55 CBS
    Crossroads   ep   Vivi Shining Bright   12.23.55 ABC
    I Love Lucy   ep   2.6.56 CBS
    Screen Directors Playhouse   ep   The Sword of Villon
      4.4.56 NBC
    West Point   ep   The Right to Choose   11.9.56 CBS
    Studio 57   ep   Palm Springs Incident   7.7.57 NN
    Perry Mason   ep   The Case of the Sleepwalker's Niece
      9.28.57 CBS
    Meet McGraw   ep   Kiss of Death   10.29.57 NBC
    December Bride   ep   12.9.57 CBS
    West Point   ep   The Right to Choose   5.27.58 ABC
    Richard Diamond   ep   5.24.59 CBS
    Lawman   ep   The Ring   5.24.59 ABC
    Father Knows Best   ep   The Great Anderson Mystery
      6.8.59 CBS
    Richard Diamond   ep   Fine Art of Murder   1.25.60 NBC
    Michael Shayne   ep   This Is It, Michael Shayne   11.18.
      60 NBC

BROOKS, GERALDINE
    Starlight Theatre   ep   Magic Wire   3.17.51 NN
    Lights Out   ep   The Chamber of Gloom   11.5.51 NBC
    Broadway Television Theatre   ep   Seventh Heaven   10.
      26.53 NN
    Armstrong Circle Theatre   ep   The Honor of Littorno
      11.3.53 NBC

Studio One   ep   A Criminal Design   1.18.54 CBS
Medallion Theatre   ep   The 39th Bomb   2.13.54 CBS
U.S. Steel Hour   ep   Goodbye...But It Doesn't Go Away
  11.9.54 ABC
Studio One   ep   Joey   11.22.54 CBS
Climax   ep   Champion   3.31.55 CBS
Appointment with Adventure   ep   The Quiet Gun   4.24.
  55 CBS
Way of the World   ep   8.22.55 NBC
Appointment with Adventure   ep   When in Rome   9.11.
  55 CBS
Studio One   ep   Manhattan Duet   2.13.56 CBS
Modern Romance   ep   3.25.57 NBC
U.S. Steel Hour   ep   This Day in Fear   11.19.58 CBS
U.S. Steel Hour   ep   No Leave for the Captain   6.17.
  59 CBS
Richard Diamond   ep   Dead to the World   1.11.60 NBC
Staccato   ep   The Only Witness   1.14.60 NBC
Have Gun Will Travel   ep   3.26.60 CBS
U.S. Steel Hour   ep   The Mating Machine   1.11.61 CBS
Adventures in Paradise   ep   Who Is Sylvia   3.13.61
  ABC
Bonanza   ep   Elizabeth, My Love   5.27.61 NBC
Bus Stop   ep   Call Back Yesterday   12.10.61 ABC
Sam Benedict   ep   Where There's a Will   12.22.62 NBC
G.E. Theatre   ep   The Troubled Heart   4.22.62 CBS
Virginian   ep   Duel at Shiloh   1.2.63 NBC
Stoney Burke   ep   Death Rides a Pale Horse   1.14.63
  ABC
Alcoa Premiere   ep   Five, Six, Pick up Sticks   1.24.
  63 ABC
Dick Powell Theatre   ep   Colossus   3.12.63 NBC
Laramie   ep   The Stranger   4.23.63 NBC
Combat   ep   The Walking Wounded   4.30.63 ABC
Defenders   ep   Everybody Else Is Dead   5.11.63 CBS
Kraft Suspense Theatre   ep   A Hero for Our Times
  10.31.63 NBC
Fugitive   ep   Ticket to Alaska   11.12.63 ABC
Nurses   ep   The Rainbow Ride   1.16.64 CBS
Ben Casey   ep   Keep Out of Reach of Adults   3.11.64
  ABC
Outer Limits   ep   Cold Hands, Warm Heart   9.26.64
  ABC
Dr. Kildare   ep   The Elusive Dik-Dik   12.3.64 NBC
Mr. Novak   ep   Love Among the Grownups   12.29.64
  NBC
Fugitive   ep   3.9.65 ABC

Ben Casey   ep   In Case of Emergency, Cry Havoc   1.
    3.66 ABC
Shenandoah   ep   A Long Way Home   1.31.66 ABC
Gunsmoke   ep   2.5.66 CBS
Hawk   ep   Thanks for the Honeymoon   9.22.66 ABC
Bonanza   ep   To Bloom for Thee   10.16.66 NBC
Run for Your Life   ep   The List of Alice McKenna
    1.23.67 NBC
Fugitive   ep   2.21.67 ABC
Ironside   tf   3.28.67 NBC
Danny Thomas Show   ep   Fame Is a Four Letter Word
    10.30.67 NBC
High Chaparral   ep   11.19.67 NBC
Name of the Game   ep   Incident in Berlin   10.25.68
    NBC
Mannix   ep   Edge of the Knife   11.9.68 CBS
Judd for the Defense   ep   Borderline Girl   1.10.69
    ABC
Outsider   ep   All the Social Graces   3.12.69 NBC
It Takes a Thief   ep   4.1.69 ABC
Dan August   ep   Circle of Lies   2.18.71 ABC
Marcus Welby, M.D.   ep   Contract   3.16.71 ABC
Ironside   ep   11.16.72 NBC
Streets of San Francisco   ep   12.16.72 ABC

BROWN, JIM
    I Spy   ep   Cops and Robbers   4.12.67 NBC

BROWN, JOE E.
    Schlitz Playhouse of Stars   ep   Meet Mr. Justice   7.
        15.55 CBS
    Screen Directors Playhouse   ep   The Silent Partner
        12.21.55 NBC
    G.E. Theatre   ep   The Golden Key   5.27.56 CBS
    Ann Sothern Show   ep   Oliver's Dream Man   2.15.60
        CBS
    Route 66   ep   Journey to Nineveh   9.22.62 CBS
    The Greatest Show on Earth   ep   You're All Right Ivy
        4.28.64 ABC

BROWN, JOHN MACK
    Perry Mason   ep   The Case of the Daring Decoy   3.29.
        58 CBS

BROWN, PAMELA
    Celanese Theatre   ep   Susan and God   10.17.51 ABC
    Playhouse 90   ep   The Violent Heart   2.6.58 CBS

BROWN, VANESSA
   Pulitzer Prize Playhouse   ep   Blockade   3.23.51 ABC
   Robert Montgomery Presents   ep   The Kimballs   11.19.
      51 NBC
   Philco Playhouse   ep   The Monument   6.29.52 NBC
   Stage 7   ep   The Legacy   2.13.55 CBS
   Climax   ep   The Box of Chocolates   2.24.55 CBS
   Justice   ep   4.21.55 NBC
   Climax   ep   The Dance   6.30.55 CBS
   My Favorite Husband   sr   10.4.55 CBS
   The Millionaire   ep   The Louise Williams Story   5.2.
      56 CBS
   Climax   ep   Hurricane Diane   12.12.57 CBS
   Wagon Train   ep   The Sally Potter Story   4.9.58 NBC
   Matinee Theatre   ep   The Man with Pointed Toes   6.17.
      58 NBC
   G.E. Theatre   ep   Silhouette   12.27.59 CBS
   Alcoa Presents   ep   The Lovers   2.16.60 ABC
   Mystery Show   ep   Murder by the Book   9.4.60 NBC

BROWNE, ROSCOE LEE
   Espionage   ep   The Whistling Shrimp   11.20.63 NBC
   Festival of the Arts   ep   Benito Cereno   10.11.65 NN
   Mannix   ep   Deadfall   1.20.68, 1.27.68 CBS
   Invaders   ep   The Vise   2.21.68 ABC
   Outcasts   ep   2.24.69 ABC
   Name of the Game   ep   The Third Choice   3.7.69 NBC
   Bonanza   ep   3.5.72 NBC

BRUCE, CAROL
   Silver Theatre   ep   Happy Marriage   1.16.50 CBS
   Musical Comedy Time   ep   Miss Liberty   1.8.51 NBC
   Curtain Call   ep   The Promise   6.20.52 NBC
   Armstrong Circle Theatre   ep   Thief of Diamonds   12.
      11.57 CBS

BRUCE, NIGEL
   Four Star Playhouse   ep   A String of Beads   1.21.54
      CBS

BRUCE, VIRGINIA
   Silver Theatre   ep   Wedding Anniversary   5.22.50 CBS
   Video Theatre   ep   Something to Live for   8.6.53 CBS
   G.E. Theatre   ep   Woman's World   10.25.53 CBS
   Loretta Young Show   ep   Week-End in Winnetka   9.4.55
      NBC
   Studio 57   ep   Who's Calling   2.12.56 NN

Matinee Theatre   ep   People in Glass   4.11.56 NBC
Lux Video Theatre   ep   Mildred Pierce   9.20.56 NBC

BRYNNER, YUL
Omnibus   ep   A Lodging for the Night   3.8.53 CBS
The Poppy Is Also a Flower   tf   4.22.66 ABC
Anna and the King of Siam   sr   9.17.72 CBS

BUCHHOLZ, HORST
Danny Thomas Show   ep   Fear Is the Chain   2.19.68
   NBC

BUJOLD, GENEVIEVE
Playhouse New York   ep   Antigone   10.7.72 NN

BULOFF, JOSEPH
Philco Playhouse   ep   Dirty Eddie   4.9.50 NBC
Philco Playhouse   ep   Anything Can Happen   6.18.50
   NBC
Two Girls Named Smith   sr   1.20.51 ABC
Philco Playhouse   ep   Justice and Mr. Pleznik   5.20.
   51 NBC
Lights Out   ep   Pit of the Dead   6.11.51 NBC
Philco Playhouse   ep   Education of a Fullback   11.4.51
   NBC
Cosmopolitan Theatre   ep   The Beautiful Time   12.4.51
   NN
Philco Playhouse   ep   The Best Laid Schemes   3.23.52
   NBC
Goodyear Playhouse   ep   Holiday Song   9.14.52 NBC
Tales of Tomorrow   ep   Invigorating Air   11.28.52 ABC
Philco Playhouse   ep   The Reluctant Citizen   2.8.53
   NBC
Goodyear Playhouse   ep   Holiday Song   9.20.53 NBC
The Web   ep   The Trouble with Diamonds   7.18.54 CBS
Center Theatre   ep   Lucky Louie   7.27.54 ABC
Suspicion   ep   Murder Me Gently   10.7.57 NBC
Wonderful Town   Sp   11.30.58 CBS
Untouchables   cp   Ain't We Got Fun   11.12.59 ABC
Naked City   ep   Go Fight City Hall   10.31.62 ABC
Ben Casey   ep   I'll Get on My Icefloe and Wave Good-
   bye   1.18.64 CBS
Medical Center   ep   Emergency in Ward E   10.8.69
   CBS

BUNCE, ALAN
Armstrong Circle Theatre   ep   The 38th President

1. 6. 53 NBC
The Web ep Dark Meeting 1.25.53 CBS
Kraft Theatre ep Autumn Story 3.18.53 NBC
Ethel and Albert sr 4.25.53 NBC
Mirror Theatre ep The Party 8.18.53 NBC
The Web ep The Bait 8.22.54 CBS
Ethel and Albert sr ret 9.4.54 NBC
Elgin Hour ep Family Meeting 1.25.55 ABC
Ethel and Albert sr ret 6.20.55 CBS
Studio One ep Operation Home 5.30.55 CBS
The Right Man Sp 10.24.60 CBS
Perry Mason ep The Case of the G Clients 6.10.61
CBS
U.S. Steel Hour ep The Perfect Accident 2.21.62
CBS
Defenders ep The Crusader 2.24.62 CBS
Stoney Burke ep Fight Night 10.8.62 ABC
Nurses ep You Could Die Laughing 4.18.63 CBS
Patty Duke Show ep Patty, the People's Voice 10.28.
64 ABC
For the People ep To Prosecute All Crimes 1.31.65
CBS

BUONO, VICTOR
Rebel ep Blind Marriage 4.17.60 ABC
Checkmate ep Moment of Truth 11.26.60 CBS
Untouchables ep Mr. Moon 4.20.61 ABC
Harrigan and Son ep The Testimonial 9.29.61 ABC
77 Sunset Strip ep Bullet for Santa 12.22.61 ABC
New Breed ep Cross the Little Line 1.9.62 ABC
Untouchables ep The Gang War 1.18.62 ABC
Perry Mason ep The Case of the Absent Artist 3.17.
62 CBS
G.E. True ep Firebug 1.27.63 CBS
77 Sunset Strip ep "f" 9.27.63 ABC
Perry Mason ep The Case of the Simple Simon 4.2.
64 CBS
Bob Hope Chrysler Theatre ep Memorandum for a
Spy 4.2.65 NBC
Perry Mason ep The Case of the Grinning Gorilla
4.29.65 CBS
Wild Wild West ep Night of the Inferno 9.17.65 CBS
Voyage to the Bottom of the Sea ep 10.10.65 ABC
The Man from U.N.C.L.E. ep The Deadly Goddess
Affair 1.14.66 NBC
I Spy ep Turkish Delight 2.9.66 NBC
Perry Mason ep The Case of the Twice-Told Twist

2. 27. 66 CBS
Batman   ep   The Curse of Tut   4. 13. 66, 4. 14. 66 ABC
Wild Wild West   ep   The Night of the Eccentrics   9. 16.
   66 CBS
Batman   ep   The Spell of Tut   9. 28. 66 ABC
Batman   ep   3. 8. 67, 3. 9. 67 ABC
The Girl from U. N. C. L. E.   ep   3. 14. 67 NBC
T. H. E. Cat   ep   3. 31. 67 NBC
Daniel Boone   ep   9. 14. 67 NBC
Danny Thomas Show   ep   The Scene   9. 25. 67 NBC
Batman   ep   10. 19. 67 ABC
Legend of Robin Hood   Sp   2. 18. 68 NBC
Batman   ep   2. 22. 68 ABC
It Takes a Thief   ep   The Three Virgins of Rome   11. 6.
   69 ABC
Get Smart   ep   1. 2. 70 CBS
Night Gallery   ep   11. 17. 71 NBC
Goodnight, My Love   tf   10. 17. 72 ABC
Assignment Vienna   ep   12. 7. 72 ABC
Mod Squad   ep   12. 21. 72 ABC

BURKE, BILLIE
   Lights Out   ep   Dr. Heidegger's Experiment   11. 20. 50
      NBC
   Bigelow Theatre   ep   Dear Amanda   3. 18. 51 CBS
   Doc Corkle   sr   10. 5. 52 NBC
   Best of Broadway   ep   Arsenic and Old Lace   1. 5. 55
      CBS
   Matinee Theatre   ep   Mother Was a Bachelor   1. 17. 56
      NBC
   Playhouse 90   ep   The Star-Wagon   1. 24. 57 CBS
   Playhouse 90   ep   Rumors of Evening   4. 10. 58 CBS
   77 Sunset Strip   ep   Publicity Brat   4. 1. 60 ABC

BURKE, PAUL
   Big Town   ep   12. 13. 54 NBC
   Big Town   ep   The Blood Profiteer   5. 16. 55 NBC
   Stage 7   ep   The Fox Hunt   9. 2. 55 CBS
   Navy Log   ep   Sky Pilot   10. 25. 55 CBS
   Matinee Theatre   ep   Hold My Hand and Run   2. 1. 56
      NBC
   Noah's Ark   sr   9. 18. 56 NBC
   Panic   ep   Courage   5. 7. 57 NBC
   Lineup   ep   The Winner Takes Nothing Case   11. 28. 58
      CBS
   M Squad   ep   Death Threat   3. 13. 59 NBC
   The Millionaire   ep   Millionaire Karl Miller   4. 22. 59
      CBS

Playhouse 90   ep   Dark December   4.30.59 CBS
Playhouse 90   ep   Seven against the Wall   7.9.59 CBS
Man and the Challenge   ep   The Sphere of No Return
   9.12.59 NBC
Men into Space   ep   Moon Probe   9.30.59 CBS
Five Fingers   sr   10.3.59 NBC
Tightrope   ep   The Money Fight   11.17.59 CBS
Black Saddle   ep   End of the Line   5.6.60 ABC
Wanted Dead or Alive   ep   9.21.60 CBS
Naked City   sr   10.12.60 ABC
Wagon Train   ep   Path of the Sergeant   2.8.61 NBC
Naked City   sr ret   fall, 1961 ABC
Naked City   sr ret   9.19.62 ABC
Eleventh Hour   ep   What Did She Mean by Good Luck
   11.13.63 NBC
Great Adventure   ep   The Special Courage of Captain
   Pratt   2.14.64 CBS
Dr. Kildare   ep   A Hundred Million Tomorrows   3.12.
   64 NBC
Eleventh Hour   ep   A Pattern of Sundays   4.8.64 NBC
12 O'Clock High   sr   9.18.64 ABC
Combat   ep   Point of View   9.29.64 ABC
Slattery's People   ep   What Is a Genius Worth This
   Week   11.16.64 CBS
12 O'Clock High   sr ret   9.13.65 ABC
12 O'Clock High   sr ret   9.9.66 ABC
Medical Center   ep   9.23.70 CBS
Crowhaven Farm   tf   11.24.70 ABC
Medical Center   ep   Undercurrent   1.20.71 CBS
Hawaii Five-O   ep   The Gun Runner   2.10.71 CBS
The Rookies   tf   3.7.72 ABC
Owen Marshall ep   10.5.72 ABC
Lt. Schuster's Wife   tf   10.11.72 ABC
Medical Center   ep   Doctor and Mr. Harper   10.25.72
   CBS

BURNETT, CAROL
Stanley   sr   9.24.56 NBC
Twilight Zone   ep   Cavender Is Coming   5.25.62 CBS
Calamity Jane   Sp   11.12.63 CBS
Once Upon a Mattress   Sp   6.3.64 CBS
The Lucy Show   ep   11.7.66 CBS
The Lucy Show   ep   3.13.67, 3.20.67 CBS
Gomer Pyle, U.S.M.C.   ep   9.22.67 CBS
Get Smart   ep   11.4.67 NBC
The Lucy Show   ep   12.4.67, 12.11.67 CBS
Here's Lucy   ep   Secretary Beautiful   3.2.70 CBS

Once Upon a Mattress   Sp (restaged)   12.12.72 CBS

BURNS, CATHERINE
    Two for the Money   tf   2.26.72 ABC
    Jigsaw   tf   9.21.72 ABC
    Night of Terror   tf   10.10.72 ABC
    Jigsaw   ep   10.12.72 ABC
    Mod Squad   ep   12.72.72 ABC

BURNS, GEORGE
    George Burns-Gracie Allen Show   sr   10.12.50 CBS
    George Burns-Gracie Allen Show   sr ret   10.51 CBS
    George Burns-Gracie Allen Show   sr ret   10.52 CBS
    George Burns-Gracie Allen Show   sr ret   10.53 CBS
    George Burns-Gracie Allen Show   sr ret   10.4.54 CBS
    George Burns-Gracie Allen Show   sr ret   10.3.55 CBS
    Bob Cummings Show   ep   Hawaii Calls   10.27.55 CBS
    George Burns-Gracie Allen Show   sr ret   10.56 CBS
    George Burns-Gracie Allen Show   sr ret   10.57 CBS
    George Burns Show   sr   10.21.58 NBC
    Bob Cummings Show   ep   Bob Butters Beck   12.2.58
        NBC
    G.E. Theatre   ep   Platinum on the Rocks   11.29.59
        CBS
    Wendy and Me   sr   9.14.64 ABC
    The Lucy Show   ep   9.12.66 CBS
    Here's Lucy   ep   11.23.70 CBS

BURNS, MICHAEL
    Alfred Hitchcock Presents   ep   Special Delivery   11.29.
        59 CBS
    Alfred Hitchcock Presents   ep   The Doubtful Doctor
        10.4.60 NBC
    Wagon Train   ep   The Alison Justis Story   10.19.60
        NBC
    G.E. Theatre   ep   Learn to Say Good-By   12.4.60 CBS
    Tales of Wells Fargo   ep   Frightened Witness   12.26.
        60 NBC
    Wagon Train   ep   The Jeremy Dow Story   12.28.60 NBC
    Loretta Young Show   ep   Quiet Desperation   2.5.61 NBC
    G.E. Theatre   ep   Louise and the Horseless Buggy   4.
        30.61 CBS
    Tall Man   ep   Ransom of a Town   5.6.61 NBC
    Twilight Zone   ep   The Shelter   9.29.61 CBS
    Alcoa Premiere   ep   Family Outing   11.14.61 ABC
    Wagon Train   ep   The Mark Minor Story   11.15.61
        NBC

Lassie ep 11.19.61 CBS
It's a Man's World sr 9.17.62 NBC
Wagon Train sr 9.16.63 ABC
Kraft Suspense Theatre ep Charlie, He Couldn't Kill
  a Fly 5.7.64 NBC
Wagon Train sr ret 9.20.64 ABC
FBI ep The Forests of the Night 1.2.66 ABC
Virginian ep Long Ride to Wind River 1.19.66 NBC
Bonanza ep The Trouble with Jamie 3.20.66 NBC
Jesse James ep A Field of Wild Flowers 4.25.66
  ABC
Off We Go pt 9.5.66 CBS
Virginian ep The Challenge 10.19.66 NBC
Dragnet ep 1.12.67 NBC
Bonanza ep 4.16.67 NBC
Dundee and the Culhane ep 10.25.67 CBS
Tarzan ep The Last of the Superman 11.3.67 NBC
Daniel Boone ep 11.23.67 NBC
Cowboy in Africa ep 1.29.68 ABC
Big Valley ep Run of the Savage 3.11.68 ABC
Gunsmoke ep 9.3.68 CBS
Outcasts ep 12.23.68 ABC
Virginian ep The Bugler 11.18.69 NBC
FBI ep Scapegoat 11.23.69 ABC
Medical Center ep Jeopardy 11.26.69 CBS
Then Came Bronson ep Pickin' and a Singin' 1.14.70
  NBC
Marcus Welby, M.D. ep Nobody Wants a Fat Jockey
  2.17.70 ABC
Gunsmoke ep 3.9.70 CBS
Hollywood Television Theatre ep The Andersonville
  Trial 5.17.70 NN
Here's Lucy ep 2.8.71 CBS
FBI ep Downfall 2.21.71 ABC
Men from Shiloh ep 2.24.71 NBC
Hawaii Five-O ep 10.19.71 CBS
Gidget Gets Married tf 1.4.72 ABC
Sarge ep 1.11.72 NBC
Love American Style ep 2.4.72 ABC

BURR, RAYMOND
Gruen Guild Playhouse ep The Tiger 4.24.52 NN
Gruen Guild Playhouse ep Face Value 9.23.52 NN
Twilight Theatre ep The Mask of Medusa 6.1.53 ABC
Ford Theatre ep The Fugitives 1.75.54 NBC
Four Star Playhouse ep The Room 6.10.54 CBS
Schlitz Playhouse of Stars ep Ordeal of Dr. Sutton

7. 1. 55 CBS
Gruen Guild Playhouse   ep   The Leather Coat   9. 9. 52
NN
Mr. Lucky at Seven   ep   Pearls from Paris   11. 10. 52
ABC
Counterpoint   ep   The Wreck   9. 17. 55 NN
20th Century-Fox Hour   ep   The Ox Bow Incident   11.
2. 55 CBS
Lux Video Theatre   ep   The Web   12. 1. 55 NBC
Ford Theatre   ep   Man without a Fear   3. 1. 56 NBC
Climax   ep   The Sound of Silence   3. 1. 56 CBS
Climax   ep   The Shadow of Evil   5. 24. 56   CBS
Lux Video Theatre   ep   Flamingo Road   10. 18. 56 NBC
Climax   ep   Savage Portrait   12. 6. 56 CBS
Playhouse 90   ep   The Greer Case   1. 31. 57 CBS
Perry Mason   sr   9. 21. 57 CBS
Playhouse 90   ep   The Lone Woman   12. 26. 57 CBS
Perry Mason   sr ret   fall, 1958 CBS
Perry Mason   sr ret   10. 3. 59 CBS
Perry Mason   sr ret   fall, 1960 CBS
Perry Mason   sr ret   fall, 1961 CBS
Perry Mason   sr ret   9. 27. 62 CBS
Perry Mason   sr ret   9. 26. 63 CBS
Perry Mason   sr ret   9. 24. 64 CBS
Perry Mason   sr ret   9. 12. 65 CBS
Ironside   tf   3. 28. 67 NBC
Ironside   sr   9. 14. 67 NBC
It Takes a Thief   ep   1. 9. 68 ABC
Ironside   sr ret   9. 19. 68 NBC
Ironside   sr ret   9. 19. 69 NBC
Ironside   sr ret   9. 17. 70 NBC
Ironside   sr ret   9. 21. 71 NBC
Ironside   sr ret   9. 14. 72 NBC
Bold Ones   ep   9. 19. 72 NBC

BURTON, RICHARD
Dupont Show of the Month   ep   Wuthering Heights   5. 9.
58 CBS
The Fifth Column   Sp   1. 29. 60 CBS
Hallmark Hall of Fame   ep   The Tempest   2. 3. 60 NBC
Here's Lucy   ep   9. 14. 70 CBS

BURTON, WENDELL
Medical Center   ep   Fatal Decision   1. 19. 72 CBS
Longstreet   ep   Please Leave the Wreck for Others to
Enjoy   1. 27. 72 ABC

BUSHMAN, FRANCIS X.
  Pepsi Cola Playhouse   ep   Hollywood, Home Sweet
    Home   4.16.54 ABC
  Schlitz Playhouse of Stars   ep   The Secret   9.10.54
    CBS
  Mr. Adams and Eve   ep   The Business Manager   3.1.
    57 CBS
  77 Sunset Strip   ep   All Our Yesterdays   11.21.58 ABC
  Danny Thomas Show   ep   10.12.59 CBS
  Dobie Gillis   ep   The Flying Millicans   2.2.60 CBS
  G.E. Theatre   ep   The Other Wise Man   12.25.60 CBS
  Theatre   ep   The Weekend Nothing Happened   2.10.61
    NBC
  Peter Gunn   ep   The Last Resort   5.15.61 ABC
  G.E. Theatre   ep   The Other Wise Man   12.25.61 CBS
  Batman   ep   Death in Slow Motion   4.27.66, 4.28.66
    ABC
  Dr. Kildare   ep   Life in the Dance Hall   9.28.65 NBC
  Voyage to the Bottom of the Sea   ep   The Terrible Toys
    10.16.66 ABC

BUTTONS, RED
  Studio One   ep   The Tale of St. Emergency   3.26.56
    CBS
  Hansel and Gretel   Sp   4.27.58 NBC
  Playhouse 90   ep   A Marriage of Strangers   5.14.59
    CBS
  G.E. Theatre   ep   The Tallest Marine   10.18.59 CBS
  Ford Star Time   ep   Something Special   12.1.59 NBC
  U.S. Steel Hour   ep   The Case of the Missing Wife
    8.10.60 CBS
  G.E. Theatre   ep   Tippy-Top   12.17.61 CBS
  Saints and Sinners   ep   All the Hard Young Men   9.24.
    62 NBC
  Eleventh Hour   ep   Sunday Father   1.8.64 NBC
  The Greatest Show on Earth   ep   The Last of the Strong-
    men 3.3.64 ABC
  Ben Casey   ep   Journeys End in Lovers' Meeting   4.19.
    65 ABC
  Double Life   sr   1.13.66 ABC
  Danny Thomas Show   ep   The Zero Man   11.27.67 NBC
  Love American Style   ep   11.10.69 ABC
  George M   Sp   9.12.70 NBC
  Breakout   tf   12.8.70 NBC

BUZZI, RUTH
  Night Gallery   ep   9.22.71 NBC

Here's Lucy   ep   12.11.72 CBS

BYINGTON, SPRING
   Bigelow Theatre   ep   Charming Billy   6.3.51 CBS
   Ford Theatre   ep   Wonderful Day for a Wedding   5.13.
      54 NBC
   December Bride   sr   10.4.54 CBS
   December Bride   sr ret   10.3.55   CBS
   Studio 57   ep   The Great Wide World   5.20.56 NN
   December Bride   sr ret   10.56 CBS
   20th Century-Fox Hour   ep   The Moneymaker   10.31.56
      CBS
   December Bride   sr ret   10.7.57 CBS
   December Bride   sr ret   10.2.58 CBS
   Goodyear Theatre   ep   The Sitter's Baby   5.9.60 NBC
   Detectives   ep   Face Down, Floating   4.29.60 ABC
   Tab Hunter Show   ep   The Matchmaker   10.23.60 NBC
   Alfred Hitchcock Presents   ep   The Man with Two Faces
      12.13.60 NBC
   Dennis the Menace   ep   Dennis' Birthday   2.19.61 CBS
   Laramie   sr   10.3.61 NBC
   Laramie   sr ret   9.25.62 NBC
   The Greatest Show on Earth   ep   This Train Doesn't
      Stop 'till It Gets There   4.14.64 ABC
   Bob Hope Chrysler Theatre   ep   The Timothy Heist
      10.30.64 NBC
   Dr. Kildare   ep   Fathers and Daughters   11.22.65, 11.
      23.65, 11.29.65, 11.30.65 NBC
   Blondie   ep   11.21.68 CBS
   Flying Nun   ep   12.19.68 ABC

BYRD, RALPH
   Fireside Theatre   ep   Operation Mona Lisa   5.2.50 NBC
   Fireside Theatre   ep   The Man without a Country   5.30.
      50 NBC
   Dick Tracy   sr   2.17.51 ABC
   Cinema Theatre   ep   The Bunker   6.17.52 NN

-C-

CAAN, JAMES
   Untouchables   ep   A Fist of Five   12.4.62 ABC
   Dr. Kildare   ep   The Mosaic   1.31.63 NBC
   Alcoa Premiere   ep   The Masked Marine 5.16.63 ABC

Ben Casey   ep   Justice to a Microbe   9.18.63 ABC
Combat   ep   Anatomy of a Patrol   11.26.63 ABC
Kraft Suspense Theatre   ep   The Hunt   12.19.63 NBC
Breaking Point   ep   Glass Flowers Never Drop Petals
    3.23.64 ABC
Channing   ep   My Son the All American   4.1.64 ABC
Alfred Hitchcock Theatre   ep   Memo from Purgatory
    12.21.64 NBC
Wagon Train   ep   1.3.65 ABC
FBI   ep   A Life in the Balance   1.19.69 ABC
Brian's Song   tf   11.30.71 ABC

CABOT, BRUCE
Stars over Hollywood   ep   Not a Bad Guy   9.27.50 NBC
Stars over Hollywood   ep   Merry Christmas from
    Sweeney   12.20.50 NBC
Video Theatre   ep   Treasure Trove   3.26.51 CBS
Gruen Guild Playhouse   ep   Driven Snow   10.4.51 ABC
Tales of Tomorrow   ep   Dune Roller   1.4.52 ABC
Tales of Tomorrow   ep   The Seeing-Eye Surgeon   9.5.
    52 ABC
Half Hour Theatre   ep   Tails for Jeb Mulcahy   7.10.53
    ABC
The Slowest Gun in the West   Sp   5.7.60 CBS
77 Sunset Strip   ep   Double Trouble   11.4.60 ABC
Bob Hope Chrysler Theatre   ep   Have Girls--Will
    Travel   10.16.64 NBC
Bonanza   ep   A Dime's Worth of Glory   11.1.64 NBC
Daniel Boone   ep   The Devil's Four   3.4.65 NBC

CABOT, SEBASTIAN
Gunsmoke   ep   12.3.55 CBS
Alfred Hitchcock Presents   ep   A Bullet for Baldwin   1.
    1.56 CBS
Fireside Theatre   ep   The Liberator   1.10.56 NBC
World of Disney   ep   Along the Oregon Trail   11.14.56
    ABC
Studio 57   ep   A Hero Returns   1.6.57 NN
Playhouse 90   ep   So Soon to Die   1.17.57 CBS
Hiram Holliday   ep   Ersatz Joe   2.13.57 NBC
Suspicion   ep   Lord Arthur Savile's Crime   1.13.58
    NBC
Meet McGraw   ep   Vivian   1.14.58 NBC
Telephone Time   ep   Recipe for Success   2.11.58 ABC
Suspicion   ep   The Way up to Heaven   4.28.58   NBC
World of Disney   ep   Boston Tea Party   11.21.58 ABC
Shirley Temple's Story Book   ep   Dick Whittington and

His Cat 3.23.58 NBC
Shirley Temple's Story Book ep The Emperor's New
    Clothes 11.25.58 NBC
Hotel de Paree ep A Fool and his Gold 11.13.59 CBS
Bonanza ep The Spanish Grant 2.6.60 NBC
Twilight Zone ep A Nice Place to Visit 4.15.60 CBS
Checkmate sr 9.17.60 CBS
Islanders ep Five O'Clock Friday 10.2.60 ABC
Checkmate sr ret 10.4.61 CBS
Beachcomber sr 2.20.62 NN
Dick Powell Theatre ep In Search of a Son 11.20.62
    NBC
Dick Powell Theatre ep The Last of the Private Eyes
    4.30.63 NBC
Suspense sh 3.25.64 CBS
Mister Ed ep 5.5.65 CBS
Family Affair sr 9.12.66 CBS
Family Affair sr ret 9.11.67 CBS
Family Affair sr ret 9.23.68 CBS
Family Affair sr ret 9.25.69 CBS
The Spy Killer tf 11.11.69 ABC
Foreign Exchange tf 1.13.70 ABC
Family Affair sr ret 9.17.70 CBS
McCloud ep Encounter with Aries 9.22.71 CBS
Ghost Story pt 3.17.72 NBC
Ghost Story sh 9.15.72 NBC

CAESAR, SID
G.E. Theatre ep The Devil You Say 1.22.61 CBS
Checkmate ep Kill the Sound 11.15.61 CBS
Danny Thomas Show ep Instant Money 9.18.67 NBC
That Girl ep 4.18.68 ABC
That's Life ep Buying a House 10.22.68 ABC
That's Life ep You Never Take Me Any Place 2.18.
    69 ABC
Love American Style ep Love and Who 10.20.69
    ABC
Love American Style ep 12.10.71 ABC

CAGNEY, JAMES
Robert Montgomery Presents ep Soldier from the Wars
    Returning 9.10.56 NBC
Christophers ep A Link in the Chain 6.30.57 ABC
Navy Log ep hos The Lonely Watch 1.9.58 ABC
Smokey the Bear Sp nar 11.23.66 NBC

CAGNEY, JEANNE
  Video Theatre ep Satan's Waitin' 6.25.59 NBC
  Drama ep A Capture 12.29.50 NN
  Bigelow Theatre ep The Big Hello 4.29.51 CBS
  The Unexpected ep Legal Tender 4.30.52 NBC
  TV Reader's Digest ep I'll Pick More Daisies 2.14.
    55 ABC

CAINE, MICHAEL
  Hamlet Sp 11.15.64 NN
  On Stage ep Male of the Species 1.3.69 NBC

CALHOUN, RORY
  Ford Theatre ep The Road Ahead 11.11.54 NBC
  Ford Theatre ep Garrity's Sons 3.24.55 NBC
  Climax ep Champion 3.31.55 CBS
  Screen Directors Playhouse ep Day Is Done 10.12.55
    NBC
  Ford Theatre ep Bet the Queen 12.8.55 NBC
  Screen Directors Playhouse ep Hot Cargo 1.4.56
    NBC
  December Bride ep 10.1.56 CBS
  Zane Grey Theatre ep Muletown Gold Strike 12.21.
    56 CBS
  Suspicion ep Meeting in Paris 2.10.58 NBC
  Telephone Time ep Trail Blazer 4.1.58 ABC
  Schlitz Playhouse of Stars ep Curfew at Midnight 5.
    27.58 CBS
  Texan sr 9.29.58 CBS
  December Bride ep 3.26.59 CBS
  Texan sr ret 9.59 CBS
  Wagon Train ep The Artie Mattewson Story 11.8.61
    NBC
  Death Valley Days ep Measure of a Man 11.16.63
    ABC
  Dick Powell Theatre ep Luxury Liner 2.12.63 NBC
  The Greatest Show on Earth ep This Train Doesn't
    Stop Till It Gets There 4.14.64 ABC
  Bonanza ep Thanks for Everything, Friend 10.11.64
    NBC
  Virginian ep A Father for Toby 11.4.64 NBC
  Burke's Law ep Who Killed Nobody Somehow 3.31.65
    ABC
  Wagon Train ep 5.2.65 ABC
  Gunsmoke ep 5.15.65 CBS
  Rawhide ep The Testing Post 11.30.65 CBS
  I Spy ep A Day Called Four Jaguar 3.9.66 NBC

Gilligan's Island ep 1.16.67 CBS
Custer ep 11.29.67 ABC
Land's End Sp 4.21.68 NBC
Alias Smith and Jones 11.4.71 ABC
Owen Marshall ep 11.16.72 ABC
Hec Ramsey ep The Green Feather 12.16.72 NBC

CALLAN, MICHAEL
   Arrest and Trial ep Tears from a Silver Dipper 9.
      29.63 ABC
   Dr. Kildare ep Quid Pro Quo 3.26.64 NBC
   Breaking Point ep 4.20.64 ABC
   12 O'Clock High ep The Suspected 12.18.64 ABC
   FBI ep Quantico 1.30.66 ABC
   12 O'Clock High ep Decoy 3.7.66 ABC
   Occasional Wife sr 9.13.66 NBC
   FBI ep 2.4.68 ABC
   Felony Squad ep The Love Victim 2.5.68 ABC
   Kiss Me, Kate! Sp 3.25.68 ABC
   Journey to the Unknown ep Girl of My Dreams 12.26.
      68 ABC
   Love American Style ep 9.29.69 ABC
   Love American Style ep 11.3.69 ABC
   FBI ep 10.19.69 ABC
   That Girl ep 11.30.69 NBC
   In Name Only tf 11.25.69 ABC
   Name of the Game ep Aquarius Descending 12.11.70
      NBC
   Love American Style ep 12.18.70 ABC
   Love American Style ep 3.12.71 ABC
   Love American Style ep 9.17.71 ABC
   Ironside ep Good Samaritan 11.23.71 NBC
   Love American Style ep 1.7.72 ABC
   Medical Center ep 2.2.72 CBS
   Marcus Welby, M.D. ep It Is So Soon that I Am Done
      for 2.8.72 ABC
   Love American Style ep 12.8.72 ABC
   FBI ep 12.17.72 ABC

CALLOWAY, CAB
   Hallmark Hall of Fame ep The Littlest Angel 12.6.69
      NBC

CALVET, CORINNE
   Video Theatre ep Legacy of Love 10.6.52 CBS
   Video Theatre ep Babette 1.19.53 CBS
   Burke's Law ep Who Killed Julian Buck 10.18.63 ABC

Ford Theatre   ep   Indirect Approach   6. 24. 54 NBC
Climax   ep   Bait for the Tiger   5. 16. 57 CBS
Studio One   ep   Balance of Terror   1. 27. 58 CBS
Richard Diamond   ep   3. 8. 59 CBS
Burke's Law   ep   10. 14. 64 ABC
Burke's Law   ep   Who Killed the 13th Clown   2. 24. 66
    ABC
Batman   ep   2. 29. 68 ABC

CAMBRIDGE, GODFREY
U. S. Steel Hour   ep   Male Call   8. 8. 62 CBS
Dick van Dyke Show   ep   The Man from My Uncle   4.
    20. 66 CBS
Daktari   ep   12. 6. 66 CBS
Night Gallery   ep   Make Me Laugh   1. 6. 71 NBC
O'Hara, U. S. Treasury   ep   2. 11. 72 CBS

CAMERON, ROD
City Detective   sr   1953 NN
Pepsi Cola Playhouse   ep   The Silence   3. 26. 54 ABC
Fireside Theatre   ep   Gusher City   9. 6. 55 NBC
Studio 57   ep   Win a Cigar   10. 16. 55 NN
Loretta Young Show   ep   Tropical Sea   11. 6. 55 NBC
Star Stage   ep   Killer on Horseback   2. 3. 56 NBC
Studio 57   ep   Tombstone for Taro   3. 25. 56 NN
Crossroads   ep   Deadly Fear   4. 13. 56 ABC
Loretta Young Show   ep   New Slant   10. 14. 56 NBC
State Trooper   sr   1957 NN
State Trooper   sr ret   1958 NN
State Trooper   sr ret   1959 NN
Coronado 9   sr   1959 NN
Laramie   ep   Men in Shadows   5. 30. 61 NBC
Laramie   ep   The Last Journey   10. 31. 61 NBC
Tales of Wells Fargo   ep   Assignment in Gloribee   1.
    27. 62 NBC
Laramie   ep   Lost Allegiance   10. 30. 62 NBC
Laramie   ep   Broken Honor   4. 9. 63 NBC
Burke's Law   ep   Who Killed Holly Howard   9. 20. 63
    ABC
Perry Mason   ep   The Case of the Bouncing Boomerang
    12. 12. 63 CBS
Bob Hope Chrysler Theatre   ep   Have Girls--Will Travel
    10. 16. 64 NBC
Bonanza   ep   Ride the Wind   1. 16. 66, 1. 24. 66 NBC
Iron Horse   ep   10. 10. 66 ABC
Hondo   ep   11. 17. 67 ABC
Name of the Game   ep   The Civilized Man 11. 28. 69 NBC

Adam-12   ep   4.1.71 NBC
Alias Smith and Jones   ep   2.3.72 ABC
Alias Smith and Jones   ep   High Lonesome Country   9.
    23.72 ABC

CAMPANELLA, JOSEPH
    Robert Montgomery Presents   ep   In a Foreign City
        10.31.55 NBC
    Kraft Theatre   ep   Anna Santonello   8.8.56 NBC
    Robert Montgomery Presents   ep   The Weather Lover
        6.17.57 NBC
    U.S. Steel Hour   ep   Haunted Harbor   9.25.57 CBS
    Modern Romance   ep   The Alibi   12.30.57 NBC
    True Story   ep   Panic   2.8.58 NBC
    Modern Romance   ep   3.24.58 NBC
    Armstrong Circle Theatre   ep   The Man with a Thou-
        sand Names   1.21.59 CBS
    Ford Star Time   ep   The Man   1.5.60 NBC
    Alcoa Premiere   ep   The Hands of Danofrio   11.29.62
        ABC
    Combat   ep   The Medal   1.8.63 ABC
    Route 66   ep   Soda Pop and Paper Flags   5.31.63 CBS
    Virginian   ep   Siege   12.18.63 NBC
    Bob Hope Chrysler Theatre   ep   Corridor 400   12.27.
        63 NBC
    Nurses   ep   The Rainbow Ride   1.16.64 CBS
    Espionage   ep   We the Hunted   2.5.64 NBC
    Eleventh Hour   ep   87 Different Kinds of Love   2.19.64
        NBC
    Lieutenant   ep   Lament for a Dead Goldbrick   3.14.64
        NBC
    Combat   ep   Command   4.7.64 ABC
    Virginian   ep   The Long Quest   4.8.64 NBC
    Fugitive   ep   The End Game   4.21.64 ABC
    Doctors/Nurses   sr   9.22.64 CBS
    For the People   ep   Act of Violence   2.21.65, 2.28.65
        CBS
    Fugitive   ep   Set Fire to a Straw Man   11.30.65 ABC
    Big Valley   ep   10.17.66 ABC
    FBI   ep   Anatomy of a Prison Break   11.27.66 ABC
    12 O'Clock High   ep   12.23.66 ABC
    Fugitive   ep   1.10.67 ABC
    Mission Impossible   ep   1.14.67 CBS
    Wild Wild West   ep   3.31.67 CBS
    Invaders   ep   4.3.67   ABC
    Mannix   sr   9.16.67 CBS
    Mission Impossible   ep   1.7.68 CBS

Name of the Game   ep   Witness   9.27.68 NBC
Gunsmoke   ep   9.30.68 CBS
FBI   ep   10.20.68 ABC
Any Second Now   tf   2.11.69 NBC
The Whole World Is Watching   tf   3.11.69 NBC
Ironside   ep   Alias Mr. Baithwaite   9.18.69 NBC
Bold Ones   sr   9.21.69 NBC
Paris 7000   ep   No Place to Hide   1.29.70 ABC
Marcus Welby, M.D.   ep   Dance to No Music   2.3.70
   ABC
Bracken's World   ep   3.6.70 NBC
A Clear and Present Danger   tf   3.21.70 NBC
Name of the Game   ep   4.10.70 NBC
Ironside   ep   The Happy Dreams of Hollow Men   10.1.
   70 NBC
Night Gallery   ep   The Nature of the Enemy   12.23.70
   NBC
Marcus Welby, M.D.   ep   A Spanish Saying I Made up
   2.16.71 ABC
Alias Smith and Jones   ep   The Fifth Victim   3.25.71
   ABC
Night Gallery   ep   9.15.71 NBC
Marcus Welby, M.D.   ep   11.2.71 ABC
Sixth Sense   ep   2.12.72 ABC
Mannix   ep   10.1.72 CBS
Gunsmoke   ep 11.6.72 CBS

CAMPBELL, WILLIAM
Schlitz Playhouse of Stars   ep   Fresh Start   11.20.53
   CBS
A Letter to Loretta   ep   Thanksgiving in Beaver Run
   11.22.53 NBC
Four Star Playhouse   ep   The Wallet   10.21.54 CBS
Loretta Young Show   ep   The Flood   1.9.55 NBC
Loretta Young Show   ep   Prison at One O'Clock   3.11.
   56 NBC
Cavalcade Theatre   ep   The Man on the Beat   3.27.56
   ABC
The Millionaire   ep   The Story of Nick Cannon   1.2.57
   CBS
Telephone Time   ep   Passport to Life   1.6.57 CBS
West Point   ep   Thicker than Water   10.22.57 ABC
Cannonball   ep   The Runaway   10.16.59 NN
The Millionaire   ep   Millionaire Tom Hampton   11.18.
   59 CBS
Goodyear Theatre   ep   Squeeze Play   3.14.60 NBC
Tales of Wells Fargo   ep   Threat of Death   4.25.60
   NBC

Philip Marlowe   ep   Murder in the Stars   2.23.60 ABC
Garlund Touch   ep   To Double, Double Vamp   12.23.60
   CBS
Combat   ep   Soldier of Fortune   11.23.65 ABC
Star Trek   ep   1.12.67 NBC
Combat   cp   Nightmare on the Red Ball Run   2.28.67
   ABC
Dundee and the Culhane   ep   11.29.67 CBS
Garrison's Gorillas   ep   The Magnificent Forger   12.
   19.67 ABC
Star Trek   ep   12.29.67 NBC
Bonanza   ep   3.3.68 NBC
It Takes a Thief   ep   3.5.68 ABC
O'Hara, U.S. Treasury   ep   9.17.71 CBS
Adam-12   ep   11.10.71 NBC

CANARY, DAVID
   Peyton Place   sr   1.65 ABC
   Bonanza   sr   9.15.68 NBC
   Bonanza   sr ret   9.14.69 NBC
   Bonanza   sr ret   9.13.70 NBC
   FBI   ep   The Last Job   9.26.71 ABC
   Bearcats   ep   Hostages   10.14.71 CBS
   Alias Smith and Jones   ep   12.16.71 ABC
   Bonanza   sr ret   9.12.72 NBC
   Alias Smith and Jones   ep   The Strange Fate of Conrad
      Meyer Zulick   12.2.72 ABC

CANNON, DYAN
   Bat Masterson   ep   Lady Luck   11.5.59 NBC
   Wanted Dead or Alive   ep   12.26.59 CBS
   Hawaiian Eye   ep   The Big Dealer   5.17.61 ABC
   Guestward Ho   ep   The Wrestler   5.18.61 ABC
   Follow the Sun   ep   The Woman Who Never Was   10.
      15.61 ABC
   Untouchables   ep   The Silent Partner   2.1.62 ABC
   77 Sunset Strip   ep   The Bridal Trail Caper   2.2.62
      ABC
   Stoney Burke   ep   Death Rides a Pale Horse   1.14.63
      ABC
   Amos Burke   ep   The Weapon   11.10.63 ABC
   Mr. Broadway   ep   Between the Rats and the Finks
      10.17.64 CBS
   Profiles in Courage   ep   Sam Houston   12.13.64 NBC
   Medical Center   ep   Victim   10.1.69 CBS

CANOVA, JUDY
 Alfred Hitchcock Presents ep Party Line 5.29.60
  CBS
 Pistols 'n Petticoats ep 2.11.67 CBS
 The Murdocks and McClays pt 9.2.70 ABC

CANTOR, EDDIE
 Eddie Cantor Theatre sh/sr 1955 ABC
 Matinee Theatre ep George Has a Birthday 6.11.56
  NBC
 Playhouse 90 ep Seidman and Son 10.18.56 CBS

CAPUCINE
 Search ep 9.13.72 NBC

CARERE, CHRISTINE
 Blue Light sr 1.12.66 ABC

CAREY, MacDONALD
 Celanese Theatre ep Yellow Jack 5.28.52 ABC
 Video Theatre ep You Be the Bad Guy 8.18.52 CBS
 Ford Theatre ep Edge of the Law 11.6.52 NBC
 Hollywood Opening Night ep 11.17.52 NBC
 Ford Theatre ep The Sermon of the Gun 1.22.53
  NBC
 Video Theatre ep The Inn of the Eagles 1.26.53 CBS
 G.E. Theatre ep Hired Mother 2.22.53 CBS
 Video Theatre ep Night Call 7.1.53 CBS
 Appointment with Adventure ep The Quiet Gun 4.24.
  55 CBS
 Climax ep Unimportant Man 6.2.55 CBS
 Climax ep Deal a Blow 8.25.55 CBS
 Stage 7 ep Where You Love Me 9.4.55 CBS
 Stage 7 ep The Hayfield 9.18.55 CBS
 Climax ep Gamble on a Thief 2.2.56 CBS
 Screen Directors Playhouse ep Cry Justice 2.15.56
  NBC
 20th Century-Fox Hour ep Times Like These 2.22.
  56 CBS
 U.S. Steel Hour ep Moments of Courage 2.29.56 CBS
 G.E. Theatre ep Easter Gift 4.1.56 CBS
 Ford Theatre ep The Kill 5.17.56 NBC
 U.S. Steel Hour ep Moment of Courage 6.20.56 CBS
 Undercurrent ep The Plug Nickel 7.28.56 CBS
 Dr. Christian sr fall, 1956 NN
 Alcoa Hour ep Flight into Danger 9.16.56 NBC
 Climax ep The Chinese Game 11.22.56 CBS

Kaiser Aluminum Hour   ep   Whereabouts Unknown   2. 26. 57 NBC

Ford Theatre   ep   Broken Barrier   3. 6. 57 ABC

On Trial   ep   Alibi for Murder   4. 26. 57 NBC

Jane Wyman Theatre   ep   Man on the 35th Floor   10. 10. 57 NBC

Zane Grey Theatre   ep   License to Kill   2. 7. 58 CBS

Wagon Train   ep   The Bill Tawnee Story   2. 12. 58 NBC

Studio One   ep   The Lonely Stage   2. 24. 58 CBS

Playhouse 90   ep   Natchez   5. 29. 58   CBS

Frank Sinatra Show   ep   The Seedling Doubt   6. 6. 58 ABC

Suspicion   ep   Eye for an Eye   6. 23. 58 NBC

Pursuit   ep   The Vengeance   10. 22. 58 CBS

Schlitz Playhouse of Stars   ep   False Impression   11. 7. 58 CBS

Rawhide   ep   Incident of the Golden Calf   3. 13. 59 CBS

Lock Up   sr   fall, 1959 NBC

Alfred Hitchcock Presents   ep   Coyote Noon   10. 18. 59 CBS

Moment of Fear   ep   The Golden Deed   7. 1. 60 NBC

Lock Up   sr ret   fall, 1960 NBC

Thriller   ep   The Devil's Ticket   4. 18. 61 NBC

U. S. Steel Hour   ep   Tangle of Truth   11. 29. 61 CBS

Checkmate   ep   Rendezvous in Washington   5. 9. 62 CBS

Alfred Hitchcock Theatre   ep   House Guest   11. 8. 62 CBS

Dick Powell Theatre   ep   The Last of the Private Eyes   4. 30. 63 NBC

Mr. Novak   ep   Pay the $2. 00   11. 26. 63 NBC

Burke's Law   ep   Who Killed Cynthia Royal   12. 13. 63 ABC

Outer Limits   ep   The Special One   4. 6. 64 ABC

Arrest and Trial   ep   Those Which Love Has Made   4. 12. 64 ABC

Burke's Law   ep   3. 13. 64 ABC

Daniel Boone   ep   The Place of 1000 Spirits   2. 4. 65 NBC

Burke's Law   ep   2. 10. 65 ABC

Run for Your Life   ep   The Girl Next Door Is a Spy   9. 20. 65 NBC

Run for Your Life   ep   Our Man in Limbo   10. 25. 65 NBC

Ben Casey   ep   The Importance of Being 65937   11. 15. 65 ABC

Bewitched   ep   10. 19. 67 ABC

Days of Our Lives   sr   1967 NBC

Gidget Gets Married   tf   1.4.72 ABC

CAREY, PHILIP
    Ford Theatre   ep   Madame 44   3.5.53 NBC
    Ford Theatre   ep   6.11.53 NBC
    Ford Theatre   ep   Gun Job   12.17.53 NBC
    Ford Theatre   ep   The Unlocked Door   6.3.54 NBC
    Ford Theatre   ep   Stars Don't Shine   1.20.55 NBC
    Pond's Theatre   ep   Billy Budd   3.10.55 ABC
    Ford Theatre   ep   Twelve to Eternity   10.27.55 NBC
    Ford Theatre   ep   Panic   6.14.56 NBC
    77th Bengal Lancers   sr   10.21.56 NBC
    Ford Theatre   ep   Duffy's Man   12.19.56 ABC
    Ford Theatre   ep   Torn   5.29.57 ABC
    Lux Playhouse   ep   A Deadly Guest   1.9.59 CBS
    Philip Marlowe   sr   10.6.59 ABC
    Michael Shayne   ep   Shoot the Works   11.11.60 NBC
    Zane Grey Theatre   ep   One Must Die   1.12.61 CBS
    Thriller   ep   Man in the Cage   1.17.61 NBC
    Stagecoach West   ep   The Root of Evil   2.28.61 ABC
    Rifleman   ep   Death Trap   5.9.61 ABC
    Asphalt Jungle   ep   The Professor   5.28.61 ABC
    Tales of Wells Fargo   ep   The Dodger   10.7.61 NBC
    Roaring 20s   ep   Kitty Goes West   10.14.61 ABC
    Cheyenne   ep   One Way Ticket   2.19.62 ABC
    Cheyenne   ep   Until Kingdom Comes   3.26.62 ABC
    77 Sunset Strip   ep   Violence for your Fires   3.30.62
       ABC
    Cheyenne   ep   Johnny Brassbuttons   12.3.62 ABC
    Gallant Men   ep   The Leathernecks   2.26.63 ABC
    77 Sunset Strip   ep   3.29.63 ABC
    G.E. True   ep   Nitro   4.28.63 CBS
    Virginian   ep   Siege   12.18.63 NBC
    Kraft Suspense Theatre   ep   My Enemy, This Town   2.
       6.64 NBC
    Virginian   ep   We've Lost a Train   4.21.65 NBC
    Laredo   sr   9.16.65 NBC
    Laredo   sr ret   9.16.66 NBC
    Daniel Boone   ep   3.9.67 NBC
    Custer   ep   10.4.67 ABC
    Felony Squad   ep   No Sad Songs for Charlie   12.25.67
       ABC
    Ironside   ep   2.29.68 NBC
    Ironside   ep   Good-By to Yesterday   9.25.69 NBC
    All in the Family   ep   2.2.71 CBS

CARLISLE, KITTY
    Airflyte Theatre   ep   Waltz Dream   1.4.51 CBS
    Holiday   Sp   6.9.56 NBC

CARLSON, RICHARD
    Pulitzer Prize Playhouse   ep   The Canton Story   10.13.
        50 ABC
    Studio One   ep   The Road to Jericho   10.23.50 CBS
    Theatre Hour   ep   Heart of Darkness   11.3.50 CBS
    Prudential Playhouse   ep   One Sunday Afternoon   3.13.51
        CBS
    Lights Out   ep   Devil in Glencairn   7.16.51 NBC
    Robert Montgomery Presents   ep   Eva? Caroline?   1.
        28.52 NBC
    Studio One   ep   Captain-General of the Armies   6.2.52
        CBS
    Celanese Theatre   ep   When Ladies Meet   6.11.52 ABC
    Schlitz Playhouse of Stars   ep   The Playwright   12.19.
        52 CBS
    Ford Theatre   ep Adventure in Connecticut   12.9.53
        NBC
    Hollywood Opening Night   ep   My Boss and I   3.23.53
        NBC
    Eye Witness   ep nar   Statement of the Accused   5.11.
        53 NBC
    Schlitz Playhouse of Stars   ep   Pursuit   5.22.53 CBS
    I Led Three Lives   sr   10.4.53 NBC
    Video Theatre   ep   All Dressed in White   1.14.54 CBS
    G.E. Theatre   ep   Pardon My Aunt   4.4.54 CBS
    Schlitz Playhouse of Stars   ep   Hemmed in   9.27.54
        CBS
    I Led Three Lives   sr ret   10.54 NBC
    Best of Broadway   ep   The Philadelphia Story   12.8.54
        CBS
    Kraft Theatre   ep   Haunted   8.24.55 NBC
    I Led Three Lives   sr ret   10.55 NBC
    Omnibus   ep   The Billy Mitchell Court-Martial   4.1.56
        CBS
    Climax   cp   Flame-Out on T-6   5.17.56 CBS
    Schlitz Playhouse of Stars   ep   The Night They Won the
        Oscar   11.9.56 CBS
    Climax   ep   The Secret Thread   11.29.56 CBS
    Crossroads   ep   The Happy Gift   2.1.57 ABC
    Crossroads   ep   Call for Help   3.1.57 ABC
    Studio One   ep   The Other Place   1.13.58 CBS
    Mackenzie's Raiders   sr   10.15.58 CBS
    Schlitz Playhouse of Stars   ep   And Practically Strangers

1. 30. 59 CBS
Riverboat ep The Faithless 11. 22. 59 NBC
Loretta Young Show ep The Best Season 4. 17. 60 NBC
Mystery Theatre ep Enough Rope 7. 31. 60 NBC
Bus Stop ep Verdict of Twelve 3. 11. 62 ABC
Going My Way ep Blessed Are the Meek 2. 27. 63
ABC
Wagon Train ep 12. 23. 63 ABC
Arrest and Trial ep Onward and Upward 1. 19. 64 ABC
Virginian ep Smile of a Dragon 2. 26. 64 NBC
Fugitive ep The Homecoming 4. 7. 64 ABC
Burke's Law ep 4. 17. 64 ABC
Voyage to the Bottom of the Sea ep The Village of
Guilt 11. 2. 64 ABC
Perry Mason ep The Case of the Tragic Trophy 11.
19. 64 CBS
Wagon Train ep The Clay Shelby Story 12. 6. 64 ABC
Virginian ep Farewell to Honesty 3. 24. 65 NBC
Rawhide ep Brush War at Buford 11. 23. 65 CBS
Perry Mason ep The Case of the Avenging Angel 3.
13. 66 CBS
Bonanza ep 1. 21. 68 NBC
It Takes a Thief ep The Naked Billionaire 1. 28. 69
ABC
FBI ep 3. 30. 69 ABC
Lancer ep 11. 18. 69 CBS
Owen Marshall ep Eighteen Years Next April 11. 4. 71
ABC
Cannon ep 2. 29. 72 CBS

CARMICHAEL, HOAGY
Gulf Playhouse ep The Whale on the Beach 11. 21. 52
On Trial ep Death in the Snow 11. 16. 56 NBC
Playhouse 90 ep The Helen Morgan Story 5. 16. 57
CBS
Telephone Time ep I Get Along Without You Very Well
11. 12. 57 ABC
Climax ep Sound of the Moon 1. 23. 58 CBS
Laramie sr 9. 15. 59 NBC
Burke's Law ep Who Killed the Jet-Setter 1. 10. 64
ABC
Burke's Law ep 3. 27. 64 ABC
Name of the Game ep Echo of a Nightmare 3. 20. 70
NBC

CARNE, JUDY
Fair Exchange sr 9. 21. 62 CBS

Fair Exchange   sr ret   3.28.63 CBS
Bonanza   ep   A Question of Strength   10.27.63 NBC
Baileys of Balboa   sr   9.24.64 CBS
The Man from U.N.C.L.E.   ep   The Ultimate Computer
    Affair   10.1.65 NBC
Gunsmoke   ep   1.15.66 CBS
I Dream of Jeannie   ep   1.22.66 NBC
Patty Duke Show   ep   4.13.66 ABC
Love on a Rooftop   sr   9.13.66 ABC
Big Valley   ep   Explosion   11.20.67, 11.27.67 ABC
The Man from U.N.C.L.E.   ep   11.27.67 NBC
Run for Your Life   ep   A Dangerous Proposal   1.3.68
    NBC
Love American Style   ep   11.17.69 ABC
Love American Style   ep   1.29.71 ABC
Alias Smith and Jones   ep   The Root of It All   4.1.71
    ABC
Love American Style   ep   1.21.72 ABC
Dead Men Tell No Tales   tf   12.17.71 CBS
Love American Style   ep   1.7.72 ABC
Cade's County   ep   1.9.72 CBS

CARNEY, ART
    Video Theatre   ep   Thanks for a Lovely Evening   1.12.
        53 CBS
    Studio One   ep   The Laugh Maker   5.18.53 CBS
    Danger   ep   I'll Be Waiting   8.4.53 CBS
    TV Sound Stage   ep   The Square Hole   9.4.53 NBC
    Studio One   ep   Confessions of a Nervous Man   11.30.
        53 CBS
    Suspense   ep   Mr. Nobody   12.29.53 NBC
    Kraft Theatre   ep   Burlesque   1.14.54 ABC
    Suspense   ep   The Return Journey   4.20.54 CBS
    Kraft Theatre   ep   Alice in Wonderland   5.5.54 NBC
    Studio One   ep   A Letter to Mr. Gubbins   6.14.54 CBS
    Kraft Theatre   ep   Uncle Harry   8.26.54 ABC
    Best of Broadway   ep   Panama Hattie   11.10.54 CBS
    Climax   ep   The Bigger They Come   1.6.55 CBS
    Studio One   ep   The Incredible World of Horace Ford
        6.13.55 CBS
    The Honeymooners   sr   10.1.55 CBS
    Star Stage   ep   The Man Who Was Irresistible to Wom-
        en   3.16.56 NBC
    Playhouse 90   ep   Charley's Aunt   3.28.57 CBS
    Playhouse 90   ep   The Fabulous Irishman   6.27.57 CBS
    Dupont Show of the Month   ep   Harvey   9.22.58 CBS
    Alfred Hitchcock Presents   ep   Safety for the Witness

11. 23. 58 CBS
Peter and the Wolf   Sp   11. 30. 58 ABC
Playhouse 90   ep   The Velvet Alley   1. 22. 59 CBS
The Sorcerer's Apprentice   Sp   4. 5. 59 ABC
Our Town   Sp   11. 13. 59 NBC
Victory   Sp   4. 8. 60 NBC
Full Moon Over Brooklyn   Sp   5. 6. 60 NBC
The Right Man   Sp   10. 24. 60 CBS
Twilight Zone   ep   The Night of the Meek   12. 23. 60
   CBS
Dupont Show of the Month   ep   A Day Like Today   4. 19.
   64 NBC
Batman   ep   Shoot a Crooked Arrow   9. 7. 66,   9. 8. 66
   ABC
Bob Hope Chrysler Theatre   ep   The Timothy Heist
   10. 30. 64 NBC
Mr. Broadway   ep   11. 28. 64 CBS
Men from Shiloh   ep   With Love, Bullets, and Valen-
   tines   10. 7. 70 NBC
The Snoop Sisters   tf   12. 18. 72 NBC

CARRADINE, DAVID
Bob Hope Chrysler Theatre   ep   The War and Eric
   Kurtz   3. 5. 65 NBC
Alfred Hitchcock Theatre   ep   Thou Still Unravished
   Bride   3. 22. 65 NBC
Trials of O'Brien   ep   The Greatest Game   3. 4. 66,
   3. 11. 66 CBS
Coronet Blue   ep   The Rebel   6. 19. 67 CBS
Shane   sr   9. 10. 66 ABC
Johnny Belinda   Sp   10. 22. 67 ABC
Ironside   ep   3. 28. 68 NBC
Name of the Game   ep   Tarot   2. 13. 70 NBC
Ironside   ep   1. 7. 71 NBC
Maybe I'll Come Home in the Spring   tf   2. 16. 71 ABC
Gunsmoke   ep   2. 22. 71 CBS
Ironside   ep   License to Kill   12. 21. 71 NBC
Kung Fu   tf   2. 22. 72 ABC
Kung Fu   sr   10. 14. 72 ABC

CARRADINE, JOHN
Crimson Circle   ep   1950 NN
Secrets of Wu Sin   ep   1950 NN
Lights Out   ep   The Half-Pint Flask   11. 6. 50 NBC
The Web   ep   Stone Cold Dead   12. 27. 50 CBS
Lights Out   ep   Meddlers   7. 9. 51 NBC
Trapped   sh   7. 15. 51 NN

Suspense ep Come into My Parlor 5.19.53 CBS
So This Is Hollywood ep 1.8.55 NBC
Climax ep The First and the Last 4.28.55 CBS
Climax ep The Adventures of Huckleberry Finn 9.1.
   55 CBS
Gunsmoke ep 12.31.55 CBS
Climax ep The Hanging Judge 1.12.56 CBS
Front Row Center ep Deadlock 2.5.56 CBS
Studio 57 ep The Rarest Stamp 3.11.56 NN
Damon Runyon Theatre ep Miracle Jones 4.14.56 CBS
Matinee Theatre ep The House of Seven Gables 8.22.
   56 NBC
Playhouse 90 ep Shoes 1.3.57 CBS
Navy Log ep The Star 3.6.57 ABC
Cheyenne ep Decision at Gunsight 4.23.57 ABC
Schlitz Playhouse of Stars ep Swith Station 10.4.57
   CBS
Dupont Show of the Month ep Prince and the Pauper
   10.28.57 CBS
Studio One ep Please Report Any Odd Characters 11.
   18.57 CBS
Telephone Time ep Novel Appeal 12.3.57 ABC
Matinee Theatre ep Daniel Webster and the Sea Ser-
   pent 1957 NBC
Wagon Train ep The Dora Gray Story 1.29.58 NBC
Suspicion ep A Touch of Evil 2.17.58 NBC
Lineup ep The Deacon Whitehall Case 4.18.58 CBS
Rough Riders ep The End of Nowhere 2.12.59 ABC
Bat Masterson ep Tumbleweed Trail 3.25.59 NBC
The Millionaire ep Millionaire Karl Miller 4.22.59
   CBS
Bat Masterson ep Tumbleweed Wagon 9.9.59 NBC
Rebel ep 10.4.59 ABC
Johnny Ringo ep 11.26.59 CBS
Overland Trail ep The Reckoning 4.29.60 NBC
Rebel ep Bequest 9.25.60 ABC
Twilight Zone ep The Howling Man 11.4.60 CBS
Harrigan and Son ep A Matter of Dignity 11.18.60
   ABC
Wagon Train ep The Colter Craven Story 11.23.60
   NBC
Maverick ep Red Dog 3.5.61 ABC
Bonanza ep Springtime 10.1.61 NBC
Thriller ep Masquerade 10.30.61 NBC
Thriller ep The Remarkable Mrs. Hawk 12.18.61
   NBC
The Lucy Show ep Lucy Goes to Art Class 1.13.64 CBS

Branded   sr   1.24.65 NBC
Alfred Hitchcock Theatre   ep   Death Scene   3.8.65 NBC
The Munsters   ep   Herman's Raise   6.3.65 CBS
Jesse James   ep   As Far as the Sea   3.21.66 ABC
Laredo   ep   Sound of Terror   4.7.66 NBC
The Girl from U.N.C.L.E.   ep   The Montori Device
    Affair   10.11.66 NBC
Green Hornet   ep   2.24.67 ABC
The Man from U.N.C.L.E.   ep   The Prince of Dark-
    ness Affair   10.2.67, 10.9.67 NBC
Hondo   ep   11.3.67 ABC
Daniel Boone   ep   1.25.68 NBC
Big Valley   ep   4.7.69 ABC
Land of the Giants   ep   11.30.69 ABC
Daughter of the Mind   tf   12.9.69 ABC
Bonanza   ep   19.69 NBC
Crowhaven Farm   tf   11.24.70 ABC
Ironside   ep   Gentle Oaks   11.25.71 NBC
Kung Fu   ep   11.11.72 ABC

CARRILLO, LEO
The Cisco Kid   sr   1.20.51 NN

CARROLL, DIAHANN
Peter Gunn   ep   Sing a Song of Murder   3.7.60 NBC
Naked City   ep   A Horse Has a Big Head   11.21.62
    ABC
Eleventh Hour   ep   And Man Created Vanity   10.23.63
    NBC
Julia   sr   9.24.68 NBC
Julia   sr ret   9.16.69 NBC
Julia   sr ret   9.15.70 NBC

CARROLL, LEO G.
Billy Rose's Playbill   ep   The Benefit of the Doubt   12.
    4.50 NN
Danger   ep   Head Print   3.27.51 CBS
Topper   sr   10.16.53 CBS
Cavalcade of America   ep   The Splendid Dream   3.16.54
    ABC
Topper   sr ret   10.54 CBS
Star Tonight   ep   Can You Coffee Pot on Ice Skates   5.
    3.56 ABC
Cheyenne   ep   6.19.56   ABC
Matinee Theatre   ep   Angel Street   5.9.58 NBC
Shirley Temple Story Book   ep   The Magic Fishbone   8.
    19.58 NBC
Studio One   ep   Bellingham   8.25.58 CBS

Alcoa Premiere   ep   The Fugitive Eye   10.17.61 ABC
U.S. Steel Hour   ep   Bury Me Twice   10.18.61 CBS
Mystery Theatre   ep   Dead on Nine   7.4.62 NBC
Going My Way   sr   10.3.62 ABC
Channing   ep   2.12.64 ABC
The Man from U.N.C.L.E.   sr   9.22.64 NBC
Hazel   ep   Hazel's Midas Touch   12.31.64 NBC
The Man from U.N.C.L.E.   sr ret   9.17.65 NBC
Bob Hope Chrysler Theatre   ep   Wind Fever   3.2.66
     NBC
The Girl from U.N.C.L.E.   sr   9.13.66 NBC
The Man from U.N.C.L.E.   sr ret   9.16.66 NBC
The Man from U.N.C.L.E.   sr ret   9.11.67 NBC
Hondo   ep   10.20.67 ABC
World of Disney   ep   A Boy Called Nuthin'   10.10.67,
     12.17.67 NBC
Ironside   ep   Little Dog, Gone   4.2.70 NBC

CARROLL, MADELEINE
Robert Montgomery Presents   ep   The Letter   1.30.50
     NBC
Philco Playhouse   ep   Women of Intrigue   9.91.51 NBC
Tales of the City   ep   7.23.53 CBS
G.E. Theatre   ep   The Bitter Choice   3.20.55 CBS

CARROLL, NANCY
Ellery Queen   ep   The Paper Tiger   4.3.59 NBC
U.S. Steel Hour   ep   The Love of Claire Ambler   4.4.
     62 CBS
U.S. Steel Hour   ep   A Man for Oona   5.2.62 CBS
Going My Way   ep   Cornelius Come Home   3.6.63 ABC

CARROLL, PAT
Pepsi Cola Playhouse   ep   The Black Purse   5.14.54
     ABC
Best Foot Forward   Sp   11.20.54 NBC
Studio 57   ep   Fish Widow   12.7.54 NN
Producers Showcase   ep   The Women   2.7.55 NBC
Kraft Theatre   ep   Gramercy Ghost   4.20.55 NBC
Damon Runyon Theatre   ep   Broadway Dateline   11.12.
     55 CBS
G.E. Theatre   ep   Signs of Love   11.8.59 CBS
June Allyson Show   ep   Night Out   11.23.59 CBS
Ann Sothern Show   ep   3.16.61 CBS
Investigators   ep   The Dead End Men   12.28.61 CBS
Danny Thomas Show   sr   10.1.62 CBS
Danny Thomas Show   sr ret   9.30.63 CBS

Interns   ep   3.18.71 CBS
My Three Sons   ep   3.20.71 CBS
Love American Style   ep   11.12.71 ABC

CARSON, JACK
Theatre Hour   ep   Room Service   3.10.50 CBS
Video Theatre   ep   No Shoes   3.19.51 CBS
Video Theatre   ep   For Heaven's Sake   1.28.52 CBS
G.E. Theatre   ep   The Marriage Fix   11.29.53 CBS
G.E. Theatre   ep   Here Comes Calvin   2.21.54 CBS
U.S. Steel Hour   ep   Goodbye ... But it Doesn't Go
    Away   11.9.54 ABC
U.S. Steel Hour   ep Man in the Corner   3.1.55 ABC
Screen Directors Playhouse   ep   Arroyo   10.26.55 NBC
U.S. Steel Hour   ep   The Gambler   7.20.55 CBS
Fireside Theatre   ep   The Director   9.13.55 NBC
Climax   ep   Portrait in Celluloid   11.24.55 CBS
Damon Runyon Theatre   ep   Broadway Dateline   5.26.
    56 CBS
Schlitz Playhouse of Stars   ep   The Trophy   10.12.56
    CBS
Ford Theatre   ep   Paris Edition   10.17.56 ABC
Playhouse 90   ep   Three Men on a Horse   4.18.57 CBS
Climax   ep   Tunnel of Fear   10.24.57 CBS
U.S. Steel Hour   ep   Huck Finn   11.20.57 CBS
Studio One   ep   The Funny-Looking Kid   5.19.58 CBS
Playhouse 90   ep   The Long March   10.16.58 CBS
Alcoa Theatre   ep   High Class Type of Mongrel   1.12.
    59 NBC
Bonanza   ep   Mr. Henry Comstock   11.7.59 NBC
Ford Star Time   ep   Something Special   12.1.59 NBC
Alcoa Theatre   ep   How's Business   12.28.59 NBC
Zane Grey Theatre   ep   Sundown Smith   3.24.60 CBS
Thriller   ep   The Big Blackout   12.6.60 NBC
Twilight Zone   ep   The Whole Truth   1.20.61 CBS
U.S. Steel Hour   ep   The Big Splash   2.8.61 CBS
Chevy Show   ep   Happiest Day   4.23.61 NBC
Dick Powell Theatre   ep   Who Killed Julie Greer   9.26.
    61 NBC
Bus Stop   ep   Man from Bootstrap   11.26.61 ABC
U.S. Steel Hour   ep   Far from the Shade Tree   1.10.62
    CBS
World of Disney   ep   Sammy, the Way-Out Seal   10.28.
    68, 11.4.62 NBC

CARSON, JOHNNY
Playhouse 90   ep   Three Men on a Horse   4.18.57 CBS

U.S. Steel Hour   ep   Queen of the Orange Bowl   1.13.
   60 CBS
U.S. Steel Hour   ep   Girl in the Gold Bathtub   5.4.60
   CBS
Johnny Come Lately   pt   8.8.60 CBS
Here's Lucy   ep   12.1.69 CBS

CARTER, JANIS
   Tales of the City   ep   6.25.53 CBS
   Suspense   ep   Point Blank   8.11.53 CBS
   Center Stage   ep   Golden Anniversary   7.13.54 ABC
   Elgin Hour   ep   Family Meeting   1.25.55 ABC

CASH, JOHNNY
   Deputy   ep   The Deathly Quiet   5.27.61 NBC

CASS, PEGGY
   The Hathaways   sr   10.6.61 ABC
   Love American Style   ep   9.22.72 ABC
   Love American Style   ep   12.22.72 ABC

CASSAVETES, JOHN
   Armstrong Circle Theatre   ep   Ladder of Lies   2.1.55
      NBC
   Elgin Hour   ep   Crime in the Street   3.8.55 ABC
   You Are There   ep   The Death of Socrates   3.13.55 CBS
   Kraft Theatre   ep   Judge Contain's Hotel   5.11.55 NBC
   Elgin Hour   ep   Combat Medic   6.14.55 ABC
   Armstrong Circle Theatre   ep   Time for Love   6.21.55
      NBC
   Pond's Theatre   ep   Coquette   7.7.55 ABC
   Philco Playhouse   ep   A Room in Paris   8.7.55 NBC
   Goodyear Playhouse   ep   The Expendable House   10.9.55
      NBC
   U.S. Steel Hour   ep   Bring Me a Dream   1.4.56 CBS
   Alfred Hitchcock Presents   ep   You Got to Have Luck
      1.15.56 CBS
   Appointment with Adventure   ep   All Through the Night
      2.5.56 CBS
   Climax   ep   No Right to Kill   8.9.56 CBS
   20th Century-Fox Hour   ep   The Last Patriarch   11.28.
      56 CBS
   Climax   ep   Savage Portrait   12.6.56 CBS
   Playhouse 90   ep   Winter Dreams   5.23.57 CBS
   Studio One   ep   Kurishiki Incident   5.12.58 CBS
   Alcoa Theatre   ep   The First Star   12.1.58 NBC
   Pursuit   ep   Calculated Risk   12.10.58 CBS

G. E. Theatre   ep   Train for Tecumseh   3. 15. 59 CBS
Lux Playhouse   ep   The Dreamer   4. 3. 59 CBS
Drama   ep   The Final Ingredient   4. 19. 59 ABC
Staccato   sr   9. 10. 59 NBC
Rawhide   ep   Incident Near Gloomy River   3. 17. 61
    CBS
Dr. Kildare   ep   The Visitors   10. 11. 62 NBC
Lloyd Bridges Theatre   ep   El Medico   9. 18. 62 CBS
Channing   ep   Message from the Tin Room   9. 18. 63
    ABC
Breaking Point   ep   There Are the Hip and There Are
    the Square   10. 14. 63 ABC
Alfred Hitchcock Theatre   ep   Murder Case   3. 6. 64 CBS
Burke's Law   ep   4. 10. 64 ABC
Burke's Law   ep   5. 1. 64 ABC
Alfred Hitchcock Theatre   ep   Water's Edge   10. 19. 64
    NBC
Profiles in Courage   ep   1. 24. 65 NBC
Bob Hope Chrysler Theatre   ep   The Fliers   2. 5. 65
    NBC
Burke's Law   ep   4. 7. 65 ABC
Burke's Law   ep   4. 28. 65 ABC
Combat   ep   9. 28. 65 ABC
Jesse James   ep   The Quest   10. 4. 65 ABC
Voyage to the Bottom of the Sea   ep   The Peacemaker
    11. 14. 65 ABC
Virginian   ep   Long Ride to Wind River   1. 19. 66 NBC
The Long Hot Summer   ep   The Intruders   2. 22. 66 ABC
Bob Hope Chrysler Theatre   ep   Free of Charge   3. 22.
    67 NBC
Alexander the Great   pt   1. 26. 68 ABC

CASSIDY, DAVID
Survivors   sr   11. 69 ABC
Ironside   ep   Stolen on Demand   12. 25. 69 NBC
Marcus Welby, M. D.   ep   Fun and Games   1. 13. 70
    ABC
Adam-12   ep   2. 14. 70 NBC
Bonanza   ep   The Law and Billy Burgess   2. 15. 70 NBC
Medical Center   ep   His Brother's Keeper   4. 1. 70 CBS
Mod Squad   ep   4. 7. 70 ABC
Partridge Family   sr   9. 25. 70 ABC
Partridge Family   sr ret   9. 23. 71 ABC
Partridge Family   sr ret   9. 15. 72 ABC

CASSIDY, JACK
Lux Video Theatre   ep   Dark Victory   2. 14. 57 NBC

U.S. Steel Hour   ep   Shadow of Evil   2.27.57 CBS
Lux Video Theatre   ep   The Last Act   9.21.57 NBC
Gunsmoke   ep   6.7.58 CBS
Cheyenne   ep   The Harrigan   12.25.61 ABC
Hawaiian Eye   ep   Concert in Hawaii   12.27.61 ABC
77 Sunset Strip   ep   The Bridal Trail Caper   2.2.62
   ABC
Surfside 6   ep   Who Is Sylvia   2.12.62 ABC
Mission Impossible   ep   2.19.62 CBS
Hennesey   ep   5.7.62 CBS
Mr. Magoo's Christmas Carol   Sp (voice only)   12.18.
   62 NBC
Dick Powell Theatre   ep   The Big Day   12.25.62 NBC
The Lucy Show   ep   11.22.65 CBS
Garry Moore Show   ep   High Button Shoes   11.20.66
   CBS
I Spy   ep   1.25.67 NBC
The Girl from U.N.C.L.E.   ep   2.14.67 NBC
Coronet Blue   ep   A Charade for Murder   7.24.67 CBS
He and She   sr   9.6.67 CBS
Bewitched   ep   10.3.68 ABC
Get Smart   ep   11.9.68 NBC
That's Life   ep   3.11.69 ABC
That Girl   ep   12.11.69, 12.18.69 ABC
Love American Style   ep   2.20.70 ABC
Bewitched   ep   3.19.70 ABC
Hollywood Television Theatre   ep   The Andersonville
   Trials   5.17.70 NN
George M   Sp   9.12.70 NBC
Matt Lincoln   ep   10.8.70 ABC
Governor and J.J.   ep   11.25.70 CBS
Night Gallery   ep   The Last Laurel   1.20.71 NBC
Love American Style   ep   1.29.71 ABC
Men at Law   ep   Marathon   2.10.71 CBS
Columbo   ep   Murder by the Book   9.15.71 NBC
Alias Smith and Jones   ep   9.23.71 ABC
Sarge   ep   11.2.71 CBS
Love American Style   ep   9.15.72 ABC
Banyon   ep   11.3.72 NBC
Your Money or Your Wife   tf   12.19.72 CBS

CASTELLANO, RICHARD
   On Stage   ep   The Choice   3.30.69 NBC
   The Super   sr   6.14.72 ABC

CATLETT, WALTER
   Climax   ep   The Adventures of Huckleberry Finn 9.1.

55 CBS
World of Disney ep Davy Crockett and the River
Pirates 12.14.55 ABC

CAULFIELD, JOAN
Drama ep Saturday's Children 10.2.50 CBS
Schlitz Playhouse of Stars ep Girl in a Million 12.
28.51 CBS
Robert Montgomery Presents ep The Longest Night
5.19.52 NBC
Ford Theatre ep Girl in the Park 10.30.52 NBC
Schlitz Playhouse of Stars ep A String of Beads 12.
26.52 CBS
My Favorite Husband sr 9.12.53 CBS
My Favorite Husband sr ret 9.11.54 CBS
Schlitz Playhouse of Stars ep The Bankmouse 7.20.
56 CBS
Lux Video Theatre ep Only Yesterday 9.27.56 NBC
Ford Theatre ep House of Glass 3.27.57 ABC
Sally sr 9.15.57 NBC
Pursuit ep Eagle in the Cage 12.3.58 CBS
G.E. Theatre ep The Lady's Choice 3.22.59 CBS
Hong Kong ep Love, Honor and Perish 3.15.61 ABC
Cheyenne ep Showdown at Oxbend 12.17.62 ABC
Burke's Law ep Who Killed the Kind Doctor 11.29.63
ABC
Burke's Law ep Who Killed the 13th Clown 2.24.66
ABC
High Chaparral ep 9.10.67 NBC

CAVETT, DICK
Alias Smith and Jones ep 1.6.72 ABC

CELI, ADOLFO
It Takes a Thief ep 12.4.69 ABC
It Takes a Thief ep 2.16.70 ABC

CHAKIRIS, GEORGE
Kismet Sp 10.24.67 ABC
Medical Center ep Trial by Terror 11.25.70 CBS
Hawaii Five-O ep 9.12.72 CBS
Medical Center ep 11.8.72 CBS

CHAMBERLAIN, RICHARD
Mr. Lucky ep 5.21.60 CBS
Deputy ep The Edge of Doubt 3.4.61 NBC
Thriller ep The Watcher 11.11.60 NBC
Dr. Kildare sr 9.28.61 NBC

Dr. Kildare   sr ret   9. 27. 62 NBC
Dr. Kildare   sr ret   9. 26. 63 NBC
Eleventh Hour   ep   Four Feet in the Morning   11. 27. 63
    NBC
Dr. Kildare   sr ret   9. 24. 64 NBC
Dr. Kildare   sr ret   9. 13. 65 NBC
Hallmark Hall of Fame   ep   11. 1. 70 NBC
Portrait: The Woman I Love   Sp   12. 17. 72 ABC

CHAMPION, GOWER
    Video Theatre   ep   Bouquet for Millie   12. 17. 53 CBS
    Three for Tonight   Sp   6. 22. 55 CBS
    G. E. Theatre   ep   The Rider on the Pale Horse   11. 4.
        56 CBS
    Marge and Gower   sr   3. 31. 57 CBS
    G. E. Theatre   ep   Mischief at Bandy Leg   11. 3. 57 CBS

CHAMPION, MARGE
    Video Theatre   ep   Bouquet for Millie   12. 17. 53 CBS
    G. E. Theatre   ep   The Rider on the Pale Horse   11. 4.
        56 CBS
    Three for Tonight   Sp   6. 22. 55 CBS
    Marge and Gower   sr   3. 31. 57 CBS
    G. E. Theatre   ep   Mischief at Bandy Leg   11. 3. 57 CBS
    N. E. T. Playhouse   ep   New Theatre for Now   11. 14. 69
        NN

CHANEY, LON, JR.
    Tales of Tomorrow   ep   Frankenstein   1. 18. 52 ABC
    Schlitz Playhouse of Stars   ep   The Trial   9. 25. 52 CBS
    Cavalcade Theatre   ep   Moonlight School   5. 18. 54 ABC
    Cavalcade Theatre   ep   Stay On, Stranger   5. 3. 55 ABC
    Telephone Time   ep   Golden Junkman   4. 7. 56 CBS
    Studio 57   ep   Ballad of Jubal Pickett   8. 12. 56 NN
    Hawkeye   sr   4. 19. 57 ABC
    Climax   ep   The Necessary Evil   9. 19. 57 CBS
    Rough Riders   ep   An Eye for an Eye   1. 15. 59 ABC
    Rawhide   ep   Incident on the Edge of Madness 2. 6. 59
        CBS
    Have Gun Will Travel   ep   The Scorched Feather   2. 14.
        59 CBS
    G. E. Theatre   ep   The Family Man   2. 22. 59 CBS
    Texan   ep   3. 9. 59 CBS
    Tombstone Territory   ep   The Black Marshal from
        Deadwood   6. 12. 59 ABC
    Wanted Dead or Alive   ep   10. 10. 59 CBS
    Adventure in Paradise   ep   The Black Pearl   10. 12. 59
        ABC

Johnny Ringo   ep   The Raffertys   3.3.60 CBS
Bat Masterson   ep   Bat Trap   10.13.60 NBC
Wagon Train   ep   The Jose Morales Story   10.26.60
NBC
Stagecoach West   ep   Not in Our Stars   2.7.61 ABC
Klondike   ep   The Hostages   2.13.61 NBC
Zane Grey Theatre   ep   A Warm Day in Heaven   3.23.
61 CBS
Deputy   ep   Brother in Arms   4.15.61 NBC
Wagon Train   ep   The Chalice   5.24.61 NBC
Surfside 6   ep   Witness for the Defense   10.23.61 ABC
Route 66   The Mud Nest   11.10.61 CBS
Rifleman   ep   Gunfire   1.15.62 ABC
Lawman   ep   The Tarnished Badge   1.28.62 ABC
Route 66   ep   Lizard's Leg and Owlet's Wing   10.26.62
CBS
Rawhide   ep   Incident at Spider Rock   1.18.63 CBS
Have Gun Will Travel   ep   2.16.63 CBS
Empire   ep   Hidden Asset   3.26.63 NBC
Route 66   ep   Come Out, Come Out   10.11.63 CBS
Route 66   ep   4.24.64 CBS
Pistols 'N Petticoats   ep   10.1.66   CBS
Monkees   ep   10.24.66 NBC

CHANNING, CAROL
Omnibus   ep   This Little Kitty Stayed Cool   10.3.53
CBS
Svengali and the Blonde   Sp   7.30.55 NBC
Playhouse 90   ep   Three Men on a Horse   4.18.57 CBS
George Burns Show   ep   1.6.59 NBC

CHAPIN, LAURIN
Father Knows Best   sr   10.3.54 CBS
Fireside Theatre   ep   The 99th Day   5.31.55 NBC
Father Knows Best   sr ret   8.31.55 NBC
Father Knows Best   sr ret   9.56 NBC
Father Knows Best   sr ret   9.57 NBC
Father Knows Best   sr ret   9.22.58 CBS
Father Knows Best   sr ret   9.59 CBS
Father Knows Best   sr ret   9.60 CBS
G.E. Theatre   ep   The Man Who Thought for Himself
9.18.60 CBS

CHAPLIN, GERALDINE
Danny Thomas Show   ep   The Scene   9.25.67 NBC

CHAPLIN, SYDNEY
    Kings Row ep 1.17.56 ABC
    Wonderful Town Sp 11.30.58 CBS
    Phil Silvers Sp 1.23.59 CBS

CHAPMAN, MARGUERITE
    Bigelow Theatre ep The Lady's Companion 4.22.51
        CBS
    Ford Theatre ep Life, Liberty and Orrin Dooley 10.
        2.52 NBC
    Schlitz Playhouse of Stars ep Girl of My Dreams 2.
        27.53 CBS
    Hollywood Opening Night ep My Boss and I 3.23.53
        NBC
    Your Play Time ep The Tin Bridge 7.5.53 CBS
    Pepsi Cola Playhouse ep When, Lovely Woman 10.
        2.53 ABC
    Mirror Theatre ep Key in the Lock 11.14.53 CBS
    Four Star Playhouse ep The Book 4.1.54 CBS
    Pepsi Cola Playhouse ep Unfair Game 6.4.54 ABC
    Studio 57 ep The Traveling Room 10.12.54 NN
    Playhouse ep Such a Nice Little Girl 10.31.54 ABC
    Four Star Playhouse ep The Contest 11.4.54 CBS
    Studio 57 ep Sauce for the Gander 12.28.54 NN
    Studio 57 ep The Will to Survive 1.18.55 NN
    Climax ep Private Worlds 4.7.55 CBS
    Studio 57 ep The Traveling Room 6.28.55 NN
    Undercurrent ep 7.15.55 CBS
    Climax ep The Healer 7.21.55 CBS
    The Whistler ep The Jubilee Earring 8.21.55 NN
    Science Fiction Theatre ep The World Below 8.26.
        55 NBC
    Fireside Theatre ep Stephen and Publius Cyrus 10.
        11.55 NBC
    Climax ep Thin Air 10.13.55 CBS
    Studio 57 ep Diagnosis of a Selfish Lady 10.23.55
        NN
    TV Reader's Digest ep The Case of the Uncertain
        Hand 2.27.56 ABC
    Turning Point ep Unfair Game 4.28.56 NBC
    Lux Video Theatre ep The Captives 7.19.56 NBC
    Ford Theatre ep Broken Barrier 3.6.57 ABC
    Eve Arden Show ep 10.29.57 CBS
    Climax ep Shadow of a Memory 12.26.57 CBS
    Studio One ep A Dead Ringer 3.10.58 CBS
    Richard Diamond ep The Bungalow Murder 5.29.58
        CBS

Pursuit   ep   Eagle in the Cage   12.3.58 CBS
Rawhide   ep   Incident with an Executioner   1.23.59
   CBS

CHARISSE, CYD
   Checkmate   ep   Dance of Death   4.22.61 CBS

CHASE, BARRIE
   Bob Hope Chrysler Theatre   ep   Think Pretty   10.2.64
   NBC

CHASE, ILKA
   Silver Theatre   ep   Concerning the Soul of Felicity   3.
      20.50 CBS
   Pulitzer Prize Playhouse   ep   Robert E. Lee   3.26.52
      ABC
   Cinderella   Sp   3.31.57 CBS
   Kraft Theatre   ep   The Spell of the Tigress   2.5.58
      NBC
   Modern Romance   ep hos   6.2.58 NBC
   Playhouse 90   ep   The Return of Ansel Gibbs   11.27.
      58 CBS
   Defenders   ep   The Boy Between   10.21.61 CBS
   New Breed   ep   I Remember Murder   12.26.61 ABC
   Patty Duke Show   ep   House Guest   9.18.63 ABC
   Trials of O'Brien   sr   9.18.65 CBS
   Cool Million   ep   11.22.72 NBC

CHATTERTON, RUTH
   Prudential Playhouse   ep   Dodsworth   10.24.50 CBS
   Celanese Theatre   ep   Old Acquaintance   11.14.51 ABC
   Kraft Theatre   ep   The Paper Moon   12.31.52 NBC
   Hallmark Hall of Fame   ep   Hamlet   4.26.53 NBC

CHEVALIER, MAURICE
   Lucille Ball-Desi Arnaz Hour   ep   Lucy Goes to Mexi-
      co   10.6.58 CBS

CHILDRESS, ALVIN
   Amos 'n Andy   sr   6.28.51 CBS

CHRISTIAN, LINDA
   Alfred Hitchcock Theatre   ep   An Out for Oscar   4.5.
      63 CBS
   Lloyd Bridges Theatre   ep   4.16.63 CBS
   Dick Powell Theatre   ep   Last of the Private Eyes   4.
      30.63 NBC

CHRISTIANS, MADY
    The Clock ep The Morning After 9.22.50 NBC

CHURCH, SANDRA
    Dupont Show of the Month ep Years Ago 4.21.60 CBS
    Eleventh Hour ep The Middle Child Gets all the Aches
        5.22.63 NBC
    Kraft Suspense Theatre ep A Hero for Our Times 10.
        31.63 NBC
    Nurses ep The Intern Syndrome 1.23.64 CBS

CHURCHILL, SARAH
    Video Theatre ep Sweet Sorrow 5.28.51 CBS
    Faith Baldwin Playhouse ep We Have These Hours 9.
        8.51 ABC
    Hallmark Hall of Fame sh/sr 4.20.52 NBC
    Hallmark Hall of Fame sh/sr ret fall, 1952 NBC
    Hallmark Hall of Fame sh/sr ret fall, 1953 NBC
    Hallmark Hall of Fame sh/sr ret fall, 1954 NBC
    Matinee Theatre ep The Old Maid 1.16.56 NBC
    Matinee Theatre ep Susan and God 2.6.56 NBC
    Matinee Theatre ep Skylark 2.27.56 NBC
    Lux Video Theatre ep Temptation 4.12.56 NBC
    Matinee Theatre ep Savrola 11.15.56 NBC
    Playhouse 90 ep Sincerely, Willis Wayde 12.13.56
        CBS
    Matinee Theatre ep The Others 2.15.57 NBC
    Matinee Theatre ep The Tone of Time 10.17.57 NBC
    Matinee Theatre ep Aesop and Rhodope 11.10.57 NBC
    Matinee Theatre ep No Time for Comedy 12.17.57
        NBC
    Matinee Theatre ep The Makropoulos Secret 1.14.58
        NBC
    Matinee Theatre ep Love out of Town 6.21.58 NBC

CIANNELLI, EDUARDO
    Studio One ep The Idol of San Vittore 10.1.51 CBS
    Celanese Theatre ep Winterset 10.31.51 ABC
    Footlights Theatre ep A Man's First Debt 9.5.52
        CBS
    Climax ep The Shadow of Evil 5.24.56 CBS
    Climax ep Throw Away the Cane 8.2.56 CBS
    Matinee Theatre ep The Fall of the House of Usher
        8.6.56 NBC
    Climax ep Island in the City 10.4.56 CBS
    I Love Lucy ep 10.29.56 CBS
    Climax ep Nine-Day Wonder 3.7.57 CBS

Schlitz Playhouse of Stars ep Carriage from Britain
3. 8. 57 CBS
On Trial ep The Secret of Polanto 5. 31. 57 NBC
Climax ep The Disappearance of Daphne 5. 15. 58
CBS
No Warning ep Nightmare 6. 29. 58 NBC
Pursuit ep The Dark Clue 12. 31. 58 CBS
Wagon Train ep The Clark Duncan Story 4. 22. 59
NBC
Playhouse 90 ep The Killers of Mussolini 6. 4. 59
CBS
Have Gun Will Travel ep Gold and Brimstone 6. 20.
59 CBS
Staccato sr 9. 10. 59 NBC
Tightrope ep Park Avenue Story 3. 8. 60 CBS
Islanders ep Forbidden Cargo 11. 27. 60 ABC
Bringing Up Buddy ep The Girls Rent a House 2. 6.
61 CBS
Detectives ep An Eye for an Eye 2. 24. 61 ABC
Tall Man ep Ransom of a Town 5. 6. 61 NBC
Naked City ep Make Believe Man 5. 17. 61 ABC
Follow the Sun ep Chicago Style 1. 7. 62 ABC
Untouchables ep The Whitey Steele Story 2. 8. 62 ABC
Alfred Hitchcock Theatre ep Strange Miracle 2. 13. 62
NBC
Alfred Hitchcock Theatre ep The Test 2. 20. 62 NBC
Dr. Kildare ep The Stepping Stones 2. 22. 62 NBC
Thriller ep The Bride Who Died Twice 3. 19. 62 NBC
New Breed ep The Man with the Other Face 4. 10. 62
ABC
Lloyd Bridges Theatre ep Little Man, Big Bridge 11.
27. 62 CBS
Gallant Men ep Signal for an End Run 12. 7. 62 ABC
Lloyd Bridges Theatre ep Without Wheat, There is No
Bread 5. 14. 63 CBS
Burke's Law ep 11. 25. 64 ABC
Slattery's People ep What Did You Do all Day Mr.
Slattery 1. 15. 65 CBS
Bob Hope Chrysler Theatre ep Cops and Robbers 2.
19. 65 NBC
The Man from U. N. C. L. E. ep The Children's Day Af-
fair 12. 10. 65 NBC
Dr. Kildare ep A Cry from the Streets 1. 24. 66, 1.
25. 66, 1. 31. 66, 2. 1. 66 NBC
Bob Hope Chrysler Theatre ep After the Lion, Jackals
1. 26. 66 NBC
Virginian ep No Drums, No Trumpets 4. 6. 66 NBC

Seven Rich Years pt 9.11.66 ABC
Fugitive ep A Clean and Quiet Town 9.27.66 ABC
Jericho ep Two for the Road 11.10.66, 11.17.66
  CBS
The Man from U.N.C.L.E. ep 11.25.66, 12.2.66
  NBC
The Girl from U.N.C.L.E. ep 1.10.67 NBC
Time Tunnel ep The Ghost of the Year 1.20.67 ABC
The Girl from U.N.C.L.E. ep 1.24.67 NBC
I Spy ep 9.18.67 NBC
Garrison's Gorillas ep 11.14.67 ABC
Mission Impossible ep 11.19.67, 11.26.67 CBS

CILENTO, DIANE
  Alcoa Hour ep The Small Servant 10.30.55 NBC
  Hallmark Hall of Fame ep The Taming of the Shrew
    3.18.56 NBC
  Family Classics ep Vanity Fair 1.12.61, 1.13.61
    CBS
  Court Martial ep La Belle France 6.10.66 ABC
  Dial M for Murder Sp 11.15.67 ABC

CLARK, DANE
  Mystery Theatre ep The Dark Door 9.19.50 ABC
  Airflyte Theatre ep I Won't Take a Minute 11.9.50
    CBS
  Airflyte Theatre ep Pearl Are a Nuisance 2.15.51
    CBS
  Video Theatre ep Not Guilty--of Much 3.5.51 CBS
  Gruen Guild Theatre ep Unfinished Business 9.27.51
    ABC
  Starlight Theatre ep Gravy Train 9.20.51 CBS
  Schlitz Playhouse of Stars ep 2.15.52 CBS
  Philco Playhouse ep The Recluse 4.12.53 NBC
  Medallion Theatre ep Columbo Discovers Italy 8.29.
    53 CBS
  Tales of the City ep 9.17.53 CBS
  Mirror Theatre ep Equal Justice 10.17.53 CBS
  Philco Playhouse ep Hangman in the Fog 1.10.54
    NBC
  P.M. Playhouse ep Up for Parole 2.4.54 CBS
  Ford Theatre ep Remember to Live 11.4.54 NBC
  Producers Showcase ep Yellow Jack 1.10.65 NBC
  Appointment with Adventure ep Rendezvous in Paris
    5.1.55 CBS
  G.E. Theatre ep Into the Night 5.8.55 CBS

Appointment with Adventure   ep   The Royal Treatment
Science Fiction Theatre   ep   Negative Man   9.16.55
    NBC
Fireside Theatre   ep   The Little Guy   9.27.55 NBC
Damon Runyon Theatre   ep   A Job for the Macarone
    11.26.55 CBS
Science Fiction Theatre   ep   Before the Beginning   12.
    16.55 NBC
Schlitz Playhouse of Stars   ep   The Baited Hook   12.
    16.55 CBS
Fireside Theatre   ep   The Liberator   1.10.56 NBC
20th Century-Fox Hour   ep   One Life   1.25.56 CBS
Ford Theatre   ep   Behind the Mask   5.10.56 NBC
Wire Service SR   10.4.56 ABC
On Trial   ep   The Fourth Witness   12.21.56 NBC
Jane Wyman Theatre   ep   Little Black Lie   1.1.57 NBC
Studio 57   ep   A Hero's Return   1.6.57 NN
Climax   ep   The Mad Bomber   4.18.57 CBS
Climax   ep   The Giant Killer   8.1.57 CBS
Playhouse 90   ep   Reunion   1.2.58 CBS
Schlitz Playhouse of Stars   ep   Heroes Never Grow Up
    2.7.58 CBS
Studio One   ep   The Enemy Within   4.7.58 CBS
Wagon Train   ep   The John Wilbot Story   6.11.58 NBC
Pursuit   ep   The House at Malibu   11.26.58 CBS
The Killers   Sp   11.19.59 CBS
Play of the Week   ep   The Closing Door   1.4.60 NN
Mystery Theatre   ep   The Last Six Blocks   7.17.60
    NBC
Rawhide   ep   Incident of the Night Visitor   11.4.60
    CBS
U.S. Steel Hour   ep   The Devil Makes Sunday   1.25.61
    CBS
Play of the Week   ep   No Exit   2.27.61 NN
Twilight Zone   ep   The Prime Mover   3.24.61 CBS
Untouchables   ep   Bird in the Hand   10.30.62 ABC
Untouchables   ep   Jake Dance   1.22.63 ABC
Ben Casey   ep   A Woods Full of Question Marks   10.
    26.64 ABC
Burke's Law   ep   10.28.64 ABC
Kraft Suspense Theatre   ep   The Safe House   5.20.65
    NBC
Ben Casey   ep   For San Diego, You Need a Different
    Bus   1.17.66 ABC
I Spy   ep   One Thousand Fine   4.27.66 NBC
Showcase   ep   The Good Lieutenant   6.5.66 NN
N.Y.P.D.   ep   Joshua Fit the Battle of Fulton Street

12.5.67 ABC
Danny Thomas Show   ep   The Last Hunters   1.29.68
   NBC
I Spy   ep   4.1.68 NBC
Name of the Game   ep   Incident in Berlin   10.25.68
   NBC
Ironside   ep   I the People   10.31.68 NBC
Ironside   ep   Good-By to Yesterday   9.2.5.69 NBC
Name of the Game   ep   10.24.69 NBC
Bracken's World   ep   Stop Date   12.19.69 NBC
Mannix   ep   Walk with a Dead Man   1.10.70 CBS
Ironside   ep   9.17.70 NBC
Mannix   ep   A Ticket to the Clipse   9.19.70 CBS
Silent Force   ep   10.12.70 ABC
Men from Shiloh   ep   The Mysterious Mr. Tate   10.
   14.70 NBC
Mannix   ep   With Intent to Kill   1.23.71 CBS
Dan August   ep   The Meal Ticket   3.18.71 ABC
Owen Marshall   ep   Legacy of Fear   9.16.71 ABC
Cade's County   ep   11.21.71 CBS
Ironside   ep   When She Was Bad   12.30.71 NBC
The Family Rico   tf   9.12.72 CBS
Rookies   ep   9.17.72 ABC
Say Goodbye, Maggie Cole   tf 9.17.72 ABC
Night Gallery   ep   Spectre in Tap Shoes   10.29.72
   NBC
Mission Impossible   ep   11.11.72 CBS
Mod Squad   ep   12.7.72 ABC

CLARK, FRED
   George Burns-Gracie Allen Show   sr   10.12.50 CBS
   George Burns-Gracie Allen Show   sr ret   fall, 1951
      CBS
   George Burns-Gracie Allen Show   sr ret   fall, 1952
      CBS
   Broadway Television Theatre   ep   Twentieth Century
      10.12.53 NN
   Lux Video Theatre   ep   Forever Female   6.23.55 NBC
   Screen Directors Playhouse   ep   Want Ad Wedding   11.
      2.55 NBC
   Studio One   ep   Circle of Guilt   2.20.56 CBS
   Alcoa Hour   ep   President   5.13.56 NBC
   Dupont Theatre   ep   Pursuit of a Princess   12.4.56
      ABC
   Kraft Theatre   ep   The Singin' Idol   1.30.57 NBC
   Lux Playhouse   ep   The Case of the Two Sisters   5.1.
      59 CBS

Untouchables   ep   Little Egypt   2.11.60 ABC
Shirley Temple Theatre   ep   Emmy Lou   11.6.60 NBC
Twilight Zone   ep   A Most Unusual Camera   12.16.60
    CBS
G.E. Theatre   ep   My Darling Judge   4.23.61 CBS
Bus Stop   ep   The Runaways   12.24.61 ABC
Naked City   ep   Bridge Party   12.27.61 ABC
G.E. Theatre   ep   The Hold-Out   1.14.62 CBS
Armstrong Circle Theatre   ep   Securities for Suckers
    1.17.62 CBS
U.S. Steel Hour   ep   Male Call   8.8.62 CBS
Wagon Train   ep   The Martin Gatsby Story   10.10.62
    ABC
Going My Way   ep   A Matter of Principle   11.21.62
    ABC
Burke's Law   ep   Who Killy Holly Howard   9.20.63 ABC
Beverly Hillbillies   sr   9.25.63 CBS
Burke's Law   ep   10.21.64 ABC
Slattery's People   ep   Bill Bailey, Why Did You Come
    Home   4.2.65 CBS
Dick van Dyke Show   ep   100 Terrible Hours   4.7.65
    CBS
Bob Hope Chrysler Theatre   ep   Mr. Governess   11.
    10.65 NBC
Addams Family   ep   11.26.65 ABC
Laredo   ep   The Land Grabbers   12.9.65 NBC
Double Life   sr   1.12.66 ABC
ABC Stage 67   ep   Olympus 7-0000   9.28.66 ABC
Beverly Hillbillies   ep   3.22.67 CBS
I Dream of Jeannie   ep   9.26.67 NBC
Off to See the Wizard   ep   Who's Afraid of Mother
    Goose   10.13.67 ABC
Bonanza   ep   1.14.68 NBC

CLARK, SUSAN
    Bob Hope Chrysler Theatre   ep   Blind Man's Bluff   2.8.
    67 NBC
    Virginian   ep   2.22.67 NBC
    Run for Your Life   ep   Cry Hard, Cry Fast   11.22.67,
    11.29.67 NBC
    Marcus Welby, M.D.   ep   Hello, Goodby, Hello   9.23.
    69 ABC
    The Challengers   tf   2.20.70 CBS
    Bold Ones   ep   11.14.71 NBC
    Columbo   ep   Lady in Waiting   12.15.71 NBC
    The Astronaut   tf   1.8.73 ABC
    Marcus Welby, M.D.   ep   Please Don't Send Flowers

10.17.72 ABC

CLARKE, MAE
  Loretta Young Show ep The Judgment 5.2.54 NBC
  Four Star Playhouse ep Man in the Cellar 9.30.54
    CBS
  Public Defender ep Gunpoint 1.20.55 CBS
  Medic ep When I Was Young 10.24.55 NBC
  Ford Theatre ep Front Page Father 12.5.56 ABC
  Jane Wyman Theatre ep Killer's Pride 2.9.57 NBC
  Loretta Young Show ep A Greater Strength 2.23.58
    NBC

CLAYTON, JAN
  Story Theatre ep The Manchester Marriage 2.2.51
    NN
  Jewelers Showcase ep Three and One-Half Musketeers
    1.27.53 CBS
  Lassie sr 9.12.54 CBS
  Lassie sr ret fall, 1955 CBS
  Lassie sr ret fall, 1956 CBS
  Matinee Theatre ep Wednesday's Child 3.5.58 NBC
  The Millionaire ep Millionaire Irene Marshall 1.21.
    59 CBS
  Deputy ep Lady with a Mission 3.5.60 NBC
  Tales of Wells Fargo ep The Bride and the Bandit
    12.12.60 NBC
  Danny Thomas Show ep 12.19.60 CBS
  Wagon Train ep The Prairie Story 2.1.61 NBC
  My Three Sons ep Romance of the Silver Pines 1.11.
    62 ABC
  Tall Man ep St. Louis Woman 1.20.62 NBC
  Wagon Train ep 1.31.64 ABC
  Gunsmoke ep 4.11.64 CBS
  Gunsmoke ep 4.24.65 CBS
  Daktari ep 3.22.66, 3.29.66 CBS
  My Three Sons ep 3.16.67 CBS

CLEVELAND, GEORGE
  Lassie sr 9.12.54 CBS
  Lassie sr ret fall, 1955 CBS
  Lassie sr ret fall, 1956 CBS

CLOONEY, ROSEMARY
  Dick Powell Theatre ep The Losers 1.15.63 NBC

COATES, PHYLLIS
    Superman   sr   1950 NN
    Superman   sr ret   1951 NN
    Jewelers Showcase   ep   The Bean Farm   3.24.53 CBS
    Jewelers Showcase   ep   Cell 14   11.10.53 NN
    Death Valley Days   ep   Solomon in all His Glory 11.17.
        53 NN
    G.E. Theatre   ep   Here Comes Calvin   2.21.54 CBS
    The Duke   sr   7.2.54 NBC
    Professional Father   sr   1.8.55 CBS
    The Millionaire   ep   The Story of Jack Martin   5.4.55
        CBS
    Frontier   ep   King of the Dakotas   11.13.55, 11.20.55,
        NBC
    TV Reader's Digest   ep   The Man Who Could Beat
        Death   1.16.56 ABC
    Navy Log   ep   Web Feet   2.21.56 CBS
    Four Star Playhouse   ep   Once to Every Woman   3.1.
        56 CBS
    It's a Great Life   ep   3.18.56 NBC
    Cavalcade Theatre   ep   The Gift of Dr. Minot 5.15.56
        ABC
    Death Valley Days   ep   Solomon in all His Glory   6.20.
        56 NBC
    Richard Diamond   ep   Another Man's Poison   4.17.58
        CBS
    Perry Mason   ep   The Case of the Black-Eyed Blonde
        6.14.58 CBS
    Desilu Playhouse   ep   Trial at Devil's Canyon   1.5.59
        CBS
    Black Saddle   ep   1.31.59 NBC
    Lux Playhouse   ep   The Case of the Two Sisters   5.1.
        59 CBS
    Rawhide   ep   Incident of the Judas Trap   6.5.59 CBS
    Hennesey   ep   12.7.59 CBS
    June Allyson Show   ep   The Trench Coat   1.11.60 CBS
    Perry Mason   ep   The Case of the Cowardly Lion   4.8.
        61 CBS
    Gunslinger   ep   Johnny Sergeant   5.4.61 CBS
    Rawhide   ep   Little Fishes   11.24.61 CBS
    Untouchables   ep   A Fist of Five   12.4.62 ABC
    Perry Mason   ep   The Case of the Ice Cold Hands   1.
        23.64 CBS

COBB, LEE J.
    Somerset Maugham Theatre   ep   The Moon and Six-
        pence   4.30.51 NBC

Tales of Tomorrow op Test Flight 10.26.51 ABC
Lights Out ep The Veil 10.29.51 NBC
Ford Theatre ep Night Visitor 4.29.54 NBC
Producers Showcase ep Darkness at Noon 5.2.55
    NBC
Medic ep Break through the Bars 7.18.55 NBC
Goodyear Playhouse ep A Patch on Faith 1.22.56
    NBC
Zane Grey Theatre ep Death Watch 11.8.56 CBS
Playhouse 90 ep Panic Button 11.28.57 CBS
Studio One ep No Deadly Medicine 12.9.57, 19.16.
    57 CBS
Zane Grey Theatre ep Legacy of a Legend 11.6.58
    CBS
Playhouse 90 ep Project Immortality 6.11.59 CBS
Dupont Show of the Month ep I, Don Quixote 11.9.
    59 CBS
G.E. Theatre ep Lear vs the Committeeman 1.17.60
    CBS
Dupont Show of the Month ep Men in White 9.30.60
    CBS
June Allyson Show ep School of the Soldier 1.30.61
    CBS
Naked City ep Take Off Your Hat When a Funeral
    Passes 9.27.61 ABC
Westinghouse Presents ep Footnote to Fame 2.3.62
    CBS
G.E. Theatre ep The Unstoppable Gray Fox 5.6.62
    CBS
Virginian sr 9.19.62 NBC
Virginian sr ret 9.18.63 NBC
Bob Hope Chrysler Theatre ep It's Mental Work 12.
    20.63 NBC
Virginian sr ret 9.16.64 NBC
Virginian sr ret 9.15.65 NBC
Death of a Salesman Sp 5.8.66 CBS
On Stage ep To Confuse the Angel 3.15.70 NBC
Young Lawyers sr 9.21.70 ABC
Heat of Anger tf 3.3.72 CBS

COBURN, CHARLES
    Pulitzer Prize Playhouse ep You Can't Take It With
        You 10.6.50 ABC
    Tales of the City ep 8.6.53 CBS
    Ford Theatre ep The World's My Oyster 11.5.53
        NBC
    Center Stage ep The Worthy Opponent 8.24.54 ABC

Best of Broadway   ep   The Royal Family   9.15.54 CBS
U.S. Steel Hour   ep   One for the Road   12.7.54 ABC
Studio One   ep   The Cuckoo in Spring   12.27.54 CBS
Ford Theatre   ep   Pretend You're You   2.10.55 NBC
Studio 57   ep   Sam   3.22.55 NN
Rheingold Theatre   ep   The Lady's Game   4.23.55 NBC
Eddie Cantor Theatre   ep   7.25.55 ABC
December Bride   ep   10.17.55 CBS
Rheingold Theatre   ep   A Difficult Age   1.21.56 NBC
Jane Wyman Theatre   ep   Kristi   2.14.56 NBC
Ford Theatre   ep   Mr. Kagle and the Baby Sitter   6.7.
    56 NBC
Ethel Barrymore Theatre   ep   Winter and Spring   12.
    14.56 NN
Danny Thomas Show   ep   Grandpa's Diet   4.6.59 CBS
Ford Star Time   ep   The Wicked Scheme of Jebel Deeks
    11.10.59 NBC
Best of the Post   ep   Six Months to Live   3.25.61 ABC

COBURN, JAMES
Restless Gun   ep   Take Me Home   12.29.58 NBC
Cheyenne   ep   Payroll of the Dead   1.27.59 ABC
Zane Grey Theatre   ep   A   Thread of Respect   2.12.59
    CBS
Trackdown   ep   3.11.59 CBS
Black Saddle   ep   3.21.59 NBC
Wanted Dead or Alive   ep   3.28.59 CBS
Restless Gun   ep   The Pawn   4.6.59 NBC
M Squad   ep   Firemaker   4.17.59 NBC
Californians   ep   One Ton of Peppercorns   5.12.59 NBC
Rough Riders   ep   Deadfall   5.21.59 ABC
Californians   ep   Act of Faith   5.26.59 NBC
Johnny Ringo   ep   10.1.59 CBS
Bonanza   ep   The Truckee Strip   11.21.59 NBC
Wyatt Earp   ep   The Noble Outlaws   11.24.59 ABC
Alfred Hitchcock Presents   ep   An Occurrence at Owl
    Creek Bridge   1.20.59 CBS
Have Gun Will Travel   ep   12.26.59 CBS
The Millionaire   ep   Millionaire Timothy Mackail   12.
    30.59 CBS
Texan   ep   1.4.60 CBS
Lawman   ep   The Showdown   1.10.60 ABC
Bronco   ep   Shadow of Jesse James   1.12.60 ABC
Wichita Town   ep   Afternoon in Town   2.17.60 NBC
Sugarfoot   ep   Blackwater Swamp   3.1.60 ABC
Men Into Space   ep   3.2.60   CBS
Peter Gunn   ep   The Murder Clause   3.28.60 NBC

Deputy   ep   The Truly Years   4. 9. 60 NBC
Tate   sr   6. 8. 60 NBC
Wanted Dead or Alive   ep   9. 21. 60 CBS
Zane Grey Theatre   ep   Desert Flight   10. 13. 60 CBS
Lawman   ep   The Catch   12. 4. 60 ABC
Klondike   sr   10. 10. 60 BNC
Aquanauts   ep   River Gold   1. 4. 61 CBS
Detectives   ep   The Frightened Ones   1. 6. 61 ABC
Perry Mason   ep   The Case of the Envious Editor   1. 7.
   61 CBS
Stagecoach West   ep   Come Home Again   1. 10. 61 ABC
Tall Men   ep   The Best Policy   1. 28. 61 NBC
Untouchables   ep   Jamaica Ginger   2. 21. 61 ABC
Outlaws   ep   Culley   2. 16. 61 NBC
Acapulco   sr   2. 27. 61 NBC
Bonanza   ep   The Dark Gate   3. 4. 61 NBC
Laramie   ep   The Mark of the Maneaters   3. 14. 61 NBC
Cheyenne   ep   Trouble Street   10. 21. 61 ABC
Rifleman   ep   The High Country   12. 18. 61 ABC
Cain's Hundred   ep   Blues for a Junkman   2. 20. 62 NBC
Untouchables   ep   Jamaica Ginger   3. 15. 62 ABC
Checkmate   ep   A Chant of Silence   3. 21. 62 CBS
Perry Mason   ep   The Case of the Angry Astronaut   4.
   7. 62 CBS
Bonanza   ep   The Long Night   5. 6. 62 NBC
Rifleman   ep   The High Country   5. 6. 63 ABC
Stoney Burke   ep   The Test   5. 13. 63 ABC
The Greatest Show on Earth   ep   Uncaged   10. 29. 63 ABC
Eleventh Hour   ep   You Shouldn't Have Done It 10. 30. 63 NBC
Twilight Zone   ep   The Old Man in the Cave   11. 8. 63 CBS
Route 66   ep   Kiss the Monster--Make Him Sleep   1. 24.
   64 CBS
Defenders   ep   The Man Who Saved His Country   5. 9. 64 CBS

COCA, IMOGENE
Imogene Coca Show   sr   10. 2. 54 NBC
U. S. Steel Hour   ep   The Funny Heart   4. 1. 56 CBS
Jane Wyman Theatre   ep   Helpmate   12. 4. 56 NBC
Playhouse 90   ep   Made in Heaven   12. 6. 56 CBS
Ruggles of Red Gap   Sp   2. 3. 57 NBC
G. E. Theatre   ep   Cab Driver   4. 14. 57 CBS
Shirley Temple Theatre   ep   Madeline 10. 16. 60 NBC
Grindl   sr   9. 15. 63 NBC
It's about Time   sr   9. 11. 66 CBS
Bewitched   ep   1. 21. 71, 1. 28. 71 ABC
Night Gallery   ep   The Cask of Amontillado 9. 22. 71 NBC
Love American Style   ep   12. 8. 72 ABC

COCHRAN, STEVE
    Studio One   ep   Letter of Love   10.19.53 CBS
    Medallion Theatre   ep   The 39th Bomb   2.13.54 CBS
    Studio One   ep   The Role of Lover   2.22.54 CBS
    Ford Theatre   ep   Trip Around the Block   10.28.54
      NBC
    Climax   ep   The After House   11.25.54 CBS
    Studio One   ep   A Most Contagious Game   10.17.55
      CBS
    Climax   ep   Fear Is the Hunter   7.13.56 CBS
    Schlitz Playhouse of Stars   ep   Outlaw's Boots   11.29.
      57 CBS
    Zane Grey Theatre   ep Debt of Gratitude   4.18.58 CBS
    Loretta Young Show   ep   4.19.59 NBC
    Naked City   ep   Debt of Honor   11.23.60 ABC
    Untouchables   ep   The Purple Gang   12.1.60 ABC
    Shirley Temple Theatre   ep   The Indian Captive   12.4.
      60 NBC
    Renegade   Sp   12.27.60 NBC
    Untouchables   ep   90-Proof Dame   6.8.61 ABC
    Bus Stop   ep   Afternoon of a Convoy   10.1.61 ABC
    Dick Powell Theatre   ep   Obituary for Mr. "X"   1.23.
      62 NBC
    Virginian   ep   West   11.28.62 NBC
    Stoney Burke   ep   Death Rides a Pale Horse   1.14.63
      ABC
    Route 66   ep   Shall Forfeit His Dog and Ten Shillings
      to the King   2.22.63 CBS
    Death Valley Days   ep   West of Heaven   3.28.64 ABC
    Mr. Broadway   ep   Keep an Eye on Emily   9.26.64
      CBS
    Burke's Law   ep   11.25.64 ABC
    Bonanza   ep   The Rap   3.28.65 NBC

COCO, JAMES
    Directions '66 ep   The Bigger They Are   5.1.66 ABC
    N.E.T. Playhouse   ep   La Mama Playwrights   1.20.67
      NN
    New York Television Theatre   ep   Apple Pie   3.14.68
      NN
    N.Y.P.D.   ep   Who's Got the Bundle   2.25.69 ABC
    Hallmark Hall of Fame   ep   The Littlest Angel   12.6.
      69 NBC
    The Trouble with People   Sp   11.12.72 NBC

COLBERT, CLAUDETTE
    Best of Broadway   ep   The Royal Family   9.15.54 CBS

Climax ep The White Carnation 12.16.54 CBS
Ford Theatre ep Magic Formula 1.6.55 NBC
Best of Broadway ep The Guardsman 3.2.55 CBS
Climax ep Private Worlds 4.7.55 CBS
Ford Theatre ep While We're Young 4.28.55 NBC
Climax ep The Deliverance of Sister Cecilia 5.5.55
    CBS
Loretta Young Show ep A Pattern of Deceit 12.4.55
    NBC
Ford Star Jubilee ep Blithe Spirit 1.14.56 CBS
Robert Montgomery Presents ep After All These Years
    9.24.56 NBC
Playhouse 90 ep One Coat of White 2.21.57 CBS
Zane Grey Theatre ep Blood in the Dust 10.11.57
    CBS
Telephone Time ep Novel Appearance 12.3.57 ABC
G.E. Theatre ep Last Town Car 2.16.58, 2.23.58
    CBS
Colgate Theatre ep 9.30.58 NBC
The Bells of St. Mary's Sp 10.27.59 CBS
Welcome to Washington pt 8.23.60 CBS
Zane Grey Theatre ep So Young the Savage Land 11.
    10.60 CBS

COLE, DENNIS
Hawaiian Eye ep 1963 ABC
Felony Squad sr 9.16.66 ABC
Felony Squad sr ret 9.11.67 ABC
Felony Squad sr ret 9.27.68 ABC
Bracken's World sr 9.19.69 NBC
Bracken's World sr ret 9.18.70 NBC
Bearcats sr 9.16.71 CBS

COLEMAN, NANCY
Kraft Theatre ep The Wind Is Ninety 7.23.50 NBC
Valiant Lady sr 1953 CBS
Tales of Tomorrow ep The End of the Cocoon 3.6.53
    ABC
Tales of Tomorrow ep The Spider Web 5.22.53 ABC
TV Sound Stage ep Wonder in Your Eyes 8.28.53 NBC
Producers Showcase ep The Barretts of Wimpole
    Street 4.2.56 NBC
Kaiser Aluminum Hour ep Member in Good Standing
    1.1.57 NBC
U.S. Steel Hour ep The Reward 2.12.58 CBS
Modern Romance ep 3.3.58 NBC
True Story ep 6.7.58 NBC

Play of the Week   ep   Black Monday   1.16.61 NN
N.E.T. Playhouse   ep   Celebration for William Jennings
    Bryan   12.6.68 NN

COLLINGE, PAT
    Celanese Theatre   ep   4.16.52 ABC
    The Web   ep   Midnight Guest   1.18.53 CBS
    Studio One   ep   The River Garden   2.9.53 CBS
    Goodyear Playhouse   ep   The Rumor   3.8.53 NBC
    Studio One   ep   Crime at Blossom's   11.2.53 CBS
    Love Story   ep   The Wedding Dress   5.18.54 NN
    Appointment with Adventure   ep   A Sword Has Two
        Edges   12.11.55 CBS
    Alfred Hitchcock Presents   ep   The Cheney Vase   12.
        25.55 CBS
    Armstrong Circle Theatre   ep   Ward Three: 4 P.M.
        to Midnight   1.10.56 NBC
    Front Row Center   ep   Hawk's Head   4.1.56 CBS
    Alfred Hitchcock Presents   ep   The Rose Garden   12.
        16.56 CBS
    Alfred Hitchcock Presents   ep   Across the Threshold
        2.28.60 CBS
    Alfred Hitchcock Theatre   ep   1.17.61 NBC
    U.S. Steel Hour   ep   Scene of the Crime   6.27.62 CBS
    Alfred Hitchcock Theatre   ep   Bonfire   12.13.62 CBS
    East Side/West Side   ep   Creeps Live Here   12.23.63
        CBS
    Alfred Hitchcock Theatre   ep   The Ordeal of Mrs.
        Snow   4.17.64 CBS

COLLINS, DOROTHY
    U.S. Steel Hour   ep   Who's Earnest   10.9.57 CBS
    Music Theatre   ep   The Sound of Murder   5.9.59 NBC

COLLINS, JOAN
    Run for Your Life   ep   The Borders of Barbarism   9.
        26.66 NBC
    The Man from U.N.C.L.E.   ep   The Galates Affair   9.
        30.66 NBC
    Star Trek   ep   The City on the Edge of Forever   4.6.67 NBC
    Batman   ep   9.21.67, 9.28.67 ABC
    Virginian   ep   The Lady from Wichita   9.27.67 NBC
    Danny Thomas Show   ep   The Demon under the Bed   10.
        9.67 NBC
    Mission Impossible   ep   3.30.69 CBS
    Persuaders   ep   2.16.72 ABC
    Hallmark Hall of Fame   ep   The Man Who Came to Dinner
        11.29.72 NBC

COLLINS, RAY
  Cavalcade of America   ep   Last Will of Daniel Webster
    11.24.53 ABC
  Climax   ep   Champion   3.31.55 CBS
  The Halls of Ivy   sr   10.19.54 CBS
  You Are There   ep   P.T. Barnum Presents Jenny Lind
    4.10.55 CBS
  20th Century-Fox Hour   ep   Miracle on 34th Street   12.
    14.55 CBS
  20th Century-Fox Hour   ep   Gun in His Hand   4.4.56
    CBS
  Ford Star Jubilee   ep   20th Century   4.7.56 CBS
  Studio One   ep   The Star Spangled Soldier   5.21.56
    CBS
  Alfred Hitchcock Presents   ep   Conversation with a
    Corpse   11.18.56 CBS
  On Trial   ep   The Trail of Mary Suratt   11.23.56 NBC
  Playhouse 90   ep   Invitation to a Gunfighter   3.7.56
    CBS
  Perry Mason   sr   9.21.57 CBS
  Perry Mason   sr ret   fall, 1958 CBS
  Perry Mason   sr ret   10.3.59 CBS
  Perry Mason   sr ret   fall, 1960 CBS
  Father Knows Best   ep   Betty Goes to College   12.13.
    60 CBS
  Perry Mason   sr ret   fall, 1961 CBS
  Perry Mason   sr ret   9.27.62 CBS
  Perry Mason   sr ret   9.26.63 CBS

COLMAN, RONALD
  Four Star Playhouse   ep   The Lost Silk Hat   10.23.52
    CBS
  Four Star Playhouse   ep   The Man Who Walked Out on
    Himself   3.26.53 CBS
  Four Star Playhouse   ep   The Ladies on His Mind   5.
    21.53 CBS
  Four Star Playhouse   ep   A String of Pearls   1.24.54
    CBS
  The Halls of Ivy   sr   10.19.54 CBS
  G.E. Theatre   ep   The Chess Game   12.16.56 CBS
  Studio 57   ep   Perfect Likeness   6.23.57 NN

COMINGORE, DOROTHY
  Easy Chair Theatre   ep   Handcuffed   10.6.52 NN

CONKLIN, CHESTER
  Make Room for Daddy   ep   The First Hollywood Show

11. 2. 54 ABC

CONKLIN, PEGGY
  Airflyte Theatre   ep   The Windfall   12. 14. 50 CBS
  Kraft Theatre   ep   The Intimate Strangers   5. 16. 51
    NBC
  Armstrong Circle Theatre   ep   Red Tape   9. 30. 52
    ABC
  Kraft Theatre   ep   The Long Road Home   6. 23. 54 NBC
  Elgin Hour   ep   Days of Grace   2. 8. 55 ABC

CONNELLY, MARC
  Broadway Television Theatre   ep   The Village Green
    5. 11. 53 NN
  Play of the Week   ep   Black Monday   1. 16. 61 NN
  Dupont Show of the Month   ep   Night of the Storm   3.
    21. 61 CBS
  Defenders   ep   Man Against Himself   1. 12. 63 CBS
  Defenders   ep   A Taste of Vengeance   4. 6. 63 CBS
  The Borgia Stick   tf   2. 25. 67 NBC

CONNERY, SEAN
  Age of Kings   ep   The Hollow Crown   1. 10. 61 NN
  Age of Kings   ep   The Road to Shrewbury   1. 31. 61 NN
  Festival of the Arts   ep   Mademoiselle Colombe   11.
    23. 62 NN
  Age of Kings   ep   The Deposing of a King   2. 12. 63 NN
  BBC Drama   ep   Anna Karenina   4. 22. 64 NN
  On Stage   ep   Male of the Species   1. 3. 69   NBC

CONNORS, CHUCK
  Dear Phoebe   sr   9. 10. 54 NBC
  G. E. Theatre   ep   The Road to Edinburgh   10. 31. 54
    CBS
  Four Star Playhouse   ep   Vote of Confidence   11. 11. 54
    CBS
  Loretta Young Show   ep   The Girl Who Knew   1. 2. 55
    NBC
  Four Star Playhouse   ep   The Good Sisters   1. 27. 55 CBS
  TV Reader's Digest   ep   3. 28. 55 ABC
  Schlitz Playhouse of Stars   ep   O'Connor and the Blue-
    Eyed Felon   6. 10. 55 CBS
  TV Reader's Digest   ep   The Manufactured Clue   8. 15.
    55 ABC
  My Favorite Husband   ep   10. 25. 55 CBS
  Screen Directors Playhouse   ep   The Brush Roper   11.
    23. 55 NBC
  Cavalcade Theatre   ep   Barbed Wire Christmas   12. 20.

55 ABC
Fireside Theatre   ep   The Thread   6.12.56 NBC
Gunsmoke   ep   6.16.56 CBS
Oh Susanna   ep   The Witch Doctor   12.8.56 CBS
Tales of Wells Fargo   ep   3.18.57 NBC
The Millionaire   ep   The Hub Grimes Story   5.1.57
   CBS
West Point   ep   Army-Navy Game   10.29.57 ABC
Wagon Train   ep   The Charles Avery Story   11.13.57
   NBC
Restless Gun   ep   Silver Threads   12.16.57 NBC
Date with the Angels   ep   Double Trouble   1.15.58 ABC
Love That Jill   ep   They Went Thataway   2.10.58 ABC
West Point   ep   The Operator   2.11.58 ABC
Jim Bowie   ep   Horse Thief   3.21.58 ABC
Zane Grey Theatre   ep   The Sharpshooter   3.27.58 CBS
Tales of Wells Fargo   ep   The Thin Rope   6.2.58 NBC
Rifleman   sr   9.30.58 ABC
Rifleman   sr ret   fall, 1959 ABC
June Allyson Show   ep   Trial by Fear   5.16.60 CBS
Rifleman   sr ret   fall, 1960 ABC
Rifleman   sr ret   fall, 1961 ABC
Rifleman   sr ret   10.1.62 ABC
Arrest and Trial   sr   9.15.63 ABC
Branded   sr   1.24.65 NBC
Hero   ep   9.8.66 NBC
Cowboy in Africa   sr   9.11.67 ABC
Men from Shiloh   ep   1.20.71 NBC
Name of the Game   ep   The Broken Puzzle   3.12.71
   CBS
The Birdmen   tf   9.18.71 ABC
Night of Terror   10.10.72 ABC
Night Gallery   ep   The Ring with the Red Velvet Ropes
   11.5.72 NBC

CONNORS, MICHAEL
Ford Theatre   ep   Yours for a Dream   4.8.54 NBC
Schlitz Playhouse of Stars   ep   The Last Out   9.30.55
   CBS
Schlitz Playhouse of Stars   ep   No Trial by July   11.11.
   55 CBS
Wyatt Earp   ep   Big Baby Contest   11.22.55 ABC
The Millionaire   ep   The Story of Victor Volante   2.22.
   56 CBS
People's Choice   ep   12.6.56 NBC
Video Theatre   ep   The Latchkey   6.27.57 CBS
Maverick   ep   Point Blank   9.29.57 ABC

M Squad   ep   Peter Loves Mary   10.11.57 NBC
Have Gun Will Travel   ep   10.19.57 CBS
Oh Susanna   ep   Mardi Gras   12.7.57 CBS
Maverick   ep   Naked Gallows   12.15.57 ABC
Wagon Train   ep   The Dora Gray Story   1.29.58 NBC
Cheyenne   ep   Dead to Rights   5.20.58 ABC
Cimarron City   ep   Hired Hand   11.15.58 NBC
Lawman   ep   Lady in Question   12.21.58 ABC
Alcoa Premiere   ep   The Aerialist   4.28.59 ABC
Tightrope!   sr   9.8.59 CBS
Rescue 8   ep   5.2.60 ABC
Expendables   pt   9.27.62 ABC
Untouchables   ep   The Eddie O'Hara Story   11.13.62
   ABC
Perry Mason   ep   The Case of the Bullied Bowler   11.
   5.64 CBS
Mannix   sr   9.16.67 CBS
Mannix   sr ret   9.28.68 CBS
Mannix   sr ret   9.27.69 CBS
Mannix   sr ret   9.19.70 CBS
Mannix   sr ret   9.14.71 CBS
Mannix   sr ret   9.17.72 CBS

CONRAD, ROBERT
Maverick   ep   Yellow River   2.8.59 ABC
Sea Hunt   ep   2.28.59 CBS
Colt .45   ep   Amnesty   5.24.59 ABC
Man and the Challenge   ep   9.19.59 NBC
Hawaiian Eye   sr   10.7.59 ABC
77 Sunset Strip   ep   Only Zeroes Count   10.2.59 ABC
Hawaiian Eye   sr ret   9.14.60 ABC
Hawaiian Eye   sr ret   9.61 ABC
Hawaiian Eye   sr ret   10.2.62 ABC
Gallant Men   ep   And Cain Cried Out   10.19.62 ABC
Temple Houston   ep   The Town that Trespassed   3.26.
   64 NBC
Wild, Wild West   sr   9.17.65 CBS
Wild, Wild West   sr ret   9.16.66 CBS
Wild, Wild West   sr ret   9.67 CBS
Wild, Wild West   sr ret   9.68 CBS
The D.A.: Murder One   tf   12.8.69 NBC
Weekend of Terror   tf   12.8.70 ABC
Five Desperate Men   tf   9.28.71 ABC
The Adventures of Nick Carter   tf   2.20.72 ABC
Mission Impossible   ep   9.16.72 CBS
Assignment Vienna   sr   9.27.72 ABC

CONRAD, WILLIAM
   Bat Masterson ep Stampede at Tent City   10.29.58
      NBC
   Aquanauts ep 1.25.61 CBS
   Bat Masterson ep Terror on the Trinity 3.9.61 NBC
   Cain's Hundred ep fall, 1961 NBC
   Have Gun Will Travel ep 3.24.62 CBS
   G.E. True ep Circle of Death 10.30.62 CBS
   Alfred Hitchcock Theatre ep The Thirty-First of Feb-
      ruary 1.4.63 CBS
   Have Gun Will Travel ep 5.4.63 CBS
   Name of the Game ep The Power   12.12.69 NBC
   High Chaparral ep 2.25.70 NBC
   Name of the Game ep The Skin Game   2.27.70 NBC
   The Brotherhood of the Bell tf 9.17.70 CBS
   Storefront Lawyers ep Survivors Will Be Prosecuted
      10.21.70 NBC
   Conspiracy to Kill tf 1.11.71 NBC
   Cannon tf 3.26.71 CBS
   O'Hara, U.S. Treasury tf 4.2.71 CBS
   Cannon sr 9.14.71 CBS
   Cannon sr ret 9.12.72 CBS

CONTE, JOHN
   Musical Comedy Time ep Anything Goes 10.2.50
      CBS
   Naughty Marietta Sp 1.15.55 NBC
   A Connecticut Yankee Sp 3.12.55 NBC
   The Merry Widow Sp 4.9.55 NBC
   The Desert Song Sp 5.7.55 NBC
   Goodyear Playhouse ep Tangled Wed 7.3.55 NBC
   Climax ep Fear Strikes Out 8.18.55 CBS
   Matinee Theatre sh/sr 10.31.55 NBC
   77 Sunset Strip ep The Positive Negative 1.27.61
      ABC
   Perry Mason ep The Case of the Blind Man's Bluff
      3.11.61 CBS
   Perry Mason ep The Case of the Injured Innocent
      11.18.61 CBS
   Perry Mason ep The Case of the Lover's Leap 4.4.
      63 CBS
   Bonanza ep The Return 5.2.65 NBC

CONTE, RICHARD
   G.E. Theatre ep The Eye of the Beholder 12.6.53
      CBS
   Ford Theatre ep Turn Back the Clock 4.1.54 NBC

Ford Theatre   ep   The Silent Strangers   2. 9. 56 NBC
20th Century-Fox Hour   ep   Overnight Haul   5. 16. 56
    CBS
20th Century-Fox Hour   ep   End of a Gun   1. 9. 57 CBS
Twilight Zone   ep   Perchance to Dream   11. 27. 59 CBS
Untouchables   ep   The Organization   1. 26. 61 ABC
Frontier Circus   ep   Naomi Champagne   3. 29. 63 CBS
Kraft Suspense Theatre   ep   The Green Felt Jungle   4.
    1. 65 NBC
Four Just Men   sr   fall, 1959 NN
Drama   ep   The Gambler, the Nun and the Radio   5. 19.
    60 CBS
Checkmate   ep   Moment of Truth   11. 26. 60 CBS
Alfred Hitchcock Theatre   ep   The Old Pro   11. 28. 61
    NBC
Bus Stop   ep   Cry to Heaven   1. 14. 62 ABC
Naked City   ep   One of the Most Important Men in the
    Whole World   1. 31. 62 ABC
Checkmate   ep   An Assassin Arrives, Andante   2. 21. 62
    CBS
Untouchables   ep   The Chess Game   10. 9. 62 ABC
Alcoa Premiere   ep   Ordeal in Darkness   11. 15. 62 ABC
Going My Way   ep   A Saint for Mama   12. 26. 62 ABC
77 Sunset Strip   ep   "5"   9. 20. 63, 9. 27. 63, 10. 4. 63,
    10. 11. 63, 10. 18. 63 ABC
Arrest and Trial   ep   Tigers Are for Jungles   3. 22. 64
    ABC
Jean Arthur Show   ep   9. 26. 66 CBS
Jean Arthur Show   ep   Fame Is a Four-letter Word   10.
    30. 67 NBC
The Challengers   tf   3. 28. 69 CBS
Bold Ones   ep   Trial of a Mafiosa   1. 4. 70 NBC
Name of the Game   ep   10. 16. 70 NBC

CONVERSE, FRANK
Hawk   ep   H Is a Dirty Letter   12. 1. 66 ABC
Coronet Blue   sr   5. 29. 67 CBS
N. Y. P. D.   sr   9. 5. 67 ABC
N. Y. P. D.   sr ret   10. 1. 68 ABC
Young Rebels   ep   Is There a Good Samaritan in the
    House   9. 21. 70 ABC
Most Deadly Game   ep   Model for Murder   12. 19. 70
    ABC
Dr. Cook's Garden   tf   1. 19. 71 ABC
FBI   ep   Death on Sunday   9. 12. 71 ABC
FBI   ep   11. 26. 72 ABC
Hollywood Television Theatre   ep   Shadow of a Gunman

12. 4. 72 NN

CONVY, BERT
   77 Sunset Strip ep Vicious Circle 12.12.58 ABC
   Alcoa Theatre ep Boden Vs Bunty 5.18.59 NBC
   Alcoa Premiere ep The Explorer 3.15.60 ABC
   Perry Mason ep The Case of the Nimble Nephew 4.
      23.60 CBS
   My Sister Eileen ep Eileen's Big Chance 11.9.60
      CBS
   Harrigan and Son ep The Comics 3.3.61 ABC
   Hawaiian Eye ep The Humuhumunukunukuapuaa Kid
      3.22.61 ABC
   77 Sunset Strip ep Vamp Till Ready 4.7.61 ABC
   Father of the Bride ep 11.17.61 CBS
   Father of the Bride ep 1.5.62 CBS
   Defenders ep Survival 3.14.64 CBS
   The Cliff Dwellers pt 8.28.66 ABC
   Hawk ep Game with a Dead End 9.29.66 ABC
   Silent Force ep 11.9.70 ABC
   Most Deadly Game ep The Lady from Praha 1.9.71
      ABC
   Night Gallery ep They're Tearing Down Tim Riley's
      Bar 9.20.71 NBC
   Death Takes a Holiday tf 10.23.71 ABC
   Mission Impossible ep 2.26.72 CBS
   Keep the Faith pt 4.14.72 CBS
   Mary Tyler Moore Show ep 11.18.72 CBS

CONWAY, SHIRL
   Joe and Mabel sr 6.25.56 CBS
   Route 66 ep Some of the People, Some of the Time
      12.1.61 CBS
   Defenders ep Gideon's Follies 12.23.61 CBS
   Nurses sr 9.27.62 CBS
   Nurses sr ret 9.26.63 CBS
   Doctors/Nurses sr ret 9.22.64 CBS
   Showcase ep The Beggar's Opera 2.5.67 NN

CONWAY, TIM
   McHale's Navy sr 10.11.62 NBC
   McHale's Navy sr ret 9.17.63 NBC
   McHale's Navy sr ret 9.64 NBC
   Mr. Broadway ep 9.20.64 ABC
   McHale's Navy sr ret 9.65 NBC
   Rango sr 1.13.67 ABC
   That's Life ep Our First Baby 11.19.68 ABC

Tim Conway Show   sr   1.30.70 CBS

CONWAY, TOM
Mystery Theatre sh/sr 10.5.51 ABC
Inspector Mark Saber Mystery Theatre sh/sr ret ABC
20th Century-Fox Hour ep Stranger in the Night 10.
17.56 CBS
Alfred Hitchcock Presents ep The Glass Eye 10.6.57
CBS
Cheyenne ep The Conspirators 10.8.57 ABC
Suspicion ep Rainy Day 12.2.57 NBC
Jane Wyman Theatre ep Not for Publication 5.15.58
NBC
Alfred Hitchcock Presents ep 3.1.59 CBS
Rawhide ep Incident of the Tumbleweed Wagon 7.3.59
CBS
Goldie ep Hollister's Mother 11.26.59 CBS
Goldie ep Art for Goldie's Sake 12.3.59 CBS
Dick Powell Theatre ep The Fifth Caller 12.19.61
NBC
Perry Mason ep The Case of the Simple Simon 4.2.
64 CBS

COOGAN, JACKIE
Racket Squad ep Christmas Caper 12.25.52 CBS
Cowboy G-Men sr 1954 NN
So This Is Hollywood ep Reunion in Hollywood 6.11.
55 NBC
Damon Runyon Theatre ep Honorary Degree 12.10.55
CBS
Matinee Theatre ep The Old Payola 8.8.56 NBC
Playhouse 90 ep The Troublemakers 11.21.57 CBS
Telephone Time ep Death of a Nobody 12.31.57 ABC
Playhouse 90 ep Forbidden Area 10.4.56 CBS
Playhouse 90 ep The Star-Wagon 1.24.57 CBS
Studio One ep Trial by Slander 1.20.58 CBS
Matinee Theatre ep The Iceman 2.4.58 NBC
Loretta Young Show ep 810 Franklin Street 3.1.59
NBC
Peter Gunn ep Keep Smiling 3.23.59 NBC
G.E. Theatre ep The Indian Giver 5.17.59 CBS
Lineup ep Wake Up to Terror 9.30.59 CBS
Loretta Young Show ep Ten Men and a Girl 11.15.59
NBC
Ozzie and Harriet ep 3.2.60 ABC
Ann Sothern Show ep 4.18.60 CBS
Ann Sothern Show ep 5.16.60 CBS

Shirley Temple Theatre   ep   Tom and Huck   10.9.60
  NBC
Tab Hunter Show   ep   I Love a Marine   10.30.60 NBC
Guestward Ho   ep   The Matchmakers   12.15.60 ABC
Klondike   ep   Halliday's Cub   12.19.60 NBC
Shirley Temple Theatre   ep   Rebel Gun   1.22.61 NBC
Best of the Post   ep   Martha   2.18.61 ABC
Outlaws   ep   Rape of Red Sky   2.23.61 NBC
Americans   ep   The Coward   5.8.61 NBC
Perry Mason   ep   The Case of the Crying Comedian
  10.14.61 CBS
Andy Griffith Show   ep   10.30.61 CBS
Outlaws   ep   The Sisters   1.11.62 NBC
Follow the Sun   ep   A Choice of Weapons   2.25.62 ABC
Joey Bishop Show   ep   A Show of His Own   5.2.62 NBC
McKeever and the Colonel   sr   9.23.60 NBC
Dick Powell Theatre   ep   Thunder in a Forgotten Town
  3.5.63 NBC
Perry Mason   ep   The Case of the Witless Witness
  5.16.63 CBS
The Lucy Show   ep   Lucy and the Military Academy
  12.9.63 CBS
Perry Mason Show   ep   The Case of the Fifty Millionth
  Frenchman   2.20.64 CBS
Addams Family   sr   9.18.64 ABC
Addams Family   sr ret   9.17.65 ABC
The Hoofer   pt   8.15.66 CBS
Wild, Wild West   ep   11.17.67 CBS
The Lucy Show   ep   1.15.68 CBS
Outsider   ep   Tell It Like It Is   12.4.68 NBC
Wild, Wild West   ep   1.17.69, 1.24.69 CBS
Hawaii Five-O   ep   1.22.69 CBS
Hawaii Five-O   ep   12.24.69 CBS
Love American Style   ep   2.6.70 ABC
Name of the Game   ep   3.6.70 NBC
Partridge Family   ep   11.20.70 ABC
Name of the Game   ep   The Glory Shouter   12.18.70
  NBC
Andy Griffith Show   ep   2.5.71 CBS
Jimmy Stewart Show   ep   11.7.71 NBC
Longstreet   ep   12.2.71 ABC
McMillan and Wife   ep   Death Is a Seven-point Favorite
  12.8.71 NBC
Adam-12   ep   2.2.72 NBC
Owen Marshall   ep   2.3.72 ABC
Love American Style   ep   2.26.72 ABC
Brady Bunch   ep   3.10.72 ABC

Alias Smith and Jones   ep   Which Way to the OK Cor-
    ral   2.10.72 ABC
Cool Million   tf   10.6.72 NBC
Emergency   ep   11.11.72 NBC
Love American Style   ep   11.17.72 ABC
Alias Smith and Jones   ep   12.9.72 ABC

COOGAN, RICHARD
    Captain Video   sr   1949-1950 NN

COOK, BARBARA
    Babes in Toyland   Sp   12.24.55 ABC
    Producers Showcase   ep   Bloomer Girl   5.28.56 NBC
    Hallmark Hall of Fame   ep   The Yeoman of the Guard
        4.10.57 NBC
    Alfred Hitchcock Presents   ep   A Little Sleep   6.16.57
        CBS
    Hansel and Gretel   Sp   4.27.58 NBC
    Play of the Week   ep   In a Garden   4.10.61 NN
    U.S. Steel Hour   ep   The Go-Between   4.18.62 CBS

COOK, DONALD
    Prudential Playhouse   ep   Skylark   1.16.51 CBS
    Video Theatre   ep   The Magnolia Touch   8.25.52 CBS
    Video Theatre   ep   One of Those Things   3.9.53 CBS
    ABC Album   sh   4.12.53 ABC
    The Doctor   ep   The Way of Hope   4.19.53 NBC
    P.M. Playhouse   ep   Make Me Happy, Make Me Sad
        1.21.54 CBS
    Goodyear Playhouse   ep   The Treasure Hunters   5.26.
        57 NBC
    Schlitz Playhouse of Stars   ep   No Answer   12.19.58
        CBS

COOK, ELISHA
    TV Hour   ep   Brandenburg Gate   12.1.53 ABC
    Treasury Men in Action   ep   The Case of the Elder
        Brother   2.10.55 ABC
    Alfred Hitchcock Presents   ep   Salvage   11.6.55 CBS
    TV Reader's Digest   ep   The Trigger Finger Clue   3.
        26.56 ABC
    The Millionaire   ep   The Story of Judge William West-
        holme   2.20.57 CBS
    Wyatt Earp   ep   The Equalizer   4.16.57 ABC
    G.E. Theatre   ep   Silent Ambush   1.26.58 CBS
    Trackdown   ep   The Trail   2.28.58 CBS
    No Warning   ep   Emergency   4.6.58 NBC

Perry Mason ep The Case of the Pint-Sized Client
   10.4.58 CBS
Bat Masterson ep Double Showdown 10.8.58 NBC
Rawhide ep Incident of a Burst of Evil 6.26.59 CBS
Bat Masterson ep No Funeral for Thorn 10.22.59
   NBC
Johnny Ringo ep Dead Wait 11.19.59 CBS
Gunsmoke ep 11.21.59 CBS
Tightrope ep The Long Odds 2.16.60 CBS
Wagon Train ep The Tracy Salder Story 3.9.60 NBC
Ford Star Time ep The Young Juggler 3.29.60 NBC
Rebel ep Bequest 9.25.60 ABC
Thriller ep The Fatal Impulse 11.29.60 NBC
Real McCoys ep The Hermit 2.16.61 ABC
G.E. Theatre ep Open House 3.5.61 CBS
Wagon Train ep The Nancy Palmer Story 3.8.61
   NBC
Surfside 6 ep Witness for the Defense 10.23.61 ABC
Outlaws ep The Dark Sunrise of Griff Kincaid 1.4.62
   NBC
Fugitive ep The Witch 9.24.63 ABC
Destry ep Law and Order Day 2.28.64 ABC
Perry Mason ep The Case of the Reckless Rockhound
   11.26.64 CBS
Bonanza ep Dollar's Worth of Trouble 5.14.66 NBC
McNab's Lab pt 7.22.66 ABC
Road West ep 11.14.66 NBC
Batman ep Ice Spy 3.29.67, 3.30.67 ABC
Bonanza ep The Weary Willies 9.27.70 NBC
Night Chase tf 11.20.70 CBS
Chicago Teddy Bears ep 11.5.71 CBS

COOMBS, FREDERICK
   Defenders ep Fires of the Mind 2.18.65 CBS

COOPER, GLADYS
   Alcoa Hour ep Sister 7.22.56 NBC
   On Trial ep The Tichborne Claimant 2.1.57 NBC
   Alfred Hitchcock Presents ep The End of Indian Sum-
      mer 2.24.57 CBS
   Playhouse 90 ep Circle of the Day 5.30.57 CBS
   Playhouse 90 ep The Mystery of 13 10.24.57 CBS
   Suspicion ep Lord Arthur Savile's Crime 1.13.58
      NBC
   Playhouse 90 ep Verdict of Three 4.24.58 CBS
   Theatre '59 ep The Stray Cat 5.27.59 NBC
   Adventures in Paradise ep Paradise Lost 5.23.60
      ABC

Twilight Zone   ep   Nothing in the Dark   1.5.62 CBS
Dick Powell Theatre   ep   In Search of a Son   11.20.62
    NBC
Fair Exchange   ep   Dorothy's Trip to Europe   11.23.
    62 CBS
Alfred Hitchcock Theatre   ep   What Really Happened
    1.11.63 CBS
Hallmark Hall of Fame   ep   Pygmalion   2.6.63 NBC
Going My Way   ep   The Custody of the Child   4.3.63
    ABC
Twilight Zone   ep   Passage on the Lady Anne   5.9.63
    CBS
Outer Limits   ep   Borderland   12.16.63 ABC
Twilight Zone   ep   Night Call   2.7.64 CBS
Rogues   sr   9.13.64 NBC
Laf Hit   ep   Consider He Was   12.28.64 NBC
Ben Casey   ep   Because of the Needle, the Haystack
    Was Lost   10.11.65 ABC
Run, Buddy, Run   ep   10.10.66 CBS
Persuaders   ep   1.1.72 ABC

COOPER, JACKIE
Tales of Tomorrow   ep   The Cocoon   9.12.52 ABC
Video Theatre   ep   A Message for Janice   9.29.52
    CBS
Robert Montgomery Presents   ep   The Fall Guy   10.
    13.52 NBC
Ford Theatre   ep   Something Old, Something New   12.
    4.52 NBC
Suspense   ep   The Invisible Killer   12.30.52 CBS
Robert Montgomery Presents   ep   The Outer Limit
    1.26.53 NBC
Schlitz Playhouse of Stars   ep   Big Jim's Boy   3.6.53
    CBS
Studio One   ep   Birthright   5.4.53 CBS
Armstrong Circle Theatre   ep   The Middle Son   5.26.
    53 NBC
Kraft Theatre   ep   The Diehard   7.1.53 NBC
Mirror Theatre   ep   A Reputation   7.28.53 NBC
Ford Theatre   ep   Something Old, Something New   8.
    13.53 NBC
Studio One   ep   Hound Dog Man   9.28.53 CBS
Armstrong Circle Theatre   ep   Tour of Duty   10.6.53
    NBC
Medallion Theatre   ep   Grand'ma Rebel   10.31.53 CBS
TV Hour   ep   Westward the Sun   11.17.53 ABC
Danger   ep   Towerman   11.24.53 CBS

Medallion Theatre   ep   Twenty-Four Men to a Plane
    12.19.53 CBS
Robert Montgomery Presents   ep   A Dreamer of Summer
    9.27.54 NBC
Elgin Hour   ep   Falling Star   12.28.54 ABC
Producers Showcase   ep   Yellow Jack   1.10.55 NBC
G.E. Theatre   ep   Yankee Peddler   1.16.55 CBS
Armstrong Circle Theatre   ep   I Found 60 Million Dol-
    lars   2.15.55 NBC
Robert Montgomery Presents   ep   It Depends on You   2.
    28.55 NBC
Philco Playhouse   ep   The Pardon-Me Boy   5.15.55
    NBC
People's Choice   sr   10.6.55 NBC
Robert Montgomery Presents   ep   End of Morning   2.
    27.56 NBC
U.S. Steel Hour   ep   The Old Lady Shows Her Medals
    5.23.56 CBS
People's Choice   sr ret   fall, 1956 NBC
Robert Montgomery Presents   ep   Really the Blues   12.
    7.56 NBC
People's Choice   sr ret   fall, 1957 NBC
Studio One   ep   The Fair-Haired Boy   3.3.58 CBS
U.S. Steel Hour   ep   Mid-Summer   10.8.58 CBS
Dupont Show of the Month   ep   The Hasty Heart   12.18.
    58 CBS
Goodyear Theatre   ep   Curtain Call   12.22.58 CBS
Hayes and Henderson   ep   A Nice Place to Hide   3.26.
    59 NBC
Hennesey   sr   9.28.59 CBS
Hennesey   sr ret   10.3.60 CBS
Hennesey   sr ret   9.25.61 CBS
Golden Showcase   ep   The Fourposter   1.13.62 CBS
Dick Powell Theatre   ep   Special Assignment   9.25.62
    NBC
Dick Powell Theatre   ep   Thunder in a Forgotten Town
    3.5.63 NBC
Twilight Zone   ep   Caesar and Me   4.10.64 CBS
Shadow on the Land   tf   12.4.68 ABC
Maybe I'll Come Home in the Spring   tf   2.16.71 ABC
Hawaii Five-O   ep   11.9.71 CBS
The Astronaut   tf   1.8.72 ABC
McCloud   ep   10.1.72 NBC
Ironside   ep   11.23.72 CBS
Ghost Story   ep   11.24.72 NBC
Of Men and Women   ep   Hot Machine   12.17.72 ABC

COOPER, MELVILLE

Musical Comedy Hour ep The Merry Widow 11.27. 50 NBC

Musical Comedy Time ep Mme. Modiste 2.5.51 NBC

Robert Montgomery Presents ep Cashel Byron's Profession 1.14.52 NBC

Broadway Television Theatre ep Angel Street 5.13.52 NN

Robert Montgomery Presents ep King of the Castle 6.30.52 NBC

Broadway Television Theatre ep Jenny Kissed Me 8. 25.52 NN

Kraft Theatre ep A Kiss for Cinderella 10.15.52 NBC

Armstrong Circle Theatre ep The Marmalade Scandal 2.10.53 NBC

Summer Studio One ep The Gathering Night 8.24.53 CBS

Kraft Theatre ep A Christmas Carol 12.24.53 ABC

Armstrong Circle Theatre ep Return to Ballygally 12.29.53 NBC

Schlitz Playhouse of Stars ep Volturio Investigates 12.3.54 CBS

Hallmark Hall of Fame ep The Corn Is Green 1.8. 56 NBC

Telephone Time ep Keely's Wonderful Machine 9.16. 56 CBS

Playhouse 90 ep Charley's Aunt 3.28.57 CBS

West Point ep Jet Flight 12.17.57 ABC

Shirley Temple's Story Book ep The Wild Swans 9. 12.58 NBC

U.S. Steel Hour ep Night of Betrayal 3.25.59 CBS

Great Mysteries ep The Datchet Diamonds 9.20.60 NBC

COPELAND, JOAN

The Web ep Turn Back 11.9.52 CBS

CORBETT, GLENN

Silver Theatre ep My Brother's Keeper 2.20.50 CBS

It's a Man's World sr 9.17.62 NBC

Route 66 sr 9.21.62 CBS

Route 66 sr ret 9.63 CBS

Kraft Suspense Theatre ep The Last Clear Chance 3. 11.65 NBC

Virginian ep The Awakening 10.13.65 NBC

Bonanza ep Might Is the Word 11.7.65 NBC

Bob Hope Chrysler Theatre   ep   In Pursuit of Excel-
    lence   6. 22. 66 NBC
Road West   sr   9. 12. 66 NBC
Garrison's Gorillas   ep   Now I Lay Me Down to Die
    10. 24. 67 ABC
Star Trek   ep   Metamorphosis   11. 10. 67 NBC
FBI   ep   12. 29. 68   ABC
World of Disney   ep   The Secret of Boyne Castle   2. 9.
    69, 2. 16. 69, 2. 23. 69 NBC
The Immortal   ep   10. 24. 70 ABC
Marcus Welby, M.D.   ep   Another Buckle for Westley
    Hill   1. 5. 71 ABC
FBI   ep   Death Watch   2. 14. 71 ABC
Bonanza   ep   Winter Ranch   3. 28. 71 NBC
Owen Marshall   ep   Legacy of Fear   9. 16. 71 ABC
Gunsmoke   ep   9. 20. 71 CBS
Night Gallery   ep   11. 3. 71 NBC
Medical Center   ep   Shock   12. 29. 71, 1. 5. 72 CBS
Alias Smith and Jones   ep   1. 6. 72 ABC
Alias Smith and Jones   ep   10. 21. 72 ABC
Mod Squad   ep   12. 21. 72 ABC
Owen Marshall   ep   12. 21. 72 ABC

CORD, ALEX
Branded   ep   Survival   1. 24. 65 NBC
Bob Hope Chrysler Theatre   ep   The Lady Is My Wife
    2. 1. 67 NBC
The Scorpio Letters   tf   2. 19. 67 ABC
Room 222   ep   Clothes Make the Boy   12. 3. 69 ABC
Night Gallery   ep   Keep in Touch   11. 24. 71 NBC
Gunsmoke   ep   11. 20. 72 CBS
Mission Impossible   ep   12. 9. 72 CBS

COREY, WENDELL
Celanese Theatre   ep   Susan and God   10. 17. 51 ABC
Drama   ep   C.O.D.   2. 21. 52 NBC
Celanese Theatre   ep   The Animal Kingdom   3. 5. 52
    NBC
Curtain Call   ep   Swell Girl   8. 1. 52 NBC
Gulf Playhouse   ep   The Duel   11. 14. 52 NBC
Hollywood Opening Night   ep   The Lucky Coin   12. 1. 52
    NBC
Plymouth Playhouse   ep   A Tale of Two Cities   5. 3. 53,
    5. 10. 53 ABC
Robert Montgomery Presents   ep   Half a Kingdom   6.
    29. 53 NBC
Tales of the City   ep   7. 9. 53 CBS

Backbone of America   ep   12. 29. 53 NBC
Robert Montgomery Presents   ep   The 17th of June
    2. 1. 54 NBC
Studio One   ep   Donovan's Brain   2. 28. 55 CBS
U. S. Steel Hour   ep   The Rack   4. 12. 55 ABC
Climax   ep   To Wake at Midnight   6. 23. 55 CBS
Alcoa Hour   ep   The Black Wings   10. 16. 55 NBC
Studio One   ep   My Son Johnny   1. 30. 56 CBS
Studio One   ep   The Arena   4. 9. 56 CBS
Climax   ep   The Lou Gehrig Story   4. 19. 56 CBS
Zane Grey Theatre   ep   Quiet Sunday in San Ardo 11.
    23. 56   CBS
20th Century-Fox Hour   ep   Man of the Law   2. 20. 57
    CBS
Harbor Command   sr   10. 11. 57 ABC
Studio One   ep   The Desperate Age   4. 21. 58 CBS
Alfred Hitchcock Presents   ep   Pison   10. 5. 58 CBS
Peck's Bad Girl   sr   5. 5. 59   CBS
Sunday Showcase   ep   One Loud Clear Voice   1. 17. 60
    NBC
Zane Grey Theatre   ep   Killer Instinct   3. 17. 60 CBS
Zane Grey Theatre   ep   The Man from Yesterday   12.
    22. 60 CBS
Westinghouse Presents   ep   1. 6. 61 NBC
Untouchables   ep   Power Play   10. 19. 61 ABC
New Breed   ep   Till Death Do Us Part   11. 7. 61 ABC
Target Corruptors   ep   Mr. Megalomonia   11. 17. 61
    ABC
Bus Stop   ep   Turn Again Home   1. 28. 62 ABC
Eleventh Hour   sr   10. 3. 62 NBC
Channing   ep   A Window on the War   12. 11. 63 ABC
Burke's Law   ep   4. 10. 64 ABC
Branded   ep   The Mission   3. 28. 65 NBC
Perry Mason   ep   The Unwelcome Well   4. 3. 66 CBS
Run for Your Life   ep   The Committee for the 25th
    10. 3. 66 NBC
Road West   ep   Piece of Tin   10. 31. 66 NBC

CORIO, ANN
    Trials of O'Brien   ep   Dead End on Fugel Street   12.
    3. 65 CBS

CORNELL, KATHARINE
    Producers Showcase   ep   The Barretts of Wimpole
        Street   4. 2. 56 NBC
    Hallmark Hall of Fame   ep   There Shall Be No Night
        3. 17. 57 NBC

CORT, BUD
  Mr. Deeds   ep   10.3.69 ABC

CORTESA, VALENTINA
  Lux Video Theatre   ep   Adam Had Four Sons   4.4.57
    NBC
  Schlitz Playhouse of Stars   ep   Night of the Stranger
    3.7.58 CBS

COSBY, BILL
  I Spy   sr   9.15.65 NBC
  I Spy   sr ret   9.14.66 NBC
  I Spy   sr ret   9.67 NBC
  Bill Cosby Show   sr   9.14.69 NBC

COSTELLO, LOU
  Abbott and Costello Show   sr   12.5.52 CBS
  G.E. Theatre   ep   Blaze of Glory   9.21.58 CBS

COTSWORTH, STAATS
  Studio One   ep   The Secret Self   8.30.54 CBS
  Hallmark Hall of Fame   ep   Macbeth   11.28.54 NBC
  Robert Montgomery Presents   ep   Death and the Sky
    Above   1.3.55 NBC

COTTEN, JOSEPH
  G.E. Theatre   ep   High Green Wall   10.3.54 CBS
  Producers Showcase   ep   State of the Union   11.15.54
    NBC
  Best of Broadway   ep   Broadway   5.4.55 CBS
  Star Stage   ep   On Trial   9.23.55 NBC
  Loretta Young Show   ep hos   Reunion   9.11.55 NBC
  20th Century-Fox Hour   sh   10.5.55 CBS
  Alfred Hitchcock Presents   ep   Breakdown   11.13.55
    CBS
  Ford Theatre   ep   Man without Fear   3.1.56 NBC
  G.E. Theatre   ep   HMS Marlborough   4.29.56 CBS
  Star Stage   ep   The Man in the Black Robe   5.18.56
    NBC
  Star Stage   ep   U.S. Vs. Alexander Holmes   6.15.56
    NBC
  On Trial   sh/sr   9.14.56 NBC
  Jane Wyman Theatre   ep   Contact   10.3.57 NBC
  Telephone Time   ep   The Man the Navy Couldn't Sink
    10.15.57 ABC
  Playhouse 90   ep   Edge of Innocence   10.31.57 CBS
  Zane Grey Theatre   ep   Man Unforgiving   1.3.58 CBS

Alfred Hitchcock Presents   ep   Together   1.12.58 CBS
Suspicion   ep   The Eye of Truth   3.17.58 NBC
Joseph Cotten Theatre   sh   7.6.59 CBS
Desilu Playhouse   ep   The Day the Town Stood Up   10.2.59 CBS
Alfred Hitchcock Presents   ep   Dead Weight   11.22.59 CBS
June Allyson Show   ep   The Blue Goose   3.21.60 CBS
June Allyson Show   ep   Dark Fear   10.13.60 CBS
Checkmate   ep   Face in the Window   10.22.60 CBS
Barbara Stanwyck Theatre   ep   The Hitch-Hiker   5.29.61 NBC
Wagon Train   ep   The Captain Dan Brady Story   9.27.61 NBC
Bus Stop   ep   Cherie   11.12.61 ABC
Theatre 62   ep   Notorious   12.10.61 NBC
Dr. Kildare   ep   The Administrator   1.11.62 NBC
Saints and Sinners   ep   The Man on the Rim   10.1.62 NBC
Wagon Train   ep   The John Augustus Story   10.17.62 ABC
Great Adventures   ep   The Death of Sitting Bull   10.4.63, 10.11.63 CBS
Cimarron Strip   ep   The Search   11.9.67 CBS
77 Sunset Strip   ep   By His Own Verdict   11.15.63 ABC
Alexander the Great   pt   1.26.68 ABC
Ironside   ep   9.26.68 NBC
Journey to the Unknown   ep   11.7.68 ABC
It Takes a Thief   ep   Hands Across the Border   11.12.68 ABC
The Lonely Profession   tf   10.21.69 NBC
It Takes a Thief   ep   To Lure a Man   12.18.69 ABC
Cutter's Trail   tf   2.6.70 CBS
Virginian   ep   A Time of Terror   2.11.70 NBC
Name of the Game   ep   The King of Denmark   2.20.70 NBC
It Takes a Thief   ep   2.23.70 ABC
Men from Shiloh   ep   Gun Quest   10.21.70 NBC
Assault on the Wayne   tf   1.12.71 ABC
Do You Take This Stranger   tf   1.18.71 NBC
The Screaming Woman   tf   1.29.72 ABC

COUGHLIN, KEVIN
Armstrong Circle Theatre   ep   For Ever and Ever   1.5.54 NBC
Goodyear Playhouse   ep   Old Tosselfoot   4.25.54 NBC
(I Remember) Mama   sr   6.11.54 CBS

Robert Montgomery Presents   ep   Don't You Ever Go
   Home?   7.12.54 NBC
Philco Playhouse   ep   Man in the Middle of the Ocean
   8.8.54 NBC
Mama   sr ret   9.3.54 CBS
Center Stage   ep   The Heart of a Clown   9.21.54 ABC
Goodyear Playhouse   ep   The Rabbit Trap   2.13.55 NBC
Mama   sr ret   10.7.55 CBS
Justice   ep   End of a Chase   12.25.55 NBC
U.S. Steel Hour   ep   Moment of Courage   6.20.56 CBS
Mama   sr ret   12.16.56 CBS
Studio One   ep   A Christmas Surprise   12.24.56 CBS
Harbourmaster   ep   Sanctuary   10.24.57 CBS
Harbourmaster   ep   Enemy Unknown   11.14.57 CBS
U.S. Steel Hour   ep   Old Marshals Never Die   8.13.58
   CBS
House on High Street   ep   10.26.59 NBC
Play of the Week   ep   The Closing Door   1.4.60 NN
Play of the Week   ep   The Climate of Eden   2.29.60
   NN
Robert Herridge Theatre   ep   A Trip to Czardis   7.7.
   60 CBS
Play of the Week   ep   My Heart's in the Highlands   11.
   7.60 NN
Armstrong Circle Theatre   ep   Runaway Road   1.31.62
   CBS
Combat   ep   The First Day   9.21.65 ABC
Virginian   ep   The Crooked Path   2.21.68 NBC
Bonanza   ep   5.2.68 NBC
Virginian   ep   Last Grave at Sorocco Creek   1.22.69
   NBC
Gunsmoke   ep   The Commandment   2.3.69 CBS
Dragnet   ep   9.25.69 NBC
Gunsmoke   ep   10.6.69 CBS
Gunsmoke   ep   11.9.70 CBS
O'Hara, U.S. Treasury   ep   Operation Time Fuse   10.
   15.71 CBS

COULOURIS, GEORGE
   Trials of O'Brien   ep   The Greatest Game   2.18.66,
      2.25.66 CBS
   Dundee and the Culhane   ep   A Lynching Brief   11.8.67
      CBS
   Search   ep   12.6.72 NBC

COWARD, NOEL
   Ford Star Jubilee   ep   Blithe Spirit   1.14.56 CBS

Ford Star Jubilee   ep   This Happy Breed   5.5.56 CBS
Androcles and the Lion   Sp   11.15.67 NBC

COX, WALLY
Danger   ep   Ask Me Another   12.6.51 CBS
Starlight Theatre   ep   I Guess There Are Other Girls
   5.3.51 CBS
Goodyear Playhouse   ep   The Copper   10.28.51 NBC
Goodyear Playhouse   ep   Tigers Don't Sing   3.30.52
   NBC
Mr. Peepers   sr   9.3.52 NBC
Mr. Peepers   sr ret   10.26.52 NBC
Mr. Peepers   sr ret   9.13.53 NBC
Mr. Peepers   sr ret   9.19.54 NBC
Babes in Toyland   Sp   12.18.54 NBC
Producers Showcase   ep Yellow Jack   1.10.55 NBC
Opera Theatre   ep   The Would-Be Gentleman   2.27.55
   NBC
G.E. Theatre   ep   When in France   5.22.55 CBS
U.S. Steel Hour   ep   The Meanest Man in the World
   7.6.55 CBS
Heidi   Sp   10.1.55 NBC
Babes in Toyland   Sp (restaged)   12.24.55 NBC
Adventures of Hiram Holiday   sr   10.3.56 NBC
Matinee Theatre   ep   The 19th Hole   3.19.57 NBC
Kraft Theatre   ep   Roaring 20th   6.5.57 NBC
Loretta Young Show   ep   The Bargain   2.16.58 NBC
Frank Sinatra Show   ep   The Green Grass of St. The-
   resa   5.16.58 ABC
Dupont Show of the Month   ep   Heaven Can Wait   11.16.
   60 CBS
Shirley Temple Theatre   ep   King Midas   1.15.61 NBC
Chevy Show   ep   Happiest Day   4.23.61 NBC
Ozzie and Harriet   ep   The Fraternity Rents out a
   Room   10.19.61 ABC
Follow the Sun   ep   The Inhuman Equation   3.11.62
Car 54 Where Are You   ep   No More Pickpockets
   3.11.62 NBC
77 Sunset Strip   ep   "5"   9.20.63, 9.27.63 ABC
Burke's Law   ep   Who Killed Purity Mather   12.6.63
   ABC
Twilight Zone   ep   From Agnes--With Love   2.14.64
   CBS
Burke's Law   ep   5.5.65 ABC
Dick van Dyke Show   ep   The Making of a Councilman
   1.26.66 CBS
Mister Roberts   ep   Undercover Cook   3.25.66 NBC

Beverly Hillbillies   ep   4.13.66 CBS
Beverly Hillbillies   ep   4.27.66 CBS
Mission Impossible   ep   9.17.66 CBS
Jean Arthur Show   ep   10.17.66 CBS
I Spy   ep   Casanova from Canarsie   3.29.67 NBC
Vacation Playhouse   ep   7.31.67 CBS
Bonanza   ep   12.24.67 NBC
It Takes a Thief   ep   1.9.68 ABC
Bonanza   ep   The Last Vote   10.20.68 NBC
Here's Lucy   ep   1.13.69 CBS
That's Life   ep   3.4.69 ABC
Love American Style   ep   1.12.70 ABC
Bill Cosby Show   ep   2.8.70 NBC
Here's Lucy   ep   2.9.70 CBS
Quarantined   tf   2.24.70 ABC
The Young Country   tf   3.17.70 ABC
World of Disney   ep   The Wacky Zoo of Morgan City
     10.18.70, 10.25.70 NBC
Here's Lucy   ep   11.16.70 CBS
McMillan and Wife   ep   The Easy Sunday Murder Case
     10.20.71 NBC
Alias Smith and Jones   ep   1.27.72 ABC
Magic Carpet   tf   11.6.72 NBC
Once Upon a Mattress   Sp   12.12.72 CBS

CRABBE, BUSTER
Philco Playhouse   ep   A Cowboy for Chris   5.18.52
     NBC
Pond's Theatre   ep   The Cornered Man   1.27.55 ABC
Captain Gallant   sr   2.13.55 NBC
Captain Gallant   sr ret   fall, 1955 NBC
Captain Gallant   sr ret   fall, 1956 NBC
Ellery Queen   ep   The Murder Comes to You Live   6.
     5.59 NBC

CRAIG, JAMES
Ford Theatre   ep   Wedding March   4.22.54 NBC
Studio 57   ep   Cubs of the Bear   11.23.54 NN
Studio 57   ep   The Westerner   2.1.55 NN
The Millionaire   ep   The Story of Jane Carr   9.19.56
     CBS
Broken Arrow   ep   Johnny Flagstaff   3.19.57 ABC
Have Gun Will Travel   ep   3.8.58 CBS

CRAIG, MICHAEL
N.E.T. Playhouse   ep   A Choice of Kings   11.24.67
     NN

CRAIN, JEANNE
    Star Stage   ep   The Girl Who Wasn't Wanted   11.25.55 NBC
    Ford Theatre   ep   Airborne Honeymoon   2.15.56 NBC
    Playhouse 90   ep   The Great Gatsby   6.26.58 CBS
    Schlitz Playhouse of Stars   ep   The Trouble with Ruth 10.24.58 CBS
    Meet Me in St. Louis   Sp   4.26.59 CBS
    Goodyear Theatre   ep   Wait Till Spring   5.25.59 NBC
    Riverboat   ep   Escape to Memphis   10.25.59   NBC
    U.S. Steel Hour   ep   The Man Who Knew Tomorrow 9.21.60 CBS
    G.E. Theatre   ep   Journal of Hope   9.25.60 CBS
    G.E. Theatre   ep   My Dark Days   3.18.62, 3.25.62 CBS
    U.S. Steel Hour   ep   The Other Woman   5.16.62 CBS
    Dick Powell Theatre   ep   Last of the Private Eyes 4.30.63 NBC
    Burke's Law   ep   Who Killed Madison Cooper   1.24.64 ABC
    Burke's Law   ep   4.24.64 ABC
    Danny Thomas Show   ep   My Pal Tony   3.4.68 NBC
    Name of the Game   ep   Fear of High Places   9.20.68 NBC
    Owen Marshall   ep   Run, Carol, Run   1.20.72 ABC

CRANE, BOB
    G.E. Theatre   ep   The $200 Parley 10.15.61 CBS
    Donna Reed Show   ep   Friends and Neighbors   4.4.63 ABC
    Donna Reed Show   ep   Out on the Town   9.17.63 ABC
    Channing   ep   Hall Full of Strangers   12.25.63 ABC
    Donna Reed Show   sr   9.17.64 ABC
    Hogan's Heroes   sr   9.17.65 CBS
    Hogan's Heroes   sr ret   9.66 CBS
    Hogan's Heroes   sr ret   9.9.67 CBS
    Hogan's Heroes   sr ret   9.28.68 CBS
    Arsenic and Old Lace   Sp   4.2.69 ABC
    Hogan's Heroes   sr ret   9.26.69 CBS
    Hogan's Heroes   sr ret   9.20.70 CBS
    Love American Style   ep   2.19.71 ABC
    Night Gallery   ep   11.17.71 NBC
    Love American Style   ep   12.17.71 ABC
    The Delphi Bureau   tf   3.6.72 ABC

CRAWFORD, BRODERICK
    Video Theatre   ep   Hunt the Man Down   4.7.52 CBS

Four Star Playhouse   ep   1.1.53 CBS
G.E. Theatre   ep   Ride the River   2.8.53 CBS
Ford Theatre   ep   Margin for Fear   2.19.53 NBC
Schlitz Playhouse of Stars   ep   The Widow Makes Three
  6.12.53 CBS
Schlitz Playhouse of Stars   ep   Desert Tragedy   9.25.53
  CBS
Schlitz Playhouse of Stars   ep   Man from Outside
  2.12.54 CBS
Producers Showcase   ep   Yellow Jack   1.10.55 NBC
Damon Runyon Theatre   ep   Dancing Dan's Christmas
  4.23.55 CBS
Highway Patrol   sr   10.24.55 NBC
Highway Patrol   sr ret   fall, 1956 NBC
Highway Patrol   sr ret   fall, 1957 NBC
Highway Patrol   sr ret   fall, 1958 NBC
Bat Masterson   ep   Two Graves for Swan Valley   6.3.
  59 NBC
King of Diamonds   sr   10.6.61 ABC
Virginian   ep   A Killer in Town   10.9.63 NBC
Arrest and Trial   ep   Flame in the Dark   10.20.63
  ABC
Burke's Law   ep   Jet-Setter   1.10.64 ABC
Destry   ep   The Solid Gold Girl   2.14.64 ABC
Rawhide   ep   The Incident at Deadhorse   4.16.64, 4.
  23.64 CBS
Burke's Law   ep   Who Killed 711   12.9.64 ABC
Burke's Law   ep   Who Killed Davidian Jones   12.30.64
  ABC
Rogues   ep   Gambit by the Golden Gate   1.10.65 NBC
Kraft Suspense Theatre   ep   The Long Ravine   5.6.65
  NBC
Bob Hope Chrysler Theatre   ep March from Camp
  Tyler   10.6.65 NBC
Bob Hope Chrysler Theatre   ep   Brilliant Benjamin
  Boggs   3.30.66 NBC
The Girl from U.N.C.L.E.   ep   2.28.67 NBC
The Man from U.N.C.L.E.   ep   9.25.67 NBC
Cimarron Strip   ep   The Blue Moon Train   10.5.67
  CBS
Name of the Game   ep   12.6.68 NBC
Ironside   ep   1.2.69 NBC
Land of the Giants   ep   9.21.69 ABC
Name of the Game   ep   Blind Man's Bluff   10.3.69
  NBC
Get Smart   ep   Treasure of C. Errol Madre   10.24.
  69 CBS

Love American Style   ep   11.3.69 ABC
Name of the Game   ep   The Power   12.12.69 NBC
Bracken's World   ep   A Perfect Piece of Casting   1.30.
70   NBC
It Takes a Thief   ep   Fortune City   2.2.70 ABC
The Challenge   tf   2.10.70 ABC
Interns   sr   9.25.70 CBS
Man and the City   ep   Disaster on Turner Street   10.
20.71 ABC
Cade's County   ep   12.12.71 CBS
The Adventures of Nick Carter   tf   2.20.72 ABC
Night Gallery   ep   You Can't Get Help Like That Any-
more   2.23.72 NBC
Banacek   10.11.72 NBC

CRAWFORD, H. MARION
Sherlock Holmes   sr   10.18.54 NBC

CRAWFORD, JOAN
Mirror Theatre   ep   Because I Love Him   9.19.53 CBS
G.E. Theatre   ep   The Road to Edinburgh   10.31.54
CBS
G.E. Theatre   ep   Strange Witness   3.23.58 CBS
G.E. Theatre   ep   And One Was Loyal   1.4.59 CBS
Della   tf   1959 NN
Zane Grey Theatre   ep   Rebel Ranger   12.3.59 CBS
Zane Grey Theatre   ep   One Must Die   1.12.61 CBS
Route 66   ep   Same   Picture, Different Frame   10.4.
63 CBS
The Man from U.N.C.L.E.   ep   3.31.67 NBC
The Lucy Show   ep   2.26.68 CBS
The Secret Storm   ep   10.68 CBS
Night Gallery   tf   11.8.69 NBC
Virginian   ep   Nightmare   1.21.70 NBC
Sixth Sense   ep   9.30.72 ABC

CRAWFORD, JOHNNY
Cavalcade Theatre   ep   The Boy Nobody Wanted   5.29.
56 ABC
Rin Tin Tin   ep   The Second Chance   6.1.56 ABC
Loretta Young Show   ep   The End of the Week   11.11.
56 NBC
Matinee Theatre   ep   From the Desk of Margaret Tyd-
ings   2.18.57 NBC
Matinee Theatre   ep   The Serpent's Tooth   2.25.57
NBC
Telephone Time   ep   Bullet Lou Kirn   4.11.57 ABC

The Millionaire ep The Story of Frank Keegan 11.
    20. 57 CBS
Loretta Young Show ep A Little Witness 11.24. 57
    NBC
Zane Grey Theatre ep Man Unforgiving 1.3. 58 CBS
Matinee Theatre ep The Iceman 2.4. 58 NBC
Wagon Train ep The Sally Potter Story 4. 9. 58 NBC
Trackdown ep The Deal 4. 25. 58 CBS
Rifleman sr 9. 30. 58 ABC
Rifleman sr ret fall, 1959 ABC
Rifleman sr ret fall, 1960 ABC
Rifleman sr ret 10. 2. 61 ABC
Donna Reed Show ep A Very Bright Boy 12. 21. 61
    ABC
Rifleman sr ret 10. 1. 62 ABC
Dick Powell Theatre ep Apples Don't Fall Far 2. 19.
    63 NBC
Mr. Novak ep Let's Dig a Little Grammar 11. 10. 64
    NBC
Branded ep Coward Steps Aside 3. 7. 65 NBC
Rawhide ep Crossing at White Feather 12. 2. 65 CBS
Hawaii Five-O ep 12. 12. 68 CBS
Big Valley ep 3. 31. 69 ABC
Cade's County ep 12. 12. 71 CBS

CRENNA, RICHARD
    Our Miss Brooks sr 10. 3. 52 CBS
    Our Miss Brooks sr ret 10. 2. 53 CBS
    Our Miss Brooks sr ret 10. 1. 54 CBS
    Our Miss Brooks sr ret 10. 7. 55 CBS
    Medic ep Don't Count the Stars 4. 9. 56 NBC
    Matinee Theatre ep Barricade on the Big Black 3. 27.
        57 NBC
    Frontier ep the Ten Days of John Leslie 4. 1. 57 NN
    Cheyenne ep Hard Bargain 5. 21. 57 ABC
    Real McCoys sr 10. 3. 57 ABC
    Sally ep 1. 5. 58 NBC
    Matinee Theatre ep The Cause 5. 12. 58 NBC
    Real McCoys sr ret fall, 1958 ABC
    Real McCoys sr ret fall, 1959 ABC
    Deputy ep A Time to Sow 4. 23. 60 NBC
    Real McCoys sr ret 9. 29. 60 ABC
    Real McCoys sr ret 9. 28. 61 ABC
    Real McCoys sr ret 9. 30. 62 CBS
    Kraft Suspense Theatre ep The Long Lost Life of Ed-
        ward Smalley 12. 12. 63 NBC
    Slattery's People sr 9. 21. 64 CBS

Slattery's People sr ret 9.17.65 CBS
Thief tf 10.9.71 ABC
Footstep tf 10.3.72 CBS

CRISP, DONALD
Crossroads ep Anatole of the Bayous 4.20.56 ABC
Playhouse 90 ep The Raider 2.19.59 CBS

CRISTAL, LINDA
Rawhide ep Incident of a Burst of Evil 6.26.59
   CBS
Tab Hunter Show ep Holiday in Spain 3.12.61 NBC
Voyage to the Bottom of the Sea 9.21.64 ABC
T.H.E. Cat ep 10.28.66 NBC
Iron Horse ep 3.6.67 ABC
High Chaparral sr 9.10.67 NBC
High Chaparral sr ret 9.20.68 NBC
High Chaparral sr ret 9.19.69 NBC
High Chaparral sr ret 9.18.70 NBC
Cade's County ep 11.28.71 CBS
Bonanza ep 12.26.71 NBC
Call Holme pt 4.24.72 NBC
Search ep 11.22.72 NBC

CRONYN, HUME
Philco Playhouse ep The Reluctant Landlord 7.2.50
   NBC
Suspense ep Strike Me Dead 11.21.50 CBS
Studio One ep Public Servant 1.29.51 CBS
Tales of the City ep 9.3.53 CBS
Omnibus ep Glory in the Flower 10.3.53 CBS
Motorola TV Hour ep The Family Man 3.9.54 ABC
The Marriage sr 7.1.54 NBC
Omnibus ep John Quincy Adams 1.23.55 CBS
Producers Showcase ep The Fourposter 7.25.55 NBC
Philco Playhouse ep Christmas 'til Closing 12.18.55
   NBC
U.S. Steel Hour ep The Great Adventure 1.18.56
   CBS
Omnibus ep 1.29.56 CBS
Climax ep The Fifth Wheel 2.9.56 CBS
Omnibus ep The Better Half 3.11.56 CBS
Alcoa Hour ep The Confidence Man 5.27.56 NBC
Alcoa Hour ep The Big Wave 9.30.56 NBC
G.E. Theatre ep 10.7.56 CBS
Studio One ep The Five Dollar Bill 1.21.57 CBS
Alcoa Hour ep No License to Kill 2.3.57 NBC

Studio One   ep   A Member of the Family   3.25.57 CBS
Schlitz Playhouse of Stars   ep   Clothes Make the Man
   4.5.57 CBS
Studio 57   ep   Little Miss Bedford   6.9.57 NN
Dupont Show of the Month   ep   The Bridge of San Luis
   Rey   1.21.58 CBS
Telephone Time   ep   War against War   3.4.58 ABC
Loretta Young Show   ep   Windfall   3.16.58 NBC
Loretta Young Show   ep   Thanks to You   4.13.58 NBC
G.E. Theatre   ep   Ah There, Beau Brummel   5.4.58
   CBS
Moon and Sixpence   Sp   10.30.59 NBC
Hallmark Hall of Fame   ep   A Doll's House   11.15.59
   NBC
Play of the Week   ep   Juno and the Paycock   2.1.60
   NN
Barbara Stanwyck Theatre   ep   Good Citizen 10.3.60
   NBC
Naked City   ep $C_3H_5 (No_3)^3$ 5.10.61 ABC
Hawaii Five-O   ep   11.25.70 CBS
Hawaii Five-O   ep   12.28.71 CBS

CROSBY, BING
   I Married Joan   ep   2.25.53 NBC
   Ford Star Jubilee   ep   High Tor   3.10.56 CBS
   Phil Silvers Show   ep   1.22.57 CBS
   Bing Crosby Show   sr   9.14.64 ABC
   Danny Thomas Show   ep   The Demon under the Bed
      10.9.67 NBC
   Dr. Cook's Garden   tf   1.19.71 ABC

CROSBY, BOB
   Climax   ep   One Night Stand   9.4.55 CBS

CROWLEY, PAT
   Television Theatre   ep   Sixteen   11.8.50 NBC
   A Date with Judy   sr   6.2.51 ABC
   Armstrong Circle Theatre   ep   The Laughing Shoes
      3.18.52 NBC
   Armstrong Circle Theatre   ep   Fairy Tale   6.3.52
      NBC
   Armstrong Circle Theatre   ep   Caprice   9.9.52 NBC
   Video Theatre   ep   The Pretext   6.17.54 CBS
   U.S. Steel Hour   ep   Two   8.31.54 ABC
   Goodyear Playhouse   ep   Guilty Is the Stranger   9.26.
      54 NBC
   G.E. Theatre   ep Bachelor's Bride   2.20.55 CBS

Lux Video Theatre   ep   Here Comes the Groom   3.1.
56 NBC
Climax   ep   The 78th Floor   8.16.56 CBS
West Point   ep   Heat of Anger   12.14.56 CBS
Schlitz Playhouse of Stars   ep   Girl with a Glow   4.19.
57 CBS
Crossroads   ep   The Deadline   6.14.57 ABC
Frank Sinatra Show   ep   A Gun at His Back   11.29.57
ABC
Loretta Young Show   ep   Blizzard   12.1.57 NBC
G.E. Theatre   ep   Time to Go Now   1.19.58 CBS
Loretta Young Show   ep   The Bargain   2.16.58 NBC
Maverick   ep   The Rivals   1.25.59 ABC
Wanted Dead or Alive   ep   1.31.59 CBS
77 Sunset Strip   ep   Conspiracy of Silence   2.6.59 ABC
Maverick   ep   Betrayal   3.22.59 ABC
Desilu Playhouse   ep   The Untouchables   4.20.59, 4.
27.59 CBS
Loretta Young Show   ep   Trouble in Fenton Valley   5.
10.59 NBC
Goodyear Theatre   ep   I Remember Caviar   5.11.59
NBC
Bronco   ep   Game at the Beacon Club   9.22.59 ABC
Riverboat   ep   Tampico Raid   1.3.60 NBC
June Allyson Show   ep   Threat of Evil   2.15.60 CBS
Goodyear Theatre   ep   All in the Family   3.28.60 NBC
Maverick   ep   A Tale of Three Cities   4.24.60 ABC
Tab Hunter Show   ep   Operation Iceberg   10.16.60 NBC
Hong Kong   ep   The Jade Necklace   10.26.60 ABC
Roaring 20s   ep   The Prairie Flower   11.12.60 ABC
Michael Shayne   ep   The Body Beautiful   3.24.61 NBC
Hong Kong   ep   The Jade Empress   4.12.61 ABC
Tales of Wells Fargo   ep   Treasure Coach   10.14.61
NBC
87th Precinct   ep   Empty Hours   11.20.61 NBC
Detectives   ep   Escort   12.15.61 NBC
Dr. Kildare   ep   A Very Present Help   4.5.62 NBC
Cain's Hundred   ep   Quick Brown Fox   5.8.62 NBC
Rawhide   ep   Incident of the Mountain Man   1.25.63
CBS
Bonanza   ep   The Actress   2.24.63 NBC
Twilight Zone   ep   Printer's Devil   2.28.63 CBS
Eleventh Hour   ep   Five Moments of Time   3.6.63 NBC
Fugitive   ep   The Witch   9.24.63 ABC
Mr. Novak   ep   Love in the Wrong Season   12.3.63
NBC
77 Sunset Strip   ep   The Toy Jungle   12.6.63 ABC

Lieutenant ep Between Music and Laughter 1.11.64 NBC

Arrest and Trial ep The Black Flower 3.1.64 CBS

Dr. Kildare ep A Sense of Tempo 5.7.64 NBC

The Man from U.N.C.L.E. ep The Vulcan Affair 9. 22.64 NBC

Bob Hope Chrysler Theatre ep Mr. Biddle's Crime Wave 12.4.64 NBC

Please Don't Eat the Daisies sr 9.14.65 NBC

The Two of Us pt 8.29.66 CBS

Please Don't Eat the Daisies sr ret 9.17.66 NBC

World of Disney ep 9.22.68, 9.29.68 NBC

Judd for the Defense ep 10.18.68 ABC

Love American Style ep Love and the American Wife 10.27.69 ABC

World of Disney ep Menace on the Mountain 2.1.70, 3.8.70 NBC

Marcus Welby, M.D. ep A Portrait of Debbie 9.21. 71 ABC

Alias Smith and Jones ep 12.30.71 ABC

Owen Marshall ep Warlock at Machine 3 1.6.72 ABC

CULP, ROBERT

Star Tonight ep The Chevigny Man 3.22.56 ABC

U.S. Steel Hour ep The Funny Heart 4.1.56 CBS

Playwrights '56 cp Nick and Letty 6.5.56 NBC

U.S. Steel Hour ep Operation Three R's 7.4.56 CBS

Zane Grey Theatre ep Badge of Honor 5.3.57 CBS

Robert Montgomery Presents ep Longing for to Go 5.6.57 NBC

Lamp Unto My Feet ep 6.2.57 CBS

Trackdown sr 10.4.57 CBS

U.S. Steel Hour ep Flint and Fire 7.16.58 CBS

Trackdown sr ret 1.28.59 CBS

June Allyson Show ep So Dim the Light 2.1.60 CBS

Zane Grey Theatre ep Calico Bait 3.31.60 CBS

Tate ep The Bounty Hunter 6.22.60 NBC

Mystery Show ep Dead Man's Walk 7.10.60 NBC

Outlaws ep Thirty a Month 9.29.60 NBC

Shirley Temple Theatre ep The House of the Seven Gables 12.11.60 NBC

Zane Grey Theatre ep Morning Incident 12.29.60 CBS

Hennesey ep The Specialist 1.23.61 CBS

Rawhide ep Incident at the Top of the World 1.27.61 CBS

Detectives ep Bad Apple 3.3.61 ABC

Barbara Stanwyck Theatre   ep   Adventure on Happiness Street   3.20.61 NBC
87th Precinct   ep   The Floater   9.25.61 NBC
Bonanza   ep   Broken Ballad   10.29.61 NBC
Target: Corruptors   ep   To Wear a Badge   12.1.61 ABC
Cain's Hundred   ep   1.2.62 NBC
Rifleman   ep   The Man from Salinas   2.12.62 ABC
Wagon Train   ep   The Baylor Crowfoot Story   3.21.62 NBC
World of Disney   ep   Sammy, The Way-out Seal   10.28.62, 11.4.62 NBC
Empire   ep   Where the Hawk Is Wheeling   1.29.63 NBC
Naked City   ep   The Highest of Prizes   2.27.63 ABC
Dr. Kildare   ep   Face of Fear   3.7.63 NBC
Outer Limits   ep   Corrupt Earthling   11.18.63 ABC
Alfred Hitchcock Theatre   ep   Goodbye, George   12.13.63 CBS
Great Adventure   ep   The Testing of Sam Houston   1.31.64 CBS
Ben Casey   ep   The Sound of One Hand Clapping   2.19.64 ABC
Ben Casey   ep   Autumn without Red Leaves   10.5.64 ABC
The Man from U.N.C.L.E.   ep   The Shark Affair   10.13.64   NBC
Outer Limits   ep   Demon with a Glass Hand   10.17.64 ABC
Gunsmoke   ep   11.14.64 CBS
The Hanged Man   tf   11.18.64 NBC
Dr. Kildare   ep   Do You Trust Our Doctor   3.4.65 NBC
I Spy   sr   9.15.65 NBC
I Spy   sr ret   9.14.66 NBC
I Spy   sr ret   9.67 NBC
On Stage   ep   Married Alive   1.23.70 NBC
Name of the Game   ep   Cynthia Is Alive and Living In Avalon   10.2.70 NBC
Name of the Game   ep   11.6.70 NBC
See the Man Run   tf   12.11.71 ABC
Columbo   ep   11.5.72 NBC

CUMMINGS, CONSTANCE
Video Theatre   ep   Lady from Washington   7.7.52 CBS
Douglas Fairbanks, Jr. Presents   ep   The Scream   8.5.53 NBC
Screen Directors Playhouse   ep   Bitter Waters   8.1.56 NBC

Schlitz Playhouse of Stars ep Night Drive 2.15.57
CBS

CUMMINGS, ROBERT
Sure as Fate ep Run from the Sun 9.19.50 ABC
Video Theatre ep the Shiny People 1.29.51 CBS
Robert Montgomery Presents ep Lila, My Love 5.
12.52 NBC
Video Theatre ep Pattern for Glory 5.26.52 CBS
My Hero (a.k.a. The Bob Cummings Show) sr 10.
8.52 NBC
TV Soundstage ep The Test Case 3.26.54 CBS
Elgin Hour ep Flood 10.5.54 ABC
Best Foot Forward Sp 11.20.54 NBC
Burns and Allen Show ep 12.27.54 CBS
Love that Bob (a.k.a. The Bob Cummings Show) sr
1.2.55 NBC
Love that Bob sr ret 10.5.55 CBS
Studio One ep Special Announcement 9.24.56 CBS
Love that Bob sr ret fall, 1956 CBS
Schlitz Playhouse of Stars ep One Left Over 2.1.57
CBS
G.E. Theatre ep Too Good with a Gun 3.24.57 CBS
Love that Bob sr ret 9.25.57 NBC
Schlitz Playhouse of Stars ep Dual Control 11.1.57
CBS
Playhouse 90 ep Bomber's Moon 5.22.58 CBS
Love that Bob sr ret 9.58 NBC
Lucille Ball-Desi Arnaz Hour ep The Ricardos Go to
Japan 11.27.59 CBS
Twilight Zone ep King Nine Will Not Return 9.30.60
CBS
Zane Grey Theatre ep The Last Bugle 11.24.60 CBS
Bob Cummings Shows sr 10.5.61 CBS
Dupont Show of the Week ep The Action in New Or-
leans 4.15.62 NBC
Dick Powell Theatre ep Last of the Private Eyes 4.
30.63 NBC
Great Adventure ep Plague 2.28.64 CBS
Bob Hope Chrysler Theatre ep The Square Peg 3.6.
64 NBC
My Living Doll sr 9.27.64 CBS
Bob Hope Chrysler Theatre ep Blind Man's Bluff 2.
8.67 NBC
Love American Style ep 9.29.69 ABC
Flying Nun ep 10.1.69 ABC
Gidget Grows Up tf 12.30.69 ABC

Green Acres   ep   1.10.70 CBS
Here Come the Brides   ep   1.30.70 ABC
Arnie   ep   1.16.71 CBS
Love American Style   ep   2.12.71 ABC
Here's Lucy   ep   2.7.72 CBS

CUMMINGS, VICKI
Philco Playhouse   ep   Leaf out of a Book   12.31.50
NBC
Robert Montgomery Presents   ep   For Love or Money
6.4.51 NBC
Broadway Television Theatre   ep   7.2.52 NN
Tales of Tomorrow   ep   Substance "X"   10.3.52 ABC
Goodyear Playhouse   ep   Before I Wake   5.21.53
ABC
The American Hour   ep   Outlaw's Reckoning   11.3.53
ABC
Broadway Television Theatre   ep   The Last of Mrs.
Cheyney   12.14.53 NN
Climax   ep   Sit Down with Death   4.26.56 CBS

CURRIE, FINLAY
Douglas Fairbanks, Jr. Presents   ep   The Witness 5.
19.54 NBC
Dupont Show of the Month   ep   The Ordeal of Dr. Shan-
non   12.16.62 NBC
Dupont Show of the Month   ep   The Last Hangman   9.
15.63 NBC
Brigadoon   Sp   10.15.66 ABC

CURTIS, DONALD
Silver Theatre   ep   The Late Mr. Beasley   2.6.50
CBS
Studio One   ep   The Survivors   3.20.50 CBS
Studio One   ep   Room Upstairs   5.22.50 CBS
Detective's Wife   sr   7.7.50 CBS
Television Theatre   ep   Sixteen   11.8.50 NBC
Prudential Playhouse   ep   Burlesque   1.2.51   CBS
Prudential Playhouse   ep   Skylark   1.16.51 CBS
Starlight Theatre   ep   Lunch at Disalvo's   8.23.51
CBS
A Letter to Loretta   ep   Secret Answer   1.17.54 NBC
Studio 57   ep   The Will to Survive   1.18.55 NN
Science Fiction Theatre   ep   The Strange Dr. Lorenz
7.15.55 NBC
Studio 57   ep   The Will to Survive   7.26.55 NN
Loretta Young Show   ep   Reunion   9.11.55 NBC

Ford Theatre   ep   Bet the Queen   12.8.55 NBC
Ford Theatre   ep   The Silent Stranger   2.9.56 NBC
Cavalcade Theatre   ep   Call Home the Heart   2.21.56
     ABC
Crossroads   ep   The Judge   5.18.56 ABC
Jane Wyman Theatre   ep   Assignment Champ   4.2.57
     NBC

CURTIS, TONY
     G.E. Theatre   ep   Cornada   11.10.57 CBS
     Schlitz Playhouse of Stars   ep   Man on a Rock   2.21.
          58 CBS
     G.E. Theatre   ep   The Stone   1.18.59 CBS
     Ford Star Time   ep   The Young Juggler   3.29.60 NBC
     Flintstones   ep (voice only)   10.1.65 ABC
     Bracken's World   ep   Fade-In   9.19.69 NBC
     The Persuaders   sr   9.18.71 ABC

CUSHING, PETER
     Spread of the Eagle   ep   The Colossus   9.16.64 NN

-D-

DAHL, ARLENE
     Pepsi Cola Playhouse   sh   10.2.53 ABC
     Ford Theatre   ep   Wedding March   4.22.54 NBC
     Lux Video Theatre   ep   September Affair   12.23.54
          NBC
     Ford Theatre   ep   All That Glitters   10.6.55 NBC
     Opening Night   sh   6.14.58 NBC
     Riverboat   ep   That Taylor Affair   9.26.60 NBC
     Burke's Law   ep   Who Killed Alex Debbs   10.25.63
          ABC
     Burke's Law   ep   Jet Setter   1.10.64 ABC
     Burke's Law   ep   10.14.64 ABC
     Burke's Law   ep   3.3.65 ABC
     Love American Style   ep   2.26.71 ABC

DAILEY, DAN
     Shower of Stars   ep   Burlesque   3.17.55 CBS
     Paris in the Springtime   Sp   1.2.56 NBC
     G.E. Theatre   ep   Bill Bailey, Won't You Please Come
          Home   1.25.59 CBS

Four Just Men sr fall, 1959 NN
Untouchables ep Come and Kill Me 11.27.62 ABC
Alfred Hitchcock Theatre ep The Tender Poisoner 12.
    20.62 CBS
Governor and J.J. sr 9.23.69 CBS
Governor and J.J. sr ret 9.23.70 CBS
Mr. and Mrs. Bo Jo Jones tf 11.16.71 ABC
Here's Lucy ep 11.22.71 CBS
World of Disney ep Michael O'Hara the 4th 3.26.72,
    4.2.72 NBC

DAILEY, IRENE
Dr. Kildare ep A Trip to Niagara 2.21.63 NBC
Eleventh Hour ep The Bride Wore Pink 12.4.63 NBC
Ben Casey ep Heap Logs and Let the Blaze Laugh Out
    4.8.64 ABC
Doctors/Nurses ep Threshold 4.6.65 CBS
Hawk ep How Close Can You Get 10.27.66 ABC
N.E.T. Playhouse ep Home 1.19.68 NN
New York Television Theatre ep The Sand Castle 4.
    7.70 NN

DALL, JOHN
Lights Out ep Pit of the Dead 6.11.51 NBC
The Clock ep A Right Smart Trick 8.31.51 NBC
Studio One ep The Doctor's Wife 10.6.52 CBS
Broadway Television Theatre ep Outward Bound 11.24.
    52 NN
Suspense ep The Invisible Killer 12.30.52 CBS
Broadway Television Theatre ep The Hasty Heart 11.
    2.53 NN
Suspense ep Tenth Reunion 3.23.54 CBS
G.E. Theatre ep The Coward of Ft. Bennett 3.16.58
    CBS
Schlitz Playhouse of Stars ep And Practically Strangers
    1.30.59 CBS
Perry Mason ep The Case of the Weary Watchdog 11.
    29.62 CBS
Perry Mason ep The Case of the Reluctant Model 10.
    31.63 CBS
Perry Mason ep The Case of the Lonely Eloper 5.27.
    65 CBS
Perry Mason ep The Case of the Laughing Lady 9.12.
    65 CBS

DALY, JAMES
The Front Page sr 1949-1950 CBS

The Web   ep   The Vanished Hours   5.28.52 CBS
Robert Montgomery Presents   ep   Til Next We Meet
   6.23.52 NBC
Studio One   ep   The Great Lady   12.15.52 CBS
Studio One   ep   To a Moment of Triumph   1.26.53 CBS
Philco Playhouse   ep   The Reluctant Citizen   2.8.53
   NBC
Suspense   ep   The Quarry   2.17.53 CBS
Studio One   ep   Edge of Evil   3.23.53 CBS
Kraft Theatre   ep   Next of Kin   4.8.53 NBC
Studio One   ep   Along Came a Spider   4.27.53 CBS
The Web   ep   The 32nd Floor   5.10.53 CBS
Studio One   ep   Fly with the Hawk   5.25.53 CBS
Foreign Intrigue   sr   10.8.53 NBC
Studio One   ep   The Strike   6.7.54 CBS
The Web   ep   Missing Person   6.27.54 CBS
Danger   ep   A Day's Pay   8.24.54 CBS
Studio One   ep   Prelude to Murder   10.4.54 CBS
Elgin Hour   ep   Family Crisis   10.19.54 ABC
Lux Video Theatre   ep   Sunset Boulevard   1.6.55 NBC
Goodyear Playhouse   ep   Doing Her Bit   1.16.55 NBC
U.S. Steel Hour   ep   Freighter   2.15.55 ABC
Kraft Theatre   ep   Jeannie   3.16.55 NBC
Omnibus   ep   The Education of Henry Adams   3.20.55
   CBS
Omnibus   ep   Uncle Tom's Cabin   4.10.55 CBS
U.S. Steel Hour   ep   Roads to Home   4.26.55 ABC
Appointment with Adventure   ep   5.8.55 CBS
Front Row Center   ep   Tender Is the Night   9.7.55 CBS
Omnibus   ep   The Renaissance   10.9.55 CBS
Climax   ep   House of Shadows   10.20.55 CBS
The Millionaire   ep   The Story of Tom Bryon   11.2.55
   CBS
Cavalcade Theatre   ep   One at a Time   11.15.55 ABC
Studio One   ep   The Strongbox   12.12.55 CBS
Appointment with Adventure   ep   A Touch of Christmas
   12.12.55 CBS
Front Row Center   ep   The Human Touch   4.15.56 CBS
Front Row Center   ep   Strange Suspicion   1.15.56 CBS
Omnibus   ep   The Billy Mitchell Court Martial   4.1.56
   CBS
Armstrong Circle Theatre   ep   Seventy-Three Seconds
   into Space   5.1.56 NBC
Kraft Theatre   ep   Death Is a Spanish Dancer   5.9.56
   NBC
Studio One   ep   The Power   6.4.56 CBS
Omnibus   ep   My Heart's in the Highlands   10.28.56 ABC

Omnibus   ep nar   The Art of Murder   12. 9. 56 ABC
Studio One   ep   Goodbye Piccadilly   12. 31. 56 CBS
Omnibus   ep   Lee at Gettysburg   1. 20. 57 ABC
Dupont Theatre   ep   One Day at a Time   3. 12. 57 ABC
Goodyear Playhouse   ep   First Love   3. 24. 57 NBC
Studio One   ep   The Furlough   6. 3. 57 CBS
Ford Theatre   ep   Cross Hairs   6. 12. 57 ABC
Studio One   ep   The Staring Match   6. 17. 57 CBS
Studio One   ep   Escape Route   12. 2. 57 CBS
Loretta Young Show   ep   Power Play   12. 29. 57 NBC
Loretta Young Show   ep   Air Stewardess   3. 30. 58 NBC
Alcoa Theatre   ep   My Wife's Next Husband   4. 21. 58
   NBC
U. S. Steel Hour   ep   Climate of Marriage   7. 30. 58
   CBS
Loretta Young Show   ep   This Is the Moment   1. 18. 59
   NBC
Our American Heritage   ep   Destiny West   1. 24. 60
   NBC
Ann Sothern Show   ep   4. 4. 60 CBS
Twilight Zone   ep   Stop at Willoughby   5. 6. 60 CBS
Roughing It   Sp   5. 13. 60 NBC
Hallmark Hall of Fame   ep   Give Us Barabbas   3. 26. 61
   NBC
Special for Women   ep   What's Wrong with Men   10. 19.
   61 NBC
Armstrong Circle Theatre   ep   The Cross and the
   Dragon   9. 26. 62 CBS
Dupont Show of the Month   ep   Two Faces of Treason
   2. 10. 63 NBC
Nurses   ep   Field of Battle   5. 30. 63 CBS
Great Adventures   ep   The Man Who Stole New York
   City   12. 13. 63 CBS
Breaking Point   ep   And if Thy Hands Offend Thee   1.
   13. 64 ABC
Nurses   ep   The Human Transition   4. 23. 64 CBS
Suspense   ep   4. 29. 64 CBS
Dupont Show of the Month   ep   Don't Go Upstairs   5. 17.
   64 NBC
Hallmark Hall of Fame   ep   The Magnificent Yankee   1.
   28. 65 NBC
Dr. Kildare   ep   With Hellfire and Thunder   10. 19. 65
   NBC
Hallmark Hall of Fame   ep   Eagle in a Cage   10. 20. 65
   NBC
Dr. Kildare   ep   Daily Flights to Olympus   10. 25. 65
   NBC
Road West   ep   The Gunfighter   9. 26. 66 NBC

FBI   ep   The Chameleon   1. 9. 66 ABC
Bob Hope Chrysler Theatre   ep   Storm Crossing   12. 7.
   66 NBC
N. E. T. Playhouse   ep   An Enemy of the People   12. 21.
   66 NN
Invaders   ep   Beachhead   1. 10. 67 ABC
Felony Squad   ep   The Night of the Shark   1. 16. 67 ABC
Felony Squad   ep   1. 23. 67 ABC
Virginian   ep   Nightmare at Ft. Killman   3. 8. 67 NBC
Gunsmoke   ep   3. 11. 67 CBS
Mission Impossible   ep   3. 25. 67 CBS
Custer   ep   9. 13. 67 ABC
FBI   ep   9. 17. 67 ABC
Mission Impossible   ep   10. 1. 67 CBS
Judd for the Defense   ep   Conspiracy   10. 13. 67 ABC
Run for Your Life   ep   10. 15. 67 NBC
Hallmark Hall of Fame   ep   St. Joan   12. 4. 67 NBC
CBS Playhouse   ep   Dear Friends   12. 6. 67 CBS
Mission Impossible   ep   12. 31. 67 CBS
Invaders   ep   The Peacemaker   2. 6. 68 ABC
World of Disney   ep   The Treasure of San Bosco   11.
   24. 68, 12. 1. 68 NBC
Judd for the Defense   ep   Punishments, Cruel and Un-
   usual   12. 6. 68 ABC
Star Trek   ep   Requiem for Methuselah   2. 14. 69 NBC
FBI   ep   Conspiracy of Silence   3. 2. 69 ABC
U. M. C.   tf   4. 17. 69 CBS
Medical Center   sr   9. 24. 69 CBS
Medical Center   sr ret   9. 16. 70 CBS
Ironside   ep   The People Against Judge McIntire   10. 8.
   70 NBC
Medical Center   sr ret   9. 15. 71 CBS
Medical Center   sr ret   9. 13. 72 CBS

DAMONE, VIC
   Alcoa Hour   ep   The Stingiest Man in Town   12. 23. 56
      NBC
   June Allyson Show   ep   Piano Man   2. 29. 60 CBS
   Rebel   ep   The Proxy   4. 16. 61 ABC
   The Dangerous Christmas of Red Riding Hood   Sp   11.
      28. 65 ABC
   Jericho   ep   11. 10. 66 CBS
   Danny Thomas Show   ep   It's Greek to Me   10. 2. 67
      NBC
   Shadows over Elveron   tf   3. 5. 68 NBC

DANA, LEORA
    Philco Playhouse   ep   A Letter to Mr. Priest   2.19.50
      NBC
    Philco Playhouse   ep   Nocturne   4.2.50 NBC
    Philco Playhouse   ep   Mr. Arcularis   4.29.51 NBC
    Goodyear Playhouse   ep   Four Meetings   6.8.52 NBC
    Curtain Call   ep   Season of Divorce   8.8.52 NBC
    Robert Montgomery Presents   ep   The Woman Who
      Hated Children   6.22.53 NBC
    The Web   ep   A Case of Escape   7.5.53 CBS
    TV Soundstage   ep   Innocent 'til Proven Guilty   7.10.53
      NBC
    Kraft Theatre   ep   Ca'n Jonas   10.7.53 NBC
    Kraft Theatre   ep   Dark Victory   3.11.54 ABC
    Armstrong Circle Theatre   ep   So Close the Stars   3.
      23.54 NBC
    Motorola TV Hour   ep   Black Chiffon   4.20.54 ABC
    Goodyear Playhouse   ep   Dear Harriet Heart-Throb
      7.18.54 NBC
    Kraft Theatre   ep   Full of the Old Harry   11.3.54 NBC
    Robert Montgomery Presents   ep   The Lost Weekend
      2.7.55 NBC
    Pond's Theatre   ep   The Forger   3.31.55 ABC
    Appointment with Adventure   ep   Priceless Cargo   5.15.
      55 CBS
    Studio One   ep   The Incredible World of Horace Ford
      6.13.55 CBS
    Kraft Theatre   ep   The Sears Girls   1.11.56 NBC
    Armstrong Circle Theatre   ep   Man in Shadow   3.6.56
      NBC
    Star Tonight   ep   The Chevigny Man   3.22.56 ABC
    Studio One   ep   The Arena   4.9.56 CBS
    Alfred Hitchcock Presents   ep   The Legacy   5.27.56
      CBS
    Kraft Theatre   ep   Babies for Sale   7.18.56 NBC
    Kraft Theatre   ep   One Way West   8.1.56 NBC
    Telephone Time   ep   Mr. and Mrs. Browning   9.30.56
      CBS
    Producers Showcase   ep   Jack and the Beanstock   11.
      12.56 NBC
    Alfred Hitchcock Presents   ep   John Brown's Body
      12.30.56 CBS
    Kraft Theatre   ep   Medallion   4.3.57 NBC
    Schlitz Playhouse of Stars   ep   The Traveling Corpse
      5.3.57 CBS
    Climax   ep   Tunnel of Fear   10.24.57 CBS
    Schlitz Playhouse of Stars   ep   Neighbors 12.6.57 CBS

U.S. Steel Hour   ep   The Bromley Touch   1.15.58
   CBS
Suspicion   ep   The Eye of Truth   3.17.58 NBC
Shirley Temple's Story Book   ep   Rip Van Winkle   5.8.
   58 NBC
U.S. Steel Hour   ep   Climate of Marriage   7.30.58 CBS
Alcoa Theatre   ep   High Class Type of Mongrel   1.12.
   59 NBC
Playhouse 90   ep   A Dream of Treason   1.21.60 CBS
Defenders   ep   The Treadmill   11.25.61 CBS
U.S. Steel Hour   ep   A Nightmare at Bleak Hill   2.7.
   62 CBS
Bust Stop   ep   The Opposite Virtues   2.18.62 ABC
Stoney Burke   ep   King of the Hill   1.21.63 ABC
Channing   ep   A Claim to Immortality   2.26.64 ABC
Lieutenant   ep   Operation Actress   3.28.64 NBC
For the People   ep   Act of Violence   2.21.65, 2.28.65
   CBS
Doctors/Nurses   ep   Act of Violence   2.23.66 CBS
N.Y.P.D.   ep   Everybody Loved Him   3.18.69 ABC

D'ANDREA, TOM
   Life of Riley   sr   1.2.53 NBC
   Appointment with Love   ep   Never Laugh at Lady   6.26.
      53 ABC
   Life of Riley   sr ret   9.18.53 NBC
   Life of Riley   sr ret   9.54 NBC
   The Soldiers   sr   6.25.55 NBC
   Life of Riley   sr ret   9.14.56 NBC

DANDRIDGE, DOROTHY
   Light's Diamond Jubilee   ep   A Chance for Adventure
      10.24.64 ABC, CBS, NBC
   Cain's Hundred   ep   Blues for a Junkman   2.20.62 NBC

DANIELL, HENRY
   Philco Playhouse   ep   The Marriages   1.22.50 NBC
   Studio One   ep   The Target   2.5.51 CBS
   Kraft Theatre   ep   The Iron Gate   12.3.52 NBC
   Fireside Theatre   ep   The Smuggler   10.25.55 NBC
   TV Reader's Digest   ep   Archer-Shee Case   10.31.55
      ABC
   Producers Showcase   ep   The Barretts of Wimpole
      Street   4.2.56 NBC
   Telephone Time   ep   The Mystery of Casper Hauser   5.
      6.56 CBS
   Playhouse 90   ep   Confession 11.29.56 CBS

On Trial   ep   Colonel Blood   1.4.57 NBC
On Trial   ep   The Freeman Case   3.15.57 NBC
Telephone Time   ep   The Gadfly   10.1.57 ABC
Californians   ep   12.10.57 NBC
Matinee Theatre   ep   The Little Minister   12.26.57
   NBC
Kraft Theatre   ep   The Spell of the Tigress   2.5.58
   NBC
Alcoa Theatre   ep   Night Caller   2.10.58 NBC
Desilu Playhouse   ep   Debut   10.27.58 CBS
Playhouse 90   ep   The Wings of the Dove   1.8.59 CBS
Maverick   ep   Pappy   9.13.59 ABC
Ford Star Time   ep   My Three Angels   12.8.59 NBC
Markham   ep   12.19.59 CBS
World of Disney   ep   Tory Vengeance   1.1.60 CBS
Wagon Train   ep   The Christine Elliott Story   3.23.60
   NBC
Wagon Train   ep   Trial for Murder   4.27.60, 5.4.60
   NBC
Peter Gunn   ep   The Crossbow   6.6.60 NBC
Shirley Temple Theatre   ep   The Black Arrow   11.27.
   60 NBC
Thriller   ep   The Cheaters   12.27.60 NBC
Islanders   ep   Escape from Kaledau   1.29.61 ABC
Thriller   ep   Well of Doom   2.28.61 NBC
Law and Mr. Jones   ep   The Quiet Town   5.12.61 ABC
Thriller   ep   God Grante that She Lye Stille   10.23.61
   NBC
77 Sunset Strip   ep   The Floating Man   11.9.62 ABC
77 Sunset Strip   ep   The Odds on Odette   12.21.62 ABC

DANNER, BLYTHE
N.Y.P.D.   ep   Day Tripper   10.15.68 ABC
On Stage   ep   To Confuse the Angel   3.15.70 NBC
George M   Sp   9.12.70 NBC
Dr. Cook's Garden   tf   1.19.71 ABC

DANTINE, HELMUT
Drama   ep   Shadow of the Cloak   6.20.51 NN
Ford Theatre   ep   The Bet   3.19.53 NBC
G.E. Theatre   ep   Flight from Tormendero   2.24.57
   CBS
Playhouse 90   ep   Clipper Ship   4.4.57 CBS
The Millionaire   ep   The Josef Marton Story   5.15.57
   CBS
On Trial   ep   The Gentle Voice of Murder   5.24.57
   NBC

Studio 57   ep   A Source of Irritation   1.19.58 NN
Schlitz Playhouse of Stars   ep   I Shot a Prowler   3.28.
    58 CBS
Thin Man   ep   Design for Murder   12.12.58 NBC
Playhouse 90   ep   The Hiding Place   3.22.60 CBS
Rogues   ep   Run for the Money   2.14.65 NBC
Run for Your Life   ep   3.6.67 NBC
Hallmark Hall of Fame   ep   The File on Devlin   11.21.
    69 NBC
Call Holme   pt   4.24.72 NBC

DANTON, RAY
Matinee Theatre   ep   Eye of the Storm   6.7.57 NBC
Sugarfoot   ep   Bunch Quitter   10.29.57 ABC
Trackdown   ep   11.8.57 CBS
Climax   ep   Sound of the Moon   1.23.58 CBS
Climax   ep   The Disappearance of Daphne   5.15.58 CBS
Decision   ep   The Danger Game   7.20.58 NBC
Desilu Playhouse   ep   Chez Rouge   2.16.59 CBS
Behind Closed Doors   ep   The Meeting   3.5.59 NBC
77 Sunset Strip   ep   A Bargain in Tombs   4.24.59 ABC
Yancy Derringer   ep   6.11.59 CBS
Sugarfoot ep   The Wild Bunch   9.29.59 ABC
Alaskans   ep   The Golden Fleece   11.29.59 ABC
Alaskans   ep   The Seal Skin-Game   2.21.60 ABC
Bourbon Street Beat   ep   Last Exit   5.2.60 ABC
Colt .45   ep   Bounty List   5.31.60 ABC
Hawaiian Eye   ep   I Wed Three Wives   9.14.60 ABC
Surfside 6   ep   Country Gentleman   10.3.60 ABC
Lawman   ep   Yawkey   10.23.60 ABC
Surfside 6   ep   The Frightened Canary   12.12.60 ABC
Maverick   ep   A State of Siege   1.1.61 ABC
Cheyenne   ep   The Buckbrier Trail   2.20.61 ABC
Roaring 20s   ep   The Vamp   3.4.61 ABC
Laramie   ep   The Fortune Hunter   10.9.62 NBC
Virginian   ep   Riff-Raff   11.7.62 NBC
Wide Country   ep   The Bravest Man in the World   12.
    6.62 NBC
Empire   ep   The Four Thumbs Story   1.8.63 NBC
Gallant Man   ep   Operation Secret   2.16.63 ABC
Mystery Theatre   ep   Talk to My Partner   8.28.63 NBC
Wagon Train   ep   The Molly Kincaid Story   9.16.63
    ABC
Redigo   ep   The Thin Line   12.3.63 NBC
Temple Houston   ep   The Case for William Gotch   2.6.
    64 NBC
Death Valley Days   ep   The Wooing of Perilous Pauline

2. 22. 64 ABC
Wagon Train   ep   4. 5. 64 ABC
Honey West   ep   The Swingin' Mrs. Jones   9. 17. 65 ABC
The Man from U. N. C. L. E.   ep   The Discotheque Affair
    10. 15. 65 NBC
Big Valley   ep   3. 4. 68 ABC
Name of the Game   ep   The Inquiry   1. 17. 69 NBC
Ironside   ep   3. 6. 69 NBC
It Takes a Thief   ep   3. 18. 69 ABC
Love American Style   ep   1. 12. 70 ABC
Dan August   ep   The Color Fury   10. 28. 70 ABC
Hawaii Five-O   ep   The Last Eden   11. 18. 70 ABC
FBI   ep   The Inheritors   12. 27. 70 ABC
Young Lawyers   ep   And the Walls Came Tumbling Down
    2. 24. 71 ABC
Banyon   tf   3. 15. 71 NBC
Nichols   ep   10. 21. 71 NBC
Hawaii Five-O   ep   2. 8. 72 CBS
McCloud   ep   10. 1. 72 NBC

DARBY, KIM
Mr. Novak   ep   10. 1. 63 NBC
Farmer's Daughter   ep   Katy and the Prince   2. 26. 64
    ABC
Eleventh Hour   ep   Does My Mother Have to Know   3. 25.
    64, 4. 1. 64 NBC
Dr. Kildare   ep   What's Different about Today?   10. 22.
    64 NBC
Wagon Train   ep   The Story of Hector Heatherington
    12. 20. 64 ABC
Mr. Novak   ep   The Silent Dissuaders   2. 16. 65 NBC
Donna Reed Show   ep   The Mysterious Smile   3. 25. 65
    ABC
John Forsythe Show   ep   Tis Better to Have Loved and
    Lost   10. 11. 65 NBC
Fugitive   ep   An Apple a Day   11. 2. 65 ABC
Fugitive   ep   Joshua's Kingdom   10. 18. 66 ABC
Star Trek   ep   Miri   10. 27. 66 NBC
Gunsmoke   ep   2. 25. 67 CBS
Road West   ep   Fair Ladies of France   2. 27. 67 NBC
Ironside   tf   3. 28. 67 NBC
The Man from U. N. C. L. E   ep   3. 31. 67, 4. 7. 67 NBC
Gunsmoke   ep   10. 2. 67, 10. 9. 67 CBS
Judd for the Defense   ep   Conspiracy   10. 13. 67 ABC
Flesh and Blood   Sp   1. 26. 68 NBC
Run for Your Life   ep   3. 6. 68 NBC
She People   tf   1. 22. 72 ABC

Streets of San Francisco   ep   9.16.72 ABC
Cool Million   ep   10.25.72 NBC

DARCEL, DENISE
Naked City   ep   The Virtue of Madame Douvay   12.5.
62 ABC
Combat   ep   A Distant Drum   11.19.63 ABC

DARIN, BOBBY
Hennesey   ep   10.5.59 CBS
Dan Raven   ep   The High Cost of Fame   9.23.60 NBC
Wagon Train   ep   10.4.64 ABC
Run for Your Life   ep   Who's Watching the Fleshpot
3.7.66 NBC
Danny Thomas Show   ep   The Cage   1.15.68 NBC
Cade's County   ep   11.28.71 CBS
Night Gallery   ep   Stop Killing Me   2.9.72 NBC

DARNELL, LINDA
20th Century-Fox Hour   ep   Deception   3.7.56 CBS
Ford Theatre   ep   All for a Man   3.8.56 NBC
Schlitz Playhouse of Stars   ep   Terror in the Streets
1.18.57 CBS
Ford Theatre   ep   Fate Travels East   3.13.57 ABC
Playhouse 90   ep   Homeward Borne   5.9.57 CBS
Climax   ep   Trial by Fire   9.5.57 CBS
Jane Wyman Theatre   ep   The Elevator   1.2.58 NBC
Wagon Train   ep   The Dora Gray Story   1.29.58 NBC
Wagon Train   ep   The Sacremento Story   9.24.58 NBC
Cimarron City   ep   Kid on a Calico Horse   11.20.58
CBS
Burke's Law   ep   2.21.64 ABC

DARREN, JAMES
Donna Reed Show   ep   April Fool   4.1.59 ABC
City Beneath the Sea   tf   1.25.71 NBC

DARRO, FRANKIE
Lineup   ep   Gremlin Grady Case   12.12.58 CBS
Peter Gunn   ep   The Jockey   12.15.58 NBC
Bat Masterson   ep   Garrison Finish   12.10.59 NBC
Alfred Hitchcock Presents   ep   I Can Take Care of My-
self   5.15.60 CBS
Checkmate   ep   Death Runs Wilde 9.17.60 CBS
Alfred Hitchcock Theatre   ep   Ten O'Clock Tiger   4.3.
62 NBC
Mister Ed   ep   The Pilgrim   11.22.62 CBS

DARVAS, LILI
   Cosmopolitan Theatre   ep   The Beautiful Time   12.14.51
      NN
   Armstrong Circle Theatre   ep   Black Wedding   1.27.53
      NBC
   Armstrong Circle Theatre   ep   Julie's Castle   10.27.53
      NBC
   TV Hour   ep   Brandenburg Gate   12.1.53 ABC
   Goodyear Playhouse   ep   Star in the Night   8.22.54 NBC
   Center Stage   ep   The Heart of a Clown   9.21.54 ABC
   Goodyear Playhouse   ep   My Lost Saints   3.13.55 NBC
   Producers Showcase   ep   Reunion in Vienna   4.4.55
      NBC
   Climax   ep   Flight 951   4.21.55 CBS
   Goodyear Playhouse   ep   End of the Mission   6.19.55
      NBC
   Kraft Theatre   ep   The Beautiful Time   10.5.55 NBC
   Appointment with Adventure   ep   Dark Memory   10.30.
      55 CBS
   Philco Playhouse   ep   The Trees   12.4.55 NBC
   G.E. Theatre   ep   Portrait of a Ballerina   1.1.56 CBS
   Matinee Theatre   ep   The American   6.5.56 NBC
   Studio One   ep   Portrait of a Citizen   12.3.56 CBS
   Goodyear Playhouse   ep   First Love   3.24.57 NBC
   Kaiser Aluminum Hour   ep   The Deadly Silence   5.21.
      57 NBC
   U.S. Steel Hour   ep   The Littlest Enemy   6.18.58 CBS
   Studio One   ep   Image of Fear   9.29.58 CBS
   Ellery Queen   ep   2.27.59 NBC
   Playhouse 90   ep   Dark December   4.30.59 CBS
   June Allyson Show   ep   1.2.61 CBS
   24 Hours in a Woman's Life   Sp   3.20.61 CBS
   Twilight Zone   ep   A Long-Distance Call   3.31.61 CBS
   Route 66   ep   Should the Sky, My Lad   3.2.62 CBS
   Saints and Sinners   ep   A Shame for a Diamond Wedding
      11.26.62 NBC
   The Man from U.N.C.L.E.   ep   The Secret Scepter Af-
      fair   2.8.65 NBC
   Good Guys   ep   12.18.68 CBS

DARVI, BELLA
   Conflict   ep   Blind Drop   1.22.57 ABC
   Dick Powell Theatre   ep   View from the Eiffel Tower
      3.13.62 NBC

DARWELL, JANE
   Hollywood Opening Night   ep   Josie   12.22.52 NBC

Ford Theatre   ep   Good of His Soul   3.4.54 NBC
Fireside Theatre   ep   Nine Quarts of Water   4.20.54
   NBC
Ford Theatre   ep   Slide, Darling, Slide   12.23.54
   NBC
Climax   ep   The Bigger They Come   1.6.55 CBS
Studio 57   ep   Center Ring   3.8.55 NN
Ford Theatre   ep   Second Sight   3.10.55 NBC
Willy   ep   3.26.55 CBS
Ford Theatre   ep   The Mumbys   6.23.55 NBC
Climax   ep   House of Shadows   10.20.55 CBS
Screen Directors Playhouse   ep   The Prima Donna   2.
   1.56 NBC
Rin Tin Tin   ep   Rin Tin Tin Meets O'Hara's Mother
   2.17.56 ABC
Dupont Theatre   ep   Woman's Work   11.20.56 ABC
Playhouse 90   ep   Sincerely, Willis Wayde   12.13.56
   CBS
Playhouse 90   ep   The Greer Case   1.13.57 CBS
Playhouse 90   ep   Three Men on a Horse   4.18.57
   CBS
Studio One   ep   A Dead Ringer   3.10.58 CBS
Matinee Theatre   ep   A Boy Grows Up   4.22.58 NBC
Buckskin   ep   Mr. Rush's Secretary   1.19.59 NBC
Wagon Train   ep   The Vivian Carter Story   3.11.59
   NBC
Wagon Train   ep   The Andrew Hale Story   6.3.59 NBC
Shirley Temple Theatre   ep   The Fawn   2.5.61 NBC
Real McCoys   ep   Back to West Virginny   9.28.61 ABC
Wagon Train   ep   The Artie Matthewson Story   11.8.61
   NBC
Follow the Sun   ep   The Far Side of Nowhere   12.17.
   61 ABC
Burke's Law   ep   Who Killed Eleanor Davis   12.20.63
   ABC
Lassie   ep   Lassie the Voyager   11.13.66 CBS

DA SILVA, HOWARD
   Silver Theatre   ep   My Heart's in the Highlands   6.12.
      50 CBS
   Defenders   ep   The Bagman   10.19.63 CBS
   East Side/West Side   ep   I Before E   10.21.63 CBS
   Hamlet   Sp   6.17.64 CBS
   Defenders   ep   The Man Who   10.29.64 CBS
   Outer Limits   ep   I Robot   11.14.64 ABC
   For the People   sr   1.31.65 CBS
   Ben Casey   ep   The Day They Stole County General

4. 26. 65 ABC
Ben Casey ep A Nightingale Named Nathan 9. 27. 65
ABC
The Man from U. N. C. L. E. ep The Foreign Legion
Affair 2. 18. 66 NBC
Loner ep To Hang a Dead Man 3. 12. 66 CBS
Fugitive ep Death Is the Door Prize 9. 20. 66 ABC
Showcase ep Trial Begins 1. 15. 67 NN
Showcase ep The Beggar's Opera 2. 5. 67 NN
N. Y. P. D. ep Old Gangsters Never Die 10. 17. 67
ABC
Gentle Ben ep 10. 29. 67 CBS
Mannix ep 2. 3. 68 CBS
Keep the Faith pt 4. 14. 72 CBS

DAUPHIN, CLAUDE
Summer Studio One ep Shadow of a Man 7. 20. 53
CBS
Video Theatre ep The Moment of the Rose 11. 19.
53 CBS
U. S. Steel Hour ep The Vanishing Point 12. 22. 53
ABC
Philco Playhouse ep The Broken Fist 3. 21. 54 NBC
Omnibus ep The Apollo of Bellac 3. 28. 54 CBS
Schlitz Playhouse of Stars ep Something Wonderful
4. 16. 54 CBS
Studio One ep Cardinal Mindszenty 5. 3. 54 CBS
Schlitz Playhouse of Stars ep How the Brigadier Won
His Medals 7. 2. 54 CBS
Studio One ep Sail with the Tide 1. 17. 55 CBS
Appointment with Adventure ep Minus Three Thousand
4. 3. 55 CBS
Paris Precinct sr 4. 3. 55 ABC
Paris Precinct sr ret 9. 25. 55 ABC
Front Row Center ep Meeting at Mayerling 9. 21. 55
CBS
Alcoa Hour ep Paris and Mrs. Perlman 4. 29. 56 NBC
G. E. Summer Originals ep The Green Parrot 8. 7. 56
ABC
Play of the Week ep Crime of Passion 11. 30. 59 NN
U. S. Steel Hour ep How to Make a Killing 4. 6. 60
CBS
Mystery Theatre ep The Problem in Cell Thirteen 8.
29. 62 NBC
Naked City ep The Virtues of Madame Douvay 12. 5.
62 ABC
Harry's Girls ep Collector's Item 12. 13. 63 NBC

World Theatre   ep   France: The Faces of Love   10.
    11.64 NN

DAVIDSON, JOHN
    Hallmark Hall of Fame   ep   The Fantasticks   10.18.64
        NBC
    Daniel Boone   ep   2.27.69 NBC
    Roberta   Sp   11.6.69 NBC
    Love American Style   ep   11.20.70 ABC
    FBI   ep   1.23.72 ABC
    Owen Marshall   ep   9.28.72 ABC

DAVIS, BETTE
    G.E. Theatre   ep   With Malice Toward One   3.10.57
        CBS
    Schlitz Playhouse of Stars   ep   For Better, For Worse
        3.22.57 CBS
    Ford Theatre   ep   Footnote on a Doll   4.24.57 ABC
    Telephone Time   ep   Stranded   5.9.57 ABC
    G.E. Theatre   ep   The Cold Touch   4.13.58 CBS
    Suspicion   ep   Fraction of a Second   4.21.58 NBC
    Studio 57   ep   The Starmaker   8.10.58 NN
    Alfred Hitchcock Theatre   ep   Out There--Darkness
        1.25.59 CBS
    Wagon Train   ep   The Ella Lindstrom Story   2.4.59
        NBC
    June Allyson Show   ep   Dark Morning   9.28.59 CBS
    Wagon Train   ep   The Elizabeth McQueeney Story   10.
        28.59 NBC
    Wagon Train   ep   The Bettina May Story   12.20.61
        NBC
    Virginian   ep   The Accomplice   12.19.62 NBC
    Perry Mason   ep   The Case of the Constant Doyle
        1.31.63   CBS
    Gunsmoke   ep   10.1.66 CBS
    It Takes a Thief   ep   Touch of Magic   1.26.70 ABC
    Madame Sin   tf   1.15.72 ABC
    The Judge and Jake Wyler   tf   12.2.72 NBC

DAVIS, GAIL
    Annie Oakley   sr   1.9.54 NN
    Annie Oakley   sr ret   fall, 1954 NN
    Annie Oakley   sr ret   fall, 1955 NN
    Andy Griffith Show   ep   11.27.61 CBS

DAVIS, JOAN
    I Married Joan   sr   10.15.52 NBC

I Married Joan   sr ret   fall, 1953 NBC
I Married Joan   sr ret   9.29.54 NBC
Mystery Show   ep   Blind Man's Bluff   9.11.60 NBC

DAVIS, NANCY

Schlitz Playhouse of Stars   ep   22 Sycamore Road   6.
   5.53 CBS
Ford Theatre   ep   First Born   9.10.53 NBC
Schlitz Playhouse of Stars   ep   The Pearl Street Inci-
   dent   5.14.54 CBS
Climax   ep   Bail Out at 43,000   12.29.55 CBS
G.E. Theatre   ep   That's the Man   4.15.56 CBS
G.E. Theatre   ep   Turkey for the President   11.23.58
   CBS
G.E. Theatre   ep   The Playoff   11.20.60 CBS
Zane Grey Theatre   ep   The Long Shadow   1.19.61
   CBS
Tall Man   ep   Shadow of the Past   10.7.61 NBC
G.E. Theatre   ep   Money and the Minister   11.26.61
   CBS
Dick Powell Theatre   ep   Obituary for Mr. "X"   1.23.
   62 NBC
87th Precinct   ep   King's Ransom   2.19.62 NBC
Wagon Train   ep   The Sam Darland Story   12.26.62
   ABC

DAVIS, OSSIE

Showtime U.S.A.   ep   Green Pastures   4.7.51 NN
Kraft Theatre   ep   The Emperor Jones   2.23.55 NBC
John Brown's Raid   Sp   10.25.60 NBC
Play of the Week   ep   Seven Times Monday   10.31.60
   NN
Defenders   ep   The Riot   10.17.61 CBS
Defenders   ep   Metamorphosis   3.2.63 CBS
Defenders   ep   The Star-Spangled Ghetto   11.1.63 CBS
Great Adventure   ep   Go Down, Moses   11.1.63 CBS
Defenders   ep   Mind Over Murder   5.16.64 CBS
Doctors/Nurses   ep   A Family Resemblance   11.17.64
   CBS
Defenders   ep   Fires of the Mind   2.18.65 CBS
Defenders   ep   Nobody Asks What Side You're On   3.
   11.65 CBS
Defenders   ep   The Sworn Twelve   3.25.65 CBS
Slattery's People   ep   What Can You Do with a Wounded
   Tiger   10.22.65 CBS
Look up and Live   ep   Continuity of Despair   2.6.66,
   2.13.66, 2.20.66 CBS

Fugitive   ep   Death Is the Door Prize   9. 20. 66 ABC
Run for Your Life   ep   A Game of Violence   11. 28. 66
   NBC
Run for Your Life   ep   1. 9. 67, 1. 16. 67 NBC
Outsider   ep   11. 21. 67 NBC
N. Y. P. D.   ep   Nothing Is Real but the Dead   3. 12. 68
   ABC
Name of the Game   ep   The Third Choice   3. 7. 69
   NBC
Bonanza   ep   The Wish   3. 9. 69 NBC
Night Gallery   tf   11. 8. 69 NBC
The Sheriff   tf   3. 30. 71 ABC

DAVIS, SAMMY, JR.
   G. E. Theatre   ep   Auf Widerschen   10. 5. 58 CBS
   Zane Grey Theatre   ep   Mission   11. 12. 59 CBS
   G. E. Theatre   ep   Memory in White   1. 8. 61 CBS
   Lawman   ep   Blue Boss and Willie Shay   3. 12. 61 ABC
   Frontier Circus   ep   Coals of Fire   1. 4. 62 CBS
   Hennesey   ep   1. 29. 62 CBS
   Dick Powell Theatre   ep   The Legend   2. 20. 62 NBC
   Rifleman   ep   The Most Amazing Man   11. 26. 62 ABC
   Ben Casey   ep   Allie   10. 2. 63 ABC
   Patty Duke Show   ep   Will the Real Sammy Davis Stand
      up   3. 3. 65 ABC
   Alice in Wonderland   Sp (voice only)   3. 30. 66 ABC
   Wild, Wild West   ep   The Night of the Returning Dead
      10. 14. 66 CBS
   I Dream of Jeannie   ep   2. 27. 67 NBC
   Danny Thomas Show   ep   The Enemy   11. 20. 67 NBC
   Mod Squad   ep   Keep the Faith, Baby   3. 25. 69 ABC
   The Pigeon   tf   11. 4. 69 ABC
   Beverly Hillbillies   ep   11. 12. 69 CBS
   Mod Squad   ep   2. 10. 70 ABC
   Mod Squad   ep   The Song of Willie   10. 20. 70 ABC
   Name of the Game   ep   I Love You Billy Baker   11. 20.
      70, 11. 27. 70 NBC
   The Trackers   tf   12. 14. 71 ABC

DAVISON, BRUCE
   Medical Center   ep   A Duel with Doom   2. 11. 70 CBS
   Owen Marshall   tf   9. 12. 71 ABC
   Marcus Welby, M. D.   ep   Love Is When They Say They
      Need You   9. 19. 72 ABC

DAWN, HAZEL
   Kraft Theatre   ep   Kitty Foyle   12. 2. 54 ABC

DAY, DENNIS
    Dennis Day Show   sr   2.8.52 NBC
    Dennis Day Show (a.k.a. RCA Victor Show)   sr 10.3.
      52 NBC
    Dennis Day Show   sr ret   10.5.53 NBC
    Babes in Toyland   Sp   12.18.54 NBC
    Babes in Toyland   Sp (restaged)   12.24.55 NBC
    Navy Log   ep hos   The Soapbox Kid   12.27.58 ABC
    Studio One   ep   The McTaggart Succession   5.5.58 CBS
    Alfred Hitchcock Presents   ep   Cheap Is Cheap   4.5.59
      CBS
    Burke's Law   ep   Who Killed Davidian Jones   12.30.64
      ABC
    Burke's Law   ep   Who Killed Rosie Sunset 1.27.65
      ABC
    Bing Crosby Show   ep   Operation Man Save   3.1.65
      CBS
    The Lucy Show   ep   10.23.67 CBS
    Love American Style   ep   11.24.69 ABC

DAY, DORIS
    Doris Day Show   sr   9.24.68 CBS
    Doris Day Show   sr ret   9.22.69 CBS
    Doris Day Show   sr ret   9.14.70 CBS
    Doris Day Show   sr ret   9.13.71 CBS
    Doris Day Show   sr ret   9.11.72 CBS

DAY, LARAINE
    Airflyte Theatre   ep   The Crisis   2.1.51 CBS
    Video Theatre   ep   Column Item   4.9.51 CBS
    Video Theatre   ep   It's a Promise   9.10.51 CBS
    Ford Theatre   ep   So Many Things Happen   12.18.52
      NBC
    G.E. Theatre   ep   Hired Mother   2.22.53 CBS
    Tales of the City   ep   7.9.53 CBS
    Video Theatre   ep   Women Who Wait   8.20.53 CBS
    Ford Theatre   ep   Double Bet   11.26.53 NBC
    Ford Theatre   ep   Turn Back the Clock   4.1.54 NBC
    Ford Theatre   ep   The Legal Beagles   11.25.54 NBC
    Lux Video Theatre   ep   Double Indemnity   12.16.54
      NBC
    Ford Theatre   ep   Too Old for Dolls   2.24.55 NBC
    Loretta Young Show   ep   Slander   10.30.55 NBC
    Screen Directors Playhouse   ep   Final Tribute   11.16.
      55 NBC
    Loretta Young Show   ep   A Pattern of Deceit   12.4.55
      NBC

Screen Directors Playhouse   ep   The Prima Donna
2. 1. 56 NBC
Lux Video Theatre   ep   Now, Voyager   10. 4. 56 NBC
Ford Theatre   ep   Woman Who Dared   11. 14. 56 ABC
Lux Video Theatre   ep   Obsessed   2. 28. 57 NBC
Ford Theatre   ep   Torn   5. 29. 57 ABC
Schlitz Playhouse of Stars   ep   Bitter Parting   10. 25.
57 CBS
Loretta Young Show   ep   Man in a Hurry   12. 15. 57
NBC
Theatre 59   ep   Alone   3. 4. 59 NBC
Playhouse 90   ep   Dark as the Night   6. 18. 59 CBS
Checkmate   ep   To the Best of My Knowledge   12. 27.
61 CBS
Follow the Sun   ep   Not Aunt Charlotte   3. 25. 62 ABC
New Breed   ep   A Motive Named Walter   5. 8. 62 ABC
Wagon Train   ep   12. 23. 63 ABC
Name of the Game   ep   The Taker   10. 4. 68 NBC
FBI   ep   10. 19. 69 ABC
Sixth Sense   ep   The Heart that Wouldn't Stay Buried
1. 22. 72 ABC

DEAN, JAMES
Summer Studio One   ep   Sentence of Death   8. 17. 53
CBS
Kraft Theatre   ep   A Long Time Till Dawn   fall, 1953
NBC
TV Sound Stage   ep   Life Sentence   10. 16. 53 NBC
Philco Playhouse   ep   Run Like a Thief   9. 5. 54 NBC
Schlitz Playhouse of Stars   ep   The Unlighted Road
5. 6. 55 CBS

DEAN, JIMMY
Daniel Boone   sr   3. 2. 67 NBC
Daniel Boone   sr ret   9. 19. 68 NBC
The Ballad of Andy Crocker   tf   11. 18. 69 ABC

DE BENNING, BURR
N. E. T. Playhouse   ep   Yes Is for a Very Young Man
3. 18. 66 NN
Iron Horse   ep   11. 21. 66 ABC
Run for Your Life   ep   3. 13. 67 NBC
Judd for the Defense   ep   10. 20. 67 ABC
Custer   ep   Breakout   11. 1. 67 ABC
Virginian   ep   The Storm Gate   11. 13. 68 NBC
FBI   ep   3. 24. 68 ABC
Ironside   ep   3. 28. 68 NBC

Outcasts   ep   9.23.68 ABC
FBI   ep   12.1.68 ABC
Lancer   ep   2.4.69 CBS
Name of the Game   ep   Wrath of Angels   2.28.69
    NBC
FBI   ep   Nightmare Road   9.21.69 ABC
Survivors   sr   11.69 ABC
Virginian   ep   Journey to Scathelock   12.10.69 NBC
Bonanza   ep   Is There any Man Here   2.8.70 NBC
Daniel Boone   ep   2.12.70 NBC
Bracken's World   ep   9.18.70 NBC
Dan August   ep   9.23.70 ABC
McCloud   ep   The Concrete Corral   9.30.70 CBS
City Beneath the Sea   tf   1.25.71 NBC
Mod Squad   ep   Is That Justice?   2.16.71 ABC
Ironside   ep   Grandmother's House   4.1.71 NBC
Mod Squad   ep   10.19.71 ABC
Cade's County   ep   11.21.71 CBS
Ironside   ep   1.27.72 NBC
FBI   ep   The Set-Up   2.13.72 ABC
Cannon   ep   3.14.72 CBS
Rookies   ep   11.27.72 ABC

DE CAMP, ROSEMARY
Life of Riley   sr   1949-1950 NBC
Ford Theatre   ep   Madame 44   3.5.53 NBC
Ford Theatre   ep   Alias Nora Hale   12.31.53 NBC
Ford Theatre   ep   Good of His Soul   3.4.54 NBC
Ford Theatre   ep   Segment   10.21.54 NBC
Love that Bob (a.k.a. The Bob Cummings Show)   sr
    1.2.55 NBC
Cavalcade Theatre   ep   Nobody's Fool   3.12.55 ABC
Love that Bob   sr ret   10.5.55 CBS
TV Reader's Digest   ep   The Sad Death of a Hero
    12.5.55 ABC
TV Reader's Digest   ep   The Old, Old Story   5.7.56
    ABC
Climax   ep   The 78th Floor   8.16.56 CBS
Love that Bob   sr ret   fall, 1956 CBS
Love that Bob   sr ret   9.25.57 NBC
Studio One   ep   Trial by Slander   1.20.58 CBS
Studio One   ep   No Place to Run   9.15.58 CBS
Love that Bob   sr ret   9.58 NBC
G.E. Theatre   ep   Night Club   10.11.59 CBS
Follow the Sun   ep   Chalk One up for Johnny   4.8.62
    ABC
Rawhide   ep   The House of the Hunter   4.20.62 CBS

Hazel   ep   Hazel's Cousin   9.20.62 NBC
Breaking Point   ep   A Little Anger Is a Good Thing
    11.25.63 ABC
Dr. Kildare   ep   Music Hath Charms   4.15.65 NBC
Amos Burke   ep   Operation Long Shadow   9.22.65
    ABC
That Girl   sr   9.8.66 ABC
That Girl   sr ret   9.7.67 ABC
Death Valley Days   ep   Canary Harris Vs the Almighty
    9.18.67 NN
Here Come the Brides   ep   3.5.69 ABC
Love American Style   ep   12.22.69 ABC
Mannix   ep   The Crime that Wasn't   1.30.71 CBS
Night Gallery   ep   12.15.71 NBC
Longstreet   ep   12.30.71 ABC
Call Holme   pt   4.24.72 NBC

DE CARLO, YVONNE
Ford Theatre   ep   Madame 44   9.24.53 NBC
Backbone of America   ep   12.29.53 NBC
Screen Directors Playhouse   ep   Hot Cargo   1.4.56
    NBC
Star Stage   ep   The Sainted General   4.6.56 NBC
Playhouse 90   ep   Verdict of Three   4.24.58 CBS
Bonanza   ep   A Rose for Lotta   9.12.59 NBC
Adventures in Paradise   ep   Isle of Eden   2.22.60 ABC
Follow the Sun   ep   The Longest Crap Game in History
    11.5.61 ABC
Follow the Sun   ep   Annie Beeler's Place   2.11.62 ABC
Virginian   ep   A Time Remembered   12.11.63 NBC
Burke's Law   ep   12.27.63 ABC
The Greatest Show on Earth   ep   3.10.64 ABC
The Munsters   sr   9.24.64 CBS
The Munsters   sr ret   9.16.65 NBC
The Girl from U.N.C.L.E.   ep   The Moulin Ruse Af-
    fair   1.17.67 NBC
Custer   ep   The Raiders   12.27.67 ABC
Virginian   ep   Crime Wave at Buffalo Springs   1.29.69
    NBC
Name of the Game   ep   Island of Gold and Precious
    Stones   1.16.70 NBC

DEE, FRANCES
Fireside Theatre   ep   Child in the House   1.30.51 NBC
Fireside Theatre   ep   The Green Convertible   6.5.51
    NBC
Ford Theatre   ep   Unbroken Promise   12.30.54 NBC

DEE, RUBY
    Play of the Week   ep   Seven Times Monday   10.31.60
        NN
    Play of the Week   ep   Black Monday   1.16.61 NN
    Alcoa Premiere   ep   Impact of an Execution   1.3.62
        ABC
    Nurses   ep   Express Stop from Lenox Avenue   5.9.63
        CBS
    Fugitive   ep   Decision in the Ring   10.22.63 ABC
    Great Adventure   ep   Go Down, Moses   11.1.63 CBS
    East Side/West Side   ep   No Hiding Place   12.2.63
        CBS
    Defenders   ep   The Sworn Twelve   3.25.65 CBS
    Look up and Live   ep   Continuity of Despair   2.6.66,
        2.13.66, 2.20.66 CBS
    Peyton Place   sr   9.68 ABC
    Deadlock   tf   2.22.69 NBC
    The Sheriff   tf   3.30.71 ABC
    N.E.T. Playhouse   ep   To Be Young, Gifted and Black
        1.22.72 NN

DEE, SANDRA
    Night Gallery   ep   Tell David   12.29.71 NBC
    The Daughters of Joshua Cabe   tf   9.12.72 ABC
    Love American Style   ep   9.15.72 ABC
    Night Gallery   ep   Spectre in Tap Shoes   10.29.72
        NBC
    Sixth Sense   ep   11.4.72 ABC

DE FORE, DON
    Silver Theatre   ep   Double Feature   4.17.50 CBS
    Silver Theatre   ep   Walt and Lavinia   6.5.50 CBS
    Hollywood Premiere Theatre   ep   Mr. and Mrs. De-
        tective   10.15.50 ABC
    Bigelow Theatre   ep   A Woman's Privilege   4.8.51
        CBS
    Bigelow-Sanford Theatre   ep   Always a Bridesmaid
        12.27.51 NN
    Schlitz Playhouse of Stars   ep   The Marriage of Lit-
        Lit   9.12.52 CBS
    Ozzie and Harriet   sr   10.10.52 ABC
    Hollywood Opening Night   ep   The Romantic Type   2.
        23.53 NBC
    Goodyear Playhouse   ep   The Power of Suggestion   8.
        29.54 NBC
    Science Fiction Theatre   ep Time Is Just a Place   4.
        15.55 NBC

Schlitz Playhouse of Stars   ep   A Gift of Life   11. 4. 55
    CBS
Ozzie and Harriet   ep   Ozzie the Treasurer   5. 1. 57
    ABC
Ford Theatre   ep   The Idea Man   5. 8. 57 ABC
Ozzie and Harriet   ep   The Ladder   12. 31. 58 ABC
G. E. Theatre   ep   The Lady's Choice   3. 22. 59 CBS
The Philadelphia Story   Sp   12. 7. 59 NBC
Ozzie and Harriet   ep   Volunteer Fireman   1. 13. 60 ABC
Loretta Young Show   ep   Plain, Unmarked Envelope   4.
    3. 60 NBC
Best of the Post   ep   Suicide Flight   12. 10. 60 ABC
Alfred Hitchcock Presents   ep   Coming Mama   4. 11. 61
    NBC
Hazel   sr   9. 28. 61 NBC
Hazel   sr ret   9. 20. 62 NBC
Ozzie and Harriet   ep   The Boys Earn Some Christmas
    Money   12. 6. 62 ABC
Hazel   sr ret   9. 19. 63 NBC
Hazel   sr ret   9. 17. 64 NBC
Hallmark Hall of Fame   ep   A Punt, a Pass, and a
    Prayer   11. 20. 68 NBC
My Three Sons   ep   3. 22. 69 CBS
Mod Squad   ep   A Place to Run   12. 2. 69 ABC
Mannix   ep   Murder Revisited   3. 7. 70 CBS
Men from Shiloh   ep   9. 16. 70 NBC

DE HAVEN, GLORIA
Musical Comedy Time   ep   Miss Liberty   1. 8. 51 NBC
Appointment with Adventure   ep   The Snow People   7.
    31. 55 CBS
Robert Montgomery Presents   ep   The Briefcase   3. 12.
    56 NBC
Mr. Broadway   Sp   5. 11. 57 NBC
Ellery Queen   ep   Body of the Crime   5. 29. 59 NBC
Johnny Ringo   ep   12. 17. 59 CBS
Wagon Train   ep   The Alison Justice Story   10. 19. 60
    NBC
Adventures in Paradise   ep   The Jonah Stone   4. 31. 61
    ABC
Defenders   ep   Gideon's Theatre Follies   12. 23. 61 CBS
Lloyd Bridges Show   ep   Gym in January   3. 19. 63 CBS
Burke's Law   ep   12. 23. 64 ABC
As the World Turns   sr   1967 CBS
Flipper   ep   1. 21. 67 NBC
Mannix   ep   9. 30. 67 CBS
Call Her Mom   tf   2. 15. 72 ABC

Jimmy Stewart Show   ep   3.5.72 NBC
Wednesday Night Out   pt   4.24.72 NBC

DE HAVILLAND, OLIVIA
ABC Stage 67   ep   Noon Wine   11.23.66 ABC
Danny Thomas Show   ep   The Last Hunters   1.29.68 NBC
The Screaming Woman   tf   1.29.72 ABC

DEKKER, ALBERT
Fireside Theatre   ep   The Human Touch   6.6.50 NBC
Pulitzer Prize Playhouse   ep   Valley Forge   2.23.51 ABC
Hollywood Opening Night   ep   The Housekeeping   2.29.52 CBS
TV Workshop   ep   The Million Dollar Trio   4.6.52 NBC
Dark Adventure   ep   The Housekeeper   4.27.53 ABC
Goodyear Playhouse   ep   The Chivington Road   3.27.55 NBC
Playwrights '56   ep   The Answer   10.4.55 NBC
Playwrights '56   ep   Flight   2.28.56 NBC
Climax   ep   Fear Is the Hunter   7.12.56 CBS
Play of the Week   ep   Emmanuel   12.19.60 NN
Witness   ep   1.5.61 CBS
Naked City   ep   A Kettle of Precious Fish   5.31.61 ABC
Westinghouse Presents   ep   The Dispossessed   10.24.61 CBS
Naked City   ep   Bridge Party   12.27.61 ABC
Defenders   ep   King of the Hill   12.30.61 CBS
Kraft Suspense Theatre   ep   The World I Want   10.1.64 NBC
Rawhide   ep   Josh   1.15.65 CBS
Trials of O'Brien   ep   Bargain Day on the Street of Regret   9.25.65 CBS
Rawhide   ep   Crossing at White Feather   12.7.65 CBS
Death of a Salesman   Sp   5.8.66 CBS
N.E.T. Playhouse   ep   Ten Blocks on the Camino Real   10.7.66 NN
The Man from U.N.C.L.E.   ep   9.11.67 NBC
Run for Your Life   ep   A Dangerous Proposal   1.3.68 NBC
Judd for the Defense   ep   1.26.88 ABC
I Spy   ep   3.4.68 NBC
Bonanza   ep   The Bottle Fighter   5.12.68 NBC

DELL, CLAUDIA
Fireside Theatre   ep   The Rivals   5.13.52 NBC

DELL, GABRIEL
  Naked City   ep   Man without a Skin   2.6.63 ABC
  Ben Casey   ep   10.25.65 ABC
  Mannix   ep   11.25.67 CBS
  Then Came Bronson   ep   Old Tigers Never Die   11.5.
      69 NBC
  Name of the Game   ep   Appointment in Palermo   2.26.
      71 NBC
  McCloud   ep   11.24.71 NBC
  Corner Bar   sr   6.21.72 ABC
  Banyon   ep   10.13.72 NBC

DELMAR, KENNY
  U.S. Steel Hour   ep   Good for You   6.8.54 ABC
  Elgin Hour   ep   The $1,000 Window   3.22.55 CBS
  U.S. Steel Hour   ep   The Meanest Man in the World
      7.6.55 CBS
  Goodyear Playhouse   ep   Suit Yourself   9.11.55 NBC
  Studio One   ep   A Most Contagious Game   10.17.55 CBS
  U.S. Steel Hour   ep   Shoot it Again   10.26.55 CBS
  Armstrong Circle Theatre   ep   Actual   11.1.55 NBC
  Kraft Theatre   ep   Paper Foxhole   4.4.56 NBC
  Kraft Theatre   ep   The Gentle Grafter   4.25.56 NBC
  Studio One   ep   The Star Spangled Soldier   5.21.56 CBS
  Playhouse 90   ep   Snow Shoes   1.3.57 CBS
  Car 54 Where Are You   ep   A Star Is Born in the
      Bronx   11.25.62 NBC

DEL RIO, DOLORES
  Schlitz Playhouse of Stars   ep   Old Spanish Custom   6.
      7.57 CBS
  U.S. Steel Hour   ep   The Public Prosecutor   4.23.58
      CBS
  I Spy   ep   Return to Glory   2.23.66 NBC
  Branded   ep   The Ghost of Murietta   3.20.66 NBC
  Marcus Welby, M.D.   ep   The Legacy   1.27.70 ABC

DENNING, RICHARD
  Mr. and Mrs. North   sr   10.3.52 CBS
  Cavalcade of America   ep   The Man Who Took a Chance
      10.29.52 NBC
  Ford Theatre   ep   The Doctor's Downfall   10.8.53 NBC
  Mr. and Mrs. North   sr ret   2.2.54 NBC
  Schlitz Playhouse of Stars   ep   Tapu   4.2.54 CBS
  Pitfall   ep   The Hot Welcome   7.18.54 NN
  Ford Theatre   ep   The Legal Beagles   11.25.54 NBC
  Mr. and Mrs. North   sr ret   2.25.55 NN

Ford Theatre ep All That Glitters 10.6.55 NBC
Crossroads ep Chinese Checkers 12.16.55 ABC
Ford Theatre ep Double Trouble 3.22.56 NBC
Ford Theatre ep On the Beach 4.12.56 NBC
Cheyenne ep 6.5.56 ABC
Ford Theatre ep The Idea Man 5.8.57 ABC
G.E. Theatre ep Eyes of a Stranger 12.8.57 CBS
G.E. Theatre ep Letters from Cairo 1.12.58 CBS
Studio One ep The Laughing Willow 2.3.58 CBS
Michael Shayne sr 9.30.60 NBC
Going My Way ep Don't Forget to Say Goodbye 1.23.
  63 ABC
Karen sr 10.5.64 NBC
Alice Through the Looking Glass 11.6.66 NBC
I Spy ep 2.5.68 NBC
Hawaii Five-O sr 9.26.68 CBS
Hawaii Five-O sr ret 9.24.69 CBS
Hawaii Five-O sr ret 9.16.70 CBS
Hawaii Five-O sr ret 9.14.71 CBS
Hawaii Five-O sr ret 9.12.72 CBS

DENNIS, SANDY
Naked City ep Idylls of a Running Back 9.26.62 ABC
Naked City ep Carrier 4.24.63 ABC
Fugitive ep The Other Side of the Mountain 10.1.63
  ABC
Arrest and Trial ep Somewhat Lower than Angels
  2.2.64 ABC
Mr. Broadway ep Don't Mention My Name in Sheboy-
  gan 10.7.64 CBS
A Hatful of Rain Sp 3.3.68 ABC
Something Evil tf 1.21.72 CBS

DENNY, REGINALD
Drama ep The Invisible Wound 12.22.50 NN
Personal Appearance Theatre ep I Wake up Smiling
  1.5.52 ABC
Cavalcade Theatre ep All's Well with Lydia 10.15.52
  NBC
Schaefer Century Theatre ep 12.14.52 NBC
Fireside Theatre ep The Deauville Bracelet 6.9.53
  NBC
Cavalcade Theatre ep The Stolen General 10.6.53
  ABC
Ford Theatre ep Mason-Dixon Line 6.10.54 NBC
Colgate Comedy Hour ep Roberta 4.10.55 NBC
Playhouse 90 ep Helen Morgan Story 5.16.57 CBS

Topper   ep The Neighbors   6.3.55 CBS
Fireside Theatre   ep The Sport   10.4.55 NBC
Climax   ep The Hanging Judge   1.12.56 CBS
Telephone Time   ep Grandpa Changes the World   7.22.
    56 CBS
Matinee Theatre   ep Perfect Alibi   8.10.56 NBC
Family Classics   ep The Scarlet Pimpernel   10.28.60
    CBS
Bringing Up Buddy   ep Cousin Jordan   1.30.61 CBS
Adventures in Paradise   ep Policeman's Holiday   1.28.
    62 ABC
Bob Hope Chrysler Theatre   ep The Timothy Heist
    10.30.64 NBC
Please Don't Eat the Daisies   ep   11.16.65 NBC
Batman   ep A Riddle a Day   2.16.66, 2.17.66 ABC

DENVER, BOB
    (The Many Loves of) Dobie Gillis   sr   9.29.59 CBS
    Dobie Gillis   sr ret fall, 1960 CBS
    Dobie Gillis   sr ret 10.10.61 CBS
    Dobie Gillis   sr ret fall, 1962 CBS
    Dr. Kildare   ep If You Can't Believe the Truth   10.10.
        63 NBC
    Farmer's Daughter   ep An Enterprising Young Man
        10.11.63 ABC
    Gilligan's Island   sr   9.26.64 ABC
    Gilligan's Island   sr ret 9.16.65 CBS
    Gilligan's Island   sr ret 9.12.66 CBS
    Good Guys   sr   9.25.68 CBS
    Good Guys   sr ret 9.26.69 CBS
    Love American Style   ep   1.30.70 ABC
    Love American Style   ep   1.22.71 ABC

DEREK, JOHN
    Ford Theatre   ep Tomorrow's Men   10.29.53 NBC
    Ford Theatre   ep Black Jack Hawk   10.31.56 ABC
    Playhouse 90   ep Massacre at Sand Creek   12.27.56
        CBS
    Zane Grey Theatre   ep There Were Four   3.15.57 CBS
    Zane Grey Theatre   ep Storm over Eden   5.4.61 CBS
    Frontier Circus   sr   10.5.61 CBS

DERN, BRUCE
    Surfside 6   ep Daphne, Girl Detective   10.9.61 ABC
    Ben Casey   ep Dark Night for Bill Harris   12.18.61
        ABC
    Detectives   ep Act of God   12.29.61 NBC

Stoney Burke   sr   10.1.62 ABC
Law and Mr. Jones   ep   Poor Eddie's Dead   10.4.62
     ABC
Wagon Train   ep   The Eli Bancroft Story   11.11.63 ABC
Kraft Suspense Theatre   ep   The Hunt   12.19.63 NBC
Outer Limits   ep   The Zanti Misfits   12.30.63 ABC
77 Sunset Strip   ep   Lovers' Lane   1.3.64 ABC
Fugitive   ep   Come Watch Me Die   1.21.64 ABC
Laf Hit   ep   Night Caller   1.31.64 CBS
The Greatest Show on Earth   ep   The Last of the Strong-
     men   3.3.64 ABC
Wagon Train   ep   Those Who Stay Behind   11.8.64 ABC
Alfred Hitchcock Theatre   ep   Lonely Place   11.16.64
     NBC
Fugitive   ep   Corner of Hell   2.9.65 ABC
12 O'Clock High   ep   The Mission   4.2.65 ABC
Wagon Train   ep   4.18.65 ABC
Rawhide   ep   Walk into Terror   9.21.65 CBS
Virginian   ep   A Little Learning   9.29.65 NBC
Gunsmoke   ep   10.9.65 CBS
Shenandoah   ep   The Verdict   11.1.65 ABC
Gunsmoke   ep   11.27.65 CBS
12 O'Clock High   ep   The Jones Boy   12.6.65 ABC
FBI   ep   Pound of Flesh   12.19.65 ABC
Big Valley   ep   2.9.66 ABC
Loner   ep   To Hang a Dead Man   3.12.66 CBS
Big Valley   ep   3.30.66 ABC
Big Valley   ep   9.12.66 ABC
Gunsmoke   ep   10.1.66 CBS
Run for Your Life   ep   The Treasure Seekers   11.14.
     66 NBC
Fugitive   ep   12.6.66 ABC
Run for Your Life   ep   10.25.67 NBC
Big Valley   ep   12.4.67 ABC
Bonanza   ep   1.7.68 NBC
Lancer   ep   10.29.68 CBS
FBI   ep   The Nightmare   11.10.68 ABC
Big Valley   ep   12.16.68 ABC
Gunsmoke   ep   The Long Night   2.17.69 CBS
Then Came Bronson   ep   Amid Splinters of the Thunder-
     bolt   10.22.69 NBC
Land of the Giants   ep   Wild Journey 3.6.70 ABC
Bonanza   ep   The Gold Mine   3.8.70 NBC
High Chaparral   ep   Only the Bad Come to Sonora   10.
     2.70 NBC
Sam Hill: Who Killed the Mysterious Mr. Foster
     tf 2.1.71 NBC

DE SICA, VITTORIO
    Four Just Men   sr   fall, 1959 NN

DESMOND, JOHNNY
    Danger   ep   Sing for Your Life   4.28.53 CBS
    Philco Playhouse   ep   Hearts and Flowers   3.6.55 NBC
    Robert Montgomery Presents   ep   Don't Do Me Any
        Favors   4.30.56 NBC
    Philco Playhouse   ep   The Miss America Story   9.4.55
        NBC
    Alcoa Hour   ep   The Stingiest Man in Town   12.23.56
        NBC
    Climax   ep   Keep Me in Mind   11.7.57 CBS
    Sally   ep   Dear Myrtle   3.30.58 NBC
    Desilu Playhouse   ep   Diamond for Carla   9.14.59 CBS
    U.S. Steel Hour   ep   Dry Rain   9.5.62 CBS

DEUEL, PETE
    Combat   ep   Vendetta   9.22.64 ABC
    Gidget   sr   9.15.65 ABC
    FBI   ep   Slow March up a Steep Hill   10.10.65 ABC
    Love on a Roof Top   sr   9.13.66 ABC
    FBI   ep   12.10.67 ABC
    Virginian   ep   The Good-Hearted Badman   2.7.68 NBC
    Ironside   ep   3.7.68 NBC
    Name of the Game   cp   11.29.68 NBC
    Virginian   ep   The Price of Love   2.12.69 NBC
    The Young Country   tf   3.17.70 ABC
    Matt Lincoln   ep   10.29.70 ABC
    Interns   ep   The Price of Life   10.30.70 CBS
    Young Lawyers   ep   The Glass Prison   11.2.70 ABC
    Bold Ones   ep   Trial of a Pfc   11.8.70 NBC
    The Psychiatrist: God Bless the Children   tf   12.14.70
        NBC
    Alias Smith and Jones   tf   1.5.71 ABC
    Alias Smith and Jones   sr   1.21.71 ABC
    Marcus Welby, M.D.   ep   A Passing of Torches   1.26.
        71 ABC
    Name of the Game   ep   The Savage Eye   2.19.71 NBC
    Alias Smith and Jones   sr ret   9.16.71 ABC
    TV Theatre   ep   The Scarecrow   1.10.72 NN

DEVINE, ANDY
    Wild Bill Hickok   sr   7.3.51 ABC
    Wild Bill Hickok   sr ret   fall, 1952 ABC
    Wild Bill Hickok   sr ret   fall, 1953 ABC
    Wild Bill Hickok   sr ret   fall, 1954 ABC

Andy's Gang   sr   9.20.55 NBC
Wagon Train   ep   The Jess MacAbbee Story   11.25.59
   NBC
Barbara Stanwyck Theatre   ep   Big Jake   6.5.61 NBC
Twilight Zone   ep   Hocus Pocus and Frisby   4.13.62
   CBS
Burke's Law   ep   Who Killed Victor Barrows   1.17.64
   ABC
My Three Sons   ep   3.25.65 ABC
Rounders   ep   11.29.66 ABC
Rounders   ep   12.20.66 ABC
Virginian   ep   1.18.67 NBC
World of Disney   ep   Ride a Northbound Horse   3.16.
   69, 3.23.69 NBC
The Over the Hill Gang   tf   10.7.69 ABC
Love American Style   ep   12.8.69 ABC
World of Disney   ep   Smoke   2.1.70, 2.18.70 NBC
Bracken's World   ep   2.6.70 NBC
The Over the Hill Gang Rides Again   tf   11.17.70 ABC
Men from Shiloh   ep   1.20.71 NBC
Alias Smith and Jones   ep   1.27.72 ABC

DEWHURST, COLLEEN
Dupont Show of the Month   ep   The Count of Monte
   Cristo   10.28.58 CBS
U.S. Steel Hour   ep   The Hours Before Dawn   9.23.59
   CBS
Drama   ep   How Long the Night   9.30.59 NN
Play of the Week   ep   Medea   10.12.59 NN
Play of the Week   ep   Burning Bright   10.26.59 NN
Dupont Show of the Month   ep   I, Don Quixote   11.9.59
   CBS
Play of the Week   ep   No Exit   2.27.61 NN
Ben Casey   ep   I Remember a Lemon Tree   10.23.61
   ABC
Focus   ep   1.21.62 NBC
Nurses   ep   The Fly Shadow   10.11.62 CBS
Eleventh Hour   ep   I Don't Belong in a White-Painted
   House   10.24.62 NBC
U.S. Steel Hour   ep   Night Run to the West   2.20.63
   CBS
Dupont Show of the Month   ep   Something to Hide   5.5.
   63 NBC
East Side/West Side   ep   Nothing but the Half Truth
   3.30.64 CBS
Dr. Kildare   ep   All Brides Should be Beautiful   3.11.
   65 NBC

FBI   ep   The Baby Sitter   2. 12. 66 ABC
Play of the Week   ep   Burning Bright   10. 19. 66 NN
The Crucible   Sp   5. 4. 67 CBS
Showcase   ep   My Mother's House   5. 7. 67 NN
Big Valley   ep   A Day of Terror   12. 12. 67 NBC
Hallmark Hall of Fame   ep   The Price   2. 3. 71 NBC
Hallmark Hall of Fame   ep   The Hands of Cormac   11.
    17. 72 NBC

DE WILDE, BRANDON

Philco Playhouse   ep   No Medals on Pop   3. 11. 51 NBC
Philco Playhouse   ep   A Cowboy for Chris   5. 18. 52
    NBC
Plymouth Playhouse   ep   Jamie   4. 26. 53 ABC
Jamie   sr   10. 5. 53 ABC
Jamie   sr ret   9. 27. 54 ABC
Light's Diamond Jubilee   ep   The Leader of the People
    10. 24. 54 ABC, CBS, NBC
Climax   ep   The Day They Gave Babies Away   12. 22. 55
    CBS
Climax   ep   An Episode of Sparrows   3. 29. 56 CBS
Star Stage   ep   Bend to the Wind   5. 4. 56 NBC
U. S. Steel Hour   ep   The Locked Door   11. 6. 57 CBS
Alcoa Hour   ep   Man of His House   3. 9. 59 NBC
Wagon Train   ep   The Danny Benedict Story   12. 2. 59
    NBC
Men from Shiplan   ep   10. 21. 60 ABC
CBS TV Workshop   ep   My Theory about Girls   11. 27.
    60 CBS
Thriller   ep   Pigeons from Hell   6. 6. 61 NBC
Wagon Train   ep   The Mark Minor Story   11. 15. 61 NBC
Virginian   ep   50 Days to Moose Jaw   12. 12. 62 NBC
Nurses   ep   Ordeal   11. 14. 63   CBS
The Greatest Show on Earth   ep   Love the Giver   4. 7.
    64 ABC
World of Disney   ep   The Tenderfoot   10. 8. 64, 10. 25.
    64, 11. 1. 64 NBC
Defenders   ep   The Objector   2. 11. 65 CBS
Combat   ep   Sudden Terror   3. 29. 66 ABC
ABC Stage 67   ep   The Confession   10. 19. 66 ABC
Virginian   ep   The Orchard   10. 2. 68 NBC
Journey to the Unknown   ep   One on a Desert Island 12.
    19. 68 ABC
Name of the Game   ep   The Bobby Currier Story   2. 21.
    69 NBC
Hawaii Five-O   ep   The King Kamehameha Blues   11.
    12. 69 CBS

Love American Style   ep   12.22.69 ABC
Young Rebels   ep   To Hang a Hero   10.11.70 ABC
Night Gallery   ep   9.22.71 NBC
Ironside   ep   10.19.71 NBC

DE WOLFE, BILLY
Imogene Coca Show   sr   10.2.54 NBC
Burke's Law   ep   2.10.65 ABC
Bob Hope Chrysler Theatre   ep   Cops and Robbers   2.
   19.65 NBC
Dick van Dyke Show   ep   The Ugliest Dog in the World
   10.6.65 CBS
That Girl   sr   9.8.66 ABC
Rango   ep   2.24.67 ABC
Good Morning World   sr   9.5.67 CBS
Queen and I   sr   1.16.69 CBS
Arsenic and Old Lace   Sp   4.2.69 ABC
Here's Debbie   ep   2.10.70 NBC
Doris Day Show   ep   3.30.70 CBS
Doris Day Show   sr   9.28.70 CBS
Doris Day Show   sr ret   9.13.71 CBS

DEXTER, BRAD
Wagon Train   ep   The Sally Potter Story   4.9.58 NBC
Jefferson Drum   ep   The Keeney Gang   10.3.58 NBC
77 Sunset Strip   ep   The Bouncing Ship   11.7.58 ABC
Zane Grey Theatre   ep   The Tall Shadow   11.20.58
   CBS
Cimarron City   ep   Return of the Dead   2.14.59 NBC
Jefferson Drum   ep   3.5.59 NBC
Yancy Derringer   ep   V as in Voodoo   5.14.59 CBS
77 Sunset Strip   ep   Thanks for Tomorrow   10.30.59
   ABC
Bronco   ep   Night Train to Denver   12.29.59 ABC
Tightrope   ep   Broken Rope   1.21.60 CBS
Bat Masterson   ep   Cattle and Cane   3.3.60 NBC
Aquanauts   ep   The Big Swim   12.14.60 CBS
Hawaiian Eye   ep   Made in Japan   1.4.61 ABC
G.E. Theatre   ep   A Possibility of Oil   2.19.61 CBS
Tales of Wells Fargo   ep   Stage from Yuma   3.20.61
   NBC
Surfside 6   ep   A Double Image   4.10.61 ABC
Investigators   ep   Murder on Order   10.5.61 CBS
Alcoa Premiere   ep   The Breaking Point   12.5.61 ABC
Mannix   ep   12.22.71 CBS
Mission Impossible   ep   The Bride   1.1.72 CBS

DICKINSON, ANGIE
   Matinee Theatre ep Technique 12.20.55 NBC
   Lineup ep 2.10.56 CBS
   G.E. Theatre ep Try to Remember 2.26.56 CBS
   It's a Great Life ep The Voice 3.4.56 NBC
   Wyatt Earp ep One of Jesse's Gang 3.13.56 ABC
   It's a Great Life ep The Raffle Ticket 4.8.56 NBC
   The Millionaire ep The Story of Jane Carr 9.19.56
     CBS
   Gunsmoke ep Sins of the Fathers 1.19.57 CBS
   Cheyenne ep War Party 2.12.57 ABC
   Meet McGraw ep Tycoon 7.9.57 NBC
   Alcoa Theatre ep Circumstantial 10.4.57 NBC
   Lineup ep 11.15.57 CBS
   M Squad ep Diamond Hard 11.29.57 NBC
   Meet McGraw ep McGraw in Reno 12.3.57 NBC
   Mike Hammer ep Letter Edged in Blackmail 1.28.58
     CBS
   Perry Mason ep The Case of the One Eyed Witness
     2.22.58 CBS
   Bob Cummings Show ep Bob and Automation 2.25.58
     NBC
   Tombstone Territory ep Geronimo 3.5.58 ABC
   Lineup ep The Harger Jameson Case 4.4.58 CBS
   Northwest Passage ep Bound Women 10.12.58 NBC
   Men into Space ep Moon Probe 9.30.59 CBS
   Checkmate ep Remembrance of Crimes Past 2.28.62
     CBS
   Alfred Hitchcock Theatre ep Captive Audience 10.18.
     62 CBS
   Bob Hope Chrysler Theatre ep A Killing at Sundial
     10.4.63 NBC
   Alfred Hitchcock Theatre ep 2.1.65 NBC
   Dr. Kildare ep Do You Trust Your Doctor 3.4.65
     NBC
   Dr. Kildare ep She Loves Me, She Loves Me Not 3.
     25.65 NBC
   The Poppy Is Also a Flower tf 4.22.66 ABC
   Virginian ep Ride to Delphi 9.21.66 NBC
   Bob Hope Chrysler Theatre ep And Baby Makes Five
     10.5.66 NBC
   A Case of Libel Sp 2.11.68 ABC
   The Love War tf 3.10.70 ABC
   Thief tf 10.9.71 ABC
   Man and the City ep 11.3.71 ABC
   See the Man Run tf 12.11.71 ABC

Ghost Story   ep   12.15.72 NBC

DILLER, PHYLLIS
Pruitts of Southampton   sr   9.13.66 ABC
That's Life   ep   3.11.69 ABC
Love American Style   ep   Love and the Phonies   10.27.
69 ABC
Night Gallery   ep   Pamela's Voice   1.13.71 NBC
Love American Style   ep   11.5.71 ABC

DILLMAN, BRADFORD
Kraft Theatre   ep   Strangers in Hiding 12.29.54 NBC
Pond's Theatre   ep   The Kingdom of Andrew Jones 5.
26.55 ABC
Hallmark Hall of Fame   ep   There Shall Be No Night
3.17.57 NBC
Omnibus   ep   Stover at Yale   10.20.57 NBC
Climax   ep   A Matter of Life and Death   11.21.57 CBS
Alcoa Premiere   ep   The Voice of Charlie Pont   10.25.
62 ABC
Eleventh Hour   ep   Eat Little Fishie, Eat   12.5.62 NBC
Naked City   ep   Her Life in Moving Pictures   1.2.63
ABC
Alfred Hitchcock Theatre   ep   To Catch a Butterfly   2.
1.63 CBS
Alcoa Premiere   ep   Chain Reaction   2.21.63 ABC
Virginian   ep   Echo from Another Day   3.27.63 NBC
Espionage   ep   A Covenant with Death   10.2.63 NBC
The Greatest Show on Earth   ep   Don't Look Down,
Don't Look Back   10.8.63 ABC
Kraft Suspense Theatre   ep   The Case against Paul
Ryker   10.10.63, 10.17.63 NBC
Wagon Train   ep   The Kitty Pryer Story   11.18.63 ABC
Dr. Kildare   ep   Night of the Beast   1.2.64 NBC
Nurses   ep   Credo   1.9.64 CBS
Ben Casey   ep   The Bark of a Three-Headed Hound   2.
12.64 ABC
Breaking Point   ep   Shadows of a Starless Night   3.9.64
ABC
Profiles in Courage   ep   3.21.65 NBC
Dr. Kildare   ep   The Atheist and the True Believer   1.
3.66, 1.4.66, 1.11.66, 1.12.66, 1.17.66, 1.18.66
NBC
12 O'Clock High   ep   25th Mission   2.14.66 ABC
FBI   ep   The Divided Man   3.20.66 ABC
Court Martial   sr   4.8.66 ABC
Hawk   ep   Death Comes Full Circle   10.6.66 ABC
Bob Hope Chrysler Theatre   ep   Crazier than Cotton

10. 12. 66 NBC
Shane ep The Great Invasion 12. 17. 66, 12. 24. 66 ABC
Bob Hope Chrysler Theatre ep The Lady Is My Wife
    2. 1. 67 NBC
FBI ep 2. 26. 67 ABC
Felony Squad ep 10. 2. 67 ABC
The Man from U. N. C. L. E. ep The Prince of Darkness
    Affair 10. 2. 67, 10. 9. 67 NBC
Big Valley ep A Noose Is Waiting 11. 13. 67 ABC
Judd for the Defense ep 1. 5. 68, 1. 12. 68 ABC
Danny Thomas Show ep Measure of a Man 1. 22. 68
    NBC
FBI ep 3. 3. 68 ABC
Wild, Wild West ep 11. 17. 67 CBS
Mission Impossible ep 3. 17. 68 CBS
Name of the Game ep The Taker 10. 4. 68 NBC
Fear No Evil tf 3. 3. 69 NBC
Bold Ones ep Crisis 12. 7. 69 NBC
Marcus Welby, M. D. ep The Chemistry of Hope 12.
    16. 69 ABC
Ironside ep 3. 26. 70 NBC
FBI ep The Traitor 9. 27. 70 ABC
Medical Center ep 10. 7. 70 CBS
Ironside ep This Could Blow Your Mind 12. 17. 70 NBC
Men from Shiloh ep The Legacy of Spencer Flats 1.
    27. 71 NBC
Longstreet tf 2. 23. 71 ABC
Five Desperate Women tf 9. 28. 71 ABC
FBI ep The Mastermind 10. 17. 71 ABC
Bonanza ep Face of Fear 11. 14. 71 NBC
Night Gallery ep Ickman's Model 12. 1. 71 NBC
Mission Impossible ep 1. 8. 72 CBS
Alias Smith and Jones ep 1. 13. 72 ABC
The Eyes of Charles Sand tf 2. 29. 72 ABC
The Delphi Bureau tf 3. 6. 72 ABC
Cannon ep 3. 7. 72 CBS
Mod Squad ep The Connection 9. 14. 72 ABC
Moon of the Wolf tf 9. 26. 72 ABC
Columbo ep 10. 15. 72 NBC

DINGLE, CHARLES
    Pulitzer Prize Playhouse ep The Late Christopher
        Bean 10. 27. 50 ABC
    Pulitzer Prize Playhouse ep Our Town 12. 1. 50 ABC
    Pulitzer Prize Playhouse ep The Just and the Unjust
        3. 30. 51 ABC
    Pulitzer Prize Playhouse ep Ice Bound 4. 13. 51 ABC

Pulitzer Prize Playhouse   ep   The Stolen City   5.25.
    51 ABC
Lights Out   ep   Dead Freight   6.18.51 NBC
Schlitz Playhouse of Stars   ep   Decision and Daniel
    Webster   11.9.51 CBS
Theatre for You   ep   Babylon Revisited   10.6.53 NN
Center Stage   ep   Lucky Louie   7.27.54 ABC
The Web   ep   The House   8.29.54 CBS
Elgin Hour   ep   The Flood   10.5.54 ABC
Road of Life   sr   12.13.54 CBS
Elgin Hour   ep   Black Eagle Pass   4.5.55 ABC
Kraft Theatre   ep   Judge Contain's Hotel   5.11.55 NBC
Philco Playhouse   ep   Incident in July   7.10.55 NBC
Studio One   ep   Like Father, Like Son   9.19.55 CBS
Philco Playhouse   ep   The Mechanical Heart   11.6.55
    NBC
Robert Montgomery Presents   ep   Lucifer   12.5.55
    NBC
Big Story   ep   Miracle in the Desert   12.9.55 NBC

DIXON, IVAN
    Dupont Show of the Month   ep   Arrowsmith   1.17.60
        CBS
    Twilight Zone   ep   Big Tall Wish   4.8.60 CBS
    Have Gun Will Travel   ep   2.4.61 CBS
    Cain's Hundred   ep   Blues for a Junkman   2.20.62
        NBC
    Target Corruptors   ep   Journey into Mourning   4.13.62
        ABC
    Dr. Kildare   ep   Something of Importance   5.3.62 NBC
    Laramie   ep   Among the Missing   9.25.62 NBC
    Defenders   ep   Man Against Himself   1.12.63 CBS
    Stoney Burke   ep   The Test   5.13.63 ABC
    Perry Mason   ep   The Case of the Nebulous Nephew
        9.26.63 CBS
    Outer Limits   ep   The Human Factor 11.11.63 ABC
    Great Adventures   ep   The Special Courage of Captain
        Pratt 2.14.64 CBS
    Twilight Zone   ep   I am the Night--Color Me Black
        3.27.64 CBS
    The Man from U.N.C.L.E   ep   The Vulcan Affair   9.
        22.64 NBC
    Fugitive   ep   Escape into Black   11.17.64 ABC
    Outer Limits   ep   The Inheritors   11.21.64, 11.28.64
        ABC
    Defenders   ep   The Non-Violent   4.1.65 CBS
    I Spy   ep   So Long, Patrick Henry   9.15.65 NBC

Hogan's Heroes   sr   9.17.65 CBS
Fugitive   ep   3.28.67 ABC
Hogan's Heroes   sr ret   9.66 CBS
Hogan's Heroes   sr ret   9.9.67 CBS
Felony Squad   ep   The Deadly Junkman   10.16.67 ABC
Ironside   ep   Backfire   11.2.67 NBC
Hogan's Heroes   sr ret   9.28.68 CBS
It Takes a Thief   ep   10.22.68 ABC
Name of the Game   ep   12.13.68 NBC
Mod Squad   ep   Return to Darkness, Return to Light 3.
    17.70 ABC
FBI   ep   The Deadly Pact   11.7.70 ABC
Love American Style   ep   11.12.71 ABC

DOMERGUE, FAITH
    Mirror Theatre   ep   Equal Justice   10.17.53 CBS
    Fireside Theatre   ep   Retribution   3.23.54 NBC
    Schlitz Playhouse of Stars   ep   The Roman and the
        Renegade   8.6.54 CBS
    Ford Theatre   ep   The Road Ahead   11.11.54 NBC
    Count of Monte Cristo   sr   3.17.56 NN
    Schlitz Playhouse of Stars   ep   No Boat for Four Months
        1.31.58 CBS
    Sugarfoot   ep   The Vultures   4.28.59 ABC
    Cheyenne   ep   The Rebellion   10.12.59 ABC
    Bourbon Street Beat   ep   Girl in Trouble   11.2.59 ABC
    Colt .45   ep   Breakthrough   3.27.60 ABC
    Bronco   ep   La Rubia   5.17.60 ABC
    Hawaiian Eye   ep   Beach Boy   6.1.60 ABC
    Exclusive   ep   10.25.60 CBS
    Tales of Wells Fargo   ep   The Jealous Man   4.10.61
        NBC
    Perry Mason   ep   The Case of the Guilty Clients   6.10.
        61 CBS
    Bonanza   ep   The Lonely House   10.15.61 NBC
    Hawaiian Eye   ep   Concert in Hawaii   12.27.61 ABC
    Have Gun Will Travel   ep   10.13.62 CBS
    Have Gun Will Travel   ep   4.13.63 CBS
    Perry Mason   ep   The Case of the Greek Goddess   4.
        18.63 CBS
    Bonanza   ep   The Companeros   4.19.64 NBC
    Combat   ep   12.20.66 ABC
    Garrison's Gorillas   ep   The Plot to Kill   2.13.68, 2.
        20.68 ABC

DONAHUE, ELINOR
    Schlitz Playhouse of Stars   ep   I Want to Be a Star

9. 19. 52 CBS
Loretta Young Show   ep   He Always Comes Home   4. 10. 55 NBC
Father Knows Best   sr   10. 3. 54 CBS
Father Knows Best   sr ret   8. 31. 55 NBC
Loretta Young Show   ep   Week-End in Winnetka   9. 4. 55 NBC
Burns and Allen Show   ep   4. 2. 56 CBS
Ford Theatre   ep   Sheila   5. 24. 56 NBC
Father Knows Best   sr ret   fall, 1956 NBC
Father Knows Best   sr ret   fall, 1957 NBC
Father Knows Best   sr ret   9. 22. 58 CBS
Father Knows Best   sr ret   9. 59 CBS
Father Knows Best   sr ret   9. 60 CBS
Dennis the Menace   ep   Dennis and the Wedding   10. 9. 60 CBS
G. E. Theatre   ep   A Voice on the Phone   11. 19. 61 CBS
77 Sunset Strip   ep   Scream Softly, Dear   1. 18. 63 ABC
U. S. Steel Hour   ep   The Secrets of Stella Crozier   3. 20. 63 CBS
Dr. Kildare   ep   Ship's Doctor   4. 18. 63 NBC
Redigo   ep   Hostage Hero Hiding   12. 10. 63 NBC
Virginian   ep   Siege   12. 18. 63 NBC
Eleventh Hour   ep   The Secret in the Stone   2. 26. 64 NBC
Many Happy Returns   sr   9. 21. 64 CBS
Shenandoah   ep   Town on Fire   11. 8. 65 ABC
Occasional Wife   ep   4. 25. 67 NBC
Star Trek   Metamorphosis   11. 10. 67 NBC
Flying Nun   ep   12. 26. 68 ABC
Mr. Deeds   ep   11. 21. 69 ABC
In Name Only   tf   11. 25. 69 ABC
Flying Nun   ep   1. 7. 70 ABC
Gidget Gets Married   tf   1. 4. 72 ABC
Odd Couple   ep   9. 15. 72 ABC

DONAHUE, TROY
    Wagon Train   ep   The Hunter Malloy Story   1. 21. 59 NBC
    Tales of Wells Fargo   ep   The Rawhide Kid   3. 16. 59 NBC
    Maverick   ep   Pappy   9. 13. 59 ABC
    Sugarfoot   ep   The Wild Bunch   9. 29. 59 ABC
    Bronco   ep   The Devil's Spawn   12. 1. 59 ABC
    77 Sunset Strip   ep   Condor's Lair   2. 21. 60 ABC
    Hawaiian Eye   ep   A Birthday Boy   3. 16. 60 ABC

Alaskans   ep   Heart of Gold   5.1.60 ABC
Lawman   ep   The Payment   5.8.60 ABC
Hawaiian Eye   ep   Beach Boy   6.1.60 ABC
Colt .45   ep   The Hothead   10.1.60 ABC
Surfside 6   sr   10.3.60 ABC
77 Sunset Strip   ep   The Hot Tamale Caper   5.26.61
   ABC
Surfside 6   sr ret   10.61 ABC
Hawaiian Eye   ep   The After Hours Heart   11.13.62
   ABC
Patty Duke Show   ep   Operation-Tonsils   9.22.65 ABC
Ironside   ep   9.26.68 NBC
Virginian   ep   4.2.69 NBC
The Lonely Profession   tf   10.21.69 NBC
The Secret Storm   sr   1970 CBS

DONLEVY, BRIAN
Pulitzer Prize Playhouse   ep   The Pharmacist's Mate
   12.22.50 ABC
Dangerous Assignment   sr   3.10.52 NBC
Video Theatre   ep   Tunnel Job   5.21.53 CBS
Robert Montgomery Presents   ep   First Vice-President
   8.21.53 NBC
Medallion Theatre   ep   Safari   4.3.54 CBS
Lux Video Theatre   ep   The Great McGinty   6.28.55
   NBC
Ford Theatre   ep   Policy of Joe Aladdin   5.12.55 NBC
Climax   ep   Pink Cloud   10.27.55 CBS
Crossroads   ep   Mr. Liberty Bell   11.18.55 ABC
Damon Runyon Theatre   ep   Barbecue   12.3.55 CBS
Kraft Theatre   ep   Home Is the Hero   1.25.56 NBC
Studio One   ep   The Laughter of Giants   3.19.56 CBS
Ford Theatre   ep   Double Trouble   3.22.56 NBC
Lux Video Theatre   ep   Impact   4.26.56 NBC
Crossroads   ep   The Judge   5.18.56 ABC
Crossroads   ep   God of Kandikur   12.5.57 ABC
Dupont Show of the Month   ep   Beyond This Place   11.
   25.57   CBS
Texan   ep   2.9.59 CBS
Wagon Train   ep   The Joseph Cato Story   3.4.59 NBC
Hotel de Paree   ep   10.9.59 CBS
Texan   ep   10.19.59 CBS
June Allyson Show   ep   Escape   2.22.60 CBS
Zane Grey Theatre   ep   The Sunday Man   2.25.60 CBS
Target: Corruptors   ep   A Man Is Waiting to Be Mur-
   dered   1.5.62 ABC
Saints and Sinners   ep   Dear George, The Siamese Cat

Is Missing 9. 17. 62 NBC
Dupont Show of the Month ep Jeremy Rabbitt the Secret Avenger 4. 5. 64 NBC
Perry Mason ep The Case of the Positive Negative
5. 1. 66 CBS

DONNELL, JEFF
Bigelow Theatre ep Make Your Bed 3. 4. 51 CBS
Schlitz Playhouse of Stars ep Girl of My Dreams 2.
27. 53 CBS
Ford Theatre ep Taming of the Shrewd 3. 25. 54 NBC
U. S. Steel Hour ep One for the Road 12. 7. 54 ABC
Counterpoint ep It Wouldn't Be Fair 1. 7. 55 NN
Cavalcade of America ep New Salem Story 2. 8. 55
ABC
Gloria Swanson Theatre ep The Antique Shop 2. 15.
55 ABC
Climax ep No Stone Unturned 5. 19. 55 CBS
Matinee Theatre ep The Old Payola 8. 8. 56 NBC
Ethel Barrymore Theatre ep The Peabodys 10. 19. 56
NN
Playhouse 90 ep Sincerely, Willis Wayde 12. 13. 56
CBS
U. S. Steel Hour ep Goodbye... but it Doesn't Go Away
12. 31. 58 CBS
U. S. Steel Hour ep Little Tin God 4. 22. 59 CBS
Ellery Queen ep The Chemistry Set 6. 19. 59 NBC
U. S. Steel Hour ep Game of Hearts 6. 1. 60 CBS
Overland Trail ep The Most Dangerous Gentleman
6. 5. 60 NBC
Ann Sothern Show ep 10. 20. 60 CBS
June Allyson Show ep A Thief or Two 1. 21. 60 CBS
Play of the Week ep Uncle Harry 12. 5. 60 NN
U. S. Steel Hour ep Tangle of Truth 11. 29. 61 CBS
Perry Mason ep The Case of the Melancholy Marks-
man 3. 24. 62 CBS
U. S. Steel Hour ep Farewell to Innocence 11. 28. 62
CBS
World of Disney ep Bristle Face 1. 26. 64, 2. 2. 64
NBC
Perry Mason ep The Case of the Bullied Bowler
11. 5. 64 CBS
Addams Family ep 2. 18. 66 ABC
Gidget ep 3. 10. 66 ABC
Julia ep 1. 26. 68 NBC
Mothers-in-Law ep 2. 11. 68 NBC
Daniel Boone ep 1. 16. 69 NBC

Bracken's World   ep   Together Again--for the Last
      Time   10.9.70 NBC
Medical Center   ep   Witch Hunt   11.11.70 CBS
Love Hate Love   tf   2.9.71 ABC
Congratulations It's a Boy   tf   9.21.71 ABC
Jimmy Stewart Show   ep   1.2.72 NBC
Jimmy Stewart Show   ep   2.13.72 NBC
Emergency   ep   4.15.72 NBC
Adam-12   ep   11.1.72 NBC
FBI   ep   12.3.72 ABC

DONNELLY, RUTH
Imogene Coca Show   sr   10.2.54 NBC
Crossroads   ep   Mother O'Brien   3.9.56 ABC
Dupont Theatre   ep   Are Trees People   2.5.57 ABC
Harris Against the World   ep   11.16.64 NBC

DORS, DIANA
Rheingold Theatre   ep   The Lovely Place   12.8.54 NBC
Phil Silvers Show   Sp   1.23.59 CBS
Straightaway   ep   The Sports Car Breed   12.8.61 ABC
Alfred Hitchcock Theatre   ep   Run for Doom   5.17.63
      CBS
Burke's Law   ep   Who Killed Alex Debbs   10.25.63 ABC
Eleventh Hour   ep   87 Different Kinds of Love   2.19.64
      NBC

D'ORSAY, FIFI
Pepsi Cola Playhouse   ep   Fie, Fie, Fifi   5.21.54 ABC
Adventures in Paradise   ep   Castaways   1.4.60 ABC
G.E. Theatre   ep   Love Is a Lion's Roar   3.19.61 CBS
Pete and Gladys   ep   Pop's Girl Friend   5.8.61 CBS
Adventures in Paradise   ep   One-Way Ticket   12.3.61
      ABC
Combat   ep   Reunion   1.1.62 ABC

DOUGLAS, KIRK
The Legend of Silent Night   Sp nar   12.25.68 ABC

DOUGLAS, MELVYN
Ford Theatre Hour   ep   Cause for Suspicion   12.29.50
      ABC
Starlight Theatre   ep   Relatively Speaking   1.11.51 CBS
Celanese Theatre   ep   Reunion in Vienna   1.9.52 ABC
Lights Out   ep   Private, Keep Out   3.3.52 NBC
Hollywood Off Beat   sr   6.12.52 ABC
Ford Theatre   ep   Letters Marked Personal   1.27.55
      NBC

Kraft Theatre   ep   The Chess Game   8. 31. 55 NBC
Alcoa Hour   ep   Thunder in Washington   11. 27. 55 NBC
Alcoa Hour   ep   Man on a Tiger   1. 8. 56 NBC
Playhouse 90   ep   The Greer Case   1. 31. 57 CBS
U. S. Steel Hour   ep   The Hill Wife   4. 10. 57 CBS
Goodyear Playhouse   ep   The Legacy   6. 30. 57 NBC
G. E. Theatre   ep   Love Came Late   11. 17. 57 CBS
Playhouse 90   ep   The Plot to Kill Stalin   9. 25. 58
    CBS
U. S. Steel Hour   ep   Second Chance   11. 5. 58 CBS
Playhouse 90   ep   The Return of Ansel Gibbs   11. 27. 58
    CBS
Frontier Justice   sh   7. 6. 59 CBS
Our American Heritage   ep   Shadow of a Soldier   2. 21.
    60 NBC
Ben Casey   ep   Rage against the Dying Light   4. 15. 63
    ABC
Bob Hope Chrysler Theatre   ep   A Killing at Sundial
    10. 4. 63 NBC
Hallmark Hall of Fame   ep   Inherit the Wind   11. 18.
    65 NBC
Fugitive   ep   The 2130   3. 29. 66 ABC
Hallmark Hall of Fame   ep   Lamp at Midnight   4. 27.
    66 NBC
The Crucible   Sp   5. 4. 67 CBS
CBS Playhouse   ep   Do Not Go Gentle into That Good
    Night   10. 16. 67 CBS
On Stage   ep   The Choice   3. 30. 69 NBC
Hunters Are for Killing   tf   3. 12. 70 CBS
Death Takes a Holiday   tf   10. 23. 71 ABC
Ghost Story   ep   11. 10. 72 NBC

DOUGLAS, MICHAEL
CBS Playhouse   ep   The Experiment   2. 25. 69 CBS
FBI   ep   The Hitchhiker   2. 28. 71 ABC
Medical Center   ep   The Albatross   11. 3. 71 CBS
Streets of San Francisco   sr   9. 16. 72 ABC

DOUGLAS, PAUL
Hollywood Opening Night   ep   The Living Image   1. 12.
    53 NBC
Omnibus   ep   The Oyster and the Pearl   2. 15. 53 CBS
ABC Album   ep   Justice   4. 12. 53 ABC
Medallion Theatre   ep   The Magic Touch   1. 9. 54 CBS
U. S. Steel Hour   ep   1. 19. 54 ABC
Lux Video Theatre   ep   Casablanca   3. 3. 55 NBC
Elgin Hour   ep   Black Eagle Pass   4. 5. 55 ABC

Request Performance   ep   Trouble with Youth   4.13.55
   NBC
Climax   ep   Flight 951   4.21.55 CBS
Damon Runyon Theatre   ep   Numbers and Figures   5.
   14.55 CBS
Playwrights '55   ep   The Answer   10.4.55 NBC
Star Stage   ep   The Man in the Black Robe   5.18.56
   NBC
20th Century-Fox Hour   ep   The Hefferan Family   6.
   13.56 CBS
Adventure Theatre   sh   6.16.56 NBC
Hallmark Hall of Fame   ep   Born Yesterday   10.28.56
   NBC
Jane Wyman Theatre   ep   Day of Glory   1.6.58 NBC
Suspicion   ep   Comfort for the Grave   1.27.58 NBC
Schlitz Playhouse of Stars   ep   The Honor System   3.
   14.58 CBS
Climax   ep   On the Take   4.3.58 CBS
Playhouse 90   ep   The Dungeon   4.17.58 CBS
Studio One   ep   The Edge of Truth   4.28.58 CBS
Studio One   ep   The Lady Died at Midnight   9.1.58 CBS
Goodyear Theatre   ep   The Chain and the River   9.29.
   58 NBC
Zane Grey Theatre   ep   Day of the Killing   1.8.59 CBS
Playhouse 90   ep   The Raider   2.19.59 CBS
Lucille Ball-Desi Arnaz Hour   ep   Lucy Wants a Career
   4.13.59 CBS
Playhouse 90   ep   Judgment at Nuremberg   4.16.59 CBS
Alfred Hitchcock Presents   ep   Touché   6.14.59 CBS
Goodyear Theatre   ep   The Incorrigibles   10.12.59 NBC

DOWLING, EDDIE
   Anywhere U.S.A.   sr   11.9.52 ABC

DOWNS, HUGH
   Riverboat   ep   The Night of the Faceless Men   3.28.60
      NBC

DOWNS, JOHNNY
   Racket Squad   ep   Fair Exchange   2.14.52 CBS

DRAKE, ALFRED
   Billy Rose's Playbill   ep   If You Can Act--Act   11.27.
      50 NN
   Somerset Maugham Theatre   ep   The French Governor
      7.9.51 NBC
   Celanese Theatre   ep   Counsellor-at-Law   11.28.51 ABC

Cameo Theatre   ep   Dark of the Moon   1. 6. 52 NBC
Naughty Marietta   Sp   1. 15. 55 NBC
Marco Polo   Sp   4. 14. 56 NBC
Alcoa Hour   ep   Key Largo   10. 14. 56 NBC
Hallmark Hall of Fame   ep   The Yeoman of the Guard
   4. 10. 57 NBC
Hallmark Hall of Fame   ep   Kiss Me, Kate!   11. 20. 58
   NBC
Play of the Week   ep   Volpone   3. 7. 60 NN
Dupont Show of the Month   ep   The Legend of Lylah
   Clare   5. 19. 63 NBC

DRAKE, BETSY
   G. E. Theatre   ep   A Question of Romance   11. 9. 58
      CBS
   Wanted Dead or Alive   ep   1. 17. 59 CBS

DRAKE, CHARLES
   Fireside Theatre   ep   Afraid to Live   9. 28. 54 NBC
   Loretta Young Show   ep   You're Driving Me Crazy   9.
      26. 54 NBC
   Robert Montgomery Presents   ep   N. Y. to L. A.   3. 21.
      55 NBC
   Best of Broadway   ep   Stage Door   4. 6. 55 CBS
   Studio One   ep   Summer Pavilion   5. 2. 55 CBS
   Robert Montgomery Presents   sr   6. 27. 55 NBC
   Appointment with Adventure   ep   When in Rome   9. 11.
      55 CBS
   Fireside Theatre   ep   Sound of Thunder   3. 27. 56 NBC
   20th Century-Fox Hour   ep   Gun in His Hand   4. 4. 56
      CBS
   Climax   ep   Spin into Darkness   4. 5. 56 CBS
   Robert Montgomery Presents   ep   The Baobab Tree   4.
      23. 56 NBC
   Loretta Young Show   ep   Casebook   4. 29. 56 NBC
   Robert Montgomery Presents   sr   7. 2. 56 NBC
   Playhouse 90   ep   Reunion   1. 2. 58 CBS
   Wagon Train   ep   The Charles Maury Story   4. 7. 58
      NBC
   Theatre '59   ep   Markheim   4. 1. 59 NBC
   Theatre '60   ep   The Big Miracle   4. 21. 60 NBC
   Laramie   ep   Ride into Darkness   10. 18. 60 NBC
   Barbara Stanwyck Theatre   ep   A Man's Game   7. 3. 61
      NBC
   Laramie   ep   The Accusers   11. 14. 61 NBC
   Checkmate   ep   The Best of My Knowledge   12. 27. 61
      CBS

Dick Powell Theatre   ep   The Clocks   3.27.62 NBC
Wagon Train   ep   The Caroline Castell Story   9.26.62
   ABC
Wagon Train   ep   The Hollister John Garrison Story
   2.6.63 ABC
Alcoa Premiere   ep   Chain Reaction   2.21.63 ABC
Eleventh Hour   ep   Everybody Knows You've Left Me
   4.10.63 NBC
Wagon Train   ep   The Myra Marshall Story   10.21.63
   ABC
Wagon Train   ep   4.13.64 ABC
Destry   ep   Ree Brady's Kid   4.24.64 ABC
The Lucy Show   ep   9.21.64 CBS
Slattery's People   ep   What Did You Do All Day, Mr.
   Slattery   1.15.65 CBS
Bob Hope Chrysler Theatre   ep   The Faceless Man   5.
   4.66 NBC
Fugitive   ep   1.17.67 ABC
F Troop   ep   4.6.67 ABC
Invaders   ep   The Saucer   9.5.67 ABC
Mannix   ep   9.23.67 CBS
The Man from U.N.C.L.E.   ep   The THRUSH Roulette
   Affair   10.23.67 NBC
Star Trek   ep   The Deadly Years   12.8.67 NBC
Daniel Boone   ep   10.31.68 NBC
The Smugglers   tf   12.24.68 NBC
Bold Ones   ep   A Good Case of Whiskey at Christmas
   Time   9.28.69 NBC
Name of the Game   ep   The Perfect Image   11.7.69
   NBC
Virginian   ep   A Woman of Stone   12.17.69 NBC
Name of the Game   ep   The Skin Game   2.27.70 NBC
Men from Shiloh   ep   9.30.70 NBC
Bracken's World   ep   For the Last Time   10.9.70 NBC
Marcus Welby, M.D.   ep   Aura of a New Tomorrow
   11.24.70 ABC
Ironside   ep   Accident   3.11.71 NBC
Man and the City   ep   11.3.71 ABC
Mission Impossible   ep   12.2.72 CBS

DRAKE, TOM
   Suspense   ep   1,000 to One for Your Money   4.4.50
      CBS
   Suspense   ep   Murder at the Mardi Gras   4.18.50 CBS
   Suspense   ep   Red Wine   5.9.50 CBS
   Lights Out   ep   The Power of the Brute   3.26.51 NBC
   Tales of Tomorrow   ep   Fountain of Youth   3.21.52 ABC

The Unexpected ep Bright Boy 10.22.52 NBC
Schlitz Playhouse of Stars ep A String of Beads 12.
  26.52 CBS
Mirror Theatre ep Lullaby 10.3.53 CBS
Schlitz Playhouse of Stars ep The Secret 9.10.54
  CBS
Climax ep The Long Goodbye 10.7.54 CBS
Ford Theatre ep Girl in Flight 12.2.54 NBC
Fireside Theatre ep No Place to Live 2.15.55 NBC
Science Fiction Theatre ep Beyond 4.5.55 NBC
Playhouse ep The Man Nobody Wanted 5.15.55 ABC
Climax ep No Stone Unturned 5.19.55 CBS
Studio One ep Rope Enough 1.15.56 NN
Studio 57 ep A Farewell Appearance 2.5.56 NN
The Millionaire ep The Story of Alan Marsh 4.3.57
  CBS
Studio 57 ep The Brotherhood of the Bell 1.6.58 CBS
Wanted Dead or Alive ep 11.22.58 CBS
Cimarron City ep Return of the Dead 2.14.59 NBC
Perry Mason ep The Case of the Jaded Joker 2.21.
  59 CBS
77 Sunset Strip ep Treehouse Caper 11.13.59 ABC
Wagon Train ep The Lita Foladaire Story 1.6.60
  NBC
Philip Marlowe ep Murder Is Dead Wrong 3.15.60
  ABC
Wichita Town ep Second Chance 3.16.60 NBC
Adventures in Paradise ep The Amazon 3.21.60 ABC
Riverboat ep Face of Courage 6.6.60 NBC
Wanted Dead or Alive ep 10.26.60 CBS
Lawman ep Dilemma 10.30.60 ABC
Stagecoach West ep The Storm 12.13.60 ABC
Rebel ep Berserk 12.18.60 ABC
Rebel ep The Last Drink 2.26.61 ABC
Follow the Sun ep The Far Side of Nowhere 12.17.61
  ABC
Hawaiian Eye ep Big Fever 1.17.62 ABC
Surfside 6 ep A Piece of Tommy Minor 3.19.62 ABC
Untouchables ep Man in the Middle 4.5.62 ABC
Cheyenne ep Trouble Street 5.14.62 ABC
77 Sunset Strip ep Dial S for Spencer 3.1.63 ABC
Lassie ep 1.31.65 CBS
Ben Casey ep Eulogy in Four Flats 3.22.65 ABC
Branded ep Very Few Heroes 4.11.65 NBC
Mr. Novak ep Once a Clown 4.27.65 NBC
Alfred Hitchcock Theatre ep Off Season 5.10.65 NBC
Branded ep Judge Not 9.12.65 NBC

Combat   ep   The Old Men   11.16.65 ABC
Wild, Wild West   ep   11.4.66 CBS
Green Hornet   ep   11.18.66 ABC
Road West   ep   12.5.66 NBC
Land of the Giants   ep   Doomsday   2.15.70 ABC
Name of the Game   ep   Echo of a Nightmare   3.20.70
   NBC
World of Disney   ep   The Boy Who Stole the Elephants
   9.20.70, 9.27.70 NBC
Young Lawyers   ep   Down at the House of Truth, I Vis-
   it   3.3.71 ABC
Mannix   ep   The Man Outside   11.24.71 CBS
Adam-12   ep   2.2.72 NBC

DREIER, ALEX
Cowboy in Africa   ep   1.29.68 ABC
It Takes a Thief   ep   4.22.69 ABC
Land of the Giants   ep   10.12.69 ABC
Mannix   ep   Missing: Sun and Sky   12.20.69 CBS
Mannix   ep   The Lost Art of Ying   10.24.70 CBS
Name of the Game   ep   The Broken Puzzle   3.12.71
   NBC

DREW, ELLEN
Footlights Theatre   ep   Crossroads   8.1.52 CBS
Ford Theatre   ep   Birth of a Hero   10.23.52 NBC
Schlitz Playhouse of Stars   ep   The Governess   4.3.53
   CBS
Ford Theatre   ep   Gun Job   12.17.53 NBC
Schlitz Playhouse of Stars   ep   Go Away a Winner   1.1.
   54 CBS
Ford Theatre   ep   Keep It in the Family   5.27.54 NBC
Schlitz Playhouse of Stars   ep   Visitor in the Night   3.
   11.55 CBS
Science Fiction Theatre   ep   Beyond 4.5.55 NBC
Science Fiction Theatre   ep   The Brain of John Emerson
   5.27.55 NBC
Ford Theatre   ep   One Man Missing   6.9.55 NBC
The Millionaire   ep   Millionaire Julia Conrad   1.28.59
   CBS
Barbara Stanwyck Theatre   ep   The Sisters   2.6.61 NBC

DRISCOLL, BOBBY
Schlitz Playhouse of Stars   ep   Early Space Conqueror
   7.18.52 CBS
Loretta Young Show   ep   Big Jim   12.5.54 NBC
Fireside Theatre   ep   His Father's Keeper   12.7.54 NBC

Fireside Theatre ep The Double Life of Barney Peters
1.18.55 NBC
Gloria Swanson Theatre ep The Best Years 2.10.55
ABC
TV Reader's Digest ep A Matter of Life and Death
2.28.55 ABC
Front Row Center ep Ah, Wilderness! 6.15.55 CBS
Medic ep Laughter Is a Boy 7.11.55 NBC
Schlitz Playhouse of Stars ep Too Late to Run 8.5.
55 CBS
Screen Directors Playhouse ep Day Is Done 10.12.55
NBC
Navy Log ep Navy Corpsman 11.29.55 CBS
Crusader ep Fear 1.13.56 CBS
Ford Theatre ep Try Me for Size 1.26.56 NBC
TV Reader's Digest ep No Horse, No Wife, No Mus-
tache 3.19.56 ABC
Studio One ep I Do 4.30.56 CBS
TV Reader's Digest ep The Smuggler 7.9.56 ABC
Zane Grey Theatre ep Death Watch 11.8.56 CBS
M Squad ep Pete Loves Mary 10.11.57 NBC
Mystery Show ep Summer Hero 6.12.60 NBC

DRIVAS, ROBERT
Armstrong Circle Theatre ep Case for Room 310
10.1.58 CBS
East Side/West Side ep Age of Consent 9.30.63 CBS
Defenders ep Claire Cheval Died in Boston 11.23.63
CBS
Fugitive ep Man in a Chariot 9.15.64 ABC
12 O'Clock High ep The Albatross 1.15.65 ABC
For the People ep 2.7.65 CBS
The Irregular Verb To Love Sp 11.12.65 NN
Run for Your Life ep Strangers at the Door 1.3.66
NBC
12 O'Clock High ep The Hollow Man 3.14.66 ABC
FBI ep The Bomb that Walked Like a Man 5.1.66
ABC
Felony Squad ep 11.7.66 ABC
FBI ep The Executioners 3.12.67, 3.19.67 ABC
Felony Squad ep 11.20.67 ABC
FBI ep 1.28.68 ABC
Bonanza ep 2.18.68 NBC
N.Y.P.D. ep Boys' Night Out 3.11.69 ABC
FBI ep 3.1.70 ABC
FBI ep The Corruptor 2.27.72 ABC
Hawaii Five-O ep 11.14.72 CBS

DRU, JOANNE
    Pulitzer Prize Playhouse ep The Silver Cord 1.26.51
      ABC
    Robert Montgomery Presents ep Betrayed 3.2.53
      NBC
    Ford Theatre ep Just What the Doctor Ordered 4.9.
      53 NBC
    Schlitz Playhouse of Stars ep Richard and the Lion
      7.3.53 CBS
    Video Theatre ep Call Off the Wedding 1.7.54 CBS
    Ford Theatre ep Yours for a Dream 4.8.54 NBC
    Rheingold Theatre ep Brief Affair 2.12.55 NBC
    Ford Theatre ep Celebrity 3.17.55 NBC
    Climax ep The Darkest Hour 3.24.55 CBS
    Summer Theatre ep A Kiss for Mr. Lincoln 7.19.55
      NBC
    Loretta Young Show ep The Waiting Game 10.8.55
      NBC
    Ford Theatre ep Passage to Yesterday 11.24.55
      NBC
    Schlitz Playhouse of Stars ep The Gentle Stranger
      2.3.56 CBS
    Fireside Theatre ep The Mirror 2.28.56 NBC
    Lux Video Theatre ep Flamingo Road 10.18.56 NBC
    Climax ep Night Shriek 11.15.56 CBS
    Playhouse 90 ep The Blackwell Story 2.28.57 CBS
    Lux Video Theatre ep Paris Calling 5.30.57 NBC
    Studio 57 ep Palm Springs Incident 7.7.57 NN
    Wagon Train ep The Nels Stack Story 10.23.57 NBC
    Studio One ep The Brotherhood of the Bell 1.6.58
      CBS
    G.E. Theatre ep All I Survey 2.2.58 CBS
    David Niven Theatre ep The Lady from Winnetka 5.
      26.59 NBC
    Adventures of a Model pt 9.6.60 CBS
    Guestward Ho! sr 9.29.60 ABC
    Burke's Law ep 4.24.64 ABC
    The Long Hot Summer ep 12.9.65 ABC
    Green Hornet ep Corpse of the Year 1.13.67, 1.20.
      67 ABC
    Bob Hope Chrysler Theatre ep To Sleep, Perchance
      to Scream 5.10.67 NBC

DRURY, JAMES
    20th Century-Fox Hour ep Times Like These 2.22.
      56 CBS
    Decision ep The Virginian 7.6.58 NBC

Texan ep Troubled Town 10.13.58 CBS
Ed Wynn Show ep A Date with Mrs. Creavy 11.20.58 NBC
Have Gun Will Travel ep 2.7.59 CBS
Richard Diamond ep 3.29.59 CBS
Gunsmoke ep 4.25.59 CBS
Gunsmoke ep 10.3.59 CBS
Men into Space ep 1.6.60 CBS
Rebel ep Fair Game 3.27.60 ABC
Bourbon Street Beat ep A Wall of Silence 3.28.60 ABC
Loretta Young Show ep Linda 10.9.60 NBC
Rebel ep Vindication 12.4.60 ABC
Gunsmoke ep 3.18.61 CBS
Loretta Young Show ep The Preliminaries 3.19.61 NBC
Rawhide ep Incident of the Boomerang 3.24.61 CBS
Michael Shayne ep No Shroud for Shayne 5.5.61 NBC
Rifleman ep Death Trap 5.9.61 ABC
Stagecoach West ep Blind Man's Bluff 5.16.61 ABC
Perry Mason ep The Case of the Missing Melody 9.30.61 CBS
Detectives ep Walk a Crooked Line 2.23.62 NBC
Wagon Train ep The Cole Crawford Story 4.11.62 NBC
Virginian sr 9.19.62 NBC
Virginian sr ret 9.18.63 NBC
Virginian sr ret 9.16.64 NBC
Virginian sr ret 9.15.65 NBC
Virginian sr ret 9.14.66 NBC
Virginian sr ret 9.13.67 NBC
It Takes a Thief ep 1.9.68 ABC
Virginian sr ret 9.18.68 NBC
Virginian sr ret 9.17.69 NBC
Men from Shiloh sr 9.16.70 NBC
Breakout tf 12.8.70 NBC
Alias Smith and Jones tf 1.5.71 ABC
Ironside ep The Professional 9.18.71 NBC
The Devil and Miss Sarah tf 12.4.71 ABC
Alias Smith and Jones ep 9.16.72 ABC

DUFF, HOWARD
Ford Theatre ep The Ming Lama 11.12.53 NBC
Ford Theatre ep A Season to Love 5.6.54 NBC
Schlitz Playhouse of Stars ep Woman Expert 12.17.54 CBS
Climax ep Escape from Fear 1.13.55 CBS

Rheingold Theatre   ep   First Offense   3. 26. 55 NBC
Science Fiction Theatre   ep   Sound of Murder   5. 20. 55
   NBC
Rheingold Theatre   ep   The Confessions of Henry Pell
   6. 11. 55 NBC
Crossroads   ep   The Mountain Angel   1. 20. 56 ABC
Rheingold Theatre   ep   Payment in Kind   1. 28. 56 NBC
Science Fiction Theatre   ep   Sound of Murder   2. 10. 56
   NBC
Front Row Center   ep   The Morals Squad   3. 11. 56 CBS
Ford Theatre   ep   The Payoff   4. 3. 56 NBC
Climax   ep   Fury at Dawn   7. 19. 56 CBS
Mr. Adams and Eve   sr   1. 4. 57 CBS
Studio 57   ep   Pride Is the Man   6. 30. 57 NN
Mr. Adams and Eve   sr ret   fall, 1957 CBS
Lucille Ball-Desi Arnaz Hour   ep Lucy's Summer Vaca-
   tion   6. 8. 59 CBS
Bonanza   ep   Enter Mark Twain   10. 10. 59 NBC
Alcoa Theatre   ep   Small Bouquet   11. 16. 59 NBC
Twilight Zone   ep   A World of Difference   3. 11. 60 CBS
Dante('s Inferno)   sr   9. 26. 60 NBC
Alfred Hitchcock Theatre   ep   The Tender Poisoner   12.
   20. 62 CBS
Sam Benedict   ep   Not Even the Gulls Shall Weep   1. 5.
   63 NBC
Virginian   ep   Distant Fury   3. 20. 63 NBC
Arrest and Trial   ep   Isn't It a Lovely View   9. 22. 63
   ABC
Eleventh Hour   ep   Prodigy   3. 18. 64 NBC
Burke's Law   ep   3. 20. 64 ABC
Mr. Novak   ep   Mountains to Climb   2. 23. 66 NBC
I Spy   ep   Crusade   to Limbo   3. 23. 66 NBC
Felony Squad   sr   9. 12. 66 ABC
Felony Squad   sr ret   9. 11. 67 ABC
Batman   ep   3. 7. 68 ABC
Felony Squad   sr ret   9. 27. 68 ABC
Bold Ones   ep   Man without a Heart   11. 8. 69 NBC
The D. A. :   Murder One   tf   12. 8. 69 NBC
The Immortal   ep   Paradise Bay   12. 10. 70 ABC
Men from Shiloh   ep   The Town Killer   3. 10. 71 NBC
Alias Smith and Jones   ep   Shootout at Diablo Station
   12. 2. 71 ABC
Medical Center   ep   3. 1. 72 CBS
The Heist   tf   11. 28. 72 ABC

DUKE, PATTY
   Kraft Theatre   ep   Big Heist   11. 13. 57 NBC

Armstrong Circle Theatre ep Have Jacket: Will Travel 11.27.57 CBS
Kitty Foyle sr 1.22.58 NBC
U.S. Steel Hour ep The Reward 2.12.58 CBS
Dupont Show of the Month ep Wuthering Heights 5.9.58 CBS
Drama ep An American Girl 6.8.58 NBC
U.S. Steel Hour ep One Red Rose for Christmas 12.17.58 CBS
U.S. Steel Hour ep Family Happiness 2.11.59 CBS
Meet Me in St. Louis Sp 4.26.59 CBS
Armstrong Circle Theatre ep The Zone of Silence 6.24.59 CBS
U.S. Steel Hour ep Seed of Guilt 8.12.59 CBS
Once Upon a Christmas Fable Sp 12.9.59 NBC
Ben Casey ep Mrs. McBroom and the Cloud Watcher 10.1.62 ABC
Power and the Glory Sp 10.29.61 CBS
U.S. Steel Hour ep The Duchess and the Mugs 12.26.62 CBS
Wide Country ep To Cindy, with Love 2.28.63 NBC
Patty Duke Show sr 9.18.63 ABC
Patty Duke Show sr ret 9.64 ABC
Patty Duke Show sr ret 9.15.65 ABC
Virginian ep 1.11.67 NBC
Journey to the Unknown ep The Last Visitor 1.2.69 ABC
My Sweet Charlie tf 1.20.70 NBC
Matt Lincoln ep 9.24.70 ABC
Two on a Bench tf 11.2.71 ABC
If Tomorrow Comes tf 12.7.71 ABC
She Waits tf 1.28.72 CBS
Deadly Harvest tf 9.26.72 CBS
Sixth Sense ep 10.14.72 ABC
Owen Marshall ep 11.9.72 ABC

DULLEA, KEIR
Mrs. Miniver Sp 1.7.60 CBS
Frontiers of Faith ep From the Dark Source 4.17.60 NBC
Naked City ep Murder Is a Face I Know 1.11.61 ABC
U.S. Steel Hour ep The Big Splash 2.8.61 CBS
Hallmark Hall of Fame ep Give Us Barabbas 3.26.61 NBC
Play of the Week ep All Summer Long 5.1.61 NN
U.S. Steel Hour ep The Golden Thirty 8.9.61 CBS

Alcoa Premiere   ep   People Need People   10.10.61
   ABC
U.S. Steel Hour   ep   Far from the Shade Tree   1.62
Alcoa Premiere   ep   Tiger   3.20.62 ABC
Mystery Theatre   ep   Cry Ruin   8.15.62 NBC
Alcoa Premiere   ep   Ordeal in Darkness 11.15.62 ABC
Eleventh Hour   ep   Cry a Little for Mary Too   11.28.
   62 NBC
Empire   ep   Stopover on the Way to the Moon   1.1.63
   NBC
U.S. Steel Hour   ep   The Young Avengers   1.9.63 CBS
Bonanza   ep   Elegy for a Hangman   1.20.63 NBC
Naked City   ep   The Apple Falls Not Far from the
   Tree   1.23.63 ABC
Going My Way   ep   One Small, Unhappy Family   2.13.
   63 ABC
Alcoa Premiere   ep   The Broken Year   4.4.63 ABC
Channing   ep   The Trouble with Girls   3.11.64 ABC
12 O'Clock High   ep   To Heinie with Love   2.5.65 ABC
Hollywood Television Theatre   ep   Montserrat   3.2.71
   NN

DUMBRILLE, DOUGLASS
   Fireside Theatre   ep   The Devil's Due   6.13.50 NBC
   Racket Squad   ep   Case of the Fabulous Mr. Jones   7.
      26.51 CBS
   China Smith   sr   5.13.53 NN
   The Millionaire   ep   The Newman Johnson Story   spring,
      1957 CBS
   Ford Theatre   ep   The Fugitives   1.7.54 NBC
   Public Defender   ep   The Do-Gooder   10.7.54 CBS
   Gloria Swanson Theatre   ep   My Last Duchess   1.4.55
      ABC
   Treasury Men in Action   ep   The Case of the Slippery
      Eel   7.1.55 ABC
   Life of Riley   ep   Ghost Town   11.18.55 NBC
   Life of Riley   ep   12.2.55 NBC
   TV Reader's Digest   ep   The Sad Death of a Hero   12.
      5.55 ABC
   Fireside Theatre   ep   Big Joe's Comin' Home   12.27.
      55 NBC
   Crossroads   ep   Through the Window   1.6.56 ABC
   Life of Riley   ep   Riley's Allergy   3.30.56 NBC
   Cavalcade Theatre   ep   Young Andy Jackson   4.10.56
      ABC
   Charlie Farrell Show   ep   7.9.56 CBS
   77th Bengal Lancers   ep   The Traitor   11.18.56 NBC

Crossroads   ep   Thanksgiving Prayer   11.23.56 ABC
Oh Susanna   ep   Desirable Alien   1.12.57 CBS
Hey Jeannie   ep   Jeannie the Wac   2.16.57 CBS
Mr. Adams and Eve   ep   The Fighter   5.24.57 CBS
Life of Riley   ep   Nobody Down Here Likes Me   11.22.57 NBC
Telephone Time   ep   Rescue   11.26.57 ABC
Alcoa Theatre   ep Souvenir   12.2.57 NBC
Life of Riley   ep   Mrs. Aircraft Industries   2.28.58 NBC
Californians   ep   The Marshal   3.11.58 NBC
Californians   ep   Murietta   5.27.58 NBC
The Millionaire   ep   The Newman Johnson Story   11.12.58 CBS
George Burns Show   ep   3.10.59 CBS
Laramie   ep   Duel at Alta Mesa   2.23.60 NBC
Loretta Young Show   ep   These Few Years   12.11.60 NBC
Bringing up Buddy   ep   12.19.60 CBS
Dobie Gillis   ep   I Was a High School Scrooge   2.21.61 CBS
Dobie Gillis   ep   Move over Perry Mason   10.24.61 CBS
Twilight Zone   ep   Self-Improvement of Salvadore Ross   1.17.64 CBS
New Phil Silvers Show   ep   My Son, The Governor   1.25.64 CBS
New Phil Silvers Show   ep   3.14.64 CBS
Perry Mason   ep   The Case of the Duplicate Case   4.22.65 CBS

DUMONT, MARGARET
Donna Reed Show   ep   Miss Lovelace Comes to Tea   5.12.59 ABC

DUNAWAY, FAYE
Trials of O'Brien   ep   The 10-Foot, 6 Inch Pole   1.14.66 CBS
Portrait: The Woman I Love   Sp   12.17.72 ABC

DUNCAN, SANDY
Funny Face   sr   9.18.71 CBS
Sandy Duncan Show   sr   9.17.72 CBS

DUNN, JAMES
Pulitzer Prize Playhouse   ep   6.29.51 ABC
Curtain Call   ep   The Summer People   8.29.52 NBC

Schlitz Playhouse of Stars   ep   I Want to be a Star
   9.19.52 CBS
Hollywood Opening Night   ep   Quite a Viking   10.27.52
   NBC
Hollywood Opening Night   ep   Josie   12.22.52 NBC
Goodyear Playhouse   ep   Medal in the Family   2.1.53
   NBC
Studio One   ep   The Show Piece   2.23.53 CBS
Studio One   ep   The Magic Lantern   4.13.53 CBS
Goodyear Playhouse   ep   Her Prince Charming   6.14.53
   NBC
First Person   ep   One Night Stand   7.31.53 NBC
Robert Montgomery Presents   ep   Paradise Cafe   3.8.
   54 NBC
Robert Montgomery Presents   ep   My Little Girl   3.
   29.54 NBC
Schlitz Playhouse of Stars   ep   The Treasure of Santa
   Domingo   6.11.54 CBS
G.E. Theatre   ep   Desert Crossing   6.20.54 CBS
It's a Great Life   sr   9.7.54 NBC
Armstrong Circle Theatre   ep   Jody and Me   9.14.54
   NBC
Robert Montgomery Presents   ep   Joe's Boy   1.24.55
   NBC
Studio One   ep   A Picture in the Paper   5.9.55 CBS
Damon Runyon Theatre   ep   A Nice Price   8.6.55 CBS
Schlitz Playhouse of Stars   ep   Nothing to Do till Next
   Fall   10.28.55 CBS
Climax   ep   The Secret of River Lane   1.26.56 CBS
Screen Directors Playhouse   ep   Cry Justice   2.15.56
   NBC
Mr. Broadway   Sp   5.11.57 NBC
World of Disney   ep   Law and Order, Inc.   fall, 1957
   ABC
Climax   ep   Keep Me in Mind   11.7.57 CBS
World of Disney   ep   Elgego--Lawman or Gunman   11.
   28.58 ABC
World of Disney   ep   Effego Baca, Attorney-at-Law
   2.6.59 ABC
Wanted Dead or Alive   ep   2.7.59 CBS
World of Disney   ep   The Griswold Murder   2.20.59
   ABC
Rawhide   ep   Incident at Red River Station   1.15.60
   CBS
Playhouse 90   ep   Journey to the Day   4.22.60 CBS
Stagecoach West   ep   The Arsonist   2.14.61 ABC
Acapulco   ep   Death Is a Smiling Man   3.27.61 NBC

Naked City   ep   Sweet Prince of Delancey Street   6.7.
   61   ABC
Route 66   ep   Bridge across Five Days   11.17.61 CBS
Bonanza   ep   The Auld Sod   2.4.62 NBC
Follow the Sun   ep   Run, Clown, Run   4.1.62 ABC
Route 66   ep   Across Walnuts and Wine   11.2.62 CBS
Going My Way   ep   Keep an Eye on Santa Claus   12.
   12.62 ABC
Ben Casey   ep   Saturday, Surgery and Stanley Schultz
   12.31.62 ABC
Swingin' Together   pt   8.26.63 CBS
Great Adventures   ep   The Death of Sitting Bull   10.4.
   63, 10.11.63 CBS
Fugitive   ep   Decision in the Ring   10.22.63 ABC
Ben Casey   ep   The Black Cyclone   11.27.63 ABC
Virginian   ep   Man of the People   12.23.64 NBC
T.H.E. Cat   ep   12.23.66 NBC
Dundee and the Culhane   ep   11.15.67 CBS
Shadow over Elveron   tf   3.5.68 NBC

DUNN, MICHAEL
   Arrest and Trial   ep   The Revenge of the Worm   3.29.
      64 ABC
   East Side/West Side   ep   Here Today   4.27.64 CBS
   Get Smart   ep   Mr. Big   9.18.65 NBC
   Wild, Wild West   ep   The Night the Wizard Shook the
      Earth   10.1.65 CBS
   Amos Burke   ep   The Prisoners of Mr. Sin   10.27.65
      ABC
   Wild, Wild West   ep   11.19.65 CBS
   Wild, Wild West   ep   The Night of the Whirring Death
      2.18.66 CBS
   Wild, Wild West   ep   The Night of the Murderous
      Spring   4.15.66 CBS
   Wild, Wild West   ep   Night of the Raven   9.30.66 CBS
   Run for Your Life   ep   The Dark Beyond the Door   10.
      10.66 NBC
   Wild, Wild West   ep   11.18.66 CBS
   Voyage to the Bottom of the Sea   ep   3.5.67 ABC
   The Monroes   ep   3.15.67 ABC
   Wild, Wild West   ep   4.7.67 CBS
   Wild, Wild West   ep   9.29.67 CBS
   Wild, Wild West   ep   3.22.68 CBS
   Star Trek   ep   Plato's Stepchildren   11.22.68 NBC
   Wild, Wild West   ep   12.13.68 CBS
   Night Gallery   ep   The Sins of the Fathers   2.23.72
      NBC

Goodnight My Love   tf   10.17.72 ABC

DUNNE, IRENE
   Schlitz Playhouse of Stars   sh   5.30.52 CBS
   Ford Theatre   ep   Sister Veronica   4.15.54 NBC
   Ford Theatre   ep   Touch of Spring   2.3.55 NBC
   Loretta Young Show   ep hos   Slander   10.30.55 NBC
   Loretta Young Show   ep hos   Tropical Secretary   11.6.
      55 NBC
   Ford Theatre   ep   On the Beach   4.12.56 NBC
   Ford Theatre   ep   Sheila   5.24.56 NBC
   June Allyson Show   ep   The Opening Door   10.5.59
      CBS
   G.E. Theatre   ep   Go Fight City Hall   1.28.62 CBS
   Saints and Sinners   ep   Source of Information   10.15.
      62 NBC

DUNNOCK, MILDRED
   Television Theatre   ep   The Last Step   9.20.50 NBC
   The Web   ep   The Handcuff   5.7.52 CBS
   Celanese Theatre   ep   On Borrowed Time   6.25.52
      ABC
   Gulf Playhouse   ep   The Rose   10.17.52 NBC
   Broadway Television Theatre   ep   11.17.52 NN
   Studio One   ep   Mark of Cain   2.2.53 CBS
   The Web   ep   The Boy in the Front Row   4.12.53 CBS
   Suspense   ep   The Queen's Ring   6.2.53 CBS
   Goodyear Playhouse   ep   The Young and the Fair   7.26.
      53 NBC
   The Web   ep   Like Father   8.2.53 CBS
   Tales of the City   ep   Miracle in the Rain   8.20.53
      CBS
   The Web   ep   Speak No Evil   8.30.53 CBS
   Inner Sanctum   ep   Guilty Secrets   2.5.54 NN
   Goodyear Playhouse   ep   Game of Hide and Seek   2.7.
      54 NBC
   Inner Sanctum   ep   The Sisters   3.26.54 NN
   Medallion Theatre   ep   Sinners   3.6.54 CBS
   Armstrong Circle Theatre   ep   Treasure Trove   4.20.
      54 NBC
   TV Soundstage   ep   The Almighty Dollar   4.23.54 NBC
   Kraft Theatre   ep   The Worried Songbirds   5.13.54
      ABC
   Kraft Theatre   ep   Uncle Harry   8.26.54 ABC
   Kraft Theatre   ep   The Happy Journey   10.28.54 ABC
   Kraft Theatre   ep   A Child Is Born   12.23.54 ABC
   Kraft Theatre   ep   The Hickory Limb   1.13.55 ABC

Philco Playhouse   ep   A Business Proposition   10.23.
    55 NBC
Alcoa Hour   ep   President   5.13.56 NBC
Alfred Hitchcock Presents   ep   None Are So Blind   10.
    28.56 CBS
Kraft Theatre   ep   The Wonderful Gifts   12.19.56 NBC
Climax   ep   Don't Touch Me   4.4.57 CBS
Studio One   ep   The Traveling Lady   4.22.57 CBS
Playhouse 90   ep   Winter Dreams   5.23.57 CBS
Alfred Hitchcock Presents   ep   The West Warlock Time
    Capsule   5.26.57 CBS
Playhouse 90   ep   The Play Room   10.10.57 CBS
Alfred Hitchcock Presents   ep   Heart of Gold   10.27.57
    CBS
Kraft Theatre   ep   The Sound of Trouble   11.20.57 NBC
Playhouse 90   ep   Diary of a Nurse   5.7.59 CBS
Robert Herridge Theatre   ep   A Trip to Cardis   7.7.60
    CBS
Tom Ewell Show   ep   12.20.60 CBS
Thriller   ep   The Cheaters   12.27.60 NBC
Dupont Theatre   ep   Night of the Story   3.21.61 CBS
Power and the Glory   Sp   10.29.61 CBS
Investigators   ep   The Mind's Own Fire   12.14.61 CBS
Westinghouse Presents   ep   The First Day   6.20.62
    CBS
Alfred Hitchcock Theatre   ep   Beyond the Sea of Death
    1.24.64 CBS
Defenders   ep   The Man Who Saved His Country   5.9.
    64 CBS
Death of a Salesman   Sp   5.8.66 CBS
Experiment in Television   ep   The Hamster of Happi-
    ness   2.25.68 NBC
FBI   ep   The Prey   12.7.69 ABC
Ghost Story   ep   11.10.72 NBC

DUPREZ, JUNE
    Robert Montgomery Presents   ep   The Last Tycoon
        2.26.51 NBC

DURANTE, JIMMY
    Danny Thomas Show   ep   11.27.61 CBS
    Alice Through the Looking Glass   Sp   11.6.66 NBC
    Frosty the Snowman   Sp nar   12.5.71 CBS

DURYEA, DAN
    Schlitz Playhouse of Stars   ep   P.G.   1.25.52 ABC
    Schlitz Playhouse of Stars   ep   Singapore Souvenir

6.6.52 CBS
Ford Theatre   ep   Double Exposure   3.26.53 NBC
China Smith   sr   5.13.53 ABC
Schlitz Playhouse of Stars   ep   O'Brien   4.15.55 CBS
Rheingold Theatre   ep   The Lie   7.2.55 NBC
Fireside Theatre   ep   Nailed Down   11.1.55 NBC
December Bride   ep   12.12.55 CBS
20th Century-Fox Hour   ep   Smoke Jumpers   11.14.56
    CBS
G.E. Theatre   ep   The Road that Led Afar   11.25.56
    CBS
Dupont Theatre   ep   The Frightened Witness   2.19.57
    ABC
Suspicion   ep   Doomsday   12.16.57 NBC
Wagon Train   ep   The Cliff Grundy Story   12.25.57
    NBC
Zane Grey Theatre   ep   This Man Must Die   1.24.58
    CBS
Climax   ep   Four Hours in White   2.6.58 CBS
U.S. Steel Hour   ep   Hour of the Rat   5.21.58 CBS
Wagon Train   ep   The Sacramento Story   9.24.58 NBC
Cimarron City   ep   Terror Town   10.18.58 NBC
Wagon Train   ep   Last Man   2.11.59 NBC
World of Disney   ep   Showdown at Sandoval   1.23.59
    ABC
Rawhide   ep   Incident with an Executioner   1.23.59 CBS
Desilu Playhouse   ep   Comeback   3.2.59 CBS
David Niven Theatre   ep   The Vengeance   6.30.59 ABC
Laramie   ep   Stage Stop   9.15.59 NBC
Twilight Zone   ep   Mr. Denton on Doomsday   10.16.59
    CBS
Adventures in Paradise   ep   Judith   2.1.60 ABC
G.E. Theatre   ep   The Road that Led Afar   2.14.60
    CBS
Riverboat   ep   The Wichita Arrows   2.29.60 NBC
Wagon Train   ep   The Joshua Gilliam Story   3.30.60
    NBC
G.E. Theatre   ep   Mystery at Malibu   4.10.60 CBS
U.S. Steel Hour   ep   Shadow of a Pale Horse   7.20.60
    CBS
Bonanza   ep   Badge without Honor   9.24.60 NBC
Shirley Temple Theatre   ep   Tom and Huck   10.9.60
    NBC
Laramie   ep   The Long Riders   10.25.60 NBC
Barbara Stanwyck Theatre   ep   Sign of the Zodiac   4.3.
    61 NBC
Zane Grey Theatre   ep   Knight of the Sun   3.9.61 CBS

Route 66 ep Don't Count Stars 4.28.61 CBS
Checkmate ep Tight as a Drum 5.13.61 CBS
Fronteir Circus ep The Shaggy Kings 10.12.61 CBS
Laramie ep The Mountainmen 10.17.61 NBC
Wagon Train ep The Wagon Train Mutiny 9.9.62
    ABC
Naked City ep Daughter, Am I in my Father's House
    10.3.62 ABC
Rawhide ep Incident of the Wolves 11.16.62 CBS
Wide Country ep Tears on a Painted Face 11.29.62
    NBC
Eleventh Hour ep Why Am I Grown so Cold 2.6.63
    NBC
Alcoa Premiere ep Blow High, Blow Clear 2.14.63
    ABC
U.S. Steel Hour ep The Many Ways of Heaven 5.1.
    63 CBS
Rawhide ep Incident of the Prophecy 11.21.63 CBS
Alfred Hitchcock Theatre ep Three Wives too Many
    1.3.64 CBS
Kraft Suspense Theatre ep Who Is Jennifer 1.16.64
    NBC
Burke's Law ep 3.20.64 ABC
Wagon Train ep 10.11.64 ABC
Bonanza ep Logan's Treasures 10.18.64 NBC
Daniel Boone ep The Sound of Fear 2.11.65 NBC
The Long Hot Summer ep The Return of the Quicks
    12.16.65 ABC
Loner ep A Little Stroll to the End of the Line 1.15.
    66 CBS
Combat ep Dateline 2.23.66 ABC
Virginian ep The Challenge 10.19.66 NBC
Combat ep 2.21.67 ABC
Winchester 73 tf 3.14.67 NBC
Peyton Place sr 9.7.67 ABC
Stranger on the Run tf 10.31.67 NBC

DURYEA, PETER
    Kraft Suspense Theatre ep Rumble on the Docks 10.
        22.64 NBC
    Defenders ep Survival 3.14.64 CBS
    Dr. Kildare ep Lullaby for an Indian Summer 1.7.65
        NBC
    Daniel Boone ep The Sound of Fear 2.11.65 NBC
    Bob Hope Chrysler Theatre ep A Time for Killing
        4.30.65 NBC
    Virginian ep Jacob Was a Plain Man 10.12.66 NBC

Combat   ep   3. 7. 67 ABC
Dragnet   ep   12. 14. 67 NBC
I Spy   ep Tag, You're It   1. 22. 68 NBC
Dragnet   ep   12. 12. 68 NBC
Family Affair   ep   1. 14. 71 CBS

DUVALL, ROBERT
Armstrong Circle Theatre   ep   The Jailbreak   10. 14. 59
   CBS
Drama   ep   Destiny's Tot   1. 24. 60 NBC
Armstrong Circle Theatre   ep   Positive Identification
   5. 25. 60 CBS
John Brown's Raid   Sp   10. 25. 60 NBC
Naked City   ep   A Hole in the City   2. 1. 61 ABC
Defenders   ep   Perjury   12. 2. 61 CBS
Alfred Hitchcock Theatre   ep   Bad Actor   1. 19. 62 NBC
Naked City   ep   The One Marked Hot Gives Cold   3. 21.
   62 ABC
Naked City   ep   Five Cranks for Winter   10. 24. 62 ABC
Naked City   ep   Torment Him   11. 7. 62 ABC
Untouchables   ep   Blues for a Gone Goose   1. 29. 63 ABC
Route 66   ep   Suppose I Saw I Was the Queen of Spain
   2. 8. 63 CBS
Twilight Zone   ep   Miniature   2. 21. 63 CBS
Defenders   ep   Metamorphosis   3. 2. 63 CBS
Virginian   ep   The Golden Door   3. 13. 63 NBC
Stoney Burke   ep   Joby   3. 18. 63 ABC
Fugitive   ep   Never Wave Goodbye   10. 8. 63,   10. 15. 63
   ABC
Arrest and Trial   ep   The Quality of Justice   11. 17. 63
   ABC
Lieutenant   ep   Lament for a Dead Goldbrick   3. 14. 64
   NBC
Kraft Suspense Theatre   ep   Portrait of an Unknown
   Man   4. 16. 64 NBC
Outer Limits   ep   The Chameleon   4. 27. 64 ABC
Outer Limits   ep   The Inheritors   11. 21. 64,   11. 28. 64
   ABC
Combat   ep   The Enemy   1. 5. 65 ABC
Voyage to the Bottom of the Sea   ep   The Invaders   1.
   25. 65 ABC
Defenders   ep   Only a Child   5. 13. 65 CBS
FBI   ep   The Giant Killer   11. 21. 65 ABC
Bob Hope Chrysler Theatre   ep   Guilty or Not Guilty
   3. 9. 66 NBC
Hawk   ep   The Theory of the Innocent Bystander   10.
   13. 66 ABC

FBI   ep   The Scourge   10.23.66 ABC
Felony Squad   ep   Death of a Dream   10.31.66 ABC
Shane   ep   Poor Tom's a-cold   11.5.66 ABC
T.H.E. Cat   ep   11.18.66 NBC
Fame Is the Name of the Game   tf   11.26.66 NBC
Combat   ep   12.20.66 ABC
T.H.E. Cat   ep   3.10.67 NBC
Combat   ep   3.14.67 ABC
Cimarron Strip   ep   The Roarer   11.2.67 CBS
Wild, Wild West   ep   11.10.67 CBS
Run for Your Life   ep   The Killing Scene   1.31.68
    NBC
Judd for the Defense   ep   3.1.68 ABC
FBI   ep   11.24.68 ABC
Mod Squad   ep   Keep the Faith Baby   3.25.69 ABC
FBI   ep   Nightmare Road   9.21.69 ABC

DVORAK, ANN
Silver Theatre   ep   Close-Up   5.29.50 CBS
Gruen Guild Theatre   ep   Ballerina   11.22.51 ABC
Bigelow-Sanford Theatre   ep   Flowers for John   12.7.
    51 NN
Celanese Theatre   ep   Street Scene   4.2.52 ABC
Broadway Television Theatre   ep   The Trial of Mary
    Dugan   4.14.52 NN

-E-

EASTWOOD, CLINT
Navy Log   ep   The Lonely Watch   1.9.58 ABC
West Point   ep   White Fury   2.4.58 ABC
Rawhide   sr   1.9.59 CBS
Rawhide   sr ret   fall, 1959 CBS
Rawhide   sr ret   fall, 1960 CBS
Rawhide   sr ret   9.29.61 CBS
Rawhide   sr ret   9.21.62 CBS
Rawhide   sr ret   9.26.63 CBS
Rawhide   sr ret   9.25.64 CBS
Rawhide   sr ret   9.14.65 CBS

EATON, SHIRLEY
The Saint   sr   9.22.63 NBC
The Scorpio Letters   tf   2.19.67 ABC

The Saint   sr ret   2.17.68 NBC
The Saint   sr ret   4.18.69 NBC

EBSEN, BUDDY
    Gruen Guild Playhouse   ep   Al Haddon's Lamp   5.8.52
        NN
    Broadway Television Theatre   ep   Burlesque   7.1.52
        NN
    Broadway Television Theatre   ep   The Nervous Wreck
        10.27.52 NN
    Broadway Television Theatre   ep   Seven Keys to Bald-
        pate   11.10.52 NN
    Schlitz Playhouse of Stars   ep   The Pussyfooting Rocks
        11.21.52 CBS
    Twilight Theatre   ep   Nor Gloom of Night   6.22.53 ABC
    Omnibus   ep   The House   3.7.54 CBS
    World of Disney   ep   Davy Crockett, Indian Fighter   12.
        15.54 ABC
    World of Disney   ep   Davy Crockett Goes to Congress
        1.26.55 ABC
    World of Disney   ep   Davy Crockett   at the Alamo   2.
        23.55 ABC
    World of Disney   ep   Davy Crockett and the Kneelboat
        Race   11.16.55 ABC
    World of Disney   ep   Davy Crockett and the River Pi-
        rates   12.14.55 ABC
    Studio 57   ep   My Baby Boy   4.29.56 NN
    Climax   ep   Tunnel of Fear   10.24.57 CBS
    Northwest Passage   sr   9.14.58 NBC
    Playhouse 90   ep   A Trip to Paradise   3.29.59 CBS
    Playhouse 90   ep   Free Weekend   7.23.59 CBS
    Black Saddle   ep   The Apprentice   3.11.60 ABC
    Rawhide   ep   Incident of the Stargazer   4.1.60 CBS
    Johnny Ringo   ep   The Killing Bug   4.28.60 CBS
    Maverick   ep   Cats of Paradise   5.1.60 ABC
    G.E. Theatre   ep   Graduation Dress   10.30.60 CBS
    Maverick   ep   The Maverick Line   11.30.60 ABC
    Gunsmoke   ep   12.24.60 CBS
    77 Sunset Strip   ep   Open and Close in One   3.17.61
        ABC
    Twilight Zone   ep   The Prime Mover   3.24.61 CBS
    Tales of Wells Fargo   ep   To Kill a Town   3.31.61
        NBC
    Gunslinger   ep   Golden Circle   4.13.61 CBS
    Have Gun Will Travel   ep   4.15.61 CBS
    Barbara Stanwyck Theatre   ep   Little Big Mouth   5.8.
        61 NBC

Gunsmoke   ep   10.28.61 CBS
Bus Stop   ep   Cherie   11.12.61 ABC
Have Gun Will Travel   ep   11.25.61 CBS
Bus Stop   ep   The Man from Bootstrap   11.26.61 ABC
Adventures in Paradise   ep   One-Way Ticket   12.3.61
    ABC
Rawhide   ep   The Pitchwagon   3.2.62 CBS
Westinghouse Presents   ep   That's Whither the Town's
    Going   4.17.62 CBS
Beverly Hillbillies   sr   9.26.62 CBS
Beverly Hillbillies   sr ret   9.25.63 CBS
Beverly Hillbillies   sr ret   9.64 CBS
Beverly Hillbillies   sr ret   9.15.65 CBS
Beverly Hillbillies   sr ret   9.14.66 CBS
Beverly Hillbillies   sr ret   9.6.67 CBS
Beverly Hillbillies   sr ret   9.24.68 CBS
Beverly Hillbillies   sr ret   9.24.69 CBS
Beverly Hillbillies   sr ret   9.15.70 CBS
Gunsmoke   ep   11.22.71 CBS
Bonanza   ep   Saddle Stiff   1.16.72 NBC
Night Gallery   ep   The Waiting Room   1.26.72 NBC
Alias Smith and Jones   ep   2.24.72 ABC
The Daughters of Joshua Cabe   tf   9.13.72 ABC
Alias Smith and Jones   ep   High Lonesome Country
    9.23.72 ABC

EDDY, NELSON
The Desert Song   Sp   5.7.55 NBC
Danny Thomas Show   ep   10.8.56 ABC

EDEN, BARBARA
West Point   ep   Decision   11.23.56 CBS
I Love Lucy   ep   4.22.57 CBS
Gunsmoke   ep   11.9.57 CBS
December Bride   ep   The Other Woman   12.9.57 CBS
Father Knows Best   ep   The Rivals   1.29.58 NBC
How to Marry a Millionaire   sr   10.7.58 NN
Perry Mason   ep   The Case of the Angry Mourner   3.
    28.59 CBS
Adventures in Paradise   ep   The Inheritance   12.24.61
    ABC
Andy Griffith Show   ep   1.22.62 CBS
Cain's Hundred   ep   Savage in Darkness   3.27.62 NBC
Saints and Sinners   ep   Daddy's Girl   11.12.62 NBC
Dr. Kildare   ep   If You Can't Believe the Truth   10.10.
    63 NBC
Burke's Law   ep   Who Killed Harris Crown   10.11.63
    ABC

Rawhide   ep   Incident at Confidence Rock   11.28.63
   CBS
Route 66   ep   Where There's a Will, There's a Way
   3.6.64, 3.13.64 CBS
Burke's Law   ep   3.20.64 ABC
Virginian   ep   The Brazos Kid   10.21.64 NBC
Burke's Law   ep   10.28.64 ABC
Rawhide   ep   Damon's Road   11.13.64, 11.20.64 CBS
Slattery's People   2.19.65 CBS
Rogues   ep   Wherefore Art Thou, Harold   3.21.65 NBC
I Dream of Jeannie   sr   9.18.65 NBC
I Dream of Jeannie   sr ret   9.12.66 NBC
I Dream of Jeannie   sr ret   9.12.67 NBC
Kismet   Sp   10.24.67 ABC
I Dream of Jeannie   sr ret   9.16.68 NBC
The Feminist and the Fuzz   tf   1.26.71 ABC

EDWARDS, JAMES
   Cavalcade Theatre   ep   Toward Tomorrow   10.4.55 ABC
   20th Century-Fox Hour   ep   The Last Patriarch   11.28.
      56 CBS
   Meet McGraw   sr   7.2.57 NBC
   Climax   ep   The Volcano Seat   4.10.58 CBS
   Desilu Playhouse   ep   Silent Thunder   12.8.58 CBS
   Peter Gunn   ep   Sing a Song of Murder   3.7.60 NBC
   Lloyd Bridges Show   ep   The Testing Ground   10.23.62
      CBS
   Fugitive   ep   Decision in the Ring   10.22.63 ABC
   East Side/West Side   ep   Where's Harry   12.9.63 CBS
   Eleventh Hour   ep   Who Chopped Down the Cherry Tree
      1.29.64 NBC
   Outcasts   ep   11.18.68 ABC
   Nurses   ep   The Courage to Be   2.6.64 CBS
   Outsider   ep   I Can't Hear You Scream   11.27.68 NBC
   Virginian   ep   12.4.68 NBC
   Mannix   ep   The Sound of Darkness   12.6.69 CBS

EDWARDS, VINCE
   Ford Theatre   ep   Garrity's Sons   3.24.55 NBC
   Fireside Theatre   ep   The Smuggler   10.25.55 NBC
   G.E. Theatre   ep   Bitter Choice   4.21.57 CBS
   Alfred Hitchcock Presents   ep   The Young One   12.1.57
      CBS
   Untouchables   ep   Mexican Standoff   11.26.59 ABC
   Laramie   ep   The Protectors   3.22.60 NBC
   Adventures in Paradise   ep   The Raft   6.6.60 ABC
   Ben Casey   sr   10.2.61 ABC

Ben Casey   sr ret   10. 1. 62 ABC
Ben Casey   sr ret   9. 18. 63 ABC
Ben Casey   sr ret   9. 14. 64 ABC
Ben Casey   sr ret   9. 13. 65 ABC
Dial Hot Line   tf   3. 8. 70 ABC
Matt Lincoln   sr   9. 24. 70 ABC
Do Not Fold, Spindle or Mutilate   tf   11. 9. 71 ABC

EGAN, EDDIE
Mannix   ep   9. 18. 72 CBS

EGAN, RICHARD
Ford Theatre   ep   Double Bet   11. 26. 53 NBC
Schlitz Playhouse of Stars   ep   Go Away a Winner   1. 1.
     54 CBS
Empire   sr   9. 25. 62 NBC
Redigo   sr   9. 24. 63 NBC
Bob Hope Chrysler Theatre   ep   Massacre at Ft. Phil
     Kearny   10. 26. 66 NBC
The House that Wouldn't Die   tf   10. 27. 70 ABC

EGGAR, SAMANTHA
Anna and the King of Siam   sr   9. 17. 72 CBS

EKBERG, ANITA
Casablanca   sr   9. 27. 55 ABC

EKLAND, BRITT
Carol for Another Christmas   tf   12. 28. 64 ABC
Trials of O'Brien   ep   The Greatest Game   2. 18. 66,
     2. 25. 66 CBS
McCloud   ep   12. 3. 72 NBC

ELDRIDGE, FLORENCE
Video Theatre   ep   The Speech   4. 30. 51 CBS
Video Theatre   ep   Ferry Crisis at Friday Point   5. 19.
     52 CBS
Dupont Show of the Month   ep   The Winslow Boy   11. 13.
     58 CBS

ELG, TAINA
Northwest Passage   ep   The Secret of the Cliff   1. 9. 59
     NBC
Wagon Train   ep   The Countess Baranof Story   5. 11. 60
     NBC
Hong Kong   ep   The Jumping Dragon   11. 2. 60 ABC
It Takes a Thief   ep   3. 19. 68 ABC

ELLINGTON, DUKE
   U.S. Steel Hour   ep   A Drum Is a Woman   5.8.57 CBS

ELLIOTT, CASS
   Love American Style   ep   10.6.72 ABC

ELLIOTT, DENHAM
   Studio One   ep   One Pair of Hands   3.5.51 CBS
   Hallmark Hall of Fame   ep   The Lark   2.10.57 NBC
   Dupont Show of the Month   ep   A Tale of Two Cities
      3.27.58 CBS
   Dupont Show of the Month   ep   Wuthering Heights   5.9.
      58 CBS
   Alfred Hitchcock Presents   ep   The Crocodile Case   5.
      25.58 CBS
   Dupont Show of the Month   ep   The Winslow Boy   11.
      13.58 CBS
   Alfred Hitchcock Presents   ep   3.1.59 CBS
   Family Classics   ep   Vanity Fair   1.12.61, 1.13.61
      CBS
   Hallmark Hall of Fame   ep   The Invincible Mr. Dis-
      raeli   4.4.63 NBC
   Hallmark Hall of Fame   ep   The Holy Terror   4.7.65
      NBC
   Dr. Jekyll and Mr. Hyde   ep   Sp   1.7.68 ABC
   Persuaders   ep   1.12.72 ABC
   Madame Sin   tf   1.15.72 ABC

ELY, RON
   Wyatt Earp   ep   The Posse   5.10.60 ABC
   Father Knows Best   ep   Crisis over a Kiss   9.12.60
      CBS
   Aquanauts   sr   1.25.61 CBS
   Thriller   ep   Waxworks   1.8.62 NBC
   Tarzan   sr   9.15.67 NBC
   Tarzan   sr ret   9.8.68 NBC
   Ironside   ep   A Killing at the Track   2.4.71 NBC

EMERSON, FAYE
   Billy Rose's Playbill   ep   George III Once Drooled in
      this Plate   10.23.50 NN
   Goodyear Theatre   ep   Catch a Falling Star   6.28.53
      NBC
   U.S. Steel Hour   ep   Hope for a Harvest   11.10.53 ABC
   Studio One   ep   Melissa   10.11.54 CBS
   U.S. Steel Hour   ep   The Fifth Wheel   10.26.54 ABC
   U.S. Steel Hour   ep   Secret in the Family   10.22.58 CBS

U. S. Steel Hour   ep   Call It a Day   5. 20. 59 CBS
U. S. Steel Hour   ep   The Oddball   4. 5. 61 CBS

ERICKSON, LEIF
   Story Theatre   ep   The Marquis   3. 9. 51 NN
   Schlitz Playhouse of Stars   ep   Say Hello to Pamela   6.
      20. 52 CBS
   Schlitz Playhouse of Stars   ep   Homecoming   9. 5. 52
      CBS
   The Unexpected   ep   Blackmail   10. 1. 52 NBC
   The Millionaire   ep   The Brian Hendricks Story   2. 8. 56
      CBS
   Climax   ep   The Gold Dress   1. 17. 57 CBS
   Playhouse 90   ep   One Coat of White   2. 21. 57 CBS
   Playhouse 90   ep   Panic Button   11. 28. 57 CBS
   Alfred Hitchcock Presents   ep   The Equalizer   2. 9. 58
      CBS
   Matinee Theatre   ep   The Vigilante   3. 4. 58 NBC
   Zane Gray Theatre   ep   The Sharpshooter   3. 7. 58 CBS
   G. E. Theatre   ep   The Cold Touch   4. 13. 58 CBS
   Rifleman   ep   The Sharpshooter   9. 30. 58 ABC
   Colgate Theatre   ep   9. 30. 58 NBC
   Playhouse 90   ep   The Raider   2. 19. 59 CBS
   June Allyson Show   ep   Dark Morning   9. 28. 59 CBS
   Hotel de Paree   ep   The High Cost of Living   10. 23. 59
      CBS
   Zane Grey Theatre   ep   The Sunday Man   2. 25. 60 CBS
   Playhouse 90   ep   The Shape of the River   5. 2. 60 CBS
   Welcome to Washington   pt   9. 23. 60 CBS
   Bonanza   ep   The Rescue   2. 25. 61 NBC
   Rawhide   ep   Incident Near Gloomy River   3. 17. 61 CBS
   Rebel   ep   Helping Hand   4. 30. 61 ABC
   New Breed   ep   Care Is No Cure   1. 23. 62 ABC
   Alcoa Premiere   ep   The Broken Year   4. 4. 63 ABC
   Arrest and Trial   ep   Whose Little Girl Are You   10.
      27. 63 ABC
   Wagon Train   ep   The Eli Bancroft Story   11. 11. 63 ABC
   Hazel   ep   Hazel and the Vanishing Hero   11. 28. 63 NBC
   Great Adventure   ep   The Outlaw and the Nun   12. 6. 63
      CBS
   The Travels of Jaimie McPheeters   ep   The Day of the
      Toll Takers   1. 5. 64 ABC
   Virginian   ep   The Drifter   1. 29. 64 NBC
   Great Adventure   ep   The President Vanishes   3. 13. 64
      CBS
   Virginian   ep   Return a Stranger   11. 18. 64 NBC
   Burke's Law   ep   12. 23. 64 ABC

Alfred Hitchcock Theatre ep Consider Her Ways 12.
  28.64 NBC
Alfred Hitchcock Theatre ep The Monkey's Paw 4.19.
  65 NBC
Daniel Boone ep 10.28.65 NBC
Bonanza ep All Ye His Saints 12.19.65 NBC
Gunsmoke ep 1.7.67 CBS
High Chaparral sr 9.10.67 NBC
Daniel Boone ep 12.15.67 NBC
High Chaparral sr ret 9.20.68 NBC
High Chaparral sr ret 9.19.69 NBC
Paris 7000 ep To Cage a Lion 2.19.70 ABC
High Chaparral sr ret 9.18.70 NBC
Name of the Game ep Seek and Destroy 2.5.71 NBC
Terror in the Sky tf 9.17.71 CBS
The Deadly Dream tf 9.25.71 ABC
Longstreet ep The Old Team Spirit 12.16.71 ABC
Sixth Sense ep The Heart that Wouldn't Stay Buried
  1.22.72 ABC
Insight ep The Governor's Mansion 3.18.72 NN
New Healers pt 3.27.72 ABC
Mod Squad ep 10.26.72 ABC
Owen Marshall ep Love Child 11.9.72 ABC
Marcus Welby, M.D. ep 11.21.72 ABC

ERICSON, JOHN
  Saturday's Children Sp 10.2.50 CBS
  Television Playhouse ep A Matter of Life and Death
    2.4.51 NBC
  Television Theatre ep Delicate Story 3.6.51 NBC
  G.E. Theatre ep Shadow on the Heart 10.30.55 CBS
  Star Stage ep The Girl Who Wasn't Wanted 11.25.55
    NBC
  Loretta Young Show ep A Ticket for May 1.1.56 NBC
  Schlitz Playhouse of Stars ep The Young and the Brave
    3.16.56 CBS
  Cavalcade Theatre ep A Life to Live By 3.20.56 ABC
  Schlitz Playhouse of Stars ep Date for Tomorrow 5.
    25.56 CBS
  Kraft Theatre ep Long Arm 7.11.56 NBC
  Climax ep The Man Who Lost His Head 7.26.56 CBS
  Playhouse 90 ep Heritage of Anger 11.15.56 CBS
  Zane Grey Theatre ep Stage for Tucson 11.16.56 CBS
  Schlitz Playhouse of Stars ep The Letter 11.23.56
    CBS
  Schlitz Playhouse of Stars ep The Enchanted 1.25.57
    CBS

Dupont Theatre ep Decision for a Hero 2.12.57 ABC
Climax ep The Long Count 2.21.57 CBS
Loretta Young Show ep Emergency 3.24.57 NBC
Climax ep Along Came a Spider 9.26.57 CBS
Climax ep The Devil's Brood 12.5.57 CBS
The Millionaire ep The Peter Barley Story 1.15.58
CBS
Zane Grey Theatre ep License to Kill 2.7.58 CBS
Shirley Temple's Story Book ep The Legend of Sleepy
Hollow 3.5.58 NBC
Restless Gun ep The Hand Is Quicker 3.17.58 NBC
Playhouse 90 ep The Innocent Sleep 6.5.58 CBS
Shirley Temple's Story Book ep Hiawatha 10.5.58
NBC
Zane Grey Theatre ep The Tall Shadow 11.20.58
CBS
The Millionaire ep The Peter Bartley Story 11.26.58
CBS
Wagon Train ep The Dick Richardson Story 12.31.58
NBC
Zane Grey Theatre ep Trail Incident 1.29.59 CBS
Rawhide ep Incident of the Chubasco 4.3.59 CBS
Restless Gun ep Four Lives 4.13.59 NBC
David Niven Theatre ep Sticks and Stone 6.23.59
NBC
Adventures in Paradise ep Safari at Sea 11.16.59
ABC
Loretta Young Show ep The Grenade 1.3.60 NBC
Mystery Show ep Blind Man's Bluff 9.11.60 NBC
Bonanza ep Breed of Violence 11.5.60 NBC
U.S. Steel Hour ep The Mating Machine 1.11.61 CBS
Rawhide ep Incident Near Gloomy River 3.17.61 CBS
Mystery Theatre ep Night Panic 7.18.62 NBC
Dick Powell Theatre ep The Sea Witch 10.23.62 NBC
Burke's Law ep 2.28.64 ABC
Burke's Law ep 4.21.65 ABC
Honey West sr 9.17.65 ABC
Profiles in Courage ep Prudence Crandall 2.21.66
NBC
Bob Hope Chrysler Theatre ep Guilty or Not Guilty
3.9.66 NBC
Bonanza ep Journey to Terror 2.5.67 NBC
Invaders ep 4.18.67 ABC
FBI ep 2.18.68 ABC
Gunsmoke ep 1.6.69 CBS
Ironside ep Beware the Wiles of the Stranger 1.22.
70 NBC

Marcus Welby, M. D.   ep   Sea of Security   3. 10. 70
ABC
Men from Shiloh   ep   The Politician   1. 13. 71 NBC
Medical Center   ep   The Albatross   11. 3. 71 CBS
Longstreet   ep   The Old Team Spirit   12. 16. 71 ABC
The Bounty Man   tf   10. 31. 72 ABC

ERSKINE, MARILYN
G. E. Theatre   ep   Woman's World   10. 25. 53 CBS
Robert Montgomery Presents   ep   The Glass Cage   4.
13. 53 NBC
Pepsi Cola Playhouse   ep   The House Nobody Wanted
11. 13. 53 ABC
U. S. Steel Hour   ep   Morning Star   3. 2. 54 ABC
Drama   ep   The Boss Comes to Dinner   6. 27. 54 NBC
Schlitz Playhouse of Stars   ep   By-Line   7. 30. 54 CBS
Lux Video Theatre   ep   So Evil My Love   1. 27. 55 NBC
Ford Theatre   ep   The Lilac Bush   3. 3. 55 NBC
Fireside Theatre   ep   It's Easy to Get Ahead   3. 29. 55
NBC
Climax   ep   Private Worlds   4. 7. 55 CBS
Damon Runyon Theatre   ep   Dancing Dan's Christmas
4. 23. 55 CBS
Schlitz Playhouse of Stars   ep   Ordeal of Dr. Sutton
7. 1. 55 CBS
Science Fiction Theatre   ep   The Frozen Sound   7. 29. 55
NBC
Schlitz Playhouse of Stars   ep   Uninhibited Female   9. 9.
55 CBS
Climax   ep   Scheme to Defraud   11. 10. 55 CBS
TV Reader's Digest   ep   Texas in New York   2. 13. 56
ABC
Loretta Young Show   ep   Tightwad Millionaire   2. 19. 56
NBC
Screen Directors Playhouse   ep   It's a Most Unusual
Day   3. 14. 56 NBC
TV Reader's Digest   ep   The Woman Who Changed Her
Mind   4. 16. 56 ABC
Ford Theatre   ep   The Kill   5. 17. 56 NBC
Lux Video Theatre   ep   A Marriage Day   7. 5. 56 NBC
Climax   ep   Fury at Dawn   7. 19. 56 CBS
20th Century-Fox Hour   ep   End of a Gun   1. 9. 57 CBS
Climax   ep   The Stalker   2. 7. 57 CBS
Ford Theatre   ep   Ringside Seat   2. 13. 57 ABC
Lux Video Theatre   ep   Black Angel   3. 28. 57 NBC
Lux Video Theatre   ep   Who Is Picasso   7. 4. 57 NBC
Playhouse 90   ep   The Playroom   10. 10. 57 CBS

Studio One   ep   The Other Place   1.13.58 CBS
Matinee Theatre   ep   The Odd Ones   2.7.58 NBC
Matinee Theatre   ep   With Love We Live   3.11.58 NBC
Climax   ep   The Big Success   5.8.58 CBS
Studio One   ep   The Undiscovered   6.30.58 NBC
Zane Grey Theatre   ep   Man Alone   3.5.59 CBS
Wichita Town   ep   Ruby Does   1.6.60 NBC
Tom Ewell Show   sr   9.27.60 CBS
Perry Mason   ep   The Case of the Careless Kidnapper
     4.30.64 CBS
Virginian   ep   Shadows of the Past   2.24.66 NBC
Perry Mason   ep   The Case of the Unwelcome Well
     4.3.66 CBS
Laredo   ep   2.24.67 NBC
Ironside   ep   1.27.72 NBC

ERWIN, STUART
Circle Theatre   ep   Jackpot   6.13.50 NBC
Trouble with Father (a.k.a. Life with the Erwins, The
     Stu Erwin Show)   sr   10.21.50 ABC
Trouble with Father   sr ret   10.51 ABC
Armstrong Circle Theatre   ep   The Lucky Suit   5.6.52
     NBC
Trouble with Father   sr ret   10.17.52 ABC
Trouble with Father   sr ret   10.53 ABC
The New Stu Erwin Show   sr c. 1955
Playhouse 90   ep   Snow Shoes   1.3.57 CBS
Crossroads   ep   Patchwork Family   6.21.57 ABC
Playhouse 90   ep   The Right Hand Man   3.20.58 CBS
Pursuit   ep   The Vengeance   11.22.58 CBS
World of Disney   ep   A Diamond Is a Boy's Best Friend
     10.2.59, 10.9.59 ABC
Father Knows Best   ep   Family Contest   4.3.60 CBS
World of Disney   ep   Wrong Way Mooche   4.15.60, 4.22.
     60 ABC
Thriller   ep   The Watcher   11.1.60 NBC
Andy Griffith Show   ep   11.28.60 CBS
Peter Loves Mary   ep   Doc Bailey Day   3.15.61 NBC
Perry Mason   ep   The Case of the Posthumous Painter
     11.11.61 CBS
Ichabod and Me   ep   Made in Japan   2.20.62 CBS
Straightaway   ep   Full Circle   3.14.62 ABC
National Velvet   ep   4.2.62 NBC
Armstrong Cirlce Theatre   ep   The Friendly Thieves
     10.24.62 CBS
Perry Mason   ep   The Case of the Double-Entry Mind
     11.1.62 CBS

Untouchables   ep   The Floyd Gibbons Story   12.11.62
  ABC
Our Man Higgins   ep   The Milkman Cometh   1.9.63
  ABC
Defenders   ep   The Poisoned Fruit Doctrine   1.19.63
  CBS
The Greatest Show on Earth   sr   9.17.63 ABC
Donna Reed Show   ep   9.19.63 ABC
Perry Mason   ep   The Case of the Scandalous Sculptor
  10.8.64 CBS
Dr. Kildare   ep   Take Care of My Little Girl   1.14.65
  NBC
Perry Mason   ep   The Case of the Impetuous Imp   10.
  10.65 CBS
Lassie   ep   12.4.66 CBS
Gunsmoke   ep   12.5.66 CBS
Bonanza   ep   Three Brides for Hoss   2.20.66 NBC
Virginian   ep   1.18.67 NBC
Big Valley   ep   11.20.67, 11.27.67 ABC
Shadow over Elveron   tf   3.5.68 NBC

ESTELITA
  I Spy   ep   There Was a Little Girl   4.6.66 NBC

EVANS, DALE
  Roy Rogers Show   sr   12.30.51 NBC
  Roy Rogers Show   sr ret   8.31.52 NBC

EVANS, EDITH (DAME)
  Hallmark Hall of Fame   ep   Time Remembered   2.7.61
    NBC
  Pursue and Destroy   pt   8.14.66 ABC
  Masterpiece Theatre   ep   The Gambler   11.14.71 NN

EVANS, MADGE
  Philco Playhouse   ep   Sense and Sensibility   6.4.50
    NBC
  Cameo Theatre   ep   Deception   7.16.51 NBC
  Video Theatre   ep   Kill That Story!   6.25.53 CBS
  Armstrong Circle Theatre   ep   Judgment   9.1.53 NBC
  Medallion Theatre   ep   The Trouble Train   10.10.53
    CBS
  Studio One   ep   Fear Is No Stranger   5.10.54 CBS
  Studio One   ep   The Magic Monday   8.2.54 CBS

EVANS, MAURICE
  Hallmark Hall of Fame   ep   Hamlet   4.26.53 NBC

Hallmark Hall of Fame ep King Richard II 1.24.54 NBC

Hallmark Hall of Fame ep Macbeth 11.28.54 NBC

Hallmark Hall of Fame ep The Devil's Disciple 11. 20.55 NBC

Hallmark Hall of Fame ep The Taming of the Shrew 3.18.56 NBC

Hallmark Hall of Fame ep Man and Superman 11.25. 56 NBC

Hallmark Hall of Fame ep Twelfth Night 12.15.57 NBC

Hallmark Hall of Fame ep Dial M for Murder 4.25. 58 NBC

G.E. Theatre ep Caesar and Cleopatra 4.12.59 CBS

U.S. Steel Hour ep No Leave for the Captain 6.17. 59 CBS

Hallmark Hall of Fame ep The Tempest 2.3.60 NBC

Hallmark Hall of Fame ep (restaged) Macbeth 11.20. 60 NBC

Westinghouse Presents ep Come Again to Carthage 12.8.61 CBS

U.S. Steel Hour ep The Loves of Claire Ambler 4. 4.62 CBS

Bewitched ep 11.19.64 ABC

Bob Hope Chrysler Theatre ep The Game 9.15.65 NBC

The Man from U.N.C.L.E. ep The Bridge of Lions Affair 2.4.66, 2.11.66 NBC

War of the Roses Sp hos 2.13.66, 2.20.66, 2.27.66 NN

Heartbreak House Sp 4.24.66 NN

Batman ep The Puzzler 12.21.66, 12.22.66 ABC

Tarzan ep Basil of the Jungle 2.10.67 NBC

Tarzan ep 4.7.67 NBC

Daniel Boone ep 10.12.67 NBC

I Spy ep Oedipus at Colonus 11.27.67 NBC

Hallmark Hall of Fame ep St. Joan 12.4.67 NBC

Tarzan ep 3.1.68, 3.8.68 NBC

FBI ep 12.1.68 ABC

Name of the Game ep 3.21.69 NBC

Bewitched ep 4.10.69 ABC

U.M.C. tf 4.17.69 CBS

Big Valley ep 4.21.69 ABC

Bewitched ep 10.23.69

Mod Squad ep 12.23.69 ABC

The Brotherhood of the Bell tf 9.17.70 CBS

Search ep 9.13.72 NBC

EVELYN, JUDITH
    Circle Theatre   ep   Green Eyes   12.12.50 NBC
    Studio One   ep   Macbeth   1.9.51 CBS
    Sure as Fate   ep   The Devil Takes A Bride   2.6.51
       CBS
    Starlight Theatre   ep   Miss Buell   3.8.51 CBS
    Drama   ep   Three in a Room   6.1.51 CBS
    Studio One   ep   Coriolanus   6.11.51 CBS
    Somerset Maugham Theatre   ep   The Letter   6.25.51
       NBC
    Armstrong Cirlce Theatre   ep   Runaway Heart   10.2.51
       NBC
    Studio One   ep (restaged)   Macbeth   10.22.51 CBS
    Suspense   ep   The Lonely Place   12.25.51 CBS
    Goodyear Playhouse   ep   3.16.52 NBC
    Studio One   ep   Abraham Lincoln   5.26.52 CBS
    Broadway Television Theatre   ep   The Enchanted Cot-
       tage   12.22.52 NN
    Broadway Television Theatre   ep   The Acquittal   1.26.
       53 NN
    Plymouth Playhouse   ep   A Tale of Two Cities   5.3.53,
       5.10.53 ABC
    Suspense   ep   The Sister   9.29.53 CBS
    Schlitz Playhouse of Stars   ep   In the Pincers   10.16.
       53 CBS
    Lamp Unto My Feet   ep   No Pets Allowed   3.20.55 CBS
    Window   ep   Rose's Boy   7.29.55 CBS
    Kraft Theatre   ep   The Failure   8.17.55 NBC
    Loretta Young Show   ep   The Bracelet   11.13.55 NBC
    Studio 57   ep   The Girl in the Bathing Suit   11.27.55
       NN
    Alfred Hitchcock Presents   ep   Guilty Witness   12.11.55
       CBS
    Front Row Center   ep   Hawk's Head   4.1.56 CBS
    Star Stage   ep   The Shadowy Third   4.20.56 NBC
    TV Reader's Digest   ep   Miss Victoria   4.30.56 ABC
    Goodyear Playhouse   ep   The Primary Colors   6.3.56
       NBC
    Climax   ep   The Gorsten Case   9.20.56 CBS
    Producers Showcase   ep   Mayerling   2.4.57 NBC
    Climax   ep   Avalanche at Devil's Pass   4.24.57 CBS
    Alfred Hitchcock Presents   ep   Martha Mason, Movie
       Star   5.19.57 CBS
    Climax   ep   The Secret of the Red Room   9.12.57 CBS
    Climax   ep   To Walk the Night   12.19.57 CBS
    Matinee Theatre   ep   2.14.58 NBC
    Schlitz Playhouse of Stars   ep   Two Lives Have I   2.28.
       58 CBS

Matinee Theatre   ep   Angel Street   5. 9. 58 NBC
Shirley Temple's Story Book   ep   The Sleeping Beauty
    6. 8. 58 NBC
Behind Closed Doors   ep   Man in the Moon   11. 6. 58
    NBC
Tales of Wells Fargo   ep   Double Reverse   10. 19. 59
    NBC
Playhouse 90   ep   Alas, Babylon   4. 3. 60 CBS
Thriller   ep   What Beckoning Ghost   9. 18. 61 NBC
Tales of Wells Fargo   ep   Who Lives by the Gun   3.
    24. 62 NBC
Eleventh Hour   ep   Cry a Little for Mary, Too   11.
    28. 62 NBC

EVERETT, CHAD
Hawaiian Eye   ep   The Kahuna Curtain   11. 9. 60 ABC
77 Sunset Strip   ep   The College Caper   1. 20. 61 ABC
77 Sunset Strip   ep   The Rival Eye Caper   9. 22. 61
    ABC
Lawman   ep   The Son   10. 8. 61 ABC
Surfside 6   ep   The Artful Deceit   1. 22. 62 ABC
Cheyenne   ep   A Man Called Ragan   4. 23. 62 ABC
Hawaiian Eye   ep   Four-Cornered Triangle   2. 14. 62
    ABC
Hawaiian Eye   ep   Cricket   5. 2. 62 ABC
Dakotas   sr   1. 7. 63 ABC
Redigo   ep   Papa-San   11. 12. 63 NBC
Route 66   ep   Come Home Greta Inger Gruenschaffen
    12. 13. 63 CBS
Lieutenant   ep   Man with an Edge   3. 21. 64 NBC
Combat   ep   Beneath the Ashes   4. 27. 65 ABC
The Man from U. N. C. L. E.   ep   9. 25. 67 NBC
FBI   ep   12. 22. 68 ABC
Journey to the Unknown   ep   Poor Butterfly   1. 9. 69
    ABC
Ironside   ep   And Be My Love   2. 20. 69 NBC
Medical Center   sr   9. 24. 69 CBS
Medical Center   sr ret   9. 16. 70 CBS
Medical Center   sr ret   9. 15. 71 CBS
Medical Center   sr ret   9. 13. 72 CBS

EWELL, TOM
Billy Rose's Playbill   ep   Whirligig of Life   1. 22. 51
    NN
Studio One   ep   Mighty Like a Rogue   10. 8. 51 CBS
Lights Out   ep   The Deal   10. 22. 51 NBC
Robert Montgomery Presents   ep   See No Evil   3. 31.
    52 NBC

Playwrights '56 ep Daisy, Daisy 11.22.55 NBC
Alfred Hitchcock Presents ep The Case of Mr. Pel-
  ham 12.4.55 CBS
Alcoa Hour ep Man on Fire 3.4.56 NBC
U.S. Steel Hour ep The Square Egghead 3.11.59 CBS
G.E. Theatre ep The Day of the Hanging 10.25.59
  CBS
Tom Ewell Show sr 9.27.60 CBS
Golden Showcase ep The Fourposter 1.13.62 CBS
Dick Powell Theatre ep The Honorable Albert Higgins
  1.1.63 NBC
Burke's Law ep Who Killed Nobody Somehow 3.31.65
  ABC
The Kwimpers of New Jersey pt 8.13.66 ABC
Governor and J.J. ep 3.24.70 CBS
Men from Shiloh ep With Love, Bullets and Valentines
  10.7.70 NBC
Name of the Game ep A Sister from Napoli 1.8.71
  NBC
Alias Smith and Jones ep The Proof of It All 4.1.71
  ABC

EYER, RICHARD
Cavalcade of America ep Spindletop 10.12.54 ABC
Playhouse ep The Woman on the Bus 12.12.54 ABC
Loretta Young Show ep Dickie 2.13.55 NBC
Ford Theatre ep Celebrity 3.17.55 NBC
Father Knows Best ep New Girl at School 10.5.55
  NBC
The Millionaire ep The Story of Victor Volante 2.22.
  56 CBS
Front Row Center ep Search for a Stranger 3.25.56
  CBS
20th Century-Fox Hour ep Overnight Haul 5.16.56
  CBS
Lux Video Theatre ep Only Yesterday 9.27.56 NBC
Dupont Theatre ep Once a Hero 12.11.56 ABC
Climax ep Strange Hostage 12.20.56 CBS
Dupont Theatre ep Shark of the Mountain 4.23.57
  ABC
Playhouse 90 ep Homeward Borne 5.9.57 CBS
Panic ep Peter and the Tiger 5.14.57 NBC
G.E. Theatre ep Mr. Kensington's Finest Hour 10.
  27.57 CBS
G.E. Theatre ep The Trail to Christmas 12.15.57
  CBS
Father Knows Best ep Kathy's Romance 10.6.58 CBS

Ed Wynn Show ep New Boy in Town 12.11.58 NBC
Desilu Playhouse ep Happy Hill 1.12.59 CBS
Lux Playhouse ep Boy on a Fence 5.15.59 CBS
Rawhide ep Incident of the Roman Candles 7.10.59
    CBS
Gunsmoke ep 11.14.59 CBS
Stagecoach West sr 10.4.60 ABC
Dr. Kildare ep A Time for Every Purpose 12.27.62
    NBC
Stoney Burke ep The Test 5.13.63 ABC
Arrest and Trial ep My Name Is Martin Burnham
    10.13.63 ABC
Great Adventure ep A Boy at War 12.20.63 CBS
Mr. Novak ep Day in the Year 3.24.64 NBC

EYTHE, WILLIAM
    Armstrong Circle Theatre ep Fog Station 11.6.51
        NBC
    Lights Out ep Perchance to Dream 12.17.51 NBC
    Tales of Tomorrow ep The Invaders 12.21.51 ABC
    Schlitz Playhouse of Stars ep The Haunted Heart 3.
        7.52 CBS
    Ford Theatre ep Indirect Approach 6.24.54 NBC

-F-

FABARES, SHELLEY
    Matinee Theatre ep Wuthering Heights 11.30.55 NBC
    Captain Midnight ep Flight into the Unknown 12.31.
        55 CBS
    Loretta Young Show ep Day of Rest 5.18.58 NBC
    Donna Reed Show sr 9.24.58 ABC
    Colgate Theatre ep 9.30.58 NBC
    Donna Reed Show sr ret 9.59 ABC
    Donna Reed Show sr ret 9.15.60 ABC
    Donna Reed Show sr ret 9.61 ABC
    Donna Reed Show sr ret 9.20.62 ABC
    Mr. Novak ep I Don't Even Live Here 10.8.63 NBC
    Donna Reed Show ep Mary Comes Home 11.7.63 ABC
    Mr. Novak ep My Name Is Not Legion 12.24.63 NBC
    Eleventh Hour ep How I Say I Love You 1.15.64 NBC
    Arrest and Trial ep An Echo of Conscience 1.26.64
        ABC

Twilight Zone   ep   Black Leather Jackets   1.31.64 CBS
Meet Me in St. Louis   pt   9.2.66 ABC
Daniel Boone   ep   2.27.69 NBC
Lancer   ep   3.11.69 CBS
U.M.C.   tf   4.17.69 CBS
Bracken's World   ep   A Package Deal   11.28.69 NBC
Love American Style   Love and Mother   12.1.69 ABC
Interns   ep   The Guardian   3.5.71 CBS
Love American Style   ep   3.12.71 ABC
Mannix   ep   A Step in Time   9.29.71 CBS
Longstreet   ep   11.4.71 ABC
Owen Marshall   ep   12.2.71 ABC
Love American Style   ep   1.7.72 ABC
McCloud   ep   Fifth Man in a String Quartet   2.2.72
   NBC
Two for the Money   tf   2.26.72 ABC
Cade's County   ep   3.26.72 CBS
Little People   sr   9.15.72 NBC

FABRAY, NANETTE
Omnibus   ep   Arms and the Man   5.3.53 CBS
High Button Shoes   Sp   11.24.56 NBC
Alcoa Hour   ep   The Original Miss Chase   3.17.57 NBC
Kaiser Aluminum Hour   ep   A Man's Game   4.23.57
   NBC
Westinghouse Playhouse   sr   1.6.61 NBC
Burke's Law   ep   3.27.64 ABC
Burke's Law   ep   10.28.64 ABC
Bob Hope Chrysler Theatre   ep   In Any Language   3.12.
   65 NBC
Alice Through the Looking Glass   Sp   11.6.66 NBC
The Girl from U.N.C.L.E.   ep   3.7.67 NBC
Love American Style   ep   1.30.70 ABC
George M   Sp   9.12.70 NBC
But I Don't Want to get Married   tf   10.6.70 ABC
Love American Style   ep   2.26.71 ABC
Love American Style   ep   12.10.71 ABC
Mary Tyler Moore Show   ep   10.28.72 CBS
Magic Carpet   tf   11.6.72 NBC
The Couple Take a Wife   tf   12.5.72 ABC

FAIRBANKS, DOUGLAS, JR.
Douglas Fairbanks Jr. Presents   sh/sr   1.7.53 NBC
Douglas Fairbanks Jr. Presents   sh/sr ret   1954 NBC
Rheingold Theatre   ep   Counterfeit   6.22.55 NBC
U.S. Steel Hour   ep   Nightmare at Bleak Hill   2.7.62
   CBS

Route 66   ep   Kiss the Maiden all Forlorn   4.13.62
   CBS
Dupont Show of the Month   ep   The Shadowed Affair
   11.4.62 NBC
Dr. Kildare   ep   An Ungodly Act   4.9.64 NBC
ABC Stage 67   ep   The Canterville Ghost   11.2.66
   ABC
Legend of Robin Hood   Sp   2.18.68 NBC
The Crooked Hearts   tf   11.8.72 ABC

FALK, PETER
Robert Montgomery Presents   ep   Return Visit   5.13.
   57 NBC
Studio One   ep   The Mother Bit   6.10.57 CBS
Studio One   ep   Rudy   8.19.57 CBS
Play of the Week   ep   The Power and the Glory   10.
   19.59 NN
Play of the Week   ep   The Emperor's Clothes   1.11.
   60 NN
Untouchables   ep   Underworld Bank   4.14.60 ABC
Islanders   ep   Hostage Island   11.6.60 ABC
Witness   ep   Kid Twist   12.22.60 CBS
Cry Vengeance   Sp   2.21.61 NBC
Malibu Run   ep   The Jeremiah Adventure   3.1.61 CBS
The Million Dollar Incident   Sp 4.21.61 CBS
Alfred Hitchcock Theatre   ep   Gratitude   4.25.61 NBC
Barbara Stanwyck Theatre   ep   The Assassin   5.15.61
   NBC
Target Corruptors   ep   The Million Dollar Dump   9.29.
   61 ABC
Untouchables   ep   The Troubleshooters   10.12.61 ABC
Twilight Zone   ep   The Mirror   10.20.61 CBS
New Breed   ep   Cross the Little Line   1.9.62 ABC
Dick Powell Theatre   ep   Price of Tomatoes   1.16.62
   NBC
87th Precinct   ep   The Pigeon   1.29.62 NBC
Naked City   ep   Lament for a Dead Indian   4.11.62
   ABC
Dick Powell Theatre   ep   The Doomsday Boys   10.16.
   62 NBC
Alfred Hitchcock Theatre   ep   Bonfire   12.13.62 CBS
Dr. Kildare   ep   The Balance and the Crucible   5.2.63
   NBC
Wagon Train   ep   The Gus Morgan Story   9.30.63 ABC
Bob Hope Chrysler Theatre   ep   Four Kings   11.1.63
   NBC
Ben Casey   ep   For Jimmy, the Best of Anything

10. 19. 64 ABC
Trials of O'Brien   sr   9. 18. 65 CBS
Brigadoon   Sp   10. 15. 66 ABC
Bob Hope Chrysler Theatre   ep   Dear Deductible   11.
    9. 66   NBC
Prescription: Murder   tf   2. 20. 68 NBC
A Hatful of Rain   Sp   3. 3. 68 ABC
Name of the Game   ep   A Sister from Napoli   1. 8. 71
    NBC
A Step Out of Line   tf   2. 26. 71 CBS
Ransom for a Dead Man   tf   3. 1. 71 NBC
Columbo   sr   9. 15. 71 NBC
Columbo   sr ret   9. 17. 72 NBC

FARENTINO, JAMES
Defenders   ep   The Last Illusion   3. 9. 63 CBS
77 Sunset Strip   ep   Bonus Baby   12. 20. 63 ABC
Reporter   ep   Super Star   11. 20. 64 CBS
Alfred Hitchcock Theatre   ep   Death Scene   3. 8. 65
    NBC
12 O'Clock High   ep   P. O. W.   4. 23. 65, 4. 30. 65 ABC
Ben Casey   ep   The Big Wheel Turns by Faith   9. 20.
    65 ABC
Laredo   ep   I See by Your Outfit   9. 23. 65 NBC
Run for Your Life   ep   11. 22. 65, 11. 29. 65 NBC
FBI   ep   All the Streets Are Silent   11. 28. 65 NBC
Virginian   ep   The Wolves up Front, the Jackals Be-
    hind   3. 23. 66 NBC
Bob Hope Chrysler Theatre   ep   The Sister and the
    Savage   4. 6. 66 NBC
Death of a Salesman   Sp   5. 8. 66 CBS
Road West   ep   1. 9. 67 NBC
Wings of Fire   tf   2. 14. 67 NBC
Fugitive   ep   3. 7. 67 ABC
Ironside   ep   Something for Nothing   2. 22. 68 NBC
The Sound of Anger   tf   12. 10. 68 NBC
The Whole World Is Watching   tf   3. 11. 69 NBC
Bold Ones   sr   9. 21. 69 NBC
Men from Shiloh   ep   The Best Man   9. 23. 70 NBC
Bold Ones   sr ret   9. 70 NBC
Marcus Welby, M. D.   ep   Brave on a Mountain Top
    12. 22. 70 ABC
Love American Style   ep   1. 22. 71 ABC
Vanished   tf   3. 8. 71, 3. 9. 71 NBC
Night Gallery   ep   Since Aunt Ada Came to Stay   9. 29.
    71 NBC
Bold Ones   sr ret   10. 7. 71 NBC

The Longest Night tf 9.12.72 ABC
The Family Rico tf 9.12.72 CBS
Night Gallery ep The Girl with the Hungry Eyes 10.
   1.72 NBC
Cool Million tf 10.16.72 NBC
Cool Million sr 10.25.72 NBC

FARMER, FRANCES
   Playhouse 90 ep Reunion 1.2.58 CBS

FARNUM, WILLIAM
   TV Playhouse ep The Vine that Grew on 50th Street
      10.8.50 NBC

FARRELL, CHARLES
   My Little Margie sr 6.16.52 CBS
   My Little Margie sr ret 10.4.52 NBC
   My Little Margie sr ret 1.1.53 CBS
   My Little Margie sr ret 9.2.53 NBC
   Charlie Farrell Show sr 7.2.56 CBS

FARRELL, GLENDA
   Silver Theatre ep Gaudy Lady 2.13.50 CBS
   Prudential Playhouse ep Ruggles of Red Gap 2.27.51
      CBS
   Tales of Tomorrow ep The Build-Box 2.6.53 ABC
   Elgin Hour ep Crime in the Streets 3.8.55 ABC
   Studio One ep Miss Turner's Decision 3.21.55 CBS
   Goodyear Playhouse ep The Expendable House 10.9.
      55 NBC
   Front Row Center ep Uncle Barney 2.26.56 CBS
   Alcoa Hour ep Doll Face 3.18.56 NBC
   Kaiser Aluminum Hour ep Cracked Money 12.4.56
      NBC
   20th Century-Fox Hour ep The Marriage Broker 6.12.
      57 CBS
   Kraft Theatre ep The Old Ticker 9.11.57 NBC
   Kraft Theatre ep Polka 12.18.57 NBC
   Studio One ep The Other Place 1.13.58 CBS
   Studio One ep The Edge of Truth 4.28.58 CBS
   Cimarron City ep A Respectable Girl 12.6.58 NBC
   Ellery Queen ep Confession of Murder 4.17.59 NBC
   G.E. Theatre ep Night Club 10.11.59 CBS
   The Killers Sp 11.19.59 CBS
   Wagon Train ep The Jess MacAbbee Story 11.25.59
      NBC
   U.S. Steel Hour ep Queen of the Orange Bowl 1.13.60
      CBS

Play of the Week   ep   A Palm Tree in a Rose Garden
    4. 4. 60 NN
Islanders   ep   The Widow from Richmond   12. 18. 60
    ABC
Our American Heritage   ep   The Invincible Teddy   1.
    13. 61 NBC
A String of Beads   Sp   2. 7. 61 NBC
Nanette Fabray Show   ep   A Tale of Two Mothers   2.
    17. 61 NBC
U. S. Steel Hour   ep   Summer Rhapsody   5. 3. 61 CBS
Frontier Circus   ep   Mighty Like Rogues   4. 5. 62 CBS
Defenders   ep   The Naked Heiress   4. 7. 62 CBS
U. S. Steel Hour   ep   The Inner Panic   9. 12. 62 CBS
Route 66   ep   Man out of Time   10. 5. 62 CBS
Empire   ep   Stopover on the Way to the Moon   1. 1. 63
    NBC
Ben Casey   ep   A Cardinal Act of Mercy   1. 14. 63,
    1. 21. 63 ABC
U. S. Steel Hour   ep   Moment of Rage   3. 6. 63 CBS
Rawhide   ep   Incident at Farragut Pass   10. 31. 63 CBS
Dr. Kildare   ep   The Exploiters   10. 31. 63 NBC
Fugitive   ep   Fatso   11. 19. 63 ABC
Bonanza   ep   The Pure Truth   3. 8. 64 NBC
Bing Crosby Show   ep   The Liberated Woman   11. 23.
    64 ABC
Directions '66   ep   The Bigger They Are   5. 1. 66 ABC
Felony Squad   ep   10. 18. 68 ABC

FARRELL, SHARON
    CBS TV Workshop   ep   Another Valley   10. 9. 60 CBS
    Saints and Sinners   sr   9. 17. 62 NBC
    Wagon Train   ep   The Orly French Story   12. 12. 62
        ABC
    Gunsmoke   ep   3. 30. 63 CBS
    Ben Casey   ep   The White Ones Are Dolphins   3. 11. 63
        ABC
    Kraft Suspense Theatre   ep   Are There Any More Out
        There Like You   11. 7. 63 NBC
    Gunsmoke   ep   11. 9. 63 CBS
    Death Valley Days   ep   12. 7. 63 ABC
    Lieutenant   ep   Alert   12. 14. 63 NBC
    Dr. Kildare   ep   Night of the Beast   1. 2. 64 NBC
    Wagon Train   ep   2. 24. 64 ABC
    Ben Casey   ep   For a Just Man Falleth Seven Times
        4. 15. 64 ABC
    The Man from U. N. C. L. E.   ep   The Double Affair
        11. 17. 64 NBC

Beverly Hillbillies   ep   1.13.65 CBS
Fugitive   ep   Corner of Hell   2.9.65 ABC
Ben Casey   ep   The Day They Stole County General
    4.26.65 ABC
Dr. Kildare   ep   Wings of Hope   5.13.65 NBC
I Dream of Jeannie   ep   The Yacht Murder Case   10.
    23.65 NBC
My Three Sons   ep   11.25.65 CBS
Dr. Kildare   ep   Something Old, Something New   12.6.
    65, 12.7.65 NBC
Run for Your Life   ep   The Night of the Terror   1.31.
    66 NBC
The Man from U.N.C.L.E.   ep   The Minus "X" Affair
    4.8.66 NBC
Run for Your Life   ep   The Sex Object   10.17.66 NBC
Iron Horse   ep   1.9.67 ABC
The Man from U.N.C.L.E.   ep   2.24.67 NBC
Virginian   ep   12.13.67 NBC
Lassiter   pt   7.8.68 CBS
Wild, Wild West   ep   The Night of the Amnesiac   2.9.
    69 CBS
Name of the Game   ep   A Hard Case of the Blues   9.
    26.69 NBC
Quarantined   tf   2.24.70 ABC
Storefront Lawyer   ep   10.28.70 CBS
Name of the Game   ep   L.A. 2017   1.15.71 NBC
D.A.   ep   10.15.71 NBC
The Eyes of Charles Sand   tf   2.29.72 ABC
Banyon   ep   10.13.72 NBC
Marcus Welby, M.D.   ep   10.17.72 ABC

FARROW, MIA
Peyton Place   sr   9.15.64 ABC
Johnny Belinda   Sp   10.22.67 ABC

FAY, FRANK
Screen Directors Playhouse   ep   Tom and Jerry   11.
    30.55 NBC

FELDON, BARBARA
East Side/West Side   ep   The Street   2.24.64 CBS
Mr. Broadway   ep   Try to Find a Spy   10.10.64 CBS
Doctors/Nurses   ep   10.27.64 CBS
The Man from U.N.C.L.E.   ep   The Never-Never Af-
    fair   3.22.65 NBC
Profiles in Courage   ep   4.4.65 NBC
Get Smart   sr   9.18.65 NBC

Get Smart   sr ret   9.17.66 NBC
Get Smart   sr ret   9.16.67 NBC
Get Smart   sr ret   9.26.69 CBS
Matt Lincoln   ep   10.22.70 ABC
Getting Away from It All   tf   1.18.72 ABC
Playmates   tf   10.3.72 ABC
Search   ep   11.8.72 NBC

FELLOWS, EDITH
Musical Comedy Time   ep   Babes in Toyland   12.25.50
NBC
Tales of Tomorrow   ep   Enemy Unknown   11.23.51
ABC
Summer Theatre   ep   The Good Companions   8.25.52
CBS
Tales of Tomorrow   ep   The Cacoon   9.12.52 ABC
Armstrong Circle Theatre   ep   The Gentle Rain   10.
28.52 NBC
Tales of Tomorrow   ep   The Glacier Giant   12.5.52
ABC
Tales of Tomorrow   ep   Homecoming   4.10.53 ABC
Medallion Theatre   ep   Flight to Fame 3.13.54 CBS

FENNELLY, PARKER
Video Theatre   ep   Bert's Wedding   1.15.50 NBC
Airflyte Theatre   ep   Fiddling Fool   3.8.51 CBS
Philco Playhouse   ep   Ephraim Tutt's Clean Hands 8.
12.51 NBC
Philco Playhouse   ep   Mr. Quimby's Christmas   12.21.
52 NBC
TV Soundstage   ep   The Golden Box   2.12.54 NBC
TV Soundstage   ep   The Almighty Dollar   4.23.54 NBC
Center Stage   ep   The Worthy Opponent   8.24.54 ABC
Studio One   ep   U.F.O.   9.6.54 CBS
Kraft Theatre   ep   The Southwest Corner   3.30.55 NBC
U.S. Steel Hour   ep   The Meanest Man in the World
7.6.55 CBS
Lamp Unto My Feet   ep   To Hold in Trust   8.14.55
CBS
Robert Montgomery Presents   ep   The Stranger   10.3.
55 NBC
American Inventory   ep   Calculated Risk   11.27.55 NBC
Robert Montgomery Presents   ep   Mr. Tutt Baits a
Hook   1.30.56 NBC
Robert Montgomery Presents   ep   Mr. Tutt Goes West
11.5.56 NBC
Have Gun Will Travel   ep   4.10.58 CBS

Father Knows Best ep The Ideal Father 1.19.59
   CBS
Play of the Week ep The Girls in 509 4.18.60 NN
The Trouble with Richard pt 8.22.60 CBS
Have Gun Will Travel ep 10.15.60 CBS
Harrigan and Son ep Pay the Two Dollars 11.11.60
   ABC
Window on Main Street ep 1.15.62 CBS
Headmaster sr 9.18.70 CBS

FERRER, JOSE
Producers Showcase ep Cyrano de Bergerac 10.17.
   55 NBC
G.E. Theatre ep Survival 11.15.59 CBS
The Greatest Show on Earth ep No Middle Ground for
   Harry Kyle 10.1.63 ABC
Kismet Sp 10.24.67 ABC
A Case of Libel Sp 2.1.68 ABC
Name of the Game ep Tarot 2.13.70 NBC
The Aquarians tf 10.24.70 NBC
Name of the Game ep 12.5.70 NBC
Banyon tf 3.15.71 NBC
Hallmark Hall of Fame ep Gideon 3.26.71 NBC
The Cable Car Mystery tf 11.19.71 CBS

FERRER, MEL
Video Theatre ep The Vigilantes 12.10.53 CBS
Omnibus ep Nature of the Beast 12.13.53 CBS
Producers Showcase ep Mayerling 2.4.57 NBC
Zane Grey Theatre ep The Ghost 12.31.59 CBS
Bob Hope Chrysler Theatre ep The Fifth Passenger
   11.29.63 NBC
Search ep 12.13.72 NBC

FIELD, BETTY
Masterpiece Playhouse ep Six Characters in Search of
   an Author 8.13.50 NBC
Pulitzer Prize Playhouse ep 10.20.50 ABC
Video Theatre ep Local Storm 5.14.51 CBS
Somerset Maugham Theatre ep Grace 10.1.51 NBC
Robert Montgomery Presents ep See No Evil 3.31.52
   NBC
Celanese Theatre ep They Knew What They Wanted
   4.3.52 ABC
Goodyear Playhouse ep Before I Wake 5.31.53 NBC
Motorola TV Hour ep The Sins of the Fathers 4.6.
   54 ABC

Elgin Hour   ep   Family Crisis   10.19.54 ABC
Producers Showcase   ep   Happy Birthday   5.25.56 NBC
Loretta Young Show   ep   Take Care of My Child   11.4.
   56 NBC
G.E. Theatre   ep   The Breach   12.9.56 CBS
Ford Theatre   ep   The Lie   6.5.57 ABC
Kraft Theatre   ep   Triumph   9.4.57 NBC
Climax   ep   Scream in Silence   1.2.58 CBS
Hallmark Hall of Fame   ep   Ah, Wilderness!   4.28.59
   NBC
Untouchables   ep   The White Slaves   3.10.60 ABC
Alfred Hitchcock Presents   ep   Very Moral Theft   10.
   11.60 NBC
Route 66   ep   Swan Bed   10.21.60 CBS
Play of the Week   ep   Uncle Harry   12.5.60 NN
Naked City   ep   Bullets Cost Too Much   1.4.61 ABC
Naked City   ep   A Memory of Crying   4.12.61 ABC
Play of the Week   ep   All Summer Long   5.1.61 NN
Route 66   ep   The Mud Nest   11.10.61 CBS
Focus   Sp   1.21.62 NBC
Ben Casey   ep   And Eve Wore a Veil of Tears   4.3.62
   ABC
Route 66   ep   Across Walnuts and Wine   11.2.62 CBS
Dr. Kildare   ep   A Time for Every Purpose   12.27.62
   NBC
Alfred Hitchcock Theatre   ep   The Star Juror   3.15.63
   CBS
Going My Way   ep   Florence, Come Home   4.10.63
   ABC
Defenders   ep   A Taste of Ashes   11.12.64 CBS
Outsider   ep   One Long-Stemmed American Beauty   11.
   20.68 NBC
Judd for the Defense   ep   Thou Shall Not Suffer a
   Witch to Live   12.13.68 ABC

FIELD, SALLY
   Gidget   sr   9.15.65 ABC
   Occasional Wife   ep   12.9.66 NBC
   Hey Landlord   ep   2.19.67 NBC
   The Flying Nun   sr   9.7.67 ABC
   The Flying Nun   sr ret   9.26.68 ABC
   The Flying Nun   sr ret   9.17.69 ABC
   Bracken's World   ep   Jenny, Who Bombs Buildings
      10.2.70 NBC
   Maybe I'll Come Home in the Spring   tf   2.16.71 ABC
   Marriage: Year One   tf   10.15.71 NBC
   Alias Smith and Jones   ep   Dreadful Sorry Clementine

11.17.71 ABC
Mongo's Back in Town   tf   12.10.71 CBS
Alias Smith and Jones   ep   The Clementine Incident
   10.7.72 ABC
Home for the Holidays   tf   11.28.72 ABC

FIELD, VIRGINIA
   Schlitz Playhouse of Stars   ep   Mr. and Mrs. Trouble
      8.22.52 CBS
   Ford Theatre   ep   So Many Things Happen   12.18.52
      NBC
   Hollywood Opening Night   ep   2.9.53 NBC
   Mirror Theatre   ep   Award Performance   11.7.53 CBS
   Ford Theatre   ep   Kiss and Forget   12.3.53 NBC
   Fireside Theatre   ep   Three Missions West   11.30.54
      NBC
   Ford Theatre   ep   Slide, Darling, Slide   12.23.54 NBC
   G.E. Theatre   ep   Bachelor's Bride   2.20.55 CBS
   Fireside Theatre   ep   No Time for Susan   3.15.55 NBC
   Ford Theatre   ep   The Mumbys   6.23.55 NBC
   G.E. Theatre   ep   Bachelor's Bride   8.7.55 CBS
   Damon Runyon Theatre   ep   A Star Lights up   11.5.55
      CBS
   Ford Theatre   ep   A Kiss for Santa   12.22.55 NBC
   Ford Theatre   ep   Autumn Fever   4.5.56 NBC
   20th Century-Fox Hour   ep   The Empty Room   5.30.56
      CBS
   Four Star Playhouse   ep   The Stand-In   7.19.56 CBS
   Schlitz Playhouse of Stars   ep   Light in the Desert   12.
      21.56 CBS
   Perry Mason   ep   The Case of the Prodigal Parent
      6.7.58 CBS
   Ed Wynn Show   ep   Aunt Lydia Comes to Town   12.4.
      58 NBC
   Man with a Camera   ep   The Last Portrait   1.2.59
      ABC
   The Millionaire   ep   Millionaire Bill Franklin   5.13.59
      CBS
   Meet the Girls   pt   9.30.60 CBS
   Perry Mason   ep   The Case of the Provocative Protege
      11.12.60 CBS
   Rebel   ep   The Actress   2.5.61 ABC
   Perry Mason   ep   The Case of the Meddling Medium
      10.21.61 CBS
   Adventures in Paradise   ep   Policeman's Holiday   11.
      28.62 ABC
   Tales of Wells Fargo   ep   Kelly's Clover Girls   12.9.
      61 NBC

New Breed   ep   I Remember Murder   12.26.61 ABC
Perry Mason   ep   The Case of the Polka Dot Pony
    12.20.62 CBS
Perry Mason   ep   The Case of the Simple Simon   4.2.
    64 CBS
Perry Mason   ep   The Case of the Tsarina's Tiara   3.
    20.66 CBS
T.H.E. Cat   ep   12.2.66 NBC
Felony Squad   ep   2.13.67 ABC

FIELDS, GRACIE
    U.S. Steel Hour   ep   The Old Lady Shows Her Medals
        5.23.56 CBS
    Goodyear Playhouse   ep   A Murder Is Announced   12.
        30.56 NBC
    Dupont Show of the Month   ep   A Tale of Two Cities
        3.27.58 CBS
    Studio One   ep   Mrs 'Arris Goes to Paris   4.14.58
        CBS

FIELDS, TOTIE
    Here's Lucy   ep   10.23.72 CBS

FISHER, EDDIE
    Light's Diamond Jubilee   ep   10.24.54 ABC, CBS, NBC

FISHER, GAIL
    Mannix   sr   9.28.68 CBS
    Mannix   sr ret   9.27.69 CBS
    Love American Style   ep   9.29.69 ABC
    Mannix   sr ret   9.19.70 CBS
    Mannix   sr ret   9.15.71 CBS
    Love American Style   ep   11.12.71 ABC
    Mannix   sr ret   9.17.72 CBS
    Room 222   ep   10.15.72 ABC
    Every Man Needs One   tf   12.13.72 ABC

FITZGERALD, BARRY
    Video Theatre   ep   The Man Who Struck It Rich   11.17.
        52 CBS
    RCA Victor Show   ep   6.26.53 NBC
    G.E. Theatre   ep   The White Steed   12.26.54 CBS
    Alfred Hitchcock Presents   ep   Santa Claus and the 10th
        Avenue Kid   12.18.55 CBS

FITZGERALD, GERALDINE
    Theatre Hour   ep   The Marble Faun   10.6.50 CBS

Robert Montgomery Presents ep To Walk the Night 10.8.51 NBC

Schlitz Playhouse of Stars ep The Daughter 2.8.52 CBS

TV Workshop ep The Gallows Tree 3.25.52 CBS

Studio One ep Pontius Pilate 4.7.52 CBS

Schlitz Playhouse of Stars ep Fear 4.25.52 CBS

Suspense ep House of Masks 5.10.52 CBS

Robert Montgomery Presents ep Summer Tempest 4.27.53 NBC

Theatre for You ep Babylon Revisited 10.6.53 NN

Suspense ep The Others 10.27.53 CBS

Studio One ep Dark Possession 2.15.54 CBS

Robert Montgomery Presents ep Love Story 4.26.54 NBC

Goodyear Playhouse ep The Lawn Party 5.23.54 NBC

Robert Montgomery Presents ep The Iron Cobweb 3.28.55 NBC

Armstrong Circle Theatre ep The Secret of Emily du Vane 4.19.55 NBC

The Barretts of Wimpole Street Sp 6.8.55 CBS

Climax ep The Healer 7.21.55 CBS

Studio One ep Like Father, Like Son 9.19.55 CBS

Robert Montgomery Presents ep Isobel 11.21.55 NBC

Studio One ep Flower of Pride 3.12.56 CBS

Producers Showcase ep Dodsworth 4.30.56 NBC

Ellery Queen ep The Murder Comes to You Live 6.5.59 NBC

Moon and Sixpence Sp 10.30.59 NBC

Shirley Temple Theatre ep The Black Sheep 12.18.60 NBC

Naked City ep Take Off Your Hat When a Funeral Passes 9.27.61 ABC

Nurses ep For the Mice and Rabbits 2.27.64 CBS

Defenders ep A Voice Loud and Clear 12.17.64 CBS

Alfred Hitchcock Theatre ep Power of Attorney 4.5.65 NBC

Our Private World sr 5.5.65 CBS

The Best of Everything sr 1970 ABC

FLEMING, ERIC

The Phil Silvers Show ep 1.3.56 CBS

Studio One ep The Strong Man 6.9.58 CBS

Rawhide sr 1.9.59 CBS

Rawhide sr ret 9.60 CBS

Rawhide sr ret 9.29.61 CBS

Rawhide sr ret 9.26.62 CBS

Rawhide   sr ret 9.21.63 CBS
Rawhide   sr ret 9.25.64 CBS
Bonanza   ep Peace Officer 3.6.65 NBC
Bonanza   ep Pursued 10.2.66, 10.9.66 NBC

FLEMING, RHONDA
    Best of Broadway ep Stage Door 4.6.55 CBS
    Ford Theatre ep South of Selanger 12.15.55 NBC
    Wagon Train ep The Jennifer Churchill Story 10.15.
        58 NBC
    Wagon Train ep The Patience Miller Story 1.11.61
        NBC
    Hong Kong ep The Woman in Gray 3.8.61 ABC
    Investigators ep Murder on Order 10.5.61 CBS
    Dick Powell Theatre ep John H. Diggs 10.17.61
        NBC
    Follow the Sun ep Marine of the Month 5.6.62 ABC
    Burke's Law ep Who Killed Wade Walter 11.15.63
        ABC
    Wagon Train ep 12.2.63 ABC
    Bob Hope Chrysler Theatre ep Have Girls--Will
        Travel 10.16.64 NBC
    Burke's Law ep Who Killed 711 12.9.64 ABC

FLETCHER, BRAMWELL
    Philco Playhouse ep 11.26.50 NBC
    Somerset Maugham Theatre ep The Moon and Six-
        pence 4.30.51 NBC
    Kraft Theatre ep A Play for Mary 5.23.51 NBC
    Robert Montgomery Presents ep When We Are Mar-
        ried 7.2.51 NBC
    Cosmopolitan Theatre ep Mr. Whittle and the Morn-
        ing Star 12.11.51 NN
    Broadway Television Theatre ep The Velvet Glove
        7.7.52 NN
    The Web ep Fatal Alibi 12.21.52 CBS
    Kraft Theatre ep Candlelight 12.31.53 ABC
    Studio One ep Dark Possession 2.15.54 CBS
    Kraft Theatre ep The Scarlet Letter 5.26.54 NBC
    Kraft Theatre ep The Bishop Misbehaves 8.12.54
        ABC
    Robert Montgomery Presents ep Hunchback of Notre
        Dame 11.1.54, 11.8.54, 11.15.54 NBC
    Robert Montgomery Presents ep It Depends on You
        2.28.55 NBC
    G.E. Theatre ep Mr. Blue Ocean 5.1.55 CBS
    Studio One ep The Voysey Inheritance 8.22.55 CBS

Lamp Unto my Feet   ep   A Fall of Stars   12.25.55
   CBS
Studio One   ep   Mr. Arcularis   6.25.56 CBS
Lamp Unto my Feet   ep   6.2.57 CBS
U.S. Steel Hour   ep   The Enemies   12.3.58 CBS
Our American Heritage   ep   Autocrat and Son   3.20.60
   NBC
Theatre 62   ep   The Paradine Case   3.11.62 NBC
Defenders   ep   Claire Cheval Died in Boston   11.23.63
   CBS
Nurses   ep   Imperfect Prodigy   2.20.64 CBS
Eternal Light   ep   The Thief and the Hangman   11.21.
   65 NBC
Coronet Blue   ep   7.17.67 CBS

FLIPPEN, JAY C.
Ford Theatre   ep   Come on Red   3.11.54 NBC
Climax   ep   Pink Cloud   10.27.55 CBS
Climax   ep   Faceless Enemy   6.7.56 CBS
Climax   ep   The Stalker   2.7.57 CBS
20th Century-Fox Hour   ep   The Man Who Couldn't
   Wait   3.20.57 CBS
Climax   ep   Mr. Runyon of Broadway   6.6.57 CBS
Goodyear Playhouse   ep   The House   9.8.57 NBC
Playhouse 90   ep   Before I Die   1.23.58 CBS
Wanted Dead or Alive   ep   10.25.58 CBS
Alcoa Theatre   ep   The Best Way to Go   6.15.59   NBC
David Niven Theatre   ep   Good Deed   7.7.59 NBC
Thriller   ep   The Guilty Men   10.18.60 NBC
Route 66   ep   Legacy for Lucia   11.25.60 CBS
Untouchables   ep   Fall Guy   1.11.62 ABC
Follow the Sun   ep   The Last of the Big Spenders   1.
   14.62 ABC
Ensign O'Toole   sr   9.23.62 NBC
Bus Stop   ep   Verdict of Twelve   3.1.62 ABC
Burke's Law   ep   Who Killed Wade Walker   11.15.63
   ABC
Gunsmoke   ep   11.23.63 CBS
Bonanza   ep   The Prime of Life   12.29.63 NBC
Rawhide   ep   Incident at Hourglass   3.12.64 CBS
Burke's Law   ep   3.27.64   ABC
Gunsmoke   ep   4.4.64 CBS
Kraft Suspense Theatre   ep   Portrait of an Unknown
   Man   4.16.64 NBC
Shenandoah   ep   The Imposter   4.4.66 ABC
Rawhide   ep   Josh   1.15.65 CBS
Virginian   ep   The Wolves up Front, The Jackals Be-

hind   3.23.66 NBC
Road West ep Charade of Justice 3.27.67 NBC
Virginian ep The Barren Ground 12.6.67 NBC
The Sound of Anger tf 12.10.68 NBC
Virginian ep Stopover 1.8.69 NBC
Judd for the Defense ep Borderline Girl 1.10.69
   ABC
Bracken's World ep 10.3.69 NBC
Name of the Game ep Chains of Command 10.17.69
   NBC
Here Come the Brides ep 1.30.70 ABC

FLYNN, ERROL
   Screen Directors Playhouse ep The Sword of Villon
      4.4.56 NBC
   Errol Flynn Theatre sh/sr 3.22.57 NN
   Playhouse 90 ep Without Incident 6.6.57 CBS
   Goodyear Theatre ep The Golden Shanty 11.9.59
      NBC

FOCH, NINA
   Suspense ep One and One's a Lonesome 5.16.50 CBS
   Armstrong Circle Theatre ep The Rose and the Sham-
      rock 6.20.50 NBC
   Video Theatre ep 10.30.50 CBS
   Airflyte Theatre ep The Case of the Calico Dog 1.
      25.51 CBS
   Pulitzer Prize Playhouse ep Ice Bound 4.13.51 ABC
   Pulitzer Prize Playhouse ep The Buccaneer 6.15.51
      ABC
   Cameo Theatre ep Betrayal 7.2.51 NBC
   Two Girls Named Smith sr 7.21.51 ABC
   Pulitzer Prize Playhouse ep The Skin of Our Teeth
      12.19.51 ABC
   Schlitz Playhouse of Stars ep World So Wide 2.22.
      52 CBS
   Tales of Tomorrow ep Bound Together 3.7.52 ABC
   Pulitzer Prize Playhouse ep The Jungle 4.9.52 ABC
   Video Theatre ep The Magnolia Touch 8.25.52 CBS
   Studio One ep The Kill 9.22.52 CBS
   Gulf Playhouse ep Double By-Line 10.3.52 NBC
   Video Theatre ep The Key 12.29.52 CBS
   Hollywood Opening Night ep Legal Affair 1.5.53 NBC
   Armstrong Circle Theatre ep Ski Story 1.13.53 NBC
   G.E. Theatre ep Trapped 3.22.53 CBS
   Danger ep Hand Me Down 4.21.53 CBS
   U.S. Steel Hour ep The Rise of Carthage 1.19.54
      ABC

Studio One   ep   A Guest at the Embassy   7. 12. 54 CBS
Loretta Young Show   ep   Reunion   9. 11. 55 NBC
Suspense   ep   Main Feature: Death   7. 27. 54 CBS
Danger   ep   See No Evil   9. 21. 54 CBS
Producers Showcase   ep   State of the Union   11. 15. 54
    NBC
Studio One   ep   Miss Turner's Decision   3. 21. 55 CBS
Colgate Hour   ep   Roberta   4. 10. 55 NBC
Climax   ep   Night of Execution   9. 22. 55 CBS
Playwrights '56   ep   The Answer   10. 4. 55 NBC
Studio One   ep   Manhattan Duet   2. 13. 56 CBS
20th Century-Fox Hour   ep   Yacht on the High Sea
    1. 11. 56 CBS
Playwrights '56   ep   The Undiscovered Country   3. 27.
    56 NBC
Studio One   ep   The Drop of a Hat   5. 7. 56 CBS
Playhouse 90   ep   Heritage of Anger   11. 15. 56 CBS
Alcoa Hour   ep   A Double Life   1. 6. 57 NBC
Kraft Theatre   ep   A Night of Rain   4. 24. 57 NBC
Climax   ep   Deadly Climate   8. 29. 57 CBS
Playhouse 90   ep   The Playroom   10. 10. 57 CBS
Wagon Train   ep   The Clara Beauchamp Story   12. 11.
    57 NBC
Studio One   ep   The Laughing Willow   2. 3. 58 CBS
G. E. Theatre   ep   God Is My Judge   4. 20. 58 CBS
Matinee Theatre   ep   Much Ado about Nothing   5. 20. 58,
    5. 21. 58 NBC
Studio One   ep   Image of Fear   9. 29. 58 CBS
Pursuit   ep   Ticket to Tangier   11. 5. 58 CBS
Playhouse 90   ep   Free Week-end   12. 4. 58 CBS
Alcoa Premiere   ep   Ten Little Indians   1. 18. 59 NBC
U. S. Steel Hour   ep   Whisper of Evil   6. 3. 59 CBS
U. S. Steel Hour   ep   The Case of Julia Walton   9. 9. 59
    CBS
Loretta Young Show   ep   The Red Dress   11. 1. 59 NBC
Play of the Week   ep   Tiger at the Gates   2. 8. 60 NN
U. S. Steel Hour   ep   A Time to Decide   11. 2. 60 CBS
Americans   ep   The Rebellious Rose   2. 13. 61 NBC
Shirley Temple Theatre   ep   The Little Mermaid   3. 5.
    61 NBC
Naked City   ep   The Fingers of Henri Tourelle   10. 18.
    61 ABC
Route 66   ep   Bridge across Five Days   11. 17. 61 CBS
Bus Stop   ep   Cry to Heaven   1. 14. 62 ABC
Dick Powell Theatre   ep   Seeds of April   2. 13. 62 CBS
G. E. Theatre   ep   Hercule Poirot 4. 1. 62 CBS
Theatre 62   ep   Rebecca   4. 8. 62 NBC

Naked City   ep   Sweetly Smiling Face of Truth   4.25.
   62 ABC
Route 66   ep   Across Walnuts and Wine   11.2.62 CBS
Virginian   ep   Vengeance Is the Spur   2.27.63 NBC
Arrest and Trial   ep   My Name is Martin Burnham   10.
   13.63 ABC
Kraft Suspense Theatre   ep   The End of the World 10.
   24.63 NBC
The Greatest Show on Earth   ep   Leaves in the Wind
   11.26.63 ABC
Outer Limits   ep   The Borderland   12.16.63 ABC
Route 66   ep   Where's a Will, There's a Way   3.6.64,
   3.13.64 CBS
Burke's Law   ep   5.8.64 ABC
Mr. Broadway   ep   Maggie, Queen of the Jungle   11.
   21.64 CBS
Shenandoah   ep   Marlee   3.14.66 ABC
The Long Hot Summer   ep   Carlotta, Come Home   3.
   30.66 ABC
Bob Hope Chrysler Theatre   ep   And Baby Makes Five
   10.5.66 NBC
I Spy   ep   Child out of Time   1.11.67 NBC
Bob Hope Chrysler Theatre   ep   A Time to Love   1.11.
   67 NBC
Bonanza   ep   4.30.67 NBC
Prescription Murder   tf   2.20.68 NBC
Name of the Game   ep   10.11.68 NBC
Mod Squad   ep   Love   12.10.68 ABC
Wild, Wild West   ep   3.21.69 CBS
Gunsmoke   ep   10.6.69 CBS
Gidget Grows Up   tf   12.30.69 ABC
Paris 7000   ep   1.29.70 ABC
FBI   ep   2.22.70 ABC
McCloud   ep   Walk in the Dark   10.14.70 NBC
Name of the Game   ep   I Love you Billy Baker   11.20.
   70, 11.27.70 NBC
Men at Law   ep   Marathon   2.10.71 CBS
Hollywood Television Theatre   ep   The Scarecrow   1.10.
   72   NN

FONDA, HENRY
   Medallion Theatre   ep   The Decision at Arrowsmith   7.
      11.53 CBS
   Rheingold Theatre   sh   1.8.55 NBC
   G.E. Theatre   ep   Clown   3.27.55 CBS
   Producers Showcase   ep   The Petrified Forest   5.30.55
      NBC

Deputy   sr   9.12.59 NBC
Deputy   sr ret   10.1.60 NBC
Dick Powell Theatre   ep   Tissue of Hate   2.26.63 NBC
Stranger on the Run   tf   10.31.67 NBC
Smith Family   sr   1.20.71 ABC
Smith Family   sr ret   9.21.71 ABC

FONDA, JANE
A String of Beads   Sp   2.7.61 NBC

FONDA, PETER
Naked City   ep   The Night the Saints Lost Their Halos
1.17.62 ABC
New Breed   ep   Thousands and Thousands of Miles
4.17.62 ABC
Wagon Train   ep   The Orly French Story   12.12.62
ABC
Defenders   ep   The Brother Killers   5.25.63 CBS
Channing   ep   An Abelisk for Benny   10.2.63 ABC
Arrest and Trial   ep   A Circle of Strangers   3.8.64
ABC
12 O'Clock High   ep   The Sound of Distant Thunder
10.16.64 ABC

FONTAINE, JOAN
Four Star Playhouse   ep   Girl on the Park Bench   12.
3.53 CBS
Four Star Playhouse   ep   Trudy   5.26.55 CBS
Loretta Young Show   ep   A Shadow Between 12.18.55
NBC
G.E. Theatre   ep   In Summer Promise   1.29.56 CBS
Ford Theatre   ep   Your Other Love   2.23.56 NBC
Star Stage   ep   The Shadowy Third   4.20.56 NBC
20th Century-Fox Hour   ep   Stranger in the Night   10.
17.56 CBS
G.E. Theatre   ep   The Victorian Chaise Lounge   3.
17.57 CBS
On Trial   ep   Fatal Charm   6.28.57 NBC
Mr. Adams and Eve   ep   10.18.57 CBS
G.E. Theatre   ep   At Miss Minner's   10.26.58 CBS
Desilu Playhouse   ep   Perilous   6.22.59 CBS
Ford Star Time   ep   Closed Set   2.16.60 NBC
G.E. Theatre   ep   The Story of Judith   2.28.60 CBS
G.E. Theatre   ep   A Possibility of Oil   2.19.61 CBS
Checkmate   ep   Voyage into Fear   5.6.61 CBS
Dick Powell Theatre   ep   The Clocks   3.27.62 NBC
Wagon Train   ep   The Naomi Taylor Story   1.30.63
ABC

Alfred Hitchcock Theatre   ep   The Paragon   2.8.63 CBS
Bing Crosby Show   ep   Operation Man Save   3.1.65 CBS

FONTANNE, LYNN
    Producers Showcase   ep   The Great Sebastians   4.1.57
      NBC
    Hallmark Hall of Fame   ep   The Magnificent Yankee   1.
      28.65 NBC

FORAN, DICK
    Studio One   ep   The Loud Red Patrick   2.6.50 CBS
    Tele-Theatre   ep   The Great Emptiness   3.27.50 NBC
    Video Theatre   ep   Treasure Trove   3.26.51 CBS
    Studio One   ep   The Old Foolishness   5.14.51 CBS
    Studio One   ep   Screwball   6.18.51 CBS
    Summer Theatre   ep   Tremolo   7.23.51 CBS
    Kraft Theatre   ep   Irish Eyes   10.3.51 NBC
    Studio One   ep   The Kill   9.22.52 CBS
    A Letter to Loretta   ep   Thanksgiving in Beaver Run
      11.22.53 NBC
    Four Star Playhouse   ep   Detective's Holiday   3.4.54
      CBS
    Studio One   ep   The Magic Monday   8.2.54 CBS
    Best of Broadway   ep   The Philadelphia Story   12.8.54
      CBS
    Shower of Stars   ep   Burlesque   3.17.55 CBS
    Stage 7   ep   Billy and the Bride   5.8.55 CBS
    Public Defender   ep   Condemned   5.19.55 CBS
    Public Defender   ep   Operation CLEAT   5.26.55 CBS
    Ford Theatre   ep   Cardboard Casanova   5.26.55 NBC
    Summer Theatre   ep   A Kiss for Mr. Lincoln   7.19.55
      NBC
    Four Star Playhouse   ep   Detective's Holiday   7.28.55
      CBS
    Damon Runyon Theatre   ep   Small Town Caper   8.13.55
      CBS
    Stage 7   ep   The Hayfield   9.18.55 CBS
    Climax   ep   Night of Execution   9.22.55 CBS
    Four Star Playhouse   ep   Face of Danger   10.13.55 CBS
    My Favorite Husband   ep   11.1.55 CBS
    20th Century-Fox Hour   ep   Miracle on 34th Street   12.
      14.55 CBS
    TV Reader's Digest   ep   When the Wise Man Appeared
      12.19.55 ABC
    Climax   ep   The Secret of River Lane   1.26.56 CBS
    Damon Runyon Theatre   ep   The Pigeon Gets Plucked
      3.3.56 CBS

Science Fiction Theatre ep The Long Sleep 4.13.56 NBC

Ford Theatre ep The Lady in His Life 4.19.56 NBC

Crossroads ep The Singing Preacher 6.15.56 ABC

Four Star Playhouse ep The Face of Danger 8.30.56 CBS

Ford Theatre ep Sweet Charlie 1.16.57 ABC

Crossroads ep Boomtown Padre 2.22.57 ABC

On Trial ep A Case of Sudden Death 5.10.57 NBC

Crossroads ep Coney Island Wedding 5.31.57 ABC

Colt .45 ep Final Payment 11.22.57 ABC

The Millionaire ep The Hugh Waring Story 12.1.57 CBS

Maverick ep The Third Rider 1.5.58 ABC

Matinee Theatre ep The Gardenia Bush 5.28.58 NBC

Have Gun Will Travel ep 11.8.58 CBS

Perry Mason ep The Case of the Bedevilled Doctor 4.4.59 CBS

Wanted Dead or Alive ep 6.20.59 CBS

Playhouse 90 ep The Sounds of Eden 10.15.59 CBS

Perry Mason ep The Case of the Garrulous Gambler 10.17.59 CBS

World of Disney ep The Swamp Fox 10.23.59 ABC

World of Disney ep The Redcoat Strategy 5.27.60

Wanted Dead or Alive ep 12.14.60 CBS

Deputy ep The Dream 2.4.61 NBC

Dante ep Aces and Eights 2.13.61 NBC

Laramie ep Bitter Glory 5.2.61 NBC

Lassie ep 11.5.61 CBS

Perry Mason ep The Case of the Renegade Refugee 12.8.61 CBS

Laramie ep The Killer Legend 12.12.61 NBC

Dr. Kildare ep Hit and Run 12.14.61 NBC

Lassie ep 1.21.62 CBS

Perry Mason ep The Case of the Garrulous Gambler 2.17.62 CBS

Lawman ep The Wanted Man 9.25.62 ABC

Laramie ep Double Eagles 11.20.62 NBC

Cheyenne ep Wanted for the Murder of Cheyenne Bodie 12.10.62 ABC

Great Adventures ep The Great Diamond Mountain 11.8.63 CBS

Lassie ep 2.3.63 CBS

Lassie ep 11.3.63 CBS

Death Valley Days ep Holy Terror 12.7.63 ABC

Death Valley Days ep Pioneer Doctor 2.29.64 ABC

Virginian ep A Man Called Kane 5.6.64 NBC

O. K. Crackerby   sr   9. 16. 65 ABC
Rawhide   ep   The Testing Post   11. 30. 65 CBS
Off We Go   pt   9. 5. 66 CBS
Daniel Boone   ep   9. 15. 66 NBC
Virginian   ep   1. 25. 67 NBC
Virginian   ep   9. 13. 67 NBC
Bonanza   ep   Mark of Guilt   12. 15. 68 NBC
Daniel Boone   ep   3. 27. 69 NBC
Mayberry RFD   ep   12. 29. 69 CBS

FORBES, RALPH
Masterpiece Playhouse   ep   The Rivals   8. 6. 50 NBC

FORD, CONSTANCE
Armstrong Circle Theatre   ep   Fog Station   11. 6. 51
   NBC
The Web   ep   The Patsy   2. 15. 53 CBS
Philco Playhouse   ep   The Recluse   4. 12. 53 NBC
Plymouth Playhouse   ep   Colonel Humphrey J. Flack   5.
   31. 53 ABC
Summer Studio One   ep   The King in Yellow   7. 27. 53
   CBS
Kraft Theatre   ep   The Blues of Joey Menetti   8. 26. 53
   NBC
Kraft Theatre   ep   Her Father's Butler   9. 16. 53 NBC
Kraft Theatre   ep   A Cup of Kindness   12. 30. 53 NBC
Studio One   ep   Experiment Perilous   8. 23. 54 CBS
Goodyear Playhouse   ep   The Big Man   9. 12. 54 NBC
Goodyear Playhouse   ep   A Case of Pure Fiction   1. 2.
   55 NBC
Kraft Theatre   ep   The Night Watchers   3. 9. 55 NBC
Cavalcade Theatre   ep   Man on the Beat   3. 15. 55 ABC
Goodyear Playhouse   ep   Beloved Stranger   4. 10. 55
   NBC
Studio One   ep   The Tall Dark Stranger   7. 25. 55 CBS
Way of the World   ep   10. 3. 55 NBC
The Phil Silvers Show   ep   11. 8. 55 CBS
Appointment with Adventure   ep   A Thief There Was   3.
   18. 56 CBS
Climax   ep   Sit Down with Death   4. 26. 56 CBS
Alfred Hitchcock Presents   ep   The Creeper   6. 17. 56
   CBS
Lux Video Theatre   ep   The Captives   7. 19. 56 NBC
The Millionaire   ep   Story of Anna Hartley   9. 26. 56
   CBS
Matinee Theatre   ep   Alumni Reunion   9. 27. 56 NBC
Zane Grey Theatre   ep   The Lariat   11. 2. 56 CBS

Climax ep The Chinese Game 11.22.56 CBS
Gunsmoke ep 12.22.56 CBS
Playhouse 90 ep The Comedian 2.14.57 CBS
20th Century-Fox Hour ep Man of the Law 2.20.57 CBS
Studio One ep Eight Feet to Midnight 4.29.57 CBS
The Phil Silvers Show ep Sgt. Bilko, the Marriage Broker 4.30.57 CBS
Matinee Theatre ep The Alumni Reunion 6.6.57 NBC
Trackdown ep Self-Defense 11.22.57 CBS
Climax ep Murder Has a Deadline 11.28.57 CBS
The Phil Silvers Show ep Bilko and the Flying Saucers 12.31.57 CBS
Have Gun Will Travel ep 2.1.58 CBS
Perry Mason ep The Case of the Deadly Double 3.1.58 CBS
Bat Masterson ep Lottery of Death 5.13.59 NBC
Plainsman ep Rabbit's Fang 3.24.60 NBC
Bat Masterson ep Stage to Nowhere 4.14.60 NBC
Thriller ep The Twisted Image 9.13.60 NBC
Thriller ep Worse than Murder 9.27.60 NBC
Alfred Hitchcock Presents ep Outlaw in Town 11.15.60 NBC
Wanted Dead or Alive ep 1.11.61 CBS
Surfside 6 ep Little Star Lost 1.26.61 ABC
Deputy ep The Lonely Road 2.18.61 NBC
Untouchables ep The Nick Acropolis Story 6.1.61 ABC
87th Precinct ep Lady in Waiting 10.2.61 NBC
Naked City ep A Wednesday Night Story 11.1.61 ABC
Target: Corruptors ep One for the Road 1.12.62 ABC
Adventures in Paradise ep The Dream Merchant 3.18.62 ABC
Frontier Circus ep Naomi Champagne 3.29.62 CBS
Father Knows Best ep Extraordinary Woman 4.23.62 CBS
Sam Benedict ep Nothing Equals Nothing 10.6.62 NBC
Rawhide ep Incident of the Buryin' Man 1.4.63 CBS
Dakotas ep Red Sky over Bismark 1.14.63 ABC
Dr. Kildare ep The Great Guy 1.17.63 NBC
Perry Mason ep The Case of the Potted Planter 5.9.63 CBS
Perry Mason ep The Case of the Shifty Shoebox 10.10.63 CBS
Twilight Zone ep Uncle Simon 11.15.63 CBS
Temple Houston ep The Dark Madonna 12.26.63 NBC
East Side/West Side ep No Hiding Place 12.2.63 CBS
Shane ep The Great Invasion 12.17.66, 12.24.66 ABC

Another World   sr   1969 NBC

FORD, ERNIE (TENNESSEE)
I Love Lucy   ep   1.24.55 CBS
I Love Lucy   ep   6.18.56, 6.25.56 CBS
Danny Thomas Show   cp   1.19.59 CBS
Tennessee Ernie Ford Show   ep   The Mikado   4.16.59
   CBS
Tennessee Ernie Ford Show   ep   H.M.S. Pinafore   1.
   14.60 NBC
Tennessee Ernie Ford Show   ep   Tennessee Ernie Meets
   King Arthur   5.10.60 NBC
The Lucy Show   ep   2.27.67 CBS
Here's Lucy   ep   3.10.69 CBS

FORD, FRANCIS
Fireside Theatre   ep   Parasol   5.9.50 NBC
Gruen Guild Theatre   ep   A Boy Wears a Gun   5.22.52
   NN

FORD, GLENN
The Brotherhood of the Bell   tf   9.17.70 CBS
Cade's County   sr   9.19.71 CBS

FORD, PAUL
Norby   ep   Overdrawn Account   1.12.55 NBC
The Phil Silvers Show   sr   9.20.55 CBS
Studio One   ep   The Tale of St. Emergency   3.26.56
   CBS
Producers Showcase   ep   Bloomer Girl   5.28.56 NBC
The Phil Silvers Show   sr ret   fall, 1956 CBS
Kaiser Aluminum Hour   ep   A Man's Game   4.23.57
   NBC
The Phil Silvers Show   sr ret   fall, 1957 CBS
Dupont Show of the Month   ep   Junior Miss   12.20.57
   CBS
The Phil Silvers Show   sr ret   fall, 1958 CBS
Play of the Week   ep   The Girls in 509   4.18.60 NN
The Right Man   Sp   10.24.60 CBS
Shirley Temple Theatre   ep   King Midas   1.15.61 NBC
G.E. Theatre   ep   Open House   3.5.61 CBS
Outlaws   ep   Outrage at Pawnee Bend   4.6.61 NBC
Alfred Hitchcock Theatre   ep   The Hat Box   10.10.61
   NBC
Hallmark Hall of Fame   ep   The Teahouse of the August
   Moon   10.26.62 NBC
Lloyd Bridges Show   ep   12.25.62 CBS

U.S. Steel Hour   ep   Don't Shake the Family Tree   5.
    15.63 CBS
Baileys of Balboa   sr   9.24.64 CBS
That's Life   ep   12.10.68 ABC
In Name Only   tf   11.25.69 ABC
Love American Style   ep   3.6.70 ABC
Love American Style   ep   10.20.72 ABC

FORD, WALLACE
    Schlitz Playhouse of Stars   ep   Come What May   10.3.52
        CBS
    Goodyear Playhouse   ep   The Happy Rest   10.4.53 NBC
    The American Hour   ep   Outlaw's Reckoning   11.3.53
        ABC
    Studio One   ep   Runaway   1.4.54 CBS
    Armstrong Circle Theatre   ep   Treasure Trove   4.20.
        54 NBC
    Death Valley Days   ep   Claim Jumping Jennie 6.15.54
        NN
    Father Knows Best   ep   12.19.54 CBS
    Climax   ep   Champion   3.31.55 CBS
    Ford Theatre   ep   Sunday Mourn   4.21.55 NBC
    Damon Runyon Theatre   ep   Tobias the Terrible   5.21.
        55 CBS
    Kings Row   ep   10.4.55 ABC
    20th Century-Fox Hour   ep   The Ox-Bow Incident   11.
        2.55 CBS
    Father Knows Best   ep   12.21.55 NBC
    Fireside Theatre   ep   Big Joe's Comin' Home   12.27.
        55 NBC
    Climax   ep   The Prowler   1.5.56 CBS
    Screen Directors Playhouse   ep   One Against Many   3.
        7.56 NBC
    Climax   ep   The Fog   9.27.56 CBS
    Playhouse 90   ep   Snow Shoes   1.3.57 CBS
    Court of Last Resort   ep   The Jim Thompson Case   1.
        21.57 NBC
    Playhouse 90   ep   The Last Man   1.9.58 CBS
    Trackdown   ep   A Stone for Benny French   10.3.58 CBS
    Father Knows Best   ep   The Christmas Story   12.2.58
        CBS
    Desilu Playhouse   ep   Silent Thunder   12.8.58 CBS
    Trackdown   ep   5.27.59 CBS
    Deputy   sr   9.12.59 NBC
    Tales of Wells Fargo   ep   Dead Man's Street   4.18.60
        NBC
    Klondike   ep   88 Keys to Trouble   11.14.60 NBC

Peter Loves Mary ep Wilma's Uncle Charlie 4.12.61
    NBC
Barbara Stanwyck Theatre ep Frightened Doll 4.24.61
    NBC
Wide Country ep Journey Down a Dusty Road 10.4.62
    NBC
Alcoa Premiere ep The Glass Palace 1.17.63 ABC
Three Wishes pt 7.29.63 CBS
Great Adventures ep The Colonel from Connecticut 1.
    10.64 CBS
World of Disney ep Bristle Face 2.2.64 NBC
The Travels of Jaimie McPheeters ep The Day of the
    Tin Trumpet 2.21.64 ABC
Lassie ep 3.8.64 CBS

FORREST, SALLY
    Schlitz Playhouse of Stars ep Barrow Street 11.28.52
        CBS
    Studio One ep Edge of Evil 3.23.53 CBS
    Ford Theatre ep Life of the Party 4.23.53 NBC
    Studio One ep Letter of Love 10.19.53 CBS
    Armstrong Circle Theatre ep Julie's Castle 10.27.53
        NBC
    U.S. Steel Hour ep P.O.W. 10.27.53 ABC
    Front Row Center ep Guest in the House 8.22.55 CBS
    Climax ep Pink Cloud 10.27.55 CBS
    Screen Directors Playhouse ep Want Ad Wedding 11.2.
        55 NBC
    Front Row Center ep The Teacher and Hector Hodge 2.
        12.56 CBS
    Climax ep The Man Who Stole the Bible 6.13.57 CBS
    Climax ep Throw Away the Cane 8.2.56 CBS
    Climax ep Burst of Fire 1.30.58 CBS
    Pursuit ep Epitaph for a Golden Girl 1.14.59 CBS
    Rawhide ep Incident of the Widowed Dove 1.30.59 CBS
    The Millionaire ep Millionaire Emily Baker 2.4.59
        CBS
    G.E. Theatre ep Strictly Solo 12.11.60 CBS
    Rawhide ep Incident of the Swindler 2.20.64 CBS
    Family Affair ep 12.5.67 CBS

FORREST, STEVE
    Climax ep Flight to Tomorrow 11.8.56 CBS
    Alfred Hitchcock Presents ep The End of Indian Sum-
        mer 2.24.57 CBS
    Climax ep Let It Be Me 3.21.57 CBS
    Playhouse 90 ep Clipper Ship 4.4.57 CBS

Lux Video Theatre ep The Armed Venus 5. 23. 57 NBC
Climax ep Mask for the Devil 10. 10. 57 CBS
Alfred Hitchcock Presents ep Post Mortem 5. 18. 58
 CBS
Schlitz Playhouse of Stars ep You'll Have to Die Now
 6. 20. 58 CBS
Schlitz Playhouse of Stars ep Third Son 12. 5. 58 CBS
Desilu Playhouse ep Ballad for a Badman 1. 26. 59 CBS
Alcoa Theatre ep Minister Accused 2. 8. 60 NBC
Zane Grey Theatre ep Setup 3. 3. 60 CBS
Outlaws ep Thirty a Month 9. 29. 60 NBC
June Allyson Show ep End of a Mission 1. 2. 61 CBS
Bus Stop ep Summer Lightning 1. 7. 62 ABC
Wide Country ep The Royce Bennett Story 9. 20. 62 NBC
Dick Powell Theatre ep Project "X" 1. 8. 63 NBC
Virginian ep The Money Cage 3. 6. 63 NBC
Twilight Zone ep The Parallel 3. 14. 63 CBS
Kraft Suspense Theatre ep A Truce to Terror 1. 9. 64
 NBC
Arrest and Trial ep Somewhat Lower than Angels 2. 2.
 64 ABC
Virginian ep The Hero 10. 7. 64 NBC
12 O'Clock High ep In Search of My Enemy 1. 8. 65
 ABC
Kraft Suspense Theatre ep That Time in Havana 2. 11.
 65 NBC
Rawhide ep Blood Harvest 2. 12. 65 CBS
Fugitive ep Last Second of a Big Dream 4. 20. 65 ABC
The Baron sr 1. 20. 66 ABC
Cimarron Strip ep Broken Wing 9. 21. 67 CBS
Bonanza ep 11. 5. 67 NBC
Cimarron Strip ep Sound of a Drum 2. 1. 68 CBS
Legend of Robin Hood Sp 2. 18. 68 NBC
Gunsmoke ep 1. 20. 69 CBS
Name of the Game ep The Bobby Currier Story 2. 21. 69
 NBC
Ironside ep Poole's Paradise 10. 2. 69 NBC
Bonanza ep To Stop a War 10. 19. 69 NBC
Gunsmoke ep 3. 2. 70 CBS
Medical Center ep Death Grip 11. 4. 70 CBS
Name of the Game ep 11. 6. 70 NBC
FBI ep The Stalking Horse 1. 10. 71 ABC
Nichols ep 11. 8. 71 ABC
Mission Impossible ep 11. 27. 71 CBS
Alias Smith and Jones ep 1. 6. 72 ABC
Night Gallery ep The Waiting Room 1. 26. 72 NBC
Sixth Sense ep Echo of a Distant Scream 4. 1. 72 ABC

Ghost Story   ep   The Summer House   10.13.72 NBC
Hec Ramsey   ep   10.29.72 NBC
Gunsmoke   ep   11.27.72 CBS

FORSTER, ROBERT
N.Y.P.D.   ep   Catch a Hero   10.31.67 ABC
Drama   ep   Higher and Higher   9.9.68 CBS
Judd for the Defense   ep   A Puff of Smoke   9.27.68
   ABC
Banyon   tf   3.15.71 NBC
Banyon   sr   9.15.72 NBC

FORSYTH, ROSEMARY
The Brotherhood of the Bell   tf   9.17.70 CBS
Name of the Game   ep   The War Merchants   10.30.70
   NBC
City Beneath the Sea   tf   1.25.71 NBC
Triple Play   tf   3.22.71 NBC
Longstreet   ep   Let the Memories Be Happy Ones   1.6.
   72 ABC
Night Gallery   ep   Deliver in the Rear   2.9.72 NBC
Cade's County   ep   3.19.72 CBS
Assignment Vienna   ep   12.7.72 ABC

FORSYTHE, JOHN
Studio One   ep   None But My Foe   2.12.51 CBS
Robert Montgomery Presents   ep   Dark Victory   3.26.51
   NBC
Danger   ep   A Clear Case of Suicide   5.22.51 CBS
Lights Out   ep   The Pattern   5.28.51 NBC
Starlight Theatre   ep   Three Hours Between Planes   6.
   28.51 CBS
Starlight Theatre   ep   In the Military Manner   7.26.51
   CBS
Schlitz Playhouse of Stars   ep   Girl in a Million   12.28.
   51 CBS
Pulitzer Prize Playhouse   ep   The Town   1.16.52 ABC
Schlitz Playhouse of Stars   ep   P.G.   1.25.52 CBS
Schlitz Playhouse of Stars   ep   World So Wide   2.22.52
   CBS
Studio One   ep   Ten Thousand Horses Singing   3.3.52
   CBS
Lights Out   ep   The Upstairs Floor   3.10.52 NBC
Studio One   ep   Hold Back the Night   4.14.52 CBS
Pulitzer Prize Playhouse   ep   The American Leonardo
   5.21.52 ABC
Philco Playhouse   ep   The Monument   6.29.52 NBC

Suspense   ep   The Beach of Falesa   9.30.52 CBS
Philco Playhouse   ep   The Winter of the Dog   11.2.52
   NBC
Studio One   ep   I am Jonathan Scrivener   12.1.52 CBS
Studio One   ep   Conflict   6.8.53 CBS
U.S. Steel Hour   ep   King's Pawn   11.23.54 ABC
Elgin Hour   ep   Driftwood   5.3.55 ABC
Studio One   ep   Operation Home   5.30.55 CBS
Climax   ep   One Night Stand   8.4.55 CBS
Alfred Hitchcock Presents   ep   Premonition   10.9.55
   CBS
Playwrights '56   ep   Return to Cassino   2.14.56 NBC
Climax   ep   Pale Horse, Pale Rider   3.22.56 CBS
Star Stage   ep   A Place to be Alone   4.27.56 NBC
Climax   ep   Journey into Fear   10.11.56 CBS
Goodyear Playhouse   ep   Stardust II   11.11.56 NBC
Schlitz Playhouse of Stars   ep   Girl with a Glow   4.19.
   57 CBS
Zane Grey Theatre   ep   Decision at Wilson's Creek   5.
   17.57 CBS
Climax   ep   Hand of Evil   5.23.57 CBS
G.E. Theatre   ep   A New Girl in His Life   5.26.57
   CBS
Bachelor Father   sr   9.15.57 CBS
Climax   ep   Shooting for the Moon   4.24.58 CBS
Schlitz Playhouse of Stars   ep   Way of the West   6.6.
   58 CBS
Bachelor Father   sr ret   9.58 CBS
Lux Playhouse   ep   The Miss and Missiles   6.12.59
   CBS
Bachelor Father   sr ret   9.17.59 NBC
Sunday Showcase   ep   What Makes Sammy Run   9.27.59,
   10.4.59 NBC
Bachelor Father   sr ret   9.15.60 NBC
Bachelor Father   sr ret   10.3.61 ABC
Alfred Hitchcock Theatre   ep   I Saw the Whole Thing
   10.11.62 CBS
Hallmark Hall of Fame   ep   Teahouse of the August
   Moon   10.26.62 NBC
Alcoa Premiere   ep   Five, Six, Pick up Sticks   1.24.63
   ABC
Dick Powell Theatre   ep   The Third Side of the Coin
   3.26.63 NBC
See How They Run   tf   10.7.64 NBC
Mystery Theatre   ep   Look at Roses   9.11.63 NBC
Kraft Suspense Theatre   ep   The Kamchatka Incident
   11.12.64 NBC

Bob Hope Chrysler Theatre   ep   In any Language   3.13.
  65 NBC
John Forsythe Show   sr   9.13.65 NBC
Run for Your Life   ep   A Choice of Evils   4.3.67 NBC
Hallmark Hall of Fame   ep   A Bell for Adano   11.11.
  67 NBC
It Takes a Thief   ep   3.12.68 ABC
Shadow on the Land   tf   12.4.68 ABC
To Rome with Love   sr   9.29.69 CBS
To Rome with Love   sr ret   9.15.70 CBS
Columbo   ep   Murder by the Book   9.15.71 NBC
Mannix   ep   Dark So Early, Dark So Long   9.15.71 CBS

FOSTER, PRESTON
    Schlitz Playhouse of Stars   ep   Manhattan Robin Hood
      2.6.53 CBS
    Ford Theatre   ep   The Lady and the Champ   5.7.53
      NBC
    G.E. Theatre   ep   The Hunter   11.15.53 CBS
    Waterfront   sr   9.28.54 NN
    Waterfront   sr ret   9.55 NN
    Star Stage   ep   The Guardian   5.11.56 NBC
    Target Corruptors   ep   Prison Empire   12.15.61 ABC
    Going My Way   ep   A Memorial for Finnegan   1.16.63
      ABC
    Eleventh Hour   ep   Cold Hands, Warm Heart   10.2.63
      NBC
    77 Sunset Strip   ep   Lovers' Lane   1.3.64 ABC

FOX, JAMES
    Espionage   ep   The Very End   11.6.63 NBC

FOX, REDD
    Here's Lucy   ep   2.7.65 CBS
    Mister Ed   ep   11.7.65 CBS
    Green Acres   ep   9.14.66 CBS
    Sanford and Son   sr   1.14.72 NBC
    Sanford and Son   sr ret   9.15.72 NBC

FRANCINE, ANNE
    Producers Showcase   ep   The Great Sebastians   4.1.57
      NBC

FRANCIOSA, TONY
    Goodyear Playhouse   ep   The Arena   8.1.54 NBC
    Studio One   ep   It Might Happen Tomorrow   1.24.55
      CBS

Hallmark Hall of Fame ep The Cradle Song 5.6.56
NBC
Goodyear Playhouse ep Country Fair Time 7.15.56
NBC
Dupont Show of the Month ep Heaven Can Wait 11.
16.60 CBS
Dick Powell Theatre ep Charlie's Duet 3.19.63 NBC
Dupont Show of the Month ep The Shark 4.7.63 NBC
Arrest and Trial ep Call It a Lifetime 9.15.63 ABC
Breaking Point ep Last Summer We Didn't Get Away
9.23.63 ABC
The Greatest Show on Earth ep An Echo of Faded
Velvet 11.13.63 ABC
Bob Hope Chrysler Theatre ep A Case of Armed Rob-
bery 4.3.64 NBC
Valentine's Day sr 9.18.64 ABC
Fame Is the Name of the Game tf 11.26.66 NBC
Name of the Game sr 9.20.68 NBC
Name of the Game sr ret 10.3.69 NBC
Virginian ep The Shiloh Years 1.28.70 NBC
Name of the Game sr ret 10.16.70 NBC
Men from Shiloh ep 12.2.70 NBC
The Deadly Hunt tf 10.1.71 CBS
Earth II tf 11.28.71 ABC

FRANCIS, ANNE
Lights Out ep Faithful Heart 4.10.50 NBC
Television Theatre ep Black Sheep 4.26.50 NBC
Television Theatre ep Good Housekeeping 6.14.50
NBC
Television Theatre ep I Like It Here 10.4.50 NBC
Ford Theatre ep The Tryst 6.17.54 NBC
Climax ep Sermon in Silence 1.2.58 CBS
Studio One ep Presence of the Enemy 2.10.58 CBS
Climax ep Deadly Tatoo 5.1.58 CBS
Kaleidoscope ep The Third Commandment 2.8.59 NBC
David Niven Theatre ep The Twist of the Key 5.12.
59 NBC
Rawhide ep Incident of the Shambling Man 10.9.59
CBS
Adventures in Paradise ep The Bamboo Curtain 12.
14.59 ABC
U.S. Steel Hour ep Queen of the Orange Bowl 1.13.
60 CBS
Ford Star Time ep Jeff McCleod, the Last Reb 3.1.
60 NBC
Our American Heritage ep Autocrat and Son 3.20.60
NBC

Untouchables   ep   The Doreen Maney Story   3.31.60
   ABC
Twilight Zone   ep   The After Hours   6.10.60 CBS
U.S. Steel Hour   ep   The Yum Yum Girl   11.30.60
   CBS
Route 66   ep   Play it Glissando   1.20.61 CBS
Hong Kong   ep   With Deadly Sorrow   2.22.61 ABC
Route 66   ep   A Month of Sundays   9.22.61 CBS
Dr. Kildare   ep   A Million Dollar Property   10.26.61
   NBC
Going My Way   ep   A Man for Mary   10.31.62 ABC
Alfred Hitchcock Theatre   ep   What Really Happened
   1.11.63 CBS
Twilight Zone   ep   Jess-Belle   2.14.63 CBS
Alfred Hitchcock Theatre   ep   Blood Bargain   10.25.63
   CBS
Ben Casey   ep   9.25.63 ABC
Arrest and Trial   ep   The Witnesses   11.3.63 ABC
Burke's Law   ep   Who Killed Wade Walker   11.15.63
   ABC
Kraft Suspense Theatre   ep   The Machine that Played
   God   12.5.63 NBC
Temple Houston   ep   Tend Rounds for Bab   1.30.64
   NBC
Death Valley Days   ep   The Last Stagecoach Robbery
   3.21.64 ABC
The Man from U.N.C.L.E.   ep   The Gluco Piano Af-
   fair   11.10.64 NBC
Virginian   ep   All Nice and Legal   11.25.64 NBC
Burke's Law   ep   4.21.65 ABC
Honey West   sr   9.17.65 ABC
World of Disney   ep   The Big Swindle   10.3.65 NBC
World of Disney   ep   The Further Adventures of Gae-
   gher   10.10.65 NBC
Alfred Hitchcock Theatre   ep   The Trap   2.22.66 ABC
Fugitive   ep   1.17.67 ABC
Invaders   ep   The Saucer   9.5.67 ABC
Name of the Game   ep   Incident in Berlin   10.25.68
   NBC
Name of the Game   ep   1.30.70 NBC
FBI   ep   3.1.70 ABC
Dan August   ep   Murder By Proxy   9.23.70 ABC
Wild Women   tf   10.20.70 ABC
Men from Shiloh   ep   Gun Quest   10.27.70 ABC
The Intruders   tf   11.10.70 NBC
The Forgotten Man   tf   9.14.71 ABC
My Three Sons   ep   9.20.71 CBS

Mongo's Back in Town tf 12.10.71 CBS
My Three Sons ep 12.13.71 CBS
Columbo ep Short Fuse 1.19.72 NBC
Ironside ep 2.24.72 NBC
Fireball Foreward tf 3.5.72 ABC
Ironside ep 3.9.72 NBC
Haunts of the Very Rich tf 9.20.72 ABC
Gunsmoke ep 10.16.72 CBS
Assignment Vienna ep 11.9.72 ABC

FRANCIS, ARLENE
Sure as Fate ep The Dancing Doll 11.28.50 CBS
Drama ep With These Hands 3.1.52 NBC
Suspense ep Her Last Adventure 8.19.52 CBS
Five Fingers ep The Man Who Got Away 11.14.59
    NBC
U.S. Steel Hour ep When in Rome 9.7.60 CBS
U.S. Steel Hour ep The Big Splash 2.8.61 CBS
Gertrude Berg Show ep The Mother Affair 2.1.62
    CBS
Laura Sp 1.24.68 ABC
Hallmark Hall of Fame ep Harvey 3.22.72 NBC

FRANCIS, CONNIE
Bob Hope Chrysler Theatre ep The Sister and the
    Savage 4.6.66 NBC

FRANCIS, KAY
Prudential Playhouse ep Call It a Day 11.7.50 CBS

FRANCISCUS, JAMES
Have Gun Will Travel ep 6.7.58 CBS
Studio One ep The Strong Man 6.9.58 CBS
Naked City sr 9.30.58 ABC
Wagon Train ep The Benjamin Burns Story 2.17.60
    NBC
Hennesey ep Annapolis Man 2.22.60 CBS
Black Saddle ep The Penalty 4.22.60 ABC
Alfred Hitchcock Presents ep Forty Detectives Later
    4.24.60 CBS
Rawhide ep Incident of the Murder Steer 5.13.60
    CBS
Deputy ep Mother and Son 10.29.60 NBC
Alfred Hitchcock Theatre ep Summer Shade 1.10.61
    NBC
June Allyson Show ep The Guilty Heart 1.16.61 CBS
G.E. Theatre ep Love Is a Lion's Roar 3.19.61 CBS

Investigators   sr   10.5.61 CBS
Ben Casey   ep   So If It Chances in Particular Men   5.
    21.62 ABC
Dr. Kildare   ep   Jail Ward   2.14.63 NBC
Eleventh Hour   ep   Hang by One Hand   3.27.63 NBC
Mr. Novak   sr   9.24.63 NBC
Mr. Novak   sr ret   9.22.64 NBC
12 O'Clock High   ep   Cross Harison Death   3.21.66
    ABC
FBI   ep   4.9.67 ABC
Judd for the Defense   ep   The Devil's Surrogate   2.23.
    68 ABC
Shadow over Elveron   tf   3.5.68 NBC
FBI   ep   9.29.68 ABC
Night Slaves   tf   9.29.70 ABC
Longstreet   tf   2.23.71 ABC
Longstreet   sr   9.16.71 ABC
Ghost Story   ep   9.29.72 NBC

FRANCKS, DON
Jericho   sr   9.15.66 CBS
Mission Impossible   ep   1.14.68 CBS
Virginian   ep   The Land Dreamer   2.26.69 NBC
Mission Impossible   ep   10.5.69 CBS
Mannix   ep   Memory Zero   11.22.69 CBS
Lancer   ep   12.30.69 CBS

FRANKLIN, PAMELA
World of Disney   ep   The Horse without a Head   9.29.
    63, 10.5.63 NBC
See How They Run   tf   10.7.64 NBC
Hallmark Hall of Fame   ep   Eagle in a Cage   10.20.65
    NBC
David Copperfield   tf   3.15.70 NBC
Name of the Game   ep   3.27.70 NBC
Medical Center   ep   Secret Heritage   2.3.71 CBS
Green Acres   ep   3.16.71 CBS
Cannon   ep   10.18.72 CBS
Ghost Story   ep   11.3.72 NBC
Sixth Sense   ep   11.11.72 ABC
Cool Million   ep   11.22.72 NBC
Bonanza   ep   First Love   12.26.72 NBC

FRANZ, ARTHUR
Ford Theatre   ep   Junior   10.9.52 NBC
Schlitz Playhouse of Stars   ep   The Devil's Other Name
    2.20.53 CBS

Fireside Theatre   ep   Grey Gardens   3.3.53 NBC
Films of Faith   ep   Three Lives   6.21.53 NN
Schlitz Playhouse of Stars   ep   Storm Warnings   7.10.
   53 CBS
Danger   ep   Help Wanted   10.6.53 CBS
Studio One   ep   Camille   11.9.53 CBS
Studio One   ep   Dry Run   12.7.53 CBS
Robert Montgomery Presents   ep   The Steady Man   1.
   4.54 NBC
Kraft Theatre   ep   The Shining Palace   1.28.54 ABC
The Web   ep   A Handful of Stars   2.7.54 CBS
Kraft Theatre   ep   Picture Window   3.10.54 NBC
Ford Theatre   ep   The Last 30 Minutes   3.18.54 NBC
Robert Montgomery Presents   ep   For These Services
   4.5.54 NBC
Schlitz Playhouse of Stars   ep   By-Line   7.30.54 CBS
Schlitz Playhouse of Stars   ep   Spangel Island   12.10.
   54 CBS
The Millionaire   ep   Millionaire Carl Nelson   1.26.55
   CBS
Fireside Theatre   ep   Not Captain Material   1.25.55
   NBC
Ford Theatre   ep   Hanrahan   3.31.55 NBC
Appointment with Adventure   ep   Priceless Cargo   5.15.
   55 CBS
TV Reader's Digest   ep   France's Greatest Detective
   5.16.55 ABC
Fireside Theatre   ep   The 99th Day   5.31.55 NBC
Philco Playhouse   ep   Total Recall   6.12.55 NBC
Climax   ep   The Healer   7.21.55 CBS
Kraft Theatre   ep   Spur of the Moment   8.2.55 NBC
Schlitz Playhouse of Stars   ep   Too Late to Run   8.5.
   55 CBS
20th Century-Fox Hour   ep   The Late George Apley
   11.16.55 CBS
Four Star Playhouse   ep   Looking Glasshouse   11.24.55
   CBS
TV Reader's Digest   ep   Emergency Case   12.12.55
   ABC
Crossroads   ep   Calvary in China   1.13.56 ABC
Four Star Playhouse   ep   Once to Every Woman   3.1.
   56 CBS
The Whistler   ep   An Actor's Life   3.4.56 NN
Crossroads   ep   The Rabbi Davis Story   6.8.56 ABC
Schlitz Playhouse of Stars   ep   Pattern for Pursuit   6.
   15.56 CBS
TV Reader's Digest   ep   The Only Way Out 7.2.56 ABC

Climax   ep   Phone Call for Matthew Quade   7.5.56
   CBS
Schlitz Playhouse of Stars   ep   The House that Jackson
   Built   10.5.56 CBS
Dupont Theatre   ep   Date with a Stranger   10.30.56
   ABC
Ford Theatre   ep   Mrs. Wane Comes to Call 1.30.57
   ABC
20th Century-Fox Hour   ep   The Man Who Couldn't Wait
   3.20.57 CBS
Crossroads   ep   The Deadline   6.14.57 ABC
Zane Grey Theatre   ep   Man of Fear   3.14.58 CBS
World of Giants   sr   1959 NN
Men into Space   ep   Moon Quake   11.11.59 CBS
Perry Mason   ep   The Case of the Golden Fraud   11.
   21.59 CBS
Wanted Dead or Alive   ep   1.23.60 CBS
Markham   ep   The Last Oasis   4.21.60 CBS
Bourbon Street Beat   ep   Deadly Persuasion   5.9.60
   ABC
Alaskans   ep   The Silent Land   5.15.60 ABC
Mystery Show   ep   Fear Is the Parent   6.26.60 NBC
Perry Mason   ep   The Case of the Larcenous Lady   12.
   17.60 CBS
Rawhide   ep   Incident of the Wanted Painter   12.23.60
   CBS
Death Valley Days   ep   The Young Gun   1.11.61 NBC
Deputy   ep   Past and Present   1.21.61 NBC
Hawaiian Eye   ep   The Trouble with Murder   3.1.61 ABC
77 Sunset Strip   ep   The Space Caper   3.10.61 ABC
Perry Mason   ep   The Case of the Married Moonlighters
   5.13.61 CBS
Law and Mr. Jones   ep   The Last Commandment   5.19.
   61 ABC
Hawaiian Eye   ep   Satan City   9.27.61 ABC
Perry Mason   ep   The Case of the Captain's Coins   1.
   13.62 CBS
Tales of Wells Fargo   ep   Portrait of Teresa   2.10.62
   NBC
Bonanza   ep   The Law Maker   3.11.62 NBC
Wagon Train   ep   The Jud Steele Story   5.2.62 NBC
Saints and Sinners   ep   Judith Was a Lady   12.3.62 NBC
Wagon Train   ep   3.13.63 ABC
77 Sunset Strip   ep   Reunion at Balboa   4.12.63 ABC
Virginian   ep   No Tears for Savannah   10.2.63 NBC
Perry Mason   ep   The Case of the Fifty Millionth
   Frenchman   2.20.64 CBS

Lassie   ep   4.26.64 CBS
Mr. Novak   ep   Little Girl Lost   10.20.64 NBC
Slattery's People   ep   What Did You Do All Day Mr.
   Slattery   1.15.65 CBS
Voyage to the Bottom of the Sea   ep   The Condemned
   4.12.65 ABC
Profiles in Courage   ep   5.2.65 NBC
Fugitive   ep   Landscape with Running Faces   11.16.65
   ABC
FBI   ep   The Conspirators   2.5.67 ABC
Tarzan   ep   4.7.67 NBC
Custer   ep   10.4.67 NBC
FBI   ep   Region of Peril   2.25.68 ABC
Invaders   ep   The Life Seekers   3.5.68 ABC
Outcasts   ep   11.18.68 ABC
Mod Squad   ep   Love   12.10.68 ABC
Land of the Giant   ep   Target Earth   3.2.69 ABC
Mod Squad   ep   Lisa   11.4.69 ABC
FBI   ep   Scapegoat   11.23.69 ABC
Hawaii Five-O   ep   The One with the Gun   1.28.70 CBS
Mission Impossible   ep   3.22.70 CBS
Owen Marshall   ep   Eulogy for a Wide Receiver   9.30.
   71 ABC
Mannix   ep   12.15.71 CBS
FBI   ep   12.19.71 ABC
McCloud   ep   Give My Regards to Broadway   2.23.72
   NBC
Owen Marshall   ep   12.7.72 ABC
Mission Impossible   ep   12.9.72 CBS

FRAWLEY, WILLIAM
   Silver Theatre   ep   The First Hundred Years   5.1.50
      CBS
   Silver Theatre   ep   Papa Romani   5.15.50 CBS
   Story Theatre   ep   The Lady or the Tiger   2.9.51 NN
   I Love Lucy   sr   10.15.51 CBS
   I Love Lucy   sr ret   9.15.52
   Demi-Tasse Tales   ep   Wedding Morning   3.3.53 CBS
   Summer Night Theatre   ep   Room for Improvement   9.
      8.54 NN
   I Love Lucy   sr ret   10.5.53 CBS
   Loretta Young Show   ep   Dear Midge   5.16.54 NBC
   I Love Lucy   sr ret   10.4.54 CBS
   Shower of Stars   ep   High Pitch   5.12.55 CBS
   Damon Runyon Theatre   ep   Bunny on the Beach   7.16.
      55 CBS
   I Love Lucy   sr ret   10.3.55 CBS

Lucille Ball-Desi Arnaz Hour   sr   11.6.57 CBS
Lucille Ball-Desi Arnaz Hour   sr ret   10.6.58 CBS
Lucille Ball-Desi Arnaz Hour   sr ret   9.25.59 CBS
Desilu Playhouse   ep   Comeback   3.2.59 CBS
Gale Storm Show   ep   The Card Sharp   10.8.59 ABC
My Three Sons   sr   9.29.60 ABC
My Three Sons   sr ret   9.61 ABC
My Three Sons   sr ret   9.20.62 ABC
My Three Sons   sr ret   9.19.63 ABC
My Three Sons   sr ret   9.17.64 ABC
The Lucy Show   ep   10.25.65 CBS

FRAZEE, JANE
    Death Valley Days   ep   The Rival Hash Houses   12.3.
        54 NN
    Eddie Cantor Theatre   ep   6.13.55 ABC
    Stage 7   ep   Yesterday's Pawnshop   8.21.55 CBS
    Matinee Theatre   ep   Tin Wedding   4.24.56 NBC

FREEMAN JR., AL
    Defenders   ep   Nobody Asks What Side You're on   3.11.
        65 CBS
    Slattery's People   ep   What's a Swan Song for a Sparrow
        4.16.65 CBS
    FBI   ep   The Enemies   11.3.68 ABC
    Judd for the Defense   ep   The View from the Ivy Tower
        3.7.69 ABC
    My Sweet Charlie   tf   1.20.70 NBC
    Mod Squad   ep   1.18.72 ABC
    N.E.T. Playhouse   ep   To Be Young, Gifted and Black
        1.22.72 NN

FREEMAN, MONA
    Ford Theatre   ep   Appointment with Destiny   5.5.55
        NBC
    Eddie Cantor Theatre   ep   V for Victoria   5.23.55 ABC
    Eddie Cantor Theatre   ep   Triple Vision   7.18.55 ABC
    Climax   ep   Fear Strikes Out   8.18.55 CBS
    Front Row Center   ep   The Ainsley Case   2.9.56 CBS
    Studio 57   ep   The Baxter Boy   3.4.56 NN
    Climax   ep   Phone Call for Matthew Quade   7.5.56 CBS
    Climax   ep   The Fog   9.27.56 CBS
    Playhouse 90   ep   Seidman and Son   10.18.56 CBS
    Damon Runyon Theatre   ep   Big Shoulders   10.30.56
        ABC
    Zane Grey Theatre   ep   Stage for Tucson   11.16.56
        CBS

20th Century-Fox Hour   Men Against Speed   12.12.56
   CBS
Ford Theatre   ep   The Marriage Plan   12.12.56 ABC
Playhouse 90   ep   Three Men on a Horse   4.18.57 CBS
Matinee Theatre   ep   The Prizewinner   3.7.57 NBC
Climax   ep   The Disappearance of Daphne   5.15.58 CBS
Climax   ep   Murder Is a Witch   8.15.57 CBS
Lux Video Theatre   ep   Christmas in Connecticut   12.
   13.56 NBC
Playhouse 90   ep   The Long March   10.16.58 CBS
Wanted Dead or Alive   ep   11.1.58 NBC
Pursuit   ep   Calculated Risk   12.10.58 CBS
Wanted Dead or Alive   ep   9.26.59 CBS
Riverboat   ep   The Boy from Pittsburgh   11.29.59 NBC
Maverick   ep   Cat of Paradise   10.11.59 ABC
June Allyson Show   ep   The Pledge   10.26.59 CBS
Maverick   ep   Cruise of the Cynthia B   1.10.60 ABC
U.S. Steel Hour   ep   The Women of Hadley   2.24.60
   CBS
U.S. Steel Hour   ep   Revolt in Hadley   3.9.60 CBS
U.S. Steel Hour   ep   The Girl Who Knew Too Much   4.
   20.60 CBS
Maverick   ep   Cats of Paradise   5.1.60 ABC
Mystery Show   ep   Fear Is the Parent   6.26.50 NBC
Thriller   ep   The Mark of the Hand   10.4.60 NBC
Michael Shayne   ep   Blood on Biscayne Bay   12.2.60
   NBC
U.S. Steel Hour   ep   Operation Northstar   12.28.60
   CBS
Checkmate   ep   Don't Believe a Word She Says   1.28.61
   CBS
U.S. Steel Hour   ep   The Two Worlds of Charlie Gordon
   2.22.61 CBS
Tall Man   ep   Petticoat Crusade   11.18.61 NBC
U.S. Steel Hour   ep   The Bitter Sex   12.27.61 CBS
Perry Mason   ep   The Case of the Lurid Letter   12.6.
   62 CBS
Perry Mason   ep   The Case of the Illicit Illusion   4.9.
   64 CBS
Perry Mason   ep   The Case of the 12th Wildcat   10.31.
   65 CBS
Branded   ep   McCord's Way   1.30.66 NBC
Welcome Home, Johnny Bristol   tf   1.30.72 CBS

FRENCH, VALERIE
   Meet McGraw   ep   Kiss of Death   10.29.57 NBC
   Trackdown   ep   11.8.57 CBS

Schlitz Playhouse of Stars   ep   The Kind Mr. Smith   4.
    25. 58 CBS
Ten Little Indians   Sp   1. 18. 59 NBC
Alaskans   ep   Odd Man Hangs   4. 17. 60 ABC

FREY, LEONARD
    Mission Impossible   ep   10. 9. 71 CBS

FROST, DAVID
    Here's Lucy   ep   11. 29. 71 CBS

FULLER, PENNY
    Women in Chains   tf   1. 25. 72 ABC
    FBI   ep   The Deadly Species   3. 5. 72 ABC

FULLER, ROBERT
    Californians   ep   Pipeline   4. 22. 58 NBC
    No Warning   ep   Survivors   5. 18. 58 NBC
    Restless Gun   ep   Shadow of a Gunfighter   1. 12. 59 CBS
    Alcoa Premiere   ep   Emergency Only   2. 4. 59 ABC
    Cimarron   ep   Blind Is the Killer   2. 21. 59 NBC
    Wagon Train   ep   The Kate Parker Story   5. 6. 59 NBC
    Lawless Years   ep   The Story of Cutie Jafie   5. 7. 59
        NBC
    Laramie   sr   9. 15. 59 NBC
    Laramie   sr ret   9. 20. 60 NBC
    Laramie   sr ret   9. 26. 61 NBC
    Cain's Hundred   ep   The Debasers   1. 16. 62 NBC
    Laramie   sr ret   9. 25. 62 NBC
    Wagon Train   sr   9. 16. 63 ABC
    Wagon Train   sr ret   9. 20. 64 ABC
    Kraft Suspense Theatre   ep   Jungle Fear   4. 22. 65 NBC
    Bob Hope Chrysler Theatre   ep   Massacre at Ft. Phil
        Kearny   10. 26. 66 NBC
    The Monroes   ep   11. 16. 66 ABC
    Virginian   ep   3. 22. 67 NBC
    Big Valley   ep   A Flock of Trouble   9. 25. 67 ABC
    Dan August   ep   The Titan   1. 6. 71 ABC
    Men from Shiloh   ep   Flight from Memory   2. 17. 71 NBC
    Emergency   tf   1. 15. 72 NBC
    Emergency   sr   1. 22. 72 NBC
    Emergency   sr ret   9. 16. 72 NBC
    Adam-12   ep   Emergency   10. 4. 72 NBC

FURNESS, BETTY
    Studio One   ep   Confessions of a Nervous Man   11. 30.
        53 CBS

Studio One   ep   Affairs of State   4.18.55 CBS
Climax   ep   Silent Decision   9.15.55 NBC
Studio One   ep   Babe in the Woods   5.13.57 CBS
Climax   ep   The Thief with the Big Blue Eyes   3.6.58
     CBS
ABC Stage 67   ep   The People Trap   11.8.66 ABC

-G-

GABOR, EVA
     Masterpiece Playhouse   ep   Uncle Vanya   9.3.50 NBC
     Story Theatre   ep   Lodging for the Night   5.11.51 NN
     Suspense   ep   This Is Your Confession   8.21.51, 8.28,
          51
     Summer Theatre   ep   At Mrs. Beam's   7.30.51 CBS
     Ellery Queen   ep   Adventures of the Twilight Zone   9.
          13.51   NN
     Tales of Tomorrow   ep   The Invaders   12.21.51 ABC
     Pulitzer Prize Playhouse   ep   The Return of Mr. Moto
          5.7.52 ABC
     Philco Playhouse   ep   The Gesture   3.15.53 NBC
     Suspense   ep   The Duel   4.21.53 CBS
     Studio One   ep   Paul's Apartment   3.29.54 CBS
     Pond's Theatre   ep   Candle Light   5.5.55 ABC
     Way of the World   ep   5.16.55 NBC
     Justice   ep   The Intruder   5.26.55 NBC
     Appointment with Adventure   ep   Notorious Woman   6.
          5.55 CBS
     Philco Playhouse   ep   One Mummy Too Many   11.20.55
          NBC
     Kraft Theatre   ep   Once a Genius   11.30.55 NBC
     Matinee Theatre   ep   Pearls of Sheba   10.2.56 NBC
     Climax   ep   Journey into Fear   10.11.56 CBS
     77th Bengal Lancers   ep   Steel Bracelet   11.11.56 NBC
     G.E. Theatre   ep   The Big Shooter   2.17.57 CBS
     Climax   ep   Jacob and the Angel   10.3.57 CBS
     Matinee Theatre   ep   The Vagabond   3.27.58 NBC
     G.E. Theatre   ep   Ah There, Beau Brummel   5.4.58
          CBS
     Matinee Theatre   ep   Nine-Finger Jack   5.19.58 NBC
     Five Fingers   ep   Station Break   10.3.59 NBC
     Adventure in Paradise   ep   Peril at Pitcairn   12.7.59
          ABC

U.S. Steel Hour   ep   How to Make a Killing   4.6.60
   CBS
Ann Sothern Show   ep   Katy and the New Girl   5.30.60
   CBS
Detectives   ep   The Retirement of Maria Muir   5.20.
   60 ABC
Great Mysteries   ep   The Great Impersonation   11.15.
   60 NBC
Harrigan and Son   ep   There's No Fool Like an Old
   Fool   12.9.60 ABC
Dick Powell Theatre   ep   The Fifth Caller   12.19.61
   NBC
Defenders   ep   Gideon's Follies   12.23.61 CBS
U.S. Steel Hour   ep   Two Black Kings   3.21.62 CBS
Mickey and the Countess   pt   8.12.63 CBS
Burke's Law   ep   Who Killed Harris Crown   10.11.63
   ABC
Green Acres   sr   9.15.65 CBS
Petticoat Junction   ep   4.26.66 CBS
Green Acres   sr ret   9.14.66 CBS
Green Acres   sr ret   9.6.67 CBS
Green Acres   sr ret   9.25.68 CBS
Here's Lucy   ep   11.11.68 CBS
Green Acres   sr ret   9.27.69 CBS
Wake Me When the War Is Over   tf   10.14.69 ABC
Green Acres   sr ret   9.15.70 CBS
Here's Lucy   ep   9.18.72 CBS

GABOR, ZSA ZSA
   Climax   ep   The Great Impersonation   3.10.55 CBS
   Climax   ep   Man of Taste   12.11.55 CBS
   G.E. Theatre   ep   The Honest Man   2.19.56 CBS
   Matinee Theatre   ep   The Tall Dark Stranger   2.28.56
      NBC
   Ford Theatre   ep   Autumn Fever   4.5.56 NBC
   Matinee Theatre   ep   The Babylonian Heart   4.19.56
      NBC
   Bob Cummings Show   ep   10.4.56 CBS
   Playhouse 90   ep   The Greer Case   1.31.57 CBS
   Playhouse 90   ep   Circle of the Day   5.30.57 CBS
   Matinee Theatre   ep   The Last Voyage   7.4.57 NBC
   Matinee Theatre   ep   The Subpoena   1.6.58 NBC
   Matinee Theatre   ep   The Two Mrs. Carrolls   4.3.58
      NBC
   Lux Playhouse   ep   This Will Do Nicely   4.17.59 CBS
   December Bride   ep   5.21.59 CBS
   Ninotchka   Sp   4.20.60 ABC

Danny Thomas Show   ep   10.31.60 CBS
G.E. Theatre   ep   The Legend that Walks Like a Man
    2.12.61 CBS
Dick Powell Theatre   ep   Charlies' Duet   3.19.63 NBC
Mister Ed   ep   Zsa Zsa   4.21.63 CBS
Burke's Law   ep   Who Killed Cable Roberts   10.4.63
    ABC
Burke's Law   ep   12.16.64 ABC
Bob Hope Chrysler Theatre   ep   Double Jeopardy   1.8.
    65 NBC
Gilligan's Island   ep   12.30.65 CBS
Alice in Wonderland   Sp (voice only)   3.30.66 ABC
Bonanza   ep   5.7.67 NBC
Batman   ep   3.14.68 ABC
Name of the Game   ep   Fear of High Places   9.20.68
    NBC
Bracken's World   ep   10.3.69 NBC
Night Gallery   ep   12.15.71 NBC

GALLAGHER, HELEN
    Kraft Theatre   ep   Pardon My Prisoner   3.24.54 NBC
    Paris in the Springtime   Sp   1.21.56 NBC

GALLAGHER, SKEETS
    Personal Appearance Theatre   ep   If Clancy Were Here
        3.22.52 ABC

GAM, RITA
    Danger   ep   Marley's Ghost   6.26.51 CBS
    Cameo Theatre   ep   Peer Gynt   2.24.52, 3.2.52 NBC
    Motorola TV Hour   ep   Nightmare in Algiers   3.23.54
        ABC
    Omnibus   ep   11.28.54 CBS
    Ford Theatre   ep   Mimi   5.19.55 NBC
    Kraft Theatre   ep   Trucks Welcome   10.12.55 NBC
    Front Row Center   ep   Deadlock   2.5.56 CBS
    Studio One   ep   The Laughter of Giants   3.19.56 CBS
    Dupont Show of the Month   ep   The Bridge of San Luis
        Rey   1.21.58 CBS
    U.S. Steel Hour   ep   The Women of Hadley   2.24.60
        CBS
    U.S. Steel Hour   ep   Revolt in Hadley   3.9.60 CBS
    Hidden Faces   sr   1969 NBC

GARDINER, REGINALD
    Best of Broadway   ep   The Man Who Came to Dinner
        10.13.54 CBS

Best of Broadway   ep   The Guardsman   3.2.55 CBS
Hallmark Hall of Fame   ep   Alice in Wonderland   10.
    23.55   NBC
20th Century-Fox Hour   ep   Mr. Belvedere   4.18.56
    CBS
The Millionaire   ep   The Story of Waldo Francis Tur-
    ner   11.14.56 CBS
Suspicion   ep   Murder Me Gently   10.7.57 NBC
Playhouse 90   ep   No Time at All   2.13.58 CBS
Behind Closed Doors   ep   Double Jeopardy   10.16.58
    NBC
Alfred Hitchcock Presents   ep   Banquo's Chair   5.3.59
    CBS
Our Man Higgins   ep   Will the Real Mr. Hargrave
    Please Stand Up   4.17.63 ABC
Laramie   ep   The Marshals   4.30.63 NBC
Burke's Law   ep   Who Killed Victor Barrows   1.17.64
    ABC
Hazel   ep   Fashion Show   1.30.64 NBC
77 Sunset Strip   ep   Dead as in Dude   1.31.64 ABC
Burke's Law   ep   Who Killed Davidian Jones   12.30.64
    ABC
Hazel   ep   Stop Rockin' our Reception   2.18.65 NBC
The Man from U.N.C.L.E.   ep   The Round-Table Af-
    fair   3.25.66 NBC
Pruitts of Southampton   sr   9.13.66 ABC
Batman   ep   3.22.67, 3.23.67 ABC
Petticoat Junction   ep   12.16.67 CBS
Monkees   ep   2.26.68 NBC

GARDNER, ED
    Duffy's Tavern   ep   4.5.54 NBC

GARDNER, ERLE STANLEY
    Perry Mason   ep   The Case of the Final Fade-Out   5.
        22.66 CBS

GARFIELD, ALLEN
    Mod Squad   ep   Welcome to our City   3.2.71 ABC
    Young Lawyers   ep   The Whimper of Whipped Dogs   3.
        10.71 ABC
    Footsteps   tf   10.3.72 CBS
    Banyon   ep   11.24.72 NBC

GARGAN, WILLIAM
    Martin Kane, Private Eye   sr   1.5.50 NBC
    Martin Kane, Private Eye   sr ret   9.7.50 NBC

Ellery Queen   sr   4. 5. 51 NBC
Playhouse   ep   Death the Hard Way   10. 17. 54 ABC
Playhouse   ep   Lost Lullaby   12. 26. 54 ABC
Ford Theatre   ep   Favorite Son   6. 16. 55 NBC
20th Century-Fox Hour   ep   Man on the Ledge   12. 28.
  55 CBS
Studio One   ep   The McTaggart Succession   5. 5. 58
  CBS

GARLAND, BEVERLY
Medic   ep   9. 13. 54 NBC
Four Star Playhouse   ep   Bourbon Street   12. 9. 54 CBS
Medic   ep   White Is the Color   1. 17. 55 NBC
The Millionaire   ep   Millionaire Carl Nelson   1. 26. 55
  CBS
Four Star Playhouse   ep   Night of Lark Cottage   3. 24.
  55 CBS
Playhouse   ep   Woman in the Mine   6. 12. 55 ABC
Schlitz Playhouse of Stars   ep   Too Late to Run   8. 5.
  55 CBS
Undercurrent   ep   Woman in the Mine   8. 5. 55 CBS
Big Town   ep   Hot Car Murder   8. 29. 55 NBC
Damon Runyon Theatre   ep   Tobias the Terrible   9. 10.
  55 CBS
Science Fiction Theatre   ep   Negative Man   9. 16. 55
  NBC
Soldiers of Fortune   ep   The Lady and the Lion   9. 16.
  55 ABC
Navy Log   ep   Family Special   11. 8. 55 CBS
Frontier   ep   Cattle Drive to Casper   11. 27. 55 NBC
Front Row Center   ep   The Morals Squad   3. 11. 56
  CBS
Crusader   ep   A Deal in Diamonds   4. 6. 56 CBS
Four Star Playhouse   ep   Touch and Go   4. 26. 56 CBS
Four Star Playhouse   ep   Second Chance   6. 14. 56
  CBS
Climax   ep   Throw Away the Cane   8. 2. 56 CBS
Climax   ep   The Fog   9. 27. 56 CBS
Zane Grey Theatre   ep   Courage Is a Gun   12. 14. 56
  CBS
Climax   ep   A Taste for Crime   6. 20. 57 CBS
Decoy   sr   fall, 1957 NN
Turn of Fate   ep   Silhouette of a Killer   9. 30. 57 NBC
Telephone Time   ep   The Other Van Gogh   10. 29. 57
  ABC
Trackdown   ep   3. 11. 59 CBS
Zane Grey Theatre   ep   Hanging Fever   3. 12. 59 CBS

Yancy Derringer   ep   The Wayward Warrior   4.16.59
   CBS
The Millionaire   ep   Louise Benson   5.20.59 CBS
Rawhide   ep   Incident of the Roman Candles   7.10.59
   CBS
World of Disney   ep   Move Along Mustangers   11.13.
   59   ABC
Hawaiian Eye   ep   Shipment from Kihei   12.16.59 ABC
World of Disney   ep   Mustang Man, Mustang Maid   11.
   20.59 ABC
Perry Mason   ep   The Case of the Mythical Monkeys
   2.27.60 CBS
Zane Grey Theatre   ep   A Small Town That Died   3.
   10.60 CBS
Riverboat   ep   Three Graves   3.14.60 NBC
Laramie   ep   Saddle and Spur   3.29.60 NBC
Tales of Wells Fargo   ep   Pearl Hunt   5.9.60 NBC
Coronado 9   sr   9.6.60 NN
Hong Kong   ep   Freebooter   10.19.60 ABC
Thriller   ep   Knock Three-One-Two   12.13.60 NBC
Stagecoach West   ep   The Storm   12.13.60 ABC
Michael Shayne   ep   Murder and the Wanton Bride   12.
   16.60 NBC
Checkmate   ep   Between Two Guns   2.11.61 CBS
Zane Grey Theatre   ep   Jericho   5.18.61 CBS
Asphalt Jungle   ep   The Nine-Twenty Hero   5.21.61
   ABC
Dr. Kildare   ep   Twenty-Four Hours   9.28.61 NBC
87th Precinct   ep   Killer's Payoff   11.6.61 NBC
Bus Stop   ep   Summer Lightning   1.7.62 ABC
Dick Powell Theatre   ep   Seeds of April   2.13.62 NBC
Cain's Hundred   ep   The Left Side of Canada   5.1.62
   NBC
Mystery Theatre   ep   In Close Pursuit   6.13.62 NBC
Dr. Kildare   ep   Hastings' Farewell   11.1.62 NBC
Rawhide   ep   Incident at Sugar Creek   11.23.62 CBS
Going My Way   ep   A Saint for Mama   12.26.62 ABC
Rawhide   ep   Incident of the Gallows Trees   2.22.63
   CBS
Sam Benedict   ep   Image of a Toad   2.23.63 NBC
Dakotas   ep   The Chooser of the Slain   4.22.63 ABC
Gunsmoke   ep   5.18.63 CBS
Fugitive   ep   Smoke Screen   10.29.63 ABC
Eleventh Hour   ep   What Did She Mean by Good Luck
   11.13.63 NBC
Kraft Suspense Theatre   ep   Charlie, He Couldn't Kill
   a Fly   5.7.64 NBC

Bing Crosby Show   sr   9.14.64 ABC
Shenandoah   ep   The Onslaught   9.13.65 ABC
Laredo   ep   Lazyfoot Where Are You   9.16.65 NBC
World of Disney   ep   Trial by Error   1.29.67, 2.5.67
   NBC
Judd for the Defense   ep   9.15.67 ABC
Wild, Wild West   ep   11.17.67 CBS
Gunsmoke   ep   1.1.68 CBS
Mannix   ep   1.20.68, 1.27.68 CBS
Gunsmoke   ep   Time of the Jackals   1.13.69 CBS
Wild, Wild West   ep   The Night of the Bleak Island
   3.14.69 CBS
My Three Sons   sr   10.4.69 CBS
Gunsmoke   ep   2.2.70 CBS
Cutter's Trail   2.6.70 CBS
My Three Sons   sr ret   9.19.70 CBS
My Three Sons   sr ret   9.13.71 CBS
Marcus Welby, M.D.   ep   A Fragile Procession   9.
   12.72 ABC
Say Goodbye, Maggie Cole   tf   9.27.72 ABC
Mod Squad   ep   10.19.72 ABC
The Weekend Nun   tf   12.20.72 ABC

GARNER, JAMES
Cheyenne   ep   6.5.56 ABC
Conflict   ep   The People Against McQuade   11.13.56
   ABC
Conflict   ep   The Man from 1997   11.27.56 ABC
Cheyenne   ep   War Party   2.12.57 ABC
Maverick   sr   9.22.57 ABC
Maverick   sr ret   9.58 ABC
Maverick   sr ret   9.13.59 ABC
Maverick   sr ret   9.18.60 ABC
Angel   ep   The French Lesson   2.23.61 CBS
Nichols (a.k.a. The James Garner Show)   sr   9.16.71
   NBC

GARNER, PEGGY ANN
Tele-Theatre   ep   Once to Every Boy   2.20.50 NBC
Family Playhouse   ep   11.7.50 CBS
Two Girls Named Smith   sr   1.20.51 ABC
Robert Montgomery Presents   ep   Claire Ambler   3.24.
   52 NBC
Video Theatre   ep   Salad Days   4.28.52 CBS
Video Theatre   ep   The Orchard   8.11.52 CBS
Studio One   ep   Plan for Escape   11.17.52 CBS
Schlitz Playhouse of Stars   ep   Mr. Thayer   12.5.52
   CBS

Mirror Theatre   ep   A Reputation   7.28.53 NBC
Robert Montgomery Presents   ep   Once Upon a Time   5.
    31.54 NBC
Danger   ep   Precinct Girl   1.4.55 CBS
Robert Montgomery Presents   ep   Deadline   1.31.55
    NBC
Best of Broadway   ep   Stage Door   4.6.55 CBS
Climax   ep   The First and the Last   4.28.55 CBS
Studio One   ep   Strange Companion   5.16.55 CBS
Stage 7   ep   The Time of Day   5.29.55 CBS
Kraft Theatre   ep   The Killer Instinct   9.18.57 NBC
Dupont Show of the Month   ep   Beyond This Place   11.
    25.57 CBS
Kraft Theatre   ep   The Velvet Trap   1.8.58 NBC
G.E. Theatre   ep   The Unfamiliar   3.30.58 CBS
Studio One   ep   Man Under Glass   7.14.58 CBS
U.S. Steel Hour   ep   We Wish on the Moon   7.29.59
    CBS
Lineup   ep   10.28.59 CBS
Zane Grey Theatre   ep   Deception   4.14.60 CBS
Tate   ep   Stopover   6.15.60 NBC
Adventure in Paradise   ep   Once Around the Circuit
    10.17.60 ABC
Alcoa Premiere   ep   Tonight at 12:17   12.6.60 ABC
Perry Mason   ep   The Case of the Constant Doyle   1.31.
    61 CBS
Naked City   ep   Button in a Haystack   2.22.61 ABC
Bonanza   ep   The Rival   4.15.61 NBC
Alcoa Premiere   ep   Impact of an Execution   1.3.62
    ABC
Have Gun, Will Travel   ep   2.10.62 CBS
Adventures in Paradise   ep   Build My Gallows Low   2.
    18.62 ABC
Alfred Hitchcock Theatre   ep   Victim Four   5.15.62 NBC
Untouchables   ep   Elegy   11.20.62 ABC
Untouchables   ep   The Giant Killer   4.9.63 ABC
Hallmark Hall of Fame   ep   The Patriots   11.15.63 NBC
Eleventh Hour   ep   Who Chopped Down the Cherry Tree
    1.29.64 NBC
The Man from U.N.C.L.E.   ep   The Project Strigas Af-
    fair   11.24.64 NBC
Batman   ep   9.21.67 ABC

GARRETT, BETTY
    Ford Theatre   ep   A Smattering of Bliss   11.17.55 NBC
    Ford Theatre   ep   The Penlands and the Poodle   1.23.57
        ABC

Lloyd Bridges Show ep Mr. Pennington's Machine
10.9.62 CBS
Fugitive ep Escape into Black 11.17.64 ABC

GARROWAY, DAVE
Babes in Toyland Sp 12.18.54 NBC
Babes in Toyland Sp (restaged) 12.24.55 NBC
Alias Smith and Jones ep 1.27.72 ABC

GARSON, GREER
Producers Showcase ep Reunion in Vienna 4.4.55
NBC
Star Stage ep Career 2.24.56 NBC
Hallmark Hall of Fame ep The Little Foxes 12.16.56
NBC
G.E. Theatre ep The Earring 1.13.57 CBS
G.E. Theatre ep The Glorious Gift of Molly Malloy
6.2.57 CBS
Telephone Time ep Revenge 9.10.57 ABC
Father Knows Best ep Kathy's Big Chance 11.13.57
NBC
Hallmark Hall of Fame ep Captain Brassbound's Con-
version 5.2.60 NBC
Dupont Show of the Month ep The Shadowed Affair 11.
4.62 NBC
Hallmark Hall of Fame ep The Invincible Mr. Dis-
raeli 4.4.63 NBC
Men from Shiloh ep Lady at the Bar 11.4.70 NBC

GARVER, KATHY
Dr. Kildare ep Fathers and Daughters 11.22.65, 11.
23.65, 11.29.65, 11.30.65 NBC
Family Affair sr 9.12.66 CBS
Family Affair sr ret 9.11.67 CBS
Family Affair sr ret 9.23.68 CBS
Big Valley ep The Royal Road 3.3.69 ABC
Family Affair sr ret 9.25.69 CBS
Family Affair sr ret 9.17.70 CBS
Adam-12 ep 12.29.71 NBC

GATES, NANCY
Playhouse ep Melody in Black 11.6.53 ABC
Pepsi Cola Playhouse ep His Brother's Girl 2.26.54
ABC
Pepsi Cola Playhouse ep Don't You Remember 3.12.
54 ABC
G.E. Theatre ep Exit for Margo 5.23.54 CBS
Lux Video Theatre ep Christmas in July 9.9.54 NBC

Studio 57   ep   Trap Mates   10. 5. 54 NN
Schlitz Playhouse of Stars   ep   Woman Expert   12. 17.
   54 CBS
Studio 57   ep   The Big Jump   1. 11. 55 NN
TV Reader's Digest   ep   Trouble on the Double   1. 24.
   55 ABC
G. E. Theatre   ep   The Big Shot   1. 30. 55 CBS
The Millionaire   ep   Millionaire Joe Iris   2. 2. 55 CBS
Treasury Men in Action   ep   The Case of the Lady in
   Hiding   3. 10. 55 ABC
Soldiers of Fortune   cp   4. 9. 55 ABC
Studio 57   ep   Rainy Night   4. 19. 55 NN
Damon Runyon Theatre   ep   All Is Not Gold   4. 30. 55
   CBS
Dear Phoebe   ep   Phoebe   5. 20. 55 NBC
Damon Runyon Theatre   ep   Bred for Battle   10. 8. 55
   CBS
G. E. Theatre   ep   Lash of Fear   10. 16. 55 CBS
The Millionaire   ep   Millionaire Irish Miller   10. 19. 55
   CBS
Alfred Hitchcock Presents   ep   Salvage   11. 6. 55 CBS
Screen Directors Playhouse   ep   Tom and Jerry   11.
   30. 55 NBC
Schlitz Playhouse of Stars   ep   Well of Anger   12. 30.
   55 CBS
Fireside Theatre   ep   Scent of Roses   3. 13. 56 NBC
Alfred Hitchcock Presents   ep   Portrait of Jocelyn   4.
   8. 56 CBS
Loretta Young Show   ep   Understanding Heart   11. 10.
   57 NBC
Kraft Theatre   ep   Code of the Corner   1. 15. 58 NBC
Loretta Young Show   ep   My Two Hands   2. 2. 58 NBC
Maverick   ep   Burial Ground of the Gods   3. 30. 58 ABC
Wagon Train   ep   The Millie Davis Story   11. 26. 58
   NBC
77 Sunset Strip   ep   The Girl Who Couldn't Remember
   1. 23. 59 ABC
Maverick   ep   Passage to Fort Doom   3. 8. 59 ABC
The Millionaire   ep   Millionaire Marcia Forrest   3. 25.
   59 CBS
Perry Mason   ep   The Case of the Crooked Candle   6.
   6. 59 CBS
Riverboat   ep   Payment in Full   9. 13. 59 NBC
Men into Space   ep   First Woman on the Moon   12. 16.
   59 CBS
Lineup   ep   Prince of Penmen   12. 30. 59 CBS
Bourbon Street Beat   ep   Kill with Kindness   1. 4. 60
   ABC

Wichita Town ep The Legend of Tom Horn 3. 30. 60 NBC
Best of the Post ep Band of Brothers 1. 21. 61 ABC
Hong Kong ep Murder by Proxy 3. 1. 61 ABC
Zane Grey Theatre ep Storm over Eden 5. 4. 61 CBS
Detectives ep A Barrel Full of Monkeys 10. 27. 61
   NBC
Tales of Wells Fargo ep Jeremiah 11. 11. 61 NBC
Adventures in Paradise ep The Fires Kanau 11. 19.
   61 ABC
Bus Stop ep Accessory by Consent 11. 19. 61 ABC
New Breed ep Wings for a Plush Horse 2. 20. 62 ABC
Wagon Train ep The Shiloh Degnan Story 11. 7. 62 ABC
Lloyd Bridges Show ep The Sound of the Angels 12.
   18. 62 CBS
Lloyd Bridges Show ep 4. 16. 63 CBS
Wagon Train ep 2. 3. 64 ABC
Perry Mason ep The Case of the Woeful Widower 3.
   26. 64 CBS
Kentucky Jones ep 2. 13. 65 NBC
Perry Mason ep The Case of the Candy Queen 9. 26.
   65 CBS
Loner ep The House Rule at Mrs. Wayne's 11. 6. 65 CBS
Amos Burke ep The Man's Men 12. 8. 65 ABC
Danny Thomas Show ep The Scene 9. 25. 67 NBC
Mod Squad ep An Eye for an Eye 10. 7. 69 ABC

GAVIN, JOHN
Alcoa Premiere ep The Jail 2. 6. 62 ABC
Alfred Hitchcock Theatre ep Run for Doom 5. 17. 63 CBS
Kraft Suspense Theatre ep A Truce to Terror 1. 9.
   64 NBC
Destry sr 2. 14. 64 ABC
Virginian ep Portrait of a Widow 12. 9. 64 NBC
Kraft Suspense Theatre ep Three Persons 12. 10. 64
   NBC
Alfred Hitchcock Theatre ep Off Season 5. 10. 65 NBC
Convoy sr 9. 16. 65 NBC
Cutter's Trail 2. 6. 70 CBS
Doris Day Show ep 3. 1. 71 CBS

GAXTON, WILLIAM
Nash Airflyte Theatre sh 9. 28. 50 CBS

GAYNOR, JANET
Medallion Theatre ep Dear Cynthia 11. 28. 53 CBS
Video Theatre ep Two Dozen Roses 5. 6. 54 CBS
G. E. Theatre ep The Flying Wife 4. 5. 59 CBS

GAZZARA, BEN
>   The Web   ep   A Case of Escape   7.5.53 CBS
>   Medallion Theatre   ep   The Alibi Kid   3.27.54 CBS
>   U.S. Steel Hour   ep   The Notebook Warrior   9.14.54
>   ABC
>   Playhouse 90   ep   The Troublemakers   11.20.57 CBS
>   Playhouse 90   ep   The Violent Heart   2.6.58 CBS
>   Kraft Theatre   ep   Three Plays by Tennessee Williams
>   4.16.58 NBC
>   Dupont Show of the Month   ep   Body and Soul   9.28.59
>   CBS
>   Cry Vengeance   Sp   2.21.61 NBC
>   Arrest and Trial   sr   9.15.63 ABC
>   Carol for Another Christmas   tf   12.28.64 ABC
>   Kraft Suspense Theatre   ep   Rapture at 240   4.15.65
>   NBC
>   Run for Your Life   sr   9.13.65 NBC
>   Run for Your Life   sr ret   9.66 NBC
>   Bob Hope Chrysler Theatre   ep   Free of Charge   3.22.
>   67 NBC
>   Run for Your Life   sr ret   9.13.67 NBC
>   When Michael Calls   tf   2.5.72 ABC
>   Fireball Forward   tf   3.5.72 ABC
>   The Family Rico   tf   9.12.72 CBS
>   Pursuit   tf   12.12.72 ABC

GEAR, LUELLA
>   The Trap   ep   The Chocolate Cobweb   6.3.50 CBS
>   Sure as Fate   ep   Tremolo   7.4.50 CBS
>   Broadway Television Theatre   ep   The Patsy   6.23.52
>   NN
>   The Web   ep   The Poison Tree   7.2.52 CBS
>   Elgin Hour   ep   Falling Star   12.28.54 ABC
>   Joe and Mabel   sr   9.20.55 CBS
>   Producers Showcase   ep   Happy Birthday   6.25.56 NBC
>   Joe and Mabel   sr ret   6.26.56 CBS
>   Play of the Week   ep   Juno and the Paycock   2.1.60
>   ABC

GEER, WILL
>   East Side/West Side   ep   Here Today   4.27.64 CBS
>   Trials of O'Brien   ep   The Ten Foot, Six Inch Pole   1.
>   14.66 CBS
>   Trials of O'Brien   ep   The Only Game in Town   3.18.66
>   CBS
>   Garrison's Gorillas   ep   10.17.67 ABC
>   I Spy   ep   Home to Judgment   1.8.68 NBC

Of Mice and Men   Sp   1.31.68 ABC
Run for Your Life   ep   The Killing Scene   1.31.68 NBC
Gunsmoke   ep   10.21.68 CBS
Bonanza   ep   3.30.69 NBC
Hawaii Five-O   ep   10.8.69 CBS
Then Came Bronson   ep   Old Tigers Never Die   11.5.
    69 NBC
Daniel Boone   ep   11.20.69 NBC
The Bold Ones   ep   The Shattered Image   2.15.70 NBC
Name of the Game   ep   One of the Girls in Research
    4.3.70 NBC
The Brotherhood of the Bell   tf   9.17.70 CBS
Young Rebels   ep   9.20.70, 9.27.70 ABC
Bold Ones   ep   The Verdict   9.27.70 NBC
Bold Ones   ep   The Day the Lion Died   10.4.70 NBC
Immortals   ep   10.8.70 ABC
Bonanza   ep   The Love Child   11.8.70 NBC
Young Rebels   ep   The Age of Independence   11.15.70
    ABC
Sam Hill: Who Killed the Mysterious Mr. Foster   tf
    2.1.71 NBC
Love American Style   ep   2.5.71 ABC
Cade's County   ep   Company Town   9.26.71 CBS
Owen Marshall   ep   Voice from a Nightmare   12.16.71
O'Hara, U.S. Treasury   ep   12.17.71 CBS
Bonanza   ep   12.19.71 NBC
Bold Ones   ep   The Letter of the Law   12.26.71 NBC
Bewitched   ep   2.26.72 ABC
Sixth Sense   ep   3.4.72 ABC
The Waltons   sr   9.14.72 CBS

GEESON, JUDY
Sam Hill: Who Killed the Mysterious Mr. Foster   2.1.
    71 NBC

GENEVIEVE
Satins and Spurs   Sp   9.12.54 NBC

GENN, LEO
Omnibus   ep   Salome   12.18.55 CBS
Screen Directors Playhouse   ep   Titanic Incident   12.28.
    55 NBC
Mrs. Miniver   Sp   1.7.60 CBS
Strange Report   ep   Shrapnel   3.19.71 NBC
Persuaders   ep   2.2.72 ABC

GEORGE, DAN (CHIEF)
   High Chaparral ep Apache Trust 11.7.69 NBC
   Bonanza ep 12.26.71 NBC
   Cade's County 4.9.72 CBS

GEORGE, GLADYS
   Bigelow-Sanford Theatre ep The Other Jessie Grant
      10.4.51 NN
   Jewelers Showcase ep Rocking Horse 1.13.53 CBS
   Playhouse ep Sal 10.3.54 ABC

GIBSON, HOOT
   I Married Joan ep 3.16.55 NBC

GIBSON, WYNNE
   The Clock ep A Right Smart Trick 8.31.51 NBC
   The Web ep Paper Doll 2.21.54 CBS
   Producers Showcase ep Happy Birthday 6.25.56 NBC

GIELGUD, JOHN (SIR)
   Dupont Show of the Month ep The Browning Version
      4.23.59 CBS
   Ages of Man Sp 1.23.66 CBS
   ABC Stage 67 ep The Love Song of Barney Kempinski
      9.14.66 ABC
   N.E.T. Playhouse ep The May Fly and the Frog 10.
      11.68 NN
   Ivanov Sp 5.30.67 CBS
   Hallmark Hall of Fame ep 11.17.70 NBC
   Home Sp 11.29.71 NN
   Probe tf 2.21.72 NBC

GIFFORD, FRANCES
   Fireside Theatre ep Grey Gardens 3.3.53 NBC
   G.E. Theatre ep My Wife, Poor Wretch 9.20.53 CBS
   Drama at Eight ep Adopted Son 9.3.53 NN

GILFORD, JACK
   The Play's the Thing ep Screwball 4.28.50 CBS
   Car 54 Where Are You ep The Curse of the Snitkins
      4.14.63 NBC
   Cowboy and the Tiger Sp 11.28.63 ABC
   Defenders ep Moment of Truth 3.21.64 CBS
   Defenders ep The Seven Hundred Year Old Gang 9.24.
      64, 10.1.64 CBS
   Mr. Broadway ep Try to Find a Spy 10.10.64 CBS
   Defenders ep No-Knock 2.25.66 CBS

T. H. E. Cat   ep   10. 14. 66 NBC
Governor and J. J.   ep   10. 21. 69 CBS
Get Smart   ep   11. 7. 69, 11. 14. 69 CBS
N. E. T. Playhouse   ep   They   4. 17. 70 NN
Of Thee I Sing   Sp   10. 24. 72 CBS
Once Upon a Mattress   Sp   12. 12. 72 CBS

GILLMORE, MARGALO
Theatre Hour   ep   School for Scandal   4. 21. 50 CBS
Robert Montgomery Presents   ep   Claire Ambler   3. 24.
   52 NBC
Philco Playhouse   ep   Uncertain Heritage   10. 19. 52 NBC
Producers Showcase   ep   Peter Pan   3. 7. 55 NBC
Producers Showcase   ep (restaged) Peter Pan   1. 9. 56
   NBC
Producers Showcase   ep   The Barretts of Wimpole Street
   4. 2. 56 NBC
Lux Video Theatre   ep   Old Witch, Old Witch   9. 5. 57
   NBC
Play of the Week   ep   The Girls in 509   4. 18. 60 NN
Peter Pan   Sp (restaged)   12. 8. 60 NBC

GILMORE, VIRGINIA
Video Theatre   ep   Blackmail   3. 19. 50 NBC
Philco Playhouse   ep   The Man in the Black Hat   4. 23.
   50 ABC
Studio One   ep   There Was a Crooked Man   6. 19. 50
   CBS
Starlight Theatre   ep   Three Hours between Planes   7.
   27. 50 ABC
Tales of Tomorrow   ep   Dune Roller   1. 4. 52 ABC
Broadway Television Theatre   ep   The Barker   6. 16. 52
   NN
Broadway Television Theatre   ep   The Night of January
   16   7. 14. 52 NN
The Doctor   ep   Googan   2. 22. 53 NBC
The Web   ep   Fair Warning   4. 19. 53 CBS
Defenders   ep   The Poisoned Fruit Doctrine   1. 19. 63
   CBS
Nurses   ep   The Human Transition   4. 23. 64 CBS

GING, JACK
Man and the Challenge   ep   The Visitors   12. 26. 59 NBC
Men into Space   ep   1. 13. 60 CBS
Black Saddle   ep   Means to an End   1. 29. 60 ABC
Wanted Dead or Alive   ep   1. 30. 60 CBS
Man and the Challenge   ep   Hurricane Mesa   3. 19. 60
   NBC

Loretta Young ep Linda 10.9.60 NBC
Wyatt Earp ep Johnny Behind the Deuce 10.11.60
  ABC
Deputy ep Three Brothers 12.10.60 NBC
Twilight Zone ep The Whole Truth 1.20.61 CBS
Perry Mason ep The Case of the Blind Man's Bluff
  3.11.61 CBS
Shirley Temple Theatre ep The Princess and the Gob-
  lins 3.19.61 NBC
Sea Hunt ep 4.22.61 CBS
Roaring 20s ep Among the Mi Sing 5.6.61 ABC
Michael Shayne ep It Takes a Heap O' Dyin' 5.12.61
  NBC
Tales of Wells Fargo ep 9.30.61 NBC
Eleventh Hour sr 10.3.62 NBC
Eleventh Hour sr ret 10.2.63 NBC
Bob Hope Chrysler Theatre ep The War and Eric
  Kurtz 3.5.65 NBC
Perry Mason ep The Case of the Lonely Eloper 5.27.
  65 CBS
Trials of O'Brien ep A Horse Called Destiny 1.28.66
  CBS
Shane ep 11.26.66 ABC
Gunsmoke ep 11.26.66 CBS
World of Disney ep Willie and the Yank 1.8.67, 1.15.
  67, 1.22.67 NBC
Bonanza ep 2.25.68 NBC
Judd for the Defense ep A Puff of Smoke 9.27.68
  ABC
Mannix ep End of the Rainbow 10.26.68 CBS
Mannix ep Medal for a Hero 1.3.70 CBS
Hawaii Five-O ep Run Johnny Run 1.14.70 CBS
Men from Shiloh ep 1.20.71 NBC
O'Hara, U.S. Treasury tf 4.2.71 CBS
Mod Squad ep I Am My Brother's Keeper 1.4.72
  ABC
Mannix ep 1.12.72 CBS
Mannix ep 2.16.72 CBS
Medical Center ep 2.23.72 CBS
O'Hara, U.S. Treasury ep Operation Smokescreen
  3.10.72 CBS
My Sister, Hank pt 3.31.72 ABC
Ironside ep 11.9.72 NBC
FBI ep 11.26.72 ABC
Mannix ep A Puzzle for One 11.26.72 CBS
Mission Impossible ep 12.2.72 CBS
Mannix ep 12.24.72 CBS

GINGOLD, HERMIONE
    Omnibus   ep   11. 28. 54 CBS
    Elgin Hour   ep   A Sting of Death   2. 22. 55 ABC
    Omnibus   ep   She Stoops to Conquer   11. 20. 55 CBS
    Alfred Hitchcock Presents   ep   The Schartz-Metterlume
        Method   6. 12. 60   CBS
    Drama   ep   Assassination Plot at Teheran   9. 23. 61,
        9. 30. 61 ABC
    Hallmark Hall of Fame   ep   A Cry of Angels   12. 15. 63
        NBC
    The Girl from U. N. C. L. E.   ep   2. 28. 67 NBC
    It Takes a Thief   ep   4. 30. 68 ABC
    Ironside   ep   Checkmate and Murder   10. 29. 70,   11. 5. 70
        NBC
    Name of the Game   ep   Aquarius Descending   12. 11. 70
        NBC
    Love American Style   ep   2. 26. 71 ABC
    Banyon   tf   3. 15. 71 NBC

GISH, DOROTHY
    Ford Theatre   ep   One Day for Keeps   2. 9. 51 CBS
    Prudential Playhouse   ep   The Bishop Misbehaves   3. 27.
        51 CBS
    Starlight Theatre   ep   The Magnificent Faker   4. 19. 51
        ABC
    Robert Montgomery Presents   ep   The Post Road   12. 1.
        52 NBC
    Goodyear Playhouse   ep   The Oil Well 5. 17. 53 NBC
    Robert Montgomery Presents   ep   Harvest 11. 23. 53
        NBC
    U. S. Steel Hour   ep   The Rise and Fall of Silas Lapham
        4. 27. 54 ABC
    Philco Playhouse   ep   The Shadow of Willie Greer   5. 30.
        54 NBC
    Elgin Hour   ep   Flood   10. 5. 54 ABC
    Lux Video Theatre   ep   Miss Susie Slagle's   11. 24. 55
        NBC
    Alcoa Hour   ep   Morning's at Seven   11. 4. 56 NBC
    Play of the Week   ep (restaged)   Morning's at Seven   4.
        25. 60 NN

GISH, LILLIAN
    Philco Playhouse   ep nar   Birth of Movies   4. 22. 51 NBC
    Robert Montgomery Presents   ep   Ladies in Retirement
        5. 7. 51 NBC
    Pulitzer Prize Playhouse   ep   Detour   6. 1. 51 ABC
    Celanese Theatre   ep   The Joyous Season   12. 26. 51 ABC

Schlitz Playhouse of Stars   ep   Grandma Moses   3.28.
   52 CBS
Philco Playhouse   ep   The Trip to Bountiful   3.1.53
   NBC
Robert Montgomery Presents   ep   The Quality of Mercy
   3.15.54 NBC
TV Soundstage   ep   The Corner Drugstore   5.28.54
   NBC
Kraft Theatre   ep   I, Mrs. Bibb   10.19.55 NBC
Playwrights '56   ep   The Sound and the Fury   12.6.55
   NBC
Ford Star Jubilee   ep   The Day Lincoln Was Shot   2.11.
   56 NBC
Alcoa Hour   ep   Morning's at Seven   11.4.56 NBC
Play of the Week   ep   The Grass Harp   3.28.60 NN
Theatre 62   ep   The Spiral Staircase   10.4.61 NBC
Defenders   ep   Grandma TNT   12.22.62 CBS
Mr. Novak   ep   Hell, Miss Phipps   11.5.63 NBC
Breaking Point   ep   The Gnu, Now Almost Extinct   12.
   16.63 ABC
Arsenic and Old Lace   Sp   4.2.69 ABC

GLEASON, JACKIE
   Life of Riley   sr   1949-1950 NBC
   Studio One   ep   The Laugh Maker   5.18.53 CBS
   Studio One   ep   Peacock City   12.6.54 CBS
   Best of Broadway   ep   The Show-off   2.2.55 CBS
   The Honeymooners   sr   10.1.55 CBS
   Studio One   ep   Uncle Ed and Circumstance   10.10.55
      CBS
   The Million Dollar Incident   Sp   4.21.61 CBS

GLEASON, JAMES
   Ford Theatre   ep   Sweet Talk Me, Jackson   5.21.53
      NBC
   Drama   ep   The Frame-Up   12.19.54 CBS
   Shower of Stars   ep   Burlesque   3.17.55 CBS
   So This Is Hollywood   ep   The Old Timer   4.23.55 NBC
   Danny Thomas Show   ep   6.14.55 ABC
   Damon Runyon Theatre   ep   The Big Umbrella   6.18.55
      CBS
   Screen Directors Playhouse   ep   Rookie of the Year   12.
      7.55 NBC
   Damon Runyon Theatre   ep   Dog about Town   12.31.55
      CBS
   Cheyenne   ep   1.3.56 ABC
   Climax   ep   The Fifth Wheel   2.9.56 CBS

The Millionaire   ep   10.3.56 CBS
Ford Theatre   ep   Try Me for Size   12.6.56 NBC
Alfred Hitchcock Presents   ep   The End of Indian Summer   2.24.57 CBS
Dupont Theatre   ep   Shark of the Mountain   4.23.57 ABC
Playhouse 90   ep   The Time of Your Life   10.9.58 CBS

GOBEL, GEORGE
Light's Diamond Jubilee   ep   10.24.54 ABC, CBS, NBC
Ford Star Time   ep   Cindy's Fella   12.15.59 NBC
G.E. Theatre   ep   They Liked Me Fine   6.5.60 CBS
Wagon Train   ep   The Horace Best Story   10.5.60 NBC
My Three Sons   ep   Lonesome George   12.1.60 ABC
G.E. Theatre   ep   A Friendly Tribe   12.31.61 CBS
Valentine's Day   ep   Hottest Game in Town   11.20.64 ABC
Bing Crosby Show   ep   The Image   2.15.65 ABC
Daniel Boone   ep   Four-Leaf Clover   3.25.65 NBC
Love American Style   ep   12.29.69 ABC

GODDARD, PAULETTE
Ford Theatre   ep   The Doctor's Downfall   10.8.53 NBC
Producers Showcase   ep   The Women   2.7.55 NBC
On Trial   ep   The Ghost of Devil's Island   3.29.57 NBC
Ford Theatre   ep   Singapore   4.17.57 ABC
Adventures in Paradise   ep   Lady from South Chicago   11.2.59 ABC
The Snoop Sisters   tf   12.18.72 NBC

GODFREY, ARTHUR
Here's Lucy   ep   3.8.65 CBS
Bob Hope Chrysler Theatre   ep   The Reason Nobody Hardly Ever Seen a Fat Outlaw   3.8.67 NBC

GOMEZ, THOMAS
Life with Luigi   sr   4.16.53 CBS
TV Hour   ep   Brandenburg Gate   12.1.53 ABC
Center Stage   ep   The Worthy Opponent   8.24.54 ABC
G.E. Theatre   ep   High Green Wall   10.3.54 CBS
Climax   ep   South of the Sun   3.3.55 CBS
Lux Video Theatre   ep   The Great McGinty   4.28.55 NBC
Playwrights '56   ep   This Business of Murder   1.31.56 NBC
Producers Showcase   ep   Caesar and Cleopatra   3.5.56 NBC
Schlitz Playhouse of Stars   ep   Lottery for Revenge

5. 30. 58 CBS
Shirley Temple's Story Book   ep   Ali Baba and the Forty
  Thieves   11. 12. 58 NBC
Rifleman   ep   Stranger at Night   6. 2. 59 ABC
Twilight Zone   ep   Escape Clause   11. 6. 59 CBS
Adventures in Paradise   ep   Mission to Manila   11. 23.
  59 ABC
Route 66   ep   A Lance of Straw   10. 14. 60 CBS
Aquanauts   ep   11. 9. 60 CBS
Islanders   ep   Forbidden Cargo   11. 27. 60 ABC
Twilight Zone   ep   Dust   1. 6. 61 CBS
Route 66   ep   Trap at Cordova   5. 26. 61 CBS
Michael Shayne   ep   Man with a Cane   6. 30. 61 NBC
Power and the Glory   Sp   10. 29. 61 CBS
Target Corruptors   ep   Bite of a Tiger   11. 3. 61 ABC
Dick Powell Theatre   ep   Open Season   12. 26. 61 NBC
Dick Powell Theatre   ep   Death in a Village   1. 2. 62
  NBC
Dr. Kildare   ep   The Good Samaritan   10. 3. 63 NBC
Amos Burke   ep   The Man with the Power   10. 13. 65
  ABC
Virginian   ep   Beyond the Border   11. 24. 65 NBC
Bob Hope Chrysler Theatre   ep Nightmare   9. 14. 66
  NBC
Shadow over Elveron   tf   3. 5. 68 NBC
It Takes a Thief   ep   9. 24. 68 ABC
FBI   ep   The Patriot   2. 2. 69 ABC
Outsider   ep   Behind God's Back   2. 5. 69 NBC
It Takes a Thief   ep   11. 27. 69 ABC

GOODMAN, DODY
Phil Silvers Show   ep   The Rich Kid   12. 27. 55 CBS

GOODWIN, BILL
Lux Video Theatre   ep   Welcome Stranger   9. 2. 54 NBC
G. E. Theatre   ep   Amelia   1. 2. 55 CBS
Public Defender   ep   A Pair of Gloves   4. 21. 55 CBS
Matinee Theatre   ep   The Serpent's Tooth   2. 25. 57 NBC
Eve Arden Show   ep   3. 11. 58 CBS

GORDON, GALE
Our Miss Brooks   sr   10. 3. 52 CBS
Our Miss Brooks   sr ret   10. 2. 53 CBS
Our Miss Brooks   sr ret   10. 54 CBS
Our Miss Brooks   sr ret   10. 7. 55 CBS
Climax   ep   A Trophy for Howard Davenport   6. 28. 56
  CBS

The Brothers   sr   10.2.56 CBS
Playhouse 90   ep   The Jet-Propelled Couch   11.14.57
   CBS
Sally   sr   2.23.58 NBC
Studio One   ep   The Award Winner   3.24.58 CBS
Playhouse 90   ep   The Male Animal   3.13.58 CBS
Danny Thomas Show   ep   12.21.59 CBS
Pete and Gladys   ep   11.21.60 CBS
Danny Thomas Show   ep   1.2.61 CBS
Danny Thomas Show   ep   Party Wrecker   5.22.61 CBS
Pete and Gladys   sr   9.18.61 CBS
Harrigan and Son   ep   On Broadway   9.22.61 ABC
Donna Reed Show   ep   Dr. Stone and His Horseless
   Car   1.11.62 ABC
The Lucy Show   sr   9.30.63 CBS
The Lucy Show   sr ret   9.21.64 CBS
The Lucy Show   sr ret   9.13.65 CBS
Where There's Money   pt   8.1.66 CBS
The Lucy Show   sr ret   9.12.66 CBS
The Lucy Show   sr ret   9.67 CBS
Here's Lucy   sr   9.23.68 CBS
Here's Lucy   sr ret   9.22.69 CBS
Here's Lucy   sr ret   9.14.70 CBS
Here's Lucy   sr ret   9.13.71 CBS
Here's Lucy   sr ret   9.11.72 CBS

GORDON, RUTH
   Prudential Playhouse   ep   Over 21   12.19.50 CBS

GORMAN, CLIFF
   N.Y.P.D.   ep   Naked in the Streets   10.1.68 ABC
   N.E.T. Playhouse   ep   Paradise Lost   2.25.71, 3.4.71
   NN

GOULET, ROBERT
   Westinghouse Presents   ep   The Enchanted Nutcracker
   12.23.61 ABC
   Joey Bishop Show   ep   4.25.64 NBC
   Kraft Suspense Theatre   ep   Operation Grief   10.8.64
   NBC
   Patty Duke Show   ep   Don't Monkey with Mendel   3.10.
   65 ABC
   Blue Light   sr   1.12.66 ABC
   Brigadoon   Sp   10.15.66 ABC
   Big Valley   ep   2.20.67 ABC
   Carousel   Sp   5.7.67 ABC
   Kiss Me, Kate   Sp   3.25.68 ABC

Name of the Game ep Keep the Doctor Away 2.14.69
  NBC
Mission Impossible ep 10.7.72 CBS

GRABLE, BETTY
  Star Stage ep Cleopatra Collins 3.9.56 NBC
  Ford Star Jubilee ep Twentieth Century 4.7.56 CBS
  Lucille Ball-Desi Arnaz Show ep Lucy Wins a Race
    Horse 2.3.58 CBS

GRAHAM, SHEILAH
  G.E. Theatre ep Nobody's Child 5.10.59 CBS

GRAHAME, GLORIA
  Harrigan and Son ep My Fair Lawyer 1.27.61 ABC
  New Breed ep Blood Money 12.19.61 ABC
  Sam Benedict ep Too Many Strangers 12.8.62 NBC
  Burke's Law ep 1.31.64 ABC
  Outer Limits ep The Guests 3.23.64 ABC
  Fugitive ep The Homecoming 4.7.64 ABC
  Burke's Law ep 4.14.65 ABC
  Iron Horse ep Appointment with an Epitaph 2.13.67
    ABC
  Then Came Bronson ep The 3:13 Arrives at Noon
    10.29.69 NBC
  Daniel Boone ep Perilous Passage 1.15.70 NBC
  Name of the Game ep The Takeover 1.23.70 NBC
  Mannix ep Duet for Three 12.19.70 CBS

GRANGER, FARLEY
  Schlitz Playhouse of Stars ep Splendid with Swords
    6.24.55 CBS
  U.S. Steel Hour ep Incident in an Alley 11.23.55
    CBS
  Producers Showcase ep Caesar and Cleopatra 3.5.56
    NBC
  Robert Montgomery Presents ep Pistolero 4.9.56
    NBC
  Climax ep Faceless Enemy 6.7.56 CBS
  Playhouse 90 ep Seidman and Son 10.18.56 CBS
  Ford Theatre ep Stand by to Dive 11.28.56 ABC
  20th Century-Fox Hour ep Men Against Speed 12.12.
    56 CBS
  Robert Montgomery Presents ep The Clay Pigeon 1.
    28.57 NBC
  U.S. Steel Hour ep The Bottle Imp 3.13.57 CBS
  Kraft Theatre ep Circle of Fear 8.14.57 NBC

Kraft Theatre   ep   Man in a Trance   10.23.57 NBC
Playhouse 90   ep   The Clouded Image   11.7.57 CBS
Wagon Train   ep   The Charles Avery Story   11.13.57
NBC
Dupont Show of the Month   ep   Beyond This Place   11.
25.57 CBS
Kraft Theatre   ep   Come to Me   12.4.57 NBC
U.S. Steel Hour   ep   The Hidden River   7.2.58 CBS
U.S. Steel Hour   ep   The Wound Within   9.10.58 CBS
Dupont Show of the Month   ep   Arrowsmith   1.17.60
CBS
Great Mysteries   ep   The Inn of the Flying Dragon   10.
18.60 NBC
Our American Heritage   ep   Born a Giant   12.2.60 NBC
Dupont Show of the Month   ep   The Prisoner of Zenda
1.18.61 CBS
Family Classics   ep   The Heiress   2.13.61 CBS
Bob Hope Chrysler Theatre   ep   Nightmare   9.14.66
NBC
Bob Hope Chrysler Theatre   ep   Blind Man's Bluff   2.8.
67 NBC
Ironside   ep   10.5.67 NBC
Hondo   ep   10.13.67 ABC
Laura   Sp   1.24.68 ABC
Outsider   ep   What Flowers Daisies Are   9.25.68 NBC
Name of the Game   ep   The Ordeal   11.22.68 NBC
Hawaii Five-O   ep   2.5.69 CBS
The Challengers   tf   3.28.69 CBS
Medical Center   ep   The Loner   12.10.69 CBS

GRANGER, STEWART
Any Second Now   tf   2.11.69 NBC
Men from Shiloh   sr   9.16.70 NBC
The Hound of the Baskervilles   tf   2.12.72 ABC

GRANT, KIRBY
Story Theatre   ep   The Celebrated Jumping Frog   4.13.
51 NN
Sky King Theatre   sr   4.13.52 NBC
Cavalcade of America   ep   Betrayal   12.8.53 ABC

GRANT, LEE
The Play's the Thing   ep   Screwball   4.28.50 CBS
Comedy Theatre   ep   Zone of Quiet   7.2.50 CBS
Danger   ep   Dark as Night   5.6.52 CBS
Danger   ep   Death to the Lonely   6.24.52 CBS
Danger   ep   The Face of Fear   8.26.52 CBS

Broadway Television Theatre   ep   The Noose   4.20.53
   NN
ABC Album   ep   Justice   4.12.53 ABC
Summer Theatre   ep   The Blonde Comes First   6.30.53
   CBS
Philco Playhouse   ep   Shadow of the Champ   3.20.55
   NBC
Pond's Theatre   ep   Death Is a Spanish Dancer   6.30.55
   ABC
Alcoa Hour   ep   Even the Weariest River   4.15.56 NBC
Playwrights '56   ep   Keyhole   5.22.56 NBC
Kraft Theatre   ep   Three Plays by Tennessee Williams
   4.16.58 NBC
Kraft Theatre   ep   Look What's Going On   3.19.58 NBC
Jewish Appeal   ep   Where Is Thy Brother?   5.18.58
   NBC
Play of the Week   ep   The House of Bernarda Alba   6.6.
   60 NN
Golden Showcase   ep   Saturday's Children   2.25.62 CBS
Defenders   ep   The Empty Heart   10.5.63 CBS
Nurses   ep   The Gift   10.17.63 CBS
East Side/West Side   ep   Not Bad for Openers   11.18.
   63 CBS
Nurses   tp   Spend, to Give, to Want   12.12.63 CBS
Fugitive   ep   Taps for a Dead War   3.17.64 ABC
Ben Casey   ep   For a Just Man Falleth Seven Times   4.
   15.64 ABC
Ben Casey   ep   For Jimmy, the Best of Anything   10.19.
   64 ABC
Defenders   ep   Nobody Asks What Side You're On   3.11.
   65 CBS
For the People   ep   With Intent to Influence   4.11.65
   CBS
Peyton Place   sr   7.65 ABC
ABC Stage 67   ep   The Love Story of Barney Kempinski
   9.14.66 ABC
ABC Stage 67   ep   The People Trap   11.9.66 ABC
Big Valley   ep   4.3.67 ABC
Bob Hope Chrysler Theatre   ep   Deadlock   5.17.67 NBC
Ironside   ep   10.5.67 NBC
Judd for the Defense   ep   The Gates of Crebecus   11.15.
   68 ABC
Mission Impossible   ep   12.1.68 CBS
Medical Center   ep   The Loner   12.10.69 CBS
Name of the Game   ep   2.13.70 NBC
Mod Squad   ep   Mother of Sorrow   2.17.70 ABC
Name of the Game   ep   9.24.70 NBC

Night Slaves tf 9. 29. 70 ABC
The Neon Ceiling tf 2. 8. 71 NBC
Ransom for a Dead Man tf 3. 1. 71 NBC
Men at Law ep Yesterday Is But a Dream 3. 31. 71
   CBS
Lt. Schuster's Wife tf 10. 11. 72 ABC

GRANVILLE, BONITA
   Bigelow Theatre ep Make Your Bed 3. 4. 51 CBS
   Video Theatre ep Not Guilty of Much 3. 5. 51 CBS
   Gruen Guild Theatre ep One Strange Day 11. 15. 51
      ABC
   Schaefer Century Theatre ep Annual Honeymoon 5.
      31. 52 NBC
   Schaefer Century Theatre ep Yesterday's World 7. 9.
      52 NBC
   Campbell Playhouse ep One Strange Day 8. 29. 52
      NBC
   Campbell Playhouse ep Hit and Run 7. 18. 52 NBC
   The Unexpected ep The Woman Who Left Herself
      9. 24. 52 NBC
   Broadway Television Theatre ep Guest in the House
      2. 23. 53 NN
   Ford Theatre ep The Son-in-Law 4. 30. 53 NBC
   Dangerous Encounter ep I Saw It Happen 2. 21. 54 NN
   Gloria Swanson Theatre ep The Antique Shop 2. 15. 55
      ABC
   Climax ep The Healer 7. 21. 55 CBS
   Climax ep The Fifth Wheel 2. 9. 56 CBS
   Ethel Barrymore Theatre ep Lady Investigator 11. 30.
      56 NN
   Bob Cummings Show ep Bob Meet Schultzy's Cousin
      3. 14. 57 CBS
   U. S. Steel Hour ep Shadow in the Sky 5. 22. 57 CBS
   Studio One ep The Fair-Haired Boy 3. 3. 58 CBS
   Playhouse 90 ep The Velvet Alley 1. 22. 59 CBS
   Lassie ep 5. 8. 60 CBS
   Best of the Post ep Valley of the Blue Mountain 3. 11.
      61 ABC

GRAVES, PETER
   Playhouse ep Melody in Black 11. 6. 53 ABC
   Fireside Theatre ep The Suitors 12. 15. 53 NBC
   Schlitz Playhouse of Stars ep Part of the Game 12. 18.
      53 CBS
   Pepsi Cola Playhouse ep Miss Darkness 1. 1. 54 ABC
   Fireside Theatre ep Beyond the Cross 4. 13. 54 NBC

Fireside Theatre   ep   Bread upon the Waters   6.8.54
   NBC
Studio 57   ep   Sauce for the Gander   12.28.54 NN
TV Reader's Digest   ep   Trouble on the Double   1.24.
   55 ABC
Fireside Theatre   ep   Bitter Grapes   4.26.55   NBC
Fury   sr   10.15.55 NBC
Studio One   ep   Circle of Guilt   2.20.56 CBS
Cavalcade Theatre   ep   The Major of St. Louis   6.5.56
   ABC
The Millionaire   ep   The Story of Anna Hartley   9.26.56
   CBS
Climax   ep   Carnival at Midnight   1.3.57 CBS
Lux Video Theatre   ep   Armed Venus   5.23.57 NBC
Climax   ep   Deadly Tattoo   5.1.58 CBS
Whiplash   sr   fall, 1961 NN
Route 66   ep   You Never Had It So Good   2.23.63 CBS
Route 66   ep   Hell Is Empty, All the Devils Are Here
   5.25.62 CBS
Alfred Hitchcock Theatre   ep   I'll Be the Judge, I'll Be
   the Jury   2.15.63
Kraft Suspense Theatre   ep   The Case Against Paul
   Ryker   10.10.63, 10.17.63 NBC
Farmer's Daughter   ep   The Playboy of Capitol Hill   2.
   12.64 ABC
Virginian   ep   A Matter of Destiny   2.19.64 NBC
Great Adventure   ep   Kentucky's Bloody Ground   4.3.64,
   4.10.64 CBS
Laredo   ep   That's Norway, Thataway   1.6.66 NBC
Branded   ep   The Assassins   3.27.66, 4.3.66 NBC
Court Martial   sr   4.8.66 ABC
Run for Your Life   ep   The Dark Beyond the Door   10.
   10.66 NBC
Daniel Boone   ep   10.20.66 NBC
World of Disney   ep   Showdown with the Sundown Kid
   10.23.66, 10.30.66 NBC
12 O'Clock High   ep   1.6.67 ABC
FBI   ep   2.12.67 ABC
Invaders   ep   4.18.67 ABC
Mission Impossible   sr   9.10.67 CBS
Call to Danger   pt   7.1.68 CBS
Mission Impossible   sr ret   9.68 CBS
Mission Impossible   sr ret   9.28.69 CBS
Mission Impossible   sr ret   9.19.70 CBS
Mission Impossible   sr ret   9.18.71 CBS
Mission Impossible   sr ret   9.16.72 CBS

GRAY, BILLY
Celanese Theatre ep On Borrowed Time 6.25.52
    ABC
Schaefer Century Theatre ep Lesson in Hot Lead 10.
    12.52 NBC
Fireside Theatre ep The First Prize 1.12.54 NBC
Cavalcade of America ep Young Andy Jackson 3.23.
    54 ABC
Father Knows Best sr 10.3.54 CBS
Father Knows Best sr ret 8.31.55 NBC
Father Knows Best sr ret fall, 1956 NBC
Father Knows Best sr ret fall, 1957 NBC
Thin Man ep Come, Darling Asta 10.11.57 NBC
Father Knows Best sr ret 9.22.58 CBS
Father Knows Best sr ret 9.59 CBS
Father Knows Best sr ret 9.60 CBS
Peter Gunn ep The Semi Private Eye 5.23.60 NBC
Stagecoach West ep Dark Return 10.18.60 ABC
Bachelor Father ep Ginger's Big Romance 12.29.60
    NBC
G.E. Theatre ep The Drop-Out 1.29.61 CBS
Deputy ep Two-Way Deal 3.11.61 NBC
G.E. Theatre ep Sis Bowls 'em Over 4.9.61 CBS
Alfred Hitchcock Theatre ep The Hat Box 10.10.61
    NBC
I Spy ep Lori 9.21.66 NBC
Bold Ones ep Memo from the Class of '76 3.8.70
    NBC

GRAY, DOLORES
U.S. Steel Hour ep Famous 5.31.61 CBS

GRAYSON, KATHRYN
G.E. Theatre ep Shadow on the Heart 10.30.55 CBS
G.E. Theatre ep The Invitation 10.21.56 CBS
Playhouse 90 ep Lone Woman 12.26.57 CBS
Lux Playhouse ep A Game of Hate 11.14.58 CBS

GREEN, MITZI
So This Is Hollywood sr 1.1.55 NBC

GREEN, NIGEL
Broadway Television Theatre ep Death Takes a Holi-
    day 1.5.53 NN

GREENE, LORNE
Studio One ep A Handful of Diamonds 4.19.54 CBS

You Are There   ep   The Torment of Beethoven   1.2.55
   CBS
Studio One   ep   The Cliff   9.13.54 CBS
Climax   ep   Private Worlds   4.7.55 CBS
Star Stage   ep   The Toy Lady   9.9.55 NBC
Studio 57   ep   Death Dream   11.13.55 NN
Alfred Hitchcock Presents   ep   Help Wanted   4.1.56
   CBS
Alcoa Hour   ep   Key Largo   10.14.56 NBC
Armstrong Circle Theatre   ep   Flareup   10.30.56 NBC
U.S. Steel Hour   ep   Survival   11.7.56 CBS
Kraft Theatre   ep   The Medallion   4.3.57 NBC
Studio One   ep   Twenty-Four Hours to Dawn   11.11.57
   CBS
Sailor of Fortune   sr   12.27.57 NN
Shirley Temple's Story Book   ep   The Little Lame
   Prince   7.15.58 NBC
Gale Storm Show   ep   Jailmates   2.28.59 CBS
Wagon Train   ep   The Vivian Carter Story   3.11.59 NBC
Cheyenne   ep   Prairie Skipper   5.5.59 ABC
Mike Hammer   ep   A Haze on the Lake   7.7.59 NBC
True Story   ep   7.25.59 NBC
Bonanza   sr   9.12.59 NBC
Bonanza   sr ret   9.10.60 NBC
Bonanza   sr ret   9.24.61 NBC
Bonanza   sr ret   9.23.62 NBC
Bonanza   sr ret   9.63 NBC
Bonanza   sr ret   9.20.64 NBC
Bonanza   sr ret   9.12.65 NBC
Bonanza   sr ret   9.11.66 NBC
Bonanza   sr ret   9.67 NBC
Bonanza   sr ret   9.15.68 NBC
Bonanza   sr ret   9.14.69 NBC
Destiny of a Spy   tf   10.27.69 NBC
Bonanza   sr ret   9.13.70 NBC
Bonanza   sr ret   9.19.71 NBC
Bonanza   sr ret   9.12.72 NBC

GREENE, RICHARD
   Prudential Playhouse   ep   Berkeley Square   2.13.51
      CBS
   Robert Montgomery Presents   ep   Stairway to Heaven
      4.9.51 NBC
   Video Theatre   ep   Sire de Maletroit's Door   5.7.51
      CBS
   Peter Ibbetson   5.18.51 CBS
   Studio One   ep   Coriolanus   6.11.51 CBS

Somerset Maugham Theatre   ep   The Fall of Edward
    Bernard   10. 29. 51 NBC
Video Theatre   ep   Stolen Years   11. 19. 51 CBS
Robert Montgomery Presents   ep   The Moonstone   2. 11.
    52 NBC
Drama   ep   A Terribly Strange Bed   9. 25. 53 CBS
G. E. Theatre   ep   The Return of Gentleman Jim   2. 6.
    55 CBS
Robin Hood   sr   9. 26. 55 CBS
Robin Hood   sr ret   9. 56 CBS
Robin Hood   sr ret   9. 57 CBS
Robin Hood   sr ret   9. 58 CBS
U. S. Steel Hour   ep   The Wayward Widow   5. 6. 59 CBS
G. E. Theatre   ep   Hot Footage   5. 15. 60 CBS
Off to See the Wizard   ep   Island of the Lost   11. 10.
    67,   11. 17. 67 ABC

GREENWOOD, CHARLOTTE
    Best of the Post   ep   The Thompson of Thunder Ridge
        4. 22. 61 ABC

GREENWOOD, JOAN
    Philco Playhouse   ep   The King and Mrs. Candle   4. 18.
        54 NBC
    Hallmark Hall of Fame   ep   Man and Superman   11. 25.
        56 NBC

GREER, JANE
    Ford Theatre   ep   Look for Tomorrow   5. 14. 53 NBC
    Mirror Theatre   ep   Summer Dance   11. 21. 53 CBS
    Playhouse 90   ep   One Man Missing   6. 9. 55 NBC
    Ford Theatre   ep   Moment of Decision   4. 10. 57 ABC
    Zane Grey Theatre   ep   A Gun for My Bride   12. 27. 57
        CBS
    Suspicion   ep   Meeting in Paris   2. 10. 58 NBC
    Playhouse 90   ep   No Time at All   2. 13. 58 CBS
    Zane Grey Theatre   ep   The Vaunted   11. 27. 58 CBS
    Alfred Hitchcock Presents   ep   A True Account   6. 7.
        59 CBS
    Bonanza   ep   The Julia Bulette Story   10. 17. 59 NBC
    Stagecoach West   ep   High Lonesome   10. 4. 60 ABC
    Thriller   ep   Portrait without a Face   12. 25. 61 NBC
    Burke's Law   ep   4. 7. 64 ABC

GREER, MICHAEL
    Ironside   ep   No Game for Amateurs   9. 24. 70 NBC

GREY, JOEL
Producers Showcase ep Jack and the Beanstock 11.
    12. 56 NBC
Telephone Time ep The Intruder 3. 3. 57 CBS
December Bride ep 10. 7. 57, 10. 14. 57 CBS
Court of Last Resort ep The Todd-Loomis Case 4.
    4. 58 NBC
Bronco ep The Masquerade 1. 26. 60 ABC
Lawman ep The Salvation of Owny O'Reilly 4. 24. 60
    ABC
Lawman ep The Return of Owny O'Reilly 10. 16. 60
    ABC
Nanette Fabray Show ep Nanette's Teen-age Suitor 2.
    24. 61 NBC
77 Sunset Strip ep Open and Close in One 3. 17. 61
    ABC
Lawman ep Owny O'Reilly, Esq. 10. 15. 61 ABC
My Lucky Penny pt 8. 8. 66 CBS
George M Sp 9. 12. 70 NBC
Ironside ep A Killing at the Track 2. 4. 71 NBC
Night Gallery ep There Aren't Any More MacBanes
    2. 16. 72 NBC
Man on a String tf 2. 18. 72 CBS

GREY, VIRGINIA
The Unexpected ep The Professional Touch 5. 21. 52
    ABC
Four Star Playhouse ep Dante's Inferno 10. 9. 52 CBS
Jewelers Showcase ep Dinner Party 12. 9. 52 CBS
Ford Theatre ep The Lady and the Champ 5. 75. 53
    NBC
Ford Theatre ep Tangier Lady 7. 1. 54 NBC
Fireside Theatre ep Three Missions West 11. 30. 54
    NBC
Fireside Theatre ep Not Captain Material 1. 25. 55
    NBC
Fireside Theatre ep The 99th Day 5. 31. 55 NBC
20th Century-Fox Hour ep Crack-Up 2. 8. 56 CBS
Climax ep Spin into Darkness 4. 5. 56 CBS
Jane Wyman Theatre ep A Point of Law 12. 18. 56
    NBC
The Millionaire ep the Marjorie Martinson Story 1. 8.
    58 CBS
Jane Wyman Theatre ep A Guilty Woman 1. 30. 58
    NBC
Wagon Train ep The Major Adams Story 4. 23. 58,
    4. 30. 58 NBC

Goodyear Theatre   ep   Taps for Jeffrey   3.31.58 NBC
Playhouse 90   ep   The Great Gatsby   6.26.58 CBS
Trackdown   ep   10.10.58 CBS
Wagon Train   ep   The Kate Parker Story   5.6.59 NBC
Yancy Derringer   ep   V as in Voodoo   5.15.59 CBS
David Niven Theatre   ep   Good Deeds   7.7.59 NBC
Desilu Playhouse   ep   The Day the Town Stood Up   10.
    2.59 CBS
G.E. Theatre   ep   R.S.V.P.   1.10.60 CBS
June Allyson Show   ep   Slip of the Tongue   4.11.60 CBS
Stagecoach West   ep   12.6.60 ABC
Wagon Train   ep   The Beth Pearson Story   2.22.61
    NBC
Peter Gunn   ep   Death Is a Four-Letter Word   6.5.61
    ABC
Bonanza   ep   The Artist   10.7.62 NBC
Virginian   ep   Nobody Said Hello   1.5.66 NBC
My Three Sons   ep   9.22.66 CBS
I Spy   ep   3.15.67 NBC
Marcus Welby, M.D.   ep   The Rebel Doctor   4.14.70
    ABC

GRIFFIES, ETHEL
Lights Out   ep   The Determined Lady   6.12.50 NBC
TV Playhouse   ep   The Gambler   10.29.50 NBC
Television Theatre   ep   Romantic Young Lady   11.22.50
    NBC
Musical Comedy Time   ep   Miss Liberty   1.8.51 NBC
U.S. Steel Hour   ep   Don't Shake the Family Tree   5.
    15.63 CBS
Doctors/Nurses   ep   A Question of Murder   1.26.65
    CBS

GRIFFITH, ANDY
U.S. Steel Hour   ep   No Time for Sergeants   3.15.55
    ABC
U.S. Steel Hour   ep   Never Know the End   1.29.58 CBS
Playhouse 90   ep   The Male Animal   3.13.58 CBS
Danny Thomas Show   ep   2.15.60 CBS
Andy Griffith Show   sr   10.3.60 CBS
Andy Griffith Show   sr ret   10.2.61 CBS
Andy Griffith Show   sr ret   9.30.63 CBS
Andy Griffith Show   sr ret   9.21.64 CBS
Andy Griffith Show   sr ret   9.13.65 CBS
Andy Griffith Show   sr ret   9.12.66 CBS
Andy Griffith Show   sr ret   9.11.67 CBS
Mayberry R.F.D.   ep   9.23.68 CBS

Mayberry R. F. D.   ep   9. 22. 69 CBS
Headmaster   sr   9. 18. 70 CBS
Andy Griffith Show   sr   1. 8. 71 CBS
The Strangers in 7A   tf   10. 14. 72 CBS
Hawaii Five-O   ep   I'm a Family Crook--Don't Shoot
    12. 19. 72 CBS

GRIMES, TAMMY
    U. S. Steel Hour   ep   The Bride Cried   8. 17. 55 CBS
    Holiday   Sp   6. 9. 56 NBC
    Studio One   ep   Babe in the Woods   5. 13. 57 CBS
    Omnibus   ep   Forty-Five Minutes from Broadway   3.
        15. 59 NBC
    Play of the Week   ep   Archy and Mehitabel   5. 16. 60
        NN
    Great Mysteries   ep   The Datchel Diamonds   9. 20. 60
        NBC
    Golden Showcase   ep   The Fourposter   1. 13. 62 CBS
    Virginian   ep   The Exiles   1. 9. 63 NBC
    Route 66   ep   Where are the Sounds of Brahms   10.
        18. 63 CBS
    Route 66   ep   Come Home Greta Inger Gruenschaffen
        12. 13. 63 CBS
    Burke's Law   ep   Who Killed Jason Shaw   1. 3. 64 ABC
    Destry   ep   The Solid Gold Girl   2. 14. 64 ABC
    Trials of O'Brien   ep   10. 30. 65 CBS
    Tarzan   ep   4. 14. 67 NBC
    Outcasts   ep   3. 10. 69 ABC
    The Other Man   tf   10. 19. 70 NBC
    Love American Style   ep   2. 26. 71 ABC

GRIZZARD, GEORGE
    Justice   ep   The Big Frame   11. 13. 55 NBC
    Appointment with Adventure   ep   Escape   12. 4. 55 CBS
    U. S. Steel Hour   ep   Bring Me a Dream   1. 4. 56 CBS
    Playwrights '56   ep   You and Me...and the Gatepost!
        4. 10. 56 NBC
    Goodyear Playhouse   ep   The Sentry   5. 6. 56 NBC
    Kaiser Aluminum Hour   ep   The Army Game   7. 3. 56
        NBC
    Goodyear Playhouse   ep   The Gene Austin Story   4. 21.
        57 NBC
    Alcoa Premiere   ep   Brainwave   10. 6. 59 ABC
    Brenner   ep   Good Friend   10. 3. 59 CBS
    Playhouse   ep   The Hidden Image   11. 12. 59 CBS
    Ford Star Time   ep   My Three Angels   12. 8. 59 NBC
    U. S. Steel Hour   ep   Act of Terror   12. 30. 59 CBS

The Millionaire ep Millionaire Jerry Mitchell 2.10.
60 CBS
Alfred Hitchcock Presents ep Across the Threshold
2.28.60 CBS
Detectives ep Armed and Dangerous 3.4.60 ABC
Twilight Zone ep The Chaser 5.13.60 CBS
Thriller ep The Twisted Image 9.13.60 NBC
A String of Beads Sp 3.7.61 NBC
Play of the Week ep In a Garden 4.10.61 NN
Alfred Hitchcock Theatre ep Act of Faith 4.10.62
NBC
Bus Stop ep I Kiss Your Shadow 5.25.62 ABC
Nurses ep The Prisoner 11.8.62 CBS
Theatre 62 ep Notorious 12.10.62 NBC
Twilight Zone ep In His Image 1.3.63 CBS
Three Wishes pt 7.29.63 CBS
Ben Casey ep 12.25.63 ABC
Dr. Kildare ep A Hundred Million Tomorrows 3.12.
64 NBC
Profiles in Courage ep 4.25.65 NBC
A Case of Libel Sp 2.11.68 ABC
Hallmark Hall of Fame ep Teacher, Teacher 2.5.69
NBC
On Stage ep The Choice 3.30.69 NBC
The Front Page Sp 1.31.70 NN
Medical Center ep Brink of Doom 9.16.70 CBS
Interns ep 10.23.70 CBS
Ironside ep This Could Blow Your Mind 12.17.70 NBC
N.E.T. Playhouse ep A Memory of Two Mondays 1.28.
71 NN
Travis Logan, D.A. tf 3.11.71 CBS
Marcus Welby, M.D. ep A Portrait of Debbie 9.21.71
ABC

GUARDINO, HARRY
Kaiser Aluminum Hour ep The Deadly Silence 5.21.57
NBC
Studio One ep The Mother Bit 6.10.57 CBS
Alfred Hitchcock Presents ep Last Request 11.24.57
CBS
Kraft Theatre ep Run, Joe, Run 1.29.58 NBC
Suspicion ep A Touch of Evil 2.17.58 NBC
Desilu Playhouse ep Chez Rouge 2.16.59 CBS
Playhouse 90 ep Made in Japan 3.5.59 CBS
Playhouse 90 ep The Killers of Mussolini 6.4.59 CBS
Naked City ep The Canvas Bullet 6.16.59 ABC
Staccato ep The Wild Reed 12.3.59 NBC

Untouchables ep One-Armed Bandit 2.4.60 ABC
Overland Trail ep Perilous Passage 2.7.60 NBC
Overland Trail ep The O'Hara's Ladies 2.14.60 NBC
Staccato ep The Wild Reed 3.10.60 NBC
Untouchables ep The Nick Moses Story 2.23.61 ABC
Checkmate ep Good-by Griff 4.15.61 CBS
Cain's Hundred ep The Left Side of Canada 5.1.62
  NBC
Mystery Theatre ep Chez Rouge 8.8.62 NBC
Dick Powell Theatre ep The Sea Witch 10.23.62 NBC
Dr. Kildare ep Hastings' Farewell 1.1.62 NBC
Alcoa Premiere ep The Masked Marine 11.8.62 ABC
Lloyd Bridges Show ep Wheresoever I Enter 9.11.62
  CBS
Route 66 ep Hey Moth, Come Eat the Flat 11.30.62
  CBS
Eleventh Hour ep Which Man Will Die 1.2.63 NBC
Eleventh Hour ep Advice to the Lovelorn and Shopworn
  1.30.63 NBC
Naked City ep No Naked Ladies in Front of Giavanni's
  House 4.17.63 ABC
The Greatest Show on Earth ep Lion on Fire 9.17.63
  ABC
Outer Limits ep The Human Factor 11.11.63 ABC
Bob Hope Chrysler Theatre ep It's Mental Work 12.
  20.63 NBC
Ben Casey ep A Falcon's Eye, a Lion's Heart, a Girl's
  Hand 2.26.64 ABC
Reporter sr 9.25.64 CBS
Virginian ep The Horse Fighter 12.15.65 NBC
Run for Your Life ep Sequenstro 3.14.66, 3.21.66
  NBC
Name of the Game ep The Revolutionary 12.27.68
  NBC
Hawaii Five-O ep A Thousand Pardons, You're Dead
  9.24.69 CBS
The Lonely Profession 10.21.69 NBC
Hawaii Five-O ep Trouble in Mind 9.23.70 CBS
FBI ep Escape to Terror 10.4.70 ABC
Men at Law ep The Dark World of Harry Anders 2.
  17.71 CBS
Name of the Game ep Appointment in Palermo 2.26.
  71 NBC
Love American Style ep 3.12.71 ABC
Night Gallery ep The Miracle 1.19.72 NBC
Medical Center ep The Torn Man 10.11.72 CBS

GUILD, NANCY
   Ford Theatre   ep   First Born   2.5.53 NBC
   Video Theatre   ep   One of Those Things   3.9.53 CBS
   Robert Montgomery Presents   ep   Death and the Sky
      Above   1.3.55 NBC

GUINNESS, ALEC (SIR)
   Ford Star Time   ep   Wicked Scheme of Jebal Deeks
      11.10.59 NBC

GUNN, MOSES
   FBI   ep   1.5.69 ABC
   Carter's Army   tf   1.27.70 ABC
   Love American Style   ep   3.12.71 ABC
   The Sheriff   tf   3.30.71 ABC
   Hawaii Five-O   ep   Nine, Ten You're Dead   11.30.71
      CBS
   McCloud   ep   A Little Plot at Tranquil Valley   1.12.72
      NBC
   ABC Theatre   ep   If You Give a Dance You Gotta Pay
      the Band   12.19.72 ABC

GURIE, SIGRID
   Gruen Guild Theatre   ep   Joe Santa Claus   12.20.51
      ABC

GWENN, EDMUND
   Ford Theatre   ep   Heart of Gold   12.25.52 NBC
   Schlitz Playhouse of Stars   ep   Guardian of the Clock
      1.23.53 CBS
   Ford Theatre   ep   Come on Red   3.11.54 NBC
   Rheingold Theatre   ep   The Great Shinin' Saucer of
      Paddy Faneen   3.12.55 NBC
   Science Fiction Theatre   ep   The Strange Dr. Lorenz
      7.15.55 NBC
   Eddie Cantor Theatre   ep   The Man Who Liked Little
      People   9.5.55 ABC
   The Phil Silvers Show   ep   The Eating Contest   11.15.
      55 CBS
   Playhouse 90   ep   The Greer Case   1.31.57 CBS
   Kaiser Aluminum Hour   ep   A Man's Game   4.23.57
      NBC
   Playhouse 90   ep   Winter Dreams   5.23.57 CBS
   Alfred Hitchcock Presents   ep   Father and Son   6.2.57
      CBS

GWYNNE, FRED
  Phil Silvers Show ep The Eating Contest 11.15.55
    CBS
  Studio One ep The Landlady's Daughter 11.26.56 CBS
  Suspicion ep Hand in Glove 10.21.57 NBC
  Kraft Theatre ep The Big Heist 11.13.57 NBC
  Dupont Show of the Month ep Harvey 9.22.58 CBS
  Dupont Show of the Month ep The Hasty Heart 12.18.
    58 CBS
  Play of the Week ep The Old Foolishness 3.6.61 NN
  Car 54 Where Are You sr 9.17.61 NBC
  Car 54 Where Are You sr ret 9.16.62 NBC
  U.S. Steel Hour ep Don't Shake the Family Tree 5.
    15.63 CBS
  The Munsters sr 9.24.64 CBS
  The Munsters sr ret 9.16.65 CBS
  New York Television Theatre ep The Lesson 10.17.66
    NN
  N.E.T. Playhouse ep Infancy 12.15.67 NN
  Guess What I Did Today pt 9.10.68 NBC
  Arsenic and Old Lace Sp 4.2.69 ABC
  Hallmark Hall of Fame ep The Littlest Angel 12.6.69
    NBC
  N.E.T. Playhouse ep Paradise Lost 2.25.71, 3.4.71
    NN
  Hollywood Television Theatre ep The Police 10.14.71
    NN
  Family Theatre ep Dames at Sea 11.15.71 NBC
  Hallmark Hall of Fame ep Harvey 3.22.71 NBC

GYNT, GRETA
  Douglas Fairbanks, Jr. Presents ep The Last Moment
    4.15.53 NBC

                              -H-

HAAS, DOLLY
  Studio One ep Riviera 1.2.50 CBS
  Armstrong Circle Theatre ep The Fugitive 3.11.54
    NBC
  Studio One ep Regarding File Number 4356 4.16.56
    CBS

HAAS, HUGO
    Story Theatre   ep   Mysterious Picture   12. 16. 51 NN
    Ford Theatre   ep   Adventure in Connecticut   1. 29. 53
        NBC
    Ford Theatre   ep   Girl in Flight   12. 2. 54 NBC
    Telephone Time   ep   The Gingerbread Man   7. 1. 56 CBS
    Telephone Time   ep   Escape   3. 24. 57 CBS
    Telephone Time   ep   Rabbi on Wheels   4. 24. 57 ABC
    Five Fingers   ep   Search for Edward Stoyan   1. 9. 60
    Bonanza   ep   Dark Star   4. 23. 60 NBC

HACKETT, BUDDY
    Stanley   sr   10. 1. 56 NBC
    Dan Raven   ep   The Mechanic   9. 30. 60 NBC
    Rifleman   ep   The Clarence Bibs Story   4. 4. 61 ABC
    Trials of O'Brien   ep   Notes on a Spanish Prisoner   10.
        2. 65 CBS
    Big Valley   ep   9. 12. 66 ABC

HACKETT, JOAN
    Ellery Queen   ep   2. 59 NBC
    Young Dr. Malone   sr   1959-1960 NBC
    Armstrong Circle Theatre   ep   12. 60 CBS
    Alfred Hitchcock Theatre   ep   Servant Problem   6. 6. 61
        NBC
    Defenders   sr   9. 16. 61 CBS
    Westinghouse Presents   ep   Come Again to Carthage   12.
        8. 61 CBS
    Ben Casey   ep   A Certain Time, a Certain Darkness
        12. 11. 61 ABC
    New Breed   ep   Cross the Little Line   1. 9. 62 ABC
    Dr. Kildare   ep   1. 62 NBC
    Twilight Zone   ep   A Piano in the House   2. 16. 62 CBS
    Gunsmoke   ep   3. 24. 62 CBS
    Theatre 62   ep   Rebecca   4. 8. 62 NBC
    Alcoa Premiere   ep   A Place to Hide   5. 22. 62 ABC
    Defenders   sr ret   9. 62 CBS
    Alcoa Premiere   ep   The Way from Darkness   12. 13. 62
        ABC
    Combat   ep   The Chateau   2. 12. 63 ABC
    Nurses   ep   The Life   2. 14. 63 CBS
    Empire   ep   Between Friday and Monday   5. 7. 63 NBC
    Great Adventure   ep   The Outlaw and the Nun   12. 6. 63
        CBS
    Channing   ep   A Rich, Famous, Glamorous Folk Singer
        Like Me   1. 8. 64 NBC
    Alfred Hitchcock Theatre   ep   Beast in View   3. 20. 64
        CBS

Bob Hope Chrysler Theatre   ep   Echo of Evil   6.5.64
   NBC
Ben Casey   ep   The Wild, Wild, Wild Waltzing World
   12.14.64 ABC
Bonanza   ep   Woman of Fire   12.29.64 NBC
Bob Hope Chrysler Theatre   ep   The Highest Fall of All
   12.1.65 NBC
Court Martial   ep   4.8.66 ABC
Run for Your Life   ep   The Sex Object   10.17.66 NBC
Danny Thomas Show   ep   It's Greek to Me   10.2.67
   NBC
Judd for the Defense   ep   12.15.67 ABC
Name of the Game   ep   Witness 9.27.68 NBC
The Young Country   tf   3.17.70 ABC
How Awful about Allan   tf   9.22.70 ABC
The Other Man   tf   10.19.70 NBC
Love American Style   ep   2.19.71 ABC
Dan August   ep   1971 ABC
Hollywood Television Theatre   ep   U.S.A.   5.4.71 NN
Five Desperate Women   tf   9.28.71 ABC
Lights Out   ep   When Widows Weep   12.30.71 NN
Bonanza   ep   Second Sight   1.9.72 NBC
Mission Impossible   ep   1.15.72 CBS
Alias Smith and Jones   ep   1972 ABC

HACKMAN, GENE
   U.S. Steel Hour   ep   Little Tin God   4.22.59 CBS
   U.S. Steel Hour   ep   Big Doc's Girl   11.4.59 CBS
   U.S. Steel Hour   ep   Bride of the Fox   8.24.60 CBS
   Defenders   ep   Quality of Mercy   9.16.61 CBS
   U.S. Steel Hour   ep   Brandenburg Gate   10.4.61 CBS
   U.S. Steel Hour   ep   Far from the Shade Tree   1.10.62
      CBS
   Defenders   ep   Judgment Eve   4.20.63 CBS
   Dupont Show of the Month   ep   Ride with Terror   12.1.
      63 NBC
   Trials of O'Brien   ep   3.18.66 CBS
   Hawk   ep   Do Not Mutilate or Spindle   9.8.66 ABC
   FBI   ep   1.15.67 ABC
   Invaders   ep   The Spores   10.17.67 ABC
   Iron Horse   ep   Leopards Try   10.28.67 ABC
   CBS Playhouse   ep   My Father and My Mother   2.13.68
      CBS
   I Spy   ep   2.26.68 NBC
   Shadow on the Land   tf   12.4.68   ABC

HADEN, SARA
Summer Night Theatre ep Room for Improvement 9. 8.53 NN
Hallmark Hall of Fame ep Of Time and the River 11. 15.53 NBC
Ford Theatre ep A Season to Love 5.6.54 NBC
Kraft Theatre ep The Long Road Home 6.23.54 NBC
Cavalcade of America ep Six Hours to Deadline 5.3. 55 ABC
Damon Runyon Theatre ep Bunny on the Beach 7.16. 55 CBS

HAGEN, JEAN
Make Room for Daddy (a.k.a. Danny Thomas Show) sr 9.29.53 ABC
Make Room for Daddy sr ret 9.54 ABC
Make Room for Daddy sr ret 9.55 ABC
Climax ep The Lou Gehrig Story 4.19.56 CBS
Alfred Hitchcock Presents ep Enough Rope for Two 11. 17.57 CBS
Desilu Playhouse ep Symbol of Authority 2.2.59 CBS
Desilu Playhouse ep Six Guns for Donegan 10.16.59 CBS
Wagon Train ep The Madie Brant Story 1.20.60 NBC
The Snows of Kilimanjaro Sp 3.25.60 CBS
June Allyson Show ep Once Upon a Knight 3.28.60 CBS
Detectives ep The Streger Affair 6.24.60 ABC
Stagecoach West 1.17.61 ABC
Zane Grey Theatre ep The Empty Shell 3.30.61 CBS
Andy Griffith Show ep 10.16.61 CBS
Ben Casey ep A Story to Be Told Softly 1.22.62 ABC
Wagon Train ep The Sarah Proctor Story 2.27.63 ABC
Dr. Kildare ep A Very Infectious Disease 3.21.63 NBC

HAGEN, UTA
Television Theatre ep Macbeth 5.10.50 NBC
Betty Crocker Star Matinee ep The Willow and I 1.5. 52 ABC
Playhouse 90 ep Out of Dust 5.21.59 CBS
Play of the Week ep A Month in the Country 11.9.59 NN
The Long Hot Summer ep Blaze of Glory 3.2.66 ABC

HAGMAN, LARRY
Dupont Show of the Month ep The Member of the Wed-
ding 6.12.58 CBS
U.S. Steel Hour ep Climate of Marriage 7.30.58 CBS
Sea Hunt ep 1.3.59 CBS
Play of the Week ep Once Around the Block 11.7.60
NN
Defenders ep The Last Day 1.11.64 CBS
Mr. Broadway ep Between the Rats and the Finks
10.17.64 CBS
I Dream of Jeannie sr 9.18.65 NBC
I Dream of Jeannie sr ret 9.66 NBC
I Dream of Jeannie sr ret 9.12.67 NBC
I Dream of Jeannie sr ret 9.16.68 NBC
Three's a Crowd tf 12.2.69 ABC
Love American Style ep 10.9.70 ABC
Marcus Welby, M.D. ep To Get Through the Night
10.20.70 ABC
Night Gallery ep The Housekeeper 12.16.70 NBC
Name of the Game ep A Capitol Affair 2.11.71 NBC
Vanished tf 3.8.71, 3.9.71 NBC
Triple Play tf 3.22.71 NBC
The Good Life sr 9.18.71 ABC
Getting Away from It All tf 1.18.72 ABC
No Place to Run tf 9.19.72 ABC

HALE, BARBARA
Ford Theatre ep The Divided Heart 11.27.52 NBC
Schlitz Playhouse of Stars ep Vacation for Ginny 5.
15.53 CBS
Ford Theatre ep Remember to Live 11.4.54 NBC
Schlitz Playhouse of Stars ep Tourists--Overnight 4.
1.55 CBS
G.E. Theatre ep The Windmill 4.24.55 CBS
Science Fiction Theatre ep The Hastings Secret sum-
mer, 1955 NBC
Climax ep The Day They Gave Babies Away 12.22.55
CBS
Loretta Young Show ep The Challenge 1.15.56 NBC
Damon Runyon Theatre ep The Good Luck Kid 1.21.
56 CBS
Ford Theatre ep Behind the Mask 5.10.56 NBC
Star Stage ep The Guardian 5.11.56 NBC
Crossroads ep Lifeline 5.11.56 ABC
The Millionaire ep The Story of Katy Munson 9.12.56
CBS
Playhouse 90 ep The Country Husband 11.1.56 CBS

Perry Mason   sr   9.21.57 CBS
Perry Mason   sr ret   fall, 1958 CBS
Perry Mason   sr ret   10.59 CBS
G.E. Theatre   ep   Night Club   10.11.59 CBS
Perry Mason   sr ret   fall, 1960 CBS
Perry Mason   sr ret   fall, 1961 CBS
Perry Mason   sr ret   9.27.62 CBS
Perry Mason   sr ret   9.26.63 CBS
Perry Mason   sr ret   9.24.64 CBS
Perry Mason   sr ret   9.12.65 CBS
Custer   ep   Death Hunt   11.22.67 ABC
Most Deadly Game   ep   Model for Murder   12.19.70
    ABC
Ironside   ep   Murder Impromptu   11.2.71 NBC
Adam-12   ep   12.29.71 NBC

HALEY, JACK
    Mirror Theatre   ep   Uncle Jack   11.28.53 CBS
    Playhouse 90   ep   No Time at All   2.13.58 CBS
    Desilu Playhouse   ep   Ballad for a Badman   1.26.59
        CBS
    Burke's Law   ep   Who Killed Beau Sparrow   12.27.63
        ABC
    Rolling Man   tf   10.4.72 ABC
    Marcus Welby, M.D.   ep   10.17.72 ABC

HALL, JON
    Ramar of the Jungle   sr   1953 NN
    Perry Mason   ep   The Case of the Festive Falcon   11.
        28.63 CBS
    Perry Mason   ep   The Case of the Feather Clock   2.11.
        65 CBS

HALL, JUANITA
    Schlitz Playhouse of Stars   ep   2.8.52 CBS

HALL, PORTER
    Footlights Theatre   ep   The Man Who Had Nothing to
        Lose   8.22.52 CBS
    Four Star Playhouse   ep   My Wife Geraldine   9.25.52
        CBS
    Fireside Theatre   ep   Moses and Mr. Aiken   1.5.54
        NBC

HALOP, BILLY
    Racket Squad   ep   Accidentally on Purpose   1.3.52 CBS
    Footlights Theatre   ep   Crossroads   8.1.52 CBS

Favorite Story   ep   The World Beyond   5.3.53 NBC
Robert Montgomery Presents   ep   The Pale Blonde of
    Sand Street   4.12.54 NBC
Favorite Story   ep   The Law and the Lady   5.10.54 NBC
Telephone Time   ep   The Jumping Parson   1.12.57 CBS
Ozzie and Harriet   ep   The Money Watchers   11.20.63
    ABC
Ozzie and Harriet   ep   David and the Mermaid   12.18.63
    ABC
Perry Mason   ep   The Case of the Antic Angel   4.16.64
    CBS
FBI   ep   To Free My Enemy   10.24.65 ABC
All in the Family   ep   2.2.71 CBS

HALOP, FLORENCE
Meet Millie   sr   10.25.52 CBS
Meet Millie   sr ret   3.16.54 CBS
Saints and Sinners   ep   A Shame for a Diamond Wedding
    11.26.62 NBC
Danny Thomas Show   ep   11.11.63 CBS
The Phil Silvers Show   ep   Las Vegas Was My Mother's
    Maiden Name   12.7.63 CBS
Hank   ep   11.5.65 NBC
The Smothers Brothers Show   ep   4.1.66 CBS
That Girl   ep   10.31.68 ABC
Love American Style   ep   11.12.71 ABC

HAMILTON, GEORGE
Donna Reed Show   ep   Have Fun   2.4.59 ABC
Cimarron City   ep   The Beauty and the Sorrow   2.7.59
    NBC
Bob Hope Chrysler Theatre   ep   The Turncoat   10.23.64
    NBC
Rogues   ep   Two of a Kind   11.8.64 NBC
Burke's Law   ep   11.11.64 ABC
Ben Casey   ep   Where Does the Boomerang Go   1.11.
    65 ABC
Burke's Law   ep   Who Killed Mother Goose   1.13.65
    ABC
Survivors   sr   9.29.60 ABC
Paris 7000   sr   1.22.70 ABC

HAMILTON, MARGARET
Silver Theatre   ep   Papa Romani   5.15.50 CBS
Studio One   ep   Man of Extinction   2.8.54 CBS
TV Sound Stage   ep   An Eye for an Eye   3.5.54 NBC
Center Stage   ep   Lucky Louise   7.27.54 ABC

U. S. Steel Hour   ep   The Fifth Wheel   10. 26. 54 ABC
Kraft Theatre   ep   The Happy Touch   8. 4. 54 NBC
Best of Broadway   ep   The Man Who Came to Dinner
    10. 13. 54 CBS
Elgin Hour   ep   Warn Clay   11. 16. 54 ABC
Studio One   ep   The Silent Women   1. 31. 55 CBS
Best of Broadway   ep   The Guardsman   3. 2. 55 CBS
Omnibus   ep   A Different Drummer   3. 13. 55 CBS
Goodyear Playhouse   ep   Beloved Stranger   4. 10. 55
    NBC
Hallmark Hall of Fame   ep   The Devil's Disciple   11.
    20. 55 NBC
Alcoa Hour   ep   Merry Christmas, Mr. Baxter   12. 2.
    56 NBC
Omnibus   ep   The Trial of Lizzie Borden   3. 24. 57 ABC
Studio One   ep   The Staring Match   6. 17. 57 CBS
Phil Silvers Show   ep   The Merry Widow   9. 17. 57 CBS
Hallmark Hall of Fame   ep   On Borrowed Time   11. 17.
    57 NBC
U. S. Steel Hour   ep   You Can't Win   12. 4. 57 CBS
Oh Susanna   ep   Susanna Takes a Husband   2. 8. 58 CBS
Once Upon a Christmas Time   Sp   12. 9. 59 NBC
Playhouse 90   ep   The Silver Whistle   12. 24. 59 CBS
Great Mysteries   ep   The Bat   3. 31. 60 NBC
Ichabod and Me   ep   10. 31. 61 CBS
Car 54 Where Are You   ep   Benny the Bookie's Last
    Chance   1. 13. 63 NBC
Car 54 Where Are You   ep   Here Comes Charlie   2. 24.
    63 NBC
Patty Duke Show   ep   Let 'em Eat Cake   2. 5. 64 ABC
Ghostbreaker   pt   9. 8. 67 NBC
Off to See the Wizard   ep   Who's Afraid of Mother
    Goose   10. 13. 67 ABC

HAMILTON, NEIL
    That Wonderful Guy   sr   1950 NBC
    Broadway Television Theatre   ep   The Night of January
        16   7. 14. 52 NN
    Best of Broadway   ep   Panama Hattie   11. 10. 54 CBS
    U. S. Steel Hour   ep   King's Pawn   11. 23. 54 ABC
    Kraft Theatre   ep   Five Minutes to Live   2. 1. 56 NBC
    Oh Susanna   ep   Mardi Gras   12. 7. 57 CBS
    Telephone Time   ep   Man of Principle   3. 25. 58 ABC
    Perry Mason   ep   The Case of the Lazy Lover   5. 31. 58
        CBS
    77 Sunset Strip   ep   Hong Kong Caper   3. 20. 59 ABC
    Lineup   ep   5. 22. 59 CBS

Colt .45   ep   The Pirate   5.31.59 NN
Perry Mason   ep   The Case of the Dubious Bridegroom
    6.13.59 CBS
Dennis O'Keefe Show   ep   On Stage, Sarge   10.13.59
    CBS
Tightrope   ep   The Penthouse Story   4.19.60 CBS
Mr. Garlund   ep   The X-27   10.28.60 CBS
Aquanauts   ep   2.22.61 CBS
Harrigan and Son   ep   Senior Goes to Hollywood   4.21.
    61 ABC
Real McCoys   ep   How to Win Friends   11.16.61 ABC
Follow the Sun   ep   Conspiracy of Silence   12.10.61
    ABC
Bus Stop   ep   Cry to Heaven   1.14.62 ABC
77 Sunset Strip   ep   Leap, My Lovely   10.19.62 ABC
Perry Mason   ep   The Case of Constant Doyle   1.31.63
    CBS
Outer Limits   ep   The Invisibles   2.3.64 ABC
Outer Limits   ep   The Bellero Shield   2.10.64 ABC
Perry Mason   ep   The Case of the Drifting Dropout   5.
    7.64 CBS
Perry Mason   ep   The Case of the Betrayed Bride   10.
    22.64 CBS
Profiles in Courage   ep   The Anne Hutchinson Story   1.
    10.65 NBC
Kraft Suspense Theatre   ep   In Darkness Waiting   1.14.
    65, 1.21.65, NBC
Mister Ed   ep   2.3.65 CBS
Cara Williams Show   ep   3.10.65 CBS
Hank   ep   1.7.66 NBC
Batman   sr   1.12.66 ABC
Batman   sr ret   9.7.66 ABC
Batman   sr ret   9.14.67 ABC
Here's Debbie   ep   12.30.69 NBC

HAMPDEN, WALTER
Theatre Hour   ep   The Traitor   9.8.50 ABC
Billy Rose's Playbill   ep   The Benefit of the Doubt   12.
    4.50 NN
Billy Rose's Playbill   ep   The Old Magician   3.13.51
    ABC
Prudential Playhouse   ep   The Bishop Misbehaves   3.27.
    51 CBS
Schlitz Playhouse of Stars   ep   Decision and Daniel Web-
    ster   11.9.51 CBS
Schlitz Playhouse of Stars   ep   Two Living and One Dead
    11.30.51 CBS

Schlitz Playhouse of Stars   ep   Billy Budd   1.11.52 CBS
Schlitz Playhouse of Stars   ep   Make Way for Teddy   3. 14.52 CBS
Schlitz Playhouse of Stars   ep   Now's the Time   4.18.52 CBS
Robert Montgomery Presents   ep   The Bench in the Park   11.3.52 NBC
Robert Montgomery Presents   ep   Such a Busy Day   3.1. 54 NBC
Motorola TV Hour   ep   The Sins of the Father   4.6.54 ABC
U.S. Steel Hour   ep   The Great Chair   5.25.54 ABC
Studio One   ep   Two Little Minks   12.20.54 CBS

HANEY, CAROL
The Bachelor   Sp   7.15.56 NBC

HARDIN, TY
Bronco   sr   9.23.58 ABC
Bronco   sr ret   9.22.59 ABC
Maverick   ep   Hadley's Hunters   9.25.60 ABC
Bronco   sr ret   9.60 ABC
77 Sunset Strip   ep   2.17.61 ABC
Bronco   sr ret   9.61 ABC

HARDING, ANN
Pulitzer Prize Playhouse   ep   Years of Grace   1.30.52 ABC
Hollywood Opening Night   ep   Quite a Viking   10.27.52 NBC
Ford Theatre   ep   There's No Place Like Home   6.4.53 NBC
Schlitz Playhouse of Stars   ep   Miracle in the Night   8. 14.53 CBS
Danger   ep   The Honeymoon Is Over   9.29.53 CBS
Schlitz Playhouse of Stars   ep   The Great Lady   3.5.54 CBS
Video Theatre   ep   The Queen's English   5.13.54 CBS
Stage 7   ep   Young Girl in an Apple Tree   4.10.55 CBS
Lux Video Theatre   ep   An Act of Murder   4.21.55 NBC
Ford Theatre   ep   P.J. and the Lady   6.2.55 NBC
Damon Runyon Theatre   ep   Lonely Heart   6.4.55 CBS
G.E. Theatre   ep   Tryout   10.2.55 CBS
Crossroads   ep   With All My Love   10.28.55 ABC
Matinee Theatre   ep   Progress and Minnie Sweeney   11. 4.55 NBC
20th Century-Fox Hour   ep   The Late George Apley   11.

16.55 CBS

Climax ep A Promise to Murder 11.17.55 CBS

Front Row Center ep Strange Suspicion 1.15.56 CBS

Playwrights '56 ep The Center of the Maze 4.24.56 NBC

G.E. Summer Originals ep The Great Lady 9.11.56 ABC

Dupont Theatre ep The House of Empty Rooms 1.8. 57 ABC

20th Century-Fox Hour ep Young Man from Kentucky 2.6.57 CBS

Kraft Theatre ep Heroes Walk on Sand 12.11.57 NBC

June Allyson Show ep 9.21.59 CBS

Our American Heritage ep Autocrat and Son 3.20.60 NBC

Play of the Week ep Morning's at Seven 4.25.60 NN

Westinghouse Present ep Come Again to Carthage 12. 8.61 CBS

Alfred Hitchcock Theatre ep A Jury of Her Peers 12. 26.61 NBC

Defenders ep A Taste of Vengeance 4.6.63 CBS

Armstrong Circle Theatre ep The Embezzler 4.10.63 CBS

Burke's Law ep Who Killed Mr. "X" 9.27.63 ABC

Eleventh Hour ep Fear Begins at 40 10.16.63 NBC

Dr. Kildare ep Never Too Old for the Circus 1.30. 64 NBC

Ben Casey ep Because of the Needle, the Haystack Was Lost 10.11.65 ABC

HARDWICKE, CEDRIC (SIR)

Schlitz Playhouse of Stars ep Crossroads 8.1.52 CBS

Omnibus ep The Trial of Mr. Pickwick 12.21.52 CBS

G.E. Theatre ep Best Seller 3.1.53 CBS

Suspense ep Death in the Passing 8.25.53 CBS

Medallion Theatre ep The Big Bow Mystery 9.26.53 CBS

Schlitz Playhouse of Stars ep In the Pincers 10.16.53 CBS

Suspense ep The Interruption 11.3.53 CBS

Armstrong Circle Theatre ep The Beard 11.24.53 NBC

Motorola TV Hour ep The Thirteen Clocks 12.29.53 ABC

Motorola TV Hour ep Black Chiffon 4.20.54 ABC

Elgin Hour ep The $1000 Window 3.22.55 CBS

Climax ep No Stone Unturned 5.19.55 CBS
The Barretts of Wimpole Street Sp 6.8.55 CBS
Cameo Theatre ep The Inca of Perusalem 7.3.55
NBC
Climax ep Dr. Jekyll and Mr. Hyde 7.28.55 CBS
TV Reader's Digest ep Archer-Shee Case 10.31.55
ABC
Climax ep The Hanging Judge 1.12.56 CBS
Four Star Playhouse ep Tunnel of Fear 1.19.56 CBS
Producers Showcase ep Caesar and Cleopatra 3.5.56
NBC
Climax ep The Man Who Lost His Head 7.16.56 CBS
Climax ep Flight to Tomorrow 11.8.56 CBS
Playhouse 90 ep Mr. and Mrs. McAdam 1.10.57 CBS
Matinee Theatre ep Shadow and Substance 3.1.57 NBC
Matinee Theatre ep Mr. Krane 3.21.57 NBC
Climax ep Strange Death at Burnleigh 5.2.57 CBS
Alfred Hitchcock Presents ep A Man Greatly Beloved
5.12.57 CBS
Dupont Show of the Month ep The Prince and the Pau-
per 10.28.57 CBS
Studio One ep The Other Place 1.13.58 CBS
U.S. Steel Hour ep The Women of Hadley 2.24.60
CBS
U.S. Steel Hour ep Revolt in Hadley 3.9.60 CBS
Our American Heritage ep Autocrat and Son 3.20.60
NBC
Mrs. G. Goes to College sr 10.4.61 CBS
Burke's Law ep Who Killed Holly Howard 9.20.63 ABC
Twilight Zone ep Uncle Simon 11.15.63 CBS
Outer Limits ep The Forms of Things Unknown 5.4.64
ABC
Nurses ep White on White 5.14.64 CBS
Doctors/Nurses ep So Some Girls Play the Cello 12.
1.64 CBS

HARRIS, BARBARA
Naked City ep Daughter, Am I in My Father's House
10.3.62 ABC
Channing ep No Wild Games for Sophie 10.9.63 ABC
Defenders ep Claire Cheval Died in Boston 11.23.63
CBS

HARRIS, JULIE
Starlight Theatre ep Bernice Bobs Her Hair 5.17.51
CBS
Goodyear Playhouse ep October Story 10.14.51 NBC

Goodyear Playhouse   ep   The Happy Rest   10. 4. 53 NBC
U. S. Steel Hour   ep   A Wind from the South   9. 14. 55
   CBS
Hallmark Hall of Fame   ep   The Good Fairy   2. 5. 56
   NBC
Hallmark Hall of Fame   ep   The Lark   2. 10. 57 NBC
Hallmark Hall of Fame   ep   Johnny Belinda   10. 13. 58
   NBC
Hallmark Hall of Fame   ep   A Doll's House   11. 15. 59
   NBC
Dupont Show of the Month   ep   Ethan Frome   2. 18. 60
   CBS
Sunday Showcase   ep   Turn the Key Softly   3. 6. 60 NBC
Family Classics   ep   The Heiress   2. 13. 61 CBS
Dupont Show of the Month   ep   Night of the Storm   3. 21.
   61 CBS
Play of the Week   ep   He Who Gets Slapped   1. 30. 61 NN
Power and the Glory   Sp   10. 29. 61 CBS
Hallmark Hall of Fame   ep   Victoria Regina   11. 30. 61
   NBC
Hallmark Hall of Fame   ep   Pygmalion   2. 6. 63 NBC
Hallmark Hall of Fame   ep   Little Moon of Alban   3. 18.
   64 NBC
Ben Casey   ep   The Only Place They Know My Name
   5. 20. 64 ABC
Kraft Suspense Theatre   ep   The Robrioz Ring   5. 28. 64
   NBC
Hamlet   Sp   6. 17. 64 CBS
Hallmark Hall of Fame   ep   The Holy Terror   4. 7. 65
   NBC
Rawhide   ep   The Calf Woman   4. 30. 65 CBS
Bob Hope Chrysler Theatre   ep   Nightmare   9. 14. 66 NBC
Tarzan   ep   3. 10. 67, 3. 17. 67 NBC
Hallmark Hall of Fame   ep   Anastasia   3. 17. 67 NBC
Garrison's Gorillas   ep   Run from Death   1. 9. 68 ABC
Run for Your Life   ep   1. 17. 68 NBC
Tarzan   ep   3. 1. 68, 3. 8. 68 NBC
Hallmark Hall of Fame ep (restaged)   Little Moon of Al-
   ban   3. 24. 68 NBC
Daniel Boone   ep   4. 4. 68 NBC
Bonanza   ep   Dream to Dream   4. 14. 68 NBC
Journey to the Unknown   ep   10. 10. 68 ABC
Big Valley   ep   A Stranger Everywhere   12. 9. 68 ABC
Name of the Game   ep   The Bobby Currier Story   2. 21.
   69 NBC
The House on Green Apple Road   tf   1. 11. 70 ABC
Name of the Game   ep   So Long, Baby, and Amen

9.18.70 NBC
How Awful About Allan   tf 9.22.70 ABC
Men from Shiloh   ep   3.17.71 NBC

HARRIS, PHIL
Manhattan Tower   Sp 10.27.56 NBC
Burke's Law   ep   9.23.64 ABC
Bing Crosby Show   ep   One for the Birds   3.8.65 ABC
The Lucy Show   ep   2.5.68 CBS

HARRIS, RICHARD
Hallmark Hall of Fame   ep   The Snow Goose   11.15.71
NBC

HARRIS, ROBERT H.
Robert Montgomery Presents   ep   The Outer Limit   1.
26.53 NBC
Tales of the City   ep   6.25.53 CBS
The Goldbergs   sr   7.3.53 NBC
Tales of the City   ep   7.23.53 CBS
Armstrong Cirlce Theatre   ep   The Honor of Littorno
11.3.53 NBC
The Purim Story   Sp   3.14.54 ABC
The Goldbergs   sr ret   4.13.54 NN
Studio One   ep   Home Again, Home Again   7.19.54 CBS
The Goldbergs   sr ret   9.22.55 NN
Alfred Hitchcock Presents   ep   Shopping for Death   1.29.
56 CBS
Alfred Hitchcock Presents   ep   The Orderly World of
Mr. Appleby   4.15.56 CBS
Kraft Theatre   ep   Profile in Courage   5.16.56 NBC
Alfred Hitchcock Presents   ep   A Hidden Thing   5.20.56
CBS
Climax   ep   No Right to Kill   8.9.56 CBS
Alfred Hitchcock Presents   ep   Toby   11.4.56 CBS
Hiram Holliday   ep   12.26.56 NBC
20th Century-Fox Hour   ep   False Witness   1.23.57
CBS
Alfred Hitchcock Presents   ep   The Dangerous People
6.23.57 CBS
Court of Last Resort   ep   The Case of Tomas Mendoza
10.11.57 NBC
Court of Last Resort   ep   The James Dawson Case   11.
29.57 NBC
Perry Mason   ep   The Case of the Lonely Heiress   2.1.
58 CBS
Studio One   ep   The Fair-Haired Boy   3.3.58 CBS

Have Gun Will Travel   ep   3.8.58 CBS
Alfred Hitchcock Presents   ep   The Safe Place   6.8.58 CBS
Rough Riders   ep   Breakout   10.9.58 ABC
Pursuit   ep   The Vengeance   10.22.58 CBS
77 Sunset Strip   ep   Hit and Run   1.2.59 ABC
Behind Closed Doors   ep   The Quemoy Street   2.12.59 NBC
Restless Gun   ep   3.9.59 NBC
Wanted Dead or Alive   ep   3.21.59 CBS
Mike Hammer   ep   The Big Drop   4.21.59 NBC
Peter Gunn   ep   Love Me to Death   4.27.59 NBC
Markham   ep   Seamark   6.6.59 CBS
Lawless Years   ep   The Maxey Gorman Story   6.25.59 NBC
Wichita Town   ep   Out of the Past   12.9.59 NBC
Alfred Hitchcock Presents   ep   Graduating Class   12.27.59 CBS
Mr. Lucky   ep   2.27.60 CBS
Tightrope   ep   First Time Out   3.1.60 CBS
Man from Blackhawk   ep   Destination Death   3.11.60 ABC
Roaring 20s   ep   Black Saturday   2.11.61 ABC
Perry Mason   ep   The Case of the Torrid Tapestry   4.22.61 CBS
Law and Mr. Jones   ep   The Broken Hand   6.2.61 ABC
Target Corruptors   ep   Silent Partner   12.8.61 ABC
Outlaws   ep   The Dark Sunrise of Griff Kincaid   1.4.62 NBC
Surfside 6   ep   Vendetta Arms   3.12.62 ABC
Alcoa Premiere   ep   Blues for a Hanging   12.27.62 ABC
Bonanza   ep   The Legacy   12.15.63 NBC
Alfred Hitchcock Theatre   ep   Consider Her Ways   12.28.64 NBC
Perry Mason   ep   The Case of the Frustrated Folk Singer   1.7.65 CBS
Ben Casey   ep   A Little Fun to Match the Sorrow   3.8.65 ABC
The Man from U.N.C.L.E.   ep   The Love Affair   3.29.65 NBC
Voyage to the Bottom of the Sea   ep   The Sky's on Fire   1.23.66 ABC
The Man from U.N.C.L.E.   ep   The Pop Art Affair   10.21.66 NBC
T.H.E. Cat   ep   11.18.66 NBC
Virginian   ep   2.28.68 NBC
Outsider   ep   Love Is under L   11.6.68 NBC

Wild, Wild West   ep   The Night of the Bleak Island   3.
    14. 69 CBS
Here's Debbie   ep   2. 24. 70 NBC
Medical Center   ep   The Torn Man   10. 11. 72 CBS

HARRIS, ROSEMARY
Studio One   ep   The Great Lady   12. 15. 52 CBS
The Doctor   ep   The World of Nancy Clark   3. 1. 53 NBC
Alfred Hitchcock Presents   ep   The Glass Eye   10. 6. 57
    CBS
Dupont Show of the Month   ep   The Prince and the Pau-
    per   10. 28. 57 CBS
Suspicion   ep   Lord Arthur Savile's Crime   1. 13. 58 NBC
Omnibus   ep   Moment of Truth   2. 23. 58 NBC
Dupont Show of the Month   ep   A Tale of Two Cities   3.
    27. 58 CBS
Hallmark Hall of Fame   ep   Dial M for Murder   4. 5. 58
    NBC
Play of the Week   ep   The Enchanted   4. 11. 60 NN
Profiles in Courage   ep   11. 15. 64 NBC
New York Television Theatre   ep   Eh Joe   7. 18. 66 NN
N. E. T. Playhouse   ep   Uncle Vanya   2. 10. 67 NN
Alfred Hitchcock Presents   ep   I Killed the Count   3. 31.
    57 CBS
CBS Playhouse   ep   Dear Friends   12. 6. 67 CBS
Hallmark Hall of Fame   ep   Twelfth Night   12. 15. 57
    NBC

HARRISON, NOEL
The Girl from U. N. C. L. E.   sr   9. 13. 66 NBC
The Man from U. N. C. L. E.   ep   The Galatea Affair   9.
    30. 66 NBC
Legend of Robin Hood   Sp   2. 18. 68 NBC
It Takes a Thief   ep   11. 26. 68 ABC
Love American Style   ep   11. 17. 69 ABC
Mission Impossible   ep   The Falcon   1. 4. 70, 1. 11. 70,
    1. 18. 70 CBS
Name of the Game   ep   The King of Denmark   2. 20. 70
    NBC
Call Holme   pt   4. 24. 72 NBC
The Deadly Gamesmen   11. 30. 72 NBC

HARRISON, REX
Tele-Theatre   ep   The Walking Stick   3. 20. 50 NBC
U. S. Steel Hour   ep   The Man in Possession   12. 8. 53
    ABC
Ford Star Time   ep   Dear Arthur   3. 22. 60 NBC

Great Mysteries   ep   The Datchet Diamonds   9.20.60
   NBC

HART, DOLORES
   Alfred Hitchcock Presents   ep   Silent Witness   11.3.57
      CBS
   Schlitz Playhouse of Stars   ep   Man on a Rack   2.21.58
      CBS
   June Allyson Show   ep   The Crossing   12.14.59 CBS
   Playhouse 90   ep   The Sound of Trumpets   2.9.60 CBS
   Virginian   ep   The Mountain of the Sun   4.17.63 NBC

HART, RICHARD
   Masterpiece Playhouse   ep   Hedda Gabler   7.23.50 NBC
   Studio One   ep   The Passionate Pilgrim   10.2.50 CBS
   Ellery Queen   sr   10.19.50 NN

HARTMAN, ELIZABETH
   Night Gallery   ep   The Dark Boy   11.24.71 NBC

HARTMAN, PAUL
   Faith Baldwin Playhouse   ep   Henry's Harem   9.22.51
      ABC
   Gulf Playhouse   ep   The Trial of Charley Christmas   12.
      19.52 NBC
   Pride of the Family   sr   10.2.53 ABC
   Studio One   ep   Twelve Angry Men   9.20.54 CBS
   Producers Showcase   ep   The Petrified Forest   5.30.55
      NBC
   Paul Hartman Show   sr   6.12.55 CBS
   Producers Showcase   ep   Our Town   9.19.55 NBC
   Goodyear Playhouse   ep   The Expendable House   10.9.55
      NBC
   Playwrights '56   ep   The Heart's a Forgotten Hotel   10.
      25.55 NBC
   Studio One   ep   My Son Johnny   1.30.56 CBS
   Kraft Theatre   ep   Good Old Charlie Fay   2.8.56 NBC
   Kraft Theatre   ep   Most Blessed Woman   1.23.57 NBC
   Kraft Theatre   ep   Sheriff's Man   3.27.57 NBC
   Kraft Theatre   ep   The Old Ticker   9.11.57 NBC
   Kraft Theatre   ep   Run, Joe, Run   1.29.58 NBC
   Hansel and Gretel   Sp   4.27.58 NBC
   Ellery Queen   ep   The Paper Tiger   4.3.59 NBC
   Alfred Hitchcock Presents   ep   Not the Running Type
      2.7.60 CBS
   Ford Star Time   Incident at a Corner   4.5.60 NBC
   Twilight Zone   ep   Back There   1.13.61 CBS

Hallmark Hall of Fame   ep   Time Remembered   2.7.61
   NBC
Alfred Hitchcock Theatre   ep   Gratitude   4.25.61 NBC
Checkmate   ep   The Thrill Seekers   5.27.61 CBS
Have Gun Will Travel   ep   11.25.61 CBS
Adventures in Paradise   ep   Once There Was a Prin-
   cess   1.14.62 ABC
Ben Casey   ep   Behold a Pale Horse   2.26.62 ABC
Alfred Hitchcock Theatre   ep   Burglar Proof   2.27.62
Defenders   ep   Along Came a Spider   5.5.62 CBS
Our Man Higgins   ep   Rules of the Road   11.7.62 ABC
Our Man Higgins   ep   My First Friend   2.13.63 ABC
The Lucy Show   ep   3.4.63 CBS
Our Man Higgins   4.17.63 ABC
Our Man Higgins   ep   The Education of Harry Barker
   5.1.63 ABC
Alfred Hitchcock Theatre   ep   Death of a Cop   5.24.63
   CBS
Farmer's Daughter   ep   The Speechmaker   9.20.63, 9.
   27.63 ABC
The Greatest Show on Earth   ep   Leaves in the Wind
   11.26.63 ABC
Alfred Hitchcock Theatre   ep   The Magic Shop   1.10.64
   CBS
For the People   ep   2.14.65 CBS
Bing Crosby Show   ep   The Test   3.22.65 ABC
Ozzie and Harriet   ep   12.8.65 ABC
Jesse James   ep   A Real Tough Town   1.24.66 ABC
John Forsythe Show   ep   The Cupid Caper   2.14.66 NBC
Family Affair   ep   9.26.66 CBS
Occasional Wife   ep   12.20.66 NBC
Bob Hope Chrysler Theatre   ep   To Sleep, Perchance to
   Scream   5.10.67 NBC
Vacation Playhouse   ep   9.30.67 CBS
Mayberry R.F.D.   sr   9.23.68 CBS
Mayberry R.F.D.   sr ret   9.22.69 CBS
Mayberry R.F.D.   sr ret   9.14.70 CBS
Of Thee I Sing   Sp   10.24.72 CBS

HARVEY, LAURENCE
   Alcoa Hour   ep   The Small Servant   10.30.55 NBC
   Alfred Hitchcock Presents   ep   Arthur   9.27.59 CBS
   Festival of the Arts   ep   A Month in the Country   12.26.
      62 NN
   Dial M for Murder   Sp   11.15.67 ABC

HASSO, SIGNE
   Celanese Theatre ep Reunion in Vienna 1.9.52 ABC
   Lights Out ep Cries the String 2.11.52 NBC
   Video Theatre ep Something to Celebrate 11.10.52
     CBS
   Robert Montgomery Presents ep Unclouded Summer 9.
     1.52 NBC
   Broadway Television Theatre ep The Two Mrs. Car-
     rolls 10.20.52 NN
   Robert Montgomery Presents ep Two Wise Women 10.
     4.54 NBC
   Kraft Theatre ep Camille 12.1.54 NBC
   Kraft Theatre ep The Diamond as Big as the Ritz 9.
     28.55 NBC
   Appointment with Adventure ep Till the End of Time
     2.19.56 CBS
   Play of the Week ep Mary Stuart 5.23.60 NN
   Play of the Week ep Duet for Two Hands 10.24.60
     NN
   Checkmate ep An Assassin Arrives, Andante 2.21.62
     CBS
   Mystery Theatre ep Dead on Nine 7.4.62 NBC
   Route 66 ep One Tiger to a Hill 9.21.62 CBS
   Alcoa Premiere ep The Contenders 12.6.62 ABC
   Bonanza ep A Stranger Passed This Way 3.3.63 NBC
   Outer Limits ep Production and Decay of Strange Par-
     ticles 4.20.64 ABC
   Run, Buddy Run ep 9.19.66 CBS
   Green Hornet ep Programmed for Death 9.23.66 ABC
   T.H.E. Cat ep 9.23.66 NBC
   Bob Hope Chrysler Theatre ep Code Name: Heraclitus
     1.4.67, 1.11.67 NBC
   Road West ep Fair Ladies of France 2.27.67 NBC
   The Girl from U.N.C.L.E. ep 3.28.67 NBC
   Coronet Blue ep 6.12.67 CBS
   Interns ep 1.29.71 CBS
   Ghost Story ep 11.3.72 NBC

HATFIELD, HURD
   Masterpiece Playhouse ep The Rivals 8.6.50 NBC
   Masterpiece Theatre ep The Importance of Being
     Earnest 9.20.50 NBC
   Story Theatre ep Mademoiselle Fifi 12.1.50 NN
   The Web ep Tiger in the Closet 10.12.52 CBS
   Studio One ep The Nativity Play 12.22.52 CBS
   Summer Studio One ep Greed 6.29.53 CBS
   Broadway Television Theatre ep Seventh Heaven 10.

26.53 NN

Broadway Television Theatre ep The Hasty Heart 11. 2.53 NN

Suspense ep The Pistol Shot 6.15.54 CBS

Robert Montgomery Presents ep The Hunchback of Notre Dame 11.8.54, 11.15.54 NBC

Kraft Theatre ep The King's Bounty 9.21.55 NBC

Armstrong Circle Theatre ep I Was Accused 12.13. 55 NBC

Climax ep The Hanging Judge 1.12.56 CBS

Alfred Hitchcock Theatre ep The Perfect Murder 3. 11.56 CBS

The Millionaire ep The Eric Vincent Story 3.21.56 CBS

Hallmark Hall of Fame ep Lamp at Midnight 4.27.66 NBC

Climax ep The Fog 9.27.56 CBS

Alfred Hitchcock Presents ep None Are So Blind 10. 28.56 CBS

Dupont Show of the Month ep 11.25.57 CBS

Playhouse 90 ep The Last Man 1.9.58 CBS

Climax ep Cabin B-13 6.26.58 CBS

Dupont Show of the Month ep The Count of Monte Cristo 10.28.58 CBS

Armstrong Circle Theatre ep The Trial of Poznan 2. 19.57 NBC

Dupont Show of the Month ep The Prince and the Pauper 10.28.57 CBS

Lux Playhouse ep Various Temptations 2.20.59 CBS

Music Theatre ep Too Bad About Sheila Troy 4.16. 59, 4.23.59 NBC

Ellery Queen ep The Curse of Adam 5.1.59 NBC

Dupont Show of the Month ep I, Don Quixote 11.9.59 CBS

Play of the Week ep Don Juan in Hell 2.15.60 NN

Hallmark Hall of Fame ep The Invincible Mr. Disraeli 4.4.63 NBC

Bob Hope Chrysler Theatre ep One Day in the Life of Ivan Denisovich 11.8.63 NBC

Hallmark Hall of Fame ep A Cry of Angels 12.15.63 NBC

Voyage to the Bottom of the Sea ep The City Beneath the Sea 9.21.64 ABC

N.E.T. Playhouse ep Ten Blocks on the Camino Real 10.7.66 NN

New York Television Theatre ep The Movers 11.14. 66 NN

Play of the Week   ep   Don Juan in Hell   11.23.66 NN
Wild, Wild West   ep   12.2.66 CBS
Thief   tf   10.9.71 ABC
FBI   ep   1.30.72 ABC
Search   ep   12.20.72 NBC

HATTON, RAYMOND
Eddie Cantor Theatre   ep   6.13.55 ABC
Schlitz Playhouse of Stars   ep   The Quitter   9.23.55
   CBS
Four Star Playhouse   ep   A Spray of Bullets   11.3.55
   CBS

HAVOC, JUNE
Somerset Maugham Playhouse   ep   Cakes and Ale   5.28.
   51 NBC
Cameo Theatre   ep   Special Delivery   6.18.51 NBC
Celanese Theatre   ep   Anna Christie   1.23.52 ABC
Pulitzer Prize Playhouse   ep   Daisy Mayme   6.4.52 ABC
Robert Montgomery Presents   ep   Fairfield Lady   9.15.
   52 NBC
Omnibus   ep   The Beat   1.4.53 CBS
Hollywood Opening Night   ep   The Romantic Type   2.23.
   53 NBC
Omnibus   ep   Aunt Sarah's History   3.22.53 CBS
Medallion Theatre   ep   Mrs. Union Station   8.8.53 CBS
Willy   sr   9.18.54 CBS
Fireside Theatre   ep   A Mother's Duty   12.28.54 NBC
Robert Montgomery Presents   ep   The Tyrant   1.16.56
   NBC
Matinee Theatre   ep   Robin Dow   3.1.56 NBC
Errol Flynn Theatre   ep   My Infallible Luck   3.22.57
   NN
Mr. Broadway   Sp   5.11.57 NBC
Studio One   ep   The Mother Bit   6.10.57 CBS
U.S. Steel Hour   ep   The Pink Burrow   7.15.59 CBS
Untouchables   ep   The Larry Fay Story   12.15.60 ABC
Burke's Law   ep   10.14.64 ABC
Outer Limits   ep   Cry of Silence   10.24.64 ABC
World of Disney   ep   The Boy Who Stole the Elephants
   9.20.70, 9.27.70 NBC
McMillan and Wife   ep   The Easy Sunday Murder Case
   10.20.71 NBC

HAWKINS, JACK
Producers Showcase   ep   Caesar and Cleopatra   3.5.56
   NBC

Four Just Men   sr   1959 NN
Dupont Show of the Month   ep   The Fallen Idol   10.14.
59 CBS
Bob Hope Chrysler Theatre   ep   Back to Back   10.27.65
NBC
Dr. Kildare   ep   The Atheist and the True Believer
1.3.66, 1.4.66, 1.10.66, 1.11.66, 1.17.66, 1.18.66
NBC
The Poppy Is Also a Flower   tf   4.22.66 ABC
Jane Eyre   Sp   3.24.71 NBC

HAWN, GOLDIE
Good Morning World   sr   9.5.67 CBS

HAWORTH, JILL
Outer Limits   ep   The Sixth Finger   5.18.64 ABC
12 O'Clock High   ep   The Sound of Distant Thunder   10.
16.64 ABC
12 O'Clock High   ep   Heinie with Love   2.5.65 ABC
Rogues   ep   Mr. White's Christmas   4.4.65 NBC
Burke's Law   ep   5.5.65 ABC
FBI   ep   To Free My Enemy   10.24.65 ABC
12 O'Clock High   ep   Runaway in the Dark   11.1.65
ABC
Rawhide   ep   Duel at Daybreak   11.16.65 CBS
Run for Your Life   ep   The Savage Season   11.8.65 NBC
The Ballad of Andy Crocker   tf   11.18.69 ABC
Most Deadly Game   ep   Witches' Sabbath   10.17.70 ABC
Mission Impossible   ep   10.25.70 CBS
Bonanza   ep   The Reluctant American   2.14.71 NBC
Home for the Holidays   tf   11.28.72 ABC

HAY, ALEXANDRA
Monkees   ep   2.27.67 ABC
CBS Playhouse   ep   Shadow Game   5.7.69 CBS
Mission Impossible   ep   10.28.69 CBS
Love American Style   ep   1.12.70 ABC
Dan August   ep   Invitation to Murder   11.4.70 ABC

HAYAKAWA, SESSUE
Kraft Theatre   ep   The Sea Is Boiling Hot   3.12.58 NBC
Studio One   ep   Kurishiki Incident   5.12.58 CBS
Wagon Train   ep   The Sakae Ito Story   12.3.58 NBC
Route 66   ep   Two Strangers and an Old Enemy   9.27.63
CBS

HAYDEN, STERLING
    Schlitz Playhouse of Stars   ep   At Ft. Bess 9.3.54
        CBS
    Zane Grey Theatre   ep   The Necessary Breed   2.15.57
        CBS
    Playhouse 90   ep   A Sound of Different Drummers
        10.3.57 CBS
    Wagon Train   ep   The Les Rand Story   10.16.57 NBC
    Playhouse 90   ep   The Last Man   1.9.58 CBS
    Schlitz Playhouse of Stars   ep   East of the Moon   2.
        14.58 CBS
    G.E. Theatre   ep   Iron Horse   6.1.58 CBS
    Playhouse 90   ep   The Long March   10.16.58 CBS
    Playhouse 90   ep   Old Man   11.20.58 CBS
    Dupont Show of the Month   ep   Ethan Frome   2.18.60
        CBS
    Carol for Another Christmas   tf   12.28.64 ABC

HAYDN, RICHARD
    Schlitz Playhouse of Stars   ep   A Quarter for Your
        Trouble   5.30.52 CBS
    World of Disney   ep   Alice in Wonderland   11.3.54 ABC
    Producers Showcase   ep   The King and Mrs. Candle
        8.22.55 NBC
    Playhouse 90   ep   Charley's Aunt   3.28.57 CBS
    Playhouse 90   cp   Heart of Darkness   11.6.58 CBS
    Shirley Temple's Story Book   ep   The Emperor's New
        Clothes   11.25.58 NBC
    Lux Playhouse   ep   This Will Do Nicely   4.17.59 CBS
    G.E. Theatre   ep   The Ugly Duckling   5.1.60 CBS
    Twilight Zone   ep   A Thing about Machines   10.28.60
        CBS
    McCloud   ep   Fifth Man in a String Quartet   2.2.72
        NBC

HAYDON, JULIE
    The Doctor   ep   The Way of Hope   4.19.53. NBC
    U.S. Steel Hour   ep   The Grand Tour   8.17.54 ABC
    Robert Montgomery Presents   ep   Autumn Crocus   10.
        11.54 NBC

HAYES, BILL
    Armstrong Circle Theatre   ep   The No-Talent Kid   12.
        16.52 NBC
    U.S. Steel Hour   ep   A Family Alliance   6.4.58 CBS
    Little Women   Sp   10.16.58 CBS
    Hallmark Hall of Fame   ep   Kiss Me, Kate!   11.20.58
        NBC

Hayes and Henderson Show sh 3.26.59 NBC
Once Upon a Mattress Sp 6.3.64 CBS
Cade's County ep Jessica 3.12.72 CBS

HAYES, HELEN
Pulitzer Prize Playhouse ep The Late Christopher
   Bean 10.27.50 ABC
Prudential Playhouse ep The Barretts of Wimpole
   Street 12.5.50 CBS
Robert Montgomery Presents ep Victoria Regina 1.
   15.51 NBC
Pulitzer Prize Playhouse ep Mary of Scotland 2.16.
   51 ABC
Schlitz Playhouse of Stars ep Not a Chance 10.5.51
   CBS
Schlitz Playhouse of Stars ep The Lucky Touch 11.2.
   51 CBS
Schlitz Playhouse of Stars ep Dark Fleece 12.21.51
   CBS
Omnibus ep The Twelve Pound Look 11.23.52 CBS
Omnibus ep The Christmas Tie 11.30.52 CBS
Omnibus ep The Happy Journey 3.1.53 CBS
Medallion Theatre ep 11.7.53 CBS
Omnibus ep Irish Linen/Mom and Leo 12.20.53 CBS
Motorola TV Hour ep Side by Side 1.26.54 ABC
The Best of Broadway ep The Royal Family 9.15.54
   CBS
Light's Diamond Jubilee ep Chance for Adventure 10.
   24.54 ABC, CBS, NBC
The Best of Broadway ep Arsenic and Old Lace 1.5.
   55 CBS
The Skin of Our Teeth Sp 9.11.55 NBC
Omnibus ep Dear Brutus 1.8.56 CBS
Omnibus ep The Christmas Tie 12.16.56 ABC
Playhouse 90 ep Four Women in Black 4.27.57 CBS
Alcoa Hour ep Mrs. Gilling and the Skyscraper 6.9.
   57 NBC
Omnibus ep Mrs. McThing 3.9.58 NBC
U.S. Steel Hour ep One Red Rose for Christmas 12.
   17.58 CBS
Hallmark Hall of Fame ep Ah, Wilderness! 4.28.59
   NBC
Play of the Week ep The Cherry Orchard 12.28.59
   NN
Great Mysteries ep The Bat 3.31.60 NBC
Hallmark Hall of Fame ep The Cradle Song 4.10.60
   NBC

Play of the Week   ep   The Velvet Glove   10.17.60 NN
Michael Shayne   ep   Murder Round My Wrist   1.20.61
   NBC
Tarzan   ep   11.17.67 NBC
Arsenic and Old Lace   Sp   4.2.69 ABC
Hollywood Television Theatre   ep   The Front Page   1.
   31.70 NN
Do Not Fold, Spindle or Mutilate   tf   11.9.71 ABC
Here's Lucy   ep   1.3.72 CBS
Hallmark Hall of Fame   ep   Harvey   3.22.72 NBC
Ghost Story   ep   Alter Ego   10.26.72 NBC
The Snoop Sisters   tf   12.18.72 NBC

HAYES, MARGARET
   Big Town   sr   10.5.50 CBS
   Robert Montgomery Presents   sr   7.14.52 NBC
   Robert Montgomery Presents   ep   The Bench in the
      Park   11.3.52 NBC
   Robert Montgomery Presents   ep   Maggie, Pack Your
      Bags   1.19.53 NBC
   Short Short Drama   ep   The Double Cross   3.17.53 NBC
   Robert Montgomery Presents   ep   Appointment in Sa-
      marra   5.11.53 NBC
   Robert Montgomery Presents   sr ret   7.6.53 NBC
   Suspense   ep   The Mascot   7.7.53 CBS
   Schlitz Playhouse of Stars   ep   The Perfect Secretary
      9.4.53 CBS
   Armstrong Circle Theatre   ep   The Tree in the Empty
      Room   12.22.53 NBC
   Hallmark Hall of Fame   ep   The Story of Ruth   4.18.54
      NBC
   Producers Showcase   ep   Tonight at 8:40   10.18.54 NBC
   Armstrong Circle Theatre   ep   Fight for Tomorrow   4.
      26.55 NBC
   Loretta Young Show   ep   Katy   10.23.55 NBC
   Loretta Young Show   ep   Across the Plaza   11.27.55
      NBC
   Matinee Theatre   ep   Letter to a Stranger   3.2.56 NBC
   20th Century-Fox Hour   ep   Mr. Belvedere   4.18.56
      CBS
   Climax   ep   The Midas Touch   10.18.56 CBS
   Wyatt Earp   ep   Reformation of Jim Kelley   10.30.56
      ABC
   Wyatt Earp   ep   So Long, Dora, So Long   11.13.56
      ABC
   Wire Service   ep   The Deep End   12.13.56 ABC
   Zane Grey Theatre   ep   No Man Living   1.11.57 CBS

Playhouse 90 ep The Star Wagon 1.24.57 CBS
G.E. Theatre ep Doctors of Pawnee Kill 1.27.57
CBS
Matinee Theatre ep From the Desk of Margaret Tyd-
ings 2.18.57 NBC
On Trial ep The Case of the Absent Man 5.3.57 NBC
Conflict ep Anything for Money 7.23.57 ABC
Zane Grey Theatre ep The Deserters 10.4.57 CBS
Perry Mason ep The Case of the Nervous Accomplice
10.5.57 CBS
Trackdown ep San Saba Incident 10.18.57 CBS
Climax ep The Great World and Timothy Colt 3.27.
58 CBS
The Millionaire ep The Martin Scott Story 10.8.58
CBS
Desilu Playhouse ep Comeback 3.2.59 CBS
Goodyear Theatre ep A Light in the Fruit Closet 4.
27.59 NBC
Perry Mason ep The Case of the Nervous Accomplice
11.29.59 CBS
Markham ep The Sitting Duck 5.5.60 CBS
Perry Mason ep The Case of the Ominous Outcast
5.21.60 CBS
Mystery Show ep I Know What I'd Have Done 7.24.60
NBC
Bonanza ep The Countess 11.19.61 NBC
New Breed ep Policemen Die Alone 1.30.62, 2.6.62
ABC
77 Sunset Strip ep Twice Dead 3.2.62 ABC
Golden Showcase ep Tonight in Smarkand 3.24.62 CBS
Target Corruptors ep The Blind Goddess 4.20.62 ABC
Life with Virginia pt 9.18.62 CBS
Perry Mason ep The Case of the Reluctant Model 10.
31.63 CBS
Defenders ep Blacklist 1.18.64 CBS
Flame in the Wind sr 12.28.64 ABC

HAYES, PETER LIND
Armstrong Circle Theatre ep The Marshal of Misery
Gulch 12.8.53 NBC
Studio One ep Side Street 3.1.54 CBS
Goodyear Playhouse ep The Way Things Happen 1.30.
55 NBC
Lux Video Theatre ep One Sunday Afternoon 1.31.57
NBC
Danny Thomas Show ep Lose Me in Las Vegas 10.7.
57 CBS

Miracle on 34th Street Sp 11.27.59 NBC
Peter Loves Mary sr 10.12.60 NBC
Outer Limits ep Behold 10.3.64 ABC

HAYMES, DICK
Ford Theatre ep National Honeymoon 10.16.52 NBC
Video Theatre ep Song for a Banjo 12.15.52 CBS
Suspense ep The Deadly Lamb 12.23.52 CBS
Ford Theatre ep Sweet Talk Me, Jackson 5.21.53
    NBC
Suspense ep Laugh It Off 12.1.53 CBS
Screen Directors Playhouse ep Cry Justice 2.15.56
    NBC
Producers Showcase ep The Lord Don't Play Favorites
    9.17.56 NBC

HAYS, KATHRYN
Hawaiian Eye ep Total Eclipse 2.21.62 ABC
Surfside Six ep Many a Slip 2.26.62 ABC
Wide Country ep The Girl from Nob Hill 3.28.63
    NBC
Route 66 ep Shadows of an Afternoon 5.17.63 CBS
Eleventh Hour ep What Did She Mean by Good Luck
    11.13.63 NBC
U.S. Steel Hour ep Moment of Rage 3.6.63 CBS
Dr. Kildare ep An Island like a Peacock 5.16.63
    NBC
Lieutenant ep Cool of the Evening 9.21.63 NBC
Nurses ep Climb a Broken Ladder 3.12.64 CBS
Mr. Novak ep One Way to Say Goodbye 2.17.64 NBC
Arrest and Trial ep He Ran for His Life 4.5.64
    ABC
Bonanza ep The Wild One 10.4.64 NBC
Rawhide ep The Backshooter 11.27.64 CBS
Defenders ep King of the Hill 11.31.64 CBS
Alfred Hitchcock Theatre ep One of the Family 2.8.65
    NBC
Virginian ep A Slight Case of Charity 2.10.65 NBC
The Man from U.N.C.L.E. ep The See Paris and Die
    Affair 3.1.65 NBC
Branded ep Very Few Heroes 4.11.65 NBC
Kraft Suspense Theatre ep Kill Me on July 20th 6.17.
    65 NBC
Run for Your Life ep The Cruel Fountain 4.4.66 NBC
Mannix ep End of the Rainbow 10.26.68 CBS
Star Trek ep The Empath 12.6.68 NBC
Here Come the Brides ep A Kiss Just for You 1.29.
    69 ABC

Mr. Deeds ep 10.24.69 ABC
Breakout tf 12.8.70 NBC
Bold Ones ep Absence of Loneliness 1.24.71 NBC
Yuma tf 3.21.71 ABC
Marcus Welby, M.D. ep In My Father's House 9.28.
71 ABC
Owen Marshall ep 11.11.71 ABC
Bearcats ep 12.23.71 CBS
Cade's County ep Ragged Edge 3.5.72 CBS
Night Gallery ep 12.24.72 NBC

HAYWARD, LOUIS
Matinee Theatre ep Beginning Now 10.31.51 NBC
Ford Theatre ep Crossed and Double-Crossed 12.11.
52 NBC
Lux Video Theatre ep So Evil My Love 1.27.55 NBC
The Lone Wolf sr 9.12.55 NN
Climax ep A Promise to Murder 11.17.55 CBS
TV Reader's Digest ep The Voyage of Captain Tom
Jones, Pirate 11.21.55 ABC
Studio One ep Balance of Terror 1.27.58 CBS
Schlitz Playhouse of Stars ep A Contest of Ladies 4.
18.58 CBS
Decision ep Stand and Deliver 9.17.58 NBC
Riverboat ep Payment in Full 9.13.59 NBC
Golden Showcase ep The Picture of Dorian Gray 12.
6.61 CBS
Mystery Theatre ep Dead on Nine 7.4.62 NBC
Alfred Hitchcock Theatre ep Day of Reckoning 11.22.
62 CBS
Burke's Law ep 4.21.65 ABC
Survivors sr 10.69 ABC
Night Gallery ep Certain Shadows on the Walls 12.30.
70 NBC

HAYWARD, SUSAN
Heat of Anger tf 3.3.72 CBS
Say Goodbye, Maggie Cole tf 9.27.72 ABC

HAYWORTH, RITA
The Poppy Is Also a Flower tf 4.22.66 ABC

HEALY, MARY
Armstrong Circle Theatre ep The Marshal of Misery
Gulch 12.18.53 NBC
Studio One ep Side Street 3.1.54 CBS
Goodyear Playhouse ep The Way Things Happen 1.30.55
NBC

Lux Video Theatre   ep   One Sunday Afternoon   1.31.57
   NBC
Danny Thomas Show   ep   Lose Me in Las Vegas   10.7.
   57 CBS
Miracle on 34th Street   Sp   11.27.59 NBC
Peter Loves Mary   sr   10.12.60 NBC

HEATHERTON, JOEY
Route 66   ep   Three Sides   11.18.60 CBS
Nurses   ep   Night Shift   9.27.62 CBS
Virginian   ep   A Distant Fury   3.20.63 NBC
Mr. Novak   ep   To Break a Camel's Back   11.12.63
   NBC
Arrest and Trial   ep   Some Weeks Are All Mondays
   12.15.63 ABC
Nurses   ep   Rally Round My Comrades   12.26.63 CBS
Bob Hope Chrysler Theatre   ep   1.10.64 NBC
Channing   ep   The Trouble with Girls   3.11.64 ABC
I Spy   ep   11.23.66 NBC
Of Mice and Men   Sp   1.31.68 ABC
It Takes a Thief   ep   2.4.69, 2.11.69 ABC
The Ballad of Andy Crocker   tf   11.17.69 ABC

HECKART, EILEEN
Television Theatre   ep   Black Sheep   4.26.50 NBC
Studio One   ep   Zone Four   6.12.50 CBS
Saturday's Children   Sp   10.2.50 CBS
Philco Playhouse   ep   Segment   1.27.52 NBC
Philco Playhouse   ep   The Best Laid Schemer   3.23.52
   NBC
Naked City   ep   Hold for Gloria Christmas   9.19.62
   ABC
Dr. Kildare   ep   The Soul Killer   11.22.62 NBC
Short Short Drama   ep   The Unknown Factor   11.27.52
   NBC
Other People's Houses   8.30.53 NBC
Goodyear Playhouse   ep   The Haven   11.1.53 NBC
TV Soundstage   ep   A Little Child Shall Lead Them   5.
   21.54   NBC
Goodyear Playhouse   ep   My Lost Saints   3.13.55 NBC
Philco Playhouse   ep   Christmas 'til Closing   12.18.55
   NBC
Kraft Theatre   ep   Anna Santonello   8.8.56 NBC
Hallmark Hall of Fame   ep   The Little Foxes   12.16.56
   NBC
Alcoa Hour   ep   No License to Kill   2.3.57 NBC
Studio One   ep   The Out-of-Towners   5.6.57 CBS

Kraft Theatre ep Success 7.31.57 NBC
Playhouse 90 ep The Blue Men 1.15.59 CBS
Playhouse 90 ep A Corner of the Garden 4.23.59
 CBS
Hallmark Hall of Fame ep A Doll's House 11.15.59
 NBC
Play of the Week ep Morning's at Seven 4.25.60 NN
Play of the Week ep The House of Bernarda Alba
 6.6.60 NN
Play of the Week ep Four by Tennessee Williams
 2.6.61 NN
Alfred Hitchcock Presents ep Coming, Mama 4.11.61
 NBC
New Breed ep Till Death Do Us Part 11.7.61 ABC
Dr. Kildare ep The Soul Killer 11.22.62 NBC
Naked City ep Her Life in Moving Pictures 1.2.63
 ABC
Ben Casey ep Dispel the Black Cyclone that Shakes
 the Throne 11.27.63 ABC
Eleventh Hour ep There Should Be an Outfit Called
 Families Anonymous 12.11.63 NBC
Defenders ep All The Silent Voices 2.1.64 CBS
Fugitive ep Angels Travel on Lonely Roads 2.25.64,
 3.3.64 ABC
Doctors/Nurses ep Night of the Witch 2.2.65 CBS
Gunsmoke ep 3.27.65 CBS
FBI ep The Insolents 10.17.65 ABC
New York Television Theatre ep Save Me a Place at
 Forest Lawn 3.7.66 NN
Felony Squad ep The Broken Badge 9.26.66 ABC
New York Television Theatre ep The Effect of Gamma
 Rays on Man-in-the-Moon Marigolds 10.3.66 NN
Fugitive ep The Breaking of a Habit 1.31.67 ABC
CBS Playhouse ep Secrets 5.15.68 CBS
Gunsmoke ep 11.24.69 CBS
Hallmark Hall of Fame ep All the Way Home 12.1.
 71 NBC
Streets of San Francisco ep 9.23.72 ABC
Banyon ep 11.24.72 NBC

HEDISON, DAVID
 Five Fingers sr 10.3.59 NBC
 Hong Kong ep 1.11.61 ABC
 Bus Stop ep Call Back Yesterday 12.10.61 ABC
 Perry Mason ep 10.25.62 CBS
 Voyage to the Bottom of the Sea sr 9.14.64 ABC
 Voyage to the Bottom of the Sea sr ret 9.19.65 ABC

Voyage to the Bottom of the Sea sr ret 9.18.66 ABC
Voyage to the Bottom of the Sea sr ret 9.17.67 ABC
Journey to the Unknown ep Somewhere in a Crown
11.14.68 ABC
Love American Style ep 12.22.69 ABC

HEFLIN, VAN
Nash Airflyte Theatre ep A Double-Dyed Deceiver 9.
21.50 ABC
Robert Montgomery Presents ep Arrowsmith 10.9.50
NBC
Playhouse 90 ep The Dark Side of the Earth 9.19.57
CBS
Playhouse 90 ep Rank and File 5.28.59 CBS
Playhouse 90 ep The Cruel Day 2.24.60 CBS
Great Adventures sh 2.27.63 CBS
A Case of Libel Sp 2.11.68 ABC
Danny Thomas Show ep Fear Is the Chain 2.19.68
NBC
Hallmark Hall of Fame ep Neither Are We Enemies
3.13.70 NBC

HELPMANN, ROBERT
Lux Video Theatre ep Two for Two 1.5.53 CBS

HEMMINGS, DAVID
N.E.T. Playhouse ep Auto Stop 1.5.68 NN

HENDERSON, FLORENCE
U.S. Steel Hour ep Huck Finn 11.20.57 CBS
U.S. Steel Hour ep A Family Alliance 6.4.58 CBS
Little Women Sp 10.16.58 CBS
Hayes and Henderson sh 3.26.59 NBC
I Spy ep The Abbe and the Nymph 4.13.66 NBC
Brady Bunch sr 9.26.69 ABC
Brady Bunch sr ret 9.25.70 ABC
Brady Bunch sr ret 9.17.71 ABC
Brady Bunch sr ret 9.25.72 ABC

HENDERSON, MARCIA
Armstrong Circle Theatre ep Mountain Song 7.30.51
NBC
Two Girls Named Smith sr 9.29.51 ABC
Dear Phoebe sr 9.10.54 NBC
20th Century-Fox Hour ep Cavalcade 10.5.55 CBS
Crossroads ep Through the Window 1.6.56 ABC
Matinee Theatre ep The Gate 1.9.56 NBC

Schlitz Playhouse of Stars ep Angels in the Sky 4.6.
56 CBS
Matinee Theatre ep Ask Me No Questions 8.24.56
NBC
Ford Theatre ep Black Jack Hawk 10.31.56 ABC
Matinee Theatre ep Arms and the Man 4.23.57 NBC
Matinee Theatre ep Liza 6.17.57 NBC
Matinee Theatre ep Forbidden Search 10.4.57 NBC
People's Choice ep Sock's Old Flame 12.26.57 NBC
M Squad ep The Black Mermaid 2.28.58 NBC
Tales of Wells Fargo ep The Reward 4.21.58 NBC
Meet McGraw ep The Florentine Shield 5.6.58 NBC
Meet McGraw ep Lady in Limbo 6.24.58 NBC
The Millionaire ep Regina Wainwright Story 12.25.
57 CBS
Northwest Passage ep The Fourth Brother 1.30.59
NBC
Colt .45 ep Point of Honor 3.22.59 ABC
Bat Masterson ep Two Graves for Swan Valley 6.3.
59 NBC
Richard Diamond ep 6.7.59 CBS
Men into Space ep Lost Missile 11.4.59 CBS
Man and the Challenge ep 12.5.59 NBC
Bat Masterson ep The Inner Circle 12.31.59 NBC
Deputy ep Silent Gun 1.23.60 NBC
Bachelor Father ep Strictly Business 3.13.62 ABC

HENDRIX, WANDA
Lux Video Theatre ep The Token 11.27.50 CBS
Drama ep Rewrite for Love 1.20.51 NN
Pulitzer Prize Playhouse ep The Happy Journey 5.4.
51 ABC
Bigelow Theatre ep A New Year for Margaret 5.27.
51 CBS
Pulitzer Prize Playhouse ep The American Leonardo
5.31.52 ABC
Robert Montgomery Presents ep Keane Vs. Keane
10.20.52 NBC
Ford Theatre ep Something Old, Something New 12.
4.52 NBC
Plymouth Playhouse ep A Tale of Two Cities 5.3.53,
5.10.53 ABC
Ford Theatre ep The Bachelor 10.22.53 NBC
Mirror Theatre ep The Surprise Party 10.24.53 CBS
Schlitz Playhouse of Stars ep Fresh Start 11.20.53
CBS
Climax ep Avalanche at Devil's Pass 4.24.57 CBS

Telephone Time ep The Immortal Eye 2.4.58 ABC
Wagon Train ep The Charles Maury Story 5.7.58
   NBC
Bat Masterson ep The Lady Plays Her Hand 12.29.
   60 NBC
Deputy ep The Lesson 11.4.61 NBC

HENREID, PAUL
   Ford Theatre ep The Jewel 5.28.53 NBC
   Ford Theatre ep Mimi 5.19.55 NBC
   Climax ep Wild Stallion 7.7.55 CBS
   Playhouse 90 ep One Coat of White 2.21.57 CBS
   Schlitz Playhouse of Stars ep Bitter Parting 10.25.
      57 CBS
   Jane Wyman Theatre ep Man of Taste 4.24.58 NBC
   Aquanauts ep 10.12.60 CBS
   It Takes a Thief ep 1.21.69 ABC
   Judd for the Defense ep Elephant in a Cigar Box
      2.28.69 ABC
   Paris 7000 ep Call Me Ellen 3.26.70 ABC
   The Failing of Raymond tf 11.27.71 ABC

HEPBURN, AUDREY
   TV Workshop ep Rainy Day in Paradise Junction 4.
      13.52 CBS
   Producers Showcase ep Mayerling 2.4.57 NBC

HERLIE, EILEEN
   Heartbreak House Sp 4.24.66 NN
   Hollywood Television Theatre ep Lemonade 10.21.71
      NN
   Portrait: The Woman I Love ep 12.17.72 ABC

HERNANDEZ, JUANO
   Studio 57 ep The Goodwill Ambassadors 6.24.57
      CBS
   Studio One ep Escape Route 12.2.57 CBS
   Play of the Week ep Black Monday 1.16.61 NN
   Adventure in Paradise ep The Good Killing 1.30.61
      ABC
   Route 66 ep Good Night, Sweet Blues 10.6.61 CBS
   Dick Powell Theatre ep Safari 4.3.62 NBC
   Defenders ep The Savage Infant 12.8.62 CBS
   Naked City ep Howard Running Bear Is a Turtle 4.3.
      63 ABC

HERSHEY, BARBARA
    Gidget ep Chivalry Is Not Dead 11.10.65 ABC
    Farmer's Daugher ep 2.11.66 ABC
    Bob Hope Chrysler Theatre ep Holloway's Daughters
        5.11.66 NBC
    The Monroes sr 9.7.66 ABC
    Daniel Boone ep 10.19.67 NBC
    Run for Your Life ep 2.7.68 NBC
    Invaders ep The Miracle 2.27.68 ABC
    High Chaparral ep 3.3.68 NBC
    CBS Playhouse ep Secrets 5.15.68 CBS

HERSHOLT, JEAN
    Dr. Christian ep 9.56 ABC

HERVEY, IRENE
    Fireside Theatre ep Touch the Earth 2.23.54 NBC
    Fireside Theatre ep Mr. Onion 2.8.55 NBC
    Public Defender ep Mama's Boy 2.10.55 CBS
    Playhouse ep The Vanishing Suitor 2.20.55 ABC
    Studio 57 ep The Haven Technique 2.22.55 NN
    Fireside Theatre ep It's Easy to Get Ahead 3.29.55
        NN
    Climax ep Flight 951 4.21.55 CBS
    Stage 7 ep The Time of Day 5.39.55 CBS
    Studio 57 ep Any Time You Need Me 5.21.55 NN
    Damon Runyon Theatre ep Small Town Caper 8.13.55
        CBS
    The Millionaire ep The Candy Caldwell Story 2.29.56
        CBS
    Matinee Theatre ep Young Hands, Young Feet 4.13.56
        NBC
    Charlie Farrell Show ep 7.23.56 CBS
    Lux Video Theatre ep The Top Rung 9.13.56 NBC
    Matinee Theatre ep Little Woman 12.25.56 NBC
    Studio One ep The Lonely Stage 2.24.58 CBS
    Playhouse 90 ep A Quiet Game of Cards 1.29.59 CBS
    Richard Diamond ep 2.15.59 CBS
    Ann Sothern Show ep The Ugly Bonnet 5.4.59 CBS
    Perry Mason ep The Case of the Black-Eyed Blonde
        2.13.60 CBS
    Bourbon Street Beat ep False Identity 5.23.60 ABC
    O'Conner's Ocean pt 12.13.60 NBC
    Peter Gunn ep Blind Item 1.23.61 ABC
    Shirley Temple Theatre ep The Princess and the Gob-
        lins 3.19.61 NBC
    Surfside 6 ep Little Mister Kelly 5.1.61 ABC

Target Corruptors   ep   One for the Road   1.12.62 ABC
Follow the Sun   ep   The Last of the Big Spenders   1.
   14.62 ABC
Straightaway   ep   The Drag Strip   1.24.62 ABC
Hawaiian Eye   ep   The Last Samurai   4.25.62 ABC
Wide Country   ep   Our Ernie Kills People   11.1.62
   NBC
Dr. Kildare   ep   An Ancient Office   12.6.62 NBC
Hawaiian Eye   ep   Kupkio Kid   1.8.63 ABC
Perry Mason   ep   The Case of the Lawful Lazarus   3.
   14.63 CBS
Hawaiian Eye   ep   Two for the Money   5.28.63 ABC
Honey West   sr   9.17.65 ABC
Love on a Rooftop   ep   3.23.67 ABC
Mod Squad   ep   12.3.68 ABC
My Three Sons   ep   3.1.69 CBS
Family Affair   ep   9.17.70 CBS

HESTON, CHARLTON
Studio One   ep   Taming of the Shrew   6.5.50 CBS
Philco Playhouse   ep   Hear My Heart Speak   6.25.50
   NBC
Studio One   ep   Letter from Cairo   12.4..50 CBS
Suspense   ep   Santa Fe Fleight   10.2.51 CBS
Studio One   ep   Macbeth   10.22.51 CBS
Studio One   ep   A Bolt of Lightning   11.12.51 CBS
Robert Montgomery Presents   ep   Cashel Bryon's Pro-
   fession   1.14.52 NBC
Studio One   ep   The Wings of the Dove   3.10.52 CBS
Curtain Call   ep   The Liar   8.22.52 NBC
Robert Montgomery Presents   ep   Dr. Gatskill's Blue
   Shoes   12.29.52 NBC
Philco Playhouse   ep   Elegy   1.25.53 NBC
Films of Faith   ep   Three Lives   6.21.53 NN
Medallion Theatre   ep   A Day in Town   12.12.53 CBS
Robert Montgomery Presents   ep   Along Came Jones
   9.26.55 NBC
Omnibus   ep   The Renaissance   10.9.55 CBS
G.E. Theatre   ep   The Seeds of Hate   12.11.55 CBS
Climax   ep   Bailout at 43,000   12.29.55 CBS
Climax   ep   The Trial of Captain Wirz   6.27.57 CBS
Schlitz Playhouse of Stars   ep   Switch Station   10.4.57
Shirley Temple's Story Book   ep   Beauty and the Beast
   1.12.58 NBC
Playhouse 90   ep   Point of No Return   2.20.58 CBS
Alcoa Premiere   ep   The Fugitive Eye   10.17.61 ABC
Repertoire Workshop   ep hos   Company K   5.19.53 CBS

Hallmark Hall of Fame   ep   The Patriots   11.15.63
NBC
Hallmark Hall of Fame   ep   Elizabeth the Queen   1.31.
68 NBC

HICKMAN, DWAYNE

Love That Bob (a.k.a.   The Bob Cummings Show)   sr
1.2.55 NBC
Love That Bob   sr ret   10.5.55 CBS
Love That Bob   sr ret   fall, 1956 CBS
Love That Bob   sr ret   9.25.57 NBC
Love That Bob   sr ret   fall, 1958 NBC
(The Many Loves of) Dobie Gillis   sr   9.29.59 CBS
Dobie Gillis   sr ret   9.27.60 CBS
Dobie Gillis   sr ret   10.10.61 CBS
Ozzie and Harriet   ep   The Kappa Sig Party   12.28.61
ABC
The Greatest Show on Earth   ep   Rosetta   3.24.64 ABC
Wagon Train   ep   The Clay Shelby Story   12.6.64 ABC
Combat   ep   Run, Sheep, Run   4.5.66 ABC
We'll Take Manhattan   pt   4.30.67 NBC
Ironside   ep   3.28.68 NBC
Flying Nun   ep   2.13.69 ABC
My Friend Tony   ep   4.13.69 NBC
World of Disney   ep   My Dog the Thief   9.21.69, 9.28.
69 NBC
Mod Squad   ep   The Healer   12.9.69 ABC

HILL, ARTHUR

Hallmark Hall of Fame   ep   Born Yesterday   10.28.56
NBC
Studio One   ep   The Morning Face   10.7.57 CBS
U.S. Steel Hour   ep   The Enemies   12.3.58 CBS
Alfred Hitchcock Presents   ep   Human Interest Story
5.24.59 CBS
Play of the Week   ep   The Closing Door   1.4.60 NN
Dupont Show of the Month   ep   Ethan Frome   2.18.60
CBS
U.S. Steel Hour   ep   The Girl Who Knew Too Much
4.20.60 CBS
Great Mysteries   ep   The Woman in White   5.23.60
NBC
U.S. Steel Hour   ep   Game of Hearts   6.1.60 CBS
Robert Herridge Theatre   ep   The Stone Boy   8.4.60
CBS
Alfred Hitchcock Presents   ep   The Man Who Found
the Money   12.27.60 NBC

Our American Heritage   ep   The Invincible Teddy   1.12.
    61 NBC
Special for Women   ep   Mother and Daughter   3.9.61
    NBC
Defenders   ep   The Boy Between   10.21.61 CBS
Ben Casey   ep   The Sweet Kiss of Madness   12.4.61
    ABC
Westinghouse Presents   ep   Come Again to Carthage
    12.8.61 CBS
Armstrong Circle Theatre   ep   The Battle of Hearts
    12.20.61 CBS
Untouchables   ep   Canada Run   1.4.62 ABC
Focus   Sp   1.21.62 NBC
U.S. Steel Hour   ep   The Big Laugh   1.24.62 CBS
Defenders   ep   The Last Six Months   3.31.62 CBS
Route 66   ep   Kiss the Maiden All Forlorn   4.13.62
    CBS
Armstrong Circle Theatre   ep   Battle of Hearts   8.1.62
    CBS
Slattery's People   ep   Remember the Dark Sins of Youth
    10.5.54 CBS
Defenders   ep   Go-Between   10.15.64 CBS
Voyage to the Bottom of the Sea   ep   The Monster from
    the Inferno   9.18.66 ABC
FBI   ep   The Plague Merchant   10.30.66 ABC
Mission Impossible   ep   11.19.66 CBS
Bob Hope Chrysler Theatre   ep   The Fatal Mistake   11.
    30.66 NBC
World of Disney   ep   3.19.67 NBC
Run for Your Life   ep   2.7.67 NBC
Fugitive   ep   Death Is a Very Small Killer   3.21.67 ABC
FBI   ep   10.22.67, 10.29.67 ABC
Desperate Hours   Sp   12.13.67 ABC
Run for Your Life   ep   1.24.68 NBC
CBS Playhouse   ep   Secrets   5.15.68 CBS
Judd for the Defense   ep   11.22.68 ABC
Lancer   ep   2.4.69 CBS
FBI   ep   2.16.69 ABC
Bracken's World   ep   11.14.69 NBC
Name of the Game   ep   Echo of a Nightmare   3.20.70
    NBC
The Other Man   tf   10.19.70 NBC
Bold Ones   ep   Giants Never Kneel   10.25.70 NBC
Name of the Game   ep   Aquarius Descending   12.11.70
    NBC
Vanished   tf   3.8.71, 3.9.71 NBC
Owen Marshall   tf   9.12.71 ABC

Owen Marshall   sr 9.16.71 ABC
Owen Marshall   sr ret   9.14.72 ABC

HILL, STEVEN
Suspense   ep   A Pocketful of Murder   9.5.50 ABC
Schlitz Playhouse of Stars   ep   The Man I Marry   1.18.
   52 CBS
Goodyear Playhouse   ep   The Inward Eye   3.14.54 NBC
The Mask   ep   The Young Dancer   3.23.54 ABC
The Mask   ep   Marked for Murder   4.6.54 ABC
Goodyear Playhouse   ep   The Arena   8.1.54 NBC
Philco Playhouse   ep   Middle of the Night   9.19.54
   NBC
Philco Playhouse   ep   Man on the Mountaintop   10.17.
   54 NBC
Playwrights '56   ep   The Sound and the Fury   12.6.55
   NBC
Playwrights '56   ep   Lost   1.17.56 NBC
Studio One   ep   The Traveling Lady   4.22.57 CBS
Seven Lively Arts   ep   The World of Nick Adams   11.
   10.57 CBS
Alfred Hitchcock   ep   Enough Rope for Two   11.17.57
   CBS
Dupont Show of the Month   ep   The Bridge of San Luis
   Rey   1.21.58 CBS
Playhouse 90   ep   For Whom the Bell Tolls   3.12.59,
   3.19.59 CBS
Sunday Showcase   ep   The American   3.27.60 NBC
Playhouse 90   ep   Journey to the Day   4.22.60 CBS
Sacco-Vanzetti Story   Sp   6.3.60, 6.10.60 NBC
Untouchables   ep   Jack Legs Diamond Story   10.20.60
   ABC
Adventures in Paradise   ep   Act of Piracy   2.13.61 ABC
Route 66   ep   A City of Wheels   2.2.66 CBS
Untouchables   ep   Downfall   5.3.62 ABC
Eleventh Hour   ep   There Are Dragons in this Forest
   10.10.62 NBC
Ben Casey   ep   Legacy from a Stranger   10.22.62 ABC
Dr. Kildare   ep   Cobweb Chain   11.15.62 NBC
Ben Casey   ep   I'll Be All Right in the Morning   1.7.63
   ABC
Naked City   ep   Barefoot on a Bed of Coals   5.29.63
   ABC
Espionage   ep   The Incurable One   10.16.63 NBC
The Greatest Show on Earth   ep   Corsicans Don't Cry
   1.14.64 ABC
Alfred Hitchcock Theatre   ep   Who Needs an Enemy

5.15.64 CBS
Route 66   ep   A City of Wheels   5.22.64 CBS
Alfred Hitchcock Theatre   ep   2.1.65 NBC
Kraft Suspense Theatre   ep   The Safe House   5.20.65
  NBC
Rawhide   ep   The Gray Rock Hotel   5.21.65 CBS
Fugitive   ep   The White Knight   3.22.66 ABC
Mission Impossible   sr   9.17.66 CBS

HILLER, WENDY
   Studio One   ep   The Travelling Lady   4.22.57 CBS
   Matinee Theatre   ep   Ann Veronica   7.29.57 NBC
   Matinee Theatre   ep   Eden End   2.17.58 NBC
   Alfred Hitchcock Presents   ep   Graduating Class   12.
      27.59 CBS
   Profiles in Courage   ep   Anne Hutchinson   1.10.65 NBC
   David Copperfield   tf   3.15.70 NBC

HILLIARD, HARRIET
   Ozzie and Harriet   sr   10.10.52 ABC
   Ozzie and Harriet   sr ret   fall, 1953 ABC
   Ozzie and Harriet   sr ret   fall, 1954 ABC
   Ozzie and Harriet   sr ret   9.23.55 ABC
   Ozzie and Harriet   sr ret   fall, 1956 ABC
   Ozzie and Harriet   sr ret   fall, 1957 ABC
   Ozzie and Harriet   sr ret   fall, 1958 ABC
   Ozzie and Harriet   sr ret   fall, 1959 ABC
   Ozzie and Harriet   sr ret   9.28.60 ABC
   Ozzie and Harriet   sr ret   9.28.61 ABC
   Ozzie and Harriet   sr ret   9.27.62 ABC
   Ozzie and Harriet   sr ret   9.18.63 ABC
   Ozzie and Harriet   sr ret   9.15.65 ABC
   Love American Style   ep   1.8.71 ABC
   Night Gallery   ep   11.12.72 NBC

HINGLE, PAT
   Studio One   ep   An Almanac of Liberty   11.8.54 CBS
   Goodyear Playhouse   ep   Do It Yourself   4.24.55 NBC
   Philco Playhouse   ep   Black Frost   6.26.55 NBC
   Appointment with Adventure   ep   The Allenson Incident
      10.2.55 CBS
   Goodyear Playhouse   ep   The Expendable House   10.9.
      55 NBC
   You'll Never Get Rich   ep   A.W.O.L.   10.18.55 CBS
   Philco Playhouse   ep   The Trees   12.4.55 NBC
   Justice   ep   End of a Chase   12.25.55 NBC
   Philco Playhouse   ep   This Land Is Mine   1.15.56 NBC

Kraft Theatre   ep   No Warning   1.16.57 NBC
U.S. Steel Hour   ep   Inspired Alibi   2.13.57 CBS
Studio One   ep   A Child Is Waiting   3.11.57 CBS
U.S. Steel Hour   ep   A Matter of Pride   4.24.57 CBS
Studio One   ep   The Human Barrier   7.19.57 CBS
Suspicion   ep   Heartbeat   11.11.57 NBC
Alfred Hitchcock Presents   ep   Night of the Execution
    12.29.57 CBS
U.S. Steel Hour   ep   The Last Autumn   11.18.59 CBS
Play of the Week   ep   Black Monday   1.16.61 NN
Defenders   ep   The Trial of Jenny Scott   11.11.61
    CBS
Cain's Hundred   ep   The Fixer   12.12.61 NBC
Route 66   ep   Burning for Burning   12.29.61 CBS
Untouchables   ep   The Case Against Eliot Ness   5.10.62
    ABC
Eleventh Hour   ep   Of Rose and Nightingales   11.7.62
    NBC
Untouchables   ep   Junk Man   2.26.63 ABC
Twilight Zone   ep   The Incredible World of Horace
    Ford   4.18.63 CBS
Dr. Kildare   ep   The Heart, an Imperfect Machine   10.
    17.63 NBC
Kraft Suspense Theatre   ep   The Name of the Game   12.
    26.63 NBC
Fugitive   ep   Search in a Windy City   2.4.64 ABC
Carol for Another Christmas   tf   12.28.64 ABC
Rawhide   ep   The Book   1.8.65 CBS
Daniel Boone   ep   The Returning   1.14.65 NBC
Defenders   ep   A Matter of Law and Disorder   4.8.65
    CBS
Andy Griffith Show   ep   1.31.66 CBS
Loner   ep   The Mourners for Johnny Sharp   2.5.66
    CBS
Shenandoah   ep   Plunder   3.7.66 ABC
Glass Menagerie   Sp   12.8.66 CBS
Mission Impossible   ep   2.25.67 CBS
Judd for the Defense   ep   9.8.67 ABC
Bob Hope Chrysler Theatre   ep   To Sleep, Perchance
    to Scream   5.10.67 NBC
Cimarron Strip   ep   Broken Wing   9.21.67 CBS
Run for Your Life   ep   The Company of Scoundrels
    10.18.67 NBC
Invaders   ep   The Prophet   11.14.67 ABC
Felony Squad   ep   1.8.68 ABC
High Chaparral   3.31.68 NBC
Bold Ones   ep   To Save a Life   9.14.69 NBC

Bonanza   ep   Silence at Stillwater   9. 28. 69 NBC
The Ballad of Andy Crocker   tf   11. 17. 69 ABC
Lancer   ep   12. 16. 69 CBS
Medical Center   ep   The Deceived   1. 7. 70 CBS
A Clear and Present Danger   tf   3. 21. 70 NBC
Young Lawyers   ep   2. 3. 71 ABC
Medical Center   ep   Crossroads   3. 10. 71 CBS
Gunsmoke   ep   10. 18. 71 CBS
Gunsmoke   ep   11. 1. 71, 11. 8. 71, 11. 15. 71 CBS
If Tomorrow Comes   tf   12. 7. 71 ABC
Hallmark Hall of Fame   ep   All the Way Home   12. 1.
   71 NBC
Ironside   ep   Find a Victim   1. 13. 72 NBC
Bold Ones   ep   The Long Morning After   1. 9. 72, 1. 16.
   72 NBC
Owen Marshall   ep   A Question of Degree   2. 24. 72 ABC

HITCHCOCK, ALFRED
Alfred Hitchcock Presents   sh   10. 2. 55 CBS
Alfred Hitchcock Presents   sh ret   fall, 1956 CBS
Alfred Hitchcock Presents   sh ret   fall, 1957 CBS
Alfred Hitchcock Presents   sh ret   fall, 1958 CBS
Alfred Hitchcock Presents   sh ret   9. 27. 59 CBS
Alfred Hitchcock Presents   sh ret   9. 27. 60 NBC
Alfred Hitchcock Theatre   sh ret   10. 10. 61 NBC
Alfred Hitchcock Theatre   sh ret   9. 20. 62 CBS
Alfred Hitchcock Theatre   sh ret   9. 27. 63 CBS
Alfred Hitchcock Theatre   sh ret   10. 5. 64 NBC

HOBBES, HALLIWELL
Alcoa Hour   ep   The Small Servant   10. 30. 55 NBC
Studio One   ep   Flower of Pride   3. 12. 56 CBS
Alcoa Hour   ep   Mrs. Gilling and the Skyscraper   6. 9.
   57 NBC

HODIAK, JOHN
Ford Theatre   ep   They Also Serve   1. 1. 53 NBC
Loretta Young Show   ep   The Last Spring   10. 16. 55
   NBC

HOEY, DENNIS
Actor's Studio   ep   Mr. Mummery's Suspicion   2. 17. 50
   CBS
Tele-Theatre   ep   The Waking Stick   3. 20. 50 NBC
Armstrong Circle Theatre   ep   The Vase   8. 5. 52 NBC

HOFFMAN, DUSTIN
    Naked City   ep   Sweet Prince of Delancey Street   6.7.
      61 ABC
    Defenders   ep   A Matter of Law and Disorder   4.8.65
      CBS
    Doctors/Nurses   ep   The Heroine   5.4.65 CBS
    N.E.T. Playhouse   ep   The Journey of the Fifth Horse
      10.14.66 NN
    N.E.T. Playhouse   ep   The Star Wagon   6.2.67 NN
    Higher and Higher   pt   9.9.68 CBS
    The Point   tf nar   2.2.71 ABC

HOFFMAN, GERTRUDE
    My Little Margie   sr   6.16.52 CBS
    My Little Margie   sr ret   10.4.52 NBC
    My Little Margie   sr ret   1.1.53 CBS
    My Little Margie   sr ret   9.2.53 NBC
    Alfred Hitchcock Presents   ep   The Long Shot   11.27.
      55 CBS

HOLBROOK, HAL
    Mr. Citizen   ep   Late for Supper   4.20.55 ABC
    Brighter Day   sr   spring, 1956 CBS
    The Glass Menagerie   Sp   12.8.66 CBS
    The Cliff Dwellers   pt   8.28.66 ABC
    Mark Twain Tonight   Sp   3.6.67 CBS
    Coronet Blue   ep   7.10.67 CBS
    FBI   ep   1.12.69 ABC
    The Whole World Is Watching   tf   3.11.69 NBC
    A Clear and Present Danger   tf   3.21.70 NBC
    Bold Ones/The Senator   sr   9.13.70 NBC
    World of Disney   ep   10.18.70, 10.27.70 NBC
    Travis Logan, D.A.   tf   3.11.71 CBS
    Suddenly Single   tf   10.19.71 ABC
    That Certain Summer   tf   11.1.72 ABC

HOLLIDAY, JUDY
    Goodyear Playhouse   ep   The Huntress   2.14.54 NBC

HOLLIMAN, EARL
    Playhouse 90   ep   The Dark Side of the Earth   9.19.57
      CBS
    Kraft Theatre   ep   The Battle for Wednesday Night   1.
      1.58 NBC
    Kraft Theatre   ep   The Sea Is Boiling Hot   3.12.58
      NBC
    Matinee Theatre   ep   The Man with Pointed Toes   6.

17.58 NBC
Studio One   ep   The Lady Died at Midnight   9.1.58
    CBS
Playhouse 90   ep   The Return of Ansel Gibbels   11.28.
    58 CBS
Desilu Playhouse   ep   Silent Thunder   12.8.58 CBS
Hotel de Paree   sr   10.2.59 CBS
Twilight Zone   ep   Where Is Everybody   10.2.59 CBS
Dick Powell Theatre   ep   Killer in the House   10.10.
    61 NBC
Westinghouse Presents   ep   The Dispossessed   10.24.
    61 CBS
Bus Stop   ep   The Stubborn Stumbos   1.21.62 ABC
Alcoa Premiere   ep   Second Chance   3.13.62 ABC
G.E. Theatre   ep   The Troubled Heart   4.22.62 CBS
Wide Country   sr   9.20.62 NBC
Our Man Higgins   ep   10.3.62 ABC
Great Adventures   ep   Teeth of the Lion   1.17.64 CBS
Bonanza   ep   The Flannel-Mouth Gun   1.31.65 NBC
Dr. Kildare   ep   Wings of Hope   5.13.65 NBC
Virginian   ep   Ring of Silence   10.27.65 NBC
Slattery's People   ep   The Hero   11.5.65 CBS
Fugitive   ep   The Good Guys and the Bad Guys   12.14.
    65 ABC
FBI   ep   Special Delivery   1.23.66 ABC
12 O'Clock High   ep   The Ticket   2.26.66 ABC
Judd for the Defense   ep   No Law Against Murder   1.
    19.68 ABC
Gunsmoke   ep   10.27.69 CBS
Marcus Welby, M.D.   ep   Neither Punch Nor Judy   12.
    23.69 ABC
It Takes a Thief   ep   Situation Red   2.9.70 ABC
FBI   ep   3.8.70 ABC
Gunsmoke   ep   3.16.70 CBS
Tribes   tf   11.10.70 ABC
Ironside   ep   The Target   1.28.71 NBC
Hollywood Television Theatre   ep   Montserrat   3.2.71
    NN
Cannon   tf   3.26.71 CBS
FBI   ep   Dynasty of Hate   10.10.71 ABC
Medical Center   ep   Suspected   11.17.71 CBS
Rookies   ep   12.18.72   ABC

HOLM, CELESTE
    Lux Video Theatre   ep   The Pacing Goose   1.27.51
        CBS
    Schlitz Playhouse of Stars   ep   Four's a Family

4. 11. 52 CBS

Hollywood Opening Night ep Mrs. Genius 1. 26. 53 NBC

Jewelers Showcase ep Heart's Desire 5. 19. 53 CBS

U. S. Steel Hour ep The Bogey Man 1. 18. 55 ABC

Climax ep The Empty Room Blues 5. 3. 56 CBS

Carolyn pt 8. 7. 56 NBC

Producers Showcase ep Jack and the Beanstock 11. 12. 56 NBC

Schlitz Playhouse ep Wedding Present 2. 22. 57 CBS

Goodyear Playhouse ep The Princess Back Home 2. 24. 57 NBC

Zane Grey Theatre ep Fugitive 3. 22. 57 CBS

Studio 57 ep The Room Next Door 3. 31. 57 NN

Hallmark Hall of Fame ep The Yeoman of the Guard 4. 10. 57 NBC

The Man in the Dog Suit Sp 1. 8. 60 NBC

The Right Man Sp 10. 24. 60 CBS

Follow the Man ep The Irresistable Miss Bullfinch 2. 18. 62 ABC

Checkmate ep So Beats My Plastic Heart 4. 11. 62 CBS

Dr. Kildare ep The Pack Rack and the Prima Donna 11. 28. 63 NBC

Burke's Law ep Who Killed the Kind Doctor 11. 29. 63 ABC

Eleventh Hour ep How Do I Say I Love You 1. 15. 64 NBC

Mr. Novak ep An Elephant Is Like a Tree 1. 12. 65 NBC

World of Disney ep Kilroy 3. 14. 65, 3. 21. 65, 3. 28. 65, 4. 2. 65 NBC

Fugitive ep The Old Man Picked a Lemon 4. 13. 65 ABC

Run for Your Life ep The Cold, Cold War of Paul Bryan 9. 13. 65 NBC

The Long Hot Summer ep Face of Fear 1. 6. 66 ABC

Cinderella Sp 2. 26. 66 CBS

Meet Me in St. Louis pt 9. 2. 66 ABC

Nancy sr 9. 17. 70 NBC

The Delphi Bureau tf 3. 6. 72 ABC

HOLT, TIM
Playhouse ep Adventure in Java 7. 8. 54 NBC

HOMOLKA, OSCAR
Robert Montgomery Presents ep Pink Hippopotamus

Television Hour ep Love Song 5.4.54 ABC
Producers Showcase ep Darkness at Noon 5.2.55
  NBC
Climax ep Carnival at Midnight 1.3.57 CBS
Dupont Theatre ep Dowry for Ilona 1.22.57 ABC
Matinee Theatre ep The Master Builder 2.14.57
  NBC
Matinee Theatre ep You Touched Me 3.4.57 NBC
Kaiser Aluminum Hour ep Murder in the House 4.9.
  57 NBC
Playhouse 90 ep The Plot to Kill Stalin 9.25.58 CBS
Playhouse 90 ep Heart of Darkness 11.6.58 CBS
Five Fingers ep Operation Ramrod 12.26.59 NBC
Alfred Hitchcock Presents ep The Ikon of Elijah 1.
  10.60 CBS
Dupont Show of the Month ep Arrowsmith 1.17.60
  CBS
Play of the Week ep A Very Special Baby 2.22.60
  NN
Playhouse 90 ep In the Presence of Mine Enemies
  5.18.60 CBS
Assassination Plot at Teheran Sp 9.23.60, 9.30.60
  ABC
Victory Sp 4.8.60 NBC
G.E. Theatre ep The Ugly Duckling 5.1.60 CBS
Alfred Hitchcock Presents ep The Hero 5.1.60 CBS
Play of the Week ep Rashomon 12.12.60 NN
Thriller ep Waxworks 1.8.62 NBC
Theatre '62 ep Spellbound 2.11.62 NBC
World of Disney ep The Mooncussers 12.2.62, 12.
  9.62 NBC
Breaking Point ep Solo for B-Flat Clarinet 9.16.63
  ABC
Burke's Law ep Who Killed Jason Shaw 1.3.64 ABC
Hazel ep A Lesson in Diplomacy 11.26.64 NBC
Rogues ep Plovonia, Hail and Farewell 11.29.64 NBC
Dr. Jekyll and Mr. Hyde Sp 1.7.68 ABC

HOOKS, ROBERT
  Profiles in Courage ep 1.31.65 NBC
  The Cliff Dwellers pt 8.28.66 ABC
  N.Y.P.D. sr 9.5.67 ABC
  N.Y.P.D. sr ret 10.1.68 ABC
  Mannix ep Last Rites for Miss Emma 3.8.69 CBS
  FBI ep 10.12.69 ABC
  Then Came Bronson ep A Long Trip to Yesterday
    12.10.69 NBC

Carter's Army   tf   1. 27. 70 ABC
Bold Ones   ep   Killer on the Loose   10. 11. 70 NBC
Vanished   tf   3. 8. 71, 3. 9. 71 NBC
Man and the City   ep   11. 17. 71 ABC
The Cable Car Mystery   tf   11. 19. 71 CBS
Two for the Money   tf   2. 26. 72 ABC

HOPE, BOB
I Love Lucy   ep   10. 1. 56 CBS
Roberta   Sp   9. 19. 58 NBC
Danny Thomas Show   ep   The Bob Hope Show   1. 6. 58
    ABC
Danny Thomas Show   ep   1. 26. 59 CBS
Danny Thomas Show   ep   4. 2. 62 CBS
Bob Hope Chrysler Theatre   sh   10. 4. 63 NBC
Bob Hope Chrysler Theatre   sh ret   fall, 1964 NBC
Bob Hope Chrysler Theatre   sh ret   9. 15. 65 NBC
Bob Hope Chrysler Theatre   sh ret   9. 14. 66 NBC
For Love or $$$ Sp   4. 11. 68 NBC
Roberta   Sp (restaged)   11. 6. 69 NBC

HOPKINS, MIRIAM
Pulitzer Prize Playhouse   ep   Ned McCobb's Daughter
    1. 12. 51 ABC
Betty Crocker Star Matinee   ep   Farewell to Love   12.
    29. 51 ABC
Video Theatre   ep   Long Distance   3. 12. 51 CBS
Video Theatre   ep   Julie   3. 24. 52 CBS
Curtain Call   ep   The Party   7. 18. 52 NBC
G. E. Theatre   ep   Desert Crossing   6. 20. 54 CBS
Lux Video Theatre   ep   Sunset Boulevard   1. 6. 55 NBC
Studio One   ep   Summer Pavilion   5. 2. 55 CBS
Matinee Theatre   ep   Woman Alone   9. 4. 57 NBC
Drama   ep   Indifferent Love   2. 25. 61 NN
Investigators   ep   11. 16. 61 CBS
G. E. Theatre   ep   A Very Special Girl   3. 11. 62 CBS
Route 66   Shadows of an Afternoon   5. 17. 63 CBS
Outer Limits   ep   Don't Open Till Doomsday   1. 20. 64
    ABC
Flying Nun   ep   Bertrille and the Silent Flicks   11. 26.
    69 ABC

HOPPER, DENNIS
Medic   ep   Boy in the Storm   1. 3. 55 NBC
Public Defender   ep   Mama's Boy   2. 10. 55 CBS
Loretta Young Show   ep   Inga   3. 20. 55 NBC
Cheyenne   ep   4. 3. 56 ABC

Conflict   ep   A Question of Loyalty   4. 2. 57 ABC
Conflict   ep   No Man's Road   4. 30. 57 ABC
Sugarfoot   ep   Brannigan's Boots   9. 17. 57 ABC
Studio One   ep   Trial by Slander   1. 20. 58 CBS
Zane Grey Theatre   ep   The Sharpshooter   3. 7. 58 CBS
Studio One   ep   The Last Summer   8. 4. 58 CBS
Rifleman   ep   The Sharpshooter   9. 30. 58 ABC
Decision   ep   High Air   9. 7. 58 NBC
Pursuit   ep   Last Night in August   12. 17. 58 CBS
Rifleman   ep   4. 21. 59 ABC
Goldie   ep   Goldie Meets Mike   3. 17. 60 CBS
The Millionaire   ep   Millionaire Julie Sherman   3. 23.
   60 CBS
Zane Grey Theatre   ep   The Sunrise Gun   5. 19. 60
   CBS
Barbara Stanwyck Theatre   ep   No One   12. 26. 60 NBC
Naked City   ep   Shoes for Vinnie Winford   3. 1. 61 ABC
87th Precinct   ep   My Friend, My Enemy   11. 27. 61
   NBC
Investigators   ep   The Mind's Own Fire   12. 14. 61 CBS
G. E. Theatre   ep   The Hold-Out   1. 14. 62 CBS
Surfside 6   ep   Vendetta Arms   3. 12. 62 ABC
Defenders   ep   The Indelible Silence   9. 29. 62 CBS
Twilight Zone   ep   He's Alive   1. 24. 63 CBS
Wagon Train   ep   The Emmett Lawton Story   3. 6. 63
   ABC
Defenders   ep   The Weeping Baboon   9. 28. 63 CBS
Espionage   ep   The Weakling   10. 9. 63 NBC
The Greatest Show on Earth   ep   The Wrecker   12. 3.
   63 ABC
Petticoat Junction   ep   1. 7. 64 CBS
Arrest and Trial   ep   People in Glass Houses   2. 9. 64
   ABC
Lieutenant   ep   To Set It Right   2. 22. 64 NBC
Bonanza   ep   The Dark Past   5. 3. 64 NBC
Gunsmoke   ep   1. 23. 65 CBS
Convoy   ep   The Many Colors of Courage   10. 8. 65 NBC
Jesse James   ep   South Wind   2. 14. 66 ABC
Courtmartial   ep   Without Spear or Sword   6. 24. 66 ABC
Combat   ep   2. 21. 67 ABC
Big Valley   ep   3. 13. 67 ABC
Guns of Will Sonnett   12. 8. 67 ABC
Big Valley   ep   12. 11. 67 ABC

HOPPER, HEDDA
Goodyear Playhouse   ep   Fadeout   8. 23. 53 NBC
I Love Lucy   ep   The Hedda Hopper Story   3. 14. 55 CBS

Playhouse 90 ep The Hostess with the Mostess 3.21. 57 CBS

Lucille Ball-Desi Arnaz Show ep Lucy Takes a Cruise to Havana 11.6.57 CBS

Beverly Hillbillies ep 10.14.64 CBS

Alice in Wonderland Sp (voice only) 3.30.66 ABC

HOPPER, WILLIAM

Casablanca ep 11.8.55 ABC

Fury ep The Hobo 1.7.56 NBC

Studio 57 ep The Magic Glass 3.18.56 NN

The Millionaire ep The Captain Carroll Story 5.16. 56 CBS

Jane Wyman Theatre ep Ten Per Cent 8.27.56 NBC

Lux Video Theatre ep The Top Rung 9.13.56 NBC

Schlitz Playhouse of Stars ep The Restless Gun 3. 29.57 CBS

Perry Mason sr 9.21.57 CBS

Perry Mason sr ret fall, 1957 CBS

Perry Mason sr ret 10.3.59 CBS

Perry Mason sr ret fall, 1960 CBS

Perry Mason sr ret fall, 1961 CBS

Perry Mason sr ret 9.27.62 CBS

Perry Mason Sr ret 9.26.63 CBS

Perry Mason sr ret 9.24.64 CBS

Perry Mason sr ret 9.12.65 CBS

HORNE, GEOFFREY

Philco Playhouse ep Anatomy of Fear 1.23.55 NBC

Robert Montgomery Presents ep The Breaking Point 2.14.55 NBC

Pond's Theatre ep Billy Budd 3.10.55 ABC

Philco Playhouse ep Gretel 8.21.55 NBC

Studio One ep Like Father, Like Son 9.19.55 CBS

Robert Montgomery Presents ep The Young and Beautiful 12.10.56 NBC

Hallmark Hall of Fame ep The Cradle Song 4.10.60 NBC

Adventures in Paradise ep Whip Fight 5.9.60 ABC

Twilight Zone ep The Gift 4.27.62 CBS

Route 66 ep 1.10.64 CBS

Great Adventures ep Rodger Young 1.24.64 CBS

Outer Limits ep The Guests 3.23.64 ABC

Alfred Hitchcock Theatre ep Completely Foolproof 3.29.65 NBC

Doctors/Nurses ep An Unweeded Garden 5.11.65 CBS

FBI ep The Baby Sitter 2.13.66 ABC
Virginian ep Harvest of Strangers 2.16.66 NBC
Road West ep Long Journey to Leavenworth 10.17.
    66 NBC
Green Hornet ep Beautiful Dreamer 10.2.66, 10.28.
    66 ABC
Run for Your Life ep Trip to the Far Side 10.11.67
    NBC
Ghost Story ep Alter Ego 10.26.72 NBC

HORTON, EDWARD EVERETT
    Magnavox Theatre ep Father, Dear Father 11.10.50
        CBS
    I Love Lucy ep 1.21.52 CBS
    Broadway Television Theatre ep The Nightcap 5.20.
        52 NN
    Broadway Television Theatre ep Whistling in the Dark
        3.9.53 NN
    Medallion Theatre ep The Bartlett Desk 9.19.53
        CBS
    Broadway Television Theatre ep The Front Page 10.
        18.53 NN
    Medallion Theatre ep The Centerville Ghost 11.21.53
        CBS
    Broadway Television Theatre ep Your Uncle Dudley
        12.7.53 NN
    Best of Broadway ep Arsenic and Old Lace 1.5.53
        CBS
    The Merry Widow Sp 4.9.55 NBC
    Damon Runyon Theatre ep A Light in France 7.30.
        55 CBS
    Shower of Stars ep Time out for Ginger 10.6.55
        CBS
    G.E. Theatre ep The Muse and Mr. Parkinson 1.22.
        56 CBS
    Damon Runyon Theatre ep A Light in France 4.21.56
        CBS
    Manhattan Tower Sp 10.27.56 NBC
    Playhouse 90 ep Three Men on a Horse 4.18.57
        CBS
    December Bride ep 12.16.57 CBS
    Real McCoys ep Teen-age Wedding 11.17.60 ABC
    Mr. Smith ep The Senator Baits a Hook 11.24.62
        ABC
    Saint and Sinners ep A Night of Horns and Bells 12.
        24.62 NBC
    Dennis the Menace ep My Uncle Ned 1.6.63 CBS

Our Man Higgins ep Who's on First? 5. 8. 63 ABC
Burke's Law ep Who Killed Eleanor Davis 12. 20. 63
ABC
Cara Williams Show ep 2. 10. 65 CBS
Valentine's Day ep For Me and My Sal 2. 19. 65 ABC
Burke's Law ep 4. 7. 65 ABC
F Troop sr 9. 14. 65 ABC
Camp Runamuck ep 12. 3. 65 NBC
Batman ep An Egg Grows in Gotham 10. 19. 66, 10.
20. 66 ABC
Love American Style ep 2. 27. 70 ABC
Governor and J. J. ep 10. 14. 70 CBS

HORTON, ROBERT
Ford Theatre ep Portrait of Lydia 12. 16. 54 NBC
Studio 57 ep The Will to Survive 1. 18. 55 NN
Public Defender ep In Memory of Murder 6. 2. 55
CBS
Your Play Time ep Call from Robert Jest 8. 6. 55
NBC
Kings Row sr 9. 13. 55 ABC
Cavalcade Theatre ep Danger at Clover Ridge 5. 8.
56 ABC
Alfred Hitchcock Presents ep The Decoy 6. 10. 56
CBS
Crossroads ep False Prophet 6. 2. 56 ABC
Alfred Hitchcock Presents ep Crack of Doom 11. 25.
56 CBS
Studio 57 ep The Road Back 12. 19. 56 NN
Alfred Hitchcock Presents ep Bottle of Wine 2. 3. 57
CBS
George Sanders Mystery Theatre ep Last Will and
Testament 7. 20. 57 ABC
Wagon Train sr 9. 18. 57 NBC
Alfred Hitchcock Presents ep Disappearing Trick 4.
6. 58 CBS
Matinee Theatre ep Much Ado about Nothing 5. 20. 58,
5. 21. 58 NBC
Studio One ep A Delicate Affair 7. 28. 58 CBS
Wagon Train sr ret 9. 24. 58 NBC
G. E. Theatre ep The Last Rodeo 12. 7. 58 CBS
Alfred Hitchcock Presents ep The Last Dark Step 2.
8. 59 CBS
Wagon Train sr ret 9. 30. 59 NBC
June Allyson Show ep No Place to Hide 12. 21. 59
CBS
Ford Star Time ep Jeff McCleod, the Last Reb

3.1.60 NBC
Barbara Stanwyck Theatre   ep   The Choice   4.17.61 NBC
Wagon Train   sr ret   9.27.61 NBC
U.S. Steel Hour   ep   The Perfect Accident   2.21.62 CBS
U.S. Steel Hour   ep   Mission of Fear   4.3.63 CBS
Shenandoah   sr   9.13.65 ABC
Dangerous Days of Kiowa Jones   tf   12.25.66 ABC
The Spy Killer   tf   11.10.69 ABC
Foreign Exchange   tf   1.13.70 ABC
Longstreet   ep   2.17.72 ABC

HOUGHTON, KATHARINE
ABC Stage 67   ep   The Confession   10.19.66 ABC
Judd for the Defense   ep   A Puff of Smoke   9.27.68 ABC

HOVEY, TIM
Lux Video Theatre   ep   The Gay Sisters   11.22.56 NBC
Playhouse 90   ep   The Family Nobody Wanted   12.20.56
   CBS
G.E. Theatre   ep   Kid at the Stick   15.58 CBS
Kraft Theatre   ep   Material Witness 2.9.58 NBC
Cimarron City   ep   Cimarron Holiday   12.20.58 NBC
Schlitz Playhouse of Stars   ep   Ivy League   3.13.59 CBS

HOWARD, KEN
Bonanza   ep   10.31.72 NBC
Medical Center   ep   The Outcast   11.15.72 CBS

HOWARD, RONALD
Sherlock Holmes   sr   10.18.54 NBC
Robin Hood   sr   9.26.55 CBS
Suspicion   ep   Lord Arthur Savile's Crime   1.13.58 NBC
Alfred Hitchcock Presents   ep   An Occurrence at Owl
   Creek Bridge   12.20.59 CBS
Alcoa Premiere   ep   The Haunting   3.8.60 ABC
Thriller   ep   Well of Doom   2.28.61 NBC
Alfred Hitchcock Theatre   ep   A Secret Life   5.30.61
   NBC
Thriller   ep   God Grante that She Lye Stille   10.23.61
   NBC
Combat   ep   What Are the Bugles Blowin' for   3.3.64,
   3.10.64 ABC

HOWARD, RONNY
Dennis the Menace   ep   Dennis by Proxy   5.22.60 CBS
Andy Griffith Show   sr   10.3.60 CBS
Pete and Gladys   ep   10.31.60 CBS

Andy Griffith Show   sr ret   10. 2. 61 CBS
G. E. Theatre   ep   Tippy-Top   12. 17. 61 CBS
Andy Griffith Show   sr ret   9. 30. 63 CBS
Eleventh Hour   ep   Is Mr. Martian Coming Back?   12.
    25. 63 NBC
Great Adventure   ep   Plague   2. 28. 64 CBS
Andy Griffith Show   sr ret   9. 21. 64 CBS
Dr. Kildare   ep   A Candle in the Window   11. 5. 64 NBC
Fugitive   ep   Cry Uncle   12. 1. 64 ABC
Andy Griffith Show   sr ret   9. 13. 65
Big Valley   ep   Night of the Wolf   12. 1. 65 ABC
Andy Griffith Show   sr ret   9. 12. 66 CBS
The Monroes   ep   3. 8. 67 ABC
World of Disney   ep   A Boy Called Nuthin'   12. 10. 67,
    12. 17. 67 NBC
FBI   ep   10. 13. 68 ABC
Lancer   ep   11. 19. 68 CBS
Judd for the Defense   ep   Between the Dark and the Day-
    light   2. 7. 69 ABC
Land of the Giants   ep   3. 9. 69 ABC
Daniel Boone   ep   4. 3. 69 NBC
Lancer   ep   The Measure of a Man   4. 8. 69 CBS
Gunsmoke   ep   11. 3. 69 CBS
World of Disney   ep   Smoke   2. 1. 70, 2. 8. 70 NBC
Headmaster   ep   10. 23. 70 CBS
Lassie   ep   11. 22. 70, 11. 29. 70 CBS
Bonanza   ep   9. 26. 72 NBC

HOWARD, TREVOR
Producers Showcase   ep   Tonight at 8:30   10. 18. 54 NBC
20th Century-Fox Hour   ep   Deception   3. 7. 56 CBS
Studio One   ep   Flower of Pride   3. 12. 56 CBS
Desilu Playhouse   ep   Murder in Gratitude   12. 11. 59
    CBS
Playhouse 90   ep   The Hiding Place   3. 22. 60 CBS
Hallmark Hall of Fame   ep   The Invincible Mr. Dis-
    raeli   4. 4. 63 NBC
Hedda Gabler   Sp   9. 20. 63 CBS
Hallmark Hall of Fame   ep   Eagle in a Cage   10. 20. 65
    NBC
The Poppy Is Also a Flower   tf   4. 22. 66 ABC

HUBER, HAROLD
I Cover Times Square   sr   10. 5. 50 ABC
The Web   ep   Trouble at San Rivera   5. 24. 53 CBS
Phil Silvers Show   ep   Bilko and the Chaplain   11. 28. 58
    CBS

HUDSON, ROCHELLE
  The Unexpected   ep   3.5.52 NBC
  That's My Boy   sr   4.10.54 CBS
  77 Sunset Strip   ep   The Legend of Leckonby   3.24.61
    ABC
  Branded   ep   The Mission   3.28.65 NBC

HUDSON, ROCK
  Once Upon a Dead Man   tf   9.17.71 NBC
  McMillan and Wife   sr   9.29.71 NBC
  McMillan and Wife   sr ret   9.24.72 NBC

HUGHES, MARY BETH
  Not for Publication   ep   Sing a Song of Six Pence   2.29.
    52 NN
  Philco Playhouse   ep   Double Jeopardy   1.4.53 NBC
  Ford Theatre   ep   The Fugitives   1.7.54 NBC
  Public Defender   ep   The Prize Fighter Story   4.8.54
    CBS
  Big Town   ep   10.11.54 NBC
  Front Row Center   ep   Dinner at Eight   6.1.55 CBS
  Big Town   ep   The Child Killer   8.17.55 NBC
  Front Row Center   ep   Guest in the House   8.22.55
    CBS
  Eve Arden Show   ep   11.5.57 CBS
  Colt .45   ep   Rebellion   12.20.57 ABC
  Playhouse 90   ep   No Time at All 2.13.58 CBS
  December Bride   ep   3.31.58 CBS
  Thin Man   ep   The Departed Doctor   4.4.58 NBC
  Studio One   ep   Birthday Present   8.18.58 CBS
  Pursuit   ep   Kiss Me Again, Stranger   11.19.58 CBS
  Rin Tin Tin   ep   Stagecoach to Phoenix   1.23.59 ABC
  Wanted Dead or Alive   ep   2.14.59 CBS
  Thin Man   ep   Mayhem to Music   3.20.59 NBC
  Rawhide   ep   Incident in No Man's Land   6.12.59 CBS
  Deputy   ep   Past and Present   1.21.61 NBC
  Rawhide   ep   Incident at Spider Rock   1.18.63 CBS

HULL, HENRY
  Armstrong Circle Theatre   ep   Ghost Town   4.10.51
    NBC
  Lights Out   ep   I, Spy   10.15.51 NBC
  Video Theatre   ep   Mr. Finchley Versus the Bomb   1.7.
    52 CBS
  Video Theatre   ep   Brigadier   7.21.52 CBS
  Danger   ep   Trial by Jungle   7.21.53 CBS
  The Web   ep   The Well   1.10.54 CBS

TV Soundstage   ep   The Test Case   3.26.54 NBC
TV Soundstage   ep   The Almighty Dollar   4.23.54 NBC
Center Stage   ep   Chivalry at Howling Creek   6.1.54
    ABC
Ray Milland Show   ep   10.14.54 CBS
U.S. Steel Hour   ep   Freighter   2.15.55 ABC
You Are There   ep   The Hatfield-McCoy Feud   3.20.55
    CBS
Appointment with Adventure   ep   Five in Judgment   4.
    10.55 CBS
Windows   ep   The Calliope Tree   8.26.55 CBS
Climax   ep   Figures in Clay   5.31.56 CBS
Trackdown   ep   12.5.58 CBS
Playhouse 90   ep   Face of a Hero   1.1.59 CBS
Wagon Train   ep   The Kitty Angel Story   1.7.59 NBC
Restless Gun   ep   The Last Gray Man   2.23.59 NBC
Naked City   ep   Fire Island   3.3.59 ABC
Restless Gun   ep   One on the House   4.20.59 NBC
Bonanza   ep   The Gunmen   1.23.60 NBC
Zane Grey Theatre   ep   Small Town that Died   3.10.60
    CBS
Goodyear Theatre   ep   All in the Family   3.28.60 NBC
Wagon Train   ep   Trial for Murder   4.27.60, 5.4.60
    NBC
Bonanza   ep   The Mission   9.17.60 NBC
Laramie   ep   Duel at Parkison Town   12.13.60 NBC
Wagon Train   ep   The Odyssey of Flint McCullough   2.
    15.61 NBC
Outlaws   ep   Culley   2.16.61 NBC
Best of the Post   ep   No Enemy   2.25.61 ABC
Play of the Week   ep   The Wooden Dish   3.20.61 NN
Alcoa Premiere   ep   The Man with the Shine on His
    Shoes   2.20.62 ABC
Laramie   ep   The Road to Helena   5.21.63 NBC
The Travels of Jaimie McPheeters   ep   12.15.63 ABC

HULL, JOSEPHINE
    Studio One   ep   Give Us Our Dream   1.16.50 CBS
    TV Playhouse   ep   Dear Ghosts and Guest   9.24.50
        NBC
    Video Theatre   ep   Grandma Was an Actress   10.1.51
        CBS
    Schlitz Playhouse of Stars   ep   Clean Sweep for Lavinia
        1.4.52 CBS
    Lights Out   ep   The Upstairs Floor   3.10.52 NBC
    Video Theatre   ep   The Wednesday Wish   3.16.53 CBS
    U.S. Steel Hour   ep   The Meanest Man in the World

7.6.55 CBS

HULL, WARREN
    Starlight Theatre   ep   With Baited Breath   8.9.51 CBS
    Public Prosecutor   sh   9.20.51 NN
    Armstrong Circle Theatre   ep   The Oldster   11.20.51
        NBC

HUNNICUT, GAYLE
    Get Smart   ep   1.7.67 NBC
    Beverly Hillbillies   ep   10.12.66 CBS
    The Smugglers   tf   12.24.68 NBC
    Love American Style   ep   2.19.71 ABC

HUNT, MARSHA
    Studio One   ep   Willow Cabin   2.13.50 CBS
    Cosmopolitan Theatre   ep   The Secret Front   12.2.51
        NN
    Ford Theatre   ep   Double Bet   11.26.53 NBC
    20th Century-Fox Hour   ep   Man of the Law   2.20.57
        CBS
    Climax   ep   A Taste for Crime   6.20.57 CBS
    Zane Grey Theatre   ep   A Gun Is for Killing   10.18.57
        CBS
    No Warning   ep   Stranded   5.4.58 NBC
    Climax   ep   Time of the Hanging   5.22.56 CBS
    Alfred Hitchcock Presents   ep   Tea Time   12.14.58 CBS
    Zane Grey Theatre   ep   Let the Man Die   12.18.58 CBS
    Zane Grey Theatre   ep   Checkmate   4.30.59 CBS
    Peck's Bad Girl   sr   5.5.59 CBS
    Laramie   ep   Circle of Fire   9.29.59 NBC
    Detectives   ep   The Prowler   4.22.60 ABC
    Zane Grey Theatre.   ep   The Man from Yesterday   12.
        22.60 CBS
    Cain's Hundred   ep   The Debasers   1.16.62 NBC
    Sam Benedict   ep   Too Many Strangers   12.8.62 NBC
    Breaking Point   ep   And James Was a Very Small Snail
        11.11.63 ABC
    Gunsmoke   ep   1.4.64 CBS
    Channing   ep   A Rich, Famous, Glamorous Folk Singer
        Like Me   1.8.64 ABC
    Outer Limits   ep   "ZZZZZ"   1.27.64 ABC
    Twilight Zone   ep   Spur of the Moment   2.21.64 CBS
    Defenders   ep   Die Laughing   4.11.64 CBS
    Profiles in Courage   ep   12.6.64 NBC
    Run for Your Life   ep   Hoodlums on Wheels   2.22.66
        NBC

My Three Sons ep   12.2.67 CBS
Accidental Family ep   12.15.67 NBC
Outsider ep Along Came a Spider 10.2.68 NBC
Fear No Evil tf 3.3.69 NBC
Ironside ep Little Dog, Gone 4.2.70 NBC
Young Lawyers ep   10.26.70 ABC
Ironside ep The Riddle in Room Six 2.25.71 NBC
Jigsaw tf 3.26.72 ABC

HUNTER, JEFFREY
Climax ep South of the Sun 3.3.55 CBS
20th Century-Fox Hour ep The Empty Room 5.30.56
  CBS
Climax ep Hurricane Diane 12.12.57 CBS
Pursuit ep Kiss Me Again Stranger 11.19.58 CBS
Our American Heritage ep Tiny West 1.24.60 NBC
World of Disney ep The Secret Mission 5.7.61, 5.14.
  61 ABC
Checkmate ep Waiting for Jock 10.25.61 CBS
Alfred Hitchcock Theatre ep Don't Look Behind You
  9.27.62 CBS
Combat ep Lost Sheep, Lost Shepherd 10.16.62 ABC
Temple Houston sr 9.19.63 NBC
Bob Hope's Chrysler Theatre ep Seven Miles of Bad
  Road 10.18.63 NBC
Death Valley Days ep Suzie 2.15.64 ABC
Bob Hope Chrysler Theatre ep Parties to the Crime
  11.27.64 NBC
Kraft Suspense Theatre ep The Trains for Silence 6.
  10.65 NBC
FBI ep The Monster 9.19.65 ABC
Jesse James ep Field of Wild Flowers 4.25.66 ABC
Star Trek ep 11.17.66, 11.24.66 NBC
Daniel Boone ep 12.1.66 NBC
Monroes ep 2.15.67 ABC
FBI ep The Enemies 11.3.68 ABC

HUNTER, KIM
Robert Montgomery Presents ep Rise up and Walk
  2.4.52 NBC
Celanese Theatre ep The Petrified Forest 2.20.52
  ABC
Omnibus ep The Trial of St. Joan 1.2.55 CBS
Appointment with Adventure ep Ride the Comet 6.19.
  55 CBS
Screen Directors Playhouse ep A Midsummer Day-
  dream 10.19.55 NBC

Climax ep Portrait in Celluloid 11. 24. 55 CBS
G. E. Theatre ep Try to Remember 2. 26. 56 CBS
U. S. Steel Hour ep Moment of Courage 2. 29. 56 CBS
G. E. Theatre ep Orphans 12. 2. 56 CBS
On Trial ep The Person and Property of Margery Hay
    12. 7. 56 NBC
Playhouse 90 ep The Comedian 2. 14. 56 CBS
Kaiser Aluminum Hour ep Whereabout Unknown 2. 26.
    57 NBC
Studio 57 ep Perfect Likeness 6. 23. 57 NN
Playhouse 90 ep The Dark Side of the Earth 9. 19. 57
    CBS
Playhouse 90 ep Before I Die 1. 23. 58 CBS
Climax ep So Deadly My Love 3. 13. 58 CBS
Studio One ep Ticket to Tahiti 6. 2. 58 CBS
Climax ep Cabin B-13 6. 26. 58 CBS
Playhouse 90 ep Free Week-End 12. 4. 58 CBS
Alcoa Theatre ep The Dark File 12. 29. 58 NBC
Playhouse 90 ep The Sounds of Eden 10. 15. 59 CBS
Adventures in Paradise ep The Haunted 12. 21. 59 ABC
Play of the Week ep The Closing Door 1. 4. 60 NN
G. E. Theatre ep Early to Die 2. 7. 60 CBS
Sunday Showcase ep The Secret of Freedom 2. 28. 60
    NBC
Playhouse 90 ep Alas, Babylon 4. 3. 60 CBS
Play of the Week ep The Sound of Murder 2. 13. 61
    NN
Hallmark Hall of Fame ep Give Us Barabas 3. 26. 61
    NBC
Naked City ep The Face of the Enemy 1. 3. 62 ABC
Dick Powell ep Tomorrow the Man 10. 2. 62 NBC
U. S. Steel Hour ep Wanted: Someone Innocent 10. 17.
    62 CBS
Eleventh Hour ep Of Roses and Nightingales and Other
    Lovely Things 11. 7. 62 NBC
Breaking Point ep Crack in an Image 10. 28. 63 ABC
Arrest and Trial ep Some Weeks Are All Monday 12.
    15. 63 ABC
Alfred Hitchcock Theatre ep The Evil of Adelaide
    Winters 2. 7. 64 CBS
Defenders ep The Unwritten Law 2. 4. 65 CBS
Dr. Kildare ep Something Old, Something New 12. 6.
    65, 12. 7. 65 NBC
Hallmark Hall of Fame ep Lamp at Midnight 4. 27. 66
    NBC
Hawk ep Wall of Silence 12. 22. 66 ABC
Mannix ep The Name is Mannix 9. 16. 67 CBS

Bonanza   ep   The Price of Salt   2.4.68 NBC
World of Disney   ep   The Young Loner   2.25.68, 3.3.
    68 NBC
CBS Playhouse   ep   The People Next Door   10.15.68
    CBS
Dial Hot Line   tf   3.8.70 ABC
Young Lawyers   ep   The Alienation Kick   10.17.70
    ABC
Bracken's World   ep   A Team of One-Legged Acrobats
    11.6.70 NBC
Mannix   ep   Deja Vu   12.12.70 CBS
Bold Ones   ep   1.3.71 NBC
In Search of America   tf   3.23.71 ABC
Gunsmoke   ep   10.18.71 CBS
Columbo   ep   11.17.71 NBC
Medical Center   ep   The Imposter   9.29.71 CBS
Night Gallery   ep   The Late Mr. Peddington   1.12.72
    NBC
Owen Marshall   ep   9.21.72 ABC

HUNTER, TAB
Ford Theatre   ep   While We're Young   4.28.55 NBC
Lux Video Theatre   ep   Lightning Strikes Twice   6.9.55
    NBC
Climax   ep   Fear Strikes Out   8.18.55 CBS
Playhouse 90   ep   Forbidden Area   10.4.56 CBS
Conflict   ep   The People Against McQuade   11.13.56
    ABC
Hallmark Hall of Fame   ep   Hans Brinker   2.9.58 NBC
Playhouse 90   ep   Portrait of a Murderer   2.27.58 CBS
Meet Me in St. Louis   Sp   4.26.59 CBS
G.E. Theatre   ep   Disaster   11.1.59 CBS
Tab Hunter Show   sr   9.19.60 NBC
Saints and Sinners   ep   Three Columns of Anger   10.22.
    66 NBC
Combat   ep   The Celebrity   11.27.62 ABC
Burke's Law   ep   3.13.64 ABC
Virginian   ep   The Gift   3.18.70 NBC
San Francisco International Airport   tf   9.29.70 ABC
World of Disney   ep   Hacksaw   9.26.71, 10.3.71 CBS
Cannon   ep   1.11.72   ABC
Owen Marshall   ep   12.7.72 ABC

HUSSEY, RUTH
Pulitzer Prize Playhouse   ep   The Magnificent Amber-
    sons   11.3.50 ABC
Video Theatre   ep   Gallant Lady   11.13.50 CBS

Celanese Theatre ep Counsellor-at-Law 11.28.51
   ABC
Drama ep The Joyful Hour 12.25.51 ABC
Ford Theatre ep This Is My Heart 1.15.53 NBC
G.E. Theatre ep Winners Never Lose 3.15.53 CBS
Video Theatre ep The Moon for Linda 10.8.53 CBS
Mirror Theatre ep Flight from Home 10.10.53 CBS
G.E. Theatre ep To Lift a Feather 5.2.54 CBS
Studio One ep The Boy Who Changed the World 10.
   18.54 CBS
Elgin Hour ep Warm Clay 11.16.54 ABC
Producers Showcase ep The Women 2.7.55 NBC
Climax ep The Unimportant Man 6.2.55 CBS
Science Fiction Theatre ep 100 Years Young 7.22.55
   NBC
Shower of Stars ep Time Out for Ginger 10.6.55
   CBS
Fireside Theatre ep Women at Sea 11.29.55 NBC
Studio 57 ep The Magic Glass 3.18.56 NN
Alfred Hitchcock Presents ep Mink 6.3.56 CBS
Climax ep A Trophy for Howard Davenport 6.28.56
   CBS
Lux Video Theatre ep Old Acquaintance 11.29.56
   NBC
Lux Video Theatre ep Payment in Kind 6.6.57 NBC
Climax ep Along Came a Spider 9.26.57 CBS
Marcus Welby, M.D. ep The Best Is Yet to Be 11.
   16.71 ABC
Jimmy Stewart Show ep 1.23.72 NBC

HUTCHINS, WILL
   Conflict ep Stranger on the Road 12.11.56 ABC
   Matinee Theatre ep The Wisp End 12.14.56 NBC
   Conflict ep Capital Punishment 3.5.57 ABC
   Conflict ep Stranger on the Road 6.11.57 ABC
   Sugarfoot sr 9.17.57 ABC
   Sugarfoot sr ret 9.58 ABC
   Sugarfoot sr ret 9.59 ABC
   77 Sunset Strip ep The Kookie Caper 10.9.59 ABC
   Sugarfoot sr ret 9.60 ABC
   Maverick ep Hadler's Hunters 9.25.60 ABC
   Maverick ep Bolt from the Blue 11.27.60 ABC
   Roaring 20s cp Pie in the Sky 2.25.61 ABC
   Gunsmoke ep 2.23.63 CBS
   Alfred Hitchcock Theatre ep The Star Juror 3.15.63
      CBS
   Perry Mason ep The Case of the Scarlet Scandal

2.20.66 CBS
Hey Landlord sr 9.11.66 NBC
Blondie sr 9.26.68 CBS
Love American Style ep 1.7.72 ABC

HUTCHINSON, JOSEPHINE
Playhouse ep The House Where Time Stopped 4.
17.55 ABC
Your Play Time ep Wait for George 8.13.55 NN
20th Century-Fox Hour ep The Man Who Couldn't Wait
3.20.57 CBS
Schlitz Playhouse of Stars ep Sister Louise Goes to
Town 5.24.57 CBS
Matinee Theatre ep Ivy Curtain 11.6.57 NBC
Perry Mason ep The Case of the Screaming Woman
4.26.58 CBS
Perry Mason ep The Case of the Spanish Cross 5.30.
59 CBS
Gunsmoke ep 10.3.59 CBS
Lineup ep Prince of Penmen 12.30.59 CBS
Wagon Train ep The Tom Tuckett Story 3.2.60 NBC
Rifleman ep The Prodigal 4.26.60 ABC
Deputy ep Mother and Son 10.29.60 NBC
Checkmate ep A Matter of Conscience 2.18.61 CBS
G.E. Theatre ep A Possibility of Oil 2.19.61 CBS
Perry Mason ep The Case of the Barefaced Witness
3.18.61 CBS
Tales of Wells Fargo ep Lady Trouble 4.24.61 NBC
New Breed ep Mr. Weltschmerz 2.13.62 ABC
Rawhide ep Grandma's Money 2.23.62 CBS
Perry Mason ep The Case of the Mystified Miner 2.
24.62 CBS
G.E. True ep The Black-Robed Ghost 3.10.63 CBS
Kraft Suspense Theatre ep The Machine that Played
God 12.5.63 NBC
Dr. Kildare ep The Last Leaves on the Tree 10.15.
64 NBC
Founders ep 12.20.66 ABC
Gunsmoke ep 3.25.67 CBS
Shadow over Elveron tf 3.5.68 NBC
Name of the Game ep 10.18.68 NBC
Then Came Bronson ep All the World and God 12.3.
69 NBC
Bold Ones ep If I Can't Sing, I'll Listen 1.18.70 NBC
Mod Squad ep A Short Course in War 1.5.71 ABC
Mannix ep Dark So Early, Dark So Long 9.15.71 CBS
Longstreet ep A World of Perfect Complicity 9.23.71
ABC

The Homecoming Sp 12.19.71 CBS
Sixth Sense ep 11.25.72 ABC

HUTTON, BETTY
   Satan and Spurs Sp 9.12.54 NBC
   Goldie sr 10.1.59 CBS
   The Greatest Show on Earth ep The Glorious Day of
      Used to Be 3.31.64 ABC
   Burke's Law ep 5.8.64 ABC
   Gunsmoke ep 5.1.65 CBS

HUTTON, JIM
   Twilight Zone ep And When the Sky Was Opened 12.
      11.59 CBS
   Father Knows Best ep Betty's Career Problem 4.25.
      60 CBS
   The Psychiatrist ep The Private World of Martin Dal-
      ton 2.10.71 NBC
   Name of the Game ep The Savage Eye 2.19.71 NBC
   The Deadly Hunt tf 10.1.71 CBS
   The Reluctant Heroes tf 11.23.71 ABC
   They Call It Murder tf 12.17.71 NBC
   Love American Style ep 2.4.72 ABC
   Call Her Mom tf 2.15.72 ABC
   Call Holme pt 4.24.72 NBC
   Wednesday Night Out pt 4.24.72 NBC

HUTTON, ROBERT
   Gruen Guild Playhouse ep Al Haddon's Lamp 5.8.52
      NN
   Campbell Playhouse ep Hit and Run 7.18.52 NBC
   Gruen Guild Playhouse ep Emergency 8.12.52 NN
   Schaefer Century Theatre ep Cafe Berlin 8.27.52
      NBC
   The Unexpected ep The Puppeteers 9.17.52 NBC
   Schaefer Century Theatre ep Portfolio Twelve 10.5.
      52 NBC
   Schlitz Playhouse of Stars ep The House of Pride
      11.14.52 CBS
   Fireside Theatre ep A Kiss for Aunt Sophie 12.30.
      52 NBC
   Jewelers Showcase ep The Bean Farm 3.24.53 CBS
   Death Valley Days ep Sego Lilies 5.19.53 NN
   Mirror Theatre ep Surprise Party 10.24.53 CBS
   Pepsi Cola Playhouse ep Vacation Wife 12.4.53 ABC
   Jewelers Showcase ep Christmas Is Magic 12.8.53
      NN

Fireside Theatre ep The Insufferable Woman 1.19.54
NBC
Dangerous Encounter ep I Saw It Happen 2.21.54
NN
G. E. Theatre ep Too Old for the Girl 9.19.54 CBS
Fireside Theatre ep Three Mission West 11.30.54
NBC
TV Reader's Digest ep Around the Horn to Matrimony
5.23.55 ABC
The Millionaire ep The Story of Don Lewis 12.7.55
CBS
Crossroads ep The Gambler 12.9.55 ABC
Ford Theatre ep That Evil Woman 3.15.56 NBC
TV Reader's Digest ep The Man Who Dreamt Winners
5.28.56 ABC
Crossroads ep The Miracle of Faith 6.7.57 ABC
Wyatt Earp ep The Toughest Judge in Arizona 5.24.
60 ABC
Hawaiian Eye ep A Touch of Velvet 1.11.61 ABC
77 Sunset Strip ep The Six out of Eight Caper 4.21.
61 ABC

HYDE-WHITE, WILFRID
Douglas Fairbanks, Jr. Presents ep The Priceless
Pocket 11.11.53 NBC
Alcoa Hour ep Mrs. Gilling and the Skyscraper 6.9.
57 NBC
Route 66 ep An Absence of Tears 3.3.61 CBS
Ben Casey ep Monument to an Aged Hunter 3.19.62
ABC
Twilight Zone ep Passage on the Lady Anne 5.9.63
CBS
Ben Casey ep Evidence of Things Not Seen 4.22.64
ABC
Ben Casey ep From Sutter's Crick 5.10.65 ABC
Ben Casey ep When Givers Prove Unkind 11.22.65,
11.29.65 ABC
Ben Casey ep Why Did the Day Go Backwards? 12.6.
65 ABC
Peyton Place sr 9.67 ABC
Mission Impossible ep 12.10.67 CBS
Daniel Boone ep 2.8.68 NBC
The Sunshine Patriot tf 12.16.68 NBC
Name of the Game ep The Suntan Gang 2.7.69 NBC
Fear No Evil tf 3.3.69 NBC
Run a Crooked Mile tf 11.18.69 ABC
It Takes a Thief ep To Lure a Man tf 12.18.69 ABC

Ritual of Evil   tf   2.23.70 NBC
Paris 7000   ep   Ordeal   2.26.70 ABC
Most Deadly Game   ep   I Said the Sparrow   1.16.71 ABC
Cool Million   ep   11.22.72 NBC
Columbo   ep   11.26.72 NBC

HYER, MARTHA
Jewelers Showcase   ep   Teacher of the Year   12.2.52
    CBS
The Curtain Rises   ep   Exit--Linda Davis   3.9.53 ABC
Four Star Playhouse   ep   Meet a Lonely Man   12.2.54
    CBS
Best of Broadway   ep   Broadway   5.4.55 CBS
Lux Video Theatre   ep   Lady Gambles   10.27.55 NBC
Lux Video Theatre   ep   Ivy   1.19.56 NBC
Lux Video Theatre   ep   Jezebel   11.8.56 NBC
Playhouse 90   ep   Reunion   1.2.58 CBS
Climax   ep   The Push-Button Giant   5.29.58 CBS
Rawhide   ep   Incident West of Lano   2.27.59 CBS
Deputy   ep   Hang the Law   1.9.60 NBC
Zane Grey Theatre   ep   Morning Incident   12.29.60 CBS
Alfred Hitchcock Theatre   ep   A Piece of the Action   9.
    20.62 CBS
Burke's Law   ep   Who Killed Wade Walker   11.15.63
    ABC
The Greatest Show on Earth   ep   The Show Must Go on
    to Orange City   1.28.64 ABC
Burke's Law   ep   1.31.64 ABC
Kraft Suspense Theatre   ep   Doesn't Anybody Know Who
    I Am   2.27.64 NBC
Burke's Law   ep   4.24.64 ABC
Burke's Law   ep   10.28.64 ABC
Farmer's Daughter   ep   The Name of the Game   10.30.
    64 ABC
Alfred Hitchcock Theatre   ep   The Crimson Witness   1.
    4.65 NBC
Burke's Law   ep   4.28.65 ABC
Branded   ep   10,000 for Durango   11.28.65 NBC
Judd for the Defense   ep   11.17.67 ABC
Family Affair   ep   12.18.67 CBS
Name of the Game   ep   The Ordeal   11.22.68 NBC
It Takes a Thief   ep   11.20.69 ABC
Men from Shiloh   ep   9.16.70 NBC
Young Lawyers   ep   The Victims   1.27.71 ABC
O'Hara, U.S. Treasury   ep   3.3.72 CBS

HYLAND, DIANA

    Play of the Week ep The Climate of Eden 2.29.60
    NN

    Play of the Week ep No Exit 2.27.61 NN

    Play of the Week ep A Cool Wind over the Living 3.
    27.61 NN

    Defenders ep The Unwanted 10.13.62 CBS

    U.S. Steel Hour ep Someone Innocent 10.17.62 CBS

    Alcoa Premiere ep The Voice of Charlie Pont 10.25.
    62 ABC

    Sam Benedict ep The Bird of Warning 11.17.62 NBC

    Dr. Kildare ep Love Is a Sad Song 1.3.63 NBC

    Alfred Hitchcock Theatre ep To Catch a Butterfly
    2.1.63 CBS

    Ben Casey ep Rigadoon for Three Pianos 3.4.63 ABC

    Stoney Burke ep To Catch the Kaiser 3.11.63 ABC

    Dupont Show of the Month ep The Shark 4.7.63 NBC

    Wagon Train ep The Kitty Pryor Story 11.18.63
    ABC

    Alfred Hitchcock Theatre ep Beyond the Sea of Death
    1.24.64 CBS

    Twilight Zone ep Spur of the Moment 2.21.64 CBS

    Eleventh Hour ep Full Moon Every Night 3.4.64
    NBC

    Dr. Kildare ep Please Let My Baby Live 1.28.65
    NBC

    Burke's Law ep 2.10.65 ABC

    Rogues ep Run for the Money 2.14.65 NBC

    Doctors/Nurses ep The April Thaw of Dr. Mai 3.30.
    65 CBS

    Hercules Sp 9.12.65 ABC

    Run for Your Life ep The Girl Next Door Is a Spy
    9.20.65 NBC

    Wackiest Ship in the Army ep 9.26.65 NBC

    Convoy ep 10.29.65 NBC

    Fugitive ep Set Fire to a Straw Man 11.30.65 ABC

    Wackiest Ship in the Army ep Wide Isthmus 12.19.65
    NBC

    Bob Hope Chrysler Theatre ep Guilty or Not Guilty
    3.9.66 NBC

    Shenandoah ep An Unfamiliar Tune 4.11.66 ABC

    Iron Horse ep Joy Unconfirmed 9.12.66 ABC

    Green Hornet ep Give 'em Enough Rope 9.16.66 ABC

    Run for Your Life ep I Am the Late Diana Hays 9.
    19.66 NBC

    12 O'Clock High ep Practice to Deceive 10.14.66
    ABC

The Man from U.N.C.L.E.   ep   The Candidate's Wife
    Affair   11.4.66 NBC
Felony Squad   ep   11.14.66 ABC
Fugitive   ep   12.6.66 ABC
Invaders   ep   1.2.67 ABC
FBI   ep   2.19.67 ABC
Fugitive   ep   3.28.67 ABC
Tarzan   ep   The Fanatics   10.27.67 NBC
Invaders   ep   The Summer Meeting   10.31.67, 11.7.67,
    ABC
FBI   ep   11.12.67 ABC
Judd for the Defense   ep   1.5.68, 1.12.68 ABC
Peyton Place   sr   3.68 ABC
Name of the Game   ep   The Perfect Image   11.7.69
    NBC
Ritual of Evil   tf   2.23.70 NBC
Bracken's World   ep   The Mary Tree   10.23.70 NBC
FBI   ep   The Stalking Horse   1.10.71 ABC
Ironside   ep   From Hruska with Love   1.21.71 NBC
Marcus Welby, M.D.   ep   2.23.71 ABC
Alias Smith and Jones   ep   Return to Devil's Hole   2.
    25.71 ABC
Dan August   ep   Days of Rage   3.25.71 ABC
Medical Center   ep   Suspected   11.17.71 CBS
Earth II   tf   11.28.71 NBC
FBI   ep   Arrangement with Terror   2.6.72 ABC
Banyon   ep   9.29.72 NBC

HYLANDS, SCOTT
    Ironside   ep   And Then There Was One   1.20.72 NBC
    The Glass House   tf   2.4.72 CBS
    Cannon   ep   9.27.72 CBS
    Sixth Sense   ep   9.30.72 ABC

-I-

INESCOURT, FRIEDA
    Fireside Theatre   ep   Hope Chest   10.17.50 NBC
    Schaefer Century Theatre   ep   From Such a Seed   6.21.
        52 NBC
    Fireside Theatre   ep   The Old Order Changeth   2.2.54
        NBC
    G.E. Theatre   ep   The Crime of Daphne Rutledge   6.13.
        54 CBS

Ray Milland Show   ep   Stagestruck   11.18.54 CBS
Climax   ep   The Dance   6.30.55 CBS
Four Star Playhouse   ep   A Place Full of Strangers
   12.8.55 CBS
Crossroads   ep   God's Healing   11.30.56 ABC
December Bride   ep   Masquerade Party   3.11.57 CBS
The Millionaire   ep   The Regina Wainwright Story   12.
   25.57 CBS
Tab Hunter Show   ep   Devil to Pay   12.1.60 NBC
Rebel   ep   Mission--Varina   5.14.61 ABC

INGELS, MARTY
   I'm Dickens...He's Fenster   sr   9.28.62 ABC

INGRAM, REX
   Kraft Theatre   ep   The Emperor Jones   2.23.55 NBC
   Your Play Time   ep   The Intolerable Portrait   9.3.55
      NBC
   Black Saddle   ep   1.24.59 NBC
   Law and Mr. Jones   ep   The Storyville Gang   11.25.60
      ABC
   Lloyd Bridges Theatre   ep   Gentlemen in Blue   12.11.
      62 CBS
   Sam Benedict   ep   A Split Week in San Quentin   4.20.
      63 NBC
   Breaking Point   ep   3.30.64 ABC
   I Spy   ep   Weight of the World   12.1.65 NBC
   Daktari   ep   2.28.67 CBS
   Daktari   ep   1.9.68 CBS
   Cowboy in Africa   ep   4.1.68 ABC
   Gunsmoke   ep   The Good Samaritans   3.10.69 CBS

IRELAND, JILL
   Ben Casey   ep   The Lonely One   3.4.64 ABC
   The Man from U.N.C.L.E.   ep   The Quadripartite Af-
      fair   10.6.64 NBC
   Voyage to the Bottom of the Sea   ep   The Price of
      Doom   10.12.64 ABC
   The Man from U.N.C.L.E.   ep   The Giuoco Piano Af-
      fair   11.10.64 NBC
   Mystery Hour   ep   The Desperate Men   3.2.65 NN
   12 O'Clock High   ep   The Hot Shot   10.18.65 ABC
   My Favorite Martian   ep   11.14.65 CBS
   The Man from U.N.C.L.E.   ep   The Tigers Are Com-
      ing Affair   11.15.65 NBC
   Wackiest Ship in the Army   ep   2.6.66 NBC
   12 O'Clock High   ep   The Survivor   2.21.66 ABC

Shane   sr   9.10.66 ABC
Star Trek   ep   3.2.67 NBC
The Man from U.N.C.L.E.   ep   3.31.67, 4.7.67 NBC
Mannix   ep   10.19.68 CBS
Daniel Boone   ep   10.30.69 NBC

IRELAND, JOHN
    Philco Playhouse   ep   Confession 1.21.51 NBC
    Schlitz Playhouse of Stars   ep   The Man I Marry   1.18.
      52 CBS
    Schlitz Playhouse of Stars   ep   Prisoner in the Town
      5.7.54 CBS
    Schlitz Playhouse of Stars   ep   Reunion at Steepler's
      Hill   9.17.54 CBS
    Philco Playhouse   ep   Time Bomb   10.3.54 NBC
    Elgin Hour   ep   The Bridge   1.11.55 ABC
    Schlitz Playhouse of Stars   ep   Murder in Paradise   1.
      28.55 CBS
    Schlitz Playhouse of Stars   ep   Ride to the West   3.18.
      55 CBS
    Damon Runyon Theatre   ep   There's No Forever   9.20.
      55 CBS
    Studio 57   ep   Lonely Man   9.18.55 NBC
    Schlitz Playhouse of Stars   ep   Dealer's Choice   1.13.
      56 CBS
    G.E. Theatre   ep   Prologue to Glory   2.12.56 CBS
    Schlitz Playhouse of Stars   ep   Ordeal   2.24.56 CBS
    Fireside Theatre   ep   This Land Is Mine   4.10.56 NBC
    Zane Grey Theatre   ep   Return to Nowhere   12.7.56
      CBS
    Lux Video Theatre   ep   Black Angel   3.28.57 NBC
    Climax   ep   Avalanche at Devil's Pass   4.24.57 CBS
    Playhouse 90   ep   Without Incident   6.6.57 CBS
    Playhouse 90   ep   A Sound of Different Drummers   10.
      3.57 CBS
    Suspicion   ep   End of Violence   1.20.58 NBC
    Riverboat   ep   The Fight Back   10.18.59 NBC
    Ford Star Time   ep   Close Set   2.16.60 NBC
    Cheaters   sr   1.30.61 NN
    Thriller   ep   Papa Benjamin   3.21.61 NBC
    Asphalt Jungle   ep   The Last Way Out   5.7.61 ABC
    Dick Powell Theatre   ep   Obituary for Mr. "X"   1.23.
      62 NBC
    Alfred Hitchcock Theatre   ep   The Matched Pearl   4.
      24.62 NBC
    Rawhide   ep   Incident of the Portrait   10.5.62 CBS
    Burke's Law   ep   Who Killed Alex Debbs   10.25.63
      ABC

Kraft Suspense Theatre   ep   A Hero for Our Times
10. 31. 63 NBC
Mr. Broadway   ep   Pay Now, Die Later   11. 26. 64
CBS
Branded   ep   Leap Upon Mountains   2. 28. 65 NBC
Burke's Law   ep   4. 14. 65 ABC
Rawhide   ep   The Spanish Camp   5. 7. 65 CBS
Rawhide   sr   9. 21. 65 CBS
Shenandoah   ep   Marlee   3. 14. 66 ABC
Branded   ep   Cowards Die Many Times   4. 17. 66 NBC
Gunsmoke   ep   11. 26. 66 CBS
Iron Horse   ep   Appointment with an Epitaph   2. 13. 67
ABC
Bonanza   ep   2. 26. 67 NBC
Daniel Boone   ep   4. 13. 67 NBC
Gunsmoke   ep   10. 2. 67, 10. 9. 67 CBS
Name of the Game   ep   The Power   12. 12. 69 NBC
Men from Shiloh   ep   9. 30. 70 NBC
Assignment Vienna   ep   Hot Potato   10. 18. 72 ABC
Mission Impossible   ep   12. 2. 72 CBS
Ghost Story   ep   12. 15. 72 NBC

IVAN, ROSALIND
Studio One   ep   Sane as a Hatter   7. 11. 55 CBS

IVES, BURL
U. S. Steel Hour   ep   To Die Alone   1. 6. 57 CBS
Playhouse 90   ep   The Miracle Worker   2. 7. 57 CBS
G. E. Theatre   ep   Absalom, My Son   12. 6. 59 CBS
Zane Grey Theatre   ep   The Ox   11. 3. 60 CBS
O. K. Crackerby   sr   9. 16. 65 ABC
Name of the Game   ep   The Taker   10. 4. 68 NBC
Hallmark Hall of Fame   ep   Pinocchio   12. 8. 68 NBC
The Sound of Anger   tf   12. 10. 68 NBC
Daniel Boone   ep   1. 16. 69 NBC
The Whole World Is Watching   tf   3. 11. 69 NBC
Daniel Boone   ep   3. 13. 69 NBC
Bold Ones   sr   9. 21. 69 NBC
Bold Ones   sr ret   9. 20. 70 NBC
The Man Who Wanted to Live Forever   tf   12. 15. 70
ABC
Alias Smith and Jones   ep   The McCreedy Bust   1. 21.
70 ABC
Bold Ones   sr ret   9. 19. 71 NBC
Alias Smith and Jones   ep   1. 13. 72 ABC
Alias Smith and Jones   ep   9. 30. 72 ABC
Night Gallery   ep   11. 19. 72 NBC

-J-

JACKSON, ANNE
  Armstrong Circle Theatre   ep   Johnny Pickup   8.28.51
    NBC
  Drama   ep   The Vanished Hours   5.28.52 CBS
  The Doctor   ep   Marti   12.14.52 NBC
  The Doctor   ep   Night Riders in Apartment A   12.28.52
    NBC
  The Doctor   ep   The Decision   2.8.53 NBC
  The Doctor   ep   No Rap Charlie   5.17.53 NBC
  Philco Playhouse   ep   The Big Deal   7.19.53 NBC
  Philco Playhouse   ep   Statute of Limitations   2.21.54
    NBC
  Goodyear Playhouse   ep   The Merry-Go-Round   9.25.55
    NBC
  G.E. Theatre   ep   O'Hoolihan and the Leprechaun   6.3.
    56   CBS
  Play of the Week   ep   Lullaby   1.18.60 NN
  G.E. Theatre   ep   Aches and Pains   5.12.62 CBS
  Untouchables   ep   Cooker in the Sky   10.2.62 ABC
  Defenders   ep   Moment of Truth   3.21.64   CBS
  CBS Playhouse   ep   Dear Friends   12.6.67 CBS
  Hollywood Television Theatre   ep   The Typists   10.10.71
    NN
  Gunsmoke   ep   2.21.72 CBS
  Marcus Welby, M.D.   ep   3.7.72 ABC

JACKSON, GLENDA
  Masterpiece Theatre   ep   Elizabeth R   sr   3.5.72 NN

JACKSON, SHERRY
  Make Room for Daddy   (a.k.a. The Danny Thomas Show)
    sr   9.29.53 ABC
  The Danny Thomas Show   sr ret   fall, 1954 ABC
  The Danny Thomas Show   sr ret   fall, 1955 ABC
  The Charlie Farrel Show   ep   7.23.56 CBS
  The Danny Thomas Show   sr ret   10.1.56 ABC
  The Danny Thomas Show   sr ret   10.7.57 CBS
  Maverick   ep   Naked Gallows   12.15.57 ABC
  Crime Detective   ep   No Woman in the Chair   12.23.57
    NN
  The Danny Thomas Show   sr ret   fall, 1958 CBS
  Lucille Ball-Desi Arnaz Hour   ep   Lucy Makes Room

for Danny   12.1.58 CBS
The Danny Thomas Show   sr ret   10.5.59 CBS
77 Sunset Strip   ep   The Kookie Caper   10.9.59 ABC
77 Sunset Strip   ep   Texas Doll   12.11.59 ABC
World of Disney   ep   Tory Vengeance   1.1.60 CBS
The Millionaire   ep   Millionaire Susan Johnson   4.6.60
   CBS
Dobie Gillis   ep   4.12.60 CBS
77 Sunset Strip   ep   The Office Caper   10.7.60 ABC
Surfside 6   ep   High Tide   10.10.60 ABC
77 Sunset Strip   ep   Trouble in the Middle East   11.11.
   60 ABC
Bringing up Buddy   ep   Buddy and Janie   6.5.61 CBS
Tall Man   ep   Apache Daughter   12.30.61 NBC
New Breed   ep   Care Is No Cure   1.23.62 ABC
Twilight Zone   ep   The Last Rites of Jeff Myrtlebank
   2.23.62 CBS
Gunsmoke   ep   10.6.62 CBS
Mr. Novak   ep   The Risk   10.29.63 NBC
Perry Mason   ep   The Case of the Festive Falcon   11.
   28.63 CBS
Wagon Train   ep   1.20.64 ABC
Virginian   ep   Show Me a Hero   11.17.65 NBC
Lost in Space   ep   The Space Croppers   3.30.66 CBS
Batman   ep   Death in Slow Motion   4.27.66, 4.28.66
   ABC
Star Trek   ep   12.22.66 NBC
Wild, Wild West   ep   2.10.67 CBS
Wild, Wild West   ep   10.25.68 CBS
Make Room for Granddaddy   sr   9.24.70 ABC
Wild Women   tf   10.20.70 ABC
The Immortal   ep   10.24.70 ABC
Love American Style   ep   12.17.71 ABC

JACOBI, LOU
Douglas Fairbanks Jr. Presents   ep   My Favorite Aunt
   7.22.53 NBC
Texan   ep   1.26.59 CBS
Playhouse 90   ep   Child of Our Time   2.5.59 CBS
Play of the Week   ep   Volpone   3.7.60 NN
Sam Benedict   ep   Season of Vengeance   3.30.63 NBC
Alfred Hitchcock Presents   ep   Ten Minutes from Now
   5.1.64 CBS
Trials of O'Brien   ep   The Trouble with Archie   11.6.
   65 CBS
That's Life   ep   10.29.68 ABC
That Girl   ep   Mission Improbable   9.18.69, 9.25.69

ABC
Love American Style   ep   Love and the Unlikely Couple
    10. 6. 69 ABC
Make Room for Granddaddy   ep   1. 28. 71 ABC
Love American Style   ep   2. 19. 71 ABC
Love American Style   ep   10. 27. 72 ABC
The Judge and Jake Wyler   tf   12. 2. 72 NBC

JACOBSSON, ULLA
    Kraft Suspense Theatre   ep   The Action of the Tiger   2.
    20. 64 NBC

JAECKEL, RICHARD
    Bigelow Theatre   ep   T. K. O.   10. 25. 51 NN
    Four Star Playhouse   ep   The Squeeze   10. 1. 53 CBS
    U. S. Steel Hour   ep   The Last Notch   3. 30. 54 ABC
    Public Defender   ep   The Prize Fighter Story   4. 8. 54
        CBS
    Goodyear Playhouse   ep   The Big Man   9. 12. 54 NBC
    Ford Theatre   ep   Daughter of Mine   10. 7. 54 NBC
    Kraft Theatre   ep   Papa Was a Sport   10. 13. 54 NBC
    Elgin Hour   ep   Flood   10. 5. 54 ABC
    The Millionaire   ep   The Story of Nancy Marlborough
        3. 9. 55 CBS
    Bob Cummings Show   ep   4. 24. 55 NBC
    Producers Showcase   ep   The Petrified Forest   5. 30. 55
        NBC
    Bob Cummings Show   ep   Advice to the Lovelorn   8. 7.
        55 NBC
    Fireside Theatre   ep   Big Joe's Coming Home   12. 27.
        55 NBC
    Front Row Center   ep   Dinner Date   3. 18. 56 CBS
    Matinee Theatre   ep   Night Must Fall   5. 4. 56 NBC
    Climax   ep   To Scream at Midnight   6. 14. 56 CBS
    20th Century-Fox Hour   ep   Smoke Jumpers   11. 14. 56
        CBS
    Schlitz Playhouse of Stars   ep   Tower Room 14A   1. 11.
        57 CBS
    West Point   ep   One Command   2. 22. 57 CBS
    Navy Log   ep   War of the Whaleboats   3. 13. 57 ABC
    Crossroads   ep   Paratroop Padre   3. 29. 57 ABC
    Crossroads   ep   The Light   4. 5. 57 ABC
    Matinee Theatre   ep   Aftermath   5. 20. 57 NBC
    Panic   ep   May Day   6. 11. 57 NBC
    Playhouse 90   ep   Ain't No Time for Glory   6. 20. 57
        CBS
    West Point   ep   The Harder Right   11. 26. 57 ABC

Alcoa Theatre ep The Days of November 2.24.58
    NBC
West Point ep One Command 6.3.58 ABC
No Warning ep Flight 6.8.58 NBC
Trackdown ep 4.1.59 CBS
Zane Grey Theatre ep Man in the Middle 2.11.60
    CBS
77 Sunset Strip ep The Office Caper 10.7.60 ABC
Untouchables ep The Otto Frick Story 12.22.60 ABC
Tall Man ep The Grudge Fight 1.21.61 NBC
Lawman ep Blue Boss and Willie Shay 3.12.61 ABC
Alfred Hitchcock Theatre ep Incident in a Small Jail
    3.21.61 NBC
Wagon Train ep The Chalice 5.24.61 NBC
Frontier Circus sr 10.5.61 CBS
The Mighty O pt 8.21.62 CBS
Have Gun Will Travel ep 11.3.62 CBS
Wagon Train ep The Lily Legend Story 2.13.63 ABC
Dakotas ep Fargo 2.25.63 ABC
Gunsmoke ep 3.16.63 CBS
Perry Mason ep The Case of the Lover's Leap 4.4.
    63 CBS
Alfred Hitchcock Theatre ep Death of a Copy 5.24.63
    CBS
Temple Houston ep The Case for William Gotch 2.6.
    64 NBC
Virginian ep A Matter of Destiny 2.19.64 NBC
Outer Limits ep Specimen Unknown 2.24.64 ABC
New Phil Silvers Show ep Keep Cool 4.4.64 CBS
Bonanza ep Between Heaven and Earth 11.15.64 NBC
Gunsmoke ep 1.22.66 CBS
Wild, Wild West ep The Night of the Grand Emir 1.
    28.66 CBS
Wild, Wild West ep The Night of the Cadre 3.24.67
    CBS
Bonanza ep 10.15.67 NBC
Name of the Game ep 11.29.68 NBC
FBI ep Death Watch 2.14.71 ABC
The Deadly Dream tf 9.25.71 ABC
O'Hara, U.S. Treasury ep 10.22.71 CBS
Mission Impossible ep Run for the Money 12.11.71
    CBS
Banyon sr 9.15.72 NBC

JAFFE, SAM
    Playhouse 90 ep The Dingaling Girl 2.26.59 CBS
    Drama ep The Final Ingredient 4.19.59 ABC

Desilu Playhouse   ep   Lepke   11.20.59 CBS
Alfred Hitchcock Presents   ep   The Ikon of Elijah   1.
   10.60 CBS
Playhouse 90   ep   The Sound of Trumpets   2.9.60 CBS
Playhouse 90   ep   In the Presence of Mine Enemies   5.
   18.60 CBS
Play of the Week   ep   Legend of Lovers   10.10.60 NN
Law and Mr. Jones   ep   No Sale   12.2.60 ABC
Shirley Temple Theatre   ep   The Terrible Clockman
   1.29.61 NBC
Islanders   ep   To Bell a Cat   2.5.61 ABC
Untouchables   ep   Augie the Banker Ciamino   2.9.61
   ABC
Naked City   ep   An Economy of Death   5.3.61 ABC
Law and Mr. Jones   ep   The Broken Hand   6.2.61 ABC
Ben Casey   sr   10.2.61 ABC
Cain's Hundred   ep   Final Judgment   12.19.61 NBC
Defenders   ep   The Bedside Murder   1.6.62 CBS
Ben Casey   sr ret   10.1.62 ABC
Ben Casey   sr ret   9.18.63 ABC
Ben Casey   sr ret   9.14.64 ABC
Daniel Boone   ep   12.9.65 NBC
Batman   ep   Walk the Straight and Narrow   9.8.66 ABC
Tarzan   ep   The Blue Stone of Heaven   10.6.67, 10.13.
   67 NBC
Night Gallery   tf   11.8.69 NBC
Nanny and the Professor   ep   2.18.70 ABC
Quarantined   tf   2.24.70 ABC
Sam Hill: Who Killed the Mysterious Mr. Foster   tf
   2.1.71 NBC
Alias Smith and Jones   ep   The Great Shell Game   2.
   18.71 ABC
Alias Smith and Jones   ep   A Fistful of Diamonds   3.4.
   71 ABC
Hollywood Television Theatre   ep   Enemies   11.11.71
   NN
Ghost Story   pt   3.17.72 NBC
Love American Style   ep   10.6.72 ABC
Owen Marshall   ep   Five Will Get You Six   10.26.72
   ABC

JAGGER, DEAN
   Gulf Playhouse   ep   Our 200 Children   12.5.52 NBC
   Video Theatre   ep   Blind Fury   5.20.54 CBS
   Cavalcade of America   ep   Night Call 12.7.54 ABC
   Schlitz Playhouse of Stars   ep   Visibility Zero   7.22.55
      CBS

Studio 57   ep   My Son Is Gone   10. 2. 55 NN
Cavalcade Theatre   ep   Night Call   1. 10. 56 ABC
20th Century-Fox Hour   ep   Smoke Jumpers   11. 14. 56
   CBS
Zane Grey Theatre   ep   There Were Four   3. 15. 57
   CBS
Playhouse 90   ep   The Dark Side of the Earth   9. 19. 57
   CBS
Loretta Young Show   ep   Seed from the East   2. 1. 59
   NBC
Twilight Zone   ep   Static   3. 10. 61 CBS
Our American Heritage   ep   Gentleman's Decision   4.
   22. 61 NBC
G. E. Theatre   ep   Mister Doc   4. 29. 62 CBS
Alfred Hitchcock Theatre   ep   The Star Juror   3. 15. 63
   CBS
Mr. Novak   sr   9. 24. 63 NBC
Mr. Novak   sr ret   9. 22. 64 NBC
Fugitive   ep   11. 29. 66 ABC
The Lonely Profession   tf   10. 21. 69 NBC
Storefront Lawyers   ep   9. 16. 70 CBS
The Brotherhood of the Bell   tf   9. 17. 70 CBS
Matt Lincoln   sr   9. 24. 70   ABC
Name of the Game   ep   11. 6. 70 NBC
Bonanza   ep   Shadow of a Hero   2. 21. 71 NBC
Incident in San Francisco   tf   2. 28. 71 ABC
Columbo   ep   11. 5. 72 NBC
Kung Fu   ep   11. 11. 72 ABC

JAMES, DENNIS
   Kraft Theatre   ep   Pardon My Prisoner   3. 24. 54 NBC

JAMES, HARRY
   Lucille Ball-Desi Arnaz Hour   ep   Lucy Wins a Race
      Horse   2. 3. 58 CBS

JAMES, SHEILA
   Life with the Erwins   (a. k. a.   Trouble with Father; The
      Stu Erwin Show)   sr   10. 21. 50 ABC
   The Stu Erwin Show   sr ret   10. 51 ABC
   The Stu Erwin Show   sr ret   10. 17. 52 ABC
   The Stu Erwin Show   sr ret   10. 53 ABC
   G. E. Theatre   ep   That Other Sunlight   8. 15. 54 CBS
   Dobie Gillis   sr   9. 29. 59 CBS
   Dobie Gillis   sr ret   9. 27. 60 CBS
   National Velvet   ep   The Beauty Contest   3. 12. 61 NBC
   Loretta Young Show   ep   Pony Tails and Politics   10.

22. 62 CBS
McHale's Navy   ep   12. 3. 63 ABC
Donna Reed Show   ep   A Touch of Glamour   12. 5. 63
    ABC
Petticoat Junction   ep   3. 24. 64 CBS
Broadside   sr   9. 20. 64 ABC
Donna Reed Show   ep   1. 6. 66 ABC
John Forsythe Show   ep   On an Island with You and
    You and You   3. 14. 66 NBC
Beverly Hillbillies   ep   1. 25. 67 CBS
Marcus Welby, M. D.   ep   The Girl from Rainbow
    Beach   11. 17. 70 ABC

JAMESON, HOUSE
Aldrich Family   sr   1949-1950 NBC
Aldrich Family   sr   fall, 1951 NBC
Aldrich Family   sr   9. 5. 52 NBC
U. S. Steel Hour   ep   Baseball Blues   9. 28. 54 ABC
Hall of Fame   ep   Macbeth   11. 28. 54 NBC
Studio One   ep   The Incredible World of Horace Ford
    6. 13. 55 CBS
Robert Montgomery Presents   sr   9. 4. 55 NBC
Way of the World   ep   9. 19. 55 NBC
Robert Montgomery Presents   ep   Lucifer   12. 5. 55
    NBC
American Inventory   ep   In These Hands   12. 11. 55 NBC
Goodyear Playhouse   ep   The Film Maker   7. 1. 56 NBC
Robert Montgomery Presents   ep   One Bright Day   10.
    29. 56 NBC
Robert Montgomery Presents   ep   Faust '57   Spring,
    1957 NBC
Modern Romance   ep   Those We Love   7. 1. 57 NBC
Studio One   ep   The Dark Intruder   9. 2. 57 CBS
Naked City   ep   Violent Circle   10. 28. 58 ABC
True Story   ep   The Logical Victim   12. 6. 58 NBC
Phil Silvers Show   ep   Bilko's Grant Hotel   1. 30. 59
    CBS
U. S. Steel Hour   ep   The Last Autumn   11. 18. 59 CBS
Play of the Week   ep   Black Monday   1. 16. 61 NN
Dupont Show of the Month   ep   The Lincoln Murder
    Case   2. 18. 61 CBS
Naked City   ep   Bridge Party   12. 27. 61 ABC
Naked City   ep   Her Life in Moving Pictures   1. 2. 63
    ABC
Defenders   ep   Claire Cheval Died in Boston   1. 4. 64
    CBS
Lamp Unto My Feet   ep   Erazmus of Rotterdam   11.

14. 65 NN
Hallmark Hall of Fame   ep   Lamp at Midnight   4. 27.
66 NBC
Coronet Blue   ep   6. 5. 67 CBS
N. Y. P. D.   ep   1. 7. 69 ABC

JANIS, CONRAD
Actors Studio   ep   Joe McSween's Atomic Machine   1.
31. 50 CBS
Television Theatre   ep   Spring Green   1. 24. 51 NBC
Suspense   ep   Killers of the City   8. 7. 51 CBS
Big Story   ep   12. 7. 51 NBC
The Doctor   ep   Time to Kill   9. 7. 52 NBC
Bonimo   sr   9. 12. 53 NBC
First Person   ep   One Night Stand   7. 31. 53 NBC
Studio One   ep   Cinderella '53   12. 21. 53 CBS
Man Behind the Badge   ep   2. 14. 54 CBS
Kraft Theatre   ep   The Dashing White Sergeant   7. 29.
54 ABC
Kraft Theatre   ep   The Day the Diner Closed   11. 4. 54
ABC
Kraft Theatre   ep   One Hill, One River   1. 5. 55 NBC
Danger   ep   Peter River Blues   4. 12. 55 CBS
Kraft Theatre   ep   Gramercy Ghost   4. 20. 55 NBC
Appointment with Adventure   ep   Ride the Comet   6. 19.
55 CBS
U. S. Steel Hour   ep   Ashton Buys a Horse   9. 28. 55
CBS

JANNEY, LEON
Mr. District Attorney   ep   The Case of the Three
Ravens   1. 21. 52 ABC
Drama   ep   A Visitor from America   4. 11. 54 NBC
Mr. Citizen   ep   For My Brother   7. 6. 55 ABC

JANSSEN, DAVID
Lux Video Theatre   ep   It Started with Eve   3. 29. 56
NBC
Zane Grey Theatre   ep   There Were Four   3. 15. 57
CBS
You Are There   ep   The End of the Dalton Gang   5. 12.
57 CBS
Richard Diamond   sr   7. 1. 57 CBS
Alcoa Theatre   ep   Cupid Wore a Badge   12. 16. 57 NBC
The Millionaire   ep   Regina Wainwright Story   12. 25. 57
CBS
Richard Diamond   sr ret   1. 2. 58 CBS

Alcoa Theatre   ep   Cupid Wore a Badge   12.16.57 NBC
The Millionaire   ep   Regina Wainwright Story   12.25.
   57 CBS
Richard Diamond   sr ret   1.2.58 CBS
The Millionaire   ep   The David Barret Story   10.1.58
   CBS
Zane Grey Theatre   ep   Trail to Nowhere   10.2.58
   CBS
Zane Grey Theatre   ep   Hang the Heart High   1.15.59
   CBS
Richard Diamond   sr ret   2.15.59 CBS
Zane Grey Theatre   ep   Trail by Fear   6.11.59 CBS
Adventures in Paradise   ep   Show Me a Hero   11.5.61
   ABC
Checkmate   ep   Ride a Wild Horse   1.24.62 CBS
Target Corruptors   ep   The Middleman   2.22.62 ABC
G.E. Theatre   ep   Shadow of a Hero   2.4.62 CBS
Naked City   ep   A Wednesday Night Story   2.21.62 ABC
Follow the Sun   ep   A Choice of Weapons   2.25.62 ABC
Cain's Hundred   ep   Inside Track   4.10.62 NBC
Mystery Theatre   ep   Two Counts of Murder   7.11.62
   NBC
Route 66   ep   One Tiger to a Hill   9.21.62 CBS
Eleventh Hour   ep   Make Me a Place   10.17.62 NBC
Naked City   ep   On the Battlefront, Every Minute Is
   Important   3.27.63 ABC
Dick Powell Theatre   ep   Thunder in a Forgotten Town
   3.5.63 NBC
Fugitive   sr   9.17.63 ABC
Fugitive   sr ret   9.15.64 ABC
Fugitive   sr ret   9.14.65 ABC
Fugitive   sr ret   9.13.66 ABC
Night Chase   tf   11.20.70 CBS
O'Hara, U.S. Treasury   tf   4.2.71 CBS
O'Hara, U.S. Treasury   sr   9.17.71 CBS
The Longest Night   tf   9.12.72 ABC
Moon of the Wolf   tf   9.26.72 ABC

JARMAN, CLAUDE, JR.
   Best of the Post   ep   Early Americana   12.13.60 ABC

JEFFREYS, ANNE
   Musical Comedy Time   ep   Revenge with Music   2.19.
      51 NBC
   Topper   sr   10.16.53 CBS
   Topper   sr ret   fall, 1954 CBS
   The Merry Widow   Sp   4.9.55 NBC

Dearest Enemy Sp 11.26.55 NBC
20th Century-Fox Hour ep City in Flames 3.6.57
CBS
Dupont Theatre ep The Widow Was Willing 3.26.57
ABC
Wagon Train ep The Julia Gage Story 12.18.57 NBC
Love That Jill sr 1.20.58 ABC
Bob Cummings Show ep 6.16.59 NBC
Dr. Kildare ep Believe and Live 4.22.65 NBC
Bonanza ep The Unwritten Commandment 4.10.66 NBC
The Man from U.N.C.L.E. ep The Abominable Snow-
man Affair 12.9.66 NBC
Ghostbreaker pt 9.8.67 NBC
Tarzan ep 9.15.67 NBC
Love American Style ep 11.3.72 ABC
Delphi Bureau sr 10.5.72 ABC

JENKINS, ALLEN
Four Star Playhouse ep The Officer and the Lady
12.18.52 CBS
G.E. Theatre ep Here Comes Calvin 2.21.54 CBS
The Duke sr 7.2.54 NBC
Topper ep 4.29.55 CBS
Damon Runyon Theatre ep Numbers and Figures 5.
14.55 CBS
Damon Runyon Theatre ep Lonely Heart 6.4.55 CBS
Damon Runyon Theatre ep Situation Wanted 10.29.55
CBS
It's a Great Life ep The Private Line 12.4.55 NBC
Damon Runyon Theatre ep Honorary Degree 12.10.
55 CBS
Damon Runyon Theatre ep The Face of Johnny Dol-
liver 2.4.56 CBS
It's Always Jan ep 3.3.56 CBS
It's a Great Life ep The Palm Spring Story 4.22.56
NBC
Hey, Jeannie! sr 9.8.56 CBS
Playhouse 90 ep Three Men on a Horse 4.18.57
CBS
Tab Hunter Show ep Sultan for a Day 3.5.61 NBC
Top Cat sr (voice only) 9.27.61 ABC
The Man from U.N.C.L.E. ep 11.25.66, 12.2.66
NBC
Batman ep 1.25.67 ABC
Bewitched ep 3.18.71 ABC
Adam-12 ep 11.17.71 NBC

JENS, SALOME
    Play of the Week   ep   The Cherry Orchard   12. 28. 59
    NN
    Play of the Week   ep   Four by Tennessee Williams   2.
    6. 61 NN
    The Million Dollar Incident   Sp   4. 21. 61   CBS
    U. S. Steel Hour   ep   Man on the Mountain Top   11. 15.
    61 CBS
    Defenders   ep   The Naked Heiress   4. 7. 62 CBS
    Stoney Burke   ep   Spin a Golden Web   11. 26. 62 ABC
    Untouchables   ep   The Man in the Cooler   3. 5. 63 ABC
    Alcoa Premiere   ep   The Dark Labryinth   3. 21. 63 ABC
    U. S. Steel Hour   ep   Mission of Fear   4. 3. 63 CBS
    Outer Limits   ep   Corpus Earthing   11. 18. 63 ABC
    Rat Patrol   ep   10. 25. 66 ABC
    Hallmark Hall of Fame   ep   Barefoot in Athens   11. 11.
    66 NBC
    I Spy   ep   A Room with a Rack   2. 8. 67 NBC
    Medical Center   ep   9. 23. 70 CBS
    Bonanza   ep   The Wagon   10. 4. 70 NBC
    Gunsmoke   ep   Captain Sligo   1. 4. 71 CBS
    Medical Center   ep   Undercurrent   1. 20. 71 CBS

JERGENS, ADELE
    Racket Squad   ep   Hearse Chasers   2. 28. 52 CBS
    Personal Appearance Theatre   ep   Angel of Mercy   3.
    29. 52 ABC
    Ford Theatre   ep   The People Vs. Johnston   6. 25. 53
    NBC
    Regal Theatre   ep   Yang Yin and Mrs. Wiswell   10. 11.
    54 NN
    I Married Joan   ep   11. 3. 54 NBC
    Damon Runyon Theatre   ep   Teacher's Pet   7. 2. 55 CBS
    Damon Runyon Theatre   ep   Judy the Jinx   1. 28. 56 CBS
    Burns and Allen Show   ep   12. 10. 56 CBS

JESSEL, GEORGE
    The Million Dollar Incident   Sp   4. 21. 61 CBS
    77 Sunset Strip   ep   "5"   9. 27. 63 ABC

JEWELL, ISABEL
    Fireside Theatre   ep   The Boxer and the Stranger   6.
    24. 52 NBC
    The Unexpected   ep   One for the Money   8. 27. 52 NBC
    Treasury Men in Action   ep   The Case of the Lady in
    Hiding   3. 10. 55 ABC
    Climax   ep   Murder Has a Deadline   11. 28. 57 CBS

Gunsmoke   ep   2.6.65 CBS

JOHNS, GLYNIS
  Studio One   ep   Lily, The Queen of the Movies   4.21.
    52 CBS
  Video Theatre   ep   Two for Tea   1.5.53 CBS
  Frank Sinatra Show   ep   Face of Fear   5.30.58 ABC
  Roaring 20s   ep   Kitty Goes West   10.14.61 ABC
  G.E. Theatre   ep   The $200 Parlay   10.15.61 CBS
  Naked City   ep   The Hot Minerva   11.29.61 ABC
  Dick Powell Theatre   ep   Safari   4.3.62 NBC
  Dr. Kildare   ep   A Very Present Help   4.5.62 NBC
  Saints and Sinners   ep   Luscious Lois   11.19.62 NBC
  Dupont Show of the Month   ep   Windfall   1.13.63 NBC
  Lloyd Bridges Show   ep   A Game for Alternate Mondays
    1.29.63 CBS
  Hide and Seek   pt   8.5.63 CBS
  Glynis   sr   9.25.63 CBS
  Burke's Law   ep   2.28.64 ABC
  Defenders   ep   The Thief   4.25.64 CBS
  12 O'Clock High   ep   The Hours Before Dawn   11.13.64
    ABC
  Mystery Hour   ep   The Spider's Web   2.2.65 NN
  Batman   ep   11.23.67, 11.30.67, 12.7.67 ABC

JOHNSON, BEN
  Ozzie and Harriet   ep   The Top Gun   4.2.58 ABC
  Alfred Hitchcock Presents   ep   And the Desert Shall
    Blossom   12.21.58 CBS
  Laramie   ep   Hour after Dawn   3.15.60 NBC
  Have Gun Will Travel   ep   9.24.60 CBS
  Route 66   ep   A Long Piece of Mischief   1.19.62 CBS
  Bonanza   ep   The Gamble   4.1.62 NBC
  Have Gun Will Travel   ep   10.28.61 CBS
  Have Gun Will Travel   ep   9.29.62 CBS
  Virginian   ep   Duel at Shiloh   1.2.63 NBC
  Gunsmoke   ep   4.27.63 CBS
  Branded   ep   McCord's Way   1.30.66 NBC
  The Monroes   sr   9.7.66 ABC
  Virginian   ep   10.11.67 NBC
  Virginian   ep   10.9.68 NBC
  World of Disney   ep   Ride a Northbound Horse   3.16.
    69 NBC
  Bonanza   ep   The Deserter   3.16.69 NBC
  Bonanza   ep   Top Hand   1.17.71 NBC
  Gunsmoke   ep   11.22.71 CBS

JOHNSON, CELIA
Celanese Theatre ep The Distaff Side 5.14.52 ABC

JOHNSON, RICHARD
Hallmark Hall of Fame ep 11.17.70 NBC

JOHNSON, RITA
Lone Wolf ep The Art Story 9.19.55 NN

JOHNSON, VAN
Loretta Young Show ep hos The Last Spring 10.16.
55 NBC
Loretta Young Show ep hos Katy 10.23.55 NBC
I Love Lucy ep 6.17.57 CBS
Pied Piper of Hamelin Sp 11.26.57 NBC
Zane Grey Theatre ep Deadfall 2.19.59 CBS
G.E. Theatre ep At Our Service 5.22.60 CBS
Ann Sothern Show ep 10.13.60 CBS
June Allyson Show ep The Woman Who 11.3.60 CBS
Batman ep The Minstrel's Shakedown 9.21.66, 9.22.
66 ABC
Danny Thomas Show ep Is Charlie Coming 12.5.67
NBC
Doomsday Flight tf 12.13.67 NBC
Name of the Game ep High on a Rainbow 12.6.68
NBC
Here's Lucy ep 12.9.68 CBS
Name of the Game ep The Brass Ring 1.9.70 NBC
San Francisco International Airport tf 9.29.70 ABC
Doris Day Show ep 11.30.70 CBS
Doris Day Show ep 1.1.71 CBS
Men from Shiloh ep The Angus Killer 2.10.71 NBC
Call Her Mom tf 2.15.72 ABC
Wheeler and Murdoch pt 3.27.72 ABC
Love American Style ep 12.17.71 ABC
Man in the Middle pt 4.14.72 CBS

JOHNSTON, JOHNNY
Philco Playhouse ep The Gift 11.30.52 NBC
TV Reader's Digest ep Dear Friends and Gentle People
9.5.55 ABC

JONES, CAROLYN
Pepsi Cola Playhouse ep Account Closed 1.15.54 ABC
Pepsi Cola Playhouse ep The Silence 3.26.54 ABC
Pepsi Cola Playhouse ep Double in Danger 6.18.54
ABC

Schlitz Playhouse of Stars   ep   Prisoner in the Town
5. 7. 54 CBS

Four Star Playhouse   ep   The Answer   12. 23. 54 CBS

Treasury Men in Action   ep   The Case of the Elder
Brother   2. 10. 55 ABC

The Millionaire   ep   The Story of Emily Short   2. 16.
55 CBS

Studio 57   ep   The Black Sheep's Daughter   4. 26. 55 NN

Your Play Time   ep   Call from Robert Jest   8. 6. 55
NBC

Treasury Men in Action   ep   The Case of the Careless
Murder   9. 16. 55 ABC

Studio 57   ep   Diagnosis of a Selfish Lady   10. 23. 55
NN

Fireside Theatre   ep   The Key   11. 15. 55 NBC

Alfred Hitchcock Presents   ep   The Cheney Vase   12.
25. 55 CBS

Four Star Playhouse   ep   The Answer   12. 29. 55 CBS

20th Century-Fox Hour   ep   The Hefferan Family   6.
13. 56 CBS

Jane Wyman Theatre   ep   Little Black Lie   1. 1. 57
NBC

Zane Grey Theatre   ep   Until the Man Dies   1. 25. 57
CBS

Wire Service   ep   Dateline Las Vegas   3. 4. 57 ABC

Schlitz Playhouse of Stars   ep   The Girl in the Grass
3. 15. 57 CBS

Panic   ep   The Airline Hostess   4. 9. 57 NBC

G. E. Theatre   ep   The Man Who Inherited Everything
5. 19. 57 CBS

Climax   ep   The Disappearance of Amanda Hale   5. 30.
57 CBS

Wagon Train   ep   The John Cameron Story   10. 2. 57
NBC

Schlitz Playhouse of Stars   ep   High Barrier   10. 18. 57
CBS

Playhouse 90   ep   The Last Man   1. 9. 58 CBS

David Niven Theatre   ep   Portrait   6. 16. 59 NBC

Zane Grey Theatre   ep   Picture of Sal   1. 28. 60 CBS

June Allyson Show   ep   Love on Credit   11. 17. 60 CBS

Zane Grey Theatre   ep   Blood Red   1. 26. 61 CBS

Dick Powell Theatre   ep   Who Killed Julie Greer   9. 26.
61 NBC

Wagon Train   ep   The Jenna Douglas Story   11. 1. 61
NBC

Dick Powell Theatre   ep   Goodbye, Hannah   11. 21. 61
NBC

Frontier Circus   ep   Stopover in Paradise   2.22.62
    CBS
Lloyd Bridges Show   ep   Just Married   10.16.62 CBS
Dr. Kildare   ep   The Mask Makers   10.18.62 NBC
Dick Powell Theatre   ep   The Sea Witch   10.23.62
    NBC
Wagon Train   ep   The Molly Kincaid Story   9.16.63
    ABC
Burke's Law   ep   Who Killed Madison Cooper   1.24.64
    ABC
Dupont Show of the Month   ep   Jeremy Rabbit, the Se-
    cret Avenger   4.5.64 NBC
Addams Family   sr   9.18.64 ABC
Addams Family   sr ret   9.17.65 ABC
Batman   ep   Marsha, Scheme of Diamonds   11.23.66,
    11.24.66 ABC
Batman   1.25.67,   2.1.67 ABC
Bracken's World   ep   10.3.69 NBC
Mod Squad   ep   11.4.69 ABC
Love American Style   ep   11.10.69 ABC
Name of the Game   ep   12.4.70 NBC
Men from Shiloh   ep   The Legacy of Spencer Flats   1.
    27.71 NBC
Ghost Story   ep   The Summer House   10.13.72 NBC

JONES, CHRIS
    (The Legend of) Jesse James   sr   9.13.65 ABC
    Judd for the Defense   ep   9.8.67 ABC
    The Man from U.N.C.L.E.   ep   9.18.67 NBC

JONES, DEAN
    Zane Grey Theatre   ep   The Sunday Man   2.25.60 CBS
    Aquanauts   ep   10.19.60 CBS
    Outlaws   ep   Beat the Drums Slowly   10.20.60 NBC
    Stagecoach West   ep   Red Sand   11.22.60 ABC
    Dick Powell Theatre   ep   Who Killed Julie Greer   9.26.
        61 NBC
    Bonanza   ep   The Friendship   11.12.61 NBC
    Tales of Wells Fargo   ep   A Killing in Calico   12.16.
        61 NBC
    Target Corruptors   ep   Play it Blue   1.19.62 ABC
    Wagon Train   ep   The Lt. Burton Story   2.28.62 NBC
    Ensign O'Toole   sr   9.23.62 NBC
    Kraft Suspense Theatre   ep   The Rise and Fall of Eddie
        Carew   6.24.65 NBC
    Chicago Teddy Bears   sr   9.17.71 CBS

JONES, HENRY
   Actors Studio   ep   The Timid Guy   1.24.50 CBS
   Danger   ep   Death Gambles   7.30.51 CBS
   The Doctor   ep   Song for a Banker   2.15.53 NBC
   Kraft Theatre   ep   So Very Young   3.11.53 NBC
   Eye Witness   ep   The Righteous   5.4.53 NBC
   The Web   ep   The Lake   9.6.53 CBS
   Center Stage   ep   Lucky Louie   7.27.54 ABC
   Kraft Theatre   ep   The Failure   8.17.55 NBC
   Kraft Theatre   ep   It's Only Money   9.14.55 NBC
   Philco Playhouse   ep   One Mummy Too Many   11.20.55
      NBC
   Studio One   ep   The Man Who Caught the Bull At Coog-
      an's Bluff   11.28.55 CBS
   Kraft Theatre   ep   A Nugget for the Sunrise   12.14.55
      NBC
   Appointment with Adventure   ep   Suburban Terror   1.15.
      56 CBS
   Kraft Theatre   ep   Man on Roller Skates   2.15.56 NBC
   Studio One   ep   Always Welcome   2.27.56 CBS
   Robert Montgomery Presents   ep   Death Insurance   4.
      2.56 NBC
   Studio One   ep   The Genie of Sutton Place   5.14.56
      CBS
   Climax   ep   Fury at Dawn   7.19.56 CBS
   Jane Wyman Theatre   ep   While There's Life   12.11.56
      NBC
   Alfred Hitchcock Presents   ep   Nightmare in 4-D   1.13.
      57 CBS
   Robert Montgomery Presents   ep   His Name was Death
      3.18.57 NBC
   Alfred Hitchcock Presents   ep   The West Warlock Time
      Capsule   5.26.57 CBS
   Kraft Theatre   ep   Fire and Ice   6.12.57 NBC
   Alcoa Hour   ep   Awake with Fear   6.23.57 NBC
   Kraft Theatre   ep   Triumph   9.4.57 NBC
   Playhouse 90   ep   The Mystery of 13   10.24.57 CBS
   Studio One   ep   Please Report any Odd Characters   11.
      18.57 CBS
   Playhouse 90   ep   The Sounds of Eden   10.15.59 CBS
   Ford Star Time   ep   The Wicked Scheme of Jebal Deeks
      11.10.59 NBC
   Playhouse 90   ep   The Silver Whistle   12.24.59 CBS
   Untouchables   ep   Portrait of a Thief   4.7.60 ABC
   Goodyear Theatre   ep   Author at Work   4.11.60 NBC
   Twilight Zone   ep   Mr. Bevis   6.3.60 CBS
   Loretta Young Show   ep   The Misfit   6.5.60 NBC

Checkmate ep Cyanide Touch 10.1.60 CBS
Adventures in Paradise ep Away from It All 10.24.
   60 ABC
Best of the Post ep The Vision of Henry Whipple 12.
   24.60 ABC
Real McCoys ep Back to West Virginny 9.28.61 ABC
Follow the Sun ep The Woman Who Never Was 10.15.
   61 ABC
Thriller ep The Weird Taylor 10.16.61 NBC
Checkmate ep Juan Moreno's Body 11.8.61 CBS
New Breed ep Sweet Bloom of Death 11.28.61 ABC
Investigators ep The Dead End Men 12.28.61 CBS
Frontier Circus ep The Courtship 2.15.62 CBS
Thriller ep Till Death Do Us Part 3.12.62 NBC
Alfred Hitchcock Theatre ep Profit-Sharing Plan 3.13.
   62 CBS
Route 66 ep Two on the House 4.20.62 CBS
Wagon Train ep The Terry Morrell Story 4.25.62
   NBC
Channing sr 9.18.63 ABC
Dupont Show of the Month ep Something to Hide 5.5.
   63 NBC
Kraft Suspense Theatre ep The Jack Is High 11.18.64
   NBC
Bonanza ep 12.20.64 NBC
Amos Burke ep Peace, It's a Gasser 1.3.65 ABC
Profiles in Courage ep 3.7.65 NBC
Alfred Hitchcock Theatre ep The World's Oldest Motive
   4.12.65 NBC
Honey West ep The Abominable Snowman 10.1.65 ABC
Shenandoah ep 11.8.65 ABC
Bewitched ep 3.17.66 ABC
Tammy Grimes Show ep 9.8.66 ABC
Voyage to the Bottom of the Sea ep Night of Terror
   10.8.66 ABC
Hawk ep 11.17.66 ABC
Big Valley ep 3.6.67 ABC
The Man from U.N.C.L.E. ep 4.14.67 NBC
Gunsmoke ep 11.20.67 CBS
Daniel Boone ep 11.23.67 NBC
Second Hundred Years ep 1.10.68 ABC
Voyage to the Bottom of the Sea ep 3.31.68 ABC
Mod Squad ep 10.8.68 ABC
Guns of Will Sonnett ep 10.11.68 ABC
Daniel Boone ep 1.2.69 NBC
Name of the Game ep Love-In at Ground Zero 1.31.69
   NBC

Outsider ep Service for One 4.9.69 NBC
Name of the Game ep Island of Gold and Precious
    Stones 1.16.70 NBC
Virginian ep No War for the Warrior 2.18.70 NBC
Gunsmoke ep 2.2.70 CBS
The Movie Murderer tf 2.2.70 NBC
Love Hate Love tf 2.9.71 ABC
Mod Squad ep 11.23.71 ABC
Gunsmoke ep No Tomorrow 1.3.72 CBS
Night Gallery ep You Can't Help Like That Anymore
    2.23.72 NBC
Bonanza ep 3.12.72 NBC
The Daughters of Joshua Cabe tf 9.13.72 ABC
Emergency ep 9.30.72 NBC
Adam-12 ep 11.8.72 NBC

JONES, JACK
Guys 'n Geishas Sp 2.10.67 NBC
Rat Patrol ep 11.6.67 ABC

JONES, JAMES EARL
East Side/West Side ep Who Do You Kill 11.4.63
    CBS
Channing ep Freedom Is a Lowsome Thing 3.4.64
    ABC
Defenders ep The Non-Violent 4.1.65 CBS
Dr. Kildare ep A Cry from the States 1.24.66, 1.25.
    66, 1.31.66, 2.1.66 NBC
The Guiding Light sr 1967 CBS
Tarzan ep 2.24.67 NBC
Tarzan ep 1.12.68 NBC
N.E.T. Playhouse ep Trumpets of the Lord 5.10.68
    NN
N.Y.P.D. ep Candy Man 2.11.69, 2.18.69 ABC

JONES, MARCIA MAE
Story Theatre ep Why Thomas Was Discharged 3.30.
    51 NN
Mona McCluskey ep 4.14.66 NBC
My Three Sons ep 3.22.69 CBS

JONES, SHIRLEY
Fireside Theatre ep Hired Girl 6.12.51 NBC
Gruen Guild Theatre ep For Life 7.3.52 NN
Playhouse 90 ep The Big Slide 11.8.56 CBS
Lux Video Theatre ep Dark Victory 2.14.57 NBC
U.S. Steel Hour ep Shadow of Evil 2.27.57 CBS

Dupont Show of the Month   ep   The Red Mill   4.19.58
   CBS
Danny Thomas Show   ep   2.16.59 CBS
Bob Hope Chrysler Theatre   ep   The Shattered Glass
   12.11.64 NBC
Out of the Blue   pt   9.12.68 CBS
Name of the Game   ep   The Third Choice   3.7.69 NBC
Silent Night, Lonely Night   tf   12.16.69 NBC
Partridge Family   sr   9.25.70 ABC
Partridge Family   sr ret   9.17.71 ABC
Partridge Family   sr ret   9.15.72 ABC

JORY, VICTOR
   Tele-Theatre   ep   The Wine of Ore Palo   2.6.50 NBC
   Philco Playhouse   ep   The Second Oldest Profession   3.
      26.50 NBC
   Sure as Fate   ep   Child's Play   9.12.50 ABC
   Two Girls Named Smith   ep   8.4.51 ABC
   Broadway Television Theatre   ep   Angel Street   5.13.52
      NN
   Tales of Tomorrow   ep   World of War   5.23.52 ABC
   Studio One   ep   Captain-General of the Armies   6.2.52
      CBS
   Studio One   ep   International Incident   6.16.52 CBS
   Footlights Theatre   ep   Sum of Seven   7.4.52 CBS
   Studio One   ep   The Hospital   12.8.52 CBS
   Schlitz Playhouse of Stars   ep   The Mirror   4.10.53
      CBS
   Medallion Theatre   ep   The Bishop's Candlesticks   11.
      14.53 CBS
   Hallmark Hall of Fame   ep   Moby Dick   5.16.54 NBC
   G.E. Theatre   ep   Exit for Margo   5.23.54 CBS
   Schlitz Playhouse of Stars   ep   The Man Who Escaped
      from Devil's Island   6.25.54 CBS
   Kraft Theatre   ep   A Connecticut Yankee in King Arthur's
      Court   7.8.54 ABC
   Climax   ep   The Box of Chocolates   2.24.55 CBS
   Kings Row   sr   9.13.55 ABC
   Climax   ep   The Secret of River Lane   1.26.56 CBS
   Omnibus   ep   One Nation   2.5.56 CBS
   TV Reader's Digest   ep   The Woman Who Changed Her
      Mind   4.16.56 ABC
   Kraft Theatre   ep   Profile in Courage   5.16.56 NBC
   TV Reader's Digest   ep   The Gigantic Banknote Swindle
      6.11.56 ABC
   Kraft Theatre   ep   Prairie Night   7.25.56 NBC
   Telephone Time   ep   I Am Not Alone   9.23.56 CBS

Alcoa Hour   ep   Key Largo   10.14.56 NBC
Matinee Theatre   ep   Savrola   11.15.56 NBC
Playhouse 90   ep   Mr. and Mrs. McAdam   1.10.57 CBS
Omnibus   ep   The Trial of Captain Kidd   3.10.57 ABC
Crossroads   ep   Lone Star Preacher   3.15.57 ABC
20th Century-Fox Hour   ep   The Still Trumpet   4.3.57
   CBS
Ford Theatre   ep   Moment of Decision   4.10.57 ABC
Kraft Theatre   ep   Flesh and Blood   5.8.57 NBC
Matinee Theatre   ep   The Starmaster   5.17.57 NBC
Kraft Theatre   ep   Ride into Danger   8.21.57 NBC
Climax   ep   The Necessary Evil   9.19.57 CBS
Playhouse 90   ep   Galvanized Yankee   12.5.57 CBS
Hallmark Hall of Fame   ep   Johnny Belinda   10.13.58
   NBC
Pursuit   ep   The Silent Night   12.24.58 CBS
Wanted Dead or Alive   ep   3.7.59 CBS
U.S. Steel Hour   ep   Night of Betrayal   3.25.59 CBS
Playhouse 90   ep   Diary of a Nurse   5.7.59 CBS
Rawhide   ep   Incident of the Dry Drive   5.22.59 CBS
Manhunt   sr   fall, 1959 NN
Dr. Kildare   ep   Oh, My Daughter   1.25.62 NBC
New Breed   ep   Policemen Die Alone   1.30.62 ABC
Untouchables   ep   Element of Danger   3.22.62 ABC
87th Precinct   ep   Dawns an Evil Day   4.23.62 NBC
Rawhide   ep   Gold Fever   5.4.62 CBS
Empire   ep   Ride to a Fall   10.16.62 NBC
Wide Country   ep   Step Over the Sky   1.10.63 NBC
Alfred Hitchcock Theatre   ep   Death of a Cop   5.24.63
   CBS
Temple Houston   ep   The Twisted Rope   9.19.63 NBC
Great Adventure   ep   The Testing of Sam Houston   1.31.
   64 CBS
Suspense   ep   I Bradford Charles   4.8.64 CBS
Virginian   ep   Dark Challenge   9.24.64 NBC
Profiles in Courage   ep   11.8.64 NBC
Farmer's Daughter   ep   Big Sultan, Little Sultan   11.
   13.64 ABC
Gunsmoke   ep   1.30.65 CBS
Kraft Suspense Theatre   ep   That Time in Havana   2.11.
   65 NBC
Who Has Seen the Wind   tf   2.19.65 ABC
Bonanza   ep   Ride   1.16.66, 1.24.66 NBC
Hazel   ep   2.7.66 NBC
I Spy   ep   Return to Glory   2.23.66 NBC
Loner   ep   The Burden of the Badge   3.5.66 CBS
Virginian   ep   The Return of Golden Tom   3.9.66 NBC

Jesse James   ep   Things Don't Just Happen   3.14.66
   ABC
Green Hornet   ep   The Frog Is a Deadly Weapon   10.7.
   66 ABC
Iron Horse   ep   10.10.66 ABC
Road West   ep   1.16.67 NBC
Voyage to the Bottom of the Sea   ep   1.17.67 ABC
Time Tunnel   ep   2.17.67 ABC
Virginian   ep   2.22.67 NBC
Virginian   ep   A Bad Place to Die   11.8.67   NBC
Ironside   ep   The Past Is Prologue   12.7.67 NBC
High Chaparral   ep   3.3.68 NBC
Name of the Game   ep   Witness   9.27.68 NBC
Virginian   ep   4.2.69 NBC
Mannix   ep   Return to Summer Grove   10.11.69 CBS
Longstreet   ep   Who's Fred Hornbeck   12.23.71 ABC
Banacek   ep   10.11.72 NBC

JOURDAN, LOUIS
   Robert Montgomery Presents   ep   Wages of Fear   5.3.
      54 NBC
   Elgin Hour   ep   Warm Clay   11.16.54 ABC
   Paris Precinct   sr   4.3.55 ABC
   Appointment with Adventure   ep   Minus Three Thousand
      4.3.55 CBS
   Studio One   ep   Passage of Arms   4.11.55 CBS
   Climax   ep   The Escape of Mendes-France   7.14.55
      CBS
   Paris Precinct   sr ret   9.25.55 ABC
   Ford Theatre   ep   Journey by Moonlight   1.5.56 NBC
   Playhouse 90   ep   Eloise   11.22.56 CBS
   Ford Theatre   ep   The Man Who Beat Lupe   2.27.57
      ABC
   G.E. Theatre   ep   The Falling Angel   11.16.58 CBS
   Bob Hope Chrysler Theatre   ep   War of Nerves   1.3.64
      NBC
   The Greatest Show on Earth   ep   A Place to Belong   2.
      11.64 ABC
   Kraft Suspense Theatre   ep   Graffiti   11.26.64 NBC
   Bob Hope Chrysler Theatre   ep   A Crash of Cymbals
      12.25.64 NBC
   FBI   ep   2.12.67 ABC
   FBI   ep   Wind It up and It Betrays You   9.22.68 ABC
   Name of the Game   ep   Lola in Lipstick   11.8.68 NBC
   Fear No Evil   tf   3.3.69 NBC
   Run a Crooked Mile   tf   11.18.69 NBC
   Ritual of Evil   tf   2.23.70 NBC

FBI   ep   The Minerva Tapes   12.5.71 ABC

JOY, LEATRICE
    Robert Montgomery Presents   ep   The Steady Man   1.4.
        54 NBC
    Studio One   ep   The Cuckoo in Spring   12.27.54 CBS

JURADO, KATY
    Mr. and Mrs. North   ep   These Latins   2.25.55 NN
    Climax   ep   Nightmare by Day   2.23.56 CBS
    Playhouse 90   ep   Four Women in Black   4.25.57 CBS
    Rifleman   ep   The Boarding House   2.24.59 ABC
    Eleventh Hour   ep   The 7th Day of Creation   10.31.62
        NBC
    Death Valley Days   ep   1.18.64 ABC
    Any Second Now   tf   2.11.69 NBC
    Men from Shiloh   ep   The Best Man   9.23.70 NBC

JURGENS, CURT
    Dick Powell Theatre   ep   The Great Anatole   10.30.62
        NBC
    Dupont Show of the Month   ep   The Hell Walkers   3.8.
        64 NBC
    The Man from U.N.C.L.E.   ep   3.31.67, 4.7.67 NBC

                              -K-

KAPLAN, MARVIN
    Meet Millie   sr   10.25.52 CBS
    Ford Theatre   ep   Double Exposure 3.26.53 NBC
    G.E. Theatre   ep   The Marriage Fix   11.29.53 CBS
    Meet Millie   sr ret   3.16.54 CBS
    Danny Thomas Show   ep   Evil Eye Schultz   1.13.58 CBS
    Sally   ep   Look Hans, No Sally   1.19.58 NBC
    Dennis O'Keefe Show   ep   1.5.60 CBS
    Tom, Dick and Harry   pt   9.20.60 CBS
    Dobie Gillis   ep   The Second Childhood of Herbert Gillis
        3.7.61 CBS
    Top Cat   sr (voice only)   9.27.61 ABC
    Maggie Brown   pt   9.23.63 CBS
    Bob Hope Chrysler Theatre   ep   The Game with Glass
        Pieces   5.1.64 NBC
    McHale's Navy   ep   4.27.65 ABC

Hank   ep   11.19.65 NBC
Gidget   ep   4.21.66 ABC
Out of the Blue   pt   8.12.68 CBS
Mod Squad   ep   Flight Five Doesn't Answer   1.21.69
   ABC
My World and Welcome to It   ep   9.15.69 NBC
Chicago Teddy Bears   sr   9.25.71 ABC
Love American Style   ep   2.11.72 ABC

KARINA, ANNA
   I Spy   ep   A Gift from Alexander   10.12.66 NBC

KARLOFF, BORIS
   Masterpiece Playhouse   ep   Uncle Vanya   9.3.50 NBC
   Lights Out   ep   The Leopard Lady   9.18.50 NBC
   Robert Montgomery Presents   ep   The Kimballs   11.19.
      51 NBC
   Studio One   ep   Mutiny on the Nicolette   12.3.51 CBS
   Suspense   ep   The Lonely Place   12.25.51 CBS
   Video Theatre   ep   The Jest of Hahalaba   12.31.51 CBS
   Tales of Tomorrow   ep   Memento   2.22.52 ABC
   Curtain Call   ep   The Soul of the Great Bell   6.27.52
      NBC
   Schlitz Playhouse of Stars   ep   Death House   7.4.52
      CBS
   Hollywood Opening Night   ep   The Invited Seven   3.2.53
      NBC
   Suspense   ep   The Black Prophet   3.17.53 CBS
   Robert Montgomery Presents   ep   Burden of Proof   3.
      30.53 NBC
   Tales of Tomorrow   ep   Past Tense   4.3.53 ABC
   Plymouth Playhouse   ep   The Chase   5.24.53 ABC
   Suspense   ep   The Signal Man   6.23.53 CBS
   Colonel March of Scotland Yard   sr   1954 ABC
   Best of Broadway   ep   Arsenic and Old Lace   1.5.55
      CBS
   Elgin Hour   ep   A Sting of Death   2.22.55 ABC
   A Connecticut Yankee   Sp   3.12.55 NBC
   G.E. Theatre   ep   Mr. Blue Ocean   5.1.55 CBS
   U.S. Steel Hour   ep   Counterfeit   8.31.55 CBS
   Alcoa Hour   ep   Even the Weariest River   4.15.56 NBC
   Hallmark Hall of Fame   ep   The Lark   2.10.57 NBC
   Lux Video Theatre   ep   The Man Who Played God   4.24.
      57 NBC
   Suspicion   ep   The Deadly Game   12.9.57 NBC
   Telephone Time   ep   Vestris   2.25.58 ABC
   Shirley Temple's Story Book   ep   The Legent of Sleepy

Hollow   3. 5. 58 NBC
Studio One   ep   The Shadow of a Genius   3.31.58 CBS
Playhouse 90   ep   Heart of Darkness   11.6.58 CBS
Gale Storm Show   ep   It's Murder, My Dear   1.31.59
  CBS
G. E. Theatre   ep   The Indian Giver   5.17.59 CBS
Playhouse 90   ep   The Sounds of Trumpet   2.9.60 CBS
Dupont Show of the Month   ep   Treasure Island   3.5.60
  CBS
Thriller   sh/sr   The Twisted Image   9.13.60 NBC
Thriller   sh/sr   ret   9.18.61 NBC
Hallmark Hall of Fame   ep   Arsenic and Old Lace   2.
  5.62 NBC
Theatre 62   ep   The Paradine Case   3.11.62 NBC
Route 66   ep   Lizard's Leg and Owlet's Wing   10.26.62
  CBS
Wild, Wild West   ep   The Night of the Golden Cobra   9.
  23.66 CBS
The Girl from U. N. C. L. E.   ep   The Mother Muffin Af-
  fair   9.27.66 NBC
I Spy   ep   2.22.67 NBC
Name of the Game   ep   11.29.68 NBC

KARNS, ROSCOE
Inside Detective   sr   1950   NN
Richard Diamond   ep   The Ed Church Case   2.6.58 CBS
December Bride   ep   10.23.58 CBS
December Bride   ep   5.14.59 CBS
Hennesey   sr   9.28.59 CBS
Hennesey   sr ret   10.3.60 CBS
Hennesey   sr   ret   9.25.61 CBS

KASZNAR, KURT
The Web   ep   6.13.54 CBS
Philco Playhouse   ep   Run Like a Thief   9.5.54 NBC
Pond's Theatre   ep   The Forger   3.31.55 ABC
Studio One   ep   The Judge and His Hangman   11.14.55
  CBS
Playwrights '56   ep   Return to Cassino   2.14.56 NBC
Lux Video Theatre   ep   A Yankee Cousin   6.28.56 NBC
Kraft Theatre   ep   One Way West   8.1.56 NBC
Jane Wyman Theatre   ep   A Place on the Bay   12.25.56
  NBC
Schlitz Playhouse of Stars   ep   The Enchanted   1.25.57
  CBS
Goodyear Playhouse   ep   Rumblin Galleries   7.28.57
  NBC

Studio 57   ep   The Customs of the Country   6.16.57 NN
Suspicion   ep   Murder Me Gently   10.7.57 NBC
Dupont Show of the Month   ep   The Bridge of San Luis
   Rey   1.21.58 CBS
Shirley Temple's Story Book   ep   Rumpelstiltskin   2.2.
   58 NBC
Play of the Week   ep   Thieves' Carnival   12.21.59 NN
Play of the Week   ep   Volpone   3.7.60 NN
Play of the Week   ep   Waiting for Godot   4.31.61 NN
Naked City   ep   The Hot Minerva   11.29.61 ABC
Mystery Theatre   ep   Chez Rouge   8.8.62 NBC
Trials of O'Brien   ep   How Do You Get to Carnegie Hall
   11.13.65 CBS
Naked City   ep   The Battlefield   3.27.63 ABC
Repertory Theatre   ep   Hideout   10.2.64 CBS
The Girl from U.N.C.L.E.   ep   The Dog-Gone Affair
   9.13.66 NBC
Hero   ep   11.17.66 NBC
Run for Your Life   ep   11.21.66 NBC
That Girl   ep   11.24.66 ABC
I Spy   ep   1.25.67 NBC
The Man from U.N.C.L.E.   ep   1.27.67 NBC
My Three Sons   ep   3.23.67 CBS
Run for Your Life   ep   The Inhuman Predicament   9.20.
   67 NBC
It Takes a Thief   ep   1.9.68 ABC
Land of the Giants   sr   9.22.68 ABC
The Smugglers   tf   12.24.68 NBC
Land of the Giants   sr ret   9.21.69 ABC
Men from Shiloh   ep   Crooked Corner   10.28.70 NBC
Once Upon a Dead Man   tf   9.17.71 NBC
The Snoop Sisters   tf   12.18.72 NBC
Search   ep   12.20.72 NBC

KAYE, DANNY
   The Lucy Show   ep   12.28.64 CBS
   The Emperor's New Clothes   Sp (voice only)   2.21.72
      ABC

KAZAN, LAINIE
   Ben Casey   ep   Why Did the Day Go Backwards   12.6.65
      ABC

KEACH, STACY
   Hamlet   Sp   6.17.64 CBS
   Actors Company   ep   Twelfth Night   1.15.68 NN
   Actors Company   ep   Macbeth   4.18.68 NN

New York Playhouse   ep   Antigone   10.7.72 NN

KEATON, BUSTER
    Douglas Fairbanks Presents   ep   The Awakening   7.14.
        54 NBC
    Best of Broadway   ep   The Man Who Came to Dinner
        10.13.54 CBS
    Eddie Cantor Theatre   ep   10.10.55 ABC
    Screen Directors Playhouse   ep   The Silent Partner   3.
        21.56 NBC
    Producers Showcase   ep   The Lord Don't Play Favorites
        9.17.56 NBC
    Playhouse 90   ep   The Innocent Sleep   6.5.58 CBS
    Donna Reed Show   ep   A Very Merry Christmas   12.24.
        58 ABC
    Sunday Showcase   ep   After Hours   2.7.60 NBC
    Twilight Zone   ep   Once Upon a Time   12.15.61 CBS
    Route 66   ep   Journey to Nineveh   9.28.62 CBS
    Mr. Smith   ep   Think Mink   1.9.63 ABC
    The Greatest Show on Earth   ep   You're All Right Ivy
        4.28.64 ABC
    Burke's Law   ep   5.8.64 ABC

KEEL, HOWARD
    Zane Grey Theatre   ep   Gift from a Gunman   12.13.57
        CBS
    Roberta   sp   9.19.58 NBC
    Tales of Wells Fargo   ep   Casket "7.3."   9.30.61 NBC
    Run for Your Life   ep   The Time of the Sharks   12.6.
        65 NBC

KEELER, RUBY
    The Greatest Show on Earth   ep   The Show Must Go on
        --to Orange City   1.28.64 ABC

KEITH, BRIAN
    TV Hour   ep   Westward the Sun   11.17.53 ABC
    The Mask   ep   2.7.54 ABC
    TV Soundstage   ep   Journey to Java   2.19.54 NBC
    Playhouse   ep   Pals to the End   2.13.55 ABC
    Studio 57   ep   The Haven Technique   2.22.55 NN
    Playhouse   ep   Passage Home   4.3.55 ABC
    Studio 57   ep   Rescue   4.5.55 NN
    Ford Theatre   ep   Sunday Mourn   4.21.55 NBC
    Elgin Hour   ep   Combat Medic   6.14.55 ABC
    Crusader   sr   10.7.55 CBS
    Fireside Theatre   ep   Man on the Window Sill   12.13.55
        NBC

Lux Video Theatre   ep   Branded   12.15.55 NBC
Lux Video Theatre   ep   Possessed   2.28.57 NBC
Climax   ep   Hurricane Diane   12.12.57 CBS
Zane Grey Theatre   ep   Trouble at Tres Acres   3.26.
   59 CBS
Alfred Hitchcock Presents   ep   Your Witness   5.17.59
   CBS
Rawhide   ep   Incident in No Man's Land   6.12.59 CBS
Alfred Hitchcock Presents   ep   No Pain   10.25.59 CBS
World of Disney   ep   Move Along Mustangers   11.13.59,
   11.20.59 ABC
Laramie   ep   The General Must Die   11.17.59 NBC
Alfred Hitchcock Presents   ep   Cell 227   6.5.60 CBS
Westerner   sr   9.30.60 NBC
Untouchables   ep   Jamaica Ginger   2.2.61 ABC
Americans   ep   The Sentry   4.10.61 NBC
Outlaws   ep   My Friend, the Horse Thief   10.19.61 NBC
Alcoa Premiere   ep   The Breaking Point   12.5.61 ABC
Follow the Sun   ep   The Dumbest Blonde   2.4.62 ABC
Alfred Hitchcock Theatre   ep   The Test   2.20.62 NBC
Target Corruptors   ep   The Organizer   5.18.62, 5.25.
   62 ABC
Alfred Hitchcock Theatre   ep   Night of the Owl   10.4.62
   CBS
Virginian   ep   Duel at Shiloh   1.2.63 NBC
World of Disney   ep   World of Johnny Shiloh   1.20.63,
   1.27.63 NBC
Sam Benedict   ep   Run Softly, Oh Softly   1.26.63 NBC
Dr. Kildare   ep   The Gift of the Koodjanuk   5.9.63 NBC
Fugitive   ep   Feat In a Desert City   9.17.63 ABC
Wagon Train   ep   The Robert Harison Clarke Story   10.
   14.63   ABC
World of Disney   ep   Bristle Face   1.26.64, 2.2.64 NBC
Great Adventures   ep   Henry Bergh Story   3.20.64 CBS
World of Disney   ep   The Tenderfoot   10.18.64, 10.25.
   64, 11.1.64 NBC
Profiles in Courage   ep   11.29.64 NBC
Family Affair   sr   9.12.66 CBS
Family Affair   sr ret   9.11.67 CBS
Family Affair   sr ret   9.23.68 CBS
Family Affair   sr ret   9.25.69 CBS
Family Affair   sr ret   9.17.70 CBS
Second Chance   tf   2.8.72 ABC
Little People   sr   9.15.72 NBC

KEITH, ROBERT
   Pulitzer Prize Playhouse   ep   Robert E. Lee   3.26.52
      ABC

Philco Playhouse   ep   The Basket Weaver   4.20.52
   NBC
Police Story   ep   The California Case   8.1.52 CBS
Armstrong Circle Theatre   ep   Judgment   9.1.53 NBC
Studio One   ep   Another Caesar   10.26.53 CBS
Television Hour   ep   Atomic Attack   5.18.54 ABC
The Great Gildersleeve   sr   9.27.55 NBC

KELLAWAY, CECIL
   Magnavox Theatre   ep   The Hurricane at Pilgrim Hill
      12.8.50 CBS
   Cavalcade of America   ep   Poor Richard   10.1.52 NBC
   Cavalcade of America   ep   Sam the Whale   9.29.53
      ABC
   Schlitz Playhouse of Stars   ep   Day of Good News   12.
      24.54 CBS
   Danny Thomas Show   ep   3.8.55 ABC
   Ford Theatre   ep   Hanrahan   3.31.55 NBC
   Schlitz Playhouse of Stars   ep   Visa for "X"   5.2.55
      CBS
   Studio One   ep   Private History   10.24.55 CBS
   Ford Theatre   ep   The Fabulous Sycamores   12.1.55
      NBC
   Crossroads   ep   Tenement Saint   12.14.56 ABC
   Crossroads   ep   Big Sombrero   4.12.57 ABC
   Studio 57   ep   A Source of Irritation   1.19.58 NN
   Playhouse 90   ep   Verdict of Three   4.24.58 CBS
   Studio One   ep   Birthday Party   8.18.58 CBS
   Ann Sothern Show   ep   Hurrah for the Irish   2.2.59,
      2.9.59 CBS
   The Millionaire   ep   Father Gilhooley   2.18.59 CBS
   Johnny Ringo   ep   12.3.59 CBS
   Twilight Zone   ep   Elegy   2.19.60 CBS
   Hennesey   ep   10.10.60 CBS
   Adventures in Paradise   ep   The Intruders   10.10.60
      ABC
   Rawhide   ep   Incident in the Middle of Nowhere   4.7.61
      CBS
   Adventures in Paradise   ep   A Touch of Genius   4.10.61
      ABC
   Adventures in Paradise   ep   The Pretender   11.12.61
      ABC
   Donna Reed Show   ep   The Fabulous O'Hara   12.7.61
      ABC
   Dick Powell Theatre   ep   A Swiss Affair   12.12.61 NBC
   New Breed   ep   Mr. Weltschmerz   2.13.62 ABC
   Follow the Sun   ep   The Inhuman Equation   3.11.62 ABC

Mr. Smith ep For Richer or Poorer 12.1.62 ABC
Twilight Zone ep Passage on the Lady Anne 5.9.63
   CBS
Ben Casey ep If Dreams Were to Sell 10.9.63 ABC
The Greatest Show on Earth ep Rosetta 3.24.64 ABC
Burke's Law ep 5.1.64 ABC
Valentine's Day ep Farrow's Last Fling 4.16.65 ABC
Kraft Suspense Theatre ep Connery's Hands 7.1.65
   NBC
Bewitched ep 12.23.65 ABC
Kismet Sp 10.24.67 ABC
My Friend Tony ep Dead Reckoning 3.9.69 NBC
World of Disney ep The Wacky Zoo of Morgan City
   10.18.70, 10.25.70 NBC

KELLERMAN, SALLY
   Cheyenne ep The Durango Brothers 9.24.62 ABC
   Dobie Gillis ep The Call of the Like Wild 5.29.63 CBS
   Outer Limits ep The Human Facotr 11.11.63 ABC
   My Three Sons ep Steve and the Viking 12.5.63 ABC
   Outer Limits ep The Bellero Shield 2.10.64 ABC
   Ben Casey ep The Bark of a Three-Headed Hound 2.
      12.64 ABC
   The Greatest Show on Earth ep This Train Doesn't
      Stop Till It Gets There 4.14.64 ABC
   Slattery's People ep What Are You Doing out There
      Waldo 10.19.64 CBS
   Bob Hope Chrysler Theatre ep Parties to the Crime
      11.27.64 NBC
   Alfred Hitchcock Theatre ep Thou Still Unravished
      Bride 3.22.65 NBC
   Ben Casey ep You Want to Know What Really Goes
      on in a Hospital 12.20.65 ABC
   Shenandoah ep 1.10.66 ABC
   I Spy ep My Mother the Spy 3.30.66 NBC
   Bonanza ep A Dollar's Worth of Trouble 5.14.66 NBC
   Star Trek ep Where No Man Has Gone Before 9.22.
      66 NBC
   Tarzan ep 3.24.67 NBC
   Dundee and the Culhane ep The Dead Man's Brief 10.
      4.67 CBS
   Invaders ep 11.21.67 ABC
   Higher and Higher pt 9.9.68 CBS
   It Takes a Thief ep The Naked Billionaire 1.28.69
      ABC
   Hawaii Five-O ep 3.19.69 CBS
   Mannix ep The Solid Gold Web 3.22.69 CBS

   Bonanza   ep   Return Engagement   3.1.70 NBC

KELLY, GENE
   Schlitz Playhouse of Stars   ep   The Life You Save   3.1.
      57 CBS
   Going My Way   sr   10.3.62 ABC
   Jack and the Beanstalk   Sp   2.26.67 NBC
   Funny Side   ep hos   11.30.71 NBC

KELLY, GRACE
   Studio One   ep   The Rockingham Tea Set   1.23.50 CBS
   Philco Playhouse   ep   Ann Rutledge   2.12.50 NBC
   Cads, Scoundrels, Ladies   ep   The Love-Sick Robber
      4.25.50   NBC
   The Play's the Thing   ep   The Swan   6.9.50 CBS
   Comedy Theatre   ep   Summer Had Better Be Good   7.9.
      50 ABC
   Big Town   ep   The Pay-Off   10.5.50 CBS
   The Web   ep   Mirror of Delusion   11.1.50 CBS
   Philco Playhouse   ep   Leaf out of a Book   12.31.50 NBC
   Prudential Playhouse   ep   Berkeley Square   2.13.51 CBS
   Danger   ep   2.5.52 CBS
   Armstrong Circle Theatre   ep   City Editor   7.1.52 NBC
   Armstrong Circle Theatre   ep   Recapture   9.2.52 NBC
   Studio One   ep   The Kill   9.22.52 CBS
   Video Theatre   ep   A Message for Janice   9.29.52 CBS
   Philco Playhouse   ep   The Way of the Eagle   6.7.53
      NBC

KELLY, JACK
   Pepsi Cola Playhouse   ep   The Sound of Silence   4.23.54
      ABC
   Pepsi Cola Playhouse   ep   Girl on the Drum   5.7.54 ABC
   Cavalcade Theatre   ep   Sunrise on a Dirty Face   5.10.55
      ABC
   TV Reader's Digest   ep   My First Bullfight   6.20.55
      ABC
   Kings Row   sr   9.13.55 ABC
   Fireside Theatre   ep   2.14.56 NBC
   Fireside Theatre   ep   Scent of Roses   3.13.56 NBC
   The Millionaire   ep   10.10.56 CBS
   Lux Video Theatre   ep   Just Across the Street   1.10.57
      NBC
   Ford Theatre   ep   The Idea Man   5.8.57 ABC
   Maverick   sr   9.22.57 ABC
   Maverick   sr ret   9.58 ABC
   Maverick   sr ret   9.13.59 ABC
   Maverick   sr ret   9.18.60 ABC
   Maverick   sr ret   9.24.61 ABC
   Wagon Train   ep   12.30.63 ABC

Kraft Suspense Theatre   ep   The Name of the Game   12.
   26.63 NBC
Bob Hope Chrysler Theatre   ep   White Snow, Red Ice
   3.13.64 NBC
Kraft Suspense Theatre   ep   Kill Me on July 20th   6.17.
   65 NBC
Laredo   ep   The Deadliest Kid in the West   3.31.66
   NBC
Bob Hope Chrysler Theatre   ep   One Embezzlement and
   Two Margaritas   5.18.66 NBC
Batman   ep   The Cat and the Fiddle   9.14.66, 9.15.66
   ABC
Bob Hope Chrysler Theatre   ep   Time of Flight   9.21.
   66 NBC
Run for Your Life   ep   Baby, the World's on Fire   2.6.
   67 NBC
Please Don't Eat the Daisies   ep   2.18.67 NBC
Bob Hope Chrysler Theatre   ep   Deadlock   5.17.67 NBC
Ironside   ep   Tapped for Murder   10.26.67 NBC
High Chaparral   ep   10.29.67 NBC
Iron Horse   ep   Dealer's Choice   12.9.67 ABC
Name of the Game   ep   1.17.69 NBC
Name of the Game   ep   The Civilized Man   11.28.69
   NBC
Alias Smith and Jones   ep   11.4.71 ABC
Marcus Welby, M.D.   ep   Solomon's Choice   3.14.72
   ABC
Ghost Story   ep   The Dead We Leave Behind   9.15.72
   NBC
Ironside   ep   12.14.72 NBC

KELLY, NANCY
   Silver Theatre   ep   Minor Incident   4.10.50 CBS
   Studio One   ep   The Fathers   4.20.53 CBS
   Studio One   ep   Conflict   6.8.53 CBS
   Medallion Theatre   ep   Voyage Back   2.20.54 CBS
   Kraft Theatre   ep   Flowers in a Book   8.5.54 ABC
   Studio One   ep   The Secret Self   8.30.54 CBS
   Philco Playhouse   ep   Time Bomb   10.3.54 NBC
   Studio One   ep   The Pilot   11.12.56 CBS
   Climax   ep   Murder Is a Witch   8.15.57 CBS
   Suspicion   ep   Four O'Clock   9.30.57 NBC
   Alcoa Theatre   ep   Office Party   11.3.58 NBC
   Thriller   ep   The Storm   1.22.62 NBC
   Sam Benedict   ep   Nothing Equals Nothing   10.6.62 NBC
   Alfred Hitchcock Theatre   ep   The Lonely Hours   3.8.63
      CBS

KELLY, PATSY
   Laramie   ep   Lily 1.26.60 NBC

Laf Hit   ep   Outlaw in Town   11.15.60 NBC
Burke's Law   ep   10.21.64 ABC
My Son, the Doctor   pt   8.22.66 CBS
Wild, Wild West   ep   Night of the Big Blast   10.7.66
   CBS
Laredo   ep   A Question of Guilt   3.10.67 NBC
Love American Style   ep   11.3.69 ABC
The Pigeon   tf   11.4.69 ABC

KELLY, PAUL
Pulitzer Prize Playhouse   ep   Melville Goodwin, U.S.A.
   2.27.52 ABC
Celanese Theatre   ep   Street Scene   4.2.52 ABC
Robert Montgomery Presents   ep   Precinct   9.29.52
   NBC
Teledrama   ep   Deadline for Murder   6.5.53 CBS
Schlitz Playhouse of Stars   ep   The Black Mate   6.18.
   54 CBS
Fireside Theatre   ep   His Father's Keeper   12.7.54
   NBC
Schlitz Playhouse of Stars   ep   Underground   1.21.55
   CBS
Lux Video Theatre   ep   One Foot in Heaven   2.3.55
   NBC
Fireside Theatre   ep   Marked for Death   2.22.55 NBC
Cavalcade Theatre   ep   How to Raise a Boy   4.26.55
   ABC
Schlitz Playhouse of Stars   ep   Jury of One   8.19.55
   CBS
Crossroads   ep   Shadow of God   10.7.55 ABC
Crossroads   ep   Two-Fisted Saint   4.6.56 ABC
Front Row Center   ep   Instant of Truth   4.8.56 CBS

KENDALL, KAY
Phil Silvers Show   ep   Bilko Stars Kay Kendall   1.21.
   58 CBS

KENDALL, SUZY
The Persuaders   ep   The Man in the Middle   10.9.71
   ABC

KENNEDY, ARTHUR
Ford Theatre   ep   Night Visitor   4.29.54 NBC
Ethel Barrymore Theatre   ep   This Is Villa   10.12.56
   NN
Zane Grey Theatre   ep   Make It Look Good   2.5.59 CBS
Kaleidoscope   ep   The Third Commandment   2.8.59 NBC

Theatre '59   ep   The Sound of Gunfire   6.3.59 NBC
G.E. Theatre   ep   The Web of Guilt   3.27.60 CBS
Playhouse 90   ep   In the Presence of Mine Enemies   5.
   18.60 CBS
Our American Heritage   ep   Not without Honor   10.21.
   60 NBC
Alcoa Premiere   ep   People Need People   10.10.61 ABC
Dupont Show of the Month   ep   The Forgery   2.4.62
   NBC
Espionage   ep   The Whistling Shrimp   11.20.63 NBC
Kraft Suspense Theatre   ep   Leviathan Five   1.30.64
   NBC
Alfred Hitchcock Theatre   ep   10.12.64 NBC
ABC Stage 67   ep   The Confession   10.19.66 ABC
CBS Playhouse   ep   Appalachian Autumn   10.7.69 ABC
The Movie Murderer   tf   2.2.70 NBC
A Death of Innocence   ep   11.26.71 CBS
Crawlspace   tf   2.11.72 CBS

KENNEDY, GEORGE
Alaskans   ep   The Golden Fleece   11.29.59 ABC
Gunsmoke   ep   9.17.60 CBS
Have Gun Will Travel   ep   9.24.60 CBS
Have Gun Will Travel   ep   12.10.60 CBS
My Sister Eileen   ep   Ebenezer Scrooge Appopolous 12.
   21.60 CBS
Gunsmoke   ep   2.11.61 CBS
Gunsmoke   ep   3.25.61 CBS
Acapulco   ep   Fisher's Daughter   4.3.61 NBC
Bonanza   ep   The Infernal Machine   4.22.61 NBC
Bat Masterson   ep   The Fourth Man   4.27.61 NBC
Have Gun Will Travel   ep   5.27.61 CBS
Have Gun Will Travel   ep   9.16.61 CBS
Have Gun Will Travel   ep   10.14.61 CBS
Tall Man   ep   Trial by Hanging   11.4.61 NBC
Rawhide   ep   The Peddler   1.19.62 CBS
Tales of Wells Fargo   ep   Assignment in Gloribee   1.
   27.62 NBC
Tall Man   ep   Three for All   3.10.62 NBC
Have Gun Will Travel   ep   3.10.62 CBS
Thriller   ep   The Innocent Bystanders   4.9.62 NBC
Father of the Bride   ep   5.18.62 CBS
Travels of Jaimie McPheeters   ep   The Day of the Long
   Night   11.10.63 ABC
Farmer's Daughter   ep   The Simple Life   12.18.63 ABC
Great Adventures   ep   Rodger Young   1.24.64 CBS
Gunsmoke   ep   5.16.64 CBS

Bonanza ep The Scapegoat 10.25.64 NBC
See How They Run tf 10.7.65 NBC
Daniel Boone ep 12.2.65 NBC
Shenandoah ep A Special Talent for Killing 12.6.65
ABC
Laredo ep Pride of the Rangers 12.16.65 NBC
Jesse James ep Return to Lawrence 1.31.66 ABC
Perry Mason ep The Case of the Greek Goddess 2.
6.66 CBS
Big Valley ep 2.16.66 ABC
Gunsmoke ep 3.26.66 CBS
Dr. Kildare ep Mercy or Murder 3.28.66, 3.29.66,
4.4.66, 4.5.66 NBC
Tarzan ep 9.29.67 NBC
Sarge: The Badge or the Cross tf 2.22.71 NBC
Sarge sr 9.21.71 NBC
A Great American Tragedy tf 10.18.72 ABC

KENNEDY, MADGE
Schlitz Playhouse of Stars ep The Secret 9.10.54
CBS
G.E. Theatre ep Star in the House 6.5.55 CBS
Studio 57 ep Christmas Every Day 12.18.55 NN

KERR, JOHN
Summer Studio One ep End of the Honeymoon 7.13.53
CBS
Suspense ep The Hunted 6.29.54 CBS
Philco Playhouse ep The Bold and the Brave 4.17.55
NBC
Elgin Hour ep Combat Medic 6.14.55 ABC
Climax ep Man of Taste 12.1.55 CBS
Alcoa Hour ep Undertow 12.11.55 NBC
Hallmark Hall of Fame ep The Corn Is Green 1.8.56
NBC
U.S. Steel Hour ep A Fair Shake 2.1.56 CBS
Climax ep Throw Away the Cane 8.2.56 CBS
Playhouse 90 ep Mr. and Mrs. McAdam 1.10.57 CBS
Jane Wyman Theatre ep Killer's Pride 1.29.57 NBC
Climax ep Nine-Day Wonder 3.7.57 CBS
Studio One ep The Years In Between 4.1.57 CBS
On Trial ep The Case of the Jealous Bomber 4.5.57
NBC
Playhouse 90 ep Rumors of Evening 4.10.58 CBS
Alcoa Theatre ep Strange Occurrence at Roksay 10.6.
58 NBC
G.E. Theatre ep A Question of Romance 11.9.58 CBS

Hallmark Hall of Fame ep Berkeley Square 2. 5. 59
   NBC
Riverboat ep The Barrier 9. 20. 59 NBC
World of Disney ep Friendly Enemies at Law 3. 18.
   60 ABC
Checkmate ep The Crimson Pool 11. 22. 61 CBS
Gunsmoke ep 2. 17. 62 CBS
Bus Stop ep Verdict of Twelve 3. 11. 62 ABC
U. S. Steel Hour ep Honor in Love 7. 25. 62 CBS
U. S. Steel Hour ep Dry Rain 9. 5. 62 CBS
Lloyd Bridges Show ep Miracles of Mesa Verde 11.
   20. 62 NBC
Defenders ep The Apostle 12. 15. 62 CBS
Virginian ep The Judgment 1. 16. 63 NBC
Wagon Train ep The Jim Whitlow Story 5. 29. 63 ABC
Profiles in Courage ep 1. 24. 65 NBC
Alfred Hitchcock Theatre ep An Unlocked Window 2.
   15. 65 NBC
12 O'Clock High ep Mutiny at 10, 000 Feet 3. 26. 65
   ABC
The Long Hot Summer sr 9. 16. 65 ABC
Peyton Place sr 9. 17. 65 ABC
Flipper ep 1. 7. 67, 1. 14. 67 NBC
FBI ep 11. 5. 67 ABC
High Chaparral ep 11. 5. 67 NBC
FBI ep 1. 7. 68 ABC
FBI ep The Homecoming 2. 11. 68 ABC
Name of the Game ep Wrath of Angels 2. 28. 69 NBC
Adam 12 ep 11. 22. 69 NBC
Name of the Game ep 12. 19. 69 NBC
Bold Ones ep The Verdict 9. 27. 70 NBC
Young Lawyers ep False Witness 1. 4. 71 ABC
Yuma tf 3. 2. 71 ABC
Owen Marshall ep Men Who Care 10. 21. 71 ABC
Mod Squad ep I Am My Brother's Keeper 1. 4. 72 ABC

KERRIGAN, J. M.
   The Unexpected ep Slightly Dead 7. 16. 52 NBC
   Easy Chair Theatre ep Twilight Song 12. 15. 52 NBC
   Lux Video Theatre ep Welcome Stranger 9. 2. 54 NBC
   G. E. Theatre ep The Martyr 1. 23. 55 CBS
   Frontier ep The Devil and Doctor O'Hara 2. 5. 56 NBC

KERT, LARRY
   Combat ep One at a Time 3. 22. 66 ABC

KEYES, EVELYN
    Video Theatre ep Wild Geese 5.21.51 CBS
    Climax ep Wild Stallion 7.7.55 CBS
    Ugliest Girl in Town ep 10.3.68 ABC

KILBURN, TERENCE
    Cavalcade of America ep Slater's Dream 5.13.53
      NBC
    Kraft Theatre ep You Touched Me 3.17.54 NBC

KILEY, RICHARD
    Robert Montgomery Presents ep The Champion 6.5.
      50 NBC
    The Web ep Journey By Night 10.25.50 CBS
    Westinghouse Theatre ep The Guinea Pigs 9.9.51
      CBS
    Danger ep The Hand of the Enemy 2.12.52 CBS
    Curtain Call ep Azaya 7.4.52 NBC
    Curtain Call ep Season of Divorce 8.8.52 NBC
    Danger ep Death Signs and Autograph 9.16.52 CBS
    Short Short Dram ep The Unknown Factor 11.27.52
      NBC
    Kraft Theatre ep The Paper Moon 12.31.52 NBC
    Tales of Tomorrow ep Two-Faced 1.31.53 ABC
    Short Short Drama ep Act of Bravery 3.5.53 NBC
    Mirror Theatre ep Salt of the Earth 6.30.53 NBC
    The Web ep The Line of Duty 7.12.53 CBS
    Danger ep Trail by Jungle 7.21.53 CBS
    Summer Studio One ep Flowers from a Stranger 8.
      10.53 CBS
    Kraft Theatre ep Her Father's Butler 9.16.53 NBC
    The Web ep Kind Stranger 10.11.53 CBS
    U.S. Steel Hour ep P.O.W. 10.27.53 ABC
    Studio One ep A Criminal Design 1.18.54 CBS
    Studio One ep Paul's Apartment 3.29.54 CBS
    Justice ep Keith's Case 4.15.64 NBC
    TV Soundstage ep The Corner Drugstore 5.28.54 NBC
    Philco Playhouse ep Write Me out Forever 6.20.54
      CBS
    Studio One ep The Small Door 7.5.54 CBS
    U.S. Steel Hour ep The Notebook Warrior 9.14.54
      ABC
    Omnibus ep A Clean Fresh Breeze 10.31.54 CBS
    Ford Theatre ep Summer Memory 11.18.54 NBC
    Studio One ep The Cuckoo in Spring 12.27.54 CBS
    Kraft Theatre ep Patterns 1.12.55 NBC
    You Are There ep The Tragedy of John Milton 1.30.

55 CBS
Kraft Theatre   ep (restaged)   Patterns   2.9.55 NBC
You Are There   ep   The Death of Socrates   3.13.55
  CBS
Elgin Hour   ep   Black Eagle Pass   4.5.55 ABC
Climax   ep   The Dance   6.10.55 CBS
G.E. Theatre   ep   The Day He Got Fired   6.19.55 CBS
Studio One   ep   A Chance at Love   8.29.55 CBS
Kraft Theatre   ep   I, Mrs. Bibb   10.19.55 NBC
Armstrong Circle Theatre   ep   Actuals   9.27.55 NBC
Studio One   ep   Shakedown Cruise   11.7.55 CBS
Kraft Theatre   ep   The Just and the Unjust   1.26.56
  NBC
Studio One   ep   The Landlady's Daughter   11.26.56
  CBS
Kraft Theatre   ep   The Discoverers   2.6.57 NBC
Kaiser Aluminum Hour   ep   The Story of a Crime   3.
  12.57 NBC
Omnibus   ep   The Trial of Lizzie Borden   3.24.57 ABC
Alcoa Hour   ep   Mechanical Manhunt   4.28.57 NBC
Playhouse 90   ep   Homeward Borne   5.9.57 CBS
U.S. Steel Hour   ep   Shadow in the Sky   5.22.57 CBS
Studio One   ep   Act of Mercy   10.14.57 CBS
Kraft Theatre   ep   The Other Wise Man   12.25.57 NBC
Playhouse 90   ep   Before I Die   1.23.58 CBS
Kraft Theatre   ep   Material Witness   2.19.58 NBC
U.S. Steel Hour   ep   Give Me My Son   3.12.58 CBS
U.S. Steel Hour   ep   The Hidden River   7.2.58 CBS
Decision   ep   Indemnity   8.10.58 NBC
Alfred Hitchcock Presents   ep   The Crooked Road   10.
  26.58 CBS
Goodyear Theatre   ep   Guy in Ward 4   11.24.58 NBC
U.S. Steel Hour   ep   The Women of Hadley   2.24.60
  CBS
U.S. Steel Hour   ep   Revolt in Hadley   3.9.60 CBS
U.S. Steel Hour   ep   Bride of the Fox   8.24.60 CBS
Play of the Week   ep Close Quarter   4.24.61 NN
U.S. Steel Hour   ep   Trial Without Jury   6.14.61 CBS
U.S. Steel Hour   ep   Brandenburg Gate   10.4.61 CBS
Defenders   ep   The Attack   12.9.61 CBS
Dr. Kildare   ep   Hit and Run   12.14.61 NBC
Cain's Hundred   ep   The Schemer   1.23.62 NBC
Alcoa Premiere   ep   The Doctor   2.27.62 ABC
Alfred Hitchcock Theatre   ep   Blood Bargain   10.25.63
  CBS
Eleventh Hour   ep   This Wonderful Mad Man Called Me
  a Beauty   11.20.63 NBC

Great Adventure   ep   The Colonel from Connecticut
    1.10.64 CBS
Defenders   ep   The Last Day   1.11.64 CBS
Ben Casey   ep   Keep out of Reach of Adults   3.11.64
    ABC
Nurses   ep   The Forever Child   3.19.64 CBS
Kraft Suspense Theatre   ep   Charlie, He Couldn't Kill a
    Fly   5.7.64 NBC
Slattery's People   ep   What Ever Happened to Ezra   10.
    12.64 CBS
Slattery's People   ep   3.26.65 CBS
The Long Hot Summer   ep   The Desperate Innocent 11.
    11.65 ABC
Coronet Blue   ep   The Rebel   6.19.67 CBS
Danny Thomas Show   ep   Measure of a Man   1.22.68
    NBC
FBI   ep   The Homecoming   2.11.68 ABC
Garrison's Gorillas   ep   The Plot to Kill   2.13.68, 2.
    20.68 ABC
Judd for the Defense   ep   2.14.69, 2.21.69 ABC
New People   ep   9.22.69 ABC
Night Gallery   ep   11.8.69 NBC
Name of the Game   ep   1.30.70 NBC
Gunsmoke   ep   9.28.70 CBS
Mod Squad   ep   Who Are the Keepers   10.6.70 ABC
Bonanza   ep   Gideon the God   10.18.70 NBC
N.E.T. Playhouse   ep   The Ceremony of Innocence   10.
    29.70 NN
FBI   ep   1.24.71 ABC
Medical Center   ep   Man in Hiding   3.3.71 CBS
Name of the Game   ep   Beware of the Watchdog   3.5.71
    NBC
Gunsmoke   ep   11.1.71 CBS
Hallmark Hall of Fame   ep   All the Way Home   12.1.71
    NBC
Night Gallery   ep   The Ghost of Sorworth Place   1.19.72
    NBC
FBI   ep   1.30.72 ABC
Jigsaw   tf   3.26.72 ABC
Gunsmoke   ep   9.25.72 CBS

KING, DENNIS
    Pulitzer Prize Playhouse   ep   Nickerbocker Holiday   11.
        17.50 ABC
    Musical Comedy Time   ep   Babes in Toyland   12.25.50
        NBC
    Somerset Maugham Theatre   ep   The Narrow Corner

6. 11. 51 NBC
Studio One   ep   The Love Letter   10. 27. 52 CBS
Motorola TV Hour   ep   Side by Side   1. 26. 54 ABC
Hallmark Hall of Fame   ep   The Devil's Disciple   11.
    20. 55 NBC
Alcoa Hour   ep   Merry Christmas, Mr. Baxter   12. 2.
    56 NBC
Hallmark Hall of Fame   ep   Twelfth Night   12. 15. 57
    NBC
Playhouse 90   ep   Not the Glory   5. 8. 58 CBS
Playhouse 90   ep   The Innocent Sleep   6. 5. 58 CBS
Play of the Week   ep   Don Juan in Hell   2. 15. 60 NN
Bell Telephone Hour   ep   The Mikado   4. 29. 60 NBC
Hallmark Hall of Fame   ep   Give Us Barabbas   3. 26. 61
    NBC
New Breed   ep   Wave Goodbye to Grandpa   11. 21. 61
    ABC
Alfred Hitchcock Theatre   ep   Act of Faith   4. 10. 62 NBC
Chronicle   ep   Four Views of Caesar   11. 6. 63 CBS

KIRK, LISA
Studio One   ep   Taming of the Shrew   6. 5. 50 CBS
TV Hour   ep   Love Song   5. 4. 54 ABC
G. E. Theatre   ep   From the Top   11. 27. 55 CBS
Front Row Center   ep   The Human Touch   4. 15. 56 CBS
Stagecoach West   ep   Come Home Again   1. 10. 61 ABC
Bewitched   ep   4. 6. 67 ABC

KIRK, PHYLLIS
Studio One   ep   Devil in Velvet   1. 7. 52 CBS
Tales of Tomorrow   ep   Age of Peril   2. 15. 52 ABC
Goodyear Playhouse   ep   Wish on the Moon   3. 29. 53
    NBC
Video Theatre   ep   Listen He's Proposing   5. 7. 53 CBS
Armstrong Circle Theatre   ep   Candle in a Bottle   5.
    12. 53 NBC
The Web   ep   The Closing Net   12. 20. 53 CBS
Goodyear Playhouse   ep   The Inward Eye   2. 14. 54 NBC
Justice   ep   Keith's Case   4. 15. 54 NBC
Goodyear Playhouse   ep   The Power of Suggestion   8. 29.
    54 NBC
The Web   ep   Crackpot   9. 5. 54 CBS
Studio One   ep   Prelude to Murder   10. 4. 54 CBS
Robert Montgomery Presents   ep   The Great Gatsby   4.
    11. 55 NBC
Appointment with Adventure   ep   Forbidden Holiday   5.
    22. 55 CBS

Studio One   ep   Heart Song   6. 20. 55 CBS
Climax   ep   Edge of Terror   8. 11. 55 CBS
Playwrights '56   ep   The Battler   10. 18. 55 NBC
Loretta Young Show   ep   Tropical Secretary   11. 6. 55
    NBC
Star Stage   ep   Foreign Wife   12. 16. 55 NBC
Studio One   ep   the Bounty Hunters   1. 16. 56 CBS
Ford Theatre   ep   Tin Can Skipper   2. 2. 56 NBC
Climax   ep   Gamble on a Thief   2. 2. 56 CBS
Schlitz Playhouse of Stars   ep   The Waiting House   3.
    23. 56 CBS
Climax   ep   Faceless Enemy   6. 7. 56 CBS
Playhouse 90   ep   Made in Heaven   12. 6. 56 CBS
Ford Theatre   ep   Duffy's Man   12. 19. 56 ABC
Ford Theatre   ep   Mrs. Wane Comes to Call   1. 30. 57
    ABC
Ford Theatre   ep   Exclusive   4. 3. 57 ABC
20th Century-Fox Hour   ep   Men in Her Life   4. 17. 57
    CBS
The Thin Man   sr   9. 20. 57 NBC
Suspicion   ep   End of Violence   1. 20. 58 NBC
The Thin Man   sr ret   9. 58 NBC
Zane Grey Theatre   ep   Setup   3. 3. 60 CBS
Name of the Game   ep   Give Till it Hurts   10. 31. 69
    NBC
FBI   ep   The Impersonator   11. 22. 70 ABC

KIRKLAND, MURIEL
TV Playhouse   ep   A Husband for Mama   10. 15. 50 NBC
Video Theatre   ep   Abe Lincoln in Illinois   2. 12. 51 CBS
The Egg and I   sr   9. 3. 51 CBS
Armstrong Circle Theatre   ep   The Vase   8. 5. 52 NBC
Modern Romance   ep   1. 20. 58 NBC
Modern Romance   ep   4. 7. 58 NBC
Play of the Week   ep   Mary Stuart   5. 23. 60 NN
Family Classics   ep   The Heiress   2. 13. 61 CBS

KIRSTEN, DOROTHY
Matinee Theatre   ep   The Legend of Jenny Lind   5. 2. 56
    NBC

KITT, EARTHA
Omnibus   ep   Salome   12. 18. 55 CBS
Playhouse 90   ep   Heart of Darkness   1. 6. 58 CBS
Play of the Week   ep   The Wingless Victory   4. 17. 61
    NN
Ben Casey   ep   A Horse Named Stravinsky   5. 17. 65 ABC

I Spy   ep   The   Loser   10. 20. 65   NBC
Mission   Impossible   ep   4. 15. 67   CBS
Batman   ep   12. 14. 67   ABC
Batman   ep   12. 28. 67   ABC
Lieutenant   Schuster's   Wife   tf   10. 11. 72   ABC

KJELIN, ALF
Fireside Theatre   ep   The Old Talbot   2. 12. 52   NBC
TV Reader's Digest   ep   Comrade Lindemann's Con-
    science   6. 26. 55   ABC
Playhouse   ep   The Nightingale   6. 26. 55   ABC
Crusader   ep   Cross on the Hill   10. 7. 55   CBS
Turning Point   ep   The Nightingale   5. 19. 56   NBC
Loretta Young Show   ep   Emergency in 114   4. 23. 61
    NBC
Alfred Hitchcock Theatre   ep   Don't Look Behind You
    9. 27. 62   CBS
Combat   ep   Just for the Record   1. 15. 63   ABC
Combat   ep   Barrage   12. 10. 63   ABC
12 O'Clock High   ep   P. O. W.   4. 23. 65, 4. 30. 65   ABC
12 O'Clock High   ep   Back to the Drawing Board   2. 7.
    66 ABC
Run for Your Life   ep   The Borders of Barbarism   9.
    26. 66   NBC
Tarzan   ep   Last of the Supermen   11. 3. 67   NBC
FBI   ep   12. 3. 67   ABC
Mission Impossible   ep   3. 3. 68   CBS
Mission Impossible   ep   Doomsday   2. 16. 69   CBS
FBI   ep   Deadly Reunion   1. 25. 70   ABC
Dan August   ep   Days of Rage   3. 25. 71   ABC
Sixth Sense   ep   Lady, Lady, Take My Life   1. 29. 72
    ABC

KLUGMAN, JACK
U. S. Steel Hour   ep   Good for You   6. 8. 54   ABC
U. S. Steel Hour   ep   Two   8. 31. 54   ABC
U. S. Steel Hour   ep   Presento   12. 21. 54   ABC
Producers Showcase   ep   The Petrified Forest   5. 30. 55
    NBC
Big Town   ep   Comic Book Murder   6. 13. 55   NBC
Treasury Men in Action   ep   6. 17. 55   ABC
Studio One   ep   A Terrible Day   7. 18. 55   CBS
Kraft Theatre   ep   Two Times Two   8. 10. 55   NBC
Appointment with Adventure   ep   9. 4. 55   CBS
Goodyear Playhouse   ep   The Expendable House   10. 9. 55
    NBC
Kraft Theatre   ep   Number Four with Flowers   11. 2. 55
    NBC

Armstrong Circle Theatre   ep   Saturday Visit 11. 15. 55
  NBC
Philco Playhouse   ep   Rise up and Walk   1. 1. 56 NBC
Armstrong Circle Theatre   ep   The Third Ear   2. 7. 56
  NBC
U. S. Steel Hour   ep   The Finny Heart   4. 11. 56 CBS
Kraft Theatre   ep   The Ninth Hour   12. 5. 56 NBC
Alcoa Hour   ep   Mrs. Gilling and the Skyscraper   6. 9.
  57 NBC
Alfred Hitchcock Presents   ep   The Mail Order Prophet
  10. 13. 57 CBS
Playhouse 90   ep   The Thundering Wave   12. 12. 57 CBS
Gunsmoke   ep   1. 11. 58 CBS
Studio One   ep   The Lonely Stage   2. 24. 58 CBS
Suspicion   ep   Protege   5. 12. 58 NBC
G. E. Theatre   ep   Young and Scared   5. 18. 58 CBS
Investigator   ep   6. 10. 58 NBC
Studio One   ep   The Man Who Asked for a Funeral   6.
  23. 58 CBS
Alfred Hitchcock Presents   ep   The Mail Order Prophet
  7. 6. 58 CBS
Kraft Theatre   ep   Night Cry   8. 13. 58 NBC
Playhouse 90   ep   The Time of Your Life   10. 9. 58 CBS
Hallmark Hall of Fame   ep   Kiss Me Kate!   11. 20. 58
  NBC
Playhouse 90   ep   The Velvet Alley   1. 22. 59 CBS
Naked City   ep   The Shield   2. 3. 59 ABC
Sunday Showcase   ep   One Loud Clear Voice   1. 17. 60
  NBC
Twilight Zone   ep   A Passage for Trumpet   5. 20. 60 CBS
The Million Dollar Incident   Sp   4. 21. 61 CBS
Twilight Zone   ep   A Game of Pool   10. 13. 61 CBS
Follow the Sun   ep   Busman's Holiday   10. 22. 61 ABC
Straightaway   ep   Die Laughing   11. 3. 61 ABC
Naked City   ep   The Tragic Success of Alfred Tiloff   11.
  8. 61 ABC
Untouchables   ep   Loophole   11. 16. 61 ABC
Defenders   ep   The Search   1. 20. 62 CBS
Ben Casey   ep   Give My Hands an Epitaph   2. 5. 62 ABC
Naked City   ep   Let Me Die before I Wake   2. 14. 62
  ABC
New Breed   ep   All the Dead Faces   3. 13. 62 ABC
Cain's Hundred   ep   Woman of Silence   4. 24. 62 NBC
Naked City   ep   King Stanislaus   12. 12. 62 ABC
Twilight Zone   ep   Death Ship   2. 7. 63 CBS
Untouchables   ep   An Eye for an Eye   2. 19. 63 ABC
Twilight Zone   ep   In Praise of Pip   9. 27. 63 CBS

Arrest and Trial   ep   The Quality of Justice   11.17.63
   ABC
Fugitive   ep   Terror at High Point   12.17.63 ABC
Virginian   ep   Roar from the Mountain   1.8.64 NBC
Defenders   ep   Blacklist   1.18.64 CBS
Great Adventure   ep   The Night Raider   2.21.64 CBS
Kraft Suspense Theatre   ep   The Threatening Eye   3.12.
   64 NBC
Harris Against the World   sr   10.5.64 NBC
Bob Hope Chrysler Theatre   ep   A Crash of Symbols
   12.25.64 NBC
Fugitive   ep   3.9.65 ABC
Ben Casey   ep   A Slave Is on the Throne   4.12.65 ABC
FBI   ep   Image in a Cracked Mirror   9.25.65   ABC
Bob Hope Chrysler Theatre   ep   A Time of Flight   9.
   21.66 NBC
Garrison's Gorillas   ep   9.26.67 ABC
Fame Is the Name of the Game   tf   11.26.66 NBC
Name of the Game   ep   Swingers Only   1.14.69 NBC
Then Came Bronson   ep   The Runner   9.17.69 NBC
Name of the Game   Blind Man's Bluff   10.3.69 NBC
FBI   ep   The Diamond Millstone   1.18.70 ABC
Bold Ones   ep   Dark Is the Rainbow, Loud the Silence
   3.1.70 NBC
Odd Couple   sr   9.24.70 ABC
Name of the Game   ep   The Time Is Now   10.23.70
   ABC
Odd Couple   sr ret   9.17.71 ABC
Odd Couple   sr ret   9.15.72 ABC
Love American Style   ep   9.22.72 ABC

KNIGHT, SHIRLEY
   Buckskin   ep   Little Heathen   2.23.59 NBC
   Staccato   ep   The Parents   9.24.59 NBC
   Texan   ep   11.2.59 CBS
   Hawaiian Eye   ep   A Dime a Dozen   12.23.59 ABC
   Bourbon Street Beat   ep   Key to the City   2.1.60 ABC
   Hawaiian Eye   ep   Fatal Cruise   2.24.60 ABC
   Playhouse 90   ep   The Shape of the River   5.2.60 CBS
   77 Sunset Strip   ep   Fraternity of Fear 5.7.60 ABC
   Hawaiian Eye   ep   The Kahumna Curtain   11.9.60 ABC
   Surfside 6   ep   Power of Suggestion   11.21.60 ABC
   Surfside 6   ep   Little Star Lost   1.2.61 ABC
   Roaring 20s   ep   Big-Town Blues   1.21.61 ABC
   Cheyenne   ep   The Invaders   1.23.61 ABC
   Maverick   ep   The Ice Man   1.29.61 ABC
   Lawman   ep   The Trial   5.7.61 ABC

Surfside 6   ep   Elegy for a Bookkeep   4.2.62 ABC
Target Corruptors   ep   A Book of Faces   4.27.62 ABC
U.S. Steel Hour   ep   You Can't Escape   6.13.62 CBS
Naked City   ep   Five Cranks for Winter   10.24.62 ABC
Virginian   ep   Man from the Sea   12.26.62 NBC
U.S. Steel Hour   ep   Fair Young Ghost   1.23.63 CBS
Alcoa Premiere   ep   The Broken Year   4.4.63 ABC
Dupont Show of the Month   ep   The Takers   10.13.63
    NBC
Eleventh Hour   ep   And Man Created Vanity   10.23.63
    NBC
Outer Limits   ep   The Man Who Was Never Born   10.
    28.63 ABC
Arrest and Trial   ep   Run Little Man, Run   12.22.63
    ABC
Fugitive   ep   The Homecoming   4.7.64 ABC
Defenders   ep   A Voice Loud and Clear   12.17.64 CBS
Virginian   ep   Lost Yesterday   2.3.65 NBC
Fugitive   ep   A.P.B.   4.6.65 ABC
Fugitive   ep   Echo of a Nightmare   1.25.66 ABC
Bob Hope Chrysler Theatre   ep   The Faceless Man   5.
    4.66 NBC
Invaders   ep   9.19.67 ABC
The Outsider   tf   11.21.67 NBC
Shadow over Elveron   tf   3.5.68 NBC
Alias Smith and Jones   ep   11.4.72 ABC

KNOTTS, DON
Andy Griffith Show   sr   10.3.60 CBS
Andy Griffith Show   sr ret   10.2.61 CBS
Andy Griffith Show   sr ret   fall, 1962 CBS
Andy Griffith Show   sr ret   9.30.63 CBS
Andy Griffith Show   sr ret   9.21.64 CBS
Andy Griffith Show   ep   1.10.66 CBS
Andy Griffith Show   ep   1.17.66 CBS
McHale's Navy   ep   3.8.66 ABC
Andy Griffith Show   ep   1.23.67 CBS
Bob Hope Chrysler Theatre   ep   The Reason Nobody
    Hardly Ever Seen a Fat Outlaw   3.8.67 NBC
Mayberry R.F.D.   ep   9.23.68 CBS
Hallmark Hall of Fame   ep   The Man Who Came to Din-
    ner   11.29.72 NBC

KNOX, ALEXANDER
The Vise   ep   One Just Man   10.1.54 ABC

KOHNER, SUSAN
    Alcoa Hour ep Long after Summer 2.5.56 NBC
    Matinee Theatre ep Letter to a Stranger 3.2.56 NBC
    Schlitz Playhouse of Stars ep Date for Tomorrow 5.
      25.56 CBS
    Climax ep Ten Minutes to Curfew 12.27.56 CBS
    Four Star Playhouse ep Desert Encounter 3.22.56
      CBS
    Schlitz Playhouse of Stars ep Dual Control 11.1.57
      CBS
    Wagon Train ep The Charles Avery Story 11.13.57
      NBC
    Alfred Hitchcock Presents ep Return of the Hero 3.
      2.58 CBS
    Suspicion ep The Flight 7.5.59 NBC
    Playhouse 90 ep In the Presence of Mine Enemies 5.
      18.60 CBS
    June Allyson Show ep The Guilty Heart 1.16.61 CBS
    Hong Kong ep The Innocent Exile 3.22.61 ABC
    Route 66 ep The Quick and the Dead 1.13.61 CBS
    Dick Powell Theatre ep Tomorrow, the Man 10.2.62
      NBC
    Nurses ep Root of Violence 12.13.62 CBS
    Going My Way ep One Small, Unhappy Family 2.13.
      63 ABC
    Route 66 ep But What Do You Do in March 5.3.63
      CBS
    Temple Houston ep Toll the Bell Slowly 10.17.63
      NBC
    Rawhide ep Incident at Ten Trees 1.2.64 CBS
    Channing ep A Bang and Whimper 3.25.64 ABC

KORVIN, CHARLES
    Drama ep Mr. Omm 4.11.50 NBC
    Studio One ep Wreath of Roses 5.8.50 CBS
    Studio One ep There Was a Crooked Man 6.19.50
      CBS
    Starlight Theatre ep Season for Marriage 4.28.51 NN
    Studio One ep A Man and Two Gods 5.24.54 CBS
    Studio One ep Fatal in My Fashion 10.25.54 CBS
    U.S. Steel Hour ep Scandal at Peppernut 3.29.55
      ABC
    Studio One ep The Judge and his Hangman 11.14.55
      CBS
    Climax ep The Passport 12.8.55 CBS
    Studio One ep The Bounty Hunters 1.16.56 CBS
    The Millionaire ep The Story of Anton Bohrman

1. 23. 57 CBS
Playhouse 90   ep   The Blackwell Story   2.28.57 CBS
Robert Montgomery Presents   ep   Last Train to Kilde-
   vil   3.11.57 NBC
Ford Theatre   ep   Singapore   4.17.57 NBC
Alcoa Hour   ep   Hostages to Fortune   7.7.57 NBC
Climax   ep   The Stranger Within   8.22.57 CBS
Studio One   ep   The Dark Intruder   9.2.57 CBS
Loretta Young Show   ep   Friends at a Distance   12.8.57
   NBC
Playhouse 90   ep   The Violent Heart   2.6.58 CBS
Loretta Young Show   ep   The Night the Doorbell Rang
   11.27.60 NBC
FBI   ep   12.18.66 ABC
FBI   ep   The Butcher   12.8.68 ABC
FBI   ep   The Replacement   2.7.71 ABC

KOSLECK, MARTIN
Robert Montgomery Presents   ep   The Sheffield Story
   10.27.52 NBC
One Man's Story   ep   Crime and Punishment   2.9.53 NN
Mono-Drama Theatre   ep   The Telltale Heart   10.5.53
   NN
TV Hour   ep   The Last Days of Hitler   1.12.54 ABC
Studio One   ep   The Expendables   3.22.54 CBS
Suspense   ep   Torment 3.30.54 CBS
Appointment with Adventure   ep   The Fateful Pilgrimage
   4.17.55 CBS
Appointment with Adventure   ep   The Helping Hand   10.
   16.55 CBS

KOTTO, YAPHET
Experiment in Terror   ep   Losers Weepers   2.19.67
   NBC
Big Valley   ep   12.25.67 ABC
High Chaparral   ep   The Buffalo Soldiers   11.22.68 NBC
Daniel Boone   ep   11.14.68 NBC
Hawaii Five-O   ep   King of the Hill   1.8.69 CBS
Mannix   ep   Death in a Minor Key   2.8.69 CBS
Daniel Boone   ep   2.13.69 NBC
Name of the Game   ep   10.23.70 NBC
Gunsmoke   ep   The Scavengers   11.16.70 CBS
Night Chase   tf   11.20.70 CBS

KOVACS, ERNIE
Playhouse 90   ep   Topaze   9.26.57 CBS
G.E. Theatre   ep   The World's Greatest Quarterback

10.19.58 CBS
Ann Sothern Show   ep   Hurrah for the Irish   2.22.59
  CBS
G.E. Theatre   ep   I Was a Blood Hound   2.15.59 CBS
Schlitz Playhouse of Stars   ep   The Salted Mine   3.27.
  59 CBS
Lucille Ball-Desi Arnaz Hour   ep   Lucy Meets the
  Moustache   4.1.60 CBS
Goodyear Theatre   ep   Author at Work   4.11.60 NBC
Silents Please   sh   3.23.61 ABC

KRUGER, OTTO
Armstrong Circle Theatre   ep   The Happy Ending   12.
  5.50 NBC
Lights Out   ep   Curtain Call   2.12.51 NBC
Somerset Maugham Theatre   ep   Outstation   2.28.51
  CBS
Video Theatre   ep   Something to Live for   8.6.53 CBS
G.E. Theatre   ep   Woman's World   10.25.53 CBS
Medallion Theatre   ep   Suitable Marriage   1.2.54 CBS
Center Stage   ep   Golden Anniversary   7.13.54 ABC
Studio One   ep   Prelude to Murder   10.4.54 CBS
G.E. Theatre   ep   The Face Is Familiar   11.21.54
  CBS
Science Fiction Theatre   ep   No Food for Thought   4.
  22.55 NBC
The Desert Song   Sp   5.7.55 NBC
Climax   ep   The 78th Floor   8.16.56 CBS
Ford Theatre   ep   Miller's Millions   5.22.57 ABC
Climax   ep   Jacob and the Angel   10.3.57 CBS
Law and Mr. Jones   ep   A Fool for a Client   4.21.61
  ABC
Perry Mason   ep   The Case of the Grumbling Grand-
  father   5.27.61 CBS
Dick Powell Theatre   ep   Up Jumped the Devil   11.28.
  61 CBS
Thriller   ep   An Attractive Family   1.1.62 NBC
Checkmate   ep   A Funny Thing Happened to Me on the
  Way to the Game   1.3.62 CBS
Perry Mason   ep   The Case of the Counterfeit Crank
  4.28.62 CBS
Dr. Kildare   ep   Gravida One   9.27.62 NBC
Sam Benedict   ep   Nothing Equals Nothing   10.6.62 NBC
Bonanza   ep   Elegy for a Hangman   1.20.63 NBC
Dick Powell Theatre   ep   The Judge   2.5.63 NBC
Perry Mason   ep   The Case of the Devious Delinquent
  12.5.63 CBS

KWAN, NANCY
 Hawaii Five-O   tf   9. 20. 68 CBS

-L-

LADD, ALAN
 G. E. Theatre   ep   Committed 12. 5. 54 CBS
 G. E. Theatre   ep   Farewell to Kennedy 11. 12. 55 CBS
 G. E. Theatre   ep   Silent Ambush 1. 26. 58 CBS

LA GALLIENNE, EVA
 The Theatre Hour   ep   Uncle Harry 2. 25. 50 CBS
 Goodyear Playhouse   ep   Roman Fever 8. 31. 52 NBC
 Kraft Theatre   ep   The Southwest Corner 3. 30. 55 NBC
 Hallmark Hall of Fame   ep   Alice in Wonderland 10.
  23. 55 NBC
 Hallmark Hall of Fame   ep   The Corn Is Green 1. 8.
  56 NBC
 Dupont Show of the Month   ep   The Bridge of San Luis
  Rey 1. 21. 58 CBS
 Studio One   ep   The Shadow of a Genius 3. 31. 58 CBS
 Play of the Week   ep   Mary Stuart 5. 23. 60 NN
 Play of the Week   ep   Therese Raquin 3. 13. 61 NN

LAHR, BERT
 Prudential Playhouse   ep   Burlesque 1. 2. 51 CBS
 Omnibus   ep   Vive 1. 18. 53 CBS
 Musical Comedy Time   ep   Flying High 3. 19. 51 NBC
 Best of Broadway   ep   The Man Who Came to Dinner
  10. 13. 54 CBS
 The Great Waltz   Sp   11. 5. 55 NBC
 Omnibus   ep   School for Wives 11. 11. 56 ABC
 Kraft Theatre   ep   The Big Heist 11. 13. 57 NBC
 U. S. Steel Hour   ep   You Can't Win 12. 4. 57 CBS
 G. E. Theatre   ep   Mr. O'Malley 12. 20. 59 CBS
 Ford Star Time   ep   The Greatest Man Alive 2. 2. 60
  NBC
 Eleventh Hour   ep   Is Mr. Martian Coming Back? 12.
  25. 63 NBC
 Hallmark Hall of Fame   ep   The Fantasticks 10. 18. 64
  NBC
 Bob Hope Chrysler Theatre   ep   Cops and Robbers 2.
  19. 65 NBC

Thompson's Ghost   pt   8.6.66 ABC

LAINE, FRANKIE
 Perry Mason   ep   The Case of the Jaded Joker   2.21.
   59 CBS
 Danny Thomas Show   ep   3.9.59 CBS

LAIRE, JUDSON
 (I Remember) Mama   sr   1.6.50 CBS
 Studio One   ep   The Rockingham Tea Set   1.23.50 CBS
 Television Theatre   ep   Valley Forge   2.22.50 NBC
 Studio One   ep   The Ambassadors   5.15.50 CBS
 Studio One   ep   Zone Four   6.12.50 CBS
 Mama   sr ret   8.4.50 CBS
 Studio One   ep   The Shadow of a Man   11.27.50 CBS
 Studio One   ep   (restaged) The Ambassadors   2.26.51
   CBS
 Studio One   ep   Here Is My Life   5.28.51 CBS
 Mama   sr ret   9.7.51 CBS
 Studio One   ep   The Other Father   1.21.52 CBS
 Mama   sr ret   9.5.52 CBS
 Mama   sr ret   9.4.53 CBS
 Mama   sr ret   9.3.54 CBS
 Kraft Theatre   ep   Kitty Foyle   12.2.54 ABC
 Mama   sr ret   10.7.55 CBS
 Mama   sr ret   12.16.56 CBS
 Studio One   ep   The Weston Strain   5.27.57 CBS
 Our American Heritage   ep   Woodrow Wilson and the
   Unknown Soldier   5.13.61 NBC
 Defenders   ep   The Treadmill   11.25.61 CBS
 Route 66   ep   To Walk with the Serpent   1.5.62 CBS
 Defenders   ep   The Search   1.20.62 CBS
 Defenders   ep   The Benefactors   4.28.62 CBS
 Stoney Burke   ep   Child of Luxury   10.15.62 ABC
 Ben Casey   ep   Legacy from a Stranger   10.22.62 ABC
 Defenders   ep   The Weeping Baboon   9.28.63 CBS
 Nurses   ep   Show Just Cause Why You Should Weep   10.
   3.63 CBS
 Dr. Kildare   ep   The Exploiters   10.31.63 NBC
 Kraft Suspense Theatre   ep   Leviathan Five   1.30.64
   NBC
 Nurses   ep   Nurse Is a Feminine Noun   2.13.64 CBS
 Defenders   ep   Death on Heels   1.28.65 CBS
 The Nurses   sr   1967 ABC
 Love Is a Many Splendored Thing   sr   1969 CBS

LAKE, ARTHUR
  Blondie   sr   1.4.57 NBC

LAKE, VERONICA
  Drama   ep   Shadow of the Heart   10.16.50 CBS
  Lights Out   ep   Beware This Woman   12.4.50 NBC
  Somerset Maugham Theatre   ep   The Facts of Life   5.
    14.51 NBC
  Video Theatre   ep   12.17.51 CBS
  Celanese Theatre   ep   Brief Moment   2.6.52 ABC
  Tales of Tomorrow   ep   Flight Overdue   3.28.52 ABC
  Goodyear Playhouse   ep   Better than Walking   10.26.52
    NBC
  Video Theatre   ep   Thanks for a Lovely Evening   1.12.
    53 CBS
  Danger   ep   3.31.53 CBS
  Broadway Television Theatre   ep   Gramercy Ghost   1.
    4.54 NN

LAMARR, HEDY
  Zane Grey Theatre   ep   Proud Woman   10.25.57 CBS

LAMAS, FERNANDO
  Lucille Ball-Desi Arnaz Hour   ep   Lucy Goes Skiing
    7.14.58 CBS
  Jane Wyman Theatre   ep   The Bravado Touch   4.17.58
    NBC
  Climax   ep   Spider Web   6.5.58 CBS
  Pursuit   ep   Eagle in the Cage   12.3.58 CBS
  Zane Grey Theatre   ep   The Last Raid   2.26.59 CBS
  Zane Grey Theatre   ep   Guns for Garibaldi   2.18.60
    CBS
  Shirley Temple Theatre   ep   Little Men   10.23.60 NBC
  Burke's Law   ep   2.14.64 ABC
  Virginian   ep   We've Lost a Train   4.21.65 NBC
  Run for Your Life   ep   Someone Who Makes Me Feel
    Beautiful   9.27.65 NBC
  Run for Your Life   ep   The Rediscovery of Charlotte
    Hude   1.24.66 NBC
  Laredo   ep   It's the End of the Road, Stanley   3.10.66
    NBC
  Combat   ep   The Brothers   10.3.66 ABC
  Run for Your Life   ep   The Sex Object   10.17.66 NBC
  The Girl from U.N.C.L.E.   ep   The Horns of the Di-
    lemma Affair   10.18.66 NBC
  The Girl from U.N.C.L.E.   ep   The UFO Affair   1.3.
    67 NBC

Run for Your Life   ep   The Inhuman Predicament   9.
    20. 67 NBC
Run for Your Life   ep   11. 8. 67 NBC
High Chaparral   12. 31. 67 NBC
Tarzan   ep   Jungle Ranson   2. 23. 68 NBC
He and She   ep   3. 6. 68 CBS
For Love or $ $ $ Sp   4. 11. 68 NBC
Mission Impossible   ep   12. 1. 68 CBS
It Takes a Thief   ep   2. 18. 69 ABC
Then came Bronson   ep   Where Will the Trumpets Be
    10. 15. 69 NBC
The Lonely Profession   tf   10. 21. 69 NBC
It Takes a Thief   ep   1. 19. 70 ABC
Mission Impossible   ep   1. 25. 70 CBS
Name of the Game   ep   3. 6. 70 NBC
Dan August   ep   The Worst Crime   2. 11. 71 ABC
Alias Smith and Jones   ep   Return to Devil's Hole   2.
    25. 71 ABC

LAMB, GIL
    Starlight Theatre   ep   Flaxen-Haired Mannequin   3. 22.
        51 CBS
    Big Town   ep   Shield of a Killer   7. 25. 55 NBC

LAMOUR, DOROTHY
    Hollywood Opening Night   ep   The Singing Years   11.
        24. 52 NBC
    Damon Runyon Theatre   ep   The Mink Doll   7. 9. 55 CBS
    Burke's Law   ep   Who Killed Madison Cooper   1. 24. 64
        ABC
    Burke's Law   ep   9. 16. 64 ABC
    I Spy   ep   10. 16. 67 NBC
    Name of the Game   ep   Chains of Command   10. 17. 69
        NBC
    Marcus Welby, M. D.   ep   Echo from Another World
        11. 9. 71 ABC

LAMPERT, ZOHRA
    Hallmark Hall of Fame   ep   The Cradle Song   4. 10. 60
        NBC
    Defenders   ep   The Prowler   12. 16. 61 CBS
    Defenders   ep   Gideon's Follies   12. 23. 61 CBS
    U. S. Steel Hour   ep   Malc Call   8. 8. 62 CBS
    Sam Benedict   ep   Hear the Mellow Wedding Bells   11.
        3. 62 NBC
    Dr. Kildare   ep   The Thing Speaks for Itself   1. 10. 63
        NBC

Dr. Kildare   ep   A Place Among the Monuments   2.28.
63 NBC
Naked City   ep   Barefoot on a Bed of Coals   5.29.63
ABC
Reporter   ep   Super Star   11.20.64 CBS
The Man from U.N.C.L.E.   ep   The Mad, Mad Tea
Party Affair   2.1.65 NBC
Slattery's People   ep   Who You Taking to the Main Event,
Eddie   3.12.65 CBS
Trials of O'Brien   ep   How Do You Get to Carnegie
Hall   11.13.65 CBS
I Spy   ep   Blackout   3.8.67 NBC
Then came Bronson   ep   10.22.69 NBC
FBI   ep   3.1.70 ABC

LANCHESTER, ELSA
Studio One   ep   Music and Mrs. Pratt   10.12.53 CBS
Omnibus   ep   Toine   11.22.53 CBS
Schlitz Playhouse of Stars   ep   The Baker of Barnbury
12.25.53 CBS
Ford Theatre   ep   Hanrahan   3.31.55 NBC
Best of Broadway   ep   Stage Door   4.6.55 CBS
Heidi   Sp   10.1.55 NBC
Hallmark Hall of Fame   ep   Alice in Wonderland   10.23.
59 NBC
Lux Video Theatre   ep   Miss Mabel   7.26.56 NBC
20th Century-Fox Hour   ep   Stranger in the Night   10.
17.56 CBS
Robert Montgomery Presents ep   Miracle at Lensham
12.17.56 NBC
Shirley Temple's Story Book   ep   Mother Goose   12.21.
58 NBC
Wanted Dead or Alive   ep   1.16.60 CBS
Adventures in Paradise   ep   The Intruders   10.10.60
ABC
G.E. Theatre   ep   Cat in the Cradle   10.1.61 CBS
Dick Powell Theatre   ep   The Fifth Caller   12.19.61
NBC
Follow the Sun   ep   A Ghost in Her Gazebo   3.18.62
ABC
Burke's Law   ep   Who Killed Eleanor Davis   12.20.63
ABC
Eleventh Hour   ep   Full Moon Every Night   3.4.64 NBC
Burke's Law   ep   9.20.64 ABC
Alfred Hitchcock Theatre   ep   The McGregory Affair 11.
23.64 NBC
Ben Casey   ep   A Boy Is Standing Outside   1.4.65 ABC

The Man from U. N. C. L. E.   ep   The Brain Killer Affair   3. 8. 65   NBC
Slattery's People   ep   What's A Swan Song for a Sparrow   4. 16. 65   CBS
John Forsythe Show   sr   9. 13. 65   NBC
World of Disney   ep   My Dog the Thief   9. 21. 69,   9. 28. 69   NBC
Then Came Bronson   ep   The Circle of Time   10. 8. 69   NBC
In Name Only   tf   11. 25. 69   ABC
It Takes a Thief   ep   12. 11. 69   ABC
Nanny and the Professor   ep   11. 15. 71   ABC
Night Gallery   ep   Green Finger   1. 5. 72   NBC
Mannix   ep   Death Is the Fifth Gear   3. 8. 72   CBS

LANDAU, MARTIN
Omnibus   ep   Salome   10. 18. 55   CBS
Harbourmaster   ep   Sanctuary   10. 24. 57   CBS
Tales of Wells Fargo   ep   Doc Holliday   5. 4. 59   NBC
Maverick   ep   High Card Hangs   5. 10. 59   ABC
Playhouse 90   ep   The Sounds of Eden   10. 15. 59   CBS
Twilight Zone   ep   Mr. Denton on Doomsday   10. 16. 59   CBS
G. E. Theatre   ep   Survival   11. 15. 59   CBS
Johnny Ringo   ep   5. 26. 60   CBS
Rawhide   ep   Incident below the Brazos   1. 1. 60   CBS
Adventures in Paradise   ep   Nightmare on Napuka   1. 18. 60   ABC
Wagon Train   ep   The Cathy Eckhardt Story   11. 9. 60   NBC
Checkmate   ep   Moment of Truth   11. 26. 60   CBS
Islanders   ep   Duel of Strangers   12. 25. 60   ABC
Tall Man   ep   Dark Moment   2. 11. 61   NBC
Acapulco   ep   The Gentleman from Brazil   3. 13. 61   NBC
Bonanza   ep   The Gift   4. 1. 61   NBC
Outlaws   ep   The Avengers   4. 12. 61   NBC
Rifleman   ep   The Vaueros   10. 2. 61   ABC
Detectives   ep   Shadow of his Brother   10. 13. 61   NBC
Untouchables   cp   Loophole   11. 16. 61   ABC
Outer Limits   ep   The Man Who Was Never Born   10. 28. 63   ABC
Mr. Novak   ep   Pay the $2. 00   11. 26. 63   NBC
Defenders   ep   The Secret   2. 8. 64   CBS
Outer Limits   ep   The Bellero Shield   2. 10. 64   ABC
The Greatest Show on Earth   ep   3. 10. 64   ABC
Twilight Zone   ep   The Jeopardy Room   4. 17. 64   CBS
I Spy   ep   Danny Was a Million Laughs   10. 27. 65   NBC

Big Valley ep 11.24.65 ABC
Shenandoah ep The Locket 11.22.65 ABC
Wild, Wild West ep The Night of the Red Eyed Mad-
   man 11.26.65 CBS
Branded ep This Stage of Fools 1.16.66 NBC
The Man from U.N.C.L.E. ep The Bat Cave Affair
   4.1.66 NBC
Mission Impossible sr 9.17.66 CBS
Gunsmoke ep 9.24.66 CBS
Mission Impossible sr ret 9.10.67 CBS
Mission Impossible sr ret 9.29.68 CBS
Welcome Home, Johnny Bristol tf 1.30.72 CBS

LANDIS, JESSIE ROYCE
Armstrong Circle Theatre ep 2.3.53 NBC
The Doctor ep A Time for Hate 4.26.53 NBC
First Person ep Comeback 7.24.53 NBC
Goodyear Playhouse ep Fadeout 8.23.53 NBC
Armstrong Circle Theatre ep Lost Tour 9.22.53 NBC
U.S. Steel Hour ep Papa Is All 2.2.54 ABC
U.S. Steel Hour ep Late Date 4.13.54 ABC
Kraft Theatre ep Account Rendered 12.15.54 NBC
Climax ep An Episode of Sparrows 3.29.66 CBS
Goodyear Playhouse ep Career Girl 4.22.56 NBC
The Man in the Dog Suit Sp 1.8.60 NBC
Alfred Hitchcock Presents ep Mother, May I Go out to
   Swim 4.10.60 CBS
U.S. Steel Hour ep A Girl in the Gold Bathtub 5.4.60
   CBS
Thriller ep The Mark of the Hand 10.4.60 NBC
Adventures in Paradise ep A Touch of Genius 4.10.61
   ABC
Ironside ep 1.23.69 NBC
Governor and J.J. ep 12.9.69 CBS
Ironside ep Grandmother's House 4.1.71 NBC
Mr. and Mrs. Bo Jo Jones tf 11.16.71 ABC
Columbo ep Lady in Waiting 12.15.71 NBC

LANDON, MICHAEL
Wire Service ep High Adventure 12.20.56 ABC
Dupont Theatre ep The Man from St. Paul 1.29.57
   ABC
Telephone Time ep Fight for the Title 3.17.57 CBS
G.E. Theatre ep Too Good with a Gun 3.24.57 CBS
Schlitz Playhouse of Stars ep The Restless Gun 3.29.
   57 CBS
Tales of Wells Fargo ep 6.10.57 NBC

Court of Last Resort ep The Forbes-Carol Case 10.
   18.57 NBC
Tales of Wells Fargo ep The Kid 11.18.57 NBC
Schlitz Playhouse of Stars ep Way of the West 6.6.
   58 CBS
Tales of Wells Fargo ep Shotgun Messenger 6.9.58
   NBC
Studio One ep Man under Glass 7.14.58 CBS
Wanted Dead or Alive ep 9.6.58 CBS
Texan ep The Hemp Tree 11.17.58 CBS
Trackdown ep 11.28.58 CBS
Wanted Dead or Alive ep 3.7.59 CBS
Playhouse 90 ep Project Immortality 6.1.59 CBS
Staccato ep The Naked Truth 9.10.59 NBC
Bonanza sr 9.12.59 NBC
Cheyenne ep White Warrior 2.22.60 ABC
Bonanza sr ret 9.10.60 NBC
Bonanza sr ret 9.23.61 NBC
Bonanza sr ret 9.23.62 NBC
Bonanza sr ret 9.63 NBC
Bonanza sr ret 9.20.64 NBC
Bonanza sr ret 9.12.60 NBC
Bonanza sr ret 9.11.66 NBC
Bonanza sr ret 9.67 NBC
Bonanza sr ret 9.15.68 NBC
Bonanza sr ret 9.14.69 NBC
Bonanza sr ret 9.13.70 NBC
Bonanza sr ret 9.19.71 NBC
Bonanza sr ret 9.12.72 NBC

LANG, JUNE
   Fireside Theatre ep The Man without a Country 5.30.
      50 NBC

LANGE, HOPE
   Playhouse 90 ep For I Have Loved Strangers 12.19.
      57 CBS
   Playhouse 90 ep Point of No Return 2.20.58 CBS
   Playhouse 90 ep The Innocent Sleep 6.5.58 CBS
   Hallmark Hall of Fame ep Cyrano de Bergerac 12.6.
      62 NBC
   Bob Hope Chrysler Theatre ep Shipwrecked 6.8.66
      NBC
   Fugitive ep The Last Oasis 9.13.66 ABC
   CBS Playhouse ep Dear Friends 12.6.67 CBS
   Ghost and Mrs. Muir sr 9.21.68 NBC
   Ghost and Mrs. Muir sr ret 9.18.69 ABC

Crowhaven Farm   tf 11. 24. 70 ABC
New Dick Van Dyke Show   sr 9. 18. 71 CBS
New Dick Van Dyke Show   sr ret 9. 17. 72 CBS
That Certain Summer   tf 11. 1. 72 ABC

LANGELLA, FRANK
Festival of the Arts   ep Benito Creno 10. 11. 65 NN
Trials of O'Brien   ep How Do You Get to Carnegie
    Hall 11. 13. 65 CBS
Experiment in Television   ep Good Day 3. 5. 67 NBC
On Stage   ep   The Choice   3. 30. 69 NBC

LANSBURY, ANGELA
Robert Montgomery Presents   ep   The Citadel 6. 19. 50
    NBC
Video Theatre   ep   The Wonderful Night   11. 6. 50 CBS
Video Theatre   ep   Stone's Throw 9. 15. 52 CBS
Robert Montgomery Presents   ep   Cakes and Ale   10.
    26. 53 NBC
Mirror Theatre   ep   Dreams Never Lie   10. 31. 53 CBS
Ford Theatre   ep   The Ming Lama 11. 12. 53 NBC
Schlitz Playhouse of Stars   ep   12. 4. 53 CBS
Four Star Playhouse   ep   A String of Beads 1. 21. 54
    CBS
G. E. Theatre   ep   The Crime of Daphne Rutledge   6.
    13. 54 CBS
Fireside Theatre   ep   The Indiscreet Mrs. Jarvis 1. 4.
    55 NBC
Drama   ep   Madeira! Madeira! 4. 14. 55 CBS
Stage 7   ep   Billy and the Bride 5. 8. 55 CBS
Rheingold Theatre   ep   The Treasure 5. 28. 55 NBC
Studio 57   ep   The Rarest Stamp 3. 11. 56 NN
Rheingold Theatre   ep   The Force of Circumstance   3.
    24. 56 NBC
Front Row Center   ep   Instant of Truth 4. 8. 56 CBS
Screen Directors Playhouse   ep   Claire 4. 25. 56 NBC
Studio 57   ep   The Brown Leather Case 6. 10. 56 NN
Climax   ep   The Devil's Brook 12. 5. 57 CBS
Playhouse 90   ep   Verdict of Three 4. 24. 58 CBS
Playhouse 90   ep   The Grey Nurse Said Nothing 11. 26.
    59 CBS
Eleventh Hour   ep   Something Crazy's Going On in the
    Back Room 4. 3. 63 NBC
The Man from U. N. C. L. E.   ep   The Deadly Toys Af-
    fair 11. 12. 65 NBC

LANSING, ROBERT
  Kraft Theatre   ep   Shadow of Suspicion   11.7.56 NBC
  U.S. Steel Hour   ep   The Square Egghead   3.11.59 CBS
  U.S. Steel Hour   ep   Case of Julia Walton   9.9.59 CBS
  U.S. Steel Hour   ep   Big Doc's Girl   11.4.59 CBS
  Great Mysteries   ep   The Burning Court   4.24.60 NBC
  U.S. Steel Hour   ep   The Great Gold Mountain   6.29.60
    CBS
  Alcoa Premiere   ep   The Voice   11.22.60 ABC
  Thriller   ep   The Fatal Impulse   11.29.60 NBC
  Outlaws   ep   The Daltons Must Die   1.26.61, 2.2.61
    NBC
  G.E. Theatre   ep   Image of a Doctor   2.26.61 CBS
  Checkmate   ep   Phantom Lover   3.4.61 CBS
  87th Precinct   sr   9.25.61 NBC
  U.S. Steel Hour   ep   Wanted: Someone Innocent   10.17.
    62 CBS
  San Benedict   ep   Maddon's Folly   10.27.62 NBC
  Saints and Sinners   ep   The Year Joan Crawford Won
    the Oscar   1.21.63 NBC
  U.S. Steel Hour   ep   Fair Young Ghost   1.23.63 CBS
  Sam Benedict   ep   Read No Evil   3.16.63 NBC
  Eleventh Hour   ep   Fear Begins at Forty   10.16.63
    NBC
  Temple Houston   ep   Gallows in Galilee   10.31.63 NBC
  Virginian   ep   The Fatal Journey   12.3.63 NBC
  Twilight Zone   ep   The Long Morrow   1.10.64 CBS
  Wagon Train   ep   1.20.64 ABC
  Eleventh Hour   ep   Prodigy   3.18.64 NBC
  12 O'Clock High   sr   9.18.64 ABC
  Virginian   ep   The Brotherhood   9.15.65 NBC
  Slattery's People   ep   11.12.65 CBS
  Daniel Boone   ep   The Tamarack Massacre Affair   12.
    30.65 NBC
  Loner   ep   The Trial in Paradise 1.22.66 CBS
  Branded   ep   Call to Glory   2.28.66, 3.6.66, 3.13.66
    NBC
  The Man Who Never Was   sr   9.7.66 ABC
  High Chaparral   ep   12.10.67 NBC
  Virginian   ep   12.13.67 NBC
  Cimarron Strip   ep   1.11.68 CBS
  Ironside   ep   The Lonely Hostage   2.1.68 NBC
  Mod Squad   ep   11.12.68 ABC
  Journey to the Unknown   ep   The Beckoning Fair One
    12.12.68 ABC
  Name of the Game   ep   Swingers Only   1.10.69 NBC
  Gunsmoke   ep   9.22.69 CBS

Medical Center ep Victim 10.1.69 CBS
Bonanza ep Danger Road 1.11.70 NBC
Mannix ep Blind Mirror 1.24.70 CBS
Flying Nun ep 2.6.70 ABC
Interns ep 1.1.71 CBS
Mannix ep The Judas Touch 1.16.71 CBS
Marcus Welby, M.D. ep False Spring 1.19.71 ABC
Killer by Night tf 1.7.72 CBS
The Astronaut tf 1.8.72 ABC

LANZA, MARIO
Shower of Stars ep Lend an Ear 10.28.54 CBS

LA PLANCHE, ROSEMARY
Hennesey ep My Daughter, the Nurse 10.23.61 CBS

LA PLANTE, LAURA
It's a Great Life ep The Movie Star 11.13.55 NBC

LA RUE, JACK
Lights Out sh 1949-1950 NBC
Racket Squad ep Hearse Chasers 2.28.52 NBC
Eddie Cantor Theatre ep 9.22.55 ABC
The Millionaire ep The Story of Victor Volante 2.22.
56 CBS

LAUGHLIN, TOM
Climax ep Edge of Terror 9.11.55 CBS
Navy Log ep The Pollywog of Yosu 12.13.55 CBS
Navy Log ep Bucket of Sand 5.15.56 CBS
Walter Winchell Theatre ep The Boy from Mason City
10.30.57 ABC
Wagon Train ep The Mary Halstead Story 11.20.57
NBC
Man with a Camera ep Second Avenue Assassin 10.
10.58 ABC
Lux Playhouse ep A Game of Hate 11.14.58 CBS
M Squad ep The Teacher 1.2.59 NBC

LAUGHTON, CHARLES
This Is Charles Laughton sr 1.6.53 NN
Ford Star Jubilee ep nar The Day Lincoln Was Shot
2.11.56 NBC
Studio 57 ep Stopover in Bombay 2.23.58 NN
G.E. Theatre ep New York Knight 3.2.58 CBS
G.E. Theatre ep The Last Lesson 2.8.59 CBS
Playhouse 90 ep In the Presence of Mine Enemies

5.18.60 CBS
Wagon Train ep The Albert Farnsworth Story 10.12.
60 NBC
Checkmate ep Terror from the East 1.7.61 CBS

LAURIE, PIPER
Best of Broadway ep Broadway 5.4.55 CBS
Robert Montgomery Presents ep Quality Town 12.19.
55 NBC
Front Row Center ep Winter Dreams 2.19.56 CBS
G.E. Theatre ep The Road that Led Afar 11.25.56
CBS
Playhouse 90 ep Mr. and Mrs. McAdam 1.10.57
CBS
Hallmark Hall of Fame ep Twelfth Night 12.15.57
NBC
Studio One ep The Deaf Heart 10.21.57 CBS
Playhouse 90 ep The Days of Wine and Roses 10.2.
58 CBS
Desilu Playhouse ep The Innocent Assassin 3.16.59
CBS
G.E. Theatre ep Caesar and Cleopatra 4.12.59 CBS
Hallmark Hall of Fame ep Winterset 10.26.59 NBC
U.S. Steel Hour ep You Can't Have Everything 1.27.
60 CBS
Play of the Week ep Legend of Lovers 10.10.60 NN
G.E. Theatre ep A Musket for Jessica 10.8.61 CBS
Westinghouse Presents ep Come Again to Carthage
12.8.61 CBS
Naked City ep Howard Running Bear Is a Turtle 4.3.
63 ABC
Bob Hope Chrysler Theatre ep Something about Lee
Wiley 10.11.63 NBC
Ben Casey ep Light up the Dark Corners 11.6.63
ABC
Eleventh Hour ep My Door is Locked and Bolted 1.
1.64 NBC
Breaking Point ep The Summer Hose 3.16.64 ABC

LAWFORD, PETER
Ford Theatre ep The Son-in-Law 4.30.53 NBC
G.E. Theatre ep Woman's World 10.25.53 CBS
Schlitz Playhouse of Stars ep At the Natchez Inn 1.
22.54 CBS
Ford Theatre ep For Value Received 2.18.54 NBC
Ford Theatre ep Mason-Dixon Line 6.10.54 NBC
Dear Phoebe sr 9.10.54 NBC

Fireside Theatre ep Stephen and Publius Cyrus 10. 11.55 NBC

Alfred Hitchcock Presents ep The Long Shot 11.27. 55 CBS

Screen Directors Playhouse ep Tom and Jerry 11. 30.55 NBC

Schlitz Playhouse of Stars ep Once upon a Time 11. 30.56 CBS

Playhouse 90 ep Sincerely, Willis Wayde 12.13.56 CBS

Ruggles of Red Gap Sp 2.3.57 NBC

Climax ep Bait for the Tiger 5.16.57 CBS

The Thin Man sr 9.20.57 NBC

Goodyear Theatre ep Point of Impact 11.23.59 NBC

Theatre '62 ep The Armer's Daughter 1.14.62 NBC

Alfred Hitchcock Theatre ep The Crimson Witness 1. 4.65 NBC

Patty Duke Show ep Will the Real Sammy Davis Stand Up 3.3.65 ABC

Bob Hope Chrysler Theatre ep March from Camp Tyler 10.6.65 NBC

Wild, Wild West ep The Night of the Returning Dead 10.14.66 CBS

Run for Your Life ep The Carnival Ends at Midnight 11.10.66 NBC

How I Spent My Summer Vacation tf 1.7.67 NBC

I Spy ep Get Thee to a Nunnery 3.1.67 NBC

A Step out of Time tf 2.26.71 CBS

Men from Shiloh ep The Town Killer 3.10.71 NBC

The Deadly Hunt tf 10.1.71 CBS

Ellery Queen: Don't Look Behind You tf 11.19.71 NBC

Doris Day Show ep 11.29.71 CBS

Bewitched ep 1.22.72 ABC

Bold Ones ep 1.30.72 NBC

Doris Day Show sr ret 9.11.72 CBS

LAWRENCE, CAROL

U.S. Steel Hour ep Night of Betrayal 3.25.59 CBS

Music Theatre ep Too Bad about Sheila Troy 4.16. 59, 4.23.59 NBC

U.S. Steel Hour ep Apple of His Eye 7.1.59 CBS

Play of the Week ep The Dybbuk 10.3.60 NN

Play of the Week ep Rashomon 12.12.60 NN

G.E. Theatre ep The Iron Silence 9.24.61 CBS

Westinghouse Presents ep The Enchanted Nutcracker 12.23.61 ABC

U.S. Steel Hour ep Honor in Love 7.25.62 CBS
Wagon Train ep The Widow O'Rourke Story 10.7.63
   ABC
Breaking Point ep There Are the Hip and There Are
   the Square 10.14.63 ABC
Kraft Suspense Theatre ep He Should Weep for Me
   11.5.64 NBC
Bob Hope Chrysler Theatre ep Mr. Governess 11.10.
   65 NBC
Run for Your Life ep Make the Angels Weep 12.13.
   65 NBC
Bob Hope Chrysler Theatre ep Terror Island 2.26.
   66 NBC
Run for Your Life ep The Day Time Stopped 9.12.66
   NBC
Garry Moore Show ep High Button Shoes 11.20.66
   CBS
Run for Your Life ep A Game of Violence 11.28.66
   NBC
Fugitive ep Death Is a Very Small Killer 3.21.67
   ABC
Kiss Me, Kate! Sp 3.25.68 ABC
Name of the Game ep Keep the Doctor Away 2.14.69
   NBC
Paris 7000 ep The Shattered Idol 3.5.70 ABC
Medical Center ep Blood Line 9.15.71 CBS
Sarge ep 11.16.71 NBC

LAWRENCE, GERTRUDE
   Prudential Playhouse ep Biography 10.10.50 CBS
   Prudential Playhouse ep Skylark 1.16.51 CBS

LAWRENCE, STEVE
   Carol for Another Christmas tf 12.28.64 ABC
   Medical Center ep The Corrupted 9.22.71 CBS
   Night Gallery ep The Dear Departed 12.1.71 NBC

LEACHMAN, CLORIS
   Philco Playhouse ep Nocturne 4.2.50 NBC
   Philco Playhouse ep Sense and Sensibility 6.4.50 NBC
   Television Playhouse ep Matter of Life and Death 2.
      4.51 NBC
   Kraft Theatre ep A Play for Mary 5.23.51 NBC
   Tales of Tomorrow ep The Last Man on Earth 8.31.
      51 ABC
   Charlie Wild sr 9.11.51 ABC
   Hallmark Hall of Fame ep Forgotten Children 6.22.52
      NBC

The Web   ep   A Handful of Stars   2.7.54 CBS
The Mask   ep   The Young Dancer   3.23.54 ABC
The Mask   ep   Marked for Murder   4.6.54 ABC
Philco Playhouse   ep   The Catamaran   9.25.54 NBC
Kraft Theatre   ep   Kitty Foyle   12.2.54 ABC
Climax   ep   One Night Stand   9.4.55 CBS
Alfred Hitchcock Presents   ep   Premonition   10.9.55
   CBS
G.E. Theatre   ep   Let It Rain   12.18.55 CBS
Star Stage   ep   Dr. Jordan   6.8.56 NBC
Zane Grey Theatre   ep   You Only Run Once   10.5.56
   CBS
Gunsmoke   ep   11.17.56 CBS
Zane Grey Theatre   ep   Hanging Tree   2.22.57 CBS
Telephone Time   ep   The Unsinkable Mrs. Brown   2.
   24.57 CBS
Lassie   sr   fall, 1957 CBS
Frank Sinatra Show   ep   Brownstone Incident   11.8.57
   ABC
Climax   ep   The Great World and Timothy Colt   3.27.
   58 CBS
Alcoa Premiere   ep   The Dark Room   2.10.59 ABC
Staccato   ep   Jessica Winthrop   2.11.60 NBC
Rawhide   ep   4.22.60 CBS
Wanted Dead or Alive   ep   11.23.60 CBS
Checkmate   ep   The Mask of Vengeance   12.3.60 CBS
Shirley Temple Theatre   ep   The Indian Captive   12.4.
   60 NBC
Loretta Young Show   ep   My Own Master   12.18.60
   NBC
Hawaiian Eye   ep   Man in a Rage   2.15.61 ABC
77 Sunset Strip   ep   Caper in E Flat   5.19.61 ABC
Loretta Young Show   ep   The Wedding   5.21.61 NBC
Gunsmoke   ep   5.27.61 CBS
Donna Reed Show   ep   Mouse at Play   10.5.61 ABC
Twilight Zone   ep   It's a Good Life   11.3.61 CBS
Untouchables   ep   Jigsaw   11.23.61 ABC
Cain's Hundred   ep   12.12.61 NBC
Alcoa Premiere   ep   The Doctor   2.27.62 ABC
Target Corruptors   ep   The Wrecker   3.2.62 ABC
Untouchables   ep   Man in the Middle   4.5.62 ABC
Route 66   ep   Love Is a Skinny Kid   4.6.62 CBS
Laramie   ep   Trial by Fire   4.10.62 NBC
G.E. Theatre   ep   The Bar Mitzvah of Major Orlovsky
   4.15.62 CBS
New Breed   ep   Judgment at San Belito   5.22.62 ABC
Mystery Theatre   ep   Night Panic   7.18.62 NBC

77 Sunset Strip ep Shadow on Your Shoulder 12.7.62 ABC
Saints and Sinners ep A Night of Horns and Bells 12. 24.62 NBC
Stoney Burke ep Cousin Eunice 12.24.62 ABC
Loretta Young Show ep Anything for a Laugh 12.24. 62 CBS
77 Sunset Strip ep 88 Bars 11.1.63 ABC
Defenders ep Conflict of Interest 10.22.64 CBS
Mr. Novak ep Faculty Follies 2.2.65, 2.9.65 NBC
Trials of O'Brien ep Good-By and Keep Cool 10.23. 65 CBS
Dr. Kildare ep The Life Machine 10.26.65, 11.16. 65 NBC
Perry Mason ep The Case of the Crafty Kidnaper 5. 15.66 CBS
Run for Your Life ep The List of Alice McKenna 1. 23.67 NBC
Virginian ep 1.25.67 NBC
Big Valley ep 3.13.67 ABC
Road West ep 4.3.67 NBC
Guns of Will Sonnett ep 12.1.67 ABC
Name of the Game ep Nightmare 10.18.68 NBC
Mannix ep 11.23.68 CBS
Judd for the Defense ep Punishments, Cruel and Un- usual 12.6.68 ABC
Lancer ep 2.25.69 CBS
Virginian ep The Land Dreamer 2.26.69 NBC
Ironside ep Good-By to Yesterday 9.25.69 CBS
Adam-12 ep 9.28.69 NBC
Silent Night, Lonely Night tf 12.16.69 NBC
Lancer ep 12.30.69 CBS
Mary Tyler Moore Show ep 9.19.70 CBS
Marcus Welby, M.D. ep A Very Special Sailfish 9. 22.70 ABC
Men at Law ep The Truth 3.31.71 CBS
Suddenly Single tf 10.19.71 ABC
Night Gallery ep You Can't Get Help Like That Any- more 2.23.72 NBC
Sixth Sense ep 3.11.72 ABC
Haunts of the Very Rich tf 9.20.72 ABC
Of Thee I Sing Sp 10.24.72 CBS
Of Men and Women Sp 12.17.72 ABC

LEDERER, FRANCIS
    TV Playhouse ep The Long Run 9.17.50 NBC
    Robert Montgomery Presents ep The Patriot from

Antibes   6.7.54 NBC
Schlitz Playhouse of Stars   ep   No Rescue   11.5.54 CBS
Elgin Hour   ep   Yesterday's Magic   12.14.54 ABC
Sally   ep   9.29.57 NBC
Studio One   ep   A Delicate Affair   7.28.58 CBS
Dupont Show of the Month   ep   Arrowsmith   1.17.60
   CBS
Sunday Showcase   ep   Turn the Key Softly   3.6.60 NBC
Untouchables   ep   The Otto Frick Story   12.22.60 ABC
Ben Casey   ep   Odyssey of a Proud Suitcase   2.19.62
   ABC
Ben Casey   ep   Every Other Minute It's the End of the
   World   1.25.65 ABC
Kraft Suspense Theatre   ep   The Safe House   5.20.65
   NBC
Blue Light   ep   Invasion by the Stars   3.9.66 ABC
Mission Impossible   ep   4.1.67 CBS
That Girl   ep   11.9.67 ABC
It Takes a Thief   ep   12.11.69 ABC

LEE, CANADA
Tele Theatre   ep   The Final Bell   1.23.50 NBC

LEE, CHRISTOPHER
Douglas Fairbanks, Jr. Presents   ep   Destination Milan
   3.2.5.53 NBC
The Vise   ep   The Final Column   1.14.55 ABC
The Vise   ep   The Stranglehold   7.8.55 ABC
Assignment Foreign Legion   ep   Anaya   12.24.57 CBS
O.S.S.   ep   Operation Firefly   1.13.58 ABC
Alcoa Premiere   ep   The Sorcerer   5.23.61 ABC
Alfred Hitchcock Theatre   ep   The Sign of Satan   5.8.64
   CBS
Avengers   ep   Never, Never Say Die   3.31.67 ABC
Avengers   ep   The Interrogators   1.20.69 ABC

LEE, GYPSY ROSE
U.S. Steel Hour   ep   Sauce for the Goose   10.10.56
   CBS
U.S. Steel Hour   ep   The Charmer   1.1.58 CBS
Modern Romances   ep hos   5.12.58 NBC
Burke's Law   ep   9.23.64 ABC
Who Has Seen the Wind   tf   2.19.65 ABC
Pruitts of Southampton   sr   9.13.66 ABC
Name of the Game   ep   Shine On, Shine On   1.1.68
   NBC
The Over the Hill Gang   tf   10.7.69 ABC

LEE, LILA
   Oh Susanna ep A Hit in Tahiti 6.15.57 CBS
   Panic ep Love Story 6.25.57 NBC

LEE, PEGGY
   G.E. Theatre ep So Deadly, So Evil 3.13.60 CBS

LEIBMAN, RON
   Dupont Show of the Month ep Ride with Terror 12.1.
      63 NBC

LEIGH, JANET
   Schlitz Playhouse of Stars ep Carriage from Britain
      3.8.57 CBS
   Bob Hope Chrysler Theatre ep Dear Deductible 11.
      9.66 NBC
   The Man from U.N.C.L.E. ep 11.25.66, 12.2.66
      NBC
   Danny Thomas Show ep 2.5.68 NBC
   For Love or $$$ Sp 4.11.68 NBC
   The Monk tf 10.21.69 ABC
   Honeymoon with a Stranger tf 12.23.69 ABC
   The House on Green Apple Road tf 1.11.70 ABC
   Men from Shiloh ep 9.30.70 NBC
   Bracken's World ep The Anonymous Star 11.13.70
      NBC
   Name of the Game ep The Man Who Killed a Ghost
      1.29.71 NBC
   The Deadly Dreams tf 9.25.71 ABC

LEIGHTON, MARGARET
   Suspicion ep The Sparkle of Diamonds 11.18.57 NBC
   Alfred Hitchcock Presents ep Tea Time 12.14.58
      CBS
   Playhouse 90 ep The Second Man 2.12.59 CBS
   Dupont Show of the Month ep The Browning Version
      4.23.59 CBS
   Westinghouse Presents ep The First Day 6.20.62
      CBS
   Festival of the Arts ep A Month in the Country 12.
      26.62 NN
   Ben Casey ep August Is the Month before Christmas
      9.14.64 ABC
   Burke's Law ep 10.14.64 ABC
   Dr. Kildare ep Lullaby for an Indian Summer 1.7.
      65 NBC
   Alfred Hitchcock Theatre ep Where the Woodbine

Twineth 1.11.65 NBC
Dr. Kildare ep Behold the Great Man 9.13.65, 9.
14.65, 9.20.65, 9.21.65 NBC
FBI ep The Chameleon 1.9.66 ABC
Heartbreak House Sp 4.24.66 NN
The Girl from U.N.C.L.E. ep 11.29.66 NBC
Judd for the Defense ep The Crystal Maze 1.3.69
ABC
Name of the Game ep The King of Denmark 2.20.70
NBC
Hallmark Hall of Fame ep Hamlet 11.7.70 NBC
N.E.T. Playhouse ep An Ideal Husband 1.14.71 NN

LEMBECK, HARVEY
The Phil Silvers Show sr 9.20.55 CBS
The Phil Silvers Show sr ret fall, 1956 CBS
The Phil Silvers Show sr ret fall, 1957 CBS
The Phil Silvers Show sr ret fall, 1958 CBS
Hallmark Hall of Fame ep Kiss Me, Kate! 11.20.58
NBC
Ensign O'Toole sr 9.23.62 NBC
Mr. Novak ep Let's Dig a Little Grammar 11.10.64
NBC
Many Happy Returns ep 3.1.65 CBS
The Man from U.N.C.L.E. ep The Discotheque Af-
fair 10.15.65 NBC
Batman ep The Penguin Goes Straight 3.23.66, 3.24.
66 ABC
Name of the Game ep Lola in Lipstick 11.8.68 NBC
Farmer's Daughter ep 12.24.65 ABC
Please Don't Eat the Daisies ep 4.12.66 NBC
It Takes a Thief ep A Sour Note 10.1.68 ABC
Night Gallery ep The Dear Departed 12.1.71 NBC

LEMMON, JACK
That Wonderful Guy sr 1949-1950 CBS
Pulitzer Prize Playhouse ep The Happy Journey 5.4.
51 ABC
Danger ep Sparrow Cop 7.24.51 CBS
Kraft Theatre ep The Easy Mark 9.5.51 NBC
Newsstand Theatre ep Size 12 Tantrum 1.23.52 ABC
Heaven for Betsy sr 9.30.52 CBS
Kraft Theatre ep Duet 1.28.53 NBC
Kraft Theatre ep Snooksie 2.18.53 NBC
Robert Montgomery Presents ep Dinah, Kip, and Mr.
Barlow 2.23.53 NBC
Armstrong Circle Theatre ep The Checkerboard Heart

3.17.53 NBC
Medallion Theatre   ep   The Grand Cross of the Crescent   7.25.53 CBS
Ford Theatre   ep   Marriageable Male   2.25.54 NBC
Ford Star Jubilee   ep   The Day Lincoln Was Shot   2.11.56 NBC
Zane Grey Theatre   ep   The Three Graves   1.4.57 CBS
Goodyear Theatre   ep   Lost and Found   10.14.57 NBC
Playhouse 90   ep   The Mystery of 13   10.24.57 CBS
Goodyear Theatre   ep   Voices in the Fog   11.11.57 NBC
Alcoa Theatre   ep   Souvenir   12.2.57 NBC
Goodyear Theatre   ep   The Victim   1.6.58 NBC
Alcoa Theatre   ep   The Days of November   2.24.58 NBC
Alcoa Theatre   ep   Loudmouth   4.7.58 NBC
Alcoa Theatre   ep   Most Likely to Succeed   5.5.58 NBC
Goodyear Theatre   ep   Disappearance   6.9.58 NBC
Playhouse 90   ep   Face of a Hero   1.1.59 CBS

LENYA, LOTTA
N.E.T. Playhouse   ep   Ten Blocks on the Camino Real   10.7.66 NN
N.E.T. Playhouse   ep   The World of Kurt Weill   2.24.67 NN

LENZ, RICK
Hec Ramsey   sr   10.8.72 NBC
Marcus Welby, M.D.   ep   Don and Denise   10.31.72 ABC

LEONARD, JACK E.
Babes in Toyland   Sp   12.18.54 NBC
Babes in Toyland   Sp (restaged)   12.24.55 NBC

LEONTOVICH, EUGENIE
Studio One   ep   Image of Fear   9.29.58 CBS
Naked City   ep   Line of Duty   10.14.58 ABC
Naked City   ep   The Deadly Guinea Pig   3.8.61 ABC
June Allyson Show   ep   Our Man in Rome   3.27.61 CBS
U.S. Steel Hour   ep   The Duchess and the Mugs   12.26.62 CBS

LESLIE, BETHEL
   The Girls (a.k.a. Young and Gay) 1949-1950 CBS
   TV Playhouse ep The Vine That Grew on 50th Street
      10.8.50 NBC
   Prudential Playhouse ep The Barretts of Wimpole
      Street 12.5.50 CBS
   Cosmopolitan Theatre ep The Sighing Sound 12.18.51
      NN
   Tales of Tomorrow ep The Chase 1.25.52, 2.1.52
      ABC
   Broadway Television Theatre ep Night Must Fall 8.
      18.52 NN
   Kraft Theatre ep Letters to Lucerne 9.10.52 NBC
   Kraft Theatre ep The Fire Below and the Devil Above
      1.7.53 NBC
   Short Short Drama ep To Whom It May Concern 2.
      24.53 NBC
   Kraft Theatre ep Smilin' Through 12.17.53 ABC
   Lux Video Theatre ep Pick of the Litter 4.8.54 CBS
   Studio One ep The Hero 7.26.54 CBS
   The Millionaire ep The Ruth Ferris Story 10.30.57
   M Squad ep Blue Indigo 1.17.58 NBC
   Studio One ep Presence of the Enemy 2.10.58 CBS
   Suspicion ep A Touch of Evil 2.17.58 NBC
   Climax ep Shooting for the Moon 4.24.58 CBS
   Perry Mason ep The Case of the Purple Woman 11.
      22.58 CBS
   Name of the Game ep 11.29.68 NBC
   December Bride ep 2.1.59 CBS
   Texan ep 5.4.59 CBS
   Richard Diamond ep 5.24.59 CBS
   Maverick ep The Thirty-Ninth Star 5.24.59 ABC
   Alcoa Premiere ep The Riddle 6.16.59 ABC
   Man and the Challenge ep Odds Against Survival 9.26.
      59 NBC
   Bat Masterson ep 10.15.59 NBC
   Man from Blackhawk ep A Matter of Conscience 12.
      11.59 ABC
   Playhouse 90 ep The Silver Whistle 12.24.59 CBS
   June Allyson Show ep The Way Home 1.18.60 CBS
   Perry Mason ep The Case of the Wayward Wife 1.23.
      60 CBS
   Wagon Train ep The Joshua Gilliam Story 3.30.60
      NBC
   Great Mysteries ep The Bat 3.31.60 NBC
   Loretta Young Show ep Plain, Unmarked Envelope
      4.3.60 NBC

Man and the Challenge   ep   Early Warning   5. 28. 60
   NBC
Thriller   ep   Child's Play   9. 20. 60 NBC
Stagecoach West   ep   Unwanted   10. 25. 60 ABC
Riverboat   ep   Trunk Full of Dreams   10. 31. 60 NBC
Route 66   ep   Layout at Glen Canyon   12. 2. 60 CBS
Hong Kong   ep   12. 14. 60 ABC
Adventures in Paradise   ep   Man Eater   2. 6. 61 ABC
Thriller   ep   The Merriweather File   2. 14. 61 NBC
Checkmate   ep   Phantom Lover   3. 4. 61 CBS
Rifleman   ep   Stopover   4. 25. 61 ABC
Hong Kong   ep   The Dragon Cup   5. 31. 61 ABC
Wagon Train   ep   The Janet Hale Story   5. 31. 61 NBC
Perry Mason   ep   The Case of the Purple Woman   6.
   3. 61 CBS
Bus Stop   ep   Afternoon of a Cowboy   10. 1. 61 ABC
Follow the Sun   ep   The Woman Who Never Was   10.
   15. 61 ABC
Investigators   ep   Style of Living   11. 9. 61 CBS
Straightaway   ep   The Stranger   11. 17. 61 ABC
Ben Casey   ep   Pavane for a Gentle Lady   11. 20. 61
   ABC
Rawhide   ep   The Long Count   1. 5. 62 CBS
Route 66   ep   A City of Wheels   2. 2. 62 CBS
Cain's Hundred   ep   Inside Track   4. 10. 62 NBC
Checkmate   ep   Referendum on Murder   4. 25. 62 CBS
Alcoa Premiere   ep   The Rules of the Game   5. 1. 62
   ABC
Gunsmoke   ep   5. 31. 62 CBS
Lloyd Bridges Show   ep   My Child Is Yet a Stranger
   9. 25. 62 CBS
Empire   ep   The Tall Shadow   11. 20. 62 NBC
Naked City   ep   Spectre of the Rose Street Gang   12.
   19. 62 ABC
Ben Casey   ep   I'll Be All Right in the Morning   1. 7.
   63 ABC
Virginian   ep   The Money Cage   3. 6. 63 NBC
Have Gun, Will Travel   ep   3. 30. 63 CBS
Richard Boone Show   sr   9. 24. 63 NBC
Bob Hope Chrysler Theatre   ep   A Case of Armed Rob-
   bery   4. 3. 64 NBC
Eleventh Hour   ep   A Pattern of Sunday   4. 8. 64 NBC
Fugitive   ep   Storm Center   4. 14. 64 ABC
Route 66   ep   A City of Wheels   5. 22. 64 CBS
Daniel Boone   ep   The Family Fluellen   10. 15. 64 NBC
Wagon Train   ep   1. 24. 65 ABC
Wagon Train   ep   2. 28. 65 ABC

Defenders ep The Merry-Go-Round Murder 3.4.65 CBS
Bob Hope Chrysler Theatre ep March from Camp Tyler 10.6.65 NBC
Loner ep Mantrap 1.8.66 CBS
The Doctors sr 1968 NBC
Virginian ep 12.17.69 NBC
Bold Ones ep This Day's Child 2.8.70 NBC
Name of the Game ep Tarot 2.13.70 NBC
Mannix ep Once Upon a Saturday 3.21.70 CBS
Dr. Cook's Garden tf 1.19.71 ABC

LESLIE, JOAN
Bigelow-Sanford Theatre ep Flowers for John 12.6. 51 NN
Fireside Theatre ep Black Savannah 12.18.51 NBC
Fireside Theatre ep The Imposter 5.27.52 NBC
Schlitz Playhouse of Stars ep The Von Linden File 6.27.52 CBS
Summer Theatre ep Dream Job 7.17.53 ABC
Ford Theatre ep The Old Man's Bride 9.17.53 NBC
Ford Theatre ep Wonderful Day for a Wedding 5.13. 54 NBC
Ford Theatre ep Girl in Flight 12.2.54 NBC
20th Century-Fox Hour ep Smoke Jumpers 11.14.56 CBS
G.E. Theatre ep The Day of the Hanging 10.25.59 CBS
Branded ep Leap Upon Mountains 2.28.65 NBC

LESTER, JERRY
Robert Montgomery Presents ep Plainfield Teachers College 11.26.56 NBC

LESTER, MARK
World of Disney ep The Boy Who Stole the Elephants 9.20.70, 9.27.70 NBC

LEVENE, SAM
With These Hands ep 3.1.52 NBC
Medallion Theatre ep The Alibi Kid 3.27.54 CBS
Douglas Fairbanks, Jr. Presents ep Johnny Blue 5. 26.54 NBC
Studio One ep The Mother Bit 6.10.57 CBS
Kraft Theatre ep The Old Ticker 9.11.57 NBC
Omnibus ep Mrs. McThing 3.9.58 NBC
Play of the Week ep The World of Sholom Aleickem

12. 14. 59 NN
Aquanauts   ep   11. 16. 60 CBS
Untouchables   ep   The Larry Fay Story   12. 15. 60 ABC
Aquanauts   ep   1. 18. 61 CBS
Bob Hope Chrysler Theatre   ep   A Small Rebellion   2.
9. 66 NBC

LEWIS, CATHY
My Friend Irma   sr   1. 8. 52 CBS

LEWIS, JERRY
Ford Star Time   ep   The Jazz Singer   10. 13. 59 NBC
Ben Casey   ep   A Little Fun to Match the Sorrow   3. 8.
65 ABC

LIBERACE
Batman   ep   The Devil's Fingers   10. 26. 66, 10. 27. 66
ABC

LIEBER, FRITZ
Kraft Theatre   ep   Full of the Old Harry   11. 3. 54 NBC

LIGON, TOM
New York Television Theatre   ep   No Way   12. 13. 65
NN
Southern Baptist Hour   ep   The Statesman   1. 16. 66 NBC
A World Apart   sr   1970 ABC
Medical Center   ep   The Loser   11. 24. 71 CBS

LINDFORS, VIVECA
Ford Theatre   ep   The Bet   3. 19. 53 NBC
Lux Video Theatre   ep   Autumn Nocturne   2. 23. 53 CBS
Suspense   ep   The Riddle of Mayerling   9. 22. 53 CBS
U. S. Steel Hour   ep   The Vanishing Point   12. 22. 53
ABC
Appointment with Adventure   ep   The Fateful Pilgrimage
4. 17. 55 CBS
Climax   ep   The Passport   12. 8. 55 CBS
Alcoa Hour   ep   Adventure in Diamonds   12. 9. 56 NBC
U. S. Steel Hour   ep   They Never Forget   1. 30. 57 CBS
Climax   ep   The Long Count   2. 21. 57 CBS
Loretta Young Show   ep   Louise   3. 10. 57 NBC
Playhouse 90   ep   The Last Tycoon   3. 14. 57 CBS
Dupont Show of the Month   ep   The Bridge of San Luis
Rey   1. 21. 58 CBS
Kraft Theatre   ep   The Spell of the Tigress   2. 5. 58
NBC

U.S. Steel Hour   ep   Dangerous Episode   1.14.59 CBS
Adventures in Paradise   ep   Castaways   1.4.60 ABC
Play of the Week   ep   The Emperor's Clothes   1.11.60
    NN
Naked City   ep   The Deadly Guinea Pig   3.8.61 ABC
Untouchables   ep   Ring of Terror   4.13.61 ABC
Defenders   ep   The Locked Room   2.10.62 CBS
Theatre   62   ep   The Paradine Case   3.11.62 NBC
Nurses   ep   Night Shirt   9.27.62 CBS
12 O'Clock High   ep   The Climate of Doubt   10.23.64
    ABC
Defenders   ep   Comeback   11.26.64 CBS
Voyage to the Bottom of the Sea   ep   Hail to the Chief
    12.28.64 ABC
Ben Casey   ep   A Dip Full of Water from a Poisoned
    Well   3.1.65 ABC
Bonanza   ep   5.16.65 NBC
Ben Casey   ep   Where Did all the Roses Go?   2.21.66
    ABC
Coronet Blue   ep   The Presence of Evil   8.7.67 CBS
FBI   ep   11.5.67 ABC
Diary of Anne Frank   Sp   11.26.67 ABC
Medical Center   ep   12.3.69 CBS
FBI   ep   The Doll Courier   12.21.69 ABC
Interns   ep   The Fever   12.4.70 CBS

LINDSAY, HOWARD
    U.S. Steel Hour   ep   Haven's End   7.6.54 ABC
    Cinderella   Sp   3.31.57 CBS

LINDSAY, MARGARET
    Masterpiece Theatre   ep   The Importance of Being
        Earnest   8.20.50 NBC
    TV Reader's Digest   ep   Ordeal at Yuba Gap   12.26.55
        ABC
    Lux Video Theatre   ep   Indiscreet   5.31.56 NBC
    Studio 57   ep   Mrs. Snyder   7.28.57 NN
    The Millionaire   ep   The Martha Crockett Story   2.12.
        58 CBS
    Buckskin   ep   The Ballad of Gabe Pruitt   6.8.59 NBC
    Five Fingers   ep   The Judas Goat   1.2.60 CBS
    Surfside 6   ep   The Old School Tie   11.20.61 ABC

LINKLETTER, ART
    G.E. Theatre   ep   The Big Shooter   2.17.57 CBS
    G.E. Theatre   ep   Kid at the Stick   1.5.58 CBS
    G.E. Theatre   ep   The Odd Ball   12.28.58 CBS

Bob Cummings Show   ep   1. 27. 59 NBC
G. E. Theatre   ep   Badge of Honor   2. 11. 62 CBS
Wagon Train   ep   The Sam Darland Story   12. 26. 62
    ABC

LIPTON, PETTY
    Mod Squad   sr   9. 24. 68 ABC
    Mod Squad   sr ret   9. 23. 69 ABC
    Mod Squad   sr ret   9. 22. 70 ABC
    Mod Squad   sr ret   9. 14. 71 ABC
    Mod Squad   sr ret   9. 14. 72 ABC

LITTLE, CLEAVON
    All in the Family   ep   10. 9. 71 CBS
    Temperatures Rising   sr   9. 12. 72 ABC
    Mod Squad   ep   The Connection   9. 14. 72 ABC

LO BIANCO, TONY
    N. Y. P. D.   ep   Cry Brute   2. 6. 68 ABC
    N. Y. P. D.   ep   2. 27. 68 ABC
    Hidden Faces   sr   1969 NBC
    N. E. T. Playhouse   ep   A Memory of Two Mondays
        1. 28. 71 NN

LOCKHART, GENE
    Lights Out   ep   Dr. Heidegger's Experiment   11. 20. 50
        NBC
    Prudential Playhouse   ep   The Barretts of Wimpole
        Street   12. 5. 50 CBS
    Airflyte Theatre   ep   The Windfall 12. 14. 50 CBS
    Video Theatre   ep   A Child Is Born   12. 25. 50 CBS
    Robert Montgomery Presents   ep   The House of Seven
        Gables   5. 21. 51 NBC
    Tales of Tomorrow   ep   The Golden Ingot   5. 9. 52 ABC
    Video Theatre   ep   Ile   9. 8. 52 CBS
    Broadway Television Theatre   ep   The Bishop Misbe-
        haves   9. 22. 52 NN
    Gulf Playhouse   ep   The Rose   10. 17. 52 NBC
    Robert Montgomery Presents   ep   The Biarritz Scandal
        11. 10. 52 NBC
    Gulf Playhouse   ep   An Afternoon in Caribou   11. 28. 52
        NBC
    Robert Montgomery Presents   ep   The Burtons   2. 16.
        53 NBC
    Ford Theatre   ep   My Daughter's Husband   3. 12. 53 NBC
    Danger   ep   But the Patient Died   10. 13. 53 CBS
    Armstrong Circle Theatre   .ep   The Bells of Cockaigne

11.17.53 NBC

Schlitz Playhouse of Stars   ep   The Closed Door   11.27.
53 CBS

Backbone of America   12.29.53 NBC

TV Soundstage   ep   The Test Case   3.26.54 NBC

Motorola TV Hour   ep   The Sins of the Fathers   4.6.
54 ABC

Armstrong Circle Theatre   ep   Treasure Trove   4.20.
54 NBC

Video Theatre   ep   The Queen's English   5.13.54 CBS

His Honor, Homer Bell   sr   1955 NN

20th Century-Fox Hour   ep   The Late Christopher Bean
11.30.55 CBS

Lux Video Theatre   ep   Has Anybody Seen My Gal?
5.3.56 NBC

Science Fiction Theatre   ep   When a Camera Falls   5.
4.56 NBC

On Trial   ep   Law Is for the Lovers   11.9.56 NBC

Lux Video Theatre   ep   It Happened on Fifth Avenue
1.3.57 NBC

Climax   ep   Don't Ever Come Back   2.28.57 CBS

LOCKHART, JUNE

Pulitzer Prize Playhouse   ep   The Just and the Unjust
3.30.51 ABC

Prudential Playhouse   ep   One Sunday Afternoon   3.13.
51 CBS

Robert Montgomery Presents   ep   The House of Seven
Gables   5.21.51 NBC

Robert Montgomery Presents   ep   For Love or Money
6.4.51 NBC

Video Theatre   ep   The Doctor's Wife   10.29.51 CBS

Robert Montgomery Presents   ep   Cashel Byron's Profession   1.14.52 NBC

Schlitz Playhouse of Stars   ep   Apple of His Eye   2.29.
52 CBS

Robert Montgomery Presents   ep   Operation Hitchhike
4.14.52 NBC

Video Theatre   ep   Happily, But Not Forever   9.22.52
CBS

Studio One   ep   The Doctor's Wife   10.6.52 CBS

Robert Montgomery Presents   ep   The Biarritz Scandal
11.10.52 NBC

Robert Montgomery Presents   ep   The Burtons   2.16.53
NBC

Studio One   ep   At Midnight on the 31st of March   3.30.
53 CBS

Robert Montgomery Presents ep The Steady Man 1.
  4.54 NBC
U.S. Steel Hour ep Goodbye ...But It Doesn't Go Away
  11.9.54 ABC
Studio One ep The Deserter 11.29.54 CBS
Elgin Hour ep Midsummer Melody 4.19.55 ABC
Kraft Theatre ep My Aunt Daisy 6.15.55 CBS
Philco Playhouse ep Rise Up and Walk 1.1.56 NBC
Appointment with Adventure ep Suburban Terror 1.15.
  56 CBS
Robert Montgomery Presents ep Jack Be Nimble 5.
  7.56 NBC
Telephone Time ep Vicksburg 5:35 P.M. 10.7.56
  CBS
Alcoa Hour ep Morning's at Seven 11.4.56 NBC
Schlitz Playhouse of Stars ep The Night They Won the
  Oscar 11.9.56 CBS
Playhouse 90 ep The Confession 11.29.56 CBS
Ford Theatre ep Fear Has Many Faces 1.2.57 ABC
Climax ep The Gold Dress 1.17.57 CBS
On Trial ep Libel in the Wax Museum 1.18.57 NBC
Robert Montgomery Presents ep The Grand Prize 2.
  11.57 NBC
Kaiser Aluminum Hour ep The Story of a Crime 3.12.
  57 NBC
Lux Video Theatre ep The Man Who Played God 4.24.
  57 NBC
Studio One ep A Matter of Guilt 7.8.57 CBS
U.S. Steel Hour ep A Loud Laugh 8.14.57 CBS
Lassie sr fall, 1957 CBS
Climax ep Jacob and the Angel 10.3.57 CBS
U.S. Steel Hour ep The Locked Door 11.6.57 CBS
Have Gun, Will Travel ep 11.30.57 CBS
U.S. Steel Hour ep Little Charlie Don't Want a Saddle
  12.18.57 CBS
Shirley Temple's Story Book ep Beauty and the Beast
  1.12.58 NBC
Studio One ep Balance of Terror 1.27.58 CBS
Matinee Theatre ep The Long, Long Laugh 2.5.58
  NBC
Gunsmoke ep 3.1.58 CBS
Wagon Train ep The Sarah Drummond Story 4.1.58
  NBC
Zane Grey Theatre ep A Handful of Ashes 5.2.58 CBS
Have Gun, Will Travel 5.17.58 CBS
Decision ep Fear Has Many Faces 8.31.58 NBC
Lassie sr ret fall, 1958 CBS

Rawhide   ep   Incident at Barker Springs   2.20.59 CBS
U.S. Steel Hour   ep   The Square Egghead   3.11.59 CBS
Cimarron City   ep   Medicine Man   4.18.59 NBC
Lassie   sr ret   fall, 1959 CBS
G.E. Theatre   ep   Night Club   10.19.59 CBS
Lassie   sr ret   9.11.60 CBS
Best of the Post   ep   The Marriage that Couldn't Suc-
    ceed   11.19.60 ABC
Perry Mason   ep   The Case of the Scandalous Sculptor
    10.8.64 CBS
Bewitched   ep   10.22.64 ABC
Voyage to the Bottom of the Sea   ep   The Ghost of Moby
    Dick   12.14.64 ABC
The Man from U.N.C.L.E.   ep   The Dove Affair   12.
    15.64 NBC
Branded   ep   Vindicated   1.31.65 NBC
Alfred Hitchcock Theatre   ep   The Second Wife   4.26.65
    NBC
Mr. Novak   ep   Once a Clown   4.27.65 NBC
Lost in Space   sr   9.15.65 CBS
Lost in Space   sr ret   9.21.66 CBS
Lost in Space   sr ret   9.6.67 CBS
Family Affair   ep   10.21.68 CBS
Petticoat Junction   sr   11.16.68 CBS
Petticoat Junction   sr ret   9.27.69 CBS
But I Don't Want to Get Married   tf   10.6.70 ABC
Man and the City   ep   Hands of Love   9.15.71 ABC

LOCKWOOD, GARY
    Follow the Sun   sr   9.17.61 ABC
    Bus Stop   ep   Cherie   11.12.61 ABC
    Saints and Sinners   ep   Dear George, the Siamese Cat
        Is Missing   9.17.62 NBC
    Perry Mason   ep   The Case of the Playboy Pugilist   10.
        11.62 CBS
    Lloyd Bridges Show   ep   My Daddy Can Lick Your Daddy
        1.22.63 CBS
    Lieutenant   sr   9.14.63 NBC
    Combat   ep   Operation Fly Trap   10.27.64 ABC
    12 O'Clock High   ep   Appointment at Liege   11.20.64
        ABC
    12 O'Clock High   ep   V for Vendetta   4.16.65 ABC
    Kraft Suspense Theatre   ep   Connery's Hands   7.1.65
        NBC
    The Long Hot Summer   ep   A Day of Trouble   1.19.66
        ABC
    Gunsmoke   ep   1.22.66 CBS

Star Trek   ep   Where No Man Has Gone Before   9.22.
    66 NBC
Medical Center   ep   10.7.70 CBS
Medical Center   ep   Men at Bay   10.14.70 CBS
Young Rebels   ep   To Kill a Traitor   1.3.71 ABC
Young Lawyers   ep   I've Got a Problem   3.25.71 ABC
Earth II   tf   11.28.71 ABC
Night Gallery   ep   The Ring with the Red Velvet Ropes
    11.5.72 NBC

LODEN, BARBARA
    Naked City   ep   Torment Him   11.7.62 ABC

LODER, JOHN
    Tele Theatre   ep   The Bone for the Shadow   4.17.50
        NBC
    Prudential Playhouse   ep   Call It a Day   11.7.50 CBS
    Billy Rose's Playbill   ep   One More Night to Go   12.
        18.50 NN
    Robert Montgomery Presents   ep   For Love or Money
        6.4.51 NBC
    The Vise   ep   The Bargain   8.5.55 ABC
    Assignment Foreign Legion   ep   The Thin Line   12.3.
        57 CBS
    Saber of London   ep   Fast Cars and Girls   12.22.57
        NBC
    Detective Diary   ep   The Visitor   3.28.59 NBC

LOM, HERBERT
    World of Disney   ep   The Horse without a Head   9.29.
        63, 10.5.63 NBC
    The Man from U.N.C.L.E.   ep 3.31.67, 4.7.67 NBC
    Mister Jerico   tf   3.3.70 ABC
    Hawaii Five-O   ep   Highest Castle   12.21.71 CBS

LONDON, JULIE
    Zane Grey Theatre   ep   A Time to Live   4.5.57 CBS
    Playhouse 90   ep   Without Incident   6.6.57 CBS
    David Niven Theatre   ep   Maggie Malone   6.9.59 NBC
    Adventures in Paradise   ep   Mission to Manila   11.23.
        59 ABC
    Laramie   ep   Queen of Diamonds   9.20.60 NBC
    Rawhide   ep   Incident at Rojo Canyon   9.30.60 CBS
    Dan Raven   ep   Tinge of Red   12.16.60 NBC
    Hong Kong   ep   Suitable for Framing   1.4.61 ABC
    Barbara Stanwyck Theatre   ep   Night Visitors   1.9.61
        NBC

Checkmate ep Good-By Griff 4.15.61 CBS
Follow the Sun ep Night Son 11.26.61 ABC
Dick Powell Theatre ep Charlie's Duet 3.19.63 NBC
Eleventh Hour ep Like a Diamond in the Sky 2.13.63
    NBC
Alfred Hitchcock Theatre ep The Crimson Witness 1.
    4.65 NBC
I Spy ep Three Hours on a Sunday Night 12.8.65 NBC
Big Valley ep 9.30.68 ABC
Emergency tf 1.15.72 NBC
Emergency sr 1.22.72 NBC
Emergency sr ret 9.16.72 NBC
Adam-12 ep Emergency 10.4.72 NBC

LONG, RICHARD
Video Theatre ep 5.27.54 CBS
TV Reader's Digest ep Holiday in Mexico 4.18.55
    ABC
Climax ep Wild Stallion 7.7.55 CBS
Matinee Theatre ep The Gate 1.9.56 NBC
U.S. Steel Hour ep The Great Adventure 1.18.56
    CBS
TV Reader's Digest ep Down on the Tennessee 5.21.
    56 ABC
Schlitz Playhouse of Stars ep Terror in the Streets 1.
    18.57 CBS
Suspicion ep Four O'Clock 9.30.57 NBC
Alcoa Theatre ep In the Dark 1.13.58 NBC
Wagon Train ep The Annie MacGregor Story 2.5.58
    NBC
The Millionaire ep The Johanna Judson Story 3.5.58
    CBS
Maverick ep Alias Bart Maverick 4.12.59 ABC
Maverick ep The Spanish Dancer 4.26.59 ABC
Sugarfoot ep The Vultures 4.28.59 ABC
Lawman ep The Ring 5.24.59 ABC
77 Sunset Strip ep One False Step 9.18.59 ABC
Bourbon Street Beat sr 10.5.59 ABC
Maverick ep The Goose-Drowner 12.13.59 ABC
77 Sunset Strip ep The President's Daughter 9.30.60
    ABC
Thriller ep An Attractive Family 1.1.62 NBC
Outlaws ep No More Horses 3.1.62 NBC
Twilight Zone ep Person or Persons Unknown 3.23.62
    CBS
77 Sunset Strip ep Nine to Five 3.8.63 ABC
Going My Way ep Hear No Evil 4.17.63 ABC

77 Sunset Strip   ep   The Fumble   12.13.63 ABC
Twilight Zone   ep   Number Twelve Looks Just Like You
   1.24.64 CBS
I Spy   ep   So Long Patrick Henry   9.15.65 NBC
Big Valley   sr   9.15.65 ABC
Kraft Suspense Theatre   ep   Streetcar Do You Read Me
   2.25.66 NBC
Big Valley   sr ret   9.12.66 ABC
Big Valley   sr ret   9.11.67 ABC
Big Valley   sr ret   9.23.68 ABC
Nanny and the Professor   sr   1.21.70 ABC
Nanny and the Professor   sr ret   9.25.70 ABC
Nanny and the Professor   sr ret   9.12.71 ABC

LOO, RICHARD
   Summer Theatre   ep   Foo Young   7.10.53 ABC
   Cavalcade of America   ep   Ordeal in Burma   11.30.54
      ABC
   Elgin Hour   ep   Combat Medic   6.14.55 ABC
   TV Reader's Digest   ep   The Brainwashing of John Hayes
      11.7.55 ABC
   Navy Log   ep   Dr. Van   1.10.56 CBS
   Four Star Playhouse   ep   Wall of Bamboo   4.19.56 CBS
   Cavalcade Theatre   ep   Diplomatic Outpost   5.1.56 ABC
   TV Reader's Digest   ep   The Smuggler   7.9.56 ABC
   Music Theatre   ep   An Almost Perfect Plan   4.2.59 NBC
   Hong Kong   ep   The Jade Empress   4.12.61 ABC
   Bonanza   ep   Day of the Dragon   12.3.61 NBC
   Hawaiian Eye   ep   Two Too Many   1.29.63 ABC
   Dakotas   ep   The Chooser of the Slain   4.22.63 ABC
   Outer Limits   ep   The Hundred Days of the Dragon   9.
      23.63 ABC
   Wagon Train   ep   The Widow O'Rourke Story   10.7.63
      ABC
   Honey West   ep   The Owl and the Eye   9.24.65 ABC
   Amos Burke   ep   Deadlier than the Male   11.17.65 ABC
   Wackiest Ship in the Army   ep   The Lamb that Hunted
      Wolves   1.2.66, 1.9.66 NBC
   I Dream of Jeannie   ep   2.12.66 NBC
   The Man from U.N.C.L.E.   ep   The Indian Affairs   4.
      15.66 NBC
   Family Affair   ep   2.27.67 CBS
   My Three Sons   ep   5.11.67 CBS
   Hawaii Five-O   ep   The 24 Karat Kill   11.14.68 CBS
   Marcus Welby, M.D.   tf   3.26.69 ABC
   Here Come the Brides   ep   4.9.69 ABC
   Kung Fu   tf   2.22.72 ABC

Sixth Sense   ep   3. 4. 72 ABC
Delphi Bureau   ep   10. 5. 72 ABC

LORD, JACK
Omnibus   ep   One Nation   2. 5. 56 CBS
Studio One   ep   An Incident of Love   7. 23. 56 CBS
Philco Playhouse   ep   This Land Is Mine   1. 15. 56 NBC
Conflict   ep   Pattern for Violence   5. 14. 57 ABC
Climax   ep   Mr. Runyon of Broadway   6. 6. 57 CBS
Playhouse 90   ep   Reunion   1. 2. 58 CBS
The Millionaire   ep   The Lee Randolph Story   11. 19. 58
   CBS
Lineup   ep   The Strange Return of Army Armitage   11.
   25. 59 CBS
Alcoa Presents   ep   Father Image   12. 15. 59 ABC
Bonanza   ep   The Outcast   1. 9. 60 NBC
Route 66   ep   Play It Glissando   1. 20. 61 CBS
Americans   ep   Half Moon Road   2. 27. 61 NBC
Outlaws   ep   The Bell   3. 9. 61 NBC
Stagecoach West   ep   House of Violence   3. 21. 61 ABC
Rawhide   ep   The Incident of His Brother's Keeper   3.
   31. 61 CBS
Checkmate   ep   The Star System   1. 10. 62 CBS
Stoney Burke   sr   10. 1. 62 ABC
The Greatest Show on Earth   ep   Man in a Hole   2. 18.
   64 ABC
Reporter   ep   How Much for a Prince   10. 9. 64 CBS
Wagon Train   ep   1. 3. 65 ABC
Kraft Suspense Theatre   ep   The Long Ravine 5. 6. 65
   NBC
Bob Hope Chrysler Theatre   ep   The Crime   9. 22. 65
   NBC
Loner   ep   The Vespers   9. 25. 65 CBS
12 O'Clock High   ep   Big Brother   10. 11. 65 ABC
Laredo   ep   1. 13. 66 NBC
Bob Hope Chrysler Theatre   ep   The Faceless Man   5.
   4. 66 NBC
12 O'Clock High   ep   Face of a Shadow   9. 23. 66 ABC
FBI   ep   11. 13. 66 ABC
Bob Hope Chrysler Theatre   ep   Storm Crossing   12. 7.
   66 NBC
Doomsday Flight   tf   2. 13. 67 NBC
Invaders   ep   2. 14. 67 ABC
Fugitive   ep   2. 28. 67 ABC
Have Gun, Will Travel   ep   9. 14. 67 CBS
Ironside   ep   Dead Man's Tale   9. 28. 67 NBC
The Man from U. N. C. L. E.   ep   The Master's Touch

10. 16. 67 NBC
High Chaparral   ep   The Kinsman   1. 28. 68 NBC
Hawaii Five-O   tf   9. 20. 68 CBS
Hawaii Five-O   sr   9. 26. 68 CBS
Hawaii Five-O   sr ret   9. 24. 69 CBS
Hawaii Five-O   sr ret   9. 16. 70 CBS
Hawaii Five-O   sr ret   9. 14. 71 CBS
Hawaii Five-O   sr ret   9. 12. 72 CBS

LORD, MARJORIE
Story Theatre   ep   The Real Thing   1. 5. 51 NN
Fireside Theatre   ep   Mirage   6. 10. 52 NBC
Fireside Theatre   ep   Visit from a Stranger   10. 28. 52
   NBC
Fireside Theatre   ep   The Visitor   2. 10. 53 NBC
Schlitz Playhouse of Stars   ep   The Devil's Other Name
   2. 20. 53 CBS
Easy Chair Theatre   ep   Brown of Calaveras   3. 2. 53
   NN
20th Century Tales   ep   Small Town Story   4. 22. 53
   ABC
Fireside Theatre   ep   The Hitchhiker   5. 5. 53 NBC
Ford Theatre   ep   The Jewel   5. 28. 53 NBC
Ford Theatre   ep   The Edge of the Law   7. 23. 53 NBC
Gold Seal Theatre   ep   The Devil's Other Hand   12. 16.
   53 ABC
G. E. Theatre   ep   That Other Sunlight   3. 14. 54 CBS
Schlitz Playhouse of Stars   ep   Her Kind of Honor   3.
   19. 54 CBS
Fireside Theatre   ep   Trial Period   5. 4. 54 NBC
Cavalcade of America   ep   The Great Gamble   10. 5. 54
   NBC
Ford Theatre   ep   Shadow of Truth   10. 14. 54 NBC
Cavalcade of America   ep   Take Off Zero   2. 1. 55 ABC
Cavalcade of America   ep   Decision for Justice   2. 15.
   55 ABC
Loretta Young Show   ep   A Shadow Between 12. 18. 55
   NBC
Omnibus   ep   The Billy Mitchell Court-Martial   4. 1. 56
   CBS
Zane Grey Theatre   ep   Decision at Wilson's Creek   5.
   17. 57 CBS
Wagon Train   ep   The Willy Moran Story   9. 18. 57 NBC
Danny Thomas Show   sr   10. 7. 57 CBS
Danny Thomas Show   sr ret   10. 58 CBS
Lucille Ball-Desi Arnaz Hour   ep   Lucy Makes Room
   for Danny   12. 15. 58 CBS

Danny Thomas Show   sr ret   10. 5. 59 CBS
Danny Thomas Show   sr ret   10. 3. 60 CBS
Danny Thomas Show   sr ret   10. 2. 61 CBS
Danny Thomas Show   sr ret   10. 1. 62 CBS
Danny Thomas Show   sr ret   9. 30. 63 CBS
Danny Thomas Show   ep   Make More Room for Daddy
    11. 6. 67 NBC
Love American Style   ep   10. 27. 69 ABC
Make Room for Granddaddy   sr   9. 23. 70 ABC

LORNE, MARION
Mr. Peepers   sr   10. 26. 52 NBC
Mr. Peepers   sr ret   9. 13. 53 NBC
Mr. Peepers   sr ret   9. 19. 54 NBC
Sally   sr   9. 15. 57 NBC
Suspicion   ep   The Way up to Heaven   4. 28. 58 NBC
Dupont Show of the Month   ep   Harvey   9. 22. 58 CBS
Bewitched   sr   9. 17. 64 ABC
Bewitched   sr ret   9. 16. 65 ABC
Bewitched   sr ret   9. 15. 66 ABC
Bewitched   sr ret   9. 7. 67 ABC

LORRE, PETER
Video Theatre   ep   Taste   3. 31. 52 CBS
Suspense   ep   The Tortured Hand   12. 16. 52 CBS
U. S. Steel Hour   ep   The Vanishing Point   12. 22. 53
    ABC
Schlitz Playhouse of Stars   ep   The Pipe   9. 24. 54 CBS
Climax   ep   Casino Royale   10. 21. 54 CBS
Best of Broadway   ep   Arsenic and Old Lace   1. 5. 55
    CBS
Producers Showcase   ep   Reunion in Vienna   4. 4. 55 NBC
Eddie Cantor Theatre   ep   The Sure Cure   5. 2. 55 ABC
Climax   ep   A Promise to Murder   11. 17. 55 CBS
Rheingold Theatre   ep   The Blue Landscape   12. 10. 55
    NBC
Screen Directors Playhouse   ep   Number Five Checked
    Out   1. 18. 56 NBC
Studio 57   ep   The Finishers   1. 29. 56 NN
Climax   ep   The Fifth Wheel   2. 9. 56 CBS
Climax   ep   The Man Who Lost His Head   7. 26. 56 CBS
Playhouse 90   ep   Seidman and Son   10. 18. 56 CBS
20th Century-Fox Hour   ep   Operation Cicero   12. 26. 56
    CBS
Playhouse 90   ep   The Last Tycoon   3. 14. 57 CBS
Climax   ep   A Taste for Crime   6. 20. 57 CBS
Playhouse 90   ep   The Jet-Propelled Couch   11. 14. 57 CBS

Alfred Hitchcock Presents ep The Diplomatic Corpse
    12. 8. 57 CBS
Five Fingers ep Thin Ice   12. 19. 59 NBC
Alfred Hitchcock Presents ep Man from the South 1.
    3. 60 CBS
Playhouse 90 ep The Cruel Day 2. 24. 60 CBS
Wagon Train ep The Alexander Portlass Story 3. 16.
    60 NBC
Rawhide ep Incident of the Slavemaster 10. 11. 60
    CBS
Checkmate ep The Human Touch 1. 14. 61 CBS
Best of the Post ep The Baron Loved His Wife 1. 21.
    61 ABC
Mrs. G. Goes to College ep 12. 6. 61 CBS
Route 66 ep Lizard's Leg and Owlet's Wing 10. 26. 62
    CBS
Dupont Show of the Month ep Diamond Fever 3. 24. 63
    NBC
77 Sunset Strip ep "5" 9. 20. 63 ABC
Kraft Suspense Theatre ep The End of the World Baby
    10. 24. 63 NBC

LORRING, JOAN
    Philco Playhouse ep The Thin Air 9. 21. 52 NBC
    The Doctor ep No Story Assignment 11. 23. 52 NBC
    Goodyear Playhouse ep The Rumor 3. 8. 53 NBC
    Motorola TV Hour ep A Dash of Bitters 2. 9. 54 ABC
    Robert Montgomery Presents ep The Pale Blond of
        Sand Street 4. 12. 54 NBC
    Studio One ep Castles in Spain 5. 17. 54 CBS
    Center Stage ep The Day Before Atlanta 9. 7. 54 ABC
    Norby sr 1. 5. 55 NBC
    Studio One ep Millions of George 3. 7. 55 CBS
    Elgin Hour ep Black Eagle Pass 4. 5. 55 ABC
    Goodyear Playhouse ep The Prizewinner 7. 3. 55 NBC
    Ponds Theatre ep Coquette 7. 7. 55 ABC
    Appointment with Adventure ep Return of the Stranger
        7. 17. 55 CBS
    Hallmark Hall of Fame ep The Corn Is Green 1. 8. 56
        NBC
    Star Stage ep Of Missing Persons 1. 13. 56 NBC
    Alfred Hitchcock Presents ep The Older Sister 1. 22.
        56 CBS
    Robert Montgomery Presents ep End of Morning 2.
        27. 56 NBC
    G. E. Theatre ep The Shunning 5. 6. 56 CBS
    For the People ep Act of Violence 2. 21. 65, 2. 28. 65
        CBS

N. E. T. Playhouse   ep   The Star Wagon   6.2.67 NN

LOUISE, ANITA
Stars over Hollywood   ep   Landing at Daybreak   11.29. 50 NBC
Ford Theatre   ep   Heart of Gold   12.25.52 NBC
Fireside Theatre   ep   The Juror   2.24.53 NBC
Ford Theatre   ep   The Fugitives   1.7.54 NBC
Ford Theatre   ep   Favorite Son   6.16.55 NBC
My Friend Flicka   sr   9.30.55 CBS
Ethel Barrymore Theatre   ep   Dear Miss Lovelace   12. 7.56 NN
The Millionaire   ep   The Story of Nancy Wellington   1. 8.57 CBS
Playhouse 90   ep   The Greer Case   1.31.57 CBS
Theatre Time   sh   7.25.57 ABC
Loretta Young Show   ep   Power Play   12.29.57 NBC
Spotlight Playhouse   sh   7.1.58 CBS
U.S. Steel Hour   ep   Far from the Shade Tree   1.10. 62 CBS

LOUISE, TINA
Studio One   ep   The Bounty Hunters   1.16.56 CBS
Appointment with Adventure   ep   All Through the Night   2.5.56 CBS
Producers Showcase   ep   Happy Birthday   6.25.56 NBC
Phil Silvers Show   ep   Bilko Goes South   3.26.57 CBS
Climax   ep   A Matter of Life and Death   12.1.57 CBS
Tales of Wells Fargo   ep   New Orleans Trackdown   12. 23.61 NBC
New Breed   ep   I Remember Murder   12.26.61 ABC
Checkmate   ep   A Funny Thing Happened to Me on the Way to the Game   1.3.62 CBS
Real McCoys   ep   Grandpa Pygmalion   9.30.62 CBS
Route 66   ep   Tex I'm Here to Kill a King   11.29.63 ABC
Gilligan's Island   sr   9.26.64 ABC
Gilligan's Island   sr ret   9.15.65 CBS
Gilligan's Island   sr ret   9.12.66 CBS
Bonanza   ep   11.5.67 NBC
Suspense Theatre   ep   The Deep End   1.11.68 ABC
It Takes a Thief   ep   2.20.68 ABC
Love American Style   ep   11.10.69 ABC
Mannix   ep   Missing: Sun and Sky   12.20.69 CBS
Ironside   ep   Beware the Wiles of the Stranger   1.22.70 NBC
But I Don't Want to Get Married   tf   10.7.70 ABC

Love American Style   ep   1.7.72 ABC

LOVEJOY, FRANK
  Video Theatre   ep   Second Meeting   9.10.53 CBS
  Four Star Playhouse   ep   Out of the Night   11.5.53
    CBS
  Four Star Playhouse   ep   Meet McGraw   2.25.54 CBS
  Four Star Playhouse   ep   Search in the Night   6.17.54
    CBS
  U.S. Steel Hour   ep   Baseball Blues   9.28.54 ABC
  Lux Video Theatre   ep   Double Indemnity   12.16.54
    NBC
  Stage 7   ep   The Deceiving Eye   1.30.55 CBS
  Rheingold Theatre   ep   Safe Journey   2.5.55 NBC
  Stage 7   ep   The Long Count   3.27.55 CBS
  Rheingold Theatre   ep   Honolulu   6.25.55 NBC
  Ford Star Jubilee   ep   The Caine Mutiny Court Martial
    11.19.55 CBS
  Climax   ep   The Passport   12.8.55 CBS
  Rheingold Theatre   ep   Act of Decision   3.10.56 NBC
  Rheingold Theatre   ep   The Whizzer   3.31.56 NBC
  Loretta Young Show   ep   Case 258   4.15.56 NBC
  Man Against Crime   sr   7.1.56 NBC
  Four Star Playhouse   ep   Yellowbelly   7.12.56 CBS
  Playhouse 90   ep   The Country Husband   11.1.56 CBS
  Zane Grey Theatre   ep   No Man Living   1.11.57 CBS
  Ford Theatre   ep   Sweet Charlie   1.16.57 ABC
  Dupont Theatre   ep   Chicago 2-1-2   4.30.57 ABC
  Meet McGraw   sr   7.2.57 NBC
  Loretta Young Show   ep   Out of Control   11.2.58 NBC
  Playhouse 90   ep   The Raider   2.19.59 CBS
  Zane Grey Theatre   ep   Hanging Fever   3.12.59 CBS
  David Niven Theatre   ep   Backtrack   4.21.59 NBC
  Loretta Young Show   ep   Circles of Panic   10.25.59
    NBC
  Zane Grey Theatre   ep   Shadows   11.5.59 CBS
  June Allyson Show   ep   Escape   2.22.60 CBS
  Wichita Town   ep   The Hanging Judge   3.9.60 NBC
  U.S. Steel Hour   ep   Shadow of a Pale Horse   7.20.60
    CBS
  Dupont Show of the Month   ep   The Battle of the Paper
    10.15.61 NBC
  Target Corruptors   ep   The Fix   12.22.61 ABC
  Bus Stop   ep   County General   3.18.62 ABC

LOWE, EDMUND
  Front Page Detective   sr   3.16.51 NN

Conflict   ep   Execution Night   5. 28. 57 ABC
Maverick   ep   The War of the Silver Kings   9. 22. 57
   ABC

LOY, MYRNA
   G. E. Theatre   ep   It Gives Me Great Pleasure   4. 3. 55
   G. E. Theatre   ep   Lady of the House   1. 20. 57 CBS
   G. E. Theatre   ep   Love Came Late   11. 17. 57 CBS
   Schlitz Playhouse of Stars   ep   No Second Helping   11.
      22. 57 CBS
   Meet Me in St. Louis   Sp   4. 26. 59 CBS
   June Allyson Show   ep   Surprise Party   4. 18. 60 CBS
   Family Affair   ep   2. 6. 67 CBS
   Virginian   ep   4. 5. 67 NBC
   Death Takes a Holiday   tf   10. 21. 71 ABC
   Do Not Fold, Spindle or Mutilate   tf   11. 9. 71 ABC
   Columbo   ep   Etude in Black   9. 17. 72 NBC

LUCE, CLARE
   Cameo Theatre   ep   Of Unsound Mind   7. 23. 51 NBC
   Tales of Tomorrow   ep   The Children's Room   2. 29. 52
      ABC
   Cameo Theatre   ep   Peer Gynt   2. 24. 52, 3. 2. 52 NBC
   Lights Out   ep   Death Trap   7. 28. 52 NBC
   Broadway Television Theatre   ep   Candlelight   2. 16. 53
      NN
   Broadway Television Theatre   ep   Interference   5. 5. 53
      NN
   Broadway Television Theatre   ep   The Thirteenth Chair
      12. 28. 53 NN
   Broadway Television Theatre   ep   Reflected Glory   1.
      18. 54 NN
   Matinee Theatre   ep   Technique   12. 20. 55 NBC
   Matinee Theatre   ep   Hold My Hand and Run   2. 1. 56
      NBC

LUCKINBILL, LAURENCE
   N. Y. P. D.   ep   Naked in the Streets   10. 1. 68 ABC
   Where the Heart Is   sr   1970 CBS
   Bold Ones   ep   The Continual Roar of Musketry   11. 22.
      70, 11. 29. 70 NBC
   Mission Impossible   ep   1. 15. 72 CBS
   Delphi Bureau   tf   3. 6. 72 ABC
   Delphi Bureau   sr   10. 5. 72 ABC

LUKAS, PAUL
   Sure as Fate   ep   Tremolo   7. 4. 50 CBS

Robert Montgomery Presents ep The Ringmaster 5.
26. 52 NBC
Armstrong Circle Theatre ep Caprice 9. 9. 52 NBC
Video Theatre ep Something to Celebrate 11. 10. 52
CBS
Orient Express ep Red Sash 12. 19. 53 CBS
U. S. Steel Hour ep The Thief 1. 4. 55 ABC
Mr. Citizen ep The Friendly Stranger 6. 8. 55 ABC
Playhouse 90 ep Judgment at Nuremberg 4. 16. 59
CBS
Sam Benedict ep Season of Vengeance 3. 30. 63 NBC
Bob Hope Chrysler Theatre ep Four Kings 11. 1. 63
NBC
FBI ep The Defector 3. 27. 66, 4. 3. 66 ABC
Run for Your Life ep The Day Time Stopped 9. 12.
66 NBC
FBI ep 2. 19. 67 ABC
The Man from U. N. C. L. E. ep 9. 18. 67 NBC
Name of the Game ep Collector's Edition 10. 11. 68
NBC
It Takes a Thief ep 2. 4. 69, 2. 11. 69 ABC
The Challenge tf 2. 10. 70 ABC

LUKE, KEYE
Fireside Theatre ep The Traitor 9. 1. 53 NBC
Fireside Theatre ep The Reign of Amelia Jo 10. 12.
54 NBC
Studio 57 ep Ring Once for Death 6. 21. 55 NN
Ray Milland Show ep Chinese Luck 7. 8. 55 CBS
My Little Margie ep The San Francisco Story 7. 13.
55 NBC
Gunsmoke ep 12. 3. 55 CBS
Crusader ep Christmas in Burma 12. 23. 55 CBS
Crossroads ep Calvary in China 1. 13. 56 ABC
Telephone Time ep Time Bomb 5. 20. 56 CBS
TV Reader's Digest ep The Smuggler 7. 9. 56 ABC
Wire Service ep No Peace at Lo Dao 3. 18. 57 ABC
Panic ep May Day 6. 11. 57 NBC
Alcoa Theatre ep In the Dark 1. 13. 58 NBC
Oh Susanna ep The Case of the Chinese Puzzle 1. 25.
58 CBS
Richard Diamond ep Chinese Honeymoon 2. 13. 58
CBS
Follow the Sun ep Little Girl Lost 11. 19. 61 ABC
Fair Exchange ep 9. 21. 62 CBS
Kentucky Jones ep 10. 24. 64 NBC
Perry Mason ep The Case of the Feather Clock 2.

11.65 CBS
I Spy   ep   Danny Was a Million Laughs   10.27.65 NBC
Wackiest Ship   ep   Last Path to Garcia   12.12.65 NBC
Andy Griffith Show   ep   2.6.67 CBS
Family Affair   ep   1.15.68 CBS
Big Valley   ep   Emperor of Rice   2.12.68 ABC
Outsider   ep   As Cold as Ashes   10.16.68 NBC
Hawaii Five-O   ep   11.26.69 CBS
Marcus Welby, M.D.   ep   2.2.71 ABC
Adam-12   ep   3.12.71 NBC
Here's Lucy   ep   1.10.72 CBS
Adam-12   ep   2.9.72 NBC
Kung Fu   tf   2.22.72 ABC
Anna and the King of Siam   sr   9.17.72 CBS

LUNA, BARBARA
Zorro   ep   An Eye for an Eye   11.20.58 ABC
Desilu Playhouse   ep   So Tender, So Profane   10.30.59
    CBS
Hawaiian Eye   ep   The Koa Man   12.30.59 ABC
Bonanza   ep   Toro Grande   1.2.60 NBC
Overland Trail   ep   Mission to Mexico   4.24.60 NBC
Tales of Wells Fargo   ep   Vasquez   5.16.60 NBC
Adventures in Paradise   ep   Away from It All   10.24.60
    ABC
Stagecoach West   ep   The Big Gun   4.25.61 ABC
Gunslinger   ep   The Death of Yellow Singer   5.11.61
    CBS
Alcoa Premiere   ep   The House of the Bath   1.16.62
    ABC
Untouchables   ep   The Death Tree   2.15.62 ABC
Gunsmoke   ep   2.24.62 CBS
Hawaiian Eye   ep   Payoff   3.28.62
Real McCoys   ep   The Love Bug Bugs Pepino   12.16.62
    CBS
Wide Country   ep   Farewell to Margarita   3.21.63 NBC
G.E. True   ep   Five Tickets to Hell   4.7.63 CBS
Death Valley Days   ep   Pete Kitchen's Wedding Night
    9.28.63 ABC
Outer Limits   ep   It Crawled out of the Woodwork   12.
    9.63 ABC
Wild, Wild West   ep   Night of the Deadly Bed   9.24.65
    CBS
Amos Burke   ep   Nightmare in the Sun   10.20.65 ABC
O.K. Crackerby   ep   11.11.65 ABC
Ben Casey   ep   The Man from Quasillia   11.29.65 ABC
Wackiest Ship   ep   Last Path to Garcia   12.12.65 NBC

FBI   ep   Special Delivery   1. 23. 66 ABC
Laredo   ep   Coup de Grace   10. 7. 66 NBC
FBI   ep   1. 29. 67 ABC
Invaders   ep   4. 3. 67 ABC
FBI   ep   4. 16. 67 ABC
Cimarron Strip   ep   9. 14. 67 CBS
Star Trek   ep   Mirror, Mirror   10. 6. 67 NBC
Tarzan   ep   10. 20. 67 NBC
The Man from U. N. C. L. E.   ep   12. 4. 67 NBC
High Chaparral   12. 31. 67 NBC
Big Valley   ep   1. 15. 68 ABC
FBI   ep   The Young Warrior   3. 9. 69 ABC
Hawaii Five-O   ep   A Thousand Pardons, You're Dead
    9. 24. 69 CBS
Mission Impossible   ep   12. 14. 69 CBS
Young Lawyers   ep   The Glass Prison   11. 2. 70 ABC
Love American Style   ep   11. 5. 71 ABC
Cannon   ep   12. 28. 71 CBS
Women in Chains   tf   1. 25. 72 ABC

LUNDIGAN, WILLIAM
    Video Theatre   ep   A Man in the Kitchen   7. 23. 53 CBS
    Ford Theatre   ep   The Bachelor   10. 22. 53 NBC
    Schlitz Playhouse of Stars   ep   Give the Guy a Break
        1. 29. 54 CBS
    G. E. Theatre   ep   To Lift a Feather   5. 2. 54 CBS
    Ford Theatre   ep   The Tryst   6. 17. 54 NBC
    Climax   sh   10. 7. 54 CBS
    Fireside Theatre   ep   The Indiscreet Mrs. Jarvis   1. 4.
        55 NBC
    Rheingold Theatre   ep   Total Recall   2. 26. 55 NBC
    Science Fiction Theatre   ep   Beyond   4. 5. 55 NBC
    Desilu Playhouse   ep   K. O. Kitty   11. 17. 58 CBS
    Playhouse 90   ep   No Time at All   2. 13. 58 CBS
    Men into Space   sr   9. 30. 59 CBS
    Dick Powell Theatre   ep   Last of the Private Eyes   4.
        30. 63 NBC
    Run for Your Life   ep   In Search of April   2. 14. 66
        NBC

LUNT, ALFRED
    Producers Showcase   ep   The Great Sebastians   4. 1. 57
        NBC
    U. S. Steel Hour   ep   The Old Lady Shows Her Medals
        6. 12. 63 CBS
    Hallmark Hall of Fame   ep   The Magnificent Yankee
        1. 28. 65 NBC

LUPINO, IDA
Four Star Playhouse   sr   12.31.53 CBS
Ford Theatre   ep   Marriageable Male   2.25.54 NBC
Ford Theatre   ep   A Season to Love   5.6.54 NBC
Four Star Playhouse   sr ret   10.28.54 CBS
Four Star Playhouse   sr ret   9.22.55 CBS
Zane Grey Theatre   ep   The Fearful Courage   10.12.
   56 CBS
Mr. Adams and Eve   sr   1.4.57 CBS
Mr. Adams and Eve   sr ret   fall, 1957 CBS
Lux Playhouse   ep   Various Temptations   2.20.59 CBS
Lucille Ball-Desi Arnaz Hour   ep   Lucy's Summer Va-
   cation   6.8.59 CBS
Twilight Zone   ep   The 16mm Shrine   10.23.59 CBS
Bonanza   ep   The Saga of Annie O'Toole   10.24.59 NBC
G.E. Theatre   ep   Image of a Doctor   2.26.61 CBS
Investigators   ep   Something for Charity   12.21.61 CBS
Sam Benedict   ep   Not Even the Gulls Shall Weep   1.5.
   62 NBC
Virginian   ep   A Distant Fury   3.20.63 NBC
Kraft Suspense Theatre   ep   One Step Down   11.14.63
   NBC
Burke's Law   ep   Who Killed Lenore Wingfield   11.4.64
   ABC
Rogues   ep   Two of a Kind   11.8.64 NBC
Virginian   ep   We've Lost a Train   4.21.65 NBC
Wild, Wild West   ep   Night of the Big Boast   10.7.66
   CBS
Judd for the Defense   ep   Kingdom of the Blind   2.9.68
   ABC
Batman   ep   3.7.68 ABC
It Takes a Thief   ep   4.2.68 ABC
Outcasts   ep   The Thin Edge   2.17.69 ABC
Mod Squad   ep   3.18.69 ABC
Name of the Game   ep   The Perfect Image   11.7.69
   NBC
Family Affair   ep   12.18.69 CBS
Bracken's World   ep   The Anonymous Star   11.13.70
   NBC
Nanny and the Professor   ep   The Balloon Ladies   2.
   12.71 ABC
Columbo   ep   Short Fuse   1.19.72 NBC
Women in Chains   tf   1.25.72 ABC
Medical Center   ep   3.1.72 CBS
The Strangers in 7A   tf   10.14.72 CBS
Bold Ones   ep   Terminal Career   12.26.72 NBC

LUPTON, JOHN
   Fireside Theatre ep The Relentless Weavers 3.30.54
     NBC
   Halls of Ivy sr 10.19.54 CBS
   My Little Margie ep The Shipboard Story 10.27.54
     NBC
   Studio 57 ep Step Lightly, Please 11.9.54 NN
   Robert Montgomery Presents ep Homecoming 11.22.
     54 NBC
   Schlitz Playhouse of Stars ep Underground 1.21.55
     CBS
   Climax ep The Mojave Kid 1.27.55 CBS
   Four Star Playhouse ep Tusitala 2.24.55 CBS
   Ford Theatre ep Dear Diane 1.12.56 NBC
   Climax ep The Fifth Wheel 2.9.56 CBS
   Schlitz Playhouse of Stars ep Top Man 2.10.56 CBS
   Studio One ep Always Welcome 2.27.56 CBS
   Matinee Theatre ep A Cowboy for Chris 3.12.56
     NBC
   20th Century-Fox Hour ep Broken Arrow 5.2.56 CBS
   Broken Arrow sr 9.25.56 ABC
   The Millionaire ep Story of Jimmy Reilly 3.13.57
     CBS
   Studio One ep The Edge of Truth 4.28.58 CBS
   Studio One ep The Undiscovered 6.30.58 NBC
   The Millionaire ep Millionaire Emily Baker 2.4.59
     CBS
   Playhouse 90 ep Second Happiest Day 6.25.59 CBS
   Wanted Dead or Alive ep 2.14.59 CBS
   Restless Gun ep Ricochet 3.9.59 NBC
   Behind Closed Doors ep 4.2.59 NBC
   Yancy Derringer ep A State of Crisis 4.30.59 CBS
   Goodyear Theatre ep Wait till Spring 5.25.59 NBC
   G.E. Theatre ep The Tallest Marine 10.18.59 CBS
   Black Saddle ep 10.30.59 ABC
   Perry Mason ep The Case of the Bartered Bikini 12.
     5.59 CBS
   Longstreet ep 11.18.71 ABC
   Owen Marshall ep Eulogy for a Wide Receiver 12.23.
     71 ABC
   The Astronaut tf 1.8.72 ABC
   Marcus Welby, M.D. ep Solomon's Choice 3.14.72
     ABC
   All My Darling Daughters tf 11.22.72 ABC

LUPUS, PETER
   I'm Dickens, He's Fenster ep Nurse Dickens 10.5.62
     ABC

Joey Bishop Show   ep   Chance of a Lifetime   12.8.62
   NBC
Mission Impossible   sr   9.17.66 CBS
Mission Impossible   sr ret   9.10.67 CBS
Mission Impossible   sr ret   9.29.68 CBS
Mission Impossible   sr ret   9.28.69 CBS
Mission Impossible   sr ret   9.19.70 CBS
Mission Impossible   sr ret   9.18.71 CBS
Mission Impossible   sr ret   9.16.72 CBS

LYNCH, PEG
Ethel and Albert   sr   4.25.53 NBC
Ethel and Albert   sr ret   9.4.54 NBC
Ethel and Albert   sr ret   6.20.55 CBS
Ethel and Albert   sr ret   10.14.55 ABC

LYNDE, PAUL
Phil Silvers Show   ep   Bilko in Outer Space   6.5.59
   CBS
Burke's Law   ep   Who Killed Cable Roberts   10.4.63
   ABC
The Munsters   ep   Low-Cal Munster   10.29.64 CBS
Grindl   ep   Twas the Week Before Christmas   12.22.
   63 NBC
The Munsters   ep   Eddie's Nickname   1.28.65 CBS
Farmer's Daughter   ep   Rich Man, Poor Man   2.19.65
   ABC
Burke's Law   ep   3.3.65 ABC
Bewitched   ep   3.25.65 ABC
Bewitched   sr   9.16.65 ABC
Farmer's Daughter   ep   Stag at Bay   9.27.65 ABC
Gidget   ep   3.10.66 ABC
F Troop   ep   9.8.66 ABC
Bob Hope Chrysler Theatre   ep   The Blue-Eyes Horse
   11.23.66 NBC
Pruitts of Southampton   ep   1.3.67 ABC
That Girl   ep   1.12.67 ABC
Flying Nun   ep   10.17.68 ABC
That's Life   ep   Buying a House   10.22.68 ABC
That's Life   ep   12.17.68 ABC
Bewitched   ep   12.25.69 ABC
Gidget Grows Up   tf   12.30.69 ABC
Love American Style   ep   1.30.70 ABC
Love American Style   ep   2.19.71 ABC
Love American Style   ep   12.17.71 ABC
Gidget Gets Married   tf   1.4.72 ABC
Paul Lynde Show   sr   9.13.72 ABC

LYNLEY, CAROL
  Goodyear Playhouse ep Grow Up 8.26.56 NBC
  Alfred Hitchcock Presents ep The Young One 12.1.
    57 CBS
  Dupont Show of the Month ep Junior Miss 12.20.57
    CBS
  G.E. Theatre ep The Young and Scared 5.18.58 CBS
  Pursuit ep The Vengeance 10.22.58 CBS
  Shirley Temple's Story Book ep Rapunzel 10.27.58
    NBC
  G.E. Theatre ep Deed of Mercy 3.1.59 CBS
  G.E. Theatre ep The Last Dance 11.22.59 CBS
  Laf Hit ep Final Vow 9.25.62 NBC
  Alcoa Premiere ep Whatever Happened to Miss Illinois
    11.22.62 ABC
  Virginian ep Man from the Sea 12.26.62 NBC
  Dick Powell Theatre ep The Rage of Silence 1.29.63
    NBC
  Bob Hope Chrysler Theatre ep The Fliers 2.5.65
    NBC
  Run for Your Life ep In Search of April 2.14.66 NBC
  Bob Hope Chrysler Theatre ep Runaway Boy 5.25.66
    NBC
  The Man from U.N.C.L.E. ep The Prince of Darkness
    Affair 10.2.67, 10.9.67 NBC
  Invaders ep 12.5.67 ABC
  Journey to the Unknown ep Eve 9.26.68 ABC
  Big Valley ep 11.18.68 ABC
  Shadow on the Land tf 12.4.68 ABC
  The Smugglers tf 12.24.68 NBC
  It Takes a Thief ep Boom at the Top 2.25.69 ABC
  The Immortal tf 9.30.69 ABC
  The Immortal ep 10.24.70 ABC
  Bold Ones ep Giants Never Kneel 10.25.70 NBC
  Most Deadly Game ep Who Killed Kindness 11.7.70
    ABC
  Weekend of Terror tf 12.8.70 ABC
  Mannix ep Voice in the Dark 2.20.71 CBS
  The Cable Car Mystery tf 11.19.71 CBS
  The Night Stalker tf 1.11.72 ABC
  Night Gallery ep Last Rites for a Dead Druid 1.26.72
    NBC
  Sixth Sense ep 2.5.72 ABC

LYNN, DIANA
  Silver Theatre ep Double Feature 4.17.50 CBS
  Silver Theatre ep Walt and Lavinia 6.5.50 CBS

Video Theatre ep Down Bayou DuBac 12.18.50 CBS
Video Theatre ep The Twinkle in Her Eye 10.22.51 CBS
Schlitz Playhouse of Stars ep The Memoirs of Aimee Durant 11.16.51 CBS
Schlitz Playhouse of Stars ep 3.21.52 CBS
Schlitz Playhouse of Stars ep Doctors Should Never Marry 5.2.52 CBS
Video Theatre ep Marriage Is the Beginning 5.12.52 CBS
Ford Theatre ep National Honeymoon 10.16.52 NBC
Robert Montgomery Presents ep Dinah, Kip, and Mr. Barlow 2.23.53 NBC
G.E. Theatre ep Best Seller 3.1.53 CBS
You Are There ep Joan of Arc 3.1.53 CBS
Robert Montgomery Presents ep World by the Tail 4.20.53 NBC
Medallion Theatre ep The Blue Serge Suit 1.23.54 CBS
U.S. Steel Hour ep Highway 2.16.54 ABC
Video Theatre ep Borrowed Wife 2.25.54 CBS
Ford Theatre ep The Unlocked Door 6.3.54 NBC
U.S. Steel Hour ep Good for You 6.8.54 ABC
U.S. Steel Hour ep The Thief 1.4.55 ABC
Lux Video Theatre ep Love Letter 1.20.55 NBC
Climax ep A Leaf out of the Book 2.3.55 CBS
Stage 7 ep Down from the Stars 4.3.55 CBS
Best of Broadway ep Stage Door 4.6.55 CBS
Climax ep A Farewell to Arms 5.26.55 CBS
Schlitz Playhouse of Stars ep O'Connor and the Blue-Eyed Felon 6.10.55 CBS
U.S. Steel Hour ep The Seventh Veil 8.3.55 CBS
Loretta Young Show ep Moment of Decision 10.2.55 NBC
Alcoa Hour ep A Girl Can Tell 11.13.55 NBC
Matinee Theatre ep Anything but Love 2.29.56 NBC
Lux Video Theatre ep Princess O'Rourke 5.17.56 NBC
Climax ep To Scream at Midnight 6.14.56 CBS
Matinee Theatre ep The Hollow Woman 8.23.56 NBC
Playhouse 90 ep Forbidden Area 10.4.56 CBS
Schlitz Playhouse of Stars ep The House That Jackson Built 10.5.56 CBS
Playhouse 90 ep The Star Wagon 1.24.57 CBS
Playhouse 90 ep A Sound of Different Drummers 10.3.57 CBS
Dupont Show of the Month ep Junior Miss 12.20.57 CBS

Playhouse 90   ep   The Return of Ansel Gibbs   11.28.
   58 CBS
Playhouse 90   ep   Marriage of Strangers   5.14.59 CBS
Lux Playhouse   ep   Boy on a Fence   5.15.59 CBS
Adventures in Paradise   ep   Safari at Sea   11.16.59
   ABC
The Philadelphia Story   Sp   12.7.59 NBC
Mystery Show   ep   Dark Possession   6.19.60 NBC
U.S. Steel Hour   ep   The Mating Machine   1.11.61 CBS
Checkmate   ep   The Deadly Silence   4.8.61 CBS
Checkmate   ep   Juan Moreno's Body   11.8.61 CBS
Investigators   ep   In a Mirror Darkly   11.16.61 CBS
Bus Stop   ep   How Does Charlie Feel   2.4.62 ABC
Burke's Law   ep   2.14.64 ABC
Nurses   ep   A Kind of Loving   4.2.64 CBS
Burke's Law   ep   11.11.64 ABC
Virginian   ep   You Take the High Road   2.17.65 NBC

LYNN, JEFFREY
   Studio One   ep   Miracle in the Rain   5.1.50 CBS
   Lights Out   ep   The Dispossessed   2.26.51 NBC
   Video Theatre   ep   Sweet Sorrow   5.28.51 CBS
   The Clock   ep   Affliction   8.24.51 NBC
   Schlitz Playhouse of Stars   ep   The Man I Marry   1.18.
      52 CBS
   Robert Montgomery Presents   ep   Happy Birthday,
      George   3.3.52 NBC
   Tales of Tomorrow   ep   Sleep No More   4.11.52 ABC
   Video Theatre   ep   Stone's Throw   9.15.52 CBS
   Philco Playhouse   ep   The Black Sheep   10.5.52 NBC
   Video Theatre   ep   Thanks for a Lovely Evening   1.12.
      53 CBS
   Suspense   ep   The Quarry   2.17.53 CBS
   Goodyear Playhouse   ep   The Accident   5.3.53 NBC
   Robert Montgomery Presents   ep   The Woman Who
      Hated Children   6.22.53 NBC
   My Son Jeep   sr   9.4.53 NBC
   Medallion Theatre   ep   The Trouble Train   10.10.53
      CBS
   Suspense   ep   Before the Fact   3.9.54 CBS
   Elgin Hour   ep   High Man   11.2.54 ABC
   Kraft Theatre   ep   The Independent   11.17.54 NBC
   Danger   ep   A Taste for Murder   12.14.54 CBS
   Robert Montgomery Presents   ep   Death and the Sky
      above   1.3.55 NBC
   True Story   ep   Dream No More   4.20.57 NBC
   U.S. Steel Hour   ep   The Case of Julia Walton   9.9.59
      CBS

Play of the Week   ep   The Magic and the Loss   2. 20.
    61 NN
Theatre 62   ep   The Spiral Staircase   10. 4. 61 NBC
The Secret Storm   sr   1969 CBS
Ironside   ep   Love My Enemy   10. 23. 69 NBC
Bold Ones   ep   Crisis   12. 7. 69 NBC
Matt Lincoln   ep   10. 22. 70 ABC

LYON, SUE
Arsenic and Old Lace   Sp   4. 2. 69 ABC
Bold Ones   ep   Crisis   12. 7. 69 NBC
Love American Style   ep   12. 29. 69 ABC
Men from Shiloh   ep   Nightmare at New Life   11. 16. 70
    NBC
Men at Law   ep   Marathon   2. 10. 71 CBS
Night Gallery   ep   9. 15. 71 NBC

LYONS, ROBERT F.
Night Gallery   ep   11. 3. 71 NBC
Medical Center   ep   Shock   12. 29. 71, 1. 5. 72 CBS
The Rookies   tf   3. 7. 72 ABC

LYTELL, BERT
One Man's Family   sr   1949-1950 NBC
One Man's Family   sr ret   9. 22. 51 NBC
Tales of Tomorrow   ep   A Child Is Crying   8. 15. 52
    ABC
Broadway Television Theatre   ep   I Like It Here   12.
    15. 52 NN
Broadway Television Theatre   ep   Janie   11. 9. 53 NN

McALLISTER, LON
    Suspense   ep   The Wisteria Cottage   6.20.50 CBS
    Video Theatre   ep   Down Bayou DuBac   12.18.50 CBS
    Tales of Tomorrow   ep   Enemy Unknown   11.23.51 ABC
    Ford Theatre   ep   My Daughter's Husband   3.12.53 NBC
    Schlitz Playhouse of Stars   ep   Operation Riviera   6.19.
        53 CBS

MacARTHUR, JAMES
    Climax   ep   Deal a Blow   8.25.55 CBS
    Studio One   ep   Tongues of Angels   3.17.58 CBS
    G.E. Theatre   ep   Young and Scared   5.18.58 CBS
    Studio One   ep   Ticket to Tahiti   6.2.58 CBS
    Desilu Playhouse   ep   The Innocent Assassin   3.16.69
        CBS
    Play of the Week   ep   Night of the Auk   5.2.60 NN
    Untouchables   ep   Death for Sale   4.27.61 ABC
    Bus Stop   ep   And the Pursuit of Evil   12.17.61 ABC
    Wagon Train   ep   Dick Pederson Story   1.10.62 NBC
    Sam Benedict   ep   Some Fires Die Slowly   2.16.63 NBC
    Great Adventures   ep   6.27.63 CBS
    Eleventh Hour   ep   La Belle Indifference   12.18.63 NBC
    Great Adventures   ep   Rodger Young   1.24.64 CBS
    Alfred Hitchcock Theatre   ep   Behind the Locked Door
        3.27.64 CBS
    Branded   ep   A Destiny Which Made Us Brothers   1.23.
        66 NBC
    12 O'Clock High   ep   The Outsider   1.31.66 ABC
    Gunsmoke   ep   3.26.66 CBS
    World of Disney   ep   Willie and the Yank   1.8.67, 1.15.
        67, 1.22.67 NBC
    Hondo   ep   10.27.67 ABC
    Tarzan   ep   Island of the Lost   11.17.67 NBC
    Bonanza   ep   12.3.67 NBC
    Lassiter   pt   7.8.68 CBS
    Hawaii Five-O   sr   9.26.68 CBS
    Hawaii Five-O   sr ret   9.23.69 CBS
    Hawaii Five-O   sr ret   9.16.70 CBS

Hawaii Five-O   sr ret   9.14.71 CBS
Hawaii Five-O   sr ret   9.12.72 CBS

McCALLA, IRISH
Sheena, Queen of the Jungle   sr   2.15.66 NN

McCALLUM, DAVID
Outer Limits   ep   The Sixth Finger   10.14.63 ABC
Perry Mason   ep   The Case of the Fifty Millionth French-
man   2.20.64 CBS
Great Adventure   ep   Kentucky's Bloody Ground   4.3.64,
4.10.64 CBS
Outer Limits   ep   The Forms of Things Unknown   5.4.
64 ABC
The Man from U.N.C.L.E.   sr   9.22.64 NBC
Profiles in Courage   ep   12.27.64 NBC
The Man from U.N.C.L.E.   sr ret   9.17.65 NBC
The Man from U.N.C.L.E.   sr ret   9.16.66 NBC
The Man from U.N.C.L.E.   sr ret   9.11.67 NBC
Hallmark Hall of Fame   ep   Teacher, Teacher   2.5.69
NBC
Hallmark Hall of Fame   ep   The File on Devlin   11.21.
69 NBC
Hauser's Memory   tf   11.24.70 NBC
Night Gallery   ep   The Phantom Farmhouse   10.21.71
NBC
Man and the City   ep   Pipe Me a Loving Tune   12.8.71
ABC
She Waits   tf   1.28.72 CBS
Marcus Welby, M.D.   ep   Just a Little Courage   2.15.
72 ABC

McCAMBRIDGE, MERCEDES
Tele-Theatre   ep   The Voice of the Cricket   1.16.50
NBC
Video Theatre   ep   The Lovely Menace   12.11.50 CBS
Video Theatre   ep   The Hill   11.24.52 CBS
Ford Theatre   ep   Crossed and Double-Crossed   12.11.
52 NBC
Tales of Tomorrow   ep   Read to Me, Herr Doktor   3.
20.53 ABC
Studio One   ep   Shadow of the Devil   4.6.53 CBS
Studio One   ep   Fly with the Hawk   5.25.53 CBS
Front Row Center   ep   Tender Is the Night   9.7.55 CBS
Climax   ep   Sailor on Horseback   9.29.55 CBS
Studio One   ep   A Public Figure   1.23.56 CBS
Loretta Young Show   ep   Father Happe   3.4.56 NBC

Front Row Center   ep   Pretend You Belong to Me   4.
   22. 56 CBS
Wire Service   sr   10. 4. 56 ABC
Wagon Train   ep   The Emily Rossiter Story   10. 30. 57
   NBC
No Warning   ep   Hear No Evil   4. 13. 58 NBC
Jane Wyman Theatre   ep   On the Brink   5. 1. 58 NBC
Schlitz Playhouse of Stars   ep   On the Brink   2. 27. 59
   CBS
Rawhide   ep   Incident of the Curious Street   4. 10. 59
   CBS
Riverboat   ep   Jessie Quinn   2. 15. 60 NBC
Overland Mail   ep   Sour Annie   5. 8. 60 NBC
Rawhide   ep   Incident of the Captive   12. 16. 60 CBS
Bonanza   ep   The Lady from Baltimore   1. 14. 62 NBC
Rawhide   ep   The Greedy Town   2. 16. 62 CBS
Dakotas   ep   Trouble at Trench Creek   1. 28. 63 ABC
Nurses   ep   Credo   1. 9. 64 CBS
Defenders   ep   The Man Who   10. 29. 64 CBS
Dr. Kildare   ep   Rome Will Never Leave You   11. 12.
   64, 11. 19. 64, 11. 26. 64 NBC
Lost in Space   ep   The Space Cropper   3. 30. 66 CBS
ABC Stage 67   ep   The People Trap   11. 8. 66 ABC
Bewitched   ep   10. 17. 68 ABC
Bonanza   ep   The Law and Billy Burgess   2. 15. 70 NBC
Medical Center   ep   A Matter of Tomorrow   2. 25. 70
   CBS
Name of the Game   ep   A Capital Affair   2. 12. 71 NBC
Gunsmoke   ep   The Lost   9. 13. 71 CBS
Killer by Night   tf   1. 7. 72 CBS
Two for the Money   tf   2. 26. 72 ABC

McCARTHY, KEVIN
   Prudential Playhouse   ep   Biography   10. 10. 50 CBS
   TV Playhouse   ep   Power Devil   11. 5. 50 NBC
   Prudential Playhouse   ep   Icebound   1. 30. 51 CBS
   Studio One   ep   Hangman's House   3. 19. 51 CBS
   Ford Theatre   ep   Sunk   11. 20. 52 NBC
   Philco Playhouse   ep   Double Jeopardy   1. 4. 53 NBC
   Summer Studio One   ep   The King in Yellow   7. 27. 53
      CBS
   Inner Sanctum   ep   The Stranger   1. 29. 54 NN
   Ford Theatre   ep   Lucky Tommy Jordan   2. 4. 54 NBC
   U. S. Steel Hour   ep   Highway   2. 16. 54 ABC
   TV Soundstage   ep   The Magnificent Lie   3. 12. 54 NBC
   Goodyear Playhouse   ep   Spring Reunion   4. 11. 54 NBC

Satin and Spurs   Sp   9. 12. 54 NBC
Goodyear Playhouse   ep   The Personal Touch   10. 10. 54
   NBC
Omnibus   ep   Antigone   11. 21. 54 CBS
Star Tonight   ep   You Need Me   2: 3. 55 ABC
Big Town   ep   Blinded Battler   9. 27. 55 NBC
Matinee Theatre   ep   Make Believe Mother   11. 1. 55
   NBC
Schlitz Playhouse of Stars   ep   Moment of Triumph   12.
   2. 55 CBS
Star Stage   ep   The Secret Place   3. 23. 56 NBC
Front Row Center   ep   Instant of Truth   4. 8. 56 CBS
Climax   ep   Flame-Out on T-6   5. 17. 56 CBS
Climax   ep   The Circular Staircase   6. 21. 56 CBS
Telephone Time   ep   The Key   7. 15. 56 CBS
G. E. Theatre   ep   Doctors of Pawnee Kill   1. 27. 57
   CBS
20th Century-Fox Hour   ep   City in Flames   3. 6. 57 CBS
Crossroads   ep   The Ice Cathedral   3. 8. 57 ABC
Telephone Time   ep   The Key   3. 10. 57 CBS
Dupont Theatre   ep   The Last Singer   4. 2. 57 ABC
Kraft Theatre   ep   The Medallion   4. 3. 57 NBC
G. E. Theatre   ep   A Question of Survival   5. 12. 57 CBS
Climax   ep   Deadly Climate   8. 29. 57 CBS
Schlitz Playhouse of Stars   ep   Lottery for Revenge   5.
   30. 58 CBS
Sunday Showcase   ep   Murder and Android   11. 8. 59 NBC
June Allyson Show   ep   The Wall Between   12. 7. 59 CBS
Twilight Zone   ep   Long Live Alter Jameson   3. 18. 60
   CBS
Armstrong Circle Theatre   ep   Moment of Panic   5. 10.
   61 CBS
Way Out   ep   The Overnight Case   6. 16. 61 CBS
Ben Casey   ep   A Few Brief Lines for Dave   11. 13. 61
   ABC
Rifleman   ep   The Shattered Idol   12. 4. 61 ABC
U. S. Steel Hour   ep   Two Black Kings   3. 21. 62 CBS
Armstrong Circle Theatre   ep   Journey to Oblivion   6.
   6. 62 CBS
Westinghouse Presents   ep   The First Day   6. 20. 62 CBS
Going My Way   ep   Ask Me No Questions   12. 5. 62 ABC
Rifleman   ep   Suspicion   1. 14. 63 ABC
Breaking Point   ep   Fire and Ice   9. 30. 63 ABC
Dr. Kildare   ep   The Backslider   12. 5. 63 NBC
Burke's Law   ep   Who Killed Madison Cooper   1. 24. 64
   ABC
Alfred Hitchcock Theatre   ep   Beast in View   3. 20. 64
   CBS

Mr. Novak   ep   Fare Thee Well   4.6.64 NBC
Nurses   ep   White on White   5.14.64 CBS
Burke's Law   cp   3.31.65 ABC
Dr. Kildare   ep   Believe and Live   4.22.65 NBC
Honey West   ep   The Gray Lady   12.10.65 ABC
Fugitive   ep   Wife Killer   1.11.66 ABC
FBI   ep   The Spy Master   2.6.66 ABC
The Man from U.N.C.L.E.   ep   The Moonglow Affair
    2.25.66 NBC
Jesse James   ep   A Burying for Rosey   5.9.66 ABC
12 O'Clock High   ep   Massacre   9.16.66 ABC
Bob Hope Chrysler Theatre   ep   Crazier than Cotton
    10.12.66 NBC
Felony Squad   ep   11.21.66 ABC
Road West   ep   3.6.67 NBC
Ghostbreaker   pt   9.8.67 NBC
Invaders   ep   9.19.67 ABC
Judd for the Defense   ep   Conspiracy   10.13.67 ABC
Felony Squad   ep   3.11.68 ABC
Judd for the Defense   ep   3.22.68 ABC
Hawaii Five-O   ep   Full Fathom Five   9.26.68 CBS
Wild, Wild West   ep   The Night of the Doomsday For-
    mula   10.4.68 CBS
Name of the Game   ep   10.25.68 NBC
High Chaparral   ep   North to Tucson   11.8.68 NBC
FBI   ep   Conspiracy of Silence   3.2.69 ABC
U.M.C.   tf   4.17.69 CBS
Survivors   sr   9.29.69 ABC
Julia   ep   2.10.70 NBC
Mission Impossible   ep   11.13.71 CBS
A Great American Tragedy   tf   10.18.72 ABC

McCLURE, DOUG
Jim Bowie   ep   Bad Medicine   4.18.58 ABC
Court of Last Resort   ep   The Todd-Loomis Case   4.4.
    58 NBC
Gale Storm Show   ep   The Honeymoon Suite   1.24.59
    CBS
Riverboat   ep   Face of Courage   12.27.59 NBC
Overland Trail   sr   2.7.60 NBC
Hennesey   ep   3.28.60 CBS
Johnny Midnight   ep   4.12.60 NBC
The Sky's the Limit   pt   8.16.60 CBS
Checkmate   sr   9.17.60 CBS
U.S. Steel Hour   ep   Street of Love   9.20.61 CBS
Checkmate   sr ret   10.4.61 CBS
Virginian   sr   9.19.62 NBC

Virginian sr ret 9.18.63 NBC
Virginian sr ret 9.16.64 NBC
Virginian sr ret 9.15.65 NBC
Virginian sr ret 9.14.66 NBC
The Longest Hundred Miles tf 1.21.67 NBC
Virginian sr ret 9.67 NBC
It Takes a Thief ep 1.9.68 ABC
Virginian sr ret 9.18.68 NBC
That's Life ep 2.11.69 ABC
Virginian sr ret 9.17.69 NBC
Men from Shiloh sr 9.16.70 NBC
Terror in the Sky tf 9.17.71 CBS
The Birdmen tf 9.18.71 ABC
Search sr 9.19.72 NBC
Playmates tf 10.3.72 ABC
Ghost Story ep 11.24.72 NBC
The Judge and Jake Wyler tf 12.2.72 NBC

McCORMACK, PATTY
Mirror Theatre ep The Party 8.18.53 NBC
TV Soundstage ep I Remember, I Remember 1.15.54
    NBC
The Web ep A Handful of Stars 2.7.54 CBS
TV Soundstage ep The Golden Box 2.12.54 NBC
Armstrong Circle Theatre ep 4.13.54 NBC
Philco Playhouse ep Somebody Special 6.6.54 NBC
(I Remember) Mama sr 9.3.54 CBS
Armstrong Circle Theatre ep Jody and Me 9.14.54
    NBC
Mama sr ret 10.7.55 CBS
Climax ep An Episode of Sparrows 3.29.56 CBS
Mama sr ret summer, 1956 CBS
G.E. Theatre ep Alien Angel 6.17.56 CBS
Playhouse 90 ep The Miracle Worker 2.7.57 CBS
Dupont Theatre ep Dan Marshall's Brat 3.19.57 ABC
Matinee Theatre ep We Won't Be Any Trouble 4.2.
    57 NBC
Playhouse 90 ep Child of Trouble 5.2.57 CBS
Kraft Theatre ep Sing a Song 8.28.57 NBC
Playhouse 90 ep The Clouded Image 11.7.57 CBS
Kraft Theatre ep The Spell of the Tigress 2.5.58
    NBC
Matinee Theatre ep The Devil's Violin 2.28.58 NBC
Playhouse 90 ep The Dungeon 4.17.58 CBS
Goodyear Theatre ep Chain and the River 9.29.58
    NBC
Wagon Train ep The Mary Ellen Thomas Story 12.

24.58 NBC
Peck's Bad Girl   sr   5.5.59 CBS
Playhouse 90   ep   Project Immortality   6.11.59 CBS
U.S. Steel Hour   ep   Rachel's Summer   10.7.59 CBS
Alcoa Premiere   ep   Make Me Not a Witch   12.22.59
    ABC
Mystery Show   ep   Summer Hero   6.12.60 NBC
Route 66   ep   Black November   10.7.60 CBS
Route 66   ep   Sleep on Four Pillows   2.24.61 CBS
New Breed   ep   Thousands and Thousands of Miles   4.
    17.62
Rawhide   ep   Incident of the Wolves   11.16.62 CBS
Rawhide   ep   Incident at Paradise   10.24.63 CBS
Farmer's Daughter   ep   Cousin Helga Came to Dinner
    1.22.64 ABC
Play of the Week   ep   Burning Bright   10.19.66 NN
Wild, Wild West   ep   1.26.68 CBS
O'Hara, U.S. Treasury   ep   2.4.72 CBS

McCORMICK, MYRON
Pursuit   ep   Kiss Me Again, Stranger   11.19.58 CBS
Play of the Week   ep   Burning Bright   10.26.59 NN
Untouchables   ep   The Frank Nitti Story   4.28.60 ABC
Alfred Hitchcock Presents   ep   I Can Take Care of My-
    self   5.15.60 CBS
Play of the Week   ep   My Heart's in the Highlands   11.
    7.60 NN
Play of the Week   ep   Iceman Cometh   11.14.60, 11.21.
    60 NN
Garland Touch   ep   12.16.60 CBS
Play of the Week   ep   Black Monday   1.16.61 NN
Naked City   ep   Landscape with Dead Figures   1.18.61
    ABC
Alfred Hitchcock Theatre   ep   Museum Piece   4.4.61
    NBC
Way Out   ep   Side Show   6.30.61 CBS
Heave Ho Harrigan   pt   9.22.61 NBC
Outlaws   ep   The Outlaw Marshalls   12.14.61 NBC
87th Precinct   ep   1.1.62 NBC
Alcoa Premiere   ep   Pattern of Guilt   1.9.62 ABC
Ben Casey   ep   The Trouble with Charlie   1.29.63 ABC
Naked City   ep   One of the Most Important Men in the
    Whole World   1.31.62 ABC
Outlaws   ep   Farewell Performance   3.15.62 NBC

McCRACKEN, JOAN
Claudia   sr   1.6.52 NBC

Mirror Theatre   ep   White Night   8.4.53 NBC

McCREA, JOEL
Wichita Town   sr   9.30.59 NBC

MacDONALD, JEANETTE
Screen Directors Playhouse   ep   The Prima Donna   2. 1.56 NBC
Playhouse 90   ep   Charley's Aunt   3.28.57 CBS

McDOWALL, RODDY
Robert Montgomery Presents   ep   When We Are Married   7.2.51 NBC
Video Theatre   ep   12.17.51 CBS
Video Theatre   ep   Salad Days   4.29.52 CBS
Broadway Television Theatre   ep   It Pays to Advertise   10.31.52 NN
Goodyear Playhouse   ep   Buy Me Blue Ribbons   2.28. 54 NBC
Armstrong Circle Theatre   ep   My Client, McDuff   4.6. 54 NBC
Robert Montgomery Presents   ep   The Reality   6.21.54 NBC
Kraft Theatre   ep   Philip Goes Forth   9.2.54 ABC
Kraft Theatre   ep   Emma   11.24.54 NBC
Elgin Hour   ep   Yesterday's Magic   12.14.54 ABC
Pond's Theatre   ep   The Silver Box   3.17.55 ABC
Hallmark Hall of Fame   ep   The Good Fairy   2.5.56 NBC
Goodyear Playhouse   ep   In the Days of Our Youth   5. 20.56 NBC
Kaiser Aluminum Hour   ep   Gwyneth   12.18.56 NBC
Matinee Theatre   ep   The Vicarious Years   3.28.57 NBC
Matinee Theatre   ep   Talk You of Killing?   4.4.57 NBC
Kraft Theatre   ep   A Night of Rain   4.24.57 NBC
Goodyear Playhouse   ep   The Treasure Hunters   5.26. 57 NBC
Matinee Theatre   ep   Rain in the Spring   6.5.57 NBC
Matinee Theatre   ep   White-Headed Boy   6.12.57 NBC
Alcoa Hour   ep   He's for Me   7.21.57 NBC
Suspicion   ep   The Woman with Red Hair   5.5.58 NBC
Kraft Theatre   ep   The Last of the Belles   6.4.58 NBC
Playhouse 90   ep   Heart of Darkness   11.6.58 CBS
U.S. Steel Hour   ep   Night of Betrayal   3.25.59 CBS
Music Theatre   ep   Too Bad about Sheila Troy   4.16.59, 4.23.59 NBC

Dupont Show of the Month   ep   Billy Budd   5. 25. 59
   CBS
Hallmark Hall of Fame   ep   Tempest   2. 3. 60 NBC
Twilight Zone   ep   People Are Alike All Over   3. 25. 60
   CBS
Our American Heritage   ep   Not without Honor   10. 21.
   60 NBC
Naked City   ep   The Fault in our Stars   3. 22. 61 ABC
Play of the Week   ep   In a Garden   4. 10. 61 NN
Power and the Glory   Sp   10. 29. 61 CBS
Hallmark Hall of Fame   ep   The Tempest   10. 20. 63
   NBC
Eleventh Hour   ep   The Only Remaining Copy Is in the
   British Museum   2. 12. 64 NBC
Bob Hope Chrysler Theatre   ep   Wake Up, Darling   2.
   21. 64 NBC
Alfred Hitchcock Theatre   ep   The Gentleman Caller
   4. 10. 64 CBS
Arrest and Trial   ep   Journey into Darkness   5. 10. 64
   ABC
Alfred Hitchcock Theatre   ep   See the Monkey Dance
   11. 9. 64 NBC
Bob Hope Chrysler Theatre   ep   Mr. Biddle's Crime
   Wave   12. 4. 64 NBC
Combat   ep   12. 15. 64 ABC
Kraft Suspense Theatre   ep   The Wine-Dark Sea   12. 31.
   64 NBC
Ben Casey   ep   When I Am Grown to Man's Estate   2. 8.
   65 ABC
12 O'Clock High   ep   Angel Baby   2. 28. 66 ABC
Run for Your Life   ep   Don't Count on Tomorrow   3. 28.
   66 NBC
Batman   ep   The Bookworm Turns   4. 21. 66 ABC
Name of the Game   ep   11. 29. 68 NBC
Bob Hope Chrysler Theatre   ep   The Fatal Mistake   11.
   30. 66 NBC
Invaders   ep   1. 17. 67 ABC
Hallmark Hall of Fame   ep   Saint Joan   12. 4. 67 NBC
Danny Thomas Show   ep (voice only)   The Cricket on the
   Hearth   12. 18. 67 NBC
Felony Squad   ep   The Flip Side of Fear   1. 15. 68, 1. 22.
   68 ABC
Journey to the Unknown   ep   The Killing Bottle   1. 23. 69
   ABC
It Takes a Thief   ep   2. 25. 69   ABC
Night Gallery   tf   11. 8. 69 NBC
Name of the Game   ep   12. 4. 70 NBC

Medical Center   ep   Crisis   12.9.70 CBS
Terror in the Sky   tf   9.17.71 CBS
No Taste of Evil   tf   10.12.71 ABC
Ironside   ep   Murder Impromptu   11.2.71 NBC
What's a Nice Girl Like You   tf   12.18.71 ABC
Columbo   ep   Short Fuse   1.19.72 NBC
Delphi Bureau   ep   10.26.72 ABC
Rookies   ep   10.30.72 ABC
Mission Impossible   ep   12.22.72 CBS
McCloud   ep   12.24.72 NBC

McGAVIN, DARREN
Crime Photographer   sr   5.3.51 CBS
Tales of Tomorrow   ep   The Duplicates   7.4.52 ABC
Goodyear Playhouse   ep   The Witness   8.17.52 NBC
Armstrong Circle Theatre   ep   Recapture   9.2.52 NBC
Goodyear Playhouse   ep   Better than Walking   10.26.52
    NBC
The Web   ep   Turn Back   11.9.52 CBS
Short Short Drama   ep   The Double Cross   3.17.53 NBC
Mirror Theatre   ep   The Enormous Radio   7.21.53 NBC
Philco Playhouse   ep   The Rainmaker   8.16.53 NBC
Suspense   ep   An Affair with a Ghost   1.26.54 CBS
TV Soundstage ep "XXXX" Isn't Everything   4.9.54
    NBC
Kraft Theatre   ep   Unequal Contest   4.29.54 ABC
Mama   ep   5.28.54 CBS
Kraft Theatre   ep   Blind Alley   6.10.54 ABC
Studio One   ep   Fandango   at War Bonnet   6.21.54 CBS
Omnibus   ep   11.28.54 CBS
It's Always Jan   ep   10.1.55 CBS
Alfred Hitchcock Presents   ep   Triggers in Leash   10.
    16.55 CBS
Armstrong Circle Theatre   ep   The Town that Refused
    to Die   11.29.55 NBC
Alfred Hitchcock Presents   ep   The Cheney Vase   12.
    25.55 CBS
Armstrong Circle Theatre   ep   Terror at My Heels   2.
    21.56 NBC
Alcoa Hour   ep   Archangel Harrigan   6.24.56 NBC
Robert Montgomery Presents   ep   Sunset Boulevard   12.
    3.56 NBC
Alcoa Hour   ep   The Original Miss Chase   3.17.57 NBC
Studio One   ep   First Prize for Murder   9.16.57 CBS
Mike Hammer   sr   1.28.58 CBS
Studio One   ep   The Fair-Haired Boy   3.3.58 CBS
Decision   ep   Man against Crime   9.21.58 NBC

Riverboat   sr   9.13.59 NBC
Riverboat   sr ret   9.19.60 NBC
Islanders   ep   Island Witness   2.6.61 ABC
Stagecoach West   ep   A Place of Still Waters   4.11.61
    ABC
Death Valley Days   ep   The Stolen City   4.12.61 NBC
Route 66   ep   The Opponent   6.2.61 CBS
Rawhide   ep   The Sendoff   10.6.61 CBS
U.S. Steel Hour   ep   Marriage Marks the Spot   11.14.
    62 CBS
Defenders   ep   Everybody Else Is Dead   5.11.63 CBS
Virginian   ep   The Intruders   3.4.64 NBC
Alfred Hitchcock Theatre   ep   A Matter of Murder   4.
    3.64 CBS
Doctors/Nurses   ep   10.27.64 CBS
Ben Casey   ep   Kill the Dream but Spare the Dreamer
    11.2.64 ABC
Defenders   ep   A Taste of Ashes   11.12.64 CBS
Bob Hope Chrysler Theatre   ep   Parties to the Crime
    11.27.64 NBC
Rogues   ep   The Diamond-Studded Pie   1.31.65 NBC
Gunsmoke   ep   4.1.65 CBS
Gunsmoke   ep   12.4.65 CBS
Dr. Kildare   ep   From Nigeria with Love   12.13.65,
    12.14.65, 12.20.65, 12.21.65 NBC
Court-Martial   ep   5.20.66 ABC
Felony Squad   ep   The Streets Are Lined with Quicksand
    9.12.66 ABC
Gunsmoke   ep   10.22.66 CBS
Cimarron Strip   ep   9.14.67 CBS
Virginian   ep   The Deadly Past   9.20.67 NBC
The Man from U.N.C.L.E.   ep   10.30.67 NBC
Mission Impossible   ep   11.5.67 CBS
The Outsider   tf   11.21.67 NBC
Outsider   sr   9.18.68 NBC
World of Disney   ep   9.22.68, 9.29.68 NBC
Name of the Game   ep   Shine on, Shine on   11.1.68
    NBC
The Challengers   tf   3.28.69 CBS
Name of the Game   ep   10.24.69 NBC
The Challenge   tf   2.10.70 ABC
Love American Style   ep   3.13.70 ABC
Mannix   ep   A Ticket to the Eclipse   9.19.70 CBS
Name of the Game   ep   10.9.70 NBC
Berlin Affair   tf   11.2.70 NBC
Tribes   tf   11.10.70 ABC
Bracken's World   ep   Infinity   11.20.70 NBC

Matt Lincoln ep 12.10.70 ABC
Banyon tf 3.15.71 NBC
Cade's County ep 9.19.71 CBS
The Night Stalker tf 1.11.72 ABC
Something Evil tf 1.21.72 CBS
The Rookies tf 3.7.72 ABC
Say Goodbye, Maggie Cole tf 9.27.72 ABC
World of Disney ep High Flying Spy 10.22.72, 10.29.
    72, 11.5.72 NBC

McGOOHAN, PATRICK
The Vise ep Gift from Heaven 12.9.55 ABC
Danger Man sr 4.5.61 CBS
World of Disney ep The Scarecrow of Romney Marsh
    2.9.64, 2.16.64, 2.23.64 NBC
Secret Agent sr 4.3.65 CBS
Secret Agent sr ret 12.4.65 CBS
Prisoner sr 6.1.68 CBS

McGRATH, LEUEEN
Theatre Hour ep School for Scandal 4.21.50 CBS
Studio One ep The Passionate Pilgrim 10.2.50 CBS
Robert Montgomery Presents ep 11.6.50 NBC
Robert Montgomery Presents ep The Lonely 5.5.52
    NBC
Kraft Theatre ep Angel Street 3.25.54 ABC
U.S. Steel Hour ep The Man with the Gun 10.12.54
    ABC
Pond's Theatre ep The Dover Road 2.17.55 ABC
Alcoa Hour ep Mrs. Gilling and the Skyscraper 6.9.
    57 NBC
Studio One ep Escape Route 12.2.57 CBS
Ellery Queen ep Castaway on a Nearby Island 4.24.59
    NBC
Play of the Week ep Tiger at the Gates 2.8.60 NN

McGRAW, CHARLES
G.E. Theatre ep The Cat with the Crimson Eyes 8.
    30.53 CBS
Casablanca sr 9.27.55 ABC
The Falcon sr 10.9.55 ABC
Cavalcade Theatre ep Breakfast at Nancy's 3.13.56
    ABC
Crossroads ep Paratroop Padre 3.29.57 ABC
Crossroads ep The Light 4.5.57 ABC
Troubleshooters ep Down Range 11.20.59 NBC
Man from Blackhawk ep Death at Noon 1.8.60 ABC

Staccato   ep   Murder for Credit   4.3.60 ABC
Untouchables   ep   Portrait of a Thief   4.7.60 ABC
Deputy   ep   Last Gunfight   4.30.60 NBC
Route 66   Playout at Glen Canyon   12.2.60 CBS
Thriller   ep   The Big Blackout   12.6.60 NBC
Shirley Temple Theatre   ep   The Fawn   2.5.61 NBC
Laramie   ep   Mark of the Maneaters   3.14.61 NBC
G.E. Theatre   ep   The Great Alberti   11.5.61 CBS
Follow the Sun   ep   Night Song   11.26.61 ABC
Dr. Kildare   ep   For the Living   11.30.61 NBC
New Breed   ep   Blood Money   12.19.61 ABC
Untouchables   ep   The Silent Partner   2.1.62 ABC
Cain's Hundred   ep   Marked by Proxy   2.6.62 NBC
87th Precinct   ep   King's Ransom   2.19.62 NBC
Wagon Train   ep   The Lieutenant Burton Story   2.28.62
    NBC
Bonanza   ep   The Gamble   4.1.62 NBC
Virginian   ep   Say Goodbye to All That   1.23.63 NBC
Alfred Hitchcock Theatre   ep   Diagnosis: Danger   3.1.
    63 CBS
Untouchables   ep   The Tornado   5.7.63 ABC
Dr. Kildare   ep   The Heart, an Imperfect Machine   10.
    17.63 NBC
Lieutenant   ep   Alert   12.14.63 NBC
77 Sunset Strip   ep   Lovers' Lane   1.3.64 ABC
Travels of Jaimie McPheeters   ep   The Day of the Search
    1.19.64 ABC
Kraft Suspense Theatre   ep   Once upon a Savage Night
    4.2.64 NBC
Destry   ep   Ride to Rio Verde   4.10.64 ABC
Gunsmoke   ep   4.11.64 CBS
Voyage to the Bottom of the Sea   ep   The Sky Is Falling
    10.19.64 ABC
Ben Casey   ep   Where Does the Boomerang Go   1.11.65
    ABC
Kraft Suspense Theatre   ep   Twixt the Cup and the Lip
    6.3.65 NBC
Bob Hope Chrysler Theatre   ep   March from Camp Tyler
    10.6.65 NBC
Run for Your Life   ep   12.19.66 NBC
Judd for the Defense   ep   Shadow of a Killer   10.6.67
    ABC
Hondo   ep   10.6.67 ABC
Gunsmoke   ep   11.13.67 CBS
Outcasts   ep   A Ride to Vengeance   9.30.68 ABC
Wild, Wild West   ep   11.8.68 CBS
Judd for the Defense   ep   Punishments, Cruel and Un-

usual 12. 6. 68 ABC
Bonanza ep 4. 6. 69 NBC
Name of the Game ep The King of Denmark 2. 20. 70
  NBC
Name of the Game ep 9. 25. 70 NBC
Mod Squad ep Time for Hyacinths 12. 1. 70 ABC
Matt Lincoln ep 12. 10. 70 ABC
Travis Logan, D. A. ep 3. 11. 71 CBS
Smith Family ep 3. 17. 71 ABC
O'Hara, U. S. Treasury tf 4. 2. 71 CBS
Man and the City ep Reprisal 10. 13. 71 ABC
The Devil and Miss Sarah tf 12. 4. 71 ABC
O'Hara, U. S. Treasury ep 1. 7. 72 CBS
Nichols ep 2. 15. 72 ABC

McGUIRE, BIFF
Tele-Theatre ep The Way I Feel 6. 12. 50 NBC
Studio One ep Side Street 3. 1. 54 CBS
Armstrong Circle Theatre ep So Close the Stars 2.
  23. 54 NBC
Kraft Theatre ep Arrowsmith 5. 6. 54 ABC
Studio One ep Castles in Spain 5. 17. 54 CBS
The Web ep I'll Buy a Dream 8. 1. 54 CBS
The Web ep Welcome Home 9. 26. 54 CBS
Kraft Theatre ep Split Level 10. 27. 54 NBC
You Are There ep The Tragedy of John Milton 1. 30.
  55 CBS
Pond's Theatre ep A Second Chance 2. 24. 55 ABC
Studio One ep The Day Before the Wedding 7. 4. 55
  CBS
Appointment with Adventure ep Number 7, Hangman's
  Lane 10. 9. 55 CBS
Justice ep Flight from Fear 10. 16. 55 NBC
American Inventory ep The Sun Watchers 11. 13. 55
  NBC
Philco Playhouse ep This Land Is Mine 1. 15. 56 NBC
Justice ep The Trapped 1. 29. 56 NBC
U. S. Steel Hour ep Command 2. 15. 56 CBS
Studio One ep The Laughter of Giants 3. 19. 56 CBS
Alfred Hitchcock Presents ep The Gentlemen from Amer-
  ica 4. 29. 56 CBS
Armstrong Circle Theatre ep Seventy-Three Seconds in-
  to Space 5. 1. 56 NBC
Alfred Hitchcock Presents ep A Hidden Thing 5. 20. 56
  CBS
Kraft Theatre ep Flying Object at 3 O'Clock High 6.
  20. 56 NBC

Armstrong Circle Theatre   ep   The Flareup   10.30.56
     NBC
Kraft Theatre   ep   Before It's Too Late   11.14.56 NBC
U.S. Steel Hour   ep   The Old Lady Shows Her Medals
     12.19.56 CBS
Alfred Hitchcock Presents   ep   Crackpot   1.6.57 CBS
Armstrong Circle Theatre   ep   Error in Judgment   2.5.
     57 NBC
True Story   ep   The Treasure   5.25.57 NBC
U.S. Steel Hour   ep   Upbeat   6.19.57 CBS
Modern Romance   ep   7.22.57 NBC
Goodyear Playhouse   ep   The Dark Side of the Moon   8.
     18.57 NBC
U.S. Steel Hour   ep   The Bromley Touch   1.15.58 CBS
True Story   ep   3.1.58 NBC
Modern Romance   ep   5.19.58 NBC
Theatre '59   ep   The Incurable Wound   4.29.59 NBC
U.S. Steel Hour   ep   Wish on the Moon   7.29.59 CBS
Diagnosis Unknown   ep   The Parasite   9.13.60 CBS
Witness   ep   Shoeless Joe   10.27.60 CBS
Witness   ep   1.26.61 CBS
Defenders   ep   The Tarnished Cross   3.17.62 CBS
Defenders   ep   The Seal of Confession   11.30.63 CBS
Directions '66   ep   Johan   10.3.65, 10.10.65, 10.17.65,
     10.24.65 ABC
New York Television Theatre   ep   Father Uxbridge Wants
     to Marry   2.17.70 NN
N.E.T. Playhouse   ep   Paradise Lost   2.25.71, 3.4.71
     NN

McGUIRE, DOROTHY
     Robert Montgomery Presents   ep   Dark Victory   3.26.51
          NBC
     U.S. Steel Hour   ep   A Garden in the Sea   7.20.54 ABC
     Lux Video Theatre   ep   To Each His Own   8.26.54 NBC
     Climax   ep   The Gioconda Smile   11.11.54 CBS
     Best of Broadway   ep   The Philadelphia Story   12.8.54
          CBS
     Climax   ep   Pale Horse, Pale Rider   3.22.56 CBS
     She Waits   tf   1.28.72 CBS
     Hollywood Television Theatre   ep   Another Part of the
          Forest   10.2.72 NN

McHUGH, FRANK
     Musical Comedy Time   ep   Mme. Modiste   2.5.51 NBC
     Tales of Tomorrow   ep   And a Little Child   4.4.52 ABC
     The Doctor   ep   No Rap Charlie   5.17.53 NBC

Plymouth Playhouse ep Colonel Humphrey J. Flack
5. 31. 53 ABC
The Web ep The Winner 11. 1. 53 CBS
Motorola TV Hour ep The Muldoon Matter 2. 23. 54
ABC
Center Stage ep The Heart of a Clown 9. 21. 54 ABC
Kraft Theatre ep The Happy Journey 10. 28. 54 ABC
Studio One ep Two Little Minks 12. 20. 54 CBS
Elgin Hour ep Falling Star 12. 28. 54 ABC
Studio One ep Miracle at Potter's Farm 12. 19. 55
CBS
Studio One ep The Silent Gun 2. 6. 56 CBS
Alcoa Hour ep Doll Face 3. 18. 56 NBC
Star Stage ep The Man in the Black Robe 5. 18. 56
NBC
U. S. Steel Hour ep The Human Pattern 1. 2. 57 CBS
Playhouse 90 ep Three Men on a Horse 4. 18. 57 CBS
Kraft Theatre ep Fire and Ice 6. 12. 57 NBC
Kraft Theatre ep Dog in a Bush Tunnel 3. 5. 58 NBC
Studio One ep The Funny-Looking Kid 5. 19. 58 CBS
The Millionaire ep Millionaire Charles Bradwell 6. 10.
59 CBS
U. S. Steel Hour ep Apple of His Eye 7. 1. 59 CBS
The Killers Sp 11. 19. 59 CBS
U. S. Steel Hour ep Queen of the Orange Bowl 1. 13. 60
CBS
Full Moon over Brooklyn Sp 5. 6. 60 NBC
Dupont Show of the Month ep Heaven Can Wait 11. 16.
60 CBS
Harrigan and Son ep 100 Proof 3. 10. 61 ABC
Outlaws ep Outrage at Pawnee Bend 4. 6. 61 NBC
Wagon Train ep The Duke Shannon Story 4. 26. 61 NBC
Cain's Hundred ep 1. 9. 62 NBC
Route 66 ep How Much a Pound Is Albatross 2. 9. 62
CBS
Dupont Show of the Week ep The Action in New Orleans
4. 15. 62 NBC
Going My Way ep Keep an Eye on Santa Claus 12. 12.
62 ABC
Route 66 ep Man Out of Time 10. 5. 62 CBS
Nurses ep Many a Sullivan 1. 17. 63 CBS
U. S. Steel Hour ep Don't Shake the Family Tree 5.
15. 63 CBS
Bing Crosby Show sr 9. 14. 64 ABC
F Troop ep Will the Real Captain Try to Stand Up 5.
10. 66 ABC
The Lucy Show ep 11. 20. 67 CBS

World of Disney   ep   Way Down Cellar   1.7.68, 1.14.68
   NBC
Lancer   ep   2.11.69 CBS

McINTIRE, JOHN
   G.E. Theatre   ep   The Windmill   4.24.55 CBS
   Cavalcade of America   ep   Six Hours to Deadline   5.24.
      55 ABC
   Front Row Center   ep   Innocent Witness   3.4.56 CBS
   Cavalcade Theatre   ep   Wild April   10.16.56 ABC
   Lux Video Theatre   ep   The Taggart Light   4.18.57
      NBC
   G.E. Theatre   ep   The Trail to Christmas   12.15.57
      CBS
   Alfred Hitchcock Presents   ep   Sylvia   1.19.58 CBS
   G.E. Theatre   ep   Strange Witness   3.23.58 CBS
   Naked City   sr   9.30.58 ABC
   Wanted Dead or Alive   ep   4.11.59 CBS
   Zane Grey Theatre   ep   Mission to Marathon   5.14.59
      CBS
   Wagon Train   ep   The Andrew Hale Story   6.2.59 NBC
   Wichita Town   ep   Drifting   10.28.59 NBC
   Laramie   ep   The Passing Kuba Smith   1.3.60 NBC
   Alfred Hitchcock Presents   ep   Hitchhike   2.21.60 CBS
   Wichita Town   ep   Paid in Full   3.23.60 NBC
   Twilight Zone   ep   The Chase   5.13.60 CBS
   Laramie   ep   The Lawbreakers   5.17.60 NBC
   Overland Trail   ep   The Most Dangerous Gentleman   6.
      5.60 NBC
   Bonanza   ep   The Bride   1.21.61 NBC
   Americans   ep   Harpers Ferry   1.23.61 NBC
   Wagon Train   sr   3.15.61 NBC
   Wagon Train   sr ret   9.27.61 NBC
   Wagon Train   sr ret   9.19.62 ABC
   Wagon Train   sr ret   9.16.63 ABC
   Arrest and Trial   ep   Run Little Man, Run   12.22.63
      ABC
   Wagon Train   sr ret   9.20.64 ABC
   Daniel Boone   ep   The Reunion   3.11.65 NBC
   FBI   ep   The Hijackers   12.26.65 ABC
   Fugitive   ep   Ill Wind   3.8.66 ABC
   Shenandoah   ep   Care of General Delivery   5.9.66 ABC
   FBI   ep   The Cave-In   10.16.66 ABC
   World of Disney   ep   Showdown with the Sundown Kid
      10.23.66, 10.30.66 NBC
   Bonanza   ep   11.6.66 NBC
   World of Disney   ep   Gallagher Goes West   1.29.67,

2. 5. 67 NBC
Dundee and the Culhane   ep   The Dead Man's Brief
10. 4. 67 CBS
World of Disney   ep   The Mystery of Edward Sims   3.
31. 68, 4. 7. 68 NBC
Virginian   sr   11. 1. 67 NBC
Virginian   sr ret   9. 18. 68 NBC
Virginian   sr ret   9. 17. 69 NBC
World of Disney   ep nar   Snow Bear   11. 1. 70, 11. 8. 70
NBC
Homewood   ep   The Plot to Overthrow Christmas   12.
26. 70 NN
World of Disney   ep   Bayou Boy   2. 7. 71, 2. 14. 71 NBC
FBI   ep   The Last Job   9. 26. 71 ABC
Love American Style   ep   11. 12. 71 ABC
Longstreet   ep   Please Leave the Wreck for Others to
Enjoy   1. 27. 72 ABC

MACKAILL, DOROTHY
Studio One   ep   The Magic Lantern   4. 13. 53 CBS

McKAY, GARDNER
Thin Man   ep   The Angel Biz   10. 4. 57 NBC
Adventures in Paradise   sr   10. 5. 59 ABC
Adventures in Paradise   sr ret   10. 3. 60 ABC
Adventures in Paradise   sr ret   10. 1. 61 ABC
A Love Affair Just for Three   pt   7. 22. 63 CBS

McKAY, SCOTT
Stage Door   sr   2. 7. 50 CBS
Suspense   ep   One and One's a Lonesome   5. 16. 50 CBS
Philco Playhouse   ep   The Lost Diplomat   1. 14. 51 NBC
Summer Theatre   ep   The Pink Hussar   8. 6. 51 CBS
Douglas Fairbanks, Jr. Presents   ep   The Heel   7. 15.
53 NBC
Medallion Theatre   ep   Mrs. Union Station   8. 8. 53 CBS
Man Behind the Badge   ep   11. 22. 53 CBS
Kraft Theatre   ep   Flowers in a Book   8. 5. 54 ABC
Honestly, Celeste   sr   10. 10. 54 CBS
Robert Montgomery Presents   ep   Reclining Figure   2.
25. 57 NBC
Goodyear Playhouse   ep   The Gene Austin Story   4. 21.
57 NBC
Alfred Hitchcock Presents   ep   Guest for Breakfast   2.
23. 58 CBS
Climax   ep   So Deadly My Love   3. 13. 58 CBS
Armstrong Circle Theatre   ep   The Innocent Killer   4. 1.

59 CBS
U.S. Steel Hour   ep   A Taste of Champagne   8.26.59
CBS
Play of the Week   ep   Grand Tour   5.30.60 NN

McKENNA, SIOBHAN
Hallmark Hall of Fame   ep   The Cradle Song   5.6.56 NBC
Dupont Show of the Month   ep   The Winslow Boy   11.13.
58 CBS
Dupont Show of the Month   ep   What Every Woman Knows
1.28.59 CBS
Play of the Week   ep   Don Juan in Hell   2.15.60 NN
Play of the Week   ep   The Rope Dancers   3.14.60 NN
Hallmark Hall of Fame   ep (restaged) The Cradle Song
4.10.60 NBC
Great Mysteries   ep   The Woman in White   5.23.60 NBC

McKENNA, VIRGINIA
N.E.T. Playhouse   ep   A Passage to India   1.26.68 NN
Hallmark Hall of Fame   ep   The Admirable Crichton
5.2.68 NBC

MacKENZIE, GISELE
Kraft Theatre   ep   Now, Where Was I   4.13.55 NBC
Justice   ep   Hard to Get   5.11.55 NBC
Studio One   ep   The Man Who Caught the Ball at Coogan's
Bluff   11.28.55 CBS
G.E. Theatre   ep   The Hat with the Roses   5.20.56 CBS
Studio One   ep   Love at First Sight   1.7.57 CBS
G.E. Theatre   ep   No Man Can Tame Me   2.1.59 CBS
Lux Playhouse   ep   The Miss and the Missiles   6.12.59
CBS
Bachelor Father   ep   The Case Against Gisele   10.1.59
NBC
Burke's Law   ep   5.8.64 ABC

McLAGLEN, VICTOR
Schlitz Playhouse of Stars   ep   Port of Call   8.29.52
CBS
Video Theatre   ep   The Exposure of Michael O'Reilly
3.18.54 CBS
Eddie Cantor Theatre   ep   The Marine Went to Town   5.
16.55 ABC
Eddie Cantor Theatre   ep   9.19.55 ABC
Fireside Theatre   ep   Big Joe's Comin' Home   12.27.55
NBC
Have Gun Will Travel   ep   3.1.58 CBS

Rawhide   ep   Incident of the Shambling Man   10.9.59
   CBS

MacLAINE, SHIRLEY
   Shirley's World   sr   9.15.71 ABC

MacMAHON, ALINE
   Pulitzer Prize Playhouse   ep   The Town   1.16.52 ABC
   Celanese Theatre   ep   Morning's at Seven   4.16.52 ABC
   Studio One   ep   The Weston Strain   5.27.57 CBS
   Frontiers of Faith   ep   Boulevard Jasmine   12.22.57
      NBC
   Studio One   ep   The Desperate Age   4.21.58 CBS
   Play of the Week   ep   Medea   10.12.59 NN
   Defenders   ep   Old Lady Ironsides   12.21.63 CBS
   Defenders   ep   King of the Hill   12.31.64 CBS
   Repertory Theatre   ep   Coriolanus   5.12.65 NN
   New York Playhouse   ep   Antigone   10.7.72 NN

MacMAHON, HORACE
   Schlitz Playhouse of Stars   ep   The Pearl Street Incident
      5.14.54 CBS
   Climax   ep   The Long Goodbye   10.7.54 CBS
   Ford Theatre   ep   Stars Don't Shine   1.20.55 NBC
   Pond's Theatre   ep   The Cornered Man   1.27.55 ABC
   Damon Runyon Theatre   ep   Situation Wanted   10.29.55
      CBS
   Studio One   ep   The Man Who Caught the Ball at Coogan's
      Bluff   11.28.55 CBS
   Star Tonight   ep   Faith and Patience   5.24.56 ABC
   Robert Montgomery Presents   ep   The Misfortunes of
      Mr. Minihan   11.19.56 NBC
   Ford Theatre   ep   Front Page Father   12.5.56 ABC
   Father Knows Best   ep   Trip to Hillsborough   2.20.57
      NBC
   20th Century-Fox Hour   ep   Threat to a Happy Ending
      5.29.57 CBS
   Suspicion   ep   Death Watch   6.2.58 NBC
   Naked City   sr   3.24.59 ABC
   Sunday Showcase   ep   What Makes Sammy Run   9.27.59,
      10.4.59 NBC
   Play of the Week   ep   Crime of Passion   11.30.59 NN
   Alaskans   ep   Counterblow   4.24.60 ABC
   77 Sunset Strip   ep   Sierra   5.27.60 ABC
   Naked City   sr ret   10.12.60 ABC
   Naked City   sr ret   9.61 ABC
   Naked City   sr ret   1.19.62 ABC

Route 66   ep   Where Are the Sounds of Celi Brahms
   10. 18. 63 CBS
Mr. Broadway   sr   9. 26. 64 CBS
For the People   ep   The Right to Kill   4. 4. 65 CBS
Family Affair   ep   1. 20. 69 CBS

MacMURRAY, FRED
   G. E. Theatre   ep   Bachelor's Bride   2. 20. 55 CBS
   Screen Directors Playhouse   ep   It's a Most Unusual
      Day   3. 14. 56 NBC
   20th Century-Fox Hour   ep   False Witness   1. 27. 57
      CBS
   Lucille Ball-Desi Arnaz Hour   ep   Lucy Hunts Uranium
      1. 3. 58 CBS
   December Bride   ep   6. 2. 58 CBS
   G. E. Theatre   ep   One Is a Wanderer   9. 28. 58 CBS
   Cimarron City   ep   I the People   10. 11. 58 NBC
   My Three Sons   sr   9. 29. 60 ABC
   My Three Sons   sr ret   9. 61 ABC
   My Three Sons   sr ret   9. 20. 62 ABC
   My Three Sons   sr ret   9. 19. 63 ABC
   My Three Sons   sr ret   9. 17. 64 ABC
   My Three Sons   sr ret   9. 16. 65 CBS
   My Three Sons   sr ret   9. 15. 66 CBS
   My Three Sons   sr ret   9. 9. 67 CBS
   My Three Sons   sr ret   9. 28. 68 CBS
   My Three Sons   sr ret   10. 4. 69 CBS
   My Three Sons   sr ret   9. 19. 70 CBS
   My Three Sons   sr ret   9. 13. 71 CBS

McNAIR, BARBARA
   Eleventh Hour   ep   Who Is to Say How the Battle Is to
      Be Fought   3. 11. 64 NBC
   I Spy   ep   Night Train to Madrid   3. 22. 67 NBC
   Hogan's Heroes   ep   11. 18. 67 CBS
   The Lonely Profession   tf   10. 21. 69 NBC
   To Rome with Love   ep   10. 27. 70 CBS
   McMillan and Wife   ep   An Elementary Case of Murder
      3. 1. 72 NBC
   Mod Squad   ep   The Connection   9. 14. 72 ABC

McNALLY, STEPHEN
   Ford Theatre   ep   The Divided Heart   11. 27. 52 NBC
   Schlitz Playhouse of Stars   ep   No Compromise   12. 11.
      53 CBS
   Schlitz Playhouse of Stars   ep   Rabbit Foot   7. 9. 54
      CBS

Goodyear Playhouse ep The Big Man 9.12.54 NBC
Medallion Theatre ep The Alibi Kid 12.7.54 CBS
Schlitz Playhouse of Stars ep The Cool Ones 1.7.55
CBS
Stage 7 ep Tiger at Noon 2.27.55 CBS
Stage 7 ep The Verdict 5.22.55 CBS
Rheingold Theatre ep The Northern 10.15.55 NBC
Star Stage ep Foreign Wife 12.16.55 NBC
Loretta Young Show ep A Shadow Between 12.18.55
NBC
Loretta Young Show ep The Wise One 3.26.56 NBC
Schlitz Playhouse of Stars ep Officer Needs Help 5.
18.56 CBS
Zane Grey Theatre ep Return to Nowhere 12.7.56 CBS
Crossroads ep The Patton Prayer 1.18.57 ABC
Ford Theatre ep Strange Disappearance 5.1.57 ABC
Crossroads ep Convict 1321 5.10.57 ABC
Loretta Young Show ep Blizzard 12.1.57 NBC
Climax ep The Devil's Brook 12.5.57 CBS
Telephone Time ep Flight for Life 1.28.58 ABC
Climax ep House of Doubt 6.19.58 CBS
Wagon Train ep The Ben Courtney Story 1.28.59 NBC
World of Disney ep The Man from Bitter Creek 3.6.
59 ABC
Zane Grey Theatre ep Mission to Marathon 5.14.59
CBS
Zane Grey Theatre ep The Reckoning 1.14.60 CBS
June Allyson Show ep Moment of Fear 1.25.60 CBS
Riverboat ep Hang the Men High 3.21.60 NBC
Barbara Stanwyck Theatre ep The Mink Coat 9.19.60
NBC
Laramie ep The Track of the Jackal 9.27.60 NBC
Best of the Post ep The Murderer 11.26.60 ABC
Zane Grey Theatre ep The Mormons 12.15.60 CBS
Michael Shayne ep The Boat Caper 4.7.61 NBC
Rawhide ep Incident of the Black Storms 5.26.61 CBS
Target: Corruptors sr 9.29.61 ABC
Burke's Law ep Who Killed Holly Howard 9.20.63
ABC
Virginian ep No Tears for Savannah 10.2.63 NBC
Kraft Suspense Theatre ep The Action of the Tiger 2.
20.64 NBC
Alfred Hitchcock Theatre ep Final Escape 2.21.64
CBS
Outer Limits ep Specimen Unknown 2.24.64 ABC
Burke's Law ep 4.17.64 ABC
Fugitive ep The Iron Maiden 12.15.64 ABC

Run for Your Life   ep   The Cold, Cold War of Paul
   Bryan   9.13.65 NBC
Ben Casey   ep   O the Big Wheel Turns by Faith   9.20.
   65, 9.27.65 ABC
Branded   ep   The Bar Sinner   10.10.65 NBC
Run for Your Life   ep   The Sadness of a Happy Time
   5.16.66 NBC
Run for Your Life   ep   The Borders of Barbarism   9.
   26.66 NBC
Iron Horse   ep   War Cloud   10.31.66 ABC
Big Valley   ep   12.19.66 NBC
Gunsmoke   ep   2.25.67 CBS
Guns of Will Sonnett   ep   11.10.67 ABC
Danny Thomas Show   ep   The Zero Man   11.27.67 NBC
Run for Your Life   ep   The Exchange   3.27.68 NBC
Braddock   pt   7.22.68 CBS
Name of the Game   ep   The Protector   11.15.68 NBC
The Lonely Profession   tf   10.21.69 NBC
Name of the Game   ep   The Perfect Image   11.7.69
   NBC
Bold Ones   ep   And Those Unborn   12.21.69 NBC
Mission Impossible   ep   12.28.69 CBS
Bracken's World   ep   2.6.70 NBC
Ironside   ep   Warrior's Return   3.5.70 NBC
Name of the Game   ep   One of the Girls in Research
   4.3.70 NBC
Bold Ones   ep   The Verdict   9.27.70 NBC
Name of the Game   ep   All the Old Familiar Faces   11.
   13.70 NBC
Vanished   tf   3.8.71, 3.9.71 NBC
Mannix   ep   11.10.71 CBS
Longstreet   ep   Anatomy of a Mayday   2.3.72 ABC
Sixth Sense   ep   Coffin, Coffin, in the Sky   9.23.72 ABC
Mission Impossible   ep   10.21.72 CBS

McNAMARA, MAGGIE
   Ben Casey   ep   12.25.63 ABC
   Twilight Zone   ep   Ring-a-Ding Girl   12.27.63 CBS
   Great Adventures   ep   The Colonel from Connecticut   1.
      10.64 CBS
   The Greatest Show on Earth   ep   2.25.64 ABC

McNEIL, CLAUDIA
   Dupont Show of the Month   ep   The Member of the Wed-
      ding   6.12.58 CBS
   Look up and Live   ep   Death   9.30.59 CBS
   Play of the Week   ep   Simply Heavenly   12.7.59 NN

Nurses   ep   Express Stop from Lenox Avenue   5. 9. 63
  CBS
Look up and Live   ep   1. 5. 64, 1. 12. 64, 1. 19. 64 CBS
Profiles in Courage   ep   1. 31. 65 NBC
CBS Playhouse   ep   Do Not Go Gentle into that Good
  Night   10. 17. 67 CBS
Incident in San Francisco   tf   2. 28. 71 ABC
N. E. T. Playhouse   ep   To Be Young, Gifted and Black
  1. 22. 72 NN
Mod Squad   ep   The Connection   9. 14. 72 ABC
Moon of the Wolf   tf   9. 26. 72 ABC

McQUADE, ARLENE
  The Goldbergs   sr   1949-1950 CBS
  The Goldbergs   sr ret   9. 25. 50 CBS
  The Goldbergs   sr ret   7. 3. 53 NBC
  The Goldbergs   sr ret   4. 13. 54 NN
  The Goldbergs   sr ret   9. 22. 55 NN
  Telephone Time   ep   Fight for the Title   3. 17. 57 CBS
  True Story   ep   Home to Mother   5. 23. 59 NBC
  Have Gun Will Travel   ep   12. 3. 60 CBS
  Hawaii Five-O   ep   Full Fathoms Deep   9. 26. 68 CBS

McQUADE, JOHN
  Tele-Theatre   ep   Welcome Jeremiah   5. 8. 50 NBC
  Sure as Fate   ep   Tremolo   7. 4. 50 CBS
  Starlight Theatre   ep   The Last Kiss   7. 10. 50 ABC
  The Web   ep   Heaven Ran Last   8. 8. 50 CBS
  Sure as Fate   sr   9. 5. 50 ABC
  Prudential Playhouse   ep   Call It a Day   11. 7. 50 CBS
  Philco Playhouse   ep   Decoy   12. 17. 50 NBC
  Prudential Playhouse   ep   Skylark   1. 16. 51 CBS
  Tales of Tomorrow   ep   The Last Man on Earth   8. 31.
    51 ABC
  Charlie Wild   sr   9. 11. 51 ABC
  Studio One   ep   I Am Jonathan Scrivener   12. 1. 52 CBS
  Tales of Tomorrow   ep   The Squeeze Play   3. 13. 53
    ABC
  Center Stage   ep   The Day Before Atlanta   9. 7. 54 ABC
  U. S. Steel Hour   ep   The Gambler   7. 20. 55 CBS
  Producers Showcase   ep   Cyrano de Bergerac   10. 17. 55
    NBC
  Kraft Theatre   ep   Night Cry   8. 13. 58 NBC
  Armstrong Circle Theatre   ep   Jailbreak   10. 14. 59 CBS

McQUEEN, BUTTERFLY
  Studio One   ep   Give Us Our Dream   1. 16. 50 CBS

Beulah   sr   10.3.50 ABC
Hallmark Hall of Fame   ep   The Green Pastures   3.23.
    59 NBC

McQUEEN, STEVE
    Goodyear Playhouse   ep   The Chivington Raid   3.27.55
        NBC
    U.S. Steel Hour   ep   Bring Me a Dream   1.4.56 CBS
    Studio One   ep   The Defender   2.23.57, 3.4.57 CBS
    West Point   ep   Ambush   3.8.57 CBS
    Climax   ep   Four Hours in White   2.6.58 CBS
    Tales of Wells Fargo   ep   Bill Longley   2.10.58 NBC
    Trackdown   ep   The Bounty Hunter   3.7.58 CBS
    Wanted, Dead or Alive   sr   9.6.58 CBS
    Alfred Hitchcock Presents   ep   Human Interest Story
        5.24.59 CBS
    Wanted, Dead or Alive   sr ret   9.59 CBS
    Alfred Hitchcock Presents   ep   Man from the South   1.
        3.60 CBS
    Wanted, Dead or Alive   sr ret   9.21.60 CBS

MacRAE, GORDON
    Colgate Comedy Hour   ep   Roberta   4.10.55 NBC
    Lux Video Theatre   sh   fall, 1956 NBC
    Lux Video Theatre   ep   One Sunday Afternoon   1.31.57
        NBC
    Lux Video Theatre   ep   Eileen   3.14.57 NBC
    Gift of the Magi   Sp   12.9.58 CBS

MACREADY, GEORGE
    Rebound   ep   The Prize   3.7.52 ABC
    Ford Theatre   ep   Edge of the Law   11.6.52 NBC
    Four Star Playhouse   ep   The Island   7.30.53 CBS
    Four Star Playhouse   ep   House for Sale   12.31.53 CBS
    Danger   ep   A Taste for Murder   12.14.54 CBS
    Studio One   ep   The Missing Men   1.3.55 CBS
    Elgin Hour   ep   Days of Grace   2.8.55 ABC
    Rheingold Theatre   ep   Louise   2.10.55 NBC
    Studio One   ep   The Conviction of Peter Shea   3.14.55
        CBS
    G.E. Theatre   ep   The Bitter Choice   3.20.55 CBS
    Appointment with Adventure   ep   The Fateful Pilgrimage
        4.17.55 CBS
    Pond's Theatre   ep   The Kingdom of Andrew Jones   5.
        26.55 ABC
    U.S. Steel Hour   ep   Hung for a Sheep   6.7.55 ABC
    Kraft Theatre   ep   The Diamond as Big as the Ritz

9. 28. 55 NBC
Alfred Hitchcock Presents ep Premonition 10. 9. 55
CBS
Appointment with Adventure ep The Helping Hand 10.
16. 55 CBS
G. E. Theatre ep The Night Goes On 3. 18. 56 CBS
Alfred Hitchcock Presents ep The Cheney Vase 12. 25.
55 CBS
TV Reader's Digest ep The General's Escape 6. 4. 56
ABC
Ford Theatre ep Panic 6. 14. 56 NBC
Goodyear Playhouse ep The Film Maker 7. 1. 56 NBC
G. E. Theatre ep Flight from Tormendero 2. 24. 57
CBS
Alfred Hitchcock Presents ep Vicious Circle 4. 14. 57
CBS
Rifleman ep Eight Hours to Die 11. 4. 58 ABC
Gunsmoke ep 11. 15. 58 CBS
Perry Mason ep The Case of the Purple Woman 11.
22. 58 CBS
Texan ep Time of the Year 12. 22. 58 CBS
Loretta Young Show ep The Portrait 2. 22. 59 NBC
Bonanza ep A Rose for Lotta 9. 12. 59 NBC
Tightrope ep The Lady 12. 8. 59 CBS
Riverboat ep Guns for Empire 12. 20. 59 NBC
Desilu Playhouse ep Thunder in the Night 2. 19. 60
CBS
Alcoa Theatre ep The Observer 4. 18. 60 NBC
Playhouse 90 ep In the Presence of Mine Enemies 5.
18. 60 CBS
Rebel ep Johnny Yuma at Appomattox 9. 18. 60 ABC
Family Classics ep The Three Musketeers 11. 30. 60,
12. 1. 60 CBS
Bat Masterson ep Tempest at Tioga Pass 1. 5. 61 NBC
Adventures in Paradise ep The Feather Cloak 2. 27. 61
ABC
Perry Mason ep The Case of the Blind Man's Bluff 3.
11. 61 CBS
Perry Mason ep The Case of the Purple Woman 6. 31.
61 CBS
Thriller ep The Weird Taylor 10. 16. 61 NBC
Adventures in Paradise ep Show Me a Hero 11. 5. 61
ABC
Perry Mason ep The Case of the Posthumous Painter
11. 11. 61 CBS
Laramie ep Handful of Fire 12. 15. 61 NBC
Dick Powell Theatre ep The Fifth Caller 12. 19. 61 NBC

Dr. Kildare   ep   Thing Speaks for Itself   1.10.63 NBC
Dakotas   ep   Mutiny at Ft. Mercy   1.21.63 ABC
Perry Mason   ep   The Case of the Elusive Element   4.
   11.63 CBS
Twilight Zone   ep   The Long Morrow   1.10.64 CBS
Outer Limits   ep   The Invisibles   2.3.64 ABC
Great Adventures   ep   The President Vanishes   3.13.
   64 CBS
Outer Limits   ep   Production and Decay of Strange
   Particles   4.20.64 ABC
Peyton Place   sr   fall, 1964 ABC
Bob Hope Chrysler Theatre   ep   Memorandum for a
   Spy   4.2.65 NBC
Kentucky Jones   ep   4.3.65 NBC
Profiles in Courage   ep   4.4.65 NBC
The Man from U.N.C.L.E.   ep   The Recollector Af-
   fair   10.22.65 NBC
Fame is the Name of the Game   tf   11.26.66 NBC
The Man from U.N.C.L.E.   ep   11.27.67 NBC
Get Smart   ep   3.2.68 NBC
Night Gallery   tf   11.8.69 NBC
Daughter of the Mind   tf   12.9.69 ABC
Lancer   ep   12.9.69 CBS

McVEY, PATRICK
   Big Town   sr   10.5.50 CBS
   Big Town   sr ret   fall, 1951 CBS
   Big Town   sr ret   fall, 1952 CBS
   Big Town   sr ret   fall, 1953 CBS
   Kraft Theatre   ep   Wish Tonight   7.7.54 NBC
   Studio One   ep   The Laughter of Giants   3.19.56 CBS
   Armstrong Circle Theatre   ep   Seventy-Three Seconds
      into Space   5.1.56 NBC
   Kaiser Aluminum Hour   ep   The Army Game   7.3.56
      NBC
   Telephone Time   ep   The Sgt. Boyd Story   12.23.56
      CBS
   Matinee Theatre   ep   Night Train to Chicago   6.14.57
      NBC
   Cheyenne   ep   Decision at Gunsight   4.23.57 ABC
   The Millionaire   ep   The John Richards Story   2.26.58
      CBS
   Cheyenne   ep   Ghost of Cimarron   3.25.58 ABC
   Sugarfoot   ep   Price on His Head   4.29.58 ABC
   Tombstone Territory   ep   Pick up the Gun   5.14.58
      ABC
   Maverick   ep   The Jail at Junction Flats   11.9.58 ABC

Maverick ep The Brasada Spur 2.22.59 ABC
Zane Grey Theatre ep Hanging Fever 3.12.59 CBS
Tombstone Territory ep Day of the Amnesty 4.3.59
    ABC
Wanted, Dead or Alive ep 4.4.59 CBS
Black Saddle ep 5.2.59 NBC
Bat Masterson ep Two Graves for Swan Valley 6.3.
    59 NBC
Perry Mason ep The Case of the Dubious Bridegroom
    6.13.59 CBS
Manhunt sr 9.59 NN

MADISON, GUY
Wild Bill Hickok sr 7.3.51 ABC
Wild Bill Hickok sr ret fall, 1952 ABC
Wild Bill Hickok sr ret fall, 1953 ABC
Light's Diamond Jubilee ep A Kiss for the Lieutenant
    10.24.54 ABC, CBS, NBC
Climax ep A Farewell to Arms 5.26.55 CBS
Ford Theatre ep Passage to Yesterday 11.24.55 NBC
Ford Theatre ep Sometimes It Happens 11.7.56 ABC
Climax ep The Man Who Stole the Bible 6.13.57 CBS
Wagon Train ep The Riley Gratton Story 12.4.57
    NBC
G.E. Theatre ep Bold Loser 5.11.58 CBS
Schlitz Playhouse of Stars ep You Can't Win 'Em All
    1.16.59 CBS
Zane Grey Theatre ep Jericho 5.18.61 CBS

MAHARIS, GEORGE
Naked City ep Fire Island 3.3.59 ABC
Naked City ep Four Sweet Corners 4.28.59 ABC
Alcoa Theatre ep Action Off Screen 1.11.60 NBC
Route 66 sr 10.7.60 CBS
Naked City ep A Death of Princes 10.12.60 ABC
Route 66 sr ret 9.22.61 CBS
Bob Hope Chrysler Theatre ep A Small Rebellion 2.
    9.66 NBC
Bob Hope Chrysler Theatre ep 12.21.66 NBC
Danny Thomas Show ep The Demon under the Bed
    10.9.67 NBC
Journey to the Unknown ep Miss Belle 10.24.68
    ABC
Escape to Mindano tf 12.7.68 NBC
Most Deadly Game sr 10.29.70 ABC
The Monk tf 10.21.69 ABC
Cade's County ep 11.14.71 CBS

Night Gallery   ep   The Hand of Borgus Weems   9.15.71
   NBC
Medical Center   ep   The Pawn   12.1.71 CBS
Cannon   ep   11.1.72 CBS
The Victim   tf   11.14.72 ABC
Of Men and Women   ep   The Brave and the Free   12.
   17.72 ABC

MAHONEY, JOCK
   The Range Rider   sr   1951 ABC
   The Range Rider   sr ret   1952 ABC
   The Range Rider   sr ret   1953 ABC
   Loretta Young Show   ep   The First Man to Ask Her
      4.4.54 NBC
   Loretta Young Show   ep   No Help Wanted   11.7.54 NBC
   Loretta Young Show   ep   Decision   1.16.55 NBC
   Loretta Young Show   ep   Option on a Wife   2.20.55
      NBC
   Loretta Young Show   ep   Tale of a Cayuse   2.27.55
      NBC
   Loretta Young Show   ep   Mink Coat   3.27.55 NBC
   Private Secretary   ep   The Boy Next Door   6.26.55 CBS
   Wagon Train   ep   The Dan Hogan Story   5.14.58 NBC
   Yancy Derringer   sr   10.2.58 CBS
   Rawhide   ep   Incident of the Sharpshooters   2.26.60 CBS
   The Millionaire   ep   Millionaire Vance Ludlow   5.11.60
      CBS
   77 Sunset Strip   ep   The Laurel Canyon Caper   10.28.60
      ABC
   Laramie   ep   Man from Kansas   1.10.61 NBC
   Rawhide   ep   Incident of the Phantom Burglar   4.14.61
      CBS
   Laramie   ep   Ladies Day   10.3.61 NBC
   Batman   ep   The Purrfect Crime   3.16.66, 3.17.66 ABC
   Tarzan   ep   The Ultimate Weapon   9.16.66 NBC
   Tarzan   ep   Deadly Silence   10.28.66, 11.4.66 NBC
   Daniel Boone   ep   12.14.67 NBC
   Emergency   ep   1.22.72 NBC

MAIN, MARJORIE
   December Bride   ep   10.15.56 CBS
   Wagon Train   ep   The Cassie Tanner Story   6.4.58 NBC
   Wagon Train   ep   The Sacramento Story   9.24.58 NBC

MAJORS, LEE
   Gunsmoke   ep   2.13.65 CBS
   Alfred Hitchcock Theatre   ep   The Monkey's Paw   4.19.
      65 NBC

Big Valley   sr   9.15.65 ABC
Big Valley   sr ret   9.12.66 ABC
Big Valley   sr ret   9.11.67 ABC
Big Valley   sr ret   9.68 ABC
The Ballad of Andy Crocker   tf   11.17.69 ABC
Bracken's World   ep   2.6.70 NBC
Weekend of Terror   tf   12.8.70 ABC
Owen Marshall   sr   9.16.71 ABC
Alias Smith and Jones   ep   1.13.72 ABC
Sixth Sense   ep   3.4.72 ABC
Owen Marshall   sr ret   9.14.72 ABC

MALDEN, KARL
Streets of San Francisco   sr   9.16.72 ABC

MALONE, DOROTHY
The Doctor   ep   The Runaways   6.21.53 NBC
Four Star Playhouse   ep   Moorings   11.12.53 CBS
TV Soundstage   ep   Surprise Party   6.18.54 NBC
Fireside Theatre   ep   Afraid to Live   9.28.54 NBC
Fireside Theatre   ep   Our Son   12.21.54 NBC
Fireside Theatre   ep   Mr. Onion   2.8.55 NBC
G.E. Theatre   ep   Clown   3.27.55 CBS
Four Star Playhouse   ep   A Study in Panic   7.14.55
  CBS
Loretta Young Show   ep   A Ticket for May   1.1.56
  NBC
Cimarron City   ep   A Respectable Girl   12.6.58 NBC
Alcoa Theatre   ep   The Last Flight Out   1.25.60 NBC
G.E. Theatre   ep   A Little White Lye   2.5.61 CBS
Route 66   ep   Fly Away Home   2.17.61 CBS
Checkmate   ep   The Heat of Passion   10.18.61 CBS
Dick Powell Theatre   ep   Open Season   12.26.61 NBC
Dr. Kildare   ep   The Administrator   1.11.62 NBC
Untouchables   ep   The Floyd Gibbons Story   12.11.62
  ABC
The Greatest Show on Earth   ep   Where the Wire Ends
  1.7.64 ABC
Peyton Place   sr   9.15.64 ABC
The Pigeon   tf   11.4.69 ABC
Bold Ones   ep   9.26.72 NBC

MANNING, IRENE
Schlitz Playhouse of Stars   ep   Make Way for Teddy
  3.14.52 CBS
Producers Showcase   ep   The King and Mrs. Candle
  9.22.55 NBC

MANSFIELD, JAYNE
    The Bachelor Sp 7.15.56 NBC
    Follow the Sun ep The Dumbest Blonde 2.4.62 ABC
    Alfred Hitchcock Theatre ep Hangover 12.6.62 CBS
    Burke's Law ep 3.27.64 ABC

MARCH, FREDRIC
    Airflyte Theatre ep The Boor 10.12.50 CBS
    Video Theatre ep The Speech 4.30.51 CBS
    Video Theatre ep Ferry Crisis at Friday Point 5.19.
      52 CBS
    Omnibus ep The Last Night of Don Juan 3.15.53 CBS
    The Best of Broadway ep The Royal Family 9.15.54
      CBS
    Shower of Stars ep A Christmas Carol 12.3.54 CBS
    Producers Showcase ep Dodsworth 4.30.56 NBC
    Dupont Show of the Month ep The Winslow Boy 11.13.
      58 CBS
    Dupont Show of the Month ep Hamlet 2.24.59 CBS

MARCH, HAL
    RCA Victor Show sr 10.3.52 NBC
    My Friend Irma sr 11.6.53 CBS
    Four Star Playhouse ep Marked Down 11.25.54 CBS
    The Soldiers sr 6.25.55 NBC
    Hallmark Hall of Fame ep Dream Girl 12.11.55 NBC
    Omnibus ep The Great Forgery 1.15.56 CBS
    The Bachelor Sp 7.15.56 NBC
    High Button Shoes Sp 11.24.56 NBC
    Studio One ep Tale of the Comet 2.4.57 CBS
    Dupont Show of the Month ep 9.22.63 NBC
    Gidget ep 2.3.66 ABC
    Trials of O'Brien ep Dead End on Flugel Street 12.
      3.65 CBS
    Hey Landlord ep 12.4.66 NBC
    The Lucy Show ep 12.5.66 CBS
    Danny Thomas Show ep My Pal Tony 3.4.68 NBC

MARCHAND, NANCY
    Studio One ep Little Women 12.18.50, 12.25.50 CBS
    Kraft Theatre ep Of Famous Memory 3.21.51 NBC
    Studio One ep The Hospital 12.8.52 CBS
    Kraft Theatre ep The Old Maid 4.8.54 ABC
    Kraft Theatre ep The Office Dance 10.6.54 NBC
    Kraft Theatre ep Career 12.8.54 NBC
    Kraft Theatre ep A Child Is Born 12.23.54 ABC
    Omnibus ep The Renaissance 10.55 CBS

Omnibus ep The Trial of Captain Kidd 3.10.57 ABC
Studio One ep Rudy 8.19.57 CBS
Kraft Theatre ep Material Witness 2.19.58 NBC
Shirley Temple's Story Book ep The Sleeping Beauty
  6.8.58 NBC
Armstrong Circle Theatre ep Miracle at Spring Hill
  2.4.59 CBS
Playhouse 90 ep Free Weekend 7.23.59 CBS
Playhouse 90 ep The Hidden Image 11.12.59 CBS
Sunday Showcase ep The Indestructible Mr. Gore 12.
  13.59 NBC
Play of the Week ep A Piece of Blue Sky 5.9.60 NN
Play of the Week ep The House of Bernarda Alba 6.
  6.60 NN
Law and Mr. Jones ep The Long Echo 12.30.60 ABC
Defenders ep The Attack 12.9.61 CBS
Repertory Theatre ep Don Juan in Hell 4.14.65 NN
Southern Baptist Theatre ep The Statesman 1.16.66
  NBC
The Lower Depths Sp 2.11.66 NN
New York Television Theatre ep Dark Lady of the
  Sonnets 10.31.66 NN
N.Y.P.D. ep What's A Nice Girl Like You 10.29.68
  ABC

MARGO

The Unexpected ep Eclipse 5.14.52 NBC
Schlitz Playhouse of Stars ep Enchanted Evening 10.
  31.52 CBS
Wagon Train ep The John Darro Story 11.6.57 NBC
Desilu Playhouse ep The Night the Phone Rang 12.
  15.58 CBS
Desilu Playhouse ep So Tender, So Profane 10.30.59
  CBS
New Breed ep My Brother's Keeper 5.1.62 ABC
Rawhide ep A Man Called Mushy 10.23.64 CBS
Perry Mason ep The Case of the Sad Sicilian 3.11.
  65 CBS

MARGOLIN, JANET

Ben Casey ep Legacy from a Stranger 10.22.62 ABC
Coronet Blue ep 6.12.67 CBS
Interns ep 3.17.71 CBS

MARKEY, ENID

Television Theatre ep The 19th Hole 3.8.50 NBC
Armstrong Circle Theatre ep Enter Rosalind 12.25.
  51 NBC

Philco Playhouse   ep   Up Above the World So High   11.
   22. 53 NBC
Kraft Theatre   ep   The Rose Garden   12. 2. 53 NBC
Goodyear Playhouse   ep   Buy Me Blue Ribbons   2. 28.
   54 NBC
TV Hour   ep   Love Song   5. 4. 54 ABC
Amstrong Circle Theatre   ep   Man Talk   5. 11. 54 NBC
Kraft Theatre   ep   Citizen Miller   6. 3. 54 NBC
Kraft Theatre   ep   The Southwest Corner   3. 30. 55 NBC
Alfred Hitchcock Presents   ep   The Legacy   5. 27. 56
   CBS
Producers Showcase   ep   Happy Birthday   6. 25. 56 NBC
Suspicion   ep   11. 18. 57 NBC
True Story   ep   The Writer   12. 14. 57 NBC
Playhouse 90   ep   The Silver Whistle   12. 24. 59 CBS
Bringing Up Buddy   sr   10. 10. 60 CBS
Defenders   ep   Grandma TNT   12. 22. 62 CBS
Repertory Theatre   ep   The Wedding   4. 21. 65 NN
Ozzie and Harriet   ep   1. 22. 66 ABC
Please Don't Eat the Daisies   ep   Who's Walking Under
   the Bed   3. 8. 66 NBC

MARLOWE, HUGH
   The Adventures of Ellery Queen   sr   1954 NN
   Schlitz Playhouse of Stars   ep   Her Kind of Honor   3.
      19. 54 CBS
   Studio One   ep   Cross My Heart   4. 4. 55 CBS
   U. S. Steel Hour   ep   Hung for a Sheep   6. 7. 55 ABC
   G. E. Theatre   ep   The Crime of Daphne Rutledge   6.
      13. 54 CBS
   The Adventures of Ellery Queen   sr ret   10. 2. 55 NN
   Crossroads   ep   Dig or Die Another Hyde   3. 30. 56
      ABC
   Alfred Hitchcock Presents   ep   John Brown's Body   12.
      30. 56 CBS
   Crossroads   ep   4. 26. 57 ABC
   Alfred Hitchcock Presents   ep   A Man Greatly Beloved
      5. 12. 57 CBS
   Lux Video Theatre   ep   Who Is Picasso?   7. 4. 57 NBC
   Alfred Hitchcock Presents   ep   Last Request   11. 24. 57
      CBS
   Jane Wyman Theatre   ep   A Reasonable Doubt   11. 28.
      57 NBC
   Studio One   ep   Balance of Terror   1. 27. 58 CBS
   Schlitz Playhouse of Stars   ep   Bluebeard's Seventh Wife
      3. 21. 58 CBS
   Matinee Theatre   ep   The 65th Floor   6. 9. 58 NBC

Perry Mason ep The Case of the Fraudulent Photo
2. 7. 59 CBS
Rawhide ep Incident of the Champagne Bottles 3. 18.
60 CBS
Perry Mason ep The Case of the Slandered Submarine
5. 14. 60 CBS
Michael Shayne ep The Poison Pen Club 6. 16. 61
NBC
Alfred Hitchcock Theatre ep Services Rendered 12.
12. 61 NBC
Law and Mr. Jones ep Poor Eddie's Dead 10. 4. 62
ABC
Dick Powell Theatre ep The Third Side of the Coin
3. 26. 63 NBC
Perry Mason ep The Case of the Nebulous Nephew
9. 26. 63 CBS
Arrest and Trial ep An Echo of Conscience 1. 26. 64
ABC
Virginian ep The Intruders 3. 4. 65 NBC
Perry Mason ep The Case of the Sleepy Slayer 10.
15. 64 CBS
Hazel ep Hazel's Day in Court 3. 4. 65
Perry Mason ep The Case of the Hasty Honeymooner
10. 24. 65 CBS
Virginian ep Trail to Ashley Mountain 11. 2. 66 NBC
The Man from U. N. C. L. E. ep The Seven Wonders of
the World Affair 1. 8. 68, 1. 15. 68 NBC
Judd for the Defense ep 3. 1. 68 ABC
Another World sr 1970 NBC

MARMONT, PERCY
Playhouse 4 ep The Five Pound Note 7. 30. 55 NBC

MARSH, MAE
Bonanza ep The Diedesheimer Story 5. 21. 60 NBC

MARSHALL, CONNIE
Halls of Ivy ep Professor Hall's Baby 8. 18. 55 CBS

MARSHALL, E. G.
Television Theatre ep The Dark Tower 1. 11. 50 NBC
Television Theatre ep Kelly 1. 25. 50 NBC
Actors Studio ep Mr. Mummery's Suspicion 2. 17. 50
CBS
Television Theatre ep Valley Forge 2. 22. 50 NBC
Tele-Theatre ep The Californian's Tale 4. 24. 50
NBC

Television Theatre   ep   Macbeth   5.10.50 NBC
The Trap   ep   Stan, the Killer   5.20.50 CBS
Philco Playhouse   ep   Semmelweis   5.28.50 NBC
Studio One   ep   My Granny Van   6.26.50 CBS
Philco Playhouse   ep   The Tentacles   7.9.50 NBC
Television Theatre   ep   Feathers in a Gale   8.9.50 NBC
TV Playhouse   ep   The Touch of a Stranger   10.1.50 NBC
Sure as Fate   ep   Nightfall   12.12.50 CBS
Television Theatre   ep   Rip Van Winkle   12.27.50 NBC
Philco Playhouse   ep   The Great Escape   1.28.51 CBS
Danger   ep   The Night Draws Tight   2.13.51 CBS
Philco Playhouse   ep   Let Them Be Sea Captains   2.18.51 NBC
Kraft Theatre   ep   On Stage   3.14.51 NBC
Philco Playhouse   ep   Adventures of Hiram Holliday   6.3.51 NBC
Lights Out   ep   Meddlers   7.9.51 NBC
Philco Playhouse   ep   By-Line for Murder   9.30.51 NBC
Philco Playhouse   ep   Without Fear or Favor   1.13.52 NBC
Kraft Theatre   ep   The Rugged Path   3.26.52 NBC
Police Story   ep   The Springfield, Massachusetts Story   5.16.52 CBS
Philco Playhouse   ep   The Monument   6.29.52 NBC
Television Theatre   ep   The Great Big Doorstep   7.16.52 NBC
Armstrong Circle Theatre   ep   The Vase   8.5.52 NBC
Short Short Drama   ep   A Portrait of General Garrity   11.25.52 NBC
Kraft Theatre   ep   Mr. Lazarus   11.26.52 NBC
Goodyear Playhouse   ep   The Oil Well   9.20.53 CBS
Goodyear Playhouse   ep   The Happy Rest   10.4.53 CBS
The Web   ep   Strange Sanctuary   10.25.53 CBS
TV Sound Stage   ep   Nemesis   10.30.53 NBC
Kraft Theatre   ep   Rip Van Winkle   12.23.53 NBC
Goodyear Playhouse   ep   Old Tosselfoot   4.25.54 NBC
Suspense   ep   Smoke   5.4.54 CBS
Armstrong Circle Theatre   ep   The First Born   9.7.54 NBC
Philco Playhouse   ep   Middle of the Night   9.19.54 NBC
Omnibus   ep   A Clean Fresh Breeze   10.31.54 CBS
Goodyear Playhouse   ep   Flight Report   11.7.54 NBC
Elgin Hour   ep   Yesterday's Magic   12.14.54 ABC
Elgin Hour   ep   Falling Star   12.28.54 ABC

Producers Showcase ep Yellow Jack 1.10.55 NBC
You Are There ep The Trial of Susan B. Anthony
    1.23.55 CBS
Armstrong Circle Theatre ep Thunder in the House
    1.25.55 NBC
Philco Playhouse ep A Sense of Justice 2.6.55 NBC
You Are There ep Washington's Farewell to His Of-
    ficers 2.27.55 CBS
Studio One ep Donovan's Brain 2.28.55 CBS
Omnibus ep The Might Case 3.6.55 CBS
You Are There ep The Death of Socrates 3.13.55
    CBS
Inner Sanctum ep Sound of the Birds 3.18.55 NN
You Are There ep The Triumph of Alexander the
    Great 3.27.55 CBS
G.E. Theatre ep O, Lonely Moon 4.17.55 CBS
Goodyear Playhouse ep Do It Yourself 4.24.55 NBC
Pond's Theatre ep Cynara 5.12.55 ABC
Elgin Hour ep Mind Over Mama 5.31.55 ABC
20th Century-Fox Hour ep The Ox-Bow Incident 11.
    2.55 CBS
Playwrights '56 ep This Business of Murder 1.31.56
    NBC
Goodyear Playhouse ep The Terrorists 2.26.56 NBC
Playwrights '56 ep Keyhole 5.22.56 NBC
G.E. Theatre ep O'Hoolihan and the Leprechaun 6.3.
    56 CBS
Hallmark Hall of Fame ep The Little Foxes 12.16.56
    NBC
Kraft Theatre ep The Duel 3.6.57 NBC
Alcoa Hour ep The Big Build Up 3.31.57 NBC
Studio One ep The Out-of-Towners 5.6.57 CBS
Playhouse 90 ep Clash by Night 6.13.57 CBS
Alcoa Hour ep Night 9.22.57 NBC
Suspicion ep Four O'Clock 9.30.57 NBC
Alfred Hitchcock Presents ep The Mail Order Prophet
    10.13.57 CBS
Studio One ep Presence of the Enemy 2.10.58 CBS
Shirley Temple's Story Book ep Rip Van Winkle 5.8.
    58 NBC
Playhouse 90 ep The Plot to Kill Stalin 9.25.58 CBS
Pursuit ep Calculated Risk 12.10.58 CBS
Playhouse 90 ep A Quiet Game of Cards 1.29.59 CBS
Drama ep Man in Orbit 5.11.59 CBS
Playhouse 90 ep Made in Japan 3.5.59 CBS
Sunday Showcase ep The Indestructible Mr. Gore 12.
    13.59 NBC

Play of the Week   ep   The Cherry Orchard   12. 28. 59
   NN
Play of the Week   ep   The Master Builder   3. 21. 60 NN
Moment of Fear   ep   The Third Party   8. 12. 60 NBC
Route 66   ep   Three Sides   11. 18. 60 CBS
Islanders   ep   Forbidden Cargo   11. 27. 60 ABC
Rawhide   ep   Incident of the Broken Word   1. 20. 61
   CBS
Dupont Show of the Month   ep   The Night of the Storm
   3. 21. 61 CBS
Defenders   sr   9. 16. 61 CBS
Defenders   sr ret   9. 62 CBS
Defenders   sr ret   9. 63 CBS
Suspense   ep   5. 6. 64 CBS
Defenders   sr ret   9. 24. 64 CBS
The Poppy Is Also a Flower   tf   4. 22. 66 ABC
A Case of Libel   Sp   2. 11. 68 ABC
On Stage   ep   This Town Will Never Be the Same   4.
   23. 69 NBC
Bold Ones   sr   9. 15. 69 NBC
Hallmark Hall of Fame   ep   The Littlest Angel   12. 6. 69
   NBC
Paris 7000   ep   1. 22. 70 ABC
Bold Ones   sr ret   9. 20. 70 NBC
Brady Bunch   ep   10. 9. 70 ABC
Men from Shiloh   ep   Lady at the Bar   11. 4. 70 NBC
Men from Shiloh   ep   1. 6. 71 NBC
Vanished   tf   3. 8. 71, 3. 9. 71 NBC
Bold Ones   sr ret   9. 19. 71 NBC
Night Gallery   ep   9. 22. 71 NBC
Ellery Queen: Don't Look Behind You   tf   11. 19. 71
   NBC
CBS Playhouse 90   ep   Look Homeward, Angel   2. 25.
   72 CBS
Ironside   ep   9. 14. 72 NBC
Bold Ones   sr ret   9. 19. 72 NBC
Pursuit   tf   12. 12. 72 ABC

MARSHALL, HERBERT
   Airflyte Theatre   ep   Municipal Report   10. 26. 50 CBS
   Robert Montgomery Presents   ep   An Inspector Calls
      11. 5. 51 NBC
   The Unexpected   sh   3. 5. 52 NBC
   Ford Theatre   ep   Girl in the Park   10. 30. 52 NBC
   December Bride   ep   11. 14. 55 CBS
   Best of Broadway   ep   The Philadelphia Story 12. 8. 54
      CBS

Lux Video Theatre   ep   The Browning Version   4.7.55
  NBC
Lux Video Theatre   ep   Now Voyager   10.4.56 NBC
Alfred Hitchcock Presents   ep   A Bottle of Wine   2.3.
  57 CBS
Loretta Young Show   ep   Louise   3.10.57 NBC
Playhouse 90   ep   The Mystery of 13   10.24.57 CBS
Studio One   ep   Balance of Terror   1.27.58 CBS
Alfred Hitchcock Presents   ep   Little White Rock   6.
  29.58 CBS
Adventures in Paradise   ep   Nightmare on Napuka   1.
  18.60 ABC
Adventures in Paradise   ep   There Is an Island   3.14.
  60 ABC
Hong Kong   ep   Colonel Cat   11.16.60 ABC
Michael Shayne   ep   Spotlight on a Corpse   1.13.61
  NBC
Zane Grey Theatre   ep   The Atoner   4.6.61 CBS
77 Sunset Strip   ep   "5"   9.20.63 ABC

MARTIN, DEAN
  Danny Thomas Show   ep   Terry's Crush   2.24.58 CBS
  Rawhide   ep   Canliss   10.30.64 CBS
  The Lucy Show   ep   2.14.66 CBS

MARTIN, DEWEY
  Playwrights '56   ep   The Battler   10.18.55 NBC
  Studio One   ep   Fair Play   12.26.55 CBS
  Climax   ep   Gamble on a Thief   2.2.56 CBS
  Front Row Center   ep   Search for a Stranger   3.25.56
    CBS
  Climax   ep   To Scream at Midnight   6.14.56 CBS
  Climax   ep   Ten Minutes to Curfew   12.27.56 CBS
  Climax   ep   The Necessary Evil   9.19.57 CBS
  Zane Grey Theatre   ep   Episode in Darkness   11.15.
    57 CBS
  Studio 57   ep   Seventh Brother, Seventh Son   12.1.57
    NN
  Climax   ep   Thieves of Tokyo   1.16.58 CBS
  Loretta Young Show   ep   The Hidden One   1.19.58 NBC
  Zane Grey Theatre   ep   Man of Fear   3.14.58 CBS
  Loretta Young Show   ep   Second Rate Citizen   4.27.58
    CBS
  June Allyson Show   ep   The Pledge   10.26.59 CBS
  Twilight Zone   ep   I Shot an Arrow into the Air   1.15.
    60 CBS
  World of Disney   ep   The Warrior's Path   12.4.60,

12.11.60 ABC
World of Disney   ep   The Wilderness Road   3.12.61
   ABC
Dick Powell Theatre   ep   Thunder in a Forgotten Town
   3.5.63 NBC
Burke's Law   ep   Who Killed the Kind Doctor   11.29.
   63 ABC
Arrest and Trial   ep   The Black Flower   3.1.64 CBS
Outer Limits   ep   The Premonition   1.9.65 ABC
I Spy   ep   11.16.66 NBC
Mannix   ep   1.17.70 CBS
Hawaii Five-O   ep   Force of Waves   10.28.70 CBS
Assault on the Wayne   tf   1.12.71 ABC
Wheeler and Murdoch   pt   3.27.72 ABC
Mission Impossible   ep   10.7.72 CBS

MARTIN, DICK
   The Lucy Show   sr   10.8.62 CBS
   Off to See the Wizard   ep   Who's Afraid of Mother
      Goose?   10.13.67 ABC

MARTIN, MARY
   Producers Showcase   ep   Peter Pan   3.7.55 NBC
   The Skin of Our Teeth   Sp   9.11.55 NBC
   Producers Showcase   ep (restaged)   Peter Pan   1.9.56
      NBC
   Hallmark Hall of Fame   ep   Born Yesterday   10.28.56
      NBC
   Annie Get Your Gun   Sp   11.27.57 NBC
   Peter Pan   Sp (restaged)   12.8.60 NBC

MARTIN, TONY
   Shower of Stars   ep   High Pitch   5.12.55 CBS
   George Burns Show   ep   12.2.58 NBC
   Donna Reed Show   ep   3.21.61 ABC
   Death Valley Days   ep   The Unshakable Man   5.1.63
      NBC
   Name of the Game   ep   I Love You, Billy Baker   11.
      20.70 NBC

MARTINELLI, ELSA
   Rogues   ep   The Real Russian Caviar   12.27.64 NBC

MARVIN, LEE
   Rebound   ep   The Mine   2.29.52 ABC
   Easy Chair Theatre   ep   Sound in the Night   2.16.53
      NN

The Doctor   ep   The Runaways   6.21.53 NBC
The American Hour   ep   Outlaw's Reckoning   11.3.53
    ABC
Pepsi Cola Playhouse   ep   Open Season   3.19.54 ABC
TV Soundstage   ep   The Psychophonic Nurse   6.25.54
    NBC
Center Stage   ep   The Day Before Atlanta   9.7.54 ABC
G.E. Theatre   ep   Mr. Death and the Redheaded Wom-
    an   11.28.54 CBS
Medic   ep   White Is the Color   1.17.55 NBC
G.E. Theatre   ep   The Martyr   1.23.55 CBS
TV Reader's Digest   ep   How Charlie Faust Won a
    Pennant for the Giants   4.11.55 ABC
Fireside Theatre   ep   The Little Guy   9.27.55 NBC
Studio One   ep   Shakedown Cruise   11.7.55 CBS
Climax   ep   Bail Out at 43,000   12.29.55 CBS
Kraft Theatre   ep   The Fool Killer   3.7.56 NBC
Front Row Center   ep   Dinner Date   3.18.56 CBS
G.E. Theatre   ep   The Doctors of Pawnee Kill   1.27.
    57 CBS
U.S. Steel Hour   ep   Shadow of Evil   2.27.57 CBS
M Squad   sr   9.20.57 NBC
G.E. Theatre   ep   All I Survey   2.2.58 CBS
Climax   ep   Time of the Hanging   5.22.58 CBS
M Squad   sr ret   9.58 NBC
Schlitz Playhouse of Stars   ep   A Fistful of Love   1.2.
    59 CBS
M Squad   sr ret   9.59 NBC
Desilu Playhouse   ep   A Man in Orbit   5.11.59 CBS
G.E. Theatre   ep   The Last Reunion   9.27.59 CBS
Sunday Showcase   ep   The American   3.27.60 NBC
G.E. Theatre   ep   Don't You Remember?   5.8.60 CBS
Wagon Train   ep   The Jose Morales Story   10.26.60
    NBC
Americans   ep   Reconnaissance   3.6.61 NBC
Wagon Train   ep   The Christopher Hale Story   3.15.61
    NBC
Checkmate   ep   Jungle Castle   4.1.61 CBS
G.E. Theatre   ep   The Joke's on Me   4.16.61 CBS
Untouchables   ep   The Nick Acropolis Story   6.1.61
    ABC
Alcoa Premiere   ep   People Need People   10.10.61
    ABC
Investigators   ep   The Oracle   10.12.61 CBS
Twilight Zone   ep   The Grave   10.27.61 CBS
Route 66   ep   Mon Petit Chou   11.24.61 CBS
Ben Casey   ep   A Story to Be Told Softly   1.22.62 ABC

Untouchables ep Lament of Danger 3.22.62 ABC
Bonanza ep Crucible 4.8.62 NBC
Dr. Kildare ep One for the Road 4.12.62 NBC
Virginian ep It Tolls for Thee 11.21.62 NBC
Untouchables ep A Fist of Five 12.4.62 ABC
Dick Powell Theatre ep The Losers 1.15.63 NBC
Dick Powell Theatre ep Epilogue 4.2.63 NBC
Combat ep The Bridge at Chalons 9.17.63 ABC
Lawbreaker sh 9.20.63 ABC
Twilight Zone ep Steel 10.4.63 CBS
Kraft Suspense Theatre ep The Case Against Paul
   Ryker 10.10.63, 10.17.63 NBC
Great Adventures ep Six Wagons to the Sea 10.18.63
   CBS
Dr. Kildare ep The Sound of a Faraway Hill 10.29.
   64 NBC
Bob Hope Chrysler Theatre ep The Loving Cup 1.29.
   65 NBC

MARX, CHICO
   Silver Theatre ep Papa Romani 1.9.50 CBS
   G.E. Theatre ep The Incredible Jewel Robbery 3.8.
      59 CBS

MARX, GROUCHO
   Bell Telephone Hour ep The Mikado 4.29.60 NBC
   G.E. Theatre ep The Holdout 1.14.62 CBS
   Bob Hope Chrysler Theatre ep Time for Elizabeth
      4.24.64 NBC

MARX, HARPO
   I Love Lucy ep 5.9.55 CBS
   Dupont Show of the Month ep nar The Red Mill 4.19.
      58 CBS
   G.E. Theatre ep The Incredible Jewel Robbery 3.
      8.59 CBS
   June Allyson Show ep Silent Panic 12.22.60 CBS

MASON, JAMES
   Lux Video Theatre sh 8.26.54 NBC
   Panic ep Marooned 4.30.57 NBC
   G.E. Theatre ep The Questioning Note 10.6.57 CBS
   Playhouse 90 ep The Thundering Wave 12.12.57 CBS
   Schlitz Playhouse of Stars ep No Boat for Four Months
      1.31.58 CBS
   Playhouse 90 ep Not the Glory 5.8.58 CBS
   Playhouse 90 ep The Second Man 2.12.59 CBS

Goodyear Theatre ep A Sword for Marius 4.13.59
     NBC
Playhouse 90 ep The Hiding Place 3.22.60 CBS
June Allyson Show ep Once Upon a Knight 3.28.60
     CBS
John Brown's Raid Sp 10.25.60 NBC
Theatre '62 ep Rebecca 4.8.62 NBC
Alfred Hitchcock Theatre ep Captive Audience 10.18.
     62 CBS
Dr. Kildare ep Behold the Great Man 9.13.65, 9.14.
     65, 9.20.65, 9.21.65 NBC
ABC Stage 67 ep Dare I Weep, Dare I Mourn 9.21.
     66 ABC
The Legend of Silent Night Sp 12.25.68 ABC

MASSEN, OSA
Robert Montgomery Presents ep Land of Happiness
     2.22.54 NBC
Waterfront ep 4.26.55 NN
Ray Milland Show ep 9.9.55 CBS
Science Fiction Theatre ep The Unexplored 11.11.55
     NBC
Telephone Time ep Time Bomb 5.20.56 CBS
Telephone Time ep Escape 3.24.57 CBS
Climax ep Strange Sanctuary 3.28.57 CBS
Ford Theatre ep Exclusive 4.3.57 ABC
Richard Diamond ep The Homicide Habit 7.22.57
     CBS
Perry Mason ep The Case of the Desperate Daughter
     3.22.58 CBS
Wagon Train ep Around the Horn 10.1.58 NBC
Perry Mason ep The Case of the Shattered Dream 1.
     3.59 CBS
Perry Mason ep The Case of the Tarnished Trade-
     mark 1.20.62 CBS

MASSEY, DANIEL
Bonanza ep The Reluctant American 2.14.71 NBC

MASSEY, ILONA
Studio One ep The Ambassadors 5.15.50 CBS
Studio One ep The Shadow of a Man 11.27.50 CBS
Video Theatre ep Purple and Fine Linen 1.15.51
     CBS
Studio One ep (restaged) The Ambassadors 2.26.51
     CBS
Cameo Theatre ep The Third Time 7.30.51 NBC

Faith Baldwin Playhouse   ep   The Sleeping Beauty   10.
   6.51 ABC
Rendezvous   sr   2.13.52 ABC
Curtain Call   ep   The Liar   8.22.52 NBC

MASSEY, RAYMOND
   Drama   ep   Laburnum Grove   1.27.50 CBS
   The Clock   ep   The Morning After   9.22.50 NBC
   Pulitzer Prize Playhouse   ep   10.20.50 ABC
   Video Theatre   ep   Abe Lincoln in Illinois   2.12.51
      CBS
   Betty Crocker Star Matinee   ep   The Linden Tree   12.
      8.51 ABC
   Robert Montgomery Presents   ep   For These Services
      4.5.54 NBC
   Producers Showcase   ep   Yellow Jack   1.10.55 NBC
   Robert Montgomery Presents   ep   The Tender Leaves
      of Hope   4.4.55 NBC
   G.E. Theatre   ep   Bounty Court Martial   10.9.55 CBS
   20th Century-Fox Hour   ep   The Late George Apley
      11.16.55 CBS
   Climax   ep   The Hanging Judge   1.12.56 CBS
   Ford Star Jubilee   ep   The Day Lincoln Was Shot   2.
      11.56 NBC
   I Spy   sh   2.17.56 NN
   Robert Montgomery Presents   ep   Adam's Son   3.5.56
      NBC
   Goodyear Playhouse   ep   All Summer Long   10.28.56
      NBC
   Climax   ep   Strange Hostage   12.20.56 CBS
   Producers Showcase   ep   Mayerling   2.4.57 NBC
   Kraft Theatre   ep   A Matter of Life   4.17.57 NBC
   Kraft Theatre   ep   The Curly-Haired Kid   6.26.57 NBC
   G.E. Theatre   ep   Hitler's Secret   10.4.59 CBS
   Alfred Hitchcock Presents   ep   Road Hog   12.6.59 CBS
   Playhouse 90   ep   The Cruel Day   2.24.60 CBS
   Zane Grey Theatre   ep   Seed of Evil   4.7.60 CBS
   Adventures in Paradise   ep   Command at Sea   6.5.61
      ABC
   Dr. Kildare   sr   9.29.61 NBC
   Mystery Theatre   ep   Two Counts of Murder   7.11.62
      NBC
   Dr. Kildare   sr ret   9.27.62 NBC
   Dr. Kildare   sr ret   9.26.63 NBC
   Eleventh Hour   ep   Four Feet in the Morning   11.27.63
      NBC
   Dr. Kildare   sr ret   9.24.64 NBC

Dr. Kildare sr ret 9.13.65 NBC
Hallmark Hall of Fame ep St. Joan 12.4.67 NBC
Wagon Train ep Princess of a Lost Tribe 11.2.70
    NBC
Night Gallery ep Clean Kills and Other Trophies 1.
    6.71 NBC
Night Gallery ep Rare Objects 10.22.72 NBC

MASTROIANNI, MARCELLO
    The Poppy Is Also a Flower tf 4.22.66 ABC

MATHERS, JERRY
    Leave It to Beaver sr 10.4.57 CBS
    Leave It to Beaver sr ret 9.58 ABC
    Leave It to Beaver sr ret 9.59 ABC
    Leave It to Beaver sr ret 9.60 ABC
    Leave It to Beaver sr ret 9.61 ABC
    Leave It to Beaver sr ret 9.62 ABC

MATHEWS, KERWIN
    Ford Theatre ep Charlie C Company 12.9.54 NBC
    Ford Theatre ep Lady in the Wind 10.20.55 NBC
    Playhouse 90 ep The Country Husband 11.1.56 CBS
    Matinee Theatre ep Show of Strength 5.6.57 NBC
    Goodyear Playhouse ep The Obenauf Story 3.16.59
        NBC
    World of Disney ep The Waltz King 10.27.63, 11.3.
        63 NBC
    Ghostbreaker pt 9.8.67 NBC
    Ironside ep Achilles' Heel 2.17.72 NBC
    Ironside ep 11.16.72 NBC

MATHIAS, BOB
    Troubleshooters sr 9.11.59 NBC

MATTHAU, WALTER
    Philco Playhouse ep The Basket Weaver 4.20.52 NBC
    Goodyear Playhouse ep Three Sundays 8.24.52 NBC
    Danger ep Hand Me Down 4.21.53 CBS
    Suspense ep F.O.B. Vienna 4.28.53 CBS
    Plymouth Playhouse ep Nightmare Number Three 5.
        24.53 ABC
    Goodyear Playhouse ep Nothing to Sneeze At 7.12.53
        NBC
    Goodyear Playhouse ep The New Process 8.23.53
        NBC
    TV Sound Stage ep Wonder in Your Eyes 8.28.53 NBC

Philco Playhouse   ep   Othello   9.6.53 NBC
Studio One   ep   Dry Run   12.7.53 CBS
Philco Playhouse   ep   The Glorification of Al Toolum
    12.27.53 NBC
U.S. Steel Hour   ep   Late Date   4.13.54 ABC
TV Hour   ep   Atomic Attack   5.18.54 ABC
Philco Playhouse   ep   Adapt or Die   6.13.54 NBC
Center Stage   ep   The Human Touch   6.29.54 ABC
Goodyear Playhouse   ep   Flight Report   11.7.54 NBC
Robert Montgomery Presents   ep   Dr. Ed   12.6.54
    NBC
Philco Playhouse   ep   Walk into the Night   1.9.55 NBC
Robert Montgomery Presents   ep   A Westerner's Race
    Prejudice   3.14.55 NBC
Justice   ep   Booby Trap   10.23.55 NBC
Robert Montgomery Presents   ep   The Lost Weekend
    2.7.55 NBC
Alcoa Hour   ep   The Big Vote   8.19.56 NBC
Goodyear Playhouse   ep   A Will to Live   5.12.57 NBC
Goodyear Playhouse   ep   The Legacy   6.30.57 NBC
Alcoa Hour   ep   The Trouble with Women   8.11.57
    NBC
Climax   ep   To Walk the Night   12.19.57 CBS
Kraft Theatre   ep   Code of the Corner   1.15.58 NBC
Alfred Hitchcock Presents   ep   Dry Run   11.8.59 CBS
Play of the Week   cp   Juno and the Paycock   2.1.60 NN
Play of the Week   ep   The Rope Dancers   3.14.60 NN
Alfred Hitchcock Theatre   ep   Very Moral Theft   10.11.
    60 NBC
Play of the Week   ep   My Heart's in the Highlands   11.
    7.60 NN
Our American Heritage   ep   Born a Giant   12.2.60
    NBC
Naked City   ep   The Man Who Bit the Diamond in Half
    12.14.60 ABC
Tallahassee 7000   sr   1.3.61 CBS
Route 66   ep   Eleven, the Hard Way   4.7.61 CBS
Target: Corruptors   ep   The Million Dollar Dump   9.
    29.61 ABC
Alfred Hitchcock Theatre   ep   Cop for a Day   10.31.61
    NBC
Target: Corruptors   ep   1.12.62 ABC
Westinghouse Presents   ep   Footnote to Fame   2.3.62
    CBS
G.E. Theatre   ep   Acres and Pains   5.12.62 CBS
Dupont Show of the Month   ep   Big Deal in Laredo   10.
    7.62 NBC

Naked City   ep   Don't Knock It Till You've Tried It
     12. 26. 62 ABC
Eleventh Hour ep   A Tumble from a High White Horse
     2. 27. 63 NBC
Dupont Show of the Month   ep   The Takers   10. 13. 63
     NBC
Bob Hope Chrysler Theatre   ep   White Snow, Red Ice
     3. 13. 64 NBC
Dupont Show of the Month   ep Jeremy Rabbitt the Se-
     cret Avenger   4. 5. 64 NBC
Rogues   ep   The Personal Touch   9. 13. 64 NBC
Dr. Kildare   ep   Man Is Rock   9. 24. 64 NBC
Profiles in Courage   ep   12. 20. 64 NBC
Profiles in Courage   ep   Andrew Johnson   2. 28. 65 NBC
Hollywood Television Theatre   ep   Awake and Sing   3.
     6. 72 NN

MATTHEWS, CARMEN
     Danger   ep   2. 5. 52 CBS
     Kraft Theatre   ep   The Rugged Path   3. 26. 52 NBC
     The Web   ep   The Dark Shore   6. 25. 52 CBS
     The Doctor   ep   Time to Kill   9. 7. 52 NBC
     Summer Theatre   ep   The Shadowy Third   9. 15. 52 CBS
     Goodyear Playhouse   ep   The Room   9. 28. 52 NBC
     Danger   ep   The Scarlet Thread   10. 7. 52 CBS
     The Web   ep   K Is for Killer   11. 2. 52 CBS
     Philco Playhouse   ep   The Old Beginning   11. 23. 52
          NBC
     Goodyear Playhouse   ep   Ernie Barger Is Fifty   8. 9. 53
          NBC
     Danger   ep   Riviera Revisited   1. 19. 54 CBS
     TV Soundstage   ep   A Time for Hope   1. 29. 54 NBC
     Kraft Theatre   ep   Icewater, Please   2. 18. 54 ABC
     Armstrong Circle Theatre   ep   Gang-Up   4. 27. 54 NBC
     Kraft Theatre   ep   The Worried Songbirds   5. 13. 54
          ABC
     Armstrong Circle Theatre   ep   Breakdown   5. 18. 54
          NBC
     Kraft Theatre   ep   Short Story   8. 25. 54 NBC
     Armstrong Circle Theatre   ep   The First Born   9. 7. 54
          NBC
     Kraft Theatre   ep   The Day the Diner Closed   11. 4. 54
          ABC
     Omnibus   ep   1. 9. 55 CBS
     You Are There   ep   The Trial of Susan B. Anthony
          1. 23. 55 CBS
     Kraft Theatre   ep   Half the World's a Bride   3. 2. 55 NBC

Pond's Theatre   ep   Autumn Crocus   3.24.55 ABC
Hallmark Hall of Fame   ep   The Corn Is Green   1.8.
    56 NBC
Alfred Hitchcock Presents   ep   The Older Sister   1.22.
    56   CBS
Studio 57   ep   The Finishers   1.29.56 NN
Star Stage   ep   The Man Who Was Irresistible to Wom-
    en   3.16.56 NBC
G.E. Theatre   ep   The Night Goes On   3.18.56 CBS
Alfred Hitchcock Presents   ep   The Baby Sitter   5.6.
    55 CBS
Producers Showcase   ep   Bloomer Girl   5.28.56 NBC
Alfred Hitchcock Presents   ep   Conversations with a
    Corpse   11.18.56 CBS
Studio One   ep   The Unmentionable Blues   8.12.57 CBS
U.S. Steel Hour   ep   Above the World So High   8.28.57
    CBS
Alfred Hitchcock Presents   ep   The Percentage   1.5.58
    CBS
Hallmark Hall of Fame   ep   Hans Brinker   2.9.58 NBC
Playhouse 90   ep   Verdict of Three   4.24.58 CBS
Alfred Hitchcock Presents   ep   Festive Season   5.4.58
    CBS
Suspicion   ep   The Velvet Vault   5.19.58 NBC
G.E. Theatre   ep   The Indian Giver   5.17.59 CBS
Play of the Week   ep   The Grass Harp   3.28.60 NN
G.E. Theatre   ep   The Drop-Out   1.29.61 CBS
Twilight Zone   ep   Static   3.10.61 CBS
Play of the Week   ep   A Cool Wind over the Living   3.
    27.61 NN
Alfred Hitchcock Theatre   ep   The Kerry Blues   4.17.
    62 NBC
Ben Casey   ep   And Eve Wore a Veil of Tears   4.23.
    62 ABC
New Breed   ep   Wherefore Art Thou, Romeo   5.15.62
    ABC
Fugitive   ep   World's End   9.22.64 ABC
FBI   ep   12.22.68 ABC
Death Takes a Holiday   tf   10.23.71 ABC
They Call It Murder   tf   12.17.71 NBC
N.E.T. Playhouse   ep   They   4.17.70 NN
Cannon   ep   3.7.72 CBS

MAUGHAM, W. SOMERSET
    Tellers of Tales (a.k.a. Somerset Maugham Theatre)
        sh   10.18.50 CBS

MAUNDER, WAYNE
    Custer   sr   9.6.67 ABC
    Lancer   sr   9.24.68 CBS
    Lancer   sr ret   9.23.69 CBS
    FBI   ep   Time Bomb   10.25.70 ABC

MAXWELL, MARILYN
    G.E. Theatre   ep   Twinkle, Twinkle, Little Star   9.6.
        53 CBS
    Best Foot Forward   Sp   11.20.54 NBC
    Shower of Stars   ep   Burlesque   3.17.55 CBS
    Ford Theatre   ep   Sunday Mourn   4.21.55 NBC
    Playhouse 90   ep   Snow Shoes   1.3.57 CBS
    77 Sunset Strip   ep   Legend of Crystal Dart   4.15.60
        ABC
    Gunsmoke   ep   5.28.60 CBS
    Adventures in Paradise   ep   Beached   5.2.60 ABC
    Adventures in Paradise   ep   The Serpent in the Garden
        4.17.61 ABC
    Bus Stop   sr   10.1.61 ABC
    77 Sunset Strip   ep   Bullets   12.22.61 ABC
    Burke's Law   ep   Who Killed Cynthia Royal   12.13.63
        ABC
    Wagon Train   ep   2.24.64 ABC
    Danny Thomas Show   ep   Moose   4.5.64 CBS
    Bob Hope Chrysler Theatre   ep   Have Girls--Will
        Travel   10.16.64 NBC
    Burke's Law   ep   4.28.65 ABC
    Outsider   ep   Tell It Like It Is   12.4.68 NBC
    Debbie Reynolds Show   ep   12.2.69 NBC
    Wild Women   tf   10.20.70 ABC
    O'Hara, U.S. Treasury   ep   10.22.71 CBS

MAY, ELAINE
    Dupont Show of the Month   ep   The Red Mill   4.19.58
        CBS

MAYEHOFF, EDDIE
    Doc Corkle   sr   10.5.52 NBC
    That's My Boy   sr   4.10.54 CBS
    Studio One   ep   The Star Spangled Soldier   5.21.56 CBS
    Playhouse 90   ep   Made in Heaven   12.6.56 CBS

MAYO, VIRGINIA
    Conflict   ep   Execution Night   5.28.57 ABC
    Loretta Young Show   ep   Operation Snowball   12.28.58
        NBC

Wagon Train ep The Beauty Jamison Story 12. 17. 58
   NBC
Lux Playhouse ep Deathtrap 2. 6. 59 CBS
Outsider ep Behind God's Back 2. 5. 69 NBC

MEADE, JULIA
   Armstrong Circle Theatre ep The Complex Mummy
      Complex 1. 8. 58 CBS
   Spotlight Playhouse sh 6. 30. 59 CBS

MEADOWS, AUDREY
   The Honeymooners sr 10. 1. 55 CBS
   Play of the Week ep Grand Tour 5. 30. 60 NN
   Laf Hit ep Mrs. Bixby and the Colonel's Coat 9. 27.
      60 NBC
   Wagon Train ep The Nancy Palmer Story 3. 8. 61 NBC
   Checkmate ep One for the Book 3. 18. 61 CBS
   G. E. Theatre ep Sis Bowls 'em over 4. 9. 61 CBS
   Dupont Show of the Week ep The Action in New Or-
      leans 4. 15. 62 NBC
   Sam Benedict ep Life Is a Lie, Love a Cheat 11. 10.
      62 NBC
   Love American Style ep 10. 13. 72 ABC

MEADOWS, JAYNE
   Robert Montgomery Presents ep Eva? Caroline? 1.
      28. 52 NBC
   The Web ep End of the Line 8. 16. 53 CBS
   Kraft Theatre ep The Old Maid 4. 8. 54 ABC
   U. S. Steel Hour ep Red Gulch 6. 21. 55 ABC
   Fireside Theatre ep The Sport 10. 4. 55 NBC
   Modern Romance ep nar 4. 21. 58 NBC
   Ann Sothern Show ep 12. 21. 59 CBS
   G. E. Theatre ep The Man Who Thought for Himself
      9. 18. 60 CBS
   Good Morning World ep 3. 19. 68 CBS
   Now You See It, Now You Don't tf 11. 11. 68 NBC
   Here Come the Brides ep 10. 17. 69 ABC
   Love American Style ep 2. 20. 70 ABC
   Medical Center ep Screen of Silence 10. 28. 70 CBS
   Medical Center ep Trial by Terror 11. 25. 70 CBS
   Here's Lucy ep 12. 28. 70 CBS
   Medical Center ep Woman in Question 1. 6. 71 CBS
   Medical Center ep The Imposter 9. 29. 71 CBS
   Medical Center ep Terror 1. 26. 72 CBS
   Temperatures Rising ep 10. 24. 72 ABC

MEARA, ANNE
  Ninotchka Sp 4.20.60 ABC
  Corner Bar ep 8.9.72 ABC
  Paul Lynde Show sr 9.27.72 ABC

MEDINA, PATRICIA
  Ford Theatre ep Tangier Lady 10.1.53 NBC
  Lux Video Theatre ep Imperfect Lady 11.4.54 NBC
  Climax ep The After Hours 11.25.54 CBS
  77 Bengal Lancers sr 10.21.56 NBC
  Ford Theatre ep Alibi 4.26.56 NBC
  Perry Mason ep The Case of the Lucky Loser 9.27.
    58 CBS
  Climax ep House of Doubt 6.19.58 CBS
  Zorro ep The Gay Caballero 1.22.59 ABC
  G.E. Theatre ep The Last Lesson 2.8.59 CBS
  Zorro ep The Legend of Zorro 2.12.59 ABC
  Have Gun Will Travel ep The Return of the Lady 2.
    21.59 CBS
  Californians ep 6.16.59 NBC
  Adventures in Paradise ep The Black Pearl 10.12.59
    ABC
  G.E. Theatre ep Absalom, My Son 12.6.59 CBS
  Bonanza ep The Spanish Grant 2.6.60 NBC
  Rebel ep Fair Game 3.27.60 ABC
  Riverboat ep The Night of the Faceless Men 3.28.60
    NBC
  Ford Star Time ep The Young Juggler 3.29.60 NBC
  Hotel de Paree ep Sundance and the Black Widow 4.
    1.60 CBS
  Black Saddle ep Change of Venue 5.27.60 ABC
  Dante ep The Feline Traveler 10.17.60 NBC
  Perry Mason ep The Case of the Lucky Loser 11.26.
    60 CBS
  Coronado 9 ep Londonderry Heiress 1.10.61 NN
  Rawhide ep Incident of the Boomerang 3.24.61 CBS
  Thriller ep The Premature Burial 10.2.61 NBC
  Cain's Hundred ep Blue Water, White Beach 10.3.61
    NBC
  Have Gun Will Travel ep 1.26.63 CBS
  Mystery Theatre ep Man without a Witness 9.25.63
    NBC
  Grindl ep Grindl, Femme Fatale 10.20.63 NBC
  Burke's Law ep 5.1.64 ABC
  Rogues ep Two of a Kind 11.8.64 NBC
  Alfred Hitchcock Theatre ep See the Monkey Dance
    11.9.64 NBC

The Man from U.N.C.L.E.   ep   The Foxes and Hounds
   Affair   10.8.65 NBC
Name of the Game   ep   3.6.70 NBC
Mannix   ep   Cold Trail   9.22.71 CBS

MEEKER, RALPH
   Kraft Theatre   ep   A Sound of Hunting   1.31.51 NBC
   Goodyear Playhouse   ep   The Darkness Below   11.9.52
   NBC
   Mirror Theatre   ep   Someone Like You   7.7.53 NBC
   Mirror Theatre   ep   The Happy Tingle   8.11.53 NBC
   Studio One   ep   Dominique   3.28.55 CBS
   Alfred Hitchcock Presents   ep   Revenge   10.2.55 CBS
   Studio One   ep   Dino   1.2.56 CBS
   Star Stage   ep   Of Missing Persons   1.13.56 NBC
   Alcoa Hour   ep   The Magic Horn   6.10.56 NBC
   Lux Video Theatre   ep   The Guilty   10.11.56 NBC
   Jane Wyman Theatre   ep   Between Jobs   10.30.56 NBC
   Studio 57   ep   The Blue Wall   12.2.56 NN
   Alfred Hitchcock Presents   ep   Malice Domestic   2.10.
   57 CBS
   Zane Grey Theatre   ep   A Time to Live   4.5.57 CBS
   Playhouse 90   ep   Four Women in Black   4.25.57 CBS
   20th Century-Fox Hour   ep   Deep Water   5.1.57 CBS
   Climax   ep   A Matter of Life and Death   11.21.57 CBS
   Climax   ep   So Deadly My Love   3.13.58 CBS
   Schlitz Playhouse of Stars   ep   Bluebeard's Seventh Wife
   3.21.58 CBS
   Wagon Train   ep   A Man Called Horse   3.26.58 NBC
   Kraft Theatre   ep   Fifty Grand   4.30.58 NBC
   Zane Grey Theatre   ep   A Time to Live   5.16.58 CBS
   Loretta Young Show   ep   I Want to Get Married   11.16.
   58 NBC
   Loretta Young Show   ep   Strange Money   12.14.58 NBC
   Loretta Young Show   ep   The Break-Off   1.4.59 NBC
   Wanted, Dead or Alive   ep   1.24.59 CBS
   Alfred Hitchcock Presents   ep   Total Loss   2.1.59 CBS
   Schlitz Playhouse of Stars   ep   The Man Who Had No
   Friends   2.13.59 CBS
   Alfred Hitchcock Presents   ep   I'll Take Care of You
   3.15.59 CBS
   Texan   ep   4.20.59 CBS
   Music Theatre   ep   The Sound of Murder   5.7.59 NBC
   Wanted, Dead or Alive   ep   5.30.59 CBS
   Not for Hire   sr   10.23.59 NN
   Drama   ep   Blue Wall   9.24.60 ABC
   Hallmark Hall of Fame   ep   A Punt, a Pass, and a

Prayer   11.20.60 NBC
Loretta Young Show   ep   Enter at Your Own Risk   1.8.
   61 NBC
World of Disney   ep   Frank Clell's in Town   4.23.61
   ABC
Route 66   ep   Two on the House   4.20.62 CBS
Going My Way   ep   The Crooked Angel   10.10.62 ABC
Empire   ep   Walk Like a King   10.30.62 NBC
U.S. Steel Hour   ep   Night Run to the West   2.20.63
   CBS
Route 66   ep   Shadows of an Afternoon   5.17.63 CBS
Breaking Point   ep   The Bull Roarer   10.21.63 ABC
Outer Limits   ep   Tourist Attraction   12.23.63 ABC
Defenders   ep   The Last Day   1.11.64 CBS
Channing   ep   Swing for the Moon   1.15.64 ABC
Doctors/Nurses   ep   The Respect of One for Another
   10.13.64 CBS
Kraft Suspense Theatre   ep   Three Persons   12.10.64
   NBC
The Long Hot Summer   ep   A Time to Die   2.16.66
   ABC
FBI   ep   The Plunderers   4.24.66 ABC
FBI   ep   1.1.67 ABC
Green Hornet   ep   1.6.67   ABC
Tarzan   ep   3.31.67 NBC
Custer   ep   9.20.67 ABC
Dundee and the Culhane   ep   10.25.67 CBS
High Chaparral   ep   11.19.67 NBC
Name of the Game   ep   The Protector   1.15.68 NBC
Ironside   ep   Price Tag Death   11.7.68 NBC
Men from Shiloh   ep   Nightmare at New Life   11.18.70
   NBC
N.E.T. Playhouse   ep   Hard Traveling   2.4.71 NN
The Reluctant Heroes   tf   11.23.71 ABC
The Night Stalker   tf   1.11.72 ABC
Police Surgeon   sr   9.12.72 NBC

MEGNA, JOHN
   Naked City   ep   A Horse Has a Big Head   11.21.62
      ABC
   Alfred Hitchcock Theatre   ep   The Magic Shop   1.10.64
      CBS
   Dr. Kildare   ep   The Sound of a Faraway Hill   10.29.
      64 NBC
   Ben Casey   ep   From Sutter's Crick   5.10.65 ABC
   Star Trek   ep   Miri   10.27.66 NBC
   I Spy   ep   10.9.67 NBC

Danny Thomas Show   ep   The Zero Man   11.27.67 NBC

MENJOU, ADOLPHE
    Favorite Story   sh/sr   1.11.53 NBC
    June Allyson Show   ep   The Secret Life of James Thur-
        ber   3.20.61 CBS

MEREDITH, BURGESS
    Robert Montgomery Presents   ep   Our Town   4.10.50
        NBC
    Studio One   ep   The Horse's Mouth   4.24.50 CBS
    Billy Rose's Playbill   ep   George III Once Drooled in
        This Plate   10.23.50 NN
    Lights Out   ep   The Martian Eyes   10.30.50 NBC
    Philco Playhouse   ep   I'm Still Alive   11.19.50 NBC
    Lights Out   ep   This Way to Heaven   12.24.51 NBC
    Video Theatre   ep   Decision   4.14.52 CBS
    Omnibus   ep   The Christmas Tie   11.30.52 CBS
    Tales of Tomorrow   ep   The Great Silence   2.20.53
        ABC
    G.E. Theatre   ep   Edison the Man   10.17.54 CBS
    Omnibus   ep   11.28.54 CBS
    U.S. Steel Hour   ep   Haunted Harbor   9.25.57 CBS
    Big Story   s nar   10.4.57 NN
    Suspicion   ep   Hand in Glove   10.21.57 NBC
    G.E. Theatre   ep   The Unfamiliar   3.30.58 CBS
    Hallmark Hall of Fame   ep   Ah, Wilderness!   4.28.59
        NBC
    Twilight Zone   ep   Time Enough at Last   11.20.59 CBS
    Twilight Zone   ep   Mr. Dingle the Strong   3.3.61 CBS
    Play of the Week   ep   Waiting for Godot   4.3.61 NN
    Twilight Zone   ep   The Obsolete Man   6.2.61 CBS
    Rawhide   ep   Little Fishes   11.24.61 CBS
    Westinghouse Presents   ep   Footnote to Fame   2.3.62
        CBS
    Naked City   ep   Hold for Gloria Christmas   9.19.62
        ABC
    Eleventh Hour   ep   Hooray, Hooray, the Circus Is Com-
        ing to Town   11.21.62 NBC
    Sam Benedict   ep   Everybody's Playing Polo   12.1.62
        NBC
    Ben Casey   ep   Pack Up All My Cares and Woe   12.17.
        62 ABC
    Twilight Zone   ep   Printer's Devil   2.28.63 CBS
    77 Sunset Strip   ep   "5"   9.20.63, 9.27.63, 10.4.63,
        10.11.63, 10.18.63 ABC
    Rawhide   ep   Incident at Paradise   10.24.63 CBS

Burke's Law ep Who Killed Alex Debbs 10.25.63 ABC

Breaking Point ep Heart of Marble, Body of Stone 12.23.63 ABC

Burke's Law ep Who Killed Jason Shaw 1.3.64 ABC

Wagon Train ep 2.3.64 ABC

Bob Hope Chrysler Theatre ep The Square Peg 3.6. 64 NBC

Rawhide ep Incident at Dead Horse 4.16.64, 4.23.64 CBS

Burke's Law ep Who Killed 711 12.9.64 ABC

Profiles in Courage ep 1.24.65 NBC

Mr. Novak sr 2.65 NBC

Laredo ep Lazyfoot, Where Are You 9.16.65 NBC

Wild, Wild West ep Night of the Human Trigger 12. 3.65 CBS

Loner ep Hunt the Man Down 12.11.65 CBS

Trials of O'Brien ep No Justice for the Judge 12.10. 65 CBS

Batman ep The Penguin's Jinx 1.19.66, 1.20.66 ABC

12 O'Clock High ep Back to the Drawing Board 2.7. 66 ABC

Batman ep The Penguin Goes Straight 3.23.66, 3.24. 66 ABC

Please Don't Eat the Daisies ep The Magnificent Muldoon 3.29.66 NBC

Branded ep Headed for Doomsday 4.10.66 NBC

Batman ep Fine Finny Fiends 5.4.66, 5.5.66 ABC

Batman ep Dizzonner the Penguin 11.2.66, 11.3.66 ABC

Batman ep The Penguin's Nest 12.7.66, 12.8.66 ABC

Batman ep The Zodiac Crimes 1.11.67, 1.12.67, 1. 18.67 ABC

Batman ep 1.25.67, 2.1.67 ABC

Invaders ep 5.2.67 ABC

Batman ep 9.14.67 ABC

Batman ep Horse of Another Color 10.12.67 ABC

Bonanza ep 11.26.67 NBC

Batman ep 1.25.68 ABC

Virginian ep The Orchard 10.2.68 NBC

Ironside ep The Macabre Mr. Micawber 11.28.68 NBC

Daniel Boone ep 2.6.69 NBC

Bold Ones ep Power Play 11.1.70 NBC

Name of the Game ep All the Old Familiar Faces 11.13.70 NBC

Night Gallery   ep   The Little Black Bag   12.23.70 NBC
Men from Shiloh   ep   Flight from Memory   2.17.71
    NBC
Lock, Stock and Barrel   tf   9.24.71 NBC
Room   222   sr   9.17.71 ABC
Love American Style   ep   10.1.71 ABC
World of Disney   ep   The Strange Monster of Strawberry
    Cove   11.6.71 NBC
Man and the City   ep   Pipe Me a Loving Tune   12.8.71
    ABC
Ironside   ep   1.6.72 ABC
McCloud   ep   A Little Plot at Tranquil Valley   1.12.72
    NBC
Getting Away from It All   tf   1.18.72 ABC
Probe   tf   2.21.72 NBC
New Healers   pt   3.27.72 ABC
Search   sr   9.13.72 NBC
Mannix   ep   10.1.72 CBS
Of Men and Women   ep   Why He Was Late to Work   12.
    17.72 ABC

MERKEL, UNA
Four Star Playhouse   ep   My Wife Geraldine   9.25.52
    CBS
Jewelers Showcase   ep   4.7.53 CBS
Studio One   ep   Two Little Minks   12.20.54 CBS
Kraft Theatre   ep   Trucks Welcome   10.12.55 NBC
Calling Terry Conway   pt   8.1.56 NBC
Playhouse 90   ep   The Greer Case   1.31.57 CBS
Climax   ep   The Secret of the Red Room   9.12.57 CBS
Dupont Show of the Month   ep   Aladdin   2.21.58 CBS
U.S. Steel Hour   ep   Flint and Fire   7.16.58 CBS
Real McCoys   ep   The New Housekeeper   11.18.62 CBS
Burke's Law   ep   Who Killed Cynthia Royal   12.13.63
    ABC
Destry   ep   Law and Order Day   2.28.64 ABC
Burke's Law   ep   4.14.65 ABC
I Spy   ep   Home to Judgment   1.8.68 NBC

MERMAN, ETHEL
Best of Broadway   ep   Panama Hattie   11.10.54 CBS
G.E. Theatre   ep   Reflected Glory   3.25.56 CBS
U.S. Steel Hour   ep   Honest in the Rain   5.9.56 CBS
Maggie Brown   pt   9.23.63 CBS
The Lucy Show   ep   Lucy Teaches Ethel Merman to Sing
    5.25.64, 6.1.64 CBS
Kraft Suspense Theatre   ep   Twixt the Cup and the Lip

6. 3. 65 NBC
Annie Get Your Gun   Sp   3. 19. 67 NBC
That Girl   ep   9. 7. 67 ABC
Batman   ep   Horse of Another Color   10. 12. 67 ABC
Tarzan   ep   Mountains of the Moon   11. 24. 67, 12. 1. 67
    NBC
That's Life   ep   10. 29. 68 ABC

MERRILL, DINA
Four Star Playhouse   ep   A Place Full of Strangers
    12. 8. 55 CBS
Playwrights '56   ep   Return to Cassino   2. 14. 56 NBC
Playwrights '56   ep   The Center of the Maze   4. 24. 56
    NBC
Matinee Theatre   ep   One for All   3. 17. 58 NBC
Climax   ep   Spider Web   6. 5. 58 CBS
Playhouse 90   ep   The Time of Your Life   10. 9. 58 CBS
Sunday Showcase   ep   What Makes Sammy Run   9. 27. 59,
    10. 4. 59 NBC
Dupont Show of the Month   ep   The Fallen Idol   10. 14.
    59 CBS
Desilu Playhouse   ep   Murder Is a Private Affair   6.
    10. 60 CBS
Dupont Show of the Month   ep   Men in White   9. 30. 60
    CBS
Hong Kong   ep   Lady Godiva   2. 8. 61 ABC
U. S. Steel Hour   ep   Brandenburg Gate   1. 4. 61 CBS
Westinghouse Presents   ep   The Dispossessed   10. 24. 61
    CBS
Investigators   ep   Style of Living   11. 9. 61 CBS
Dick Powell Theatre   ep   Obituary for Mr. "X"   1. 23.
    62 NBC
Westinghouse Presents   ep   Footnote to Fame   2. 3. 62
    CBS
Dr. Kildare   ep   Oh, My Daughter   2. 5. 62 NBC
Expendables   pt   9. 27. 62 ABC
Dick Powell Theatre   ep   The Court-Martial of Captain
    Wycliff   12. 11. 62 NBC
Alfred Hitchcock Theatre   ep   Bonfire   12. 13. 62 CBS
Eleventh Hour   ep   Everybody Knows You've Left Me
    4. 10. 63 NBC
Burke's Law   ep   Who Killed Mr. "X"   9. 27. 63 ABC
Bob Hope Chrysler Theatre   ep   The Candidate   12. 6.
    63 NBC
Rogues   ep   The Personal Touch   9. 13. 64 NBC
Mickey Rooney Show   ep   9. 16. 64 ABC
Kraft Suspense Theatre   ep   The Gun   12. 24. 64 NBC

Rogues   ep   A Daring Step Backward   4.18.65 NBC
Bob Hope Chrysler Theatre   ep   The Game 9.15.65
    NBC
FBI   ep   The Monster   9.19.65 ABC
Daniel Boone   ep   The Tamarack Massacre Affair   12.
    30.65 NBC
12 O'Clock High   ep   Which Way the Wind Blows   1.24.
    66 ABC
Daktari   ep   2.8.66 CBS
Shenandoah   ep   Macauley's Cure   5.16.66 ABC
Bonanza   ep   Pursued   10.2.66, 10.9.66 NBC
Run for Your Life   ep   3.20.67 NBC
Batman   ep   2.1.68, 2.8.68 ABC
The Sunshine Patriot   tf   12.16.68 NBC
The Lonely Profession   tf   10.21.69 NBC
Seven in Darkness   tf   9.23.69 ABC
Mission Impossible   ep   10.12.69, 10.19.69 CBS
Name of the Game   ep   The Glory Shouter   12.18.70
    NBC
Men from Shiloh   ep   The Angus Killer   2.10.71 NBC
Medical Center   ep   Perfection of Vices   2.24.71 CBS
Mr. and Mrs. Bo Jo Jones   tf   11.16.71 ABC
FBI   ep   10.8.72 ABC
Family Flight   tf   10.25.72 ABC

MERRILL, GARY
    Tales of the City   ep   6.25.53 CBS
    Tales of the City   ep   7.23.53 CBS
    U.S. Steel Hour   ep   P.O.W.   10.27.53 ABC
    Robert Montgomery Presents   ep   No Picnic at Mt. Ken-
        ya   11.2.53 NBC
    Justice   sh/sr   1954 NBC
    The Mask   sr   1.10.54 ABC
    U.S. Steel Hour   ep   The Great Chair   5.25.54 ABC
    Justice   ep   Timid Thief   10.7.54 NBC
    U.S. Steel Hour   ep   The Man with the Gun   10.12.54
        ABC
    Alcoa Hour   ep   Adventure in Diamonds   12.9.56 NBC
    Alfred Hitchcock Presents   ep   Manacles   1.27.57 CBS
    Schlitz Playhouse of Stars   ep   Wedding Present   2.22.
        57 CBS
    Alcoa Hour   ep   The Last Train to Pusan   3.3.57 NBC
    Playhouse 90   ep   If You Knew Elizabeth   4.11.57 CBS
    Schlitz Playhouse of Stars   ep   Hey Mac   4.26.57 CBS
    Zane Grey Theatre   ep   Badge of Honor   5.3.57 CBS
    Zane Grey Theatre   ep   The Promise   11.8.57 CBS
    Loretta Young Show   ep   Understanding Heart   11.10.57
        NBC

Suspicion   ep   The Deadly Game   12. 9. 57 NBC
Loretta Young Show   ep   My Two Hands   2. 2. 58 NBC
G. E. Theatre   ep   God Is My Judge   4. 20. 58 CBS
Jane Wyman Theatre   ep   The Last Test   5. 8. 58 NBC
Zane Grey Theatre   ep   Utopia, Wyoming   6. 6. 58 CBS
Alfred Hitchcock Presents   ep   Flight to the East   3.
    23. 58 CBS
Studio 57   ep   The Starmaker   9. 10. 58 NN
Studio One   ep   The Lady Died at Midnight   9. 1. 58 CBS
Alfred Hitchcock Presents   ep   Man with a Problem
    11. 16. 58 CBS
Pursuit   ep   The Dark Cloud   12. 31. 58 CBS
Playhouse 90   ep   A Quiet Game of Cards   1. 29. 59
    CBS
Cimarron City   ep   Medicine Man   4. 18. 59 NBC
Playhouse 90   ep   A Corner of the Garden   4. 23. 59
    CBS
Alcoa Theatre   ep   The Best Way to Go   6. 15. 59 NBC
Alfred Hitchcock Presents   ep   Invitation to an Accident
    6. 21. 59 CBS
Laramie   ep   The Lonesome Gun   12. 15. 59 NBC
Alfred Hitchcock Theatre   ep   Oh, Youth and Beauty
    11. 22. 60 NBC
Checkmate   ep   A Matter of Conscience   2. 18. 61 CBS
Outlaws   ep   Blind Spot   3. 30. 61 NBC
Zane Grey Theatre   ep   The Release   4. 27. 61 CBS
New Breed   ep   To None a Deadly Drug   10. 24. 61 ABC
Twilight Zone   ep   Still Valley   11. 24. 61 CBS
G. E. Theatre   ep   Money and the Minister   11. 26. 61
    CBS
Dick Powell Theatre   ep   Obituary for Mr. "X"   1. 23.
    62 NBC
Bus Stop   ep   Put Your Dreams Away   2. 11. 62 ABC
Alcoa Premiere   ep   Tiger   3. 20. 62 ABC
Ben Casey   ep   Neon for My Epitaph   1. 28. 63 ABC
Sam Benedict   ep   The Boiling Point   1. 12. 63 NBC
Alfred Hitchcock Theatre   ep   The Paragon   2. 8. 63 CBS
Combat   ep   The Walking Wounded   4. 30. 63 ABC
Alfred Hitchcock Theatre   ep   Nothing Ever Happens in
    Linvale   11. 8. 63 CBS
Outer Limits   ep   The Human Factor   11. 1. 63 ABC
Kraft Suspense Theatre   ep   The Machine that Played
    God   12. 5. 63 NBC
Suspense   ep   The Hunter   5. 30. 64 CBS
Reporter   sr   9. 25. 64 CBS
Doctors/Nurses   ep   A Dangerous Silence   3. 2. 65 CBS
For the People   ep   The Right to Kill   4. 4. 65 CBS

Bob Hope Chrysler Theatre   ep   The Highest Fall of
  All   12.1.65 NBC
Branded   ep   Romany Roundup   12.5.65, 12.12.65 NBC
Voyage to the Bottom of the Sea   ep   The Menfish   3.
  6.66 ABC
Time Tunnel   ep   Rendezvous with Yesterday   9.9.66
  ABC
The Dangerous Day of Kiowa Jones   tf   12.25.66 ABC
N.E.T. Playhouse   ep   They   4.17.70 NN
Marcus Welby, M.D.   ep   The Worth of a Man   9.29.
  70   ABC
Earth II   tf   11.28.71 NBC
Young Dr. Kildare   sr   9.14.72 CBS

MICHAEL, GERTRUDE
  Fireside Theatre   ep   No Strings Attached   4.18.50 NBC
  Fireside Theatre   ep   Stopover   9.5.50 NBC
  Fireside Theatre   ep   Judas   11.7.50 NBC
  Fireside Theatre   ep   Shifting Sands   3.13.51 NBC
  Fireside Theatre   ep   The Green Convertible   6.5.51
    NBC
  Fireside Theatre   ep   Solitaire   9.18.51 NBC
  Fireside Theatre   ep   His Name Is Jason   9.22.53 NBC
  Cavalcade Theatre   ep   Major Pauline   12.1.53 ABC
  Pepsi Cola Playhouse   ep   The Grey and Gold Dress   4.
    2.54 ABC
  Fireside Theatre   ep   Lost Perspectives   11.9.54 NBC
  Schlitz Playhouse of Stars   ep   Woman Expert   12.17.
    54 CBS
  Ford Theatre   ep   Unbroken Promise   12.30.54 NBC
  Four Star Playhouse   ep   Tusitala   2.24.55 CBS
  Fireside Theatre   ep   Return in Triumph   3.1.55 NBC
  Counterpoint   ep   The Honeymoon   8.27.55 NN
  Matinee Theatre   ep   The Gate   1.9.56 NBC
  Schlitz Playhouse of Stars   ep   The Traveling Corpse
    5.3.57 CBS

MILES, SYLVIA
  Route 66   ep   The Mud Nest   4.24.64 CBS
  N.Y.P.D.   ep   To Catch a Hero   10.31.67 ABC

MILES, VERA
  Schlitz Playhouse of Stars   ep   The Sail   10.30.53 CBS
  G.E. Theatre   ep   Walking John Stopped Here   1.24.54
    CBS
  Pepsi Cola Playhouse   ep   The Grey and Gold Dress   4.
    2.54 ABC

Ford Theatre   ep   The Tryst   6.17.54 NBC
Four Star Playhouse   ep   My Own Dear Dragon   11.18.
   54 CBS
Medic   ep   The Wild Intruder   12.6.54 NBC
Four Star Playhouse   ep   Championship Affair   12.16.
   54 CBS
Gloria Swanson Theatre   ep   This Day Is Yours   12.21.
   54 ABC
Playhouse   ep   The Golden Flower   1.9.55 ABC
Playhouse   ep   The House Where Time Stopped   4.17.55
   ABC
The Millionaire   ep   The Story of Merle Roberts   5.18.
   55 CBS
Ford Theatre   ep   P.J. and the Lady   6.2.55 NBC
Lux Video Theatre   ep   Inside Story   6.16.55 NBC
Undercurrent   ep   7.15.55 CBS
Medic   ep   The Wild Intruder   8.8.55 NBC
Alfred Hitchcock Presents   ep   Revenge   10.2.55 CBS
Screen Directors Playhouse   ep   Rookie of the Year
   12.7.55 NBC
20th Century-Fox Hour   ep   Man on the Ledge   12.28.55
   CBS
G.E. Summer Originals   ep   The Great Lady   9.11.56
   ABC
Schlitz Playhouse of Stars   ep   The Letter   11.23.56
   CBS
Lux Video Theatre   ep   The Taggart Light   4.18.57
   NBC
Climax   ep   Hand of Evil   5.23.57 CBS
Playhouse 90   ep   Panic Button   11.28.57 CBS
Studio 57   ep   Emergency Call   1.12.58 NN
Climax   ep   Sound of the Moon   1.23.58 CBS
Climax   ep   House of Doubt   6.19.58 CBS
Wagon Train   ep   The Sister Tia Story   3.25.59 NBC
G.E. Theatre   ep   Nora   5.3.59 CBS
Riverboat   ep   About Roger Mowbray   9.27.59 NBC
Zane Grey Theatre   ep   Miss Jenny   1.7.60 CBS
Twilight Zone   ep   Mirror Image   2.26.60 CBS
Ford Star Time   ep   Incident at a Corner   4.5.60 NBC
Laramie   ep   Three Rode West   10.4.60 NBC
G.E. Theatre   ep   The Camel's Foot   10.23.60 CBS
Asphalt Jungle   ep   The Lady and the Lawyer   4.9.61
   ABC
Checkmate   ep   The Crimson Pool   11.22.61 CBS
Detectives   ep   Three Blind Mice   4.6.62 NBC
Alfred Hitchcock Theatre   ep   Don't Look Behind You
   9.27.62 CBS

Eleventh Hour   ep   Ann Costigan's Duel on a Field of
  White   10.3.62 NBC
Sam Benedict   ep   Maddon's Folly   10.27.62 NBC
Route 66   ep   Where Is Chick Lorimer   12.14.62 CBS
Dick Powell Theatre   ep   Crazy Sunday   12.18.62 NBC
Virginian   ep   The Man Who Couldn't Die   1.30.63 NBC
Eleventh Hour   ep   Beauty Playing a Mandolin under a
  Willow Tree   2.20.63 NBC
Fugitive   ep   Fear in a Desert City   9.17.63 ABC
Arrest and Trial   ep   Isn't it a Lovely View   9.22.63
  ABC
Kraft Suspense Theatre   ep   The Case against Paul Ry-
  ker   10.10.63, 10.17.63 NBC
Outer Limits   ep   The Forms of Things Unknown   5.4.
  64 ABC
Wagon Train   ep   The Bob Stuart Story   9.20.64 ABC
The Hanged Man   tf   11.18.64 NBC
Virginian   ep   Portrait of a Widow   12.9.64 NBC
Slattery's People   ep   How Long is the Shadow of a Man
  1.1.65 CBS
Alfred Hitchcock Theatre   ep   Death Scene   3.8.65 NBC
Mr. Novak   ep   There's a Penguin in My Garden   4.6.
  65 NBC
My Three Sons   ep   9.16.65, 9.23.65, 9.30.65 CBS
I Spy   ep   Affair in T-sien-Cha   12.29.65 NBC
The Man from U.N.C.L.E.   ep   The Bridge of Lions
  Affair   2.4.66, 2.11.66 NBC
Bonanza   ep   Four Sisters from Boston   10.30.66 NBC
ABC Stage 67   ep   The People Trap   11.9.66 ABC
Run for Your Life   ep   The Inhuman Predicament   9.20.
  67 NBC
Judd for the Defense   ep   Everybody Loved Harlan But
  His Wife   12.29.67 ABC
Ironside   ep   2.29.68 NBC
Name of the Game   ep   The Revolutionary   12.27.68
  NBC
Name of the Game   ep   Keep the Doctor Away   2.14.69
  NBC
Ironside   ep   Good-by to Yesterday   9.25.69 NBC
FBI   ep   9.28.69 ABC
Mannix   ep   Return to Summer Grove   10.11.69 CBS
Marcus Welby, M.D.   ep   The Merely Syndrome   3.3.
  70 ABC
Name of the Game   ep   3.6.70 NBC
Gunsmoke   ep   10.5.70 CBS
Medical Center   ep   The Clash   10.14.70 CBS
Men from Shiloh   ep   Nightmare at New Life   11.18.70
  NBC

Dan August   ep   When the Shooting Dies   11. 25. 70 ABC
Hawaii Five-O   ep   2. 17. 71 CBS
Bonanza   ep   A Time to Die   3. 21. 71 NBC
In Search of America   tf   3. 23. 71 ABC
Cannon   tf   3. 26. 71 CBS
Owen Marshall   tf   9. 12. 71 ABC
Alias Smith and Jones   ep   The Posse that Wouldn't
   Quit   10. 14. 71 ABC
Ironside   ep   10. 19. 71 NBC
Gunsmoke   ep   12. 20. 71 CBS
Medical Center   ep   12. 29. 71, 1. 5. 72 CBS
Jigsaw   tf   3. 26. 72 ABC
A Great American Tragedy   tf   10. 18. 72 ABC

MILJAN, JOHN
Public Defender   ep   End of the Line   4. 28. 55 CBS
Schlitz Playhouse of Stars   ep   The Gentle Stranger
   2. 3. 56 CBS
Frontier   ep   Captivity of Joe Long   2. 12. 56 NBC

MILLAND, RAY
Meet Mr. McNutley   sr   9. 17. 53 CBS
Ray Milland Show   sr   9. 16. 54 CBS
Screen Directors Playhouse   ep   Markheim   4. 11. 56
   NBC
G. E. Theatre   ep   That's The Man   4. 15. 56 CBS
Ford Theatre   ep   Catch at Straws   10. 3. 56 NBC
G. E. Theatre   ep   Never Turn Back   1. 6. 57 CBS
Schlitz Playhouse of Stars   ep   The Girl in the Grass
   3. 15. 57 CBS
G. E. Theatre   ep   Angel of Wrath   5. 5. 57 CBS
Suspicion   ep   Eye for an Eye   6. 23. 58 NBC
G. E. Theatre   ep   Battle for a Soul   11. 2. 58 CBS
Goodyear Theatre   ep   A London Affair   2. 2. 59 NBC
Markham   sr   5. 2. 59 CBS
Alcoa Premiere   ep   Pattern of Guilt   1. 9. 62 ABC
Alfred Hitchcock Theatre   ep   Home Away from Home
   9. 27. 63 CBS
Dupont Show of the Month   ep   The Silver Burro   11. 3.
   63 NBC
Bracken's World   ep   10. 10. 69 NBC
Daughter of the Mind   tf   12. 9. 69 ABC
Name of the Game   ep   9. 25. 70 CBS
River of Gold   tf   3. 9. 71 ABC
Black Noon   tf   11. 5. 71 CBS
Columbo   ep   10. 15. 72 NBC
Cool Million   ep   10. 25. 72 NBC

MILLER, ANN
    Family Theatre   ep   Dames at Sea   11.15.71 NBC
    Love American Style   ep   11.17.72 ABC

MILLER, KRISTINE
    Story Theatre   ep   The Celebrated Jumping Frog   4.13.
       51 NN
    Gruen Guild Theatre   ep   Driven Snow   10.4.51 ABC
    Fireside Theatre   ep   The People's Choice   10.14.52
       NBC
    Mr. Lucky at Seven   ep   A Letter from Home   12.5.52
       ABC
    Fireside Theatre   ep   Mission to Algiers   4.21.53 NBC
    TV Sound Stage   ep   Innocent 'til Proven Guilty   7.10.
       53 NBC
    Stage 7   ep   The Magic Hat   4.24.55 CBS
    Science Fiction Theatre   ep   The Strange Dr. Lorenz
       7.15.55 NBC
    Summer Theatre   ep   A Kiss for Mr. Lincoln   7.19.55
       NBC
    Stories of the Century   ep   Rube Burrows   9.10.55 CBS
    Lone Wolf   ep   Memo: Wife   1.2.56 NN
    Cavalcade Theatre   ep   Call Home the Heart   2.21.56
       ABC
    The Millionaire   ep   The Larry Parker Story   10.23.57
       CBS
    Restless Gun   ep   The Torn Flag   3.31.58 NBC
    M Squad   ep   The Case of the Double Face   5.23.58
       NBC
    Wagon Train   ep   The Rex Montana Story   5.28.58 NBC
    Father Knows Best   ep   It's a Small World   3.23.59
       CBS
    Texan   ep   6.8.59 CBS
    Tales of Wells Fargo   ep   Prince Jim   3.27.61 NBC

MILLS, JOHN
    Dupont Show of the Month   ep   The Interrogator   9.23.
       62 NBC
    Dupont Show of the Month   ep   The Hell Walkers   3.8.
       64 NBC
    Dundee and the Culhane   sr   9.6.67 CBS
    Nanny and the Professor   ep   1971 ABC

MILNER, MARTIN
    Schlitz Playhouse of Stars   ep   Rim of Violence   1.8.54
       CBS
    Stuart Erwin Show   ep   12.29.54 ABC

Schlitz Playhouse of Stars   ep   Mr. Schoomarm   2.11.
  55 CBS
Life of Riley   ep   1.6.56 NBC
Life of Riley   ep   Train Trip   2.24.56 NBC
TV Reader's Digest   ep   The Old, Old Story   5.7.56
  ABC
Life of Riley   ep   House for Sale   5.18.56 NBC
Charles Farrell Show   ep   8.27.56 CBS
Telephone Time   ep   The Churchill Club   10.14.56 CBS
Crossroads   ep   Timberland Preacher   11.16.56 ABC
Navy Log   ep   Incident at Formosa   12.5.56 ABC
West Point   ep   No Reason   11.12.57 ABC
Wagon Train   ep   The Sally Potter Story   4.9.58 NBC
Desilu Playhouse   ep   Debut   10.27.58 CBS
Desilu Playhouse   ep   Chain of Command   3.23.59 CBS
Hotel de Paree   ep   Vein of Ore   10.16.59 CBS
Twilight Zone   ep   Mirror Image   2.26.60 CBS
Route 66   sr   10.7.60 CBS
Route 66   sr ret   9.22.61 CBS
Route 66   sr ret   9.21.62 CBS
Route 66   sr ret   9.63 CBS
Slattery's People   ep   What Is a Requiem for a Loser
  12.14.64 CBS
Bob Hope Chrysler Theatre   ep   The War and Eric
  Kurtz   3.5.65 NBC
Virginian   ep   Timberland   3.10.65 NBC
Gidget   ep   The Great Kahuna   9.29.65 ABC
Laredo   ep   Yahoo   9.30.65 NBC
Bob Hope Chrysler Theatre   ep   When Hell Froze   2.2.
  66 NBC
Kraft Suspense Theatre   ep   Streetcar, Do You Read
  Me   2.25.66 NBC
Shenandoah   ep   Requiem for the Second   5.2.66 ABC
Virginian   ep   Trail to Ashley Mountain   11.2.66 NBC
Run for Your Life   ep   Rendezvous in Tokyo   2.13.67
  NBC
Rat Patrol   ep   2.27.67 ABC
Run for Your Life   ep   4.17.67 NBC
Felony Squad   ep   11.6.67 ABC
12 O'Clock High   ep   Six Feet Under   12.16.67 ABC
Land's End   Sp   4.21.68 NBC
Adam-12   sr   9.21.68 NBC
Adam-12   sr ret   9.20.69 NBC
Adam-12   sr ret   9.19.70 NBC
Adam-12   sr ret   9.15.71 NBC
Emergency   tf   1.15.72 NBC
Adam-12   sr ret   9.13.72 NBC

MIMIEUX, YVETTE
   Alcoa Premiere   ep   The Clown   3.22.60 ABC
   Dr. Kildare   ep   Tyger, Tyger   1.16.64, 1.23.64 NBC
   Desperate Hours   Sp   12.13.67 ABC
   Most Deadly Game   sr   10.10.70 ABC
   Death Takes a Holiday   tf   10.23.71 ABC
   Black Noon   tf   11.5.71 CBS

MINEO, SAL
   Big Town   ep   Juvenile Gangs   11.1.55 NBC
   Philco Playhouse   ep   The Trees   12.4.55 NBC
   Frontiers of Faith   ep   The Man on the 6:02   12.25.55
      NBC
   Studio One   ep   Dino   1.2.56 CBS
   Look up and Live   ep   Nothing to Do   1.15.56 CBS
   Screen Directors Playhouse   ep   The Dream   5.16.56
      NBC
   Alcoa Hour   ep   The Magic Horn   6.10.56 NBC
   Climax   ep   Island in the City   10.4.56 CBS
   Kraft Theatre   ep   Drummer Man   5.1.57 NBC
   Kraft Theatre   ep   Barefoot Soldier   10.2.57 NBC
   Dupont Show of the Month   ep   Aladdin   2.21.58 CBS
   Pursuit   ep   The Vengeance   10.22.58 CBS
   Ann Sothern Show   ep   11.2.59 CBS
   Cry Vengeance   Sp   2.21.61 NBC
   The Greatest Show on Earth   ep   The Loser   10.22.63
      ABC
   Dr. Kildare   ep   Tomorrow Is a Fickle Girl   3.19.64
      NBC
   Burke's Law   ep   4.14.65 ABC
   Mona McCluskey   ep   1.27.66 NBC
   Combat   ep   Nothing to Lose   2.1.66 ABC
   Run for Your Life   ep   Sequenstro   3.14.66, 3.21.66
      NBC
   Court Martial   ep   The House Where He Lived   4.29.66
      ABC
   Combat   ep   The Brothers   10.3.66 ABC
   The Dangerous Days of Kiowa Jones   tf   12.25.66 ABC
   Bob Hope Chrysler Theatre   ep   A Song Called Revenge
      3.1.67 NBC
   Stranger on the Run   tf   10.31.67 NBC
   Hawaii Five-O   ep   10.10.68 CBS
   The Challengers   tf   3.28.69 CBS
   Name of the Game   ep   A Hard Case of the Blues   9.
      26.69 NBC
   Name of the Game   ep   So Long Baby, and Amen   9.
      18.70 NBC

Mission Impossible   ep   Flip Side   9. 26. 70 CBS
Immortals   ep   Sanctuary   1. 7. 71 ABC
Dan August   ep   The Worst Crime   2. 11. 71 ABC
In Search of America   tf   3. 23. 71 ABC
The Family Rico   tf   9. 12. 72 CBS

MINNELLI, LIZA
Mr. Broadway   ep   Nightingale for Sale   10. 24. 64 NBC
The Dangerous Christmas of Red Riding Hood   Sp   11.
   28. 65 ABC
That's Life   ep   12. 17. 68 ABC

MINTZ, ELI
The Goldbergs   sr   1949-1950 CBS
The Goldbergs   sr ret   9. 25. 50 CBS
Studio One   ep   The Little Black Bag   9. 24. 51 CBS
The Doctor   ep   Jules   1. 25. 53 NBC
The Goldbergs   sr ret   7. 3. 53 NBC
The Goldbergs   sr ret   4. 13. 54 NN
Kraft Theatre   ep   The Man Most Likely   6. 30. 54 NBC
Studio One   ep   An Almanac of Liberty   11. 8. 54 CBS
The Goldbergs   sr ret   9. 22. 55 NN
Studio One   ep   Three Empty Rooms   9. 26. 55 CBS
Playhouse 90   ep   The Fabulous Irishman   6. 27. 57 CBS
Lamp Under My Feet   ep   Nachshon's Leap   3. 30. 58
   CBS
Play of the Week   ep   The Dybbuk   10. 3. 60 NN
U. S. Steel Hour   ep   Honor in Love   7. 25. 62 CBS
Ben Casey   ep   Saturday, Surgery and Stanley Schultz
   12. 31. 62 ABC
New York Television Theatre   ep   Whisper in My Good
   Ear   11. 29. 65 NN

MIRANDA, ISA
The Baron   ep   The Legions of Ammak   4. 14. 66 ABC
Avengers   ep   4. 14. 67 ABC
N. E. T. Playhouse   ep   The May Play and the Frog   10.
   11. 68 NN

MITCHELL, CAMERON
Hollywood Opening Night   ep   The Kirby's   1. 25. 52 CBS
Hollywood Opening Night   ep   Prison Doctor   3. 14. 52
   CBS
Campbell Playhouse   ep   Return to Vienna   6. 27. 52
   NBC
Video Theatre   ep   Kill that Story!   6. 25. 53 CBS
20th Century-Fox Hour   ep   The Ox-Bow Incident   11. 2.

55 CBS
20th Century-Fox Hour   ep   Man on the Ledge   12.28.
     55 CBS
Climax   ep   The Prowler   1.5.56 CBS
Studio One   ep   The Bounty Hunter   1.16.56 CBS
U.S. Steel Hour   ep   Command   2.15.56 CBS
Climax   ep   Payment for Judas   7.11.57 CBS
Studio One   ep   The Brotherhood of the Bell   1.6.58
     CBS
U.S. Steel Hour   ep   The Bromley Touch   1.15.58 CBS
Kraft Theatre   ep   Dog in a Bush Tunnel   3.5.58 NBC
Zane Grey Theatre   ep   The Doctor Keeps a Promise
     3.21.58 CBS
Pursuit   ep   Last Night in August   12.17.58 CBS
Zane Grey Theatre   ep   Rail Incident   1.29.59 CBS
David Niven Theatre   ep   Fortune's Folly   4.7.59 NBC
Untouchables   ep   Ain't We Got Fun   11.12.59 ABC
Zane Grey Theatre   ep   The Grubstake   12.24.59 CBS
Goodyear Theatre   ep   Omaha Beach--Plus 15   1.4.60
     NBC
Desilu Playhouse   ep   Meeting at Appalachia   1.22.60
     CBS
Beachcomber   sr   2.20.62 NN
Court-Martial   ep   Where There's No Echo   7.22.66 ABC
Daniel Boone   ep   2.17.66 NBC
Daniel Boone   ep   11.10.66 NBC
High Chaparral   sr   9.10.67 NBC
Lassiter   pt   7.8.68 CBS
High Chaparral   sr ret   9.20.68 NBC
High Chaparral   sr ret   9.19.69 NBC
Hollywood Television Theatre   ep   The Andersonville
     Trials   5.17.70 NN
High Chaparral   sr ret   9.18.70 NBC
Mod Squad   ep   Home Is the Street   9.26.71 ABC
Cade's County   ep   10.31.71 CBS
McCloud   ep   11.24.71   NBC
Thief   tf   10.9.71 ABC
The Reluctant Heroes   tf   11.23.71 ABC
FBI   ep   Bitter Harbor   12.12.71 ABC
Night Gallery   ep   Green Fingers   1.5.72 NBC
Bold Ones   ep   Short Flight to a Distant Star   1.23.72
     NBC
Cutter   tf   1.26.72 NBC
Alias Smith and Jones   ep   Which Way to the O.K. Cor-
     ral   2.10.72 ABC
Delphi Bureau   tf   3.6.72 ABC
The Rookies   tf   3.7.72 ABC

McMillan and Wife   ep   9.24.72 NBC
Ironside   ep   11.16.72 NBC

MITCHELL, THOMAS
 Celanese Theatre   ep   Ah, Wilderness   10.3.51 ABC
 Tales of Tomorrow   ep   The Crystal Egg   10.12.51
  ABC
 Armstrong Circle Theatre   ep   The Long View   10.23.
  51 NBC
 Video Theatre   ep   Confession   11.5.51 CBS
 Pulitzer Prize Playhouse   ep   The Skin of Our Teeth
  12.19.51 ABC
 Video Theatre   ep   A Child Is Born   12.24.51 CBS
 Robert Montgomery Presents   ep   The Farmer's Hotel
  1.7.52 NBC
 Tales of Tomorrow   ep   The Chase   1.25.52, 2.1.52
  ABC
 Lights Out   ep   The Eyes from San Francisco   2.18.52
  NBC
 Video Theatre   ep   Promotion   3.10.52 CBS
 Pulitzer Prize Playhouse   ep   The Fascinating Stranger
  4.23.52 ABC
 Studio One   ep   The Square Peg   9.29.52 CBS
 Video Theatre   ep   The Country Lawyer   10.20.52 CBS
 Gulf Playhouse   ep   Mr. Nothing   10.31.52 NBC
 Suspense   ep   A Time of Innocence   12.2.52 CBS
 The Doctor   ep   Desk of Matthew Day   1.4.53 NBC
 Omnibus   ep   Nobody's Fool   1.3.53 CBS
 Drama   ep   Country Editor   2.13.53 ABC
 Hallmark Hall of Fame   ep   Of Time and the River   11.
  15.53 NBC
 Backbone of America   ep   12.29.53 NBC
 Medallion Theatre   ep   The Gentle Deception   1.16.54
  CBS
 Ford Theatre   ep   The Good of His Soul   3.4.54 NBC
 U.S. Steel Hour   ep   The Rise and Fall of Silas Lep-
  ham   4.27.54 ABC
 G.E. Theatre   ep   Too Old for the Girl   9.19.54 CBS
 Fireside Theatre   ep   Afraid to Live   9.28.54 NBC
 Light's Diamond Jubilee   ep   Chance for Adventure
  10.24.54 ABC, CBS, NBC
 Ford Theatre   ep   Shadow of Truth   10.14.54 NBC
 U.S. Steel Hour   ep   Freight   2.15.55 ABC
 Rheingold Theatre   ep   The Unforgivable   4.16.55 NBC
 Ford Theatre   ep   P.J. and the Lady   6.2.55 NBC
 Mayor of the Town   sr   6.4.55 NBC
 Damon Runyon Theatre   ep   It Comes up Money   6.11.
  55 CBS

Lux Video Theatre   ep hos   6.16.55 NBC
Climax   ep   The Adventures of Huckleberry Finn   9.1.
    55 CBS
Schlitz Playhouse of Stars   ep   The Last Out   9.30.55
    CBS
Rheingold Theatre   ep   The Man Who Was Dead   11.12.
    55 NBC
Screen Directors Playhouse   ep   Final Tribute   11.16.55
    NBC
Alcoa Hour   ep   Undertow   12.11.55 NBC
20th Century-Fox Hour   ep   Miracle on 34th Street   12.
    14.55 CBS
G.E. Theatre   ep   The Ballad of Mender McClure   1.
    15.56 CBS
Ford Theatre   ep   Try Me for Size   1.26.56   NBC
Rheingold Theatre   ep   They   3.3.56 NBC
Web of Circumstances   ep   3.9.56 CBS
Lux Video Theatre   ep   It Started with Eve   3.29.56
    NBC
Telephone Tide   ep   Grandpa Changes the World   7.22.56
    CBS
O'Henry Theatre   sh   1.23.57 NN
Ford Theatre   ep   Millier's Millions   5.22.57 ABC
Telephone Time   ep   The Gadfly   10.1.57 ABC
Kraft Theatre   ep   The Velvet Trap   1.8.58 NBC
Shirley Temple's Story Book   ep   The Nightingale   2.19.
    58 NBC
Zane Grey Theatre   ep   Handful of Ashes   5.2.58 CBS
Playhouse 90   ep   Natchez   5.29.58 CBS
Zane Greu Theatre   ep   Man Alone   3.5.59 CBS
Laramie   ep   Dark Verdict   11.24.59 NBC
Goodyear Theatre   ep   Lady Bug   12.21.59 NBC
Sunday Showcase   ep   The Secret of Freedom   2.28.60
    NBC
Untouchables   ep   Underworld Bank   4.14.60 ABC
The Right Man   Sp   10.24.60 CBS
Islanders   ep   Deadly Tomorrow   12.11.60 ABC
Our American Heritage   ep   The Invincible Teddy   1.13.
    61 ABC
Zane Grey Theatre   ep   A Warm Day in Heaven   3.23.
    61 CBS
Adventures in Paradise   ep   A Penny a Day   4.24.61
    ABC
Hallmark Hall of Fame   ep   The Oke and the Valley   5.
    5.61 NBC

MOOREHEAD, AGNES

Mirror Theatre   ep   Lullaby   10.3.53 CBS
Colgate Comedy Hour   ep   Roberta   4.10.55 NBC
Matinee Theatre   ep   Greybeards and Witches   5.1.56
    NBC
Studio 57   ep   Teacher   10.28.56 NN
Schlitz Playhouse of Stars   ep   The Life You Save   3.
    1.57 CBS
Climax   ep   False Witness   7.4.57 CBS
Wagon Train   ep   The Mary Halstead Story   11.20.57
    NBC
Dupont Show of the Month   ep   A Tale of Two Cities
    3.27.58 CBS
Playhouse 90   ep   The Dungeon   4.17.58 CBS
Suspicion   ep   Protege   5.12.58 NBC
Shirley Temple's Story Book   ep   Rapunzel   10.27.58
    NBC
G.E. Theatre   ep   Deed of Mercy   3.1.59 CBS
Alcoa Theatre   ep   Man of His House   3.9.59 NBC
Rebel   ep   12.6.59 ABC
Ford Star Time   ep   Closed Set   2.16.60 NBC
The Millionaire   ep   Millionaire Katherine Boland   4.20.
    60 CBS
Mystery Show   ep   Trial by Fury   8.7.60 NBC
Shirley Temple Theatre   ep   The Land of Oz   9.18.60
    NBC
Adventures in Paradise   ep   The Irishmen   10.31.60
    ABC
Harrigan and Son   ep   There's No Fool Like an Old
    Fool   12.9.60 ABC
Shirley Temple Theatre   ep   The House of the Seven
    Gables   12.11.60 NBC
Rifleman   ep   Miss Bertie   12.27.60 ABC
My Sister Eileen   ep   Aunt Harriet's Way   3.1.61 CBS
My Sister Eileen   ep   The Protectors   3.29.61 CBS
Poor Mr. Campbell   pt   8.7.62 CBS
Burke's Law   ep   Who Killed Beau Sparrow   12.27.63
    ABC
Channing   ep   Freedom Is a Lovesome Thing   3.4.64
    ABC
The Greatest Show on Earth   ep   This Train Doesn't
    Stop Till It Gets There   4.14.64 ABC
Burke's Law   ep   5.1.64 ABC
Bewitched   sr   9.17.64 ABC
Burke's Law   ep   4.7.65 ABC
Bewitched   sr ret   9.16.65 ABC
Bewitched   sr ret   9.15.66 ABC

Alice Through the Looking Glass   Sp   11.6.66 NBC
Wild, Wild West   ep   Night of the Vicious Valentine
    2.10.67 CBS
Bewitched   sr ret   9.7.67 ABC
Custer   ep   Spirit Woman   12.13.67 ABC
Bewitched   sr ret   9.26.68 ABC
Bewitched   sr ret   9.18.69 ABC
Love American Style   ep   9.29.69 ABC
The Ballad of Andy Crocker   tf   11.18.69 ABC
Barefoot in the Park   ep   9.24.70 ABC
Bewitched   sr ret   9.24.70 ABC
Night Gallery   ep   Certain Shadows on the Walls   12.30.
    70 NBC
Bewitched   sr ret   9.15.71 ABC
Night Gallery   ep   9.22.71 NBC
Marriage: Year One   tf   10.15.71 NBC
Suddenly Single   tf   10.19.71 ABC
World of Disney   ep   The Strange Monster of Strawberry
    Cove   11.6.71 NBC
Marcus Welby, M.D.   ep   10.17.72 ABC

MONTALBAN, RICARDO
    Climax   ep   The Mojave Kid   1.27.55 CBS
    Ford Theatre   ep   Cardboard Casanova   5.26.55 NBC
    Loretta Young Show   ep   Gina   9.25.55 NBC
    G.E. Theatre   ep   Estaban's Legacy   1.8.56 CBS
    Ford Theatre   ep   The Lady in His Life   4.19.56 NBC
    Loretta Young Show   ep   The Cardinal's Secret   4.22.
        56 NBC
    20th Century-Fox Hour   ep   Broken Arrow   5.2.56 CBS
    Climax   ep   Island in the City   10.4.56 CBS
    Loretta Young Show   ep   Rhubarb in Apartment 7-8
        12.2.56 NBC
    20th Century-Fox Hour   ep   Operation Cicero   12.26.55
        CBS
    Loretta Young Show   ep   The Man on Top   4.28.57 NBC
    Playhouse 90   ep   Child of Trouble   5.2.57 CBS
    Wagon Train   ep   The Jean LeBec Story   9.25.57 NBC
    Loretta Young Show   ep   Each Man's Island   3.29.59
        NBC
    Playhouse 90   ep   Target for Three   10.15.59 CBS
    Riverboat   ep   A Night at Trapper's Landing   11.8.59
        NBC
    Adventures in Paradise   ep   The Derelict   11.9.59 ABC
    Loretta Young Show   ep   The Hired Hand   2.7.60 NBC
    Ford Star Time   ep   Jeff McCleod, the Last Reb   3.1.
        60 NBC

Loretta Young Show   ep   At the Edge of the Desert   9. 25. 60 NBC

Bonanza   ep   Day of Reckoning   10. 22. 60 NBC

Loretta Young Show   ep   Margin for Error   11. 13. 60 NBC

Alfred Hitchcock Theatre   ep   Outlaw in Town   11. 15. 60 NBC

Play of the Week   ep   Rashomon   12. 12. 60 NN

World of Disney   ep   Auld Acquaintance   4. 2. 61 ABC

Loretta Young Show   ep   The Man Who Couldn't Smile   4. 9. 61 NBC

Untouchables   ep   Stranglehold   5. 4. 61 ABC

Virginian   ep   The Big Deal   10. 10. 62 NBC

Lloyd Bridges Theatre   ep   War Song 10. 30. 62 CBS

Alcoa Premiere   ep   The Glass Palace   1. 17. 63 ABC

Dick Powell Theatre   ep   Epilogue   4. 2. 63 NBC

Great Adventures   ep   The Death of Sitting Bull   10. 4. 63, 10. 11. 63 CBS

Ben Casey   ep   Six Impossible Things before Breakfast   11. 13. 63 ABC

The Greatest Show on Earth   ep   The Hanging Man   11. 19. 63 ABC

Lieutenant   ep   Tour of Duty   3. 7. 64 NBC

Great Adventures   ep   The Pirate and the Patriot   5. 1. 64 CBS

Hallmark Hall of Fame   ep   The Fantasticks   10. 18. 64 NBC

Slattery's People   ep   What Became of the White Tortilla   10. 26. 64 CBS

Burke's Law   ep   11. 11. 64 ABC

Defenders   ep   Whitewash   12. 10. 64 CBS

The Man from U. N. C. L. E.   ep   The Dove Affair   12. 15. 64 NBC

Rogues   ep   Mugger-Mugger by the Sea   12. 20. 64 NBC

Dr. Kildare   ep   A Few Hearts, a Few Flowers   2. 7. 66, 2. 8. 66, 2. 14. 66, 2. 15. 66 NBC

Bob Hope Chrysler Theatre   ep   In Any Language   3. 12. 65 NBC

The Man from U. N. C. L. E.   ep   The King of Diamonds Affair   3. 11. 66 NBC

The Long Hot Summer   ep   Man with Two Faces   4. 13. 66 ABC

Alice Through the Looking Glass   Sp   11. 6. 66 NBC

Bob Hope Chrysler Theatre   ep   Code Name: Heraclitus   1. 4. 67, 1. 11. 67 NBC

The Longest Hundred Miles   tf   1. 21. 67 NBC

Star Trek   ep   2. 16. 67 NBC

Mission Impossible   ep   2.18.67 CBS
I Spy   ep   3.15.67 NBC
Felony Squad   ep   Blueprint for Dying   3.20.67 ABC
Bob Hope Chrysler Theatre   ep   To Sleep, Perchance
     to Scream   5.10.67 NBC
Danny Thomas Show   ep   2.5.68 NBC
High Chaparral   ep   2.25.68 NBC
Felony Squad   ep   9.27.68 ABC
Ironside   ep   The Sacrifice   10.3.68 NBC
Virginian   ep   Wind of Outrage   10.16.68 NBC
It Takes a Thief   ep   The Thingamabob Heist   10.15.68
     ABC
Hawaii Five-O   ep   Samurai   10.17.68 CBS
It Takes a Thief   ep   The Galloping Skin Game   12.3.68
     ABC
High Chaparral ep   Our Lady of Guadalupe   12.20.68
     NBC
Name of the Game   ep   Wrath of Angels   2.28.69 NBC
Bracken's World   ep   10.31.69 NBC
The Pigeon   tf   11.4.69 ABC
Name of the Game   ep   Echo of a Nightmare   3.20.70
     NBC
Gunsmoke   ep   9.14.70 CBS
McCloud   ep   The Concrete Corral   9.30.70 NBC
Bracken's World   ep   Hey Gringo, Hey Chol   10.13.70
     NBC
The Aquarians   tf   10.24.70 NBC
Marcus Welby   ep   The Labyrinth   11.10.70 ABC
Men from Shiloh   ep   Last of the Comancheros   12.9.
     70 NBC
Sarge: The Badge or the Cross   tf   2.22.71 NBC
Nichols   ep   The Siege   9.23.71 NBC
O'Hara, U.S. Treasury   ep   1.14.72 CBS
Fireball Forward   tf   3.5.72 ABC
Hawaii Five-O   ep   9.19.72 CBS

MONTEALEGRE, FELICIA
     Philco Playhouse   ep   The Second Oldest Profession   3.
          26.50 NBC
     Philco Playhouse   ep   Semmelweis   5.28.50 NBC
     TV Playhouse   ep   High Tor   9.10.50 NBC
     Sure as Fate   ep   Mary Had a Little Lad   9.26.50 CBS
     Television Theatre   ep   Michael and Mary   12.13.50
          NBC
     Television Theatre   ep   Delicate Story   3.7.51 NBC
     Lights Out   ep   Leda's Portrait   3.12.51 NBC

Studio One   ep   The Case of Karen Smith   3.26.51 CBS
Circle Theatre   ep   The Mistake   8.7.51 NBC
Suspense   ep   8.14.51 CBS
Kraft Theatre   ep   The Divine Drudge   10.29.52 NBC
Goodyear Playhouse   ep   Crown of Shadows   2.17.52
   NBC
Studio One   ep   The Wings of the Dove   3.10.52 CBS
Studio One   ep   I Am Jonathan Scrivener   12.1.52 CBS
The Web   ep   Encore   6.28.53 CBS
Mirror Theatre   ep   The Enormous Radio   7.21.53 NBC
Goodyear Playhouse   ep   Moment of Panic   1.3.54 NBC
Kraft Theatre   ep   The Barn   2.10.54 NBC
Kraft Theatre   ep   Emma   11.24.54 NBC
Kraft Theatre   ep   The Little Stone God   12.22.54 NBC
Kraft Theatre   ep   Five Minutes to Live   2.1.56 NBC
Studio One   ep   Flower of Pride   3.12.56 CBS
Studio One   ep   This Will Do Nicely   4.2.56 CBS
Play of the Week   ep   The Sound of Murder   2.13.61
   NN

MONTGOMERY, DOUGLASS
Cameo Theatre   ep   Peer Gynt   2.24.52, 3.2.52 NBC
Armstrong Circle Theatre   ep   Way of Courage   4.1.52
   NBC
Hallmark Hall of Fame   ep   Crusade to Liberty   1.10.
   54 NBC
Pepsi Cola Playhouse   ep   Open Season   3.19.54 ABC
Kraft Theatre   ep   Full of the Old Harry   11.3.54 NBC
Matinee Theatre   ep   Dr. Jekyll and Mr. Hyde   8.16.
   57 NBC

MONTGOMERY, ELIZABETH
Robert Montgomery Presents   ep   Top Secret   12.3.51
   NBC
Armstrong Circle Theatre   ep   The Right Approach   6.
   2.53 NBC
Robert Montgomery Presents   sr   7.6.53 NBC
Armstrong Circle Theatre   ep   Millstone   1.19.54 NBC
Robert Montgomery Presents   ep   Our Hearts Were
   Young and Gay   2.15.54 NBC
Robert Montgomery Presents   ep   Once Upon a Time
   5.31.54 NBC
Robert Montgomery Presents   sr   6.28.54 NBC
Kraft Theatre   ep   The Lift Is Cold   9.22.54 NBC
Studio One   ep   Summer Pavilion   5.2.55 CBS
Kraft Theatre   ep   The Diamond as Big as the Ritz   9.
   28.55 NBC

Appointment with Adventure ep Relative Stranger 11. 20. 55 CBS
Warner Bros. Presents ep Siege 2. 14. 56 ABC
Robert Montgomery Presents ep The Baobab Tree 4. 23. 56 NBC
Climax ep The Shadow of Evil 5. 24. 56 CBS
Kraft Theatre ep The Duel 3. 6. 57 NBC
Studio One ep A Dead Ringer 3. 10. 58 CBS
Suspicion ep The Velvet Vault 5. 19. 58 NBC
Dupont Show of the Month ep Harvey 9. 22. 58 CBS
Cimarron City ep Hired Hand 11. 15. 58 NBC
Alfred Hitchcock Presents ep Man with a Problem 11. 16. 58 CBS
Loretta Young Show ep Marriage Crisis 2. 15. 59 NBC
Riverboat ep The Barrier 9. 20. 59 NBC
Wagon Train ep The Vittorio Bottecelli Story 12. 16. 59 NBC
Tab Hunter Show ep For Love or Money 9. 25. 60 NBC
Alcoa Premiere ep The Death Watch 10. 4. 60 ABC
Untouchables ep The Rusty Heller Story 10. 13. 60 ABC
Theatre '62 ep The Spiral Staircase 10. 4. 61 NBC
Thriller ep Masquerade 10. 30. 61 NBC
Frontier Circus ep Karina 11. 9. 61 CBS
Checkmate ep The Star System 1. 10. 62 CBS
Alcoa Premiere ep Mr. Lucifer 11. 1. 62 ABC
Saints and Sinners ep The Home-Coming Bit 1. 7. 63 NBC
Boston Terrier pt 6. 11. 63 ABC
Rawhide ep Incident at El Crucero 10. 10. 63 CBS
Eleventh Hour ep The Bronze Locust 11. 6. 63 NBC
77 Sunset Strip ep White Lie 10. 25. 63 ABC
Burke's Law ep 2. 21. 64 ABC
Bewitched sr 9. 17. 64 ABC
Bewitched sr ret 9. 16. 65 ABC
Bewitched sr ret 9. 15. 66 ABC
Bewitched sr ret 9. 7. 67 ABC
Bewitched sr ret 9. 26. 68 ABC
Bewitched sr ret 9. 18. 69 ABC
Bewitched sr ret 9. 24. 70 ABC
Bewitched sr ret 9. 15. 71 ABC
The Victim tf 11. 14. 72 ABC

MONTGOMERY, GEORGE
Stage 7 ep The Traveling Salesman 6. 12. 55 CBS
Screen Directors Playhouse ep Claire 4. 25. 56 NBC
Jane Wyman Theatre ep Ten Per Cent 8. 27. 56 NBC

Ford Theatre   ep   The Quiet Stranger   1.9.57 ABC
G.E. Theatre   ep   Thousand Dollar Gun   10.20.57 CBS
Wagon Train   ep   The Jessie Cowan Story   1.8.58 NBC
Life of Riley   ep   Movie Struck   1.24.58 NBC
Cimarron City   sr   10.11.58 NBC
Bob Cummings Show   ep   Bob Goes Western   3.24.59
     CBS
Hawaiian Eye   ep   Boar Hunt   2.5.63 ABC
FBI   ep   The Code   2.13.66 NBC
I Spy   ep   A Day Called Four Jaguar   3.9.66 NBC

MONTGOMERY, ROBERT
     Robert Montgomery Presents   sh/sr   1.30.50 to 6.24.
     57 NBC

MOODY, RON
     Shirley's World   ep   12.1.71 ABC

MOORE, CLAYTON
     The Lone Ranger   sr   fall, 1952 ABC
     The Lone Ranger   sr ret   fall, 1953 ABC
     The Lone Ranger   sr ret   fall, 1954 ABC
     The Lone Ranger   sr ret   fall, 1955 ABC
     The Lone Ranger   sr ret   fall, 1956 ABC
     Lassie   ep   5.10.59 CBS

MOORE, CONSTANCE
     My Three Sons   ep   1.12.67 CBS

MOORE, DICKIE
     Man Behind the Badge   1.24.54 CBS
     The Web   ep   Top Gun   6.6.54 CBS

MOORE, GARRY
     Mr. Broadway   Sp   5.11.57 NBC

MOORE, JUANITA
     Soldiers of Fortune   ep   Walk Wide of Lions   9.9.55
          ABC
     Alfred Hitchcock Theatre   ep   The Lonely Hours   3.8.
          63 CBS
     Wagon Train   ep   The Blane Wessels Story   4.17.63
          ABC
     Alfred Hitchcock Theatre   ep   The Gentleman Caller   4.
          10.64 CBS
     Mr. Novak   ep   Boy under Glass   11.24.64 NBC
     Alfred Hitchcock Theatre   ep   Where the Woodbine

Twineth 1.11.65 NBC
Farmer's Daughter ep Why Don't They Ever Pick Me
    3.13.65 ABC
Slattery's People ep 11.12.65 CBS
Gentle Ben ep 1.28.68 CBS
Outsider ep I Can't Hear You Scream 11.27.68 NBC
Bold Ones ep The Crowd Pleaser 11.2.69 NBC
On Being Black ep Fare Thee Well, Rev. Taylor 12.
    8.69 NN
Mannix ep Time out of Mind 10.3.70 CBS
Ironside ep Accident 3.11.71 NBC
Marcus Welby, M.D. ep Once There Was a Bantu
    Prince 2.29.72 ABC

MOORE, MARY TYLER
Bourbon Street Beat ep The Black Magnolia 12.21.
    59 ABC
Staccato ep The Mask of Jason 3.3.60 NBC
77 Sunset Strip ep The Fix 4.8.60 ABC
Hawaiian Eye ep The Typhoon 4.27.60 ABC
The Millionaire ep Millionaire Vance Ludlow 5.11.60
    CBS
Wanted, Dead or Alive ep 10.19.60 CBS
Hawaiian Eye ep Vanessa Vanishes 11.2.60 ABC
Deputy ep Day of Fear 12.17.60 NBC
Aquanauts ep 1.25.61 CBS
Hawaiian Eye ep The Comics 4.19.61 ABC
Dick Van Dyke Show sr 10.3.61 CBS
Hawaiian Eye ep Two for the Money 12.6.61 ABC
Straightaway ep Sound of Fury 2.7.62 ABC
Thriller ep Men of Mystery 4.2.62 NBC
Dick Van Dyke Show sr ret 9.26.62 CBS
Dick Van Dyke Show sr ret 9.25.63 CBS
Dick Van Dyke Show sr ret 9.23.64 CBS
Dick Van Dyke Show sr ret 9.65 CBS
Love American Style tf 11.18.69 ABC
Mary Tyler Moore Show sr 9.19.70 CBS
Mary Tyler Moore Show sr ret 9.18.71 CBS
Mary Tyler Moore Show sr ret 9.16.72 CBS

MOORE, ROGER
Goodyear Playhouse ep A Murder Is Announced 12.
    30.56 NBC
Lux Video Theatre ep The Taggar Light 4.18.57 NBC
Matinee Theatre ep The Remarkable Mr. Jerome 7.
    8.57 NBC
Ivanhoe sr 1958 NN

Maverick   ep   The Rivals   1.25.59 ABC
Alfred Hitchcock Presents   ep   The Avon Emeralds   3.
  22.59 CBS
Alaskans   sr   10.4.59 ABC
Maverick   sr   9.18.60 ABC
77 Sunset Strip   ep   Tiger by the Tail   3.3.61 ABC
Roaring 20s   ep   Right off the Boat   5.13.61, 5.20.61
  ABC
The Saint   sr   9.22.63 NBC
Trials of O'Brien   ep   What Can Go Wrong   10.16.65
  CBS
The Saint   sr ret   2.17.68 NBC
The Saint   sr ret   4.18.69   NBC
The Persuaders   sr   9.18.71 ABC

MOORE, TERRY
Ford Theatre   ep   It Happened in a Pawn Shop   1.8.53
  NBC
U.S. Steel Hour   ep   Scandal at Peppernut   3.29.55
  ABC
Climax   ep   No Right to Kill   8.9.56 CBS
20th Century-Fox Hour   ep   The Moneymaker   10.31.56
  CBS
Climax   ep   Flight to Tomorrow   11.8.56 CBS
G.E. Theatre   ep   The Shadow Outside   12.30.56 CBS
Playhouse 90   ep   The Clouded Image   11.7.57 CBS
Climax   ep   Secret Love of Johnny Spain   2.20.58 CBS
Studio One   ep   The Man Who Asked for a Funeral   6.
  23.58 CBS
Rawhide   ep   Incident of the Tumbleweed Wagon   7.3.59
  CBS
Checkmate   ep   The Princess in the Tower   12.31.60
  CBS
Empire   sr   9.25.62 NBC
Burke's Law   ep   Who Killed Eleanor Davis   12.20.63
  ABC
Bob Hope Chrysler Theatre   ep   The Highest Fall of All
  12.1.65 NBC
Batman   ep   The Zodiac Crimes   1.11.67, 1.12.67, 1.
  18.67 ABC
Quarantined   tf   2.24.70 ABC
Bonanza   ep   Gideon the God   10.18.70 NBC

MOORE, TIM
Amos 'n Andy   sr   6.28.51 CBS

MOORE, VICTOR
  Musical Comedy Time   ep   Louisiana Purchase   1.22.
    51 NBC
  Medallion Theatre   ep   A Time for Heroes   10.17.53
    CBS
  So This Is Hollywood   ep   1.22.55 NBC
  Best of Broadway   ep   Stage Door   4.6.55 CBS

MORELAND, MANTAN
  Hallmark Hall of Fame   ep   The Green Pastures   3.23.
    59 NBC
  Bill Cosby Show   ep   1.18.70 ABC

MORENO, RITA
  Fireside Theatre   ep   Saint and Senorita   1.1.52 NBC
  Fireside Theatre   ep   M'Liss   3.4.52 NBC
  G.E. Theatre   ep   The Cat with the Crimson Eyes   8.
    30.53 CBS
  Ford Theatre   ep   Wonderful Day for a Wedding   5.13.
    54 NBC
  20th Century-Fox Hour   ep   Broken Arrow   5.2.56 CBS
  Climax   ep   The Chinese Game   11.22.56 CBS
  Climax   ep   Strange Sanctuary   3.28.57 CBS
  Matinee Theatre   ep   The Daughter of Mata Hari   4.3.
    57 NBC
  Climax   ep   The Stranger Within   8.22.57 CBS
  Climax   ep   Spider Web   6.5.58 CBS
  G.E. Theatre   ep   The Stone   1.18.59 CBS
  Tales of Wells Fargo   ep   Lola Montez   2.16.59 NBC
  Trackdown   ep   2.18.59 CBS
  Zane Grey Theatre   ep   The Last Raid   2.26.59 CBS
  The Millionaire   ep   Millionaire Alicia Osante   3.18.59
    CBS
  Cimarron City   ep   The Town Is a Prisoner   3.28.59
    NBC
  Playhouse 90   ep   Alas, Babylon   4.3.60 CBS
  World of Disney   ep   El Bandito   10.30.60, 11.6.60
    ABC
  Michael Shayne   ep   No Shroud for Shayne   5.5.61 NBC
  Adventures in Paradise   ep   Vendetta   10.15.61 ABC
  Father Knows Best   ep   Fair Exchange   4.16.62 CBS
  Burke's Law   ep   Who Killed Julian Buck   10.18.63 ABC
  Trials of O'Brien   ep   Dead End on Flugel Street   12.
    3.65 CBS
  Run for Your Life   ep   Who's Che Guevara   9.13.67
    NBC

MORGAN, CLAUDIA
    Celanese Theatre   ep   When Ladies Meet   6.1.52 ABC
    Goodyear Playhouse   ep   Leaf out of a Book   7.6.52
    NBC
    Kraft Theatre   ep   One Sunday Afternoon   11.11.54 ABC
    Pond's Theatre   ep   The Dover Rose   2.17.55 ABC
    Big Story   ep   Born--A Son   6.17.55 NBC
    Kraft Theatre   ep   The Mob   6.29.55 NBC

MORGAN, DENNIS
    G.E. Theatre   ep   Atomic Love   11.22.53 CBS
    Pepsi Cola Playhouse   ep   Open Season   3.19.54 ABC
    Fireside Theatre   ep   Not Captain Material   1.25.55
    NBC
    Ford Theatre   ep   Celebrity   3.17.55 NBC
    Stage 7   ep   Press Conference   3.20.55 ABC
    Best of Broadway   ep   Stage Door   4.6.55 CBS
    Stage 7   ep   The Fox Hunt   9.25.55 CBS
    Star Stage   ep   Dr. Jordan   6.8.56 NBC
    Telephone Time   ep   Line Chief   6.11.57 ABC
    Alfred Hitchcock Presents   ep   Bull in a China Shop   3.
    30.58 CBS
    21 Beacon Street   sr   9.2.59 NBC
    Saints and Sinners   ep   Source of Information   10.15.62
    NBC
    Dick Powell Theatre   ep   The Old Man and the City   4.
    23.63 NBC

MORGAN, HARRY
    December Bride   sr   10.4.54 CBS
    December Bride   sr ret   10.3.55 CBS
    Cavalcade Theatre   ep   Who Is Byington   5.22.56 ABC
    December Bride   sr ret   10.56 CBS
    December Bride   sr ret   10.7.57 CBS
    December Bride   sr ret   10.2.58 CBS
    Have Gun Will Travel   ep   11.22.58 CBS
    Alfred Hitchcock Presents   ep   Anniversary Gift   11.1.
    59 CBS
    Pete and Gladys   sr   9.19.60 CBS
    Pete and Gladys   sr ret   9.18.61 CBS
    Going My Way   ep   Like My Own Brother   11.7.62 ABC
    Untouchables   ep   Double Cross   12.18.62 ABC
    Have Gun Will Travel   ep   2.2.63 CBS
    Virginian   ep   Strangers at Sundown   4.3.63 NBC
    Richard Boone Show   sr   9.24.63 NBC
    Kentucky Jones   sr   9.19.64 NBC
    Wackiest Ship in the Army   ep   The Lady and the Lulusi

11. 21. 65 NBC
Dr. Kildare ep Tent-Dwellers 11. 29. 65, 11. 30. 65
    NBC
Dragnet sr 1. 12. 67 NBC
Dragnet sr ret 9. 19. 68 NBC
Dragnet tf 1. 27. 69 NBC
Dragnet sr ret 9. 18. 69 NBC
But I Don't Want to get Married 10. 6. 70 ABC
Gunsmoke ep The Witness 11. 23. 70 CBS
The Feminist and the Fuzz tf 1. 26. 71 ABC
The D. A. sr 9. 17. 71 NBC
Ellery Queen: Don't Look Behind You tf 11. 19. 71 NBC
Night Gallery ep The Late Mr. Peddington 1. 12. 72
    NBC
Hec Ramsey ep 10. 8. 72 NBC
Gunsmoke ep 11. 6. 72 CBS

MORGAN, MICHELE
    Studio One ep Silent the Song 10. 5. 53 CBS
    Studio One ep Camille 11. 9. 53 CBS

MORGAN, RALPH
    Celanese Theatre ep On Borrowed Time 6. 25. 52 ABC

MORGAN, ROBIN
    (I Remember) Mama sr 1949-1950 CBS
    Mama sr ret 8. 4. 50 CBS
    Mama sr ret 9. 7. 51 CBS
    Suspense ep The Lonely Place 12. 25. 51 CBS
    Mama sr ret 9. 5. 52 CBS
    Mama sr ret 9. 4. 53 CBS
    Kraft Theatre ep 40 Weeks of Uncle Tom 7. 22. 54
        NBC
    Mama sr ret 9. 3. 54 CBS
    Robert Montgomery Presents ep Halfway House 2. 21.
        55 NBC
    Robert Montgomery Presents ep The Tall, Dark Man
        4. 25. 55 NBC
    Mama sr ret 10. 7. 55 CBS
    Alcoa Hour ep Kiss and Tell 8. 5. 56 NBC

MORGAN, WESLEY
    Life of Riley sr 1. 2. 53 NBC
    Life of Riley sr ret 9. 18. 53 NBC
    Life of Riley sr ret 9. 54 NBC
    Life of Riley sr ret 9. 55 NBC
    Life of Riley sr ret 9. 14. 56 NBC

MORISON, PATRICIA
Robert Montgomery Presents ep Rio Rita 11.13.50 NBC
Airflyte Theatre ep Trial by Jury 11.30.50 CBS
Pulitzer Prize Playhouse ep Light up the Sky 1.19. 51 ABC
Cases of Eddie Drake sr 3.6.52 NN
Celanese Theatre ep When Ladies Meet 6.11.52 ABC
Four Star Playhouse ep The Man in the Box 2.26.53 CBS
Four Star Playhouse ep The Ladies on His Mind 5. 21.53 CBS
Video Theatre ep The Moment of the Rose 11.19.53 CBS
Screen Directors Playhouse ep Dream 5.16.56 NBC
Schlitz Playhouse of Stars ep The Trophy 10.12.56 CBS
Hallmark Hall of Fame ep Kiss Me Kate 11.20.58 NBC
U.S. Steel Hour ep The Secrets of Stella Crozier 3. 20.63 CBS

MORLEY, ROBERT
U.S. Steel Hour ep Edward My Son 12.7.55 CBS
Playhouse 90 ep Misalliance 10.29.59 CBS
Dupont Show of the Month ep Oliver Twist 12.4.59 CBS
Alfred Hitchcock Presents ep Specialty of the House 12.13.59 CBS
Dupont Show of the Month ep Heaven Can Wait 11.16. 60 CBS
Dick Powell Theatre ep The Big Day 12.25.62 NBC
Espionage ep The Life of a Friendly Star 12.4.63 NBC

MORRIS, CHESTER
NBC Showcase ep The Great Merlini 5.23.50 NBC
Gang Busters sh 1951 NN
Starlight Theatre ep Act of God Notwithstanding 9. 6.51 CBS
Schlitz Playhouse of Stars ep Billy Budd 1.11.52 CBS
Tales of Tomorrow ep Exile 6.6.52 ABC
Video Theatre ep Welcome Home, Lefty 6.23.52 CBS
Robert Montgomery Presents ep The Law-Abiding 9. 8.52 NBC

Robert Montgomery Presents   ep   The Big Night   3.23.
53 NBC
Kraft Theatre   ep   Final Edition   5.13.53 NBC
Suspense   ep   Point Blank   8.11.53 CBS
Danger   ep   Towerman   11.24.53 CBS
Robert Montgomery Presents   ep   The Greatest Man in
the World   12.28.53 NBC
The Web   ep   Rock-Bound   2.14.54 CBS
Studio One   ep   Jack Sparling, 46   4.12.54 CBS
Studio One   ep   Death and Life of Larry Benson   5.31.
54 CBS
Appointment with Adventure   ep   Time Bomb   11.27.55
CBS
Studio One   ep   Blow up at Cortland   12.5.55 CBS
Studio One   ep   The Arena   4.9.56 CBS
Kraft Theatre   ep   Time Lock   11.28.56 NBC
Zane Grey Theatre   ep   Black Is for Grief   4.12.57
CBS
Playhouse 90   ep   Child of Trouble   5.2.57 CBS
Kraft Theatre   ep   Men of Prey   5.22.57 NBC
Music Theatre   ep   Too Bad about Sheila Troy   4.23.59
NBC
U.S. Steel Hour   ep   Whisper of Evil   6.3.59 CBS
Play of the Week   ep   Morning's at Seven   4.25.60 NN
Diagnosis: Unknown   sr   7.5.60   CBS
Rawhide   ep   Incident on the Road to Yesterday   11.18.
60 CBS
A String of Beads   Sp   2.7.61 NBC
Naked City   ep   Make Believe Man   5.17.61 ABC
Checkmate   ep   Portrait of a Man Running   10.4.61 CBS
Ben Casey   ep   An Expensive Glass of Water   10.30.61
ABC
Defenders   ep   The Empty Chute   2.17.64 CBS
Alcoa Premiere   ep   The Contenders   12.6.62 ABC
Eleventh Hour   ep   Along about Late in the Afternoon
12.26.62 NBC
Alcoa Premiere   ep   The Glass Palace   1.17.63 ABC
Route 66   ep   Soda Pop and Paper Flags   5.31.63 CBS
Defenders   ep   The Bagman   10.19.63 CBS
Route 66   ep   Child of a Night   1.3.64 CBS
Espionage   ep   Castles in Spain   2.19.64 NBC
East Side/West Side   ep   The Name of the Game   3.23.
64 CBS
Kraft Suspense Theatre   ep   Knight's Gambit   3.26.64
NBC
Dr. Kildare   ep   5.21.64 NBC
Bob Hope Chrysler Theatre   ep   The Fliers   2.5.65 NBC

Suspense   ep   The Hunger   5.20.64 CBS
Mr. Broadway   ep   Don't Mention My Name in Sheboygan   10.7.64 CBS
Defenders   ep   A Matter of Law and Disorder   4.8.65 CBS
Coronet Blue   ep   5.29.67 CBS
Gentle Ben   ep   Busman's Holiday   4.27.69 CBS

MORRIS, GREG
Dr. Kildare   ep   The Gift of the Koodjanuk   5.9.63 NBC
Dick Van Dyke Show   ep   That's My Bob   9.25.63 CBS
Ben Casey   ep   Allie   10.2.63 ABC
Dick Van Dyke Show   ep   Bupkiss   3.10.65 CBS
Fugitive   ep   Wings of an Angel   9.14.65 ABC
Branded   ep   Fill No Glass Forms   11.14.65 NBC
Mission Impossible   sr   9.17.66 CBS
I Spy   ep   Lori   9.21.66 NBC
Mission Impossible   sr ret   9.10.67 CBS
Mission Impossible   sr ret   9.29.68 CBS
Mission Impossible   sr ret   9.28.69 CBS
Love American Style   ep   2.20.70 ABC
Mission Impossible   sr ret   9.19.70 CBS
Mission Impossible   sr ret   9.18.71 CBS
Killer by Night   tf   1.7.72 CBS
Mission Impossible   sr ret   9.16.72 CBS

MORRIS, WAYNE
Damon Runyon Theatre   ep   The Mink Doll   7.9.55 CBS
Ford Theatre   ep   The Clay Pigeon   5.31.56 NBC
Gunsmoke   ep   3.1.58 CBS
Maverick   ep   Prey of the Cat   12.7.58 ABC
Wagon Train   ep   The Tent City Story   12.10.58 NBC
Alfred Hitchcock Presents   ep   A Personal Matter   1.18.59 CBS
Wanted, Dead or Alive   ep   2.14.59 CBS
Bat Masterson   ep   Battle of the Pass   2.25.59 NBC
Ellery Queen   ep   Confession of Murder   4.17.59 NBC
Troubleshooters   ep   Lower Depths   10.2.59 NBC
Adventures in Paradise   ep   Archer's Ring   1.11.60 ABC
They Went Thataway   pt   8.15.60 CBS

MORROW, DORETTA
Pulitzer Prize Playhouse   ep   Knickerbocker Holiday   11.17.50 ABC
Marco Polo   Sp   4.14.56 NBC
Holiday   Sp   6.9.56 NBC

MORSE, ROBERT
Goodyear Playhouse ep Man on Spikes 7.17.55 NBC
Matinee Theatre ep Rain in the Morning 3.31.58 NBC
Omnibus ep Forty-Five Minutes from Broadway 3.15.
59 NBC
Play of the Week ep Thieves' Carnival 12.21.59 NN
Alfred Hitchcock Presents ep Hitchhike 2.21.60 CBS
Play of the Week ep The Velvet Glove 10.17.60 NN
Shirley Temple Theatre ep Rebel Gun 1.22.61 NBC
Naked City ep Sweet Prince of Delancey Street 6.7.
61 ABC
That's Life sr 9.24.68 ABC
Alias Smith and Jones 9.16.71 ABC

MOSTEL, ZERO
Play of the Week ep Waiting for Godot 4.3.61 NN

MOVITA
G.E. Theatre ep Esteban's Legacy 1.8.56 CBS
Conflict ep Silent Journey 12.25.56 ABC

MOWBRAY, ALAN
Stars over Hollywood ep Small Town Story 12.6.50
NBC
Bigelow Theatre ep Agent from Scotland Yard 2.11.
51 CBS
Robert Montgomery Presents ep The Young in Heart
3.12.51 NBC
Gruen Guild Theatre ep Unfinished Business 9.27.51
ABC
Schaefer Century Theatre ep Annual Honeymoon 5.31.
52 NBC
The Unexpected ep Confidentially Yours 10.29.52
NBC
Mr. Lucky at Seven ep It Happened in Heaven 12.3.
52 ABC
Plymouth Playhouse ep Colonel Humphrey J. Flack
5.31.53 ABC
Colonel Humphrey Flack sr 10.7.53 NN
Four Star Playhouse ep The House Always Wins 4.
28.55 CBS
Four Star Playhouse ep Alias Mr. Hepp 5.12.55 CBS
My Favorite Husband ep The Great Waldo 12.20.55
CBS
Four Star Playhouse ep No Limit 2.16.56 CBS
Four Star Playhouse ep A Long Way from Texas 5.
3.56 CBS

Crossroads ep The Man Who Walked on Water 1.4.
57 ABC
Schlitz Playhouse of Stars ep A Contest of Ladies 4.
18. 58 CBS
Meet McGraw ep 5. 24. 59 ABC
Maverick ep The Misfortune Teller 3.6.60 ABC
Gale Storm Show ep It's Magic 3.17.60 ABC
Ford Star Time ep Tennessee Ernie Meets King
Arthur 5.10.60 NBC
Dante sr 10.3.60 NBC
Burke's Law ep 10.14.64 ABC
Profiles in Courage ep Anne Hutchinson 1.10.65 NBC
Mister Roberts ep 3.11.66 NBC
Beverly Hillbillies ep 9.25.68 CBS
Flying Nun ep 1.23.69 ABC

MUIR, JEAN
Philco Playhouse ep The Sudden Guest 2.5.50 NBC
Naked City ep Hey, Teach! 2.17.59 ABC
Route 66 ep Bridge Across Five Days 11.17.61 CBS

MULDAUR, DIANA
Dr. Kildare ep The Taste of Crow 2.22.66, 2.28.66,
3.1.66, 3.7.66, 3.8.66 NBC
Hawk ep The Man Who Owned Everyone 10.20.66 ABC
T.H.E. Cat ep 10.21.66 NBC
New York Television Theatre ep Dark Lady of the
Sonnets 10.31.66 NN
Run for Your Life ep Cry Hard, Cry Fast 11.22.67
NBC
Mannix ep 11.25.67 CBS
FBI ep 1.21.68 ABC
I Spy ep 2.5.68 NBC
Invaders ep The Life Seekers 3.5.68 ABC
Outcasts ep A Ride to Vengeance 9.30.68 ABC
Bonanza ep The Passing of a King 10.13.68 NBC
Star Trek ep Is There No Truth in Beauty 10.18.68
NBC
Felony Squad ep The Distant Shore 12.20.68 ABC
Courtship of Eddie's Father ep 10.1.69 ABC
Survivors sr 11.69 ABC
McCloud tf 2.17.70 NBC
Mod Squad ep 4.7.70 ABC
McCloud ep 9.16.70, 9.23.70 NBC
Dan August ep Murder by Proxy 9.23.70 ABC
Hawaii Five-O ep Time and Memories 10.7.70 CBS
Men from Shiloh ep The Politician 1.13.71 NBC

Mannix ep A Gathering of Ghosts 2.6.71 CBS
Alias Smith and Jones ep The Great Shell Game 2.
   18.71 ABC
Name of the Game ep Beware of the Watchdog 3.5.
   71 NBC
Marcus Welby, M.D. ep The Tender Comrad 9.14.
   71 ABC
McCloud ep 12.29.71 NBC
Hawaii Five-O ep 9.19.72 CBS
McCloud ep 10.1.72 NBC
Medical Center ep Doctor and Mr. Harper 10.25.72
   CBS
Banyon ep 11.3.72 NBC
Owen Marshall ep 11.16.72 ABC
Bold Ones ep The Velvet Trap 12.19.72 NBC

MULHALL, JACK
Public Defender ep The Bad Ones 6.9.55 CBS
Playhouse 90 ep The Big Slide 11.8.56 CBS
Dragnet ep 2.21.57 NBC
Lineup ep The Louie Lawrence Case 3.7.58 CBS
Goodyear Theatre ep I Remember Caviar 5.11.59
   NBC
77 Sunset Strip ep Strange Girl in Town 5.29.59 ABC

MULHARE, EDWARD
Kraft Theatre ep Night of the Plague 3.20.57 NBC
Kraft Theatre ep The First and the Last 7.10.57
   NBC
U.S. Steel Hour ep Who's Earnest? 10.9.57 CBS
Ghost and Mrs. Muir sr 9.21.68 NBC
Ghost and Mrs. Muir sr ret 9.18.69 ABC
Gidget Grows Up tf 12.30.69 ABC
Streets of San Francisco ep 10.28.72 ABC

MUNI, PAUL
Ford Theatre ep The People Vs. Johnston 6.25.53
   NBC
G.E. Theatre ep Letter from the Queen 3.4.56 CBS
Playhouse 90 ep Last Clear Chance 3.6.58 CBS
Saints and Sinners ep A Shame for a Diamond Wedding
   11.26.62 NBC

MUNSEL, PATRICE
Omnibus ep The Merry Widow 12.26.54 CBS
Naughty Marietta Sp 1.15.55 NBC
The Great Waltz Sp 11.5.55 NBC

Alcoa Hour   ep   The Stingiest Man in Town   12. 23. 56
NBC
Checkmate   ep   The Gift   3. 11. 61 CBS

MUNSON, ONA
Broadway Television Theatre   ep   Craig's Wife   11. 17.
52 NN
TV Sound Stage   ep   Nemesis   10. 30. 53 NBC
Armstrong Circle Theatre   ep   The Right Approach   11.
10. 53 NBC

MURPHY, AUDIE
G. E. Theatre   ep   Incident   2. 9. 58 CBS
Suspicion   ep   The Flight   7. 5. 59 NBC
Ford Startime   ep   The Man   1. 5. 60 NBC
Whispering Smith   sr   5. 8. 61 NBC

MURPHY, GEORGE
MGM Parade   sh   9. 14. 55 ABC

MURRAY, DON
Philco Playhouse   ep   5. 13. 51 NBC
The Skin of Our Teeth   Sp   9. 11. 55 NBC
Philco Playhouse   ep   The Man Is 10 Feet Tall   10. 2. 55
NBC
U.S. Steel Hour   ep   Moment of Courage   2. 29. 56 CBS
Playhouse 90   ep   For I Have Loved Strangers   12. 19.
57 CBS
Dupont Show of the Month   ep   The Hasty Heart   12. 18.
58 CBS
Dupont Show of the Month   ep   Billy Budd   5. 25. 59 CBS
Hallmark Hall of Fame   ep   Winterset   10. 26. 59 NBC
Playhouse 90   ep   Alas, Babylon   4. 3. 60 CBS
The Borgia Stick   tf   2. 25. 67 NBC
Outcasts   sr   9. 23. 68 ABC
Daughter of the Mind   tf   12. 9. 69 ABC
The Intruders   tf   11. 10. 70 NBC
World of Disney   ep   Justin Morgan Had a Horse   2. 6.
72, 2. 13. 72 NBC

MURRAY, JAN
Cowboy in Africa   ep   1. 15. 68, 1. 22. 68 ABC

MUSANTE, TONY
Dupont Show of the Month   ep   Ride with Terror   12. 1.
63 NBC
Bob Hope Chrysler Theatre   ep   A Wind of Hurricane

2. 7. 64 NBC
Trials of O'Brien ep   9. 25. 65 CBS
Fugitive ep   12. 20. 66 ABC

MUSE, CLARENCE
Four Star Playhouse ep Bourbon Street 12. 9. 54 CBS
Casablanca sr 9. 27. 55 ABC

MYERS, CARMEL
Studio One ep The Magic Lantern 4. 13. 53 CBS

MYERS, PAULINE
G. E. Theatre ep Train for Tecumseh 3. 15. 59 CBS

MYRTIL, ODETTE
Summer Studio One ep The Paris Feeling 6. 22. 53
CBS

-N-

NABORS, JIM
Andy Griffith Show ep 2. 25. 63 CBS
Mr. Smith ep To Be or Not to Be 3. 9. 63 ABC
Gomer Pyle, U. S. M. C. sr 9. 25. 64 CBS
Gomer Pyle, U. S. M. C. sr ret 9. 17. 65 CBS
Gomer Pyle, U. S. M. C. sr ret 9. 14. 66 CBS
The Lucy Show ep 11. 14. 66 CBS
Gomer Pyle, U. S. M. C. sr ret 9. 8. 67 CBS
Gomer Pyle, U. S. M. C. sr ret 9. 27. 68 CBS

NADER, GEORGE
Fireside Theatre ep The Lady Wears a Star 1. 27. 53
NBC
Jewelers Showcase ep Heart's Desire 5. 19. 53 CBS
Your Play Time ep The Tin Bridge 9. 5. 53 CBS
A Letter to Loretta ep Kid Stuff 11. 8. 53 NBC
Fireside Theatre ep Appointment with Death 11. 17. 53
NBC
A Letter to Loretta ep Hotel Irritant 12. 27. 53 NBC
Pepsi Cola Playhouse ep Account Closed 1. 15. 54 ABC
Pepsi Cola Playhouse ep His Brother's Girl 2. 26. 54
ABC
Loretta Young Show ep The Clara Schumann Story 3.

21.54 NBC
Loretta Young Show   ep   The Enchanted Schoolteacher
   4.25.54 NBC
Loretta Young Show   ep   Oh, My Aching Heart   5.9.54
   NBC
Private Secretary   ep   12.19.54 CBS
Sergeant Preston   ep   6.14.56 CBS
Drama   ep   The Boundary Line   9.25.56 NN
Lux Video Theatre   ep   The Glass Web   11.15.56 NBC
Lux Video Theatre   ep   One Way Street   2.21.57 NBC
Climax   ep   The Stranger Within   8.22.57 CBS
The Further Adventures of Ellery Queen   sr   9.26.58
   NBC
Man and the Challenge   sr   9.12.59 NBC
Laramie   ep   .45 Calibre   11.15.60 NBC
Loretta Young Show   ep   The Choice   2.26.61 NBC
Andy Griffith Show   ep   The New Doctor   3.27.61 CBS
Alfred Hitchcock Theatre   ep   Self-Defense   5.23.61
   NBC
Shannon   sr   6.61 ABC
Burke's Law   ep   4.21.65 ABC
Owen Marshall   ep   Warlock at Machine   3.16.72 ABC
FBI   ep   11.5.72 ABC

NAGEL, CONRAD
Silver Theatre   ep   The First Show of 1950   1.2.50
   CBS
Studio One   ep   Wreath of Roses   5.8.50 CBS
Robert Montgomery Presents   ep   A Star Is Born   2.
   12.51 NBC
Broadway Television Theatre   ep   Interference   5.5.53
   NN
Conrad Nagel Theatre   sh   1.20.55 NN
Playwrights '55   ep   The Answer   10.4.55 NBC
Kraft Theatre   ep   Hit and Run   10.31.56 NBC
Kraft Theatre   ep   The Wonderful Gift   12.19.56 NBC
Studio One   ep   The Dark Corner   1.14.57 CBS
Kraft Theatre   ep   The Duel   3.6.57 NBC
Crossroads   ep   The Last Strand   3.22.57 ABC
20th Century-Fox Hour   ep   The Great American Hoax
   5.15.57 CBS
Studio One   ep   The Weston Strain   5.27.57 CBS
Climax   ep   Secret Love of Johnny Spain   2.20.58 CBS
Bat Masterson   ep   Sharpshooter   2.11.59 NBC
Ellery Queen   ep   The Chemistry Set   6.19.59 NBC
Thriller   ep   The Fatal Impulse   11.29.60 NBC
Route 66   ep   A Fury Stinging Fame   12.30.60 CBS

Naked City ep Landscape with Dead Figures 1.18.61
  ABC
Perry Mason ep The Case of the Torrid Tapestry
  4.22.61 CBS
Route 66 ep A Month of Sundays 9.22.61 CBS
Westinghouse Presents ep The Dispossessed 10.24.61
  CBS
Defenders ep The Naked Heiress 4.7.62 CBS
Ben Casey ep An Uncommonly Innocent Killing 5.7.62
  ABC
Route 66 ep Lizard's Leg and Owlet's Wing 10.26.62
  CBS
Car 54 Where Are You ep Here We Go Again 2.3.63
  NBC
Defenders ep The Brother Killers 5.25.63 CBS
Lieutenant ep Interlude 2.1.64 NBC
Dr. Kildare ep Believe and Live 4.22.65 NBC

NAISH, J. CARROL
  Life with Luigi sr 9.22.52 CBS
  G.E. Theatre ep 2.1.53 CBS
  G.E. Theatre ep Wedding Day 9.23.53 CBS
  Video Theatre ep A Medal for Benny 11.25.54 CBS
  Cavalcade of Stars ep Mississippi Days 6.11.55 ABC
  Schlitz Playhouse of Stars ep Wild Call 9.16.55 CBS
  Climax ep An Episode of Sparrows 3.29.56 CBS
  Schlitz Playhouse of Stars ep The Mysterious Cargo
    4.20.56 CBS
  Crossroads ep The White Carnation 4.27.56 ABC
  Alcoa Hour ep Key Largo 10.14.56 NBC
  Crossroads ep With Charity for All 11.9.56 ABC
  Shirley Temple's Story Book ep Hiawatha 10.5.58
    NBC
  Texan ep The First Notch 10.20.58 CBS
  Desilu Playhouse ep My Father, the Fool 11.3.58
    CBS
  Wanted, Dead or Alive ep 11.22.58 CBS
  Charlie Chan sr 11.25.58 NN
  Cimarron City ep The Bloodline 12.13.58 NBC
  Restless Gun ep Red Blood of Courage 2.2.59 NBC
  Wagon Train ep The Old Man Charvanaugh Story 2.
    18.59 NBC
  Untouchables ep 10.29.59 ABC
  Untouchables ep The Noise of Death 1.14.60 ABC
  Wagon Train ep The Benjamin Burns Story 2.17.60
    NBC
  Guestward Ho sr 9.29.60 ABC

Route 66   ep   And Make Thunder His Tribute   11.1.63
   CBS
The Hanged Man   tf   11.18.64 NBC
The Man from U.N.C.L.E.   ep   The Super Colossal Af-
   fair   10.7.66 NBC
For Love or $$$ Sp   4.11.68 NBC
Get Smart   ep   10.12.68 NBC
Cutter's Trail   ep   2.6.70 CBS

NAMATH, JOE
   Here's Lucy   ep   10.9.72 CBS

NATWICK, MILDRED
   Suspense   ep   The Horizontal Man   1.24.50 CBS
   Lights Out   ep   The Queen Is Dead   4.3.50 NBC
   Philco Playhouse   ep   The Feast   5.7.50 NBC
   Suspense   ep   Listen, Listen   5.30.50 CBS
   Studio One   ep   My Granny Van   6.26.50 CBS
   Suspense   ep   The Rose Garden   1.30.51 CBS
   Pulitzer Prize Playhouse   ep   2.16.51 ABC
   Studio One   ep   One Pair of Hands   3.5.51 CBS
   Philco Playhouse   ep   A Secret Island   5.6.51 NBC
   Somerset Maugham Theatre   ep   The Mother   9.17.51
      NBC
   Cosmopolitan Theatre   ep   Mr. Pratt and the Triple
      Horror Bill   10.30.51 NN
   Big Town   ep   The Three R's   11.18.51 CBS
   Pulitzer Prize Playhouse   ep   The Skin of Our Teeth
      12.19.51 ABC
   Kraft Theatre   ep   The Grass Harp   9.17.52 NBC
   Philco Playhouse   ep   Tempest of Tick Creek   12.14.52
      NBC
   Armstrong Circle Theatre   ep   The Marmalade Scandal
      2.10.53 NBC
   Suspense   ep   The Suitor   5.5.53 CBS
   Tales of Tomorrow   ep   Ink   5.15.53 ABC
   The Doctor   ep   The Rocking Chair   5.24.53 NBC
   First Person   ep   The Death of the Old Man   7.17.53
      NBC
   Medallion Theatre   ep   The Bartlett Desk   9.19.53 CBS
   Goodyear Playhouse   ep   The Happy Rest   10.4.53 NBC
   Armstrong Circle Theatre   ep   Tom O'Shanter   3.9.54
      NBC
   TV Soundstage   ep   The Almighty Dollar   4.23.54 NBC
   Kraft Theatre   ep   Mr. Simmons   7.1.54 ABC
   U.S. Steel Hour   ep   A Garden in the Sea   7.20.54
      ABC

Studio One   ep   Uncle Ed and Circumstances   10.10.55
   CBS
Ford Star Jubilee   ep   Blithe Spirit   1.14.56 CBS
Studio One   ep   Always Welcome   2.27.56 CBS
Alfred Hitchcock Presents   ep   The Perfect Murder   3.
   11.56 CBS
Loretta Young Show   ep   Hapless Holiday   4.8.56 NBC
Kraft Theatre   ep   The Big Heist   11.13.57 NBC
Play of the Week   ep   The Waltz of the Toreadors   11.
   16.59 NN
Playhouse 90   ep   Eloise   11.22.56 CBS
Alfred Hitchcock Presents   ep   Miss Bracegirdle Does
   Her Duty   2.2.58 CBS
Naked City   ep   Take and Put   6.21.61 ABC
Hallmark Hall of Fame   ep   Arsenic and Old Lace   2.
   5.62 NBC
Bonanza   ep   1.19.69 NBC
Most Deadly Game   ep   I Said the Sparrow   1.16.71 ABC
Do Not Fold, Spingle or Mutilate   tf   11.9.71 ABC
The House without a Christmas   Sp   12.3.72 CBS
The Snoop Sisters   tf   12.18.72 NBC

NEAL, PATRICIA
   Goodyear Playhouse   ep   Spring Reunion   4.11.54 NBC
   Studio One   ep   A Handful of Diamonds   4.19.54 CBS
   Omnibus   ep   Salome   12.18.55 CBS
   Playhouse 90   ep   The Playroom   10.10.57 CBS
   Suspicion   ep   Someone Is After Me   1.6.58 NBC
   Playhouse 90   ep   The Gentleman from Seventh Avenue
      1.30.58 CBS
   Pursuit   ep   The Silent Night   12.24.58 CBS
   Play of the Week   ep   The Stronger   1.25.60 NN
   Play of the Week   ep   The Magic and the Loss   2.20.61
      NN
   Special for Women   ep   Mother and Daughter   3.9.61
      NBC
   Checkmate   ep   The Yacht Club Gang   1.31.62 CBS
   Untouchables   ep   The Maggie Storm Story   3.29.62
      ABC
   Westinghouse Presents   ep   That's Where the Town's Go-
      ing   4.17.62 CBS
   Ben Casey   ep   My Enemy Is a Bright Green Sparrow
      4.29.63 ABC
   Espionage   ep   The Weakling   10.9.63 NBC
   The Homecoming   Sp   12.19.71 CBS
   Ghost Story   ep   12.22.72 NBC

NEAL, TOM
    Racket Squad ep Skin Game 9.27.51 CBS

NEAR, HOLLY
    Room 222 ep 10.7.70 ABC
    Bold Ones ep Power Play 11.1.70 NBC
    All in the Family ep 2.9.71 CBS

NELSON, BARRY
    Suspense ep My Old Man's Badge 3.21.50 CBS
    Suspense ep The Gentleman from America 4.25.50
      CBS
    Starlight Theatre ep The Roman Kid 5.14.50 CBS
    Suspense ep A Pocketful of Murder 9.5.50 ABC
    TV Playhouse ep Dear Ghosts and Guests 9.24.50
      NBC
    Pulitzer Prize Playhouse ep The End Game 11.24.50
      ABC
    The Hunter sr 9.3.52 CBS
    Tales of the City ep 6.25.53 CBS
    My Favorite Husband sr 9.12.53 CBS
    My Favorite Husband sr ret 9.11.54 CBS
    Climax ep Casino Royale 10.21.54 CBS
    Schlitz Playhouse of Stars ep The Uninhibited Female
      9.9.55 CBS
    My Favorite Husband sr ret 10.4.55 CBS
    Producers Showcase ep Happy Birthday 6.25.56 NBC
    Climax ep The Push-Button Giant 5.29.58 CBS
    Lux Playhouse ep Drive a Desert Road 12.12.58 CBS
    Alfred Hitchcock Presents ep The Waxwork 4.12.59
      CBS
    David Niven Show ep Life Line 4.14.59 NBC
    June Allyson Show ep Threat of Evil 2.15.60 CBS
    Zane Grey Theatre ep Deception 4.14.60 CBS
    U.S. Steel Hour ep A Time to Decide 11.2.60 CBS
    Dupont Show of the Month ep The Bachelor Game 9.
      29.63 NBC
    Ben Casey ep My Love, My Love 12.4.63 ABC
    Bob Hope Chrysler Theatre ep Wake Up Darling 2.21.
      64 NBC
    Alfred Hitchcock Theatre ep Anyone for Murder 3.13.
      64 CBS
    The Greatest Show on Earth ep There Are No Problems,
      Only Opportunities 4.21.64 ABC
    Twilight Zone ep Stopover in a Quiet Town 4.24.64
      CBS
    Dr. Kildare ep Maybe Love Will Save My Apartment

House   10. 1. 64 NBC
Kraft Suspense Theatre   ep   The Siege   12. 3. 64 NBC
Alfred Hitchcock Theatre   ep   Misadventure   12. 7. 64
   NBC
The Borgia Stick   tf   2. 25. 67 NBC
Heaven Help Us   pt   8. 14. 67 CBS
Hondo   ep   12. 22. 67 ABC
CBS Playhouse   ep   Secrets   5. 15. 68 CBS
Name of the Game   ep   Break Out to a Fast Buck   3.
   14. 69 NBC
Seven in Darkness   tf   9. 23. 69 ABC
FBI   ep   12. 28. 69 CBS
Owen Marshall   ep   a Piece of God   12. 14. 72 ABC
Climb an Angry Mountain   tf   12. 23. 72 NBC

NELSON, DAVID
   Ozzie and Harriet   sr   10. 10. 52 ABC
   Ozzie and Harriet   sr ret   fall, 1953 ABC
   Ozzie and Harriet   sr ret   fall, 1954 ABC
   Ozzie and Harriet   sr ret   9. 23. 55 ABC
   Ozzie and Harriet   sr ret   fall, 1956 ABC
   Ozzie and Harriet   sr ret   fall, 1957 ABC
   Ozzie and Harriet   sr ret   fall, 1958 ABC
   Ozzie and Harriet   sr ret   fall, 1959 ABC
   Ozzie and Harriet   sr ret   fall, 1960 ABC
   Ozzie and Harriet   sr ret   9. 28. 61 ABC
   Ozzie and Harriet   sr ret   9. 27. 62 ABC
   Ozzie and Harriet   sr ret   9. 18. 63 ABC
   Ozzie and Harriet   sr ret   9. 64 ABC
   Ozzie and Harriet   sr ret   9. 15. 65 ABC
   D. A.   ep   11. 12. 71 NBC

NELSON, GENE
   Shower of Stars   ep   Lend an Ear   10. 28. 54 CBS
   G. E. Theatre   ep   Tryout   10. 2. 55 CBS
   Studio One   ep   The Missing Men   1. 3. 55 CBS
   Best of Broadway   ep   Broadway   5. 4. 55 CBS
   Ford Theatre   ep   A Kiss for Santa   12. 22. 55 NBC
   Matinee Theatre   ep   Fiddlin' Man   4. 9. 56 NBC
   Kaiser Aluminum Hour   ep   A Man's Game   4. 23. 57
      NBC
   Kraft Theatre   ep   The Woman of High Hollow   2. 26.
      58 NBC
   Maverick   ep   Trail West to Fury   7. 27. 58 ABC
   Northwest Passage   ep   The Fourth Brother   1. 30. 59
      NBC
   Have Gun Will Travel   ep   The Return of the Lady

2. 21. 59 CBS
The Millionaire ep Millionaire Marcia Forrest 3. 25. 59 CBS
Bat Masterson ep Brunette Bombshell 4. 1. 59 NBC
Gunsmoke ep 6. 6. 59 CBS
Rawhide ep Incident of the Shambling Man 10. 9. 59 CBS
Philip Marlowe ep Murder Is a Grave Affair 3. 8. 60 ABC
Plainsman ep Trojan Horse 5. 5. 60 NBC
Men into Space 5. 11. 60 CBS
Tom, Dick, and Harry pt 9. 20. 60 CBS
Gunsmoke ep 10. 1. 60 CBS
Hallmark Hall of Fame ep Shangri-La 10. 24. 60 NBC
Detectives ep Duty Date 5. 12. 61 ABC
Follow the Sun ep Not Aunt Charlotte 3. 25. 62 ABC
77 Sunset Strip ep "5" 10. 4. 63, 10. 18. 63 ABC
Burke's Law ep Who Killed Harris Crown 10. 11. 63 ABC
Burke's Law ep 9. 23. 64 ABC
Mod Squad ep Find Tara Chapman 11. 19. 68 ABC
Family Flight tf 10. 25. 72 ABC

NELSON, KENNETH
Aldrich Family sr 3. 28. 52 NBC
Kraft Theatre ep One Sunday Afternoon 11. 11. 54 ABC

NELSON, OZZIE
Ozzie and Harriet sr 10. 10. 52 ABC
Ozzie and Harriet sr ret fall, 1953 ABC
Ozzie and Harriet sr ret fall, 1954 ABC
Ozzie and Harriet sr ret 9. 23. 55 ABC
Fireside Theatre ep Shoot the Moon 3. 20. 56 NBC
Ozzie and Harriet sr ret fall, 1956 ABC
Ozzie and Harriet sr ret fall, 1957 ABC
Ozzie and Harriet sr ret fall, 1958 ABC
Ozzie and Harriet sr ret fall, 1959 ABC
Ozzie and Harriet sr ret 9. 28. 60 ABC
Ozzie and Harriet sr ret 9. 28. 61 ABC
Ozzie and Harriet sr ret 9. 27. 62 ABC
Ozzie and Harriet sr ret 9. 18. 63 ABC
Ozzie and Harriet sr ret 9. 64 ABC
Ozzie and Harriet sr ret 9. 15. 65 ABC
Mothers-in-Law ep 12. 22. 68 NBC
Love American Style ep 1. 8. 71 ABC
Adam-12 ep 9. 29. 71 NBC
Night Gallery ep 11. 12. 72 NBC

NELSON, RICKY
    Ozzie and Harriet   sr   10.10.52 ABC
    Ozzie and Harriet   sr ret   fall, 1953 ABC
    Ozzie and Harriet   sr ret   fall, 1954 ABC
    Ozzie and Harriet   sr ret   9.23.55 ABC
    Ozzie and Harriet   sr ret   fall, 1956 ABC
    Ozzie and Harriet   sr ret   fall, 1957 ABC
    Ozzie and Harriet   sr ret   fall, 1958 ABC
    Ozzie and Harriet   sr ret   fall, 1959 ABC
    Ozzie and Harriet   sr ret   9.28.60 ABC
    Ozzie and Harriet   sr ret   9.28.61 ABC
    G.E. Theatre ep The Wish Book 10.22.61 CBS
    Ozzie and Harriet   sr ret   9.27.62 ABC
    Ozzie and Harriet   sr ret   9.18.63 ABC
    Ozzie and Harriet   sr ret   9.64 ABC
    Ozzie and Harriet   sr ret   9.15.65 ABC
    ABC Stage 67 ep On the Flip Side 12.7.66 ABC
    Hondo ep 11.3.67 ABC
    The Over the Hill Gang tf 10.7.69 ABC
    Owen Marshall ep Victim in Shadow 12.7.72 ABC
    McCloud ep 10.1.72 NBC

NESBITT, CATHLEEN
    Philco Playhouse ep The Mother 4.4.54 NBC
    Studio One ep You're Only Young Twice 1.10.55 CBS
    Producers Showcase ep Reunion in Vienna 4.4.55 NBC
    Studio One ep Strange Companion 5.16.55 CBS
    Studio One ep Split Level 10.31.55 CBS
    Alcoa Hour ep Undertow 12.11.55 NBC
    Lamp Unto My Feet ep 5.6.56 CBS
    Goodyear Playhouse ep The Primary Colors 6.3.56
      NBC
    Alcoa Hour ep Sister 7.22.56 NBC
    Studio One ep The Playwright and the Star 4.8.57 CBS
    Alcoa Hour ep No License to Kill 9.1.57 NBC
    Suspicion ep Hand in Glove 10.21.57 NBC
    Studio One ep Bend in the Road 11.4.57 CBS
    U.S. Steel Hour ep The Reward 2.12.58 CBS
    Dupont Show of the Month ep Wuthering Heights 5.9.58
      CBS
    Playhouse 90 ep Heart of Darkness 11.6.58 CBS
    Wagon Train ep The Matthew Lowry Story 4.1.59 NBC
    Play of the Week ep Thieves' Carnival 12.21.59 NN
    Mrs. Miniver Sp 1.7.60 CBS
    Bronco ep The Masquerade 1.26.60 ABC
    Play of the Week ep The House of Bernardo Alba 6.
      6.60 NN

U. S. Steel Hour   ep   A Time to Decide   11.2.60 CBS
Family Classics   ep   Vanity Fair   1.12.61, 1.13.61
   CBS
Shirley Temple Theatre   ep   The Little Mermaid   3.5.
   61 NBC
Play of the Week   ep   The Wingless Victory   4.17.61
   NN
Adventures in Paradise   ep   Flamin' Lady   5.22.61 NBC
Naked City   ep   Dead on the Field of Honor   10.4.61
   ABC
Feathertop   Sp   10.19.61 ABC
Dr. Kildare   ep   A Million Dollar Property   10.26.61
   NBC
New Breed   ep   Sweet Bloom of Death   11.28.61 ABC
Theatre '62   ep   Notorious   12.10.61 NBC
Adventures in Paradise   ep   The Inheritance   12.24.61
   ABC
U. S. Steel Hour   ep   Fair Young Ghost   1.23.63 CBS
Empire   ep   Pressure Lock   12.4.62 NBC
U. S. Steel Hour   ep   The Old Lady Shows Her Medals
   6.12.63 CBS
Mystery Theatre   ep   Go Look at Roses   9.11.63 NBC
T. H. E. Cat   ep   2.24.67 CBS
The Crucible   Sp   5.4.67 CBS
Farmer's Daughter   sr   9.20.63 ABC
Nurses   ep   The Third Generation   2.7.63 CBS
U. S. Steel Hour   ep   The Many Ways of Heaven   5.1.63
   CBS
Farmer's Daughter   sr ret   9.64 ABC
Farmer's Daughter   sr ret   9.13.65 ABC

NETTLETON, LOIS
   Camera Three   ep   Rendezvous   1.29.56 CBS
   Studio One   ep   An Incident of Love   7.23.56 CBS
   Armstrong Circle Theatre   ep   The Complex Mummy
      Company Complex   1.8.58 CBS
   Armstrong Circle Theatre   ep   Accused of Murder   5.
      14.58 CBS
   Meet Me in St. Louis   Sp   4.26.59 CBS
   True Story   ep   Suspicion Island   5.16.59 NBC
   U. S. Steel Hour   ep   Seed of Guilt   8.12.59 CBS
   True Story   ep   9.12.59 NBC
   Great Mysteries   ep   The Woman in White   5.23.60 NBC
   Play of the Week   ep   Duet for Two Hands   10.24.60
      NN
   Naked City   ep   Debt of Honor   11.23.60 ABC
   CBS TV Workshop   ep   The Mind's Eye   12.11.60 CBS

Play of the Week   ep   Emmanuel   12.19.60 NN
Naked City   ep   To Dream without Sleep   5.24.61 ABC
Route 66   ep   The Opponent   6.2.61 CBS
Twilight Zone   ep   The Midnight Sun   11.17.61 CBS
Route 66   ep   Some of the People, Some of the Time
   12.1.61 CBS
Naked City   ep   A Run for the Money   3.14.62 ABC
Dupont Show of the Month   ep   The Shadowed Affair
   11.4.62 NBC
Route 66   ep   Suppose I Said I Was the Queen of Spain
   2.8.63 CBS
Alfred Hitchcock Theatre   ep   Dark Pool   5.3.63 CBS
Eleventh Hour   ep   Oh, You Shouldn't Have Done It   10.
   30.63 NBC
Nurses   ep   The Guilt of Molly Kane   11.21.63 CBS
East Side/West Side   ep   No Hiding Place   12.2.63 CBS
Dr. Kildare   ep   Speak Not in Angry Whispers   5.14.64
   NBC
Fugitive   ep   Man on a String   9.29.64 ABC
Doctors/Nurses   ep   A Messenger to Everyone   12.29.
   64 CBS
Mr. Novak   ep   Where Is There to Go Billie But up
   3.9.65 NBC
FBI   ep   11.20.66 ABC
Fugitive   ep   Death Is the Door Prize   9.20.66 ABC
Heartbreak House   Sp   4.24.66 NN
Virginian   ep   Nobility of Kings   11.10.65 NBC
Gunsmoke   ep   2.18.67 CBS
Accidental Family   sr   9.14.67 NBC
Bonanza   ep   Pursued   10.2.66, 10.9.66 NBC
Fugitive   ep   In a Plain Paper Wrapper   4.19.66 ABC
Actors Company   ep   Macbeth   4.18.68 NN
Virginian   ep   Wind of Outrage   10.16.68 NBC
Any Second Now   tf   2.11.69 NBC
Outsider   ep   4.2.69 NBC
Then Came Bronson   ep   All the World and God   12.3.
   69 NBC
Bold Ones   ep   And Those Unborn   12.21.69 NBC
Medical Center   ep   Scream of Silence   10.28.70 CBS
FBI   ep   The Innocent   11.1.70 ABC
Name of the Game   ep   All the Old Familiar Faces   11.
   13.70 NBC
Weekend of Terror   tf   12.8.70   ABC
Interns   ep   Metamorphosis   2.5.71 CBS
Terror in the Sky   tf   9.17.71 CBS
The Forgotten Man   tf   9.14.71 ABC
Gunsmoke   ep   12.16.71 CBS

Man and the City   ep   12. 29. 71 ABC
Women in Chains   tf   1. 25. 72 ABC
Night Gallery   ep   I'll Never Leave You Ever   2. 16. 72
   NBC
Cannon   ep   11. 22. 72 CBS
Medical Center   ep   No Way Out   12. 6. 72 ABC

NEWILL, JAMES
Renfrew of the Royal Mounted   sr   5. 24. 53 CBS

NEWLAND, JOHN
Philco Playhouse   ep   Little Boy Lost   1. 1. 50 NBC
Philco Playhouse   ep   The American   4. 30. 50 NBC
The Trap   ep   Three Blind Mice   6. 17. 50 CBS
Lights Out   ep   The Dark Corner   9. 10. 50 NBC
Television Theatre   ep   Michael and Mary   12. 13. 50
   NBC
Armstrong Circle Theatre   ep   The Partnership   3. 6. 51
   NBC
Philco Playhouse   ep   Birth of the Movies   4. 22. 51 NBC
Kraft Theatre   ep   Until Death Us Do Part   5. 9. 51 NBC
The Web   ep   Checkmate   6. 13. 51 CBS
Armstrong Circle Theatre   ep   Runaway Heart   10. 2. 51
   NBC
Tales of Tomorrow   ep   Frankenstein   1. 18. 52 ABC
Kraft Theatre   ep   The Mollusk   2. 20. 52 NBC
Philco Playhouse   ep   Dusty Portrait   3. 9. 52 NBC
Kraft Theatre   ep   The Bride the Sun Shines on   3. 19.
   52 NBC
Kraft Theatre   ep   The Last Mile   4. 9. 52 NBC
Armstrong Circle Theatre   ep   The Dark Room   4. 15. 52
   NBC
Robert Montgomery Presents   ep   The Longest Night   5.
   19. 52 NBC
Robert Montgomery Presents   sr   7. 14. 52 NBC
Robert Montgomery Presents   ep   The Christmas Cards
   12. 22. 52 NBC
Broadway Television Theatre   ep   The Gold Diggers   12.
   29. 52 NN
Schlitz Playhouse of Stars   ep   The Unopened Letter   1.
   9. 53 CBS
Kraft Theatre   ep   One Bright Day   1. 14. 53 NBC
Tales of Tomorrow   ep   The Picture of Dorian Gray   1.
   23. 53 ABC
Schlitz Playhouse of Stars   ep   Allen of Harper   4. 24. 53
   CBS
Kraft Theatre   ep   The Man in Half Moon Street   4. 30.
   53 NBC

Robert Montgomery Presents   ep   Linda   5.4.53 NBC
The Web   5.17.53 CBS
Eye Witness   ep   Youth from Vienna   6.1.53 NBC
Robert Montgomery Presents   sr   7.6.53 NBC
Schlitz Playhouse of Stars   ep   The Perfect Secretary
   9.4.53 CBS
Robert Montgomery Presents   ep   What about Christ-
   mas?   12.21.53 NBC
Robert Montgomery Presents   ep   Richard Said No   1.
   25.54 NBC
Robert Montgomery Presents   ep   Land of Happiness   2.
   22.54 NBC
Robert Montgomery Presents   ep   Love Story   4.26.54
   NBC
Robert Montgomery Presents   sr   6.28.54 NBC
Schlitz Playhouse of Stars   ep   Square Shootin'   10.15.
   54 CBS
Robert Montgomery Presents   ep   The Great Gatsby   4.
   11.55 NBC
Robert Montgomery Presents   ep   Lucifer   12.5.55 NBC
Loretta Young Show   ep   The Secret   1.29.56 NBC
Loretta Young Show   ep   His Inheritance   3.18.56 NBC
Schlitz Playhouse of Stars   ep   The Bitter Land   4.13.
   56 CBS
Robert Montgomery Presents   sr   5.7.56 NBC
Loretta Young Show   ep   The Years Between   10.7.56
   NBC
Robert Montgomery Presents   ep   September Affair   10.
   8.56 NBC
Loretta Young Show   ep   Goodbye, Goodbye   10.21.56
   NBC
Loretta Young Show   ep   My Favorite Monster   1.13.57
   NBC
Robert Montgomery Presents   ep   The Grand Prize   2.
   11.57 NBC
Loretta Young Show   ep   Tension   2.17.57 NBC
Loretta Young Show   ep   Legacy   4.21.57 NBC
Loretta Young Show   ep   Faraway Island   1.26.58 NBC
Loretta Young Show   ep   Conflict   3.2.58 NBC
Loretta Young Show   ep   Time of Decision   3.23.58
   NBC
G.E. Theatre   ep   At Miss Miner's   10.26.58 CBS
Loretta Young Show   ep   The Woman Between   1.23.58
   NBC
Alcoa Presents   sh   1.20.59 ABC
Loretta Young Show   ep   Good-Bye, Good-Bye   5.17.59
   NBC

Alcoa Premiere   sh ret   9.27.60 ABC
Loretta Young Show   ep   The Seducer   11.6.60 NBC
Loretta Young Show   ep   Unconditional Surrender   11.
  20.60 NBC
Thriller   ep   The Return of Andrew Bentley   12.11.61
  NBC
Thriller   ep   Portrait without a Face   12.25.61 NBC
Dr. Kildare   ep   Tyger, Tyger   1.23.64 NBC

NEWMAN, PAUL

The Web   ep   The Bells of Damon   7.19.53 CBS
The Web   ep   One for the Road   9.20.53 CBS
The Mask   ep   Party Night   4.11.54 ABC
Goodyear Playhouse   ep   Guilty Is the Stranger   9.26.
  54 NBC
Danger   ep   Knife in the Dark   12.7.54 CBS
Appointment with Adventure   ep   Five in Judgment   4.10.
  55 CBS
Appointment with Adventure   ep   Bridge of the Devil   6.
  26.55 CBS
Philco Playhouse   ep   The Death of Billy the Kid   7.24.
  55 NBC
Producers Showcase   ep   Our Town   9.19.55 NBC
Playwrights '56   ep   The Battler   10.18.55 NBC
Kaiser Aluminum Hour   ep   The Army Game   7.3.56
  NBC
U.S. Steel Hour   ep   The Five Fathers of Pepi   9.29.56
  CBS
U.S. Steel Hour   ep   Bang the Drum Slowly   9.26.56
  CBS
Kaiser Aluminum Hour   ep   The Rag Jungle   11.20.56
  NBC
Playhouse 90   ep   The 80 Yard Run   1.16.58 CBS

NEWTON, ROBERT

Hollywood Opening Night   ep   Mr. Barber's Love Affair
  3.16.53 NBC
G.E. Theatre   ep   Confession   10.18.53 CBS
Schlitz Playhouse of Stars   ep   The Baker of Barnbury
  12.25.53 CBS
Climax   ep   The First and the Last   4.28.55 CBS
Schlitz Playhouse of Stars   ep   The Argonauts   5.27.55
  CBS
Lux Video Theatre   ep   The Suspect   6.2.55 NBC
Long John Silver   sr   9.22.55 NN
Alfred Hitchcock Presents   ep   The Derelicts   2.5.56
  CBS

NEWTON, THEODORE
Sure as Fate ep Ten Days to Spring 11.14.50 CBS
The Doctor ep 9.21.52 NBC

NICHOLS, BARBARA
U.S. Steel Hour ep Good for You 6.8.54 ABC
Center Stage ep The Heart of a Clown 9.21.54 ABC
Armstrong Circle Theatre ep Fred Allen's Sketchbook
11.9.54 NBC
Danger ep Peter River Blues 4.12.55 CBS
Bob Cummings ep The Con Man 4.5.56 CBS
It's a Great Life ep 4.15.56 NBC
The Brothers ep 2.12.57 CBS
Thin Man ep The Unwelcome Alibi 12.27.57 NBC
Maverick ep The Third Rider 1.5.58 ABC
Love That Jill sr 1.20.58 ABC
Climax ep The Push-Button Giant 5.29.58 CBS
Desilu Playhouse ep The Untouchables 4.20.59, 4.27.
59 CBS
Untouchables ep The Empty Chair 10.15.59 ABC
Real McCoys ep The Politician 12.3.59 ABC
Twilight Zone ep Twenty-Two 2.10.61 CBS
G.E. Theatre ep The Small Elephants 3.12.61 CBS
Michael Shayne ep Marriage Can Be Fatal 3.31.61
NBC
Detectives ep 5.12.61 ABC
Dick Powell Theatre ep No Strings Attached 4.24.62
NBC
Alcoa Premiere ep Five, Six, Pick up Sticks 1.24.
63 ABC
Arrest and Trial ep Isn't It a Lovely View 9.22.63
ABC
Beverly Hillbillies sr 9.25.63 CBS
Grindl ep Grindl, Witness for the Defense 11.3.63
NBC
Kraft Suspense Theatre ep My Enemy, This Town 2.
6.64 NBC
The Travels of Jaimie McPheeters ep The Day of the
Dark Deeds 3.8.64 ABC
Laredo ep A Question of Discipline 10.28.65 NBC
Wild, Wild West ep The Night of the Whirring Death
2.18.66 CBS
Batman ep Shoot a Crooked Arrow 9.7.66, 9.8.66
ABC
Green Acres ep 2.8.67 CBS
The Girl from U.N.C.L.E. ep 3.14.67 NBC
Hawaii Five-O ep A Thousand Pardons, You're Dead

9. 24. 69 CBS
Adam-12 ep 11. 3. 71 NBC
Adam-12 ep 11. 22. 72 NBC

NICHOLS, MIKE
Dupont Show of the Month ep The Red Mill 4. 19. 58 CBS
Playhouse 90 ep Journey to the Day 4. 22. 60 CBS

NICHOLSON, JACK
Tales of Wells Fargo ep The Washburn Girl 2. 13. 61 NBC
Hawaiian Eye ep Total Eclipse 2. 21. 62 ABC
Dr. Kildare ep The Taste of Crow 2. 22. 66, 2. 28. 66, 3. 1. 66, 3. 7. 66, 3. 8. 66 NBC
Andy Griffith Show ep 11. 21. 66 CBS

NICOL, ALEX
A Letter to Loretta ep 12. 6. 53 NBC
Schlitz Playhouse of Stars ep Groundloop 3. 12. 54 CBS
Lux Video Theatre ep Christmas in July 9. 9. 54 NBC
TV Reader's Digest ep The Great Armored Car Robbery 4. 25. 55 ABC
Damon Runyon Theatre ep Earthquake 8. 27. 55 CBS
Climax ep Shadow of a Memory 12. 26. 57 CBS
Alfred Hitchcock Presents ep The Percentage 1. 5. 58 CBS
Kraft Theatre ep Run Joe, Run 1. 29. 58 NBC
Schlitz Playhouse of Stars ep Heroes Never Grow up 2. 7. 58 CBS
Climax ep Cabin B-13 6. 26. 58 CBS
Alcoa Theatre ep Medals for Harry 6. 1. 59 NBC
Cain's Hundred ep Quick Brown Fox 5. 8. 62 NBC
Twilight Zone ep Young Man's Fancy 5. 11. 62 CBS
Dr. Kildare ep The Dark Side of the Mirror 3. 28. 63 NBC
Outer Limits ep Moonstone 3. 9. 64 ABC
FBI ep The Game of Terror 11. 7. 71 ABC

NIELSEN, LESLIE
Actor's Studio ep Hannah 1. 3. 50 CBS
Studio One ep The Survivors 3. 20. 50 CBS
The Trap ep Sentence of Death 5. 27. 50 CBS
Television Theatre ep The Luck of Guldeford 5. 31. 50 NBC
Studio One ep Zone Four 6. 12. 50 CBS

Television Playhouse   ep   The Touch of a Stranger   10.
   1. 50 NBC
Studio One   ep   Spectre of Alexander Wolff   10.9.50 CBS
Studio One   ep   The Last Cruise   11.13.50 CBS
Television Theatre   ep   Best Years   1.17.51 NBC
Sure as Fate   ep   The Devil Takes a Bride   2.6.51
   CBS
Suspense   ep   A Rap at the Door   8.14.51 CBS
Armstrong Circle Theatre   ep   Flame-Out   9.18.51
   NBC
Goodyear Playhouse   ep   October Story   10.14.51 NBC
Goodyear Playhouse   ep   Crown of Shadows   2.17.52
   NBC
Philco Playhouse   ep   Sisters   12.30.51 NBC
Tales of Tomorrow   ep   Black Planet   5.16.52 ABC
Tales of Tomorrow   ep   Appointment to Mars   6.27.52
   ABC
Armstrong Circle Theatre   ep   For Worse   7.15.52
   NBC
Lights Out   ep   Death Trap   7.28.52 NBC
Kraft Theatre   ep   A Kiss for Cinderella   10.15.52
   NBC
Studio One   ep   The Hospital   12.8.52 CBS
Tales of Tomorrow   ep   Another Chance   2.13.53 ABC
Goodyear Playhouse   ep   The Rumor   3.8.53 NBC
Danger   ep   The Missing Night   7.28.53 CBS
Armstrong Circle Theatre   ep   A Story to Whisper   9.
   15.53 NBC
Armstrong Circle Theatre   ep   The Beard   11.24.53
   NBC
Medallion Theatre   ep   Twenty-Four Men to a Plane
   12.19.53 CBS
Man Behind the Badge   1.24.54 CBS
Studio One   ep   Dark Possession   2.15.54 CBS
Studio One   ep   Beyond a Reasonable Doubt   3.8.54 CBS
Studio One   ep   Castles in Spain   5.17.54 CBS
Kraft Theatre   ep   The Scarlet Letter   5.26.54 NBC
Man Behind the Badge   ep   The Case of the Yankee II
   6.27.54 CBS
Studio One   ep   A Guest at the Embassy   7.12.54 CBS
Studio One   ep   The Man Who Owned the Town   11.1.54
   CBS
Robert Montgomery Presents   ep   End of a Mission   12.
   13.54 NBC
Playhouse 90   ep   The Right Hand Man   3.20.58 CBS
Alfred Hitchcock Presents   ep   The Two-Million Dollar
   Defense   11.2.58 CBS

Playhouse 90 ep The Velvet Alley 1. 22. 59 CBS
G. E. Theatre ep Nora 5. 3. 59 CBS
World of Disney ep The Swamp Fox 10. 23. 59 ABC
World of Disney ep Tory Vengeance 1. 1. 60 ABC
Rawhide ep Incident Below the Brazos 1. 1. 60 CBS
World of Disney ep Redcoat Strategy 1. 15. 60 ABC
World of Disney ep A Case of Treason 1. 22. 60 ABC
Untouchables ep Three Thousand Suspects 3. 24. 60
    ABC
World of Disney ep Brother against Brother 5. 6. 60
    ABC
Moment of Fear ep Total Recall 7. 29. 60 NBC
Thriller ep The Twisted Image 9. 13. 60 NBC
G. E. Theatre ep Journal of Hope 9. 25. 60 CBS
Naked City ep Down the Long Night 11. 2. 60 ABC
Wagon Train ep The Jeremy Dow Story 12. 28. 60
    NBC
Route 66 ep A Fury Stinging Flame 12. 30. 60 CBS
World of Disney ep A Woman's Courage 1. 8. 61 ABC
Islanders ep Willy's Millionaire 2. 12. 61 ABC
New Breed sr 10. 3. 61 ABC
Route 66 ep Poor Little Kangaroo Rat 11. 23. 62 CBS
Ben Casey ep He Thought He Saw an Albatros 2. 4. 63
    ABC
Channing ep Exercise in a Shark Tank 9. 25. 63 ABC
Kraft Suspense Theatre ep One Step Down 11. 14. 63
    NBC
Fugitive ep The Glass Tightrope 12. 3. 63 ABC
Alfred Hitchcock Theatre ep The Magic Shop 1. 10. 64
    CBS
Defenders ep Survival 3. 14. 64 CBS
Virginian ep Ryker 9. 16. 64 NBC
Fugitive ep Tiger Left, Tiger Right 10. 20. 64 ABC
Wagon Train ep 10. 25. 64 ABC
Defenders ep Death on Wheels 1. 28. 65 CBS
Dr. Kildare ep Do You Trust Our Doctor 3. 4. 65 NBC
Voyage to the Bottom of the Sea ep The Creature 3.
    22. 65 ABC
Dr. Kildare ep She Loves Me, She Loves Me Not 3.
    25. 65 NBC
Kraft Suspense Theatre ep The Green Felt Jungle 4.
    1. 65 NBC
Ben Casey ep A War of Nerves 9. 13. 65 ABC
Loner ep The Kingdom of McComb 10. 9. 65 CBS
Dr. Kildare ep The Life Machine 10. 26. 65, 11. 1. 65,
    11. 2. 65, 11. 9. 65, 11. 16. 65 NBC
Convoy ep Sink U-116 11. 12. 65 NBC

FBI   ep   Pound of Flesh   12.19.65 ABC
Bob Hope Chrysler Theatre   ep   When Hell Froze   2.2.
   66 NBC
Bob Hope Chrysler Theatre   ep   Guilty or Not Guilty
   3.9.66 NBC
Virginian   ep   No Drums, No Trumpets   4.6.66 NBC
Bob Hope Chrysler Theatre   ep   Code Name Heraclitus
   1.4.67, 1.11.67 NBC
Judd for the Defense   ep   9.15.67 ABC
Cimarron Strip   ep   11.30.67 CBS
Virginian   ep   12.27.67 NBC
The Man from U.N.C.L.E.   ep   The Seven Wonders of
   the World Affair   1.8.68, 1.15.68 NBC
It Takes a Thief   ep   1.9.68 ABC
Shadow over Elveron   tf   3.5.68 NBC
Hawaii Five-O   tf   9.20.68 CBS
Companions in Nightmare   tf   11.23.68 NBC
Gunsmoke   ep   Time of the Jackals   1.13.69 CBS
Deadlock   tf   2.22.69 NBC
Big Valley   ep   4.7.69 ABC
Virginian   ep   9.17.69 NBC
Bold Ones   sr   9.28.69 NBC
Name of the Game   ep   4.10.70 NBC
Bracken's World   sr   9.18.70 NBC
Night Slaves   tf   9.29.70 ABC
The Aquarians   tf   10.24.70 NBC
Hauser's Memory   tf   11.24.70 NBC
Incident in San Francisco   tf   2.28.71 ABC
Sarge   ep   11.9.71 NBC
Bearcats   ep   12.2.71 CBS
Medical Center   ep   Conspiracy   12.8.71 CBS
Columbo   ep   Lady in Waiting   12.15.71 NBC
They Call It Murder   tf   12.17.71 NBC
Mod Squad   ep   1.11.72 ABC
Assignment: Vienna   ep   9.28.72 ABC

NIGH, JANE
   Big Town   sr   4.3.52 CBS
   Ford Theatre   ep   The Lady in His Life   4.19.56 NBC
   The Millionaire   ep   The Rose Russell Story   3.27.57
      CBS
   Tales of Wells Fargo   ep   The General   12.16.57 NBC
   Rawhide   ep   Incident of the Judas Trap   6.5.59 CBS
   Wichita Town   ep   Second Chance   3.16.60 NBC
   Dennis the Menace   ep   Dennis the Campaign Manager
      1.15.61 CBS

NILSSON, ANNA Q.
  Fireside Theatre ep The Old Talbot 2.12.52 NBC

NIMOY, LEONARD
  West Point ep His Brother's Fist 11.16.58 CBS
  West Point ep Cold Peril 4.12.57 CBS
  Sea Hunt ep 1.24.59 CBS
  M Squad ep The Firemakers 4.17.59 NBC
  Rough Riders ep Gunpoint Persuasion 4.30.59 ABC
  M Squad ep Badge for a Coward 5.24.60 NBC
  Tate ep Commanche Scalps 8.10.60 NBC
  Tall Man ep A Bounty for Billy 10.15.60 NBC
  Rebel ep The Hunted 11.16.60 ABC
  Sea Hunt ep 12.3.60 CBS
  Bonanza ep The Ape 12.17.60 NBC
  Wagon Train ep The Tiburcio Mendez Story 3.22.61
    NBC
  87th Precinct ep The Very Hard Sell 12.14.61 NBC
  Gunsmoke ep 12.30.61 CBS
  Laramie ep The Runt 2.20.62 NBC
  Perry Mason ep The Case of the Shoplifter's Shoe 1.
    3.63 CBS
  Combat ep The Wounded Don't Cry 10.22.63 ABC
  Eleventh Hour ep La Belle Indifference 12.18.63 NBC
  Virginian ep Man of Violence 12.25.63 NBC
  Lieutenant ep In the Highest Tradition 2.29.64 NBC
  Kraft Suspense Theatre ep The World I Want to Know
    10.1.64 NBC
  Outer Limits ep I, Robot 11.14.64 ABC
  The Man from U.N.C.L.E. ep The Project Strigas Af-
    fair 11.24.64 NBC
  Laramie ep The Runt 1.23.65 ABC
  Virginian ep Show Me a Hero 11.17.65 NBC
  Shenandoah ep Run, Killer, Run 1.10.66 ABC
  Daniel Boone ep 1.13.66 NBC
  Get Smart ep 1.22.66 NBC
  Gunsmoke ep 4.16.66 CBS
  Star Trek sr 9.8.66 NBC
  Star Trek sr ret 9.15.67 NBC
  Star Trek sr ret 9.20.68 NBC
  Mission Impossible sr 9.28.69 CBS
  Assault on the Wayne tf 1.12.71 ABC
  Night Gallery ep 12.24.72 NBC

NIVEN, DAVID
  Schlitz Playhouse of Stars ep Not a Chance 10.5.51
    CBS

Celanese Theatre   ep   The Petrified Forest   2.20.52
    ABC
Robert Montgomery Presents   ep   The Sheffield Story
    10.27.52 NBC
Four Star Playhouse   sr   12.4.52 CBS
Hollywood Opening Night   ep   Sword Play   12.15.52 NBC
Four Star Playhouse   sr ret   9.24.53 CBS
Four Star Playhouse   sr ret   10.7.54 CBS
Light's Diamond Jubilee   ep   The Girls in their Summer
    Dresses   10.24.54 ABC, CBS, NBC
Four Star Playhouse   sr ret   9.15.55 CBS
Four Star Playhouse   sr ret   9.20.56 CBS
Zane Grey Theatre   ep   Village of Fear   3.1.57 CBS
Alcoa Theatre   ep   Circumstantial   10.4.57 NBC
Goodyear Theatre   ep   The Tinhorn   12.23.57 NBC
Alcoa Theatre   ep   In the Dark   1.13.58 NBC
Alcoa Theatre   ep   Night Caller   2.10.58 NBC
Goodyear Theatre   ep   The Fatal Charm   3.3.58 NBC
Goodyear Theatre   ep   Taps for Jeffrey   3.31.58 NBC
Alcoa Theatre   ep   My Wife's Next Husband   4.21.58
    NBC
Goodyear Theatre   ep   Decision by Terror   5.26.58 NBC
Zane Grey Theatre   ep   The Accused   10.30.58 CBS
The David Niven Show   sh/sr   4.7.59 NBC
June Allyson Show   ep   The Trench Coat   1.11.60 CBS
Zane Grey Theatre   ep   Village of Fear   4.19.62 CBS
Rogues   sr   9.13.64 NBC

NOLAN, KATHY
    Jamie   sr   10.5.53 ABC
    Producers Showcase   ep   Peter Pan   3.7.55 NBC
    Elgin Hour   ep   Midsummer Melody   4.19.55 ABC
    Producers Showcase   ep (restaged)   Peter Pan   1.9.56
        NBC
    The Millionaire   ep   The Story of Waldo Francis Turner
        11.14.56 CBS
    Conflict   ep   Stranger on the Road   12.11.56 ABC
    Those Whiting Girls   ep   7.29.57 CBS
    Real McCoys   sr   10.3.57 ABC
    Real McCoys   sr ret   fall, 1958 ABC
    Real McCoys   sr ret   fall, 1959 ABC
    Real McCoys   sr ret   9.29.60 ABC
    Real McCoys   sr ret   9.28.61 ABC
    Saints and Sinners   ep   10.1.62 NBC
    Untouchables   ep   Blues for a Gone Goose   1.29.63 ABC
    Ben Casey   ep   Hang No Hats on Dreams   5.13.63 ABC
    Burke's Law   ep   Who Killed Cynthia Royal   12.13.63
        ABC

Lloyd Bridges Show ep The Rising of the Moon 12.19. 63 CBS
Gunsmoke ep 3.7.64 CBS
Alfred Hitchcock Theatre ep Beast in View 3.20.64 CBS
Breaking Point ep Confounding Her Astronomers 4.6. 64 ABC
Broadside sr 9.20.64 ABC
Big Valley ep 3.23.66 ABC
Bewitched ep 10.13.66 ABC
Name of the Game ep Seek and Destroy 2.5.71 NBC
Love American Style ep 12.10.71 ABC

NOLAN, LLOYD
Theatre Hour ep The Barker 1.13.50 CBS
Martin Kane sr 8.30.51 NBC
Ford Theatre ep Protect Her Honor 11.13.52 NBC
Climax ep Sailor on Horseback 9.29.55 CBS
Ford Star Jubilee ep The Caine Mutiny Court Martial 11.19.55 CBS
Playhouse 90 ep Galvanized Yankee 12.5.57 CBS
Zane Grey Theatre ep Homecoming 10.23.58 CBS
Wagon Train ep The Hunter Malloy Story 1.21.59 NBC
Hallmark Hall of Fame ep Ah, Wilderness! 4.28.59 NBC
Special Agent 7 sr 6.8.59 NN
Laramie ep The Star Trail 10.13.59 NBC
Desilu Playhouse ep Six Guns for Donegan 10.16.59 CBS
Father Knows Best ep Bud Branches Out 11.2.59 CBS
Lawless Years ep The Billy Boy Rockabye Creel Story 11.5.59 NBC
Ford Star Time ep nar Crime, Inc. 1.19.60 NBC
Bonanza ep The Stranger 2.27.60 NBC
Laramie ep The Star Trail 5.3.60 NBC
Untouchables ep The George Bugs Moran Story 6.23. 60 ABC
Barbara Stanwyck Theatre ep The Seventh Miracle 10. 17.60 NBC
Zane Grey Theatre ep Knife of Hate 12.8.60 CBS
Bus Stop ep The Glass Jungle 11.5.61 ABC
G.E. Theatre ep Call to Danger 12.10.61 CBS
Outlaws ep Buck Breeson Rides Again 1.25.62 NBC
Laramie ep Deadly Is the Night 5.15.62 NBC
Dick Powell Theatre ep Special Assignment 9.25.62 NBC

Dupont Show of the Month   ep   Two Faces of Treason
    2. 10. 63 NBC
Great Adventure   ep   The Death of Sitting Bull   10. 4.
    63, 10. 11. 63 CBS
Kraft Suspense Theatre   ep   The Case against Paul Ry-
    ker   10. 10. 63, 10. 17. 63 NBC
77 Sunset Strip   ep   "5"   10. 4. 63, 10. 11. 63, 10. 18. 63
    ABC
Virginian   ep   It Takes a Big Man   10. 23. 63 NBC
Outer Limits   ep   Soldier   9. 19. 64 ABC
Bob Hope Chrysler Theatre   ep   Mr. Biddle's Crime
    Wave   12. 4. 64 NBC
Virginian   ep   The Payment   12. 16. 64 NBC
Daniel Boone   ep   The Price of Friendship   2. 18. 65
    NBC
Bing Crosby Show   ep   What's a Buddy for   4. 5. 65 ABC
Slattery's People   ep   10. 15. 65 CBS
Road West   ep   1. 30. 67 NBC
Wing of Fire   tf   2. 14. 67 NBC
Mannix   ep   The Name is Mannix   9. 16. 67 CBS
Virginian   ep   10. 18. 67 NBC
Danny Thomas Show   ep   The Cage   1. 15. 68 NBC
Judd for the Defense   ep   2. 23. 68 ABC
I Spy   ep   The Name of the Game   3. 11. 68 NBC
Julia   sr   9. 24. 68 NBC
Julia   sr ret   9. 16. 69 NBC
Julia   sr ret   9. 15. 70 NBC
Owen Marshall   ep   A Question of Degree   2. 24. 72 ABC
Bold Ones   ep   A Nation of Pin Cushions   10. 3. 72 NBC

NOLTE, CHARLES
    Kraft Theatre   ep   Noah   6. 21. 50 NBC
    Schlitz Playhouse of Stars   ep   Billy Budd   1. 11. 52 CBS
    Summer Studio One   ep   The King in Yellow   7. 27. 53
        CBS

NOONAN, TOMMY
    Rebel   ep   Shriek of Silence   3. 19. 61 ABC
    Perry Mason   ep   The Case of the Crying Comedian   10.
        14. 61 CBS
    Real McCoys   ep   3. 17. 63 CBS
    My Three Sons   ep   12. 8. 66 CBS
    Gomer Pyle, U. S. M. C.   ep   9. 8. 67 CBS

NORTH, JAY
    Wanted, Dead or Alive   ep   12. 20. 58 CBS
    Sugarfoot   ep   The Giant Killer   3. 3. 59 ABC

Dennis the Menace   sr   10. 4. 59 CBS
Wanted, Dead or Alive   ep   12. 19. 59 CBS
Rescue 8   ep   5. 31. 60 ABC
Dennis the Menace   sr ret   10. 60 CBS
Dennis the Menace   sr ret   10. 1. 61 CBS
Dennis the Menace   sr ret   10. 62 CBS
77 Sunset Strip   ep   Eyewitness   5. 20. 64 ABC
Wagon Train   ep   Those Who Stay Behind   11. 8. 64 ABC
The Man from U. N. C. L. E.   ep   The Deadly Toys Affair   11. 12. 65 NBC
My Three Sons   ep   2. 10. 66 CBS
My Three Sons   ep   10. 6. 66 CBS
Jericho   ep   Eric, the Redhead   11. 3. 66 CBS
Maya   sr   9. 16. 67 NBC

NORTH, SHEREE
Shower of Stars   ep   Lend an Ear   10. 28. 54 CBS
Playhouse 90   ep   Topaz   9. 26. 57 CBS
Breaking Point   ep   Solo for B-Flat Clarinet   9. 16. 63 ABC
Gunsmoke   ep   10. 5. 63 CBS
Burke's Law   ep   Who Killed the Kind Doctor   11. 29. 63 ABC
Eleventh Hour   ep   There Should Be an Outfit Called Families Anonymous   12. 11. 63 NBC
Breaking Point   ep   Don't Cry, Baby, Don't Cry   12. 30. 63 ABC
Great Adventure   ep   Wild Bill Hickock   1. 3. 64 CBS
Virginian   ep   Walk in Another's Footsteps   3. 11. 64 NBC
Ben Casey   ep   Dress My Doll Pretty   3. 18. 64 ABC
The Greatest Show on Earth   ep   This Train Doesn't Stop Till It Gets There   4. 14. 65 ABC
Burke's Law   ep   Who Killed Davidian Jones   12. 30. 64 ABC
Burke's Law   ep   Who Killed Rosie Sunset   1. 27. 65 ABC
Bob Hope Chrysler Theatre   ep   The Crime   9. 25. 65 NBC
Fugitive   ep   An Apple a Day   11. 2. 65 ABC
Loner   ep   Escort for a Dead Man   12. 18. 65 CBS
Virginian   ep   That Saunders Woman   3. 30. 66 NBC
Big Valley   ep   The Man from Nowhere   11. 14. 66 ABC
Iron Horse   ep   12. 19. 66 ABC
Bob Hope Chrysler Theatre   ep   Code Name: Heraclitus   1. 4. 67, 1. 11. 67 NBC
Fugitive   ep   4. 4. 67 ABC
Mannix   ep   10. 5. 68 CBS

Here Come the Brides   ep   10.23.68 ABC
Then Came Bronson   tf   3.24.69 NBC
Name of the Game   ep   One of the Girls in Research
   4.3.70 NBC
Most Deadly Game   ep   Who Killed Kindness?   11.7.70
   ABC
Interns   ep   The Challengers   2.12.71 CBS
Vanished   tf   3.8.71, 3.9.71 NBC
Smith Family   ep   10.13.71 ABC
Medical Center   ep   Shock   12.29.71, 1.5.72 CBS
Alias Smith and Jones   ep   1.27.72 ABC
Rolling Man   tf   10.4.72 ABC
Cannon   ep   10.11.72 CBS
Jigsaw   ep   12.21.72 ABC

NOVAK, KIM
   Light's Diamond Jubilee   ep   A Kiss for the Lieutenant
      10.24.54 ABC, CBS, NBC

NOVARRO, RAMON
   World of Disney   ep   Elfego-Lawman or Gunman   11.28.
      58 ABC
   World of Disney   ep   Law and Order Inc.   12.12.58 ABC
   Dr. Kildare   ep   Rome Will Never Leave You   11.12.64,
      11.19.64, 11.26.64 NBC
   Bonanza   ep   The Brass Box   9.26.65 NBC
   Combat   ep   Finest Hour   12.21.65 ABC
   Wild, Wild West   ep   9.22.67 CBS

NUGENT, ELLIOTT
   Robert Montgomery Presents   ep   Mr. Whittle and the
      Morning Star   2.8.54 NBC
   Motorola TV Hour   ep   The Sins of the Fathers   4.6.54
      ABC
   Robert Montgomery Presents   ep   Pilgrim's Pride   5.10.
      54 NBC
   Goodyear Playhouse   ep   Pencil Sketch   7.29.54 NBC
   Studio One   ep   The Unmentionable Blues   8.12.57 CBS
   U.S. Steel Hour   ep   Crisis in Coroma   10.23.57 CBS
   Kraft Theatre   ep   Heroes Walk on Sand   12.11.57 NBC
   U.S. Steel Hour   ep   Be My Guest   8.27.58 CBS

NUYEN, FRANCE
   Hong Kong   ep   Clear for Action   9.28.60 ABC
   Adventures in Paradise   ep   One Little Pearl   11.28.60
      ABC
   The Man from U.N.C.L.E.   ep   The Cherry Blossom Af-

fair 11.19.65 NBC
I Spy   ep   Tiger 1.5.66 NBC
I Spy   ep   Always Say Goodby 1.26.66 NBC
Gunsmoke   ep   3.5.66 CBS
Gunsmoke   ep   10.22.66 CBS
I Spy   ep   3.15.67 NBC
I Spy   ep   An American Empress 12.25.67 NBC
Medical Center   ep   The Battle of Lily 10.22.69 CBS
Hawaii Five-O   ep   Highest Castle, Deepest Grave 9.
    14.71 CBS

NYPE, RUSSELL
    Summer Studio One   ep   Look Homeward, Hayseed 9.7.
    53 CBS

                    -O-

OAKIE, JACK
    Shower of Stars   ep   Burlesque 3.17.55 CBS
    Studio One   ep   The Award Winner 3.24.58 CBS
    New Breed   ep   I Remember Murder 12.26.61 ABC
    Target: Corruptors   ep   Viva Vegas 2.9.62 ABC
    Real McCoys   ep   The Skeleton in the Closet 4.14.63
        CBS
    Real McCoys   ep   Uncle Rightly and the Musical Milker
        4.21.63 CBS
    Real McCoys   ep   Up to their Ears in Corn 4.28.63
        CBS
    Breaking Point   ep   A Child of the Center Ring 2.24.64
        ABC
    Daniel Boone   ep   9.29.66 NBC
    Night Gallery   ep   12.24.72 NBC

OATES, WARREN
    Studio One   ep   The Night America Trembled 9.9.57
        CBS
    Wanted, Dead or Alive   ep   12.6.58 CBS
    Gunsmoke   ep   12.20.58 CBS
    Trackdown   ep   1.28.59 CBS
    Wanted, Dead or Alive   ep   3.7.59 CBS
    Tombstone Territory   ep   Whipsaw 3.13.59 ABC
    Trackdown   ep   3.18.59 CBS
    Black Saddle   ep   3.21.59 NBC
    Buckskin   ep   4.6.59 NBC
    Rough Riders   ep   The Rifle 5.7.59 ABC
    Wanted, Dead or Alive   ep   5.9.59 CBS

Bat Masterson ep Lottery of Death 5. 13. 59 NBC
Playhouse 90 ep Seven against the Wall 7. 9. 59 CBS
Rin Tin Tin ep The Epidemic 7. 10. 59 ABC
Trackdown ep 9. 9. 59 CBS
Wanted, Dead or Alive ep 1. 9. 60 CBS
77 Sunset Strip ep Blackout 3. 11. 60 ABC
Johnny Ringo ep 5. 12. 60 CBS
Tate ep Before Sunup 8. 17. 60 NBC
Rifleman ep Miss Silly 11. 15. 60 ABC
Lawman ep The Second Sun 11. 27. 60 CBS
Wanted, Dead or Alive ep 1. 11. 61 CBS
Laramie ep Two for the Gallows 4. 11. 61 NBC
Bat Masterson ep Meeting at Mimbers 4. 13. 61 NBC
Gunsmoke ep 12. 23. 61 CBS
Thriller ep The Hollow Watcher 2. 12. 62 NBC
Rifleman ep Day of Reckoning 4. 9. 62 ABC
Bonanza ep The Mountain Girl 5. 12. 62 NBC
Stoney Burke sr 10. 1. 62 ABC
77 Sunset Strip ep Terror in a Small Town 10. 26. 62
   ABC
The Travels of Jaimie McPheeters ep The Day of the
   First Sailor 9. 29. 63 ABC
Rawhide ep Incident of the Prophecy 11. 21. 63 CBS
Virginian ep Stopover in a Western Town 11. 27. 63
   ABC
Twilight Zone ep The 7th Is Made Up of Phantoms
   12. 6. 63 CBS
Combat ep The Pillbox 1. 7. 64 ABC
Fugitive ep Rat in a Corner 2. 18. 64 ABC
Gunsmoke ep 2. 22. 64 CBS
Outer Limits ep The Mutant 3. 16. 64 ABC
Rawhide ep The Race 9. 25. 64 CBS
Fugitive ep Devil's Carnival 12. 22. 64 ABC
Gunsmoke ep 2. 6. 65 CBS
Bob Hope Chrysler Theatre ep The War and Eric Kurtz
   3. 5. 65 NBC
Branded ep Judge Not 9. 12. 65 NBC
Shenendoah ep The Fort 9. 27. 65 ABC
Gunsmoke ep 10. 9. 65 CBS
Slattery's People ep 10. 15. 65 CBS
12 O'Clock High ep The Hotshot 10. 18. 65 ABC
Virginian ep Ride to Delphia 9. 21. 66 NBC
The Monroes ep The Forest Devil 9. 28. 66 ABC
Shane ep An Echo of Anger 10. 1. 66 ABC
Gunsmoke ep 10. 8. 66 NBC
Big Valley ep 11. 21. 66 ABC
Dundee and the Culhane ep The Turn the Other Cheek
   Brief 9. 6. 67 CBS
Gunsmoke ep 9. 11. 67 CBS
Cimarron Strip ep 9. 28. 67 CBS

Run for Your Life   ep   1.10.68 NBC
World of Disney   ep   The Mystery of Edward Sims   3.
    31.68, 4.7.68 NBC
Lancer   ep   3.25.69 CBS
Name of the Game   ep   The Showdown   3.19.71 NBC
The Reluctant Heroes   tf   11.23.71 ABC

OBERON, MERLE
Four Star Playhouse   ep   Sound Off, My Love   2.12.53
    CBS
Ford Theatre   ep   Allison, Ltd.   4.16.53 NBC
Four Star Playhouse   ep   The Journey   7.17.53 CBS
Best of Broadway   ep   The Man Who Came to Dinner
    10.13.54 CBS
Ford Theatre   ep   Second Night   3.10.55 NBC
Four Star Playhouse   ep   The Frightened Woman   6.23.
    55 CBS
Loretta Young Show   ep   Moment of Decision   10.2.55
    NBC
Loretta Young Show   ep   The Bracelet   11.13.55 NBC
G.E. Theatre   ep   I Will Not Die   4.28.57 CBS
Assignment Foreign Legion   sh   10.1.57 CBS

O'BRIAN, HUGH
Fireside Theatre   ep   Going Home   2.20.51 NBC
Royal Playhouse   ep   Shifting Sands   5.29.52 NN
Loretta Young Show   ep   Guest in the House   8.29.54
    NBC
Loretta Young Show   ep   Double Trouble   9.12.54 NBC
Loretta Young Show   ep   Three Minutes Too Late   12.26.
    54 NBC
Studio 57   ep   The Engagement Ring   2.15.55 NN
Loretta Young Show   ep   Feeling No Pain   4.17.55 NBC
Stage 7   ep   Billy and the Bride   5.8.55 CBS
Damon Runyon Theatre   ep   A Light in France   7.30.55
    CBS
Wyatt Earp   sr   9.6.55 ABC
Matinee Theatre   ep   Tall Dark Stranger   2.28.56 NBC
Ford Theatre   ep   Ringside Seat   2.13.57 ABC
Playhouse 90   ep   Invitation to a Gunfighter   3.7.57 CBS
Playhouse 90   ep   Reunion   1.2.58 CBS
Desilu Playhouse   ep   Chain of Command   3.23.59 CBS
Desilu Playhouse   ep   Circle of Evil   3.18.60 CBS
G.E. Theatre   ep   Graduation Dress   10.30.60 CBS
Our American Heritage   ep   The Secret Rebel   3.11.61
    NBC
Play of the Week   ep   The Wingless Victory   4.17.61 NN

Feathertop   Sp   10.19.61 ABC
Dick Powell Theatre   ep   Jumped the Devil   11.28.61
   NBC
Theatre '62   ep   Spellbound   2.11.62 NBC
Alcoa Premiere   ep   The Rules of the Games   5.1.62
   ABC
Alfred Hitchcock Theatre   ep   Ride the Nightmare   11.
   29.62 CBS
The Greatest Show on Earth   ep   Garve   10.15.63 ABC
Bob Hope Chrysler Theatre   ep   Runaway   1.10.64 NBC
Perry Mason   ep   The Case of the Two-Faced Turnabout
   2.14.60 CBS
Great Bible Adventures: Seven Rich Years   pt   9.11.66
   ABC
Dial M for Murder   Sp   11.15.67 ABC
Hallmark Hall of Fame   ep   11.20.68 NBC
Wild Women   tf   10.20.70 ABC
Harpy   tf   3.13.71 CBS
Probe   tf   2.21.72 NBC
Search   sr   9.13.72 NBC

O'BRIEN, EDMOND
   Stars over Hollywood   ep   Not a Bad Guy   9.27.50 NBC
   Pulitzer Prize Playhouse   ep   Ice Bound   4.13.51 ABC
   Video Theatre   ep   Hit and Run   4.23.51 CBS
   Video Theatre   ep   A Matter of Life   9.24.51 CBS
   Video Theatre   ep   Ceylon Treasure   1.14.52 CBS
   Robert Montgomery Presents   ep   Ricochet   1.12.53
      NBC
   Ford Theatre   ep   To any Soldier   4.2.53 NBC
   Schlitz Playhouse of Stars   ep   Lineman's Luck   11.6.53
      CBS
   Ford Theatre   ep   Charlie C Company   1.29.54 NBC
   Schlitz Playhouse of Stars   ep   The Net Draws Tight   10.
      8.54 CBS
   Climax   ep   12.2.54 CBS
   Rheingold Theatre   ep   Dark Stranger   1.8.55 NBC
   Stage 7   ep   Debt of Honor   2.20.55 CBS
   Damon Runyon Theatre   ep   Old Lem's Kentucky Home
      5.28.55 CBS
   Playwrights 56   ep   The Heart's a Forgotten Hotel   10.
      25.55 NBC
   Rheingold Theatre   ep   End of Flight   10.29.55 NBC
   Screen Directors Playhouse   ep   A Ticket for Thaddeus
      5.9.56 NBC
   Climax   ep   Figures in Clay   5.31.56 CBS
   Schlitz Playhouse of Stars   ep   Tower Room 14-A   1.11.
      57 CBS

Lux Video Theatre   ep   To Have and Have Not   1.17.57
NBC
Playhouse 90   ep   The Comedian   2.14.57 CBS
Zane Grey Theatre   ep   A Gun Is for Killing   10.18.57
CBS
Playhouse 90   ep   The Male Animal   3.13.58 CBS
Schlitz Playhouse of Stars   ep   The Town that Slept with
the Lights On   5.16.58 CBS
Suspicion   ep   Death Watch   6.2.58 NBC
Lux Playhouse   ep   Coney Island Winter   11.28.58 CBS
Playhouse 90   ep   The Blue Men   1.15.59 CBS
Laramie   ep   The Iron Captain   10.27.59 NBC
Zane Grey   ep   Lonesome Road   11.19.59 CBS
Johnny Midnight   sr   3.15.60 NBC
Dick Powell Theatre   ep   Killer in the House   10.10.61
NBC
Target Corruptors   ep   The Invisible Government   10.20.
61 ABC
Sam Benedict   sr   9.15.62 NBC
The Greatest Show on Earth   ep   2.25.64 ABC
Breaking Point   ep   Tides of Darkness   3.2.64 ABC
The Hanged Man   tf   11.18.64 NBC
World of Disney   ep   Gallegher   1.24.65, 1.31.65, 2.7.
65 NBC
The Long Hot Summer   sr   9.16.65 ABC
World of Disney   ep   The Further Adventures of Galle-
gher   9.26.65, 10.3.65, 10.10.65 NBC
Doomsday Flight   tf   2.13.67 NBC
Virginian   ep   Ah Sing vs. Wyoming   10.25.67 NBC
The Outsider   tf   11.21.67 NBC
Flesh and Blood   Sp   1.26.68 NBC
Mission Impossible   ep   2.4.68 CBS
It Takes a Thief   ep   3.25.69 ABC
The Intruders   tf   11.10.70 NBC
Young Lawyers   ep   MacGillicuddy Always Was a Pain in
the Neck   12.11.70 ABC
Name of the Game   ep   L.A. 2017   1.15.71 NBC
High Chaparral   ep   The Hostage   3.5.71 NBC
River of Mystery   tf   10.1.71 NBC
What's a Nice Girl Like You   tf   12.18.71 ABC
Cade's County   ep   1.23.72 CBS
Jigsaw   tf   3.26.72 ABC
Streets of San Francisco   ep   9.23.72 ABC
McMillan and Wife   ep   11.19.72 NBC

O'BRIEN, GEORGE
Studio 57   ep   Typhoon   9.8.57 NN

O'BRIEN, MARGARET
    Robert Montgomery Presents   ep   The Canterville Ghost
        11. 20. 50 NBC
    Video Theatre   ep   To Lovely Margaret 2. 19. 51   CBS
    Video Theatre   ep   The White Gown   2. 2. 53 CBS
    Studio One   ep   A Breath of Air   3. 16. 53 CBS
    Ford Theatre   ep   Daughter of Mine   10. 7. 54 NBC
    Climax   ep   South of the Sun   3. 3. 55 CBS
    Matinee Theatre   ep   Midsummer   11. 21. 55 NBC
    Front Row Center   ep   Innocent Witness 3. 4. 56 CBS
    Climax   ep   Nine-Day Wonder   3. 7. 57 CBS
    Matinee Theatre   ep   Winter in April   4. 22. 57 NBC
    Climax   ep   The Necessary Evil 9. 19. 57 CBS
    Playhouse 90   ep   The Mystery of Thirteen   10. 24. 57
        CBS
    Suspicion   ep   The Story of Margery Reardon   10. 28. 57
        NBC
    Jane Wyman Theatre   ep   Roadblock Number Seven   11.
        7. 57 NBC
    Kraft Theatre   ep   Come to Me   12. 4. 57 NBC
    G. E. Theatre   ep   The Young Years   12. 22. 57 CBS
    Matinee Theatre   ep   The Little Minister   12. 26. 57 NBC
    Studio One   ep   Trial by Slander   1. 20. 58 CBS
    Studio One   ep   Tongues of Angels   3. 17. 58 CBS
    Wagon Train   ep   The Sacramento Story   9. 24. 58 NBC
    Pursuit   ep   Kiss Me Again, Stranger   11. 19. 58 CBS
    Rawhide   ep   Incident of the Town in Terror   3. 6. 59
        CBS
    Playhouse 90   ep   Second Happiest Day   6. 25. 59 CBS
    U. S. Steel Hour   ep   Big Doc's Girl   11. 4. 59 CBS
    June Allyson Show   ep   Escape   2. 22. 60 CBS
    Maggie   pt   8. 29. 60 CBS
    Checkmate   ep   Deadly Shadow   11. 12. 60 CBS
    Aquanauts   ep   River Gold   1. 4. 61 CBS
    Adventures in Paradise   ep   The Trial of Adam Troy
        12. 17. 61 ABC
    Dr. Kildare   ep   The Dragon   2. 15. 62 NBC
    Dupont Show of the Month   ep   The Betrayal   10. 21. 62
        NBC
    Perry Mason   ep   The Case of the Shoplifter's Shoe   1.
        3. 63 CBS
    Bob Hope Chrysler Theatre   ep   The Turncoat   10. 23. 64
        NBC
    Combat   ep   Entombed   1. 3. 67 ABC
    Ironside   ep   9. 26. 68 NBC
    Love American Style   ep   Love and the Letter   10. 6. 69
        ABC

Marcus Welby, M.D.   ep   12.19.72 ABC

O'BRIEN, PAT
   Video Theatre   ep   The Irish Drifter   2.26.51 CBS
   Video Theatre   ep   Tin Badge   12.3.51 CBS
   Drama   ep   The Joyful Hour   12.25.51 ABC
   Schlitz Playhouse of Stars   ep   A Man's World   7.25.52
    CBS
   Video Theatre   ep   The Face of Autumn   11.3.52 CBS
   G.E. Theatre   ep   Winners Never Lose   3.15.53 CBS
   Video Theatre   ep   One for the Road   3.23.53 CBS
   Schlitz Playhouse of Stars   ep   Second Sight   10.23.53
    CBS
   Ford Theatre   ep   Tomorrow's Men   10.29.53 NBC
   Lux Video Theatre   ep   The Chase   12.30.54 NBC
   Climax   ep   The Box of Chocolates   2.24.55 CBS
   Stage 7   ep   The Great Man in the World   3.13.55 CBS
   Rheingold Theatre   ep   Newspaper Man   5.21.55 NBC
   Front Row Center   ep   Dinner at Eight   6.1.55 CBS
   Climax   ep   Thin Air   10.13.55 CBS
   Climax   ep   The Prowler   1.5.56 CBS
   Studio 57   ep   Who's Calling   2.12.56 NN
   Crossroads   ep   Strange Bequest   2.17.56 ABC
   U.S. Steel Hour   ep   Thirty-Year Man   3.28.56 CBS
   Studio 57   ep   Exit Laughing   4.1.56 NN
   Crossroads   ep   Holiday for Father Jim   6.22.56 ABC
   Studio 57   ep   Strange Query   2.17.57 NN
   Playhouse 90   ep   Invitation to a Gunfighter   3.7.57 CBS
   Crossroads   ep   Riot   4.19.57 ABC
   Crossroads   ep   Circus Priest   7.12.57 ABC
   Studio One   ep   The Brotherhood of the Bell   1.6.58 CBS
   Kraft Theatre   ep   Eddie   1.22.58 NBC
   World of Disney   ep   I Captured the King of the Lepre-
    chauns   5.29.59 ABC
   Harrigan and Son   sr   10.14.60 ABC
   Dick Powell Theatre   ep   Thunder in a Forgotten Town
    3.5.63 NBC
   Going My Way   ep   Boss of the War   3.13.63 ABC
   Virginian   ep   The Fortunes of Jimerson Jones   1.15.64
    NBC
   Kraft Suspense Theatre   ep   Threatening Eye   3.12.64
    NBC
   Bob Hope Chrysler Theatre   ep   4.3.64 NBC
   Kraft Suspense Theatre   ep   The Jack Is High   11.19.64
    NBC
   Bob Hope Chrysler Theatre   ep   The Crime   9.22.65 NBC
   Hazel   ep   1.10.66 CBS

Branded   ep   The Greatest Coward on Earth   11.21.65
   NBC
Virginian   ep   1.18.67 NBC
My Friend Tony   ep   4.13.69 NBC
The Over the Hill Gang   tf   10.7.69 ABC
Alias Smith and Jones   ep   Shootout at Diablo Station
   12.2.71 ABC
Welcome Home, Johnny Bristol   tf   1.30.72 CBS
The Adventures of Nick Carter   tf   2.20.72 ABC
Banyon   ep   9.29.72 NBC

O'CONNELL, ARTHUR
   Comedy Theatre   ep   Summer Had Better Be Good   7.9.
      50 ABC
   Philco Playhouse   ep   O for 37   1.27.53 NBC
   Kraft Theatre   ep   All Our Yesterdays   5.20.54 ABC
   Kraft Theatre   ep   Mr. Simmons   7.1.54 ABC
   Kraft Theatre   ep   Knight in a Business Suit   7.21.54
      NBC
   Lamp Unto My Feet   ep   The Gift Horse   2.20.55 CBS
   Studio One   ep   A Terrible Day   7.18.55 CBS
   Philco Playhouse   ep   The Outsiders   9.18.55 NBC
   Omnibus   ep   The Blue Hotel   11.25.56 ABC
   Zane Grey Theatre   ep   The Broken Wing   2.9.61 CBS
   Stagecoach West   ep   Songs My Mother Told Me   2.21.
      61 ABC
   Window on Main Street   ep   5.9.62 CBS
   New Breed   ep   Judgment at San Belito   5.22.62 ABC
   Empire   ep   Green, Green Hills   12.25.62 NBC
   Breaking Point   ep   A Little Anger Is a Good Thing   11.
      25.63 ABC
   Arrest and Trial   ep   The Best There Is   2.16.64 ABC
   The Greatest Show on Earth   ep   Blood, Sawdust and a
      Bucket of Tears   3.17.64 ABC
   Burke's Law   ep   3.27.64 ABC
   The Human Comedy   pt   9.19.64 CBS
   Fugitive   ep   Tug of War   10.27.64 ABC
   Wagon Train   ep   The Silver Lady   4.25.65 ABC
   Big Valley   ep   10.13.65 ABC
   FBI   ep   Hijackers   10.26.65 ABC
   Fugitive   ep   An Apple a Day   11.2.65 ABC
   Petticoat Junction   ep   12.21.65 CBS
   Voyage to the Bottom of the Sea   ep   The Mechanical Man
      3.13.66 ABC
   Shenandoah   ep   4.18.66 ABC
   Second Hundred Years   sr   9.7.67 ABC
   Gunsmoke   ep   10.30.67 CBS

My Three Sons   ep   10.19.68 CBS
Ironside   ep   1.23.69 NBC
Name of the Game   ep   3.14.69 NBC
Seven in Darkness   tf   9.23.69 ABC
Men from Shiloh   ep   3.17.71 NBC
Bonanza   ep   Fallen Woman   9.26.71 NBC
A Taste of Evil   tf   10.12.71 ABC
Cannon   ep   No Pockets in a Shroud   11.23.71 CBS
Night Gallery   ep   12.15.71 NBC
McCloud   ep   12.29.71 NBC
Room 222   ep   12.31.71 ABC
Alias Smith and Jones   ep   3.2.72 ABC
Ghost Story   ep   Elegy for a Vampire   12.1.72 NBC

O'CONNOR, CARROLL
Sacco-Vanzetti Story   Sp   6.3.60, 6.10.60 NBC
Armstrong Circle Theatre   ep   Full Disclosure   7.6.60
    CBS
U.S. Steel Hour   ep   Shadow of a Pale Horse   7.20.60
    CBS
Armstrong Circle Theatre   ep   Engineer of Death   10.12.
    60 CBS
Adventures in Paradise   ep   Hangman's Island   11.21.60
    ABC
Shirley Temple Theatre   ep   The Black Arrow   11.27.60
    NBC
Play of the Week   ep   He Who Gets Slapped   1.30.61 NN
Americans   ep   The Coward   5.8.61 NBC
Untouchables   ep   Power Play 10.19.61 ABC
Dr. Kildare   ep   The Burning Sky   10.4.62 NBC
Untouchables   ep   Bird in the Hand   10.30.62 ABC
Ben Casey   ep   Behold, They Walk an Ancient Road   11.
    5.62 ABC
Defenders   ep   The Hidden Jungle   12.1.62 CBS
Dick Powell Theatre   ep   Pericles on 31st Street   12.4.
    62 NBC
Naked City   ep   Spectre of the Rose Street Gang   12.19.
    62 ABC
Dick Powell Theatre   ep   Luxury Liner   2.12.63 NBC
Stoney Burke   ep   Web of Fear   2.18.63 ABC
Alcoa Premiere   ep   The Dark Labyrinth   3.21.63 ABC
Eleventh Hour   ep   Pressure Breakdown   5.15.63 NBC
Bonanza   ep   The Boss   5.19.63 NBC
East Side/West Side   ep   Age of Consent   9.30.63 CBS
Defenders   ep   Conspiracy of Silence   10.26.63 CBS
Dupont Show of the Month   ep   Silver Burro   11.3.63
    NBC

Great Adventure   ep   The Man Who Stole New York City
    12.13.63 CBS
Outer Limits   ep   Controlled Experiment   1.13.64 ABC
Great Adventure   ep   The Pathfinder   3.6.64 CBS
Fugitive   ep   Flight from the Final Demon   3.10.64 ABC
Bob Hope Chrysler Theatre   ep   The Turncoat   10.23.64
    NBC
The Man from U.N.C.L.E.   ep   The Green Opal Affair
    10.27.64 NBC
Voyage to the Bottom of the Sea   ep   Long Live the King
    12.21.64 ABC
Slattery's People   ep   What Did You Do All Day, Mr.
    Slattery   1.15.65 CBS
Ben Casey   ep   Three Li'l Lambs   3.29.65 ABC
Profiles in Courage   ep   4.4.65 NBC
Dr. Kildare   ep   The Time Buyer   4.8.65 NBC
Slattery's People   ep   A Sitting Duck Named Slattery   9.
    17.65 CBS
I Spy   ep   It's All Done with Mirrors   4.13.66 NBC
Bob Hope Chrysler Theatre   ep   Massacre at Ft. Phil
    Kearney   10.26.66 NBC
Gunsmoke   ep   10.29.66 CBS
Wild, Wild West   ep   The Night of the Ready Made Corpse
    11.25.66 CBS
Dundee and the Culhane   ep   11.1.67 CBS
A Walk in the Night   pt   7.15.68 NBC
Fear No Evil   tf   3.3.69 NBC
World of Disney   ep   Ride a Northbound Horse   3.16.69,
    3.23.69 NBC
Governor and J.J.   ep   9.23.69 CBS
All in the Family   sr   1.12.71 CBS
All in the Family   sr ret   9.18.71 CBS
All in the Family   sr ret   9.16.72 CBS
Of Thee I Sing   Sp   10.24.72 CBS

O'CONNOR, DONALD
    Playhouse 90   ep   The Jet-Propelled Couch   11.14.57
        CBS
    Dupont Show of the Month   ep   The Red Mill   4.19.58
        CBS
    Bob Hope Chrysler Theatre   ep   Brilliant Benjamin Boggs
        3.30.66 NBC
    The Hoofer   pt   8.15.66 CBS
    ABC Stage 67   ep   Olympus 7-0000   9.28.66 ABC

O'DONNELL, CATHY
    Lights Out   ep   To See Ourselves   9.17.51 NBC

Center Stage   ep   Chivalry at Howling Creek   6.1.54
ABC
Best of Broadway   ep   The Show-Off   2.2.55 CBS
Climax   ep   Flight 951   4.21.55 CBS
Matinee Theatre   ep   Greybeards and Witches   5.1.56
NBC
Zane Grey Theatre   ep   Sundown at Bitter Creek   2.14.
58 CBS
Californians   ep   Skeleton in the Closet   4.8.58 NBC
Detectives   ep   The Trap   2.5.60 ABC
Rebel   ep   You Steal My Eyes   3.20.60 ABC
Tate   ep   Quiet after the Storm   9.7.60 NBC
Rebel   ep   12.25.60 ABC
Cheyenne   ep   Angel   3.6.61 ABC

O'HARA, MAUREEN
Mrs. Miniver   Sp   1.7.60 CBS
Family Classics   ep   The Scarlet Pimpernel   10.28.60
CBS
Theatre '62   ep   Spellbound   2.11.62 NBC
Hallmark Hall of Fame   ep   A Cry of Angels   12.15.63
NBC
Garry Moore Show   ep   High Button Shoes   11.20.66 CBS
Off to See the Wizard   ep   Who's Afraid of Mother Goose
10.13.67 ABC

O'HERLIHY, DAN
Cavalcade of America   ep   11.12.52 NBC
G.E. Theatre   ep   Trapped   3.22.53 CBS
G.E. Theatre   ep   The Wine of St. Albans   8.2.53 CBS
Cavalcade of America   ep   Betrayal   12.8.53 ABC
U.S. Steel Hour   ep   Oberstrasse Forty-Nine   8.3.54
ABC
G.E. Theatre   ep   The White Steed   12.26.54 CBS
Cavalcade of America   ep   A Romance to Remember   1.
11.55 ABC
Lux Video Theatre   ep   Love Letter   1.20.55 NBC
Stage 7   ep   Appointment in Highbridge   2.6.55 CBS
Schlitz Playhouse of Stars   ep   Log the Man Innocent
3.25.55 CBS
Climax   ep   No Stone Unturned   5.19.55 CBS
U.S. Steel Hour   ep   The Seventh Veil   8.3.55 CBS
Screen Directors Playhouse   ep   Final Tribute   11.16.55
NBC
Fireside Theatre   ep   Man on the Window Sill   12.13.55
NBC
Schlitz Playhouse of Stars   ep   Christmas Guest   12.23.
55 CBS

Screen Directors Playhouse   ep   Final Tribute   1.25.56
   NBC
Playhouse 90   ep   The Blackwell Story   2.28.57 CBS
Kraft Theatre   ep   The Duel   3.6.57 NBC
On Trial   ep   The Deadly Chain   6.7.57 NBC
Kraft Theatre   ep   Fire and Ice   6.12.57 NBC
Zane Grey Theatre   ep   The Bitter Land   12.6.57 CBS
Road West   ep   12.12.67 NBC
G.E. Theatre   ep   Robbie and His Mary   4.19.59 CBS
June Allyson Show   ep   Edge of Fury   1.4.60 CBS
Playhouse 90   ep   To the Sounds of Trumpets   2.9.60
   CBS
Untouchables   ep   The Big Squeeze   2.18.60 ABC
Best of the Post   ep   I'm No Hero   11.5.60 ABC
Rawhide   ep   Incident at Dragoon Crossing   10.21.60
   CBS
Americans   ep   The Escape   3.13.61 NBC
Adventures in Paradise   ep   Adam Sam   5.1.61 ABC
Target: Corruptors   ep   The Platinum Highway   10.13.
   61 ABC
U.S. Steel Hour   ep   Bury Me Twice   10.18.61 CBS
Dr. Kildare   ep   Season to Be Jolly   12.21.61 NBC
Route 66   ep   To Walk with the Serpent   1.5.62 CBS
Adventures in Paradise   ep   The Secret Place   2.25.62
   ABC
Dr. Kildare   ep   3.15.62 NBC
Checkmate   ep   Referendum on Murder   4.25.62 CBS
Bonanza   ep   The Artist   10.7.62 NBC
Sam Benedict   ep   The View from an Ivory Tower   11.
   24.62 NBC
Empire   ep   The Earth Mover   11.27.62 NBC
Combat   ep   The Chateau   2.12.63 ABC
Dr. Kildare   ep   A Very Infectious Disease   3.21.63
   NBC
Ben Casey   ep   For I Will Plait Thy Hair with Gold   3.
   25.63 ABC
The Travels of Jaimie McPheeters   sr   9.15.63 ABC
Alfred Hitchcock Theatre   ep   Forecast: Low Clouds
   and Coastal Fog   1.18.63 CBS
Profiles in Courage   ep   12.6.64 NBC
Bob Hope Chrysler Theatre   ep   The Shattered Glass
   12.11.64 NBC
Dr. Kildare   ep   Believe and Live   4.22.65 NBC
The Long Hot Summer   sr   1.6.66 ABC
Big Valley   ep   1.9.67 ABC
The Man from U.N.C.L.E.   ep   The Ho-Ho-Ho and a
   Bottle of Rum Affair   1.20.67 NBC

Mission Impossible   ep   9.17.67 CBS
High Chaparral   ep   10.22.67 NBC
Hondo   ep   12.8.67 ABC
The Man from U.N.C.L.E.   ep   The Seven Wonders of
    the World Affair   1.8.68, 1.15.68 NBC
The People   tf   1.22.72 ABC

O'KEEFE, DENNIS
Airflyte Theatre   ep   Scandalous Conduct   3.1.51 CBS
Video Theatre   ep   Route Nineteen   10.8.51 CBS
Gulf Playhouse   ep   Double By-Line   10.3.52 NBC
Video Theatre   ep   A Time for Heroes   3.2.53 CBS
Robert Montgomery Presents   ep   Head for Moonlight
    6.8.53 NBC
Climax   ep   The Thirteenth Chair   10.14.54 CBS
Producers Showcase   ep   Yellow Jack   1.10.55 NBC
Climax   ep   Edge of Terror   8.11.55 CBS
Lux Video Theatre   ep   The Human Jungle   10.20.55
    NBC
Climax   ep   Scheme to Defraud   11.10.55 CBS
Screen Directors Playhouse   ep   It's Always Sunday   1.
    11.56 CBS
Kraft Theatre   ep   Five Minutes to Live   2.1.56 NBC
Studio One   ep   Manhattan Duet   2.13.56 CBS
Climax   ep   A Trophy for Howard Davenport   6.28.56
    CBS
Schlitz Playhouse of Stars   ep   The Traveling Corpse
    5.3.57 CBS
Suspicion   sh   9.30.57 NBC
Suspicion   ep   The Woman with Red Hair   5.5.58 NBC
Dennis O'Keefe Show   sr   9.22.59 CBS
Joey Bishop Show   ep   The Bachelor   10.25.61 NBC
Follow the Sun   ep   The Longest Crap Game in History
    11.5.61 ABC
Dick Powell Theatre   ep   Open Season   12.26.61 NBC
Follow the Sun   ep   Annie Beeler's Place   2.11.62 ABC

OLIVIER, LAURENCE (LORD OLIVIER)
Moon and Sixpence   Sp   10.30.59 NBC
Power and the Glory   Sp   10.29.61 CBS
N.E.T. Playhouse   ep   Uncle Vanya   2.10.67 NN
On Stage   ep   hos/nar   Male of the Species   1.3.69 NBC
David Copperfield   tf   3.15.70 NBC

OLIVER, SUSAN
Goodyear Playhouse   ep   The Prize Winner   7.3.55 NBC
Kaiser Aluminum Hour   ep   So Short a Season   2.12.57
    NBC

U.S. Steel Hour   ep   The Bottle Imp   3.13.57 CBS
Matinee Theatre   ep   End of the Rope   4.1.57 NBC
Crossroads   ep   9:30 Action   5.24.57 ABC
Wagon Train   ep   The Emily Rossiter Story   10.30.57
   NBC
Climax   ep   Two Tests for Tuesday   11.14.57 CBS
Playhouse 90   ep   The Thundering Wave   12.12.57 CBS
Kraft Theatre   ep   The Woman at High Hollow   2.26.58
   NBC
Playhouse 90   ep   A Trip to Paradise   3.26.59 CBS
David Niven Theatre   ep   The Last Room   6.2.59 NBC
Lineup   ep   Run to the City   11.11.59 CBS
Alcoa Theatre   cp   The Long House on Avenue A   12.
   14.59 NBC
Bonanza   ep   The Outcast   1.9.60 NBC
Playhouse 90   ep   A Dream of Treason   1.21.60 CBS
June Allyson Show   ep   The Blue Goose   3.21.60 CBS
Twilight Zone   ep   People Are Alike All Over   3.25.60
   CBS
Wanted, Dead or Alive   ep   3.26.60 CBS
Wagon Train   ep   The Maggie Hamilton Story   4.6.60
   NBC
Adventures in Paradise   ep   Whip Fight   5.9.60 ABC
Wrangler   ep   Incident at the Bar M   8.4.60 NBC
Deputy   ep   The Deadly Breed   9.24.60 NBC
Wagon Train   ep   The Cathy Eckhardt Story   11.9.60
   NBC
Zane Grey Theatre   ep   Knife of Hate   12.8.60 CBS
Barbara Stanwyck Theatre   ep   No One   12.26.60 NBC
Thriller   ep   Choose a Victim   1.24.61 NBC
Untouchables   ep   The Organization   1.26.61 ABC
Michael Shayne   ep   The Heiress   2.3.61 NBC
Aquanauts   ep   The Storm Adventure   2.8.61 CBS
Best of the Post   ep   No Enemy   2.25.61 ABC
Rawhide   ep   Incident of His Brother's Keeper   3.31.61
   CBS
Americans   ep   The Gun   4.3.61 NBC
Naked City   ep   A Memory of Crying   4.12.61 ABC
Zane Grey Theatre   ep   Image of a Drawn Sword   5.11.
   61 CBS
Adventures in Paradise   ep   Hill of Ghosts   5.15.61
   ABC
Checkmate   ep   The Thrill Seeker   5.27.61 CBS
Untouchables   ep   The Organization   10.5.61 ABC
Adventures in Paradise   ep   The Reluctant Hero   10.8.
   61 ABC
Dick Powell Theatre   ep   Somebody's Waiting   11.7.61
   NBC

Golden Showcase ep The Picture of Dorian Gray 12.6. 61 CBS

Ozzie and Harriet ep Ricky, the Milkman 12.14.61 ABC

Laramie ep Shadows in the Dusk 1.16.62 NBC

Cain's Hundred ep The Cost of Living 3.20.62 NBC

Checkmate ep Beats My Plastic Heart 4.11.62 CBS

Route 66 ep Between Hello and Goodbye 5.11.62 CBS

Alfred Hitchcock Theatre ep Annabel 11.1.62 CBS

Rawhide ep Incident at Spider Rock 1.18.63 CBS

Wagon Train ep The Lily Legend Story 2.13.63 ABC

Dick Powell Theatre ep Thunder in a Forgotten Town 3.5.63 NBC

Route 66 ep Fifty Miles from Home 3.22.63 CBS

77 Sunset Strip ep Your Fortune for a Penny 5.31.63 ABC

Nurses ep No Score 9.26.63 CBS

Fugitive ep Never Wave Goodbye 10.8.63, 10.15.63 ABC

Dr. Kildare ep The Eleventh Commandment 11.14.63 NBC

Burke's Law ep Who Killed the Kind Doctor 11.29.63 ABC

Rogues ep Money Is for Burning 1.3.64 NBC

The Travels of Jaimie McPheeters ep 3.15.64 ABC

Defenders ep The Hidden Fury 3.28.64 ABC

Destry ep One Hundred Bibles 5.8.64 ABC

The Man from U.N.C.L.E. ep The Bow-Wow Affair 2.15.65 NBC

Virginian ep A Little Learning 9.29.65 NBC

FBI ep Courage of a Conviction 11.7.65 ABC

Dr. Kildare ep Perfect Is Hard to Be 12.27.65, 12.28.65 NBC

Shenandoah ep Rope's End 1.17.66 ABC

Gomer Pyle, U.S.M.C. ep 3.25.66 CBS

I Spy ep One Thousand Fine 4.27.66 NBC

Peyton Place sr spring, 1966 ABC

Star Trek ep 11.17.66, 11.24.66 NBC

My Three Sons ep 12.1.66 CBS

Tarzan ep 1.13.67 NBC

Invaders ep The Ivy Curtain 3.21.67 ABC

T.H.E. Cat ep 3.24.67 NBC

Wild, Wild West ep 9.29.67 CBS

Virginian ep 12.20.67 NBC

Invaders ep 3.26.68 ABC

Virginian ep The Storm Gate 11.13.68 NBC

Name of the Game ep 11.29.68 NBC

Outsider   ep   The Land of the Fox   12.18.68 NBC
Big Valley   ep   2.24.69 ABC
Carter's Army   tf   1.27.70 ABC
Men from Shiloh   ep   12.30.70 NBC
Name of the Game   ep   Seek and Destroy   2.5.71 NBC
Love American Style   ep   2.12.71 ABC
Dan August   ep   Prognosis   4.1.71 ABC
Primus   ep   9.20.71 ABC
Longstreet   ep   12.30.71 ABC
Sarge   ep   A Kept Woman   1.4.72 NBC
Smith Family   ep   1.5.72 ABC
Night Gallery   ep   Tune in Dan's Cafe   1.5.72 NBC
Gunsmoke   ep   10.30.72 CBS

OLSON, NANCY
Ford Theatre   ep   For the Love of Kitty   2.11.54 NBC
Video Theatre   ep   Spent in Silence   3.25.54 ABC
Best of Broadway   ep   The Royal Family   9.15.54 CBS
Producers Showcase   ep   The Women   2.7.55 NBC
Ford Star Jubilee   ep   High Tor   3.10.56 CBS
U.S. Steel Hour   ep   Second Chance   11.5.58 CBS
G.E. Theatre   ep   The Last Rodeo   12.7.58 CBS
Alfred Hitchcock Presents   ep   Total Loss   2.1.59 CBS
Ford Star Time   ep   The Greatest Man Alive   2.2.60
   NBC
Alcoa Premiere   ep   Family Outing   11.14.61 ABC
Channing   ep   Collision Course   11.6.63 ABC
Big Valley   ep   Night of the Wolf   12.1.65 ABC
Name of the Game   ep   Beware of the Watchdog   3.5.
   71 NBC
Gunsmoke   ep   2.7.72 CBS

O'NEAL, FREDERICK
Playwrights '56   ep   The Battler   10.18.55 NBC
Playwrights '56   ep   The Undiscovered Man   3.27.56
   NBC
Phil Silvers Show   ep   Love that Guardhouse   1.15.57
   CBS
Armstrong Circle Theatre   ep   Trail of Diamonds   4.
   15.59 CBS
Hallmark Hall of Fame   ep   The Green Pastures   10.
   17.57 NBC
The Killers   Sp   11.19.59 CBS
Play of the Week   ep   Simply Heavenly   12.7.59 NN
CBS TV Workshop   ep   My Theory about Girls   11.27.
   60 CBS
Hallmark Hall of Fame   ep   The Patriots   11.15.63 NBC

Breaking Point   ep   3.30.64 ABC
Kraft Suspense Theatre   ep   In Darkness Waiting   1.14.
   65, 1.21.65 NBC
Profiles in Courage   ep   1.31.65 NBC
Tarzan   ep   9.22.67 NBC

O'NEAL, PATRICK
Hallmark Hall of Fame   ep   The Road to Tara   3.14.54
   NBC
Cavalcade of America   ep   The Paper Sword   4.27.54
   ABC
Pepsi Cola Playhouse   ep   The Black Purse   5.14.54
   ABC
Pepsi Cola Playhouse   ep   Dear Little Fool   7.4.54
   ABC
Philco Playhouse   ep   The Catamaran   7.25.54 NBC
Studio One   ep   Sue Ellen   8.9.54 CBS
The Web   ep   The Bait   8.22.54 CBS
Playhouse   ep   Death the Hard Way   10.17.54 ABC
Goodyear Playhouse   ep   Do It Yourself   4.24.55 NBC
Treasury Men in Action   ep   Case of the Still Waters
   7.22.55 ABC
Appointment with Adventure   ep   Design for Trouble   8.
   28.55 CBS
Matinee Theatre   ep   The Catamaran   5.10.56 NBC
Alcoa Hour   ep   The Piper of St. James   7.8.56 NBC
The Millionaire   ep   The Story of Harvey Borden   11.
   28.56 CBS
Matinee Theatre   ep   Strong Medicine   12.28.56 NBC
On Trial   ep   The Deadly Chain   6.7.57 NBC
Dick and the Duchess   sr   9.28.57 CBS
Alcoa Premiere   ep   The Return of Mitchell Campion
   4.7.59 ABC
Ann Sothern Show   ep   Springtime for Katy   5.18.59
   CBS
The Millionaire   ep   Millionaire Elizabeth Tander   1.6.
   60 CBS
Diagnosis: Unknown   sr   7.5.60 CBS
Special for Women   ep   The Single Woman   2.9.61 NBC
Play of the Week   ep   The Magic and the Loss   2.20.61
   NN
Look up and Live   ep   The Interior Life   3.12.61 CBS
Look up and Live   ep   The Moment   3.19.61 CBS
Naked City   ep   The Sweetly Smiling Face of Truth   4.
   25.62 ABC
Defenders   ep   1.26.63 CBS
Nurses   ep   The Perfect Nurse   2.28.63 CBS

Eleventh Hour   ep   Five Moments out of Time   3.6.63
   NBC
Alcoa Premiere   ep   The Dark Labyrinth   3.21.63 ABC
Dr. Kildare   ep   Ship's Doctor   4.18.63 NBC
Route 66   ep   Same Picture, Different Frame   10.4.63
   CBS
Twilight Zone   ep   A Short Drink from a Certain Foun-
   tain   12.13.63 CBS
Defenders   ep   Fugue for Trumpet and Small Boy   12.
   28.63 CBS
Route 66   ep   Where There's a Will, There's a Way
   3.6.64, 3.13.64 CBS
Alfred Hitchcock Theatre   ep   Bed of Roses   5.22.64
   CBS
Defenders   ep   The Man Who   10.29.64 CBS
Bob Hope Chrysler Theatre   ep   The Loving Cup   1.29.
   65 NBC
FBI   ep   The Spy Master   2.6.66 ABC
Bob Hope Chrysler Theatre   ep   Dead Wrong   4.5.67
   NBC
Coronet Blue   ep   Six Months to Mars   8.14.67 CBS
Companions in Nightmare   tf   11.23.68 NBC
Alias Smith and Jones   ep   12.16.71 ABC
McCloud   ep   12.29.71 NBC
Columbo   ep   Blueprint for Murder   2.9.72 NBC
Marcus Welby, M.D.   ep   10.10.72 ABC
Cannon   ep   10.11.72 CBS
Cool Million   tf   10.16.72 NBC
FBI   ep   11.5.72 ABC
McCloud   ep   12.3.72 NBC

O'NEAL, RYAN
   Dobie Gillis   ep   The Hunger Strike   1.26.60 CBS
   Vikings   ep   spring, 1960 ABC
   G.E. Theatre   ep   The Playoff   11.20.60 CBS
   Nanette Fabray Show   ep   Nanette's Teen-age Suitor   2.
      24.61 NBC
   Bachelor Father   ep   Bentley and the Great Debate   4.
      13.61 NBC
   Nanette Fabray Show   ep   Nancy Comes Home   5.26.61
      NBC
   My Three Sons   ep   Chug and Robbie   5.17.62 ABC
   Empire   sr   9.25.62 NBC
   Our Man Higgins   ep   It's Higgins, Sir   10.3.62 ABC
   Virginian   ep   It Takes a Big Man   10.23.63 NBC
   Perry Mason   ep   The Case of the Bountiful Beauty   2.
      6.64 CBS

Peyton Place   sr   9.15.64 ABC
Wagon Train   ep   11.22.64 ABC
The Search   pt   7.29.68 CBS
Under the Yum Yum Tree   pt   9.2.69 ABC
Love Hate Love   tf   2.9.71 ABC

O'NEIL, BARBARA
Studio One   ep   Dark Possession   2.15.54 CBS
Studio One   ep   Romney   4.26.54 CBS
Philco Playhouse   ep   The Catamaran   7.25.54 NBC
Studio One   ep   Sue Ellen   8.9.54 CBS
Philco Playhouse   ep   Run Like a Thief   9.5.54 NBC
Studio One   ep   The Day Before the Wedding   7.4.55
   CBS
U.S. Steel Hour   ep   The Bride Cried   8.17.55 CBS
Studio One   ep   The Pilot   11.12.56 CBS
Studio One   ep   First Prize for Murder   9.16.57 CBS

OPATOSHU, DAVID
Studio One   ep   Riviera   1.2.50 CBS
Philco Playhouse   ep   The Big Deal   7.19.53 NBC
Bonimo   sr   9.12.53 NBC
Philco Playhouse   ep   The Mother   4.4.54 NBC
Philco Playhouse   ep   The Man in the Middle of the
   Ocean   8.8.54 NBC
U.S. Steel Hour   ep   Six O'Clock Call   2.1.55 ABC
Philco Playhouse   ep   A Business Proposition   10.23.55
   NBC
Philco Playhouse   ep   One Mummy Too Many   11.20.55
   NBC
Alcoa Hour   ep   Finkle's Comet   4.1.56 NBC
Studio One   ep   The Hollywood Complex   2.18.57 CBS
Studio One   ep   The Rice Sprout Song   4.15.57 CBS
Zane Grey Theatre   ep   Wire   1.31.58 CBS
Alfred Hitchcock Presents   ep   On the Nose   2.16.58
   CBS
Walter Winchell Show   ep   Silent City   3.7.58 ABC
G.E. Theatre   ep   No Hiding Place   4.6.58 CBS
Court of Last Resort   ep   The Allen Cutler Case   4.11.
   58 NBC
Jewish Appeal   ep   Where Is Thy Brother?   5.18.58
   NBC
Decision   ep   Man Against Crime   9.21.58 NBC
Behind Closed Doors   ep   3.5.59 NBC
Ann Sothern Show   ep   The Square Peg   6.29.59 CBS
Sunday Showcase   ep   What Makes Sammy Run   9.27.59,
   10.4.59 NBC

Adventures in Paradise ep The Bamboo Curtain 12.
  14.59 ABC
Alcoa Premiere ep Earthquake 1.12.60 ABC
Play of the Week ep He Who Gets Slapped 1.30.61
  NN
Alfred Hitchcock Theatre ep Strange Miracle 2.13.62
  NBC
Alcoa Premiere ep The Potentate 12.20.62 ABC
Twilight Zone ep Valley of the Shadow 1.17.63 CBS
Nurses ep The Saturday Evening of Time 3.14.63
  CBS
Dr. Kildare ep Hour of Decision 11.15.63 NBC
Alfred Hitchcock Theatre ep The Magic Shop 1.10.64
  CBS
Bob Hope Chrysler Theatre ep Two Is the Number 1.
  31.64 NBC
Outer Limits ep A Feasibility Study 4.13.64 ABC
Voyage to the Bottom of the Sea ep The Price of
  Doom 10.12.64 ABC
Profiles in Courage ep Robert Taft 1.3.65 NBC
Defenders ep The Unwritten Law 2.4.65 CBS
Perry Mason ep The Case of the Feather Clock 2.11.
  65 CBS
The Man from U.N.C.L.E. ep The Alexander the
  Greater Affair 9.17.65, 9.24.65 NBC
Dr. Kildare ep The Life Machine 10.26.65, 11.1.65,
  11.2.65, 11.9.65, 11.16.65 NBC
Run for Your Life ep A Girl Named Sorrow 11.22.65
  NBC
Loner ep Westward the Shoemaker 11.27.65 CBS
McHale's Navy ep 4.5.66 ABC
Time Tunnel ep 11.18.66 ABC
FBI ep 11.20.66 ABC
Mr. Terrific ep 1.23.67 ABC
Star Trek ep 2.23.67 NBC
Felony Squad ep Arrangement with Death 12.11.67,
  12.18.67 ABC
Daniel Boone ep 12.14.67 NBC
Maya cp 1.6.68 NBC
FBI ep The Homecoming 2.11.68 ABC
Name of the Game ep The Ordeal 11.22.68 NBC
The Smugglers tf 11.24.68 NBC
Mannix ep A Pittance of Faith 1.11.69 CBS
Hawaii Five-O ep 1.22.69 CBS
Mod Squad ep Captain Greer Call Surgery 4.1.69
  ABC
Mission Impossible ep Fool's Gold 10.26.69 CBS

It Takes a Thief ep 11.13.69 ABC
Ironside ep L'Chayim 12.4.69 NBC
The D.A.: Murder One tf 12.8.69 NBC
FBI ep 2.1.70 ABC
Mission Impossible ep 2.15.70 CBS
Daniel Boone ep 4.9.70 NBC
Incident in San Francisco tf 2.28.71 ABC
Hawaii Five-O ep 11.23.71 CBS
Medical Center ep The Corrupted 9.22.71 CBS
Streets of San Francisco ep 9.23.72 ABC
FBI ep 10.15.72 ABC

ORBACH, JERRY
Annie Get Your Gun Sp 3.19.67 NBC

O'SHEA, MICHAEL
Mirror Theatre ep Dreams Never Lie 10.31.53 CBS
Schlitz Playhouse of Stars ep Four Things He'd Do
2.5.54 CBS
It's a Great Life sr 9.7.54 NBC
Damon Runyon Theatre ep The Big Fix 7.23.55 CBS
Adventures in Paradise ep The Wonderful Nightingale
3.27.61 ABC

O'SHEA, MILO
Playhouse ep Do You Know the Milky Way 1.11.67
NN
Journey to the Unknown ep The New People 10.3.68
ABC
N.E.T. Playhouse ep Silent Song 1.24.69 NN
The Protectors ep 11.26.72 CBS

O'SULLIVAN, MAUREEN
Hollywood Opening Night ep The Lucky Coin 12.1.52
Ford Theatre ep They Also Serve 1.1.53 NBC
Schlitz Playhouse of Stars ep Parents' Week-End 3.
20.53 CBS
Ford Theatre ep The Trestle 6.11.53 NBC
Video Theatre ep Message in a Bottle 9.3.53 CBS
Four Star Playhouse ep The Gift 12.24.53 CBS
Ford Theatre ep Daughter of Mine 10.7.54 NBC
Fireside Theatre ep Brian 2.2.55 NBC
Climax ep The Great Impersonation 3.10.55 CBS
Casablanca ep 11.8.55 ABC
The Whistler ep Trademark 3.18.56 NN
Dupont Theatre ep The Blessed Midnight 12.18.56
ABC

Lux Video Theatre   ep   Michael and Mary   12. 27. 56
   NBC
Crossroads   ep   The Man Who Walked on Water   1. 4.
   57 ABC
Climax   ep   Let It Be Me   3. 21. 57 CBS
Playhouse 90   ep   Edge of Innocence   10. 31. 57 CBS
Alcoa Premiere   ep   Moment of Decision   10. 31. 57 CBS
Ben Casey   ep   A Boy Is Standing outside the Door   1.
   4. 65 ABC
The Crooked Hearts   tf   11. 8. 72 ABC

O'TOOLE, PETER
   Present Laughter   Sp   2. 28. 68 ABC

OWEN, REGINALD
   Alcoa Premiere   ep   The Dream   3. 3. 59 ABC
   World of Disney   ep   A Diamond Is a Boy's Best Friend
      10. 21. 59 ABC
   World of Disney   ep   From Ticonderoga to Disneyland
      11. 27. 60 ABC
   Thriller   ep   Trio for Terror   3. 14. 61 NBC
   Maverick   ep   A Technical Error   11. 26. 61 ABC
   Adventures in Paradise   ep   The Quest of Ambrose
      Feather   2. 11. 62 ABC
   Kentucky Jones   ep   3. 27. 65 NBC
   Camp Runamuck   ep   Spiffy Quits   12. 3. 65 NBC
   Run for Your Life   ep   The Borders of Barbarism   9.
      26. 66. NBC
   Bewitched   ep   11. 10. 66 ABC
   Bewitched   ep   2. 15. 68 ABC
   Queen and I   ep   1. 16. 69 CBS

-P-

PAAR, JACK
   Joey Bishop Show   ep   9. 27. 61 NBC

PACE, JUDY
   Tarzan   ep   1. 26. 68 NBC
   Mod Squad   ep   Bad Man on Campus   10. 1. 68 ABC
   N. Y. P. D.   ep   Deadly Circle of Violence   11. 12. 68
      ABC
   The Young Lawyers   tf   10. 28. 69 ABC
   New People   ep   The Prisoner of Bonamo   12. 29. 69 ABC
   The Young Lawyers   sr   9. 21. 70 ABC
   Oh, Nurse   pt   3. 17. 72 CBS

PAGE, GALE

    Goodyear Playhouse   ep   Buy Me Blue Ribbons   2.28.54 NBC

    Robert Montgomery Presents   ep   For These Services 4.5.54 NBC

    Robert Montgomery Presents   ep   Death and the Sky Above   13.55 NBC

    Robert Montgomery Presents   ep   Fourth of July   7.4. 55 NBC

    Robert Montgomery Presents   ep   The Tyrant   1.16.56 NBC

    Robert Montgomery Presents   ep   All Expenses Paid   5. 21.56 NBC

    Robert Montgomery Presents   ep   One Minute to Ditch 3.25.57 NBC

    Robert Montgomery Presents   ep   The Last Trip of the Hindenburg   6.10.57 NBC

    U.S. Steel Hour   ep   Crisis in Corona   10.23.57 CBS

    Eleventh Hour   ep   My Door Is Locked and Bolted   1.1. 64 NBC

PAGE, GERALDINE

    Summer Theatre   ep   The Shadowy Third   9.15.52 CBS

    Robert Montgomery Presents   ep   The Fall Guy   10.13. 52 NBC

    Philco Playhouse   ep   Miss Look-alike   5.9.54 NBC

    Omnibus   ep   The Turn of the Screw   2.13.55 CBS

    Windows   ep   A Domestic Dilemma   8.5.55 CBS

    U.S. Steel Hour   ep   Shoot It Again   10.26.55 CBS

    U.S. Steel Hour   ep   The Hill Wife   4.10.57 CBS

    Kraft Theatre   ep   Fire and Ice   6.12.57 NBC

    Playhouse 90   ep   Portrait of a Murderer   2.27.58 CBS

    G.E. Theatre   ep   No Hiding Place   4.6.58 CBS

    Playhouse 90   ep   Old Man   11.20.58 CBS

    Sunday Showcase   ep   People Kill People   9.20.59 NBC

    The Long Hot Summer   ep   Evil Angel   1.12.66 ABC

    Hallmark Hall of Fame   ep   Barefoot in Athens   11.11. 66 NBC

    A Christmas Memory   Sp   12.21.66 ABC

    The Thanksgiving Visitor   Sp   11.28.68 ABC

    Name of the Game   ep   A Sister from Napoli   1.8.71 NBC

    Hollywood Television Theatre   ep   Montserrat   3.21.71 NN

    Night Gallery   ep   Deliveries in the Rear   2.9.72 NBC

    Night Gallery   ep   The Sins of the Father   2.23.72 NBC

    CBS Playhouse   ep   Look Homeward, Angel 2.25.72 CBS

Medical Center   ep   10.18.72 CBS
Ghost Story   ep   12.8.72 NBC

PAGE, PATTI
Appointment with Adventure   ep   Paris Venture   2.26.56
    CBS
U.S. Steel Hour   ep   Upbeat   6.18.57 CBS
Bachelor Father   ep   A Song Is Born   12.12.61 ABC

PAGET, DEBRA
20th Century-Fox Hour   ep   Gun in His Hand   4.4.56
    CBS
Climax   ep   The Man Who Lost His Head   7.26.56 CBS
Climax   ep   Carnival at Midnight   1.3.57 CBS
Wagon Train   ep   The Marie Dupree Story   3.19.58 NBC
Cimarron City   ep   The Beauty and the Sorrow   2.7.59
    NBC
Wagon Train   ep   The Stagecoach Story   9.30.59 NBC
Man and the Challenge   ep   Invisible Force   10.17.59
    NBC
June Allyson Show   ep   No Place to Hide   12.21.59 CBS
Johnny Ringo   ep   1.7.60 CBS
The Millionaire   ep   Millionaire Mara Robinson   4.27.60
    CBS
Tales of Wells Fargo   ep   Man of Another Breed   12.2.
    61 NBC
Burke's Law   ep   Who Killed Eleanor Davis   12.20.63
    ABC
Burke's Law   ep   2.3.65 ABC

PAIGE, JANIS
It's Always Jan   sr   9.10.55 CBS
Lux Video Theatre   ep   The Latch Key   6.27.57 NBC
Schlitz Playhouse of Stars   ep   Home Again   1.7.58 CBS
Roberta   Sp   9.19.58 NBC
Desilu Playhouse   ep   Chez Rouge   2.16.59 CBS
Ann Sothern Show   ep   10.20.60 CBS
Wagon Train   ep   The Nellie Jefferson Story   4.5.61
    NBC
Chevy Show   ep   Happiest Day   4.23.61 NBC
87th Precinct   ep   4.30.62 NBC
Mystery Theatre   ep   Chez Rouge   8.8.62 NBC
Alcoa Premiere   ep   Blues for a Hanging   12.27.62 ABC
Dick Powell Theatre   ep   Last of the Private Eyes   4.
    30.63 NBC
Fugitive   ep   Ballad for a Ghost   12.29.64 ABC
Roberta   Sp (restaged)   11.6.69 NBC

Columbo   ep   Blueprint for Murder   2.9.72 NBC
Banacek   ep   11.15.72 NBC

PAIGE, MABEL
Fireside Theatre   ep   A Grand Grandma   10.7.52 NBC
Alan Young Show   sr   2.15.53 CBS
Omnibus   ep   The House   3.7.54 CBS
I Married Joan   ep   Mothers-in-Law   9.8.54 NBC

PAIGE, ROBERT
Bigelow Theatre   ep   The Lady's Companion   4.22.51
  CBS
Gruen Guild Playhouse   ep   The Bachelor's Week-end
  3.27.52 NN
Fireside Theatre   ep   The Rivals   5.13.52 NBC
The Unexpected   ep   Lifeline   6.11.52 NBC
Fireside Theatre   ep   The Serpent's Tongue   6.17.52
  NBC
Schaefer Century Theatre   ep   Mansion for Jimmy   8.
  6.52 NBC
Schaefer Century Theatre   ep   The Juvenile Genius   11.
  2.52 NBC
Fireside Theatre   ep   The Gift Horse   5.12.53 NBC
Lux Video Theatre   ep   The Lovely Day   8.13.53 CBS
Playhouse   ep   Melody in Black   11.6.53 ABC
Cavalcade of America   ep   Major Pauline   12.1.53 ABC
Pepsi Cola Playhouse   ep   Vacation Wife   12.4.53 ABC
Four Star Playhouse   ep   Lady of the Orchids   3.18.54
  CBS
Crossroads   ep   Coney Island Wedding   5.31.57 ABC
The Millionaire   ep   Millionaire Whitney Ames   1.20.60
  CBS
Barbara Stanwyck Theatre   ep   Size 10   1.16.61 NBC

PALANCE, JACK
Lights Out   ep   The Man Who Couldn't Remember   4.
  24.50 NBC
Studio One   ep   Little Man, Big World   10.13.52 CBS
Gulf Playhouse   ep   Necktie Party   10.24.52 NBC
The Web   ep   The Last Chance   2.22.53 CBS
Suspense   ep   The Kiss-Off   3.3.53 CBS
Suspense   ep   Cagliostro and the Chess Player   12.15.
  53 CBS
Playhouse 90   ep   Requiem for a Heavyweight   10.11.
  56 CBS
Zane Grey Theatre   ep   The Lariat   11.2.56 CBS
Playhouse 90   ep   The Last Tycoon   3.14.57 CBS

Playhouse 90   ep   The Death of Manolete   9. 12. 57 CBS
Rivak the Barbarian   Sp   10. 4. 60 NBC
The Greatest Show on Earth   sr   9. 17. 63 ABC
Convoy   ep   The Many Colors of Courage   10. 8. 65 NBC
Run for Your Life   ep   I Am the Late Diana Hays   9. 19.
    66 NBC
Alice Through the Looking Glass   Sp   11. 6. 66 NBC
The Man from U. N. C. L. E.   ep   11. 25. 66,   12. 2. 66 NBC
Dr. Jekyll and Mr. Hyde   Sp   1. 7. 68 ABC

PALMER, BETSY
    Summer Studio One   ep   Sentence of Death   8. 17. 53 CBS
    Summer Studio One   ep   Look Homeward, Hayseed   9. 7.
        53 CBS
    TV Sound Stage   ep   Too Little a Kiss   12. 11. 53 NBC
    Studio One   ep   The Role of Lover   2. 22. 54 CBS
    U. S. Steel Hour   ep   Haven's End   7. 6. 54 ABC
    Studio One   ep   A Guest at the Embassy   7. 12. 54 CBS
    Goodyear Playhouse   ep   Dear Harriet Heart-Throb   7.
        18. 54 NBC
    Goodyear Playhouse   ep   Recoil   8. 15. 54 NBC
    The Web   ep   The Bait   8. 22. 54 CBS
    Philco Playhouse   ep   The Ghost Writer   5. 29. 55 NBC
    Appointment with Adventure   ep   The Secret of Juan Val-
        dez   6. 12. 55 CBS
    Goodyear Playhouse   ep   The Prizewinner   7. 3. 55 NBC
    U. S. Steel Hour   ep   The Meanest Man in the World   7.
        6. 55 CBS
    Appointment with Adventure   ep   Dangerous Mayhen   8.
        18. 55 CBS
    Armstrong Circle Theatre   ep   Actuals   9. 27. 55 NBC
    Front Row Center   ep   Strange Suspicion   1. 15. 56 CBS
    G. E. Theatre   ep   Summer Promise   1. 29. 56 CBS
    Goodyear Playhouse   ep   Career Girl   4. 22. 56 NBC
    Kraft Theatre   ep   The Girl Who Saw Too Much   8. 29.
        56 NBC
    Climax   ep   Burst of Violence   9. 13. 56 CBS
    Studio One   ep   Goodbye Piccadilly   12. 31. 56 CBS
    Alcoa Hour   ep   Protege   5. 19. 57 NBC
    Goodyear Playhouse   ep   Rumbling Galleries   7. 28. 57
        NBC
    Studio One   ep   Mutiny on the Shark   9. 23. 57,   9. 30. 57
        CBS
    Kraft Theatre   ep   The Category Is Murder   11. 6. 57
        NBC
    Climax   ep   A Matter of Life and Death   11. 21. 57 CBS
    Playhouse 90   ep   No Time at All   2. 13. 58 CBS

U.S. Steel Hour   ep   Give Me My Son   3.12.58 CBS
U.S. Steel Hour   ep   Climate of Marriage   7.30.58
    CBS
Playhouse 90   ep   The Time of Your Life   10.9.58 CBS
U.S. Steel Hour   ep   The Enemies   12.3.58 CBS
U.S. Steel Hour   ep   The Wayward Widow   5.6.59 CBS
The Ballad of Louie the Louse   Sp   10.17.59 CBS
U.S. Steel Hour   ep   Game of Hearts   6.1.60 CBS
U.S. Steel Hour   ep   Shame the Devil   12.14.60 CBS
Hallmark Hall of Fame   ep   A Punt, a Pass, and a
    Prayer   11.20.68 NBC
Love American Style   ep   12.8.72 ABC

PALMER, LILI
    Lux Video Theatre   ep   Three Hours Between Planes
        10.27.52 CBS
    U.S. Steel Hour   ep   The Manin Possession   12.8.53
        ABC
    Four Star Playhouse   ep   Lady of the Orchids   3.18.54
        CBS
    Hallmark Hall of Fame   ep   The Taming of the Shrew
        3.18.56 NBC
    Lili Palmer Theatre   sh/sr   1956 NN
    Diary of Anne Frank   Sp   11.26.67 ABC
    Hauser's Memory   tf   11.24.70 NBC

PALMER, MARIA
    Schaefer Century Theatre   ep   12.14.52 NBC
    The Turning Point   ep   Autumn Flames   2.19.53 ABC
    Fireside Theatre   ep   Unexpected Wife   3.24.53 NBC
    Schlitz Playhouse of Stars   ep   19 Rue Marie   3.13.53
        CBS
    Appointment with Love   ep   Joe Santa Claus   4.24.53 ABC
    Life of Riley   ep   7.9.54 NBC
    Four Star Playhouse   ep   The Wallet   10.21.54 CBS
    TV Reader's Digest   ep   Comrade Lindemann's Consci-
        ence   6.26.55 ABC
    Brave Eagle   ep   The Storm Fool   2.29.56 CBS
    Charlie Farrell Show   ep   8.13.56 CBS
    Desilu Playhouse   ep   Debut   10.27.58 CBS
    Gale Storm Show   ep   Susanna the Matchmaker   11.22.
        58 CBS
    Alcoa Presents   ep   The Secret   4.21.59 ABC
    Hawaiian Eye   ep   The Pretty People   5.10.61 ABC
    FBI   ep   12.3.67 ABC
    Rawhide   ep   The Immigrants   3.16.62 CBS
    Perry Mason   ep   The Case of the Borrowed Baby   4.

14. 62 CBS
Perry Mason ep The Case of the Lawful Lazarus 3.
14. 63 CBS
Hawaiian Eye ep The Pretty People 5. 7. 63 ABC

PAPAS, IRENE
Climax ep The Disappearance of Daphne 5. 15. 58 CBS

PARKER, ELEANOR
Drama ep The Gambler, the Nun and the Radio 5. 19.
60 CBS
Checkmate ep The Renaissance of Gussie Hill 1. 17.
62 CBS
Eleventh Hour ep Why Am I Grown So Cold 2. 6. 63
NBC
Bob Hope Chrysler Theatre ep Seven Miles of Bad
Roads 10. 18. 63 NBC
Breaking Point ep A Land More Cruel 1. 27. 64 ABC
Kraft Suspense Theatre ep Knight's Gambit 3. 26. 64
NBC
Convoy ep Lady on the Rock 10. 15. 65 NBC
The Man from U. N. C. L. E. ep The Seven Wonders of
the World Affair 1. 8. 68, 1. 15. 68 NBC
Bracken's World sr 9. 19. 69 NBC
Hans Brinker Sp 12. 13. 69 NBC
Maybe I'll Come Home in the Spring tf 2. 16. 71 ABC
Vanished tf 3. 8. 71, 3. 9. 71 NBC
Ghost Story ep 11. 3. 72 NBC
Home for the Holidays tf 11. 28. 72 ABC

PARKER, FESS
World of Disney ep Davy Crockett, Indian Fighter 12.
15. 54 ABC
World of Disney ep Davy Crockett Goes to Congress
1. 26. 55 ABC
World of Disney ep Davy Crockett at the Alamo 2. 23.
55 ABC
My Little Margie ep The All American 6. 15. 55 NBC
World of Disney ep Davy Crockett and the Keelboat
Race 11. 16. 55 ABC
World of Disney ep Davy Crockett and the River Pi-
rates 12. 14. 55 ABC
Death Valley Days ep Kickapoo Run 8. 29. 56 NBC
World of Disney ep Along the Oregon Trail 2. 20. 57
ABC
Playhouse 90 ep Turn Left at Mt. Everest 4. 3. 58 CBS
Schlitz Playhouse of Stars ep The Hasty Hanging 10.

10. 58 CBS
G. E. Theatre ep Aftermath 4. 17. 60 CBS
World of Disney ep Ambush at Wagon Gap 2. 18. 61,
    2. 26. 61 ABC
World of Disney ep Whiteman's Medicine 2. 26. 61 ABC
World of Disney ep The Secret Mission 5. 7. 61, 5.
    14. 61 ABC
Mr. Smith (Goes to Washington) sr 9. 29. 62 ABC
Alfred Hitchcock Theatre ep Nothing Ever Happens in
    Linsvale 11. 8. 63 CBS
Destry ep Destry Has a Little Lamb 2. 21. 64 ABC
Daniel Boone sr 9. 24. 64 NBC
Daniel Boone sr ret 9. 16. 65 NBC
Daniel Boone sr ret 9. 15. 66 NBC
Daniel Boone sr ret 9. 14. 67 NBC
Daniel Boone sr ret 9. 19. 68 NBC
Daniel Boone sr ret 9. 16. 69 NBC
Climb an Angry Mountain tf 12. 23. 72 NBC

PARKER, JEAN
Pulitzer Prize Playhouse ep Wisdom Tooth 3. 2. 51
    ABC
Starlight Theatre ep Be Nice to Mr. Campbell 12. 5.
    51 CBS
Damon Runyon Theatre ep Barbecue 12. 3. 55 CBS
Matinee Theatre ep Dinner at Antoine's 3. 5. 56 NBC
Private Secretary ep 3. 18. 56 CBS

PARKER, SUZY
Playhouse 90 ep The Death of Manolete 9. 12. 57 CBS
Burke's Law ep Who Killed Holly Howard? 9. 20. 63
    ABC
Burke's Law ep Who Killed Alex Debbs 10. 25. 63
    ABC
Twilight Zone ep Number 12 Looks Just Like You 1.
    24. 64 CBS
Dr. Kildare ep Maybe Love Will Save My Apartment
    House 10. 1. 64 NBC
Rogues ep Fringe Benefits 11. 22. 64 NBC
Tarzan ep 12. 2. 66 NBC
Bob Hope Chrysler Theatre ep Free of Charge 3. 22.
    67 NBC
It Takes a Thief ep 1. 30. 68 ABC
Night Gallery ep The Housekeeper 12. 16. 70 NBC

PARKER, WILLARD
Schlitz Playhouse of Stars ep Mr. and Mrs. Trouble

8. 22. 52 CBS
Schlitz Playhouse of Stars ep 22 Sycamore Road 6.5.
    53 CBS
Ford Theatre ep Kiss and Forget 12.3.53 NBC
Schlitz Playhouse of Stars ep Little War in San Dede
    5. 28. 54 CBS
Fireside Theatre ep A Mother's Duty 12.28.54 NBC
Schlitz Playhouse of Stars ep Visitor in the Night 3.
    11. 55 CBS
Ford Theatre ep The Mumbys 6.23.55 NBC
Tales of the Texas Rangers sr 9.3.55 CBS

PARKINS, BARBARA
Leave It to Beaver ep No Time for Babysitters 10.7.
    61 ABC
Wagon Train ep The Mark Minor Story 11.15.61 NBC
G. E. Theatre ep We're Holding Your Son 12.3.61
    CBS
G. E. Theatre ep A Friendly Tribe 12.31.61 CBS
Perry Mason ep The Case of the Unsuitable Uncle
    11. 8. 62 CBS
Dr. Kildare ep The Soul Killer 11.22.62 NBC
Laramie ep The Wedding Party 1.39.63 NBC
Wide Country ep The Lucky Punch 4.18.63 NBC
Peyton Place sr 9.15.64 ABC
A Taste of Evil tf 10.12.71 ABC
Double Play ep Ghost Story 3.17.62 NBC

PARKS, BERT
Burke's Law ep 2.21.64 ABC
Burke's Law ep 3.3.65 ABC

PARKS, LARRY
Ford Theatre ep The Happiest Day 1.21.54 NBC
Ford Theatre ep Wedding March 4.22.54 NBC
Ford Theatre ep Tomorrow We'll Love 2.17.55 NBC
Ford Theatre ep A Smattering of Bliss 11.17.55
    NBC
Ford Theatre ep The Penlands and the Poodle 1.23.
    57 ABC
Suspicion ep Diagnosis: Death 3.31.58 NBC
Straightaway ep Pledge a Nightmare 12.1.61 ABC
Untouchables ep The Lily Dallas Story 3.16.61 ABC
Dr. Kildare ep Breakdown 11.8.62 NBC

PARKS, MICHAEL
Detectives ep Personal Enemy 2.10.61 ABC

Asphalt Jungle   ep   The Sniper   4.30.61 ABC
Stoney Burke   ep   The Riders   10.29.62 ABC
Sam Benedict   ep   Too Many Strangers   12.8.62 NBC
Perry Mason   ep   The Case of Constant Doyle   1.31.63
   CBS
77 Sunset Strip   ep   Crashout   2.1.63 ABC
Alfred Hitchcock Theatre   ep   Diagnosis: Danger   3.1.
   63 CBS
Ben Casey   ep   Father Was an Intern   4.1.63 ABC
Wagon Train   ep   Heather and Hamish   4.10.63 ABC
Eleventh Hour   ep   Pressure Breakdown   5.15.63 NBC
Gallant Men   ep   A Place to Die   6.1.63 ABC
The Greatest Show on Earth   ep   The Hanging Man   11.
   19.63 ABC
Alfred Hitchcock Theatre   ep   The Cadaver   11.29.63
   CBS
Wagon Train   ep   The Michael Malone Story   1.6.64
   ABC
Channing   ep   Another Kind of Music   1.22.64 ABC
Route 66   ep   Cries of Persons Close to One   1.31.64
   CBS
Bob Hope Chrysler Theatre   ep   A Time for Killing
   4.30.65 NBC
Stranger on the Run   tf   10.31.67 NBC
A Hatful of Rain   Sp   3.3.68 ABC
Then Came Bronson   tf   3.24.69 NBC
Then Came Bronson   sr   9.17.69 NBC
The Young Lawyers   tf   10.28.69 ABC

PARRISH, HELEN
   Racket Squad   ep   Bill of Sale   11.29.51 CBS
   Fireside Theatre   ep   The Critic   1.20.53 NBC
   20th Century Tales   ep   Step Daughter   2.25.53 ABC
   The Curtain Rises   ep   Yang, Yin and Mrs. Wiswell
      3.16.53 ABC
   Cavalcade of America   ep   John Yankee   6.10.53 NBC
   TV Reader's Digest   ep   If I Were Rich   11.28.55 ABC
   Crossroads   ep   God in the Street   5.25.56 ABC

PARSONS, ESTELLE
   Dupont Show of the Month   ep   The Gambling Heart   2.
      23.64 NBC
   Patty Duke Show   ep   The Con Artists   2.26.64 ABC
   The Front Page   Sp   1.31.70 NN
   N.E.T. Playhouse   ep   A Memory of Two Mondays   1.
      28.71 NN
   Medical Center   ep   9.13.72 CBS

Medical Center   ep   10.4.72 CBS

PATTERSON, ELIZABETH
Pulitzer Prize Playhouse   ep   Our Town   12.1.50 ABC
G.E. Theatre   ep   The Marriage Fix   11.29.53 CBS
Pitfall   ep   The Hot Welcome   7.18.54 NN
Four Star Playhouse   ep   Vote of Confidence   11.11.54
   CBS
Stage 7   ep   The Legacy   2.13.55 CBS
Climax   ep   The Adventures of Huckleberry Finn   9.1.55
   CBS
Playwrights '56   ep   The Day the Trains Stopped Run-
   ning   1.3.56 NBC
Climax   ep   Gamble on a Thief   2.2.56 CBS
Front Row Center   ep   Search for a Stranger   3.25.56
   CBS
Ford Theatre   ep   On the Beach   4.12.56 NBC
Playhouse 90   ep   Mr. and Mrs. McAdam   1.10.57 CBS
Climax   ep   Don't Ever Come Back   2.28.57 CBS
Ford Theatre   ep   Cross Hairs   6.12.57 ABC
Playhouse 90   ep   Portrait of a Murderer   2.27.58 CBS
Alfred Hitchcock Presents   ep   Bull in a China Shop   3.
   30.58 CBS
77 Sunset Strip   ep   Pasadena Caper   3.13.59 ABC
Staccato   ep   Evil   10.29.59 NBC
Playhouse 90   ep   Tomorrow   3.7.60 CBS
Barbara Stanwyck Theatre   ep   Big Career   2.13.61
   NBC

PATTERSON, NEVA
Video Theatre   ep   Second Generation   1.8.50 NBC
Television Theatre   ep   The Silent Room   2.15.50 NBC
Philco Playhouse   ep   Confession   1.21.51 NBC
The Web   ep   Checkmate   6.13.51 CBS
Philco Playhouse   ep   A Little Night Music   11.18.51
   NBC
Betty Crocker Star Matinee   ep   The Shining Hour   12.
   15.71 ABC
Goodyear Playhouse   ep   Tour of Duty   2.3.52 NBC
Goodyear Playhouse   ep   The Lantern Copy   5.25.52
   NBC
The Doctor   ep   Night Riders in an Apartment   12.28.52
   NBC
Goodyear Playhouse   ep   The Power of Suggestion   8.29.
   54 NBC
Satins and Spurs   Sp   9.12.54 NBC
Elgin Hour   ep   High Man   11.2.54 ABC

Best of Broadway   ep   The Philadelphia Story   12.8.54
   CBS
Philco Playhouse   ep   Walk into the Night   1.9.55 NBC
Kraft Theatre   ep   Departure   2.16.55 NBC
You Are There   ep   The Triumph of Alexander the
   Great   3.27.55 CBS
G.E. Theatre   ep   O, Lonely Moon   4.17.55 CBS
Doctors/Nurses   ep   Night of the Witch   2.2.65 CBS
Danger   ep   Wire Top   3.15.55 CBS
Studio One   ep   Cross My Heart   4.4.55 CBS
G.E. Theatre   ep   A Man with a Vengeance   5.15.55
   CBS
U.S. Steel Hour   ep   Obsession   10.12.55 CBS
Appointment with Adventure   ep   Stranger in Rio   10.23.
   55 CBS
Omnibus   ep   Dear Brutus   8.56 CBS
Studio One   ep   My Son Johnny   1.30.56 CBS
Alcoa Hour   ep   Man on Fire   3.4.56 NBC
Omnibus   ep   The Billy Mitchell Courtmartial   4.1.56
   CBS
Goodyear Playhouse   ep   Your Every Wish   6.16.57
   NBC
Matinee Theatre   ep   The Tender Leaves   12.20.57 NBC
Playhouse 90   ep   Reunion   1.2.58 CBS
The Man in the Dog Suit   Sp   1.8.60 NBC
Our American Heritage   ep   Millionaire's Mite   4.10.60
   NBC
Moment of Fear   ep   Total Recall   7.29.60 NBC
Ben Casey   ep   An Expensive Glass of Water   10.30.61
   ABC
Defenders   ep   The Empty Chute   2.17.62 CBS
U.S. Steel Hour   ep   The White Lie   10.3.62 CBS
Naked City   ep   Color Schemes Like Never Before   5.1.
   63 ABC
Nurses   ep   Express Stop from Lenox Avenue   5.9.63
   CBS
Lieutenant   ep   Mother Enemy   4.4.64 NBC
Patty Duke Show   ep   My Cousin, the Hero   5.12.65
   ABC
Felony Squad   ep   The Fatal Hour   11.29.68 ABC
Governor and J.J.   sr   9.23.69 CBS
Governor and J.J.   sr ret   9.23.70 CBS
Nichols   sr   9.16.71 NBC
Hollywood Television Theatre   ep   The Police   10.14.71
   NN
Owen Marshall ep   Who Saw Him Die   11.2.72 ABC
Cannon   ep   12.13.72 CBS

PAVAN, MARISSA
    Fireside Theatre   ep   10.26.54 NBC
    Studio One   ep   Dominique   3.28.55 CBS
    Front Row Center   ep   Meeting at Mayerling   9.21.55
      CBS
    Alfred Hitchcock Presents   ep   You Got to Have Luck
      1.15.56 CBS
    Kaiser Aluminum Hour   ep   Antigone   9.11.56 NBC
    Climax   ep   Keep Me in Mind   11.7.57 CBS
    Frank Sinatra Show   ep   The Man on the Stairs   3.21.
      58 ABC
    Playhouse 90   ep   Target for Three   10.1.59 CBS
    Desilu Playhouse   ep   Come Back to Sorrento   11.6.59
      CBS
    U.S. Steel Hour   ep   Girl in the Gold Bathtub   5.4.60
      CBS
    Hallmark Hall of Fame   ep   Shangri-La   10.24.60 NBC
    Naked City   ep   Requiem for a Sunday Afternoon   12.6.
      61 ABC
    Breaking Point   ep   Bird and Snake   10.7.63 ABC
    Naked City   ep   No Naked Ladies in Front of Giovanni's
      House   4.17.63 ABC
    Combat   ep   Ambush   12.3.63 ABC
    Bob Hope Chrysler Theatre   ep   A Wind of Hurricane
      Force   2.7.64 NBC
    FBI   ep   The Exiles   11.14.65 ABC
    Cutter's Trail   2.6.70 CBS

PAYNE, JOHN
    Schlitz Playhouse of Stars   ep   The Name Is Bellingham
      10.12.51 CBS
    Schlitz Playhouse of Stars   ep   Exit   12.14.51 CBS
    Robert Montgomery Presents   ep   The Deep Six   11.16.
      53 NBC
    Best of Broadway   ep   The Philadelphia Story   12.8.54
      CBS
    G.E. Theatre   ep   Lash of Fear   10.16.55 CBS
    Hallmark Hall of Fame   ep   Alice in Wonderland   10.23.
      55 NBC
    Studio 57   ep   Deadline   2.26.56 NN
    Zane Grey Theatre   ep   Until the Man Dies   1.25.57
      CBS
    Schlitz Playhouse of Stars   ep   The Restless Gun   3.29.
      57 CBS
    The Restless Gun   sr   9.23.57 NBC
    The Restless Gun   sr ret   9.58 NBC
    O'Conner's Ocean   pt   12.13.60 NBC

G. E. Theatre ep The Little Hours 1.21.62 CBS
Name of the Game ep Fear of High Places 9.20.68
NBC
Gunsmoke ep 10.12.70 CBS
Cade's County ep 12.12.71 CBS

PECK, GREGORY
Dick Powell Theatre ep hos 1.8.63 NBC

PEPPARD, GEORGE
Kraft Theatre ep Flying Object at Three O'Clock High
6.20.56 NBC
Studio One ep A Walk in the Forest 2.11.57 CBS
Alcoa Hour ep The Big Buildup 3.31.57 NBC
Matinee Theatre ep Aftermath 5.20.57 NBC
Kraft Theatre ep The Long Flight 6.3.57 NBC
Alfred Hitchcock Presents ep The Diplomatic Corpse
12.8.57 CBS
Suspicion ep The Eye of Truth 3.17.58 NBC
Hallmark Hall of Fame ep Little Moon of Alban 3.24.
58 NBC
Matinee Theatre ep End of the Rope 3.24.58 NBC
Ford Star Time ep Incident at a Corner 4.5.60 NBC
Our American Heritage ep The Invincible Teddy 1.13.
61 NBC
Bob Hope Chrysler Theatre ep The Game with Glass
Pieces 5.1.64 NBC
The Bravos tf 1.9.72 ABC
Banacek tf 3.20.72 NBC
Banacek sr 9.13.72 NBC

PERKINS, MILLIE
Wagon Train ep The Will Santee Story 5.3.61 NBC
U.S. Steel Hour ep Street of Love 9.20.61 CBS
Breaking Point ep Solo for B-Flat Clarinet 9.16.63
ABC
Reporter ep Rope's End 10.16.64 CBS

PERKINS, TONY
Kraft Theatre ep The Missing Year 2.3.54 NBC
Armstrong Circle Theatre ep The Fugitive 3.16.54
NBC
Man Behind the Badge ep The Case of the Narcotics
Rackets 9.5.54 CBS
G. E. Theatre ep Mr. Blue Ocean 5.1.55 CBS
Windows ep The World Out There 7.22.55 CBS
Kraft Theatre ep Home Is the Hero 1.25.56 NBC

Studio One   ep   The Silent Gun   2.6.56 CBS
Front Row Center   ep   Winter Dreams   2.19.56 CBS
Goodyear Playhouse   ep   Joey   3.25.56 NBC
ABC Stage 67   ep   Evening Primrose   11.16.66 ABC
How Awful About Allan   tf   9.22.70 ABC

PERREAU, GIGI
Video Theatre   ep   The Girl Who Couldn't Cry   4.15.54
    CBS
Ford Theatre   ep   Unbroken Promise   12.30.54 NBC
Gloria Swanson Theatre   ep   Was It Red   1.11.55 ABC
Four Star Playhouse   ep   The Wild Bunch   2.17.55 CBS
Studio One   ep   I Do   4.30.56 CBS
Ford Theatre   ep   The Lie   6.5.57 ABC
Perry Mason   ep   The Case of the Desperate Daughter
    3.22.58 CBS
Goldie   sr   10.1.59 CBS
Alfred Hitchcock Presents   ep   Graduating Class   12.27.
    59 CBS
Rifleman   ep   2.23.60 ABC
Islanders   ep   Flight from Terror   10.9.60 ABC
Stagecoach West   ep   The Land Beyond   10.11.60 ABC
Laramie   ep   The Dark Trail   11.1.60 NBC
Rebel   ep   Don Gringo   11.20.60 ABC
Rawhide   ep   Incident at Poco Tiempo   12.9.60 CBS
Rebel   ep   The Promise   1.15.61 ABC
Roaring 20s   ep   The Twelfth Hour   3.18.61 ABC
Surfside 6   ep   Spring Training   4.3.61 ABC
Hawaiian Eye   ep   It Ain't Cricket   4.12.61 ABC
Rifleman   ep   Death Trap   5.9.61 ABC
Lassie   ep   2.22.64 CBS
Lassie   ep   3.1.64 CBS
Perry Mason   ep   The Case of the Sleepy Slayer   10.15.
    64 CBS
Many Happy Returns   ep   1.25.65 CBS
My Three Sons   ep   2.4.65 ABC
Gomer Pyle, U.S.M.C.   ep   1.21.66 CBS
Tarzan   ep   The Prodigal Puma   10.21.66 NBC
Iron Horse   ep   Death by Triangulation   3.20.67 ABC

PETERS, BROCK
The Snows of Kilimanjaro   Sp   3.25.60 CBS
Sam Benedict   ep   Accomplice   3.9.63 NBC
Great Adventure   ep   Go Down, Moses   11.1.63 CBS
Eleventh Hour   ep   Who Is to Say How the Battle Is to Be
    Fought   3.11.64 NBC
Doctors/Nurses   ep   A Family Resemblance   11.17.64
    CBS

Rawhide   ep   The Spanish Camp   5.7.65 CBS
Loner   ep   The Homecoming of Lemuel Stove   11.20.65
   CBS
Trials of O'Brian   ep   The Only Game in Town   3.18.66
   CBS
Run for Your Life   ep   Night Train from Chicago   4.11.
   66 NBC
The Girl from U.N.C.L.E.   ep   1.20.66 NBC
Mission Impossible   ep   10.29.67 CBS
Tarzan   ep   The Last of the Supermen   11.3.67 NBC
Judd for the Defense   ep   12.1.67 ABC
It Takes a Thief   ep   12.31.68 ABC
Judd for the Defense   ep   The Law and Order Blues   1.
   31.69 ABC
Felony Squad   ep   1.31.69 ABC
Outcasts   ep   Act of Faith   2.10.69 ABC
Gunsmoke   ep   The Good Samaritan   3.10.69 CBS
Mannix   ep   Time Out of Mind   10.3.70 CBS
Longstreet   ep   Elegy in Brass   10.14.71 ABC
Mod Squad   ep   Death of a Nobody   12.7.71 ABC
Welcome Home, Johnny Bristol   tf   1.30.72 CBS

PETERS, SUSAN
Miss Susan   sr   3.5.51 NBC

PETTET, JOANNE
Doctors/Nurses   ep   A Dangerous Silence   3.2.65 CBS
Trials of O'Brien   ep   Picture Me a Murder   11.27.65
   CBS
Fugitive   ep   Shadow of the Swan   2.8.66 ABC
Dr. Kildare   ep   The Taste of Crow   2.21.66, 2.22.66,
   3.1.66, 3.7.66, 3.8.66 NBC
Three for Danger   pt   9.8.67 NBC
Night Gallery   ep   The House   12.30.70 NBC
Mannix   ep   A Button for General D   11.17.71 CBS
Night Gallery   ep   Keep in Touch   11.24.71 NBC
The Delphi Bureau   tf   3.6.72 ABC
Miss Stewart   pt   3.31.72 CBS
Banacek   ep   9.27.72 NBC
Night Gallery   ep   The Girl with the Hungry Eyes   10.
   1.72 NBC
Footsteps   tf   10.3.72 CBS
The Weekend Nun   tf   12.20.72 ABC

PHILLIPS, MARGARET
Philco Playhouse   ep   1.22.50 NBC
Starlight Theatre   ep   White Mail   4.24.50 CBS

Studio One   ep   Wreath of Roses   5.8.50 CBS
Masterpiece Theatre   ep   Hedda Gabler   7.23.50 NBC
Masterpiece Theatre   ep   The Importance of Being
    Earnest   8.20.50 NBC
Kraft Theatre   ep   Interference   10.24.51 NBC
Goodyear Playhouse   ep   Eleventh War   11.25.51 NBC
Robert Montgomery Presents   ep   Top Secret   12.3.51
    NBC
Kraft Theatre   ep   The Iron Gate   12.3.52 NBC
Robert Montgomery Presents   ep   Victory   12.15.52
    NBC
Tales of Tomorrow   ep   The Evil Within   5.1.53 ABC
Kraft Theatre   ep   Corinth House   8.12.53 NBC
Summer Studio One   ep   The Gathering Night   8.24.53
    CBS
Robert Montgomery Presents   ep   Breakdown   10.5.53
    NBC
Omnibus   ep   King Lear   10.18.53 CBS
Danger   ep   The Educated Heart   11.17.53 CBS
Inner Sanctum   ep   Identity Unknown   4.2.54 NN
U.S. Steel Hour   ep   Oberstrasse 49   8.3.54 ABC
Robert Montgomery Presents   ep   Judith   11.29.54 NBC
Studio One   ep   Mr. Brimmer Did It   4.25.55 CBS
Appointment with Adventure   ep   Career   3.11.56 CBS
Climax   ep   The Volcano Seat   4.10.58 CBS
Five Fingers   ep   Search for Evard Stoyan   1.9.60 NBC
Alcoa Premiere   ep   Call from Tomorrow   1.26.60
    ABC
Rawhide   ep   Incident of the Dusty Flower   3.4.60 CBS
Golden Showcase   ep   The Picture of Dorian Gray   12.
    6.61 CBS
Checkmate   ep   The Sound of Nervous Laughter   2.14.
    62 CBS
Route 66   ep   Love Is a Skinny Kid   4.6.62 CBS

PIAZZA, MARGUERITE
    Airflyte Theatre   ep   The Box Supper   10.19.50 CBS
    Musical Comedy Time   ep   Mme. Modiste   2.5.51 NBC
    Shower of Stars   ep   High Pitch   5.12.55 CBS

PICKENS, JANE
    U.S. Steel Hour   ep   To Die Alone   1.16.57 CBS

PICKENS, SLIM
    Wagon Train   ep   The Tent City Story   12.10.58 NBC
    Overland Trail   ep   Sour Annie   5.8.60 NBC
    Americans   ep   The Escape   3.13.61 NBC

Outlaws   sr   10.5.61 NBC
Route 66   ep   A Long Piece of Mischief   1.19.62 CBS
Wide Country   ep   Tears on a Painted Face   11.29.62
    NBC
Wagon Train   ep   The Eve Newhope Story   12.5.62 NBC
Wide Country   ep   Memory of a Filly   1.3.63 NBC
Wide Country   ep   Don't Cry for Johnny Devlin   1.24.63
    NBC
Bonanza   ep   Half a Rogue   1.27.63 NBC
Wide Country   ep   Speckled Bird   1.31.63 NBC
Wide Country   ep   The Man Who Runs Away   2.7.63
    NBC
The Travels of Jaimie McPheeters   ep   The Day of the
    Homeless   12.7.63 ABC
Gunsmoke   ep   2.1.64 CBS
Bonanza   ep   King of the Mountain   2.23.64 NBC
The Man from U.N.C.L.E.   ep   The Iowa Scuba Affair
    9.29.64 ABC
Virginian   ep   Big Image, Little Man   10.28.64 NBC
Rawhide   ep   The Backshooter   11.27.64 CBS
Gunsmoke   ep   1.15.66 CBS
Daniel Boone   ep   1.20.66 NBC
Jesse James   ep   Wanted: Dead Only   5.2.66 ABC
Daniel Boone   ep   9.15.66 NBC
Run for Your Life   ep   3.13.67 NBC
Custer   sr   9.6.67 ABC
Cimarron Strip   ep   The Assassins   1.11.68 CBS
Gentle Ben   ep   3.24.68 CBS
Outcasts   ep   9.23.68 ABC
Bonanza   ep   10.27.68 NBC
Mannix   ep   1.18.69 CBS
Ironside   ep   Good-by to Yesterday   9.25.69 NBC
Medical Center   ep   The Professional   3.11.70 CBS
Bonanza   ep   What Are Pardners For   4.2.70 NBC
Name of the Game   ep   11.6.70 NBC
Gunsmoke   ep   The Scavengers   11.16.70 CBS
Alias Smith and Jones   ep   Exit from Wickenburg   1.28.
    71 ABC
Alias Smith and Jones   ep   The Man Who Murdered Him-
    self   3.18.71 ABC
Alias Smith and Jones   ep   9.16.71 ABC
The Devil and Miss Sarah   tf   12.4.71 ABC
Gunsmoke   ep   9.11.72, 9.18.72 CBS
Alias Smith and Jones   ep   The Strange Fate of Conrad
    Meyer Zulick   12.2.72 ABC

PICON, MOLLY
  Startime   ep   The Jazz Singer   10.13.59 NBC
  Car 54 Where Are You   ep   I Won't Go   10.15.61 NBC
  Car 54 Where Are You   ep   Occupancy, August 1   10.
    21.62 NBC
  Car 54 Where Are You   ep   Joan Crawford Didn't Say
    No   3.17.63 NBC
  Dr. Kildare   ep   The Eleventh Commandment   11.14.63
    NBC
  My Friend Tony   ep   5.18.69 NBC

PIDGEON, WALTER
  Zane Grey Theatre   ep   Pressure Point   12.4.58 CBS
  Meet Me in St. Louis   Sp   4.26.59 CBS
  Zane Grey Theatre   ep   King of the Valley   11.26.59
    CBS
  Checkmate   ep   Death Beyond Recall   2.7.62 CBS
  Rawhide   ep   The Reunion   4.6.62 NBC
  Perry Mason   ep   The Case of the Surplus Suitor   2.28.
    63 CBS
  Breaking Point   ep   The Gnu, Now Almost Extinct   12.
    16.63 ABC
  Daniel Boone   ep   Not in Our Stars   12.31.64 NBC
  Dr. Kildare   ep   Never Too Old for the Circus   1.30.
    64 NBC
  Burke's Law   ep   Who Killed Mother Goose   1.13.65
    ABC
  Cinderella   Sp   2.22.66 CBS
  How I Spent My Summer Vacation   tf   1.7.67 NBC
  FBI   ep   The Executioners   3.12.67, 3.19.67 ABC
  Danny Thomas Show   ep   My Pal Tony   3.4.68 NBC
  Medical Center   ep   12.3.69 CBS
  The House on Green Apple Road   tf   1.11.70 ABC
  The Mask of Sheba   tf   3.9.70 NBC
  Marcus Welby, M.D.   ep   A Passing of Torches   1.26.
    71 ABC
  Dan August   ep   The Law   2.4.71 ABC
  The Screaming Woman   tf   1.29.72 ABC

PINZA, EZIO
  Robert Montgomery Presents   ep   The Valari Special
    11.24.52 NBC
  Hollywood Opening Night   ep   Interlude   1.19.53 NBC
  Bonino   sr   9.12.53 NBC
  G.E. Theatre   ep   The Half-Promised Land   6.12.55
    CBS

PITTS, ZASU
  G. E. Theatre   ep   Pardon My Aunt   4.4.54 CBS
  Kraft Theatre   ep   The Happy Touch   8.4.54 NBC
  Best of Broadway   ep   The Man Who Came to Dinner
      10.13.54 CBS
  Screen Directors Playhouse   ep   The Silent Partner   12.
      21.55 NBC
  20th Century-Fox Hour   ep   Mr. Belvedere   4.18.56
      CBS
  Oh Susanna   sr   9.29.56 CBS
  Oh Susanna   sr ret   9.57 CBS
  The Gale Storm Show   sr   8.9.58 CBS
  Dennis O'Keefe Show   ep   4.12.60 CBS
  Perry Mason   ep   The Case of the Absent Artist   3.17.
      62 CBS
  Burke's Law   ep   Who Killed Holly Howard?   9.20.63
      ABC

PLEASANCE, DONALD
  Robin Hood   sr   9.26.55 CBS
  Alcoa Premiere   ep   The Confession   4.11.61 ABC
  World of Disney   ep   The Horsemasters   10.1.61, 10.
      8.61 NBC
  Outer Limits   ep   The Man with the Power   9.30.63
      ABC
  Espionage   ep   The Liberators   3.11.64 NBC
  Defenders   ep   Fire of the Mind   2.18.65 CBS
  Fugitive   ep   With Strings Attached   3.15.66 ABC
  Diary of Anne Frank   Sp   11.26.67 ABC
  Hawaii Five-O   ep   1.18.72 CBS

PLESHETTE, SUZANNE
  Harbourmaster   ep   Night Rescue   12.5.57 CBS
  Have Gun Will Travel   ep   Death of a Gunfighter   3.14.
      59 CBS
  Black Saddle   ep   10.16.59 ABC
  Adventures in Paradise   ep   Lady from South Chicago
      11.2.59 ABC
  Alfred Hitchcock Presents   ep   Hitchhiker   2.21.60 CBS
  Play of the Week   ep   The House of Bernarda Alba   6.
      6.60 NN
  Riverboat   ep   The Two Faces of Grey Holden   10.3.60
      NBC
  Route 66   ep   The Strengthening Angels   11.4.60 CBS
  Naked City   ep   The Pedigree Sheet   10.19.60 ABC
  Islanders   ep   Forbidden Cargo   11.27.60 ABC
  Hong Kong   ep   Lesson in Fear   1.11.61 ABC

Tab Hunter Show ep Weekend on Ice 1.15.61 NBC
G.E. Theatre ep Love Is a Lion's Roar 3.19.61 CBS
Route 66 ep Blue Murder 9.29.61 CBS
Dr. Kildare ep Shining Image 10.12.61 NBC
Target Corruptors ep Viva Vegas 2.9.62 ABC
Ben Casey ep Behold a Pale Horse 2.26.62 ABC
Dick Powell Theatre ep Days of Glory 11.4.62 NBC
Dr. Kildare ep The Soul Killer 11.22.62 NBC
Alcoa Premiere ep The Contenders 12.6.62 ABC
Wagon Train ep The Myra Marshal Story 10.21.63
   ABC
Channing ep The Potato Bash World 10.30.63 ABC
Bob Hope Chrysler Theatre ep Corridor 400 12.27.
   63 NBC
Dr. Kildare ep Goodbye Mr. Jersey 2.20.64 NBC
Fugitive ep World's End 9.22.64 ABC
Wild, Wild West ep Night of the Inferno 9.17.65 CBS
Fugitive ep All The Scared Rabbits 10.26.65 ABC
Bob Hope Chrysler Theatre ep After the Lion, Jack-
   als 1.26.66 NBC
FBI ep 12.18.66 ABC
Invaders ep The Mutation 1.24.67 ABC
Run for Your Life ep Baby, the World's on Fire 2.
   6.67 NBC
Wings of Fire tf 2.14.67 NBC
Cimarron Strip ep 11.16.67 CBS
Flesh and Blood ep 1.26.68 NBC
FBI ep 4.28.68 ABC
It Takes a Thief ep A Sour Note 10.1.68 ABC
Name of the Game ep The Suntan Gang 2.7.69 NBC
Name of the Game ep The Skin Game 2.27.70 NBC
Along Came a Spider tf 2.3.70 ABC
Hunters Are for Killing tf 3.12.70 CBS
Love American Style ep 3.13.70 ABC
Gunsmoke ep 9.28.70 CBS
Marcus Welby, M.D. ep Daisy in the Shadow 10.27.
   70 ABC
FBI ep The Inheritors 12.27.70 ABC
Name of the Game ep A Capitol Affair 2.12.71 NBC
River of Gold tf 3.9.71 ABC
In Broad Daylight tf 10.16.71 ABC
Medical Center ep Conspiracy 12.8.71 CBS
Ironside ep When She Was Bad 12.30.71 NBC
Bob Newhart Show sr 9.16.72 CBS

PLOWRIGHT, JOAN
   School for Scandal Sp 4.8.66 NN

N.E.T. Playhouse   ep   Uncle Vanya   2.10.67 NN

PLUMMER, CHRISTOPHER
  Summer Studio One   ep   The Gathering Night   8.24.53
    CBS
  Broadway Television Theatre   ep   Dark Victory   11.16.
    53 NN
  The Web   ep   Sheep's Clothing   3.7.54 CBS
  Kraft Theatre   ep   The Dashing White Sergeant   7.29.
    54 ABC
  Kraft Theatre   ep   The King's Bounty   9.21.55 NBC
  Producers Showcase   ep   Cyrano de Bergerac   10.17.55
    NBC
  Appointment with Adventure   ep   A Thief There Was
    3.18.56 CBS
  Alcoa Hour   ep   Even the Weariest River   4.15.56 NBC
  Omnibus   ep   Oedipus Rex   1.6.57 ABC
  Dupont Show of the Month   ep   The Prince and the
    Pauper   10.28.57 CBS
  Hallmark Hall of Fame   ep   Little Moon of Alban   3.24.
    58 NBC
  Omnibus   ep   The Lady's Not for Burning   4.6.58 NBC
  Hallmark Hall of Fame   ep   Johnny Belinda   10.13.58
    NBC
  Omnibus   ep   Prince Ore Test   1.4.59 NBC
  Hallmark Hall of Fame   ep   Doll's House   11.15.59
    NBC
  The Philadelphia Story   Sp   12.7.59 NBC
  Sunday Showcase   ep   After Hours   2.7.60 NBC
  Our American Heritage   ep   Autocrat and Son   3.20.60
    NBC
  Hallmark Hall of Fame   ep   Captain Brassbound's Con-
    version   5.2.60 NBC
  Dupont Show of the Month   ep   The Prisoner of Zenda
    1.18.61 CBS
  Hallmark Hall of Fame   ep   Time Remembered   2.7.61
    NBC
  Hallmark Hall of Fame   ep   Cyrano de Bergerac   12.6.
    62 NBC
  Hamlet   Sp   11.15.64 NN

POITIER, SIDNEY
  Pond's Theatre   ep   Fascinating Stranger   6.23.55 ABC
  Philco Playhouse   ep   The Man Is Ten Feet Tall   10.2.
    55 NBC

POLLARD, MICHAEL J.
Alfred Hitchcock Presents   ep   Anniversary Gift   11.1.
  59 CBS
Ford Star Time   ep   The Man   1.5.60 NBC
Sunday Showcase   ep   The Secret of Freedom   2.28.60
  NBC
Going My Way   ep   Tell Me When You Get to Heaven
  1.2.63 ABC
Route 66   ep   And Make Thunder His Tribute   10.25.63
  CBS
Here's Lucy   ep   Chris Goes Steady   1.20.64 CBS
Baileys of Balboa   cp   1.28.65 CBS
Baileys of Balboa   ep   2.11.65 CBS
Mr. Novak   ep   Honor and All That   3.23.65 NBC
Honey West   ep   The Princess and the Paupers   10.29.
  65 ABC
Virginian   ep   The Wolves up Front, the Jackals Behind
  3.23.66 NBC
I Spy   ep   Trial by Treehouse   10.19.66 NBC
Star Trek   ep   Miri   10.27.66 NBC
Danny Thomas Show   ep   The Scene   9.25.67 NBC
Cimarron Strip   ep   10.12.67 CBS
The Smugglers   tf   12.24.68 NBC

PORTER, DON
Private Secretary   sr   2.1.53 CBS
Private Secretary   sr ret   9.20.53 CBS
Private Secretary   sr ret   9.12.54 CBS
Private Secretary   sr ret   9.11.55 CBS
Ann Sothern Show   sr   3.9.59 CBS
Ann Sothern Show   sr ret   10.5.59 CBS
Ann Sothern Show   sr ret   10.6.60 CBS
I Love My Doctor   pt   9.14.62 CBS
Gidget   sr   9.15.65 ABC
Judd for the Defense   ep   Epitaph on a Computer Card
  1.17.69 ABC
Love American Style   ep   10.27.69 ABC
Mod Squad   ep   The Judas Trap   12.8.70 ABC
Love American Style   ep   2.26.71 ABC
Green Acres   ep   3.16.71 CBS
Banacek   ep   11.1.72 NBC
Rookies   ep   11.27.72 ABC

PORTER, NYREE DAWN
Forsyte Saga   sr   10.5.69 NN
Jane Eyre   Sp   3.24.71 NBC

The Protectors   sr   9.17.72 CBS

PORTMAN, ERIC
   Lili Palmer Theatre   ep   Mr. Betts Runs Away   11.28.
      56 NN
   Alcoa Hour   ep   A Double Life   1.6.57 NBC
   Dupont Show of the Month   ep   A Tale of Two Cities
      3.27.58 CBS
   Dupont Show of the Month   ep   Oliver Twist   12.4.59
      CBS
   Victory   Sp   4.8.60 NBC
   Alfred Hitchcock Presents   ep   The Hero   5.1.60 CBS
   Naked City   ep   The Pedigree Sheet   10.19.60 ABC
   Play of the Week   ep   Duet for Two Hands   10.24.60
      NN
   Shirley Temple Theatre   ep   The Terrible Clockman   1.
      29.61 NBC

POSTON, TOM
   Goodyear Playhouse   ep   Tangled Web   7.3.55 NBC
   Playwrights '56   ep   You Sometimes Get Rich   5.8.56
      NBC
   Robert Montgomery Presents   ep   Who   5.28.56 NBC
   U.S. Steel Hour   ep   The Change in Chester   7.31.57
      CBS
   Play of the Week   ep   The Enchanted   4.11.60 NN
   Hallmark Hall of Fame   ep   The Tempest   10.20.63
      NBC

POWELL, DICK
   Four Star Playhouse   sr   10.9.52 CBS
   Four Star Playhouse   sr ret   9.10.53 CBS
   Four Star Playhouse   sr ret   9.23.54 CBS
   Climax   ep   The Long Goodbye   10.7.54 CBS
   Four Star Playhouse   sr ret   9.11.55 CBS
   Zane Grey Theatre   sh/sr   10.5.56 CBS
   Zane Grey Theatre   sh/sr ret   10.4.57 CBS
   Zane Grey Theatre   sh/sr ret   10.2.58 CBS
   Zane Grey Theatre   sh/sr ret   10.1.59 CBS
   June Allyson Show   ep   A Summer's Ending   10.12.59
      CBS
   June Allyson Show   ep   The Doctor and the Redhead
      4.25.60 CBS
   Zane Grey Theatre   sh/sr ret   10.6.60 CBS
   Tom Ewell Show   ep   12.6.60 CBS
   Law and Mr. Jones   ep   Everybody vs. Timmy Dayton
      3.17.61 ABC

Dick Powell Theatre   sh/sr   9.26.61 NBC
Dick Powell Theatre   sh/sr ret   9.25.62 NBC
Ensign O'Toole   ep   Operation Benefit   10.14.62 NBC

POWELL, JANE
   Ruggles of Red Gap   Sp   2.3.57 NBC
   Alcoa Theatre   ep   Encounter on a Second Class Coach
      10.21.57 NBC
   Goodyear Theatre   ep   Hurricane   11.25.57 NBC
   Alcoa Theatre   ep   Cupid Wore a Badge   12.16.57 NBC
   Goodyear Theatre   ep   Music in the Night   2.3.58 NBC
   Goodyear Theatre   ep   Fix a Frame for Mourning   4.
      14.58 NBC
   Goodyear Theatre   ep   The Lady Takes the Stand   5.12.
      58 NBC
   Meet Me in St. Louis   Sp   4.26.59 CBS
   Feathertop   Sp   10.19.61 ABC
   Dick Powell Theatre   ep   View from the Eiffel Tower
      3.13.62 NBC
   Wheeler and Murdoch   tf   3.27.72 ABC

POWERS, MALA
   Appointment with Adventure   ep   Minus Three Thousand
      4.3.55 CBS
   Undercurrent   ep   8.19.55 CBS
   Ford Theatre   ep   Husband   10.13.55 NBC
   Ford Theatre   ep   The Face   3.29.56 NBC
   On Trial   ep   The Fourth Witness   12.21.56 NBC
   Mr. Adams and Eve   ep   2.1.57 CBS
   Crossroads   ep   The Last Strand   3.22.57 ABC
   Zane Grey Theatre   ep   Black Is for Grief   4.12.57
      CBS
   Wagon Train   ep   The Ruttledge Munroe Story   5.21.58
      NBC
   Wanted, Dead or Alive   ep   11.8.58 CBS
   Restless Gun   ep   The Lady and the Gun   1.19.59 NBC
   Perry Mason   ep   The Case of the Deadly Toy   5.16.59
      CBS
   Restless Gun   ep   Take Home   7.6.59 NBC
   Bourbon Street Beat   ep   The Golden Beetle   12.14.59
      ABC
   Hawaiian Eye   ep   Kim Quixote   3.30.60 ABC
   Bronco   ep   Montana Passage   4.5.60 ABC
   Perry Mason   ep   The Case of the Crying Cherub   4.9.
      60 CBS
   Man and the Challenge   ep   Shooter McLaine   5.21.60
      NBC

Bonanza   ep   The Dede Sheimer Story   5.21.60 NBC
World of Disney   ep   The Warrior's Path   12.4.60, 12.
  11.60 ABC
World of Disney   ep   The Wilderness Road   3.12.61
  NBC
G.E. Theatre   ep   The Joke's on Me   4.16.61 CBS
Lawman   ep   Blind Hate   5.14.61 ABC
Cheyenne   ep   Trouble Street   10.2.61 ABC
Bob Cummings Show   ep   Very Warm for Mayan   10.12.
  61 CBS
Thriller   ep   The Bride Who Died Twice   3.19.62 NBC
Hawaiian Eye   ep   The Meeting at Molokai   3.21.62
  ABC
77 Sunset Strip   ep   Violence for Your Furs   3.30.62
  ABC
Cheyenne   ep   Trouble Street   5.14.62 ABC
Perry Mason   ep   The Case of the Weary Watchdog   11.
  29.62 CBS
Gallant Men   ep   Signals for an End Run   12.7.62 ABC
Hawaiian Eye   ep   Maybe Menehunes   1.15.63 ABC
Wide Country   ep   The Man Who Runs Away   2.7.63
  NBC
Rawhide   ep   A Woman's Place   5.17.63 CBS
Gallant Men   ep   Signals for an End Run   5.18.63 ABC
Perry Mason   ep   The Case of the Frightened Fisherman
  2.27.64 CBS
Arrest and Trial   ep   Those Which Love Has Made   4.
  12.64 ABC
Kraft Suspense Theatre   ep   Portrait of an Unknown
  Man   4.16.64 NBC
Hazel   ep   Hazel's Second Week   9.20.65 CBS
Hazel   ep   11.22.65 CBS
The Man from U.N.C.L.E.   ep   The Virtue Affair   12.
  3.65 NBC
Hazel   ep   1.17.66 CBS
Perry Mason   ep   The Case of the Scarlet Scandal   2.
  20.66 CBS
Wild, Wild West   ep   Night of the Big Blast   10.7.66
  10.7.66 CBS
Jericho   ep   Long Journey Across a Short Street   1.28.
  66 CBS
Mission Impossible   ep   1.14.67 CBS
Gentle Ben   ep   9.10.67 CBS
Bewitched   ep   12.26.68 ABC
Ironside   ep   The People Against Judge McIntire   10.
  8.70 NBC
Silent Force   ep   11.9.70 ABC

Man and the City   sr   9.15.71 ABC

POWERS, STEFANIE
    Swingin' Together   pt   8.26.63 CBS
    Bonanza   ep   Calamity over the Comstock   11.3.63 NBC
    The Girl from U.N.C.L.E.   sr   9.13.66 NBC
    Lancer   ep   1.21.69 CBS
    Lancer   tf   9.30.69 CBS
    It Takes a Thief   ep   Fortune City   2.2.70 ABC
    Medical Center   ep   Man at Bay   12.16.70 CBS
    Love American Style   ep   2.5.71 ABC
    Love American Style   ep   9.17.71 ABC
    Five Desperate Women   tf   9.28.71 ABC
    McCloud   ep   11.3.71 NBC
    Paper Man   tf   11.12.71 CBS
    Love American Style   ep   12.17.71 ABC
    Medical Center   ep   Double Jeopardy   12.22.71 CBS
    Owen Marshall   ep   Victim in Shadow   12.27.72 ABC
    Hardcase   tf   2.1.72 ABC
    Sixth Sense   ep   Echo of a Distant Scream   4.1.72 ABC
    Banacek   ep   Let's Hear It for a Living Legend   9.13.
        72 NBC
    Mod Squad   ep   The Connection   9.14.72 ABC
    No Place to Run   tf   9.19.72 ABC
    Search   ep   9.20.72 NBC
    Bold Ones   ep   10.24.72 ABC
    Streets of San Francisco   ep   10.28.72 ABC
    Cannon   ep   11.1.72 CBS
    Sixth Sense   ep   If I Should Die Before I Wake   12.2.72
        ABC

PREMINGER, OTTO
    Suspense   ep   Operation Barracuda   4.13.54 CBS
    Batman   ep   Green Ice   11.9.66, 11.10.66 ABC

PRENTISS, PAULA
    He and She   sr   9.6.67 CBS
    The Couple Take a Wife   tf   12.5.72 ABC

PRESLE, MICHELINE
    Combat   ep   Just for the Record   1.15.63 ABC

PRESTON, ROBERT
    Pulitzer Prize Playhouse   ep   Blockade   3.23.51 ABC
    Man against Crime   sr   6.29.51 CBS
    Video Theatre   ep   Cafe Ami   10.15.51 CBS
    Schlitz Playhouse of Stars   ep   The Nymph and the Lamp

12. 7. 51 CBS
Video Theatre   ep   Kelly   2. 4. 52 CBS
Pulitzer Prize Playhouse   ep   The Juggler   4. 9. 52 ABC
Curtain Call   ep   The Promise   6. 20. 52 NBC
Lux Video Theatre   ep   Happily, But Not Forever   9. 22.
52 CBS
Anywhere, U. S. A.   sr   11. 9. 52 ABC
Medallion Theatre   ep   The Quiet Village   8. 22. 53 CBS
U. S. Steel Hour   ep   Hope for a Harvest   11. 10. 53
ABC
TV Soundstage   ep   Al Toolum and His Buddy Leo   4.
30. 54 NBC
U. S. Steel Hour   ep   The End of Paul Dane   5. 11. 54
ABC
Omnibus   ep   1. 9. 55 CBS
U. S. Steel Hour   ep   The Bogey Man   1. 18. 55 ABC
Climax   ep   The Box of Chocolates   2. 24. 55 CBS
Elgin Hour   ep   Crime in the Streets   3. 8. 55 ABC
G. E. Theatre   ep   It Gives Me Great Pleasure   4. 3. 55
CBS
Kraft Theatre   ep   Drop on the Devil   6. 22. 55 NBC
Woman in the Window   Sp   9. 12. 55 NBC
Alcoa Hour   ep   Long After Summer   2. 5. 56 NBC
20th Century-Fox Hour   ep   Child of the Regiment   10.
3. 56 CBS
Goodyear Playhouse   ep   Missouri Legend   10. 7. 56 NBC
Climax   ep   The Midas Touch   10. 18. 56 CBS
Playhouse 90   ep   Made in Heaven   12. 6. 56 CBS
Alcoa Hour   ep   The Animal Kingdom   2. 17. 57 NBC
Omnibus   ep   The Trial of Lizzie Borden   3. 24. 57 ABC
The Bells of St. Mary's   Sp   10. 27. 59 CBS
Dupont Show of the Month   ep   Years Ago   4. 21. 60 CBS

PRICE, VINCENT
Video Theatre   ep   The Promise   6. 25. 51 CBS
Lights Out   ep   The Third Door   1. 28. 52 NBC
Video Theatre   ep   The Game of Chess   2. 11. 52 CBS
Pulitzer Prize Playhouse   ep   Monsieur Beaucaire   3. 12.
52 ABC
Schlitz Playhouse of Stars   ep   The Human Touch   3. 21.
52 CBS
Gruen Guild Playhouse   ep   Dream Man   4. 10. 52 NN
Summer Theatre   ep   Dream Job   7. 17. 53 ABC
Schlitz Playhouse of Stars   ep   Sheila   8. 21. 53 CBS
Playhouse   ep   Bullet for a Stranger   11. 5. 53 CBS
Climax   ep   Night of Execution   9. 22. 55 CBS
TV Reader's Digest   ep   The Brainwashing of John

Hayes   11.7.55 ABC
G.E. Theatre   ep   The Ballad of Mender McClure   1.
   15.56 CBS
Science Fiction Theatre   ep   Operation Flypaper   2.3.56
   NBC
Crossroads   ep   The Rebel   3.2.56 ABC
Climax   ep   Spin into Darkness   4.5.56 CBS
Alcoa Hour   ep   Sister   7.22.56 NBC
Science Fiction Theatre   ep   One Thousand Eyes   9.7.
   56 NBC
Playhouse 90   ep   Forbidden Area   10.4.56 CBS
Crossroads   ep   God's Healing   11.30.56 ABC
Schlitz Playhouse of Stars   ep   The Blue Hotel   4.12.57
   CBS
Climax   ep   Avalanche at Devil's Pass   4.24.57 CBS
Schlitz Playhouse of Stars   ep   High Barrier   10.18.57
   CBS
Alfred Hitchcock Presents   ep   The Perfect Crime   10.
   20.57 CBS
Playhouse 90   ep   The Clouded Image   11.7.57 CBS
G.E. Theatre   ep   The Iron Rose   11.24.57 CBS
Jane Wyman Theatre   ep   The Perfect Alibi   12.12.57
   NBC
Playhouse 90   ep   Lone Woman   12.26.57 CBS
G.E. Theatre   ep   Angel in the Air   3.9.58 CBS
Schlitz Playhouse of Stars   ep   The Kind Mr. Smith   4.
   25.58 CBS
Matinee Theatre   ep   Angel Street   5.9.58 NBC
Have Gun, Will Travel   ep   The Moor's Revenge   12.27.
   58 CBS
Riverboat   ep   Witness to Evil   11.1.59 NBC
Adventures in Paradise   ep   The Color of Venom   2.8.
   60 ABC
Ford Star Time   ep   Tennessee Ernie Ford Meets King
   Arthur   5.10.60 NBC
Mystery Show   ep   Run-Around   8.14.60 NBC
Mystery Show   ep hos   9.18.60 NBC
Family Classics   ep   The Three Musketeers 11.30.60,
   12.1.60 CBS
U.S. Steel Hour   ep   Shame the Devil   12.14.60 CBS
The Man from U.N.C.L.E.   ep   The Foxes and Hounds
   Affair   10.8.65 NBC
Batman   ep   An Egg Grows in Gotham   10.19.66, 10.
   20.66 ABC
Batman   ep   11.2.67, 11.9.67 ABC
Daniel Boone   ep   1.30.69 NBC
Love American Style   ep   11.6.70 ABC

Mod Squad ep A Time for Hyacinths 12.1.70 ABC
Night Gallery ep 9.22.71 NBC
What's a Nice Girl Like You tf 12.18.71 ABC
Jimmy Stewart Show ep 2.13.72 NBC
Night Gallery ep 9.24.72 NBC

PRINCE, WILLIAM
Philco Playhouse ep The Second Oldest Profession 3.
  26.50 NBC
Starlight Theatre ep The M. P. and the Mouse 4.16.
  50 CBS
Starlight Theatre ep Season for Marriage 4.28.51 NN
Suspense ep A Killing in Abilene 6.19.51 CBS
Philco Playhouse ep Pretend I Am a Stranger 7.22.
  51 NBC
Philco Playhouse ep Night of the Vulcan 8.26.51 NBC
Goodyear Playhouse ep The Dusty Drawer 8.3.52
  NBC
Armstrong Circle Theatre ep A Man and His Con-
  science 8.19.52 NBC
Suspense ep The Waxworks 9.16.52 CBS
Armstrong Circle Theatre ep A Volcano Is Dancing
  Here 11.18.52 CBS
Broadway Television Theatre ep 1.19.53 NN
Broadway Television Theatre ep Wuthering Heights
  4.6.53 NN
Tales of Tomorrow ep Lazarus Walks 5.29.53 ABC
The Doctor ep The Researcher 5.31.53 NBC
Danger ep Trial by Jungle 7.21.53 CBS
Tales of the City ep Miracle in the Rain 8.20.53 CBS
Armstrong Circle Theatre ep Two Prisoners 9.8.53
  NBC
Theatre for You ep Babylon Revisited 10.6.53 NN
The Mask sr 1.10.54 ABC
Inner Sanctum ep Identity Unknown 4.2.54 NN
Best of Broadway ep The Man Who Came to Dinner
  10.13.54 CBS
Appointment with Adventure ep The Fateful Pilgrimage
  4.17.55 CBS
Appointment with Adventure ep Crash Landing 7.10.55
  CBS
Justice sr 10.2.55 NBC
Modern Romances ep 5.7.56 NBC
Crossroads ep The Man Who Walked on Water 1.4.57
  ABC
True Story ep The Accident 5.4.57 NBC
Modern Romances ep Mrs. Rocky King 5.13.57 NBC

True Story   ep   Fog   9. 7. 57 NBC
Armstrong Circle Theatre   ep   John Doe #154   11. 13.
   57 CBS
Armstrong Circle Theatre   ep   The Meanest Crime in
   the World   3. 19. 58 CBS
Modern Romances   ep   4. 21. 58 NBC
Kraft Theatre   ep   All the King's Men   5. 14. 58, 5. 21.
   58 NBC
Young Dr. Malone   sr   1960 NBC
Nurses   ep   A Kind of Loving   4. 2. 64 CBS
Hawk   ep   Thanks for the Honeymoon   9. 22. 66 ABC
N. E. T. Playhouse   ep   An Enemy of the People   12. 21.
   66 NN
New York Television Theatre   ep   Father Uxbridge
   Wants to Marry   2. 17. 70 NN
A World Apart   sr   1970 ABC

PRINE, ANDREW
   U. S. Steel Hour   ep   Little Charlie Doesn't Want a Sad-
      dle   12. 18. 57 CBS
   Look up and Live   ep   Death   8. 30. 59 CBS
   Playhouse 90   ep   Tomorrow   3. 7. 60 CBS
   Alcoa Premiere   ep   The Peter Hurkos Story   4. 26. 60
      ABC
   Overland Mail   ep   Sour Annie   5. 8. 60 NBC
   Roughing It   Sp   5. 13. 60 NBC
   Peter Gunn   ep   Letter of the Law   5. 30. 60 NBC
   Have Gun, Will Travel   ep   11. 26. 60 CBS
   Play of the Week   ep   Black Monday   1. 16. 61 NN
   Dupont Show of the Month   ep   The Lincoln Murder Case
      2. 18. 61 CBS
   Have Gun, Will Travel   ep   3. 4. 61 CBS
   Alcoa Premiere   ep   The End of a World   12. 19. 61 ABC
   Alfred Hitchcock Theatre   ep   Faith of Aaron Menefee
      1. 30. 62 NBC
   Defenders   ep   The Point Shaver   2. 3. 62 CBS
   Alcoa Premiere   ep   Second Chance   3. 12. 62 ABC
   New Breed   ep   Echoes of Hate   4. 3. 62 ABC
   Ben Casey   ep   An Uncommonly Innocent Killing   5. 7.
      62 ABC
   Gunsmoke   ep   12. 22. 62 CBS
   Gunsmoke   ep   10. 26. 63 CBS
   Lieutenant   ep   Fall from a White Horse   11. 30. 63 NBC
   Great Adventures   ep   The Outlaw and the Nun   12. 6. 63
      CBS
   Look up and Live   ep   1. 5. 64, 1. 12. 64, 1. 19. 64 CBS
   Fugitive   ep   Home Is the Hunter   1. 7. 64 ABC

Suspense   ep   I Bradford Charles   4. 8. 64 CBS
Wagon Train   ep   The Bob Stuart Story   9. 20. 64 ABC
Dr. Kildare   ep   Catch a Crooked Mouse   12. 17. 64
    NBC
Profiles in Courage   ep   12. 27. 64 NBC
Virginian   ep   Hideout   1. 13. 65 NBC
Wagon Train   ep   1. 31. 65 ABC
Combat   ep   Billy the Kid   4. 6. 65 ABC
Kraft Suspense Theatre   ep   The Long Ravine   5. 6. 65
    NBC
Bonanza   ep   Jonah   5. 9. 65 NBC
Virginian   ep   The Brothers   9. 15. 65 NBC
Dr. Kildare   ep   The Bell in the Schoolhouse Tolls for
    Thee, Kildare   9. 27. 65, 9. 28. 65, 10. 4. 65, 10. 5. 65,
    10. 11. 65, 10. 12. 65 NBC
Convoy   ep   Admiral D--Right   11. 5. 65 NBC
12 O'Clock High   ep   The Jones Boys   12. 6. 65 ABC
Fugitive   ep   End of the Line   12. 21. 65 ABC
Virginian   ep   A Bald-Faced Boy   4. 13. 66 NBC
Road West   sr   9. 12. 66 NBC
Tarzan   ep   The Ultimate Weapon   9. 16. 66 NBC
Invaders   ep   Dark Outpost   10. 24. 67 ABC
Daniel Boone   ep   3. 28. 68 NBC
FBI   ep   3. 31. 68 ABC
Ironside   ep   9. 26. 68 NBC
Lancer   ep   12. 17. 68 CBS
Name of the Game   ep   Pineapple Rose   12. 20. 68 NBC
Virginian   ep   10. 8. 69 NBC
Love American Style   ep   12. 8. 69 ABC
Lancer   ep   The Lion and the Lamb   2. 3. 70 CBS
Along Came a Spider   tf   2. 3. 70 ABC
Name of the Game   ep   Echo of a Nightmare   3. 20. 70
    NBC
Night Slaves   tf   9. 27. 70 ABC
Matt Lincoln   ep   11. 5. 70 ABC
Most Deadly Game   ep   Who Killed Kindness?   11. 7. 70
    ABC
Dan August   ep   The Union Forever   11. 11. 70 ABC
FBI   ep   Death on Sunday   9. 12. 71 ABC
Hollywood Television Theatre   ep   Another Part of the
    Forest   10. 2. 72 NN
World of Disney   ep   High Flying Spy   10. 22. 72, 10. 29.
    72, 11. 5. 72 NBC

PROVINE, DOROTHY
    The Millionaire   ep   The David Barrett Story   10. 1. 58
        CBS

Lawman   ep   Lady in Question   12.21.58 ABC
Real McCoys   ep   The McCoys Visit Hollywood   1.8.59
   ABC
Alfred Hitchcock Presents   ep   The Morning After   1.
   11.59 CBS
Sugarfoot   ep   The Giant Killer   3.3.59 ABC
Texan   ep   4.20.59 CBS
Colt .45   ep   The Confession   4.26.59 ABC
Cheyenne   ep   Red Water North   6.16.59 ABC
Alaskans   sr   10.4.59 ABC
Roaring 20s   sr   10.15.60 ABC
Hawaiian Eye   ep   A Likely Story   3.14.62 ABC
Hawaiian Eye   ep   A Night with Nora Stewart   11.27.62
   ABC
Gallant Men   ep   Tommy   3.30.63 ABC
Dr. Kildare   ep   Music Hath Charms   4.15.65 NBC
The Man from U.N.C.L.E.   ep   The Alexander the
   Greater Affair   9.17.65, 1.24.65 NBC
Danny Thomas Show   ep   My Pal Tony   3.4.68 NBC
FBI   ep   11.17.68 ABC
The Sound of Anger   tf   12.10.68 NBC
Love American Style   ep   1.23.70 ABC

PROVOST, JON
   Lassie   sr   fall, 1957 CBS
   Lassie   sr ret   fall, 1958 CBS
   Lassie   sr ret   fall, 1959 CBS
   Lassie   sr ret   9.11.60 CBS

PROWSE, JULIET
   Adventures in Paradise   ep   A Whale of a Tale   11.7.
      60 ABC
   Burke's Law   ep   Who Killed Harris Crown   10.11.63
      ABC
   Burke's Law   ep   11.25.64 ABC
   Mona McCluskey   sr   9.16.65 NBC
   Danny Thomas Show   ep   It's Greek to Me   10.2.67
      NBC
   Name of the Game   ep   Shine on, Shine on   11.1.68
      NBC
   Second Chance   tf   2.8.72 ABC

PRUD'HOMME, CAMERON
   Robert Montgomery Presents   ep   Of Lena Geyer   6.16.
      52 NBC
   Tales of Tomorrow   ep   The Vault   5.8.53 ABC
   Big Story   ep   6.19.53 NBC

Kraft Theatre   ep   Old MacDonald Had a Curve   8.5.53
NBC
Philco Playhouse   ep   The Rainmaker   8.16.53 NBC
Kraft Theatre   ep   Her Father's Butler   9.16.53 NBC
Man Behind the Badge   ep   The Case of the Slightly Used
   Car   8.18.54 CBS
Pond's Theatre   ep   Death Is a Spanish Dancer   6.30.55
   ABC
Pond's Theatre   ep   Coquette   7.7.55 ABC
Appointment with Adventure   ep   The Allenson Incident
   10.2.55 CBS
Justice   ep   Flight from Fear   10.16.55 NBC
Kraft Theatre   ep   The Ticket and the Tempest   11.9.55
NBC
U.S. Steel Hour   ep   Incident in an Alley   11.23.55 CBS
Armstrong Circle Theatre   ep   I Was Accused   12.13.55
NBC
Alcoa Hour   ep   Long After Summer   2.5.56 NBC
Studio One   ep   American Primitive   10.29.56 CBS
Alcoa Hour   ep   Adventure in Diamonds   12.9.56 NBC
Climax   ep   The Gold Dress   1.17.57 CBS
U.S. Steel Hour   ep   Old Marshals Never Die   8.13.58
CBS
Playhouse 90   ep   The Blue Men   1.15.59 CBS
Music Theatre   ep   The Sound of Murder   5.7.59 NBC
Playhouse 90   ep   Rank and File   5.28.59 CBS
The Valley of Decision   Sp   3.20.60 NBC
Best of the Post   ep   Groper in the Dark   4.8.61 ABC
New Breed   ep   Echoes of Hate   4.3.62 ABC
U.S. Steel Hour   ep   Young Avengers   1.9.63 CBS

PURDOM, EDMUND
Sword of Freedom   sr   10.28.57 NN
It Takes a Thief   ep   The Three Virgins of Rome   11.6.
   69 ABC

-Q-

QUALEN, JOHN
Hollywood Opening Night   ep   Son of the Rock   8.31.51
CBS
Celanese Theatre   ep   Anna Christie   1.23.52 ABC
Schaefer Century Theatre   ep   Portrait of Toby   5.24.52
NBC

G. E. Theatre   ep   Thirteen O'Clock   7. 19. 53 CBS
Omnibus   ep   The House   3. 7. 54 CBS
Public Defender   ep   The Prize Fighter Story   4. 8. 54
   CBS
Schlitz Playhouse of Stars   ep   The Whale on the Beach
   6. 4. 54 CBS
Philco Playhouse   ep   Adapt or Die   6. 13. 54 NBC
Ford Theatre   ep   Girl in Flight   12. 2. 54 NBC
Science Fiction Theatre   ep   Death at 2 A. M.   6. 10. 55
   NBC
Alfred Hitchcock Presents   ep   Shopping for Death   1.
   29. 56 CBS
Danny Thomas Show   ep   Like Father, Like Son   2. 7.
   56 NBC
Father Knows Best   ep   The Bus to Nowhere   2. 8. 56
   NBC
Crossroads   ep   Dig or Die, Brother Hyde   3. 30. 56
   ABC
Alfred Hitchcock Presents   ep   Help Wanted   4. 1. 56
   CBS
Crossroads   ep   Anatole of the Bayous   4. 20. 56 ABC
The Millionaire   ep   10. 3. 56 CBS
December Bride   ep   Royalty   1. 7. 57 CBS
Cheyenne   ep   Deadline   2. 26. 57 ABC
Yancy Derringer   ep   Gallatin Street   10. 9. 58 CBS
Sugarfoot   ep   Funeral at Forty Miles   5. 24. 60 ABC
Lawman   ep   Old Stefano   12. 25. 60 ABC
Klondike   ep   Queen of the Klondike   1. 2. 61 NBC
Barbara Stanwyck Theatre   ep   Big Jake   6. 5. 61 NBC
Bonanza   ep   Springtime   10. 1. 61 NBC
Maverick   ep   The Golden Fleecing   10. 8. 61 ABC
Mr. Ed   ep   Ed's New Shoes   12. 24. 61 CBS
Andy Griffith Show   ep   1. 29. 62 CBS
Real McCoys   ep   Cupid Wore a Tail   1. 13. 63 CBS
Wide Country   ep   Whose Hand at My Throat   2. 14. 63
   NBC
Ben Casey   ep   The White Ones Are Dolphins   3. 11. 63
   ABC
Ben Casey   ep   A Horse Named Stravinsky   5. 17. 65
   ABC
Donna Reed Show   ep   1. 6. 66 ABC
Hazel   ep   4. 11. 66 CBS
Jericho   ep   Dutch and Go   9. 15. 66 CBS
Shane   ep   The Hant   9. 17. 66 ABC
The Girl from U. N. C. L. E.   ep   12. 20. 66 NBC
I Spy   ep   10. 30. 67 NBC
Green Acres   ep   10. 23. 68 CBS

The Odd Couple   ep   2. 26. 71 ABC
The Partridge Family   ep   2. 4. 72 ABC

QUINN, ANTHONY
Schlitz Playhouse of Stars   ep   Dark Fleece   12. 21. 51
CBS
Schlitz Playhouse of Stars   ep   The Long Trail   11. 19.
54 CBS
The Vise   ep   The Very Silent Traveler   12. 10. 54 ABC
Schlitz Playhouse of Stars   ep   Bandit's Hideout   10. 7.
55 CBS
Man and the City   sr   9. 15. 71 ABC

-R-

RAE, CHARLOTTE
U.S. Steel Hour   ep   Two   8. 31. 54 ABC
Armstrong Circle Theatre   ep   Fred Allen's Sketchbook
11. 9. 54 NBC
Pond's Theatre   ep   30, Honey, 30   2. 3. 55 ABC
Opera Theatre   ep   The Would-be Gentleman   2. 27. 55
NBC
Appointment with Adventure   ep   Stranger on a Plane
5. 29. 55 CBS
Philco Playhouse   ep   The Miss America Story   9. 4. 55
Dupont Show of the Month   ep   Harvey   9. 22. 58 CBS
Play of the Week   ep   The World of Sholom Aleichem
12. 14. 59 NN
Way Out   ep   Death Wish   6. 9. 61 CBS
Car 54   ep   The Courtship of Sylvia Schnauser   3. 25. 62
NBC
Car 54   ep   One Sleepy People   9. 23. 62 NBC
Dupont Show of the Month   ep   Holdup   9. 22. 63 NBC
Defenders   ep   Comeback   11. 26. 64 CBS
New York Television Theatre   ep   The Immovable Gor-
dons   11. 14. 66 NN
New York Television Theatre   ep   Apple Pie   3. 14. 68
NN
Hallmark Hall of Fame   ep   Pinocchio   12. 8. 68 NBC
N.E.T. Playhouse   ep   Foul   11. 26. 70 NN
Love American Style   ep   11. 3. 72 ABC

RAFFERTY, CHIPS
  Gunsmoke   ep   4. 9. 66 CBS
  Daktari   ep   4. 19. 66 CBS
  The Girl from U. N. C. L. E.   ep   11. 22. 66 NBC
  Tarzan   ep   1. 20. 67 NBC
  Tarzan   ep   3. 24. 67 NBC

RAFFERTY, FRANCES
  Stars over Hollywood   ep   This Little Pig Cried 11. 15.
    50 NBC
  Racket Squad   ep   C. O. D.   Honeymoon   3. 6. 52 CBS
  Schlitz Playhouse of Stars   ep   The White Cream Pitcher
    12. 12. 52 CBS
  Drama at Eight   ep   Uncle Charley   7. 30. 53 NN
  G. E. Theatre   ep   Confession   10. 18. 53 CBS
  Pepsi Cola Playhouse   ep   Vacation Wife   12. 4. 53 ABC
  Jewelers Showcase   ep   Christmas Is Magic   12. 8. 53
    NN
  Pepsi Cola Playhouse   ep   Who Is Sylvia   12. 25. 53 ABC
  Four Star Playhouse   ep   The Test   1. 7. 54 CBS
  Schlitz Playhouse of Stars   ep   Give the Guy a Break
    1. 29. 54 CBS
  Cavalcade of America   ep   Crazy Judah   4. 13. 54 ABC
  Pepsi Cola Playhouse   ep   Terror Train   6. 11. 54 ABC
  Four Star Playhouse   ep   Search in the Night   6. 17. 54
    CBS
  Fireside Theatre   ep   Crusade without Conscience   9. 7.
    54 NBC
  December Bride   sr   10. 4. 54 CBS
  Schlitz Playhouse of Stars   ep   Mystery of Murder   11.
    26. 54 CBS
  Gloria Swanson Theatre   ep   Up Ferguson Way   1. 6. 55 ABC
  Public Defender   ep   In Memory of Murder   6. 2. 55 CBS
  Stage 7   ep   Where You Love Me   9. 4. 55 CBS
  Schlitz Playhouse of Stars   ep   The Quitter   9. 23. 55 CBS
  December Bride   sr ret   10. 3. 55 CBS
  The Lone Wolf   ep   Memo: The Plantation   2. 3. 56 NN
  Ellery Queen   ep   Blackjack   4. 8. 56 NN
  The Millionaire   ep   The Story of Olivia Grainger   5. 30.
    56 CBS
  G. E. Summer Originals   ep   The Unwilling Witness   7.
    24. 56 ABC
  December Bride   sr ret   10. 56 CBS
  December Bride   sr ret   10. 7. 57 CBS
  Alcoa Theatre   ep   The Perfectionist   5. 19. 58 NBC
  December Bride   sr ret   10. 2. 58 CBS
  World of Disney   ep   Ticonderoga to Disneyland   11. 27.
    60 ABC

Perry Mason ep The Case of the Grumbling Grand-
father 5. 27. 61 CBS
Pete and Gladys ep 3. 12. 62 CBS
Pete and Gladys ep 4. 2. 62, 4. 9. 62 CBS
Alcoa Premiere ep This Will Kill You 4. 11. 63 ABC
Perry Mason ep The Case of the Devious Delinquent
12. 5. 63 CBS

RAFT, GEORGE
I Am the Law sr 2. 9. 53 NN
I Am the Law sr ret 9. 8. 53 NN
Chicago Teddy Bears ep 12. 10. 71 ABC

RAINER, LUISE
Rosalind Sp 10. 9. 50 CBS
Schlitz Playhouse of Stars ep Love Came Late 5. 23. 52
CBS
Lux Video Theatre ep Bouquet for Caroline 2. 9. 53
CBS
Suspense ep Torment 3. 30. 54 CBS
Combat ep Our Finest Hour 12. 21. 65 ABC

RAINES, ELLA
Robert Montgomery Presents ep The Phantom Lady 4.
24. 50 NBC
Pulitzer Prize Playhouse ep You Can't Take It with
You 10. 6. 50 ABC
Lights Out ep The Ides of April 8. 28. 50 NBC
Janet Dean, Registered Nurse sr 3. 23. 54 NBC

RAINS, CLAUDE
Medallion Theatre ep The Man Who Liked Dickens 8.
1. 53 CBS
Medallion Theatre ep The Archer Case 10. 3. 53 CBS
Alfred Hitchcock Presents ep And So Died Riabouch-
inska 2. 12. 56 CBS
Kraft Theatre ep nar A Night to Remember 3. 28. 56
NBC
Alcoa Hour ep President 5. 13. 56 NBC
Kaiser Aluminum Hour ep Antigone 9. 11. 56 NBC
Alfred Hitchcock Presents ep The Cream of the Jest
3. 10. 57 CBS
Hallmark Hall of Fame ep On Borrowed Time 11. 17.
57 NBC
The Pied Piper of Hamelin Sp 11. 26. 57 NBC
Alfred Hitchcock Presents ep The Diamond Necklace
2. 22. 59 CBS
Playhouse 90 ep Judgment at Nuremberg 4. 16. 59 CBS

Once Upon a Christmas Time Sp 12.9.59 NBC
Naked City ep To Walk in Silence 11.9.60 ABC
Alfred Hitchcock Theatre ep The Door without a Key
 1.16.62 NBC
Rawhide ep Incident of Judgment Day 2.8.62 CBS
Wagon Train ep The Daniel Clay Story 2.21.62 NBC
Sam Benedict ep Nor Practice Makes Perfect 9.29.
 62 NBC
Bob Hope Chrysler Theatre ep Something About Lee
 Wiley 10.11.63 NBC
Dupont Show of the Month ep The Takers 10.13.63
 NBC
Dr. Kildare ep Why Won't Anybody Listen 2.27.64
 NBC
The Reporter ep A Time to Be Silent 12.4.64 CBS
Bob Hope Chrysler Theatre ep Cops and Robbers 2.
 19.65 NBC

RAITT, JOHN
 Pulitzer Prize Playhouse ep Knickerbocker Holiday
  11.17.50 ABC
 Musical Comedy Time ep Revenge with Music 2.19.
  51 NBC
 The Web ep The Dark Shore 6.25.52 CBS
 Motorola TV Hour ep The Thirteen Clocks 12.29.53
  ABC
 Annie Get Your Gun Sp 11.27.57 NBC
 Shirley Temple's Story Book ep Rumpelstiltskin 2.21.
  58 NBC
 G.E. Theatre ep No Man Can Take Me 2.1.59 CBS
 Shirley Temple Theatre ep The Reluctant Dragon 11.
  12.60 NBC

RALSTON, ESTHER
 Kraft Theatre ep September Tide 2.7.52 NBC
 Tales of Tomorrow ep All the Time in the World 6.
  13.52 ABC
 Broadway Television Theatre ep The Noose 4.20.53
  NN

RAMBEAU, MARJORIE
 G.E. Theatre ep Atomic Love 11.22.53 CBS
 Ford Theatre cp The Blue Ribbon 11.10.55 NBC
 G.E. Theatre ep Prologue to Glory 2.12.56 CBS
 Ford Theatre ep That Evil Woman 3.15.56 NBC

RAMBO, DACK
 New Loretta Young Show sr 9.24.62 CBS

Guns of Will Sonnett sr 9.8.67 ABC
Guns of Will Sonnett sr ret 9.27.68 ABC
Gunsmoke ep The Witness 11.23.70 CBS
Gunsmoke ep Pike 3.1.71, 3.8.71 CBS
River of Gold tf 3.9.71 ABC
Man and the City ep Disaster on Turner Street 10.20.71 ABC
Cannon ep 11.30.71 CBS

RANDALL, TONY
Philco Playhouse ep A Little Something in Reserve 5.10.53 NBC
The Web ep The Badger Game 7.26.53 CBS
Kraft Theatre ep In Albert's Room 8.19.53 NBC
Mr. Peepers sr 9.53 NBC
Playhouse ep When, Lovely Woman 10.2.53 ABC
Goodyear Playhouse ep The Huntress 2.14.54 NBC
Motorola TV Hour ep Nightmare in Algiers 3.23.54 ABC
Armstrong Circle Theatre ep The Beautiful Wife 8.31.54 NBC
Mr. Peepers sr ret 9.19.54 NBC
Appointment with Adventure ep 9.4.55 CBS
Philco Playhouse ep One Mummy Too Many 11.20.55 NBC
Alcoa Hour ep Man on a Tiger 1.8.56 NBC
Studio One ep The Hollywood Complex 2.18.57 CBS
Playhouse 90 ep The Playroom 10.10.57 CBS
Goodyear Playhouse ep Coogan's Reward 1.5.59 NBC
Desilu Playhouse ep Martin's Folly 2.23.59 CBS
Playhouse 90 ep Second Happiest Day 6.25.59 CBS
Goodyear Playhouse ep Hello, Charlie 9.28.59 NBC
Sunday Showcase ep The Secret of Freedom 2.28.60 NBC
G.E. Theatre ep Strictly Solo 12.11.60 CBS
Checkmate ep The Button-Down Break 10.11.61 CBS
Hallmark Hall of Fame ep Arsenic and Old Lace 2.5.62 NBC
Alfred Hitchcock Theatre ep Hangover 12.6.62 CBS
Love American Style ep 1.23.70 ABC
The Odd Couple sr 9.24.70 ABC
Here's Lucy ep 9.20.71 CBS
The Odd Couple sr ret 9.17.71 ABC
Hallmark Hall of Fame ep The Littlest Angel 12.12.71 NBC
The Odd Couple sr ret 9.15.72 ABC

RANDELL, RON
    The Doctor ep Escape from the Past 5.3.53 NBC
    Ford Theatre ep Ever Since the Day 12.24.53 NBC
    The Vise sh fall, 1954 ABC
    Douglas Fairbanks Presents ep The Apple 7.21.54
      NBC
    Rheingold Theatre ep The Lovely Place 12.8.54 NBC
    Cavalcade Theatre ep Swamp Mutiny 10.25.55 ABC
    Crusader ep The Waif 6.15.56 CBS
    20th Century-Fox Hour ep Man of the Law 2.20.57
      CBS
    O.S.S. sr 9.26.57 ABC
    The Millionaire ep The Rafe Peterson Story 4.23.58
      CBS
    Gunsmoke ep 10.18.58 CBS
    Richard Diamond ep 2.15.59 CBS
    Adventures in Paradise ep The Siege of Troy 3.7.60
      ABC
    Alcoa Premiere ep Contact 5.24.60 ABC
    Overland Trail ep The Most Dangerous Gentleman 6.
      5.60 NBC
    The Millionaire ep Maggie Dalton Story 6.10.60 CBS
    Americans ep Harpers Ferry: 1861 1.23.61 NBC
    Checkmate ep The Someday Man 5.2.62 CBS
    Tales of Wells Fargo ep The Gold Witch 5.5.62 NBC
    Espionage ep Some Other Kind of World 3.18.64 NBC
    Perry Mason ep The Case of the Illicit Illusion 4.9.
      64 CBS
    Outer Limits ep The Duplicate Man 12.19.64 ABC
    Alfred Hitchcock Theatre ep Thou Still Unravished
      Bride 3.22.65 NBC
    Bonanza ep 5.16.65 NBC
    Wild, Wild West ep Night of the Fatal Trap 12.24.65
      CBS
    Bewitched ep 1.4.68 ABC
    Mission Impossible ep 10.6.68, 10.13.68 CBS
    Mannix ep Last Rites for Miss Emma 3.8.69 CBS
    Young Rebels ep Valley of the Guns 11.29.70 ABC

RASUMNY, MIKHAIL
    Silver Theatre ep The Great Nikoli 1.23.50 CBS
    Bigelow Theatre ep Lady with Ideas 3.25.51 CBS
    Elgin Hour ep Hearts and Hollywood 11.30.54 ABC
    Kraft Theatre ep Departure 2.16.55 NBC
    Producers Showcase ep Darkness at Noon 5.2.55 NBC
    Front Row Center ep Finley's Fan Club 1.8.56 CBS

RATHBONE, BASIL
    Tele-Theatre ep Queen of Spades 3.6.50 NBC
    NBC Showcase ep Sherlock Holmes 5.30.50 NBC
    Airflyte Theatre ep The Kind Mr. Smith 12.28.50
      CBS
    Video Theatre ep 1.15.51 CBS
    Suspense ep Dr. Jekyll and Mr. Hyde 3.5.51 CBS
    Lights Out ep Dead Man's Coat 5.14.51 NBC
    Video Theatre ep Masquerade 5.5.52 CBS
    Broadway Television Theatre ep Criminal at Large
      2.2.53 NN
    Broadway Television Theatre ep The Firebrand 3.2.
      53 NN
    Suspense ep The Adventure of the Black Baronet 5.
      26.53 CBS
    Danger ep The Educated Heart 11.17.53 CBS
    Motorola Television Hour ep The Thirteen Clock 12.
      29.53 ABC
    Studio One ep The House of Gair 8.16.54 CBS
    Schlitz Playhouse of Stars ep Volturio Investigates 12.
      3.54 CBS
    Shower of Stars ep A Christmas Carol 12.23.54 CBS
    World of Disney ep nar The Reluctant Dragon 2.2.55
      ABC
    Svengali and the Blonde 7.30.55 NBC
    Star Tonight ep nar The Selfish Giant 12.22.55 ABC
    Kraft Theatre ep Five Minutes to Live 2.1.56 NBC
    Alcoa Hour ep The Stingiest Man in Town 12.23.56
      NBC
    Hallmark Hall of Fame ep The Lark 2.10.57 NBC
    Hallmark Hall of Fame ep Soldier in Love 4.26.57
      NBC
    U.S. Steel Hour ep Huck Finn 11.20.57 CBS
    Kraft Theatre ep Heroes Walk on Sand 12.11.57 NBC
    Hallmark Hall of Fame ep Hans Brinker 2.9.58 NBC
    Dupont Show of the Month ep Aladdin 2.21.58 CBS
    Hallmark Hall of Fame ep Victoria Regina 11.30.61
      NBC
    Burke's Law ep 4.7.65 ABC
    Dr. Kildare ep Perfect Is Hard to Be 12.27.65, 12.
      28.65 NBC
    The Pirates of Flounder Bay pt 8.26.66 ABC

RAY, ALDO
    Desilu Playhouse ep K.O. Kitty 11.17.58 CBS
    Riverboat ep Payment in Full 9.13.59 NBC
    Naked City ep Idylls of a Running Back 9.26.62 ABC

Virginian ep Big Day, Great Day 10.24.62 NBC
Alcoa Premiere ep Lollipop Louie 1.10.63 ABC
Ben Casey ep Little Drops of Water, Little Grains of
    Sand 10.30.63 ABC
Burke's Law ep 3.13.64 ABC
Bonanza ep The Wild One 10.4.64 NBC
Bob Hope Chrysler Theatre ep Have Girls--Will
    Travel 10.16.64 NBC
Virginian ep Jacob Was a Plain Man 10.12.66 NBC
Run for Your Life ep 1.30.67 NBC
Danny Thomas Show ep Fame Is a Four Letter Word
    10.30.67 NBC
Suspense Theatre ep The Deep End 1.11.68 ABC
Outsider ep The Old School Tie 1.22.69 NBC
Deadlock tf 2.22.69 NBC
Love American Style ep 10.10.69 ABC
Bonanza ep 10.3.72 NBC

RAY, JOHNNIE
    G.E. Theatre ep The Big Shot 1.30.55 CBS

RAYE, MARTHA
    Musical Comedy Time ep Anything Goes 10.2.50 NBC
    Burke's Law ep 2.10.65 ABC
    Bugaloos sr 9.12.70 NBC

RAYMOND, GENE
    Pulitzer Prize Playhouse ep The Pharmacist's Mate
        12.22.50 ABC
    Tales of Tomorrow ep Plague from Space 4.25.52
        ABC
    Pulitzer Prize Playhouse ep The American Leonardo
        5.21.52 ABC
    Footlights Theatre ep Mechanic on Duty 8.29.52 CBS
    Tales of Tomorrow ep Many Happy Returns 10.24.52
        ABC
    Broadway Television Theatre ep The Letter 11.3.52
        NN
    Broadway Television Theatre ep This Thing Called
        Love 12.1.52 NN
    Schlitz Playhouse of Stars ep The Girl that I Married
        5.29.53 CBS
    Video Theatre ep Some Call It Love 8.27.53 CBS
    Fireside Theatre sh/sr 9.1.53 NBC
    Schlitz Playhouse of Stars ep Dawn at Damascus 4.
        22.54 CBS
    Fireside Theatre sh/sr ret 8.31.54 NBC

Kraft Theatre ep The Hickory Limb 1.13.55 ABC
Loretta Young Show ep Week-End in Winnetka 9.4.55 NBC
Ford Theatre ep Dear Diane 1.12.56 NBC
Fireside Theatre ep The Double Life of Barney Peters 1.18.55 NBC
Matinee Theatre ep Skylark 2.26.56 NBC
TV Reader's Digest Theatre ep Go Fight City Hall 6.18.56 ABC
Matinee Theatre ep Heart of a Husband 10.4.56 NBC
Ethel Barrymore Theatre ep Lady Investigator 11.30.56 NN
Matinee Theatre ep The Wisp End 12.14.56 NBC
Matinee Theatre ep Ivy Curtain 11.6.57 NBC
Climax ep Secret Love of Johnny Spain 2.20.58 CBS
Climax ep House of Doubt 6.19.58 CBS
U.S. Steel Hour ep Big Doc's Girl 11.4.59 CBS
Johnny Ringo ep 1.14.60 CBS
Barbara Stanwyck Theatre ep Big Career 2.13.61 NBC
U.S. Steel Hour ep The Shame of Paula Marsten 4.19.61 CBS
U.S. Steel Hour ep The Haven 6.28.61 CBS
Sam Benedict ep 9.15.62 NBC
Route 66 ep Journey to Nineveh 9.28.62 CBS
Dick Powell Theatre ep The Old Man and the City 4.23.63 NBC
Defenders ep The Brother Killers 5.25.63 CBS
Channing ep Dragon in the Den 10.23.63 ABC
Outer Limits ep The Borderland 12.16.63 ABC
Burke's Law ep 4.17.64 ABC
The Man from U.N.C.L.E. ep The Secret Sceptor Affair 2.8.65 NBC
Defenders ep The Non-Violent 4.1.65 CBS
Laredo ep The Land Slickers 10.14.66 NBC
The Girl from U.N.C.L.E. ep The Fountain of Youth Affair 2.7.67 NBC
Judd for the Defense ep Death from a Flower Girl 11.3.67 ABC
Hondo ep 11.17.67 ABC
Ironside ep Desperate Encounter 10.24.68 NBC
Julia ep 4.8.69 NBC
Bold Ones ep To Save a Life 9.14.69 NBC
Name of the Game ep High Card 12.5.69 NBC
Name of the Game ep The Power 12.12.69 NBC
Mannix ep Missing: Sun and Sky 12.20.69 CBS
Paris 7000 ep No Place to Hide 1.29.70 ABC

Paris 7000 ep Call Me Lee 2. 5. 70 ABC
Interns ep The Price of Love 10. 30. 70 CBS
FBI ep The Inheritors 12. 27. 70 ABC
D. A. ep 11. 12. 71 NBC

RAYMOND, PAULA
  Story Theatre ep The Million Pound Bank Note 7. 30.
    51 NBC
  Fireside Theatre ep Let the Cards Decide 1. 6. 53
    NBC
  Ford Theatre ep Lucky Tommy Jordan 2. 4. 54 NBC
  Four Star Playhouse ep The Doctor and the Countess
    4. 29. 54 CBS
  Willy ep 11. 27. 54 CBS
  Fireside Theatre ep It's Easy to Get Ahead 3. 29. 55
    NBC
  Fireside Theatre ep Three Missions West 11. 30. 54
    NBC
  Cavalcade of America ep Petticoat Doctor 1. 25. 55
    ABC
  Cavalcade of America ep The Rescue of Dr. Beanes
    6. 21. 55 ABC
  Californians ep Shanghai Queen 6. 3. 58 NBC
  M Squad ep The Woman from Paris 6. 6. 58 NBC
  Schlitz Playhouse of Stars ep You'll Have to Die Now
    6. 20. 58 CBS
  Yancy Derringer ep Gallatin Story 10. 9. 58 CBS
  Peter Gunn ep The Torch 12. 8. 58 NBC
  Schlitz Playhouse of Stars ep Practically Strangers
    1. 30. 59 CBS
  Bachelor Father ep 2. 15. 59 CBS
  Bat Masterson ep A Matter of Honor 4. 29. 59 NBC
  Alcoa Premiere ep Emergency Only 6. 23. 59 ABC
  Markham ep Vendetta in Venice 6. 27. 59 CBS
  Hawaiian Eye ep Waikiki Widow 10. 14. 59 ABC
  G. E. Theatre ep Signs of Love 11. 8. 59 CBS
  Deputy ep Backfire 1. 2. 60 NBC
  Bat Masterson ep Mr. Fourpaws 2. 18. 60 NBC
  Have Gun Will Travel ep 4. 9. 60 CBS
  Tightrope ep Borderline 5. 17. 60 CBS
  M Squad ep Open Season 5. 31. 60 NBC
  Bat Masterson ep The Last of the Night Riders 11.
    24. 60 NBC
  Cheyenne ep Home Is the Brave 12. 5. 60 ABC
  Aquanauts ep The Cave Divers 12. 7. 60 CBS
  77 Sunset Strip ep A Face in the Window 2. 24. 61
    ABC

Michael Shayne   ep   Four Lethal Ladies   2.17.61 NBC
Law and Mr. Jones   ep   The Concert   3.10.61 ABC
Perry Mason   ep   The Case of the Torrid Tapestry   4.
   22.61 CBS
Surfside 6   ep   5.15.61 ABC
Maverick   ep   The Golden Fleecing   10.8.61 ABC

REAGAN, RONALD
Airflyte Theatre   ep   Disappearance of Mrs. Gordon
   12.7.50 CBS
Hollywood Opening Night   ep   The Priceless Gift   12.
   29.52 NBC
Ford Theatre   ep   First Born   2.5.53 NBC
Medallion Theatre   ep   A Job for Jimmy Valentine   7.
   18.53 CBS
Schlitz Playhouse of Stars   ep   The Doctor Goes Home
   7.31.53 CBS
Video Theatre   ep   Message in a Bottle   9.3.53 CBS
Mirror Theatre   ep   Next Stop Bethlehem   12.5.53 CBS
Ford Theatre   ep   And Suddenly You Knew   12.10.53
   NBC
Video Theatre   ep   A Place in the Sun   1.28.54 CBS
Schlitz Playhouse of Stars   ep   The Jungle Trap   2.19.
   54 CBS
Schlitz Playhouse of Stars   ep   The Edge of Battle   3.
   26.54 CBS
Ford Theatre   ep   Beneath These Waters   5.20.54 NBC
G.E. Theatre   sh/sr   9.26.54 CBS
G.E. Theatre   sh/sr   ret 10.2.55 CBS
G.E. Theatre   sh/sr   ret 9.30.56 CBS
G.E. Theatre   sh/sr   ret fall, 1957 CBS
G.E. Theatre   sh/sr   ret fall, 1958 CBS
G.E. Theatre   sh/sr   ret fall, 1959 CBS
G.E. Theatre   sh/sr   ret fall, 1960 CBS
Zane Grey Theatre   ep   The Long Shadow   1.19.61 CBS
G.E. Theatre   sh/sr   ret 9.24.61 CBS
Dick Powell Theatre   ep   Who Killed Julie Greer?   9.
   26.61 NBC
Wagon Train   ep   The Fort Pierce Story   9.23.63 ABC
Kraft Suspense Theatre   ep   Cruel and Unusual Night
   6.4.64 NBC
Death Valley Days   sh   1965 NN

REDFORD, ROBERT
Deputy   ep   Last Gunfight   4.30.60 NBC
Playhouse 90   ep   In the Presence of Mine Enemies
   5.18.60 CBS

Hallmark Hall of Fame   ep   Captain Brassbound's Con-
   version   5. 2. 60 NBC
Tate   ep   The Bounty Hunter   6. 22. 60 NBC
Tate   ep   Comanche Scalps   8. 10. 60 NBC
Perry Mason   ep   The Case of the Treacherous Toupee
   9. 17. 60 CBS
Play of the Week   ep   The Iceman Cometh   11. 14. 60,
   11. 21. 60 NN
Our American Heritage   ep   Born a Giant   12. 2. 60 NBC
Play of the Week   ep   Black Monday   1. 16. 61 NN
Naked City   ep   Tombstone for a Derelict   4. 5. 61 ABC
Americans   ep   The Coward   5. 8. 61 NBC
Whispering Smith   ep   5. 8. 61 NBC
Route 66   ep   First Class Mouliak   10. 20. 61 CBS
Bus Stop   ep   The Covering Darkness   10. 22. 61 ABC
Alfred Hitchcock Theatre   ep   The Right Kind of Medi-
   cine   12. 19. 61 NBC
Twilight Zone   ep   Nothing in the Dark   1. 5. 62 CBS
Alfred Hitchcock Theatre   ep   A Piece of the Action
   9. 20. 62 CBS
Dr. Kildare   ep   The Burning Sky   10. 4. 62 NBC
Alcoa Premiere   ep   The Voice of Charlie Post   10. 25.
   62 ABC
Untouchables   ep   Snowball   1. 15. 63 ABC
Dick Powell Theatre   ep   The Last of the Big Spenders
   4. 16. 63 ABC
Breaking Point   ep   Bird and Snake   10. 7. 63 ABC
Virginian   ep   The Evil that Men Do   10. 16. 63 NBC
Defenders   ep   The Siege   12. 3. 64 CBS

REDGRAVE, MICHAEL
   Omnibus   ep   My Brother Henry   12. 28. 52 CBS
   Omnibus   ep   The Bear   1. 4. 53 CBS
   Omnibus   ep   She Stoops to Conquer   11. 20. 55 CBS
   Ruggles of Red Gap   Sp   2. 3. 57 NBC
   Hedda Gabler   Sp   9. 20. 63 CBS
   ABC Stage 67   ep   The Canterville Ghost   11. 2. 66 ABC
   N. E. T. Playhouse   ep   Uncle Vanya   2. 10. 67 NN
   Heidi   Sp   11. 17. 68 NBC
   David Copperfield   tf   3. 15. 70 NBC
   Hallmark Hall of Fame   ep   11. 17. 70 NBC

REED, DONNA
   Ford Theatre   ep   Portrait of Lydia   12. 16. 54 NBC
   G. E. Theatre   ep   Flight from Tormendero   2. 24. 57
   CBS
   Suspicion   ep   The Other Side of the Curtain   10. 14. 57
   NBC

Donna Reed Show   sr   9. 24. 58 ABC
Donna Reed Show   sr ret   9. 59 ABC
Donna Reed Show   sr ret   9. 15. 60 ABC
Donna Reed Show   sr ret   9. 61 ABC
Donna Reed Show   sr ret   9. 20. 62 ABC
Donna Reed Show   sr ret   9. 19. 63 ABC
Donna Reed Show   sr ret   9. 17. 64 ABC
Donna Reed Show   sr ret   9. 16. 65 ABC

REED, FLORENCE
Pulitzer Prize Playhouse   ep   The Royal Family   3. 16. 51 ABC
Broadway Television Theatre   ep   Suspect   10. 6. 52 NN
Armstrong Circle Theatre   ep   Black Wedding   1. 27. 63 NBC
Omnibus   ep   Iliad   4. 3. 55 CBS
The Skin of Our Teeth   Sp   9. 11. 55 NBC
U. S. Steel Hour   ep   You Can't Have Everything   1. 27. 60 CBS

REED, OLIVER
Court Martial   ep   La Belle France   6. 10. 66 ABC

REED, ROBERT
Father Knows Best   ep   The Imposter   10. 26. 59 CBS
Men into Space   ep   1. 27. 60 CBS
Bronco   ep   Volunteers from Aberdeen   2. 9. 60 ABC
Defenders   sr   9. 16. 61 CBS
Defenders   sr ret   9. 62 CBS
Defenders   sr ret   9. 63 CBS
Dr. Kildare   ep   11. 15. 63 NBC
Defenders   sr ret   9. 24. 64 CBS
Dr. Kildare   ep   The Life Machine   10. 26. 65, 11. 1. 65, 11. 2. 65 NBC
Bob Hope Chrysler Theatre   ep   The Admiral   12. 29. 65 NBC
Somewhere in Italy, Company B   pt   8. 21. 66 ABC
Hondo   ep   9. 29. 67 ABC
Ironside   ep   Light at the End of the Journey   11. 9. 67 NBC
Journey to the Unknown   ep   The New People   10. 3. 68 ABC
Mannix   ep   3. 29. 69 CBS
Brady Bunch   sr   9. 26. 69 ABC
Mannix   sr   9. 27. 69 CBS
Love American Style   ep   11. 17. 69 ABC
Brady Bunch   sr ret   9. 25. 70 ABC

Mannix   sr ret   9.26.70 CBS
Love American Style   ep   1.29.71 ABC
Mannix   sr ret   9.15.71 CBS
Brady Bunch   sr ret   9.17.71 ABC
Assignment Munich   tf   4.30.72 ABC
Mod Squad   ep   The Connection   9.14.72 ABC
Mannix   sr ret   9.17.72 CBS
Brady Bunch   sr ret   9.25.72 ABC
Mission Impossible   ep   11.11.72 CBS

REEVES, GEORGE
   Superman   sr   1950 NN
   Silver Theatre   ep   The First Show of 1950   1.2.50
      CBS
   Television Theatre   ep   Kelly   1.25.50 NBC
   Television Theatre   ep   Storm in a Teacup   5.17.50
      NBC
   The Trap   ep   Sentence of Death   5.27.50 CBS
   Kraft Theatre   ep   The Wind Is 90   7.23.50 NBC
   Television Theatre   ep   Feathers in a Gale   8.9.50
      NBC
   Superman   sr ret   1951 NN
   Fireside Theatre   ep   Hurry, Hurry   3.25.52 NBC
   Kraft Theatre   ep   Six by Six   8.6.52 NBC
   Footlights Theatre   ep   Heart of Gold   7.31.53 CBS
   Superman   sr ret   4.15.53 ABC
   Superman   sr ret   fall, 1953 ABC
   Superman   sr ret   fall, 1954 ABC
   Ray Bolger Show   ep   12.17.54 ABC
   Superman   sr ret fall, 1955 ABC
   Superman   sr ret fall, 1956 ABC

REID, KATE
   Hallmark Hall of Fame   ep   Abe Lincoln in Illinois   2.
      5.54 NBC
   Hallmark Hall of Fame   ep   The Holy Terror   4.7.65
      NBC
   N.E.T. Playhouse   ep   An Enemy of the People   12.2.
      66 NN
   Hallmark Hall of Fame   ep   Neither Are We Enemies
      3.13.70 NBC
   Lassie   ep   Any Heart in a Storm   12.13.70 CBS

REMICK, LEE
   Kraft Theatre   ep   Double in Ivory   9.9.53 NBC
   Robert Montgomery Presents   ep   My Little Girl   3.29.
      54 NBC

Studio One   ep   Death and Life of Larry Benson   5.31.
  54 CBS
Robert Montgomery Presents   ep   It Depends on You
  2.28.55 NBC
Kraft Theatre   ep   The Diamond as Big as the Ritz .9.
  28.55 NBC
Robert Montgomery Presents   ep   Man Lost   10.24.55
  NBC
Robert Montgomery Presents   ep   Three Men from To-
  morrow   1.2.56 NBC
Robert Montgomery Presents   ep   All Expenses Paid
  5.21.56 NBC
Studio One   ep   The Landlady's Daughter   11.26.56 CBS
Robert Montgomery Presents   ep   The Young and Beau-
  tiful   12.10.56 NBC
Playhouse 90   ep   The Last Tycoon   3.14.57 CBS
Kraft Theatre   ep   Circle of Fear   8.14.57 NBC
Playhouse 90   ep   Last Clear Chance   3.6.58 CBS
Hallmark Hall of Fame   ep   The Tempest   2.3.60 NBC
Theatre '62   ep   The Farmer's Daughter   1.14.62 NBC
Damn Yankees   Sp   4.8.67 NBC
Hallmark Hall of Fame   ep   The Man Who Came to Din-
  ner   11.29.72 NBC
Of Men and Women   Sp   12.17.72 ABC

RENALDO, DUNCAN
  The Cisco Kid   sr   1.20.51 NN

RENNIE, MICHAEL
  Climax   ep   The Great Impersonation   3.10.55 CBS
  Climax   ep   Dr. Jekyll and Mr. Hyde   7.28.55 CBS
  Climax   ep   Man of Taste   12.1.55 CBS
  Climax   ep   Strange Sanctuary   3.28.57 CBS
  Climax   ep   Stranger Death at Burnleigh   5.2.57 CBS
  Playhouse 90   ep   Circle of the Day   5.30.57 CBS
  Climax   ep   A Taste for Crime   6.20.57 CBS
  Climax   ep   The Mystery of the Red Room   9.12.57
    CBS
  Wagon Train   ep   The John Cameron Story   10.2.57
    NBC
  Alfred Hitchcock Presents   ep   Foghorn   3.16.58 CBS
  Frank Sinatra Show   ep   The Man on the Stairs   3.21.
    58 ABC
  Zane Grey Theatre   ep   Three Days to Death   4.4.58
    CBS
  Decision   ep   The Tall Man   7.27.58 NBC
  Lux Playhouse   ep   The Connoisseur   10.31.58 CBS

Zane Grey Theatre ep Living Is a Lonesome Thing
   1.1.59 CBS
Pursuit ep Epitaph for a Golden Girl 1.14.59 CBS
Zane Grey Theatre ep Man in the Middle 2.11.60
   CBS
Man from Blackhawk ep The Ghost of Lafitte 2.26.
   60 ABC
Shirley Temple Theatre ep Kim 9.25.60 NBC
Third Man sr 9.29.60 NBC
Family Classics ep The Scarlet Pimpernel 10.28.60
   CBS
Americans ep Rebellion at Blazing Rock 1.30.61 NBC
Barbara Stanwyck Theatre ep The Sisters 2.6.61 NBC
Route 66 ep Fly Away Home 2.17.66 CBS
Dick Powell Theatre ep The Fifth Caller 12.19.61
   NBC
Alfred Hitchcock Theatre ep Silk Petticoat 1.2.62
   NBC
Dick Powell Theatre ep Project "X" 1.8.63 NBC
Perry Mason ep The Case of the Libelous Locket 2.
   7.63 CBS
Virginian ep Vengeance Is the Spur 2.27.63 NBC
Alfred Hitchcock Theatre ep Long Silence 3.21.63
   CBS
Hallmark Hall of Fame ep The Invincible Mr. Dis-
   raeli 4.4.63 NBC
Wagon Train ep The Robert Harrison Clark Story 10.
   14.63 ABC
Great Adventures ep The Treasure Train of Jefferson
   Davis 11.15.63 CBS
Daniel Boone ep The Sound of Wings 11.12.64 NBC
Kraft Suspense Theatre ep Rapture at 240 4.15.65
   NBC
Branded ep Salute the Soldier Briefly 10.24.65 NBC
12 O'Clock High ep The Slaughter Pen 1.10.66 ABC
Bob Hope Chrysler Theatre ep One Embezzlement and
   Two Margaritas 5.18.66 NBC
Time Tunnel ep Rendezvous with Yesterday 9.9.66
   ABC
Daniel Boone ep 10.13.66 NBC
FBI ep The Conspirators 2.5.67 ABC
Bob Hope Chrysler Theatre ep Blind Man's Bluff 2.
   8.67 NBC
Iron Horse ep 2.20.67 ABC
Invaders ep The Innocent 3.14.67 ABC
Hondo ep 9.15.67 ABC
I Spy ep Laya 9.25.67 NBC

The Man from U. N. C. L. E.   ep   The Thrush Roulette
  Affair   10. 23. 67 NBC
Danny Thomas Show   ep   Fame Is a Four Letter Word
  10. 30. 67 NBC
Invaders   ep   The Summer Meeting   10. 31. 67, 11. 7. 67
  ABC
FBI   ep   1. 14. 68 ABC
The Search   pt   7. 28. 68 CBS
FBI   ep   Caesar's Wife   1. 26. 69 ABC

RETTIG, TOMMY
Your Play Time   ep   The Tin Bridge   7. 5. 53 CBS
Footlights Theatre   ep   Heart of Gold   7. 31. 53 CBS
Your Play Time   ep   Long Long Ago   8. 2. 53 CBS
Four Star Playhouse   ep   No Identity   8. 27. 53 CBS
Ford Theatre   ep   First Born   9. 10. 53 NBC
Omnibus   ep   Nothing so Monster   1. 24. 54 CBS
Ford Theatre   ep   Good of His Soul   3. 4. 54 NBC
Lassie   sr   9. 12. 54 CBS
Schlitz Playhouse of Stars   ep   Mr. Ears   4. 8. 66 CBS
Lassie   sr ret   fall, 1955 CBS
Lassie   sr ret   fall, 1956 CBS
Lassie   sr ret   fall, 1957 CBS
Studio One   ep   No Place to Run   9. 15. 58 CBS
Lawman   ep   The Town Boys   9. 18. 60 ABC
Wagon Train   ep   Weight of Command   1. 25. 61 NBC
Peter Gunn   ep   I Know It's Murder   2. 13. 61 ABC
Cheyenne   ep   Trouble at Sand Springs   4. 17. 61 ABC
Death Valley Days   ep   Davy's Friend   12. 28. 63 ABC
Many Happy Returns   ep   1. 25. 65 CBS
Fugitive   ep   Trial by Fire   10. 5. 65 ABC

REVERE, ANN
Play of the Week   ep   The House of Bernarda Alba   6.
  6. 60 NN
Play of the Week   ep   Four by Tennessee Williams   2.
  6. 61 NN
Repertory Theatre   ep   The Trojan Women   5. 5. 65 NN
Two for the Money   tf   2. 26. 72 ABC

REY, ALEJANDRO
Perry Mason   ep   The Case of the Injured Innocent   11.
  18. 61 CBS
Thriller   ep   La Strega   1. 15. 62 NBC
Dick Powell Theatre   ep   Price of Tomatoes   1. 16. 62
  NBC
Outlaws   ep   A Day to Kill   2. 22. 62 NBC

Real McCoys   ep   Made in Italy   4.5.62 ABC
Lloyd Bridges Show   ep   Wheresoever I Enter   9.11.62
   CBS
Wide Country   ep   Who Killed Eddie Gannon   10.11.62
   NBC
Dick Powell Theatre   ep   The Doomsday Boys   10.16.62
   NBC
Dobie Gillis   ep   Who Did William Tell   1.2.63 CBS
Naked City   ep   Bringing Far Places Together   2.20.63
   ABC
Route 66   ep   Peace, Pity, Pardon   4.12.63 CBS
Fugitive   ep   Smoke Screen   10.29.63 ABC
The Greatest Show on Earth   ep   Where the Wire Ends
   1.7.64 ABC
Arrest and Trial   ep   The Best There Is   2.16.64 ABC
Alfred Hitchcock Theatre   ep   The Life and Work of
   Juan Diaz   10.26.64 NBC
Slattery's People   sr   9.17.65 CBS
Trials of O'Brien   ep   The Only Game in Town   3.18.66
   CBS
I Spy   ep   My Mother, The Spy   3.30.66 NBC
Daniel Boone   ep   3.13.66 NBC
The Girl from U.N.C.L.E.   ep   The Horns of the Di-
   lemma Affair   10.18.66 NBC
Run for Your Life   ep   Edge of the Volcano   10.31.66
   NBC
FBI   ep   The Gray Passenger   1.29.67 ABC
My Three Sons   ep   2.16.67 CBS
Iron Horse   ep   3.6.67 ABC
That Girl   ep   4.6.67 ABC
Flying Nun   sr   9.7.67 ABC
Three for Danger   pt   9.8.67 NBC
Cowboy in Africa   ep   1.15.68, 1.22.68 ABC
Flying Nun   sr ret   9.68 ABC
It Takes a Thief   ep   Guess Who's Coming to Rio   1.7.
   69 ABC
FBI   ep   2.23.69 ABC
Outcasts   ep   And Then There Was One   3.3.69 ABC
Flying Nun   sr ret   9.17.69 ABC
Seven in Darkness   tf   9.23.69 ABC
High Chaparral   ep   9.18.70 NBC
Cannon   ep   1.11.71 CBS
Owen Marshall   ep   Eighteen Years Next April   11.4.71
   ABC
Gunsmoke   ep   11.29.71 CBS
Gunsmoke   ep   The Bullett   12.6.71, 12.13.71 CBS
Alias Smith and Jones   ep   The Clementine Incident

10. 7. 72 ABC

REYNOLDS, BURT
    M Squad ep The Teacher 1. 2. 59 NBC
    Schlitz Playhouse of Stars ep You Can't Win 'em All
      1. 16. 59 CBS
    Riverboat sr 9. 13. 59 NBC
    Lawless Years ep The Payoff 6. 11. 59 NBC
    Playhouse 90 ep Alas, Babylon 4. 3. 60 CBS
    Johnny Ringo ep The Stranger 5. 19. 60 CBS
    Aquanauts ep The Big Swim 12. 14. 60 CBS
    Michael Shayne ep The Boat Caper 4. 7. 61 NBC
    Zane Grey Theatre ep Man from Everywhere 4. 13. 61
      CBS
    Malibu Run ep Kidnap Adventure 5. 17. 61 CBS
    Route 66 ep Love Is a Skinny Kid 4. 6. 62 CBS
    Gunsmoke sr 9. 29. 62 CBS
    Branded ep Now Join the Human Race 9. 19. 65 NBC
    Flipper ep 9. 25. 65, 10. 2. 65 NBC
    FBI ep All the Streets Are Silent 11. 28. 65 ABC
    12 O'Clock High ep The Jones Boy 12. 6. 65 ABC
    Hawk sr 9. 8. 66 ABC
    Gentle Ben ep 10. 8. 67 CBS
    FBI ep 1. 21. 68 ABC
    Lassiter pt 7. 8. 68 CBS
    Run, Simon, Run 1. 21. 70 tf ABC
    Love American Style ep 2. 6. 70 ABC
    Hunters Are for Killing tf 3. 12. 70 CBS
    Dan August sr 9. 23. 70 ABC

REYNOLDS, DEBBIE
    Here's Debbie sr 9. 16. 69 NBC
    Bracken's World ep 10. 17. 69 NBC
    Bracken's World ep It's the Power Structure Baby 12.
      5. 69 NBC

REYNOLDS, MARJORIE
    Bigelow Theatre ep A Case of Marriage 1. 28. 51 CBS
    Gruen Guild Theatre ep Peril in the House 11. 1. 51
      ABC
    Drama ep The Haircut 3. 1. 52 ABC
    The Unexpected ep The Slide Rule Blonde 4. 2. 52
      NBC
    Campbell Playhouse ep Luckiest Guy in the World 8.
      15. 52 NBC
    Life of Riley sr 1. 2. 53 NBC
    Life of Riley sr ret 9. 18. 53 NBC

Life of Riley   sr ret   9.54 NBC
The Millionaire   ep   The Story of Fred Malcolm   4.20.
  55 CBS
Life of Riley   sr ret   9.16.55 NBC
Life of Riley   sr ret   9.14.56 NBC
The Millionaire   ep   Millionaire Dixon Cooper   5.4.60
  CBS
Shirley Temple Theatre   ep   Emmy Lou   11.6.60 NBC
Leave It to Beaver   ep   Chuckie's New Shoes   12.10.60
  ABC
Alcoa Premiere   ep   The Cake Baker   1.2.62 ABC
Leave It to Beaver   ep   Beaver, the Babysitter   4.7.62
  ABC
Tales of Wells Fargo   ep   Don't Wake a Tiger   5.12.62
  NBC
Our Man Higgins   ep   The Milkman Cometh   1.9.63
  ABC
Our Man Higgins   ep   3.6.63 ABC
Wide Country   ep   The Quest of Jacob Blaufus   3.7.63
  NBC
Leave It to Beaver   ep   The All-Night Party   5.30.63
  ABC
Good Guys   ep   3.12.69 CBS

REYNOLDS, WILLIAM
  Pete Kelly's Blues   sr   4.5.59 NBC
  Wagon Train   ep   The Clara Duncan Story   4.22.59 NBC
  Maverick   ep   Holiday at Hollow Rock   7.5.59 ABC
  Maverick   ep   Cure for Johnny Rain   12.20.59 ABC
  The Millionaire   ep   Millionaire Timothy Mackail   12.
    30.59 CBS
  The Islanders   sr   10.2.60 ABC
  Roaring 20s   ep ° Nobody's Millions   10.21.61 ABC
  Gallant Men   sr   10.5.62 ABC
  Temple Houston   ep   The Siege at Thayer's Bluff   11.7.
    63 NBC
  O.K. Crackerby   ep   1.6.66 ABC
  FBI   ep   Anatomy of a Prison Break   11.27.66 ABC
  Dragnet   ep   4.12.67 NBC
  FBI   sr   9.17.67 ABC
  FBI   sr ret   9.22.68 ABC
  FBI   sr ret   9.14.69 ABC
  FBI   sr ret   9.20.70 ABC
  FBI   sr ret   9.12.71 ABC
  FBI   sr ret   9.17.72 ABC

RHODES, ERIK
    Appointment with Adventure   ep   The House on Gellen
        Street   5. 8. 55 CBS
    Phil Silvers Show   ep   Bilko the Male Model   3. 14. 58
        CBS

RICHARDS, BEAH
    Dr. Kildare   ep   A Cry from the Streets   1. 24. 66,   1.
        25. 66,   1. 31. 66,   2. 1. 66 NBC
    Big Valley   ep   9. 12. 66 ABC
    I Spy   ep   Cops and Robbers   4. 12. 67 NBC
    Hawaii Five-O   ep   2. 26. 69 CBS
    Ironside   ep   Alias Mr. Baithwaite   9. 18. 69 NBC
    Room 222   ep   12. 31. 69 ABC
    It Takes a Thief   ep   2. 23. 70 ABC
    On Stage   ep   To Confuse the Angel   3. 15. 70 NBC
    Sanford and Son   ep   9. 15. 72 NBC
    Footsteps   tf   10. 3. 72 CBS

RICHARDSON, RALPH (SIR)
    Hedda Gabler   Sp   9. 20. 63 CBS
    David Copperfield   tf   3. 15. 70 NBC
    Home   Sp   11. 29. 71 NN

RICHMAN, MARK
    Goodyear Playhouse   ep   Star in the Night   8. 22. 54
        NBC
    Philco Playhouse   ep   Middle of the Night   9. 19. 54
        NBC
    Goodyear Playhouse   ep   Backfire   2. 27. 55 NBC
    Philco Playhouse   ep   The Bold and the Brave   4. 17.
        55 NBC
    Playwrights '56   ep   The Center of the Maze   4. 24. 56
        NBC
    U. S. Steel Hour   ep   The Partners   7. 18. 56 NBC
    Kraft Theatre   ep   Sheriff's Man   3. 27. 57 NBC
    Goodyear Playhouse   ep   The House   9. 8. 57 NBC
    Jane Wyman Theatre   ep   Roadblock Number Seven   11.
        7. 57 NBC
    Playhouse 90   ep   The Last Man   1. 9. 58 CBS
    Schlitz Playhouse of Stars   ep   Home Again   1. 17. 58
        CBS
    Kraft Theatre   ep   Death Wears Many Faces   7. 30. 58
        NBC
    Alfred Hitchcock Presents   ep   Man with a Problem   11.
        16. 58 CBS
    Zane Grey Theatre   ep   Mission to Marathon   5. 14. 59
        CBS

June Allyson Show   ep   Ruth and Naomi   9.21.59 CBS
U.S. Steel Hour   ep   The Hours Before Dawn   9.23.59
   CBS
U.S. Steel Hour   ep   Act of Terror   12.30.59 CBS
Alfred Hitchcock Presents   ep   The Cure   1.24.60 CBS
Moment of Fear   ep   Fire by Night   7.22.60 NBC
Play of the Week   ep   Emmanuel   12.19.60 NN
A Question of Chairs   1.15.61 CBS
Play of the Week   ep   Therese Raquin   3.13.61 NN
U.S. Steel Hour   ep   Shame of Paula Marsten   4.19.61
   CBS
Cain's Hundred   sr   9.19.61 NBC
U.S. Steel Hour   ep   You Can't Escape   6.13.62 CBS
Stoney Burke   ep   The Journey   5.20.63 ABC
Breaking Point   ep   Crack in an Image   10.28.63 ABC
Virginian   ep   Marie Valonne   11.6.63 NBC
Ben Casey   ep   From Too Much Love of Living   12.11.
   63 ABC
Outer Limits   ep   The Borderland   12.16.63 ABC
Combat   ep   The Hostages   1.28.64 ABC
Virginian   ep   The Girl from Yesterday   11.11.64 NBC
Fugitive   ep   Ballad for a Ghost   12.29.64 ABC
Profiles in Courage   ep   3.7.65 NBC
FBI   ep   The Problem of the Honorable Wife   10.31.65
   ABC
Wild, Wild West   ep   11.5.65 CBS
12 O'Clock High   ep   The Jones Boy   12.6.65 ABC
Combat   ep   Counterplay   1.25.66 ABC
Voyage to the Bottom of the Sea   ep   Web of Destruction
   2.26.66 ABC
Blue Light   ep   The Friendly Enemy   3.16.66 ABC
Fugitive   ep   The Last Oasis   9.13.66 ABC
T.H.E.   Cat   ep   10.28.66 NBC
Jericho   ep   Two for the Road   11.10.66, 11.17.66 CBS
Virginian   ep   2.8.67 NBC   .
Iron Horse   ep   3.6.67 ABC
Daniel Boone   ep   9.28.67 NBC
Ironside   ep   The Taker   10.12.67 NBC
The Man from U.N.C.L.E.   ep   The Seven Wonders of
   the World Affair   1.8.68, 1.15.68 NBC
It Takes a Thief   ep   1.16.68 ABC
Gunsmoke   ep   2.26.68 CBS
Invaders   ep   3.26.68 ABC
FBI   ep   4.7.68 ABC
FBI   ep   11.17.68 ABC
Name of the Game   ep   Pineapple Rose   12.20.68 NBC
Bonanza   ep   A World Full of Cannibals   12.22.68 NBC

My Friend Tony   ep   1. 5. 69 NBC
It Takes a Thief   ep   1. 28. 69 ABC
Hawaii Five-O   ep   Golden Boy in Black Trunks   2. 12.
    69 CBS
Lancer   ep   2. 25. 69 CBS
Name of the Game   ep   12. 19. 69 NBC
Mannix   ep   Walk with a Dead Man   1. 10. 70 CBS
The House on Green Apple Road   tf   1. 11. 70 ABC
Mission Impossible   ep   2. 1. 70 CBS
FBI   ep   Return to Power   2. 15. 70 ABC
McCloud   tf   2. 17. 70 NBC
Silent Force   ep   10. 5. 70 ABC
Mission Impossible   ep   10. 25. 70 CBS
Longstreet   sr   9. 16. 71 ABC

RICKLES, DON
Stage 7   ep   A Note of Fear   5. 15. 55 CBS
Four Star Playhouse   ep   The Listener   2. 2. 56 CBS
Burke's Law   ep   Who Killed Harris Crown   10. 11. 63
    ABC
Addams Family   ep   10. 30. 64 ABC
Burke's Law   ep   2. 10. 65 ABC
Munsters   ep   Dance with Me, Herman   2. 18. 65 CBS
Dick Van Dyke Show   ep   The Alan Brady Show Goes to
    Jail   11. 4. 64, 11. 11. 64 CBS
Gomer Pyle, U. S. M. C.   ep   3. 12. 65 CBS
Wild, Wild West   ep   The Night of the Druid's Blood
    3. 25. 66 CBS
The Lucy Show   ep   2. 20. 67 CBS
I Spy   ep   Night Train to Madrid   3. 22. 67 NBC
I Dream of Jeannie   ep   10. 10. 67 NBC

RIGG, DIANA
Avengers   sr   3. 28. 66 ABC
Avengers   sr ret   1. 20. 67 ABC
Avengers   sr ret   1. 10. 68 ABC
N. E. T. Playhouse   ep   Women Beware Women   11. 1. 68
    NN
On Stage   ep   Married Alive   1. 23. 70 NBC

RISDON, ELISABETH
Footlight Theatre   ep   The Other Jesse Grant   9. 12. 52
    CBS
Summer Theatre   ep   The Man with Nothing to Lose   7.
    31. 53 ABC
Schlitz Playhouse of Stars   ep   Sheila   8. 21. 53 CBS
Ford Theatre   ep   Letters Marked Personal   1. 27. 55
    NBC

Treasury Men in Action   ep   The Case of the Only Son
4.28.55 ABC
Damon Runyon Theatre   ep   Bunny on the Beach   7.16.
55 CBS
Ford Theatre   ep   All for a Man   3.8.56 NBC

RITCHARD, CYRIL
Prudential Family Playhouse   ep   Ruggles of Red Gap
2.27.51 CBS
Kraft Theatre   ep   Mrs. Dane's Defense   4.11.51 NBC
Goodyear Playhouse   ep   Treasure Chest   3.2.52 NBC
Studio One   ep   Pontius Pilate   4.7.52 CBS
Philco Playhouse   ep   Two for One   1.18.53 NBC
Goodyear Playhouse   ep   Here's Father   1.17.54 NBC
Philco Playhouse   ep   The King and Mrs. Candle   4.18.
54 NBC
Omnibus   ep   11.28.54 CBS
Omnibus   ep   The Merry Widow   12.26.54 CBS
Mr. Peepers   ep   1.23.55 NBC
Mr. Peepers   ep   2.6.55, 2.13.55 NBC
Producers Showcase   ep   Peter Pan   3.7.55 NBC
Goodyear Playhouse   ep   Visit to a Small Planet   5.8.
55 NBC
Studio One   ep   The Spongers   6.6.55 CBS
Producers Showcase   ep   The King and Mrs. Candle   8.
22.55 NBC
Dearest Enemy   Sp   11.26.55 NBC
Producers Showcase   ep (restaged) Peter Pan   1.9.56
NBC
Hallmark Hall of Fame   ep   The Good Fairy   2.5.56
NBC
Playwrights '56   ep   The Undiscovered Man   3.27.56
NBC
Producers Showcase   ep   Rosalinda   7.23.56 NBC
Producers Showcase   ep   Jack and the Beanstalk   11.12.
56 NBC
Dupont Show of the Month   ep   Aladdin   2.21.58 CBS
Omnibus   ep   H.M.S. Pinafore   5.10.59 NBC
Peter Pan   Sp (restaged)   12.8.60 NBC
Dr. Kildare   ep   A Sense of Tempo   5.7.64 NBC
Irregular Verb to Love   Sp   11.12.65 NN
The Dangerous Christmas of Red Riding Hood   Sp   11.
28.65 ABC
Hans Brinker   Sp   12.13.69 NBC
N.E.T. Playhouse   ep   Foul   11.26.70 NN

RITTER, TEX
  Zane Grey Theatre ep Sundown at Bitter Creek 2.14.
    58 CBS
  Rebel ep The Ballad of Danny Brown 4.9.61 ABC

RITTER, THELMA
  Best of Broadway ep The Show-Off 2.2.55 CBS
  Goodyear Playhouse ep The Catered Affair 5.22.55
    NBC
  20th Century-Fox Hour ep The Late Christopher Bean
    11.30.55 CBS
  Alfred Hitchcock Presents ep The Baby Sitter 5.6.56
    CBS
  U.S. Steel Hour ep The Human Pattern 1.2.57 CBS
  Telephone Time ep Plot to Save a Boy 2.17.57 CBS
  G.E. Theatre ep Sarah's Laughter 1.2.60 CBS
  Ford Startime ep The Man 1.5.60 NBC
  Frontier Circus ep Journey from Hannibal 11.16.61
    CBS
  Wagon Train ep The Madame Sagittarius Story 10.3.
    62 ABC

RIVA, MARIA
  Studio One ep Portrait by Rembrandt 4.30.51 CBS
  Studio One ep A Chance for Happiness 5.21.51 CBS
  Summer Theatre ep The Swan 7.2.51 CBS
  Summer Theatre ep The Rabbit 8.13.51 CBS
  Studio One ep Angelic Avengers 9.17.51 CBS
  Studio One ep The Idol of San Vittore 10.1.51 CBS
  Video Theatre ep Cafe Ami 10.15.51 CBS
  Studio One ep The Dangerous Years 11.26.51 CBS
  Studio One ep The Innocence of Pastor Muller 12.17.
    51 CBS
  Video Theatre ep Ceylon Treasure 1.14.52 CBS
  Danger ep Hello, Mr. Lutz 4.22.52 CBS
  Summer Theatre ep I Lift My Lamp 8.17.52 NBC
  Philco Playhouse ep The Last Hour 9.7.52 NBC
  Armstrong Circle Theatre ep The Betrayal 10.14.52
    NBC
  Robert Montgomery Presents ep The Davidian Report
    11.17.52 NBC
  Studio One ep I Am Jonathan Scrivener 12.1.52 CBS
  Studio One ep To a Moment of Triumph 1.26.53 CBS
  Suspense ep Kiss Me Again, Stranger 4.14.53 CBS
  Omnibus ep The Abracadabra Kid 4.19.53 CBS
  Robert Montgomery Presents ep Linda 5.4.53 NBC
  Mirror Theatre ep The Bottle Party 9.1.53 NBC

Medallion Theatre   ep   10.24.53 CBS
TV Hour   ep   Brandenburg Gate   12.1.53 ABC
Hallmark Hall of Fame   ep   The Story of Ruth   4.18.
   54 NBC
The Web   ep   Hurricane Warning   6.13.54 CBS
Studio One   ep   The Cliff   9.13.54 CBS
Studio One   ep   The Education of H*Y*M*A*N K*A*P*-
   L*A*N   9.27.54 CBS
Robert Montgomery Presents   ep   Woman in the Window
   9.12.55 NBC
Stage 7   ep   End of the Line   6.19.55 CBS
Climax   ep   To Wake at Midnight   6.23.55 CBS
Appointment with Adventure   ep   Desperate Game   7.24.
   55 CBS
20th Century-Fox Hour   ep   Operation Cicero   12.26.56
   CBS

ROARKE, ADAM
Alfred Hitchcock Theatre   ep   The Sign of Satan   5.8.
   64 CBS
Mod Squad   ep   The Guru   12.31.68 ABC

ROBARDS JR., JASON
Studio One   ep   A Picture in the Paper   5.9.55 CBS
Studio One   ep   The Incredible World of Horace Ford
   6.13.55 CBS
Philco Playhouse   ep   The Death of Billy the Kid   7.24.
   55 NBC
Philco Playhouse   ep   The Outsiders   9.18.55 NBC
Appointment with Adventure   ep   Destination Freedom
   9.25.55 CBS
Armstrong Circle Theatre   ep   Lost: $2 Billion--Diary
   of Diane   10.11.55 NBC
Justice   ep   Decision by Panic   10.30.55 NBC
Big Story   ep   Miracle in the Desert   12.9.55 NBC
Appointment with Adventure   ep   A Thief There Was
   3.18.56 CBS
Justice   ep   Pattern of Lies   3.25.56 NBC
Alcoa Hour   ep   Even the Weariest River   4.15.56 NBC
Goodyear Playhouse   ep   Proud Passage   8.12.56 NBC
Goodyear Playhouse   ep   Nobody's Town   1.27.57 NBC
Alcoa Hour   ep   The Big Build-Up   3.31.57 NBC
Alcoa Hour   ep   Night   9.22.57 NBC
Studio One   ep   Twenty-Four Hours to Dawn   11.11.57
   CBS
Omnibus   ep   Moment of Truth   2.23.58 NBC
Playhouse 90   ep   For Whom the Bell Tolls   3.12.59,

3.19.59 CBS
Dupont Show of the Month ep Billy Budd 5.25.59 CBS
Sunday Showcase ep People Kill People 9.20.59 NBC
Hallmark Hall of Fame ep A Doll's House 11.15.59
    NBC
Great Mysteries ep The Bat 3.31.60 NBC
Play of the Week ep The Iceman Cometh 11.14.60,
    11.21.60 NN
Westinghouse Presents ep That's Where the Town's
    Going 4.17.62 CBS
Bob Hope Chrysler Theatre ep One Day in the Life of
    Ivan Denisovich 11.8.63 NBC
Hallmark Hall of Fame ep Abe Lincoln in Illinois 2.
    5.64 NBC
Bob Hope Chrysler Theatre ep Shipwrecked 6.8.66
    NBC
ABC Stage 67 ep Noon Wine 11.23.67 ABC
Ghost Story ep The Dead We Leave Behind 9.15.72
    NBC
The House without a Christmas Sp 12.3.72 CBS

ROBELING, PAUL
Hallmark Hall of Fame ep Anastasia 3.17.67 NBC

ROBERTS, LYNNE
Hollywood Opening Night ep Pretty Boy 10.12.51 CBS
Fireside Theatre ep Not a Bit Like Jason 11.27.51
    NBC
Fireside Theatre ep Hunt for Death 1.8.52 NBC
Electric Theatre ep Uncle Marty and Marie 4.13.52
    NN
Schaeffer Century Theatre ep Portrait of Toby 5.24.
    52 NBC
Royal Playhouse ep Eleventh Hour 6.12.52 NN
Schaefer Century Theatre ep Shooting Star 6.14.52
    NBC
Teledrama ep Secret Service Investigator 6.19.53 CBS
Wyatt Earp ep Shanghai Pierce 11.15.55 ABC
Wyatt Earp ep King of the Cattle Trail 5.1.56 ABC

ROBERTS, TONY
Trials of O'Brien ep Charlie Has All the Luck 11.20.
    65 CBS
Edge of Night sr 1967 CBS
Storefront Lawyers ep Where Are You At? 11.4.70
    CBS
Night Gallery ep The Messiah on Mott Street 12.15.71
    NBC

ROBERTSON, CLIFF
 Short Short Drama   ep   A Portrait of General Garrity
 11.25.52 NBC
 Rod Brown of the Rocket Rangers   sr   4.18.53 CBS
 Armstrong Circle Theatre   ep   The use of Dignity   5.
 25.54 NBC
 Robert Montgomery Presents   ep   Pilgrim's Pride   5.
 10.54 NBC
 Robert Montgomery Presents   ep   The Decision   6.28.
 54 NBC
 Robert Montgomery Presents   ep   The Expert   7.5.54
 NBC
 Robert Montgomery Presents   ep   Home Town   8.2.54
 NBC
 Robert Montgomery Presents   ep   Ten-Minute Alibi   9.
 13.54 NBC
 U.S. Steel Hour   ep   A Fair Shake   2.1.56 CBS
 Kraft Theatre   ep   Vengeance   9.25.57 NBC
 Playhouse 90   ep   Natchez   5.29.58 CBS
 Playhouse 90   ep   The Days of Wine and Roses   10.2.
 58 CBS
 Wagon Train   ep   The Liam Fitzmorgan Story   10.29.58
 NBC
 Alcoa Theatre   ep   Goodbye, Johnny   2.9.59 NBC
 Desilu Playhouse   ep   The Hard Road   3.30.59 CBS
 Alcoa Theatre   ep   Shadow of Evil   11.30.59 NBC
 Untouchables   ep   Underground Railway   12.31.59 ABC
 Playhouse 90   ep   The Cruel Day   2.24.60 CBS
 Riverboat   ep   End of a Dream   9.19.60 NBC
 U.S. Steel Hour   ep   The Man Who Knew Tomorrow   9.
 21.60 CBS
 Outlaws   ep   Ballad for a Badman   10.6.60 NBC
 U.S. Steel Hour   ep   The Two Worlds of Charlie Gordon
 2.22.61 CBS
 G.E. Theatre   ep   The Small Elephants   3.12.61 CBS
 Twilight Zone   ep   A Hundred Yards over the Rim   4.7.
 61 CBS
 Outlaws   ep   The Connie Masters Story   10.12.61 NBC
 Dick Powell Theatre   ep   The Geetas Box   11.14.61
 NBC
 U.S. Steel Hour   ep   Man on the Mountaintop   11.15.61
 CBS
 Outlaws   ep   The Dark Sunrise of Griff Kincaid   1.4.62
 NBC
 Bus Stop   ep   How Does Charlie Feel?   2.4.62 ABC
 Golden Showcase   ep   Saturday's Children   2.25.62 CBS
 Alcoa Premiere   ep   Second Chance   3.13.62 ABC

Twilight Zone   ep   The Dummy   5.4.62 CBS
Ben Casey   ep   For the Ladybug, One Dozen Roses   9.
24.62 ABC
Eleventh Hour   ep   The Man Who Came Home Late   5.
8.63 NBC
Outer Limits   ep   The Galaxy Being   9.16.63 ABC
The Greatest Show on Earth   ep   The Circus Never
Came to Town   11.5.63 ABC
Breaking Point   ep   So Many Pretty Girls, So Little
Time   2.17.64 ABC
Bob Hope Chrysler Theatre   ep   The Game   9.15.65
NBC
Bob Hope Chrysler Theatre   ep   And Baby Makes Five
10.5.66 NBC
Batman   ep   Come Back, Shame   11.30.66, 12.1.66
ABC
Bob Hope Chrysler Theatre   ep   Verdict for Terror   3.
29.67 NBC
Batman   ep   2.1.68, 2.8.68 ABC
Bracken's World   ep   Stop Date   12.19.69 NBC

ROBERTSON, DALE
Ford Theatre   ep   The Face   3.29.56 NBC
Schlitz Playhouse of Stars   ep   A Tale of Wells Fargo
12.14.56 CBS
20th Century-Fox Hour   ep   The Still Trumpet   4.3.57
CBS
Climax   ep   Circle of Destruction   1.24.57 CBS
Tales of Wells Fargo   sr   3.18.57 NBC
Tales of Wells Fargo   sr ret   9.9.57 NBC
Tales of Wells Fargo   sr ret   9.58 NBC
Tales of Wells Fargo   sr ret   9.59 NBC
Tales of Wells Fargo   sr ret   9.60 NBC
Tales of Wells Fargo   sr ret   9.30.61 NBC
Iron Horse   sr   9.12.66 ABC
Iron Horse   sr ret   9.16.67 ABC

ROBINSON, EDWARD G.
Lux Video Theatre   ep   Witness for the Prosecution   9.
17.53 CBS
Climax   ep   Epitaph for a Spy   12.9.54 CBS
For the Defense   pt   1954 NN
Ford Theatre   ep   ...And Son   1.13.55 NBC
Ford Theatre   ep   A Set of Values   12.29.55 NBC
Playhouse 90   ep   Shadows Tremble   10.23.58 CBS
Goodyear Theatre   ep   A Good Name   3.2.59 NBC
Zane Grey Theatre   ep   Heritage   4.2.59 CBS

The Devil and Daniel Webster   Sp   2. 14. 60 NBC
The Right Man   Sp   10. 24. 60 CBS
G. E. Theatre   ep   The Drop-Out   1. 29. 61 CBS
Detectives   ep   The Legend of Jim Riva   10. 6. 61 NBC
Who Has Seen the Wind   tf   2. 19. 65 ABC
U. M. C.   tf   4. 17. 69 CBS
Bracken's World   ep   9. 26. 69 NBC
The Old Man Who Cried Wolf   10. 13. 70 ABC
Bracken's World   ep   The Mary Tree   11. 23. 70 NBC
Night Gallery   ep   The Messiah on Mott Street   12. 15. 71
   NBC

ROCKWELL, ROBERT
   Schaefer Century Theatre   ep   Yesterday's World   7. 9.
      52 NBC
   Campbell Playhouse   ep   The Little Pig Cried   8. 22. 52
      NBC
   Our Miss Brooks   sr   10. 3. 52 CBS
   Our Miss Brooks   sr ret   10. 2. 53 CBS
   Our Miss Brooks   sr ret   10. 1. 54 CBS
   Our Miss Brooks   sr ret   10. 7. 55 CBS
   Telephone Time   ep   She Sette Her Little Foote   10. 21.
      56 CBS
   The Millionaire   ep   The Story of Professor Amberson
      Adams   2. 13. 57 CBS
   Private Secretary   ep   The Reunion   4. 16. 57 CBS
   Tales of Wells Fargo   ep   4. 22. 57 NBC
   Meet McGraw   ep   The Texas Story   9. 17. 57 NBC
   Oh Susanna   ep   The Phantom Valise   11. 9. 57 CBS
   Loretta Young Show   ep   Dear Milkman   2. 9. 58 NBC
   Eve Arden Show   ep   3. 25. 68 CBS
   Navy Log   ep   Fire at Sea   4. 24. 58 ABC
   Loretta Young Show   ep   Day of Rest   5. 18. 58 NBC
   Loretta Young Show   ep   In the Gold Old Summertime
      10. 19. 58 NBC
   The Millionaire   ep   The Lee Randolph Story   11. 19. 58
      CBS
   Desilu Playhouse   ep   Comeback   3. 2. 59 CBS
   Gunsmoke   ep   4. 4. 59 NBC
   Perry Mason   ep   The Case of the Deadly Toy   5. 16. 59
      CBS
   The Man from Blackhawk   sr   10. 16. 59 ABC
   Roaring 20s   ep   Champagne, Lady   10. 22. 60 ABC
   Maverick   ep   Substitute Gun   4. 2. 61 ABC
   Perry Mason   ep   The Case of the Misguided Missile   5.
      6. 61 CBS
   Perry Mason   ep   The Case of the Shapely Shadow   1. 6.
      62 CBS

Cheyenne   ep   A Town that Lived and Died   4.9.62 ABC
Perry Mason   ep   The Case of the Lurid Letter   12.6.
   62 CBS
Perry Mason   ep   The Case of the Candy Queen   9.26.
   65 CBS
Thompson's Ghost   pt   8.6.66 ABC
Lassie   ep   1.22.67 CBS
Lassie   ep   3.24.68 CBS
Lassie   ep   11.3.68 CBS
Lassie   ep   3.30.69 CBS
Bill Cosby Show   ep   Killer Instinct or Star Billing   11.
   9.69 NBC
Lassie   ep   Lassie's Saga   9.27.70, 10.4.70, 10.11.70
   CBS

RODRIGUEZ, PERCY
Nurses   ep   11.28.63 CBS
Carol for Another Christmas   tf   12.28.64 ABC
Slattery's People   ep   Who You Taking to the Main Event
   Eddie   3.12.65 CBS
Ben Casey   ep   A Horse Named Stravinsky   5.17.65 ABC
Daktari   ep   1.18.66 CBS
Wild, Wild West   ep   The Night of the Situation Normal
   10.28.66 CBS
Mission Impossible   ep   10.29.66 CBS
Fugitive   ep   3.7.67 ABC
Bob Hope Chrysler Theatre   ep   Deadlock   5.17.67 NBC
Tarzan   ep   9.22.67   NBC
Mission Impossible   ep   10.8.67, 10.15.67 CBS
Mannix   ep   Catalog of Sins   12.2.67 CBS
Peyton Place   sr   9.68 ABC
Name of the Game   ep   A Hard Case of the Blues   9.
   26.69 NBC
Then Came Bronson   ep   Two Per Cent of Nothing   11.
   26.69 NBC
Marcus Welby, M.D.   ep   Let Ernest Come Over   12.9.
   69 ABC
Mannix   ep   Tooth of the Serpent   12.27.69 CBS
Medical Center   ep   Moment of Decision   1.14.70 CBS
Mission Impossible   ep   1.25.70 CBS
Silent Force   sr   9.21.70 ABC
Name of the Game   ep   10.9.70 NBC
The Old Man Who Cried Wolf   tf   10.13.70 ABC
World of Disney   ep   Bayou Boy   2.14.71 NBC
The Forgotten Man   tf   9.14.71 ABC
Medical Center   ep   Blood Line   9.15.71 CBS
Ironside   ep   And Then There Was One   1.20.72 NBC

Banacek   ep   9. 27. 72 NBC
Owen Marshall   ep   10. 5. 72 ABC
Streets of San Francisco   ep   10. 14. 72 ABC
Sixth Sense   ep   10. 14. 72 ABC
Sixth Sense   ep   12. 23. 72 ABC

ROGERS, CHARLES "BUDDY"
The Lucy Show   ep   12. 4. 67,   12. 11. 67 CBS

ROGERS, GINGER
Producers Showcase   ep   Tonight at 8:30   10. 18. 54 NBC
June Allyson Show   ep   The Tender Shoot   10. 19. 59 CBS
Zane Grey Theatre   ep   Never Too Late   2. 4. 60 CBS
A Love Affair Just for Three   pt   7. 22. 63 CBS
Cinderella   Sp   2. 22. 66 CBS
Bob Hope Chrysler Theatre   ep   Terror Island   2. 26. 66
    NBC
Here's Lucy   ep   11. 8.71 CBS

ROGERS, ROY
Roy Rogers Show   sr   12. 30. 51 NBC
Roy Rogers Show   sr ret   8. 31. 52 NBC
Roy Rogers Show   sr ret   fall, 1953 NBC
Roy Rogers Show   sr ret   fall, 1954 NBC
Cavalcade of America   ep   A Medal for Miss Walker
    12. 14. 54 ABC
Roy Rogers Show   sr ret   fall, 1955 NBC
Roy Rogers Show   sr ret   fall, 1956 NBC

ROGERS JR., WILL
Ford Theatre   ep   Life, Liberty and Orrin Dooley   10.
    2. 52 NBC
Ford Theatre   ep   Lucky Tommy Jordan   2. 4. 54 NBC
Schlitz Playhouse of Stars   ep   Gift of the Devil   8. 13.
    54 CBS
Schlitz Playhouse of Stars   ep   Mr. Schoolmarm   2. 11.
    55 CBS
Schlitz Playhouse of Stars   ep   A Mule for Santa Fe   6.
    17. 55 CBS
Schlitz Playhouse of Stars   ep   2. 17. 56 CBS

ROLAND, GILBERT
Ford Theatre   ep   The Arden Woodsman   1. 14. 54 NBC
Fireside Theatre   ep   The Smuggler   10. 25. 55 NBC
Playhouse 90   ep   Invitation to a Gunfighter   3. 7. 57
    CBS
Schlitz Playhouse of Stars   ep   Rich Man, Poor Man

    12.20.57 CBS
Wagon Train   ep   The Bernal Sierra Story   3.12.58 NBC
Desilu Playhouse   ep   Border Justice   11.13.59 CBS
World of Disney   ep   El Bandido   10.30.60 ABC
World of Disney   ep   Adios el Cuchilo   11.6.60 ABC
Dick Powell Theatre   ep   Death in a Village   1.2.62 NBC
Frontier Circus   ep   Quick Shuffle   2.1.62 CBS
The Greatest Show on Earth   ep   Don't Look Down, Don't Look Back   10.8.63 ABC
Alfred Hitchcock Theatre   ep   Death and the Joyful Women   4.12.63 CBS
Gunsmoke   ep   Extradition   12.7.63, 12.14.63 CBS
Fugitive   ep   Somebody to Remember   3.24.64 ABC
Combat   ep   The Convict   2.16.65 ABC
Death Valley Days   ep   Kingdom for a Horse   2.19.65 NN
Bonanza   ep   The Lonely Runner   10.10.65 NBC
The Poppy Is Also a Flower   tf   4.22.66 ABC
Fugitive   ep   3.14.67 ABC
Land's End   pt   4.21.68 NBC
FBI   ep   The Patriot   2.2.69 ABC
High Chaparral   ep   The New Line of Sonora   2.19.71 NBC
Night Gallery   ep   The Waiting Room   1.26.72 NBC
McCloud   ep   10.1.72 NBC
Medical Center   ep   11.8.72 CBS

ROMAN, RUTH
Story Theatre   ep   Mme. Fifi   9.13.51 NBC
Lux Video Theatre   ep   The Chase   12.30.54 NBC
Ford Theatre   ep   The Lilac Bush   3.3.55 NBC
Producers Showcase   ep   Darkness at Noon   5.2.55 NBC
G.E. Theatre   ep   Into the Night   5.8.55 CBS
Climax   ep   Spin into Darkness   4.5.56 CBS
Ford Theatre   ep   Panic   6.14.56 NBC
Jane Wyman Theatre   ep   He Came for the Money   2.13.58 NBC
Bonanza   ep   Magnificent Adah   11.14.59 NBC
The Philadelphia Story   Sp   12.7.59 NBC
G.E. Theatre   ep   The Book of Silence   3.6.60 CBS
Naked City   ep   The Human Trap   11.30.60 ABC
Untouchables   ep   Man Killer   12.7.61 ABC
Bus Stop   ep   Turn Again Home   1.28.62 ABC
Alfred Hitchcock Theatre   ep   What Really Happened   1.11.63 CBS

Sam Benedict ep Green Room, Grey Morning 1.19.
    63 NBC
Eleventh Hour ep Advice to the Lovelorn and Shop-
    worn 1.30.63 NBC
Route 66 ep In the Closing of a Trunk 3.8.63 CBS
The Greatest Show on Earth ep Silent Love, Secret
    Love 9.24.63 ABC
Burke's Law ep Who Killed Harris Crown 10.11.63
    ABC
Dr. Kildare ep Four Feet in the Morning 11.21.63
    NBC
Eleventh Hour ep 11.27.63 NBC
Breaking Point ep Who Is Mimi--What Is She 12.2.
    63 ABC
Bob Chrysler Theatre ep The Candidate 12.6.63 NBC
Outer Limits ep Moonstone 3.9.64 ABC
Dr. Kildare ep A Candle in the Window 11.5.64 NBC
Bing Crosby Show ep Real Estate Venture 4.19.65
    ABC
The Long Hot Summer sr 9.16.65 ABC
FBI ep 1.15.67 ABC
The Girl from U.N.C.L.E. ep 2.21.67 NBC
Tarzan ep 3.31.67 NBC
I Spy ep Let's Kill Karlovassi 12.8.67 NBC
Name of the Game ep Witness 9.27.68 NBC
Mission Impossible ep 11.24.68 CBS
Outcasts ep The Town that Wouldn't 3.31.69 ABC
Gunsmoke ep 10.6.69 CBS
Marcus Welby, M.D. ep Diagnosis: Fear 12.30.69
    ABC
The Old Man Who Cried Wolf tf 10.13.70 ABC
Mannix ep The Judas Touch 1.16.71 CBS
Men from Shiloh ep The Angus Killer 2.10.71 NBC
Incident in San Francisco tf 2.28.71 ABC
Gunsmoke ep 9.27.71 NBC
Ironside ep Gentle Oaks 11.25.71 NBC
Sixth Sense ep 10.28.72 ABC
Mod Squad ep 12.7.72 ABC

ROMERO, CESAR
    Bigelow Theatre ep The Big Hello 4.29.51 CBS
    Campbell Playhouse ep The Cavorting Statue 6.20.52
        NBC
    Schlitz Playhouse of Stars ep Tango 11.7.72 CBS
    Mr. Lucky at Seven ep A Letter from Home 12.5.52
        ABC
    Ford Theatre ep All's Fair in Love 2.26.53 NBC

Pepsi Cola Playhouse ep The Police Arrive 6.25.54
ABC
Passport to Danger sr fall, 1954 NN
Climax ep The Long Goodbye 10.7.54 CBS
Passport to Danger sr ret fall, 1955 NN
Damon Runyon Theatre ep Situation Wanted 10.29.55
CBS
Manhattan Tower Sp 10.27.56 NBC
Climax ep Strange Sanctuary 3.28.57 CBS
Schlitz Playhouse of Stars ep Old Spanish Custom 6.7.
57 CBS
Studio 57 ep Mrs. Snyder 7.28.57 NN
Matinee Theatre ep Father Came Home 10.15.57 NBC
Lucille Ball-Desi Arnaz Hour ep Lucy Takes a Cruise
to Havana 11.6.57 CBS
Wagon Train ep The Honorable Don Charlie Story 1.
22.58 NBC
Zane Grey Theatre ep Threat of Violence 5.23.58
CBS
Studio One ep Birthday Present 8.18.58 CBS
Zorro ep The Gay Caballero 1.22.59 ABC
Texan ep 4.13.59 CBS
Rawhide ep Incident of the Stalking Death 11.13.59
CBS
Love and Marriage ep Jealousy 1.11.60 NBC
Zane Grey Theatre ep The Reckoning 1.14.60 CBS
Mystery Show ep The Suicide Club 9.18.60 NBC
Pete and Gladys ep Crime of Passion 9.26.60 CBS
Stagecoach West ep A Time to Run 11.15.60 ABC
Ann Sothern Show ep 11.17.60 CBS
Zane Grey Theatre ep Man from Everywhere 4.13.61
CBS
Stagecoach West ep The Big Gun 4.25.61 ABC
Dupont Show of the Month ep The Battle of the Paper
Bullets 10.15.61 NBC
Target Corruptors ep My Native Land 3.16.62 ABC
Follow the Sun ep A Ghost in Her Hazebo 3.18.62
ABC
Rawhide ep The Child-Woman 3.23.62 CBS
Dick Powell Theatre ep Charlie's Duet 3.19.63 NBC
Rawhide ep Incident at Rio Doloroso 5.10.63 CBS
Burke's Law ep Jet-Setter 1.10.64 ABC
Dr. Kildare ep Onions, Garlic and Flowers that Bloom
in the Spring 2.6.64 NBC
Burke's Law ep 5.1.64 ABC
Branded ep The Mission 3.14.65, 3.21.65, 3.28.65
NBC

The Man from U.N.C.L.E. ep The Never-Never Affair 3.22.65 NBC
Ben Casey ep Did Your Mother Come from Ireland
    5.3.65 ABC
Rawhide ep The Vasquez Woman 10.26.65 CBS
Daniel Boone ep 1.16.66 NBC
Batman ep The Joker Is Wild 2.2.66, 2.3.66 ABC
Bonanza ep The Deadliest Game 2.21.66 NBC
Batman ep 3.2.66, 3.3.66 ABC
Batman ep The Joker Trumps an Ace 4.6.66, 4.7.
    66 ABC
Batman ep The Impractical Joker 11.16.66, 11.17.
    66 ABC
T.H.E. Cat ep 1.6.67 NBC
Batman ep The Zodiak Crimes 1.11.67, 1.12.67, 1.
    18.67 ABC
Batman ep 2.15.67, 2.16.67 ABC
Batman ep 3.22.67, 3.23.67 ABC
Daniel Boone ep 3.30.67 NBC
Batman ep 11.16.67 ABC
Batman ep 12.28.67 ABC
Batman ep 2.29.68 ABC
Daniel Boone ep 11.13.69 NBC
It Takes a Thief ep Beyond a Treasonable Doubt 3.
    16.70 ABC
Julia ep Half Past Sick 9.22.70 NBC
Bewitched ep Salem, Here We Come 10.1.70 ABC
Julia ep 11.10.70 NBC
Alias Smith and Jones ep The McCreedy Bust 1.21.71
    ABC
Nanny ep 1.29.71 ABC
Alias Smith and Jones ep 1.13.72 ABC
Mod Squad ep The Connection 9.14.72 ABC
Alias Smith and Jones ep 9.30.72 ABC

ROONEY, MICKEY
    Celanese Theatre ep Saturday's Children 3.10.52 ABC
    Hey, Mulligan (a.k.a. The Mickey Rooney Show) sr 8.
        24.54 NBC
    Schlitz Playhouse of Stars ep The Lady Was a Flop 1.
        4.57 CBS
    Playhouse 90 ep The Comedian 2.14.57 CBS
    Mr. Broadway Sp 5.11.57 NBC
    Pinocchio Sp 10.13.57 NBC
    December Bride ep 4.14.58 CBS
    Alcoa Theatre ep Eddie 11.17.58 NBC
    Wagon Train ep The Greenhorn Story 10.7.59 NBC

Wagon Train ep Wagons Ho 9.28.60 NBC
G.E. Theatre ep The Money Driver 12.18.60 CBS
Checkmate ep The Paper Killers 3.25.61 CBS
Hennessey ep Shore Patrol Revisited 5.8.61 CBS
Dick Powell Theatre ep Who Killed Julie Greer? 9.
    26.61 NBC
Investigators ep I Thee Kill 10.26.61 CBS
Dick Powell Theatre ep Somebody's Waiting 11.7.61
    NBC
Naked City ep Offus Goofus 12.13.61 ABC
Dick Powell Theatre ep Special Assignment 9.25.62
    NBC
Dick Powell Theatre ep Everybody Loves Sweeney 1.
    22.63 NBC
Alcoa Premiere ep Five, Six, Pickup Sticks 5.30.63
    ABC
Twilight Zone ep The Last Night of a Jockey 10.25.
    63 CBS
Kraft Suspense Theatre ep The Hunt 12.19.63 NBC
Arrest and Trial ep Funny Man with a Monkey 1.5.
    64 ABC
Bob Hope Chrysler Theatre ep The Seven Little Foys
    1.24.64 NBC
Burke's Law ep 2.21.64 ABC
Rawhide ep Incident of the Odyssey 3.26.64 CBS
Mickey Rooney Show sr 9.16.64 ABC
Combat ep Silver Service 10.13.64 ABC
Bob Hope Chrysler Theatre ep Kicks 10.13.65 NBC
This'll Kill You 1.18.66 ABC
The Lucy Show ep 1.24.66 CBS
Jean Arthur Show ep 9.12.66 CBS
Name of the Game ep Cynthia Is Alive and Living in
    Avalon 10.2.70 NBC
Dan August ep The Manufactured Man 3.11.71 NBC
Santa Claus Is Coming to Town Sp (voice only) 12.3.
    71 ABC
Evil Roy Slade tf 2.18.72 NBC
Night Gallery ep Rare Objects 10.22.72 NBC

ROSAY, FRANCOISE
    Orient Express ep The Diamond 2.13.54 CBS

ROSS, DIANA
    Tarzan ep 1.12.68 NBC

ROSS, KATHARINE
    Kraft Suspense Theatre ep Are There Any More Out

There Like You   11.7.63 NBC
Lieutenant   ep   Fall from a White Horse   11.30.63 NBC
Alfred Hitchcock Theatre   ep   The Dividing Wall   12.6.
   63 CBS
Arrest and Trial   ep   Signs of an Ancient Fire   1.12.64
   ABC
Ben Casey   ep   Evidence of Things Not Seen   4.22.64
   ABC
Virginian   ep   Dark Challenge   9.23.64 NBC
Gunsmoke   ep   3.27.65 CBS
Run for Your Life   ep   The Cold, Cold War of Paul Bry-
   an   9.13.65 NBC
Big Valley   ep   Winner Loses All   10.27.65 ABC
Loner   ep   Widow on the Evening Stage   10.30.65 CBS
Seven Rich Years   pt   9.11.66 ABC
Road West   ep   11.28.66 NBC
The Longest Hundred Miles   tf   1.21.67 NBC
Suspense Theatre   ep   2.1.68 ABC

ROSS, SHIRLEY
Matinee Theatre   ep   Technique   12.20.55 NBC

ROTH, LILLIAN
U.S. Steel Hour   ep   Outcast   11.9.55 CBS
Playhouse 90   ep   Child of Trouble   5.2.57 CBS
Witness   ep   12.29.60 CBS

ROWAN, DAN
Off to See the Wizard   ep   Who's Afraid of Mother Goose
   10.13.67 ABC

ROWLANDS, GENA
Goodyear Playhouse   ep   Do It Yourself   4.24.55 NBC
Robert Montgomery Presents   ep   The Great Gatsby
   5.9.55 NBC
Armstrong Circle Theatre   ep   Time for Love   6.21.55
   NBC
Studio One   ep   A Chance at Love   8.29.55 CBS
Appointment with Adventure   cp   9.4.55 CBS
U.S. Steel Hour   ep   Ashton Buys a Horse   9.28.55 CBS
Goodyear Playhouse   ep   The Expendable House   10.9.55
   NBC
G.E. Theatre   ep   The Girl with the Flaxen Hair   12.14.
   58 CBS
Staccato   ep   Fly, Baby, Fly   11.12.59 NBC
Markham   ep   12.5.59 CBS
Riverboat   ep   Guns for Empire   12.20.59 NBC

Adventures in Paradise   ep   The Death-Divers   4.25.60
ABC
Alfred Hitchcock Theatre   ep   The Doubtful Doctor _ 10.
4.60 NBC
Tab Hunter Show   Double Trouble   11.6.60 NBC
Islanders   ep   Island Witness   2.26.61 ABC
87th Precinct   sr   9.25.61 NBC
Target Corruptors   ep   The Poppy Vendor   10.27.61
ABC
Alfred Hitchcock Theatre   ep   Ride the Nightmare   11.
29.62 CBS
Dick Powell Theatre   ep   Project "X"   1.8.63 NBC
Lloyd Bridges Show   ep   A Personal Matter   2.5.63
CBS
Alfred Hitchcock Theatre   ep   The Lonely Hours   3.8.
63 CBS
77 Sunset Strip   ep   Flight 307   3.29.63 ABC
Virginian   ep   No Tears for Savannah   10.2.63 NBC
Kraft Suspense Theatre   ep   One Step Down   11.14.63
NBC
Bob Hope Chrysler Theatre   ep   It's Mental Work   12.
20.63 NBC
Breaking Point   ep   Heart of Marble, Body of Stone   12.
23.63 ABC
Burke's Law   ep   Who Killed Victor Barrows   1.17.64
ABC
Dr. Kildare   ep   To Walk in Grace   2.13.64 NBC
Alfred Hitchcock Theatre   ep   Murder Case   3.6.64 CBS
Burke's Law   ep   4.10.64 ABC
Run for Your Life   ep   Rediscovery of Charlotte Hyde
1.24.66 NBC
The Long Hot Summer   ep   From This Day Forward   2.
9.66 ABC
Road West   ep   1.16.67 NBC
The Girl from U.N.C.L.E.   ep   2.7.67 NBC
Peyton Place   sr   8.67 ABC
Garrison's Gorillas   ep   The Frame Pup   2.27.68 ABC
Medical Center   ep   Man in Hiding   3.3.71 CBS
Ghost Story   ep   9.22.72 NBC

ROWLES, POLLY
Philco Playhouse   ep   We Were Children   5.4.52 NBC
Jamie   sr   10.5.53 ABC
Center Stage   ep   The Human Touch   6.29.54 ABC
Kraft Theatre   ep   Forty Weeks of Uncle Tom   7.22.54
ABC
Jamie   sr ret   9.27.54 ABC

Elgin Hour   ep   Family Meeting   1.25.55 ABC
Robert Montgomery Presents   ep   The Iron Cobweb   3.
   28.55 NBC
Alcoa Hour   ep   Man on a Tiger   1.8.56 NBC
Alfred Hitchcock Presents   ep   The Older Sister   1.22.
   56 CBS
Studio One   ep   The Genie of Sutton Place   5.14.56 CBS
Armstrong Circle Theatre   ep   Case for Room 310   10.
   1.58 CBS
U.S. Steel Hour   ep   Apple of His Eye   7.1.59 CBS
U.S. Steel Hour   ep   When in Rome   9.7.60 CBS
Play of the Week   ep   Legend of Lovers   10.10.60 NN
Family Classics   ep   The Three Musketeers   11.30.60,
   12.1.60 CBS
Naked City   ep   Tombstone for a Derelict   4.5.61 ABC
Defenders   sr   9.16.61 CBS
Nurses   ep   White on White   5.14.64 CBS
Nurses   ep   A Postcard from Yucatan   5.21.65 CBS
Doctors/Nurses   ep   Time for You and Time for Me
   11.24.64 CBS
Doctors/Nurses   ep   The Patient Nurse   1.12.65 CBS
For the People   ep   The Right to Kill   4.4.65 CBS

ROXANNE
   Broadway Television Theatre   ep   The Patsy   1.25.54
   NN

ROYLE, SELENA
   Story Theatre   ep   The Treasure of Ranchard   1.12.51
   NN
   Story Theatre   ep   An Old, Old Story   3.2.51 NN
   Ethel Barrymore Theatre   ep   The Daughters of Mars
   10.5.56 NN

RUBINSTEIN, JOHN
   Bold Ones   ep   A Thing Not of God   2.1.70 NBC
   Young Lawyers   ep   We May Be Better Strangers   10.
   26.70 ABC
   The Psychiatrist: God Bless the Children   tf   12.14.70
   NBC
   Matt Lincoln   ep   1.14.71 ABC
   Men at Law   ep   Hostage   2.24.71 CBS
   The Psychiatrist   ep   Ex-Sgt. Randell   3.3.71 NBC

RUDIE, EVELYN
   Ford Theatre   ep   The Woman at Fog Point   4.14.55
   NBC

Playhouse 90   ep   Eloise   11.22.56 CBS
Playhouse 90   ep   The Hostess with the Mostess   3.21.
57 CBS
Alfred Hitchcock Presents   ep   A Man Greatly Beloved
5.12.57 CBS
Dupont Show of the Month   ep nar   The Red Mill   4.19.
58 CBS
Wagon Train   ep   The Millie Davis Story   11.26.58
NBC
G.E. Theatre   ep   Nobody's Child   5.10.59 CBS
77 Sunset Strip   ep   Publicity Brat   4.1.60 ABC

RUGGLES, CHARLES
Charlie Ruggles Show   sr   1950 ABC
Medallion Theatre   ep   The Consul   8.15.53 CBS
Studio One   ep   Runaway   1.4.54 CBS
The World of Mr. Sweeney   sr   6.30.54 NBC
Motorola TV Hour   ep   The Muldoon Matter   2.23.54
ABC
The World of Mr. Sweeney   sr ret   10.4.54 NBC
Matinee Theatre   ep   The Luck of Amos Currie   6.6.
56 NBC
Conflict   ep   The Man from 1997   11.27.56 ABC
Climax   ep   Let It Be Me   3.21.57 CBS
U.S. Steel Hour   ep   Crisis in Coroma   10.23.57
Life of Riley   ep   2.7.58 NBC
Playhouse 90   ep   The Male Animal   3.13.58 CBS
Studio One   ep   A Delicate Affair   7.28.58 CBS
Once Upon a Christmas Time   Sp   12.9.59 NBC
Goodyear Theatre   ep   The Sitter's Baby   5.9.60 NBC
The Bells of St. Mary's   Sp   10.27.59 CBS
Best of the Post   ep   The Little Terror   11.12.60 ABC
Chevy Show   ep   Happiest Day   4.23.61 NBC
Follow the Sun   ep   The Highest Wall   10.1.61 ABC
Real McCoys   ep   Hassie's European Trip   11.9.61 ABC
Frontier Circus   ep   Mr. Grady Regrets   1.25.62 CBS
Saints and Sinners   ep   11.5.62 NBC
Dick Powell Theatre   ep   The Old Man and the City   4.
23.63 NBC
Burke's Law   ep   Who Killed Mr. X   9.27.63 ABC
Burke's Law   ep   Who Killed Purity Mather   12.6.63
ABC
Ben Casey   ep   I'll Get on My Icefloe and Wave Good-
bye   1.18.64 CBS
Destry   ep   Deputy for a Day   4.3.64 ABC
Wagon Train   ep   2.14.65 ABC
The Man from U.N.C.L.E.   ep   The Ultimate Computer

Affair   10.1.65 NBC
Laredo   ep   A Taste of Money   4.28.66 NBC
Bonanza   ep   Horse of a Different Hue   9.18.66 NBC
Pistols 'n Petticoats   ep   The Triangle   10.22.66 CBS
Beverly Hillbillies   ep   11.23.66 CBS
Carousel   Sp   5.7.67 ABC
Danny Thomas Show   ep   One for My Baby   2.5.68 NBC

RUICK, BARBARA
Public Defender   ep   Destiny   10.28.54 CBS
Climax   ep   The Mojave Kid   1.27.55 CBS
20th Century-Fox Hour   ep   Crack-Up   2.8.56 CBS

RULE, JANICE
Goodyear Playhouse   ep   The Brownstone   1.31.54 NBC
TV Soundstage   ep   A Kiss to Conquer   4.16.54 NBC
Studio One   ep   Home Again, Home Again   7.19.54
   CBS
Goodyear Playhouse   ep   The Arena   8.1.54 NBC
U.S. Steel Hour   ep   The Bride Cried   8.17.55 CBS
Appointment with Adventure   ep   Design for Trouble   8.
   28.55 CBS
Alcoa Hour   ep   Archangel Harrigan   6.24.56 NBC
Schlitz Playhouse of Stars   ep   The Life You Save   3.
   1.57 CBS
The Millionaire   ep   Story of Jimmy Reilly   3.13.57
   CBS
Playhouse 90   ep   Four Women in Black   4.25.57 CBS
Have Gun, Will Travel   ep   9.14.57 CBS
Danny Thomas Show   ep   Is Charlie Coming   12.2.57
   NBC
Frank Sinatra Show   ep   The Feeling Is Mutual   12.27.
   57 ABC
M Squad   ep   Dolly's Bar   2.7.58 NBC
G.E. Theatre   ep   Angel in the Air   3.9.58 CBS
Suspicion   ep   A World Full of Strangers   3.10.58 NBC
Suspicion   ep   Death Watch   6.2.58 NBC
Kraft Theatre   ep   The Last of the Belles   6.4.58 NBC
G.E. Theatre   ep   Train for Tecumseh   3.15.59 CBS
The Snows of Kilimanjaro   Sp   3.25.60 CBS
Playhouse 90   ep   Journey to the Day   4.22.60 CBS
Twilight Zone   ep   Face Down, Floating   4.29.60 ABC
Route 66   ep   A Lance of Straw   10.14.60 CBS
Checkmate   ep   The Mask of Vengeance   12.3.60 CBS
Route 66   ep   Once to Every Man   10.27.61 CBS
Adventures in Paradise   ep   Hurricane Audrey   1.7.62
   ABC

Golden Showcase   ep   Tonight in Samaarkand   3. 24. 62
CBS
U. S. Steel Hour   ep   The Love of Claire Ambler   4. 4.
62 CBS
Alcoa Premiere   ep   Of Struggle and Flight   3. 28. 63
ABC
Route 66   ep   But What Do You Do in March   5. 3. 63
CBS
Dr. Kildare   ep   Whoever Heard of a Two-Headed Doll
9. 26. 63 NBC
Breaking Point   ep   Fire and Ice   9. 30. 63 ABC
Burke's Law   ep   Jet-Setter   1. 10. 64 ABC
Defenders   ep   Drink Like a Lady   2. 29. 64 CBS
Dr. Kildare   ep   The Hand that Hurts, the Hand that
Heals   10. 8. 64 NBC
Reporter   ep   Super Star   11. 20. 64 CBS
Slattery's People   ep   Did He Who Made the Lamb Make
Thee   3. 5. 65 CBS
Fugitive   ep   4. 4. 67 ABC
Fugitive   ep   Wife Killer   1. 11. 66 ABC
Profiles in Courage   ep   Prudence Crandall   2. 21. 66
NBC
Judd for the Defense   ep   2. 2. 68 ABC
Run for Your Life   ep   The Exchange   3. 27. 68 NBC
Shadow on the Land   tf   12. 4. 68 ABC
Journey to the Unknown   ep   1. 1. 69 ABC
Name of the Game   ep   Lady on the Rocks   9. 19. 69
NBC
Dan August   ep   The King's Dead   10. 14. 70 ABC
The Devil and Miss Sarah   tf   12. 4. 71 ABC
Man and the City   ep   A Hundred Black Pages   9. 22. 71
ABC
Streets of San Francisco   ep   9. 30. 72 ABC
Banyon   ep   12. 22. 72 NBC

RUSH, BARBARA
Video Theatre   ep   Gavin's Darling   4. 22. 54 CBS
Lux Video Theatre   ep   Shadow of a Doubt   3. 24. 55 NBC
Lux Video Theatre   ep   The Amazing Mrs. Holliday   10.
6. 55 NBC
Lux Video Theatre   ep   Night Song   2. 16. 56 NBC
Playhouse 90   ep   The Troublemakers   11. 21. 57 CBS
Suspicion   ep   5. 26. 58 NBC
Lux Video Theatre   ep   The Connoisseur   10. 31. 58 CBS
Sunday Showcase   ep   What Makes Sammy Run   9. 27. 59,
10. 4. 59 NBC
Playhouse 90   ep   Alas, Babylon   4. 3. 60 CBS

Checkmate   ep   The Dark Divide   11.19.60 CBS
Our American Heritage   ep   Born a Giant   12.2.60 NBC
Theatre 62   ep   Notorious   12.10.61 NBC
G.E. Theatre   ep   A Very Special Girl   3.11.62 CBS
Saints and Sinners   sr   9.17.62 NBC
Eleventh Hour   ep   Make Me a Place   10.17.62 NBC
Dick Powell Theatre   ep   The Honorable Albert Higgins
   1.1.63 NBC
Saints and Sinners   ep   The Home-Coming Bit   1.7.63
   NBC
Ben Casey   ep   From too Much Love of Living   12.11.
   63 ABC
Outer Limits   ep   The Forms of Things Unknown   5.4.
   64 ABC
Kraft Suspense Theatre   ep   In Darkness, Waiting   1.
   14.65, 1.21.65 NBC
Convoy   ep   The Many Colors of Courage   10.8.65 NBC
Dr. Kildare   ep   With Hellfire and Thunder   10.19.65
   NBC
Dr. Kildare   ep   Daily Flights to Olympus   10.25.65
   NBC
Dr. Kildare   ep   Toast the Golden Couple   11.1.65 NBC
Fugitive   ep   Landscape with Running Figures   11.16.65
   ABC
Bob Hope Chrysler Theatre   ep   Storm Crossing   12.7.
   66 NBC
Custer   ep   12.20.67 ABC
Peyton Place   sr   5.68 ABC
Mannix   ep   A Copy of Murder   11.2.68 CBS
Marcus Welby, M.D.   ep   10.14.69 ABC
Medical Center   ep   A Life Is Waiting   10.15.69 CBS
Mod Squad   ep   Kicks, Incorporated   1.12.71 ABC
Ironside   ep   Ring of Prayer   10.12.71 NBC
Suddenly Single   tf   10.19.71 ABC
Night Gallery   ep   Cool Air   12.8.71 NBC
Cutter   tf   1.26.72 NBC
Marcus Welby, M.D.   ep   Don't Talk about Darkness
   2.22.72 ABC
Medical Center   ep   2.23.72 CBS
The Eyes of Charles Sand   tf   2.29.72 ABC
Cade's County   ep   Jessica   3.12.72 CBS
Owen Marshall   ep   Words of Summer   9.14.72 ABC
Moon of the Wolf   tf   9.26.72 ABC
Ironside   ep   12.14.72 NBC

RUSSELL, GAIL
Rebel   ep   Noblesse Oblige   2.14.60 ABC

RUSSELL, JANE
   Colgate Theatre   ep   MacCready's Woman   9. 23. 58 NBC‐
   Desilu Playhouse   ep   Ballad for a Badman   1. 26. 59
    CBS

RUSSELL, JOHN
   Soldiers of Fortune   sr   4. 9. 55 ABC
   Oh Susanna   ep   It's Only Money   10. 12. 57 CBS
   Maverick   ep   A Rage for Vengeance   1. 12. 58 ABC
   Cheyenne   ep   The Empty Gun   2. 25. 58 ABC
   Cheyenne   ep   Dead to Rights   5. 20. 58 ABC
   Lawman   sr   10. 5. 58 ABC
   Northwest Passage   ep   The Killers   3. 13. 59 NBC
   Lawman   sr ret   fall, 1959 ABC
   Lawman   sr ret   9. 18. 60 ABC
   Maverick   ep   Hadley's Hunters   9. 25. 60 ABC
   Alias Smith and Jones   ep   12. 16. 72 ABC

RUSSELL, ROSALIND
   Schlitz Playhouse of Stars   ep   Never Wave at a WAC
    10. 19. 51 CBS
   Loretta Young Show   ep hos   Fear Me Not   8. 28. 55 NBC
   Loretta Young Show   ep hos   Week-end in Winnetka   9.
    4. 55 NBC
   G. E. Theatre   ep   The Night Goes on   3. 18. 56 CBS
   Wonderful Town   Sp   11. 30. 58 CBS
   The Crooked Hearts   tf   11. 8. 72 ABC

RUTHERFORD, ANN
   Gruen Guild Playhouse   ep   Unfinished Business   9. 27.
    51 ABC
   Hollywood Opening Night   ep   The Kirby's   1. 25. 52 CBS
   Campbell Playhouse   ep   The Cavorting Statue   6. 20. 52
    NBC
   Suspense   ep   Portrait of Constance   3. 24. 53 CBS
   Tales of the City   ep   6. 25. 53 CBS
   Appointment with Love   ep   Never Laugh at a Lady   6.
    26. 53 ABC
   Perry Mason   ep   The Case of the Tandem Target   5.
    14. 64 CBS
   Climax   ep   Public Pigeon Number One   ep   9. 8. 55 CBS
   Climax   ep   Pale Horse, Pale Rider   3. 22. 56 CBS
   Kraft Theatre   ep   Success   7. 31. 57 NBC
   Climax   ep   Four Hours in White   2. 6. 58 CBS
   Playhouse 90   ep   The Male Animal   3. 13. 58 CBS
   No Warning   ep   Fire Lookout Post   4. 20. 58 NBC
   Perry Mason   ep   The Case of the Howling Dog   4. 11. 59
    CBS

Perry Mason ep The Case of the Vilent Village 1.2.
60 CBS
Perry Mason ep The Case of the Melancholy Marks-
man 3.24.62 CBS

RUTHERFORD, MARGARET
Dick and the Duchess ep The Kissing Bandit 11.2.57
CBS

RYAN, IRENE
The Whistler ep Lucky Night 9.4.55 NN
Front Row Center ep Uncle Barney 2.26.56 CBS
Matinee Theatre ep One of the Family 8.17.56 NBC
Restless Gun ep The Battle of Tower Rock 4.28.58
NBC
Bringing Up Buddy ep The Singer 1.23.61 CBS
Bringing Up Buddy ep Cynthia's Boyfriend 3.20.61
CBS
My Three Sons ep Romance of the Silver Pines 1.11.
62 ABC
Wagon Train ep The Malachi Hobart Story 1.24.62
NBC
Beverly Hillbillies sr 9.26.62 CBS
Beverly Hillbillies sr ret 9.25.63 CBS
Beverly Hillbillies sr ret 9.64 CBS
Beverly Hillbillies sr ret 9.15.65 CBS
Mister Ed ep Love and the Single Horse 10.10.65
CBS
Beverly Hillbillies sr ret 9.14.66 CBS
Beverly Hillbillies sr ret 9.6.67 CBS
Beverly Hillbillies sr ret 9.24.68 CBS
Beverly Hillbillies sr ret 9.24.69 CBS
Beverly Hillbillies sr ret 9.15.70 CBS
Love American Style ep 10.27.72 ABC

RYAN, ROBERT
Screen Directors Playhouse ep Lincoln's Doctor's Bag
12.14.55 NBC
Zane Grey Theatre ep You Only Run Once 10.5.56
CBS
Zane Grey Theatre ep The Hanging Tree 2.22.57 CBS
Turn of Fate ep Silhouette of a Killer 9.30.57 NBC
Alcoa Theatre ep On Edge 11.18.57 NBC
Goodyear Theatre ep The Crowd Pleaser 12.9.57
NBC
Alcoa Theatre ep The Face of Truth 12.30.57 NBC
Alcoa Theatre ep Hidden Witness 1.27.58 NBC

Goodyear Theatre   ep   White Flag   2.17.58 NBC
Goodyear Theatre   ep   The Seventh Letter   3.17.58 NBC
Goodyear Theatre   ep   The Giant Step   4.28.58 NBC
Alcoa Theatre   ep   The Perfectionist   5.19.58 NBC
Playhouse 90   ep   The Great Gatsby   6.26.58 CBS
Zane Grey Theatre   ep   To Sit in Judgment   11.13.58
     CBS
Zane Grey Theatre   ep   Trial by Fear   6.11.59 CBS
Zane Grey Theatre   ep   Interrogation   10.1.59 CBS
The Snows of Kilimanjaro   Sp   3.25.60 CBS
Wagon Train   ep   The John Bernard Story   11.21.62
     ABC
Kraft Suspense Theatre   ep   Are There Any More out
     There Like You   11.7.63 NBC
Breaking Point   ep   Better Than a Dead Lion   1.20.64
     ABC
Eleventh Hour   ep   Who Chopped Down the Cherry Tree
     1.29.64 NBC
Wagon Train   ep   The Bob Stuart Story   9.20.64 ABC
Bob Hope Chrysler Theatre   ep   Guilty or Not Guilty
     3.9.66 NBC
Suspense Theatre   ep   2.1.68 ABC
The Front Page   Sp   1.31.70 NN

RYAN, SHEILA
The Unexpected   ep   False Colors   6.18.52 NBC
Damon Runyon Theatre   ep   Earthquake   8.27.55 CBS

-S-

SAINT, EVA MARIE
One Man's Family   sr   1950 NBC
One Man's Family   sr ret   9.22.51 NBC
The Web   ep   The Last Chance   2.22.53 CBS
Goodyear Playhouse   ep   Wish on the Moon   3.29.53
     NBC
The Web   ep   A Fair Exchange   5.17.53 CBS
Summer Studio One   ep   End of the Honeymoon   7.13.
     53 CBS
Mirror Theatre   ep   The Happy Tingle   8.11.53 NBC
Philco Playhouse   ep   O for 37   9.27.53 NBC
Kraft Theatre   ep   The Old Maid   4.8.54 ABC

Philco Playhouse   ep   The Joker   5.2.54 NBC
Philco Playhouse   ep   Write Me out Forever   6.20.54
    NBC
Philco Playhouse ep Middle of the Night 1.19.54 NBC
Omnibus ep A Clean Fresh Breeze 10.31.54 CBS
G.E. Theatre   ep   Mr. Death and the Redheaded Wom-
    an 11.28.54 CBS
Producers Showcase   ep   Yellow Jack 1.10.55 NBC
Producers Showcase   ep   Our Town 9.19.55 NBC
Bob Hope Chrysler Theatre   ep Her School for Bach-
    elors   3.20.64 NBC
Carol for Another Christmas   tf 12.28.64 ABC

ST. JACQUES, RAYMOND
Slattery's People   ep   How Do You Catch a Cool Bird of
    Paradise 2.12.65 CBS
Rawhide sr 9.14.65 CBS
Wackiest Ship in the Army   ep   4.17.66 NBC
I Spy ep Trial by Treehouse 10.19.66 NBC
Daniel Boone ep 11.3.66 NBC
The Girl from U.N.C.L.E.   ep   11.22.66 NBC
Tarzan ep 12.29.67 NBC
Invaders ep The Vise 2.21.68 ABC
Name of the Game ep 12.13.68 NBC
The Monk tf 10.21.69 ABC

ST. JAMES, SUSAN
Fame Is the Name of the Game tf 11.26.66 NBC
Ironside ep Girl in the Night 12.21.67 NBC
It Takes a Thief ep 1.9.68, 1.16.68 ABC
Ironside ep Something for Nothing 1.22.68 NBC
It Takes a Thief ep 2.27.68 ABC
Name of the Game sr 9.20.68 NBC
Name of the Game sr ret 9.19.69 NBC
It Takes a Thief ep 11.13.69 ABC
It Takes a Thief ep The Suzie Simone Caper 3.2.70
    ABC
Name of the Game sr ret 9.18.70 NBC
McCloud ep Walk in the Dark 10.14.70 NBC
Alias Smith and Jones tf 1.5.71 ABC
Love American Style ep 2.12.71 ABC
Once Upon a Dead Man tf 9.17.71 NBC
McMillan and Wife sr 9.29.71 NBC
McMillan and Wife sr ret 9.24.72 NBC
Magic Carpet tf 11.6.72 NBC

ST. JOHN, JILL
 Dupont Show of the Month ep Junior Miss 12.50.57 CBS
 Bob Hope Chrysler Theatre ep The House Next Door
   11.15.63 NBC
 Bob Hope Chrysler Theatre ep Have Girls--Will Travel
   10.16.64 NBC
 Burke's Law ep Who Killed Merlin the Great 12.2.64 ABC
 Rogues ep The Pigeons of Paris 3.7.65 NBC
 Batman ep Hey Diddle Diddle 1.12.66, 1.13.66 ABC
 Big Valley ep 2.16.66 ABC
 Fame Is the Name of the Game tf 11.26.66 NBC
 How I Spent My Summer Vacation tf 1.7.67 NBC
 The Spy Killer tf 11.11.69 ABC
 Foreign Exchange tf 1.13.70 ABC

SAKALL, S. Z.
 Ford Theatre ep Yours for a Dream 4.8.54 NBC

SALINGER, PIERRE
 Batman ep 12.28.67, 1.4.68 ABC

SALMI, ALBERT
 U.S. Steel Hour ep Noon on Doomsday 4.25.56 CBS
 Studio One ep The Open Door 10.15.56 CBS
 U.S. Steel Hour ep Survival 11.7.56 CBS
 Kraft Theatre ep Most Blessed Woman 1.23.57 NBC
 U.S. Steel Hour ep The Hill Wife 4.10.57 CBS
 Climax ep The Volcano Seat 4.10.58 CBS
 Studio One ep Man Under Glass 7.14.58 CBS
 Alfred Hitchcock Presents ep The Jokester 10.19.58
   CBS
 G.E. Theatre ep The Family Man 2.22.59 CBS
 Adventures in Paradise ep Somewhere South of Suva
   12.28.59 ABC
 Twilight Zone ep Execution 4.1.60 CBS
 Alcoa Premiere ep The Peter Hurkos Story 4.19.60,
   4.26.60 ABC
 Hotel de Paree ep Sundance and the Delayed Gun 6.3.
   60 CBS
 Bonanza ep Silent Thunder 12.10.60 NBC
 Rawhide ep Incident of the Captive 12.16.60 CBS
 Have Gun Will Travel ep 12.31.60 CBS
 Naked City ep Button in a Haystack 2.22.61 ABC
 Play of the Week ep The Old Foolishness 3.6.61 NN
 Wagon Train ep Wagon to Fort Anderson 6.7.61 NBC
 Untouchables ep 10.19.61 ABC
 Tales of Wells Fargo ep Jeremiah 11.11.61 NBC

Investigators ep Panic Wagon 12.7.61 CBS
Route 66 ep A Long Piece of Mischief 1.19.62 CBS
Saints and Sinners ep Three Columns of Anger fall 62 NBC
Virginian ep It Tolls for Thee 11.21.62 NBC
Combat ep Cat and Mouse 12.4.62 ABC
Defenders ep The Postle 12.15.62 CBS
Alfred Hitchcock Theatre ep I'll Be Judge, I'll Be Jury 2.15.63 CBS
Rawhide ep Incident of the Pale Rider 3.15.63 CBS
Twilight Zone ep Of Late I think of Cliffordville 4.11.63 CBS
Route 66 ep Who Will Cheer My Bonnie Bride 5.10.63 CBS
Travels of Jaimie McPheeters ep The Day of the First Settler 9.29.63 ABC
Virginian ep My Brother Thaddeus 10.30.63 NBC
Redigo ep Man in a Blackout 11.5.63 NBC
Route 66 ep 93 Percent Is Smiling 12.20.63 CBS
Fugitive ep Angels Travel on Lonely Roads 2.25.64, 3.3.64 ABC
Daniel Boone sr 9.24.64 NBC
Profiles in Courage ep 11.15.64 NBC
Virginian ep A Little Learning 9.29.65 NBC
I Spy ep Weight of the World 12.1.65 NBC
Laredo ep Jinx 12.2.65 NBC
Shenandoah ep The Accused 1.3.66 ABC
Gunsmoke ep 1.8.66 CBS
Big Valley ep 2.9.66 ABC
Voyage ep Dead Men's Dubloons 2.13.66 ABC
FBI ep The Plunderers 4.24.66 ABC
Jericho ep Have Traitor, Will Travel 10.6.66 CBS
12 O'Clock High ep The Pariah 11.4.66 ABC
Gunsmoke ep 3.18.67 CBS
Road West ep 5.1.67 NBC
Gentle Ben ep 10.1.67 CBS
Custer ep Dangerous Prey 12.6.67 ABC
Cimarron Strip ep 12.14.67 CBS
Virginian ep 1.3.68 NBC
Bonanza ep 1.21.68 NBC
Judd for the Defense ep 2.2.68 ABC
That Girl ep 3.7.68 ABC
World of Disney ep Menace on the Mountain 3.1.70, 3.8.70 NBC
McCloud ep The Concrete Corral 9.30.70 NBC
Interns ep 10.9.70 CBS
San Francisco International Airport ep 12.2.70 NBC
Hawaii Five-O ep The Payoff 12.9.70 CBS
Gunsmoke ep 12.14.70 CBS

High Chaparral ep Man to Match the Land 3.12.71 NBC
Name of the Game ep The Showdown 3.19.71 NBC
FBI ep Three Way Split 3.21.71 ABC
Night Gallery ep The Waiting Room 1.26.72 NBC
Bonanza ep 2.20.72 NBC
Kung Fu tf 2.22.72 ABC
Bonanza ep 10.24.72 NBC
FBI ep 11.26.72 ABC

SANDERS, GEORGE
20th Century-Fox Hour ep Laur 10.19.55 CBS
Ford Theatre ep Autumn Fever 4.5.56 NBC
Screen Directors Playhouse ep Dream 5.16.56 NBC
Screen Directors Playhouse ep Bitter Waters 8.1.56 NBC
G.E. Theatre ep The Charlatan 11.11.56 CBS
G.E. Theatre ep The Man Who Inherited Everything
5.19.57 CBS
George Sanders Mystery Theatre sh 6.22.57 NBC
Schlitz Playhouse of Stars ep Night of the Stranger
3.7.58 CBS
G.E. Theatre ep The Small Elephants 3.12.61 CBS
Checkmate ep Sound of Nervous Laughter 2.14.62 CBS
The Man from U.N.C.L.E. ep The Gazebo in the Maze
Affair 4.5.65 NBC
Rogues ep A Daring Step Backward 4.18.65 NBC
Voyage to the Bottom of the Sea ep The Traitor 4.
19.65 ABC
The Man from U.N.C.L.E. ep The Yukon Affair 12.
24.65 NBC
Daniel Boone ep 1.27.66 NBC
Laura Sp 1.24.68 ABC
Mission Impossible ep 3.13.71 CBS

SANDS, DIANA
East Side/West Side ep Who Do You Kill 11.4.63
CBS
Outer Limits ep The Ice 1.6.64 ABC
Nurses ep Nurse Is a Feminine Noun 2.13.64 CBS
Nurses ep Imperfect Prophecy 2.20.64 CBS
Breaking Point ep 3.30.64 ABC
Doctors/Nurses ep A Family Resemblance 11.17.64
CBS
Dr. Kildare ep A Cry from the Streets 1.24.66, 1.
25.66, 1.31.66, 2.1.66 NBC
I Spy ep Turkish Delight 2.9.66 NBC
Fugitive ep 3.28.67 ABC
Julia ep 3.17.70, 3.24.70 NBC

Julia   cp   1.12.71 NBC
Medical Center   ep   The Nowhere Child   12.15.71 CBS

SANDS, DOROTHY
The Trap   ep   Lonely Boy   5.6.50 CBS
TV Playhouse   ep   The Vine That Grew on 50th Street
10.8.50 NBC
Television Theatre   ep   Best Years   1.17.51 NBC
Philco Playhouse   ep   The Man Who Bought a Town   2.
25.51 NBC
TV Sound Stage   ep   The Square Hole   9.4.53 NBC
Man Behind the Badge   ep   11.22.53 CBS
Studio One   ep   U.F.O.   9.6.54 CBS
Kraft Theatre   ep   Guest in the House   9.16.54 ABC
Elgin Hour   ep   Flood   10.5.54 ABC
Road of Life   sr   12.13.54 CBS
The Goldbergs   ep   Dreams   11.10.55 NN
Omnibus   ep   Dear Brutus   1.8.56 CBS
Omnibus   ep   1.29.56 CBS
Alcoa Hour   ep   The Confidence Man   5.27.56 NBC
U.S. Steel Hour   ep   Family Happiness   2.11.59 CBS
Armstrong Circle Theatre   ep   The White Collar Bandit
3.4.59 CBS
Hallmark Hall of Fame   ep   Pygmalian   2.6.63 NBC
Southern Baptist Hour   ep   1.26.64 NBC

SANDS, TOMMY
Kraft Theatre   ep   The Singin' Idol   1.30.57 NBC
Kraft Theatre   ep   Flesh and Blood   5.8.57 NBC
Zane Grey Theatre   ep   The Promise   11.8.57 CBS
Studio One   ep   The Left-Handed Welcome   6.16.58
CBS
Wagon Train   ep   The Larry Hanify Story   1.27.60
NBC
U.S. Steel Hour   ep   The Inner Panic   9.12.62 CBS
Wagon Train   ep   The Davey Baxter Story   1.9.63 ABC
Alcoa Premiere   ep   Blow High, Blow Clear   2.14.63
ABC
Wagon Train   ep   The Gus Morgan Story   9.30.63 ABC
Laramie   ep   Trapped   5.14.63 NBC
Wagon Train   ep   The Bob Stuart Story   9.20.64 ABC
Slattery's People   ep   Why the Lonely   9.28.64 CBS
Kraft Suspense Theatre   ep   Rumble on the Docks   10.
22.64 NBC
Mr. Novak   ep   Let's Dig a Little Grammar   11.10.64
NBC
Combat   ep   More Than a Soldier   1.26.65 ABC

Mr. Novak   ep   And Then I Wrote   4.20.65 NBC
Branded   ep   That the Brave Endure   4.25.65 NBC
Bonanza   ep   The Debt   9.12.65 NBC
Hawaii Five-O   ep   12.5.68 CBS

SANTONI, RENI
Hawk   ep   Thanks for the Honeymoon   9.22.66 ABC
Trials of O'Brien   ep   A Gaggle of Girls   10.30.65
   CBS
Look Up and Live   ep   Gold, Frankincense and Myrrh
   1.9.66 CBS
Love American Style   ep   Love and the Letter   10.6.69
   ABC
Odd Couple   ep   1.14.71 ABC
Bold Ones   ep   George Washington Is a Liar   2.7.71
   NBC
The Psychiatrist   ep   The Longer Trail   2.24.71 NBC
FBI   ep   10.15.72 ABC

SARRAZIN, MICHAEL
The Doomsday Flight   tf   2.13.67 NBC
Virginian   ep   1967 NBC
Bob Hope Chrysler Theatre   ep   Verdict for Terror
   3.29.67 NBC

SAVAGE, ANN
Fireside Theatre   ep   Polly   8.29.50 NBC
Fireside Theatre   ep   Judas   11.7.50 NBC
Schlitz Playhouse of Stars   ep   Tango   11.7.52 CBS
Ford Theatre   ep   Magic Formula   1.6.55 NBC

SAVALAS, TELLY
Kraft Suspense Theatre   ep   The Watchman   5.14.64
   NBC
Armstrong Circle Theatre   ep   House of Cards   2.18.59
   CBS
Armstrong Circle Theatre   ep   35 Rue du Marche   10.
   28.59 CBS
Diagnosis Unknown   ep   Gina, Gina   9.6.60 CBS
Witness   ep   9.29.60 CBS
Armstrong Circle Theatre   ep   Engineer of Death   10.
   12.60 ABC
Naked City   ep   To Walk in Silence   11.9.60 ABC
U.S. Steel Hour   ep   Operation North Star   12.28.60
   CBS
Aquanauts   ep   The Storm Adventure   2.8.61 CBS
Untouchables   ep   The Antidote   3.9.61 ABC

New Breed ep Compulsion to Confess 10.31.61 ABC
Untouchables ep The Matt Bass Story 11.9.61 ABC
Cain's Hundred ep On the Balance 11.28.61 NBC
Dick Powell Theatre ep Three Soldiers 12.5.61 NBC
Detectives ep Escort 12.15.61 NBC
Ben Casey ep A Dark Nite for Billy Harris 12.18.61
    ABC
Cain's Hundred ep Savage in Darkness 3.27.62 NBC
Alcoa Premiere ep The Hands of Danofria 11.29.62
    ABC
Untouchables ep The Speculator 1.8.63 ABC
Eleventh Hour ep A Tumble from a High White Horse
    2.27.63 NBC
Dakotas ep 4.1.63 ABC
Empire ep Arrow in the Blue 4.9.63 NBC
Grindl ep The Gruesome Basement 9.15.63 NBC
Twilight Zone ep The Living Doll 11.1.63 CBS
Burke's Law ep Who Killed Purity Mather 12.6.63
    ABC
Fugitive ep Where the Action Is 1.28.64 ABC
Kraft Suspense Theatre ep The Action of the Tiger
    2.20.64 NBC
Burke's Law ep 2.21.64 ABC
Channing ep A Claim to Immortality 2.26.64 ABC
Arrest and Trial ep The Revenge of the Worm 3.29.
    64 ABC
Alfred Hitchcock Theatre ep A Matter of Murder 4.
    2.64 CBS
Breaking Point ep My Hands Are Clearn 4.27.64 ABC
Combat ep Vendetta 9.22.64 ABC
Rogues ep Viva Diaz 10.4.64 NBC
Bonanza ep Own the World 4.18.65 NBC
Run for Your Life ep How to Sell Your Soul for Fun
    and Profit 10.18.65 NBC
Virginian ep Men with Guns 1.12.66 NBC
Fugitive ep Stroke of Genius 2.1.66 ABC
Combat ep 1.24.67 NBC
FBI ep The Executioners ep 3.12.67, 3.19.67 ABC
The Man from U.N.C.L.E. ep 3.31.67, 4.7.67 NBC
Bob Hope Chrysler Theatre ep 4.19.67 NBC
Cimarron Strip ep 9.28.67 CBS
Mongo's Back in Town tf 12.10.71 CBS
Visions tf 10.10.72 CBS

SAXON, JOHN
    Medic ep Walk with Lions 9.12.55 NBC
    G.E. Theatre ep Cat in the Cradle 10.1.61 CBS

Dick Powell Theatre ep A Time to Die 1.9.62 NBC
Burke's Law ep Who Killed Cable Roberts 10.4.63
    ABC
Gunsmoke ep 4.3.65 CBS
Gunsmoke ep 12.18.65 CBS
Bob Hope Chrysler Theatre ep After the Lion, Jack-
    als 1.26.66 NBC
Dr. Kildare ep The Art of Taking a Powder 3.14.66,
    3.5.166 NBC
Gunsmoke ep 11.11.66 CBS
Bonanza ep 1.22.67 NBC
Virginian ep The Modoc Kid 2.1.67 NBC
The Doomsday Flight tf 2.13.67 NBC
Time Tunnel ep 3.10.67 ABC
Winchester 73 tf 3.14.67 NBC
Cimarron Strip ep Journey to a Hanging 9.7.67 CBS
Bonanza ep 10.1.67 NBC
Gunsmoke ep 11.6.67 CBS
It Takes a Thief ep 1.9.68 ABC
Virginian ep 10.9.68 NBC
Name of the Game ep Collector's Edition 10.11.68
    NBC
Istanbul Express tf 10.22.68 NBC
Bold Ones sr 9.15.69 NBC
Ironside ep Ransom 2.19.70 NBC
Bold Ones sr ret 9.70 NBC
The Intruders tf 11.10.70 NBC
Men from Shiloh ep 3.3.71 NBC
Bold Ones sr ret 9.71 NBC
Sixth Sense ep Lady, Lady, Take My Life 1.29.72
    ABC
Night Gallery ep I'll Never Leave You--Ever 2.16.72
    NBC
Banyon ep 10.27.72 NBC

SCALA, GIA
Goodyear Playhouse ep A London Affair 2.2.59 NBC
Alfred Hitchcock Presents ep Mother, May I Go Out to
    Swim 4.10.60 CBS
Islanders ep Duel of Strangers 12.25.60 ABC
Hong Kong ep The Runaway 3.29.61 ABC
Alfred Hitchcock Theatre ep Deathmate 4.18.61 NBC
Alfred Hitchcock Theatre ep A Sign of Satan 5.8.64
    CBS
Rogues ep 11.15.64 NBC
Convoy ep Passage to Liverpool 9.17.65 NBC
Voyage to the Bottom of the Sea ep Jonah and the

Whale   9.19.65 ABC
12 O'Clock High   ep   RX for a Sick Bird   9.20.65 ABC
Run for Your Life   ep   How to Sell Your Soul for Fun
    and Profit   10.18.65 NBC
Jericho   ep   Upbeat and Underground   9.29.66 CBS
Name of the Game   ep   The Inquiry   1.17.69 NBC
It Takes a Thief   ep   1.21.69 ABC

SCARDINO, DON
    CBS Playhouse   ep   The People Next Door   10.15.68
    CBS
    Name of the Game   ep   The Glory Shouter   12.18.70
    NBC

SCHEFF, FRITZI
    Musical Comedy Time   ep   Mme. Modiste   2.5.51 NBC
    Armstrong Circle Theatre   ep   Recording Date   2.17.52
    NBC

SCHELL, MARIA
    Playhouse 90   ep   Word from a Sealed-Off Box   10.30.
    58 CBS
    Playhouse 90   ep   For Whom the Bells Toll   3.12.59,
    3.19.59 CBS
    Who Has Seen the Wind   tf   2.19.65 ABC

SCHELL, MAXIMILIAN
    Playhouse 90   ep   Child of Our Time   2.5.59 CBS
    Playhouse 90   ep   Judgment at Nuremberg   4.16.59 CBS
    Desilu Playhouse   ep   Perilous   6.22.59 CBS
    The Fifth Column   Sp   1.29.60 CBS
    Sunday Showcase   ep   Turn the Key Softly   3.6.60 NBC
    Alcoa Theatre   ep   The Observer   4.18.60 NBC
    Family Classics   ep   The Three Musketeers   11.30.60,
    12.1.60 CBS
    Bob Hope Chrysler Theatre   ep   A Time to Love   1.11.
    67 NBC

SCHILDKRAUT, JOSEPH
    The Theatre Hour   ep   Uncle Harry   2.24.50 CBS
    Masterpiece Playhouse   ep   Six Characters in Search of
    an Author   8.13.50 NBC
    Sure as Fate   ep   One in a Million   3.6.51 CBS
    Somerset Maugham Theatre   ep   Appearances and Reality
    9.3.51 NBC
    Cosmopolitan Theatre   ep   Be Just and Fear Not   10.9.
    51 NN

Personal Appearance   ep   The Professor   2.9.52 ABC
Schlitz Playhouse of Stars   ep   Point of Honor   1.31.53
    CBS
The Web   ep   A Time for Dying   3.8.53 CBS
Omnibus   ep   The Last Night of Don Juan   3.15.53 CBS
Hallmark Hall of Fame   ep   Hamlet   4.26.53 NBC
Joseph Schildkraut Theatre   sh/sr   10.28.53 NN
Hallmark Hall of Fame   ep   The Hammer and the Sword
    6.5.55 NBC
Cameo Theatre   ep   The Man from the South   8.14.55
    NN
Twilight Zone   ep   Death's Head Revisited   11.10.61
    CBS
Dr. Kildare   ep   The Stepping Stones   2.22.62 NBC
Twilight Zone   ep   The Trade-In   4.20.62 CBS
77 Sunset Strip   ep   "5"   9.20.63 ABC
Sam Benedict   ep   Hear the Mellow Wedding Bells   11.
    3.62 NBC
Arrest and Trial   ep   Whose Little Girl Are You   10.
    27.63 ABC

SCOTT, GEORGE C.
Dupont Show of the Month   ep   A Tale of Two Cities   3.
    27.58 CBS
Kraft Theatre   ep   We Haven't Seen Her Lately   8.20.58
    NBC
Omnibus   ep   The Empty Chair   12.7.58 NBC
U.S. Steel Hour   ep   Trap for a Stranger   2.25.59 CBS
Sunday Showcase   ep   People Kill People   9.20.59 NBC
Playhouse 90   ep   Target for Three   10.1.59 CBS
Hallmark Hall of Fame   ep   Winterset   10.26.59 NBC
Play of the Week   ep   Don Juan in Hell   2.15.60 NN
Great Mysteries   ep   The Burning Court   4.24.60 NBC
Ben Casey   ep   I Remember a Lemon Tree   10.23.61
    ABC
The Power and the Glory   Sp   10.29.61 CBS
Golden Showcase   ep   The Picture of Dorian Gray   12.6.
    61 CBS
Naked City   ep   Strike a Statue   5.16.52 ABC
Virginian   ep   The Brazen Bell   10.17.62 NBC
Eleventh Hour   ep   I Don't Belong in a White Painted
    House   10.24.62 NBC
East Side/West Side   sr   9.23.63 CBS
Bob Hope Chrysler Theatre   ep   A Time for Killing   4.
    30.65 NBC
Road West   ep   This Savage Land   9.12.66, 9.19.66
    NBC

The Crucible   Sp   5.4.67 CBS
On Stage   ep   Mirror, Mirror on the Wall   11.21.69
NBC
Hallmark Hall of Fame   ep   The Price   2.3.71 NBC
Jane Eyre   Sp   3.24.71 NBC
The Trouble with People   Sp   11.12.72 NBC

SCOTT, LIZABETH
Studio 57   ep   I'll Always Love You Natalie   12.11.55 NN
20th Century-Fox Hour   ep   Overnight Haul   5.16.56
CBS
Eddie Cantor Playhouse   ep   A Hunting We Will Go   4.
26.59 NN
Adventure in Paradise   ep   The Amazon   3.21.60 ABC
The Third Man   ep   1960 NBC
Burke's Law   ep   Who Killed Cable Roberts   10.4.63
ABC

SCOTT, MARTHA
Airflyte Theatre   ep   The Cut Glass Bowl   11.2.50 CBS
Lux Video Theatre   ep   The Choir Rehearsal   2.5.51
CBS
Robert Montgomery Presents   ep   4.23.51 NBC
Lights Out   ep   Cat's Cradle   5.21.51 NBC
The Clock   ep   Journey Along the River   7.6.51 NBC
The Web   ep   Dear Sister   6.7.53 CBS
Mirror Theatre   ep   Salt of the Earth   6.30.53 NBC
Tales of the City   ep   8.6.53 CBS
Medallion Theatre   ep   The Scent of Rose   9.5.53 CBS
Suspense   ep   The Sister   9.29.53 CBS
Modern Romances   sh   10.4.54 NBC
Center Stage   ep   The Desdemona Murder Case   8.10.
54 ABC
Omnibus   ep   A Different Drummer   3.13.55 CBS
Goodyear Playhouse   ep   Footlight Frenzy   4.8.56 NBC
Kraft Theatre   ep   Prairie Night   7.25.56 NBC
Robert Montgomery Presents   ep   Give and Take   1.14.
57 NBC
Robert Montgomery Presents   ep   Last Train to Kildevil
3.11.57 NBC
Matinee Theatre   ep   The Gardenia Bush   5.28.58 NBC
Modern Romances   sh ret   6.23.58 NBC
Playhouse 90   ep   A Trip to Paradise   3.26.59 CBS
Markham   ep   Grave and Present Danger   9.19.59 CBS
U.S. Steel Hour   ep   Rachel's Summer   10.7.59 CBS
Play of the Week   ep   The Wooden Dish   3.20.61 NN
Follow the Sun   ep   Ghost Story   1.21.62 ABC

Route 66   ep   Where Is Chick Lorimer   12. 14. 62 CBS
Dupont Show of the Month   ep   Two Faces of Treason
    2. 10. 63 NBC
Nurses   ep   A Dark World   4. 11. 63 CBS
The Greatest Show on Earth   ep   No Middle Ground for
    Harry Kyle   10. 1. 63 ABC
Cimarron Strip   ep   11. 9. 67 CBS
FBI   ep   11. 12. 67 ABC
Ironside   ep   The Prophecy   2. 6. 69 NBC
Paris 7000   ep   The Last Grand Tour   3. 19. 70 ABC
Longstreet   ep   So Who's Fred Hornbeck   10. 23. 71 ABC
Hollywood Television Theatre   ep   Lemonade   10. 21. 71
    NN
Delphi Bureau   ep   10. 5. 72 ABC

SCOTT, RANDOLPH
Films of Faith   ep   Three Lives   6. 21. 53 NN

SCOTT, ZACHARY
Robert Montgomery Presents   ep   The Big Sleep   9. 25.
    50 NBC
Armstrong Circle Theatre   ep   Roundup   10. 3. 50 NBC
Video Theatre   ep   The Valiant   10. 23. 50 CBS
Tales of Tomorrow   ep   Sneak Attack   12. 7. 51 ABC
Betty Crocker Star Matinee   ep   Shining Hour   12. 15.
    51 ABC
Suspense   ep   3. 31. 53 CBS
Studio One   ep   King Coffin   5. 11. 53 CBS
Mirror Theatre   ep   Award Performance   11. 7. 53 CBS
Schlitz Playhouse of Stars   ep   Pearl-Handled Guns   1.
    15. 54 CBS
TV Soundstage   ep   Break the Mirror   2. 26. 54 NBC
Motorola TV Hour   ep   A Dash of Bitters   2. 9. 54 ABC
Robert Montgomery Presents   ep   Skyblock   5. 17. 54
    NBC
Star Theatre   ep   Award Performance   7. 9. 54 CBS
U. S. Steel Hour   ep   The Grand Tour   8. 17. 54 ABC
Omnibus   ep   The Man with the Diamond   10. 24. 54
    CBS
Climax   ep   The Darkest Hour   3. 24. 55 CBS
G. E. Theatre   ep   It Gives Me Great Pleasure   4. 3. 55
    CBS
Rheingold Theatre   ep   Hand to Hand   5. 14. 55 NBC
Robert Montgomery Presents   ep   The Drifter   5. 23. 55
    NBC
Science Fiction Theatre   ep   Beyond Return   12. 9. 55
    NBC

Rheingold Theatre ep Point of Honor 1.7.56 NBC
G.E. Summer Originals ep The Unwilling Witness 7.
   24.56 ABC
Pursuit ep Ticket to Tangier 11.5.58 CBS
Spotlight Playhouse sh 6.30.59 CBS
Diagnosis Unknown ep Sudden Stillness 7.19.60 CBS
Mystery Show ep Summer Hero 6.12.60 NBC
Family Classics ep The Scarlet Pimpernel 10.28.60
   CBS
Play of the Week ep The Sound of Murder 2.13.61
   NN
Family Classics ep Jane Eyre 4.27.61 CBS
Rawhide ep Incident Before Black Pass 5.19.61 CBS
New Breed ep Policemen Die Alone 1.30.62, 2.6.62
   ABC
Defenders ep The Locked Room 2.10.62 CBS
Expendables pt 9.27.62 ABC
Dupont Show of the Month ep Big Deal in Laredo 10.
   7.62 NBC
Nurses ep Show Just Cause Why You Should Weep 10.
   3.63 CBS
Arrest and Trial ep He Ran for His Life 4.5.64 ABC
Rogues ep Bow to a Master 2.7.65 NBC

SEGAL, GEORGE
   Play of the Week ep The Closing Door 1.4.60 NN
   Armstrong Circle Theatre ep Ghost Bomber 2.3.60
      CBS
   Armstrong Circle Theatre ep The Friendly Thieves
      10.24.62 CBS
   Nurses ep Root of Violence 1.10.63 CBS
   Naked City ep Man Without a Skin 2.6.63 ABC
   Alfred Hitchcock Theatre ep A Nice Touch 10.4.63
      CBS
   Channing ep A Patron Saint for the Cargo Cult 11.13.
      63 ABC
   Nurses ep Climb a Broken Ladder 3.12.64 CBS
   Death of a Salesman Sp 5.8.66 CBS
   Desperate Hours Sp 12.13.67 ABC
   Of Mice and Men Sp 1.31.68 ABC

SEGAL, VIVIENNE
   Studio One ep Here Is My Life 5.28.51 CBS
   Alfred Hitchcock Theatre ep Apex 3.20.62 NBC
   Perry Mason ep The Case of the Tsarina's Tiara 3.
      20.66 CBS

SELLERS, PETER
    Carol for Another Christmas tf 12.28.64 ABC
    It Takes a Thief ep 10.2.69 ABC

SELWART, TONIA
    Philco Playhouse ep The Sudden Guest 2.5.50 NBC
    Philco Playhouse ep The American 4.30.50 NBC
    Family Playhouse ep Biography 10.10.50 CBS
    Elgin Hour ep The Bridge 1.11.55 ABC
    Appointment with Adventure ep Five Star Crisis 8.
        21.55 CBS

SERLING, ROD
    Twilight Zone sh 10.2.59 CBS
    Twilight Zone sh ret fall, 1960 CBS
    Twilight Zone sh ret fall, 1961 CBS
    Ichabod and Me ep 3.20.62 CBS
    Twilight Zone sh ret fall, 1962 CBS
    Twilight Zone sh ret 1.3.63 CBS
    Twilight Zone sh ret fall, 1963 CBS
    Night Gallery sh 12.16.70 NBC
    Night Gallery sh ret 9.15.71 NBC
    Night Gallery sh ret 9.17.72 NBC

SERNAS, JACQUES
    Conflict ep The Man from 1997 11.27.56 ABC
    Telephone Time ep Fortunatus 12.9.56 CBS
    Matinee Theatre ep The Pursuit of Happiness 4.5.57
        NBC

SEYRIG, DELPHINE
    Sherlock Holmes ep The Case of the Singing Violin
        8.22.55 NBC
    Pete and Gladys ep 9.19.60 CBS

SHARIF, OMAR
    Bracken's World ep Fade-In 9.19.69 NBC

SHATNER, WILLIAM
    Goodyear Playhouse ep All Summer Long 10.28.56
        NBC
    Omnibus ep School for Wives 11.11.56 ABC
    Kaiser Aluminum Hour ep Gwyneth 12.18.56 NBC
    Omnibus ep Oedipus Rex 1.6.57 ABC
    Studio One ep The Defenders 2.25.57, 3.4.57 CBS
    Kaiser Aluminum Hour ep The Deadly Silence 5.21.
        57 NBC

Alfred Hitchcock Presents ep The Glass Eye 10.6.57
   CBS
Studio One ep The Deaf Heart 10.21.57 CBS
Studio One ep No Deadly Medicine 12.9.57, 12.16.57
   CBS
Kraft Theatre ep The Velvet Trap 1.8.58 NBC
U.S. Steel Hour ep Walk with a Stranger 2.26.58 CBS
U.S. Steel Hour ep A Man in Hiding ep 5.7.58 CBS
Suspicion ep Protege 5.12.58 NBC
Climax ep Time of the Hanging 5.22.58 CBS
Playhouse 90 ep A Town Has Turned to Dust 6.19.58
   CBS
U.S. Steel Hour ep Old Marshal Never Die 8.13.58
   CBS
Sunday Showcase ep The Indestructible Mr. Gore 12.
   13.59 NBC
Alfred Hitchcock Presents ep Mother, May I Go Out to
   Swim 4.10.60 CBS
Play of the Week ep Night of the Auk 5.2.60 NN
Robert Herridge Theatre ep A Story of a Gunfighter 8.
   25.60 CBS
Family Classics ep The Scarlet Pimpernel 10.28.60
   CBS
Twilight Zone ep Nick of Time 11.18.60 CBS
Alcoa Premiere ep The Promise 11.29.60 ABC
Outlaws ep Starfall 11.24.60, 12.1.60 NBC
Thriller ep The Hungry Glass 1.3.61 NBC
Dr. Kildare ep Admitting Service 11.27.61 NBC
Naked City ep Portrait of a Painter 1.10.62 ABC
Naked City ep Without Stick or Sword 3.28.62 ABC
Defenders ep The Invisible Badge 11.24.62 CBS
Nurses ep A Difference of Years 1.3.63 CBS
Dick Powell Theatre ep Colossus 3.12.63 NBC
Nurses ep A Question of Mercy 3.21.63 CBS
Alcoa Premiere ep Million Dollar Hospital 4.18.63
   ABC
77 Sunset Strip ep "5" 9.20.63, 9.21.63 ABC
Twilight Zone ep Nightmare at 2,000 Feet 10.11.63
   CBS
Channing ep Dragon in the Den 10.23.63 ABC
Defenders ep The Cruel Hook 11.2.63 CBS
Arrest and Trial ep Onward and Upward 1.19.64 ABC
Burke's Law ep 2.14.64 ABC
Outer Limits ep Cold Hands, Warm Hearts 9.26.64,
   9.26.64 ABC
The Man from U.N.C.L.E. ep The Project Strigas Af-
   fair 11.24.64 NBC

Bob Hope Chrysler Theatre   ep   The Shattered Glass
    12.11.64 NBC
Defenders   ep   Whipping Boy   1.7.65 CBS
For the People   sr   1.31.65 CBS
Virginian   ep   The Claim   10.6.65 NBC
12 O'Clock High   ep   I Am the Enemy   11.8.65 ABC
Big Valley   ep   1.19.66 ABC
Dr. Kildare   ep   The Encroachment   2.21.66, 2.22.66,
    2.28.66, 3.1.66 NBC
Bob Hope Chrysler Theatre   ep   Wind Fever   3.2.66
    NBC
Star Trek   sr   9.8.66 NBC
Star Trek   sr ret   9.15.67 NBC
Alexander the Great   pt   1.26.68 ABC
Star Trek   sr ret   9.20.68 NBC
Virginian   ep   12.31.69 NBC
CBS Playhouse   ep   Shadow Game   5.7.69 CBS
Name of the Game   ep   Tarot   2.13.70 NBC
Paris 7000   ep   The Shattered Idol   3.5.70 ABC
Ironside   ep   3.12.70 NBC
Medical Center   ep   The Combatants   3.18.70 CBS
Hollywood Television Theatre   ep   The Andersonville
    Trial   5.17.70 NN
FBI   ep   Antennae of Death   11.29.70 ABC
Name of the Game   ep   The Glory Shouter   12.18.70
    NBC
Vanished   tf   3.8.71, 3.9.71 NBC
Owen Marshall   tf   9.12.71 ABC
Mission Impossible   ep   Encore   9.25.71 CBS
Cade County   ep   The Armageddon Contract   11.7.71
    CBS
The People   tf   1.22.72 ABC
The Hound of the Baskerville   tf   2.12.72 ABC
Sixth Sense   ep   2.26.72 ABC
Hawaii Five-O   ep   9.26.72 CBS
Mission Impossible   ep   10.21.72 CBS
Owen Marshall   ep   Five Will Get You Six   10.26.72
    ABC
Marcus Welby, M.D.   ep   Heartbeat for Yesterday   12.
    12.72 ABC

SHEEN, MARTIN
    Defenders   ep   The Attack   12.9.61 CBS
    Route 66   ep   And the Cat Jumped over the Moon   12.
        15.61 CBS
    Defenders   ep   The Tarnished Cross   3.17.62 CBS
    Armstrong Circle Theatre   ep   Assignment: Teen-aged

Junkies 7.18.62 CBS
U.S. Steel Hour ep The Inner Panic 9.12.62 CBS
U.S. Steel Hour ep Night Run to the West 2.20.63
   CBS
U.S. Steel Hour ep The Soldier Ran Away 4.17.63
   CBS
Outer Limits ep Nightmare 12.2.63 ABC
Nurses ep The Witch of the East Wing 12.19.63 CBS
East Side/West Side ep You Can't Beat the System
   5.11.64 CBS
Doctors/Nurses ep The Suspect 10.6.64 CBS
Defenders ep A Taste of Ashes 11.12.64 CBS
For the People ep 2.7.65 CBS
Trials of O'Brien ep Charlie Has All the Luck 11.20.
   65 CBS
Hawk ep Death Comes Full Circle 10.6.66 ABC
N.E.T. Playhouse ep Ten Blocks in the Camino Real
   10.7.66 NN
Catholic Hour ep A Sense of Loss 5.7.67 NBC
Catholic Hour ep An Abundance of Perspectives 5.14.
   67 NBC
Catholic Hour ep A Father's Death 5.21.67 NBC
FBI ep 1.7.68 ABC
N.Y.P.D. ep 12.3.68 ABC
Mission Impossible ep 2.23.69 CBS
Lancer ep 3.18.69 CBS
Then Came Bronson tf 3.24.69 NBC
Mod Squad ep The Loser 11.30.71 ABC
Mongo's Back in Town tf 12.10.71 CBS
Naked City ep The Night the Saints Lost Their Haloes
   1.17.62 ABC
Hawaii Five-O ep Cry Lie! 2.4.70 CBS
Medical Center ep A Duel with Doom 2.11.70 CBS
Medical Center ep A Duel with Doom 2.11.70 CBS
Bracken's World ep 2.27.70 NBC
Hollywood Television Theatre ep The Andersonville
   Trials 5.17.70 NN
FBI ep The Condemned 9.20.70 ABC
Ironside ep No Game for Amateurs 9.24.70 NBC
Matt Lincoln ep 10.7.70 ABC
Hawaii Five-O ep Time and Memories 10.7.70 CBS
Interns ep The Secret 1.22.71 CBS
Hollywood Television Theatre ep Montserrat 3.21.71
   NN
Sarge ep 9.28.71 NBC
Cannon ep 1.4.72 CBS
FBI ep A Second Life 1.9.72 ABC

Welcome Home, Johnny Bristol   tf 1.30.72 CBS
Cannon   ep   2.22.72 CBS
Mannix   ep   10.29.72 CBS
That Certain Summer   tf   11.1.72 ABC
Pursuit   tf   12.12.72 ABC

SHEFFIELD, REGINALD
Fireside Theatre   ep   No Strings Attached   4.18.50 NBC
Fireside Theatre   ep   The Man Without a Country   5.
30.50 NBC

SHELLEY, BARBARA
12 O'Clock High   ep   In Search of My Enemy   1.8.65
ABC
The Man from U.N.C.L.E.   ep   The Odd Man Affair
4.19.65 NBC
Hazel   ep   Temper, Temper   4.22.65 NBC
Wackiest Ship in the Army   ep   A Shade of Kaiser Bill
11.28.65 NBC
Donna Reed Show   ep   2.5.66 ABC
Somewhere in Italy, Company B   pt   8.21.66 ABC

SHERIDAN, ANN
Ford Theatre   ep   Malaya Incident   6.18.53 NBC
Lux Video Theatre   ep   The Lovely Day   8.13.53 CBS
Schlitz Playhouse of Stars   ep   The Prize   10.2.53 CBS
Eddie Cantor Theatre   ep   9.26.55 ABC
Calling Terry Conway   pt   8.14.56 NBC
U.S. Steel Hour   ep   Hunted   12.5.56 CBS
Lux Video Theatre   ep   The Hard Way   5.2.57 NBC
Playhouse 90   ep   Without Incident   6.6.57 CBS
Ford Theatre   ep   Cross Hairs   6.12.57 ABC
Pursuit   ep   The Dark Cloud   12.31.58 CBS
U.S. Steel Hour   ep   The Imposter   6.15.60 CBS
Wagon Train   ep   The Mavis Grant Story   10.24.62
ABC
Pistols 'n Petticoats   sr   9.17.66 CBS

SHERMAN, BOBBY
FBI   ep   3.31.68 ABC
Here Come the Brides   sr   9.24.68 ABC
Here Come the Brides   sr ret   9.26.69 ABC
Getting Together   sr   9.18.71 ABC
Mod Squad   ep   9.21.72 ABC

SHERMAN, HIRAM
Tele-Theatre   ep   The Verandah   6.26.50 NBC

Family Playhouse   ep   Biography   10.10.50 CBS
Prudential Family Playhouse   ep   Three Men on a Horse
    11.21.50 CBS
Studio One   ep   A Bargain with God   11.16.53 CBS
Star Tonight   ep   The Happy Journey   2.9.56 ABC
Paris in the Springtime   Sp   1.21.56 NBC
Alcoa Hour   ep   The Original Miss Chase   3.17.57 NBC
Studio One   ep   In Love with a Stranger   7.22.57 CBS
Alcoa Hour   ep   The Trouble with Women   8.11.57 NBC
Accent   ep   Interview at Weehawken   2.24.62 CBS
Hallmark Hall of Fame   ep   2.5.64 NBC
Tammy Grimes Show   sr   9.8.66 ABC

SHERWOOD, GALE
A Connecticut Yankee in King Arthur's Court   Sp   3.12.
    55 NBC
The Desert Song   Sp   5.7.55 NBC

SHERWOOD, MADELEINE
You Are There   ep   The Hatfield-McCoy Feud   3.20.55
    CBS
Studio One   ep   Rudy   8.19.57 CBS
Play of the Week   ep   Miss Julie   1.25.60 NN
Naked City   ep   The One Marked Hot Gives Gold   3.21.
    62 ABC
Nurses   ep   The Perfect Nurse   2.28.63 CBS
Naked City   ep   The South American Dream   5.8.63
    ABC
Fugitive   ep   The Witch   9.24.63 ABC
Ben Casey   ep   When I Am Grown to Man's Estate   2.
    8.65 ABC
The Flying Nun   sr   9.7.67 ABC
The Flying Nun   sr ret   9.26.68 ABC
Outcasts   ep   The Candidates   1.27.69 ABC
The Flying Nun   sr ret   9.17.69 ABC
Name of the Game   ep   1.30.70 NBC
Bonanza   ep   For a Young Lady   12.27.70 NBC
N.E.T. Playhouse   ep   Harriet   2.3.72 NN
Love American Style   ep   10.20.72 ABC
Owen Marshall   ep   11.30.72 ABC

SHERWOOD, ROBERTA
Mr. Broadway   Sp   5.11.57 NBC
Donna Reed Show   ep   Donna Meets Roberta   5.3.62
    ABC

SHIELDS, ARTHUR
Story Theatre sh 12.1.50 NN
Personal Appearance ep Luck of O'Leary 2.2.52 ABC
Jewelers Showcase ep The Woman of Bally Bunion 2. 24.53 CBS
Omnibus ep Nothing So Monster 1.24.54 CBS
Kraft Theatre ep The Ticket and the Tempest 11.9. 55 NBC
Crossroads ep Through the Window 1.6.56 ABC
Crossroads ep Mother O'Brien 3.9.56 ABC
Perry Mason ep The Case of the Screaming Woman 4.26.58 CBS
Bat Masterson ep The Conspiracy 6.17.59, 6.24.59 NBC
Alcoa Premiere ep The Stonecutter 12.8.59 ABC
Rawhide ep Incident of the Dust Flower 3.4.60 CBS
Wagon Train ep The Amos Gibbon Story 4.12.60 NBC
Maverick ep The Bond Feninan Men 12.18.60 ABC

SHIGETA, JAMES
Music Theatre ep An Almost Perfect Plan 4.2.59 NBC
Alcoa Premiere ep The Fortress 10.24.61 ABC
Naked City ep The Contract 1.24.62 ABC
Dr. Kildare ep 11.7.63 NBC
Outer Limits ep Nightmare 12.2.63 ABC
Burke's Law ep 3.20.64 ABC
Lieutenant ep To Kill a Man 4.18.64 NBC
Ben Casey ep Evidence of Things Not Seen 4.22.64 ABC
Outer Limits ep The Inheritors 11.21.64, 11.28.64 ABC
Carol for Another Christmas tf 12.28.64 ABC
Bing Crosby Show ep That's the Way the Suki Yaki 2.1.65 ABC
Perry Mason ep The Case of the Wrongful Writ 5.6. 65 CBS
Ben Casey ep No More Cried the Rooster 11.8.65 ABC
I Spy ep Three Hours on a Sunday Night 12.8.65 NBC
It Takes a Thief ep 3.12.68 ABC
Escape to Mindango tf 12.7.68 NBC
Hawaii Five-O ep Death Watch 12.25.68 CBS
U.M.C. tf 3.17.69 CBS
Ironside ep Love My Enemy 10.23.69 NBC

Medical Center   ep   The Loner   12.10.69 CBS
Medical Center   ep   The V.D. Story   3.25.70 CBS
Mission Impossible   ep   10.3.70 CBS
Ironside   ep   No Motive for Murder   12.23.71 NBC
Medical Center   ep   3.1.72 CBS

SHORE, DINAH
Loretta Young Show   ep hos   Across the Plaza   11.27.
   55 NBC
Danny Thomas Show   ep   5.26.58 CBS
Danny Thomas Show   ep   12.8.58 CBS
Cimarron City   ep   Cimarron Holiday   12.20.58 NBC
Dinah Shore Show   ep   Brief Encounter   3.26.61 NBC

SHRINER, HERB
Screen Directors Playhouse   ep   Meet the Governor
   10.5.55 NBC

SIDNEY, SYLVIA
Schlitz Playhouse of Stars   ep   Experiment   4.4.52 CBS
Tales of Tomorrow   ep   Time to Go   4.18.52 ABC
Lux Video Theatre   ep   Pattern for Glory   5.26.52 CBS
Broadway TV Theatre   ep   Theatre   9.29.52 NN
Broadway TV Theatre   ep   The Letter   11.3.52 NN
Broadway TV Theatre   ep   Climax   5.18.53 NN
Broadway TV Theatre   ep   Dark Victory   11.16.53 NN
Ford Theatre   ep   As the Flame Dies   11.19.53 NBC
Broadway TV Theatre   ep   Kind Lady   11.30.53 NN
Broadway TV Theatre   ep   Angel Street   12.21.53 NN
Philco Playhouse   ep   Catch My Boy on Sunday   12.12.
   54 NBC
Kraft Theatre   ep   The Hickory Limb   1.12.55 ABC
Climax   ep   Leaf out of the Book   2.3.55   CBS
Ford Theatre   ep   Reception   4.7.55 NBC
Star Stage   ep   The Toy Lady   9.9.55 NBC
Playwrights '56   ep   The Heart's a Forgotten Hotel   10.
   25.55 NBC
20th Century-Fox Hour   ep   Man on the Ledge   12.28.
   55 CBS
Climax   ep   The Gold Dress   1.17.57 CBS
Playhouse 90   ep   Helen Morgan   5.16.57 CBS
Kraft Theatre   ep   Circle of Fear   8.14.57 NBC
Playhouse 90   ep   The Gentleman from Seventh Avenue
   1.30.58 CBS
G.E. Theatre   ep   The Committeeman   1.17.60 CBS
June Allyson Show   ep   Escape   2.22.60 CBS
Naked City   ep   A Hole in the City   2.1.61 ABC

Route 66   ep   Like a Motherless Child   3.17.61 CBS
Defenders   ep   Madman   10.20.62, 10.27.62 CBS
Eleventh Hour   ep   Five Moments Out of Time   3.6.63
NBC
Yom Kippur Special   ep   In the Last Place   9.29.63
CBS
Route 66   Child of a Night   1.3.64 CBS
Nurses   ep   To All My Friends on Shore   5.7.64 CBS
My Three Sons   ep   4.19.69 ABC
Do Not Fold, Spindle, or Mutilate   tf   11.9.71 ABC

SIGNORET, SIMONE
G.E. Theatre   ep   Don't You Remember?   5.8.60 CBS
Bob Hope Chrysler Theatre   ep   A Small Rebellion   2.
9.66 NBC

SILVA, HENRY
Producers Showcase   ep   Darkness at Noon   5.2.55 NBC
Alfred Hitchcock Presents   ep   A Better Bargain   12.9.
56 CBS
West Point   ep   Heat of Anger   12.14.56 CBS
Suspicion   ep   The Story of Margery Reardon   10.28.57
NBC
Climax   ep   Don't Touch Me   4.4.57 CBS
Climax   ep   Deadly Torot   5.1.58 CBS
Alcoa Theatre   ep   The Long House on Avenue A   12.
14.59 NBC
Adventures in Paradise   ep   Forbidden Sea   4.4.60 ABC
Hotel de Paree   ep   Sundance and the Delayed Gun   6.3.
60 CBS
Untouchables   ep   The Mark of Cain   11.17.60 ABC
Islanders   ep   The Twenty-Six Paper   1.8.61 ABC
Stagecoach West   ep   The Raider   5.9.61 ABC
Thriller   ep   Dark Legacy   5.30.61 NBC
Joey Bishop Show   ep   Ring-a-Ding-Ding   11.22.61 NBC
Untouchables   ep   The Whitey Steel Story   2.8.62 ABC
Dr. Kildare   ep   Jail Ward   2.14.63 NBC
Alfred Hitchcock Theatre   ep   An Out for Oscar   4.5.63
CBS
Stoney Burke   ep   Weapons Man   4.8.63 ABC
Wagon Train   ep   The Robert Harrison Clarke Story   10.
14.63 ABC
Outer Limits   ep   Tourist Attraction   12.23.63 ABC
Outer Limits   ep   The Mice   1.6.64 ABC
Arrest and Trial   ep   People in Glass Houses   2.9.64
ABC
Breaking Point   ep   My Hands Are Clean   4.27.64 ABC

Voyage to the Bottom of the Sea   ep   The Enemies   3.
  29. 65 ABC
Wagon Train   ep   The Silver Lady   4. 25. 65 ABC
Daniel Boone   ep   9. 30. 65 NBC
Run for Your Life   ep   The Savage Season   11. 8. 65
  NBC
Tarzan   ep   12. 23. 66 NBC
Cimarron Strip   ep   Journey to a Hanging   9. 7. 67 CBS
Danny Thomas Show   ep   The Enemy   11. 20. 67 NBC
FBI   ep   11. 26. 67 ABC
High Chaparral   ep   12. 17. 67 NBC
I Spy   ep   Any Place I Hang My Hat   1. 15. 68 NBC
High Chaparral   ep   3. 2. 69 NBC
Mission Impossible   ep   4. 20. 69 CBS
Hawaii Five-O   ep   Savage Sunday   10. 20. 69 CBS
It Takes a Thief   ep   11. 27. 69 ABC
San Francisco International Airport   ep   11. 11. 70 NBC
Night Gallery   ep   The Doll   1. 13. 71 NBC
FBI   ep   Dynasty of Hate   10. 10. 71 ABC
Black Noon   tf   11. 5. 71 CBS

SILVERA, FRANK
The Skin of Our Teeth   Sp   9. 11. 55 NBC
Studio One   ep   Guitar   8. 26. 57 CBS
Wanted, Dead or Alive   ep   11. 29. 58 CBS
Ellery Queen   ep   The Hollow Man   12. 26. 58 NBC
Alfred Hitchcock Presents   ep   A Personal Matter   1. 8.
  69 NBC
Playhouse 90   ep   Seven Against the Wall   7. 9. 59 CBS
Lineup   ep   My Son Is a Stranger 10. 14. 59 ABC
Law and Mr. Jones   ep   Music to Hurt By   10. 14. 60
  ABC
Thriller   ep   The Guilty Men   10. 18. 60 NBC
Hong Kong   ep   Freebooter 10. 19. 60 ABC
Mr. Garlund   ep   10. 21. 60 CBS
Rebel   ep   Death Watch   10. 23. 60 ABC
Bonanza   ep   The Fugitive   2. 4. 61 NBC
Twilight Zone   ep   Person or Persons Unknown   3. 23.
  62 CBS
Defenders   ep   The Last Illusion   3. 9. 63 CBS
The Travels of Jaimie McPheeters   ep   The Day of the
  Taboo Men   10. 27. 63 ABC
Channing   ep   Memory of a Firing Squad   1. 1. 64 ABC
Bonanza   ep   The Companeros   4. 19. 64 NBC
Great Adventures   ep   The Pirate and the Patriot   5. 1.
  64 CBS
Alfred Hitchcock Theatre   ep   The Life and Work of

Juan Diaz 10.26.64 NBC
Mr. Novak ep Boy under Glass 11.24.64 NBC
Kraft Suspense Theatre ep That Time in Havana 2.11.
65 NBC
Profiles in Courage ep 3.7.65 NBC
Rawhide ep El Hombre Bravo 5.14.65 CBS
Gunsmoke ep 1.8.66 CBS
I Spy ep Crusade to Limbo 3.23.66 NBC
Rat Patrol ep The Chain of Death Raid 10.10.66 ABC
High Chaparral sr 9.10.67 NBC
Dundee and the Culhane ep 9.13.67 CBS
Wild, Wild West ep 10.6.67 CBS
World of Disney ep The Young Loner 2.25.68, 3.3.68
NBC
High Chaparral sr ret 9.20.68 NBC
High Chaparral sr ret 9.26.69 NBC
Marcus Welby, M.D. ep 11.11.69 ABC
Hawaii Five-O ep 12.3.69 CBS
High Chaparral sr ret 9.18.70 NBC
Hawaii Five-O ep Paniolo 12.30.70 CBS
World of Disney ep Bayou Boy 2.14.71 NBC

SILVERS, PHIL
You'll Never Get Rich (a.k.a. The Phil Silvers Show)
sr 9.20.55 CBS
The Phil Silvers Show sr ret fall, 1956 CBS
The Phil Silvers Show sr ret fall, 1957 CBS
The Phil Silvers Show sr ret fall, 1958 CBS
The Ballad of Louie the Louse Sp 10.17.59 CBS
The Slowest Gun in the West Sp 5.7.60 CBS
The New Phil Silvers Show sr 9.28.63 CBS
Damn Yankees Sp 4.8.67 NBC
Beverly Hillbillies ep 10.29.69 CBS
Beverly Hillbillies ep 3.18.70 CBS
Beverly Hillbillies ep 9.22.70, 9.29.70 CBS

SIM, ALASTAIR
Masterpiece Theatre ep Cold Comfort Farm 1.8.72
NN

SIMMONS, JEAN
Bob Hope Chrysler Theatre ep Crazier than Cotton
10.12.66 NBC
Bob Hope Chrysler Theatre ep The Lady Is My Wife
2.1.67 NBC
Hallmark Hall of Fame ep Soldier in Love 4.26.67
NBC

Heidi   Sp   11.17.68 NBC

SIMPSON, RUSSELL
  Personal Appearance   ep   Grandpa Cries Wolf   1.26.52
    ABC
  Cavalcade Theatre   ep   Night Strike   10.19.54 ABC

SINATRA, FRANK
  Producers Showcase   ep   Our Town   9.19.55 NBC
  Frank Sinatra Show   sh/sr   10.18.57 ABC
  Dick Powell Theatre   ep hos   1.22.63 NBC
  Burke's Law   ep   Who Killed Wade Walker   11.15.63
    ABC
  Make Room for Granddaddy   ep   11.18.70 ABC

SINATRA JR., FRANK
  Sam Benedict   ep   Read No Evil   3.16.63 NBC
  Adam-12   ep   2.16.72 NBC
  Alias Smith and Jones   ep   9.16.72 ABC
  Adam-12   ep   9.20.72 NBC

SINATRA, NANCY
  Virginian   ep   You Have Tears   2.13.63 NBC

SINCLAIR, MARY
  Studio One   ep   Beyond Reason   1.9.50 CBS
  Studio One   ep   The Scarlet Letter   4.3.50 CBS
  Starlight Theatre   ep   The Sire de Maletroit's Door   4.
    30.50 CBS
  Studio One   ep   Room Upstairs   5.22.50 CBS
  Studio One   ep   Zone Four   6.12.50 CBS
  Starlight Theatre   ep   The Last Kiss   7.10.50 ABC
  Lights Out   ep   The Dark Corner   9.10.50 NBC
  Fireside Theatre   ep   Hope Chest   10.17.50 NBC
  Fireside Theatre   ep   The Amber Gods   10.24.50 NBC
  Studio One   ep   Wuthering Heights   10.30.50 CBS
  Studio One   ep   Little Women   12.18.50, 12.25.50 CBS
  Fireside Theatre   ep Miggles   12.19.50   NBC
  Studio One   ep   No Tears for Hilda   5.7.51 CBS
  Suspense   ep   Vamp Till Deaf   5.29.51 CBS
  Royal Playhouse   ep   The Case of Marina Goodwin   5.31.
    51 NN
  Summer Theatre   ep   Lonely Boy   6.25.51 CBS
  Studio One   ep   Angelic Avengers   9.17.51 CBS
  Danger   ep   Passage for Christmas   12.25.51 CBS
  The Web   ep   The Joke   3.15.53 CBS
  Tales of Tomorrow   ep   The Rivals   4.17.53 ABC

Robert Montgomery Presents ep No Head for Moon-
light 6. 8. 53 NBC
Kraft Theatre ep Candlelight 12. 31. 53 ABC
Robert Montgomery Presents ep The Hunchback of
Notre Dame 11. 8. 54, 11. 15. 54 NBC
Sherlock Holmes ep Case of the Perfect Husband 7.
25. 55 NBC
Climax ep Dr. Jekyll and Mr. Hyde 7. 28. 55 CBS
Climax ep Sailor on Horseback 9. 29. 55 CBS
Loretta Young Show ep Gino 9. 25. 55 NBC
Loretta Young Show ep A Shadow Between 12. 18. 55
NBC
Climax ep The Sound of Silence 3. 1. 56 CBS
U. S. Steel Hour ep The Change in Chester 7. 31. 57
CBS
U. S. Steel Hour ep The Wound Within 9. 10. 58 CBS
New York Confidential ep Law Is for Suckers 3. 11.
59 CBS
Wichita Town ep The Frontiersman 3. 2. 60 NBC
June Allyson Show ep The Blue Goose 3. 21. 60 CBS
Alcoa Premiere ep The Gift 1. 31. 61 ABC
Peter Gunn ep The Most Deadly Angel 5. 1. 61 ABC
Laramie ep The Barefoot Kid 1. 9. 62 NBC
Director '66 ep David and Nathan 10. 24. 65 ABC
Masterpiece Theatre ep Cold Comfort Farm 12. 26. 71
NN

SINGLETON, PENNY
Ford Theatre ep Cause for Suspicion 12. 29. 50 ABC
Jetsons sr (voice only) 9. 23. 62 ABC
Death Valley Days ep 12. 7. 63 ABC
Twilight Zone ep Sounds and Silences 4. 3. 64 CBS
Bonanza ep 3. 26. 67 NBC

SKALA, LILIA
Summer Studio One ep The Paris Feeling 6. 22. 53
Kraft Theatre ep The Light Is Cold 9. 22. 54 NBC
Kraft Theatre ep Papa Was a Sport 10. 13. 54 NBC
Kraft Theatre ep Camille 12. 1. 54 NBC
Kraft Theatre ep The King's Bounty 9. 21. 55 NBC
Kraft Theatre ep Once a Genius 11. 30. 55 NBC
Front Row Center ep Finley's Fan Club 1. 8. 56 CBS
Omnibus ep With Liberty and Justice for All 3. 4. 56
CBS
Robert Montgomery Presents ep Honored Guest 6. 4.
56 NBC
Phil Silvers Show ep A. W. O. L. 1. 1. 57 CBS

Lux Video Theatre   ep   The Last Act   9.12.57 NBC
U.S. Steel Hour   ep   The Love of Claire Ambler   4.4.
    62 CBS
Naked City   ep   And If Any Are Frozen   5.9.62 ABC
Defenders   ep   The Trial of Twenty-Two   5.18.63 CBS
Suspense   ep   I, Christopher Bell   4.1.64 CBS
Kraft Suspense Theatre   ep   Their Own Executioner   4.
    23.64 NBC
Alfred Hitchcock Theatre   ep   One of the Family   2.8.
    65 NBC
Who Has Seen the Wind   tf   2.19.65 ABC
12 O'Clock High   ep   12.23.66 ABC
I Spy   ep   Get Thee to a Nunnery   3.1.67 NBC
Ironside   ep   9.26.68 NBC
Name of the Game   ep   11.29.68 NBC
The Sunshine Patriot   tf   12.16.68 NBC
Green Acres   ep   10.4.69 CBS
McCloud   ep   Fifth Man in a String Quartet   2.2.72
    NBC
Probe   ep   2.21.72 NBC

SKELTON, RED
    Climax   ep   Public Pigeon Number One   9.8.55 CBS
    Playhouse 90   ep   The Big Slide   11.8.56 CBS
    Lucille Ball-Desi Arnaz Hour   ep   Lucy Goes to Alaska
        2.9.59 CBS
    Desilu Playhouse   ep   The Man in the Funny Suit   4.15.
        60 CBS

SKINNER, CORNELIA OTIS
    Dearest Enemy   Sp   11.26.55 NBC
    Alcoa Hour   ep   Merry Christmas, Mr. Baxter   12.2.
        56 NBC
    Theatre '62   ep   The Farmer's Daughter   1.14.62 NBC
    Irregular Verb to Love   Sp   11.12.65 NN
    N.E.T. Playhouse   ep   They   4.17.70 NN

SKULNIK, MENASHA
    The Goldbergs   sr   9.8.53 NBC
    U.S. Steel Hour   ep   Ashton Buys a Horse   9.28.55
        CBS

SLEZAK, WALTER
    Studio One   ep   Collector's Item   1.1.51 CBS
    Danger   ep   The Knave of Diamonds   6.19.51 CBS
    Suspense   ep   Dr. Anonymous   9.25.51 CBS
    Studio One   ep   The Innocence of Pastor Muller   12.
        17.51 CBS

Danger   ep   11.18.52 CBS
Danger   ep   Footfalls   12.2.52 CBS
Schlitz Playhouse of Stars   ep   12.12.52 CBS
Omnibus   ep   Arms and the Man   5.3.53 CBS
Omnibus   ep   11.22.53 CBS
U.S. Steel Hour   ep   Papa Is All   2.2.54 ABC
Hallmark Hall of Fame   ep   The Good Fairy   2.5.56
   NBC
Robert Montgomery Presents   ep   Honored Guest   6.4.
   56 NBC
20th Century-Fox Hour   ep   The Last Patriarch   11.28.
   56 CBS
Studio One   ep   Portrait of a Citizen   12.3.56 CBS
Goodyear Playhouse   ep   The Best Wine   9.29.57 NBC
Pinocchio   Sp   10.12.57 NBC
Playhouse 90   ep   The Gentleman from Seventh Avenue
   1.30.58 CBS
Telephone Time   ep   Recipe for Success   2.11.58 ABC
U.S. Steel Hour   ep   Beaver Patrol   4.9.58 CBS
U.S. Steel Hour   ep   The Public Prosecutor   4.23.58
   CBS
Alcoa Theatre   ep   The Slightly Fallen Angel   5.4.59
   NBC
Ford Startime   ep   My Three Angels   12.8.59 NBC
Loretta Young Show   ep   Alien Love   12.13.59 NBC
Great Mysteries   ep   The Woman in White   5.23.60
   NBC
Great Mysteries   ep hos   5.29.60 NBC
Great Mysteries   ep   The Inspector Vanishes   8.21.60
   NBC
Outlaws   ep   Masterpiece   12.21.61 NBC
Cain's Hundred   ep   The Cost of Living   3.20.62 NBC
Rawhide   ep   Incident of the Black Ace   4.12.63 CBS
77 Sunset Strip   ep   "5"   9.20.63, 10.11.63, 10.18.63
   ABC
Hallmark Hall of Fame   ep   A Cry of Angels   12.15.63
   NBC
Dr. Kildare   ep   Never in a Long Day   12.31.64 NBC
Batman   ep   The Clock King's Crazy Crimes   10.12.66,
   10.13.66 ABC
I Spy   ep   12.18.67 NBC
Legend of Robin Hood   Sp   2.18.68 NBC
Heidi   Sp   11.17.68 NBC

SLOANE, EVERETT
   Philco Playhouse   ep   Vincent Van Gogh   3.5.50 NBC
   Philco Playhouse   ep   Semmelweis   5.28.50 NBC

Philco Playhouse ep The Great Escape 1.28.51 CBS
Danger ep Mad Man of Middletown 8.28.51 CBS
Philco Playhouse ep Perspective 12.16.51 NBC
Lights Out ep The Verdict 9.1.52 NBC
Studio One ep Mark of Caine 2.2.53 CBS
Studio One ep A Breath of Air 3.16.53 CBS
Tales of Tomorrow ep Read to Me, Herr Doktor 3.
  20.53 ABC
Studio One ep Birthright 5.4.53 CBS
Summer Studio One ep Flowers from a Stranger 8.
  10.53 CBS
Suspense ep Accusing 10.12.53 CBS
Playhouse ep Man Versus Town 11.12.53 CBS
Inner Sanctum ep Never Die Again 2.12.54 NN
Suspense ep The Terror Begins 4.27.54 CBS
Studio One ep The Secret Self 8.30.54 CBS
Danger ep Cornered 9.28.54 CBS
Inner Sanctum ep Face of the Dead 12.7.54 NN
Omnibus ep The Trial of St. Joan 1.2.55 CBS
Kraft Theatre ep Patterns 1.12.55 NBC
Studio One ep The Silent Women 1.31.55 CBS
Kraft Theatre ep (restaged) Patterns 2.9.55 NBC
Kraft Theatre ep The Emperor Jones 2.23.55 NBC
Front Row Center ep Dinner at Eight 6.1.55 CBS
Studio One ep Heart Song 6.20.55 CBS
Kraft Theatre ep The King's Bounty 9.21.55 NBC
Omnibus ep The Renaissance 10.9.55 CBS
Alfred Hitchcock Presents ep Our Cook's a Treasure
  11.20.55 CBS
Alfred Hitchcock Presents ep Place of Shadows 2.26.
  56 CBS
Ford Star Jubilee ep High Tor 3.10.56 CBS
U.S. Steel Hour ep Noon on Doomsday 4.25.56 CBS
Alcoa Hour ep President 5.13.56 NBC
Studio One ep Family Protection 5.28.56 CBS
Kraft Theatre ep Flying Object at Three O'Clock 6.
  20.56 NBC
Climax ep Phone Call for Matthew Quade 7.5.56 CBS
Climax ep The Gorsten Case 9.20.56 CBS
20th Century-Fox Hour ep Child of the Regiment 10.
  3.56 CBS
On Trial ep Law Is for the Lovers 11.9.56 NBC
Studio One ep Rachel 12.10.56 CBS
On Trial ep The Jameson Case 12.14.56 NBC
Playhouse 90 ep Massacre at Sand Creek 12.27.56
  CBS
Schlitz Playhouse of Stars ep Night Drive 2.15.57 CBS

Climax   ep   Don't Ever Come Back   2.28.57 CBS
Ford Theatre   ep   Exclusive   4.3.57 ABC
No Warning   ep   Ashley and Son   4.27.58 NBC
Studio 57   ep   The Customs of the Country   6.16.57 NN
Climax   ep   Trial of Captain Wirz   6.27.57 CBS
Kraft Theatre   ep   Success!   7.31.57 NBC
Official Detective   sh/nar   10.18.57 NN
Climax   ep   Thieves of Tokyo   1.16.58 CBS
Schlitz Playhouse of Stars   ep   Man on a Rack   2.21.58
   CBS
Jane Wyman Theatre   ep   Hide and Seek   5.22.58 NBC
Climax   ep   The Push-Button Giant   5.29.58 CBS
Studio One   ep   The Strong Man   6.9.58 CBS
Goodyear Theatre   ep   The Spy   11.10.58 NBC
Cimarron City   ep   The Ratman   3.7.59 NBC
Alfred Hitchcock Presents   ep   The Waxwork   4.12.59
   CBS
Zorro   ep   Exposing the Tyrant   4.23.59 ABC
Suspicion   ep   The Flight   7.5.59 NBC
Laramie   ep   Stage Stop   9.15.59 NBC
G.E. Theatre   ep   Hitler's Secret   10.4.59 CBS
Playhouse 90   ep   The Sounds of Eden   10.15.59 CBS
Loretta Young Show   ep   Shower of Ashes   12.27.59
   NBC
Twilight Zone   ep   The Fever   1.29.60 CBS
Bonanza   ep   Blood on the Land   2.13.60 NBC
Loretta Young Show   ep   Crisis in 114   3.6.60 NBC
Playhouse 90   ep   Alas, Babylon   4.3.60 CBS
Zane Grey Theatre   ep   The Sunrise Gun   5.19.60 CBS
Mystery Show   ep   The Machine Calls It Murder   5.29.
   60 NBC
Mystery Show   ep   Murder Me Nicely   7.30.60 NBC
Mystery Show   ep   Run-Around   8.14.60 NBC
Mystery Show   ep   The Suicide Club   9.18.60 NBC
Route 66   ep   Black November   10.7.60 CBS
Michael Shayne   ep   A Night with Nora   10.7.60 NBC
Thriller   ep   The Guilty Men   10.18.60 NBC
Best of the Post   ep   Command   10.22.60 ABC
Aquanauts   ep   11.9.60 CBS
A Question of Chairs   nar   1.15.61 CBS
Wagon Train   ep   The Same Elder Story   1.18.61 NBC
Checkmate   ep   Melody for Murder   2.25.61 CBS
The Million Dollar Incident   Sp   4.21.61 CBS
Asphalt Jungle   ep   The Gomez Affair   4.23.61 ABC
Target Corruptors   ep   The Silent Partner   12.8.61 ABC
G.E. Theatre   ep   The Wall Between   1.7.62 CBS
Andy Griffith Show   ep   1.8.62 CBS

Perry Mason   ep   The Case of the Poison Pen Pal   2.
    10. 62 CBS
Cain's Hundred   ep   Blood Money   2.13. 62 NBC
Dick Powell Theatre   ep   The Legend   2. 20. 62 NBC
Bus Stop   ep   Verdict of Twelve   3. 11. 62 ABC
Mystery Theatre   ep   The Problem in Cell 13   8. 29. 62
    NBC
Saints and Sinners   ep   9. 24. 62 NBC
Rawhide   ep   Incident at Sugar Creek   11. 23. 62 CBS
Sam Benedict   ep   The Target over the Hill   12. 29. 62
    NBC
Saints and Sinners   ep   The Home-Coming Bit   1. 7. 63
    NBC
Eleventh Hour   ep   Like a Diamond in the Sky   2. 13. 63
    NBC
Dakota   ep   Justice at Eagle's Nest   3. 11. 63 ABC
Dick Van Dyke Show   ep   3. 13. 63 CBS
Dick Van Dyke Show   ep   3. 27. 63 CBS
Temple Houston   ep   Toll the Bell Slowly   10. 17. 63
    NBC
Virginian   ep   No Tears for Savannah   10. 2. 63 NBC
Gunsmoke   ep   11. 9. 63 CBS
Rawhide   ep   Incident of the Pied Piper   2. 6. 64 CBS
Wagon Train   ep   2. 10. 64 ABC
Voyage to the Bottom of the Sea   ep   Hotline   11. 9. 64
    ABC
Bonanza   ep   Right Is the Fourth R   3. 7. 65 NBC
Rawhide   ep   The Empty Sleeve   4. 2. 65 CBS
Gunsmoke   ep   4. 10. 65 CBS
Ben Casey   ep   A Horse Named Stravinsky   5. 17. 65
    ABC
Hercules   Sp nar   9. 12. 65 ABC
Honey West   ep   In the Bag   11. 5. 65 ABC

SMITH, ALEXIS
    Rheingold Theatre   ep   The Back of Beyond   3. 5. 55 NBC
    Stage 7   ep   To Kill a Man   3. 6. 55 CBS
    20th Century-Fox Hour   ep   The Hefferan Family   6. 13.
        56 CBS
    Robert Montgomery Presents   ep   September Affair   10.
        8. 56 NBC
    Lux Video Theatre   ep   The Gay Sisters   1. 22. 56 NBC
    Schlitz Playhouse of Stars   ep   I Shot a Prowler   3. 28.
        58 CBS
    U. S. Steel Hour   ep   The Last Autumn   11. 18. 59 CBS
    Adventures in Paradise   ep   Somewhere South of Suva
        12. 28. 59 ABC

Route 66 ep Incident on a Bridge 6.16.61 CBS
Governor and J.J. ep 1.6.70 CBS
Marcus Welby, M.D. ep The Windfall 3.23.71 ABC

SMITH, KATE
Hallmark Hall of Fame ep nar The Small One 12.21.
52 NBC
Once Upon a Christmas Time Sp 12.9.59 NBC

SMITH, KEELY
Mister Roberts ep 3.11.66 NBC

SMITH, KENT
Philco Playhouse ep The End Is Known 4.16.50 NBC
Lights Out ep The Half-Pint Flask 11.6.50 NBC
Robert Montgomery Presents ep Victoria Regina 1.15.
51 NBC
Lights Out ep And Adam Begot 7.2.51 NBC
Philco Playhouse ep Wayward Season 9.16.51 NBC
Armstrong Circle Theatre ep Airtight Case 12.4.51
NBC
Studio One ep Waterfront Boss 1.14.52 CBS
Lux Video Theatre ep The Sound of Waves Breaking
1.21.52 CBS
Pulitzer Prize Playhouse ep The Jungle 4.9.52 ABC
Robert Montgomery Presents ep The Lost and Found
9.14.53 NBC
P.M. Playhouse sh 10.8.53 CBS
Hallmark Hall of Fame ep King Richard II 1.24.54
NBC
Motorola TV Hour ep The Muldoon Matter 2.23.54
ABC
Front Row Center ep Dark Victory 7.27.55 CBS
Science Fiction Theatre ep The Unexplored 11.11.55
NBC
Crossroads ep Vivi Shining Bright 12.23.55 ABC
Robert Montgomery Presents ep Give and Take 1.14.
57 NBC
Armstrong Circle Theatre ep Slow Assassination 4.
16.57 NBC
Kraft Theatre ep Success! 7.31.57 NBC
Wagon Train ep The Ruth Owens Story 10.9.57 NBC
Armstrong Circle Theatre ep Crisis on Tangier Is-
land 10.16.57 CBS
Have Gun, Will Travel ep 11.16.57 CBS
M Squad ep Lovers' Lane Killing 2.14.58 NBC
G.E. Theatre ep Last Town Car 2.16.58, 2.23.58
CBS

Matinee Theatre   ep   The Cause   5.12.58 NBC
The Millionaire   ep   Bill Franklin   5.13.59 CBS
Alfred Hitchcock Presents   ep   A True Account   6.7.59
   CBS
Wagon Train   ep   The Lita Folsdaire Story   1.6.60 NBC
Dan Raven   ep   The Night Is Numbered   11.11.60 NBC
Michael Shayne   ep   Shoot the Works   11.11.60 NBC
Have Gun Will Travel   ep   1.28.61 CBS
Adventures in Paradise   ep   Man Eater   2.6.61 ABC
Americans   ep   The Regular   2.6.61 NBC
Barbara Stanwyck Theatre   cp   The Golden Acres   3.13.
   61 NBC
Perry Mason   ep   The Case of the Meddling Medium   10.
   21.61 CBS
Lawman   ep   The Appointment   11.26.61 ABC
Defenders   ep   The Prowler   12.16.61 CBS
Adventures in Paradise   ep   Please Believe Me   2.4.62
   ABC
Cheyenne   ep   Trail of Hatred   2.5.62 ABC
Checkmate   ep   Death Beyond Recall   2.7.62 CBS
Have Gun Will Travel   ep   4.21.62 CBS
Alfred Hitchcock Theatre   ep   I Saw the Whole Thing
   10.11.62 CBS
Perry Mason   ep   The Case of the Prankish Professor
   1.17.63 CBS
Wide Country   ep   The Judas Goat   2.21.63 NBC
Going My Way   ep   Blessed Are the Meek   2.27.63 ABC
Gunsmoke   ep   3.16.63 CBS
Untouchables   ep   The Carlie Argos Story   4.16.63 ABC
Arrest and Trial   ep   Inquest into a Bleeding Heart   11.
   10.63 ABC
Outer Limits   ep   It Crawled out of the Woodworks   12.
   9.63 ABC
Gunsmoke   ep   1.4.64 CBS
Great Adventures   ep   The Testing of Sam Houston   1.
   31.64 CBS
Outer Limits   ep   The Children of Spider County   2.17.
   64 ABC
Eleventh Hour   ep   To Love Is to Live   4.15.64 NBC
Great Adventure   ep   The Pirate and the Patriot   5.1.64
   CBS
Peyton Place   sr   10.13.64 ABC
Beverly Hillbillies   ep   2.17.65 CBS
Profiles in Courage   ep   3.21.65 NBC
I Spy   ep   Always Say Goodbye   1.26.66 NBC
Felony Squad   ep   2.13.67 ABC
Mission Impossible   ep   2.25.67 CBS

Daniel Boone   ep   3.23.67 NBC
Invaders   ep   4.18.67 ABC
FBI   ep   10.8.67 ABC
Wild, Wild West   ep   11.24.67 CBS
Invaders   sr   12.5.67 ABC
FBI   ep   Conspiracy of Silence   3.2.69 ABC
Governor and J.J.   ep   12.9.69 CBS
Governor and J.J.   ep   From Her to Maternity   12.30.
    70 CBS
The Night Stalker   tf   1.11.72 ABC
Night Gallery   ep   Deliveries in the Rear   2.9.72 NBC
Probe   tf   2.21.72 NBC
Hollywood Television Theatre   ep   Another Part of the
    Forest   10.2.72 NN
Delphi Bureau   ep   10.5.72 ABC
The Crooked Hearts   tf   11.8.72 ABC
Owen Marshall   ep   11.16.72 ABC
Cool Million   ep   12.6.72 NBC

SMITH, LOIS
Studio One   ep   Jack Sparling   4.12.54 CBS
Star Tonight   ep   A Matter of Life   3.22.55 ABC
Justice   ep   The Girl without a Name   11.27.55 NBC
Robert Montgomery Presents   ep   Second Day of Christ-
    mas   12.26.55 NBC
U.S. Steel Hour   ep   Bring Me a Dream   1.4.56 CBS
U.S. Steel Hour   ep   Noon on Doomsday   4.25.56 CBS
Ford Startime   ep   Cindy's Fella   12.15.59 NBC
Play of the Week   ep   Miss Julie   1.25.60 NN
Play of the Week   ep   The Master Builder   3.21.60 NN
Victory   Sp   4.8.60 NBC
Dupont Show of the Month   ep   Men in White   9.30.60
    CBS
Loretta Young Show   ep   When Queens Ride By   3.12.61
    NBC
Route 66   ep   Go Read the River   3.16.62 CBS
Naked City   ep   Strike a Statue   5.16.62 ABC
Defenders   ep   The Invisible Badge   11.24.62 CBS
Route 66   ep   Only by Cunning Glimpses   12.7.62 CBS
Dr. Kildare   ep   Each His Prison   5.23.63 NBC
Route 66   ep   Who in His Right Mind Needs a Nice Girl
    2.7.64 CBS
Eleventh Hour   ep   A Pattern of Sunday   4.8.64 NBC
CBS Playhouse   ep   Do Not Go Gentle into That Good
    Night   10.17.67 CBS
N.E.T. Playhouse   ep   Dragon Country   12.3.70 NN
N.E.T. Playhouse   ep   Talk to Me Like the Rain   1.9.71
    NN

SMITH, MAGGIE
    Kraft Theatre   ep   Night of the Plague   3. 20. 57 NBC
    Much Ado About Nothing   Sp   3. 11. 71, 3. 18. 71 NN

SMITH, ROGER
    Ford Theatre   ep   Never Lend Money to a Woman   1.
      19. 56 NBC
    Ford Theatre   ep   Stand by to Dive   11. 28. 56 ABC
    West Point   ep   M-24   11. 19. 57 ABC
    Father Knows Best   ep   The Rivals   1. 29. 58 NBC
    Wagon Train   ep   The Ralph Barrister Story   4. 16. 58
      NBC
    77 Sunset Strip   sr   10. 18. 58 ABC
    77 Sunset Strip   sr ret   fall, 1959 ABC
    Hawaiian Eye   ep   I Wed Three Wives   9. 14. 60 ABC
    77 Sunset Strip   sr ret   9. 16. 60 ABC
    77 Sunset Strip   sr ret   9. 22. 61 ABC
    Surfside 6   ep   Love Song for a Deadly Redhead   4. 30.
      62 ABC
    77 Sunset Strip   sr ret   10. 12. 62 ABC
    Kraft Suspense Theatre   ep   Knight's Gambit   3. 26. 64
      NBC
    Farmer's Daughter   ep   The One-Eyed Sloth   4. 1. 64
      CBS
    Mr. Roberts   sr   9. 17. 65 NBC

SMOTHERS, DICK
    The Smothers Brothers Show   sr   9. 17. 65 CBS
    Alice Through the Looking Glass   Sp   11. 6. 66 NBC
    It Takes a Thief   ep   1. 19. 70 ABC

SMOTHERS, TOMMY
    The Smothers Brothers Show   sr   9. 17. 65 CBS
    Alice Through the Looking Glass   Sp   11. 6. 66 NBC
    Love American Style   ep   Love and the Kidnapper   1. 1.
      71 ABC

SNODGRASS, CARRIE
    Virginian   ep   Crime Wave at Buffalo Springs   1. 29. 69
      NBC
    Judd for the Defense   ep   The Crystal Maze   1. 3. 69
      ABC
    Outsider   ep   The Flip Side   2. 26. 69 NBC
    The Whole World's Watching   tf   3. 11. 69 NBC
    Silent Night, Lonely Night   tf   12. 16. 69 NBC
    Medical Center   ep   1. 7. 70 CBS

SOMMER, ELKE
    Probe   tf   2.21.72 NBC

SONDERGAARD, GALE
    It Takes a Thief   ep   12.25.69 ABC
    Get Smart   ep   Rebecca of Funny Folk Farm   1.23.70
       CBS
    The Best of Everything   sr   1971 ABC
    Bold Ones   ep   The Letter of the Law   12.26.71 NBC

SOTHERN, ANN
    Schlitz Playhouse of Stars   ep   Lady with a Will   2.1.
       52 CBS
    Hollywood Opening Night   ep   Let George Do It.   10.13.
       52 NBC
    Private Secretary   sr   2.1.53 CBS
    Private Secretary   sr ret   9.20.53 CBS
    Private Secretary   sr ret   9.12.54 CBS
    Private Secretary   sr ret   9.11.55 CBS
    Loretta Young Show   ep hos   Man in the Ring   12.11.55
       NBC
    Ford Theatre   ep   With No Regrets   2.20.57 ABC
    Lucille Ball-Desi Arnaz Hour   ep   Lucy Take a Cruise
       to Havana   11.6.57 CBS
    Ann Sothern Show   sr   10.6.58 CBS
    Ann Sothern Show   sr ret   10.5.59 CBS
    June Allyson Show   ep   Night Out   11.23.59 CBS
    Ann Sothern Show   sr ret   10.6.60 CBS
    Alfred Hitchcock Theatre   ep   Water's Edge   10.19.64
       NBC
    Here's Lucy   ep   2.7.65 CBS
    Here's Lucy   ep   3.1.65 CBS
    My Mother the Car   sr (voice only)   9.14.65 NBC
    The Lucy Show   ep   10.25.65 CBS
    The Lucy Show   ep   11.8.65 CBS
    The Lucy Show   ep   11.22.65 CBS
    Jesse James   ep   The Widow Fay   12.20.65 ABC
    The Girl from U.N.C.L.E.   ep   2.14.67 NBC
    The Outsider   tf   11.30.67 NBC
    Family Affair   ep   1.8.68 CBS
    Love American Style   ep   12.22.69 ABC
    Men from Shiloh   ep   The Legacy of Spencer Flats   1.
       27.71 NBC
    Congratulations, It's a Boy   tf   9.21.71 ABC
    A Death of Innocence   ep   11.26.71 CBS
    Chicago Teddy Bears   ep   12.10.71 CBS
    Alias Smith and Jones   ep   12.16.71 ABC
    The Weekend Nun   tf   12.20.72 ABC

SPARV, CAMILLA
    Rogues ep A Daring Step Backward 4.18.65 NBC

STACK, ROBERT
    Video Theatre ep Inside Story 6.18.51 CBS
    Lights Out ep Will-o'-the-Wisp 10.1.51 NBC
    Lux Video Theatre ep Route 19 10.8.51 CBS
    Hollywood Opening Night ep Thirty Days 11.10.52
        NBC
    Schlitz Playhouse of Stars ep Storm Warnings 7.10.
        53 CBS
    Ford Theatre ep Ever Since the Day 12.24.53 NBC
    Ford Theatre ep Indirect Approach 6.24.54 NBC
    20th Century-Fox Hour ep Laura 10.19.55 CBS
    Producers Showcase ep The Lord Don't Play Favorites
        9.17.56 NBC
    Playhouse 90 ep Panic Button 11.28.57 CBS
    Desilu Playhouse ep The Untouchables 4.20.59, 4.27.
        59 CBS
    Untouchables sr 10.15.59 ABC
    Lawless Years ep The Billy Boy Rockabye Creel Story
        11.5.59 NBC
    Untouchables sr ret 10.13.60 ABC
    Untouchables sr ret 10.12.61 ABC
    Untouchables sr ret 9.25.62 ABC
    Bob Hope Chrysler Theatre ep The Command 5.22.
        64 NBC
    Bob Hope Chrysler Theatre ep Memorandum for a Spy
        4.2.65, 4.9.65 NBC
    The Lucy Show ep 3.14.66 CBS
    Danny Thomas Show ep The Scene 9.25.67 NBC
    Laura Sp 1.24.68 ABC
    Name of the Game sr 9.27.68 NBC
    Name of the Game sr 9.26.69 NBC
    Name of the Game sr 9.18.70 NBC

STACY, JAMES
    Ozzie and Harriet ep Code of Honor 4.23.58 ABC
    Ozzie and Harriet ep The Buckingham 9.9.59 ABC
    Ozzie and Harriet ep Father's Night at the Fraternity
        House 12.2.59 ABC
    Ozzie and Harriet ep A Question of Suits and Ties 4.
        5.61 ABC
    Ozzie and Harriet ep The High Cost of Dating 10.5.
        61 ABC
    Have Gun, Will Travel ep 1.21.62 CBS
    Donna Reed Show ep Donna's Prima Donna 2.1.62
        ABC

Donna Reed Show ep The Make-Over Man 12.6.62 ABC

Ozzie and Harriet ep Rick and the Boat Model 1.3. 63 ABC

Hazel ep The Baby Came C.O.D. 11.14.63 NBC

Perry Mason ep The Case of the Simple Demon 4.2. 64 CBS

Donna Reed Show ep Indoor Outing 4.8.65 ABC

Perry Mason ep The Case of the Final Fade-Out 5. 22.66 CBS

Baby Crazy pt 9.1.66 ABC

The Monroes ep Ride with Terror 9.21.66 ABC

The Monroes ep 4.5.67 ABC

Gunsmoke ep 10.2.67, 10.9.67 CBS

Lancer sr 9.24.68 CBS

Storefront Lawyers ep Murph Collins vs. Tomorrow 9.30.70 CBS

Paper Man tf 11.12.71 CBS

Gunsmoke ep 2.7.72 CBS

Love American Style ep 2.18.72 ABC

Heat of Anger tf 3.3.72 CBS

Medical Center ep 9.20.72 CBS

Streets of San Francisco ep 10.14.72 ABC

Marcus Welby, M.D. ep 11.28.72 ABC

Owen Marshall ep 12.7.72 ABC

STANLEY, KIM

The Trap ep Sentence of Death 5.27.50 CBS

Danger ep The Anniversary 1.30.51 CBS

Goodyear Playhouse ep The Witness 8.17.52 NBC

Philco Playhouse ep A Young Lady of Property 4.5. 53 NBC

First Person ep The Tears of My Sister 8.14.53 NBC

Philco Playhouse ep The Strong Women 11.29.53 NBC

Goodyear Playhouse ep The Brownstone 1.31.54 NBC

Kraft Theatre ep The Scarlet Letter 5.26.54 NBC

Philco Playhouse ep Somebody Special 6.6.54 NBC

Elgin Hour ep The Bridge 1.11.55 ABC

Playwrights '56 ep The Witing Place 12.20.55 NBC

Playwrights '56 ep Flight 2.28.56 NBC

Goodyear Playhouse ep Conspiracy of Hearts 3.11.56 NBC

Goodyear Playhouse ep Joey 3.25.56 NBC

Kraft Theatre ep Death is a Spanish Dancer 5.9.56 NBC

Goodyear Playhouse ep In the Days of our Youth 5. 20.56 NBC

Studio One   ep   The Traveling Lady   4. 22. 57 CBS
Kraft Theatre   ep   The Glass Wall   5. 15. 57 NBC
Playhouse 90   ep   Clash by Night   5. 13. 57 CBS
Playhouse 90   ep   Tomorrow   3. 7. 60 CBS
Westinghouse Presents   ep   That's Where the Town's
    Going   4. 17. 62 CBS
Ben Casey   ep   A Cardinal Act of Mercy   1. 14. 63, 1.
    21. 63 ABC
Eleventh Hour   ep   Does My Mother Have to Know   3.
    25. 64, 4. 1. 64 NBC
Flesh and Blood   Sp   1. 26. 68 NBC
U. M. C.   tf   4. 17. 69 CBS
N. E. T. Playhouse   ep   I Can't Imagine Tomorrow   1. 9.
    71 NN
Name of the Game   ep   The Man Who Killed a Ghost   1.
    29. 71 NBC
Medical Center   ep   Secret Heritage   2. 3. 71 CBS

STANWYCK, BARBARA
    Loretta Young Show   ep hos   My Uncles O'More   9. 18.
        55 NBC
    Loretta Young Show   ep hos   The Waiting Game   10. 9.
        55 NBC
    Zane Grey Theatre   ep   The Freighter   1. 17. 58 CBS
    Goodyear Theatre   ep   Three Dark Years   6. 23. 58 NBC
    Decision   ep   Sudden Silence   8. 3. 58 NBC
    Zane Grey Theatre   ep   Trail to Nowhere   10. 2. 58 CBS
    Jack Benny Show   ep   Autolight   1. 11. 59 CBS
    Zane Grey Theatre   ep   Hang the Heart High   1. 15. 59
        CBS
    Zane Grey Theatre   ep   Lone Woman   10. 8. 59 CBS
    Barbara Stanwyck Theatre   sh/sr   9. 19. 60 NBC
    Joey Bishop Show   ep   A Windfall for Mom   10. 4. 61
        NBC
    Wagon Train   ep   The Maud Frazer Story   10. 11. 61 NBC
    Rawhide   ep   The Captain's Wife   1. 12. 62 CBS
    Dick Powell Theatre   ep   Special Assignment   9. 25. 62
        NBC
    Wagon Train   ep   The Caroline Casteel Story   9. 26. 62
        ABC
    Untouchables   ep   Elegy   11. 20. 62 ABC
    Untouchables   ep   Search for a Dead Man   1. 1. 63 ABC
    Wagon Train   ep   The Molly Kincaid Story   9. 16. 63
        ABC
    Wagon Train   ep   The Kate Crawley Story   1. 27. 64 ABC
    Big Valley   sr   9. 15. 65 ABC
    Big Valley   sr ret   9. 12. 66 ABC

Big Valley sr ret 9.11.67 ABC
Big Valley sr ret 9.23.68 ABC
The House That Wouldn't Die tf 10.27.70 ABC
A Taste of Evil tf 10.12.71 ABC

STAPLETON, JEAN
Philco Playhouse ep A Business Proposition 10.23.
55 NBC
True Story ep 4.23.60 NBC
Dr. Kildare ep The Patient 11.23.61 NBC
Nurses ep The Barbara Bowers Story 10.18.62 CBS
Defenders ep The Hidden Jungle 12.1.62 CBS
Car 54 Where Are You ep J'Adore Muldoon 12.30.62
NBC
Eleventh Hour ep The Bride Wore Pink 12.4.63 NBC
Patty Duke Show ep The Raffle 1.27.65 ABC
All in the Family sr 1.12.71 CBS
All in the Family sr ret 9.18.71 CBS
All in the Family sr ret 9.16.72 CBS

STAPLETON, MAUREEN
Curtain Call ep Carrie Marr 9.19.52 NBC
Goodyear Playhouse ep The Accident 5.3.53 NBC
Philco Playhouse ep The Mother 4.4.54 NBC
Philco Playhouse ep Incident in July 7.10.55 NBC
Armstrong Circle Theatre ep Actual 11.1.55 NBC
Justice ep Track of Fear 12.11.55 NBC
Armstrong Circle Theatre ep 6.12.56 NBC
Studio One ep Rachel 12.10.56 CBS
Alcoa Hour ep No License to Kill 9.1.57 NBC
Kraft Theatre ep All the King's Men 5.14.58, 5.21.
58 NBC
Playhouse 90 ep For Whom the Bell Tolls 3.12.59,
3.19.59 CBS
CBS TV Workshop ep Tessie Malfitano 4.3.60 CBS
A Question of Chairs 1.15.61 CBS
Play of the Week ep Four by Tennessee Williams 2.
6.61 NN
Car 54 Where Are You ep The Gypsy Curse 11.12.
61 NBC
Naked City ep Offus Goofus 12.13.61 ABC
Naked City ep Kill Me While I'm Young So I Can Die
Happy 10.17.62 ABC
Dupont Show of the Month ep The Betrayal 10.21.62
NBC
East Side/West Side ep One Drink at a Time 1.27.
64 CBS

New York Television Theatre   ep   Save Me a Place at
    Forest Lawn   3. 7. 66 NN
Among the Paths to Eden   Sp   12. 17. 67 ABC
On Stage   ep   Mirror, Mirror Off the Wall   11. 21. 69
    NBC

STEELE, BARBARA
    Adventures in Paradise   ep   Daughter of Illusion   12. 12.
        60 ABC

STEIGER, ROD
    Goodyear Playhouse   ep   Raymond Schindler, Case One
        1. 20. 52 NBC
    Kraft Theatre   ep   Marty   5. 24. 53 NBC
    First Person   ep   Desert Cafe   7. 3. 53 NBC
    Suspense   ep   The Dutch Schultz Story   7. 14. 53 CBS
    Philco Playhouse   ep   Other People's Houses   8. 30. 53
        NBC
    Philco Playhouse   ep   Smokescreen   12. 4. 54 NBC
    Kraft Theatre   ep   The Man Most Likely   6. 30. 54 NBC
    Producers Showcase   ep   Yellow Jack   1. 10. 55 NBC
    Philco Playhouse   ep   Anatomy of Fear   1. 23. 55 NBC
    Screen Directors Playhouse   ep   Markheim   4. 11. 56
        NBC
    Schlitz Playhouse   ep   The Lonely Wizard   11. 15. 57
        CBS
    Suspicion   ep   The Bull Skinner   4. 7. 58 NBC
    Playhouse 90   ep   A Town Has Turned to Dust   6. 19. 58
        CBS
    G. E. Theatre   ep   The Book of Silence   3. 6. 60 CBS
    Wagon Train   ep   The Saul Bevins Story   4. 12. 61 NBC
    Ben Casey   ep   In the Name of Love   10. 15. 62 ABC
    Route 66   ep   Welcome to the Wedding   11. 9. 63 CBS

STEPHENSON, HENRY
    Studio One   ep   Trial of John Peter Zenger   1. 22. 51
        CBS
    Pulitzer Prize Playhouse   ep   The Just and the Unjust
        3. 30. 51 ABC
    Studio One   ep   Sara Crew   12. 24. 51 CBS

STERLING, JAN
    Medallion Theatre   ep   Book Overdue   1. 30. 54 CBS
    Ford Theatre   ep   Trip around the Block   10. 28. 54 NBC
    Rheingold Theatre   ep   Ferry to Fox Island   1. 29. 55
        NBC
    Stage 7   ep   A Note of Fear   5. 15. 55 CBS

Rheingold Theatre ep Desert Story 6.4.55 NBC
Lux Video Theatre ep The Unfaithful 1.12.56 NBC
Front Row Center ep Hawk's Head 4.1.56 CBS
Climax ep The Shadow of Evil 5.24.56 CBS
Lux Video Theatre ep She Married Her Boss 6.7.56
NBC
Lux Video Theater ep Rebuke Me Not 8.9.56 NBC
Playhouse 90 ep Requiem for a Heavyweight 10.11.56
CBS
Kaiser Aluminum Hour ep Whereabouts Unknown 2.26.
57 NBC
Lux Video Theatre ep The Great Lie 3.21.57 NBC
Playhouse 90 ep Clipper Ship 4.4.57 CBS
Loretta Young Show ep Rummage Sale 4.14.57 NBC
Climax ep Mask for the Devil 10.10.57 CBS
Suspicion ep Comfort for the Grave 1.27.58 NBC
Kraft Theatre ep Run, Joe, Run 1.29.58 NBC
Jane Wyman Theatre ep A Guilty Woman 1.30.58
NBC
Alfred Hitchcock Presents ep On the Nose 2.16.58
CBS
Pursuit ep The House at Malibu 11.26.58 CBS
Wagon Train ep The Annie Griffith Story 2.25.59 NBC
Alcoa Theatre ep Chinese Finale 3.7.60 NBC
Riverboat ep Strange Request 5.16.60 NBC
G.E. Theatre ep At Your Service 5.22.60 CBS
Untouchables ep Kiss of Death Girl 12.8.60 ABC
Bonanza ep The Blood Line 12.31.60 NBC
Adventures in Paradise ep Errand of Mercy 5.29.61
ABC
Wagon Train ep The Selena Hartnell Story 10.18.61
NBC
Dick Powell Theatre ep Doyle Against the House 10.
24.61 NBC
Naked City ep The Tragic Success of Alfred Tiloff 11.
8.61 ABC
Mystery Theatre ep In Close Pursuit 6.13.62 NBC
Alfred Hitchcock Theatre ep The Tender Poisoner 12.
20.62 CBS
Dick Powell Theatre ep Luxury Liner 2.12.63 NBC
Burke's Law ep Who Killed Alex Debbs 10.25.63 ABC
Breaking Point ep Millions of Faces 12.9.63 ABC
Burke's Law ep 4.21.65 ABC
Run for Your Life ep The Cruel Fountain 4.4.66 NBC
Mannix ep The Falling Star 1.6.68 CBS
Name of the Game ep Love In at Ground Zero 1.31.
69 NBC

Name of the Game   ep   10. 24. 69 NBC
The Guiding Light   sr   1970 CBS
Bracken's World   ep   1. 9. 70 NBC
Medical Center   ep   Crossroads   3. 10. 71 CBS

STERLING, ROBERT
Studio One   ep   The Ambassadors   5. 15. 50 CBS
Studio One   ep   The Man Who Had Influence   5. 29. 50
    CBS
Video Theatre   ep   The Choir Rehearsal   2. 5. 51 CBS
Studio One   ep (restaged)   The Ambassadors   2. 26. 51
    CBS
Lights Out   ep   The Faceless Man   8. 6. 51 NBC
Video Theatre   ep   Stolen Years   11. 19. 51 CBS
Celanese Theatre   ep   Brief Moment   2. 6. 52 ABC
Robert Montgomery Presents   ep   The Lonely   5. 5. 52
    NBC
Robert Montgomery Presents   ep   Candles for Therese
    6. 2. 52 NBC
The Web   ep   Homecoming   10. 5. 52 CBS
Suspense   ep   The Man Who Had Seven Hours   10. 21. 52
    CBS
Robert Montgomery Presents   ep   The Davidian Report
    11. 17. 52 NBC
Gulf Playhouse   ep   The Scream of the Crowd   12. 12. 52
    NBC
The Web   ep   Fatal Alibi   12. 21. 52 CBS
Robert Montgomery Presents   ep   Keep Your Head Up,
    Mr. Putnam   1. 5. 53 NBC
Video Theatre   ep   Autumn Nocturne   2. 23. 53 CBS
Topper   sr   10. 16. 53 CBS
Topper   sr ret   fall, 1954 CBS
Front Row Center   sh   fall, 1955 CBS
Climax   ep   Thin Air   10. 13. 55 CBS
Dearest Enemy   Sp   11. 26. 55 NBC
Loretta Young Show   ep   Tightwad Millionaire   2. 19. 56
    NBC
Lux Video Theatre   ep   Here Comes the Groom   3. 1. 56
    NBC
Ford Theatre   ep   Clay Pigeon   5. 31. 56 NBC
20th Century-Fox Hour   sh   fall, 1956 CBS
Ford Theatre   ep   The Man Across the Hall   3. 20. 57
    ABC
Dupont Theatre   ep   The Widow Was Willing   3. 26. 57
    ABC
Wagon Train   ep   The Julia Gage Story   12. 18. 57 NBC
Love That Jill   sr   1. 20. 58 ABC

U.S. Steel Hour   ep   The Yum Yum Girl   11.30.60 CBS
Ichabod and Me   sr   9.26.61 CBS
Alfred Hitchcock Theatre   ep   House Guest   11.8.62 CBS
Twilight Zone   ep   Printer's Devil   2.28.63 CBS
Naked City   ep   Alive and Still a Second Lieutenant   3.
   6.63 ABC
Bold Ones   ep   Dagger in the Mind   12.19.71 NBC
Love American Style   ep   11.3.72 ABC

STERLING, TISHA
   Dr. Kildare   ep   Lullaby for an Indian Summer   1.7.65
      NBC
   The Long Hot Summer   ep   A Time for Living   9.23.65
      ABC
   Slattery's People   ep   11.12.65 CBS
   Frank Merriwell   pt   7.25.66 CBS
   Get Smart   ep   2.4.67 NBC
   Run for Your Life   ep   It Could Only Happen in Rome
      12.20.67 NBC
   Bonanza   ep   Star Crossed   3.10.68 NBC
   It Takes a Thief   ep   3.19.68 ABC
   Name of the Game   ep   The Bobby Currier Story   2.21.
      69 NBC
   CBS Playhouse   ep   The Experiment   2.25.69 CBS
   Bold Ones   ep   10.5.69 NBC
   Night Slaves   tf   9.29.70 ABC
   Bold Ones   ep   This Will Really Kill You   9.20.70 NBC
   Men from Shiloh   ep   Flight from Memory   2.17.71 NBC
   A Death of Innocence   tf   11.26.71 CBS
   Sixth Sense   ep   Lady, Lady, Take My Life   1.29.72
      ABC
   Medical Center   ep   3.8.72 CBS
   Ironside   ep   12.7.72 NBC

STEVENS, CONNIE
   Sugarfoot   ep   Misfire   12.10.57 ABC
   Bob Cummings Show   ep   Bob Goes Hillbilly   1.28.58
      NBC
   Maverick   ep   Two Tickets to Ten Strike   3.15.59 ABC
   77 Sunset Strip   ep   Honey from the Bea   4.10.59 ABC
   Hawaiian Eye   sr   10.7.59 ABC
   Hawaiian Eye   sr ret   9.14.60 ABC
   Hawaiian Eye   sr ret   9.27.61 ABC
   Sugarfoot   ep   The Wild Bunch   9.29.60 ABC
   Hawaiian Eye   sr ret   10.2.62 ABC
   Cheyenne   ep   Reprieve   4.26.63 ABC
   Temple Houston   ep   The Town that Trespassed   3.26.
      64 NBC

Wendy and Me   sr   9. 14. 64 ABC
Love American Style   ep   Love and the Legal Agreement   10. 20. 69 ABC
Hallmark Hall of Fame   ep   The Littlest Angel   12. 6. 69 NBC
Mister Jerico   tf   3. 3. 70 ABC
Call Her Mom   tf   2. 15. 72 ABC
Playmates   tf   10. 3. 72 ABC
Every Man Needs One   tf   12. 13. 72 ABC

STEVENS, CRAIG
Fireside Theatre   ep   The Imposter   5. 27. 52 NBC
Gruen Guild Theatre   cp   The Corner Shop   7. 29. 52 NN
Fireside Theatre   ep   Let the Cards Decide   1. 6. 53 NBC
Playhouse   ep   The Night Light at Vorden's   10. 16. 53 ABC
Mirror Theatre   ep   Surprise Party   10. 24. 53 CBS
Pepsi Cola Playhouse   ep   The House Nobody Wanted   11. 13. 53 ABC
Four Star Playhouse   ep   Girl on the Park Bench   12. 3. 53 CBS
Studio 57   ep   No Great Hero   9. 28. 54 NN
Loretta Young Show   ep   Let Columbus Discover You   4. 3. 55 NBC
Ford Theatre   ep   Mason-Dixon Line   6. 10. 54 NBC
Playhouse   ep   The Lady Challenges   4. 24. 55 ABC
The Millionaire   ep   The Story of Vickie Lawson   6. 8. 55 CBS
Four Star Playhouse   ep   The Frightened Woman   6. 23. 55 CBS
Studio One   ep   The Day Before the Wedding   7. 4. 55 CBS
Those Whiting Girls   ep   7. 11. 55 CBS
Studio 57   ep   Christmas Every Day   12. 18. 55 NN
Matinee Theatre   ep   Man and a Maid   5. 8. 56 NBC
Four Star Playhouse   ep   Beneath the Surface   5. 31. 56 CBS
On Trial   ep   Law is for the Lovers   11. 9. 56 NBC
Matinee Theatre   ep   2. 18. 57 NBC
Ford Theatre   ep   Fate Travels East   3. 13. 57 ABC
Jane Wyman Theatre   ep   The Man in the Car   4. 30. 57 NBC
Lux Video Theatre   ep   Diagnosis Homicide   8. 22. 57 NBC
Meet McGraw   ep   The Texas Story   9. 17. 57 NBC
Alfred Hitchcock Presents   ep   The Deadly   12. 15. 57 CBS

Jane Wyman Theatre   ep   The Man in the Car   12.19.
57 NBC
Loretta Young Show   ep   Mr. and Mrs. Devan   1.5.58
NBC
Eve Arden Show   ep   1.21.58 CBS
Schlitz Playhouse of Stars   ep   I Shot a Prowler   3.28.
58 CBS
Peter Gunn   sr   9.22.58 NBC
Gale Storm Show   ep   Sing, Susanna Sing   2.14.59 CBS
Eddie Cantor Playhouse   ep   A Hunting We Will Go
4.26.59 NN
Loretta Young Show   ep   The Demon and Mrs. Demon
6.21.59 NBC
Chevy Show   ep   Happiest Day   4.23.61 NBC
The Mighty   pt   8.21.62 CBS
Mr. Broadway   sr   9.26.64 CBS
Name of the Game   ep   The Emissary   10.10.69 NBC
The Bold Ones   ep   Shriek of Silence   11.30.69 NBC
McCloud   tf   2.17.70 NBC
Governor and J.J.   ep   9.30.70 CBS
My Three Sons   ep   10.3.70 CBS
To Rome with Love   ep   11.17.70 CBS
Men from Shiloh   ep   2.24.71 NBC
Marcus Welby, M.D.   ep   The Windfall   3.23.71 ABC
Alias Smith and Jones   ep   12.30.71 ABC
Medical Center   ep   2.23.72 CBS
Rookies   ep   10.16.72 ABC
Here's Lucy   ep   11.13.72 CBS
Love American Style   ep   11.24.72 ABC
The Snoop Sisters   tf   12.18.72 NBC
Ghost Story   ep   12.22.72 NBC

STEVENS, INGER
Studio One   ep   Sue Ellen   8.9.54 CBS
Kraft Theatre   ep   Strangers in Hiding   12.29.54 NBC
Robert Montgomery Presents   ep   A Night for Dreaming
1.10.55 NBC
Studio One   ep   The Conviction of Peter Shea   3.14.55
CBS
The Millionaire   ep   The Story of Betty Perkins   12.26.
56 CBS
Alfred Hitchcock Presents   ep   My Brother Richard   1.
20.57 CBS
Climax   ep   The Giant Killer   8.1.57 CBS
Playhouse 90   ep   Diary of a Nurse   5.7.59 CBS
Bonanza   ep   The Newcomers   9.26.59 NBC
Sunday Showcase   ep   The Indestructible Mr. Gore   12.
13.59 NBC

Zane Grey Theatre   ep   Calico Bait   3.31.60 CBS
Moment of Fear   ep   Total Recall   7.29.60 NBC
Twilight Zone   ep   The Hitchhiker   8.12.60 CBS
Checkmate   ep   Interrupted Honeymoon   9.24.60 CBS
Hong Kong   ep   Pearl Flower   10.12.60 ABC
Twilight Zone   ep   The Lateness of the Hour   12.2.60
    CBS
Route 66   ep   The Beryllim Eater   12.9.60 CBS
Dupont Show of the Month   ep   The Prisoner of Zenda
    1.18.61 CBS
Adventures in Paradise   ep   Angel of Death   3.6.61 ABC
Detectives   ep   Song of the Guilty Heart   12.8.61 NBC
Route 66   ep   Burning for Burning   12.29.61 CBS
Follow the Sun   ep   The Girl from the Brandenburg Gate
    12.31.61 ABC
Dick Powell Theatre   ep   Price of Tomatoes   1.16.62
    NBC
Golden Showcase   ep   Saturday's Children   2.25.62 CBS
Eleventh Hour   ep   The Blues My Baby Gave to Me   12.
    12.62 NBC
Sam Benedict   ep   The Target Over the Hill   12.29.62
    NBC
Alfred Hitchcock Theatre   ep   Forecast: Low Clouds
    and Coastal Fog   1.18.63 CBS
Nurses   ep   Party Girl   3.28.63 CBS
Dick Powell Theatre   ep   The Last of the Big Spenders
    4.16.63 ABC
Empire   ep   Duet for Eight Wheels   4.30.63 NBC
Farmer's Daughter   sr   9.20.63 ABC
Farmer's Daughter   sr ret   9.18.64 ABC
Farmer's Daughter   sr ret   9.13.65 ABC
The Borgia Stick   tf   2.25.67 NBC
Run, Simon, Run   tf   1.21.70 ABC
The Mask of Sheba   tf   3.9.70 NBC

STEVENS, MARK
Story Theatre   ep   Mysterious Picture   12.16.51 NN
Schlitz Playhouse of Stars   ep   5.9.52 CBS
Ford Theatre   ep   Birth of a Hero   10.23.52 NBC
Hollywood Opening Night   ep   Alicia   11.3.52 NBC
Ford Theatre   ep   This Is My Heart   1.15.53 NBC
Schlitz Playhouse of Stars   ep   Knave of Hearts   7.24.
    53 CBS
G.E. Theatre   ep   Confession   10.18.53 CBS
Martin Kane   sr   10.22.53 NBC
Ford Theatre   ep   Kiss and Forget   12.3.53 NBC
Big Town   sr   10.11.54 NBC

Big Town   sr ret   10.11.55 NBC
Schlitz Playhouse of Stars   ep   Washington Incident   12.
7.56 CBS
Wagon Train   ep   The Nels Stack Story   10.23.57 NBC
Loretta Young Show   ep   The Defense   10.27.57 NBC
Studio 57   ep   The Face of a Killer   10.27.57 NN
Jane Wyman Theatre   ep   A Reasonable Doubt   11.28.
57 NBC
Zane Grey Theatre   ep   The Stranger   2.28.58 CBS
Decision   ep   Man on a Raft   9.28.58 NBC
Loretta Young Show   ep   For Better or for Worse   10.
12.58 NBC
Stagecoach West   ep   The Saga of Jeremy Boone   11.
29.60 ABC
Bus Stop   ep   The Ordeals of Kevin Brooke   2.25.62
ABC
Rawhide   ep   9.28.62 CBS

STEVENS, RISE
Chocolate Soldier   Sp   6.4.55 NBC
Hansel and Gretel   Sp   4.27.58 NBC
Little Women   Sp   10.16.58 CBS

STEVENS, STELLA
Johnny Ringo   ep   Uncertain Vengeance   3.10.60 CBS
G.E. Theatre   ep   Graduation Dress   10.30.60 CBS
Hawaiian Eye   ep   Kakus Woman   11.23.60 ABC
Bonanza   ep   Silent Thunder   12.10.60 NBC
Riverboat   ep   Zigzag   12.26.60 NBC
G.E. Theatre   ep   The Great Alberti   11.5.61 CBS
Follow the Sun   ep   Conspiracy of Silence   12.10.61
ABC
Frontier Circus   ep   The Balloon Girl   1.11.62 CBS
Hawaiian Eye   ep   Hatau Woman   4.23.63 ABC
Ben Casey   sr   9.14.64 ABC
In Broad Daylight   tf   10.16.71 ABC
Ghost Story   ep   The Dead We Leave Behind   9.15.72
NBC
Climb an Angry Mountain   tf   12.23.72 NBC

STEWART, JAMES
G.E. Theatre   ep   The Windmill   4.24.55 CBS
G.E. Theatre   ep   The Town Is Past   2.10.57 CBS
G.E. Theatre   ep   The Trail to Christmas   12.15.57
CBS
Ford Startime   ep   Cindy's Fella   12.15.59 NBC
Alcoa Premiere   ep   Flashing Spikes   10.4.62 ABC

Jimmy Stewart Show   sr   9.19.71 NBC
Hallmark Hall of Fame   ep   Harvey   3.22.72 NBC

STEWART, PAUL
   Prudential Playhouse   ep   Over 21   12.19.50 CBS
   Lights Out   ep   The Man with the Astrakan Hat   3.5.51
      NBC
   TV Reader's Digest   ep   3.28.55 ABC
   TV Reader's Digest   ep   The Only Way Out   6.2.56 ABC
   Playhouse 90   ep   Confession   11.29.56 CBS
   Climax   ep   The Long Count   2.21.57 CBS
   On Trial   ep   The Secret of Polatno   5.31.57 NBC
   Climax   ep   Mask for the Devil   10.10.57 CBS
   No Warning   ep   Fingerprints   6.22.58 NBC
   Alcoa Theatre   ep   The First Star   12.1.58 NBC
   Deadline   sh/nar   9.19.59 NN
   Staccato   ep   2.4.60 NBC
   Alfred Hitchcock Presents   ep   Craig's Will   3.6.60
      CBS
   Cain's Hundred   ep   Cain's Final Judgment   12.19.61
      NBC
   Breaking Point   ep   Crack in an Image   10.28.63 ABC
   Bob Hope Chrysler Theatre   ep   A Case of Armed Rob-
      bery   4.3.64 NBC
   Dr. Kildare   ep   Rome Will Never Leave You   11.12.64,
      11.19.64, 11.26.64 NBC
   Wagon Train   ep   1.10.65 ABC
   Profiles in Courage   ep   Woodrow Wilson   2.14.65 NBC
   Mannix   ep   Pressure Point   10.12.68 CBS
   Perry Mason   ep   The Case of the Tragic Trophy   11.
      19.64 CBS
   Perry Mason   ep   The Case of the Avenging Angel   3.
      13.66 CBS
   T.H.E. Cat   ep   10.7.66 NBC
   The Man who Never Was   ep   11.9.66 ABC
   The Man who Never Was   ep   1.4.67 ABC
   Accidental Family   ep   1.5.68 NBC
   New Adventures of Huck Finn   sr   11.24.68 NBC
   Name of the Game   ep   Swingers Only   1.10.69 NBC
   Ironside   ep   The Prophecy   2.6.69 NBC
   Outsider   ep   Handle with Care   3.5.69 NBC
   Mannix   ep   A Sleep in the Deep   11.8.69 CBS
   Mission Impossible   ep   11.30.69 CBS
   Name of the Game   ep   High Card   12.5.69 NBC
   Survivors   sr   12.22.69 ABC
   It Takes a Thief   ep   1.15.70 ABC
   Governor and J.J.   ep   9.23.70 CBS

Storefront Lawyers   ep   The Emancipation of Bessie
   Gray   10.14.70 CBS
Bold Ones   ep   The Continual Roar of Musketry   11.29.
   70 NBC
Name of the Game   ep   12.4.70 NBC
Mannix   ep   Deja Vu   12.12.70 CBS
Silent Force   ep   1.4.71, 1.11.71 ABC
Name of the Game   ep   Los Angeles 2017   1.15.71
   NBC
Medical Center   ep   11.10.71 CBS

STICKNEY, DOROTHY
   Lights Out   ep   I Spy   10.15.51 NBC
   Robert Montgomery Presents   ep   The Cypress Tree   1.
      17.55 NBC
   Alcoa Hour   ep   Morning's at Seven   11.4.56 NBC
   Alfred Hitchcock Presents   ep   Conversation with a
      Corpse   11.18.56 CBS
   Cinderella   Sp   3.31.57 CBS
   Alfred Hitchcock Presents   ep   Miss Paisley's Cat   12.
      22.57 CBS
   G.E. Theatre   ep   The Young Years   12.22.57 CBS
   Telephone Time   ep   Abby, Julia and the Seven Pet
      Cows   1.7.58 ABC
   Hallmark Hall of Fame   ep   Arsenic and Old Lace   2.
      5.62 NBC
   ABC Stage 67   ep   Evening Primrose   11.16.66 ABC
   The Homecoming   Sp   12.19.71 CBS

STILLER, JERRY
   Paul Lynde Show   sr   9.27.72 ABC

STIRLING, LINDA
   Playhouse   ep   The Woman on the Bus   12.12.54 ABC
   Medic   ep   My Child's Keeper   4.25.55 NBC
   Cavalcade Theatre   ep   the Secret Life of Joe Swedie
      2.7.56 ABC
   Wyatt Earp   ep   The Suffragette   3.27.56 ABC

STOCKWELL, DEAN
   Front Row Center   ep   Innocent Witness   3.4.56 CBS
   Matinee Theatre   ep   Class of '58   7.9.56 NBC
   Matinee Theatre   ep   Horse Power   10.30.56 NBC
   Matinee Theatre   ep   Julie   12.5.56 NBC
   Schlitz Playhouse of Stars   ep   Washington Incident   12.
      7.56 CBS
   Climax   ep   Murder Is a Witch   8.15.57 CBS

Wagon Train ep The Ruth Owens Story 10. 9. 57 NBC
Matinee Theatre ep Fight the Whole World 12. 27. 57
    NBC
G. E. Theatre ep God Is My Judge 4. 20. 58 CBS
Cimarron City ep Kid on a Calico Horse 11. 20. 58
    CBS
G. E. Theatre ep The Family Man 2. 22. 59 CBS
Playhouse 90 ep Made in Japan 3. 5. 59 CBS
Cimarron City ep Kid on a Calico Horse 5. 2. 59 NBC
Wagon Train ep The Rodney Lawrence Story 6. 10. 50
    NBC
Staccato ep The Nature of the Night 10. 15. 59 NBC
The Killers Sp 11. 19. 59 CBS
Checkmate ep The Cyanide Touch 10. 1. 60 CBS
June Allyson Show ep The Dance Man 10. 6. 60 CBS
Alfred Hitchcock Theatre ep The Landlady 1. 17. 61
    NBC
Outlaws ep Assassin 2. 9. 61 NBC
Wagon Train ep The Will Santee Story 5. 3. 61 NBC
Hallmark Hall of Fame ep 5. 5. 61 NBC
Bus Stop ep Afternoon of a Cowboy 10. 1. 61 ABC
Dick Powell Theatre ep The Geetas Box 11. 14. 61
    NBC
Alfred Hitchcock Theatre ep Annabel 11. 1. 62 CBS
Dick Powell Theatre ep In Search of a Son 11. 20. 62
    NBC
The Greatest Show on Earth ep The Wrecker 12. 3. 63
    ABC
Defenders ep Climate of Evil 12. 7. 63 CBS
Eleventh Hour ep To Love Is to Live 4. 15. 64 NBC
Kraft Suspense Theatre ep Their Own Executioners
    4. 23. 64 NBC
Burke's Law ep Who Killed Lenore Wingfield 11. 4. 64
    ABC
Wagon Train ep The Richard Bloodgood Story 11. 29.
    64 ABC
Dr. Kildare ep The Bell in the Schoolhouse Tolls for
    Thee 9. 27. 65, 9. 28. 65, 10. 4. 65, 10. 11. 65, 10. 12.
    65, 10. 18. 65 NBC
Danny Thomas Show ep The Cage 1. 15. 68 NBC
FBI ep The Quarry 10. 6. 68 ABC
Bonanza ep The Medal 10. 26. 69 NBC
Mannix ep A Step in Time 9. 29. 71 CBS
The Failing of Raymond tf 11. 27. 71 ABC
The Adventures of Nick Carter tf 2. 20. 72 ABC
FBI ep Till Death Do Us Part 10. 22. 72 ABC
Columbo ep 11. 5. 72 NBC

STOCKWELL, GUY
    Men into Space   ep   12.30.59 CBS
    Gunsmoke   ep   12.3.60 CBS
    Gunsmoke   ep   12.17.60 CBS
    Thriller   ep   Man in the Cage   1.17.61 NBC
    Roaring 20s   ep   Scandal Sheet   4.22.61 ABC
    Surfside 6   ep   Vengeance Is Bitter   4.24.61 ABC
    Lawman   ep   No Contest   2.4.62 ABC
    Gallant Men   ep   The Dogs of War   1.19.63 ABC
    Richard Boone Show   sr   9.24.63 NBC
    World of Disney   ep   The Ballad of Hector   1.5.64, 1.
        12.64 NBC
    Combat   ep   Rescue   3.31.64 ABC
    Bonanza   ep   Invention of a Gunfighter   9.20.64 NBC
    Perry Mason   ep   The Case of the Betrayed Bride   10.
        22.64 CBS
    Ironside   ep   11.23.67 NBC
    The Sound of Anger   tf   12.10.68 NBC
    Wild, Wild West   ep   3.21.69 CBS
    Lancer   ep   3.25.69 CBS
    Bonanza   ep   10.12.69 NBC
    The Virginian   ep   10.22.69 NBC
    Matt Lincoln   ep   12.31.70   ABC
    Mannix   ep   Dark So Early, Dark So Long   9.15.71
        CBS
    FBI   ep   The Last Job   9.26.71 ABC
    Mod Squad   ep   I Am My Brother's Keeper   1.4.72 ABC
    Return to Peyton Place   sr   1972 ABC

STODDARD, HAILA
    Studio One   ep   Beyond Reason   1.9.50 CBS
    Philco Playhouse   ep   Murder at the Stork Club   1.15.
        50 NBC
    Philco Playhouse   ep   The Reluctant Landlord   7.2.50
        NBC
    Studio One   ep   Away from It All   9.25.50 CBS
    Philco Playhouse   ep   I'm Still Alive   11.19.50 NBC
    Prudential Playhouse   ep   Burlesque   1.2.51 CBS
    Prudential Playhouse   ep   Skylark   1.16.51 CBS
    Summer Theatre   ep   Tremolo   7.23.51 CBS
    Goodyear Playhouse   ep   Tigers Don't Sing   3.30.52 NBC
    Goodyear Playhouse   ep   The Room   9.29.52 NBC
    Kraft Theatre   ep   Hilda McKay   11.12.52 NBC
    Studio One   ep   A Criminal Design   1.18.54 CBS
    Secret Storm   2.1.54 CBS
    The Web   ep   The Cat and the Canaries   5.30.54 CBS
    U.S. Steel Hour   ep   A Wind from the South   9.14.55
        CBS

Robert Montgomery Presents   ep   Storm over Swan Lake
    6. 11. 56 NBC
The Secret Storm   sr   1967 CBS

STONE, GEORGE E.
    It's a Great Life   ep   1. 1. 56 NBC
    Alfred Hitchcock Presents   ep   The Big Switch   1. 8. 56
        CBS
    Damon Runyon Theatre   ep   Judy the Jinx   1. 28. 56 CBS

STONE, MILBURN
    Gunsmoke   sr   9. 10. 55 CBS
    Front Row Center   ep   The Morals Squad   3. 11. 56 CBS
    Gunsmoke   sr ret   9. 56 CBS
    Gunsmoke   sr ret   9. 57 CBS
    Climax   ep   The Great World and Timothy Colt   3. 27.
        58 CBS
    Gunsmoke   sr ret   9. 58 CBS
    Gunsmoke   sr ret   9. 59 CBS
    Gunsmoke   sr ret   9. 60 CBS
    Gunsmoke   sr ret   9. 30. 61 CBS
    Gunsmoke   sr ret   9. 15. 62 CBS
    Gunsmoke   sr ret   9. 63 CBS
    Gunsmoke   sr ret   9. 26. 64 CBS
    Gunsmoke   sr ret   9. 18. 65 CBS
    Gunsmoke   sr ret   9. 17. 66 CBS
    Gunsmoke   sr ret   9. 11. 67 CBS
    Gunsmoke   sr ret   9. 23. 68 CBS
    Gunsmoke   sr ret   9. 22. 69 CBS
    Gunsmoke   sr ret   9. 14. 70 CBS
    Gunsmoke   sr ret   9. 13. 71 CBS
    Gunsmoke   sr ret   9. 11. 72 CBS

STORM, GALE
    Hollywood Premiere Theatre   ep   Mr. and Mrs. Detec-
        tive   10. 15. 50 ABC
    Bigelow Theatre   ep   Mechanic on Duty   9. 6. 51 NN
    My Little Margie   sr   6. 16. 52 CBS
    The Unexpected   ep   The Puppeteers   9. 17. 52 NBC
    My Little Margie   sr ret   10. 4. 52 NBC
    My Little Margie   sr ret   1. 1. 53 CBS
    My Little Margie   sr ret   9. 2. 53 NBC
    Pitfall   ep   The Hot Welcome   7. 18. 54 NN
    My Little Margie   sr ret   fall, 1954 NBC
    Robert Montgomery Presents   ep   Tomorrow is Forever
        10. 17. 55 NBC
    Ford Theatre   ep   Johnny, Where Are You?   11. 3. 55
        NBC

Oh, Susanna   sr   9. 29. 56 CBS
Oh, Susanna   sr ret   9. 57 CBS
The Gale Storm Show   sr   8. 9. 58 CBS
Burke's Law   ep   2. 21. 64 ABC
Burke's Law   ep   2. 3. 65 ABC

STOSSEL, LUDWIG
Public Defender   ep   Destiny   10. 28. 54 CBS
December Bride   ep   1. 24. 55 CBS
Casablanca   sr   9. 27. 55 ABC
TV Reader's Digest   ep   A Bell for Okinawa   1. 23. 56
ABC
Crusader   ep   Man of Medicine   2. 24. 56 CBS

STRAIGHT, BEATRICE
Studio One   ep   A Chill on the Wind   3. 12. 51 CBS
Lights Out   ep   Gray Reminder   4. 30. 51 NBC
Armstrong Circle Theatre   ep   Image 2. 5. 52 NBC
Hallmark Hall of Fame   ep   The Magnificent Failure
5. 25. 52 NBC
Kraft Theatre   ep   Thorn in the Flesh   6. 25. 52 NBC
Armstrong Circle Theatre   ep   The Betrayal   9. 23. 52
NBC
Kraft Theatre   ep   The Iron Gate   12. 3. 52 NBC
Omnibus   ep   King Lear   10. 18. 53 CBS
Kraft Theatre   ep   Gavin   11. 25. 53 NBC
You Are There   ep   The Crisis of Anne Boleyn   6. 20.
54 CBS
Omnibus   ep   Antigone   11. 21. 54 CBS
Inner Sanctum   ep   Pattern of Fear   12. 28. 54 NN
You Are There   ep   The Torment of Beethoven   1. 2. 55
CBS
Danger   ep   The Dark Curtain   2. 1. 55 CBS
U.S. Steel Hour   ep   Roads to Home   4. 26. 55 ABC
Studio One   ep   Act of Mercy   10. 14. 57 CBS
U.S. Steel Hour   ep   Top Secret Mission   3. 26. 58 CBS
Play of the Week   ep   The Waltz of the Toreadors   11.
16. 59 NN
Alfred Hitchcock Presents   ep   Special Delivery   11. 29.
59 CBS
Alfred Hitchcock Presents   ep   The Cuckoo Clock   4. 17.
60 CBS
Route 66   ep   Most Vanquished, Most Victorious   4. 14.
61 CBS
Dr. Kildare   ep   For the Living   11. 30. 61 NBC
Nurses   ep   The Lady Made of Stone   11. 29. 62 CBS
Eleventh Hour   ep   Where Have You Been, Lord Ran-

dall, My Son   1.9.63 NBC
Ben Casey   ep   Rigadoon for Three Pianos   3.4.63
   ABC
Mission Impossible   ep   11.26.66 CBS
Felony Squad   ep   11.20.67 ABC
Matt Lincoln   ep   11.12.70 ABC

STRASBERG, SUSAN
   Goodyear Playhouse   ep   Catch a Falling Star   6.28.53
      NBC
   Kraft Theatre   ep   Romeo and Juliet   6.9.54 NBC
   The Marriage   sr   9.1.54 NBC
   G.E. Theatre   ep   Mr. Blue Ocean   5.1.59 CBS
   Omnibus   ep   Dear Brutus   1.8.56 CBS
   Desilu Playhouse   ep   Debut   10.27.58 CBS
   Play of the Week   ep   The Cherry Orchard   12.28.59
      NN
   Our American Heritage   ep   Destiny West   1.24.60 NBC
   Dr. Kildare   ep   A Game for Three   10.24.63 NBC
   Bob Hope Chrysler Theatre   ep   Four Kings   11.1.63
      NBC
   Breaking Point   ep   A Child of the Center Ring   2.24.
      64 ABC
   Burke's Law   ep   4.24.64 ABC
   Rogues   ep   The Stefanini Dowry   9.27.64 NBC
   Run for Your Life   ep   The Voice of Gina Milan   11.29.
      65 NBC
   Virginian   ep   The Captive   9.28.66 NBC
   Invaders   ep   Quantity Unknown   3.7.67 ABC
   FBI   ep   The Executioners   3.12.67, 3.19.67 ABC
   Big Valley   ep   Night in a Small Town   10.9.67 ABC
   FBI   ep   The Quarry   10.6.68 ABC
   Lancer   ep   10.29.68 CBS
   Name of the Game   ep   Pineapple Rose   12.20.68 NBC
   CBS Playhouse   ep   The Experiment   2.23.69 CBS
   Marcus Welby, M.D.   tf   3.26.69 ABC
   McCloud   ep   10.21.70 NBC
   Men from Shiloh   ep   Crooked Corner   10.28.70 NBC
   Hauser's Memory   tf   11.24.70 NBC
   Alias Smith and Jones   ep   Exit from Wickenburg   1.28.
      71 ABC
   Young Lawyers   ep   The Whimper of Whipped Dogs   3.
      10.71 ABC
   McCloud   ep   Encounter with Aries   9.22.71 CBS
   Night Gallery   ep   11.3.71 NBC
   Medical Center   ep   The Loser   11.24.71 CBS
   Owen Marshall   ep   2.10.72 ABC
   Sixth Sense   ep   10.28.72 ABC

STRITCH, ELAINE
> Goodyear Playhouse ep Nothing to Sneeze at 7.12.53 NBC
> Goodyear Playhouse ep Here's Father 1.17.54 NBC
> Motorola TV Hour ep The Family Man 3.9.54 ABC
> Appointment with Adventure ep The House on Gellen Street 5.8.55 CBS
> Alcoa Hour ep He's for Me 7.21.57 NBC
> Dupont Show of the Month ep The Red Mill 4.19.58 CBS
> Climax ep The Disappearance of Daphne 5.15.58 CBS
> Studio One ep The Left-Handed Welcome 6.16.58 CBS
> Wagon Train ep The Tracy Salder Story 3.9.60 NBC
> Full Moon over Brooklyn Sp 5.6.60 NBC
> Alcoa Theatre ep You Should Meet My Sister 5.16.60 NBC
> Adventures in Paradise ep The Haunted 6.20.60 ABC
> My Sister Eileen sr 10.5.60 CBS
> Nurses ep The Witch of the East Wing 12.19.63 CBS
> Repertory Theatre ep The Wedding 4.21.65 NN
> Trials of O'Brien sr 9.18.65 CBS
> New York Television Theatre ep Pins and Needles 7.11.66 NN

STRODE, WOODY
> Soldiers of Fortune ep Drums of Far Island 8.12.55 ABC
> Man from Blackhawk ep The Savage 1.15.60 ABC
> Thriller ep The Mark of the Hand 10.4.60 NBC
> Rawhide ep Incident of the Buffalo Soldier 1.6.61 CBS
> Rawhide ep Incident of the Boomerang 3.24.61 CBS
> Lieutenant ep To Set It Right 2.22.64 NBC
> Farmer's Daughter ep My Son, the Athlete 5.13.64 ABC
> Daniel Boone ep 9.29.66 NBC
> Tarzan ep The Deadly Silence 11.4.66 NBC
> Batman ep Marsha, Scheme of Diamonds 11.23.66, 11.24.66 ABC
> Tarzan ep 2.17.67 NBC
> Tarzan ep 2.16.68 NBC

STROUD, DON
> Bob Hope Chrysler Theatre ep Wipeout 4.26.67 NBC
> Ironside ep An Inside Job 10.19.67 NBC
> Virginian ep 11.22.67 NBC
> Run for Your Life ep 12.27.67 NBC

A Hatful of Rain   Sp   3.3.68 ABC
Virginian   ep   Image of an Outlaw   10.23.68 NBC
Outsider   ep   A Time to Run   10.30.68 NBC
Name of the Game   ep   Pineapple Rose   12.20.68 NBC
Marcus Welby, M.D.   ep   The Other Side of the Chart
     2.24.70 ABC
FBI   ep   The Savage Wilderness   10.8.70 ABC
Hawaii Five-O   ep   The Late John Louisiana   11.11.70
     CBS
Breakout   tf   12.8.70 NBC
Conspiracy to Kill   tf   1.11.71 NBC
Dan August   ep   The Meal Ticket   3.18.71 ABC
Bold Ones   ep   The Convicts   11.21.71 NBC
McMillan and Wife   ep   Death Is a Seven Point Favor-
     ite   18.8.71 NBC
O'Hara, U.S. Treasury   ep   Operation Smokescreen   3.
     10.72 CBS
The Daughters of Joshua Cabe   tf   9.13.72 ABC
The Deadly Dream   tf   9.25.72 ABC
Rolling Man   tf   10.4.72 ABC
Jigsaw   ep   1.12.72 ABC
Ironside   ep   11.9.72 NBC
Adam-12   ep   11.15.72 NBC

STRUDWICK, SHEPPERD
TV Playhouse   ep   Portrait in Smoke   10.22.50 NBC
Philco Playhouse   ep   Dr. Hudson's Secret Journal   6.
     24.51 NBC
Armstrong Circle Theatre   ep   City Editor   7.1.52 NBC
Summer Theatre   ep   The Last Thing I Do   7.28.52
     CBS
Curtain Call   ep   Season of Divorce   8.8.52 NBC
Studio One   ep   Little Man, Big World   10.13.52 CBS
Kraft Theatre   ep   Hilda McKay   11.12.52 NBC
Philco Playhouse   ep   Pride's Way   1.11.53 NBC
Studio One   ep   The Fathers   4.20.53 CBS
Goodyear Playhouse   ep   Catch a Falling Star   6.28.53
     NBC
Mirror Theatre   ep   The Party   8.18.53 NBC
Studio One   ep   Fatal in My Fashion   10.25.54 CBS
Omnibus   ep   Antigone   11.21.54 CBS
You Are There   ep   2.6.55 CBS
You Are There   ep   The Tragic Hour of Dr. Semmel-
     weis   2.13.55 CBS
You Are There   ep   The Death of Socrates   3.13.55
     CBS
Philco Playhouse   ep   The Ghost Writer   5.29.55 NBC

Studio One   ep   The Fathers   4.20.53 CBS
Goodyear Playhouse   ep   Catch a Falling Star   6.28.53
     NBC
Mirror Theatre   ep   The Party   8.18.53 NBC
Studio One   ep   Fatal in My Fashion   10.25.54 CBS
Omnibus   ep   Antigone   11.21.54 CBS
You Are There   ep   2.6.55 CBS
You Are There   ep   The Tragic Hour of Dr. Semmel-
     weis   2.13.55 CBS
You Are There   ep   The Death of Socrates   3.13.55
     CBS
Philco Playhouse   ep   The Ghost Writer   5.29.55 NBC
You Are There   ep   The Signing of the Declaration of
     Independence   7.3.55 CBS
Studio One   ep   Julius Caesar   8.1.55 CBS
Studio One   ep   A Public Figure   1.23.56 CBS
Climax   ep   Flame-Out on T-6   5.17.56 CBS
Studio One   ep   The Power   6.4.56 CBS
Climax   ep   Dark Wall   8.30.56 CBS
Wire Service   ep   Conspiracy   11.8.56 ABC
Studio One   ep   Career   12.17.56 CBS
Playhouse 90   ep   The Hostess with the Mostess   3.21.
     57 CBS
Climax   ep   The Giant Killer   8.1.57 CBS
Harbourmaster   ep   Night Rescue   12.5.57 CBS
Wagon Train   ep   The Clara Beauchamp Story   12.11.
     57 NBC
Climax   ep   So Deadly My Love   3.13.58 CBS
Meet McGraw   ep   The Long Aloha   3.18.58 NBC
Schlitz Playhouse of Stars   ep   The Town that Slept with
     the Lights on   5.16.58 CBS
Investigator   ep   6.10.58 NBC
Kraft Theatre   ep   Death for Sale   8.6.58 NBC
77 Sunset Strip   ep   10.10.58 ABC
Armstrong Circle Theatre   ep   Boy on Page One   12.
     23.59 CBS
Have Gun Will Travel   ep   1.2.60 CBS
Great Mysteries   ep   The Bat   3.31.60 NBC
June Allyson Show   ep   Surprise Party   4.18.60 CBS
Twilight Zone   ep   Nightmare as a Child   4.29.60 CBS
Play of the Week   ep   Night of the Auk   5.2.60 NN
U.S. Steel Hour   ep   Bride of the Fox   8.24.60 CBS
Barbara Stanwyck Theatre   ep   House in Order   11.7.
     60 NBC
U.S. Steel Hour   ep   Tangle of Truth   11.29.61 CBS
Westinghouse Presents   ep   Footnote to Fame   2.3.62
     CBS

Car 54 Where Are You ep Toody and the Art World
    2. 11. 62 NBC
U.S. Steel Hour ep The Perfect Accident 2.21.62
    CBS
Defenders ep The Indelible Silence 9.29.62 CBS
Doctors/Nurses ep The Suspect 10.6.64 CBS
Mr. Broadway ep Bad Little Rich Girl 12.5.64 CBS
Another World sr 1967 NBC
Name of the Game ep A Sister from Napoli 1.8.71
    NBC
McMillan and Wife ep The Easy Sunday Murder Case
    10. 20. 71 NBC

STUART, RANDY
    Schaefer Century Theatre ep The Red Balloon 7.30.
        59 NBC
    Gruen Guild Playhouse ep The Leather Coat 9.9.52
        NN
    Biff Baker, U.S.A. sr 11.6.52 CBS
    Cavalcade of America ep A Matter of Honor 2.18.53
        NBC
    Video Theatre ep Women Who Wait 8.20.53 CBS
    Omnibus ep Nothing So Monster 1.24.54 CBS
    Ford Theatre ep Come On Read 3.11.54 NBC
    Schlitz Playhouse of Stars ep Groundloop 3.12.54
        CBS
    Fireside Theatre ep Smoke and Fire 9.14.54 NBC
    Stage 7 ep Yesterday's Pawnshop 6.5.55 CBS
    Colt .45 ep Blood Money 12.21.58 ABC
    Wyatt Earp ep Little Gray Home in the West 5.5.59
        ABC
    Adventure Showcase ep Brock Callahan 8.11.59 CBS
    Wyatt Earp ep The Perfidy of Shotgun Gibbs 10.12.59
        ABC
    Wyatt Earp ep A Murderer's Return 1.5.60, 1.12.60
        ABC
    Wyatt Earp ep Silver Dollar 2.2.60 ABC
    Cheyenne ep White Warrior 2.22.60 ABC
    Bourbon Street Beat ep Neon Nightmarc 3.21.60 ABC
    Wyatt Earp ep Salvation of Emma Clanton 4.5.60 ABC
    Bronco ep Tangled Trail 5.3.60 ABC
    Wyatt Earp ep The Confidence Man 5.17.60 ABC
    Alcoa Premiere ep Anniversary of a Murder 9.27.60
        ABC
    Lawman ep The Frame-Up 1.15.61 ABC
    Roaring 20s ep Two a Day 2.4.61 ABC
    Bonanza ep The Duke 3.11.61 NBC

Maverick ep Benefit of Doubt 4. 9. 61 ABC
Peter Gunn ep Last Resort 5. 15. 61 ABC
77 Sunset Strip ep The Reluctant Spy 10. 12. 62 ABC
Hawaiian Eye ep Passport 4. 2. 63 ABC
Cheyenne ep Two Trails to Santa Fe 5. 10. 63 ABC

SULLAVAN, MARGARET

Ford Theatre ep Touchstone 3. 25. 51 ABC
Schlitz Playhouse of Stars ep Still Life 10. 26. 51 CBS
Schlitz Playhouse of Stars ep The Nymph and the
   Lamp 12. 7. 51 CBS
Producers Showcase ep State of the Union 11. 15. 54
   NBC

SULLIVAN, BARRY

Ford Theatre ep As the Flame Dies 11. 19. 53 NBC
Ford Theatre ep The Fugitives 1. 7. 54 NBC
Medallion Theatre ep Book Overdue 1. 30. 54 CBS
Studio One ep It Might Happen Tomorrow 1. 24. 55
   CBS
The Merry Widow Sp 4. 9. 55 NBC
G. E. Theatre ep Man with a Vengeance 5. 15. 55 CBS
Climax ep The Healer 7. 21. 55 CBS
Ford Theatre ep Husband 10. 12. 55 NBC
Ford Star Jubilee ep The Caine Mutiny Court Martial
   11. 19. 55 CBS
The Man Called X sr 4. 4. 56 NN
Ford Star Jubilee ep A Bell for Adano 6. 1. 56 CBS
Studio One ep Career 12. 17. 56 CBS
Playhouse 90 ep Snow Shoes 1. 3. 57 CBS
Lux Video Theatre ep One Way Passage 3. 7. 57 NBC
Mission Impossible ep 4. 22. 57 CBS
Playhouse 90 ep Ain't No Time for Glory 6. 20. 57
   CBS
Studio One ep Tide of Corruption 2. 17. 58 CBS
Zane Grey Theatre ep Shadow of a Dead Man 4. 11.
   58 CBS
Playhouse 90 ep Nightmare at Ground Zero 5. 15. 58
   CBS
Climax ep Cabin B 13 6. 26. 58 CBS
Alfred Hitchcock Presents ep The Two-Million Dollar
   Defense 11. 2. 58 CBS
Pursuit ep Ticket to Tangier 11. 5. 58 CBS
U. S. Steel Hour ep This Day in Fear 11. 19. 58 CBS
Zane Grey Theatre ep Bury Me Dead 12. 11. 58 CBS
G. E. Theatre ep Bill Bailey, Won't You Please Come
   Home 1. 25. 59 CBS

Playhouse 90   ep   A Quiet Game of Cards   1.29.59 CBS
Desilu Playhouse   ep   The Hard Road   3.30.59 CBS
Playhouse 90   ep   Dark December   4.30.59 CBS
Bonanza   ep   The Sun Mountain Herd   9.19.59 NBC
Zane Grey Theatre   ep   The Lonely Gun   10.22.59 CBS
Ford Startime   ep   My Three Angels   12.8.59 NBC
June Allyson Show   ep   The Crossing   12.14.59 CBS
Desilu Playhouse   ep   City in Bondage   5.13.60 CBS
Tall Man   sr   9.10.60 NBC
U.S. Steel Hour   ep   Operation Northstar   12.28.60
    CBS
Dupont Show of the Month   ep nar   The World's Great-
    est Robbery   4.29.62 NBC
U.S. Steel Hour   ep   Night of the Fourth   7.11.62 CBS
Wagon Train   ep   The Caroline Casteel Story   9.26.62
    ABC
Alfred Hitchcock Theatre   ep   Day of Reckoning   11.22.
    62 CBS
Dick Powell Theatre   ep   Crazy Sunday   12.18.62 NBC
Route 66   ep   A Bunch of Lonely Pagliaccis   1.4.63
    CBS
Sam Benedict   ep   Some Fires Die Slowly   2.16.63 NBC
Virginian   ep   Woman from White Wing   5.15.63 NBC
Ben Casey   ep   The Echo of a Silent Cheer   10.16.63,
    10.23.63 ABC
Great Adventure   ep   The Great Diamond Mountain   11.
    8.63 CBS
Great Adventure   ep   The President Vanishes   3.13.64
    CBS
Slattery's People   ep   Who Is Honor   11.23.64 CBS
Kraft Suspense Theatre   ep   The Last Clear Chance   3.
    11.65 NBC
Run for Your Life   ep   Never Pick Up a Stranger   10.
    11.65 NBC
12 O'Clock High   ep   Grant Me No Favor   11.15.65
    ABC
Loner   ep   The Oath   12.4.65 CBS
The Poppy Is Also a Flower   tf   4.22.66 ABC
Road West   sr   9.12.66 NBC
Bonanza   ep   10.8.67 NBC
Johnny Belinda   Sp   10.22.67 ABC
Danny Thomas Show   ep   Fame Is a Four Letter Word
    10.30.67 NBC
Garrison's Gorillas   ep   10.31.67 ABC
The Man from U.N.C.L.E.   ep   The Seven Wonders of
    the World Affair   1.8.68, 1.15.68 NBC
That Girl   ep   9.26.68 ABC

Name of the Game   ep   The Inquiry   1.17.69 NBC
It Takes a Thief   ep   Boom at the Top   2.25.69 ABC
CBS Playhouse   ep   The Experiment   2.25.69 CBS
On Stage   ep   This Town Will Never Be the Same   4.
    23.69 NBC
The Immortal   tf   9.30.69 ABC
Virginian   ep   10.8.69 NBC
Name of the Game   ep   High Card   12.5.69 NBC
The House on Green Apple Road   tf   1.11.70 ABC
It Takes a Thief   ep   2.9.70 ABC
Bracken's World   ep   3.27.70 NBC
High Chaparral   ep   A Matter of Survival   10.16.70
    CBS
Medical Center   ep   Deadly Encounter   11.18.70 CBS
High Chaparral   ep   A Matter of Vengeance   11.27.70
    NBC
Dan August   ep   The Titan   1.6.71 ABC
Name of the Game   ep   Los Angeles 2017   1.15.71 NBC
Hallmark Hall of Fame   ep   The Price   2.3.71 NBC
Yuma   tf   3.21.71 ABC
Cannon   tf   3.26.71 CBS
McCloud   ep   11.24.71 NBC
Longstreet   ep   12.2.71 ABC
Marcus Welby, M.D.   ep   12.7.71 ABC
Mannix   ep   Cry Pigeon   1.26.72 ABC
Kung Fu   tf   2.22.72 ABC
Hollywood Television Theatre   ep   Another Part of the
    Forest   10.2.72 NN
Cool Million   ep   12.6.72 NBC
Sixth Sense   12.9.72 ABC

SULLIVAN, ED
The Million Dollar Incident   4.21.61 CBS

SULLIVAN, FRANCIS L.
TV Playhouse   ep   The Man Who Got Away with It   11.
    12.50   NBC
Sure as Fate   sh   1.23.51 CBS
Lights Out   ep   The Man with the Watch   8.13.51 NBC
Lux Video Theatre   ep   Stolen Years   11.19.51 CBS
Schlitz Playhouse of Stars   ep   Mr. Thayer   12.5.52
    CBS
G.E. Theatre   ep   Trapped   3.22.53 CBS
Ford Theatre   ep   The Ming Lama   11.12.53 NBC
First Person   ep   August Heat   8.7.53 NBC
Robert Montgomery Presents   ep   The Soprano and the
    Piccolo Player   11.30.53 NBC

Cavalcade of America   ep   Margin for Victory   2.16.54
  ABC
Motorola TV Hour   ep   Nightmare in Algiers   3.23.54
  ABC
Armstrong Circle Theatre   ep   The Three Tasks   4.13.
  54 NBC
G.E. Theatre   ep   Bounty Court Martial   10.9.55 CBS

SUSANN, JACQUELINE
  Suspense   ep   Pigeons in the Cave   7.21.53 CBS
  Danger   ep   A Day's Pay   8.24.54 CBS
  Mannix   ep   The Crime that Wasn't   1.30.71 CBS

SUTHERLAND, DONALD
  Court-Martial   ep   All Is a Dream to Me   6.17.66 ABC
  The Saint   ep   7.9.67 NBC
  Man in a Suitcase   ep   Day of Execution   5.17.68 ABC
  The Sunshine Patriot   tf   12.16.68 NBC
  Name of the Game   ep   The Suntan Gang   2.7.69 NBC

SWANSON, GLORIA
  Hollywood Opening Night   ep   The Pattern   2.16.53 NBC
  Gloria Swanson Show   sh/sr   fall, 1954 ABC
  Straightaway   ep   A Toast to Yesterday   12.15.61 ABC
  Dr. Kildare   ep   The Good Luck Charm   2.7.63 NBC
  Burke's Law   ep   Who Killed Purity Mather   12.6.63
  ABC
  Alfred Hitchcock Theatre   ep   Behind the Locked Door
  3.27.64 CBS
  Kraft Suspense Theatre   ep   Who Is Jennifer   1.16.64
  NBC
  Burke's Law   ep   9.23.64 ABC
  Beverly Hillbillies   ep   11.30.66 CBS

SWEET, BLANCHE
  Thin Man   ep   Pack My Gat, Beulah   11.7.58 NBC
  Dobie Gillis   ep   5.10.60 CBS

SWENSON, INGA
  Goodyear Playhouse   ep   The Best Wine   9.29.57 NBC
  Playhouse 90   ep   Heart of Darkness   11.6.58 CBS
  U.S. Steel Hour   ep   Goodbye...But It Doesn't Go Away
  12.31.58 CBS
  Playhouse 90   ep   The Wings of the Dove   1.8.59 CBS
  Dupont Show of the Month   ep   Oliver Twist   12.4.59
  CBS
  Hallmark Hall of Fame   ep   Victoria Regina   11.30.61
  NBC

Defenders   ep   The Locked Room   2.10.62 CBS
Bonanza   ep   Inga, My Love   4.15.62 NBC
Dr. Kildare   ep   Breakdown   11.8.62 NBC
Nurses   ep   Party Girl   3.28.63 CBS
Bonanza   ep   Journey Remembered   11.10.63 NBC
CBS Playhouse   ep   My Father and My Mother   2.13.68
    CBS
Medical Center   ep   The Deceived   1.7.70 CBS
N.E.T. Playhouse   ep   The Tape Recorder   11.19.70
    NN
Medical Center   ep   Secret Heritage   2.3.71 CBS
Earth II   tf   11.28.71 NBC

SWINBURNE, NORA
O.S.S.   ep   Buried Alive   3.3.58 ABC

SWITZER, CARL
Science Fiction Theatre   ep   Negative Man   9.16.55
    NBC
Roy Rogers Show   ep   Dead End Trail   7.8.56 NBC
Roy Rogers Show   ep   Quick Draw   7.15.56 NBC

-T-

TABORI, KRISTOFFER
Hallmark Hall of Fame   ep   Neither Are We Enemies
    3.13.70 NBC
N.E.T. Playhouse   ep   A Memory of Two Mondays   1.
    28.71 NN
James Garner Show   ep   The One-Eyed Mules Time Has
    Come   11.23.71 NBC
The Glass House   tf   2.4.72 CBS
Medical Center   ep   9.13.72 CBS
Medical Center   ep   10.4.72 CBS
Family Flight   tf   10.25.72 ABC

TALBOT, NITA
Suspense   ep   The Whispering Killer   11.25.52 CBS
Man Against Crime   ep   Three Cents Worth of Murder
    10.25.53   NN
Omnibus   ep   The Man Who Married a Dumb Wife   10.
    24.54 CBS
Omnibus   ep   The Contrast   12.12.54 CBS

Producers Showcase ep The Women 2.7.55 NBC
Best of Broadway ep Stage Door 4.6.55 CBS
Studio One ep Operation Home 5.30.55 CBS
Joe and Mabel sr 9.20.55 CBS
Robert Montgomery Presents ep The Secret 3.19.56
    NBC
Joe and Mabel sr ret 6.26.56 CBS
Climax ep Mask for the Devil 10.10.57 CBS
Jane Wyman Theatre ep Prime Suspect 2.27.58 NBC
Thin Man ep Pack My Gat, Beulah 11.7.58 NBC
Gunsmoke ep 11.8.58 CBS
Peter Gunn ep Murder on the Midway 2.2.59 NBC
Markham ep 7.4.59 CBS
Lineup ep Lonesome at Midnight 11.18.59 CBS
Bourbon Street Beat ep Find My Face 1.18.60 ABC
Lawless Years ep The Muddy Kasoff Street 2.4.60
    NBC
Bourbon Street Beat ep The 10 Percent Blues 2.8.60
    ABC
Maverick ep The Resurrection of Joe November 2.
    28.60 ABC
Mr. Lucky ep 3.5.60 CBS
Maverick ep Easy Mark 4.10.60 ABC
Gunsmoke ep 5.14.60 CBS
Man from Blackhawk ep In His Steps 5.20.60 ABC
Jim Backus Show sr 9.28.60 ABC
Tab Hunter Show ep Be My Guest 10.9.60 NBC
Untouchables ep The Night They Shot Santa Claus 9.
    25.62 ABC
Rawhide ep Incident of White Eyes 5.3.63 CBS
Lieutenant ep Capp's Lady 2.8.64 NBC
Fugitive ep This'll Kill You 1.18.66 ABC
Virginian ep Ride a Cock-Horse to Laramie Cross 2.
    23.66 NBC
John Forsythe Show ep If I Were a Prince 3.28.66
    NBC
Hogan's Heroes ep 11.18.66, 11.25.66 CBS
FBI ep 1.1.67 ABC
Mannix ep 12.9.67 CBS
Hogan's Heroes ep 12.15.67 CBS
Bonanza ep 12.17.67 NBC
Second Hundred Years ep 12.27.67 ABC
Gomer Pyle, U.S.M.C. ep 11.15.68 CBS
Here's Debbie ep To and From Russia with Love 11.
    4.69, 11.11.69 NBC
The Movie Murderer tf 2.2.70 NBC
Love American Style ep 10.1.71 ABC

Arnie   ep   11.22.71 CBS
Funny Face   ep   12.11.71 CBS
They Call It Murder   tf   12.17.71 NBC
McCloud   ep   12.29.71 NBC
Mannix   ep   1.5.72 CBS

TALMAN, WILLIAM
Lux Video Theatre   ep   Pick of the Litter   4.8.54 CBS
Cavalcade Theatre   ep   Texas Rangers   9.27.55 ABC
TV Reader's Digest   ep   Old Master Detective   10.24.55 ABC
Ford Theatre   ep   South of Selanger   12.15.55 NBC
Directors Playhouse   ep   Number 5 Checked Out   1.18.56 NBC
Climax   ep   Sit Down with Death   4.26.56 CBS
Climax   ep   Dark Wall   8.30.56 CBS
Telephone Time   ep   12.16.56 CBS
Perry Mason   sr   9.21.57 CBS
Wagon Train   ep   The Sarah Drummond Story   4.1.58 NBC
Goodyear Theatre   ep   Disappearance   6.9.58 NBC
Cimarron City   ep   To Become a Man   10.25.58 NBC
Perry Mason   sr ret   10.3.59 CBS
Perry Mason   sr ret fall, 1960 CBS
Have Gun will Travel   ep   2.4.61 CBS
Perry Mason   sr ret fall, 1961 CBS
Perry Mason   sr ret   9.27.62 CBS
Perry Mason   sr ret   9.26.63 CBS
Perry Mason   sr ret   9.12.65 CBS
Invaders   ep   Quantity Unknown   3.7.67 ABC

TAMBLYN, RUSS
The Greatest Show on Earth   ep   Silent Love, Secret Love   9.24.63 ABC
Channing   ep   The Last Testament of Buddy Crown   12.18.63 ABC
Burke's Law   ep   Who Killed Rosie Sunset   1.27.65 ABC
Iron Horse   ep   2.27.67 ABC
Name of the Game   ep   A Hard Case of the Blues   9.26.69 NBC
Cade's County   ep   Ragged Edge   3.5.72 CBS

TAMIROFF, AKIM
Schlitz Playhouse of Stars   ep   Trouble on Pier 12   10.10.52 CBS
Best of Broadway   ep   Broadway   5.4.55 CBS

Climax   ep   To Wake at Midnight   5.23.55 CBS
Chocolate Soldier   Sp   6.4.55 NBC
Four Star Playhouse   ep   One Forty-Two   5.24.56 CBS
Ethel Barrymore Theatre   ep   This Is Villa   10.12.56
   NBC
Playhouse 90   ep   The Miracle Worker   2.7.57 CBS
June Allyson Theatre   ep   Love Is a Headache   11.2.
   59 CBS
Desilu Playhouse   ep   Thunder in the Night   2.19.60
   CBS
Wagon Train   ep   The Joe Muharich Story   4.19.61 NBC
Naked City   ep   And If Any Are Frozen   5.9.62 ABC
Dick Powell Theatre   ep   View from the Eiffel Tower
   3.13.62 NBC
Breaking Point   ep   A Pelican in the Wilderness   11.4.
   63 ABC
Naked City   ep   The Highest of Prizes   2.27.63 ABC
Defenders   ep   The Trial of Twenty-Two   5.18.63 CBS
The Man from U.N.C.L.E.   ep   12.23.66 NBC
Then Came Bronson   tf   2.24.69 NBC

TANDY, JESSICA
Masterpiece Playhouse   ep   Hedda Gabler   7.23.50 NBC
Prudential Family Playhouse   ep   Icebound   1.30.51 CBS
Studio One   ep   Hangman's House   3.19.51 CBS
Omnibus   ep   Glory in the Flower   10.4.53 CBS
The Marriage   sr   7.1.54 NBC
Omnibus   ep   John Quincy Adams   1.23.55 CBS
TV Reader's Digest   ep   The End of Blackbeard the Pi-
   rate   7.25.55 ABC
Philco Playhouse   ep   Christmas 'til Closing   12.18.55
   NBC
U.S. Steel Hour   ep   The Great Adventure   1.18.56 CBS
Omnibus   ep   1.29.56 CBS
Star Stage   ep   The School Mistress   2.17.56 NBC
Omnibus   ep   The Better Half   3.11.56 CBS
Alcoa Hour   ep   The Confidence Man   5.27.56 NBC
G.E. Theatre   ep   10.7.56 CBS
Alfred Hitchcock Presents   ep   Toby   11.4.56 CBS
Goodyear Playhouse   ep   A Murder Is Announced   12.30.
   56 CBS
Studio One   ep   The Five Dollar Bill   1.21.57 CBS
Schlitz Playhouse of Stars   ep   Clothes Make the Man
   4.5.57 CBS
Studio 57   ep   Little Miss Bedford   6.9.57 NN
Alfred Hitchcock Presents   ep   The Glass Eye   10.6.57
   CBS

Suspicion   ep   Murder Me Gently   10.7.57 NBC
Telephone Time   ep   War Against War   3.4.58 ABC
Alfred Hitchcock Presents   ep   The Canary Sedan   6.15.
   58 CBS
Dupont Show of the Month   ep   The Fallen Idol   10.14.
   59 CBS
Moon and Sixpence   Sp   10.30.59 NBC
Breaking Point   ep   Glass Flowers Never Drop Petals
   3.23.64 ABC
Judd for the Defense   ep   Punishments, Cruel and Un-
   usual   12.6.68 ABC
O'Hara, U.S. Treasury   ep   2.4.72 CBS
FBI   ep   The Set-Up   2.13.72 ABC

TATE, SHARON
   Beverly Hillbillies   ep   11.6.63 CBS
   Beverly Hillbillies   ep   1.8.64 CBS

TAYLOR, DON
   Ford Theatre   ep   Taming of the Shrewd   3.25.54 NBC
   Schlitz Playhouse of Stars   ep   Decision at Sea   4.30.54
      CBS
   Schlitz Playhouse of Stars   ep   The Best of Everything
      10.22.54 CBS
   Robert Montgomery Presents   ep   Homecoming   11.22.54
      NBC
   U.S. Steel Hour   ep   Presento   12.21.54 ABC
   Lux Video Theatre   ep   Penny Serenade   1.14.55 NBC
   Schlitz Playhouse of Stars   ep   Who's The Blonde?   4.
      22.55 CBS
   Stage 7   ep   Yesterday's Pawnshop   6.5.55 CBS
   Schlitz Playhouse of Stars   ep   Three Months to Re-
      member   9.2.55 CBS
   Crossroads   ep   Hostage   11.11.55 ABC
   Climax   ep   Portrait in Celluloid   11.24.55 CBS
   Schlitz Playhouse of Stars   ep   The Careless Cadet   11.
      25.55 CBS
   Star Stage   ep   The Recluse   12.23.55 NBC
   Front Row Center   ep   The Teacher and Hector Hodge
      2.12.56 CBS
   Lux Video Theatre   ep   Only Yesterday   9.27.56 NBC
   Dupont Theatre   ep   Innocent Bystander   11.13.56 ABC
   Crossroads   ep   Our First Christmas   12.21.56 ABC
   Alfred Hitchcock Presents   ep   Silent Witness   11.3.57
      CBS
   Schlitz Playhouse of Stars   ep   Home Again   1.17.58
      CBS

G. E. Theatre ep All I Survey 2. 2. 58 CBS
Climax ep The Great World and Timothy Colt 3. 27.
  58 CBS
Best of the Post ep No Visitors 2. 11. 61 ABC
Zane Grey Theatre ep The Silent Sentry 2. 16. 61 CBS
Checkmate ep The Someday Man 5. 2. 62 CBS
Burke's Law ep 2. 28. 64 ABC

TAYLOR, ELIZABETH
  Here's Lucy ep 1. 14. 70 CBS

TAYLOR, KENT
  Bigelow Theatre ep A Case of Marriage 1. 28. 51
    CBS
  Boston Blackie sr 9. 9. 51 NBC
  Teledrama ep Deadline for Murder 6. 5. 53 CBS
  Damon Runyon Theatre ep Judy the Jinx 1. 28. 56 CBS
  Crossroads ep Lifeline 5. 11. 56 ABC
  On Trial ep The Case of the Absent Man 5. 3. 57 NBC
  Wells Fargo ep Alias Jim Hardie 3. 10. 58 NBC
  Zorro ep The Man with the Whip 5. 8. 58 ABC
  Rough Riders sr 10. 2. 58 ABC
  Bronco ep The Last Resort 11. 17. 59 ABC
  Ann Sothern Show ep Queen for a Night 11. 30. 59 CBS
  Tightrope ep The Neon Wheel 12. 22. 59 CBS
  Laramie ep Lily 1. 26. 60 NBC
  Riverboat ep The Treasure of Hawk Hill 2. 8. 60 NBC
  Colt . 45 ep Last Chance 3. 6. 60 ABC
  Bat Masterson ep Three Bullets for Bat 3. 24. 60 NBC
  Sugarfoot ep Funeral at Forty Miles 5. 24. 60 ABC
  Peter Gunn ep Sepi 12. 19. 60 ABC
  Hawaiian Eye ep Man from Manila 3. 8. 61 ABC
  Cheyenne ep Stage to the Sky 4. 24. 61 ABC
  Hawaiian Eye ep Tusitala 12. 13. 61 ABC
  Voyage to the Bottom of the Sea ep And Five of Us
    Are Left 10. 3. 65 ABC

TAYLOR, ROBERT
  Detectives sr 10. 16. 59 ABC
  Detectives sr ret 9. 16. 60 ABC
  Detectives sr ret 9. 29. 61 NBC
  Death Valley Days sh fall 1966 NN
  Death Valley Days sh ret fall 1967 NN
  Hondo ep 9. 15. 67 ABC

TAYLOR, ROD
  Lux Video Theatre ep The Browning Version 4. 7. 55
    NBC

Studio 57   ep   Killer Whale   6.7.55 NN
Studio 57   ep   The Last Day on Earth   9.6.55 NN
Suspicion   ep   The Story of Margery Reardon   10.28.57
   NBC
G.E. Theatre   ep   The Young Years   12.22.57 CBS
Playhouse 90   ep   Verdict of Three   4.24.58 CBS
Playhouse 90   ep   The Great Gatsby   6.26.58 CBS
Lux Playhouse   ep   The Best House in the Valley   10.
   3.58 CBS
Playhouse 90   ep   The Long March   10.16.58 CBS
Playhouse 90   ep   The Raider   2.19.59 CBS
Playhouse 90   ep   Misalliance   10.29.59 CBS
Twilight Zone   ep   And When the Sky Was Opened   12.
   11.59 CBS
Zane Grey Theatre   ep   Picture of Sal   1.28.60 CBS
Goodyear Theatre   ep   Capital Gains   2.1.60 NBC
G.E. Theatre   ep   Early to Die   2.7.60 CBS
Desilu Playhouse   ep   Thunder in the Night   2.19.60
   CBS
Hong Kong   sr   9.28.60 ABC
Bus Stop   ep   Portrait of a Hero   10.29.61 ABC
Dupont Show of the Month   ep   The Ordeal of Dr. Shan-
   non   12.16.62 NBC
Bearcats   sr   9.16.71 CBS
Family Flight   tf   10.25.72 ABC

TAYLOR-YOUNG, LEIGH
   Peyton Place   sr   10.19.66 ABC
   Under the Yum Yum Tree   pt   9.2.69 ABC

TEMPLE, SHIRLEY
   Shirley Temple's Story Book   sh/sr   1.12.58 NBC
   Shirley Temple Theatre   sh   9.18.60 NBC

TERRY-THOMAS
   Burke's Law   ep   Who Killed Julian Buck   10.18.63
      ABC
   Burke's Law   ep   Who Killed Madison Cooper   1.24.64
      ABC
   The Man from U.N.C.L.E.   ep   3.31.67, 4.7.67 NBC
   That's Life   ep   10.29.58 ABC
   Persuaders   ep   The Man in the Middle   10.9.71 ABC

THAXTER, PHYLLIS
   Tales of the City   ep   Miracle in the Rain   8.20.53
      CBS
   U.S. Steel Hour   ep   Tin Wedding   11.24.53 ABC

Ford Theatre   ep   The Ardent Woodsman   1.14.54 NBC
Robert Montgomery Presents   ep   Richard Said No   1.
  25.54 NBC
Video Theatre   ep   The Girl Who Couldn't Cry   4.15.54
  CBS
TV Hour   ep   Atomic Attack   5.18.54 ABC
Lux Video Theatre   ep   Penny Serenade   1.13.55 NBC
Schlitz Playhouse of Stars   ep   Man Out of the Rain   1.
  14.55 CBS
Shower of Stars   ep   The Dark Fleece   6.16.55 CBS
Climax   ep   Deal a Blow   8.25.55 CBS
Loretta Young Show   ep   Fear Me Not   8.28.55 NBC
Stage 7   ep   The Hayfield   9.18.55 CBS
U.S. Steel Hour   ep   Obsession   10.12.55 CBS
Climax   ep   Scheme to Defraud   11.10.55 CBS
Loretta Young Show   ep   Man in the Ring   12.11.55 NBC
Fireside Theatre   ep   The Velvet Trap   1.31.56 NBC
Loretta Young Show   ep   Hapless Holiday   4.8.56 NBC
Alfred Hitchcock Presents   ep   Never Again   4.22.56
  CBS
Schlitz Playhouse of Stars   ep   Dara   6.28.46 CBS
Alfred Hitchcock Presents   ep   Fog Closing In   10.7.56
  CBS
Studio 57   ep   Mr. Cinderella   11.25.56 NN
Studio One   ep   The Dark Corner   1.14.57 CBS
Alfred Hitchcock Presents   ep   Malice Domestic   2.10.
  57 CBS
Climax   ep   Payment for Judas   7.11.57 CBS
Alfred Hitchcock Presents   ep   The Deadly   12.15.57
  CBS
Frank Sinatra Show   ep   The Seedling Doubt   6.6.58 ABC
Alfred Hitchcock Presents   ep   Murder Me Twice   12.7.
  58 CBS
Wagon Train   ep   The Vivian Carter Story   3.11.59 NBC
Lux Playhouse   ep   Frederick   3.20.59 CBS
G.E. Theatre   ep   The House of Truth   12.13.59 CBS
Playhouse 90   ep   The Cruel Day   2.24.60 CBS
Wagon Train   ep   The Christine Elliott Story   3.23.60
  NBC
Outlaws   ep   The Quiet Killer   12.29.60 NBC
U.S. Steel Hour   ep   Bury Me Twice   10.18.61 CBS
Thriller   ep   The Last of the Somervilles   11.6.61 NBC
Rawhide   cp   The Blue Spot   12.8.61 CBS
Twilight Zone   ep   Young Man's Fancy   5.11.62 CBS
Alfred Hitchcock Theatre   ep   The Long Silence   3.22.
  63 CBS
Alfred Hitchcock Theatre   ep   Nothing Even Happens in

Linvale   11.8.63 CBS
Kraft Suspense Theatre   ep   The Threatening Eye   3.12.
   64 NBC
Alfred Hitchcock Theatre   ep   10.12.64 NBC
Defenders   ep   Go-Between   10.15.64 CBS
FBI   ep   The Conspirators   2.5.67 ABC
Coronet Blue   ep   7.10.67 CBS
FBI   ep   10.15.67 ABC
Invaders   ep   The Peacemaker   2.6.68 ABC
Lancer   ep   11.12.68 CBS
Bonanza   ep   2.9.69 NBC
Medical Center   ep   Junkie   9.30.70 CBS
FBI   ep   The Replacement   2.7.71   ABC
Incident in San Francisco   tf   2.28.71 ABC
The Longest Night   tf   9.12.72 ABC
Cannon   ep   The Predators   10.18.72 CBS

THINNES, ROY
Dupont Theatre   ep   Chicago   2-1-2   4.30.57 ABC
Meet McGraw   ep   McGraw Meets McGinley   1.7.58
   NBC
Peter Gunn   ep   The Man with the Scar   11.24.58 NBC
Untouchables   ep   A Fist of Five   12.4.62 ABC
Gunsmoke   ep   5.25.63 CBS
12 O'Clock High   ep   In Search of My Enemy   1.8.65
   ABC
The Long Hot Summer   sr   9.16.65 ABC
FBI   ep   the Escape   10.2.66 ABC
12 O'Clock High   ep   A Distant Cry   10.7.66 ABC
Fugitive   ep   Wine Is a Traitor   11.1.66 ABC
Invaders   sr   1.10.67 ABC
Invaders   sr ret   9.5.67 ABC
The Other Man   tf   10.19.70 NBC
The Psychiatrist   sr   12.14.70 NBC
Black Noon   tf   11.5.71 CBS

THOMAS, DANNY
Make Room for Daddy   (a.k.a.   Danny Thomas Show)
   sr   9.29.53 ABC
Make Room for Daddy   sr ret   fall 1954 ABC
Make Room for Daddy   sr ret   fall 1955 ABC
The Danny Thomas Show   sr   10.1.56 ABC
The Danny Thomas Show   sr ret 10.7.57 CBS
The Danny Thomas Show   sr ret   fall, 1958 CBS
Lucille Ball-Desi Arnaz Hour   ep   Lucy Makes Room
   for Danny   12.1.58 CBS
The Danny Thomas Show   sr ret   10.5.59 CBS

Zane Grey Theatre   ep   A Thread of Respect   2.12.59
   CBS
The Danny Thomas Show   sr ret   10.3.60 CBS
Zane Grey Theatre   ep   Honor Bright   2.2.61 CBS
The Danny Thomas Show   sr ret   10.2.61 CBS
The Danny Thomas Show   sr ret   10.1.62 CBS
The Danny Thomas Show   sr ret   9.30.63 CBS
The Joey Bishop Show   ep   4.25.64 NBC
Guys 'n Geishas   Sp   2.10.67 NBC
The Danny Thomas Show   sh/sr   9.11.67 NBC
Make Room for Granddaddy   sr   9.23.70 ABC

THOMAS, MARLO
   Dobie Gillis   ep   The Hunger Strike   1.26.60 CBS
   Zane Grey Theatre   ep   Honor Bright   2.2.61 CBS
   Thriller   ep   The Ordeal of Dr. Cordell   6.27.61 NBC
   Joey Bishop Show   sr   9.20.61 NBC
   Arrest and Trial   ep   Tigers Are for Jungles   3.22.64
      ABC
   Bonanza   ep   Pink Cloud Comes from Old Cathay   4.12.
      64 NBC
   Valentine's Day   ep   Follow the Broken Pretzel   1.1.65
      ABC
   Donna Reed Show   ep   Guests, Guest, Who Needs Guests
      3.11.65 ABC
   Ben Casey   ep   Three Li'l Lambs   3.29.65 ABC
   That Girl   sr   9.8.66 ABC
   That Girl   sr ret   9.7.67 ABC
   That Girl   sr ret   9.26.68 ABC
   That Girl   sr ret   9.18.69 ABC
   That Girl   sr ret   9.25.70 ABC

THOMAS, RICHARD
   Medical Center   ep   Runaway   1.21.70 CBS
   Love American Style   ep   3.6.70 ABC
   Bonanza   ep   9.27.70 NBC
   Marcus Welby, M.D.   ep   12.15.70 ABC
   FBI   ep   The Game of Terror   11.17.71 ABC
   The Homecoming   Sp   12.19.71 CBS
   The Waltons   sr   9.14.72 CBS

THOMPSON, KAY
   Playhouse 90   ep   Eloise   11.22.56 CBS

THOMPSON, MARSHALL
   Fireside Theatre   ep   Visit from a Stranger   10.28.52
      NBC

Fireside Theatre   ep   Ward of the Golden Gate   12.23.
    52 ABC
Ford Theatre   ep   Life of the Party   4.23.53 NBC
Summer Studio One   ep   The Paris Feedling   6.22.53
    CBS
Robert Montgomery Presents   ep   Red Robin Rides
    Again   9.10.53 ABC
Favorite Story   ep   What Happened at Three Oaks   4.5.
    54 NBC
U.S. Steel Hour   ep   The Rack   4.12.55 ABC
Science Fiction Theatre   ep   Stranger in the Desert   5.
    13.55 NBC
Private Secretary   ep   The Root of All Evil   6.19.55
    CBS
Science Fiction Theatre   ep   The Frozen Sound   7.29.
    55 NBC
Schlitz Playhouse of Stars   ep   The Case for the State
    8.26.55 CBS
Science Fiction Theatre   ep   Target Hurricane   10.28.55
    NBC
U.S. Steel Hour   ep   Command   2.15.56 CBS
TV Reader's Digest   ep   The Woman Who Changed Her
    Mind   4.16.56 ABC
Matinee Theatre   ep   The House of Seven Gables   8.22.
    56 NBC
The Millionaire   ep   The Story of Valerie Hunt   12.5.56
    CBS
20th Century-Fox Hour   ep   Young Man from Kentucky
    2.6.57 CBS
Playhouse 90   ep   The Blackwell Story   2.28.57 CBS
Matinee Theatre   ep   Bread Upon the Waters   3.12.57
    NBC
Ford Theatre   ep   Moment of Decision   4.10.57 ABC
Panic   ep   Botulism   6.18.57 NBC
Those Whiting Girls   ep   The Feminine Touch   7.22.57
    CBS
Matinee Theatre   ep   The Fall of the House of Usher
    11.5.57 NBC
Zane Grey Theatre   ep   The Open Cell   11.22.57 CBS
Court of Last Resort   ep   The Lester Arnold Case   2.
    14.58 NBC
Gunsmoke   ep   5.10.58 CBS
World of Giants   sr   fall, 1959 NN
The Millionaire   ep   Millionaire Maureen Reynolds   11.
    4.59 CBS
Bronco   ep   The Last Resort   11.17.59 ABC
Loretta Young Show   ep   Vengeance Is Thine   11.29.59
    NBC

Perry Mason   ep   The Case of the Wayward Wife   1.
  23. 60 CBS
Ford Startime   ep   Jeff McCleod, the Last Rebel   3. 1.
  60 NBC
Wagon Train   ep   The Trial for Murder   4. 27. 60, 5. 4.
  60 NBC
Angel   sr   10. 6. 60 CBS
Wagon Train   ep   2. 3. 64 ABC
Daktari   sr   1. 11. 66 CBS
Daktari   sr ret   9. 13. 66 CBS
Daktari   sr ret   9. 12. 67 CBS
Flipper   ep   2. 11. 68 NBC
Daktari   sr ret   9. 25. 68 CBS

THOMPSON, REX
Robert Montgomery Presents   ep   The Promise   6. 14.
  54 CBS
Center Street   ep   The Desdemona Murder Case   8. 10.
  54 ABC
Goodyear Playhouse   ep   The Personal Touch   10. 10. 54
  NBC
Robert Montgomery Presents   ep   David Copperfield   12.
  20. 54, 12. 27. 54 NBC
Omnibus   ep   The Turn of the Screw   2. 13. 55 CBS
Kraft Theatre   ep   The Rugged Mountain   1. 20. 55 ABC
Goodyear Playhouse   ep   The Treasure Hunters   5. 26.
  57 NBC
Studio One   ep   The Morning Face   10. 7. 57 CBS
Dupont Show of the Month   ep   The Prince and the
  Pauper   10. 28.57 CBS
Shirley Temple's Story Book   ep   The Little Lame
  Prince   7. 15. 58 NBC
Dupont Show of the Month   ep   The Winslow Boy   11. 13.
  58 CBS
Fugitive   ep   With Strings Attached   3. 15. 66 ABC

THOR, JEROME
Foreign Assignment   sr   10. 4. 51 NBC
Medallion Theatre   ep   Contact with the West   3. 20. 54
  CBS
Appointment with Adventure   ep   Forbidden Holiday   5.
  22. 55 CBS
U. S. Steel Hour   ep   Hung for a Sheep   6. 7. 55 ABC
Philco Playhouse   ep   The Starlet   1. 29. 56 NBC
Alcoa Theatre   ep   Man on Fire   3. 4. 56 NBC
77 Sunset Strip   ep   Dark Vengeance   1. 30. 59 ABC
Hong Kong   ep   The Jumping Dragon   11. 2. 60 ABC

Barbara Stanwyck Theatre   ep   Along the Barbary Coast
   2. 27. 61 NBC
The Man from U. N. C. L. E.   The Arabian Affair   10. 29.
   65 NBC
Adam-12   ep   3. 22. 69 NBC
It Takes a Thief   ep   3. 25. 69 ABC
O'Hara, U. S. Treasury   4. 2. 71 CBS

THULIN, INGRID
   Theatre 62   ep   Intermezzo   11. 19. 61 NBC
   Espionage   ep   The Incurable One   10. 16. 63 NBC

TIBBETT, LAWRENCE
   Circle Theatre   ep   Close Harmony   6. 19. 51 NBC

TIERNEY, GENE
   G. E. Theatre   ep   Journey to a Wedding   11. 27. 60 CBS
   FBI   ep   Conspiracy of Silence   3. 2. 69 ABC
   Daughter of the Mind   tf   12. 9. 69 ABC

TIFFIN, PAMELA
   Fugitive   ep   The Girl from Little Egypt   12. 24. 63 ABC

TINY TIM
   Love American Style   ep   1. 29. 71 ABC

TODD, ANN
   Life with the Erwins   (a. k. a.   Trouble with Father)   sr
      10. 21. 50 ABC
   Alcoa Hour   ep   The Black Wings   10. 16. 55 NBC
   U. S. Steel Hour   ep   Edward My Son   12. 7. 55 CBS
   Climax   ep   Shadow of a Memory   12. 26. 57 CBS
   G. E. Theatre   ep   Letters from Cairo   1. 12. 58 CBS
   Alfred Hitchcock Theatre   ep   Sylvia   1. 19. 58 CBS
   Playhouse 90   ep   Not the Glory   5. 8. 58 CBS
   Playhouse 90   ep   The Grey Nurse Said Nothing   11. 26.
      59 CBS
   The Snows of Kilimanjaro   Sp   3. 25. 60 CBS
   Thriller   ep   Letter to a Lover   11. 13. 61 NBC

TODD, RICHARD
   Danny Thomas Show   ep   The Last Hunters   1. 29. 68
      NBC

TOLAN, MICHAEL
   The Purim Storm   3. 14. 54 ABC
   Studio One   ep   Julius Caesar   8. 1. 55 CBS

Kraft Theatre   ep   Spur of the Moment   8.3.55 NBC
Kraft Theatre   ep   Teddy Bear   12.12.56 NBC
Studio One   ep   The Hollywood Complex   2.18.57 CBS
Naked City   ep   Stakeout   11.4.58 ABC
Play of the Week   ep   The Dybbuk   10.3.60 NN
Omnibus   cp   He Shall Have Power   11.13.60 NBC
U.S. Steel Hour   ep   The Big Splash   2.8.61 CBS
Special for Women   ep   The Single Woman   2.9.61 NBC
Play of the Week   ep   The Wingless Victory   4.17.61
   NN
Armstrong Circle Theatre   ep   Briefing from Room 103
   4.26.61 CBS
Naked City   ep   The Fingers of Henri Tourelle   10.18.
   61 ABC
Armstrong Circle Theatre   ep   Merchants of Evil   3.28.
   62 CBS
U.S. Steel Hour   ep   You Can't Escape   6.13.62 CBS
Route 66   ep   Peace, Pity, Pardon   4.12.63 CBS
Dupont Show of the Month   ep   The Legend of Lylah
   Claire   5.19.63 NBC
Eleventh Hour   ep   The Middle Child Gets All the Aches
   5.22.63 NBC
Nurses   ep   The Helping Hand   11.7.63 CBS
Outer Limits   ep   The Zanti Misfits   12.30.63 ABC
Nurses   ep   Is There Room for Edward   1.30.64 CBS
Nurses   ep   Imperfect Prodigy   2.20.64 CBS
Espionage   ep   The Liberators   3.11.64 NBC
Doctors/Nurses   sr   9.22.64 CBS
N.E.T. Playhouse   ep   The Journey of the Fifth Horse
   10.14.66 NN
Bob Hope Chrysler Theatre   ep   12.21.66 NBC
Tarzan   ep   Hurricane Hotel   11.10.67 NBC
Rat Patrol   ep   12.11.67 ABC
Invaders   ep   Possessed   1.2.68 ABC
Mannix   ep   1.20.68, 1.27.68 CBS
FBI   ep   Wind It Up and It Betrays You   9.22.68 ABC
Journey to the Unknown   ep   Paper Dolls   11.21.68 ABC
Mission Impossible   ep   12.8.68 CBS
FBI   ep   Blood Knots   11.9.69 ABC
Mission Impossible   ep   2.15.70 CBS
N.E.T. Playhouse   ep   The Tape Recorder   11.19.70
   NN
Dan August   ep   Passing Fair   12.30.70 ABC
Owen Marshall   ep   A Lonely Stretch of Beach   9.23.71
   ABC
Nichols   ep   9.30.71 NBC
Medical Center   ep   2.16.72 CBS

Cannon   ep   9.13.72 CBS
FBI   ep   Edge of Desperation   9.24.72 ABC
Ghost Story   ep   10.6.72 NBC
Owen Marshall   ep   12.21.72 ABC

TONE, FRANCHOT
Philco Playhouse   ep   Murder at the Stork Club   1.15.
   50 NBC
Studio One   ep   Walk the Dark Streets   4.10.50 CBS
Suspense   ep   Black Bronze   6.6.50 CBS
Lux Video Theatre   ep   Goodnight, Please   11.20.50
   CBS
Starlight Theatre   ep   Lunch at Disalvo's   8.23.51 CBS
Tales of Tomorrow   ep   3.14.52   ABC
Tales of Tomorrow   ep   The Horn   10.10.52 ABC
Suspense   ep   All Hallow's Eve   10.28.52 CBS
Hollywood Opening Night   ep   1.5.53 NBC
Mirror Theatre   ep   One Summer's Rain   8.25.53 NBC
Studio One   ep   12 Angry Men   9.20.54 CBS
U.S. Steel Hour   ep   The Fifth Wheel   10.26.54 ABC
Climax   ep   The Gioconda Smile   11.11.54 CBS
Elgin Hour   ep   Days of Grace   2.8.55 ABC
Ford Theatre   ep   Too Old for Dolls   2.24.55 NBC
Best of Broadway   ep   The Guardsman   3.2.55 CBS
U.S. Steel Hour   ep   Red Gulch   6.21.55 NBC
Four Star Playhouse   ep   Award   6.30.55 CBS
Climax   ep   Silent Decision   9.15.55 NBC
Tales of Tomorrow   ep   The Horn   9.26.55 NN
Robert Montgomery Presents   ep   Man Lost   10.24.55
   NBC
Playwrights '56   ep   The Sound and the Fury   12.6.55
   NBC
Omnibus   ep   Dear Brutus   1.8.56 CBS
G.E. Theatre   ep   Steimetz   3.11.56 CBS
Alcoa Hour   ep   Even the Weariest River   4.15.56 NBC
U.S. Steel Hour   ep   Survival   11.7.56 CBS
Hallmark Hall of Fame   ep   The Little Foxes   12.16.
   56 NBC
Kaiser Aluminum Hour   ep   Throw Me a Rope   1.29.
   57 NBC
Alcoa Hour   ep   Night   9.22.57 NBC
Studio One   ep   Bend in the Road   11.4.57 CBS
Playhouse 90   ep   The Thundering Wave   12.12.57
   NBC
Studio One   ep   Trial by Slander   1.20.58 CBS
Studio One   ep   Ticket to Tahiti   6.2.58 CBS
Playhouse 90   ep   The Thundering Wave   7.10.58 CBS

Pursuit   ep   Last Night in August   12. 17. 58 CBS
Desilu Playhouse   ep   The Crazy Hunter   12. 29. 58
  CBS
Playhouse 90   ep   A Quiet Game of Cards   1. 29. 59 CBS
Alfred Hitchcock Presents   ep   The Impossible Dream
  4. 19. 59 CBS
Dupont Show of the Month   ep   Body and Soul   9. 28. 59
  CBS
Playhouse 90   ep   Hidden Image   11. 12. 59 CBS
Goodyear Theatre   ep   The Ticket   2. 15. 60 NBC
Playhouse 90   ep   The Shape of the River   5. 2. 60 CBS
Bonanza   ep   Denver McKee   10. 15. 60 NBC
Twilight Zone   ep   The Silence   4. 28. 61 CBS
Ben Casey   ep   A Memory of Candy Stripes   1. 8. 62
  ABC
Dupont Show of the Month   ep   The Betrayal   10. 21. 62
  NBC
Eleventh Hour   ep   Along about Late in the Afternoon
  12. 26. 62 NBC
Wagon Train   ep   The Malachi Hobart Story   12. 4. 62
  NBC
Dupont Show of the Month   ep   Jeremy Rabbitt, the Se-
  cret Avenger   4. 5. 64 NBC
See How They Run   tf   10. 7. 64 NBC
The Reporter   ep   The Man Behind the Badge   11. 6. 64
  CBS
Virginian   ep   3. 31. 65 NBC
Ben Casey   sr   9. 13. 65 ABC
Run for Your Life   ep   11. 15. 67 NBC
Shadow over Elveron   tf   3. 5. 68 NBC

TOOMEY, REGIS
  Bigelow-Sanford Theatre   ep   T. K. O.   10. 25. 51 NN
  Four Star Playhouse   ep   Dante's Inferno   4. 9. 53 CBS
  Schlitz Playhouse of Stars   ep   The Ledge   6. 26. 53
    CBS
  Four Star Playhouse   ep   The Hard Way   9. 10. 53 CBS
  Backbone of America   ep   12. 29. 53 NBC
  Ford Theatre   ep   For Value Received   2. 18. 54 NBC
  Hey, Mulligan   sr   8. 28. 54 NBC
  Fireside Theatre   ep   Lost Perspectives   1. 19. 54 NBC
  Cavalcade of America   ep   American Thanksgiving   11.
    23. 54 ABC
  Stage 7   ep   Young Girl in an Apple Tree   4. 10. 55 CBS
  Four Star Playhouse   ep   The House Always Wins   4. 28.
    55 CBS
  Schlitz Playhouse of Stars   ep   The Last Out   9. 30. 55
    CBS

Schlitz Playhouse of Stars   ep   The Careless Cadet   11. 25. 55 CBS

Loretta Young Show   ep   The Challenge   1. 15. 56 NBC

Cheyenne   ep   2. 7. 56 ABC

Four Star Playhouse   ep   No Limit   2. 16. 56 CBS

Matinee Theatre   ep   Young Hands, Young Feet   4. 13. 56 NBC

Producers Showcase   ep   Dodsworth   4. 30. 56 NBC

Four Star Playhouse   ep   A Long Way from Texas   5. 3. 56 CBS

Crossroads   ep   Lifeline   5. 11. 56 ABC

Cheyenne   ep   The Storm Riders   6. 25. 56 ABC

20th Century-Fox Hour   ep   Men Against Speed   12. 12. 56 CBS

Loretta Young Show   ep   Bad Apple   2. 3. 57 NBC

20th Century-Fox Hour   ep   The Still Trumpet   4. 3. 57 CBS

Cheyenne   ep   Hard Bargain   5. 21. 57 ABC

Richard Diamond   sr   7. 1. 57 CBS

Danny Thomas Show   ep   12. 23. 57 ABC

Navy Log   ep   One Grand Marine   3. 20. 58 ABC

Loretta Young Show   ep   South American Uncle   5. 4. 58 NBC

Broken Arrow   ep   Transfer   6. 24. 58 ABC

Trackdown   ep   10. 17. 58 ABC

Loretta Young Show   ep   Strange Money   12. 14. 58 NBC

Kaleidoscope   ep   The Third Commandment   2. 8. 59 NBC

Lux Playhouse   ep   Frederick   3. 20. 59 CBS

Maverick   ep   Shady Deal at Sunny Acres   4. 5. 59 ABC

David Niven Theatre   ep   Maggie Malone   6. 9. 59 NBC

Restless Gun   ep   Hill of Death   6. 22. 59 NBC

Markham   ep   The Long Haul   10. 10. 59 CBS

Rawhide   ep   Incident of the Stalking Death   11. 13. 59 CBS

Loretta Young Show   ep   Ten Men and a Girl   11. 15. 59 NBC

Tightrope   ep   Broken Rope   1. 12. 60 CBS

Bronco   ep   Volunteers from Aberdeen   2. 9. 60 ABC

World of Disney   ep   Apache Friends   2. 19. 60 ABC

Loretta Young Show   ep   The Trial   3. 20. 60 NBC

June Allyson Show   ep   The Doctor and the Redhead   4. 25. 60 CBS

G. E. Theatre   ep   The Playoff   11. 20. 60 CBS

Tall Men   ep   The Beast   11. 26. 60 NBC

Perry Mason   ep   The Case of the Loquacious Liar   12. 3. 60 CBS

Peter Gunn   ep   Dream Big, Dream Deadly   12. 12. 60 ABC

Route 66   ep   The Quick and the Dead   1.13.61 CBS
Cheyenne   ep   Shepherd with a Gun   2.6.61 ABC
Shannon   sr   6.61 ABC
Cain's Hundred   ep   Murder by Proxy   2.26.62 NBC
Cheyenne   ep   The Vanishing Breed   11.19.62   ABC
Burke's Law   sr   9.20.63 ABC
Going My Way   ep   A Tough Act to Follow   4.24.63
   ABC
Burke's Law   sr ret   9.16.64 ABC
Voyage to the Bottom of the Sea   ep   The Left-Handed
   Man   10.24.65 ABC
Perry Mason   ep   The Case of the 12th Wildcat 10.31.
   65 CBS
Farmer's Daughter   ep   11.5.65 ABC
Green Acres   ep   2.2.66 CBS
Jesse James   ep   Things Don't Just Happen   3.14.66
   ABC
Time Tunnel   ep   2.17.67 ABC
Petticoat Junction   sr   9.29.68 CBS
Virginian   ep   12.18.68 NBC
Ghost Story   ep   The Summer House   10.13.72 NBC
FBI   ep   Till Death Do Us Part   10.22.72 ABC
Jigsaw   ep   12.21.72 ABC

TORN, RIP
   Omnibus   ep   The Blue Hotel   11.25.56 ABC
   Kaiser Aluminum Hour   ep   So Short a Season   2.12.57
      NBC
   Alfred Hitchcock Presents   ep   Number 22   2.17.57
      CBS
   U.S. Steel Hour   ep   The Little Bullfighter   6.5.57 CBS
   Alcoa Hour   ep   Hostages to Fortune   7.7.57 NBC
   Kraft Theatre   ep   The Killer Instinct   9.18.57 NBC
   Restless Gun   ep   Jody   11.4.57 NBC
   U.S. Steel Hour   ep   The Charm   1.1.58 CBS
   Playhouse 90   ep   Bomber's Moon   5.22.58 CBS
   Hallmark Hall of Fame   ep   Johnny Belinda   10.13.58
      NBC
   Sunday Showcase   ep   Murder and Android   11.8.59 NBC
   Playhouse 90   ep   Face of a Hero   1.1.59 CBS
   Pursuit   ep   Epitaph for a Golden Girl   1.14.59 CBS
   Playhouse 90   ep   The Tunnel   12.10.59 CBS
   Thriller   ep   The Purple Room   10.25.60 NBC
   Untouchables   ep   The Masterpiece   1.19.61 ABC
   Alfred Hitchcock Presents   ep   The Kiss-Off   3.7.61
      NBC
   Twenty-Four Hours in a Woman's Life   Sp   3.20.61 CBS

Frontier Circus   ep   The Hunter and the Hunted   11.2.
   61 CBS
Naked City   ep   A Case Study of Two Savages   2.7.62
   ABC
Dr. Kildare   ep   The Chemistry of Anger   4.26.62
   NBC
Dick Powell Theatre   ep   Crazy Sunday   12.18.62 NBC
Untouchables   ep   The Spoiler   3.26.63 ABC
Route 66   ep   Who Will Cheer My Bonnie Bride?   5.10.
   63 CBS
Lieutenant   ep   The Proud and the Angry   9.28.63 NBC
Channing   ep   A Doll's House with Pompons and Tro-
   phies   12.4.63 ABC
Breaking Point   ep   Millions of Faces   12.9.63 ABC
Eleventh Hour   ep   The Secret in the Stone   2.26.64
   NBC
Ben Casey   ep   But Who Shall Beat the Drums   9.28.
   64 ABC
Combat   ep   A Gift of Hope   12.1.64 ABC
Dr. Kildare   ep   An Exchange of Gifts   12.24.64 NBC
The Man from U.N.C.L.E.   ep   The Alexander the
   Greater Affair   9.19.65, 9.24.65 NBC
Hollywood Television Theatre   ep   Monserrat   3.21.71
   NN
Bonanza   ep   Blind Hunch   11.21.71 NBC
Mannix   ep   9.17.72 CBS
Ghost Story   ep   12.8.72 NBC

TOTTER, AUDREY
Ford Theatre   ep   Ever Since the Day   12.24.53 NBC
Four Star Playhouse   ep   Meet McGraw   2.25.54 CBS
Science Fiction Theatre   ep   Spider, Incorporated   6.3.
   55 NBC
Ford Theatre   ep   One Man Missing   6.9.55 NBC
Climax   ep   Portrait in Celluloid   11.24.55 CBS
20th Century-Fox Hour   ep   One Life   1.25.56 CBS
Climax   ep   The Gorsten Case   9.20.56 CBS
Zane Grey Theatre   ep   Return to Nowhere   12.7.56
   CBS
On Trial   ep   The Case of the Jealous Bomber   4.5.57
   NBC
Californians   ep   12.10.57 NBC
Suspicion   ep   A Touch of Evil   2.17.58 NBC
Climax   ep   The Secret Love of Johnny Spain   2.20.58
   CBS
Cheyenne   ep   The Empty Gun   2.25.58 ABC
Cimarron City   sr   10.11.58 NBC

Wagon Train   ep   The Tent City Story   12.10.58 NBC
Alfred Hitchcock Presents   ep   Mme. Mystery   3.27.60
   CBS
G. E. Theatre   ep   Mystery at Malibu   4.10.60 CBS
Ann Sothern Show   ep   5.9.60 CBS
Loretta Young Show   ep   The Glass Cage   10.30.60
   NBC
G. E. Theatre   ep   My Darling Judge   4.23.61 CBS
Alfred Hitchcock Theatre   ep   Self-Defense   5.23.61
   NBC
Route 66   ep   A Long Piece of Mischief   1.19.62 CBS
Rawhide   ep   Abilene   9.21.62 CBS
Our Man Higgins   sr   10.3.62 ABC
Kraft Suspense Theatre   ep   A Cause of Anger   3.19.64
   NBC
Perry Mason   ep   The Case of the Reckless Rockhound
   11.26.64 CBS
Dr. Kildare   ep   Fathers and Daughter   11.22.65, 11.
   23.65, 11.29.65, 11.30.65 NBC
Dr. Kildare   ep   New Doctor in Town   4.5.66 NBC
Bonanza   ep   A Time to Step Down   9.25.66 NBC
Virginian   ep   1.18.67 NBC
The Outsider   tf   11.21.67 NBC
Run for Your Life   ep   The Rape of Lucrece   1.17.68
   NBC
Ironside   ep   Seeing is Believing   10.30.69 NBC
Virginian   ep   11.26.69 NBC
Bold Ones   ep   The Shattered Image   2.15.70 NBC

TRACY, LEE
   Theatre Hour   ep   The Traitor   9.8.50 ABC
   Danger   ep   Green and Gold String   10.17.50 CBS
   Billy Rose's Playbill   ep   If You Can Act--Act   11.27.
      60 NN
   Lights Out   ep   Men on the Mountain   12.18.50 NBC
   Pulitzer Prize Playhouse   ep   Light Up the Sky   1.19.
      51 ABC
   Billy Rose's Playbill   ep   Sugar O'Hara   1.30.51 ABC
   Amazing Mr. Malone   sr   9.24.51 ABC
   Cosmopolitan Theatre   ep   The Secret Front   10.2.51
      NN
   Kraft Theatre   ep   Good Old Charlie Fay   2.8.56 NBC
   New York Confidential   sr   1958 CBS
   Follow the Sun   ep   The Last of the Big Spenders   1.14.
      62 ABC
   87th Precinct   ep   Square Cop   3.12.62 NBC
   Wagon Train   ep   The George B. Hanrahan Story   3.28.
      62 NBC

Going My Way   ep   Cornelius Come Home   3.6.63 ABC
Profiles in Courage   ep   Robert Taft   1.3.65 NBC
Ben Casey   ep   Eulogy in Four Flats   3.22.65 ABC

TRAUBEL, HELEN
Bell Telephone Hour   ep   The Mikado   4.29.60 NBC
Valentine's Day   ep   10.30.64 ABC

TRAVERS, BILL
Kraft Theatre   ep   A Cook for Mr. General   10.16.57
NBC
Our American Heritage   ep   Born a Giant   12.2.60
NBC
Rawhide   ep   Incident at Two Graves   11.7.63 CBS
Espionage   ep   A Camel to Ride   11.27.63 NBC
Hallmark Hall of Fame   ep   The Admirable Crichton
5.2.68 NBC

TRAVIS, RICHARD
Story Theatre   ep   The Manchester Marriage   2.2.51
NN
Teledrama   ep   Danger Zone   7.24.53 CBS
Letter to Loretta   ep   The One That Got Away   11.1.
53 NBC
Schlitz Playhouse of Stars   ep   Go Away a Winner   1.1.
54 CBS

TREACHER, ARTHUR
Philco Playhouse   ep   Uncle Dynamite   1.29.50 CBS
Philco Playhouse   ep   The Room Next Door   4.6.52
NBC
Goodyear Playhouse   ep   It's a Small World   6.22.52
NBC
Philco Playhouse   ep   Mr. Pettengill Here   2.15.53
NBC
Armstrong Circle Theatre   ep   Tom O'Shanter   3.9.54
NBC
Armstrong Circle Theatre   ep   The Three Tasks   4.13.
54 NBC
Kraft Theatre   ep   Alice in Wonderland   5.5.54 NBC
Climax   ep   The Fifth Wheel   2.9.56 CBS
Play of the Week   ep   The Enchanted   4.11.60 NN
Shirley Temple Theatre   ep   The Land of Oz   9.18.60
NBC

TREVOR, CLAIRE
Ford Theatre   ep   Alias Nora Hale   12.31.53 NBC

G. E. Theatre ep Foggy Night 2. 14. 54 CBS
Willy sr 9. 19. 54 CBS
Ford Theatre ep Summer Memory 11. 18. 54 NBC
Lux Video Theatre ep No Sad Songs for Me 4. 14. 55
  NBC
Stage 7 ep Billy and the Bride 5. 8. 55 CBS
Climax ep The Prowler 1. 5. 56 CBS
Schlitz Playhouse of Stars ep Foolproof 1. 6. 56 CBS
Playhouse 90 ep If You Knew Elizabeth 4. 11. 57 CBS
Producers Showcase ep Dodsworth 4. 30. 56 NBC
G. E. Theatre ep Emergency Call 6. 24. 56 CBS
Desilu Playhouse ep Happy Hill 1. 12. 59 CBS
Wagon Train ep The C. L. Harding Story 10. 14. 59
  NBC
Untouchables ep 10. 22. 59 ABC
U. S. Steel Hour ep The Revolt of Judge Lloyd 10. 5.
  60 CBS
Alfred Hitchcock Theatre ep A Crime for Mothers 1.
  24. 61 NBC
Investigators ep New Sound for the Blues 10. 19. 61
  CBS

TRUEX, ERNEST
  The Truex Family sr 1. 5. 50 NN
  Starlight Theatre ep Much Ado about Spring 7. 3. 50
    CBS
  Ford Theatre ep The Ghost Patrol 3. 9. 51 CBS
  Danger ep Final Rejection 10. 23. 51 CBS
  Cameo Theatre ep The Canon's Curtains 3. 16. 52 NBC
  Broadway Television Theatre ep Angel in the Pawn-
    shop 5. 5. 52 NN
  Broadway Television Theatre ep Outward Bound 11.
    24. 52 NN
  Philco Theatre ep Mr. Quimby's Christmas 12. 21. 52
    NBC
  The Doctor ep Googan 2. 22. 53 NBC
  Armstrong Circle Theatre ep Anchorage 2. 24. 53 NBC
  Broadway Television Theatre ep George and Margaret
    3. 30. 53 NN
  Plymouth Playhouse ep Jamie 4. 26. 53 ABC
  Kraft Theatre ep The Rainy Day 6. 24. 53 NBC
  Medallion Theatre ep The Grand Cross of the Cres-
    cent 7. 25. 53 CBS
  Goodyear Playhouse ep The New Process 8. 23. 53
    NBC
  Jamie sr 10. 5. 53 ABC
  Inner Sanctum ep The Yellow Parakeet 3. 12. 54 NN

Kraft Theatre   ep   Alice in Wonderland   5.5.54 NBC
Mr. Peepers   ep   5.23.54 NBC
Mr. Peepers   sr   fall, 1954 NBC
Jamie   sr ret   9.27.54 ABC
Armstrong Cirlce Theatre   ep   Fred Allen's Sketchbook
    11.9.54 NBC
Pond's Theatre   ep   30, Honey, 30   2.3.55 ABC
Elgin Hour   ep   Midsummer Melody   4.19.55 ABC
Lux Video Theatre   ep   Make Way for Tomorrow   5.19.
    55 NBC
Studio One   ep   The Spongers   6.6.55 CBS
Producers' Showcase   ep   Our Town   9.19.55 NBC
Climax   ep   House of Shadows   10.20.55 CBS
Star Tonight   ep   Have Faith in Your Agent   11.24.55
    ABC
Justice   ep   Eyewitness   1.1.56 NBC
Matinee Theatre   ep   The Middle Son   2.13.56 NBC
Lux Video Theatre   ep   It Happened on Fifth Avenue   1.
    3.57 NBC
Playhouse 90   ep   If You Knew Elizabeth   4.11.57 CBS
The Millionaire   ep   Story of Andrew Sterling   4.30.58
    CBS
Ann Sothern Show   ep   10.6.58 CBS
Tom Ewell Show   ep   12.20.60 CBS
June Allyson Show   ep   Silent Panic   12.22.60 CBS
Dennis the Menace   ep   The Christmas Horse   12.25.
    60 CBS
Alfred Hitchcock Theatre   ep   A Pearl Necklace   5.2.
    61 NBC
Father Knows Best   ep   Grandpa Retires   5.9.61 CBS
Dick Powell Theatre   ep   A Time to Die   1.9.62 NBC
Twilight Zone   ep   Kick the Can   2.9.62 CBS
Alfred Hitchcock Theatre   ep   The Matched Pearl   4.24.
    62 NBC
Farmer's Daughter   ep   One Rainy Night   11.29.63 ABC
Bonanza   ep   Square Deal Sam   11.8.64 NBC
Petticoat Junction   ep   1.26.65 CBS
The Kwimpers of New Jersey   pt   8.13.66 ABC
Petticoat Junction   ep   9.13.66 CBS

TRUMAN, MARGARET
Matinee Theatre   ep   Autumn Crocus   6.8.56 NBC
Matinee Theatre   ep   Iris   11.14.57 NBC
Modern Romance   ep hos   5.19.58 NBC
CBS TV Workshop   ep   Flight of Fancy   12.4.60 CBS

TRYON, TOM

    Way of the World   ep   3.28.55 NBC

    Frontier   ep   King of the Dakotas   11.13.55, 11.20.55
    NBC

    Fireside Theatre   ep   Not What She Pretended   2.7.56
    NBC

    Fireside Theatre   ep   The Mirror   2.28.56 NBC

    Matinee Theatre   ep   The Fall of the House of Usher
    8.6.56 NBC

    20th Century-Fox Hour   ep   Young Man from Kentucky
    2.6.57 CBS

    Playhouse 90   ep   Charley's Aunt   3.28.57 CBS

    Matinee Theatre   ep   Wuthering Heights   4.8.57 NBC

    Zane Grey Theatre   ep   Black Is for Grief   4.12.57
    CBS

    Matinee Theatre   ep   Elementals   10.31.57 NBC

    Wagon Train   ep   The Mark Hanford Story   2.26.58
    NBC

    Kraft Suspense Theatre   ep   Nobody Will Ever Know   3.
    2.58 NBC

    Restless Gun   ep   Sheriff Billy   3.10.58 NBC

    G.E. Theatre   ep   Strange Witness   3.23.58 CBS

    The Millionaire   ep   The Tony Drummond Story   4.9.58
    CBS

    World of Disney   ep   Texas John Slaughter   10.31.58
    ABC

    World of Disney   ep   Ambush at Laredo   11.14.58 ABC

    World of Disney   ep   The Slaughter Trail   3.20.59 ABC

    World of Disney   ep   The Robber Stallion   12.4.59 ABC

    World of Disney   ep   Geronimo's Revenge   3.4.60 ABC

    World of Disney   ep   The End of the Trail   1.29.61
    ABC

    World of Disney   ep   A Trip to Tucson   4.16.61 ABC

    World of Disney   ep   Frank Celle's in Town   4.23.61
    ABC

    Virginian   ep   Man from the Sea   1.22.62 NBC

    Dr. Kildare   ep   The Mosaic   1.31.63 NBC

    Bob Hope Chrysler Theatre   ep   Mr. Governess   11.10.
    65 NBC

    Big Valley   ep   4.13.66 ABC

    Winchester 73   tf   3.14.67 NBC

    Road West   ep   Charade of Justice   3.27.67 NBC

    Bob Hope Chrysler Theatre   Wipeout   4.26.67 NBC

    Virginian   ep   10.4.67 NBC

    Men from Shiloh   ep   The Price of the Hanging   11.11.
    70 NBC

TUCKER, FORREST
   Tele-Theatre ep The Hoosier School-Master 2.13.50
      NBC
   Schlitz Playhouse of Stars ep Blizzard-Bound 5.21.54
      CBS
   Crunch and Des sr 1955 NN
   Appointment with Adventure ep Two Falls for Satan
      4.1.56 CBS
   Robert Montgomery Presents ep The Right Thing 5.
      14.56 NBC
   Lux Video Theatre ep Rebuke Me Not 8.9.56 NBC
   Kaiser Aluminum Hour ep Member in Good Standing
      1.1.57 NBC
   Ford Theatre ep The Quiet Stranger 1.9.57 ABC
   Lux Video Theatre ep The Softest Music 7.11.57 NBC
   Climax ep Trial by Fire 9.5.57 CBS
   G.E. Theatre ep The Cold Touch 4.13.58 CBS
   Wagon Train ep The Rex Montana Story 5.28.58 NBC
   Wide Country ep Speckle Bird 1.31.63 NBC
   Dr. Kildare ep Island Like a Peacock 5.16.63 NBC
   Channing ep Collision Course 11.6.63 ABC
   Burke's Law ep 5.1.64 ABC
   Gunsmoke ep 1.2.65 CBS
   Virginian ep Hideout 1.13.65 NBC
   Slattery's People ep Bill Bailey, Why Did You Come
      Home 4.2.65 CBS
   F Troop sr 9.14.65 ABC
   Gunsmoke ep 9.25.65 CBS
   F Troop sr ret 9.8.66 ABC
   Daniel Boone 9.14.67 NBC
   Gunsmoke ep 9.18.67 CBS
   Hondo ep 11.3.67 ABC
   World of Disney ep A Boy Called Nuthin' 12.10.67,
      12.17.67 NBC
   Daniel Boone ep 12.12.68 NBC
   Gunsmoke ep 1.5.70 CBS
   Medical Center ep The Professional 3.11.70 CBS
   Love American Style ep 3.13.70 ABC
   Bracken's World ep 9.18.70 NBC
   Ironside ep Too Many Victims 11.12.70 NBC
   Gunsmoke ep 12.14.70 CBS
   Alias Smith and Jones tf 1.5.71 ABC
   Name of the Game ep Seek and Destroy 2.5.71 NBC
   Love American Style ep 2.5.71 ABC
   Medical Center ep The Imposter 9.29.71 CBS
   Night Gallery ep 11.17.71 NBC
   Cade's County ep The Alien Land 12.19.71 CBS

Bonanza   ep   12.26.71 NBC
Welcome Home, Johnny Bristol   tf   1.30.72 CBS
Gunsmoke   ep   2.7.72 CBS
Columbo   ep   Blueprint for Murder   2.9.72 NBC

TUFTS, SONNY
    Damon Runyon Theatre   ep   A Tale of Two Citizens
        3.17.56 CBS
    Virginian   ep   Ride a Dark Trail   9.18.63 NBC
    Bob Hope Chrysler Theatre   ep   Have Girls--Will
        Travel   10.16.64 NBC
    Land's End   Sp   4.21.68 NBC

TULLY, TOM
    Personal Appearance Theatre   ep   The Death Clause
        3.15.52 ABC
    Cavalcade of America   ep   In This Crisis   12.24.52
        NBC
    Ford Theatre   ep   The Lady and the Champ   5.7.53
        NBC
    Schlitz Playhouse of Stars   ep   Showdown at Sunset   7.
        16.54 CBS
    The Lineup   sr   10.1.54 CBS
    Philco Playhouse   ep   The Bold and the Brave   4.17.55
        NBC
    The Lineup   sr ret   9.30.55 CBS
    Front Row Center   ep   Uncle Barney   2.26.56 CBS
    Ford Theatre   ep   The Clay Pigeon   5.31.56 NBC
    Telephone Time   ep   The Mountain that Moved   12.30.
        56 CBS
    Zane Grey Theatre   ep   Black Is for Grief   4.12.57
        CBS
    Zane Grey Theatre   ep   Badge of Honor   5.3.57 CBS
    The Lineup   sr   fall 1957   CBS
    The Lineup   sr   9.26.58 CBS
    Alfred Hitchcock Presents   ep   Backwards   3.1.60 CBS
    U.S. Steel Hour   ep   Summer Rhapsody   5.3.61 CBS
    Tales of Wells Fargo   ep   Defiant at the Gate   11.25.
        61 NBC
    Empire   ep   Long Past, Long Remembered   10.23.62
        NBC
    Untouchables   ep   A Taste for Pineapple   5.21.63 ABC
    Perry Mason   ep   The Case of the Arrogant Arsonist
        3.5.64 CBS
    Perry Mason   ep   The Case of the Nautical Knot   10.
        29.64 CBS
    Dick Van Dyke Show   ep   Pink Pills and Purple Parents

11. 25. 64 CBS
Virginian ep The Hour of the Tiger 12. 30. 64 NBC
Rawhide ep Blood Harvest 2. 12. 65 CBS
Bonanza ep The Dilemma 9. 19. 65 NBC
Loner ep Hunt the Man Down 12. 11. 65 CBS
Shane sr 9. 10. 66 ABC
Hey Landlord ep 2. 19. 67 NBC
Guns of Will Sonnett ep 11. 10. 67 ABC
Bonanza ep The Sure Thing 11. 12. 67 NBC
Guns of Will Sonnett ep 1. 3. 69 ABC
High Chaparral ep 1. 24. 69 NBC
Any Second Now tf 2. 11. 69 NBC
Mod Squad ep A Place to Run 12. 2. 69 ABC

TURNER, LANA
Survivors sr 9. 29. 69 ABC

TYRELL, SUSAN
Mr. Novak ep Beyond a Reasonable Doubt 12. 22. 64
   NBC
Experiment in Terror ep The Hamster of Happiness
   2. 25. 68 NBC
Bonanza ep Fallen Woman 9. 26. 71 NBC
James Garner Show ep 12. 28. 71 NBC

TYSON, CICELY
East Side/West Side sr 9. 23. 63 CBS
Slattery's People ep Who You Taking to the Main
   Event, Eddie 3. 12. 65 CBS
I Spy ep So Long 9. 15. 65 NBC
I Spy ep Trial by Treehouse 10. 19. 66 NBC
The Guiding Light sr 1967 CBS
Cowboy in Africa ep 11. 20. 67 ABC
FBI ep The Enemies 11. 3. 68 ABC
Medical Center ep The Last Ten Yards 9. 24. 69 CBS
FBI ep 10. 12. 69 ABC
On Being Black ep Johnny Ghost 10. 13. 69 NN
Courtship of Eddie's Father ep 10. 29. 69 ABC
Here Come the Brides ep 12. 26. 69 ABC
Here Come the Brides ep 1. 9. 70 ABC
Mission Impossible ep 3. 15. 70 CBS
Gunsmoke ep The Scavengers 11. 16. 70 CBS
Marriage: Year One tf 10. 15. 71 NBC
Emergency ep 4. 15. 72 NBC
Wednesday Night Pout pt 4. 24. 72 NBC

-U-

UGGAMS, LESLIE
    The Girl from U.N.C.L.E.   ep   12.20.66 NBC
    Mod Squad   ep   1.18.72 ABC

ULRIC, LENORE
    Television Theatre   ep   Once a Gentleman   4.10.50
        NBC

UMECKI, MIYOSKI
    Donna Reed Show   ep   Geisha Girl   2.16.61 ABC
    Donna Reed Show   ep   Aloha, Kimi   1.25.62 ABC
    Sam Benedict   ep   Tears for a Nobody Doll   10.13.62
        NBC
    Hallmark Hall of Fame   ep   Teahouse of the August
        Moon   10.26.62 NBC
    Dr. Kildare   ep   11.7.63 NBC
    Rawhide   ep   Incident of the Geisha   12.19.63 CBS
    Virginian   ep   Smile of a Dragon   2.26.64 NBC
    Burke's Law   ep   3.21.64 ABC
    Courtship of Eddie's Father   sr   9.17.69 ABC
    Courtship of Eddie's Father   sr ret   9.23.70 ABC
    Courtship of Eddie's Father   sr ret   9.15.71 ABC

URE, MARY
    Omnibus   ep   The Lady's Not for Burning   4.6.58 NBC

USTINOV, PETER
    Omnibus   ep   Moment of Truth   2.23.58 NBC
    Omnibus   ep   The Empty Chair   12.7.58 NBC
    Hallmark Hall of Fame   ep   Barefoot in Athens   11.11.
        66 NBC
    Babar the Elephant   Sp nar   4.21.69 NBC
    Hallmark Hall of Fame   ep   A Storm in Summer   2.6.
        70 NBC
    Hallmark Hall of Fame   ep   Gideon   3.26.71 NBC

-V-

VACCARO, BRENDA
    The Greatest Show on Earth ep Don't Look Down,
        Don't Look Back   10.8.63 ABC
    Fugitive ep See Hollywood and Die   11.5.63 ABC
    Defenders ep The Sworn Twelve   3.25.65 CBS
    Doctors/Nurses ep The Heroine   5.4.65 CBS
    My Luck Penny pt 8.8.66 CBS
    Coronet Blue ep A Charade for Murder   7.24.67 CBS
    FBI ep Scapegoat   11.23.69 ABC
    The Psychiatrist ep 2.17.71 NBC
    Name of the Game ep Appointment in Palermo   2.26.
        71 NBC
    Travis Logan, D.A.   tf 3.11.71 CBS
    What's a Nice Girl Like You tf 12.18.71 ABC
    Marcus Welby, M.D.   ep 10.10.72 ABC
    Banacek ep 11.15.72 NBC
    McCloud ep The Park Avenue Rustlers 12.24.72 NBC

VAGUE, VERA
    Oh Susanna ep 1.18.58 CBS

VALLEE, RUDY
    Eddie Cantor Theatre ep The Playboy   8.29.55 ABC
    December Bride ep 1.23.56 CBS
    Matinee Theatre ep Jenny Kissed Me   12.7.56 NBC
    Lucille Ball-Desi Arnaz Show ep Lucy Takes a Cruise
        to Havana   11.6.57 CBS
    Kraft Theatre ep The Battle for Wednesday Night 1.1.
        58 NBC
    Hansel and Gretel Sp 4.27.58 NBC
    Batman ep 11.23.70, 11.30.67, 12.7.67 ABC
    Death Valley Days ep The Friend 2.11.68 NN
    Chicago Teddy Bears ep 9.17.71 CBS
    Alias Smith and Jones ep Dreadful Sorry, Clementine
        11.17.71 ABC

VALLI, ALIDA
    Combat ep Doughboy 10.29.63 ABC
    Dr. Kildare ep Rome Will Never Leave You ep 11.
        12.64, 11.19.64, 11.26.64 NBC

VANCE, VIVIAN
    I Love Lucy sr 10.15.51 CBS

I Love Lucy sr ret 9. 15. 52 CBS
I Love Lucy sr ret 10. 5. 53 CBS
I Love Lucy sr ret 10. 4. 54 CBS
Shower of Stars ep High Pitch 5. 12. 55 CBS
I Love Lucy sr ret 10. 3. 55 CBS
Lucille Ball-Desi Arnaz Hour sr 10. 6. 58 CBS
Lucille Ball-Desi Arnaz Hour sr ret 9. 25. 59 CBS
Deputy ep Land Greed 12. 12. 59 NBC
The Lucy Show sr 10. 1. 62 CBS
The Lucy Show sr ret 9. 30. 63 CBS
The Lucy Show sr ret 9. 21. 64 CBS
The Lucy Show ep 1. 9. 67 CBS
The Lucy Show ep 1. 1. 68 CBS
The Lucy Show ep 2. 26. 68 CBS
Here's Lucy ep 12. 16. 68 CBS
Love American Style ep 12. 29. 69 ABC
Here's Lucy ep 1. 19. 70, 1. 26. 70 CBS
The Front Page sp 1. 31. 70 NN
Here's Lucy ep 2. 15. 71, 2. 22. 71 CBS
Getting Away from It All tf 1. 18. 72 ABC
Here's Lucy ep 2. 21. 72 CBS

VAN CLEEF, LEE
    Schlitz Playhouse of Stars ep Four Things He'd Do
        2. 5. 54 CBS
    Cavalcade of America ep Duel at the OK Corral 3. 9.
        54 ABC
    Man Behind the Badge ep The Case of the Desperate
        Moment 6. 25. 55 CBS
    Brave Eagle ep Shield of Honor 1. 11. 56 CBS
    Studio 57 ep Deadline 2. 26. 56 NN
    Wire Service ep The Night of August 7th 11. 1. 56
        ABC
    Crossroads ep Sky Pilot of the Cumberlands 11. 2. 56
        ABC
    Tales of Wells Fargo ep Alder Gulch 4. 8. 57 NBC
    Schlitz Playhouse of Stars ep The Blue Hotel 4. 12. 57
        CBS
    Trackdown ep The Town 12. 13. 57 CBS
    Colt .45 ep Dead Reckoning 1. 24. 58 ABC
    Rifleman ep The Deadly Wait ep 3. 24. 59 ABC
    Tombstone Territory ep The Hostage 5. 1. 59 ABC
    Yancy Derringer ep Outlaw at Liberty 5. 7. 59 CBS
    Real McCoys ep Grandpa Fights the Air Force 11.
        26. 59 ABC
    Hotel de Paree ep Sundance and The Man in Room
        Seven 2. 12. 60 CBS

Untouchables   ep   The Unhired Assassin   ep   2.25.60,
   3.3.60 ABC
Alaskans   ep   Peril at Caribou Crossing   2.28.60 ABC
Deputy   ep   Palace of Chance   5.21.60 NBC
Gunsmoke   ep   5.28.60 CBS
77 Sunset Strip   ep   The Attic   9.16.60 ABC
Lawman   ep   The Return of Owny O'Reilly   10.16.60
   ABC
Laramie   ep   .45 Calibre   11.15.60 NBC
Bonanza   ep   The Blood Line   12.31.60 NBC
Hawaiian Eye   ep   The Stanhope Brand   2.22.61 ABC
Maverick   ep   Red Dog   3.5.61 ABC
Rifleman   ep   The Clarence Bibs Story   4.14.61 ABC
Joey Bishop Show   ep   Double Exposure   2.7.62 NBC
Cheyenne   ep   One Evening in Abilene   3.19.62 ABC
Cheyenne   ep   Trouble Street   5.14.62 ABC
Rifleman   ep   Death Never Rides Alone   10.29.62 ABC
Have Gun Will Travel   ep   12.29.62 CBS
Ripcord   ep   The Money Mine   1.3.63 NBC
Dakota   ep   Thunder in Pleasant Valley   2.4.63 ABC
Have Gun Will Travel   ep   4.20.63 CBS
Destry   ep   Destry Has a Little Lamb   2.21.64 ABC
Rawhide   ep   Piney   10.9.64 CBS
Laredo   ep   Quarter Past Eleven   3.24.66 NBC
Gunsmoke   ep   4.23.66 CBS

VANDERBILT, GLORIA
   Kraft Theatre   ep   Dog in a Bush Tunnel   3.5.58 NBC

VAN DOREN, MAMIE
   Meet the Girls   pt   8.30.60 CBS

VAN DYKE, DICK
   Joe and Mabel   sr   9.20.55 CBS
   Joe and Mabel   sr ret   6.26.56 CBS
   The Phil Silvers Show   ep   Bilko's Cousin   1.28.58 CBS
   True Story   ep   The Imperfect Secretary   10.11.58 NBC
   U.S. Steel Hour   ep   Trap for a Stranger   2.25.59
      CBS
   Alfred Hitchcock Presents   ep   Craig's Will   3.6.60
      CBS
   New Comedy Showcase   ep   The Trouble with Richard
      8.22.60 CBS
   Dick Van Dyke Show   sr   10.3.61 CBS
   Dick Van Dyke Show   sr ret   9.26.62 CBS
   Dick Van Dyke Show   sr ret   9.25.63 CBS
   Dick Van Dyke Show   sr ret   9.23.64 CBS

Dick Van Dyke Show   sr ret   9.15.65 CBS
New Dick Van Dyke Show   sr   9.18.71 CBS
New Dick Van Dyke Show   sr   ret   9.17.72 CBS

VAN EYCK, PETER
   Your Play Time   ep   The Intolerable Portrait   9.3.55
      NBC
   Casablanca   ep   10.18.55 ABC
   Alfred Hitchcock Presents   ep   Safe Conduct   2.19.56
      CBS
   Casablanca   ep   4.24.56 ABC

VAN FLEET, JO
   Philco Playhouse   ep   The Thin Air   9.21.52 NBC
   U.S. Steel Hour   ep   Morning Star   3.2.54 ABC
   Suspense   ep   Before the Act   3.9.54 CBS
   The Mask   ep   Party Night   4.11.54 ABC
   Inner Sanctum   ep   Hour of Darkness   11.23.54 NN
   Robert Montgomery Presents   ep   Joe's Boy   1.24.55
      NBC
   Star Tonight   ep   Concerning Death   2.17.55 ABC
   Philco Playhouse   ep   Assassin   2.20.55 NBC
   Heidi   Sp   10.1.55 NBC
   Philco Playhouse   ep   A Business Proposition   10.23.
      55 NBC
   Alfred Hitchcock Presents   ep   Shopping for Death   1.
      29.56 CBS
   Desilu Playhouse   ep   The Crazy Hunter   12.29.58 CBS
   Alcoa Theatre   ep   30 Pieces of Silver   1.26.59 NBC
   Dupont Show of the Month   ep   The Human Comedy   3.
      28.59 CBS
   G.E. Theatre   ep   Disaster   11.1.59 CBS
   Play of the Week   ep   Volpone   3.7.60 NN
   Play of the Week   ep   Four by Tennessee Williams   2.
      6.61 NN
   Dupont Show of the Month   ep   The Night of the Storm
      3.21.61 CBS
   Alfred Hitchcock Presents   ep   Servant Problem   6.6.61
      CBS
   Thriller   ep   The Remarkable Mrs. Hawk   12.18.61
      NBC
   Frontier Circus   ep   The Courtship   2.15.62 CBS
   77 Sunset Strip   ep   Don't Wait for Me   11.8.63 ABC
   Route 66   ep   The Stone Guest   11.8.63 CBS
   Summer Playhouse   ep   Satan's Waitin'   9.12.64 CBS
   Kraft Suspense Theatre   ep   The World I Want to Know
      10.1.64 NBC

Cinderella Sp 2.22.66 CBS
Virginian ep Legacy of Hate 9.14.66 NBC
Experiment in TV ep Good Day 3.5.67 NBC
Bob Hope Chrysler Theatre ep Verdict for Terror
    3.29.67 NBC
Suspense ep 6.13.68 ABC
Wild, Wild West ep The Night of the Tycoons 3.28.
    69 CBS
Bonanza ep 1.25.70 NBC
Mod Squad ep A Is for Annie 10.15.70 ABC
N.E.T. Playhouse ep Paradise Lost 2.25.71, 3.4.71
    NN
Bonanza ep The Stillness Within 3.14.71 NBC
Medical Center ep 11.10.71 CBS
The Family Rico tf 9.12.72 CBS

VARCONI, VICTOR
Tele-Theatre ep Once a Gentleman 4.10.50 NBC
Summer Studio One ep The Roman Kid 9.3.53 CBS

VARSI, DIANA
Playhouse 90 ep The Dingaling Girl 2.26.59 CBS
Dr. Kildare ep A Sometime Distant Spring 3.21.66,
    3.22.66 NBC
The People tf 1.22.72 ABC

VAUGHN, ROBERT
Medic ep Black Friday 11.21.55 NBC
Big Town ep Marine Story 5.29.56 NBC
West Point ep The Operator and the Martinet 10.12.
    56 CBS
The Millionaire ep Story of Jay Powers 11.21.56
    CBS
Father Knows Best ep Betty Goes Steady 12.5.56
    NBC
Zane Grey Theatre ep Courage Is a Gun 12.14.56
    CBS
Telephone Time ep The Consort 1.27.57 CBS
Zane Grey ep A Gun Is for Killing 10.18.57 CBS
Tales of Wells Fargo ep Billy the Kid 10.21.57 NBC
Gunsmoke ep 11.9.57 CBS
Playhouse 90 ep The Troublemakers 11.21.57 CBS
Dragnet ep 5.1.58 NBC
Wagon Train ep The John Wilbot Story 6.11.58 NBC
Cheyenne ep Borrowed Glory 2.24.59 ABC
Playhouse 90 ep Made in Japan 3.5.59 CBS
Riverboat ep About Roger Mowbray 9.27.59 NBC

Lineup ep Prelude to Violence 11.4.59 CBS
Wichita Town ep Passage to the Enemy 12.2.59 NBC
Plainsman ep The Dude 12.3.59 NBC
Alcoa Theatre ep The Last Flight Out 1.25.60 NBC
Rebel ep Noblesse Oblige 2.14.60 ABC
Men into Space ep 2.17.60 CBS
Checkmate ep Interrupted Honeymoon 9.24.60 CBS
Laramie ep The Dark Trail 11.1.60 NBC
Garlund Touch ep The Awakening 11.18.60 CBS
June Allyson Show ep Emergency 12.8.60 CBS
Wagon Train ep The Roger Bigelow Story 12.21.60
  NBC
Stagecoach West ep Object: Matrimony 1.3.61 ABC
Thriller ep The Ordeal of Dr. Cordell 3.7.61 NBC
Malibu Run ep The Lanslide Adventure 5.10.61 CBS
Tales of Wells Fargo ep Treasure Coach 10.14.61
  NBC
Target: Corruptors ep To Wear a Badge 12.1.61
  ABC
Follow the Sun ep The Far Side of Nowhere 12.17.
  61 ABC
87th Precinct ep 12.18.61 NBC
Cain's Hundred ep The Debasers 1.16.62 NBC
Dick Powell Theatre ep The Boston Terrier 4.10.62
  NBC
Mystery Theatre ep Death of a Dream 6.20.62 NBC
Bonanza ep The Way Station 10.28.62 NBC
The Eleventh Hour ep The Blues My Baby Gave to
  Me 12.12.62 NBC
G.E. Theatre ep Defendant: Clarence Darrow 1.13.
  63 CBS
Empire ep No Small Wars 2.5.63 NBC
Virginian ep If You Have Tears 2.13.63 NBC
Untouchables ep The Charlie Argos Story 4.16.63
  ABC
77 Sunset Strip ep Your Fortune for a Penny 5.31.
  63 ABC
Boston Terrier pt 6.11.63 ABC
Lieutenant sr 9.14.63 NBC
The Eleventh Hour ep The Silence of Good Men 10.
  9.63 NBC
The Man from U.N.C.L.E.   sr 9.22.64 NBC
The Man from U.N.C.L.E.   sr ret 9.17.65 NBC
The Man from U.N.C.L.E.   sr ret 9.16.66 NBC
The Girl from U.N.C.L.E.   ep The Mother Muffin Af-
  fair 9.27.66 NBC
The Man from U.N.C.L.E.   sr ret 9.11.67 NBC
Protectors sr 9.17.72 CBS

VERA-ELLEN
 Ford Theatre ep The Man Across the Hall 3. 20. 57
 ABC

VERDON, GWEN
 Goodyear Playhouse ep Native Dancer 3. 28. 54 NBC
 N. E. T. Playhouse ep Foul 11. 26. 70 NN
 Love American Style ep 9. 29. 72 ABC

VERDUGO, ELENA
 Meet Millie sr 10. 25. 52 CBS
 Cavalcade of America ep Arrow and the Bow 1. 7. 53
 NBC
 Meet Millie sr ret 3. 16. 54 CBS
 Wanted Dead or Alive ep 2. 7. 59 CBS
 Bob Cummings Show ep 6. 2. 59 NBC
 Route 66 ep Kiss the Maiden All Forlorn 4. 13. 62
 CBS
 New Phil Silvers Show sr 9. 28. 63 CBS
 Redigo sr 9. 24. 63 NBC
 77 Sunset Strip ep Paper Chase 12. 27. 63 ABC
 Many Happy Returns sr 9. 21. 64 CBS
 Mona McCluskey ep 10. 28. 65 NBC
 Mona McCluskey ep 2. 17. 66 NBC
 Iron Horse ep 1. 23. 67 ABC
 Ironside ep The Sacrifice 10. 3. 68 NBC
 Daniel Boone ep 1. 30. 69 NBC
 Marcus Welby, M. D. tf 3. 26. 69 ABC
 Marcus Welby, M. D. sr 9. 23. 69 ABC
 Love American Style ep Love and the Modern Wife
 10. 27. 69 ABC
 Marcus Welby, M. D. sr ret 9. 22. 70 ABC
 Marcus Welby, M. D. sr ret 9. 14. 71 ABC
 Marcus Welby, M. D. sr ret 9. 12. 72 ABC

VERNE, KAREN
 Fireside Theatre ep Member of the Jury 10. 5. 54
 NBC

VICKERS, MARTHA
 G. E. Theatre ep That Other Sunlight 3. 14. 54 CBS
 Ford Theatre ep The Last 30 Minutes 3. 18. 54 NBC
 Ford Theatre ep Night Visitor 4. 29. 54 NBC
 G. E. Theatre ep The Eye of the Beholder 7. 25. 54
 CBS
 Fireside Theatre ep The Indiscreet Mrs. Jarvis 1.
 4. 55 NBC

Fireside Theatre   ep   No Place to Live   2. 15. 54 NBC
The Whistler   ep   Sleep My Pretty One   10. 9. 55 NN
The Millionaire   ep   The Ed Murdock Story   4. 25. 56
   CBS
Perry Mason   ep   The Case of the Jaded Joker   2. 21.
   59 CBS
Rebel   ep   The Rattler   3. 13. 60 ABC
Rebel   ep   Vindication   12. 4. 60 ABC

VILLELLA, EDWARD
   Brigadoon   Sp   10. 15. 66 ABC
   The Nutcracker   Sp   12. 20. 68 CBS

VOIGHT, JON
   Naked City   ep   Alive and Still a Second Lieutenant   3.
      6. 63 ABC
   Defenders   ep   The Brother Killers   5. 25. 63 CBS
   Gunsmoke   ep   12. 3. 66 CBS
   Coronet Blue   ep   The Rebel   6. 19. 67 CBS
   Gunsmoke   ep   11. 13. 67 CBS
   N. Y. P. D.   ep   12. 12. 67 ABC
   Gunsmoke   ep   3. 17. 69 CBS

VON FURSTENBERG, BETSY
   Pulitzer Prize Playhouse   ep   Second Threshhold   4. 27.
      51 ABC
   Armstrong Circle Theatre   ep   The Checkerboard Heart
      3. 17. 53 NBC
   TV Sound Stage   ep   No Scar   7. 24. 53 NBC
   Medallion Theatre   ep   Gran'ma Rebel   10. 31. 53 CBS
   Omnibus   ep   The Renaissance   10. 9. 55 CBS
   Appointment with Adventure   ep   All Through the Night
      2. 5. 56 CBS
   Robert Montgomery Presents   ep   Don't Do Me Any
      Favors   4. 30. 56 NBC
   Kraft Theatre   ep   Most Blessed Woman   1. 23. 57 NBC
   Have Gun Will Travel   ep   2. 22. 58 CBS
   Alfred Hitchcock Presents   ep   Disappearing Trick   4.
      6. 58 CBS
   Playhouse 90   ep   Word From a Sealed-Off Box   10. 30.
      58 CBS
   Alfred Hitchcock Presents   ep   The Diamond Necklace
      2. 22. 59 CBS
   U.S. Steel Hour   ep   Trouble-In-Law   4. 8. 59 CBS
   Alcoa Presents   ep   Reunion   11. 24. 59 ABC
   Play of the Week   ep   Crime of Passion   11. 30. 59 NN
   The Fifth Column   Sp   1. 29. 60 CBS

Mystery Show   ep   The Machine Calls It Murder   5.29.
  60 NBC
Alcoa Presents   ep   Reunion   7.19.60 ABC
Adventures in Paradise   ep   The Big Surf   12.5.60
  ABC
Golden Show   ep   Tonight in Samarkand   3.24.62 ĊBS
Defenders   ep   The Last Illusion   3.9.63 CBS
Your Money or Your Wife   tf   12.19.72 CBS

VON SYDOW, MAX
The Diary of Anne Frank   Sp   11.26.67 ABC
N.E.T. Playhouse   ep   A Search for Strinberg   3.23.72
  NN

-W-

WAGNER, ROBERT
20th Century-Fox Hour   ep   The Ox-Bow Incident   11.
  2.55 CBS
20th Century-Fox Hour   ep   Gun in His Hand   4.4.56
  CBS
Eleventh Hour   ep   And Man Created Vanity   10.23.63
  NBC
Bob Hope Chrysler Theatre   ep   The Enemy on the
  Beach   1.5.66 NBC
Bob Hope Chrysler Theatre   ep   Runaway Bay   5.25.66
  NBC
How I Spent My Summer Vacation   tf   1.7.67 NBC
It Takes a Thief   sr   1.9.68 ABC
It Takes a Thief   sr ret   9.24.68 ABC
It Takes a Thief   sr ret   9.25.69 ABC
Name of the Game   10.30.69 NBC
City Beneath the Sea   tf   1.25.71 NBC
Name of the Game   ep   The Man Who Killed a Ghost
  1.29.71 NBC
The Cable Car Mystery   tf   11.19.71 CBS
Killer by Night   tf   1.7.72 CBS
Madame Sin   tf   1.15.72 ABC
Streets of San Francisco   ep   9.16.72 ABC

WALBURN, RAYMOND
Lux Video Theatre   ep   Christmas in July   9.9.54 NBC
U.S. Steel Hour   ep   Be My Guest   8.27.58 CBS

WALKER, CLINT
    Cheyenne   sr   9.20.55 ABC
    Cheyenne   sr ret   fall, 1956 ABC
    Cheyenne   sr ret   fall, 1957 ABC
    Cheyenne   sr ret   fall, 1958 ABC
    Cheyenne   sr ret   fall, 1959 ABC
    Cheyenne   sr ret   fall, 1960 ABC
    Maverick   ep   Hadley's Hunters   9.25.60 ABC
    Cheyenne   sr ret   9.25.61 ABC
    Cheyenne   sr ret   9.24.62 ABC
    77 Sunset Strip   ep   "5"   9.27.63 ABC
    Kraft Suspense Theatre   ep   Portrait of an Unknown Man
        4.16.64 NBC
    The Lucy Show   ep   11.15.65 CBS
    Yuma   tf   3.21.71 ABC
    Hardcase   tf   2.1.72 ABC
    The Bounty Man   tf   10.31.72 ABC

WALKER, NANCY
    Medallion Theatre   ep   Voyage Back   2.20.54 CBS
    Playwrights '56   ep   Nick and Letty   6.5.56 NBC
    Kraft Theatre   ep   Code of the Corner   1.15.58 NBC
    Play of the Week   ep   The World of Sholom Aleichem
        12.14.59 NN
    Play of the Week   ep   The Girls in 509   4.18.60 NN
    Tab Hunter Show   ep   I Love a Marine   10.30.60 NBC
    Mary Tyler Moore Show   ep   10.24.70 CBS
    Love American Style   ep   2.5.71 ABC
    Mary Tyler Moore Show   ep   3.27.71 CBS
    McMillan and Wife   sr   9.29.71 NBC
    Keep the Faith   pt   4.14.72 CBS
    Medical Center   ep   9.20.72 CBS
    McMillan and Wife   sr ret   9.24.72 NBC
    Bridget Loves Bernie   ep   11.18.72 CBS
    Every Man Needs One   tf   12.13.72 ABC

WALKER JR. , ROBERT
    Golden Showcase   ep   The Picture of Dorian Gray   12.
        6.61 CBS
    Route 66   ep   Across Walnuts and Wine   11.2.62 CBS
    Ben Casey   ep   And Even Death Shall Die   11.19.62
        ABC
    Naked City   ep   Dust Devil on a Quiet Street   11.28.62
        ABC
    Dupont Show of the Month   ep   Mutiny   12.2.62 NBC
    Eleventh Hour   ep   Try to Keep Alive Until Next Tues-
        day   4.17.63 NBC

Dr. Kildare   ep   Quid Pro Quo   3.26.64 NBC
Bob Hope Chrysler Theatre   ep   The Command   5.22.64
   NBC
Defenders   ep   Eyewitness   1.14.65 CBS
Mr. Novak   ep   The Student Who Never Was   3.30.65
   NBC
Big Valley   ep   11.3.65 ABC
12 O'Clock High   ep   Underground   1.17.66 ABC
Quantico   ep   1.30.66 ABC
Trials of O'Brien   ep   The Only Game in Town   3.18.
   66 CBS
Star Trek   ep   Charlie "X"   9.15.66 NBC
Combat   ep   9.27.66 ABC
Road West   ep   10.25.66 NBC
12 O'Clock High   ep   11.4.66 ABC
Time Tunnel   ep   2.10.67 ABC
Invaders   ep   4.11.67 ABC
Bonanza   ep   10.29.67 NBC
FBI   ep   3.17.68 ABC

WALLACE, JEAN
   Schlitz Playhouse of Stars   ep   So Help Me   8.8.52
   G.E. Theatre   ep   The Blond Dog   3.6.65 NBC

WALLACE, MIKE
   Suspense   ep   7.7.53 CBS
   Summer Studio One   ep   The Roman Kid   8.3.53 CBS
   Studio One   ep   For the Defense   6.27.55 CBS

WALLACH, ELI
   Lights Out   ep   Rappaccini's Daughter   9.24.51 NBC
   Summer Theatre   ep   Stan, The Killer   9.1.52 CBS
   The Web   ep   Deadlock   9.28.52 CBS
   Philco Playhouse   ep   The Baby   9.13.53 NBC
   Goodyear Playhouse   ep   The Brownstone   1.31.54 NBC
   Philco Playhouse   ep   Shadow of the Champ   3.20.55
      NBC
   G.E. Theatre   ep   Mr. Blue Ocean   5.1.55 CBS
   Philco Playhouse   ep   The Outsiders   9.18.55 NBC
   Kaiser Aluminum Hour   ep   A Fragile Affair   9.28.56
   Hallmark Hall of Fame   ep   The Lark   2.10.57 NBC
   Studio One   ep   The Man Who Wasn't Himself   5.20.57
      CBS
   Seven Lively Arts   ep   The World of Nick Adams   11.
      10.57 CBS
   Climax   ep   Albert Anastasia   2.27.58 CBS
   Jewish Appeals Special   ep   Where Is Thy Brother?

5. 18. 58 NBC
Playhouse 90   ep   The Plot to Kill Stalin   9. 25. 58 CBS
Desilu Playhouse   ep   My Father, the Fool   11. 3. 58
   CBS
Shirley Temple's Story Book   ep   The Emperor's New
   Clothes   11. 25. 58 NBC
Playhouse 90   ep   For Whom the Bells Toll   3. 12. 59,
   3. 19. 59 CBS
Desilu Playhouse   ep   My Father the Fool   6. 1. 59 CBS
Sunday Showcase   ep   The Margaret Bourke-White Story
   1. 3. 60 NBC
Goodyear Theatre   ep   Birthright   1. 18. 60 NBC
Play of the Week   ep   Lullaby   1. 18. 60 NN
Robert Herridge Theatre   ep   Hope Is the Thing with
   Feathers   9. 22. 60 CBS
Naked City   ep   Death of Princes   10. 12. 60 ABC
Outlaws   ep   A Bit of Glory   2. 1. 62 NBC
Naked City   ep   A Run for the Money   3. 14. 62 ABC
Dick Powell Theatre   ep   Tomorrow the Man   10. 2. 62
   NBC
The Poppy Is Also a Flower   tf   4. 22. 66 ABC
Batman   ep   Ice Spy   3. 29. 67, 3. 30. 67 ABC
CBS Playhouse   ep   Dear Friends   12. 6. 67 CBS
Young Lawyers   ep   1. 20. 71 ABC
N. E. T. Playhouse   ep   Paradise Lost   2. 25. 71, 3. 4. 71
   NN
Hollywood Television Theatre   ep   The Typists   10. 10.
   71 NN

WALSTON, RAY
Studio One   ep   The Hero   7. 26. 54 CBS
Hallmark Hall of Fame   ep   There Shall Be No Night
   3. 17. 57 NBC
Playhouse 90   ep   Shadows Tremble   10. 23. 58 CBS
Ellery Queen   ep   The Murder Comes to You Live   6. 5.
   59 NBC
The Killers   Sp   11. 19. 59 CBS
Outlaws   ep   Beat the Drums Slowly   10. 20. 60 NBC
Play of the Week   ep   Uncle Harry   12. 5. 60 NN
Aquanauts   ep   The Armored-Truck Adventure   2. 15. 61
   CBS
Americans   ep   The Bounty Jumpers   4. 17. 61 NBC
Outlaws   ep   The Cut Pups   10. 26. 61 NBC
Target: Corruptors   ep   Touch of Evil   11. 10. 61 ABC
Adventures in Paradise   ep   A Bride for the Captain
   3. 11. 62 ABC
Saints and Sinners   ep   Judgment in Jazz Alley   10. 8. 62
   NBC

Ben Casey   ep   The White Ones Are Dolphins   3.11.63
    ABC
Going My Way   ep   The Reformation of Willie   3.27.63
    ABC
My Favorite Martian   sr   9.29.63 CBS
Satan's Waitin'   pt   9.12.64 CBS
My Favorite Martian   sr ret   9.27.64 CBS
My Favorite Martian   sr ret   9.12.65 CBS
Wild, Wild West   ep   10.27.67 CBS
Garrison's Gorillas   ep   12.5.67 ABC
Custer   ep   Breakout   11.1.67 ABC
Love American Style   ep   1.12.70 ABC
Mod Squad   ep   A Double for Danger   2.23.71 ABC
Ironside   ep   Ring of Prayer   10.12.71 NBC
Love American Style   ep   1.21.72 ABC
Mission Impossible   ep   10.14.72 CBS

WALTER, JESSICA
Route 66   ep   A Long Way from St. Louis   12.6.63 CBS
East Side/West Side   ep   Take Sides with the Sun   3.16.
    64 CBS
Alfred Hitchcock Theatre   ep   The Ordeal of Mrs. Snow
    4.17.64 CBS
Ben Casey   ep   August Is the Month Before Christmas
    9.14.64 ABC
Flipper   ep   9.19.64 NBC
Nurses/Doctors   ep   The Suspect   ep   9.29.64, 10.6.
    64 CBS
Rogues   ep   House of Cards   10.11.64 NBC
For the People   sr   1.31.65 CBS
Defenders   ep   The Unwritten Law   ep   2.4.65 CBS
Trials of O'Brien   ep   Picture Me a Murder   11.27.65
    CBS
Fugitive   ep   The White Knight   ep   3.22.66 ABC
Pursue and Destroy   pt   8.14.66 ABC
FBI   ep   2.12.67 ABC
Kiss Me, Kate   Sp   3.25.68 ABC
FBI   ep   10.20.68 ABC
Name of the Game   ep   The Ordeal   11.22.68 NBC
It Takes a Thief   ep   3.18.69 ABC
The Immortal   tf   9.30.69 ABC
Then Came Bronson   ep   Where Will the Trumpets Be
    10.15.69 NBC
Three's a Crowd   tf   12.2.69 ABC
Mannix   ep   Who Is Sylvia   2.7.70 CBS
Mission Impossible   ep   3.1.70 CBS
Most Deadly Game   ep   Breakdown   10.31.70 ABC

Love American Style ep Love and the Kidnaper 1.1.
71 ABC
Medical Center ep Web of Darkness 1.13.71 CBS
Men at Law ep Let the Doer Beware 3.17.71 CBS
Name of the Game ep The Showdown 3.19.71 NBC
Hollywood Television Theatre ep Montserrat 3.21.71
NN
Marcus Welby, M.D. ep The House of Alquist 3.30.
71 ABC
Love American Style ep 11.12.71 ABC
Alias Smith and Jones ep 12.16.71 ABC
FBI ep 12.19.71 ABC
Mannix ep Moving Target 1.19.72 CBS
Sixth Sense ep The Heart That Wouldn't Stay Buried
1.22.72 ABC
Women in Chains tf 1.25.72 ABC
Banyon ep 9.22.72 NBC
Cannon ep 10.4.72 CBS
Home for the Holidays tf 11.28.72 ABC
Medical Center ep A Game for One Player 12.13.72
CBS

WARFIELD, WILLIAM
Hallmark Hall of Fame ep The Green Pastures 3.23.
59 NBC

WARNER, DAVID
War of the Roses Sp 2.13.66, 2.20.66, 2.27.66 NN

WASHBOURNE, MONA
Home Sp 11.29.71 NN

WASHBURN, BEVERLY
The Cinema Theatre ep Hired Girl 6.24.52 NN
A Letter to Loretta ep Big Little Lie 1.24.54 NBC
Cavalcade of America ep Crazy Judah 4.13.54 ABC
Ray Milland Show ep 12.23.54 CBS
Professional Father sr 1.8.54 CBS
Fireside Theatre ep Marked for Death 2.22.55 NBC
Treasury Men in Action ep The Case of the Swindler's
Gold 2.24.55 ABC
Loretta Young Show ep Katy 10.23.55 NBC
The Millionaire ep The Rita Hanley Story 3.14.56
CBS
Studio 57 ep The Magic Glass 3.18.56 NN
Four Star Playhouse ep Autumn Carousel 4.12.56
CBS

Telephone Time   ep   The Man with the Beard   4.15.56
CBS
Star Stage   ep   The Guardian   5.11.56 NBC
Telephone Time   ep   The Key   7.15.56 CBS
Loretta Young Show   ep   Take Care of My Child   11.4.
56 NBC
G.E. Theatre   ep   The Road That Led Afar   11.25.56
CBS
Zane Grey Theatre   ep   Stars Over Texas   12.28.56
CBS
Schlitz Playhouse of Stars   ep   One Left Over   2.1.57
CBS
Jane Wyman Theatre   ep   2.19.57 NBC
20th Century-Fox Hour   ep   Men in Her Life   4.17.57
CBS
Wagon Train   ep   The Willy Moran Story   9.18.57 NBC
Shirley Temple's Story Book   ep   Rip Van Winkle   5.8.
58 NBC
G.E. Theatre   ep   Stopover   4.27.58 CBS
Alcoa Presents   ep   Premonition   3.10.59 ABC
Law and Mr. Jones   ep   A Question of Guilt   12.16.60
ABC
Best of the Post   ep   Martha   2.18.61 ABC
Father Knows Best   ep   The Spelling Bee   4.4.61 CBS
New Loretta Young Show   sr   9.24.62 CBS
77 Sunset Strip   ep   Lovers' Lane   1.3.64 ABC
Gidget   ep   Chivalry Is Not Dead   11.10.65 ABC
Patty Duke Show   ep   12.15.65 ABC
Gidget   ep   3.10.66 ABC
Star Trek   ep   The Deadly Years   12.8.67 NBC

WATERMAN, DENNIS
Fair Exchange   sr   9.21.62 CBS
Fair Exchange   sr ret   9.28.63 CBS
Journey to the Unknown   ep   Eve   9.26.68 ABC

WATERS, ETHEL
Beulah   sr   10.3.50 ABC
Favorite Playhouse   ep   Speaking to Hannah   1.23.55
CBS
Climax   ep   The Dance   6.30.55 CBS
G.E. Theatre   ep   Winner by Decision   11.6.55 CBS
Playwrights '56   ep   The Sound and the Fury   12.6.55
NBC
Matinee Theatre   ep   Sing for Me   10.21.57 NBC
Route 66   ep   Good Night, Sweet Blues   10.6.61 CBS
Great Adventures   ep   Go Down, Moses   11.1.63 CBS
Owen Marshall   ep   Run, Carol, Run   1.20.72 ABC

WATSON, DOUGLAS
 Starlight Theatre   ep   The Sire de Maletroit's Door   4.
    30.50 CBS
 Masterpiece Playhouse   ep   Richard III   7.30.50 NBC
 Kraft Theatre   ep   Brief Candle   5.2.51 NBC
 Robert Montgomery Presents   ep   The Young and Beau-
    tiful   12.10.56 NBC

WATSON, LUCILE
 Armstrong Circle Theatre   ep   The Chair   6.27.50 NBC
 Airflyte Theatre   ep   The Case of the Calico Dog   1.25.
    51 CBS
 Armstrong Circle Theatre   ep   The Partnership   3.6.51
    NBC
 Pulitzer Prize Playhouse   ep   Years of Grace   1.30.52
    ABC
 Studio One   ep   A Favor for a Friend   1.25.64 CBS

WAYNE, DAVID
 Studio One   ep   The Dreams of Jasper Hornby   3.6.50
    CBS
 Omnibus   ep   The Sojourner   12.27.53 CBS
 Norby   sr   1.5.55 NBC
 Producers Showcase   ep   Darkness at Noon   5.2.55 NBC
 Alcoa Hour   ep   Morning's at Seven   1.14.56 NBC
 Ruggles of Red Gap   Sp   2.3.57 NBC
 Alfred Hitchcock Presents   ep   One More Mile to Go
    4.7.57 CBS
 Suspicion   ep   Heartbeat   11.11.57 NBC
 Playhouse   ep   The Jet-Propelled Couch   11.14.57 CBS
 Frank Sinatra Show   ep   The Feeling Is Mutual   12.27.
    57 ABC
 Strawberry Blonde   Sp   10.18.59 NBC
 Twilight Zone   ep   Escape Clause   11.6.59   CBS
 The Devil and Daniel Webster   Sp   2.14.60 NBC
 Overland Trail   ep   Escort Detail   5.22.60 NBC
 Our American Heritage   ep   Millionaire's Mite   4.10.60
    NBC
 Outlaws   ep   No More Pencils--No More Books   3.16.
    61 NBC
 Outlaws   ep   Roly   11.23.61 NBC
 Alcoa Premiere   ep   Delbert, Texas   12.12.61 ABC
 Route 66   ep   Aren't You Surprised to See Me   2.16.62
    CBS
 Golden Showcase   ep   The Devil and Daniel Webster   4.
    30.62 CBS
 U.S. Steel Hour   ep   The White Lie   10.3.62 CBS

Hallmark Hall of Fame   ep   Teahouse of the August
   Moon   10. 26. 62 NBC
Alfred Hitchcock Theatre   ep   The Thirty-First of Feb-
   ruary   1. 4. 63 CBS
Sam Benedict   ep   The Boiling Point   1. 12. 63 NBC
Dick Powell Theatre   ep   Apples Don't Fall Far   2. 19.
   63 NBC
Virginian   ep   The Small Parade   2. 20. 63 NBC
Channing   ep   The Last Testament of Buddy Crown   12.
   18. 63 ABC
Mr. Broadway   ep   Pay Now, Die Later   12. 26. 64 CBS
Hallmark Hall of Fame   ep   Lamp at Midnight   4. 27. 66
   NBC
Bob Hope Chrysler Theatre   ep   Holloway's Daughter
   5. 11. 66 NBC
Batman   ep   1. 4. 67, 1. 5. 67 ABC
CBS Playhouse   ep   Dear Friends   12. 6. 67 CBS
Arsenic and Old Lace   Sp   4. 2. 69 ABC
World of Disney   ep   The Boy Who Stole the Elephants
   9. 20. 70, 9. 27. 70 NBC
Matt Lincoln   ep   11. 12. 70 ABC
Name of the Game   ep   A Sister from Napoli   1. 8. 71
   NBC
The Good Life   pt   3. 22. 71 NBC
Men at Law   ep   3. 31. 71 CBS
Cade's County   ep   One Small Acceptable Death   1. 16. 72
   CBS
Streets of San Francisco   ep   11. 25. 72 ABC

WAYNE, JOHN
   I Love Lucy   ep   10. 10. 55 CBS
   Screen Directors Playhouse   ep   Rookie of the Year   12.
      7. 55 NBC
   The Lucy Show   ep   11. 21. 66 CBS

WEAVER, DENNIS
   Schlitz Playhouse of Stars   ep   Underground   1. 21. 55
      CBS
   Dragnet   ep   1. 27. 55 NBC
   Gunsmoke   sr   9. 10. 55 CBS
   Big Town   ep   Crime in the City Room   5. 15. 56 NBC
   Gunsmoke   sr ret   fall, 1956 CBS
   Gunsmoke   sr ret   fall, 1957 CBS
   Climax   ep   Burst of Fire   1. 30. 58 CBS
   Playhouse 90   ep   The Dungeon   4. 17. 58 CBS
   Gunsmoke   sr ret   fall, 1958 CBS
   Gunsmoke   sr ret   fall, 1959 CBS
   Alfred Hitchcock Presents   ep   Insomnia   5. 8. 60 CBS

Gunsmoke   sr ret   fall, 1960 CBS
Twilight Zone   ep   Sandow Play   5.15.61 CBS
Gunsmoke   sr ret   9.30.61 CBS
Gunsmoke   sr ret   9.15.62 CBS
Gunsmoke   sr ret   fall, 1963 CBS
Kentucky Jones   sr   9.19.64 NBC
Dr. Kildare   ep   A Reverence for Life   4.29.65 NBC
Combat   ep   The Farmer   10.12.65 ABC
World of Disney   ep   Showdown with the Sundown Kid
    10.23.66, 10.30.66 NBC
Gentle Ben   sr   9.19.67 CBS
Gentle Ben   sr ret   9.29.68 CBS
Judd for the Defense   ep   The View from the Ivy Tower
    3.7.69 ABC
Name of the Game   ep   Play Till It Hurts   10.31.69
    NBC
Virginian   ep   2.4.70 NBC
McCloud   tf   2.17.70 NBC
McCloud   sr   9.16.70 NBC
The Forgotten Man   tf   9.14.71 ABC
McCloud   sr ret   9.22.71 CBS
McCloud   sr ret   10.1.72 CBS
Rolling Man   tf   10.4.72 ABC

WEAVER, FRITZ
Omnibus   ep   She Stoops to Conquer   11.20.55 CBS
U.S. Steel Hour   ep   We Must Kill Toni   9.12.56 CBS
Studio One   ep   The Playwright and the Star   4.8.57
    CBS
Dupont Show of the Month   ep   Beyond This Place   11.
    25.57 CBS
Omnibus   ep   Moment of Truth   2.23.58 NBC
Armstrong Circle Theatre   ep   The New Class   2.5.58
    CBS
Dupont Show of the Month   ep   A Tale of Two Cities   3.
    27.58 CBS
U.S. Steel Hour   ep   Little Tin God   4.22.59 CBS
Playhouse 90   ep   Out of Dust   5.21.59 CBS
Twilight Zone   ep   Third from the Sun   1.8.60 CBS
U.S. Steel Hour   ep   The Devil Makes Sunday   1.25.61
    CBS
Dupont Show of the Month   ep   The Night of the Storm
    3.21.61 CBS
Family Classics   ep   Jane Eyre   4.27.61 CBS
Twilight Zone   ep   The Obsolete Man   6.2.61 CBS
Asphalt Jungle   ep   The Dark Night   9.17.61 ABC
Defenders   ep   The Riot   10.7.61 CBS

New Breed ep Death of a Ghost 10.17.61 ABC
Power and the Glory Sp 10.29.61 CBS
Nurses ep The Seeing Heart 1.2.64 CBS
Espionage ep Medal for a Turned Coat 1.15.64 NBC
Great Adventures ep Escape 4.17.64 CBS
The Man from U.N.C.L.E. ep The Vulcan Affair 9.
  22.64 NBC
Rogues ep The Stefani Dowry 9.27.64 NBC
Rawhide ep Damon's Road 11.13.64, 11.20.64 CBS
12 O'Clock High ep The Hours Before Dawn 11.13.
  64 ABC
Cain's Hundred ep The Manipulators 1.30.62 NBC
U.S. Steel Hour ep The Duchess and the Mugs 12.
  26.62 CBS
Dr. Kildare ep The Thing Speaks for Itself 1.10.62
  NBC
Defenders ep The Traitor 2.16.63 CBS
Fugitive ep A Taste of Tomorrow 4.12.66 ABC
Showcase ep The Good Lieutenant 6.5.66 NN
Mission Impossible ep 10.1.66 CBS
Combat ep The Chapel at Able-Five 10.1.66 ABC
Experiment in Television ep The Questions 4.9.67
  NBC
The Crucible Sp 5.4.67 CBS
Room 222 ep We Hold These Truths 1.28.67 ABC
The Borgia Stick tf 2.25.67 NBC
Mission Impossible ep 11.21.67 CBS
Invaders ep 11.28.67 ABC
Big Valley ep 12.4.67 ABC
Gentle Ben ep 2.25.68 CBS
N.Y.P.D. ep Nothing Is Real but the Dead 3.12.68
  ABC
FBI ep 4.28.68 ABC
CBS Playhouse ep The People Next Door 10.15.68
  CBS
Mannix ep Edge of the Knife 11.9.68 CBS
Outcasts ep The Man from Bennington 12.16.68 ABC
Felony Squad ep Conspiracy of Power 1.10.69, 1.17.
  69 ABC
Big Valley ep 3.10.69 ABC
Mission Impossible ep 4.13.69 CBS
FBI ep The Challenge 11.2.69 ABC
Ironside ep Ransom 2.19.70 NBC
Berlin Affair tf 11.2.70 NBC
Dan August ep Prognosis 4.1.71 ABC
Mission Impossible ep 11.6.71 CBS
Cannon ep The Nowhere Man 12.14.71 CBS

Owen Marshall   ep   3.2.72 ABC
Heat of Anger   tf   3.3.72 CBS
Hunter   tf   3.10.72 CBS
Banyon   ep   10.6.72 NBC
Playhouse New York   ep   Antigone   10.7.72 NN
Mod Squad   ep   11.30.72 ABC

WEBB, JACK
Dragnet   sr   12.16.51 NBC
Dragnet   sr ret   fall, 1952 NBC
Dragnet   sr ret   fall, 1953 NBC
Dragnet   sr ret   fall, 1954 NBC
Dragnet   sr ret   9.1.55 NBC
G.E. True   sh/sr   9.30.62 CBS
Dragnet   sr   1.12.67 NBC
Dragnet   sr ret   fall, 1967 NBC
Dragnet   sr ret   9.19.68 NBC
Dragnet   tf   1.27.69 NBC
Dragnet   sr ret   9.18.69 NBC
Partners   ep   12.18.71 NBC

WEBB, RICHARD
The Web   ep   Journey by Night   10.25.50 CBS
Studio One   ep   The Last Cruise   11.13.50 CBS
Suspense   ep   The Whispering Killer   11.25.52 CBS
The Web   ep   The Beast   1.11.53 CBS
Broadway Television Theatre   ep   Guest in the House   2.23.53 NN
Broadway Television Theatre   ep   The Kick-In   3.16.53 NN
The Web   ep   Somewhere in Korea   5.3.53 CBS
Ford Theatre   ep   As the Flame Dies   11.19.53 CBS
Captain Midnight   sr   9.4.54 CBS
One Man Missing   ep   6.9.55 NBC
Captain Midnight   sr ret   10.1.55 CBS
Screen Directors Playhouse   ep   Want Ad Wedding   11.2.55 NBC
Loretta Young Show   ep   Across the Plaza   11.27.55 NBC
Ford Theatre   ep   Exclusive   4.3.57 ABC
Ford Theatre   ep   Miller's Millions   5.22.57 ABC
Maverick   ep   The Long Hunt   10.20.57 ABC
Colt .45   Dead Reckoning   1.24.58 ABC
Jefferson Drum   ep   Wheel of Fortune   6.27.58 NBC
U.S. Border Patrol   sr   5.26.59 ABC
Alaskans   ep   Calico   5.22.60 ABC
Cheyenne   ep   Two Trails to Santa Fe   11.28.60 ABC

My Sister Eileen   ep   Aunt Harriet's Way   3.1.61 CBS
My Sister Eileen   ep   Ruth's Fella   3.8.61 CBS
Rawhide   ep   Little Fishes   11.24.61 CBS
Cheyenne   ep   The Bad Penny   3.12.62 ABC
Cheyenne   ep   Wanted for the Murder of Cheyenne Bodie
    12.10.62 ABC
Saints and Sinners   ep   New Lead Berlin   1.28.63 NBC
Death Valley Days   ep   The Peacemaker   11.2.63 ABC
Death Valley Days   ep   Measure of a Man   11.16.63
    ABC
Breaking Point   ep   And If Thy Hand Offends Thee   1.
    13.64 ABC
Daniel Boone   ep   12.14.67 NBC
Smith Family   ep   10.13.71 ABC

WEISSMULLER, JOHNNY
    Jungle Jim   sr   10.14.55 NBC

WELCH, RAQUEL
    Wendy and Me   ep   2.1.65 ABC
    Baileys of Balboa   ep   2.11.65 CBS
    Bewitched   ep   2.18.65 ABC
    Bracken's World   ep   Fade-In   9.19.69 NBC

WELD, TUESDAY
    Ozzie and Harriet   ep   The Other Guy's Girl   4.8.59
        ABC
    Dobie Gillis   sr   9.29.59 CBS
    77 Sunset Strip   ep   Secret Island   12.4.59 ABC
    Ozzie and Harriet   ep   Rick Gets Even   12.16.59 ABC
    77 Sunset Strip   ep   Condor's Lair   2.12.60 ABC
    The Millionaire   ep   Millionaire Katherine Boland   4.20.
        60 CBS
    Tab Hunter Show   ep   The Doll in the Bathing Suit   11.
        13.60 NBC
    Zane Grey Theatre   ep   The Mormons   12.15.60 CBS
    Follow the Sun   ep   The Highest Wall   10.1.61 ABC
    Bus Stop   ep   Cherie   11.12.61 ABC
    Dick Powell Theatre   ep   A Time to Die   1.9.62 NBC
    Adventures in Paradise   ep   The Velvet Trap   1.21.62
        ABC
    Naked City   ep   A Case Study of Two Savages   2.7.62
        ABC
    Dick Powell Theatre   ep   Run Till It's Dark   10.9.62
        NBC
    Eleventh Hour   ep   Something Crazy's Going on in the
        Back Room   4.3.63 NBC

Dupont Show of the Month   ep   The Legend of Lylah
    Claire   5.19.63 NBC
The Greatest Show on Earth   ep   Silent Love, Secret
    Love   9.24.63 ABC
Mr. Broadway   ep   Keep an Eye on Emily   9.26.64
    CBS
Fugitive   ep   Dark Corner   11.10.64 ABC
The Crucible   Sp   5.4.67 CBS
Cimarron Strip   ep   1.18.68 CBS

WELLES, ORSON
    Omnibus   ep   King Lear   10.18.53   CBS
    Ford Star Jubilee   ep   Twentieth Century   4.7.56 CBS
    I Love Lucy   ep   10.15.56 CBS
    Colgate Theatre   ep nar   Fountain of Youth   9.16.58
    NBC
    Name of the Game   ep nar   9.30.70 NBC
    Hallmark Hall of Fame   ep   The Man Who Came to Din-
    ner   11.29.72 NBC

WEST, ADAM
    Sugarfoot   ep   The Mysterious Stranger   2.17.59 ABC
    Maverick   ep   Two Tickets to Ten Strike   3.15.59 ABC
    Colt .45   ep   The Escape   4.5.59 ABC
    Lawman   ep   The Wayfarer   6.7.59 ABC
    Maverick   ep   Pappy   9.13.59 ABC
    77 Sunset Strip   ep   Thanks for Tomorrow   10.30.59
    ABC
    Maverick   ep   A Fellow Brother   11.22.59 ABC
    Hawaiian Eye   ep   Quick Return   12.2.59 ABC
    Desilu Playhouse   ep   Murder Is a Private Affair   6.10.
    60 CBS
    Tales of Wells Fargo   ep   The Has-Been   1.16.61 NBC
    Bonanza   ep   The Bride   1.21.61 NBC
    Perry Mason   ep   The Case of the Barefaced Witness
    3.18.61 CBS
    Rifleman   ep   Stopover   4.25.61 ABC
    Guestward Ho   ep   Bill the Fireman   4.27.61 ABC
    Detectives   sr   9.29.61 NBC
    Perry Mason   ep   The Case of the Bogus Books   9.27.
    62 CBS
    Real McCoys   ep   The Crop Dusters   1.6.63 CBS
    Laramie   ep   The Betrayers   1.22.63 NBC
    Outer Limits   ep   The Invisible Enemy   10.31.64 ABC
    Virginian   ep   Legend for a Lawman   3.3.65 NBC
    Batman   sr   1.12.66 ABC
    Batman   sr ret   9.7.66 ABC

Batman sr ret 9.14.67 ABC
Alexander the Great pt 1.26.68 ABC
Big Valley ep In Silent Battle 9.23.68 ABC
Love American Style ep 1.30.70 ABC
Night Gallery ep With Apologies to Mr. Hyde 9.29.71
    NBC
Alias Smith and Jones ep 1.27.72 ABC
The Eyes of Charles Sand tf 2.29.72 ABC
Mannix ep Puzzle for One 11.26.72 CBS

WEST, MAE
Mr. Ed ep 3.22.64 NBC
Mr. Ed ep Mae Goes West 1965 NBC

WHEELER, BERT
Robert Montgomery Presents ep Rio Rita 11.13.50
    NBC

WHELAN, ARLENE
Tele-Theatre ep Death Comes by Night 4.3.50 NBC
Video Theatre ep Second Meeting 9.10.53 CBS
Schlitz Playhouse of Stars ep Night Ride to Butte 2.
    26.54 CBS
Playwrights '56 ep The Heart's a Forgotten Hotel 10.
    25.55 NBC
Lux Video Theatre ep The Web 12.1.55 NBC
G.E. Theatre ep Shadow of a Hero 2.4.62 CBS

WHITE, BETTY
Life with Elizabeth sr 10.18.53 NN
Date with the Angels sr 5.10.57 ABC
Modern Romances ep hos 8.11.58 NBC
U.S. Steel Hour ep Scene of the Crime 6.27.62 CBS
That's Life ep Buying a House 10.22.68 ABC

WHITE, CAROL
N.E.T. Playhouse ep Cathy Come Home 3.28.69 NN

WHITEHEAD, O.Z.
Suspense ep Nightmare at Ground Zero 8.18.53 CBS
Studio One ep The Remarkable Incident at Carson
    Corners 1.11.54 CBS
Cavalcade of America ep Arrow and the Bow 4.20.54
    ABC

WHITING, BARBARA
Silver Theatre ep The First Hundred Years 5.1.50
    CBS

Jewelers Showcase   ep   Operation E. S. P.   11. 18. 52
   CBS
Jewelers Showcase   ep   Weekend with Wal'tuh   5. 5. 53
   CBS
Those Whiting Girls   sr   7. 4. 55 CBS

WHITING, LEONARD
   World of Disney   ep   The Legend of Young Dick Turpin
      2. 13. 66, 2. 20. 66 NBC

WHITING, MARGARET
   Those Whiting Girls   sr   7. 4. 55 CBS
   Colt . 45   ep   Martial Law   5. 17. 60 ABC

WHITMAN, STUART
   Four Star Playhouse   ep   Desert Encounter   3. 22. 56
      CBS
   Gunsmoke   ep   12. 29. 56 CBS
   Zane Grey Theatre   ep   Until the Man Dies   1. 25. 57
      CBS
   Alcoa Theatre   ep   Encounter on a Second Class Coach
      10. 21. 57 NBC
   Court of Last Resort   ep   The Westland Case   1. 3. 58
      NBC
   Have Gun Will Travel   ep   1. 25. 58 CBS
   Trackdown   ep   The Town   6. 27. 58 CBS
   Bob Hope Chrysler Theatre   ep   A Killing Sundial   10.
      4. 63 NBC
   ABC Stage 67   ep   The People Trap   11. 8. 66 ABC
   Cimarron Strip   sr   9. 7. 67 CBS
   Bracken's World   ep   Murder--Off Campus   9. 25. 70
      NBC
   FBI   ep   The Impersonator   11. 22. 70 ABC
   The Man who Wanted to Live Forever   tf   12. 15. 70 ABC
   City Beneath the Sea   tf   1. 25. 71 NBC
   FBI   ep   10. 31. 71 ABC
   Night Gallery   ep   Lindemann's Catch   1. 12. 72 NBC
   Ghost Story   ep   9. 22. 72 NBC
   Night Gallery   ep   10. 15. 72 NBC
   World of Disney   ep   High Flying   10. 22. 72, 10. 29. 72,
      11. 5. 72 NBC
   Night Gallery   ep   12. 10. 72 NBC

WHITMORE, JAMES
   Ford Theatre   ep   For Value Received   2. 18. 54 NBC

Crossroads   ep   The Good Thief   11. 25. 55 ABC
Damon Runyon Theatre   ep   The Blonde Mink   1. 7. 56
  CBS
Schlitz Playhouse   ep   The Big Payday   1. 20. 56 CBS
Playwrights '56   ep   This Business of Murder   1. 31. 56
  NBC
Fireside Theatre   ep   The Velvet Trap   1. 31. 56 NBC
Studio One   ep   A Favor for Sam   3. 5. 56 CBS
Kraft Theatre   ep   Profile in Courage   5. 16. 56 NBC
Climax   ep   The Fog   9. 27. 56 CBS
Ford Theatre   ep   Fear Has Many Faces   1. 2. 57 ABC
Climax   ep   The Stalker   2. 7. 57 CBS
Panic   ep   The Priest   3. 5. 57 NBC
Alcoa Hour   ep   Nothing to Lose   4. 14. 57 NBC
Zane Grey Theatre   ep   Fearful Courage   4. 19. 57 CBS
20th Century-Fox Hour   ep   Deep Water   5. 1. 57 CBS
Playhouse 90   ep   Galvanized Yankee   12. 5. 57 CBS
Wagon Train   ep   The Gabe Carswell Story   1. 15. 58
  NBC
Zane Grey Theatre   ep   Debt of Gratitude   4. 18. 58 CBS
Playhouse 90   ep   Galvanized Yankee   7. 3. 58 CBS
Playhouse 90   ep   Free Week-End   12. 4. 58 CBS
Zane Grey Theatre   ep   Checkmate   4. 30. 59 CBS
Playhouse 90   ep   Dark December   4. 30. 59 CBS
Playhouse 90   ep   The Sounds of Eden   10. 15. 59 CBS
Desilu Playhouse   ep   The Hanging Judge   12. 4. 59 CBS
Zane Grey Theatre   ep   Wayfarers   1. 21. 60 CBS
Our American Heritage   ep   Shadow of a Soldier   2. 21.
  60 NBC
Mystery Show   ep   Thunder of Silence   6. 5. 60 NBC
Law and Mr. Jones   sr   10. 7. 60 ABC
Alcoa Presents   ep   The Witch Next Door   11. 28. 61
  ABC
Checkmate   ep   Nice Guys Finish Last   12. 13. 61 CBS
Detectives   ep   Act of God   12. 29. 61 NBC
Focus   Sp   1. 21. 62 NBC
Rawhide   ep   The Incident of the Dogfaces   11. 9. 62 CBS
U. S. Steel Hour   ep   Big Day for Ascrambler   12. 12.
  62 CBS
Going My Way   ep   Tell Me When You Get to Heaven
  1. 2. 63 ABC
Route 66   ep   A Gift for a Warrior   1. 18. 63 CBS
Ben Casey   ep   Father Was an Intern   4. 1. 63 ABC
Twilight Zone   ep   On Thursday We Leave for Home
  5. 2. 63 CBS
Rawhide   ep   Incident of Iron Bull   10. 3. 63 CBS
The Travels of Jaimie McPheeters   ep   The Day of

the Golden Fleece   10.7.63 ABC
Dr. Kildare   ep   If You Can't Believe the Truth   10.10.
63 NBC
Arrest and Trial   ep   My Name Is Martin Burnham   10.
13.63 ABC
Kraft Suspense Theatre   ep   The Long, Long Life of Ed-
ward Smalley   12.12.63 NBC
The Greatest Show on Earth   ep   Love the Giver   4.7.
64 ABC
Suspense   ep   4.15.64 CBS
Slattery's People   ep   What Is Truth?   9.21.64 CBS
Kraft Suspense Theatre   ep   Rumble on the Docks   10.
22.64 NBC
World of Disney   ep   The Tenderfoot   10.18.64, 10.25.
64, 11.1.64 NBC
Combat   ep   The Cossack   1.12.65 ABC
Gunsmoke   ep   4.3.65 CBS
For the People   ep   Any Benevolent Purpose   5.2.65
CBS
Gunsmoke   ep   11.6.65 CBS
Run for Your Life   ep   This Town for Sale   11.15.65
NBC
Virginian   ep   Nobody Said Hello   1.5.66 NBC
Loner   ep   The Mourners for Johnny Sharp   2.12.66
CBS
Big Valley   ep   The Death Merchant   2.23.66 ABC
T.H.E. Cat   ep   10.14.66 NBC
The Monroes   ep   10.26.66 ABC
Big Valley   ep   10.31.66 ABC
12 O'Clock High   ep   12.9.66 ABC
Invaders   ep   Quantity Unknown   3.7.67 ABC
Tarzan   ep   9.15.67 NBC
Big Valley   ep   Night in a Small Town   10.9.67 ABC
Judd for the Defense   ep   11.17.67 ABC
Virginian   ep   11.22.67 NBC
Custer   ep   Spirit Woman   12.13.67 ABC
Cowboy in Africa   ep   1.29.68 ABC
Big Valley   ep   Shadow of a Giant   1.29.68 ABC
Danny Thomas Show   ep   My Pal Tony   3.4.68 NBC
Bonanza   ep   To Die in Darkness   5.5.68 NBC
My Friend Tony   sr   1.5.69 NBC
Virginian   ep   A Flash of Darkness   9.24.69 NBC
Name of the Game   ep   10.24.69 NBC
Then Came Bronson   ep   2.18.70 NBC
Men from Shiloh   ep   Lady at the Bar   11.4.70 NBC
If Tomorrow Comes   tf   12.7.71 ABC
Temperatures Rising   sr   9.12.72 ABC

WIDMARK, RICHARD
    I Love Lucy   ep   The Tour   5. 20. 55 CBS
    Vanished   tf   3. 8. 71, 3. 9. 71 NBC
    Madigan   sr   9. 20. 72 NBC

WILCOXON, HENRY
    Big Valley   ep   Winner Lose All   10. 27. 65 ABC
    Daniel Boone   ep   3. 10. 66 NBC
    Pursue and Destroy   pt   8. 14. 66 ABC
    Road West   ep   11. 14. 66 NBC
    Cimarron Strip   ep   10. 12. 67 CBS
    It Takes a Thief   ep   A Matter of Royal Larceny   4. 23.
        68 ABC
    Wild, Wild West   ep   The Night of the Pistoleros   2.
        21. 69 CBS
    Marcus Welby, M. D.   ep   Flags Flying   10. 21. 69 ABC
    Gunsmoke   ep   9. 28. 70 CBS
    Sarge: The Badge or the Cross   tf   2. 22. 71 NBC

WILDE, CORNEL
    G. E. Theatre   ep   The Blond Dog   3. 6. 55 CBS
    Alcoa Theatre   ep   Coast to Coast   10. 20. 58 NBC
    Chevy Show   ep   Around the World with Nellie Bly   1.
        3. 60 NBC
    Father Knows Best   ep   An Evning to Remember   10. 4.
        60 CBS
    G. E. Theatre   ep   The Great Alberti   11. 5. 61 CBS
    The Greatest Show on Earth   ep   Big Man from Nairobi
        1. 21. 64 ABC
    Kraft Suspense Theatre   ep   Doesn't Anyone Know Who
        I Am   2. 27. 64 NBC
    Suspense Theatre   ep   2. 13. 69 ABC
    Night Gallery   ep   Deliveries in the Rear   2. 9. 72 NBC
    Gargoyles   tf   11. 21. 72 CBS

WILDER, GENE
    Hollywood Television Theatre   ep   The Scarecrow   1. 10.
        72 NN
    The Trouble with People   Sp   11. 12. 72 NBC

WILDING, MICHAEL
    20th Century-Fox Hour   ep   Cavalcade   10. 5. 55 CBS
    20th Century-Fox Hour   ep   Stranger in the Night   10.
        17. 56 CBS
    On Trial   ep   Colonel Blood   1. 4. 57 NBC
    Climax   ep   The Volcano Seat   4. 10. 58 CBS
    Playhouse 90   ep   Verdict of Three   4. 24. 58 CBS

Lux Playhouse ep The Case of the Two Sisters 4.1.
   59 CBS
Playhouse 90 Dark as the Night 5.18.59 CBS
Saints and Sinners ep 12.24.62 NBC
Alfred Hitchcock Theatre ep Last Seen Wearing Blue
   Jeans 4.19.63 CBS
The Girl from U.N.C.L.E. ep 11.29.66 NBC
Bob Hope Chrysler Theatre ep The Fatal Mistake
   11.30.66 NBC
Mannix ep 12.14.68 CBS

WILLIAMS, BILL
   The Adventures of Kit Carson sr 1951 NN
   Bigelow Theatre ep Make Your Bed 3.4.51 CBS
   Twilight Theatre ep Crew Cut 7.27.53 ABC
   Science Fiction Theatre ep The Hastings Secret sum-
      mer, 1955 NBC
   Schlitz Playhouse of Stars ep Well of Angels 12.30.
      55 CBS
   Schlitz Playhouse of Stars ep Angels in the Sky 4.6.
      56 CBS
   Damon Runyon Theatre ep Miracle Jones 4.14.56
      CBS
   Date with the Angels sr 5.10.57 ABC
   M Squad ep Girl Lost 3.21.58 NBC
   Yancy Derringer ep Ticket to Natchez 10.23.58 CBS
   World of Disney ep The Man from Bitter Creek 3.6.
      59 ABC
   G.E. Theatre ep The Flying Wife 4.5.59 CBS
   Desilu Playhouse ep The Untouchables 4.20.59. 4.27.
      59 CBS
   The Millionaire ep Millionaire Martha Halloran 5.27.
      59 CBS
   Bachelor Father ep East Meets West 10.22.59 CBS
   Men into Space ep Asteroid 11.25.59 CBS
   Assignment: Underwater sr 9.9.60 NN
   My Sister Eileen ep Marty's Best Friend 4.5.61 CBS
   Primus ep 9.27.61 ABC
   Lawman ep Get Out of Town 5.20.62 ABC
   77 Sunset Strip ep The Snow-Job Caper 12.28.62 ABC
   Perry Mason ep The Case of the Bluffing Blast 1.10.
      63 CBS
   Rawhide ep The Last Herd 10.16.64 CBS
   Wild, Wild West ep 10.15.65 CBS
   Perry Mason ep The Case of the Twelfth Wildcat
      10.31.65 CBS
   Lassie ep 9.11.66 CBS

World of Disney   ep   Trial by Error   1.29.67, 2.5.67
    NBC
Dragnet   ep   10.19.67 NBC
Daniel Boone   ep   11.23.67 NBC
Lassie   ep   A Chance to Live   10.13.68 CBS
Marcus Welby, M.D.   ep   12.8.70 ABC
Adam-12   ep   12.29.71 NBC
Ironside   ep   11.9.72 NBC

WILLIAMS, CARA
The Trap   ep   Lonely Boy   5.6.50 CBS
Armstrong Circle Theatre   ep   Man and Wife   10.31.50
    NBC
Broadway TV Theatre   ep   Within the Law   6.2.52 NN
Matinee Theatre   ep   Beyond a Reasonable Doubt   11.8.
    55 NBC
Alfred Hitchcock Presents   ep   The Decoy   6.10.56 CBS
Alfred Hitchcock Presents   ep   De Mortius   10.14.56
    CBS
Jane Wyman Theatre   ep   Harbor Patrol   4.23.57 NBC
Alfred Hitchcock Presents   ep   Last Request   11.24.57
    CBS
Desilu Playhouse   ep   Meeting Appalachia   1.22.60 CBS
Alfred Hitchcock Presents   ep   The Cure   1.24.60 CBS
Zane Grey Theatre   ep   Seed of Evil   4.7.60 CBS
Pete and Gladys   sr   9.19.60 CBS
Pete and Gladys   sr ret   9.18.61 CBS
Cara Williams Show   sr   9.23.64 CBS

WILLIAMS, CLARENCE, III
Daktari   ep   9.26.67 CBS
Danny Thomas Show   ep   Measure of a Man   1.22.68
    NBC
Mod Squad   sr   9.24.68 ABC
Mod Squad   sr ret   9.23.69 ABC
Mod Squad   sr ret   9.22.70 ABC
Mod Squad   sr ret   9.14.71 ABC
Mod Squad   sr ret   9.14.72 ABC

WILLIAMS, EMLYN
Festival of the Arts   ep   The Wild Duck   11.2.62 NN
Defenders   ep   Mind over Murder   5.16.64 CBS
David Copperfield   tf   3.15.70 NBC

WILLIAMS, ESTHER
Lux Video Theatre   ep   The Armed Venus   5.23.57
    NBC

Donna Reed Show   ep   Career Woman   4.28.60 ABC
Zane Grey Theatre   ep   The Black Wagon   12.1.60
   CBS

WILLIAMS, GUY
   Zorro   sr   10.10.57 ABC
   Lost in Space   sr   9.15.65 CBS
   Lost in Space   sr ret   fall, 1966 CBS
   Lost in Space   sr ret   9.6.67 CBS

WILLIAMS, SPENCE
   Amos 'n Andy   sr   6.28.51 CBS

WILLIAMSON, NICOL
   Of Mice and Men   Sp   1.31.68 ABC
   Outsider   ep   The Flip Side   2.26.69 NBC
   Julia   ep   Ready, Aim, Fired   9.15.70 NBC

WILLS, CHILL
   Alfred Hitchcock Presents   ep   Don't Interrupt   10.12.
      58 CBS
   Wagon Train   ep   The Bije Wilcox Story   11.19.58 NBC
   Trackdown   ep   2.18.59 CBS
   Texan   ep   2.23.59 CBS
   Playhouse 90   ep   Tomorrow   3.7.60 CBS
   Frontier Circus   sr   10.5.61 CBS
   Gunsmoke   ep   11.24.62 CBS
   Route 66   ep   Where There's a Will, There's a Way
      3.6.64, 3.13.64 CBS
   Rawhide   ep   The Incident at Deadhorse   4.16.64 CBS
   The Rounders   sr   9.13.66 ABC
   Gunsmoke   ep   10.16.67 CBS
   Judd for the Defense   ep   10.20.67 ABC
   Tarzan   ep   2.16.68 NBC
   Gunsmoke   ep   3.4.68 CBS
   The Over the Hill Gang   tf   10.7.69 ABC
   The Over the Hill Gang Rides Again   tf   11.17.70 ABC
   Marcus Welby, M.D.   ep   Another Buckle for Wesley
      Hill   1.5.71 ABC
   The Men from Shiloh   ep   The Angus Killer   2.10.71
      NBC
   Alias Smith and Jones   ep   The Biggest Game in the
      West   2.3.72 ABC

WILSON, FLIP
   Love American Style   ep   9.29.69 ABC
   Here's Lucy   ep   9.13.71 CBS
   Here's Lucy   ep   3.6.72 CBS

WILSON, LOIS
The Aldrich Family   sr   1950 NBC
Armstrong Circle Theatre   ep   The Diet   12.19.50
NBC
Philco Playhouse   ep   The Girl with the Stop Watch   10.
25.53 NBC
My Three Sons   ep   Caribbean Cruise   9.17.64 ABC

WILSON, MARIE
My Friend Irma   sr   1.8.52 CBS
My Friend Irma   sr ret   10.3.52 CBS
My Friend Irma   sr ret   10.2.53 CBS
Empire   ep   Hidden Asset   3.26.63 NBC
Burke's Law   ep   2.28.64 ABC
Burke's Law   ep   2.3.65 ABC
Love American Style   ep   10.6.72 ABC

WILSON, NANCY
I Spy   ep   Lori   9.21.66 NBC
Room   222   ep   1.14.70 ABC

WINDOM, WILLIAM
Masterpiece Playhouse   ep   Richard III   7.30.50 NBC
Omnibus   ep   The Education of Henry Adams   3.20.55
CBS
Robert Montgomery Presents   ep   The Drifter   5.23.55
NBC
Robert Montgomery Presents   ep   Tomorrow Is Forever
10.17.55 NBC
Hallmark Hall of Fame   ep   Dial M for Murder   4.25.
68 NBC
Checkmate   ep   Through a Dark Glass   11.1.61 CBS
Ben Casey   ep   The Sweet Kiss of Madness   12.4.61
ABC
Twilight Zone   ep   Five Characters in Search of an Ex-
it   12.22.61 CBS
Gunsmoke   ep   12.16.61 CBS
77 Sunset Strip   ep   Mr. Bailey's Honeymoon   1.12.62
ABC
Bus Stop   ep   The Ordeal of Kevin Brooke   2.25.62 ABC
Thriller   ep   Man of Mystery   4.2.62 NBC
Gallant Men   ep   10.5.62 ABC
Surfside 6   ep   Anniversary Special   1.29.62 ABC
Gertrude Berg Show   ep   Goodbye, Mr. Howell   2.15.
62 CBS
Mystery Theatre   ep   In Close Pursuit   6.13.62 NBC
The Lucy Show   ep   10.8.62 CBS

Stoney Burke   ep   Master of Pride   11.5.62 ABC
Gunsmoke   ep   12.22.62 CBS
Twilight Zone   ep   Miniature   2.21.63 CBS
Farmer's Daughter   sr   9.20.63 ABC
Farmer's Daughter   sr ret   9.18.64 ABC
Farmer's Daughter   sr ret   9.13.65 ABC
12 O'Clock High   ep   9.9.66 ABC
Wild, Wild West   ep   The Night of the Flying Pie Plate
   10.21.66 CBS
Iron Horse   ep   12.5.66 ABC
Run for Your Life   ep   The List of Alice McKenna   1.
   23.67 NBC
Fugitive   ep   2.21.67 ABC
Invaders   ep   Doomsday Minus One   2.28.67 ABC
Mission Impossible   ep   3.18.67 CBS
The Girl from U.N.C.L.E.   ep   4.11.67 NBC
Bob Hope Chrysler Theatre   ep   Wipeout   4.26.67 NBC
Mission Impossible   ep   9.10.67 CBS
Star Trek   ep   The Doomsday Machine   10.20.67 NBC
FBI   ep   10.22.67, 10.29.67 ABC
Invaders   ep   The Summit Meeting   10.31.67, 11.7.67
   ABC
Custer   ep   Under Fire   11.15.67 ABC
Gentle Ben   ep   11.19.67 CBS
Dundee and the Culhane   ep   11.22.67 CBS
Virginian   ep   11.29.67 NBC
Judd for the Defense   ep   12.1.67 ABC
Prescription Murder   tf   2.20.68 NBC
Bonanza   ep   Star Crossed   3.10.68 NBC
Mannix   ep   The Girl in the Frame   3.16.68 CBS
Ironside   ep   Trip to Hashbury   3.21.68 NBC
Virginian   ep   The Orchard   10.2.68 NBC
FBI   ep   The Nightmare   11.10.68 ABC
Mannix   ep   Shadow of a Man   1.25.69 CBS
Lancer   ep   3.4.69 CBS
U.M.C.   tf   4.7.69 CBS
Outcasts   ep   The Stalking Devil   4.7.69 ABC
Outsider   ep   Service for One   4.9.69 NBC
CBS Playhouse   ep   Shadow Game   5.7.69 CBS
My World and Welcome to It   sr   9.15.69 NBC
Virginian   ep   Halfway Back from Hell   10.1.69 NBC
Hawaii Five-O   ep   12.24.69 CBS
Love American Style   ep   10.23.70 ABC
Hollywood Television Theatre   ep   Big Fish, Little Fish
   1.5.71 NN
Men from Shiloh   ep   The Politician   1.13.71 NBC
Night Gallery   ep   They're Tearing Down Tim Riley's

Bar 1.20.71 NBC
Alias Smith and Jones ep The Wrong Train to Brim-
stone 2.4.71 ABC
Men at Law ep Let the Doer Beware 3.17.71 CBS
Is There a Doctor in the House pt 3.22.71 NBC
Medical Center ep Blood Line 9.15.71 CBS
Cannon ep Death Chain 9.21.71 CBS
Marriage: Year One tf 10.15.71 NBC
Man and the City ep 11.10.71 ABC
Mission Impossible ep 11.20.71 CBS
The Homecoming Sp 12.19.71 CBS
Cade's County ep 12.26.71 CBS
Columbo ep Short Fuse 1.19.72 NBC
Second Chance tf 2.8.72 ABC
Ironside ep Achilles' Heel 2.17.72 NBC
New Healers pt 3.27.72 ABC
Banacek ep 9.27.72 NBC
Gunsmoke ep 10.2.72 CBS
Ghost Story ep The Summer House 10.13.72 NBC
Rookies ep 10.16.72 ABC
A Great American Tragedy tf 10.18.72 ABC
Streets of San Francisco 10.7.72 ABC
Banacek ep 11.15.72 NBC
Love American Style ep 12.8.72 ABC
FBI ep 12.10.72 ABC
Pursuit ep 12.12.72 ABC

WINDSOR, MARIE
The Unexpected ep Blackmail 10.1.52 NBC
Ford Theatre ep For Value Received 2.18.54 NBC
Pepsi Cola Playhouse ep Live a Little 2.19.54 ABC
Science Fiction Theatre ep Time Is Just a Place 4.
15.55 NBC
Screen Directors Playhouse ep Tom and Jerry 11.30.
55 NBC
Charlie Farrell Show ep 7.2.56 CBS
Climax ep Savage Portrait 12.6.56 CBS
Ford Theatre ep House of Glass 3.27.57 ABC
Cheyenne ep Decision at Gunsight 4.23.57 ABC
Cheyenne ep The Mutton Puncher 10.22.57 ABC
Maverick ep The Quick and the Dead 12.8.57 ABC
Meet McGraw ep The Joshua Tree 12.17.57 NBC
Perry Mason ep The Case of the Daring Decoy 3.29.
58 CBS
Yancy Derringer ep Ticket to Natchez 10.23.58 CBS
Bat Masterson ep The Fighter 11.4.58 NBC
Pursuit ep The House at Malibu 11.26.58 CBS

Rawhide   ep   Incident on the Edge of Madness   2.6.59
   CBS
Schlitz Playhouse of Stars   ep   The Salted Mine   3.27.
   59 CBS
Deputy   ep   Back to Glory   9.26.59 NBC
Alaskans   ep   Winter Song   11.22.59 ABC
77 Sunset Strip   ep   Collector's Item   1.8.60 ABC
Rebel   ep   1.24.60 ABC
Perry Mason   ep   The Case of the Madcap Modiste   4.
   30.60 CBS
New Comedy Showcase   ep   Johnny Come Lately   8.8.60
   CBS
Lassie   ep   11.27.60 CBS
Hawaiian Eye   ep   The Comics   4.19.61 ABC
Wyatt Earp   ep   Wyatt Earp's Baby   4.25.61 ABC
Rawhide   ep   Incident of the Painted Lady   5.12.61 CBS
Hawaiian Eye   ep   The Final Score   11.29.61 ABC
Perry Mason   ep   The Case of the Tarnished Trademark
   1.20.62 CBS
Maverick   ep   Epitaph for a Gambler   2.11.62 ABC
Lawman   ep   The Wanted Man   4.8.62 ABC
Hawaiian Eye   ep   Day in the Sun   10.2.62 ABC
Lloyd Bridges Show   ep   12.25.62 CBS
Rawhide   ep   Incident of the Rusty Shotgun   1.9.64 CBS
Branded   ep   The Brave Endure   4.25.65 NBC
Jesse James   ep   The Quest   10.4.65 ABC
Bonanza   ep   Five Sundowns to Sun Up   12.5.65 NBC
Batman   ep   Green Ice   11.9.66, 11.10.66 ABC
Outsider   ep   One Long Stemmed American Beauty   11.
   20.68 NBC
Mannix   ep   11.23.68 CBS
Bracken's World   ep   Move in for a Close-Up   12.12.69
   NBC
Bracken's World   ep   Stop Date   12.19.69 NBC
Wild Women   tf   10.20.70 ABC
Bracken's World   ep   The Anonymous Star   11.13.70
   NBC
Adam-12   ep   3.11.71 NBC
Alias Smith and Jones   ep   High Lonesome Country   9.
   23.72 ABC

WINNINGER, CHARLES
   Schlitz Playhouse of Stars   ep   The Whale on the Beach
      6.4.54 CBS
   I Love Lucy   ep   10.11.54 CBS
   Best of Broadway   ep   The Philadelphia Story   12.8.54
      CBS

Fireside Theatre   ep   His Maiden Voyage   11.22.55
  NBC
Charlie Farrell Show   sr   7.2.56 CBS
The Millionaire   ep   Millionaire Terrance Costigan
  1.14.59 CBS

WINTERS, JONATHAN
  Shirley Temple Theatre   ep   The Land of Oz   9.18.60
    NBC
  Shirley Temple Theatre   ep   Babes in Toyland   12.25.
    60 NBC
  Twilight Zone   ep   A Game of Pool   10.13.61 CBS
  Guys 'n Geishas   Sp   2.10.67 NBC
  Now You See It, Now You Don't   tf   11.11.68 NBC

WINTERS, ROLAND
  Doorway to Danger   sr   7.4.52 NBC
  Meet Millie   sr   10.25.52 CBS
  Meet Millie   sr ret   3.16.54 CBS
  Star Playhouse   ep   Mr. Greentree and Friend   4.17.55
    NN
  Video Theatre   ep   The Wayward Saint   8.30.56 CBS
  Kaiser Aluminum Hour   ep   Throw Me a Rose   1.29.57
    ABC
  Broken Arrow   ep   Powder Keg   2.19.57 ABC
  20th Century-Fox Hour   ep   City in Flame   3.6.57 CBS
  Kraft Theatre   ep   The Duel   3.6.57 NBC
  You Are There   ep   The Attempt to Assassinate Theo-
    dore Roosevelt   6.2.57 CBS
  Kraft Theatre   ep   The Roaring 20th   6.5.57 NBC
  Goodyear Playhouse   ep   The Legacy   6.30.57 NBC
  Matinee Theatre   ep   The Remarkable Mr. Jerome   7.
    8.57 NBC
  Studio One   ep   The Unmentionable Blues   8.12.57 CBS
  Studio One   ep   The Dark Intruder   9.2.57 CBS
  Kraft Theatre   ep   A Cook for Mr. General   10.16.57
    NBC
  Schlitz Playhouse of Stars   ep   Outlaw's Boots   11.29.
    57 CBS
  Date with the Angels   ep   Double Trouble   1.15.58 ABC
  The Millionaire   ep   The Doris Winslow Story   1.29.58
    CBS
  Ford Star Time   ep   The Wicked Scheme of Jebal Deeks
    11.10.59 CBS
  Play of the Week   ep   A Piece of Blue Sky   5.9.60 NN
  Adventures of a Model   pt   9.6.60 CBS
  Omnibus   ep   He Shall Have Power   11.13.60 NBC

Play of the Week   ep   The Iceman Cometh   11.14.60,
   11.21.60 NN
A String of Beads   Sp   2.7.61 NBC
Naked City   ep   Take and Put   6.21.61 ABC
Defenders   ep   The Crusaders   2.24.62 CBS
Alcoa Premiere   ep   The Rules of the Game   5.1.62
   ABC
Alfred Hitchcock Theatre   ep   Captive Audience   10.18.
   62 CBS
Dennis the Menace   ep   Henry's New Job   12.2.62 CBS
Defenders   ep   Climate of Evil   12.7.63 CBS
Here's Lucy   ep   Lucy's College Reunion   12.16.63
   CBS
Hazel   ep   Scheherazade and Her Frying Pan   1.23.64
   NBC
Burke's Law   ep   2.14.64 ABC
Farmer's Daughter   ep   The Turkish Delight   3.18.64
   ABC
Bob Hope Chrysler Theatre   ep   Time for Elizabeth   4.
   24.64 NBC
Cara Williams Show   ep   1.27.65 CBS
Perry Mason   ep   The Case of the Telltale Tap   2.4.65
   CBS
Profiles in Courage   ep   4.11.65 NBC
The Smothers Brothers Show   sr   9.15.65 CBS
Mister Roberts   ep   Bookser's Honeymoon   9.7.65 NBC
Green Acres   ep   11.17.65 CBS
Here's Debbie   ep   9.16.69 NBC

WINTERS, SHELLEY
   Ford Theatre   ep   Mantrap   1.28.54 NBC
   Climax   ep   Sorry, Wrong Number   11.4.54 CBS
   Producers Showcase   ep   The Women   2.7.55 NBC
   Climax   ep   Dark Wall   8.30.56 CBS
   Alcoa Hour   ep   A Double Life   1.6.57 NBC
   U.S. Steel Hour   ep   Inspired Alibi   2.13.57 CBS
   Climax   ep   Don't Touch Me   4.4.57 CBS
   Wagon Train   ep   The Ruth Owens Story   10.9.57 NBC
   Schlitz Playhouse of Stars   ep   Smarty   10.11.57 CBS
   Dupont Show of the Month   ep   Beyond This Place   11.
      25.57 CBS
   Kraft Theatre   ep   Polka   12.18.57 NBC
   Alcoa Premiere   ep   The Cake Baker   1.2.62 ABC
   Alcoa Premiere   ep   The Way from Darkness   12.13.62
      ABC
   Bob Hope Chrysler Theatre   ep   Two Is the Number
      1.31.64 NBC

Ben Casey ep A Disease of the Heart Called Love
    11. 23. 64 ABC
Bob Hope Chrysler Theatre ep Back to Back 10. 27.
    65 NBC
Batman ep The Greatest Mother of Them All 10. 5. 66,
    10. 6. 66 ABC
That's Life ep The Ninth Month 11. 26. 68 ABC
A Death of Innocence tf 11. 26. 71 CBS
The Adventures of Nick Carter tf 2. 20. 72 ABC

WINWOOD, ESTELLE
Lights Out ep Masque 12. 11. 50 NBC
Suspense ep The Rose Garden 1. 30. 51 CBS
Broadway Television Theatre ep Outward Bound 11.
    24. 52 NN
Broadway Television Theatre ep Criminal at Large
    2. 2. 53 NN
Kraft Theatre ep Miss Mabel 3. 25. 53 NBC
Studio One ep Birthright 5. 4. 53 CBS
Studio One ep A Bargain with God 11. 16. 53 CBS
Broadway Television Theatre ep The Bat 11. 23. 53
    NN
Motorola TV Hour ep A Dash of Bitter 2. 9. 54 ABC
Robert Montgomery Presents ep The Promise 6. 14.
    54 NBC
Robert Montgomery Presents ep The Reality 6. 21. 54
    NBC
Producers Showcase ep Tonight at 8:30 10. 18. 54 NBC
Playwrights '56 ep Adam and Evening 3. 13. 56 NBC
Alfred Hitchcock Presents ep There Was an Old Wom-
    an 3. 18. 56 CBS
Climax ep The Mad Bomber 4. 18. 57 CBS
Matinee Theatre ep The Conversation Table 12. 2. 57
    NBC
Kraft Theatre ep The Woman at High Hollow 2. 26. 58
    NBC
Alfred Hitchcock Presents ep Bull in a China Shop 3.
    30. 58 CBS
Shirley Temple's Story Book ep The Magic Fishbone
    8. 19. 58 NBC
Donna Reed Show ep Miss Lovelace Comes to Tea 5.
    13. 59 ABC
Twilight Zone ep Long Live Walter Jameson 3. 18. 60
    CBS
Ann Sothern Show ep 4. 25. 60 CBS
Adventures in Paradise ep A Penny a Day 4. 24. 61
    ABC

Thriller   ep   Dialogs with Death   12.4.61 NBC
Dennis the Menace   ep   Calling All Birdlovers   1.14.62
  CBS
Dr. Kildare   ep   The Last Leaves on the Tree   10.15.
  64 NBC
Rogues   ep   Wherefore Art Thous, Harold   3.21.65
  NBC
FBI   ep   The Monster   9.19.65 ABC
Perry Mason   ep   The Case of the Final Fade-Out   5.
  22.66 CBS
The Man from U.N.C.L.E.   ep   Her Master's Voice Af-
  fair   9.16.66 NBC
ABC Stage 67   ep   The People Trap   11.9.66 ABC
Batman   ep   Marsha, Queen of Diamonds   11.23.66,
  11.24.66 ABC
Batman   ep   1.26.67, 1.27.67 ABC
Name of the Game   ep   The Taker   10.4.68 NBC
Doris Day Show   ep   10.8.68 CBS
Doris Day Show   ep   11.12.68 CBS
Outsider   ep   The Secret of Mareno Bay   1.15.69 NBC
Love American Style   ep   Love and the Living Doll   10.
  6.69 ABC
CBS Playhouse   ep   Appalachian Autumn   10.7.69 CBS
Love American Style   ep   10.20.72 ABC

WISEMAN, JOSEPH
  Drama   cp   With These Hands   3.1.52 NBC
  Lights Out   ep   Man in the Dark   7.21.52 NBC
  Armstrong Circle Theatre   ep   The Honor of Littorno
    11.3.53 NBC
  TV Hour   ep   Brandenburg Gate   12.1.53 ABC
  Medallion Theatre   ep   Contact with the West   3.20.54
    CBS
  Kraft Theatre   ep   Arrowsmith   5.6.54 ABC
  Kraft Theatre   ep   Death Takes a Holiday   12.30.54
    ABC
  Pond's Theatre   ep   Billy Budd   3.10.55 ABC
  Producers Showcase   ep   Darkness at Noon   5.2.55 NBC
  On Trial   ep   Twice in Pe-li   10.19.56 NBC
  Jane Wyman Show   ep   The Marked Bullet   11.20.56
    NBC
  Suspicion   ep   The Deadly Game   12.9.57 NBC
  Shirley Temple's Story Book   ep   The Wild Swans   9.12.
    58 NBC
  Theatre '59   ep   Alone   3.4.59 NBC
  Loretta Young Show   ep   Mr. Wilson's Wife   4.5.59,
    4.12.59 NBC

Desilu Playhouse   ep   Lepke   11. 20. 59 CBS
CBS Workshop   ep   4. 3. 60 CBS
Adventures in Paradise   ep   The Derelict 5. 30. 60 ABC
Shirley Temple Theatre   ep   Kim   9. 25. 60 NBC
Untouchables   ep   The Tommy Karpeles Story   12. 29. 60
    ABC
G. E. Theatre   ep   A Possibility of Oil   2. 19. 61 CBS
Untouchables   ep   The Antidote   3. 9. 61 ABC
Twilight Zone   ep   One More Pallbearer   1. 12. 62 CBS
New Breed   ep   Wherefore Art Thou Romeo   5. 15. 62
    ABC
Wagon Train   ep   3. 30. 64 ABC
Jesse James   ep   The Last Stand of Captain Hammel
    4. 4. 66 ABC
Bob Hope Chrysler Theatre   ep   The Faceless Man   5.
    4. 66 NBC
Great Bible Adventures   ep   Seven Rich Years   9. 11. 66
    ABC
Showcase   ep   Escurial   4. 2. 67 NN
Coronet Blue   ep   The Presence of Evil   8. 7. 67 CBS
The Outsider   tf   11. 21. 67 NBC
N. E. T. Playhouse   ep   They   4. 17. 70 NN
FBI   ep   Bitter Harbor   12. 12. 71 ABC
O'Hara, U. S. Treasury   ep   1. 28. 72 CBS
McCloud   ep   Fifth Man in a String Quartet   2. 2. 72
    NBC
Pursuit   tf   12. 12. 72 ABC

WITHERS, JANE
U. S. Steel Hour   ep   The Pink Burro   7. 15. 59 CBS
Pete and Gladys   ep   5. 14. 62 CBS
Alfred Hitchcock Theatre   ep   How to Get Rid of Your
    Rich Wife   12. 20. 63 CBS
Munsters   ep   Pike's Pique   10. 22. 64 CBS
Munsters   ep   2. 3. 66 CBS

WITHERSPOON, CORA
Royal Playhouse   ep   Polly   8. 11. 53 NN
Kraft Theatre   ep   A Touch of Summer   5. 19. 54 NBC

WOLFIT, DONALD
The Vise   ep   Two of a Kind   10. 14. 55 ABC

WONG, ANNA MAY
Gallery of Mme. Liu-Tsong   sr   10. 17. 51 NN
Climax   ep   The Chinese Game   11. 22. 56 CBS
Climax   ep   Deadly Tattoo   5. 1. 58 CBS

Wyatt Earp   ep   China Mary   3. 15. 60 ABC
Barbara Stanwyck Show   ep   By the Tail   1. 30. 61 NBC
Danger Man   ep   The Journey Ends Halfway   5. 24. 61
   CBS

WOOD, NATALIE
Schaefer Century Theatre   ep   Playmates   8. 20. 52 NBC
Pride of the Family   sr   10. 2. 53 ABC
Studio 57   ep   The Plot Against Miss Pomeroy   10. 19.
   54 NN
Four Star Playhouse   ep   The Wild Bunch   2. 17. 55 CBS
Ford Theatre   ep   Too Old for Dolls   2. 24. 55 NBC
Paul Hartman Show   sr   6. 12. 55 CBS
Heidi   Sp   10. 11. 55 NBC
Mayor of the Town   ep   The Old Triangle   9. 24. 55 NBC
Studio One   ep   Miracle at Potter's Farm   12. 19. 55
   CBS
G. E. Theatre   ep   Feathertop   12. 4. 55 CBS

WOOD, PEGGY
Mama   sr   1949-1950 CBS
Mama   sr ret   8. 4. 50 CBS
Mama   sr ret   9. 7. 51 CBS
Pulitzer Prize Playhouse   ep   The Skin of Our Teeth
   12. 19. 51 ABC
Mama   sr ret   9. 5. 52 CBS
Mama   sr ret   9. 4. 53 CBS
Mama   sr ret   9. 3. 54 CBS
Mama   sr ret   10. 7. 55 CBS
Mama   sr ret   12. 16. 56 CBS
Zane Grey Theatre   ep   The Bitter Land   12. 6. 57 CBS
U. S. Steel Hour   ep   Seed of Guilt   8. 12. 59 CBS
Dr. Kildare   ep   An Ancient Office   12. 6. 62 NBC
Nurses   ep   The Saturday Evening of Time   3. 14. 63
   CBS
For the People   ep   2. 7. 65 CBS
New York Television Theatre   ep   Opening Night   1966
   NN

WOODWARD, JOANNE
Robert Montgomery Presents   ep   Penny   6. 9. 52 NBC
Omnibus   ep   New Salem   1. 11. 53 CBS
Goodyear Playhouse   ep   The Young and the Fair   7. 26.
   53 NBC
Philco Playhouse   ep   The Dancers   3. 7. 54 NBC
Studio One   ep   Stir Mugs   4. 5. 54 CBS
Kraft Theatre   ep   Unequal Contest   4. 29. 54 ABC

Four Star Playhouse   ep   Interlude   10. 14. 54 CBS
Ford Theatre   ep   Segment   10. 21. 54 NBC
The Web   ep   Welcome Home   9. 26. 54 CBS
Elgin Hour   ep   High Man   11. 2. 54 ABC
Robert Montgomery Presents   ep   Homecoming   11. 22.
   54 NBC
Rheingold Theatre   ep   Dark Stranger   1. 8. 55 NBC
Pond's Theatre   ep   Cynara   5. 12. 55 ABC
Four Star Playhouse   ep   Full Circle   10. 27. 55 CBS
20th Century-Fox Hour   ep   The Late George Apley
   11. 16. 59 CBS
U. S. Steel Hour   ep   White Gloves   12. 21. 55 CBS
G. E. Theatre   ep   Prologue to Glory   2. 12. 56 CBS
Alfred Hitchcock Presents   ep   Momentum   5. 24. 56
   CBS
Studio One   ep   Family Protection   4. 28. 56 CBS
Four Star Playhouse   ep   Watch the Sunset   6. 7. 56 CBS
Playhouse 90   ep   The 80 Yard Run   1. 16. 58 CBS
Hallmark Hall of Fame   ep   All the Way Home   12. 1. 71
   NBC

WOOLEY, SHEB
   Zane Grey Theatre   ep   Vengeance Canyon   11. 30. 56
      CBS
   Ford Theatre   ep   Fate Travels East   3. 13. 57 ABC
   Wyatt Earp   ep   Indian Wife   12. 10. 57 ABC
   Rawhide   sr   1. 9. 59 CBS

WOOLLEY, MONTY
   Best of Broadway   ep   The Man Who Came to Dinner
      10. 13. 54 CBS
   Christmas Story Hour   Sp   12. 25. 54 CBS
   Playhouse 90   ep   Eloise   11. 22. 56 CBS
   Five Fingers   ep   The Man with the Triangle Heads
      10. 31. 59 NBC

WORLOCK, FREDERIC
   Omnibus   ep   King Lear   10. 18. 53 CBS
   Studio One   ep   Camille   11. 9. 53 CBS
   Hallmark Hall of Fame   ep   King Richard I   1. 24. 54
      NBC
   Medallion Theatre   ep   The 39th Bomb   2. 13. 54 CBS
   Robert Montgomery Presents   ep   Love Story   4. 26. 54
      NBC
   Kraft Theatre   ep   Kidnapped   9. 1. 54 NBC
   The Precious Heritage   ep   A Rhode Island Refuge   9.
      5. 54 CBS

U.S. Steel Hour   ep   The Man with the Gun   10.12.54
    ABC
Robert Montgomery Presents   ep   Hunchback of Notre
    Dame 11.8.54, 11.15.54 NBC
Robert Montgomery Presents   ep   David Copperfield
    12.27.54 NBC
Producers Showcase   ep   Reunion in Vienna   4.4.55
    NBC
Robert Montgomery Presents   ep   Bella Fleace Gave a
    Party 5.2.55 NBC
Robert Montgomery Presents   ep   The Great Gatsby   5.
    9.55 NBC
Kraft Theatre   ep   The Mob   6.29.55 NBC
Studio One   ep   Sane as a Hatter   7.11.55 CBS
Studio One   ep   The Voysey Inheritance   8.22.55 CBS
Star Tonight   ep   Success Story   9.8.55 ABC
U.S. Steel Hour   ep   The Great Adventure   1.18.56
    CBS
Robert Montgomery Presents   ep   The Man Who Van-
    ished 2.13.56 NBC
Alfred Hitchcock Presents   ep   Father and Son   6.2.57
    CBS
Suspicion   ep   Lord Arthur Savile's Crime   1.13.58
    NBC
Alfred Hitchcock Presents   ep   3.1.59 CBS
Markham   ep   The Counterfeit Stamps   7.25.59 CBS
Hong Kong   ep   Murder Royal   10.5.60 ABC
Hallmark Hall of Fame   ep   The Invincible Mr. Dis-
    raeli 4.4.63 NBC

WRAY, FAY
    Pride of the Family   sr   10.2.53 ABC
    Paul Hartman Show   sr   6.12.55 CBS
    Damon Runyon Theatre   ep   There's No Forever   8.20.
        55 CBS
    Studio 57   ep   My Son Is Gone   10.2.55 NN
    Screen Directors Playhouse   ep   It's Always Sunday   1.
        11.56 NBC
    20th Century-Fox Hour   ep   Times Like These   2.22.
        56 CBS
    Studio 57   ep   Exit Laughing   4.1.56 NN
    Jane Wyman Theatre   ep   Killer's Bride   1.29.57 NBC
    G.E. Theatre   ep   The Iron Horse   11.24.57 CBS
    Telephone Time   ep   Alice's Wedding Gown   11.19.57
        ABC
    Kraft Theatre   ep   Eddie   1.22.58 NBC
    Alfred Hitchcock Presents   ep   A Dip in the Pool

6. 1. 58 CBS
Perry Mason   ep   The Case of the Prodigal Parent   6.
    7. 58 CBS
David Niven Show   ep   The Promise   5. 5. 59 NBC
Playhouse 90   ep   Second Happiest Day   6. 25. 59 CBS
Perry Mason   ep   The Case of the Watery Witness   10.
    10. 59 CBS
Hawaiian Eye   ep   Bequest of Arthur Goodwin   3. 9. 60
    ABC
Islanders   ep   Flight from Terror   10. 9. 60 ABC
Real McCoys   ep Theatre in the Barn   5. 18. 61 ABC
G. E. Theatre   ep   Money and the Minister   11. 26. 61
    CBS
Wagon Train   ep   The Cole Crawford Story   4. 11. 62
    NBC
Eleventh Hour   ep   You're So Smart   1. 22. 64 NBC
Perry Mason   ep   The Case of the Fatal Fetish   3. 4.
    65 CBS

WRIGHT, TERESA
Video Theatre   ep   The Sound of Waves Breaking   1. 21.
    52 CBS
Robert Montgomery Presents   ep   And Never Come
    Back   4. 21. 52 NBC
Schlitz Playhouse of Stars   ep   Dress in the Window   6.
    13. 52 CBS
Hollywood Opening Night   ep   Alicia   11. 3. 52 NBC
Ford Theatre   ep   And Suddenly You Knew   12. 10. 53
    NBC
Ford Theatre   ep   The Happiest Day   1. 21. 54 NBC
U. S. Steel Hour   ep   The End of Paul Dane   5. 11. 54
    ABC
Climax   ep   The Long Goodbye   10. 7. 54 CBS
Ford Theatre   ep   Stars Don't Shine   1. 20. 55 NBC
Four Star Playhouse   ep   The Good Sisters   1. 27. 55
    CBS
G. E. Theatre   ep   Love Is Eternal   2. 13. 55 CBS
Rheingold Theatre   ep   Her Crowning Glory   4. 9. 55
    NBC
Elgin Hour   ep   Driftwood   5. 3. 55 ABC
U. S. Steel Hour   ep   Red Gulch   6. 21. 55 ABC
Your Play Time   ep   Intolerable Portrait   9. 3. 55 NBC
Loretta Young Show   ep   My Uncle O'More   9. 18. 55
    NBC
Ford Theatre   ep   Lady in the Wind   10. 20. 55 NBC
Hallmark Hall of Fame   ep   The Devil's Disciple   11.
    20. 55 NBC

Alcoa Hour   ep   Undertow   12.11.55 NBC
20th Century-Fox Hour   ep   Miracle on 34th Street   12.
     14.55 CBS
Screen Directors Playhouse   ep   Number Five Checked
     Out   1.18.56 NBC
Four Star Playhouse   ep   Once to Every Woman   3.1.
     56 CBS
Climax   ep   The Gay Illiterate   3.8.56 CBS
Star Stage   ep   The Secret Place   3.23.56 NBC
Rheingold Theatre   ep   The Lonely Ones   4.7.56 NBC
Studio 57   ep   The Faithful Heart   5.27.56 NN
Schlitz Playhouse of Stars   ep   Witness to Condemn   6.
     22.56 CBS
20th Century-Fox Hour   ep   Child of the Regiment   10.
     3.56 CBS
Playhouse 90   ep   The Miracle Worker   2.7.57 CBS
Schlitz Playhouse of Stars   ep   Sister Louise Goes to
     Town   5.24.57 CBS
Playhouse 90   ep   Edge of Innocence   10.31.57 CBS
U.S. Steel Hour   ep   Trap for a Stranger   2.25.59
     CBS
U.S. Steel Hour   ep   The Hours before Dawn   9.23.59
     CBS
Adventures in Paradise   ep   Pit of Silence   10.5.59
     ABC
Sunday Show   ep   The Margaret Bourke-White Story   1.
     3.60 NBC
Our American Heritage   ep   Shadow of a Soldier   2.21.
     60 NBC
Theatre 62   ep   Intermezzo   11.19.61 NBC
U.S. Steel Hour   ep   The Big Laugh   1.24.62 CBS
Dupont Show of the Month   ep   Big Deal in Laredo   10.
     7.62 NBC
Alfred Hitchcock Theatre   ep   Three Wives Too Many
     1.3.64 CBS
Bonanza   ep   My Son, My Son   1.19.64 NBC
Defenders   ep   The Pill Man   2.22.64 CBS
Alfred Hitchcock Theatre   ep   Lonely Place   11.16.64
     NBC
Defenders   ep   The Prosecutor   4.29.65 CBS
Desperate Hours   Sp   12.13.67 ABC
CBS Playhouse   ep   Appalachian Autumn   10.7.69 ABC
Crawlspace   tf   2.11.72 CBS

WYATT, JANE
     Robert Montgomery Presents   ep   Kitty Foyle   2.13.50
        NBC

Robert Montgomery Presents ep The Awful Truth 9.
  11. 50 NBC
Airflyte Theatre ep The Lipstick 1. 11. 51 CBS
Robert Montgomery Presents ep The Wall 3. 17. 52
  NBC
Studio One ep Lovers and Friends 6. 9. 52 CBS
Schlitz Playhouse of Stars ep A Southern Lady 7. 11.
  52 CBS
Ford Theatre ep Protect Her Honor 11. 13. 52 NBC
Fireside Theatre ep Love without Wings 12. 16. 52
  NBC
Robert Montgomery Presents ep The Inward Eye 12.
  8. 52 NBC
Studio One ep The Walsh Girls 2. 16. 53 CBS
The American Hour ep Outlaw's Reckoning 11. 3. 53
  ABC
P. M. Playhouse ep To Love and to Cherish 12. 31.
  53 CBS
Motorola TV Hour ep The Family Man 3. 9. 54 ABC
Father Knows Best sr 10. 3. 54 CBS
Father Knows Best sr ret 8. 31. 55 NBC
Playwrights '56 ep Daisy, Daisy 11. 22. 55 NBC
Father Knows Best sr ret fall, 1956 NBC
Father Knows Best sr ret fall, 1957 NBC
Studio One ep The Laughing Willow 2. 3. 58 CBS
Father Knows Best sr ret 9. 22. 58 CBS
Father Knows Best sr ret fall, 1959 CBS
Father Knows Best sr ret fall, 1960 CBS
Play of the Week ep The Wingless Victory 4. 17. 61
  NN
U. S. Steel Hour ep My Little Lost Sheep 11. 1. 61
  CBS
Going My Way ep Don't Forget to Say Goodbye 1. 23.
  63 ABC
Alcoa Premiere ep Blow High, Blow Clear 2. 14. 63
  ABC
Virginian ep The Secret of Brynmar Hall 4. 1. 64
  NBC
See How They Run tf 10. 7. 64 NBC
Alfred Hitchcock Theatre ep The Monkey's Paw 4.
  19. 65 NBC
Bob Hope Chrysler Theatre ep When Hell Froze 2. 2.
  66 NBC
Star Trek ep 11. 17. 67 NBC
CBS Playhouse ep My Father and My Mother 2. 13.
  68 CBS
Love American Style ep 9. 29. 69 ABC

Here Come the Brides   ep   4.3.70 ABC
Men from Shiloh   ep   The Price of the Hanging   11.11.
   70 NBC
Weekend of Terror   tf   12.8.70 ABC
Alias Smith and Jones   ep   11.11.71 ABC

WYCHERLY, MARGARET
   Philco Playhouse   ep   The Feast   5.7.50 NBC
   Philco Playhouse   ep   Wayward Season   9.16.51 NBC
   Kraft Theatre   ep   The Scarlet Letter   5.26.54 NBC
   Studio One   ep   The Deserter   11.29.54 CBS
   G.E. Theatre   ep   O, Lonely Moon   4.17.55 CBS

WYLER, GRETCHEN
   Phil Silvers Show   ep   Bilko's Honeymoon   4.11.58 CBS
   Modern Romances   ep hos   4.14.58 NBC
   Diagnosis Unknown   ep   A Sudden Stillness   7.19.60
      CBS

WYMAN, JANE
   G.E. Theatre   ep   Amelia   1.2.55 CBS
   Fireside Theatre   sh/sr   8.30.55 NBC
   Jane Wyman Theatre   sh/sr   8.27.56 NBC
   Jane Wyman Theatre   sh/sr   ret 9.26.57 NBC
   Lux Playhouse   ep   A Deadly Guest   1.9.59 CBS
   Checkmate   ep   Lady on the Brink   10.15.60 CBS
   G.E. Theatre   ep   Labor of Love   3.26.61 CBS
   Investigators   ep   Death Leaves a Tip   11.30.61 CBS
   Rawhide   ep   Twenty-Five Santa Clauses   12.22.61
      CBS
   Wagon Train   ep   The Wagon Train Mutiny   9.19.62
      ABC
   Naked City   ep   The S.A. American Dream   5.8.63
      ABC
   The Falling of Raymond   tf   11.27.71 ABC
   Bold Ones   ep   3.5.72 NBC
   Sixth Sense   ep   If I Should Die Before I Wake   12.2.
      72 ABC

WYNN, ED
   World of Disney   ep   Alice in Wonderland   11.3.54
      ABC
   Playhouse 90   ep   Requiem for a Heavyweight   10.11.
      56 CBS
   20th Century-Fox Hour   ep   The Great American Hoax
      5.15.57 CBS
   Alcoa Hour   ep   Protege   5.19.57 NBC

Hallmark Hall of Fame   ep   On Borrowed Time   11.17.
     57 NBC
December Bride   ep   3.10.58 CBS
Ed Wynn Show   sr   9.25.58 NBC
Meet Me in St. Louis   Sp   4.26.59 CBS
G.E. Theatre   ep   Miracle at the Opera   9.20.59 CBS
Twilight Zone   ep   One for the Angels   10.9.59 CBS
Wagon Train   ep   The Cappy Darrin Story   11.11.59
     NBC
Miracle on 34th Street   Sp   11.27.59 NBC
Ford Star Time   ep   The Greatest Man Alive   2.2.60
     NBC
Desilu Playhouse   ep   The Man in the Funny Suit   4.15.
     60 CBS
77 Sunset Strip   ep   "5"   9.20.63 ABC
Twilight Zone   ep   Ninety Years without Slumbering   12.
     20.63 CBS
World of Disney   ep   Treasure in the Haunted House   3.
     15.64 NBC
Slattery's People   ep   What Ever Happened to Ezra   10.
     12.64 CBS
Bonanza   ep   2.7.65 NBC

WYNN, KEENAN
U.S. Steel Hour   ep   The Rack   4.12.55 ABC
Best of Broadway   ep   Broadway   5.4.55 CBS
Studio One   ep   Like Father, Like Son   9.19.55 CBS
Fireside Theatre   ep   The Sport   10.4.55 NBC
Schlitz Playhouse of Stars   ep   Two-Bit Gangster   10.
     14.55 CBS
G.E. Theatre   ep   Lash of Fear   10.16.55 CBS
Screen Directors Playhouse   ep   A Midsummer Day-
     dream   10.19.55 NBC
Alcoa Hour   ep   Man on a Tiger   1.8.56 NBC
Damon Runyon Theatre   ep   Cleo   2.18.56 CBS
Studio One   ep   Circle of Guilt   2.20.56 CBS
Ford Star Jubilee   ep   Twentieth Century   4.7.56 CBS
Fireside Theatre   ep   The Sport   5.29.56 NBC
Playhouse 90   ep   Requiem for a Heavyweight   10.11.56
     CBS
Studio 57   ep   The Ballad of Jubal Pickett   8.12.56 NN
On Trial   ep   Death in the Snow   11.16.56 NBC
Playhouse 90   ep   The Last Tycoon   3.14.57 CBS
G.E. Theatre   ep   Cab Driver   4.14.57 CBS
Ford Theatre   ep   The Gentle Deceiver   5.15.57 ABC
Playhouse 90   ep   The Troublemakers   11.21.57 CBS
Schlitz Playhouse of Stars   ep   Outlaw's Boots   11.29.
     57 CBS

Wagon Train   ep   The Luke O'Malley Story   1.1.58
    NBC
Playhouse 90   ep   No Time at All   2.13.58 CBS
Alfred Hitchcock Presents   ep   A Dip in the Pool   6.1.
    58 CBS
Schlitz Playhouse of Stars   ep   No Answer   12.19.58
    CBS
Omnibus   ep   Malice in Wonderland   1.18.59 NBC
Goodyear Theatre   ep   Afternoon of the Beast   1.19.59
    NBC
Desilu Playhouse   ep   The Untouchables   ep   4.20.59,
    4.27.59 CBS
Theatre 59   ep   The Ledge   7.1.59 NBC
Troubleshooters   sr   9.11.59 NBC
June Allyson Show   ep   Piano Man   2.29.60 CBS
Desilu Playhouse   ep   The Man in the Funny Suit   4.15.
    60 CBS
Theatre 60   ep   Don't Look Down   6.9.60 NBC
Aquanauts   ep   10.5.60 CBS
Islanders   ep   The Cold War of Adam Smith   12.4.60
    ABC
Untouchables   ep   Augie the Banker Ciamino   2.9.61
    ABC
Naked City   ep   The Day It Rained Mink   2.15.61 ABC
Hallmark Hall of Fame   ep   Joke and the Valley   5.5.
    61 NBC
Roaring 20's   ep   Standing Room Only   10.28.61 ABC
Power and the Glory   Sp   10.29.61 CBS
Route 66   ep   Some of the People, Some of the Time
    12.1.61 CBS
Bus Stop   ep   And the Pursuit of Evil   12.17.61 ABC
New Breed   ep   The Valley of the Three Charlies   12.
    15.61 ABC
Follow the Sun   ep   Chicago Style   1.7.62 ABC
Dick Powell Theatre   ep   Seeds of April   2.13.62 NBC
Ben Casey   ep   Behold a Pale Horse   2.26.62 ABC
Naked City   ep   A Run for the Money   3.14.62 ABC
Target Corruptors   ep   4.13.62 ABC
Rawhide   ep   Incident at Cactus Wells   10.12.62 CBS
Combat   ep   The Prisoner   12.25.62 ABC
Dick Powell Theatre   ep   The Losers   1.15.63 NBC
Eleventh Hour   ep   Where Ignorant Armies Clash by
    Night   1.23.63 NBC
Nurses   ep   You Could Die Laughing   4.18.63 CBS
Dick Powell Theatre   ep   Last of the Private Eyes   4.
    30.63 NBC
77 Sunset Strip   ep   "5"   9.20.63 ABC

Littlest Hobo   ep   Die Hard   9. 25. 63 NN
Burke's Law   ep   Who Killed Cable Roberts   10. 4. 63
   ABC
Burke's Law   ep   Who Killed Julian Buck   10. 18. 63
   ABC
Burke's Law   ep   Who Killed Jason Shaw   1. 3. 64 ABC
Bob Hope Chrysler Theatre   ep   Runaway   1. 10. 64
   NBC
Travels of Jaimie McPheeters   ep   The Day of the
   Search   1. 19. 64 ABC
Bonanza   ep   Alias Joe Cartwright   1. 26. 64 NBC
Kraft Suspense Theatre   ep   Charlie, He Couldn't Kill
   a Fly   5. 7. 64 NBC
Combat   ep   The Flying Machine   2. 21. 66 ABC
Wild, Wild West   ep   The Night of the Freebooters   4.
   1. 66 CBS
The Pirates of Flounder Bay   pt   8. 26. 66 ABC
Road West   ep   No Sanctuary   2. 6. 67 NBC
Name of the Game   ep   Love-In at Ground Zero   1. 31.
   69 NBC
Then Came Bronson   ep   The Old Motorcycle Fiasco
   9. 24. 69 NBC
Lancer   ep   Blue Skies for Willie Sharpe   1. 13. 70 CBS
Name of the Game   ep   10. 9. 70 NBC
Medical Center   ep   Crisis   12. 9. 70 CBS
Assault on the Wayne   tf   1. 12. 71 ABC
Alias Smith and Jones   ep   Stagecoach Seven   3. 11. 71
   ABC
Cannon   tf   3. 26. 71 CBS
Terror in the Sky   tf   9. 17. 71 CBS
Alias Smith and Jones   ep   Dreadful Sorry, Clementine
   11. 17. 71 ABC
Mod Squad   ep   11. 23. 71 ABC
Santa Claus Is Coming to Town   Sp (voice only)   12. 3.
   71 ABC
Owen Marshall   ep   Run, Carol, Run   1. 20. 72 ABC
Cannon   ep   2. 8. 72 CBS
Assignment: Munich   tf   4. 30. 72 ABC
Alias Smith and Jones   ep   10. 28. 72 ABC
Hawaii Five-O   ep   Journey out of Limbo   10. 31. 72
   CBS

WYNTER, DANA
Suspense   ep   Operation Barracuda   4. 13. 54 CBS
U. S. Steel Hour   ep   The Man with the Gun   10. 12. 54
   ABC
Studio One   ep   It Might Happen Tomorrow   12. 4. 55
   CBS

20th Century-Fox Hour ep Laura 10.19.55 CBS
Playhouse 90 ep Winter Dreams 5.23.57 CBS
Playhouse 90 ep The Violent Heart 2.6.58 CBS
Playhouse 90 ep The Wings of the Dove 1.8.59 CBS
Wagon Train ep The Lizabeth Ann Calhoun Story 12.
    6.61 NBC
Dick Powell Theatre ep The Great Anatole 10.30.62
    NBC
Wagon Train ep The Lisa Rinacloud Story 10.31.62
    ABC
Virginian ep If You Have Tears 2.13.63 NBC
Burke's Law ep Who Killed Wade Walter? 11.15.63
    ABC
Bob Hope Chrysler Theatre ep The Fifth Passenger
    11.29.63 NBC
Wagon Train ep The Barbara Lindquist Story 10.18.
    64 ABC
12 O'Clock High ep Interlude 11.27.64 ABC
Kraft Suspense Theatre ep That Time in Havana 2.
    11.65 NBC
Alfred Hitchcock Theatre ep Unlocked Window 2.15.
    65 NBC
12 O'Clock High ep The Cry of Fallen Birds 4.9.65
    ABC
Bob Hope Chrysler Theatre ep The Crime 9.22.65
    NBC
Convoy ep Flight from Norway 9.24.65 NBC
My Three Sons ep 1.13.66 CBS
Ben Casey ep Smile, Baby, Smile 1.24.66 ABC
Wild, Wild West ep The Night of the Two-Legged Buf-
    falo 3.11.66 CBS
FBI ep The Defector 3.27.66, 4.3.66 ABC
The Man Who Never Was sr 9.7.66 ABC
FBI ep 11.5.67 ABC
Gunsmoke ep 11.27.67 CBS
Invaders ep 11.28.67 ABC
Dundee and the Culhane ep The Widow's Weeds Brief
    11.29.67 CBS
Name of the Game ep Lola in Lipstick 1.18.68 NBC
Companions in Nightmare tf 11.23.68 NBC
It Takes a Thief ep Guess Who's Coming to Rio? 1.
    7.69 ABC
Any Second Now tf 2.11.69 NBC
Get Smart ep 10.17.69 CBS
Love American Style ep 11.24.69 ABC
Ironside ep Beyond a Shadow 12.11.69 NBC
FBI ep Deadly Reunion 1.25.70 ABC

Medical Center   ep   Witch Hunt   11.11.70 CBS
To Rome with Love   ep   11.24.70 CBS
Marcus Welby, M.D.   ep   False Spring   1.19.71 ABC
Owen Marshall   tf   9.12.71 ABC
Owen Marshall   ep   Until Proven Innocent   12.9.71 ABC
Hawaii Five-O   ep   The Ninety Second War   1.11.72
  CBS
O'Hara, U.S. Treasury   ep   2.18.72 CBS

WYNYARD, DIANA
  Producers Showcase   ep   Mayerling   2.4.57 NBC
  Playhouse 90   ep   The Second Man   2.12.59 CBS

-Y-

YAMAGUCHI, SHIRLEY
  U.S. Steel Hour   ep   Presento   12.21.54 ABC
  Robert Montgomery Presents   ep   The Enemy   3.4.57
    NBC

YORK, DICK
  Goodyear Playhouse   ep   Visit to a Small Planet   5.8.
    55 NBC
  Kraft Theatre   ep   Million Dollar Rookie   5.25.55 NBC
  Mr. Citizen   ep   One for the Padre   6.15.55 ABC
  Kraft Theatre   ep   Drop on the Devil   6.22.55 NBC
  Philco Playhouse   ep   Incident in July   7.10.55 NBC
  Justice   ep   Fatal Payment   12.18.55 NBC
  Playwrights '56   ep   Honor   6.19.56 NBC
  Kaiser Aluminum Hour   ep   A Real Fine Cutting Edge
    1.15.57 NBC
  Alfred Hitchcock Presents   ep   Vicious Circle   4.14.57
    CBS
  Studio One   ep   The Weston Strain   5.27.57 CBS
  Kraft Theatre   ep   Ride into Danger   8.21.57 NBC
  Playhouse 90   ep   Last Clear Chance   3.6.58 CBS
  U.S. Steel Hour   ep   Beaver Patrol   4.9.58 CBS
  Climax   ep   Shooting for the Moon   4.24.58 CBS
  The Millionaire   ep   The Ken Leighton Story   9.24.58
    CBS
  Playhouse 90   ep   The Time of Your Life   10.9.58 CBS
  Father Knows Best   ep   Betty, Pioneer Woman   11.17.
    58 CBS

Playhouse 90   ep   Made in Japan   3. 5. 59 CBS
Playhouse 90   ep   Out of Dust   5. 21. 59 CBS
Alfred Hitchcock Presents   ep   The Dusty Drawer   5.
    31. 59 CBS
Twilight Zone   ep   The Purple Testament   2. 12. 60 CBS
The Millionaire   ep   Millionaire Sandy Newell   2. 17. 60
    CBS
Untouchables   ep   The White Slaves   3. 10. 60 ABC
Alcoa Theatre   ep   The Glorious 4th   4. 4. 60 NBC
Alfred Hitchcock Theatre   ep   The Doubtful Doctor   10.
    4. 60 NBC
Stagecoach West   ep   Three Wise Men   12. 20. 60 ABC
Naked City   ep   Bullets Cost Too Much   1. 4. 61 ABC
Rawhide   ep   Incident of the Broken Word   1. 20. 61 CBS
June Allyson Theatre   ep   School of the Soldier   1. 30.
    61 CBS
Twilight Zone   ep   A Penny for Your Thoughts   2. 3. 61
    CBS
Americans   ep   The War Between the States   5. 1. 61
    NBC
Frontier Circus   ep   The Shaggy Kings   10. 5. 61 CBS
Adventures in Paradise   ep   The Reluctant Hero   10. 8.
    61 ABC
G. E. Theatre   ep   A Musket for Jessica   10. 8. 61 CBS
Wagon Train   ep   The Clementine Jones Story   10. 25.
    61 NBC
Dr. Kildare   ep   The Lonely Ones   11. 9. 61 NBC
Alfred Hitchcock Theatre   ep You Can't Be a Little
    Girl All Your Life   11. 21. 61 NBC
Thriller   ep   The Incredible Doctor Markesan   2. 26. 62
    NBC
Outlaws   ep   Night Riders   5. 3. 62 NBC
Going My Way   sr   10. 3. 62 ABC
Alfred Hitchcock Theatre   ep   Terror in Northfield   10.
    11. 63 CBS
Rawhide   ep   Incident at Confidence Creek   11. 28. 63
    CBS
Wagon Train   ep   The Michael Malone Story   1. 6. 64
    ABC
Bewitched   sr   9. 17. 64 ABC
Bewitched   sr ret   9. 16. 65 ABC
Bewitched   sr ret   9. 15. 66 ABC
Bewitched   sr ret   9. 7. 67 ABC
Bewitched   sr ret   9. 26. 68 ABC

YORK, MICHAEL
    Wild, Wild West   ep   The Night of the Golden Cobra

9.23.66 CBS
The Forsyte Saga ep The Challenge 12.7.69 NN

YORK, SUSANNAH
Festival of the Arts ep The First Gentleman 11.30.
62 NN
Jane Eyre Sp 3.24.71 NBC

YOUNG, ALAN
The Alan Young Show sr 2.15.53 CBS
G.E. Theatre ep Wild Luke's Boy 5.16.54 CBS
Studio One ep The Man Who Caught the Ball at Coo-
gan's Bluff 11.28.55 CBS
Studio One ep This Will Do Nicely 4.2.56 CBS
Matinee Theatre ep Ask Me No Questions 4.20.56
NBC
Ford Startime ep Tennessee Ernie Meets King Arthur
5.10.60 NBC
Mr. Ed sr 1.5.61 NBC
Mr. Ed sr ret 10.1.61 CBS
Mr. Ed sr ret 9.27.62 CBS
Mr. Ed sr ret fall, 1963 CBS
Mr. Ed sr ret 9.27.64 CBS
Mr. Ed sr ret 9.12.65 CBS

YOUNG, GIG
Silver Theatre ep Lady with Ideas 5.8.50 CBS
Theatre ep Rewrite for Love 1.20.51 NN
Robert Montgomery Presents ep The Sunday Punch 10.
19.53 NBC
Schlitz Playhouse of Stars ep Part of the Game 12.18.
53 CBS
Producers' Showcase ep Tonight at 8:30 10.18.54
NBC
Warner Bros. Presents ep 9.27.55 ABC
U.S. Steel Hour ep Sauce for the Goose 10.10.56
CBS
Climax ep Jacob and the Angel 10.3.57 CBS
Studio One ep A Dead Ringer 3.10.58 CBS
Goodyear Theatre ep The Spy 11.10.58 NBC
Twilight Zone ep A Walking Distance 10.30.59 CBS
The Philadelphia Story Sp 10.7.59 NBC
Ninotchka Sp 4.20.60 ABC
Shirley Temple Story Book ep The Prince and the
Pauper 10.30.60 NBC
Theatre 62 ep The Spiral Staircase 10.4.61 NBC
Alfred Hitchcock Presents ep A Piece of the Action

9. 20. 62 CBS
Kraft Suspense Theatre   ep   The End of the World   10.
24. 63 NBC
The Rogues   sr   9. 13. 64 NBC
Companions in Nightmare   tf   11. 23. 68 NBC
The Neon Ceiling   tf   2. 8. 71 NBC

YOUNG, LORETTA
A Letter to Loretta   sh/sr   9. 20. 53 NBC
The Loretta Young Show   sh/sr   8. 2. 54 NBC
The Loretta Young Show   sh/sr   ret fall, 1955 NBC
The Loretta Young Show   sh/sr   ret 8. 26. 56 NBC
The Loretta Young Show   sh/sr   ret 10. 20. 57 NBC
The Loretta Young Show   sh/sr   ret 10. 5. 58 NBC
The Loretta Young Show   sh/sr   ret 9. 20. 59 NBC
The Loretta Young Show   sh/sr   ret 9. 18. 60 NBC
The New Loretta Young Show   sr   9. 24. 62 CBS

YOUNG, ROBERT
Ford Theatre   ep   Keep It in the Family   5. 27. 54 NBC
Father Knows Best   sr   10. 3. 54 CBS
Climax   ep   The Valiant Men   2. 10. 55 CBS
Father Knows Best   sr ret   8. 31. 55 CBS
Father Knows Best   ep   Stage to Yuma   12. 7. 55 NBC
Father Knows Best   sr ret   fall, 1956 NBC
Father Knows Best   sr ret   fall, 1957 NBC
Father Knows Best   sr ret   9. 22. 58 CBS
Father Knows Best   sr ret   9. 59 CBS
Father Knows Best   sr ret   9. 60 CBS
Window on Main Street   sr   10. 2. 61 CBS
Dr. Kildare   ep   Lullaby for an Indian Summer   1. 7. 65
NBC
Bob Hope Chrysler Theatre   ep   The Admiral   12. 29.
65 NBC
Bob Hope Chrysler Theatre   ep   Holloway's Daughters
5. 11. 66 NBC
Name of the Game   ep   The Protector   11. 15. 68 NBC
Marcus Welby, M. D.   tf   3. 26. 69 ABC
Marcus Welby, M. D.   sr   9. 23. 69 ABC
Marcus Welby, M. D.   sr ret   9. 22. 70 ABC
Vanished   tf   3. 8. 71, 3. 9. 71 NBC
Marcus Welby, M. D.   sr ret   9. 14. 71 ABC
Owen Marshall   ep   Men Who Care   10. 21. 71 ABC
Marcus Welby, M. D.   sr ret   9. 12. 72 ABC

YOUNG, ROLAND
Westinghouse Theatre   ep   Mr. Mummery's Suspicion

9. 3. 51 CBS
The Doctor   ep   Song for a Banker   2. 15. 53 NBC
Hollywood Opening Night   ep   Uncle Fred Flits By   3.
    9. 53 NBC

YURKA, BLANCHE
    Masterpiece Playhouse   ep   Richard III   7. 30. 50 NBC
    The Web   ep   The Poison Tree   7. 2. 52 CBS
    Kraft Theatre   ep   The New Tenant   10. 8. 52 NBC
    Medallion Theatre   ep   Crimson Velvet   12. 5. 53 CBS
    Kraft Theatre   ep   Alice in Wonderland   5. 5. 54 NBC
    Kraft Theatre   ep   Philip Goes Forth   9. 2. 54 ABC

                        -Z-

ZERBE, ANTHONY
    The Big Valley   ep   12. 8. 65 ABC
    Mission Impossible   ep   12. 17. 67 CBS
    Gunsmoke   ep   1. 22. 68 CBS
    Virginian   ep   The Good-Hearted Badman   2. 7. 68 NBC
    Mannix   ep   Death in a Minor Key   2. 8. 69 CBS
    Mission Impossible   ep   2. 23. 69 CBS
    Bonanza   ep   5. 11. 69 NBC
    N. E. T. Playhouse   ep   New Theatre for Now   11. 14. 69
        NN
    Mission Impossible   ep   11. 14. 70 CBS
    Gunsmoke   ep   The Noonday Devil   12. 7. 70 CBS
    Storefront Lawyers   ep   Where Were We, Waldo?   12.
        9. 70 CBS
    Ironside   ep   The Bar Savage Story   9. 20. 72 NBC
    Mannix   ep   9. 24. 72 CBS

ZETTERLING, MAI
    Studio One   ep   Sail with the Tide   1. 17. 55 CBS
    Danger Man   ep   The Sisters   4. 26. 61 CBS
    Eleventh Hour   ep   There Are Dragons in This Forest
        10. 10. 63 NBC

ZIMBALIST JR., EFRAM
    Concerning Miss Marlowe   sr   1955 CBS
    Goodyear Playhouse   ep   The Film Maker   7. 1. 56 NBC
    U. S. Steel Hour   ep   Stover at Sublimity   8. 1. 56 CBS
    Phil Silvers Show   ep   The Blue Blood Bilko   1. 8. 57
        CBS

Conflict   ep   Execution Night   5.28.57 ABC
Conflict   ep   Anything for Money   7.23.57 ABC
Maverick   ep   Stampede   5.25.58 ABC
Maverick   ep   Trail West to Fury   7.27.58 ABC
77 Sunset Strip   sr   10.10.58 ABC
Sugarfoot   ep   The Wizard   10.14.58 ABC
Maverick   ep   High Card Hangs   10.19.58 ABC
Maverick   ep   The Jail at Junction Flats   11.9.58 ABC
Maverick   ep   Shady Deal at Sunny Acres   4.5.59 ABC
77 Sunset Strip   sr ret   fall, 1959 ABC
Alaskan   ep   The Trail of Reno McKee   1.10.60 ABC
Hawaiian Eye   ep   I Wed Three Wives   9.14.60 ABC
77 Sunset Strip   sr ret   9.16.60 ABC
77 Sunset Strip   sr ret   9.22.61 ABC
Cheyenne   ep   The Prince of Darkness   11.6.61 ABC
77 Sunset Strip   sr ret   10.12.62 ABC
77 Sunset Strip   sr ret   9.20.63 ABC
Alfred Hitchcock Theatre   ep   See the Money Dance   11.
    9.64 NBC
Reporter   ep   Super Star   11.20.64 CBS
Rawhide   ep   The Last Order   4.9.65 CBS
FBI   sr   9.19.65 ABC
FBI   sr ret   9.18.66 ABC
FBI   sr ret   9.17.67 ABC
FBI   sr ret   9.22.68 ABC
FBI   sr ret   9.14.69 ABC
FBI   sr ret   9.20.70 ABC
FBI   sr ret   9.12.71 ABC
FBI   sr ret   9.17.72 ABC

ZUCCO, GEORGE
    Teledrama   ep   Secret Service Investigator   6.19.53
        CBS